American Casebook Series
Hornbook Series and Basic Legal Texts
Black Letter Series and Nutshell Series

of

WEST PUBLISHING COMPANY
P.O. Box 64526
St. Paul, Minnesota 55164–0526

Accounting

FARIS' ACCOUNTING AND LAW IN A NUT-SHELL, 377 pages, 1984. Softcover. (Text)

FIFLIS, KRIPKE AND FOSTER'S TEACHING MATERIALS ON ACCOUNTING FOR BUSINESS LAWYERS, Third Edition, 838 pages, 1984. (Casebook)

SIEGEL AND SIEGEL'S ACCOUNTING AND FINANCIAL DISCLOSURE: A GUIDE TO BASIC CONCEPTS, 259 pages, 1983. Softcover. (Text)

Administrative Law

BONFIELD AND ASIMOW'S STATE AND FEDERAL ADMINISTRATIVE LAW, 826 pages, 1989. Teacher's Manual available. (Casebook)

GELLHORN AND LEVIN'S ADMINISTRATIVE LAW AND PROCESS IN A NUTSHELL, Third Edition, 479 pages, 1990. Softcover. (Text)

MASHAW AND MERRILL'S CASES AND MATERIALS ON ADMINISTRATIVE LAW—THE AMERICAN PUBLIC LAW SYSTEM, Second Edition, 976 pages, 1985. (Casebook) 1989 Supplement.

ROBINSON, GELLHORN AND BRUFF'S THE ADMINISTRATIVE PROCESS, Third Edition, 978 pages, 1986. (Casebook)

Admiralty

HEALY AND SHARPE'S CASES AND MATERIALS ON ADMIRALTY, Second Edition, 876 pages, 1986. (Casebook)

MARAIST'S ADMIRALTY IN A NUTSHELL, Second Edition, 379 pages, 1988. Softcover.

(Text)

SCHOENBAUM'S HORNBOOK ON ADMIRALTY AND MARITIME LAW, Student Edition, 692 pages, 1987 with 1989 pocket part. (Text)

Agency—Partnership

DEMOTT'S FIDUCIARY OBLIGATION, AGENCY AND PARTNERSHIP: DUTIES IN ONGOING BUSINESS RELATIONSHIPS, Approximately 750 pages, April, 1991 Pub. (Casebook)

FESSLER'S ALTERNATIVES TO INCORPORATION FOR PERSONS IN QUEST OF PROFIT, Second Edition, 326 pages, 1986. Softcover. Teacher's Manual available. (Casebook)

HENN'S CASES AND MATERIALS ON AGENCY, PARTNERSHIP AND OTHER UNINCORPORATED BUSINESS ENTERPRISES, Second Edition, 733 pages, 1985. Teacher's Manual available. (Casebook)

REUSCHLEIN AND GREGORY'S HORNBOOK ON THE LAW OF AGENCY AND PARTNERSHIP, Second Edition, 683 pages, 1990. (Text)

SELECTED CORPORATION AND PARTNERSHIP STATUTES, RULES AND FORMS. Softcover. 727 pages, 1989.

STEFFEN AND KERR'S CASES ON AGENCY-PARTNERSHIP, Fourth Edition, 859 pages, 1980. (Casebook)

STEFFEN'S AGENCY-PARTNERSHIP IN A NUT-SHELL, 364 pages, 1977. Softcover. (Text)

Agricultural Law

MEYER, PEDERSEN, THORSON AND DAVIDSON'S AGRICULTURAL LAW: CASES AND MATERIALS, 931 pages, 1985. Teacher's Manual avail-

Agricultural Law—Cont'd

able. (Casebook)

Alternative Dispute Resolution

KANOWITZ' CASES AND MATERIALS ON ALTERNATIVE DISPUTE RESOLUTION, 1024 pages, 1986. Teacher's Manual available. (Casebook) 1990 Supplement.

RISKIN AND WESTBROOK'S DISPUTE RESOLUTION AND LAWYERS, 468 pages, 1987. Teacher's Manual available. (Casebook)

RISKIN AND WESTBROOK'S DISPUTE RESOLUTION AND LAWYERS, Abridged Edition, 223 pages, 1987. Softcover. Teacher's Manual available. (Casebook)

American Indian Law

CANBY'S AMERICAN INDIAN LAW IN A NUTSHELL, Second Edition, 336 pages, 1988. Softcover. (Text)

GETCHES AND WILKINSON'S CASES AND MATERIALS ON FEDERAL INDIAN LAW, Second Edition, 880 pages, 1986. (Casebook)

Antitrust—see also Regulated Industries, Trade Regulation

FOX AND SULLIVAN'S CASES AND MATERIALS ON ANTITRUST, 935 pages, 1989. Teacher's Manual available. (Casebook)

GELLHORN'S ANTITRUST LAW AND ECONOMICS IN A NUTSHELL, Third Edition, 472 pages, 1986. Softcover. (Text)

HOVENKAMP'S BLACK LETTER ON ANTITRUST, 323 pages, 1986. Softcover. (Review)

HOVENKAMP'S HORNBOOK ON ECONOMICS AND FEDERAL ANTITRUST LAW, Student Edition, 414 pages, 1985. (Text)

OPPENHEIM, WESTON AND MCCARTHY'S CASES AND COMMENTS ON FEDERAL ANTITRUST LAWS, Fourth Edition, 1168 pages, 1981. (Casebook) 1985 Supplement.

POSNER AND EASTERBROOK'S CASES AND ECONOMIC NOTES ON ANTITRUST, Second Edition, 1077 pages, 1981. (Casebook) 1984–85 Supplement.

SULLIVAN'S HORNBOOK OF THE LAW OF ANTITRUST, 886 pages, 1977. (Text)

Appellate Advocacy—see Trial and Appellate Advocacy

Architecture and Engineering Law

SWEET'S LEGAL ASPECTS OF ARCHITECTURE, ENGINEERING AND THE CONSTRUCTION PROCESS, Fourth Edition, 889 pages, 1989. Teacher's Manual available. (Casebook)

Art Law

DUBOFF'S ART LAW IN A NUTSHELL, 335 pages, 1984. Softcover. (Text)

Banking Law

BANKING LAW: SELECTED STATUTES AND REGULATIONS. Softcover. Approximately 265 pages, 1991.

LOVETT'S BANKING AND FINANCIAL INSTITUTIONS LAW IN A NUTSHELL, Second Edition, 464 pages, 1988. Softcover. (Text)

SYMONS AND WHITE'S BANKING LAW: TEACHING MATERIALS, Third Edition, approximately 775 pages, 1991. Teacher's Manual available. (Casebook)

Statutory Supplement. *See Banking Law: Selected Statutes*

Business Planning—see also Corporate Finance

PAINTER'S PROBLEMS AND MATERIALS IN BUSINESS PLANNING, Second Edition, 1008 pages, 1984. (Casebook) 1990 Supplement.

Statutory Supplement. *See Selected Corporation and Partnership*

SELECTED CORPORATION AND PARTNERSHIP STATUTES, RULES AND FORMS. 727 pages, 1989. Softcover.

Civil Procedure—see also Federal Jurisdiction and Procedure

AMERICAN BAR ASSOCIATION SECTION OF LITIGATION—READINGS ON ADVERSARIAL JUSTICE: THE AMERICAN APPROACH TO ADJUDICATION, 217 pages, 1988. Softcover. (Coursebook)

CLERMONT'S BLACK LETTER ON CIVIL PROCEDURE, Second Edition, 332 pages, 1988. Softcover. (Review)

COUND, FRIEDENTHAL, MILLER AND SEXTON'S CASES AND MATERIALS ON CIVIL PROCEDURE, Fifth Edition, 1284 pages, 1989. Teacher's Manual available. (Casebook)

COUND, FRIEDENTHAL, MILLER AND SEXTON'S CIVIL PROCEDURE SUPPLEMENT. 460 pages,

Civil Procedure—Cont'd

1990. Softcover. (Casebook Supplement)

FEDERAL RULES OF CIVIL PROCEDURE—EDUCATIONAL EDITION. Softcover. 632 pages, 1990.

FRIEDENTHAL, KANE AND MILLER'S HORNBOOK ON CIVIL PROCEDURE, 876 pages, 1985. (Text)

KANE AND LEVINE'S CIVIL PROCEDURE IN CALIFORNIA: STATE AND FEDERAL 498 pages, 1989. Softcover. (Casebook Supplement)

KANE'S CIVIL PROCEDURE IN A NUTSHELL, Second Edition, 306 pages, 1986. Softcover. (Text)

KOFFLER AND REPPY'S HORNBOOK ON COMMON LAW PLEADING, 663 pages, 1969. (Text)

MARCUS, REDISH AND SHERMAN'S CIVIL PROCEDURE: A MODERN APPROACH, 1027 pages, 1989. Teacher's Manual available. (Casebook)

MARCUS AND SHERMAN'S COMPLEX LITIGATION–CASES AND MATERIALS ON ADVANCED CIVIL PROCEDURE, 846 pages, 1985. Teacher's Manual available. (Casebook) 1989 Supplement.

PARK'S COMPUTER-AIDED EXERCISES ON CIVIL PROCEDURE, Second Edition, 167 pages, 1983. Softcover. (Coursebook)

SIEGEL'S HORNBOOK ON NEW YORK PRACTICE, Second Edition, Student Edition, approximately 900 pages, 1991. (Text)

Commercial Law

BAILEY AND HAGEDORN'S SECURED TRANSACTIONS IN A NUTSHELL, Third Edition, 390 pages, 1988. Softcover. (Text)

EPSTEIN, MARTIN, HENNING AND NICKLES' BASIC UNIFORM COMMERCIAL CODE TEACHING MATERIALS, Third Edition, 704 pages, 1988. Teacher's Manual available. (Casebook)

HENSON'S HORNBOOK ON SECURED TRANSACTIONS UNDER THE U.C.C., Second Edition, 504 pages, 1979, with 1979 pocket part. (Text)

MURRAY'S COMMERCIAL LAW, PROBLEMS AND MATERIALS, 366 pages, 1975. Teacher's Manual available. Softcover. (Coursebook)

NICKLES' BLACK LETTER ON COMMERCIAL PAPER, 450 pages, 1988. Softcover. (Review)

NICKLES, MATHESON AND DOLAN'S MATERIALS FOR UNDERSTANDING CREDIT AND PAYMENT SYSTEMS, 923 pages, 1987. Teacher's Manual available. (Casebook)

NORDSTROM, MURRAY AND CLOVIS' PROBLEMS AND MATERIALS ON SALES, 515 pages, 1982. (Casebook)

NORDSTROM, MURRAY AND CLOVIS' PROBLEMS AND MATERIALS ON SECURED TRANSACTIONS, 594 pages, 1987. (Casebook)

RUBIN AND COOTER'S THE PAYMENT SYSTEM: CASES, MATERIALS AND ISSUES, 885 pages, 1989. Teacher's Manual Available. (Casebook)

SELECTED COMMERCIAL STATUTES. Softcover. 1776 pages, 1990.

SPEIDEL'S BLACK LETTER ON SALES AND SALES FINANCING, 363 pages, 1984. Softcover. (Review)

SPEIDEL, SUMMERS AND WHITE'S COMMERCIAL LAW: TEACHING MATERIALS, Fourth Edition, 1448 pages, 1987. Teacher's Manual available. (Casebook)

SPEIDEL, SUMMERS AND WHITE'S COMMERCIAL PAPER: TEACHING MATERIALS, Fourth Edition, 578 pages, 1987. Reprint from Speidel et al., Commercial Law, Fourth Edition. Teacher's Manual available. (Casebook)

SPEIDEL, SUMMERS AND WHITE'S SALES: TEACHING MATERIALS, Fourth Edition, 804 pages, 1987. Reprint from Speidel et al., Commercial Law, Fourth Edition. Teacher's Manual available. (Casebook)

SPEIDEL, SUMMERS AND WHITE'S SECURED TRANSACTIONS: TEACHING MATERIALS, Fourth Edition, 485 pages, 1987. Reprint from Speidel et al., Commercial Law, Fourth Edition. Teacher's Manual available. (Casebook)

STOCKTON'S SALES IN A NUTSHELL, Second Edition, 370 pages, 1981. Softcover. (Text)

STONE'S UNIFORM COMMERCIAL CODE IN A NUTSHELL, Third Edition, 580 pages, 1989. Softcover. (Text)

WEBER AND SPEIDEL'S COMMERCIAL PAPER IN

Commercial Law—Cont'd

A NUTSHELL, Third Edition, 404 pages, 1982. Softcover. (Text)

WHITE AND SUMMERS' HORNBOOK ON THE UNIFORM COMMERCIAL CODE, Third Edition, Student Edition, 1386 pages, 1988. (Text)

Community Property

MENNELL AND BOYKOFF'S COMMUNITY PROPERTY IN A NUTSHELL, Second Edition, 432 pages, 1988. Softcover. (Text)

VERRALL AND BIRD'S CASES AND MATERIALS ON CALIFORNIA COMMUNITY PROPERTY, Fifth Edition, 604 pages, 1988. (Casebook)

Comparative Law

BARTON, GIBBS, LI AND MERRYMAN'S LAW IN RADICALLY DIFFERENT CULTURES, 960 pages, 1983. (Casebook)

GLENDON, GORDON AND OSAKWE'S COMPARATIVE LEGAL TRADITIONS: TEXT, MATERIALS AND CASES ON THE CIVIL LAW, COMMON LAW AND SOCIALIST LAW TRADITIONS, 1091 pages, 1985. (Casebook)

GLENDON, GORDON AND OSAKWE'S COMPARATIVE LEGAL TRADITIONS IN A NUTSHELL. 402 pages, 1982. Softcover. (Text)

LANGBEIN'S COMPARATIVE CRIMINAL PROCEDURE: GERMANY, 172 pages, 1977. Softcover. (Casebook)

Computers and Law

MAGGS AND SPROWL'S COMPUTER APPLICATIONS IN THE LAW, 316 pages, 1987. (Coursebook)

MASON'S USING COMPUTERS IN THE LAW: AN INTRODUCTION AND PRACTICAL GUIDE, Second Edition, 288 pages, 1988. Softcover. (Coursebook)

Conflict of Laws

CRAMTON, CURRIE AND KAY'S CASES–COMMENTS–QUESTIONS ON CONFLICT OF LAWS, Fourth Edition, 876 pages, 1987. (Casebook)

HAY'S BLACK LETTER ON CONFLICT OF LAWS, 330 pages, 1989. Softcover. (Review)

SCOLES AND HAY'S HORNBOOK ON CONFLICT OF LAWS, Student Edition, 1085 pages, 1982, with 1988–89 pocket part. (Text)

SIEGEL'S CONFLICTS IN A NUTSHELL, 470 pages, 1982. Softcover. (Text)

Constitutional Law—Civil Rights—see also Foreign Relations and National Security Law

ABERNATHY'S CASES AND MATERIALS ON CIVIL RIGHTS, 660 pages, 1980. (Casebook)

BARRON AND DIENES' BLACK LETTER ON CONSTITUTIONAL LAW, Third Edition, approximately 400 pages, 1991. Softcover. (Review)

BARRON AND DIENES' CONSTITUTIONAL LAW IN A NUTSHELL, Second Edition, approximately 475 pages, 1991. Softcover. (Text)

ENGDAHL'S CONSTITUTIONAL FEDERALISM IN A NUTSHELL, Second Edition, 411 pages, 1987. Softcover. (Text)

FARBER AND SHERRY'S HISTORY OF THE AMERICAN CONSTITUTION, 458 pages, 1990. Softcover. Teacher's Manual available. (Text)

GARVEY AND ALEINIKOFF'S MODERN CONSTITUTIONAL THEORY: A READER, 494 pages, 1989. Softcover. (Reader)

LOCKHART, KAMISAR, CHOPER AND SHIFFRIN'S CONSTITUTIONAL LAW: CASES–COMMENTS–QUESTIONS, Sixth Edition, 1601 pages, 1986. (Casebook) 1990 Supplement.

LOCKHART, KAMISAR, CHOPER AND SHIFFRIN'S THE AMERICAN CONSTITUTION: CASES AND MATERIALS, Sixth Edition, 1260 pages, 1986. Abridged version of Lockhart, et al., Constitutional Law: Cases–Comments–Questions, Sixth Edition. (Casebook) 1990 Supplement.

LOCKHART, KAMISAR, CHOPER AND SHIFFRIN'S CONSTITUTIONAL RIGHTS AND LIBERTIES: CASES AND MATERIALS, Sixth Edition, 1266 pages, 1986. Reprint from Lockhart, et al., Constitutional Law: Cases–Comments–Questions, Sixth Edition. (Casebook) 1990 Supplement.

MARKS AND COOPER'S STATE CONSTITUTIONAL LAW IN A NUTSHELL, 329 pages, 1988. Softcover. (Text)

NOWAK, ROTUNDA AND YOUNG'S HORNBOOK ON CONSTITUTIONAL LAW, Third Edition, 1191 pages, 1986 with 1988 pocket part. (Text)

ROTUNDA'S MODERN CONSTITUTIONAL LAW:

Constitutional Law—Civil Rights—Cont'd

CASES AND NOTES, Third Edition, 1085 pages, 1989. (Casebook) 1990 Supplement.

SHIFFRIN AND CHOPER'S FIRST AMENDMENT, CASES—COMMENTS—QUESTIONS, Approximately 700 pages, April, 1991 Pub. (Casebook)

VIEIRA'S CONSTITUTIONAL CIVIL RIGHTS IN A NUTSHELL, Second Edition, 322 pages, 1990. Softcover. (Text)

WILLIAMS' CONSTITUTIONAL ANALYSIS IN A NUTSHELL, 388 pages, 1979. Softcover. (Text)

Consumer Law—see also Commercial Law

EPSTEIN AND NICKLES' CONSUMER LAW IN A NUTSHELL, Second Edition, 418 pages, 1981. Softcover. (Text)

SELECTED COMMERCIAL STATUTES. Softcover. 1776 pages, 1990.

SPANOGLE, ROHNER, PRIDGEN AND RASOR'S CASES AND MATERIALS ON CONSUMER LAW, Second Edition, approximately 900 pages, 1991. (Casebook)

Contracts

CALAMARI AND PERILLO'S BLACK LETTER ON CONTRACTS, Second Edition, 462 pages, 1990. Softcover. (Review)

CALAMARI AND PERILLO'S HORNBOOK ON CONTRACTS, Third Edition, 1049 pages, 1987. (Text)

CALAMARI, PERILLO AND BENDER'S CASES AND PROBLEMS ON CONTRACTS, Second Edition, 905 pages, 1989. Teacher's Manual Available. (Casebook)

CORBIN'S TEXT ON CONTRACTS, One Volume Student Edition, 1224 pages, 1952. (Text)

FESSLER AND LOISEAUX'S CASES AND MATERIALS ON CONTRACTS—MORALITY, ECONOMICS AND THE MARKET PLACE, 837 pages, 1982. Teacher's Manual available. (Casebook)

FRIEDMAN'S CONTRACT REMEDIES IN A NUTSHELL, 323 pages, 1981. Softcover. (Text)

FULLER AND EISENBERG'S CASES ON BASIC CONTRACT LAW, Fifth Edition, 1037 pages, 1990. (Casebook)

HAMILTON, RAU AND WEINTRAUB'S CASES AND MATERIALS ON CONTRACTS, 830 pages, 1984. (Casebook)

JACKSON AND BOLLINGER'S CASES ON CONTRACT LAW IN MODERN SOCIETY, Second Edition, 1329 pages, 1980. Teacher's Manual available. (Casebook)

KEYES' GOVERNMENT CONTRACTS IN A NUTSHELL, Second Edition, 557 pages, 1990. Softcover. (Text)

SCHABER AND ROHWER'S CONTRACTS IN A NUTSHELL, Third Edition, 457 pages, 1990. Softcover. (Text)

SUMMERS AND HILLMAN'S CONTRACT AND RELATED OBLIGATION: THEORY, DOCTRINE AND PRACTICE, 1074 pages, 1987. Teacher's Manual available. (Casebook)

Copyright—see Patent and Copyright Law

Corporate Finance

HAMILTON'S CASES AND MATERIALS ON CORPORATION FINANCE, Second Edition, 1221 pages, 1989. (Casebook)

Corporations

HAMILTON'S BLACK LETTER ON CORPORATIONS, Second Edition, 513 pages, 1986. Softcover. (Review)

HAMILTON'S CASES AND MATERIALS ON CORPORATIONS—INCLUDING PARTNERSHIPS AND LIMITED PARTNERSHIPS, Fourth Edition, 1248 pages, 1990. Teacher's Manual available. (Casebook) 1990 Statutory Supplement.

HAMILTON'S THE LAW OF CORPORATIONS IN A NUTSHELL, Third Edition, approximately 500 pages, 1991. Softcover. (Text)

HENN'S TEACHING MATERIALS ON THE LAW OF CORPORATIONS, Second Edition, 1204 pages, 1986. Teacher's Manual available. (Casebook)

Statutory Supplement. *See Selected Corporation and Partnership*

HENN AND ALEXANDER'S HORNBOOK ON LAWS OF CORPORATIONS, Third Edition, Student Edition, 1371 pages, 1983, with 1986 pocket part. (Text)

SELECTED CORPORATION AND PARTNERSHIP STATUTES, RULES AND FORMS. Softcover. 727 pages, 1989.

SOLOMON, SCHWARTZ AND BAUMAN'S MATERI-

Corporations—Cont'd

ALS AND PROBLEMS ON CORPORATIONS: LAW AND POLICY, Second Edition, 1391 pages, 1988. Teacher's Manual available. (Casebook) 1990 Supplement.

    Statutory Supplement. *See Selected Corporation and Partnership*

Corrections

KRANTZ' THE LAW OF CORRECTIONS AND PRISONERS' RIGHTS IN A NUTSHELL, Third Edition, 407 pages, 1988. Softcover. (Text)

KRANTZ AND BRANHAM'S CASES AND MATERIALS ON THE LAW OF SENTENCING, CORRECTIONS AND PRISONERS' RIGHTS, Fourth Edition, approximately 625 pages, 1991. (Casebook)

ROBBINS' CASES AND MATERIALS ON POST-CONVICTION REMEDIES, 506 pages, 1982. (Casebook)

Creditors' Rights

BANKRUPTCY CODE, RULES AND OFFICIAL FORMS, LAW SCHOOL EDITION. 829 pages, 1990. Softcover.

EPSTEIN'S DEBTOR-CREDITOR LAW IN A NUTSHELL, Fourth Edition, approximately 400 pages, 1991. Softcover. (Text)

EPSTEIN, LANDERS AND NICKLES' CASES AND MATERIALS ON DEBTORS AND CREDITORS, Third Edition, 1059 pages, 1987. Teacher's Manual available. (Casebook)

LOPUCKI'S PLAYER'S MANUAL FOR THE DEBTOR-CREDITOR GAME, 123 pages, 1985. Softcover. (Coursebook)

NICKLES AND EPSTEIN'S BLACK LETTER ON CREDITORS' RIGHTS AND BANKRUPTCY, 576 pages, 1989. (Review)

RIESENFELD'S CASES AND MATERIALS ON CREDITORS' REMEDIES AND DEBTORS' PROTECTION, Fourth Edition, 914 pages, 1987. (Casebook) 1990 Supplement.

WHITE'S CASES AND MATERIALS ON BANKRUPTCY AND CREDITORS' RIGHTS, 812 pages, 1985. Teacher's Manual available. (Casebook) 1987 Supplement.

Criminal Law and Criminal Procedure—see also Corrections, Juvenile Justice

ABRAMS' FEDERAL CRIMINAL LAW AND ITS ENFORCEMENT, 866 pages, 1986. (Casebook)

1988 Supplement.

AMERICAN CRIMINAL JUSTICE PROCESS: SELECTED RULES, STATUTES AND GUIDELINES. 723 pages, 1989. Softcover.

CARLSON'S ADJUDICATION OF CRIMINAL JUSTICE: PROBLEMS AND REFERENCES, 130 pages, 1986. Softcover. (Casebook)

DIX AND SHARLOT'S CASES AND MATERIALS ON CRIMINAL LAW, Third Edition, 846 pages, 1987. (Casebook)

GRANO'S PROBLEMS IN CRIMINAL PROCEDURE, Second Edition, 176 pages, 1981. Teacher's Manual available. Softcover. (Coursebook)

HEYMANN AND KENETY'S THE MURDER TRIAL OF WILBUR JACKSON: A HOMICIDE IN THE FAMILY, Second Edition, 347 pages, 1985. (Coursebook)

ISRAEL, KAMISAR AND LaFAVE'S CRIMINAL PROCEDURE AND THE CONSTITUTION: LEADING SUPREME COURT CASES AND INTRODUCTORY TEXT. 747 pages, 1990 Edition. Softcover. (Casebook)

ISRAEL AND LaFAVE'S CRIMINAL PROCEDURE—CONSTITUTIONAL LIMITATIONS IN A NUTSHELL, Fourth Edition, 461 pages, 1988. Softcover. (Text)

JOHNSON'S CASES, MATERIALS AND TEXT ON CRIMINAL LAW, Fourth Edition, 759 pages, 1990. Teacher's Manual available. (Casebook)

JOHNSON'S CASES AND MATERIALS ON CRIMINAL PROCEDURE, 859 pages, 1988. (Casebook) 1990 Supplement.

KAMISAR, LaFAVE AND ISRAEL'S MODERN CRIMINAL PROCEDURE: CASES, COMMENTS AND QUESTIONS, Seventh Edition, 1593 pages, 1990. (Casebook) 1990 Supplement.

KAMISAR, LaFAVE AND ISRAEL'S BASIC CRIMINAL PROCEDURE: CASES, COMMENTS AND QUESTIONS, Seventh Edition, 792 pages, 1990. Softcover reprint from Kamisar, et al., Modern Criminal Procedure: Cases, Comments and Questions, Seventh Edition. (Casebook) 1990 Supplement.

LaFAVE'S MODERN CRIMINAL LAW: CASES, COMMENTS AND QUESTIONS, Second Edition, 903 pages, 1988. (Casebook)

Criminal Law and Criminal Procedure—
Cont'd

LaFave and Israel's Hornbook on Criminal Procedure, Second Edition, Student Edition, approximately 1200 pages, June, 1991 Pub. (Text)

LaFave and Scott's Hornbook on Criminal Law, Second Edition, 918 pages, 1986. (Text)

Langbein's Comparative Criminal Procedure: Germany, 172 pages, 1977. Softcover. (Casebook)

Loewy's Criminal Law in a Nutshell, Second Edition, 321 pages, 1987. Softcover. (Text)

Low's Black Letter on Criminal Law, Revised First Edition, 443 pages, 1990. Softcover. (Review)

Saltzburg's Cases and Commentary on American Criminal Procedure, Third Edition, 1302 pages, 1988. Teacher's Manual available. (Casebook) 1990 Supplement.

Uviller's The Processes of Criminal Justice: Investigation and Adjudication, Second Edition, 1384 pages, 1979. (Casebook) 1979 Statutory Supplement. 1986 Update.

Vorenberg's Cases on Criminal Law and Procedure, Second Edition, 1088 pages, 1981. Teacher's Manual available. (Casebook) 1990 Supplement.

Decedents' Estates—see Trusts and Estates

Domestic Relations

Clark's Hornbook on Domestic Relations, Second Edition, Student Edition, 1050 pages, 1988. (Text)

Clark and Glowinsky's Cases and Problems on Domestic Relations, Fourth Edition. 1150 pages, 1990. Teacher's Manual available. (Casebook)

Krause's Black Letter on Family Law, 314 pages, 1988. Softcover. (Review)

Krause's Cases, Comments and Questions on Family Law, Third Edition, 1433 pages, 1990. (Casebook)

Krause's Family Law in a Nutshell, Second Edition, 444 pages, 1986. Softcover. (Text)

Krauskopf's Cases on Property Division at Marriage Dissolution, 250 pages, 1984. Softcover. (Casebook)

Economics, Law and—see also Antitrust, Regulated Industries

Goetz' Cases and Materials on Law and Economics, 547 pages, 1984. (Casebook)

Malloy's Law and Economics: A Comparative Approach to Theory and Practice, 166 pages, 1990. Softcover. (Text)

Education Law

Alexander and Alexander's The Law of Schools, Students and Teachers in a Nutshell, 409 pages, 1984. Softcover. (Text)

Yudof, Kirp and Levin's Educational Policy and the Law, Third Edition, approximately 975 pages, April, 1991 Pub. (Casebook)

Employment Discrimination—see also Women and the Law

Estreicher and Harper's Cases and Materials on the Law Governing the Employment Relationship, 962 pages, 1990. Teacher's Manual available. (Casebook) Statutory Supplement.

Jones, Murphy and Belton's Cases and Materials on Discrimination in Employment, (The Labor Law Group). Fifth Edition, 1116 pages, 1987. (Casebook) 1990 Supplement.

Player's Federal Law of Employment Discrimination in a Nutshell, Second Edition, 402 pages, 1981. Softcover. (Text)

Player's Hornbook on Employment Discrimination Law, Student Edition, 708 pages, 1988. (Text)

Player, Shoben and Lieberwitz' Cases and Materials on Employment Discrimination Law, 827 pages, 1990. Teacher's Manual available. (Casebook)

Energy and Natural Resources Law—see also Oil and Gas

Laitos' Cases and Materials on Natural Resources Law, 938 pages, 1985. Teacher's Manual available. (Casebook)

Selected Environmental Law Statutes—Educational Edition. Softcover. 1020 pages, 1990.

Environmental Law—see also Energy and Natural Resources Law; Sea, Law of

BONINE AND MCGARITY'S THE LAW OF ENVIRONMENTAL PROTECTION: CASES—LEGISLATION—POLICIES, 1076 pages, 1984. Teacher's Manual available. (Casebook)

FINDLEY AND FARBER'S CASES AND MATERIALS ON ENVIRONMENTAL LAW, Second Edition, 813 pages, 1985. (Casebook) 1988 Supplement.

FINDLEY AND FARBER'S ENVIRONMENTAL LAW IN A NUTSHELL, Second Edition, 367 pages, 1988. Softcover. (Text)

RODGERS' HORNBOOK ON ENVIRONMENTAL LAW, 956 pages, 1977, with 1984 pocket part. (Text)

SELECTED ENVIRONMENTAL LAW STATUTES—EDUCATIONAL EDITION. Softcover. 1020 pages, 1990.

Equity—see Remedies

Estate Planning—see also Trusts and Estates; Taxation—Estate and Gift

LYNN'S AN INTRODUCTION TO ESTATE PLANNING IN A NUTSHELL, Third Edition, 370 pages, 1983. Softcover. (Text)

Evidence

BROUN AND BLAKEY'S BLACK LETTER ON EVIDENCE, 269 pages, 1984. Softcover. (Review)

BROUN, MEISENHOLDER, STRONG AND MOSTELLER'S PROBLEMS IN EVIDENCE, Third Edition, 238 pages, 1988. Teacher's Manual available. Softcover. (Coursebook)

CLEARY, STRONG, BROUN AND MOSTELLER'S CASES AND MATERIALS ON EVIDENCE, Fourth Edition, 1060 pages, 1988. (Casebook)

FEDERAL RULES OF EVIDENCE FOR UNITED STATES COURTS AND MAGISTRATES. Softcover. 381 pages, 1990.

FRIEDMAN'S PROBLEMS AND MATERIALS FOR AN INTRODUCTORY COURSE IN EVIDENCE, Approximately 290 pages, April, 1991 Pub. (Coursebook)

GRAHAM'S FEDERAL RULES OF EVIDENCE IN A NUTSHELL, Second Edition, 473 pages, 1987. Softcover. (Text)

LEMPERT AND SALTZBURG'S A MODERN AP-PROACH TO EVIDENCE: TEXT, PROBLEMS, TRANSCRIPTS AND CASES, Second Edition, 1232 pages, 1983. Teacher's Manual available. (Casebook)

LILLY'S AN INTRODUCTION TO THE LAW OF EVIDENCE, Second Edition, 585 pages, 1987. (Text)

MCCORMICK, SUTTON AND WELLBORN'S CASES AND MATERIALS ON EVIDENCE, Sixth Edition, 1067 pages, 1987. (Casebook)

MCCORMICK'S HORNBOOK ON EVIDENCE, Third Edition, Student Edition, 1156 pages, 1984, with 1987 pocket part. (Text)

ROTHSTEIN'S EVIDENCE IN A NUTSHELL: STATE AND FEDERAL RULES, Second Edition, 514 pages, 1981. Softcover. (Text)

Federal Jurisdiction and Procedure

CURRIE'S CASES AND MATERIALS ON FEDERAL COURTS, Fourth Edition, 783 pages, 1990. (Casebook)

CURRIE'S FEDERAL JURISDICTION IN A NUTSHELL, Third Edition, 242 pages, 1990. Softcover. (Text)

FEDERAL RULES OF CIVIL PROCEDURE—EDUCATIONAL EDITION. Softcover. 632 pages, 1990.

REDISH'S BLACK LETTER ON FEDERAL JURISDICTION, Second Edition, approximately 230 pages, 1991. Softcover. (Review)

REDISH'S CASES, COMMENTS AND QUESTIONS ON FEDERAL COURTS, Second Edition, 1122 pages, 1989. (Casebook) 1990 Supplement.

VETRI AND MERRILL'S FEDERAL COURTS PROBLEMS AND MATERIALS, Second Edition, 232 pages, 1984. Softcover. (Coursebook)

WRIGHT'S HORNBOOK ON FEDERAL COURTS, Fourth Edition, Student Edition, 870 pages, 1983. (Text)

Foreign Relations and National Security Law

FRANCK AND GLENNON'S FOREIGN RELATIONS AND NATIONAL SECURITY LAW, 941 pages, 1987. (Casebook)

Future Interests—see Trusts and Estates

Health Law—see Medicine, Law and

Human Rights—see International Law

Immigration Law

ALEINIKOFF AND MARTIN'S IMMIGRATION: PROCESS AND POLICY, Interim Second Edition, approximately 1075 pages, 1991. (Casebook)

Statutory Supplement. *See Immigration and Nationality Laws*

IMMIGRATION AND NATIONALITY LAWS OF THE UNITED STATES: SELECTED STATUTES, REGULATIONS AND FORMS. Softcover. 400 pages, 1990.

WEISSBRODT'S IMMIGRATION LAW AND PROCEDURE IN A NUTSHELL, Second Edition, 438 pages, 1989, Softcover. (Text)

Indian Law—see American Indian Law

Insurance Law

DEVINE AND TERRY'S PROBLEMS IN INSURANCE LAW, 240 pages, 1989. Softcover. Teacher's Manual available. (Coursebook)

DOBBYN'S INSURANCE LAW IN A NUTSHELL, Second Edition, 316 pages, 1989. Softcover. (Text)

KEETON'S CASES ON BASIC INSURANCE LAW, Second Edition, 1086 pages, 1977. Teacher's Manual available. (Casebook)

KEETON'S COMPUTER-AIDED AND WORKBOOK EXERCISES ON INSURANCE LAW, 255 pages, 1990. Softcover. (Coursebook)

KEETON AND WIDISS' INSURANCE LAW, Student Edition, 1359 pages, 1988. (Text)

WIDISS AND KEETON'S COURSE SUPPLEMENT TO KEETON AND WIDISS' INSURANCE LAW, 502 pages, 1988. Softcover. Teacher's Manual available. (Casebook)

WIDISS' INSURANCE: MATERIALS ON FUNDAMENTAL PRINCIPLES, LEGAL DOCTRINES AND REGULATORY ACTS, 1186 pages, 1989. Teacher's Manual available. (Casebook)

YORK AND WHELAN'S CASES, MATERIALS AND PROBLEMS ON GENERAL PRACTICE INSURANCE LAW, Second Edition, 787 pages, 1988. Teacher's Manual available. (Casebook)

International Law—see also Sea, Law of

BUERGENTHAL'S INTERNATIONAL HUMAN RIGHTS IN A NUTSHELL, 283 pages, 1988. Softcover. (Text)

BUERGENTHAL AND MAIER'S PUBLIC INTERNA-TIONAL LAW IN A NUTSHELL, Second Edition, 275 pages, 1990. Softcover. (Text)

FOLSOM, GORDON AND SPANOGLE'S INTERNATIONAL BUSINESS TRANSACTIONS—A PROBLEM-ORIENTED COURSEBOOK, 1160 pages, 1986. Teacher's Manual available. (Casebook) 1989 Documents Supplement.

FOLSOM, GORDON AND SPANOGLE'S INTERNATIONAL BUSINESS TRANSACTIONS IN A NUTSHELL, Third Edition, 509 pages, 1988. Softcover. (Text)

HENKIN, PUGH, SCHACHTER AND SMIT'S CASES AND MATERIALS ON INTERNATIONAL LAW, Second Edition, 1517 pages, 1987. (Casebook) Documents Supplement.

JACKSON AND DAVEY'S CASES, MATERIALS AND TEXT ON LEGAL PROBLEMS OF INTERNATIONAL ECONOMIC RELATIONS, Second Edition, 1269 pages, 1986. (Casebook) 1989 Documents Supplement.

KIRGIS' INTERNATIONAL ORGANIZATIONS IN THEIR LEGAL SETTING, 1016 pages, 1977. Teacher's Manual available. (Casebook) 1981 Supplement.

WESTON, FALK AND D'AMATO'S INTERNATIONAL LAW AND WORLD ORDER—A PROBLEM-ORIENTED COURSEBOOK, Second Edition, 1335 pages, 1990. Teacher's Manual available. (Casebook) Documents Supplement.

Interviewing and Counseling

BINDER AND PRICE'S LEGAL INTERVIEWING AND COUNSELING, 232 pages, 1977. Teacher's Manual available. Softcover. (Coursebook)

BINDER, BERGMAN AND PRICE'S LAWYERS AS COUNSELORS: A CLIENT–CENTERED APPROACH, Approximately 425 pages, 1991. Softcover. (Coursebook)

SHAFFER AND ELKINS' LEGAL INTERVIEWING AND COUNSELING IN A NUTSHELL, Second Edition, 487 pages, 1987. Softcover. (Text)

Introduction to Law—see Legal Method and Legal System

Introduction to Law Study

HEGLAND'S INTRODUCTION TO THE STUDY AND PRACTICE OF LAW IN A NUTSHELL, 418 pages,

Introduction to Law Study—Cont'd

1983. Softcover. (Text)

KINYON'S INTRODUCTION TO LAW STUDY AND LAW EXAMINATIONS IN A NUTSHELL, 389 pages, 1971. Softcover. (Text)

Judicial Process—see Legal Method and Legal System

Jurisprudence

CHRISTIE'S JURISPRUDENCE—TEXT AND READINGS ON THE PHILOSOPHY OF LAW, 1056 pages, 1973. (Casebook)

Juvenile Justice

FOX'S CASES AND MATERIALS ON MODERN JUVENILE JUSTICE, Second Edition, 960 pages, 1981. (Casebook)

FOX'S JUVENILE COURTS IN A NUTSHELL, Third Edition, 291 pages, 1984. Softcover. (Text)

Labor and Employment Law—see also Employment Discrimination, Social Legislation

FINKIN, GOLDMAN AND SUMMERS' LEGAL PROTECTION OF INDIVIDUAL EMPLOYEES, (The Labor Law Group). 1164 pages, 1989. (Casebook)

GORMAN'S BASIC TEXT ON LABOR LAW—UNIONIZATION AND COLLECTIVE BARGAINING, 914 pages, 1976. (Text)

LESLIE'S LABOR LAW IN A NUTSHELL, Second Edition, 397 pages, 1986. Softcover. (Text)

NOLAN'S LABOR ARBITRATION LAW AND PRACTICE IN A NUTSHELL, 358 pages, 1979. Softcover. (Text)

OBERER, HANSLOWE, ANDERSEN AND HEINSZ' CASES AND MATERIALS ON LABOR LAW—COLLECTIVE BARGAINING IN A FREE SOCIETY, Third Edition, 1163 pages, 1986. Teacher's Manual available. (Casebook) Statutory Supplement.

RABIN, SILVERSTEIN AND SCHATZKI'S LABOR AND EMPLOYMENT LAW: PROBLEMS, CASES AND MATERIALS IN THE LAW OF WORK, (The Labor Law Group). 1014 pages, 1988. Teacher's Manual available. (Casebook) 1988 Statutory Supplement.

Land Finance—Property Security—see Real Estate Transactions

Land Use

CALLIES AND FREILICH'S CASES AND MATERIALS ON LAND USE, 1233 pages, 1986. (Casebook) 1988 Supplement.

HAGMAN AND JUERGENSMEYER'S HORNBOOK ON URBAN PLANNING AND LAND DEVELOPMENT CONTROL LAW, Second Edition, Student Edition, 680 pages, 1986. (Text)

WRIGHT AND GITELMAN'S CASES AND MATERIALS ON LAND USE, Fourth Edition, approximately 1225 pages, 1991. Teacher's Manual available. (Casebook)

WRIGHT AND WRIGHT'S LAND USE IN A NUTSHELL, Second Edition, 356 pages, 1985. Softcover. (Text)

Legal History—see also Legal Method and Legal System

PRESSER AND ZAINALDIN'S CASES AND MATERIALS ON LAW AND JURISPRUDENCE IN AMERICAN HISTORY, Second Edition, 1092 pages, 1989. Teacher's Manual available. (Casebook)

Legal Method and Legal System—see also Legal Research, Legal Writing

ALDISERT'S READINGS, MATERIALS AND CASES IN THE JUDICIAL PROCESS, 948 pages, 1976. (Casebook)

BERCH AND BERCH'S INTRODUCTION TO LEGAL METHOD AND PROCESS, 550 pages, 1985. Teacher's Manual available. (Casebook)

BODENHEIMER, OAKLEY AND LOVE'S READINGS AND CASES ON AN INTRODUCTION TO THE ANGLO-AMERICAN LEGAL SYSTEM, Second Edition, 166 pages, 1988. Softcover. (Casebook)

DAVIES AND LAWRY'S INSTITUTIONS AND METHODS OF THE LAW—INTRODUCTORY TEACHING MATERIALS, 547 pages, 1982. Teacher's Manual available. (Casebook)

DVORKIN, HIMMELSTEIN AND LESNICK'S BECOMING A LAWYER: A HUMANISTIC PERSPECTIVE ON LEGAL EDUCATION AND PROFESSIONALISM, 211 pages, 1981. Softcover. (Text)

KEETON'S JUDGING, 842 pages, 1990. Softcover. (Coursebook)

KELSO AND KELSO'S STUDYING LAW: AN IN-

Legal Method and Legal System—Cont'd

TRODUCTION, 587 pages, 1984. (Coursebook)

KEMPIN'S HISTORICAL INTRODUCTION TO ANGLO-AMERICAN LAW IN A NUTSHELL, Third Edition, 323 pages, 1990. Softcover. (Text)

REYNOLDS' JUDICIAL PROCESS IN A NUTSHELL, 292 pages, 1980. Softcover. (Text)

Legal Research

COHEN'S LEGAL RESEARCH IN A NUTSHELL, Fourth Edition, 452 pages, 1985. Softcover. (Text)

COHEN, BERRING AND OLSON'S HOW TO FIND THE LAW, Ninth Edition, 716 pages, 1989. (Text)

COHEN, BERRING AND OLSON'S FINDING THE LAW, 570 pages, 1989. Softcover reprint from Cohen, Berring and Olson's How to Find the Law, Ninth Edition. (Coursebook)

> Legal Research Exercises, 3rd Ed., for use with Cohen, Berring and Olson, 229 pages, 1989. Teacher's Manual available.

ROMBAUER'S LEGAL PROBLEM SOLVING—ANALYSIS, RESEARCH AND WRITING, Fourth Edition, 424 pages, 1983. Teacher's Manual with problems available. (Coursebook)

STATSKY'S LEGAL RESEARCH AND WRITING, Third Edition, 257 pages, 1986. Softcover. (Coursebook)

TEPLY'S LEGAL RESEARCH AND CITATION, Third Edition, 472 pages, 1989. Softcover. (Coursebook)

> Student Library Exercises, 3rd ed., 391 pages, 1989. Answer Key available.

Legal Writing

CHILD'S DRAFTING LEGAL DOCUMENTS: MATERIALS AND PROBLEMS, 286 pages, 1988. Softcover. Teacher's Manual available. (Coursebook)

DICKERSON'S MATERIALS ON LEGAL DRAFTING, 425 pages, 1981. Teacher's Manual available. (Coursebook)

FELSENFELD AND SIEGEL'S WRITING CONTRACTS IN PLAIN ENGLISH, 290 pages, 1981. Softcover. (Text)

GOPEN'S WRITING FROM A LEGAL PERSPEC-

TIVE, 225 pages, 1981. (Text)

MELLINKOFF'S LEGAL WRITING—SENSE AND NONSENSE, 242 pages, 1982. Softcover. Teacher's Manual available. (Text)

PRATT'S LEGAL WRITING: A SYSTEMATIC APPROACH, 468 pages, 1990. Teacher's Manual available. (Coursebook)

RAY AND RAMSFIELD'S LEGAL WRITING: GETTING IT RIGHT AND GETTING IT WRITTEN, 250 pages, 1987. Softcover. (Text)

SQUIRES AND ROMBAUER'S LEGAL WRITING IN A NUTSHELL, 294 pages, 1982. Softcover. (Text)

STATSKY AND WERNET'S CASE ANALYSIS AND FUNDAMENTALS OF LEGAL WRITING, Third Edition, 424 pages, 1989. Teacher's Manual available. (Text)

TEPLY'S LEGAL WRITING, ANALYSIS AND ORAL ARGUMENT, 576 pages, 1990. Softcover. Teacher's Manual available. (Coursebook)

WEIHOFEN'S LEGAL WRITING STYLE, Second Edition, 332 pages, 1980. (Text)

Legislation

DAVIES' LEGISLATIVE LAW AND PROCESS IN A NUTSHELL, Second Edition, 346 pages, 1986. Softcover. (Text)

ESKRIDGE AND FRICKEY'S CASES AND MATERIALS ON LEGISLATION: STATUTES AND THE CREATION OF PUBLIC POLICY, 937 pages, 1988. Teacher's Manual available. (Casebook) 1990 Supplement.

NUTTING AND DICKERSON'S CASES AND MATERIALS ON LEGISLATION, Fifth Edition, 744 pages, 1978. (Casebook)

STATSKY'S LEGISLATIVE ANALYSIS AND DRAFTING, Second Edition, 217 pages, 1984. Teacher's Manual available. (Text)

Local Government

FRUG'S CASES AND MATERIALS ON LOCAL GOVERNMENT LAW, 1005 pages, 1988. (Casebook)

McCARTHY'S LOCAL GOVERNMENT LAW IN A NUTSHELL, Third Edition, 435 pages, 1990. Softcover. (Text)

REYNOLDS' HORNBOOK ON LOCAL GOVERNMENT LAW, 860 pages, 1982, with 1990 pocket part. (Text)

Local Government—Cont'd

VALENTE'S CASES AND MATERIALS ON LOCAL GOVERNMENT LAW, Third Edition, 1010 pages, 1987. Teacher's Manual available. (Casebook) 1989 Supplement.

Mass Communication Law

GILLMOR, BARRON, SIMON AND TERRY'S CASES AND COMMENT ON MASS COMMUNICATION LAW, Fifth Edition, 947 pages, 1990. (Casebook)

GINSBURG, BOTEIN, DIRECTOR AND RICE'S REGULATION OF BROADCASTING: LAW AND POLICY TOWARDS RADIO, TELEVISION AND CABLE COMMUNICATIONS, Second Edition, approximately 750 pages, April, 1991 Pub. (Casebook)

ZUCKMAN, GAYNES, CARTER AND DEE'S MASS COMMUNICATIONS LAW IN A NUTSHELL, Third Edition, 538 pages, 1988. Softcover. (Text)

Medicine, Law and

FISCINA, BOUMIL, SHARPE AND HEAD'S MEDICAL LIABILITY, 487 pages, 1991. Teacher's Manual available. (Casebook)

FURROW, JOHNSON, JOST AND SCHWARTZ' HEALTH LAW: CASES, MATERIALS AND PROBLEMS, Second Edition, approximately 1200 pages, June, 1991 Pub. Teacher's Manual available. (Casebook)

HALL AND ELLMAN'S HEALTH CARE LAW AND ETHICS IN A NUTSHELL, 401 pages, 1990. Softcover (Text)

JARVIS, CLOSEN, HERMANN AND LEONARD'S AIDS LAW IN A NUTSHELL, Approximately 350 pages, 1991. Softcover. (Text)

KING'S THE LAW OF MEDICAL MALPRACTICE IN A NUTSHELL, Second Edition, 342 pages, 1986. Softcover. (Text)

SHAPIRO AND SPECE'S CASES, MATERIALS AND PROBLEMS ON BIOETHICS AND LAW, 892 pages, 1981. (Casebook)

Military Law

SHANOR AND TERRELL'S MILITARY LAW IN A NUTSHELL, 378 pages, 1980. Softcover. (Text)

Mortgages—see Real Estate Transactions

Natural Resources Law—see Energy and Natural Resources Law, Environmental Law

Negotiation

GIFFORD'S LEGAL NEGOTIATION: THEORY AND APPLICATIONS, 225 pages, 1989. Softcover. (Text)

WILLIAMS' LEGAL NEGOTIATION AND SETTLEMENT, 207 pages, 1983. Softcover. Teacher's Manual available. (Coursebook)

Office Practice—see also Computers and Law, Interviewing and Counseling, Negotiation

HEGLAND'S TRIAL AND PRACTICE SKILLS IN A NUTSHELL, 346 pages, 1978. Softcover (Text)

MUNNEKE'S LAW PRACTICE MANAGEMENT, MATERIALS AND CASES, May, 1991 Pub. (Casebook)

STRONG AND CLARK'S LAW OFFICE MANAGEMENT, 424 pages, 1974. (Casebook)

Oil and Gas—see also Energy and Natural Resources Law

HEMINGWAY'S HORNBOOK ON OIL AND GAS, Second Edition, Student Edition, 543 pages, 1983, with 1989 pocket part. (Text)

KUNTZ, LOWE, ANDERSON AND SMITH'S CASES AND MATERIALS ON OIL AND GAS LAW, 857 pages, 1986. Teacher's Manual available. (Casebook) Forms Manual. Revised.

LOWE'S OIL AND GAS LAW IN A NUTSHELL, Second Edition, 465 pages, 1988. Softcover. (Text)

Partnership—see Agency—Partnership

Patent and Copyright Law

CHOATE, FRANCIS AND COLLINS' CASES AND MATERIALS ON PATENT LAW, INCLUDING TRADE SECRETS, COPYRIGHTS, TRADEMARKS, Third Edition, 1009 pages, 1987. (Casebook)

MILLER AND DAVIS' INTELLECTUAL PROPERTY—PATENTS, TRADEMARKS AND COPYRIGHT IN A NUTSHELL, Second Edition, 437 pages, 1990. Softcover. (Text)

NIMMER, MARCUS, MYERS AND NIMMER'S CASES AND MATERIALS ON COPYRIGHT AND OTHER ASPECTS OF ENTERTAINMENT LITIGA-

Patent and Copyright Law—Cont'd

TION ILLUSTRATED—INCLUDING UNFAIR COMPETITION, DEFAMATION AND PRIVACY, Fourth Edition, Approximately 1,000 pages, April, 1991 Pub. (Casebook)

Products Liability

FISCHER AND POWERS' CASES AND MATERIALS ON PRODUCTS LIABILITY, 685 pages, 1988. Teacher's Manual available. (Casebook)

NOEL AND PHILLIPS' CASES ON PRODUCTS LIABILITY, Second Edition, 821 pages, 1982. (Casebook)

PHILLIPS' PRODUCTS LIABILITY IN A NUTSHELL, Third Edition, 307 pages, 1988. Softcover. (Text)

Professional Responsibility

ARONSON, DEVINE AND FISCH'S PROBLEMS, CASES AND MATERIALS IN PROFESSIONAL RESPONSIBILITY, 745 pages, 1985. Teacher's Manual available. (Casebook)

ARONSON AND WECKSTEIN'S PROFESSIONAL RESPONSIBILITY IN A NUTSHELL, Second Edition, approximately 500 pages, April, 1991 Pub. Softcover. (Text)

MELLINKOFF'S THE CONSCIENCE OF A LAWYER, 304 pages, 1973. (Text)

PIRSIG AND KIRWIN'S CASES AND MATERIALS ON PROFESSIONAL RESPONSIBILITY, Fourth Edition, 603 pages, 1984. Teacher's Manual available. (Casebook)

ROTUNDA'S BLACK LETTER ON PROFESSIONAL RESPONSIBILITY, Second Edition, 414 pages, 1988. Softcover. (Review)

SCHWARTZ AND WYDICK'S PROBLEMS IN LEGAL ETHICS, Second Edition, 341 pages, 1988. (Coursebook)

SELECTED STATUTES, RULES AND STANDARDS ON THE LEGAL PROFESSION. Softcover. 678 pages, 1990.

SMITH AND MALLEN'S PREVENTING LEGAL MALPRACTICE, 264 pages, 1989. Reprint from Mallen and Smith's Legal Malpractice, Third Edition. (Text)

SUTTON AND DZIENKOWSKI'S CASES AND MATERIALS ON PROFESSIONAL RESPONSIBILITY FOR LAWYERS, 839 pages, 1989. Teacher's Manual available. (Casebook)

WOLFRAM'S HORNBOOK ON MODERN LEGAL ETHICS, Student Edition, 1120 pages, 1986. (Text)

Property—see also Real Estate Transactions, Land Use, Trusts and Estates

BERNHARDT'S BLACK LETTER ON PROPERTY, 318 pages, 1983. Softcover. (Review)

BERNHARDT'S REAL PROPERTY IN A NUTSHELL, Second Edition, 448 pages, 1981. Softcover. (Text)

BOYER, HOVENKAMP AND KURTZ' THE LAW OF PROPERTY, AN INTRODUCTORY SURVEY, Fourth Edition, approximately 640 pages, April, 1991 Pub. (Text)

BROWDER, CUNNINGHAM, NELSON, STOEBUCK AND WHITMAN'S CASES ON BASIC PROPERTY LAW, Fifth Edition, 1386 pages, 1989. Teacher's Manual available. (Casebook)

BRUCE, ELY AND BOSTICK'S CASES AND MATERIALS ON MODERN PROPERTY LAW, Second Edition, 953 pages, 1989. Teacher's Manual available. (Casebook)

BURKE'S PERSONAL PROPERTY IN A NUTSHELL, 322 pages, 1983. Softcover. (Text)

CUNNINGHAM, STOEBUCK AND WHITMAN'S HORNBOOK ON THE LAW OF PROPERTY, Student Edition, 916 pages, 1984, with 1987 pocket part. (Text)

DONAHUE, KAUPER AND MARTIN'S CASES ON PROPERTY, Second Edition, 1362 pages, 1983. Teacher's Manual available. (Casebook)

HILL'S LANDLORD AND TENANT LAW IN A NUTSHELL, Second Edition, 311 pages, 1986. Softcover. (Text)

KURTZ AND HOVENKAMP'S CASES AND MATERIALS ON AMERICAN PROPERTY LAW, 1296 pages, 1987. Teacher's Manual available. (Casebook) 1988 Supplement.

MOYNIHAN'S INTRODUCTION TO REAL PROPERTY, Second Edition, 239 pages, 1988. (Text)

Psychiatry, Law and

REISNER AND SLOBOGIN'S LAW AND THE MENTAL HEALTH SYSTEM, CIVIL AND CRIMINAL ASPECTS, Second Edition, 1117 pages, 1990. (Casebook)

Real Estate Transactions

BRUCE'S REAL ESTATE FINANCE IN A NUT-SHELL, Second Edition, 262 pages, 1985. Softcover. (Text)

MAXWELL, RIESENFELD, HETLAND AND WARREN'S CASES ON CALIFORNIA SECURITY TRANSACTIONS IN LAND, Third Edition, 728 pages, 1984. (Casebook)

NELSON AND WHITMAN'S BLACK LETTER ON LAND TRANSACTIONS AND FINANCE, Second Edition, 466 pages, 1988. Softcover. (Review)

NELSON AND WHITMAN'S CASES ON REAL ESTATE TRANSFER, FINANCE AND DEVELOPMENT, Third Edition, 1184 pages, 1987. (Casebook)

NELSON AND WHITMAN'S HORNBOOK ON REAL ESTATE FINANCE LAW, Second Edition, 941 pages, 1985 with 1989 pocket part. (Text)

Regulated Industries—see also Mass Communication Law, Banking Law

GELLHORN AND PIERCE'S REGULATED INDUSTRIES IN A NUTSHELL, Second Edition, 389 pages, 1987. Softcover. (Text)

MORGAN, HARRISON AND VERKUIL'S CASES AND MATERIALS ON ECONOMIC REGULATION OF BUSINESS, Second Edition, 666 pages, 1985. (Casebook)

Remedies

DOBBS' HORNBOOK ON REMEDIES, 1067 pages, 1973. (Text)

DOBBS' PROBLEMS IN REMEDIES. 137 pages, 1974. Teacher's Manual available. Softcover. (Coursebook)

DOBBYN'S INJUNCTIONS IN A NUTSHELL, 264 pages, 1974. Softcover. (Text)

FRIEDMAN'S CONTRACT REMEDIES IN A NUTSHELL, 323 pages, 1981. Softcover. (Text)

LEAVELL, LOVE AND NELSON'S CASES AND MATERIALS ON EQUITABLE REMEDIES, RESTITUTION AND DAMAGES, Fourth Edition, 1111 pages, 1986. Teacher's Manual available. (Casebook)

MCCORMICK'S HORNBOOK ON DAMAGES, 811 pages, 1935. (Text)

O'CONNELL'S REMEDIES IN A NUTSHELL, Second Edition, 320 pages, 1985. Softcover. (Text)

SCHOENBROD, MACBETH, LEVINE AND JUNG'S CASES AND MATERIALS ON REMEDIES: PUBLIC AND PRIVATE, 848 pages, 1990. Teacher's Manual available. (Casebook)

YORK, BAUMAN AND RENDLEMAN'S CASES AND MATERIALS ON REMEDIES, Fourth Edition, 1029 pages, 1985. Teacher's Manual available. (Casebook)

Sea, Law of

SOHN AND GUSTAFSON'S THE LAW OF THE SEA IN A NUTSHELL, 264 pages, 1984. Softcover. (Text)

Securities Regulation

HAZEN'S HORNBOOK ON THE LAW OF SECURITIES REGULATION, Second Edition, Student Edition, 1082 pages, 1990. (Text)

RATNER'S SECURITIES REGULATION IN A NUTSHELL, Third Edition, 316 pages, 1988. Softcover. (Text)

RATNER AND HAZEN'S SECURITIES REGULATION: CASES AND MATERIALS, Fourth Edition, approximately 1,075 pages, 1991. (Casebook) Problems and Sample Documents Supplement.

Statutory Supplement. *See Securities Regulation, Selected Statutes*

SECURITIES REGULATION, SELECTED STATUTES, RULES, AND FORMS. Softcover. Approximately 1,300 pages, 1991.

Social Legislation—see Workers' Compensation

Sports Law

SCHUBERT, SMITH AND TRENTADUE'S SPORTS LAW, 395 pages, 1986. (Text)

Tax Practice and Procedure

GARBIS, STRUNTZ AND RUBIN'S CASES AND MATERIALS ON TAX PROCEDURE AND TAX FRAUD, Second Edition, 687 pages, 1987. (Casebook)

MORGAN'S TAX PROCEDURE AND TAX FRAUD IN A NUTSHELL, 400 pages, 1990. Softcover. (Text)

Taxation—Corporate

KAHN AND GANN'S CORPORATE TAXATION, Third Edition, 980 pages, 1989. Teacher's Manual available. (Casebook)

Taxation—Corporate—Cont'd

WEIDENBRUCH AND BURKE'S FEDERAL INCOME TAXATION OF CORPORATIONS AND STOCKHOLDERS IN A NUTSHELL, Third Edition, 309 pages, 1989. Softcover. (Text)

Taxation—Estate & Gift—see also Estate Planning, Trusts and Estates

MCNULTY'S FEDERAL ESTATE AND GIFT TAXATION IN A NUTSHELL, Fourth Edition, 496 pages, 1989. Softcover. (Text)

PENNELL'S CASES AND MATERIALS ON INCOME TAXATION OF TRUSTS, ESTATES, GRANTORS AND BENEFICIARIES, 460 pages, 1987. Teacher's Manual available. (Casebook)

Taxation—Individual

DODGE'S THE LOGIC OF TAX, 343 pages, 1989. Softcover. (Text)

GUNN AND WARD'S CASES, TEXT AND PROBLEMS ON FEDERAL INCOME TAXATION, Second Edition, 835 pages, 1988. Teacher's Manual available. (Casebook) 1990 Supplement.

HUDSON AND LIND'S BLACK LETTER ON FEDERAL INCOME TAXATION, Third Edition, 406 pages, 1990. Softcover. (Review)

KRAGEN AND MCNULTY'S CASES AND MATERIALS ON FEDERAL INCOME TAXATION—INDIVIDUALS, CORPORATIONS, PARTNERSHIPS, Fourth Edition, 1287 pages, 1985. (Casebook)

MCNULTY'S FEDERAL INCOME TAXATION OF INDIVIDUALS IN A NUTSHELL, Fourth Edition, 503 pages, 1988. Softcover. (Text)

POSIN'S HORNBOOK ON FEDERAL INCOME TAXATION, Student Edition, 491 pages, 1983, with 1989 pocket part. (Text)

ROSE AND CHOMMIE'S HORNBOOK ON FEDERAL INCOME TAXATION, Third Edition, 923 pages, 1988, with 1989 pocket part. (Text)

SELECTED FEDERAL TAXATION STATUTES AND REGULATIONS. Softcover. 1558 pages, 1991.

SOLOMON AND HESCH'S PROBLEMS, CASES AND MATERIALS ON FEDERAL INCOME TAXATION OF INDIVIDUALS, 1068 pages, 1987. Teacher's Manual available. (Casebook)

Taxation—International

DOERNBERG'S INTERNATIONAL TAXATION IN A NUTSHELL, 325 pages, 1989. Softcover.

(Text)

KAPLAN'S FEDERAL TAXATION OF INTERNATIONAL TRANSACTIONS: PRINCIPLES, PLANNING AND POLICY, 635 pages, 1988. (Casebook)

Taxation—Partnership

BERGER AND WIEDENBECK'S CASES AND MATERIALS ON PARTNERSHIP TAXATION, 788 pages, 1989. Teacher's Manual available. (Casebook)

BISHOP AND BROOKS' FEDERAL PARTNERSHIP TAXATION: A GUIDE TO THE LEADING CASES, STATUTES, AND REGULATIONS, 545 pages, 1990. Softcover. (Text)

Taxation—State & Local

GELFAND AND SALSICH'S STATE AND LOCAL TAXATION AND FINANCE IN A NUTSHELL, 309 pages, 1986. Softcover. (Text)

HELLERSTEIN AND HELLERSTEIN'S CASES AND MATERIALS ON STATE AND LOCAL TAXATION, Fifth Edition, 1071 pages, 1988. (Casebook)

Torts—see also Products Liability

CHRISTIE AND MEEKS' CASES AND MATERIALS ON THE LAW OF TORTS, Second Edition, 1264 pages, 1990. (Casebook)

DOBBS' TORTS AND COMPENSATION—PERSONAL ACCOUNTABILITY AND SOCIAL RESPONSIBILITY FOR INJURY, 955 pages, 1985. Teacher's Manual available. (Casebook) 1990 Supplement.

KEETON, KEETON, SARGENTICH AND STEINER'S CASES AND MATERIALS ON TORT AND ACCIDENT LAW, Second Edition, 1318 pages, 1989. (Casebook)

KIONKA'S BLACK LETTER ON TORTS, 339 pages, 1988. Softcover. (Review)

KIONKA'S TORTS IN A NUTSHELL: INJURIES TO PERSONS AND PROPERTY, 434 pages, 1977. Softcover. (Text)

MALONE'S TORTS IN A NUTSHELL: INJURIES TO FAMILY, SOCIAL AND TRADE RELATIONS, 358 pages, 1979. Softcover. (Text)

PROSSER AND KEETON'S HORNBOOK ON TORTS, Fifth Edition, Student Edition, 1286 pages, 1984 with 1988 pocket part. (Text)

ROBERTSON, POWERS AND ANDERSON'S CASES

Torts—Cont'd

AND MATERIALS ON TORTS, 932 pages, 1989. Teacher's Manual available. (Casebook)

Trade Regulation—see also Antitrust, Regulated Industries

MCMANIS' UNFAIR TRADE PRACTICES IN A NUTSHELL, Second Edition, 464 pages, 1988. Softcover. (Text)

OPPENHEIM, WESTON, MAGGS AND SCHECHTER'S CASES AND MATERIALS ON UNFAIR TRADE PRACTICES AND CONSUMER PROTECTION, Fourth Edition, 1038 pages, 1983. Teacher's Manual available. (Casebook) 1986 Supplement.

SCHECHTER'S BLACK LETTER ON UNFAIR TRADE PRACTICES, 272 pages, 1986. Softcover. (Review)

Trial and Appellate Advocacy—see also Civil Procedure

APPELLATE ADVOCACY, HANDBOOK OF, Second Edition, 182 pages, 1986. Softcover. (Text)

BERGMAN'S TRIAL ADVOCACY IN A NUTSHELL, Second Edition, 354 pages, 1989. Softcover. (Text)

BINDER AND BERGMAN'S FACT INVESTIGATION: FROM HYPOTHESIS TO PROOF, 354 pages, 1984. Teacher's Manual available. (Coursebook)

CARLSON AND IMWINKELRIED'S DYNAMICS OF TRIAL PRACTICE: PROBLEMS AND MATERIALS, 414 pages, 1989. Teacher's Manual available. (Coursebook) 1990 Supplement.

DESSEM'S PRETRIAL LITIGATION: LAW, POLICY AND PRACTICE, Approximately 615 pages, March, 1991 Pub. Softcover. (Coursebook)

GOLDBERG'S THE FIRST TRIAL (WHERE DO I SIT? WHAT DO I SAY?) IN A NUTSHELL, 396 pages, 1982. Softcover. (Text)

HAYDOCK, HERR, AND STEMPEL'S FUNDAMENTALS OF PRE-TRIAL LITIGATION, 768 pages, 1985. Softcover. Teacher's Manual available. (Coursebook)

HAYDOCK AND SONSTENG'S TRIAL: THEORIES, TACTICS, TECHNIQUES, 711 pages, 1991. Softcover. (Text)

HEGLAND'S TRIAL AND PRACTICE SKILLS IN A NUTSHELL, 346 pages, 1978. Softcover.

(Text)

HORNSTEIN'S APPELLATE ADVOCACY IN A NUTSHELL, 325 pages, 1984. Softcover. (Text)

JEANS' HANDBOOK ON TRIAL ADVOCACY, Student Edition, 473 pages, 1975. Softcover. (Text)

LISNEK AND KAUFMAN'S DEPOSITIONS: PROCEDURE, STRATEGY AND TECHNIQUE, Law School and CLE Edition. 250 pages, 1990. Softcover. (Text)

MARTINEAU'S CASES AND MATERIALS ON APPELLATE PRACTICE AND PROCEDURE, 565 pages, 1987. (Casebook)

NOLAN'S CASES AND MATERIALS ON TRIAL PRACTICE, 518 pages, 1981. (Casebook)

SONSTENG, HAYDOCK AND BOYD'S THE TRIALBOOK: A TOTAL SYSTEM FOR PREPARATION AND PRESENTATION OF A CASE, 404 pages, 1984. Softcover. (Coursebook)

WHARTON, HAYDOCK AND SONSTENG'S CALIFORNIA CIVIL TRIALBOOK, Law School and CLE Edition. 148 pages, 1990. Softcover. (Text)

Trusts and Estates

ATKINSON'S HORNBOOK ON WILLS, Second Edition, 975 pages, 1953. (Text)

AVERILL'S UNIFORM PROBATE CODE IN A NUTSHELL, Second Edition, 454 pages, 1987. Softcover. (Text)

BOGERT'S HORNBOOK ON TRUSTS, Sixth Edition, Student Edition, 794 pages, 1987. (Text)

CLARK, LUSKY AND MURPHY'S CASES AND MATERIALS ON GRATUITOUS TRANSFERS, Third Edition, 970 pages, 1985. (Casebook)

DODGE'S WILLS, TRUSTS AND ESTATE PLANNING–LAW AND TAXATION, CASES AND MATERIALS, 665 pages, 1988. (Casebook)

KURTZ' PROBLEMS, CASES AND OTHER MATERIALS ON FAMILY ESTATE PLANNING, 853 pages, 1983. Teacher's Manual available. (Casebook)

MCGOVERN'S CASES AND MATERIALS ON WILLS, TRUSTS AND FUTURE INTERESTS: AN INTRODUCTION TO ESTATE PLANNING, 750 pages, 1983. (Casebook)

Trusts and Estates—Cont'd

MCGOVERN, KURTZ AND REIN'S HORNBOOK ON WILLS, TRUSTS AND ESTATES–INCLUDING TAXATION AND FUTURE INTERESTS, 996 pages, 1988. (Text)

MENNELL'S WILLS AND TRUSTS IN A NUT-SHELL, 392 pages, 1979. Softcover. (Text)

SIMES' HORNBOOK ON FUTURE INTERESTS, Second Edition, 355 pages, 1966. (Text)

TURANO AND RADIGAN'S HORNBOOK ON NEW YORK ESTATE ADMINISTRATION, 676 pages, 1986. (Text)

UNIFORM PROBATE CODE, OFFICIAL TEXT WITH COMMENTS. 615 pages, 1989. Soft-cover.

WAGGONER'S FUTURE INTERESTS IN A NUT-SHELL, 361 pages, 1981. Softcover. (Text)

WATERBURY'S MATERIALS ON TRUSTS AND ES-TATES, 1039 pages, 1986. Teacher's Manu-al available. (Casebook)

Water Law—see also Energy and Natural Resources Law, Environmental Law

GETCHES' WATER LAW IN A NUTSHELL, Sec-ond Edition, 459 pages, 1990. Softcover.

(Text)

SAX AND ABRAMS' LEGAL CONTROL OF WATER RESOURCES: CASES AND MATERIALS, 941 pages, 1986. (Casebook)

TRELEASE AND GOULD'S CASES AND MATERI-ALS ON WATER LAW, Fourth Edition, 816 pages, 1986. (Casebook)

Wills—see Trusts and Estates

Women and the Law—see also Employ-ment Discrimination

KAY'S TEXT, CASES AND MATERIALS ON SEX–BASED DISCRIMINATION, Third Edition, 1001 pages, 1988. (Casebook) 1990 Supplement.

THOMAS' SEX DISCRIMINATION IN A NUT-SHELL, 399 pages, 1982. Softcover. (Text)

Workers' Compensation

HOOD, HARDY AND LEWIS' WORKERS' COM-PENSATION AND EMPLOYEE PROTECTION LAWS IN A NUTSHELL, Second Edition, 361 pages, 1990. Softcover. (Text)

MALONE, PLANT AND LITTLE'S CASES ON WORKERS' COMPENSATION AND EMPLOYMENT RIGHTS, Second Edition, 951 pages, 1980. Teacher's Manual available. (Casebook)

STATE AND FEDERAL ADMINISTRATIVE LAW

By

Arthur Earl Bonfield

John Murray Professor of Law University of Iowa

and

Michael Asimow

Professor of Law University of California, Los Angeles

AMERICAN CASEBOOK SERIES

WEST PUBLISHING CO.
ST. PAUL, MINN., 1989

COPYRIGHT © 1989 By WEST PUBLISHING CO.
                        50 West Kellogg Boulevard
                        P.O. Box 64526
                        St. Paul, MN 55164–0526

Library of Congress Cataloging-in-Publication Data

Bonfield, Arthur Earl.
    State and federal administrative law / by
Arthur Earl Bonfield and Michael R. Asimow.
        p.   cm. — (American casebook series)
    Includes index.
    ISBN 0–314–50388–9
    1. Administrative law—United States—Cases.
    2. Administrative law—United States—States—Cases.   I. Asimow,
Michael.   II. Title.   III. Series.
    KF5402.A4B66   1989
    342.73'06—dc19
    [347.3026]   88–36679
                                                            CIP

        (B. & A.) State & Fed'l Admin.Law ACB
        1st Reprint—1991

To
Doris and Lauren
and
Bobbi, Danny, Ian, Paul, Hillary and Courtney

*

Preface

There are many other administrative law coursebooks already on the market. What new contribution could another book possibly make?

This book is different from the other books in at least one major respect. That difference is immediately apparent from the name of the book: STATE AND FEDERAL ADMINISTRATIVE LAW. All of the other books concentrate primarily or exclusively on federal law. They either ignore state administrative law entirely or mention it only in a superficial way. This book, on the other hand, has committed itself to take state administrative law as seriously as federal law and to treat both as an integrated whole.

We believe that students will benefit from a sustained exposure to state administrative law and to continuing comparisons between state and federal law. As further explained in § 1.3, *infra,* we see two important advantages from an integrated study of state and federal administrative law.

First, there is much to be learned from a study of state law that cannot be learned from a study of federal law alone. State and federal law often differ; and the circumstances surrounding state and federal administrative processes often differ. These differences add a dimension to the study of administrative law that cannot be understood or evaluated by studying either state or federal law or their respective administrative processes separately. The reason for this is that a comparative state-federal approach to the study of our subject suggests problems or solutions to problems in the administrative process that are not otherwise apparent.

Second, most law students will deal with state administrative agencies in their practice more frequently than with federal agencies. The reason for this is that the largest *number* of licensing problems, public contract problems, business regulatory problems, and benefit problems faced by individuals and entities in this country are a product of state or local agency action rather than federal agency action. As a result, for most students there is a clear professional advantage to a study of state law as well as federal law.

In another respect this book is more traditional. It is a book about administrative procedure. Unlike some other books in the field, it does not attempt to combine administrative procedure with a study of one or more regulated industries. Instead, the goal of this book is to teach the administrative process: adjudication, rulemaking, political controls of agency action, freedom of information, and judicial review. The substantive law that agencies apply is left for other courses such as environmental law, labor law, unfair trade practices, or the like.

The straight-procedure approach utilized in this book is based on our belief that the processes of all agencies have enough in common to make the study of administrative law meaningful. This approach makes it possible to organize the course much more clearly and to use all available classroom hours for study of traditional administrative process subjects.

Of course, the disadvantage of the straight-procedure approach is that students may sometimes feel that the course is too theoretical, that it appears to jump around between cases that describe wildly dissimilar agencies and functions, and that it does not adequately take account of the important relationship between procedure and substantive law.

To offset this disadvantage, our book makes extensive use of problems and questions. For the most part, the problems are practical and professionally-oriented. They take the student into the law office or into an agency where he or she must deal with a client with a particular problem in a specific context. Problems can help to bring the subject down to earth, root it in real experience, and demonstrate the important relationship between substantive law and procedure. A substantial number of questions used in this book seek also to accomplish the same result: they raise issues calculated to ensure that procedures are considered in relation to specific contexts as well as in relation to general principles.

In this book we have attempted to accomplish three other major objectives. First, we have attempted to induce our readers to engage in a "cost-benefit" examination of the procedures used by agencies. We discuss this function more fully in § 1.6, *infra*. Consequently, we have tried, throughout this book, to articulate clearly the values that administrative procedure issues place in conflict. For example, in administrative law there is frequently a struggle between such worthy values as efficiency and effectiveness of agency operation and the adequate protection of private interests. We cannot satisfy all of the demands of private parties for exhaustive procedures to protect their interests and also satisfy all of the demands of agencies for authority to act swiftly and economically so as to implement effectively and efficiently public policies mandated by the legislature. When values of this kind conflict, we have tried to force them to the surface, and to be as explicit as possible about the costs and benefits of particular procedures.

Another major theme that pervades this book is the political accountability of agencies. Throughout the book we ask whether particular procedural requirements or substantive limits imposed on agencies are likely to ensure that the agencies are responsive to the wishes of the body politic and whether there are more effective and efficient means by which to accomplish that result. We also devote a substantial portion of the book to the examination of legislative and executive techniques for checking agency action. On this subject, particularly, the states can teach some lessons to the federal government.

Finally, this book seeks to examine the mechanics of the rulemaking process in some detail and, therefore, devotes proportionately more space to that subject than do other coursebooks. This reflects our conviction that rules and the rulemaking process have become much more important during the last twenty five years than they were previously, and that there have been many recent state and federal developments in the mechanics of the rulemaking process that deserve careful examination in a current course on administrative law.

Cases and other quoted materials used in the book have been heavily edited in the interest of concise presentation. We have indicated deletions from the text of these materials by using three dots, but we have cut out citations and footnotes without any notation. In order to save space we have also refrained from using parallel citations to the many state cases used in this book, citing them only by reference to the widely available regional reporters.

ARTHUR EARL BONFIELD
MICHAEL ASIMOW

December, 1988

*

Acknowledgments

Many people helped us with this book. A number deserve special thanks. Jan Barnes of the University of Iowa Law School typed and retyped large portions of the manuscript. Her help deserves special mention and appreciation because of her tireless efforts, great attention to detail, patience, and happy disposition. Keith Dotseth and Bradley Kragel, students at the University of Iowa Law School also made significant contributions as source checkers and researchers. Rita Saavedra at the UCLA Law School contributed significant secretarial help with parts of the manuscript. Nargis Choudry, Mary O'Connell, and Janet Rich, students at the UCLA Law School, also made significant contributions as source checkers and researchers.

L. Harold Levinson of Vanderbilt Law School deserves special thanks for the many substantive suggestions and research leads he provided.

Finally, we want to thank the following publishers, authors, and journals, for their generous permission to reprint excerpts from their copyrighted publications indicated below:

(1) ABA Journal: The Lawyer's Magazine, published by the American Bar Association: Cooper, "Administrative Law: The 'Substantial Evidence' Rule," 44 A.B.A.J. 945 (1958); Segal, "The Administrative Law Judge," 62 A.B.A.J. 1424 (1976).

(2) Administrative Law Review, published by the Section of Administrative Law, American Bar Association: Minow, "Letter to President Kennedy," 15 Administrative Law Review 146 (1963); Abrams, "Administrative Law Judge Systems: The California View," 29 Administrative Law Review 487 (1977); Sullivan, "Independent Adjudication and Occupational Safety and Health Policy: A Test for Administrative Court Theory," 31 Administrative Law Review 177 (1979); Lubbers, "Federal Administrative Law Judges: A Focus on our Invisible Judiciary," 33 Administrative Law Review 109 (1981); O'Reilly, "Regaining a Confidence: Protection of Business Confidential Data Through Reform of the Freedom of Information Act," 34 Administrative Law Review 263 (1982); Stevenson, "Protecting Business Secrets Under the Freedom of Information Act: Managing Exemption 4," 34 Administrative Law Review 207 (1982); Rochvarg, "State Adoption of Federal Law—Legislative Abdication or Reasoned Policymaking," 36 Administrative Law Review 277 (1984); The Section of Administrative Law, "Restatement of Scope-of-Review Doctrine," 38 Administrative Law Review 235 (1986); Breyer, "Judicial Review of Questions of Law and Policy," 38 Administrative Law Review 363 (1986); Perritt, "Nego-

tiated Rulemaking and Administrative Law," 38 Administrative Law Review 471 (1986); Bonfield, "Chairman's Message," 40 Administrative Law Review iii (Winter 1988). Reprinted with permission from the Administrative Law Review, published by the Section of Administrative Law, American Bar Association, copyright 1963, 1977, 1979, 1981, 1982, 1984, 1986, 1988, American Bar Association.

(3) American Enterprise Institute, publisher of Regulation: Scalia, "Two Wrongs Make a Right: The Judicialization of Standardless Rulemaking," Regulation 38 July–Aug. (1977); Scalia, "Perspectives on Current Developments: On Cable T.V. and 'Lobbying' before the Agencies," Regulation 4 July–Aug. (1977); Scalia, "A Note on the Benzine Case," Regulation 27 July–Aug. (1980); Kelman, "Cost-Benefit Analysis: An Ethical Critique," Regulation 33 Jan.–Feb. (1981); Butters, Calfee, and Ippolito, "Defending Cost-Benefit Analysis," Regulation 41 Mar.–Apr. (1981); DeLong, "Defending Cost-Benefit Analysis," Regulation 39 Mar.–Apr. (1981); Scalia, "The Freedom of Information Act Has No Clothes," Regulation 15 Mar.–Apr. (1982). Copyright 1977, 1980, 1981, 1982, The American Enterprise Institute. Reprinted with permission.

(4) Center for the Study of Federalism: Levinson, "The Decline of the Legislative Veto: Federal/State Comparisons and Interactions," 17 Publius: The Journal of Federalism 115 (1987).

(5) University of Chicago Law Review: K. Davis, "A New Approach to Delegation," 36 University of Chicago Law Review 713 (1969).

(6) Cornell Law Review and Fred B. Rothman & Co.: Fuchs, "The Hearing Officer Problem," 40 Cornell L.Q. 281 (1955). Copyright 1955 by Cornell University. All rights reserved.

(7) Kenneth C. Davis, ADMINISTRATIVE LAW TREATISE (2d Ed. 1979).

(8) Environmental Law: W. Funk, "When Smoke Gets In Your Eyes: Regulatory Negotiation And The Public Interest—EPA's Woodstove Standards," 18 Environmental Law 55 (1987).

(9) Harvard Law Review: Stewart, "The Reformation of American Administrative Law," 88 Harvard Law Review 1667 (1975); Gellhorn, "Adverse Publicity by Administrative Agencies," 86 Harvard Law Review 1380 (1973). Copyright 1975, 1973, The Harvard Law Review Association.

(10) Iowa Law Review: Bonfield, "The Definition of Formal Agency Adjudication Under The Iowa Administrative Procedure Act," 63 Iowa Law Review 285 (1977).

(11) John Marshall Law Review: Ehlke, "The Privacy Act After a Decade," 18 John Marshall Law Review 829 (1985).

(12) Little Brown & Co.: A. Bonfield, STATE ADMINISTRATIVE RULE MAKING (1986); L. Jaffe, JUDICIAL CONTROL OF ADMINISTRATIVE ACTION (1965).

(13) Minnesota Law Review: Auerbach, "Administrative Rulemaking in Minnesota," 63 Minnesota Law Review 151 (1979).

(14) Northwestern University Law Review: Auerbach, "Informal Rule Making: A Proposed Relationship Between Administrative Procedures and Judicial Review," 72 Northwestern University Law Review 15 (1977).

(15) University of Pennsylvania Law Review and Fred B. Rothman & Co.: Robinson, "The Making of Administrative Policy: Another Look at Rulemaking and Adjudication and Administrative Procedure Reform," 118 University of Pennsylvania Law Review 485 (1970).

(16) Prentice Hall, Inc.: M. Weidenbaum, BUSINESS, GOVERNMENT, AND THE PUBLIC, (3rd ed. 1986). Copyright 1986, Prentice Hall, Inc. Reprinted by permission of Prentice Hall, Inc., Englewood Cliffs, N.J.

(17) Russell Sage Foundation: J. Handler, THE CONDITIONS OF DISCRETION (1986). Reprinted from THE CONDITIONS OF DISCRETION, by Joel Handler, copyright 1986, The Russell Sage Foundation. Used with permission of the Russell Sage Foundation.

(18) Virginia Law Review and Fred B. Rothman & Co.: Bonfield, "The Federal APA and State Administrative Law," 72 Virginia Law Review 297 (1986).

(19) Western New England Law Review: Zankel, "A Unified Corps of Federal Administrative Law Judges is not Needed," 6 W.N. England Law Review 723 (1984).

(20) Wisconsin Law Review: Sargentich, "The Reform of the American Administrative Process: The Contemporary Debate," Wisconsin Law Review 385 (1984); Auerbach, "Some Thoughts on the Hector Memorandum," 1960 Wisconsin Law Review 183. Copyright 1984, 1960, University of Wisconsin.

(21) Yale Law Journal and Fred B. Rothman & Co.: Handler, "Discretion in Social Welfare: The Uneasy Position in the Rule of Law," 92 Yale Law Journal 1279 (1983). Reprinted by permission of The Yale Law Journal Company and Fred B. Rothman & Co. from the Yale Law Journal, Vol. 92, p. 1270.

(22) Yale University Press: M. McCubbins, R. Noll, and B. Weingast, "Administrative Procedures as Instruments of Political Control," 3 Journal of Law Economics and Organization 243 (1987); copyright 1987, Yale University Press, reprinted with permission. J. Mashaw, BUREAUCRATIC JUSTICE (1983); copyright 1983, Yale University Press, reprinted with permission.

*

Summary of Contents

		Page
PREFACE		xxiii
ACKNOWLEDGEMENTS		xxvii
TABLE OF CASES		xliii

Chapter 1. Introduction 1

§ 1.1 Administrative Agencies and Administrative Law 1

§ 1.2 Reasons for Studying Administrative Law 2

§ 1.3 State and Federal Administrative Law 3

§ 1.4 Administrative Procedure Acts 4

§ 1.5 A Snapshot of the Administrative Process 6

§ 1.6 Costs and Benefits of Administrative Procedure and Procedural Reform 11

§ 1.7 Agency Legitimacy and Administrative Law: A Theory 14

§ 1.8 Problems 18

PART I. AGENCY PROCEDURES

Chapter 2. The Constitutional Right to a Hearing 22

§ 2.1 Hearings and Welfare Termination: Due Process and Mass Justice 24

§ 2.2 Interests Protected by Due Process: Liberty and Property 37

§ 2.3 Timing of Trial–Type Hearings 62

§ 2.4 Elements of a Hearing 76

§ 2.5 The Rulemaking–Adjudication Distinction 93

Chapter 3. Administrative Adjudication: Fundamental Problems 105

§ 3.1 Statutory Rights to a Hearing in Adjudication 106

§ 3.2 Circumventing Hearing Requirements Through Rulemaking 121

§ 3.3 The Conflict Between Institutional and Judicialized Decision–Making 131

§ 3.4 Administrative Law Judges and Decisional Independence 175

Chapter 4. The Process of Administrative Adjudication 191

§ 4.1 The Pre–Hearing Phase: Parties, Investigation and Discovery 191

§ 4.2 The Hearing Phase 209

§ 4.3 The Decision Phase: Finding Facts and Stating Reasons 219

§ 4.4 Effect of Decision: Res Judicata, Stare Decisis, Estoppel 227

Page

Chapter 5. The Relationship Between Rulemaking and Adjudication _____ 244

§ 5.1 Definition of "Rule" _____ 244
§ 5.2 Rule–Order Dichotomy: Justification _____ 254
§ 5.3 Agency Lawmaking: Advantages and Disadvantages of Rulemaking and Adjudication _____ 258
§ 5.4 Discretion to Choose Rulemaking or Adjudication _____ 261

Chapter 6. Rulemaking Procedures _____ 282

§ 6.1 The Objectives of Rulemaking Procedure _____ 282
§ 6.2 Initiating Rulemaking Proceedings _____ 286
§ 6.3 Public Participation _____ 299
§ 6.4 Good Cause Exemptions _____ 319
§ 6.5 Regulatory Analysis _____ 325
§ 6.6 Agency Decisionmakers, Ex Parte Communications, Bias, and Personal Involvement _____ 338
§ 6.7 Findings and Reasons _____ 360
§ 6.8 Exclusivity of the Agency Rulemaking Record _____ 372
§ 6.9 Publication of Rules and Deferred Effective Date _____ 379
§ 6.10 Petition for Adoption, Amendment, or Repeal of Rules _____ 388
§ 6.11 Categorical Exemptions to Rulemaking Requirements _____ 395

PART II. NONJUDICIAL CONTROL OF AGENCY ACTION

Chapter 7. Control of Agencies by the Political Branches of Government _____ 420

§ 7.1 Introduction _____ 420
§ 7.2 Defining the Scope and Limits of Agency Authority _____ 422
§ 7.3 Delegation of Legislative Power to Agencies _____ 431
§ 7.4 Delegation of Adjudicatory Power to Agencies _____ 461
§ 7.5 Legislative and Executive Controls of Agency Action _____ 478
§ 7.6 Political Control: Appraising Means _____ 531

Chapter 8. Freedom of Information and Other Open Government Laws _____ 536

§ 8.1 Freedom of Information _____ 536
§ 8.2 The Sunshine and Advisory Committee Acts _____ 554
§ 8.3 Privacy Act _____ 559

PART III. JUDICIAL REVIEW

Chapter 9. Scope of Judicial Review _____ 562

§ 9.1 Scope of Review of Agency Findings of Basic Fact _____ 562
§ 9.2 Scope of Review of Issues of Legal Interpretation _____ 586
§ 9.3 Scope of Review of Application of Law to Facts _____ 598
§ 9.4 Judicial Review Under the Arbitrary and Capricious Standard _____ 607

Page

Chapter 10. Remedies and Reviewability of Agency Decisions _____ **628**

§ 10.1 Judicial Remedies _____ 629

§ 10.2 Damage Actions as a Form of Judicial Review _____ 637

§ 10.3 Recovery of Fees _____ 659

§ 10.4 Preclusion of Judicial Review_____ 667

§ 10.5 Commitment to Agency Discretion_____ 673

Chapter 11. Standing to Seek Judicial Review and the Timing of Judicial Review _____ **683**

§ 11.1 Standing to Seek Review _____ 683

§ 11.2 Timing of Judicial Review _____ 703

Appendices

App.

A. Federal Administrative Procedure Act United States Code, Title 5 Chapter 5—Administrative Procedure_____ 742

B. Model State Administrative Procedure Act (1981) _____ 761

INDEX _____ 813

*

Table of Contents

	Page
PREFACE	xxiii
ACKNOWLEDGEMENTS	xxvii
TABLE OF CASES	xliii

Chapter 1. Introduction 1

§ 1.1 Administrative Agencies and Administrative Law 1
§ 1.2 Reasons for Studying Administrative Law 2
§ 1.3 State and Federal Administrative Law 3
§ 1.4 Administrative Procedure Acts 4
§ 1.5 A Snapshot of the Administrative Process 6
§ 1.6 Costs and Benefits of Administrative Procedure and Procedural Reform 11
§ 1.7 Agency Legitimacy and Administrative Law: A Theory ... 14
      McCubbins, Noll, Weingast, "Administrative Procedures as Instruments of Political Control" 16
§ 1.8 Problems 18

PART I. AGENCY PROCEDURES

Chapter 2. The Constitutional Right to a Hearing 22

§ 2.1 Hearings and Welfare Termination: Due Process and Mass Justice 24
      Goldberg v. Kelly 26
§ 2.2 Interests Protected by Due Process: Liberty and Property 37
    § 2.2.1 "Liberty" and "Property According to *Roth*" ... 38
        Board of Regents v. Roth 38
    § 2.2.2 Defining "Liberty" 47
        Hewitt v. Helms 47
    § 2.2.3 Defining "Property" 56
        Cleveland Board of Education v. Loudermill 56
§ 2.3 Timing of Trial–Type Hearings 62
      Mathews v. Eldridge 63
§ 2.4 Elements of a Hearing 76
      Hewitt v. Helms 77
      Walters v. National Ass'n of Radiation Survivors 83
§ 2.5 The Rulemaking–Adjudication Distinction 93
      Londoner v. Denver 94
      Bi–Metallic Inv. Co. v. State Board of Equalization 95
      Atkins v. Parker 99

	Page
Chapter 3. Administrative Adjudication: Fundamental Problems	105
§ 3.1 Statutory Rights to a Hearing in Adjudication	106
§ 3.1.1 Federal Law—Right to a Hearing Under the APA	106
City of West Chicago v. United States Nuclear Regulatory Commission	106
§ 3.1.2 Rights to a Hearing Under State Law	115
Milwaukee Metropolitan Sewerage District v. Wisconsin Department of Natural Resources	116
§ 3.2 Circumventing Hearing Requirements Through Rulemaking	121
American Airlines, Inc. v. Civil Aeronautics Board	122
§ 3.3 The Conflict Between Institutional and Judicialized Decision–Making	131
§ 3.3.1 Personal Responsibility of Decisionmakers	133
§ 3.3.2 Separation of Functions and Internal Agency Communications	141
§ 3.3.2a Constitutional Implications of Combination of Functions	142
Withrow v. Larkin	142
§ 3.3.2b Statutory Solutions to Combination of Functions	148
§ 3.3.2c Internal Agency Communications	149
§ 3.3.2d Command Influence	153
§ 3.3.2e The Principle of Necessity	153
§ 3.3.3 Bias: Personal Interest, Prejudgment, Personal Animus	153
Andrews v. Agricultural Labor Relations Board	154
§ 3.3.4 Ex Parte Contacts, Decision on the Record, and Legislative Pressure	163
Professional Air Traffic Controllers Organization (PATCO) v. Federal Labor Relations Authority (FLRA)	164
§ 3.4 Administrative Law Judges and Decisional Independence	175
§ 3.4.1 Selection and Appointment of ALJs	177
Lubbers, "Federal Administrative Law Judges: A Focus on Our Invisible Judiciary"	177
§ 3.4.2 ALJs: The Central Panel Issue	181
Segal, "The Administrative Law Judge"	181
Abrams, "Administrative Law Judge Systems: The California View"	182
Zankel, "A Unified Corps of Federal Administrative Law Judges is not Needed"	184
§ 3.4.3 ALJs: The Administrative Court Issue	188
Minow, Letter to President Kennedy	186
Auerbach, "Some Thoughts on the Hector Memorandum"	187

Page

§ 3.4 Administrative Law Judges and Decisional Independence—Continued

Sullivan, "Independent Adjudication and Occupational Safety and Health Policy: A Test for Administrative Court Theory" 189

Chapter 4. The Process of Administrative Adjudication 191

§ 4.1 The Pre–Hearing Phase: Parties, Investigation and Discovery 191

§ 4.1.1 Parties and Intervention 191

§ 4.1.2 Investigation and Discovery: An Agency's Power to Obtain Information 196

Appeal of FTC Line of Business Report Litigation 197

§ 4.2 The Hearing Phase 209

§ 4.2.1 Right to Closed or Open Hearing 209

§ 4.2.2 Evidence at the Hearing 209

Trujillo v. Employment Security Commission 209

§ 4.2.3 Official Notice 212

Franz v. Board of Medical Quality Assurance ... 213

§ 4.3 The Decision Phase: Finding Facts and Stating Reasons 219

Matlovich v. Secretary of the Air Force 219

§ 4.4 Effect of Decision: Res Judicata, Stare Decisis, Estoppel 227

§ 4.4.1 Res Judicata 227

University of Tennessee v. Elliott 227

§ 4.4.2 Consistent Decisionmaking: Stare Decisis 234

International Union, United Automobile Workers of America v. NLRB 234

§ 4.4.3 Estoppel 237

Foote's Dixie Dandy, Inc. v. McHenry 237

Chapter 5. The Relationship Between Rulemaking and Adjudication 244

§ 5.1 Definition of "Rule" 244

Acus, A Guide to Federal Agency Rulemaking 244

Anaconda Co. v. Ruckelshaus 251

§ 5.2 Rule–Order Dichotomy: Justification 254

§ 5.3 Agency Lawmaking: Advantages and Disadvantages of Rulemaking and Adjudication 258

§ 5.4 Discretion to Choose Rulemaking or Adjudication 261

NLRB v. Bell Aerospace Co., Division of Textron, Inc. 261

Megdal v. Oregon State Board of Dental Examiners 267

National Labor Relations Board v. Wyman–Gordon Co. 274

Chapter 6. Rulemaking Procedures 282

§ 6.1 The Objectives of Rulemaking Procedure 282

Bonfield, State Administrative Rule Making 282

§ 6.2 Initiating Rulemaking Proceedings 286

§ 6.2.1 Formulation of Proposed Rules 286

Page

§ 6.2   Initiating Rulemaking Proceedings—Continued
                Perritt, "Negotiated Rulemaking and Administra-
                    tive Law" _____ 288
                W. Funk, "When Smoke Gets In Your Eyes: Regu-
                    latory Negotiation and the Public Interest—
                    EPA's Woodstove Standards" _____ 290
         § 6.2.2   Notice of Proposed Rulemaking _____ 291
                Acus, a Guide to Federal Agency Rulemaking ____ 291
§ 6.3   Public Participation _____ 299
         § 6.3.1   Informal and Hybrid Rulemaking _____ 299
         § 6.3.2   Formal Rulemaking Requirements _____ 307
                United States v. Florida East Coast Railway Co. 307
         § 6.3.3   Judicial Imposition of Additional Procedures in
                    Rulemaking _____ 312
                Vermont Yankee Nuclear Power Corp. v. Natural
                    Resources Defense Council, Inc. [NRDC] _____ 312
§ 6.4   Good Cause Exemptions _____ 319
         ACUS, a Guide to Federal Agency Rulemaking _____ 319
§ 6.5   Regulatory Analysis _____ 325
         Kelman, "Cost–Benefit Analysis: An Ethical Critique" __ 332
§ 6.6   Agency Decisionmakers, Ex Parte Communications, Bias,
         and Personal Involvement _____ 338
         § 6.6.1   Ex Parte Communications and Political Influ-
                    ence in Rulemaking _____ 338
                Home Box Office, Inc. v. FCC _____ 339
                Sierra Club v. Costle _____ 348
         § 6.6.2   Role of Agency Heads _____ 356
         § 6.6.3   Bias of Agency Heads _____ 357
                Association of National Advertisers v. FTC ____ 357
§ 6.7   Findings and Reasons _____ 360
         California Hotel & Motel Ass'n v. Industrial Welfare Com'n 360
         Iowa Bankers Ass'n v. Iowa Credit Union Dept. _____ 370
§ 6.8   Exclusivity of the Agency Rulemaking Record _____ 372
§ 6.9   Publication of Rules and Deferred Effective Date _____ 379
         United States v. Gavrilovic _____ 381
§ 6.10   Petition for Adoption, Amendment, or Repeal of Rules 388
         WWHT, Inc. v. F.C.C. _____ 391
§ 6.11   Categorical Exemptions to Rulemaking Requirements __ 395
         § 6.11.1   Proprietary Matters _____ 396
                Humana of South Carolina v. Califano _____ 397
         § 6.11.2   Military and Foreign Affairs Functions _____ 400
         § 6.11.3   Agency Management and Personnel _____ 400
         § 6.11.4   Procedural Rules _____ 401
                United States Department of Labor v. Kast Metals
                    Corp. _____ 401
         § 6.11.5   Interpretive Rules and Policy Statements _____ 405
                § 6.11.5a Interpretive Rules _____ 405
                    Chamber of Commerce v. Osha _____ 405

§ 6.11 Categorical Exemptions to Rulemaking Requirements—Continued

§ 6.11.5b Policy Statements 411
Mada–Luna v. Fitzpatrick 411

PART II. NONJUDICIAL CONTROL OF AGENCY ACTION

Chapter 7. Control of Agencies by the Political Branches of Government 420
§ 7.1 Introduction 420
§ 7.2 Defining the Scope and Limits of Agency Authority 422
Kent v. Dulles 423
Boreali v. Axelrod 425
§ 7.3 Delegation of Legislative Power to Agencies 431
§ 7.3.1 The Nondelegation Doctrine and Federal Agencies 431
§ 7.3.1a From Field to the New Deal 432
§ 7.3.1b From the New Deal to the Present 436
§ 7.3.1c Revival of the Delegation Doctrine 437
Amalgamated Meat Cutters and Butcher Workmen v. Connally 437
Industrial Union Department, AFL–CIO v. American Petroleum Institute 440
§ 7.3.2 The Non–Delegation Doctrine and State Agencies 451
Thygesen v. Callahan 451
Warren v. Marion County 454
§ 7.4 Delegation of Adjudicatory Power to Agencies 461
§ 7.4.1 Generally 461
Commodity Futures Trading Commission v. Schor 462
§ 7.4.2 Delegation of Authority to Penalize or Fine.. 471
§ 7.4.2a Authority to Decide Whether Conduct Is Criminal 471
United States v. Grimaud 471
§ 7.4.2b Power of Agencies to Adjudicate Penalties 474
Waukegan v. Pollution Control Board 474
§ 7.5 Legislative and Executive Controls of Agency Action ... 478
§ 7.5.1 Desirability of Legislative and Executive Review of Agency Action 478
Bonfield, State Administrative Rule Making 478
§ 7.5.2 Legislative Veto: Introduction 479
Levinson, "The Decline of the Legislative Veto: Federal/State Comparisons and Interactions" 480
§ 7.5.3 Legislative Veto: Constitutional Problems 482
Immigration And Naturalization Service [INS] v. Chadha 482

§ 7.5   Legislative and Executive Controls of Agency Action—
         Continued
                   Bonfield, State Administrative Rule Making 495
         § 7.5.4   Other Legislative Controls 498
         § 7.5.5   Executive Control of Agency Action 502
         § 7.5.6   Executive Oversight and the Appointments
                    Power 508
                    § 7.5.6a   The Chief Executive's Appointment
                                Power 509
                    § 7.5.6b   The Chief Executive's Discharge
                                Power 512
                                Morrison v. Olson 513
§ 7.6   Political Control: Appraising Means 531
         *McCubbins, Noll, Weingast, "Administrative Procedures as
         Instruments of Political Control"* 531

**Chapter 8.   Freedom of Information and Other Open Gov-
               ernment Laws** **536**
§ 8.1   Freedom of Information 536
         § 8.1.1   FOIA Exemptions 539
                    *National Labor Relations Board v. Sears, Roe-
                    buck & Co.* 539
         § 8.1.2   Confidential Private Information: § 552(b)(4)   547
                    Chrysler Corporation v. Brown 547
§ 8.2   The Sunshine and Advisory Committee Acts 554
         § 8.2.1   Sunshine Act 554
         § 8.2.2   Federal Advisory Committee Act (FACA) 557
§ 8.3   Privacy Act 559

                PART III.   JUDICIAL REVIEW

Chapter 9.   Scope of Judicial Review **562**
§ 9.1   Scope of Review of Agency Findings of Basic Fact 562
         § 9.1.1   The Substantial Evidence and Clearly Errone-
                    ous Tests 564
                    Universal Camera Corp. v. NLRB 564
                    Defries v. Association of Owners, 999 Wilder 569
         § 9.1.2   Independent Judgment and De Novo Review   577
                    § 9.1.2a   Federal Decisions 577
                    § 9.1.2b   State Decisions 581
                                Frink v. Prod 583
§ 9.2   Scope of Review of Issues of Legal Interpretation 586
         Madison v. Alaska Dept. of Fish and Game 587
         Chevron U.S.A., Inc. v. Natural Resources Defense Council   589
§ 9.3   Scope of Review of Application of Law to Facts 598
         McPherson v. Employment Division 598
§ 9.4   Judicial Review Under the Arbitrary and Capricious
         Standard 607

Page

§ 9.4   Judicial Review Under the Arbitrary and Capricious
        Standard—Continued
        *Motor Vehicle Manufacturers Ass'n v. State Farm Mutual
        Automobile Ins. Co.* _____ 607
        Borden, Inc. v. Commissioner of Public Health _____ 615

**Chapter 10. Remedies and Reviewability of Agency Deci-
        sions** _____ **628**
§ 10.1 Judicial Remedies _____ 629
        § 10.1.1 Judicial Jurisdiction _____ 629
        § 10.1.2 Cause of Action and Remedy _____ 633
                  § 10.1.2a Injunction and Declaratory Judg-
                          ment _____ 633
                  § 10.1.2b Mandamus _____ 634
                  § 10.1.2c Certiorari _____ 636
                  § 10.1.2d Other Writs _____ 637
§ 10.2 Damage Actions as a Form of Judicial Review _____ 637
        § 10.2.1 Tort Liability of Government _____ 638
                  § 10.2.1a The Federal Tort Claims Act _____ 638
                  § 10.2.1b State and Local Government Liabili-
                          ty _____ 640
                          *Commonwealth of Kentucky, Depart-
                          ment of Banking and Securities v.
                          Brown* _____ 640
        § 10.2.2 Tort Liability of Officials _____ 644
                  § 10.2.2a Bases of Liability _____ 644
                  § 10.2.2b Immunity From Liability _____ 646
                          Butz v. Economou _____ 647
§ 10.3 Recovery of Fees_____ 659
        *Pennsylvania v. Delaware Valley Citizens' Council for Clean
        Air* _____ 659
§ 10.4 Preclusion of Judicial Review _____ 667
        Bowen v. Michigan Academy of Family Physicians _____ 667
§ 10.5 Commitment to Agency Discretion _____ 673
        *Heckler v. Chaney*_____ 673

**Chapter 11. Standing to Seek Judicial Review and the Tim-
        ing of Judicial Review** _____ **683**
§ 11.1 Standing to Seek Review_____ 683
        § 11.1.1 Standing to Seek Review in the Federal
                  Courts: Historical Introduction _____ 684
        § 11.1.2 Injury in Fact and Zone of Interest Tests_____ 686
                  *Association of Data Processing Service Orgs. v.
                  Camp* _____ 686
                  Iowa Bankers Ass'n v. Iowa Credit Union Dept. 689
        § 11.1.3 Causal Connection and Public Actions _____ 693
                  *Allen v. Wright*_____ 693
§ 11.2 Timing of Judicial Review _____ 703

Page

§ 11.2   Timing of Judicial Review—Continued
         § 11.2.1   Introduction _____ 703
         § 11.2.2   The Final Order Rule _____ 705
                    Federal Trade Commission v. Standard Oil Co. of
                    California _____ 705
         § 11.2.3   Ripeness _____ 711
                    Abbott Laboratories v. Gardner _____ 711
         § 11.2.4   Exhaustion of Administrative Remedies _____ 719
                    Myers v. Bethlehem Shipbuilding Corp. _____ 719
                    New Jersey Civil Service Ass'n (NJCSA) v. State 720
         § 11.2.5   Primary Jurisdiction _____ 729
                    Nader v. Allegheny Airlines, Inc. _____ 729
                    Foree v. Crown Central Petroleum Corp. _____ 734

Appendices

App.

A.   Federal Administrative Procedure Act United States Code,
     Title 5 Chapter 5—Administrative Procedure _____ 742
B.   Model State Administrative Procedure Act (1981) _____ 761
INDEX _____ 813

Table of Cases

The principal cases are in bold type. Cases cited or discussed in the text are roman type. References are to pages. Cases cited in principal cases and within other quoted materials are not included.

Abbott Laboratories v. Gardner, 711, 714, 715, 716, 717, 718
Action for Children's Television v. F. C. C., 348
Adamo Wrecking Co. v. United States, 672
Agnew v. City of Culver City, 460
Agosto v. Immigration and Naturalization Service, 579
Ahearn v. Bailey, 529
Airhart v. Iowa Dept. of Social Services, 417
Air Lines Pilots Association, International v. Quesada, 130
A.L.A. Schechter Poultry Corporation v. United States, 435, 436, 437, 462
Allen v. Wright, 693, 699, 700, 701, 702, 703
Altman v. Pace, 139
Alyeska Pipeline Service Co. v. Wilderness Soc., 663
Amalgamated Meat Cutters and Butcher Workmen of North America, AFL CIO v. Connally, 437, 444, 448, 450
American Airlines, Inc. v. C. A. B., 122, 128, 130, 249, 258
American Bankers Life Assur. Co. of Florida v. Division of Consumer Counsel, Office of Atty. Gen., 294
American Beauty Homes Corp. v. Louisville and Jefferson County Planning Commission, 581
American Cetacean Soc. v. Baldrige, 636
American Cyanamid Co. v. F. T. C., 161, 162
American Federation of Government Emp., AFL CIO v. Block, 395
American Federation of Labor and Congress of Indus. Organizations v. Donovan, 295
American Paper Institute, Inc. v. American Elec. Power Service Corp., 625
American School of Magnetic Healing v. McAnnulty, 633, 635
American Textile Mfrs. Institute, Inc. v. Donovan, 190, 331, 444
American Trading Transp. Co., Inc. v. United States, 112
Anaconda Co. v. Ruckelshaus, 251, 252, FZJ377

Andrade v. Lauer, 726, 727
Andresen v. Maryland, 204
Andrews v. Agricultural Labor Relations Bd., 154, 162, 163
Appeal of (see name of party)
Application of (see name of party)
Aqua Slide 'N' Dive Corp. v. Consumer Product Safety Commission, 317, 625
Arlington Heights, Village of v. Metropolitan Housing Development Corp., 701
Arthurs v. Stern, 75
Ashbacker Radio Corp. v. Federal Communications Com'n, 113
Askew v. Cross Key Waterways, 454
Associated Indem. Corp. v. Shea, 580
Association of Data Processing Service Organizations, Inc. v. Board of Governors of Federal Reserve System, 625
Association of Data Processing Service Organizations, Inc. v. Camp, 686, 687, 691
Association of Nat. Advertisers, Inc. v. F. T. C., 357, 359, 360
Atascadero State Hosp. v. Scanlon, 944
Atchison, T. & S.F. Ry. Co. v. Scarlett, 249
Athlone Industries, Inc. v. Consumer Product Safety Com'n, 727
Atkins v. Parker, 99, 121, 254
Atlas Roofing Company, Inc., v. Occupational Safety and Health Review Commission, 470, 471
Automobile Club v. Commissioner of Int. Rev., 243
Automotive Parts & Accessories Ass'n v. Boyd, 365

Bailey v. Richardson, 43
Baker v. Cameron, 603, 605
Balsam v. Department of Health and Rehabilitative Services, 250
Baltimore Gas and Elec. Co. v. Natural Resources Defense Council, Inc., 317, 623
Bargmann v. Helms, 389
Barker, State ex rel. v. Manchin, 496
Barlow v. Collins, 688
Barr v. Matteo, 646, 647, 656
Barry v. Barchi, 60, 72
BASF Wyandotte Corp. v. Costle, 293
Bates v. Sponberg, 140

Batterton v. Marshall, 251

Bekiaris v. Board of Ed. of City of Modesto, 580

Bell v. Wolfish, 53

Bellis v. United States, 203300

Bennett, State ex rel. Schneider v., 511, 512

Berkovitz v. United States, 639

Better Government Ass'n v. Department of State, 717, 718

B. F. Goodrich Co. v. Department of Transp., 298

Bi–Metallic Inv. Co. v. State Board of Equalization, 95, 97, 98, 99, 121, 254

Bio–Medical Applications of Clearwater, Inc. v. Department of Health and Rehabilitative Services, Office of Community Medical Facilities, 113

Bishop v. Wood, 59

Biswell, United States v., 197

Bivens v. Six Unknown Named Agents of Federal Bureau of Narcotics, 645, 656

Bixby v. Pierno, 582, 586

Blanding v. Sports & Health Club, Inc., 577

Blinder, Robinson & Co., Inc. v. S.E.C., 149

Board of Curators of University of Missouri v. Horowitz, 83, 249

Board of Pardons v. Allen, 53, 54

Board of Regents of State Colleges v. Roth, 38, 43, 44, 46, 47, 53, 54, 55, 56, 59

Bob Jones University v. United States, 693

Bone, State ex rel. Wallace v., 511

Book v. State Office Bldg. Commission, 511

Bookwalter v. Brecklein, 243

Borden, Inc. v. Commissioner of Public Health, 360, 370, 379, **615,** 620, 622, 623, 624

Boreali v. Axelrod, 425, 429, 430

Bowen v. City of New York, 725

Bowen v. Kendrick, 701

Bowen v. Michigan Academy of Family Physicians, 667, 670, 671

Bowsher v. Synar, 523, 527, 528

Bradford Central School Dist. v. Ambach, 692

Braswell v. United States, 293

Brock v. Roadway Exp., Inc., 60, 74

Brown Exp., Inc. v. United States, 404

Buckley v. Valeo, 509, 511

Bureau of Alcohol, Tobacco and Firearms v. Federal Labor Relations Authority, 592, 593, 597

Butz v. Economou, 152, 647, 656, 657, 658

Butz v. Glover Livestock Commission Co., Inc., 607

Cabais v. Egger, 409

California, Dept. of Educ., State of v. Bennett, 728

Califano v. Sanders, 632

California Hotel and Motel Ass'n v. Industrial Welfare Commission, 360, 364, 366, 367, 370, 372

Camp v. Pitts, 140, 225, 367, 374, 377, 378, 620, 621

Carlson v. Green, 656

Carson–Truckee Water Conservancy Dist. v. Secretary of the Interior, 664

Carter v. American Tel. & Tel. Co., 741

Carter v. Carlson, 646

Carter v. Carter Coal Co., 459

Casey v. People, 472

Center for Auto Safety v. Peck, 330, 624

Cervase v. Office of Federal Register, 384

Chamber of Commerce of United States v. Occupational Safety and Health Administration., 405, 408, 409

Chapman v. National Aeronautics and Space Admin., 560

Charles A. Field Delivery Service, Inc., Matter of, 236

Chevron, U.S.A., Inc. v. Natural Resources Defense Council, Inc., 408, 411, 417, 587, **589,** 592, 593, 595, 597, 605, 620, 623

Chisholm v. Georgia, 643

Chrysler Corp. v. Brown, 207, 539, **547,** 551

Cinderella Career & Finishing Schools, Inc. v. F. T. C., 359, 360

Citizens for a Better Environment v. California Dept. of Food and Agriculture, 545

Citizens for Sensible Zoning, Inc. v. Department of Natural Resources, Columbia County, 254

Citizens to Preserve Overton Park, Inc. v. Volpe, 139, 140, 225, 343, 373, 374, 377, 378, 607, 618, 620, 621, 622, 679, 680

City Council of Watertown v. Carbone, 672

City of (see name of city)

Civil Aeronautics Board v. Hermann, 202

Clardy v. Levi, 114

Clarke v. Securities Industry Ass'n, 691

Cleavinger v. Saxner, 657

Cleburne, Tex., City of v. Cleburne Living Center, 45

Cleveland Bd. of Educ. v. Loudermill, 56, 59, 73, 74, 82

CNA Financial Corp. v. Donovan, 552

Codd v. Velger, 82

Collison v. State ex rel. Green, 530

Colonnade Catering Corp. v. United States, 197

Commonwealth of (see name of commonwealth)

Commissioner of Agriculture v. Plaquemines Parish Com'n Council, 454

Commodity Futures Trading Com'n v. Schor, 425, 462, 467, 468, 477

Common Cause v. Nuclear Regulatory Commission, 555, 557

Community Action Research Group v. Iowa State Commerce Commission, 394, 395

Connecticut Bd. of Pardons v. Dumschat, 53

Connecticut Light and Power Co. v. Nuclear Regulatory Commission, 293, 297

Consumer Energy Council of America v. Federal Energy Regulatory Commission, 493

Consumers Union of United States, Inc. v. F. T. C., 493

Contra Costa County v. State, 724

Corn Products Co. v. Department of Health, Ed. and Welfare, Food and Drug Administration, 303

Cort v. Ash, 740

Couch v. United States, 203, 204

County Council for Montgomery County v. Investors Funding Corp., 476

Cox Enterprises, Inc. v. Board of Trustees of Austin Independent School Dist., 556

Crow v. Industrial Commission, 137

Crowell v. Benson, 462, 466, 467, 579, 581, 582

Cull, People v., FZJ574

Cuomo v. Nuclear Regulatory Com'n, 718

Curtiss–Wright Export Corporation, United States v., 450

Cusano v. Dunn, 113

Cutright, State v., 473, 474

Dairylea Cooperative, Inc. v. Walkley, 691

Daniels v. Williams, 61, 645

Davis v. City of Lubbock, 581

Davis v. Passman, 656

Davis v. Scherer, 657

Davis & Randall, Inc., v. United States, 217

D. C. Federation of Civic Associations v. Volpe, 355

Defries v. Association of Owners, 999 Wilder, 562, 569, 575

Degge v. Hitchcock, 637

Department of Air Force v. Rose, 553

Detroit Base Coalition for Human Rights of Handicapped v. Michigan Dept. of Social Services, 83

Dodge v. Department of Social Services, 700

Doe, United States v., 204

Downing v. Lebritton, 92

Duke Power Co. v. Carolina Environmental Study Group, Inc., 691, 699

Dunlop v. Bachowski, 224, 225, 680

Eagle–Picher Industries, Inc. v. United States E.P.A., 719

Edelman v. Jordan, 644

Edwards, State ex rel. McLeod v., 512

E & E Hauling, Inc. v. Pollution Control Bd., 175

E.E.O.C. v. Tempel Steel Co., 201

Elizondo v. State, Dept. of Revenue, Motor Vehicle Division, 270, 271

Elk Run Tel. Co. v. General Tel. Co. of Iowa, 456

Ellis, State ex rel. v. Kelly, 153

El Rancho Grande, Inc., Application of, 691

Endicott Johnson Corporation v. Perkins, 201

Enourato v. New Jersey Bldg. Authority, 496

Environmental Defense Fund, Inc. v. Hardin, 711

Environmental Defense Fund, Inc. v. Ruckelshaus, 711

Erika, Inc., United States v., 670

Essling, State ex rel. Todd v., 530

Estep v. United States, 467, 563, 671, 728

Ettinger v. Board of Medical Quality Assur., Dept. of Consumer Affairs, 575

Eubank v. City of Richmond, 459

Excelsior Underwear, Inc., 275, 279, 280, 281

Farmworker Justice Fund, Inc. v. Brock, 681

F.C.C. v. ITT World Communications, Inc., 556

Federal Commun. Com'n v. Allentown Broad. Corp., 576

Federal Communications Com'n v. Sanders Bros. R.S., 685

Federal Crop Ins. Corporation v. Merrill, 240

Federal Deposit Ins. Corp. v. Mallen, 72, 74, 82

Federal Election Com'n v. Rose, 666

Federal Power Com'n v. Hope Natural Gas Co., 578

Federal Radio Commission v. General Electric Co., 581

Federal Radio Com'n v. Nelson Bros. B. & M. Co., 433

Federal Trade Commission v. American Tobacco Co, 201

Federal Trade Commission v. Cement Institute, 153, 161, 162

Federal Trade Commission v. Gratz, 433

Field v. Clark, 432, 433, 434

First Sav. & Loan Ass'n of Borger v. Vandygriff, 171

Fisher v. United States, 204

Fitanides v. Crowley, 454

Fitzgerald v. Hampton, 209

Fitzgerald v. Pan Am. World Airways, 740

Flast v. Cohen, 700, 701

Florida Cities Water Co. v. Florida Public Service Commission, 274

Florida East Coast Ry. Co., United States v., 97, 111, **307**, 310, 311

Florida Power & Light Co. v. United States, 293

Foote's Dixie Dandy, Inc. v. McHenry, 237, 240, 242

Ford Motor Co. v. F. T. C., 264, 265, 266

Foree v. Crown Central Petroleum Corp., 734, 737, 738

Foundation on Economic Trends v. Heckler, 19

Fox v. Wisconsin Dept. of Health and Social Services, 691, 701

Franz v. Board of Medical Quality Assur., 213, 217

Friedman v. Rogers, 161, 509
Frink v. Prod, 583, 586
F. T. C. v. Atlantic Richfield Co., 206
F. T. C. v. Standard Oil Co. of California, 705
FTC Line of Business Report Litigation, Appeal of, 197, 201, 202, 205, 207
F. T. C. v. Cinderella Career & Finishing Schools, Inc., 206

Gagnon v. Scarpelli, 53
Garces v. Department of Registration and Ed., 461
Gardner v. Toilet Goods Ass'n, 714, 715, 717, 718
Gavrilovic, United States v., 381, 386
General Assembly of State of N. J. v. Byrne, 496
General Dynamics Corp., United States v., 738
Georgetown University Hosp. v. Bowen, 247, 248
Gerst v. Nixon, 581
Gestuvo v. District Director of United States Immigration and Naturalization Service, 240
Gibson v. Berryhill, 160
Gold v. Lomenzo, 457
Goldberg v. Kelly, 24, **26,** 34, 35, 36, 38, 43, 62, 72, 73, 76, 81, 92, 113, 133, 148, 150, 153, 195, 219, FZJ63
Goldsmith v. United States Board of Tax Appeals, 46
Goss v. Lopez, 60, 81, 92, 93
Gott v. Walters, 671
Grand Jury Subpoena Duces Tecum Served Upon Underhill, In re, 204
Gray Panthers v. Schweiker, 61
Great Northern Ry. Co. v. Merchants' Elevator Co., 738
Greenfield Const. Co. Inc. v. Michigan Dept. of State Highways, 250
Greenholtz v. Inmates of Nebraska Penal and Correctional Complex, 53, 54
Greer v. State of Georgia, 511
Grein v. Board of Educ. of School Dist. of Fremont, Dodge County, 557
Grimaud, United States v., 471, 472
Grolier Inc. v. F. T. C., 148, 151, 152
Guardian Federal Sav. and Loan Ass'n v. Federal Sav. and Loan Ins. Corp., 388
Guardian Life Ins. Co. v. Bohlinger, 672
Gumbhir v. Kansas State Bd. of Pharmacy, 461

Halley v. Lavine, 138
Hannah v. Larche, 55
Hansen, State ex rel. Pearson v., 529
Hardin v. Kentucky Utilities Co., 685
Harlow v. Fitzgerald, 657
Harmon v. Brucker, 671
Harris v. Mechanicville Central School Dist., 626

Heckler v. Chaney, 394, **673,** 679, 680, 681, 682
Heckler v. Community Health Services of Crawford County, Inc., 241
Heckler v. Day, 710
Heckler v. Ringer, 725
Hercules, Inc. v. Environmental Protection Agency, 348
Hewitt v. Helms, 47, 52, 54, 76, **77,** 81, 82, 93
H. F. Wilcox Oil & Gas Co. v. Walker, 294
Hillman v. Northern Wasco County People's Utility Dist., 460
Hinderliter v. Humphries, 559
Hladys v. Commonwealth, 148
Hodel v. Virginia Surface Min. and Reclam. Ass'n, Inc., 72
Holmes v. New York City Housing Authority, 270
Home Box Office, Inc. v. F.C.C., 339, 342, 343, 344, 346, 348, 353, 355
Homemakers North Shore, Inc. v. Bowen, 594
Hornsby v. Allen, 270
Hortonville Joint School Dist. No. 1 v. Hortonville Ed. Ass'n, 161
Hovey Concrete Products Co., State ex rel. v. Mechem, 468, 469
Howard, United States v., 249
Howard v. Wyman, 598
Hudson v. Palmer, 61, 645
Hughes v. Rowe, 664
Humana of South Carolina, Inc. v. Califano, 397, 399
Humane Soc. of United States, New Jersey Branch, Inc. v. New Jersey State Fish and Game Council, 509
Humphrey's Ex'r v. United States, 523, 524, 526
Hutchins v. Mayo, 457

Independent United States Tanker Owners Committee v. Lewis, 112
Indian Towing Company v. United States, 640
Industrial Safety Equipment Ass'n, Inc. v. E.P.A., 405
Industrial Union Dept., AFL-CIO v. American Petroleum Institute, 190, **440,** 444, 448, 450
Ingraham v. Wright, 61
In re (see name of party)
I.N.S. v. Chadha, 482, 493, 494, 495, 497, 528
I.N.S. v. Lopez-Mendoza, 197
International Harvester Co. v. Bowling, 162
International Harvester Co. v. Ruckelshaus, 317
International Union, United Auto., Aerospace and Agr. Implement Workers of America v. N.L.R.B., 234, 236
Interstate Commerce Commission v. Brimson, 200, 201, 477

Iowa Bankers Ass'n v. Iowa Credit Union Dept., 370, 689, 691
Iron Workers Local No. 67 v. Hart, 456, 477
Irval Realty Inc. v. Board of Public Utility Com'rs, 537

Jackson v. Concord Co., 476
Jackson County Public Hospital v. Public Employment Relations Bd., 576
Janis, United States v., 197
Japan Whaling Ass'n v. American Cetacean Soc., 691
Jayvee Brand, Inc. v. United States, 657
Jeffries v. Georgia Residential Finance Authority, 76
Jenkins v. McKeithen, 55
Johnson v. Robison, 670, 671
Johnston, Matter of, 148
Jonal Corp. v. District of Columbia, 153
Jones v. Morris, 136
Ju Toy, United States v., 578
J. W. Hampton, Jr., & Co. v. United States, 433

Kansas House of Representatives, State ex rel. Stephan v., 496
Kantrowitz, People v., 472
Kelly, State ex rel. Ellis v., 153
Kendall v. United States ex rel. Stokes, 635
Kennecott Copper Corp. v. Environmental Protection Agency, 369
Kent v. Dulles, 423, 425, 429, 430, 444
Kentucky v. Graham, 644
Kentucky, Dept. of Banking and Securities, Commonwealth of v. Brown, 640, 643
Koniag, Inc., Village of Uyak v. Andrus, 195
Kordel, United States v., 75

Laird v. Nelms, 638
Lambert, State v., 472
Larson v. Domestic & Foreign Commerce Corporation, 632
LaSalle Nat. Bank, United States v., 202
L. A. Tucker Truck Lines, United States v., 727
Leek v. Theis, 509
Legislative Research Com'n By and Through Prather v. Brown, 497
Leone v. Mobil Oil Corp., 406, 408
Levin v. Murawski, 202, 203
Lewis v. Weinberger, 386
Lewis Consol. School Dist. of Cass County v. Johnston, 456
Lincoln Dairy Co. v. Finigan, 472, 473, 474
Logan v. Zimmerman Brush Co., 60
Londoner v. City & County of Denver, 94, 97, 98, 254
Lopez v. Heckler, 232, 233
Lopez v. Henry Phipps Plaza South, Inc., 76

Mada–Luna v. Fitzpatrick, 411, 415
Madison v. Alaska Dept. of Fish and Game, 587, 592, 597
Madora v. Board of Ed. of City of New York, 92
Maitrejean, State v., 472
Malek–Marzban v. Immigration and Naturalization Service, 399
Manchin, State ex rel. Barker v., 496
Marbury v. Madison, 635
Marcello v. Bonds, 153
Marchetti v. United States, 204
Market St. Ry. Co. v. Railroad Commission, 217
Markgraf, United States v., 682
Marshall v. Barlow's Inc., 196, 401
Maryland Com'n on Human Relations v. Baltimore Gas & Elec. Co., 709
Mason v. Thetford School Bd., 673
Mathews v. Eldridge, 62, 63, 72, 73, 74, 76, 93, 103, 114, 323, 710, 725
Matlovich v. Secretary of the Air Force, 219, 223, 224, 225, 318, 364
Matter of (see name of party)
Mazza v. Cavicchia, 137
McAvoy v. H. B. Sherman Co., 673
McCarthy v. Industrial Commission, 217
McDonald v. Department of Banking and Finance, 274
McGee v. United States, 728, 729
McKart v. United States, 728, 729
McKee v. Likins, 250
McLeod, State ex rel. v. Edwards, 512
McPherson v. Employment Division, 598, 603, 605, 606
Meachum v. Fano, 53
Mechem, State ex rel. Hovey Concrete Products Co. v., 468, 469
Megdal v. Oregon State Bd. of Dental Examiners, 267, 267, 270, 271, 272, 418
Memphis Light, Gas and Water Division v. Craft, 60
Mendoza, United States v., 232, 233
Mendoza–Lopez, United States v., 672
Merz v. Leitch, 555
Meyer v. Nebraska, 44
Michigan, State of v. Thomas, 330
Milford v. Gilb, 545
Miller v. California, 580
Miller v. Fenton, 580, 603
Miller v. Horton, 646, 647
Milwaukee Metropolitan Sewerage Dist. v. Wisconsin Dept. of Natural Resources, 116, 119
Missouri Power & Light Co., State ex rel. v. Riley, 673
Moberg v. Independent School Dist. No. 281, 555
Moore v. East Cleveland, Ohio, 44
Morgan, (Morgan II), United States v., 313 U.S. 409, pp. 137, 138, 139, 149, 150, 153, 310

Morgan, (Morgan I), United States v., 298 U.S. 468, pp. 133, 135, 138, 139, 140, 310, 356

Morgan v. United States, 304 U.S. 1, p. 149

Morgan v. United States, 298 U.S. 468, pp. 133, 135, 138, 139, 140, 310, 356

Morrison v. Olson, 510, 511, **513,** 523, 524, 525, 527

Morrissey v. Brewer, 53

Mortensen v. Pyramid Sav. & Loan Ass'n of Milwaukee, 692

Morton v. Ruiz, 266, 385, 537

Morton v. W.C.A.B., 201, 477

Morton, State ex rel. Thompson v., 529

Morton Salt Co., United States v., 201, 203

Motor Vehicle Mfrs. Ass'n of United States, Inc. v. State Farm Mut. Auto. Ins. Co., 366, 367, **607,** 618, 619, 620, 621, 622, 623, 624, 625, 681

Mt. Healthy City School Dist. Bd. of Ed. v. Doyle, 644

Muller Optical Co. v. E.E.O.C., 495

Muskopf v. Corning Hospital District, 640

Myers v. Bethlehem Shipbuilding Corporation, 719, 724, 725

Myers v. United States, 513, 523

Nader v. Allegheny Airlines, Inc., 729, 737, 738, 739

Nader v. Baroody, 558, 559

National Ass'n of Farmworkers Organizations v. Marshall, 325

National Ornament & Elec. Light Christmas Ass'n, Inc. v. Consumer Product Safety Commission, 404

National Parks and Conservation Ass'n v. Morton, 551, 552

National Petroleum Refiners Ass'n v. F. T. C., 410

National Welfare Rights Organization v. Finch, 194, 196

Natural Resources Defense Council, Inc. v. Herrington, 558, 559

Natural Resources Defense Council, Inc. v. Securities and Exchange Commission, 622, 681

Neuberger v. City of Portland, 104

Nevada Airlines, Inc. v. Bond, 711

New Jersey v. T.L.O., 197

New Jersey Civil Service Ass'n v. State, 720

Newman v. Piggie Park Enterprises, Inc., 664

New York v. Burger, 197

Neyland v. Board of Educ. of Town of Redding, 673

Ng Fung Ho v. White, 578, 579, 580

Nixon v. Fitzgerald, 643, 657

Nixon, United States v., 249, 547, 593

N. L. R. B. v. Bell Aerospace Co. Division of Textron, Inc., 261, 264, 265, 318

National Labor Relations Bd. v. MacKay Radio & Telegraph Co., 137

N.L.R.B. v. Hearst Publications, 603, 604, 605

N. L. R. B. v. International Medication Systems, Ltd., 201

National Labor Relations Board v. Donnelly Garment Co., 161

N. L. R. B. v. Sears, Roebuck & Co., 526, 537, **539,** 545

NLRB v. Universal Camera Corp., 190 F.2d 429, p. 576

National Labor Rel. Bd. v. Universal Camera Corp., 179 F.2d 749, p. 576

N. L. R. B. v. Wyman–Gordon Co., 274, 279, 280

N. L. R. B. v. Yeshiva University, 604, 605

North American Cold Storage Co. v. Chicago, 72

Northern Pipeline Const. Co. v. Marathon Pipe Line Co., 461, 466, 467, 580

Northside Sanitary Landfill, Inc. v. Thomas, 366

O'Bannon v. Town Court Nursing Center, 60

Odell v. Village of Hoffman Estates, 636

Ohio Valley Water Co. v. Ben Avon Borough, 578, 580, 581, 582

Oklahoma Press Pub. Co. v. Walling, 201, 203

Olim v. Wakinekona, 54

1000 Friends of Oregon v. Wasco County Court, 160

Opinion of the Justices, In re, 468, 469

Opinion of the Justices, 497

Orr, Application of, 250

Owen v. City of Independence, Mo., 658

Pacific Legal Foundation v. California Coastal Com'n, 717

Pacific States Box & Basket Co. v. White, 621

Panama Refining Co. v. Ryan, 434, 436, 437, 462

Parratt v. Taylor, 61

Patsy v. Board of Regents of State of Fla., 729

Paul v. Davis, 55, 59

Pearson, State ex rel. v. Hansen, 529

Pell v. Board of Ed. of Union Free School Dist. No. 1 of Towns of Scarsdale and Mamaroneck, Westchester County, 626

Pennsylvania v. Delaware Valley Citizens' Council for Clean Air, 659, 663, 664

Pennsylvania State Bd. of Pharmacy v. Cohen, 270

People v. ___(see opposing party)

Perry v. Sindermann, 44, 46, 59

Pickus v. United States Bd. of Parole, 311

Pierce v. Underwood, 665, 666

Pillsbury Co. v. F. T. C., 173

Playboy Enterprises, Inc. v. Meese, 659

Pollack v. Simonson, 113

Portland Cement Ass'n v. Ruckelshaus, 296, 297, 318

Professional Air Traffic Controllers Organization v. Federal Labor Relations Authority, 164, 171, 172, 173

Public Citizen Health Research Group v. Tyson, 627

Railroad Commission v. Rowan & Nichols Oil Co., 311 U.S. 570, p. 578

Railroad Commission v. Rowan & Nichols Oil Co., 310 U.S. 573, p. 578

Realty Group, Inc. v. Department of Revenue, 250

Regents of University of Cal. v. Superior Court of Los Angeles County, 700

Renegotiation Bd. v. Bannercraft Clothing Co., Inc., 546

Retail, Wholesale and Dept. Store Union, AFL–CIO v. N. L. R. B., 264, 265

R. H. Johnson & Co. v. Securities & Exchange Commission, 460

Ricci v. Chicago Mercantile Exchange, 738

Richardson v. Perales, 212

Riley, State ex rel. Missouri Power & Light Co. v., 673

Riverside, City of v. Rivera, 664

Rodway v. United States Dept. of Agriculture, 366, 399

Roe v. Wade, 44

Rollins Environmental Services, Inc., Matter of, 162

Rosenthal v. Hartnett, 478

Rosenthal & Co. v. Commodity Futures Trading Commission, 709

Rowell v. Andrus, 384

Ryan v. New York Telephone Co., 231

Salk v. Weinraub, 673

Sangamon Valley Television Corp. v. United States, 342, 343

Savarese v. United States Dept. of Health, Ed. and Welfare, 560

Savoy Club v. Board of Sup'rs for Los Angeles County, 75, 203

Schlegel v. Bebout, 657

Schmitt v. Iowa Dept. of Social Services, 499

Schneider, State ex rel. v. Bennett, 511, 512

School Committee of Greenfield v. Greenfield Ed. Ass'n, 738

Schweiker v. Hansen, 240, 242

S & D Maintenance Co., Inc. v. Goldin, 62

Seacoast Anti–Pollution League v. Costle, 310

Securities and Exchange Commission v. Chenery Corp., 332 U.S. 194, p. 226

Securities and Exchange Commission v. Chenery Corp., 318 U.S. 80, pp. 279, 389

Securities and Exchange Commission v. Dresser Industries, Inc., 75, 203

S.E.C. v. Jerry T. O'Brien, Inc., 202

Serrano v. Priest, 663

Service v. Dulles, 250

Shapiro v. United States, 204

Shaughnessy v. Pedreiro, 671

Shell Oil Co. v. Federal Power Commission, 304

Sherman v. Board of Regents of University of State of N. Y., 607

Ship Creek Hydraulic Syndicate v. State, Dept. of Transp. and Public Facilities, 224, 225

Shively v. Stewart, 206

Shuttlesworth v. Birmingham, Ala., 444, 457

Sierra Club v. Costle, 348, 353, 355, 620

Sierra Club v. Morton, 699

Silver v. McCamey, 75

Sims, People v., 234

Small Refiner Lead Phase–Down Task Force v. E.P.A., 330

Soglin v. Kauffman, 271

Spilotro v. State, ex rel. Nevada Gaming Com'n, 226

Springfield Ed. Ass'n v. Springfield School Dist. No. 19, 592

Spruytte v. Walters, 56

State v. ____(see opposing party)

State ex rel. v. ____(see opposing party and relator)

State of (see name of state)

State Tax Com'n v. Administrative Hearing Com'n, 469, 470

Stauffer Chemical Co., United States v., 232

Steadman v. Securities and Exchange Commission, 575

Stephan, State ex rel. v. Kansas House of Representatives, 496

St. Joseph Stock Yards Co. v. United States, 578, 580, 581, 582, 670

St. Louis, City of v. Praprotnik, 645

Superintendent, Massachusetts Correctional Institution, Walpole v. Hill, 77

Supreme Court of Virginia v. Consumers Union of United States, Inc., 657

Sutton v. City of Milwaukee, 73

Tabor v. Joint Bd. for Enrollment of Actuaries, 367

Tennessee Electric Power Co. v. Tennessee Valley A., 684, 685, 686

Tenney v. Brandhove, 657

Tew v. City of Topeka Police and Fire Civil Service Com'n, 249

Texaco, Inc. v. F. T. C., 130, 163

13th Regional Corp. v. United States Dept. of Interior, 635

Thompson, State ex rel., v. Morton, 529

Thygesen v. Callahan, 451, 454, 476

Tijerina v. Walters, 559

Tite v. State Tax Commission, 476

Todd, State ex rel. v. Essling, 530

Todd & Co., Inc. v. Securities and Exchange Commission, 460

Tower v. Glover, 657

Traynor v. Turnage, 673
Trebesch v. Employment Div., 272
Tri–State Generation and Transmission
  Ass'n, Inc. v. Environmental Quality
  Council, 370
Troutman v. Shriver, 693
**Trujillo v. Employment Sec. Commis-
  sion of New Mexico, 209, 212**
Tull v. United States, 471
Tumey v. State of Ohio, 159
Turmon, People v., 472

United Air Lines, Inc. v. C.A.B., 410
United Church of Christ v. F. C. C., 193,
  196, 686, 699
**United States v. ____(see opposing par-
  ty)**
**United States Dept. of Labor v. Kast
  Metals Corp., 401, 404**
United States Gypsum Co., United States
  v., 562
United States Lines, Inc. v. Federal Mari-
  time Commission, 112
United Steelworkers of America, AFL CIO
  CLC v. Marshall, 348
**Universal Camera Corp. v. National La-
  bor Rel. Bd., 563, 564, 570, 573, 575, 593**
University of Kansas Faculty, Matter of,
  138
**University of Tennessee v. Elliott, 227,
  231**

Vail v. Board of Educ. of Paris Union
  School Dist. No. 95, 62
Vandygriff v. First Sav. and Loan Ass'n of
  Borger, 171, 172, 173
Varig Airlines, United States v., 639
**Vermont Yankee Nuclear Power Corp.
  v. Natural Resources Defense Coun-
  cil, Inc., 112, 129, 223, 225, 312, 316, 317,
  318, 343, 356, 366, 367, 374, 377, 404,
  622, 623**
Vietnam Veterans of America v. Secretary
  of the Navy, 250
Village of (see name of village)
Vitarelli v. Seaton, 250
Vitek v. Jones, 53

Wallace v. Commissioner of Taxation, 457
Wallace, State ex rel. v. Bone, 511
**Walters v. National Ass'n of Radiation
  Survivors, 83, 91, 92, 114, 133, 671**
Ward v. Village of Monroeville, Ohio, 159
Warren v. Marion County, 454
Warth v. Seldin, 701
Washington ex rel. Seattle Title Trust Co.
  v. Roberge, 459

Washington Research Project, Inc. v. De-
  partment of Health, Ed. and Welfare,
  554
Washington State Farm Bureau v. Mar-
  shall, 325
Wasson v. Trowbridge, 92
Watson v. Pennsylvania Turnpike Commis-
  sion, 530
**Waukegan, City of v. Pollution Control
  Bd., 474, 476**
Webster v. Doe, 671, 679, 680
Weeks v. Personnel Bd. of Review of Town
  of North Kingstown, 581
Weinberger v. Hynson, Westcott & Dun-
  ning, Inc., 129, 130
**West Chicago, Ill., City of v. United
  States Nuclear Regulatory Com'n, 106**
Western Pac. R. Co., United States v., 738
Westfall v. Erwin, 646
Whispering Pines Mobile Home Park, Ltd.
  v. City of Scotts Valley (Dickerman), 219
White v. Roughton, 271
Wiener v. United States, 523, 524, 526, 527
Wilderness Soc. v. Morton, 663
Williamson v. Lee Optical of Oklahoma, 45
Wisconsin v. Constantineau, 55
Wisconsin Elec. Power Co. v. Costle, 389
**Withrow v. Larkin, 142, 147, 148, 150,
  153, 154, 162**
WKAT, Inc. v. F. C. C., 342
Wolff v. McDonnell, 53, 54, 76, 92, 114, 233
Wong Wing v. United States, 474
Wong Yang Sung v. McGrath, 114, 115, 119
Woodby v. Immigration and Naturalization
  Service, 575
Woodland Hills Residents Ass'n, Inc. v. Los
  Angeles City Council, 175
Wright v. Central Du Page Hospital Ass'n,
  468, 469, 476
Wright v. Plaza Ford, 477
WWHT, Inc. v. F. C. C., 391, 394, 395, 682

Yakus v. United States, 436, 437, 672
Yellow Freight System, Inc., United States
  v., 738
Yerardi's Moody Street Restaurant and
  Lounge, Inc. v. Board of Selectmen of
  Randolph, 637
Young, Ex parte, 644
Young Plumbing and Heating Co. v. Iowa
  Natural Resources Council, 280, 281
Youngstown Sheet & Tube Co. v. Sawyer,
  507, 508, 526

Zablocki v. Redhail, 44
Zaharakis v. Heckler, 385
Zions First Nat. Bank, N.A. v. Taylor, 140

STATE AND FEDERAL ADMINISTRATIVE LAW

*

Chapter 1

INTRODUCTION

---

§ 1.1 ADMINISTRATIVE AGENCIES AND ADMINISTRATIVE LAW

Administrative agencies are governmental bodies other than the legislature and the courts that affect the rights or duties of individuals or entities. They typically perform missions entrusted to them by statutes that authorize them to take certain kinds of actions for specified purposes. In short, agencies administer or execute law. All levels of government, federal, state, and local, have administrative agencies.

Administrative agencies may be headed by a single official or by a collegiate body, and may be called a department, bureau, division, section, commission, board, administration, or another name. Some agencies have only a single mission while other agencies have multiple purposes. Most agencies are part of the executive branch of government but others are said to be independent bodies. While the heads of most agencies are appointed by the chief executive, in the states some agency heads are directly elected.

Agencies vary in size from bodies with no full time officials or employees and minuscule budgets to bodies with many thousands of employees and budgets in the billions of dollars. Some agencies make millions of determinations each year (such as medicare and social security determinations) while others make only a handful of determinations annually. Agencies are specialists. Some specialize in a particular problem wherever it occurs, like labor-management relations, while others specialize in problems arising in particular industries or contexts, like transportation.

There are many thousands of administrative agencies in the various levels of government in this country, and their spheres of action embrace almost every human endeavor. Many agencies are regulatory in the sense that they enforce a mandatory scheme of prohibitions or obligations. Other agencies are benefactory, meaning that they disburse benefits. To carry out these diverse missions, agencies are

1

authorized to investigate, to prosecute, to make law, to adjudicate, to license, and to perform various other kinds of functions.

Administrative law deals with the legal principles common to all administrative agencies. These principles govern the authority of agencies, the processes and procedures they use to perform their functions, and the validity of their actions. It includes an analysis of the law defining the role of the courts, the legislature, and the chief executive, vis-à-vis agencies and their activities. So, this course deals with the source and legitimacy of agency authority, the proper procedure for agency actions in investigating and prosecuting law violators and for making rules and adjudicating individual rights, and the proper procedure for obtaining judicial review of agency action. It does not deal with the *substantive* law enforced by agencies. Substantive issues relating to taxation, labor relations, social security, welfare, securities law, or environmental law, for instance, are handled in courses on those particular subjects.

A course in administrative law, therefore, has much in common with a course on civil procedure. It cuts across many substantive law areas and assumes that administrative agencies are sufficiently distinct and have enough in common to make meaningful a study of the bases of their authority and the principles governing their processes and procedures. In short, administrative law is basically a course in procedural law rather than a course in substantive law.

§ 1.2 REASONS FOR STUDYING ADMINISTRATIVE LAW

The reasons for studying administrative law are compelling. Our society may fairly be characterized as an administrative state. Agency administered law regulates or affects almost all aspects of our lives on a daily basis. Consequently, virtually every lawyer will encounter state and federal administrative agencies in his or her practice. If you are doing real estate work, you will have to deal with the administrative agencies administering the local zoning and land use planning laws. If you practice tax, immigration, or labor law, you will be in intimate contact with administrative bureaucracies at every stage of your practice. A general business lawyer deals with many different agencies— agencies that license professionals, supervise securities regulation, enforce anti-discrimination laws, administer consumer protection laws, oversee environmental protection laws, and apply safety in the workplace laws. If you represent hospitals or banks, you have to deal with a maze of regulatory agencies. If you represent clients receiving social security or welfare payments or involved in government contracting or seeking government grants, you will have to deal with the agencies administering those programs. The handling of a driver's license problem requires you to deal with an agency. Every time this happens, you will, of course, have to know the applicable substantive law; but you will also have to know administrative procedure law. So a knowledge of administrative law is as essential as a knowledge of civil procedure.

§ 1.3 STATE AND FEDERAL ADMINISTRATIVE LAW

In one major respect, this coursebook on administrative law differs from other such books. Other coursebooks use exclusively, or almost exclusively, federal materials to introduce students to the subject. Throughout this book, however, an effort has been made to integrate illustrative state materials with federal materials. That effort is justified on two grounds. First, an integrated study of both state and federal administrative law broadens and deepens the study of administrative law and enriches it in a way that would otherwise not be possible. The reason for this is that there are many differences as well as similarities between the federal and state administrative processes. There are also many differences as well as similarities between federal and state administrative law. As a result, consideration of state administrative law is essential because it stimulates important insights into problems and solutions in the administrative process that cannot be obtained from wholly federal materials. Consideration of state law is also essential because we can learn much from comparing different solutions to similar problems as well as from seeking to devise workable solutions for different problems.

Among the differences between federal and state agencies that may present different challenges for their respective schemes of administrative law are the following: Federal agencies are, in general, much larger and better financed and staffed than state agencies. On the whole, state agencies deal with less affluent, less influential, and less well educated people than federal agencies, and handle matters of smaller economic value than those handled by federal agencies. Persons dealing with state agencies are also less likely to be represented by a lawyer than persons dealing with federal agencies. State agencies are closer to the people and usually have smaller constituencies that can more easily communicate with them than federal agencies. In addition, state constitutions often differ significantly from the federal Constitution in important particulars that relate to their respective administrative processes. State and federal constitutions often differ in the way in which they create administrative units within their governments, allocate authority among units, and impose procedural or substantive limits on those units. For example, some state agencies are created directly by their state constitution; and some state agency heads are directly elected by the people. However, all federal agencies (and most state agencies) are created by statute or executive order; and all federal agency heads (and most state agency heads) are appointed.

These many differences between federal and state agencies present many different challenges for state as opposed to federal administrative law that need to be considered by students of this subject; they are also responsible for many differences between federal and state administrative law that cannot be understood or adequately evaluated without studying both of them.

There is a second reason for the inclusion of state administrative process materials throughout this book. A study of both state and federal administrative process materials better prepares law students to deal with the realities of law practice. Most lawyers in this country confront state and local agencies at least as often, and probably more often, than they deal with federal agencies. Furthermore, state law materials provide examples that better illustrate some problems or solutions in the administrative process than do existing federal materials. Finally, most students have a greater opportunity to observe first hand, or to be personally involved with, the operation of state and local government agencies than the operation of federal agencies. Therefore, a study of state administrative law examples may often be more meaningful to students and less abstract than a study confined wholly to more remote federal law examples.

As a result, this book proceeds from the conviction that significant intellectual and practical reasons require state law and federal law materials to be wholly integrated in the teaching of administrative law. State law materials are, therefore, included throughout this book to the extent necessary "to examine adequately those intellectual and practical problems and solutions in the administrative process that are not satisfactorily raised, eliminated, or solved, by a consideration of federal law alone," and to the extent necessary "to assure that students are equipped to function effectively in the various state administrative processes as well as in the federal process." *See* Bonfield, "State Law in the Teaching of Administrative Law: A Critical Analysis of the Status Quo," 61 Tex.L.Rev. 95, 136 (1982).

As you examine each aspect of administrative law you should ascertain from the materials whether state law on that subject is the same or different from federal law, and seek to identify the explanation and justification for those similarities or differences. You should also consider whether each similarity or dissimilarity in state and federal law is rational, functional, and desirable, in light of the respective circumstances of our state and federal governments. Finally, you should decide, in instances where state and federal law differ, whether one of them would be wise in emulating the law of the other.

§ 1.4 ADMINISTRATIVE PROCEDURE ACTS

The principal sources of administrative law include federal and state constitutions, statutes, and judge-made common law, as well as agency rules and precedent. Of special importance are administrative procedure acts (APAs). The federal government and about two thirds of the states have general and comprehensive APAs. *See* 14 U.L.A. 157 (Supp.1988). These statutes are *general* in the sense that they are applicable to all or most agencies rather than to only one or a select number of agencies; and they are *comprehensive* in the sense that they deal with the four main subjects of public access to agency information, agency rulemaking procedure, agency adjudication procedure, and judicial review of agency action.

Some people opposed the enactment of general and comprehensive APAs. They stressed the many divergent missions of agencies and divergent contexts within which agencies operated and concluded that for optimum efficiency the administrative process of each agency should be specially adapted to its particular situation. They contended that any code of administrative procedure generally applicable to all agencies was undesirable and practically unfeasible. However, others believed that the benefits of a single statutory procedural code binding on all agencies were substantial, and that such a *minimum* code that dealt only with *general and fundamental principles* rather than with details was both desirable and feasible. Their support of an APA was premised on the assumption that the arguments against a general and comprehensive statutory code of administrative procedure were based upon a misunderstanding of the nature and scope of such an APA, and too lightly dismissed the advantages that such an act would bring without creating the disadvantages feared by the opponents of such acts. Once the federal APA was adopted, most states became convinced of the desirability and feasibility of such acts, and followed its example. *See* Bonfield, "The Federal APA and State Administrative Law," 72 Va. L.Rev. 297, 303–308 (1986).

The federal APA was enacted in 1946. Most state APAs were enacted between 1955 and 1980. *The APAs of more than half of the states are based in whole or in part on the 1961 Model State APA (MSAPA). See* 14 U.L.A. 357 (1980). That model act was drafted by the National Conference of Commissioners on Uniform State Laws. In 1981 the Commissioners on Uniform State Laws adopted an entirely new MSAPA—the 1981 MSAPA. That new model act is now before the several states for their consideration and a number of states have already adopted some of its provisions. Throughout this book, an effort has been made to cite relevant provisions of the federal APA, the 1981 MSAPA, and the 1961 MSAPA on which most current state acts are based. The first two acts are contained in the Appendix to this book. You might also consult the relevant provisions of the APA of your own state as you read this book.

Note that the federal APA, the 1981 MSAPA, and the 1961 MSAPA, define the agencies to which those acts apply. These definitions are all inclusive. According to federal APA § 551(1), that act applies to every "authority of the Government of the United States" other than "the Congress; [and] the courts;" according to 1981 MSAPA § 1–102(1), that act applies to every "board, commission, department, officer or other administrative unit" of the state other than "the [legislature] or the courts[, or the governor] . . .;" and according to 1961 MSAPA § 1(1), that act applies to "each state [board, commission, department or officer], other than the legislature or the courts. . . ." The federal APA does not apply to the agencies of the District of Columbia, and the MSAPAs do not apply to agencies of local as distinguished from state government. The circumstances of administrative bodies of local governments are sufficiently different from those of the administrative bodies of federal and state governments as to make infeasible or impracticable application to the former of APAs that were drafted in light of the respective circumstances of the latter. Of course, this does not mean that APAs for local government agencies are undesirable or unnecessary; it only means that different APAs drafted in light of the special circumstances of local government agencies should govern their activities.

The federal act and both MSAPAs provide that a subsequent statute may exclude an otherwise covered federal or state agency from their respective provisions only if it does so expressly. *See* federal APA § 559; 1981 MSAPA § 1–103(a)–(b); 1961 MSAPA § 19. The 1981 MSAPA and the federal APA also indicate specifically that they apply to an otherwise qualifying body whether or not that body is within another agency or subject to the authority or review of another agency. *See* federal APA § 551(1); 1981 MSAPA § 1–102(1).

§ 1.5 A SNAPSHOT OF THE ADMINISTRATIVE PROCESS

A snapshot introductory glimpse of the administrative process may be provided by an example. Suppose that the state legislature has been deluged with complaints about unfair practices in the automobile insurance industry. It is not sure exactly how to solve the problem, so it enacts a rather vaguely worded statute prohibiting unfair and discriminatory automobile insurance practices. This statute, of course, is not self-enforcing. So the legislature creates an agency called the Automobile Insurance Commission (AIC) to enforce it, and authorizes the AIC to engage in a variety of activities to secure that result. According to statute, the AIC will have a director (or perhaps several agency heads), a staff, and a budget.

What techniques are available to the AIC in carrying out this mission?

i. *Research and publicity.* One relatively uncontroversial function that the AIC will be authorized to perform is to find out what the problems are and what solutions are available. For this purpose it may simply serve as a central clearing house for information on the subject of automobile insurance. On the other hand, the AIC may find that it needs more information so it may commission research—either by its staff or by outside consultants. AIC might also decide to publicize the results of its findings. For example, it might publish a directory of automobile insurance premiums or a study of consumer complaints against such insurance companies. Publicity of this kind can be an important aid to consumers in making their own economic decisions and thus can help the free market work more efficiently.

ii. *Rulemaking.* We have assumed the legislature was not certain of the precise scope of the automobile insurance problem or how it should be solved. Often, a statute of this sort can be enacted only by a compromise between proponents and opponents which resolves very few of the hard issues. Instead, the responsibility for solving those issues is passed to an agency. The political process, which was not completed in the legislature, will then resume in the agency when it takes up these issues.

The agency enabling act will probably authorize it to adopt rules which set forth the specific types of automobile insurance practices that are allowed and the specific types that are forbidden. For instance, suppose AIC believes that it is unfair for insurers to charge different premiums to consumers with different ZIP codes. It will first study the problem. Then it will propose, and later adopt, rules prohibiting such conduct. Rules are agency statements of *general* applicability and future effect that implement, interpret, or prescribe law or policy.

In practical effect, agency rules are just like statutes because they determine the legal rights or duties of described classes of individuals in specified circumstances. So the agency has engaged in a type of legislation. The typical APA carefully regulates the agency rulemaking process, imposing a number of requirements on the issuance of most, but not all, types of rules. This means that the AIC would probably have to give advance notice to the public of its intention to adopt these rules, allow the public to comment on the proposals, consider and respond to those comments, publish the rules in their final adopted form, and allow a period of grace after adoption of the rules before they become effective.

Administrative rules and regulations (the two words mean the same thing) are a very important part of the legal landscape today. Consider the fact that there are rules relating to taxation, safety in the workplace, welfare benefits, air and water pollution, social security and medicare benefits, food additives and adulteration, automobile safety, civil rights, and much, much more. Next time you are in the law library, look at the many bookshelves containing the Code of Federal Regulations (C.F.R.). While the official United States Code is contained in perhaps two dozen volumes, C.F.R., containing the rules of federal agencies, comprises almost two hundred volumes. And those volumes contain only *federal* regulations—the published rules of your state and city agencies would fill many more volumes and probably also greatly surpass in size the relevant state statutory codes and city ordinances. In addition to these published rules, agencies issue many documents called guidelines, interpretations, manuals, bulletins, circulars, or policy statements, to guide the public and their own staff in interpreting the law and in determining how agency discretion will be exercised.

These documents may be subject to different legal requirements or may have different legal effects than other documents called rules.

iii. *Licensing.* A license is a form of permission authorizing a particular individual or entity to engage in a specified activity. It is likely that AIC will also be authorized by its enabling act to regulate automobile insurance by licensing, meaning that in order to write insurance in the state, insurance companies will first need to obtain a license from AIC. Automobile insurance brokers may also be required to have licenses. The AIC will issue rules specifying the qualifications for obtaining a license (financial qualifications, education, experience, an exam etc.) and rules specifying what licensees may and may not do. It will also issue rules providing when and how licenses may be revoked or suspended.

Licensing schemes have many benefits. They help to assure that consumers are served only by properly qualified people who are subject to disciplinary rules. But such schemes also have many costs. They are a barrier to entry, often requiring licensees to have more education and experience than is needed. In that case, licensing tends to decrease competition and increase prices without compensating public benefit. Thus a licensing scheme may really be a conspiracy to use the power of government to keep competitors out and profits up. A regulated industry may have "captured" an agency so that the agency power is turned against the interests of the public rather than the regulated industry. For these reasons, we suggest the use of close scrutiny when analyzing the desirability of licensing schemes.

Permits are a form of license. An agency may be authorized to require a permit before specified action may occur. If AIC adopted a permit system, for example, an automobile insurance company might be required to secure permission from that agency before changing its rates or changing the terms of any of its policies. Permits are often required before a power plant may be built, before a new bank may be opened, and before new drugs or pesticides may be sold.

A less drastic approach is sometimes referred to as a clearance system. Under that approach, an agency requires certain steps to be taken by the regulated party before that party may proceed with a specified type of action. However, the agency need not affirmatively approve the action by issuing a permit before the regulated party may proceed. For example, the filing of an environmental impact statement with an agency may be required before an individual may take certain types of action that could be detrimental to the environment. Or a corporation may be required to file disclosure documents and issue a prospectus before selling securities. Under this approach, the AIC might require automobile insurance companies to notify AIC before changing the rates or the terms of any of their policies.

Permit systems are sometimes necessary, as in the case of an extremely dangerous activity like building a nuclear power plant or selling a new drug. However, they are costly to administer, usually entail long delays, may be harmful to the competitive system (which requires competitors to respond promptly to market conditions), and may in practice allow an administrator to substitute his or her wisdom for that of the market. And note that a staff member who must make a decision to grant a permit is likely to be conservative and cautious; that might mean that some products are never approved and never become available. For example, many drugs are available in Europe but not in the United States, because our system of regulation is more restrictive. The wisdom of this result is, of course, debatable.

iv. *Investigation and law enforcement.* Once the agency is authorized to enforce a statute and the rules it issues pursuant to that statute, it needs to ensure that those subject to the statute and rules follow them. The agency must keep in touch with its licensees and other regulated parties to make sure that they understand their responsibilities. It must also be prepared to receive complaints from the public, and needs a staff to investigate those complaints. To be effective in this role, it must have formal investigatory powers to subpoena documents, inspect premises, and obtain routine reports from its licensees or other regulated parties. In the end, if it believes it has uncovered a law violation, the agency must initiate some enforcement action against the offender because statutes and rules will not enforce themselves, and members of the public often do not have the resources, the will, or the information necessary for the effective initiation of enforcement actions on their own. For practical purposes, therefore, an agency functions much like a police department *and* a prosecuting office.

v. *Adjudication.* An adjudication is an agency determination of *particular* applicability that purports to settle the legal rights or duties of a specified person based upon his or her individual circumstances. The AIC will inevitably be engaged in adjudication. Does a particular applicant qualify for an AIC license to write automobile insurance in the state or to act as an automobile insurance broker? Should the license of a particular insurance company or broker be suspended or revoked because of a violation of AIC rules? Has a particular individual violated an AIC rule prohibiting specified unfair insurance practices? The AIC might also be empowered to resolve disputes between consumers and their insurance companies over questions of coverage, rates, or unjust cancellation. That is, sometimes agencies are authorized to decide disputes that would ordinarily be decided in the courts. Examples include disputes between employers and employees over job related injuries—workers' compensation—and disputes between commodity brokers and their customers.

State and federal APAs closely regulate the most significant types of agency adjudication. In addition, constitutional conceptions of due process impose significant constraints on agency adjudications. So, when an agency like AIC adjudicates the kinds of issues indicated above, it will typically be required to afford the parties involved a trial-type hearing of some sort. That hearing will normally be conducted by a person called a hearing officer or administrative law judge (ALJ). His or her decision may be appealed to the agency head. This part of administrative law may seem familiar because it is not unlike civil procedure. But the differences between courts and adjudicating agencies are profound.

Because the agency is obligated to execute the law and to achieve its objectives it is an interested party on one side of the dispute. A court, on the other hand, is a wholly uninvolved arbiter between two conflicting sides. In addition, an agency specializes in its particular regulatory process. As a result, it possesses a great deal of specialized experience and technical expertise. Judges, on the other hand, are usually generalists, not specialists. Finally, an agency makes the rules, investigates violations, prosecutes cases, and adjudicates cases; a court only adjudicates cases and, therefore, unlike an agency, is not subject to conflicts between potentially inconsistent obligations. All of these factors raise serious problems in assuring fair and impartial agency adjudication.

vi. *Ratemaking.* Assuming its enabling act has authorized AIC to do so, AIC might also set automobile insurance premiums. If automobile insurance rates are to be set by law, it must be done by an agency, and not by the legislature, because the process is extremely time-consuming, and the rates require constant adjustment as market conditions change.

Administrative price fixing is a common technique, particularly in situations of natural monopoly (local phones, gas, electricity, cable TV) or when market failures of one sort or another are thought to prevent the market from functioning properly. In the recent past we have partially or completely abandoned government price fixing of transportation (trucking, airlines, busses, railroads, pipelines) and financial services (banking, stock brokerage). Some price fixing, however, still continues, such as gas and electric utility rate regulation and rent control in some places.

In order to fix prices on either an industry-wide or a company-specific basis, AIC must observe appropriate procedures. Depending on whether the rates are industry-wide or company-specific, the appropriate process may look more like rulemaking or adjudication. Either way, the process will be a lengthy one since the rates can be set only after detailed economic information is collected and analyzed, and a fair rate of return is determined. In any case, one may question whether rate fixing is needed or even useful in a market like automobile insurance.

vii. *Judicial review.* Judicial review of administrative action occurs very frequently. Unlike other countries (such as France), in this country the same courts that resolve ordinary private law disputes also conduct judicial review of agency action. Broadly speaking, courts will review agency action, including agency rules and final adjudicatory orders, for errors of law and for reasonableness in finding facts or exercising discretion. A typical challenge to agency action may include allegations that the action was not within the authority delegated to the agency, that it was procedurally improper, that it was unconstitutional or inconsistent with the applicable substantive law, or that it was otherwise arbitrary or capricious.

As a result, it is inevitable that if AIC adopts rules that either consumers or the insurance industry do not like, the procedural and substantive validity of the rules will be challenged in court. Similarly, if AIC revokes a license, it is likely that the licensee will seek judicial review of that action to ensure that the proper procedures were followed, the proper legal criteria were applied, the action was supported by substantial evidence, and the AIC acted reasonably and within the scope of its authority.

viii. *Legislative and executive review.* The courts are not the only branch of government that scrutinizes the actions of agencies. The legislature performs a continuing oversight function, investigating agency action and amending agency enabling acts when it deems that desirable. In some states, the legislature has other powers to control agencies such as a power to delay or even veto agency rules or other actions. The chief executive (the governor in our example) will appoint the director or directors of AIC and will also follow its activities. The chief executive may also have the authority to remove those officials for good cause or for any reason. A statute may also give the chief executive authority to delay or veto agency rules. In practice, legislative and executive control over the agency's annual budget will also provide opportunities for effective oversight of its activities.

The above snapshot of the administrative process is meant only to convey a general idea of the nature of the process with which administrative law must deal. In fact, the administrative process is very diverse. Each agency, for good reasons, has its own way of doing business. In addition to looking at general principles of administrative law common to all agencies, therefore, a lawyer dealing with an agency must always consult, at the outset, the enabling act of that particular agency, its rules, and its precedential law.

§ 1.6 COSTS AND BENEFITS OF ADMINISTRATIVE PROCEDURE AND PROCEDURAL REFORM

In studying the legal requirements surrounding the administrative process you should consider the desirability of each requirement and the possible alternatives to that requirement. To make that determination you must first consider the principal objectives of sound agency administration. Agencies should act lawfully, be responsive to the wishes of the body politic, make accurate and sound determinations, and treat affected persons fairly. Agencies should also act in an efficient, effective, and economical manner. Sometimes realization of some of these objectives may conflict with the realization of other of these objectives. In such situations, there must be an acceptable accommodation between those competing objectives.

As to each procedural requirement imposed on agencies you should ask whether its costs are excessive in light of its potential benefits. Three steps are necessary to answer that question. First, you should determine the benefits of the requirement by asking whether it is likely to achieve one or more of the objectives posited for optimum agency administration. This inquiry should also include an estimate of the value of those objectives. Second, you should determine the costs of that requirement by asking about the extent to which it interferes with one or more of the objectives posited for optimum agency administration. This inquiry should also include an estimate of the value of those objectives. Finally, you should determine whether the total of the benefits of the particular requirement outweighs the total of its costs. As an aid in answering the third inquiry, you should determine whether the requirement in question maximizes, to the greatest extent possible, each of the potentially competing objectives of good agency administration. Of course, this determination must be made in light of any alternatives to the requirement that might achieve the objectives sought at a lesser cost.

In the end, there is no scientific answer to such a cost-benefit inquiry. It is value laden at every turn and, therefore, must be resolved by an exercise of judgment. While empirical data may help advance such an inquiry by specifying more clearly some of the benefits and costs involved, data of that kind cannot finally resolve the inquiry. The defensibility of the cost-benefit judgment depends on the quality of the arguments marshalled in its support rather than on the basis of any equation seeking to reduce disparate costs, benefits, and values, to a single common denominator, so that they may be mechanically compared. *See* A. Bonfield, STATE ADMINISTRATIVE RULE MAKING § 7.1 (1986).

A cost-benefit analysis of the kind noted above will require you to think about procedural requirements in the administrative process as overhead, the costs of which may compete, in some situations, with the quantity of the substantive results that may be delivered. Such an analysis should also induce you to think about the extent to which agency discretion should be fettered by the courts, the legislature, or the agency itself. Agencies always have a range of permissible choices to make in administering the law. This range of choice is called "discretion." One of the great tasks of administrative law is to find the optimum degree to which agency discretion should be fettered in each context. Unfettered discretion gives agencies maximum flexibility to deal with unforeseen or changing problems, but it also allows them to act in irresponsible or arbitrary ways. Fettered discretion denies agencies flexibility in dealing with unforeseen or changing problems and limits their opportunities to act in irresponsible or arbitrary ways. Determining the optimum degree to which agency discretion should be fettered in each context, therefore, will not be easy.

Another problem you will have to face in evaluating the desirability of specific legal requirements imposed on the administrative process relates to the essential nature and inherent problems of bureaucracies. The question is whether legal requirements can effectively prevent a bureaucracy that is created to advance the public interest from becoming captured by the groups it is intended to regulate, from taking action primarily to serve the self interest of the bureaucracy rather than the interests of the public, or from becoming rigid, wasteful, ineffective, and generally counter-productive. This, too, is a hard question.

Critics of the administrative process claim it suffers from many ills. They complain that the process is often unresponsive to the public will, slow and cumbersome, ineffective and inefficient, and unfair because it does not adequately protect private interests against improper governmental action. They have also argued that the administrative process is often defective because it does not sufficiently adjust the overhead costs of procedure to the varying importance of the many different substantive matters with which the process deals, and that it does not adequately ensure that the bureaucratic interests of administrators are subordinated to the public interest. Even proponents of the process agree that there is merit to one or more of these complaints in many parts of the process. And while many critics of the administrative process see deregulation—the withdrawal of governmental involvement in various aspects of our lives—as a major solution to many of these process problems, most critics and proponents of the process agree that it can at least be improved through procedural reform.

Procedural reform is seen as helpful because of a belief in our capacity to at least marginally improve (if not to perfect) the operation of our institutions through experience and experiment, and a belief that the administrative process, its problems, and the matters with which it deals, are variable and multifaceted rather than constant and uniform. In reality there is no single administrative process; there are many administrative processes, each of them operating in different contexts, and with different problems and possible solutions to those problems. Of course, at some level of generality, there are also common problems, and solutions to those problems, among the many administrative processes operating in this country.

The strong American belief in administrative procedure reform is evidenced by the constant tinkering with the administrative process in this country by our many state, federal, and local legislative bodies, and the agencies themselves. This tinkering appears endless and substantial societal resources are expended in its pursuit. On the state level, the important role in such reform of the National Conference of Commissioners on Uniform State Laws and its various MSAPAs has already been noted. At the federal level special note should be taken of the work of the Administrative Conference of the United States (cited throughout this book as ACUS). It is a federal governmental body whose sole mission is to propose improvements in the federal administrative process. ACUS recommendations are often cited in the body of this book.

Throughout this course, you should consider the extent to which administrative procedure reform is possible and realistic in particular contexts, and the specific shape it might take on the basis of a cost-benefit analysis of the kind discussed earlier.

§ 1.7 AGENCY LEGITIMACY AND ADMINISTRATIVE LAW: A THEORY

In general, there is agreement that administrative law should seek to ensure that agency processes are lawful, fair, effective, and efficient. It also should seek to ensure that agency functions are legitimate—that is—are executed in a manner that is consistent with the political will of the community at large. This subsection discusses some possible theories for the legitimacy of unelected agencies and the role of administrative law. These theories are discussed at length in a very important article by Richard Stewart, "The Reformation of American Administrative Law," 88 Harv.L.Rev. 1667 (1975). An understanding of these theories can help you explain and evaluate the many facets of administrative law you will encounter as a student and practicing lawyer.

The traditional model of administrative law assumed that the activities of unelected agencies could be legitimated if they were viewed as a "transmission belt" for implementing statutes enacted by the elected legislature that contained specific directions to the agencies. According to this model, the role of administrative law was to keep agencies within statutory bounds and, thereby, to limit official intrusions on private liberty or property to those specifically intended by the politically responsible legislature. However, as indicated in § 7.3, *infra,* most legislative delegations to agencies today are extremely vague and broad, providing agencies with great discretion that is virtually unfettered by specific statutory language. Consequently, the "transmission belt" model is insufficient to justify the role of agencies in modern government or to provide an adequate theory for current administrative law.

During the 1930's, a new model of administrative law emerged as a response to the economic disorganization of the times. Agencies were expected to solve the nation's economic problems on the basis of their special expertise. It was assumed that the resolution by agency bureaucrats of technical problems solely on the basis of their special expertise would channel and cabin the broad discretion vested in agencies and ensure that agency actions were consistent with the specific wishes of the elected legislature for a technocratic resolution of the problems facing the nation. The role of administrative law was to facilitate the development and use of agency expertise and to protect that expertise from unwarranted intrusion by purely political considerations. However, our faith in expertise as a legitimating instrument for agency lawmaking declined as it became clear that many of the problems to be solved by agencies were primarily political, rather than technocratic. Consequently, the "expertise" model also failed to provide an adequate theory for the legitimacy of agency discretionary powers and the role of administrative law.

Today, a model of administrative law based on interest representation has emerged. This model views the activities of unelected agencies as legitimate to the extent agencies engage in a political process that mirrors the legislative process. The assumption is that all special interests concerned with a problem should be represented in the administrative process that seeks its resolution, and that a desirable outcome is one that reconciles the claims of these interests in a way that best reflects their varying political influences in the governance of the community as a whole. In the interest representation model, therefore, the role of administrative law is to provide a process for the operation of agencies that approximates the political milieu surrounding elected officials, thereby ensuring the political responsibility of unelected administrative bureaucrats.

However, there are a number of serious problems with the interest representation theory for administrative law. It may not be practical or appropriate to mandate agency procedures that facilitate or ensure interest representation in all administrative proceedings. We also may not be prepared to accept the election of agency members to represent various special interest constituencies because this would often assure deadlock or domination of public administrative processes by private interests. Furthermore:

> In many fields of administration, the widespread effects of governmental decisions or the need for swift, decisive action may render formal schemes of representation for all affected interests intolerably burdensome. Even where these imperatives are absent, the case for interest representation may be doubtful if we are to give weight to policy outcomes as well as to processes of decision. A measure of deregulation seems eminently desirable in many sectors, yet interest groups that have become formally enmeshed in agency administration are unlikely to call for the agency's abolition. In other areas, it would be desirable for agencies to adopt policies designed to maximize allocational efficiency, but such policies are unlikely to emerge from a formalized process of bargaining among affected interests that will generate pressures for compromise and an "equitable" division of burdens and benefits.

Stewart, *supra,* at 1804–05.

These criticisms mean that while the interest representation model of administrative law may have great utility, this model, like the transmission belt and expertise models, does not provide a fully adequate or comprehensive theory for the current role of administrative law in our society.

Nevertheless, it is clear that a principal function of administrative law is to ensure that agency decisions are legitimate in the sense that they are responsive to the interests and preferences of the body politic. Some measures to ensure political control of administrative action involve the imposition on agencies of direct sanctions, such as legislative hearings, the firing of administrators, appropriations, and legislation. Such direct means of political control of agency action require extensive monitoring, are costly, and cannot be used very often in practice. Appropriate administrative procedures can also serve the objective of ensuring that agencies implement the legislative will; and they can do so at a much lower cost than direct monitoring or sanctions by the elected legislature or chief executive. The following excerpt provides an interesting explanation of the role of administrative procedure in securing the political accountability of agency decisionmaking.

McCUBBINS, NOLL, WEINGAST, "ADMINISTRATIVE PROCEDURES AS INSTRUMENTS OF POLITICAL CONTROL"

3 Journal of Law, Economics, & Organization 243, 253–55, 273–74 (1987).*

Administrative procedures can . . . [help to ensure agency compliance with the political will of the community] only if procedures actually affect the outcomes of decisionmaking processes. . . . [E]laborate procedures can serve at least two other ends. First, . . . procedures may be ends in their own right. Regardless of the outcome, people may derive greater value from processes that treat them respectfully and give the appearance of rationality than from processes that are perceived to be cruel, unfair, and arbitrary. Second, procedures may be a ruse aimed at the electorate in that they have no effect on outcomes but transfer apparent responsibility for decisions from elected political officials to agencies or courts. . . .

While both lines of argument point to plausible features of administrative processes, . . . we assume that the details of administrative law as applied to any given decision problem will affect the outcome. The basis for this assumption [that procedures do affect outcomes] is the presumption that decisions depend on the information that underpins them, and on the means for relating that information to decisions that are permissible according to the strictures of administrative law. If decisionmakers must take account of all of the relevant information that is available to them, and if participants in an administrative process can be relied upon to provide information that is, on balance, favorable to their interests, then . . . [certain procedural rules imposed by administrative law] will affect the range of decisions available to an agency. . . .

[Administrative procedures seek to solve] . . . two general forms of [political] control problems. First, *political principals in both branches of government suffer an informational disadvantage with respect to the bureaucracy.* . . . We argue that many . . . [required administrative procedures are calculated to] solve this asymmetric information problem. Second, *the coalition that forms to create an agency—the committee that drafted the legislation, the chamber majorities that approved it, and the . . . [chief executive] who signed it into law—will seek to ensure that the bargain struck among the members of the coalition does not unravel once the coalition disbands.* Specifically, the coalition will seek to combine sanctions with an institutional structure to create pressures on agencies that replicate the political pressures applied when the relevant legislation was enacted. Here, the point of administrative procedures is *not* to preselect specific policy outcomes, but to create a decisionmaking environment that mirrors the political circumstances that gave rise to the establishment of the policy. Whereas political officials may not know what specific policy outcome they will want in the future, they will know which interests ought to influence a decision and what distributive outcomes will be consistent with the original coalitional arrangement. In other words, [through the imposition of appropriate procedures] the coalition "stacks the deck" in the agency's decisionmaking to enhance the durability of the bargain struck among members of the coalition. . . .

If these uses of administrative process are effective, the agency, without any need for input, guidance, or attention from political principals, is directed towards the decisions its principals would make on their own, even if the principals are unaware, ex ante, of what that outcome would be. By structuring the rules of the game for the agency, administrative procedures sequence agency activity, regulate its information collection and dissemination, limit its available choices, and define its strategic advantage. Moreover, an important feature of this system is that constituents, agencies, and the courts bear much of the costs of ensuring compliance. Indeed, courts are the key, for without them political actors could not rely on decentralized enforcement. . . .

[In conclusion, administrative procedures are an especially effective means of securing agencies' compliance with the will of their political overseers] . . . because they ameliorate the problem of asymmetric information. . . . They reduce the informational costs of following agency activities and especially facilitate . . . monitoring through constituencies affected by an agency's policies. They also sharpen decisions to punish [agencies] by facilitating the assessment of the extent and importance of noncompliance. Thus, by lowering the costs of monitoring and sharpening sanctions, administrative procedures produce an equilibrium in which compliance is greater than it otherwise would be.

A second role of administrative procedures is that they can be used by agencies to avoid inadvertent noncompliance of such a magnitude that it would lead to sanctions. In politics, sanctions are costly to both the principal and the agent. . . .

Hence, sanctions impose a net loss that all sides have a common interest to avoid. Administrative procedures aid an agency in avoiding sanctions in three ways. By stacking the deck to benefit favored political interests, they channel decisions in directions preferred by political overseers. By mirroring the political environment faced by the agency's overseers, an agency's processes give it information about which constituencies, if any, might threaten the agency politically should they be dissatisfied with its policies. And by facilitating early dissemination of information about further feasible policy decisions, administrative procedures increase the chance that the "fire alarm" will be sounded by an offended constituency before an agency is fully committed to a policy. Thus, administrative procedures reduce the likelihood that sanctions will actually have to be used.

Together, the legal constraints imposed by procedures and the incentives created by threat of sanction establish a decisionmaking environment that channels agency policy choices in favor of constituencies important to political overseers. Thus, the administrative system is automatic. The infrequency of visible oversight activities (and especially sanctions) does not mean that there is an absence of political control . . . .

————

As you study *each specific requirement* of administrative law consider the extent to which it is consistent or inconsistent with the theory proposed by McCubbins, Noll, and Weingast. To the extent any requirement is inconsistent with their theory, consider what other theories might explain that requirement.

§ 1.8 PROBLEMS

1. *Enforcement of civil rights statutes.* The year is 1960. There are no existing state or federal laws that comprehensively prohibit discrimination on the basis of race, sex, ethnicity, and religion, in employment, housing, and places of public accommodation. The leadership of both parties in the state legislature decides to enact comprehensive civil rights legislation prohibiting such discrimination. They want that legislation to be effective, but they are in doubt about the precise means they should provide for its enforcement.

Such legislation might simply provide criminal penalties for violation of the substantive provisions of such an act; or it could provide for civil enforcement through the courts; or it could provide some type of administrative enforcement; or it could provide for an enforcement mechanism combining elements of all of the above.

You are a member of the staff of the state legislature. The leadership asks you to draft an ideal scheme for the effective enforcement of such legislation. Obviously, whatever scheme you propose must be as economical, efficient, and fair as possible. What kind of scheme would you recommend? If an administrative process should be used either alone or in some combination with any of the other processes, you should decide whether the agency created for enforcing this law should be single-headed or multi-headed, independent or part of the executive branch, single or multiple purposed, appointed or elected, and full or part time. You should also consider what specific kinds of powers should be delegated to the agency, and what procedures it should observe.

For a general discussion of these questions *see* Bonfield, "State Civil Rights Statutes: Some Proposals," 49 Iowa L.Rev. 1067, 1110–1119 (1964); Bonfield, "An Institutional Analysis of the Agencies Administering Fair Employment Practices Laws," 42 N.Y.U.L.Rev. 823, 828–67 (1967).

2. *Regulation of new technology.* You are a member of the staff of a state legislator who is the chair of the Technology Subcommittee. You have been meeting with representatives of several companies engaged in genetic engineering research and the production of genetically engineered products. In particular, one of the companies wants to begin testing a manufactured virus which it claims will lower the freezing point of unpicked oranges and thus preserve the oranges from deadly frosts.

Assume that at present there is no state or federal regulation of bio-engineered products (unless they are foods or drugs). The technology obviously is dangerous and there is a lot of community resistance to the proposed tests. Yet the benefit to mankind, and to the manufacturing companies, of a successful product would be enormous.

Is this an area in which there should be regulation? Should there be a new agency to deal with the problem? What powers should the agency have?

See Comment, "Regulating the Environmental Release of Genetically Engineered Organisms," 12 Fla.St.L.Rev. 891 (1985); *Foundation on Economic Trends v. Heckler,* 756 F.2d 143 (D.C.Cir.1985).

*

Part I

AGENCY PROCEDURES

In this Part we examine the procedures used by agencies in the performance of their functions affecting private rights. Consequently, the primary focus of this Part is on agency *adjudication,* the administrative process for determining the legal rights of specified individuals based on their particular circumstances, and on *rulemaking,* the administrative process for making legal determinations of general applicability. A consideration of the agency procedures utilized in these processes involves an examination of constitutional, statutory, and common law requirements.

Chapter 2

THE CONSTITUTIONAL RIGHT
TO A HEARING

The fifth amendment to the Constitution, which applies to the federal government, provides that no person shall "be deprived of life, liberty, or property, without due process of law." Section 1 of the fourteenth amendment, which applies to state government, contains similar language. These constitutional amendments guarantee some level of *process* before government deprives a person of life, liberty, or property. State constitutions may guarantee more protection than is provided by the federal Constitution.

This chapter is about "procedural due process" in administrative law. In other words, when a government agency seeks to deprive a person of important interests, must it provide some form of process? If so, what kind? And when must it be provided?

You are familiar with the *judicial* procedures required before the state imposes a criminal sanction or a civil remedy. However, a vast number of governmental decisions which have a negative impact on individuals are not administered through courts (although courts usually can *review* these decisions). Here are some examples of the sort of decisions which involve the vital interests of literally millions of people every year:

i. *Benefit decisions.* An agency refuses to grant, or it reduces or terminates, social security old age or disability payments, welfare benefits, or food stamps.

ii. *Access to services.* A state educational institution suspends or expels a student, asserting poor academic performance or violation of rules. A municipal utility cuts off a customer, claiming nonpayment of bills.

iii. *Licenses.* An agency suspends a driver's license, or it prevents a lawyer or doctor from practicing his or her profession.

iv. *Jobs or contracts.* Government fires an employee or it terminates a contract.

v. *Taxes.* An agency asserts that a taxpayer owes more in taxes than the taxpayer believes is correct.

vi. *Institutional decisions.* A prisoner is denied parole or placed in solitary confinement because of alleged violation of prison rules.

If such disputes are not resolved informally (as most of them are), the individual may wish to have an impartial decision-maker adjudicate the conflict. Through a right to hearing provided by statute or by the constitution, such persons may be able to obtain a decision through a structured hearing process conducted by someone who is not involved in the dispute.

This chapter is intended to introduce several themes which recur throughout the book. These are:

i. *Administrative law matters.* The availability of some type of hearing is extremely important to persons who believe they are victims of wrong decisions taken by a clumsy and insensitive bureaucracy. If such persons have a right to hearing, they can seize government's attention and get the dispute settled by an impartial decision-maker.

ii. *Administrative law is about discretion.* A person has "discretion" when he or she can legally choose between several alternatives. Government frequently has a vast discretion in discharging administrative functions. Much of administrative law can be viewed as a study of the rules and institutions which limit that discretion. In this chapter, we consider whether a hearing is a good way to limit and structure an agency's discretionary power over individuals.

For example, suppose that a violent student demonstration occurs at a state university. The dean suspects that a particular student was involved and wishes to impose discipline. The university must hold a hearing to determine the facts—what was the student's role in the demonstration? But the hearing should also focus on the discretionary decision—what sort of discipline is appropriate? Expulsion? Suspension? For how long? Or is a reprimand in the files sufficient?

iii. *Administrative procedure is costly.* Take welfare hearings— the subject considered next. Giving people hearings before cutting them off the rolls costs welfare agencies money and reduces the funds available for helping poor people. It delays the removal of unqualified people from the welfare rolls and encourages people to appeal just to delay the termination of their payments. Hearings take up a lot of time and energy which case-workers could spend helping their clients. Are these costs always worth it?

iv. *Issues of administrative law involve fundamental value conflicts.* Your position will be determined largely by your own philosophical and political viewpoint, but a study of administrative law can inform these positions. Some of the conflicts that this chapter illuminates are: Should non-traditional forms of property and liberty (like welfare benefits or a student's interest in staying in school) receive as much procedural protection as we give to traditional kinds of property or liberty? Where should the line be drawn between full procedural protection and conflicting administrative interests, like the need to operate efficiently or to conserve scarce budgetary resources? How much of the limited resources of the courts should be invested in judicial review of administrative decisions? Is traditional adversary judicialized procedure the best way to protect people's interests against detrimental administrative action?

The chapter opens with an important and dramatic administrative law decision. The majority and dissenting opinions in *Goldberg v. Kelly* illuminate these value conflicts with stirring rhetoric in a setting of immense practical importance: the conflict between an individual and a state welfare bureaucracy. Much of the material which follows in this chapter is a reaction to Justice Brennan's opinion in *Goldberg* — largely a retreat from it. Did Justice Brennan have his priorities straight in *Goldberg*? Or did he promise more than our government can deliver?

§ 2.1 HEARINGS AND WELFARE TERMINATION: DUE PROCESS AND MASS JUSTICE

Before turning to the seminal *Goldberg* decision, we supply some background about welfare. Aid for Families with Dependent Children (AFDC) is the most important of several need-based welfare systems. Established in 1935, AFDC furnishes federal money to the states; the states provide additional funds, set their own level of benefits, and administer the program (within the constraints of federal law). In 1985, there were 3.7 million families on AFDC, representing almost eleven million recipients, receiving more than one billion dollars per month. The great majority of recipients are single-parent households with one or more children.

Qualification for AFDC is based on need, and the welfare bureaucracy must constantly assess and reassess the need of vast numbers of people. Although welfare varies from state to state, even in the most generous states a family must be nearly destitute before it qualifies for aid. In contrast to prior years, the determination of need and resources is based on relatively routinized standards, allowing for little judgment on the part of the caseworker and little consideration of a recipient family's special circumstances.

AFDC may be denied, reduced, or terminated for various reasons, such as a failure to meet the needs standard because of a change in resources. In addition, welfare can be terminated if a qualified parent does not cooperate in obtaining support from an absent parent or when other rule violations are detected. *Goldberg v. Kelly,* which follows, addresses the question of what sort of appeal procedure must be provided when the recipient does not agree with the welfare department's decision to terminate the benefit.

For flavor, here is Professor Joel Handler's sketch of welfare today:

Volume [of recipients] is a brutal fact of the welfare state . . . vast numbers of people in our society, as presently organized, will need financial and other assistance. This is especially true for the client group on which we focus: female-headed households. Volume is the cardinal enemy of discretion, professional judgment, individualization; heavy caseloads force routinization . . .

Values and attitudes toward the poor are varied, long-standing, and greatly affect how the poor are treated. Society has always distinguished between the deserving and undeserving poor, those whose poverty is blameless and those who are blameworthy. In a prior age, the blind, the halt, and the lame were in the former category; those who could work but failed were in the latter. Today, the aged and the disabled have joined the former, but the nonaged—the childless adults, and the female-headed households—are still the undeserving. It is not only the failure of work that draws the community's hostility; fueling the furies are race, sex, and various forms of deviant behavior and life style.

. . . Programs for the undeserving are very different [from Social Security]. They are state and local, discretionary, decentralized, and subject to a great many moralistic and punitive practices . . .

The final cause of the ills of public assistance programs is the distribution of wealth and power. One can never forget that the people we are talking about are extremely dependent. They are ill-prepared to effectively participate in public programs, and, in particular, to understand the procedural systems designed to secure benefits and rights for them. The bureaucracy has control over the information, the resources, the staying power, the power of retaliation; workers, even if well-meaning, are pressed for time, short of money, and, in all honesty, feel that they know what is best for the clients . . .

Two additional comments: the utter chaos that one witnesses in the public assistance offices—the crowds, the waiting, the shouting, the maze of cubicles, the forms, the fear and resignation of the applicants, and the anger and frustration of the workers; second, that by forcing public assistance recipients to supplement their welfare grants by resorting to General Assistance and private charity—where available—the recipients are now confronting the most discretionary, moralistic public and private programs, in which there are virtually no legal protections.

"Discretion in Social Welfare: The Uneasy Position of the Rule of Law," 92 Yale L.J. 1270, 1271–74 (1983).

GOLDBERG v. KELLY

397 U.S. 254 (1970).

MR. JUSTICE BRENNAN delivered the opinion of the Court.

The question for decision is whether a State that terminates public assistance payments to a particular recipient without affording him the opportunity for an evidentiary hearing prior to termination denies the recipient procedural due process in violation of the Due Process Clause of the Fourteenth Amendment.

This action was brought in the District Court for the Southern District of New York by residents of New York City receiving financial aid under the federally assisted program of Aid to Families with Dependent Children (AFDC) or under New York State's general Home Relief program.[1] Their complaint alleged that the New York State and New York City officials administering these programs terminated, or were about to terminate, such aid without prior notice and hearing, thereby denying them due process of law. At the time the suits were filed there was no requirement of prior notice or hearing of any kind before termination of financial aid. However, the state and city adopted procedures for notice and hearing after the suits were brought, and the plaintiffs, appellees here, then challenged the constitutional adequacy of those procedures. . . .

A caseworker who has doubts about the recipient's continued eligibility must first discuss them with the recipient. If the caseworker concludes that the recipient is no longer eligible, he recommends termination of aid to a unit supervisor. If the latter concurs, he sends the recipient a letter stating the reasons for proposing to terminate aid and notifying him that within seven days he may request that a higher official review the record, and may support the request with a written statement prepared personally or with the aid of an attorney or other person. If the reviewing official affirms the determination of ineligibility, aid is stopped immediately and the recipient is informed by letter of the reasons for the action. Appellees' challenge to this procedure emphasizes the absence of any provisions for the personal appearance of the recipient before the reviewing official, for oral presentation of evidence, and for confrontation and cross-examination of adverse witnesses. However, the letter does inform the recipient that he may request a post-termination "fair hearing." This is a proceeding before an independent state hearing officer at which the recipient may appear personally, offer oral evidence, confront and cross-examine the witnesses against him, and have a record made of the hearing. If the recipient prevails at the "fair hearing" he is paid all funds erroneously withheld.

1. [One plaintiff lost AFDC payments for refusing to cooperate with the city in suing her estranged husband. She contended that the cooperation requirement was inapplicable to the facts of her case. Another was dropped because he refused to accept counseling for drug addiction. He maintained that he does not use drugs.]

A recipient whose aid is not restored by a "fair hearing" decision may have judicial review . . .

I

The constitutional issue to be decided, therefore, is the narrow one whether the Due Process Clause requires that the recipient be afforded an evidentiary hearing *before* the termination of benefits. The District Court held that only a pre-termination evidentiary hearing would satisfy the constitutional command, and rejected the argument of the state and city officials that the combination of the post-termination "fair hearing" with the informal pre-termination review disposed of all due process claims. The court said: "While post-termination review is relevant, there is one overpowering fact which controls here. By hypothesis, a welfare recipient is destitute, without funds or assets. . . . Suffice it to say that to cut off a welfare recipient in the face of . . . 'brutal need' without a prior hearing of some sort is unconscionable, unless overwhelming considerations justify it." The court rejected the argument that the need to protect the public's tax revenues supplied the requisite "overwhelming consideration." "Against the justified desire to protect public funds must be weighed the individual's overpowering need in this unique situation not to be wrongfully deprived of assistance. . . . While the problem of additional expense must be kept in mind, it does not justify denying a hearing meeting the ordinary standards of due process. Under all the circumstances, we hold that due process requires an adequate hearing before termination of welfare benefits, and the fact that there is a later constitutionally fair proceeding does not alter the result." . . .

Appellant does not contend that procedural due process is not applicable to the termination of welfare benefits. Such benefits are a matter of statutory entitlement for persons qualified to receive them.[8] Their termination involves state action that adjudicates important rights. The constitutional challenge cannot be answered by an argument that public assistance benefits are "a 'privilege' and not a 'right.'" Relevant constitutional restraints apply as much to the withdrawal of public assistance benefits as to disqualification for unem-

[8.] It may be realistic today to regard welfare entitlements as more like "property" than a "gratuity." Much of the existing wealth in this country takes the form of rights that do not fall within traditional common-law concepts of property. It has been aptly noted that "[s]ociety today is built around entitlement. The automobile dealer has his franchise, the doctor and lawyer their professional licenses, the worker his union membership, contract, and pension rights, the executive his contract and stock options; all are devices to aid security and independence. Many of the most important of these entitlements now flow from government: subsidies to farmers and businessmen, routes for airlines and channels for television stations; long term contracts for defense, space, and education; social security pensions for individuals. Such sources of security, whether private or public, are no longer regarded as luxuries or gratuities; to the recipients they are essentials, fully deserved, and in no sense a form of charity. It is only the poor whose entitlements, although recognized by public policy, have not been effectively enforced." Reich, Individual Rights and Social Welfare: The Emerging Legal Issues, 74 Yale LJ 1245, 1255 (1965). See also Reich, The New Property, 73 Yale LJ 733 (1964).

ployment compensation, . . . or to discharge from public employ-ment. . . . [The extent to which procedural due process must be afforded the recipient is influenced by the extent to which he may be "condemned to suffer grievous loss,"] Joint Anti–Fascist Refugee Committee v. McGrath, 341 US 123 (1951) (Frankfurter, J., concurring), and depends upon whether the recipient's interest in avoiding that loss outweighs the governmental interest in summary adjudication. Accordingly, as we said in Cafeteria & Restaurant Workers Union v. McElroy, 367 US 886 (1961), "consideration of what procedures due process may require under any given set of circumstances must begin with a determination of the precise nature of the government function involved as well as of the private interest that has been affected by governmental action."

It is true, of course, that some governmental benefits may be administratively terminated without affording the recipient a pre-termination evidentiary hearing.[10] But we agree with the District Court that when welfare is discontinued, only a pre-termination eviden-tiary hearing provides the recipient with procedural due process.

For qualified recipients, welfare provides the means to obtain essential food, clothing, housing, and medical care. Thus the crucial factor in this context—a factor not present in the case of the black-listed government contractor, the discharged government employee, the taxpayer denied a tax exemption, or virtually anyone else whose governmental entitlements are ended—is that termination of aid pend-ing resolution of a controversy over eligibility may deprive an *eligible* recipient of the very means by which to live while he waits. Since he lacks independent resources, his situation becomes immediately desper-ate. His need to concentrate upon finding the means for daily subsis-tence, in turn, adversely affects his ability to seek redress from the welfare bureaucracy.

Moreover, important governmental interests are promoted by af-fording recipients a pre-termination evidentiary hearing. From its founding the Nation's basic commitment has been to foster the dignity and well-being of all persons within its borders. . . . Welfare, by meeting the basic demands of subsistence, can help bring within the reach of the poor the same opportunities that are available to others to participate meaningfully in the life of the community. At the same time, welfare guards against the societal malaise that may flow from a

---

10. One Court of Appeals has stated: "In a wide variety of situations, it has long been recognized that where harm to the public is threatened, and the private inter-est infringed is reasonably deemed to be of less importance, an official body can take summary action pending a later hearing." R.A. Holman & Co. v. SEC, 299 F.2d 127 (1962) (suspension of exemption from stock registration requirement). See also, for ex-ample, Ewing v. Mytinger & Casselberry, Inc., 339 U.S. 594 (1950) (seizure of misla-beled vitamin product); North American Cold Storage Co. v. Chicago, 211 U.S. 306 (1908) (seizure of food not fit for human use); . . . In Cafeteria & Restaurant Workers Union v. McElroy, supra, summa-ry dismissal of a public employee was up-held because "[i]n [its] proprietary military capacity, the Federal Government . . . has traditionally exercised unfettered con-trol," and because the case involved the Government's "dispatch of its own internal affairs."

widespread sense of unjustified frustration and insecurity. Public assistance, then, is not mere charity, but a means to "promote the general Welfare, and secure the Blessings of Liberty to ourselves and our Posterity." The same governmental interests that counsel the provision of welfare, counsel as well its uninterrupted provision to those eligible to receive it; pre-termination evidentiary hearings are indispensable to that end.

Appellant does not challenge the force of these considerations but argues that they are outweighed by countervailing governmental interests in conserving fiscal and administrative resources. These interests, the argument goes, justify the delay of any evidentiary hearing until after discontinuance of the grants. Summary adjudication protects the public fisc by stopping payments promptly upon discovery of reason to believe that a recipient is no longer eligible. Since most terminations are accepted without challenge, summary adjudication also conserves both the fisc and administrative time and energy by reducing the number of evidentiary hearings actually held.

We agree with the District Court, however, that these governmental interests are not overriding in the welfare context. The requirement of a prior hearing doubtless involves some greater expense, and the benefits paid to ineligible recipients pending decision at the hearing probably cannot be recouped, since these recipients are likely to be judgment-proof. But the State is not without weapons to minimize these increased costs. Much of the drain on fiscal and administrative resources can be reduced by developing procedures for prompt pre-termination hearings and by skillful use of personnel and facilities. Indeed, the very provision for a post-termination evidentiary hearing in New York's Home Relief program is itself cogent evidence that the State recognizes the primacy of the public interest in correct eligibility determinations and therefore in the provision of procedural safeguards. Thus, the interest of the eligible recipient in uninterrupted receipt of public assistance, coupled with the State's interest that his payments not be erroneously terminated, clearly outweighs the State's competing concern to prevent any increase in its fiscal and administrative burdens. . . .

II

We also agree with the District Court, however, that the pre-termination hearing need not take the form of a judicial or quasi-judicial trial. We bear in mind that the statutory "fair hearing" will provide the recipient with a full administrative review.[14] Accordingly, the pre-termination hearing has one function only: to produce an initial determination of the validity of the welfare department's grounds for discontinuance of payments in order to protect a recipient against an erroneous termination of his benefits. Thus, a complete

---

14. Due process does not, of course, require two hearings. If, for example, a State simply wishes to continue benefits until after a "fair" hearing there will be no need for a preliminary hearing.

record and a comprehensive opinion, which would serve primarily to facilitate judicial review and to guide future decisions, need not be provided at the pre-termination stage. We recognize, too, that both welfare authorities and recipients have an interest in relatively speedy resolution of questions of eligibility, that they are used to dealing with one another informally, and that some welfare departments have very burdensome caseloads. These considerations justify the limitation of the pre-termination hearing to minimum procedural safeguards, adapted to the particular characteristics of welfare recipients, and to the limited nature of the controversies to be resolved. We wish to add that we, no less than the dissenters, recognize the importance of not imposing upon the States or the Federal Government in this developing field of law any procedural requirements beyond those demanded by rudimentary due process. . . .

The hearing must be "at a meaningful time and in a meaningful manner."

In the present context these principles require that a recipient have timely and adequate notice detailing the reasons for a proposed termination, and an effective opportunity to defend by confronting any adverse witnesses and by presenting his own arguments and evidence orally. These rights are important in cases such as those before us, where recipients have challenged proposed terminations as resting on incorrect or misleading factual premises or on misapplication of rules or policies to the facts of particular cases.[15]

We are not prepared to say that the seven-day notice currently provided by New York City is constitutionally insufficient per se, although there may be cases where fairness would require that a longer time be given. Nor do we see any constitutional deficiency in the content or form of the notice. New York employs both a letter and a personal conference with a caseworker to inform a recipient of the precise questions raised about his continued eligibility. Evidently the recipient is told the legal and factual bases for the Department's doubts. This combination is probably the most effective method of communicating with recipients.

The city's procedures presently do not permit recipients to appear personally with or without counsel before the official who finally determines continued eligibility. Thus a recipient is not permitted to present evidence to that official orally, or to confront or cross-examine adverse witnesses. These omissions are fatal to the constitutional adequacy of the procedures.

The opportunity to be heard must be tailored to the capacities and circumstances of those who are to be heard. It is not enough that a welfare recipient may present his position to the decisionmaker in

---

15. This case presents no question requiring our determination whether due process requires only an opportunity for written submission, or an opportunity both for written submission and oral argument, where there are no factual issues in dispute or where the application of the rule of law is not intertwined with factual issues.

writing or secondhand through his caseworker. Written submissions are an unrealistic option for most recipients, who lack the educational attainment necessary to write effectively and who cannot obtain professional assistance. Moreover, written submissions do not afford the flexibility of oral presentations; they do not permit the recipient to mold his argument to the issues the decisionmaker appears to regard as important. Particularly where credibility and veracity are at issue, as they must be in many termination proceedings, written submissions are a wholly unsatisfactory basis for decision. The secondhand presentation to the decisionmaker by the caseworker has its own deficiencies; since the caseworker usually gathers the facts upon which the charge of ineligibility rests, the presentation of the recipient's side of the controversy cannot safely be left to him. Therefore a recipient must be allowed to state his position orally. Informal procedures will suffice; in this context due process does not require a particular order of proof or mode of offering evidence.

In almost every setting where important decisions turn on questions of fact, due process requires an opportunity to confront and cross-examine adverse witnesses. . . . Welfare recipients must therefore be given an opportunity to confront and cross-examine the witnesses relied on by the department.

"The right to be heard would be, in many cases, of little avail if it did not comprehend the right to be heard by counsel." We do not say that counsel must be provided at the pre-termination hearing, but only that the recipient must be allowed to retain an attorney if he so desires. Counsel can help delineate the issues, present the factual contentions in an orderly manner, conduct cross-examination, and generally safeguard the interests of the recipient. We do not anticipate that this assistance will unduly prolong or otherwise encumber the hearing. . . . Finally, the decisionmaker's conclusion as to a recipient's eligibility must rest solely on the legal rules and evidence adduced at the hearing. To demonstrate compliance with this elementary requirement, the decisionmaker should state the reasons for his determination and indicate the evidence he relied on, though his statement need not amount to a full opinion or even formal findings of fact and conclusions of law. And, of course, an impartial decisionmaker is essential. We agree with the District Court that prior involvement in some aspects of a case will not necessarily bar a welfare official from acting as a decisionmaker. He should not, however, have participated in making the determination under review.

Affirmed.

Mr. Justice Black, dissenting. . . .

The Court [today] relies upon the Fourteenth Amendment and in effect says that failure of the government to pay a promised charitable instalment to an individual deprives that individual of *his own property,* in violation of the Due Process Clause of the Fourteenth Amendment. It somewhat strains credulity to say that the government's promise of charity to an individual is property belonging to that individual when the government denies that the individual is honestly entitled to receive such a payment.

I would have little, if any, objection to the majority's decision in this case if it were written as the report of the House Committee on Education and Labor, but as an opinion ostensibly resting on the language of the Constitution I find it woefully deficient. Once the verbiage is pared away it is obvious that this Court today adopts the views of the District Court "that to cut off a welfare recipient in the face of . . . 'brutal need' without a prior hearing of some sort is unconscionable," and therefore, says the Court, unconstitutional. The majority reaches this result by a process of weighing "the recipient's interest in avoiding" the termination of welfare benefits against "the governmental interest in summary adjudication." Today's balancing act requires a "pre-termination evidentiary hearing," yet there is nothing that indicates what tomorrow's balance will be. Although the majority attempts to bolster its decision with limited quotations from prior cases, it is obvious that today's result does not depend on the language of the Constitution itself or the principles of other decisions, but solely on the collective judgment of the majority as to what would be a fair and humane procedure in this case. . . .

The Court apparently feels that this decision will benefit the poor and needy. In my judgment the eventual result will be just the opposite. While today's decision requires only an administrative, evidentiary hearing, the inevitable logic of the approach taken will lead to constitutionally imposed, time-consuming delays of a full adversary process of administrative and judicial review. In the next case the welfare recipients are bound to argue that cutting off benefits before judicial review of the agency's decision is also a denial of due process. Since, by hypothesis, termination of aid at that point may still "deprive an *eligible* recipient of the very means by which to live while he waits," I would be surprised if the weighing process did not compel the conclusion that termination without full judicial review would be unconscionable. After all, at each step, as the majority seems to feel, the issue is only one of weighing the government's pocketbook against the actual survival of the recipient, and surely that balance must always tip in favor of the individual. Similarly today's decision requires only the opportunity to have the benefit of counsel at the administrative hearing, but it is difficult to believe that the same reasoning process would not require the appointment of counsel, for otherwise the right to counsel is a meaningless one since these people are too poor to hire their own advocates. Thus the end result of today's decision may well be that the government, once it decides to give welfare benefits, cannot reverse that decision until the recipient has had the benefits of full administrative and judicial review, including, of course, the opportunity to present his case to this Court. Since this process will usually entail a delay of several years, the inevitable result of such a constitutionally imposed burden will be that the government will not put a claimant on the rolls initially until it has made an exhaustive investigation to determine his eligibility. While this Court will perhaps have insured that no needy person will be taken off the rolls without a full "due process" proceeding, it will also have insured that many will never get on the rolls, or at least that they will remain destitute during the lengthy proceedings followed to determine initial eligibility.

For the foregoing reasons I dissent from the Court's holding. The operation of a welfare state is a new experiment for our Nation. For this reason, among others, I feel that new experiments in carrying out a welfare program should not be frozen into our constitutional structure. They should be left, as are other legislative determinations, to the Congress and the legislatures that the people elect to make our laws.

MR. CHIEF JUSTICE BURGER, with whom MR. JUSTICE BLACK joins, dissenting. . . .

The Court's action today seems another manifestation of the now familiar constitutionalizing syndrome: once some presumed flaw is observed, the Court then eagerly accepts the invitation to find a constitutionally "rooted" remedy. If no provision is explicit on the point, it is then seen as "implicit" or commanded by the vague and nebulous concept of "fairness." . . .

I would wait until more is known about the problems before fashioning solutions in the rigidity of a constitutional holding.

By allowing the administrators to deal with these problems we leave room for adjustments if, for example, it is found that a particular hearing process is too costly. The history of the complexity of the administrative process followed by judicial review as we have seen it for the past 30 years should suggest the possibility that new layers of procedural protection may become an intolerable drain on the very funds earmarked for food, clothing, and other living essentials.[3]

Aside from the administrative morass that today's decision could well create, the Court should also be cognizant of the legal precedent it may be setting. The majority holding raises intriguing possibilities concerning the right to a hearing at other stages in the welfare process which affect the total sum of assistance, even though the action taken might fall short of complete termination. For example, does the Court's holding embrace welfare reductions or denial of increases as opposed to terminations, or decisions concerning initial applications or requests for special assistance? The Court supplies no distinguishable considerations and leaves these crucial questions unanswered.

[JUSTICE STEWART also dissented].

---

3. We are told, for example, that Los Angeles County alone employs 12,500 welfare workers to process grants to 500,000 people under various welfare programs. The record does not reveal how many more employees will be required to give this newly discovered "due process" to every welfare recipient whose payments are terminated for fraud or other factors of ineligibility or those whose initial applications are denied.

Notes and Questions

1. *The Goldberg decision.* Because just about everything that follows in this chapter is a reaction to Goldberg, be clear on the issues determined:

 i. The right to a continued flow of welfare benefits is an interest which is protected by procedural due process. What analysis did the Court employ to come to that conclusion? Will that analysis furnish predictable results in future cases?

 ii. The demands of procedural due process are flexible and contextual rather than rigid and noncontextual. Application of that concept requires a balancing of interests in light of the particular circumstances. Is a court competent to make such judgments?

 iii. Due process requires a hearing before welfare benefits are terminated. A post-termination hearing is not sufficient. Why did the Court require a hearing before the benefits stop? Must hearings always occur before the government deprives an individual of liberty or property?

 iv. A pre-termination hearing must include specified ingredients. What are those ingredients and how do they differ from those required in a post-termination hearing? Did the Court hold that this combination of ingredients must be provided in every situation in which a person's property is adversely affected by government action?

 Justice Black predicted that judicial review of a pre-termination decision would also become a requisite; however, even today it remains unclear precisely when a statute can constitutionally preclude judicial review of administrative determinations. *See* § 10.4, *infra.*

2. *The Purpose of Due Process.* In thinking about the due process issues presented in this chapter, a good starting point is to ask what interests might be served by trial-type hearings. Due process decisions, and commentators on those decisions, have claimed many possible advantages for such hearings. Evaluate each of the following propositions in the context of welfare, prison discipline, license revocation, dismissal from a government job, or imposition of civil penalties for violation of an order to clean up toxic wastes.

 i. A trial-type hearing serves a *dignitary* function. It treats the individual as important, worthy of careful consideration, not just a cog in a giant machine. It affirms the value of fair procedure *for its own sake.*

 ii. A trial-type hearing helps the individual *to understand and accept* a negative government decision. Therefore it tends to enhance people's satisfaction with government and to diminish their desire to resist or undermine it.

iii. A trial-type hearing is a good way to reach an *accurate* decision—to find out exactly what happened and to apply law and policy correctly. Therefore, it protects individuals against factually or legally erroneous decisions by agencies.

iv. Hearings create a system of agency precedents which decision-makers follow in later cases. This helps to assure that agency decisions are *consistent* with each other—that persons in like circumstances are treated alike.

v. A right to a trial-type hearing serves an *empowerment* function. Demanding a hearing is a good way for recipients to *seize the attention* of a bureaucratic institution and to prevent their problems from being ignored or slipping through the cracks. On a practical level, having a right to demand a time-consuming hearing helps a person to negotiate a settlement.

vi. If people have a right to a trial-type hearing before an impartial decision-maker, officials are more likely to act *seriously and reflectively.* Or, to examine the other side of the coin, will the bother of a hearing deter officials from acting boldly and decisively?

vii. A trial-type hearing is a good way to help government exercise *discretion* wisely. Decision-makers usually have some latitude (such as whether a prisoner who engages in fighting should be punished and, if so, how and for how long). We call this latitude *discretion* and recognize that discretionary decisions are sometimes unwise.

viii. The use of trial-type hearings may *serve the purposes* of the substantive programs in which they occur. For instance, in the welfare context, hearings may help assure that the right people get benefits. Hearings may also help identify recurring problems and thus improve the system. For example, they may suggest that a problem might better be solved by adopting a rule or a guideline, rather than continued resolution on a case-by-case basis.

ix. A trial-type hearing facilitates *judicial review* because it produces a decision based exclusively on a record made at the hearing and results in a written decision. Thus a reviewing court can focus on precisely what the agency did and why.

Are you persuaded that trial-type hearings really have some or all of these advantages? What are the *disadvantages* that should be set off against these advantages?

3. *In the wake of Goldberg.* Apparently, *Goldberg* triggered a massive increase in the number of AFDC hearings. The decision occurred in March, 1970. According to the government's periodic statistical bulletins, there were 5400 requests for hearings in the AFDC program between January and June, 1970. In the second half of 1970 there were 7400 requests. In the first half of 1971 there were 17,200 requests; in the second half of 1971, there were 31,090. By 1982 the

number increased to 136,555. During this period the number of people on welfare and the number of applications denied both increased, but the rate of increase was nowhere near the rate of increase in the number of requested hearings. Still, the number of hearings is small compared with the 11,000,000 recipients of AFDC. Indeed, only about 2% of all appealable decisions in social welfare programs are actually appealed.

According to published figures, about 90% of welfare recipients represent themselves in AFDC hearings. Still, the hearings appear to produce results: in one recent year, claimants were successful in 49% of the hearings. However, when a hearing was requested but not actually held (because there was a compromise or one side gave up), claimants achieved a favorable result in only 21% of the cases.

Do these figures tend to confirm the empirical predictions of Justice Brennan or those of Justice Black and Chief Justice Burger? Do they suggest that many recipients asked for hearings solely to keep their checks coming a little longer?

4. *Consequences of Goldberg.* Considering the consequences likely to flow from the decision, was *Goldberg* an unambiguous victory for persons who are or may be in the future dependent on welfare? In practice, where is the money to pay for the hearings likely to come from? Who are likely to be the primary beneficiaries of the decision? How would welfare officials be likely to deal with the consequences of the decision?

5. *Adversariness and mass justice.* The fundamental question raised by *Goldberg* is whether adversary trial-type hearings are the best way, or even a good way, to protect the rights of people who depend on government for benefits. This problem is addressed in *Walters v. Radiation Survivors*, § 2.4, *infra.* Compare these views:

> [Compared to the pressures on welfare administrators to cut costs] virtually no pressure . . . is ordinarily exerted on behalf of the welfare client. It is in this context that the lawyer who represents the impoverished client introduces a new element. By fighting for his client, by carrying the issue involved in his client's cause into the judicial or quasi-judicial process, the lawyer not only creates the possibility of reversing an improper interpretation of law which may affect others in comparable straits but increases the administrator's potential for effecting humane policy.

Sparer, "The Role of the Welfare Client's Lawyer," 12 U.C.L.A.L.Rev. 361, 375 (1965).

> . . . [R]eliance on the complaining client is virtually fatal. In order for the due process system to be invoked, the following conditions have to be met: clients have to be aware that an injury has occurred; they have to think that the agency is at fault; they have to be aware of the existence of a remedy; they have to have the resources with which to pursue that remedy; and finally, they have to make a calculation that the benefits of pursuing the remedy outweigh its

costs. Two things must be noted about these conditions. All of them have to be satisfied if the due process procedures are to be utilized; if there is a failure in any one of them, then the process will not be used. And, each and every one of the conditions is a difficult hurdle to negotiate for the average person dealing with a large-scale public organization. . . .

The final step in the process of invoking due process is to calculate whether the benefits of pursuing the remedy outweigh the costs . . . [such as] the time and energy of the complainant and the costs of seeking help. Another cost deals with the relationship between the victim and the harmdoer. [Asserting one's rights to due process] are hostile acts. This is particularly so if the claim is made in a formal setting such as a court or administrative hearing with professional advocacy help . . . For some types of decisions, there is no relationship to speak of and the potential benefits of claiming will outweigh the costs . . . In many other situations there are continuing relationships and considerable potential for at least the fear, if not the fact, of retaliation

. . . [I]t was found that 90% of all welfare documents required an eighth grade reading level. Yet the mean level of education for the aged poor is 7.5 years; and more than 20% of the SSI non-participants had less than five years of schooling, the amount considered to be functionally literate. More than 20 percent were foreign born, so that English as a second language might be a problem . . .

. . . People approach these programs, then, in a vulnerable personal situation, and are confronted with ambiguous information. At this point, they face a hostile government bureaucracy—waiting rooms, offices, receptionists, officials, paper, forms, questions . . .

J. Handler, THE CONDITIONS OF DISCRETION 22–32 (1986).*

§ 2.2 INTERESTS PROTECTED BY DUE PROCESS: LIBERTY AND PROPERTY

There are two principal means by which courts attempt to insure that the procedural requirements imposed by due process are not excessive. The first approach, addressed in this section, entirely excludes certain interests from the categories of "liberty" and "property." As to such interests, government is constitutionally free to pursue its substantive objectives without any process. The second approach is to describe due process requirements as variable rather than fixed and dependent on the particular context in which they arise. That technique will be addressed in §§ 2.3 and 2.4.

The language of the fifth and fourteenth amendments is clear: to be entitled to procedural due process, a person must be deprived by government of "liberty" or "property." The application of those majestic terms to particular cases has proved to be difficult. Recall how the Court dealt with the issue of whether a continued flow of welfare payments is protectable under due process in *Goldberg v. Kelly*.

§ 2.2.1 "LIBERTY" AND "PROPERTY ACCORDING TO *ROTH*"

In *Board of Regents v. Roth*, which follows, the Court reconceptualized the terms "liberty" and "property." Is the approach taken in the *Roth* case more theoretically satisfactory than the approach used in *Goldberg?* Is it easier to apply to actual cases?

BOARD OF REGENTS v. ROTH
408 U.S. 564 (1972).

STEWART, J.

In 1968 the respondent, David Roth, was hired for his first teaching job as assistant professor of political science at Wisconsin State University–Oshkosh. He was hired for a fixed term of one academic year. The notice of his faculty appointment specified that his employment would begin on September 1, 1968, and would end on June 30, 1969. The respondent completed that term. But he was informed that he would not be rehired for the next academic year.

The respondent had no tenure rights to continued employment. Under Wisconsin statutory law a state university teacher can acquire tenure as a "permanent" employee only after four years of year-to-year employment. Having acquired tenure, a teacher is entitled to continued employment "during efficiency and good behavior." A relatively new teacher without tenure, however, is under Wisconsin law entitled to nothing beyond his one-year appointment. There are no statutory or administrative standards defining eligibility for re-employment. State law thus clearly leaves the decision whether to rehire a nontenured teacher for another year to the unfettered discretion of university officials.

The procedural protection afforded a Wisconsin State University teacher before he is separated from the University corresponds to his job security. As a matter of statutory law, a tenured teacher cannot be "discharged except for cause upon written charges" and pursuant to certain procedures. A nontenured teacher, similarly, is protected to some extent *during* his one-year term. Rules promulgated by the Board of Regents provide that a nontenured teacher "dismissed" before the end of the year may have some opportunity for review of the "dismissal." But the Rules provide no real protection for a nontenured teacher who simply is not re-employed for the next year. He must be informed by February 1 "concerning retention or non-retention for the ensuing year." But "no reason for non-retention need be given. No review or appeal is provided in such case."

In conformance with these Rules, the President of Wisconsin State University–Oshkosh informed the respondent before February 1, 1969, that he would not be rehired for the 1969–1970 academic year. He gave the respondent no reason for the decision and no opportunity to challenge it at any sort of hearing.

The respondent then brought this action in Federal District Court alleging that the decision not to rehire him for the next year infringed his Fourteenth Amendment rights. He attacked the decision both in substance and procedure. First, he alleged that the true reason for the decision was to punish him for certain statements critical of the University administration, and that it therefore violated his right to freedom of speech. Second, he alleged that the failure of University officials to give him notice of any reason for nonretention and an opportunity for a hearing violated his right to procedural due process of law.

The District Court granted summary judgment for the respondent on the procedural issue, ordering the University officials to provide him with reasons and a hearing. The Court of Appeals, with one judge dissenting, affirmed this partial summary judgment. The only question presented to us at this stage in the case is whether the respondent had a constitutional right to a statement of reasons and a hearing on the University's decision not to rehire him for another year. We hold that he did not.

I

The requirements of procedural due process apply only to the deprivation of interests encompassed by the Fourteenth Amendment's protection of liberty and property. When protected interests are implicated, the right to some kind of prior hearing is paramount.[7] But the range of interests protected by procedural due process is not infinite.

The District Court decided that procedural due process guarantees apply in this case by assessing and balancing the weights of the particular interests involved. It concluded that the respondent's interest in re-employment at Wisconsin State University–Oshkosh outweighed the University's interest in denying him re-employment summarily. Undeniably, the respondent's re-employment prospects were of major concern to him—concern that we surely cannot say was insignificant. And a weighing process has long been a part of any determination of the *form* of hearing required in particular situations by procedural due process. But, to determine whether due process requirements apply in the first place, we must look not to the "weight" but to the *nature* of the interest at stake. We must look to see if the interest is within the Fourteenth Amendment's protection of liberty and property.

7. Before a person is deprived of a protected interest, he must be afforded opportunity for some kind of a hearing, "except for extraordinary situations where some valid governmental interest is at stake that justifies postponing the hearing until after the event." . . .

"Liberty" and "property" are broad and majestic terms. They are among the "[g]reat [constitutional] concepts . . . purposely left to gather meaning from experience. . . . For that reason, the Court has fully and finally rejected the wooden distinction between "rights" and "privileges" that once seemed to govern the applicability of procedural due process rights. The Court has also made clear that the property interests protected by procedural due process extend well beyond actual ownership of real estate, chattels, or money. By the same token, the Court has required due process protection for deprivations of liberty beyond the sort of formal constraints imposed by the criminal process.

Yet, while the Court has eschewed rigid or formalistic limitations on the protection of procedural due process, it has at the same time observed certain boundaries. For the words "liberty" and "property" in the Due Process Clause of the Fourteenth Amendment must be given some meaning. . . .

II

"While this court has not attempted to define with exactness the liberty . . . guaranteed [by the Fourteenth Amendment], the term has received much consideration and some of the included things have been definitely stated. Without doubt, it denotes not merely freedom from bodily restraint but also the right of the individual to contract, to engage in any of the common occupations of life, to acquire useful knowledge, to marry, establish a home and bring up children, to worship God according to the dictates of his own conscience, and generally to enjoy those privileges long recognized . . . as essential to the orderly pursuit of happiness by free men." Meyer v. Nebraska, 262 U.S. 390, 399. In a Constitution for a free people, there can be no doubt that the meaning of "liberty" must be broad indeed.

There might be cases in which a State refused to re-employ a person under such circumstances that interests in liberty would be implicated. But this is not such a case.

The State, in declining to rehire the respondent, did not make any charge against him that might seriously damage his standing and associations in his community. It did not base the nonrenewal of his contract on a charge, for example, that he had been guilty of dishonesty, or immorality. Had it done so, this would be a different case. For "[w]here a person's good name, reputation, honor, or integrity is at stake because of what the government is doing to him, notice and an opportunity to be heard are essential." Wisconsin v. Constantineau, 400 U.S. 433, 437. In such a case, due process would accord an opportunity to refute the charge before University officials.[12] In the

---

12. The purpose of such notice and hearing is to provide the person an opportunity to clear his name. Once a person has cleared his name at a hearing, his employer, of course, may remain free to deny him future employment for other reasons.

present case, however, there is no suggestion whatever that the respondent's "good name, reputation, honor, or integrity" is at stake.

Similarly, there is no suggestion that the State, in declining to reemploy the respondent, imposed on him a stigma or other disability that foreclosed his freedom to take advantage of other employment opportunities. The State, for example, did not invoke any regulations to bar the respondent from all other public employment in state universities. Had it done so, this, again, would be a different case. For "[t]o be deprived not only of present government employment but of future opportunity for it certainly is no small injury. . . ." The Court has held, for example, that a State, in regulating eligibility for a type of professional employment, cannot foreclose a range of opportunities "in a manner . . . that contravene[s] . . . Due Process," and, specifically, in a manner that denies the right to a full prior hearing. In the present case, however, this principle does not come into play.[13]

To be sure, the respondent has alleged that the nonrenewal of his contract was based on his exercise of his right to freedom of speech. But this allegation is not now before us. The District Court stayed proceedings on this issue, and the respondent has yet to prove that the decision not to rehire him was, in fact, based on his free speech activities.

Hence, on the record before us, all that clearly appears is that the respondent was not rehired for one year at one university. It stretches the concept too far to suggest that a person is deprived of "liberty" when he simply is not rehired in one job but remains as free as before to seek another.

III

The Fourteenth Amendment's procedural protection of property is a safeguard of the security of interests that a person has already acquired in specific benefits. These interests—property interests—may take many forms.

Thus, the Court has held that a person receiving welfare benefits under statutory and administrative standards defining eligibility for them has an interest in continued receipt of those benefits that is safeguarded by procedural due process. Goldberg v. Kelly. Similarly, in the area of public employment, the Court has held that a public

13. The District Court made an *assumption* "that non-retention by one university or college creates concrete and practical difficulties for a professor in his subsequent academic career." And the Court of Appeals based its affirmance of the summary judgment largely on the premise that "the substantial adverse effect non-retention is likely to have upon the career interests of an individual professor" amounts to a limitation on future employment opportunities sufficient to invoke procedural due process guarantees. But even assuming, *arguendo,* that such a "substantial adverse effect" under these circumstances would constitute a state-imposed restriction on liberty, the record contains no support for these assumptions. There is no suggestion of how nonretention might affect the respondent's future employment prospects. Mere proof, for example, that his record of nonretention in one job, taken alone, might make him somewhat less attractive to some other employers would hardly establish the kind of foreclosure of opportunities amounting to a deprivation of "liberty."

college professor dismissed from an office held under tenure provisions, and college professors and staff members dismissed during the terms of their contracts have interests in continued employment that are safeguarded by due process. . . .

Certain attributes of "property" interests protected by procedural due process emerge from these decisions. To have a property interest in a benefit, a person clearly must have more than an abstract need or desire for it. He must have more than a unilateral expectation of it. He must, instead, have a legitimate claim of entitlement to it. It is a purpose of the ancient institution of property to protect those claims upon which people rely in their daily lives, reliance that must not be arbitrarily undermined. It is a purpose of the constitutional right to a hearing to provide an opportunity for a person to vindicate those claims.

Property interests, of course, are not created by the Constitution. Rather, they are created and their dimensions are defined by existing rules or understandings that stem from an independent source such as state law—rules or understandings that secure certain benefits and that support claims of entitlement to those benefits. Thus, the welfare recipients in Goldberg v. Kelly had a claim of entitlement to welfare payments that was grounded in the statute defining eligibility for them. The recipients had not yet shown that they were, in fact, within the statutory terms of eligibility. But we held that they had a right to a hearing at which they might attempt to do so.

Just as the welfare recipients' "property" interest in welfare payments was created and defined by statutory terms, so the respondent's "property" interest in employment at Wisconsin State University–Oshkosh was created and defined by the terms of his appointment. Those terms secured his interest in employment up to June 30, 1969. But the important fact in this case is that they specifically provided that the respondent's employment was to terminate on June 30. They did not provide for contract renewal absent "sufficient cause." Indeed, they made no provision for renewal whatsoever.

Thus, the terms of the respondent's appointment secured absolutely no interest in re-employment for the next year. They supported absolutely no possible claim of entitlement to re-employment. Nor, significantly, was there any state statute or University rule or policy that secured his interest in re-employment or that created any legitimate claim to it. In these circumstances, the respondent surely had an abstract concern in being rehired, but he did not have a *property* interest sufficient to require the University authorities to give him a hearing when they declined to renew his contract of employment.

IV

Our analysis of the respondent's constitutional rights in this case in no way indicates a view that an opportunity for a hearing or a statement of reasons for nonretention would, or would not, be appropriate or wise in public colleges and universities. For it is a written Constitution that we apply. Our role is confined to interpretation of that Constitution.

We must conclude that the summary judgment for the respondent should not have been granted, since the respondent has not shown that he was deprived of liberty or property protected by the Fourteenth Amendment. The judgment of the Court of Appeals, accordingly, is reversed and the case is remanded for further proceedings consistent with this opinion.

[JUSTICE DOUGLAS dissented, arguing that Roth was entitled to a hearing because he alleged that the dismissal was based upon expression protected by the first amendment. Also dissenting, JUSTICE MARSHALL contended that due process requires a statement of reasons and, if need be, a hearing whenever the government denies an individual a job. He argued that the job is "property" and that "liberty" protects the right to work.]

Notes and Questions

1. *The right-privilege doctrine.* A government job was once considered a "privilege" and not a "right," meaning that a deprivation of the job triggered no right to procedural due process. The leading case was *Bailey v. Richardson,* 182 F.2d 46 (D.C.Cir.1950), *aff'd by equally divided court,* 341 U.S. 918 (1951). Clearly reflecting the cold war attitudes of the time, *Bailey* is a landmark of the McCarthy era.

Ms. Bailey was dismissed from her "non-sensitive" job in the U.S. Employment Service on the asserted basis that reasonable grounds existed for the belief that she was disloyal. She received a hearing but was not allowed to confront the unnamed FBI informants who stated that there was reason to believe she was a member of the Communist Party. She denied this under oath, affirmed her loyalty to the United States, and placed a great deal of evidence of her loyalty on record. The Court of Appeals held that a government job is not property and that a dismissal for disloyalty is not an infringement of liberty, despite its stigmatic effect. Consequently, the government need not provide any procedure at all, much less confrontation of informants.

In addition to government jobs, many other relationships between private parties and government were treated as "privileges." Among them were licenses to do business which the state could prohibit entirely (like selling liquor), subsidies, welfare benefits, and the ability to contract with the government. The theory of the right-privilege distinction was that since government did not have to give a person a job, a license, or a contract, due process did not apply to the withdrawal of these benefits.

Goldberg v. Kelly was a critical turning point on the road to discarding the right-privilege distinction. In a footnote in *Roth* (not reproduced in the text), the Court finally declared *Bailey* to be deceased. But as you read the following materials, consider whether the right-privilege distinction is really dead. Is it struggling to be reborn? What is wrong with the right-privilege distinction as a basis for applying the requirements of procedural due process?

2. *Definition of "property."* Procedural due process has always protected a person's interest in traditional forms of property (such as the right to own and use goods). Justice Stewart's definition of property breaks new ground. Under *Roth,* the right to receive welfare benefits is a statutory "entitlement" and thus property. Similarly, *Perry* (*infra* note 6) held that a professor's right under implied contract to keep his job is "property." Would you have defined these sorts of interests as "property" before you knew about the *Roth* decision? Can you sell these interests or transfer them to another?

As Stewart makes clear, the existence of a property right depends upon some *entitlement* created and defined by an *independent source* such as state or federal law. This "positivist" approach to identifying property has profound consequences for the application of the requirements of procedural due process. If a property right wholly depends upon an entitlement created by an independent source of law, the state can modify or eliminate the right by modifying or repealing its positive law source. Or are there some constitutional limits on such subsequent state action?

3. *What is "liberty?"* Did *Roth* define "liberty" in a positive law or a natural law mold? Why did the refusal to rehire Roth not deprive him of liberty? Is a "liberty" interest something identified in state law? Or is "liberty" something that everyone has without regard to whether the state provided it?

Stewart relied upon the open-ended natural law analysis of *Meyer v. Nebraska* in sketching the contours of liberty. *Meyer* was a 1923 decision which declared invalid a Nebraska law prohibiting the teaching of foreign languages to young children. Note that *Meyer* was a *substantive* due process case, not a *procedural* one. The state law was invalid, not because of the procedures which Nebraska used, but because it "materially" interfered "with the calling of modern language teachers, with the opportunities of pupils to acquire knowledge, and with the power of parents to control the education of their own." *Roth* establishes that this definition of "liberty" applies to *both* procedural and substantive due process.

Elements of substantive due process survive in cases which limit the state's power to interfere with people's "fundamental" interests such as control over their bodies or their family relations. *See, e.g., Roe v. Wade,* 410 U.S. 113 (1973) (right to abortion); *Moore v. East Cleveland,* 431 U.S. 494 (1977) (right of closely related family members to live together); *Zablocki v. Redhail,* 434 U.S. 374 (1978) (right to marry).

In the economic area, there is little left of substantive due process (or of its close counterpart, substantive equal protection); courts are largely precluded from second-guessing statutes which limit economic rights. *See, e.g., Williamson v. Lee Optical Co.,* 348 U.S. 483 (1955) (imagining reasons why state law regulating optometry might be rational). However, it remains true that a-wholly-irrational decision is substantively invalid under the due process or equal protection clauses. This loophole allows courts to overturn decisions which they find substantively outrageous even when there is no procedural defect. *See, e.g. City of Cleburne v. Cleburne Living Center,* 473 U.S. 432 (1985). In the *Cleburne* case, a city denied a zoning permit for operation of a group home for the mentally retarded. Its primary reason was that the neighbors did not want it there. The Court held that the mentally retarded were not entitled to any special protection under the equal protection clause, but it invalidated the city's action just the same because the home did not threaten *any* legitimate interest. Since other group homes (like fraternities) received permits, an irrational prejudice against retarded people was not a sufficient reason to single them out for special treatment.

This chapter concerns *procedural,* not *substantive* due process. Although remnants of substantive due process still exist, as explained in the preceding paragraphs and in the next text note, procedural due process is accorded far more protection under current law than substantive due process *in* in the economic area. In that case, does reliance on *Meyer* for a definition of liberty still make sense? As we will see, the Court has retreated from it.

4. *Free speech rights.* Roth argued that he lost his job because the University disapproved of speeches which were constitutionally protected. However, the majority believed that issue was not before the Court and thus did not reach it. Does government invade liberty if it discharges an employee for making a protected speech? If so, why should it not be required to provide an administrative hearing on this claim? Would such a hearing preclude a later suit in court for damages? Or is a right to a trial of the free speech issue in a federal district court (without a prior administrative hearing) a better remedy?

Roth's claim was plausible. Of 442 non-tenured teachers, only four were not renewed. Roth had been involved in demonstrations against the Vietnam War and had caustically criticized the university administration. Roth ultimately prevailed on his first amendment claim in the district court. He was awarded $6746 in damages; by that time he had another teaching job at Purdue. Chronicle of Higher Education, Nov. 26, 1973.

5. *Discretion and due process.* The Court held that Wisconsin infringed no liberty or property rights so Roth was entitled to no process. Nevertheless, the effect of a non-renewal decision upon the career of a young professor is quite drastic—often academically terminal. Do you think that there should be a right to a hearing whenever government exercises discretionary power in a way which drastically and negatively affects a person's life? If so, how could you interpret

the language of the fifth and fourteenth amendments to reach this result?

6. *De facto tenure. Perry v. Sindermann,* 408 U.S. 593 (1972), decided the same day as *Roth,* was factually similar but with one vital difference: Sindermann was not protected by a formal tenure system but he alleged a right to reemployment based on *implied contract.* The contract arose from guidelines on which he had relied during his ten-year teaching career and on the practices of the institution.

The Court stated:

> We have made clear in *Roth* that "property" interests subject to procedural due process protection are not limited by a few rigid, technical forms. Rather "property" denotes a broad range of interests that are secured by "existing rules or understandings." A person's interest in a benefit is a "property" interest for due process purposes if there are such rules or mutually explicit understandings that support his claim of entitlement to the benefit and that he may invoke at a hearing.

> A written contract with an explicit tenure provision clearly is evidence of a formal understanding that supports a teacher's claim of entitlement to continued employment unless sufficient "cause" is shown. Yet absence of such an explicit contractual provision may not always foreclose the possibility that a teacher has a "property" interest in re-employment. For example, the law of contracts in most, if not all, jurisdictions long has employed a process by which agreements, though not formalized in writing, may be "implied." . . . [Sindermann] must be given an opportunity to prove the legitimacy of his claim of such entitlement in light of the policies and practices of the institution. Proof of such a property interest would not, of course, entitle him to reinstatement. But such proof would obligate college officials to grant a hearing at his request, where he could be informed of the grounds for his nonretention and challenge their sufficiency.

7. *Deprivation.* Note that the Constitution requires due process only if a person is "deprived" of life, liberty, or property. Is there a constitutional distinction between being "deprived" of what one already has and being "denied" something which one wants but does not yet have? Is such a distinction justifiable?

Language in *Roth* suggests that this distinction may be important. Stewart wrote: "The Fourteenth Amendment's procedural protection of property is a safeguard of the security of interests that a person has *already acquired* in specific benefits . . . [emphasis added]" Contrast this with *Goldsmith v. United States Board of Tax Appeals,* 270 U.S. 117, 123 (1926): "We think that the petitioner having shown by his application that . . . he was within the class of those entitled to be admitted to practice under the board's rules, he should not have been rejected upon charges of his unfitness without giving him an opportunity by notice for hearing and answer . . . as would constitute due process." But the Court has yet to rule definitively on this issue.

§ 2.2.2 DEFINING "LIBERTY"

After *Board of Regents v. Roth,* the Court encountered difficulty in deciding whether particular administrative decisions deprived persons of "liberty." For example, does a person sentenced to prison have any "liberty" left? As you read *Hewitt,* consider whether the Court has furnished clear guidance to lower courts, whether individuals harmed by government receive sufficient procedural protection under current law, and whether the costs (monetary and non-monetary) of additional procedures are acceptable.

HEWITT v. HELMS

459 U.S. 460 (1983).

[Respondent Helms was a prisoner at the State Correctional Institution at Huntington, Pa. (SCIH), the warden of which is petitioner. Helms was confined to "administrative segregation," meaning that he was deprived of vocational, educational, and recreational programs. In addition, he could exercise only five or ten minutes a day, three days a week, and receive clean clothes only once or twice a week. Helms was mostly confined to his cell whereas other prisoners are out of their cells 14 hours a day.

SCIH imposes "administrative segregation" when an inmate poses a security threat, when disciplinary charges are pending against him, or when he needs protection. In contrast, "disciplinary segregation" is imposed for misconduct. Both forms of segregation amount to solitary confinement.

In an uprising at SCIH on December 3, 1978, several guards were injured. Officials believed Helms played a part in the riot and he was administratively confined. On December 8, a hearing committee considered misconduct charges against Helms, reached no findings about his guilt, but continued his confinement. The record was unclear whether Helms appeared personally before the committee.

On December 11, the state filed criminal charges against Helms. On January 2, 1979, another committee continued his confinement for three reasons: Helms was considered a danger to staff and other inmates if placed back in the general population, he was to be arraigned the following day on criminal charges, and the committee was awaiting further information about his role in the riot.

On January 22, another committee, considering a new misconduct charge, gave Helms a hearing, found that he had taken part in the riot, and placed him in *disciplinary* segregation for six months. The state then dropped its criminal charges.

Helms contended that his confinement without a hearing in administrative segregation between December 8 and January 22 deprived him

of liberty without due process.   The District Court granted the state's
motion for summary judgment but the Court of Appeals reversed.]

REHNQUIST, J.:

[W]e agree with the Court of Appeals that the Pennsylvania statutory framework governing the administration of state prisons gave rise
to a liberty interest in respondent, but we conclude that the procedures
afforded respondent were "due process" under the Fourteenth Amendment.

While no State may "deprive any person of life, liberty, or property, without due process of law," it is well-settled that only a limited
range of interests fall within this provision.   Liberty interests protected
by the Fourteenth Amendment may arise from two sources—the Due
Process Clause itself and the laws of the States.   *Meachum v. Fano,* 427
U.S. 215, 223–227 (1976).   Respondent argues, rather weakly, that the
Due Process Clause implicitly creates an interest in being confined to a
general population cell, rather than the more austere and restrictive
administrative segregation quarters.   While there is little question on
the record before us that respondent's confinement added to the restraints on his freedom, we think his argument seeks to draw from the
Due Process Clause more than it can provide.

We have repeatedly said both that prison officials have broad
administrative and discretionary authority over the institutions they
manage and that lawfully incarcerated persons retain only a narrow
range of protected liberty interests.   As to the first point, we have
recognized that broad discretionary authority is necessary because the
administration of a prison is "at best an extraordinarily difficult
undertaking," *Wolff v. McDonnell,* 418 U.S. 539, and have concluded
that "to hold . . . that *any* substantial deprivation imposed by prison
authorities triggers the procedural protections of the Due Process
Clause would subject to judicial review a wide spectrum of discretionary
actions that traditionally have been the business of prison administrators rather than of the federal courts."   As to the second point, our
decisions have consistently refused to recognize more than the most
basic liberty interests in prisoners.   "Lawful incarceration brings about
the necessary withdrawal or limitation of many privileges and rights, a
retraction justified by the considerations underlying our penal system."
Thus, there is no "constitutional or inherent right" to parole, *Greenholtz v. Nebraska Penal Inmates,* 442 U.S. 1, 7 (1979), and "the Constitution itself does not guarantee good-time credit for satisfactory behavior
while in prison," *Wolff v. McDonnell, supra,* despite the undoubted
impact of such credits on the freedom of inmates.   Finally, in *Meachum
v. Fano, supra,* the transfer of a prisoner from one institution to
another was found unprotected by "the Due Process Clause in and of
itself," even though the change of facilities involved a significant
modification in conditions of confinement, later characterized by the
Court as a "grievous loss."   As we have held previously, these decisions
require that "[a]s long as the conditions or degree of confinement to

which the prisoner is subjected is within the sentence imposed upon him and is not otherwise violative of the Constitution, the Due Process Clause does not in itself subject an inmate's treatment by prison authorities to judicial oversight."

It is plain that the transfer of an inmate to less amenable and more restrictive quarters for nonpunitive reasons is well within the terms of confinement ordinarily contemplated by a prison sentence. . . . Accordingly, administrative segregation is the sort of confinement that inmates should reasonably anticipate receiving at some point in their incarceration. . . .

Despite this, respondent points out that the Court has held that a State may create a liberty interest protected by the Due Process Clause through its enactment of certain statutory or regulatory measures. Thus, in *Wolff*, where we rejected any notion of an interest in good-time credits inherent in the Constitution, we also found that Nebraska had created a right to such good credits. . . .

Respondent argues that Pennsylvania, in its enactment of regulations governing the administration of state prisons, has created a liberty interest in remaining free from the restraints accompanying confinement in administrative segregation. . . . [We] have never held that statutes and regulations governing daily operation of a prison system conferred any liberty interest in and of themselves. . . .

There are persuasive reasons why we should be loath to transpose all of the reasoning in the cases just cited to the situation where the statute and regulations govern the day to day administration of a prison system. The deprivations imposed in the course of the daily operations of an institution are likely to be minor when compared to the release from custody at issue in parole decisions and good time credits. Moreover, the safe and efficient operation of a prison on a day to day basis has traditionally been entrusted to the expertise of prison officials. These facts suggest that regulations structuring the authority of prison administrators may warrant treatment, for purposes of creation of entitlements to "liberty," different from statutes and regulations in other areas. Nonetheless, we conclude in the light of the Pennsylvania statutes and regulations here in question, the relevant provisions of which are set forth in full in the margin,[6] that respondent did

---

6. Section 95.104(b)(1) of Title 37 of the Pennsylvania Code provides that:

An inmate who has allegedly committed a Class I Misconduct may be placed in Close or Maximum Administrative Custody upon approval of the officer in charge of the institution, not routinely but based upon his assessment of the situation and the need for control pending application of procedures under § 95.103 of this title.

Section 95.103(b)(3) of the same title provides:

An inmate may be temporarily confined to Close or Maximum Administrative Custody in an investigative status upon approval of the officer in charge of the institution where it has been determined that there is a threat of a serious disturbance or a serious threat to the individual or others. The inmate shall be notified in writing as soon as possible that he is under investigation and that he will receive a hearing if any disciplinary action is being considered after the investigation is completed. An investigation shall begin immediately to determine

acquire a protected liberty interest in remaining in the general prison population.

Respondent seems to suggest that the mere fact that Pennsylvania has created a careful procedural structure to regulate the use of administrative segregation indicates the existence of a protected liberty interest. We cannot agree. The creation of procedural guidelines to channel the decisionmaking of prison officials is, in the view of many experts in the field, a salutary development. It would be ironic to hold that when a State embarks on such desirable experimentation it thereby opens the door to scrutiny by the federal courts, while States that choose not to adopt such procedural provisions entirely avoid the strictures of the Due Process Clause. The adoption of such procedural guidelines, without more, suggests that it is these restrictions alone, and not those federal courts might also impose under the Fourteenth Amendment, that the State chose to require.

Nonetheless, in this case the Commonwealth had gone beyond simple procedural guidelines. It has used language of an unmistakably mandatory character, requiring that certain procedures "shall," "will," or "must" be employed, see note 6 *supra,* and that administrative segregation will not occur absent specified substantive predicates—*viz.,* "the need for control," or "the threat of a serious disturbance." Petitioner argues, with considerable force, that these terms must be read in light of the fact that the decision whether to confine an inmate to administrative segregation is largely predictive, and therefore that it is not likely that the State meant to create binding requirements. But on balance we are persuaded that the repeated use of explicitly mandatory language in connection with requiring specific substantive predicates demands a conclusion that the State has created a protected liberty interest. . . .

[The Court went on to hold that SCIH had provided Helms with due process. This portion of the opinion is reproduced at § 2.4 *infra.* Accordingly the judgment of the Court of Appeals was reversed.]

On the issue of whether Helms had a liberty interest without regard to the regulations, JUSTICES STEVENS, MARSHALL and BRENNAN dissented. JUSTICE STEVENS wrote: . . .

. . . Petitioners argue that a transfer into solitary confinement is merely one example of various routine decisions made on a day-to-day

whether or not a behavior violation has occurred. If no behavior violation has occurred, the inmate must be released as soon as the reason for the security concern has abated but in all cases within ten days.

Finally, a State Bureau of Correction Administrative Directive states that when the State Police have been summoned to an institution: Pending arrival of the State Police, the institutional representative shall:

1. Place all suspects and resident witnesses or complainants in such custody, protective or otherwise, as may be necessary to maintain security. A hearing complying with [37 Pa.Code § 95.103] will be carried out after the investigation period. Such hearing shall be held within four (4) days unless the investigation warrants delay and in the case as soon as possible.

basis by prison authorities, regarding "place of confinement, both as to which facility is appropriate and within the appropriate facility which cell block or housing unit is appropriate; his job assignment; the potential for freedom of movement; and the possibility and variety of educational and vocational opportunities available to him." According to petitioners, operational decisions such as these do not raise any constitutional question because prison officials need wide latitude to operate their institutions in a safe and efficient manner.

The Court properly rejects the contention that the Due Process Clause is simply inapplicable to transfers of inmates into administrative segregation. It holds that respondent's transfer from the general population into administrative confinement was a deprivation of liberty that must be accompanied by due process of law. The majority's reasoning in support of this conclusion suffers, however, from a fundamental flaw. In its view, a "liberty interest" exists only because Pennsylvania's written prison regulations display a magical combination of "substantive predicates" and "explicitly mandatory language." This analysis attaches no significance either to the character of the conditions of confinement or to actual administrative practices in the institution. . . . .

This approach, although consistent with some of the Court's recent cases, is dramatically different from the analysis in *Wolff v. McDonnell,* 418 U.S. 539 (1974). In *Wolff,* the Court squarely held that every prisoner retains a significant residuum of constitutionally protected liberty following his incarceration. . . . .

The source of the liberty recognized in *Wolff* is not state law, nor even the Constitution itself. Rather, it is plain that:

"neither the Bill of Rights nor the laws of sovereign States create the liberty which the Due Process Clause protects. . . . .

"I had thought it self-evident that all men were endowed by their Creator with liberty as one of the cardinal unalienable rights. It is that basic freedom which the Due Process Clause protects, rather than the particular rights or privileges conferred by specific laws or regulations." *Meachum v. Fano.*

Identifying the "liberty" that survives in a closely-controlled prison environment is understandably more difficult than in the world at large. For it is obvious that "[l]awful imprisonment makes unavailable many rights and privileges of the ordinary citizen, a 'retraction justified by the considerations underlying our penal system.'" But I remain convinced that an inmate "has a protected right to pursue his limited rehabilitative goals, or at the minimum, to maintain whatever attributes of dignity are associated with his status in a tightly controlled society. It is unquestionably within the power of the State to change that status, abruptly and adversely; but if the change is sufficiently grievous, it may not be imposed arbitrarily. In such case due process must be afforded."

Thus, the relevant question in this case is whether transfer into administrative segregation constitutes a "sufficiently grievous" change in a prisoner's status to require the protection of "due process." . . .

Thus, for a prisoner as for other persons, the grievousness of any claimed deprivation of liberty is, in part, a relative matter: one must compare the treatment of the particular prisoner with the customary, habitual treatment of the population of the prison as a whole. In general, if a prisoner complains of an adverse change in conditions which he shares with an entire class of his fellow prisoners as part of the day-to-day operations of the prison, there would be no reason to find that he has been deprived of his constitutionally-protected liberty. But if a prisoner is singled out for disparate treatment and if the disparity is sufficiently severe, his liberty is at stake.

In this case, by definition, the institutional norm is confinement in the "general prison population." The deprivation of which respondent complains is transfer to "administrative segregation"—that is, solitary confinement—which by its nature singles out individual prisoners. That confinement was not specified by the terms of his initial criminal sentence. Not only is there a disparity, the disparity is drastic. It is concededly as serious as the difference between confinement in the general prison population and "disciplinary segregation." . . .

In this case, the Court's exclusive focus on written regulations happens to lead it to the conclusion that there is a "liberty interest." I agree that the regulations are relevant: by limiting the substantive reasons for a transfer to administrative segregation and by establishing prescribed procedures, these regulations indicate that the State recognizes the substantiality of the deprivation. They therefore provide evidentiary support for the conclusion that the transfer affects a constitutionally-protected interest in liberty. But the regulations do not *create* that interest. Even in their absence, due process safeguards would be required when an inmate's liberty is further curtailed by a transfer into administrative custody that is the functional equivalent of punitive isolation.

. . .

Notes and Questions

1. *The Helms majority.* Does the majority opinion in this case seem internally inconsistent? Why does it recognize a liberty interest after arguing that due process is inappropriate in prison? In the portion of the *Helms* decision reproduced in § 2.4, the Court held that very little process was due. Does that help to explain the majority's willingness to find that the regulations created a liberty interest?

2. *How much liberty does a prisoner retain?* The Court's decisions concerning procedural due process rights of prisoners, parolees, and others who are confined against their will, are difficult to reconcile. As *Helms* illustrates, the Justices have serious philosophical differences on this issue. Can you make any sense of these decisions?

After *Roth,* the Court identified several liberty interests which prisoners retain. Thus prisoners are entitled to due process when:

i.   Deprived of "good time credits" toward early release because of flagrant or serious misconduct. *Wolff v. McDonnell,* 418 U.S. 539 (1974) (state law created a right to "good time" and took it away as a sanction for major misconduct).

ii.   Parole or probation is revoked by reason of violation of the terms of conditional liberty. *Morrissey v. Brewer,* 408 U.S. 471 (1972) (parole); *Gagnon v. Scarpelli,* 411 U.S. 778 (1973) (probation).

iii.   A prisoner is transferred from prison to a mental hospital for treatment of a mental disease. *Vitek v. Jones,* 445 U.S. 480 (1980). *Vitek* held that transfer to a mental hospital imposes a stigma on the transferred prisoner which could have adverse social consequences. In addition, treatment in the hospital by mandatory behavior modification techniques goes well beyond the range of conditions generally expected in prison. The transfer invaded a liberty interest without regard to any state law or regulation defining the conditions of such transfers.

iv.   An application for parole is denied, provided the statute or regulation constrains the discretion of the parole board. *Board of Pardons v. Allen,* 107 S.Ct. 2415 (1987); *Greenholtz v. Inmates of Nebraska Penal,* 442 U.S. 1 (1979).

According to most recent decisions, however, various unwelcome events occurring to prisoners are not deprivations of liberty. Consequently, there is no right to a hearing when:

i.   A prisoner is transferred from a medium-security to a maximum-security prison. *Meachum v. Fano,* 427 U.S. 215 (1976) (although suspicion that prisoner was involved in setting fires was the primary reason for transfer, state law left transfers wholly to discretion of prison officials).

ii.   An application for parole is denied and the statute gives the parole board complete discretion. *See* dictum in *Allen* and *Greenholtz, supra. Greenholtz* distinguished *Morrissey* and *Gagnon, supra,* involving termination of parole or probation, since there is a crucial distinction between "losing what one has and not getting what one wants."

iii.   An application for commutation of a life sentence is denied (even though similar applications are granted 75% of the time). *Connecticut Bd. of Pardons v. Dumschat,* 452 U.S. 458 (1981) (rejecting claims that a de facto liberty interest in a pardon could arise from prior practice).

iv.   A pretrial detainee is subjected to various indignities such as overcrowded cells, limitations on gifts, and body cavity searches after seeing visitors. *Bell v. Wolfish,* 441 U.S. 520 (1979) (liberty interests subordinated to institution's security and administrative concerns).

3. *Disciplinary segregation.* Considering *Hewitt* and *Wolff v. McDonnell,* discussed in the *Hewitt* dissent (requiring due process when a prisoner's "good time credits" are cancelled for disciplinary reasons), do you think that Mr. Helms was deprived of "liberty" on January 22, 1979 when he was assigned to six months in disciplinary segregation?

4. *Liberty and the Pennsylvania regulations.* Assuming a prisoner is not automatically deprived of "liberty" when placed in administrative segregation, do you agree that the Pennsylvania regulations created a liberty interest? What language in the regulations had this effect?

5. *Liberty by statute or regulation.* Under the *Hewitt* case, confinement in administrative segregation deprives a prisoner of liberty only because of discretion-limiting language in the prison regulations. Similarly, in *Allen* and *Greenholtz, supra,* the Court found that a prisoner had a right to a hearing before rejection of his application for parole because a statute said a prisoner "shall" be released unless some vague criteria were fulfilled ("a reasonable probability that no detriment will result to him or the community").

Recall the definition of "liberty" in *Roth,* which drew upon the open-ended approach of *Meyer v. Nebraska.* Are later cases consistent with that approach?

How can you tell whether a statute or regulation sufficiently controls discretion to create a protectable liberty interest? Consider *Olim v. Wakinekona,* 461 U.S. 238 (1983): A prisoner was transferred for security reasons from Hawaii to the mainland (likened by the dissent to "banishment beyond the seas"). The regulations provided that a prisoner's classification "should be in the best interests of the individual, the State, and the community. In short, classification is a continuing evaluation of each individual to ensure he is given the optimum placement within the Corrections Division." Did this regulation create a liberty interest?

In an earlier case involving a different prisoner, the Hawaii Supreme Court had interpreted the regulation in a way that left a transfer decision purely a matter of the warden's discretion. In *Olim,* the United States Supreme Court deferred to the state court interpretation and found that the regulations created no liberty interest.

The regulation in *Olim* also provided for a trial-type hearing on issues of transfer which involved a "grievous loss" to an inmate. Petitioner contended that the hearing did not meet due process standards. The Supreme Court held that violation of *procedural rights* in a state statute or regulation did not rise to the level of a due process violation.

If you were counsel to a state prison agency, how would you advise it to draft and interpret its regulations relating to transfer or discipline of prisoners, solitary confinement, or parole? Do you think that decisions like *Hewitt, Allen, Greenholtz,* and *Olim* place too much weight on accidental choice of phrases in the regulations? Defer excessively to judicial or administrative interpretations of statutes or regulations? Are overly concerned with prison security problems?

6. *Stigma as deprivation of liberty.* Recall that the Court held that Mr. Roth had not been stigmatized by the discharge. The state "did not base the nonrenewal of his contract on a charge, for example, that he had been guilty of dishonesty, or immorality. Had it done so, this would be a different case. For '[w]here a person's good name, reputation, honor, or integrity is at stake because of what the government is doing to him, notice and an opportunity to be heard are essential.' *Wisconsin v. Constantineau,* 400 U.S. 433 . . ." The *Constantineau* case held that a person was entitled to a prior hearing before the state posted his name as a "public drunkard."

In later decisions, however, the Court has held that state imposition of a stigma, by itself, is not an invasion of liberty so that no prior hearing is required. In *Paul v. Davis,* 424 U.S. 693 (1976), the police circulated a flyer bearing Davis' photo and labelling him as an "active shoplifter." The Court held that Davis was not entitled to a hearing. The police might have defamed him but had not deprived him of liberty. The issue of whether Davis could have sued the chief of police for defamation in state court is addressed in § 10.2.2, *infra.*

The Court distinguished the *Roth* dictum by holding that liberty might be invaded by the imposition of a stigma *plus some other change of status*—such as discharge from a job. Similarly, it distinguished *Constantineau* because a "public drunkard" could not purchase alcoholic beverages. Thus this case also met the "stigma-plus" test.

In dissent, Justice Brennan argued that, under the majority view, the state could convene a commission to conduct ex parte trials of individuals so long as the only official judgment was a public condemnation and branding of the person as a Communist, traitor, murderer or any other mark that "merely" carries social opprobrium.

7. *Investigatory hearings.* Brennan's dissenting comments in *Paul* raise the question of whether due process applies to administrative investigations which may result in conclusions that are harmful to the persons investigated. In *Hannah v. Larche,* 363 U.S. 420 (1960), the Court held that voting registrars summoned to testify before the Civil Rights Commission had no right to cross-examine their accusers since the proceedings of the Commission were purely investigatory. The Commission was seeking information in order to advise Congress and the executive branch about civil rights problems. It could not issue orders or impose any sanctions. However, in a later case, the Court limited *Hannah.* It held that due process did apply to state investigative proceedings that sought to uncover and publicize criminal activity by unions and brand individuals as criminals. *Jenkins v. McKeithen,* 395 U.S. 411 (1969). Under these cases and the majority view in *Paul v. Davis,* was Brennan's assessment correct?

8. *Problem.* A Michigan Department of Corrections regulation provides that a prisoner "may receive any book, periodical, or other

publication which does not present a threat to the order or security of the institution." A local trial court (in an earlier case involving a different plaintiff) interpreted this rule (in accordance with the warden's long-time practice) to allow inmates to receive only new books shipped directly from publishers; whether inmates could receive any other book is left to the warden's discretion. The warden is concerned that used books, or new books sent by friends, require individual inspection to make sure there are no concealed drugs or weapons— which would be a serious administrative burden. Angela, a prisoner at Marquette Prison, is not permitted to receive a new dictionary sent to her by her brother. The warden refused to inspect the book or provide a hearing. Has the prison invaded Angela's interest in liberty? *See Spruytte v. Walters*, 753 F.2d 498 (6th Cir.1985).

§ 2.2.3 DEFINING "PROPERTY"

The *Roth* case held that a continued flow of welfare benefits is "property" while the job of an untenured professor is not. According to *Roth*, property interests are created and limited by positive law such as state statutes. Does it follow that a statute that creates "property" can also prescribe the procedure for taking it away?

CLEVELAND BOARD OF EDUCATION v. LOUDERMILL

470 U.S. 532 (1985).

[Respondents worked for cities in Ohio. One was a security guard; the other was a bus mechanic. By law, they could be discharged only for cause. They were discharged without any opportunity to respond to the charges against them prior to the discharge. One was discharged for lying on his employment application; the other failed an eye examination. As a result, they claimed they were denied liberty or property without due process. Ohio law provided no pre-termination hearing, but it did provide for a post-termination hearing and for judicial review. The post-termination hearing occurred about nine months after the discharge.]

WHITE, J.:

. . .

II

Respondents' federal constitutional claim depends on their having had a property right in continued employment. *Board of Regents v. Roth.* If they did, the State could not deprive them of this property without due process.

Property interests are not created by the Constitution, "they are created and their dimensions are defined by existing rules or understandings that stem from an independent source such as state law. . . ." The Ohio statute plainly creates such an interest. Respondents were "classified civil service employees," entitled to retain their positions "during good behavior and efficient service," who could not be dismissed "except . . . for . . . misfeasance, malfeasance, or nonfeasance in office." The statute plainly supports the conclusion, reached by both lower courts, that respondents possessed property rights in continued employment. Indeed, this question does not seem to have been disputed below.

The Parma Board argues, however, that the property right is defined by, and conditioned on, the legislature's choice of procedures for its deprivation. The Board stresses that in addition to specifying the grounds for termination, the statute sets out procedures by which termination may take place. The procedures were adhered to in these cases. According to petitioner, "[t]o require additional procedures would in effect expand the scope of the property interest itself."

This argument, which was accepted by the District Court, has its genesis in the plurality opinion in *Arnett v. Kennedy,* 416 U.S. 134 (1974). *Arnett* involved a challenge by a former federal employee to the procedures by which he was dismissed. The plurality reasoned that where the legislation conferring the substantive right also sets out the procedural mechanism for enforcing that right, the two cannot be separated:

> "The employee's statutorily defined right is not a guarantee against removal without cause in the abstract, but such a guarantee as enforced by the procedures which Congress has designated for the determination of cause.

> ". . . [W]here the grant of a substantive right is inextricably intertwined with the limitations on the procedures which are to be employed in determining that right, a litigant in the position of appellee must take the bitter with the sweet."

This view garnered three votes in *Arnett,* but was specifically rejected by the other six Justices. Since then, this theory has at times seemed to gather some additional support. More recently, however, the Court has clearly rejected it. . . . In light of these holdings, it is settled that the "bitter with the sweet" approach misconceives the constitutional guarantee. If a clearer holding is needed, we provide it today. The point is straightforward: the Due Process Clause provides that certain substantive rights—life, liberty, and property—cannot be deprived except pursuant to constitutionally adequate procedures. The categories of substance and procedure are distinct. Were the rule otherwise, the Clause would be reduced to a mere tautology. "Property" cannot be defined by the procedures provided for its deprivation any more than can life or liberty. The right to due process "is conferred, not by legislative grace, but by constitutional guarantee. While the legislature may elect not to confer a property interest in [public] employment, it may not constitutionally authorize the deprivation of such an interest, once conferred, without appropriate procedural safeguards."

In short, once it is determined that the Due Process Clause applies, "the question remains what process is due." *Morrissey v. Brewer,* 408 U.S. 471, 481 (1972). The answer to that question is not to be found in the Ohio statute. . . .

[The Court found that Ohio's pre-termination procedures did not provide due process. See § 2.3 note 4, *infra.*]

JUSTICE REHNQUIST, dissenting.

In *Arnett v. Kennedy,* six Members of this Court agreed that a public employee could be dismissed for misconduct without a full hearing prior to termination. A plurality of Justices agreed that the employee was entitled to exactly what Congress gave him, and no more. . . . Here, as in *Arnett,* "[t]he employee's statutorily defined right is not a guarantee against removal without cause in the abstract, but such a guarantee as enforced by the procedures which [the Ohio legislature] has designated for the determination of cause." We stated in *Board of Regents v. Roth:*

> "Property interests, of course, are not created by the Constitu- tion. Rather, they are created and their dimensions are defined by existing rules or understandings that stem from an independent source such as state law—rules or understandings that secure certain benefits and that support claims of entitlement to those benefits."

We ought to recognize the totality of the State's definition of the property right in question, and not merely seize upon one of several paragraphs in a unitary statute to proclaim that in that paragraph the State has inexorably conferred upon a civil service employee something which it is powerless under the United States Constitution to qualify in the next paragraph of the statute. This practice ignores our duty under *Roth* to rely on state law as the source of property interests for purposes of applying the Due Process Clause of the Fourteenth Amend- ment. While it does not impose a federal definition of property, the Court departs from the full breadth of the holding in *Roth* by its selective choice from among the sentences the Ohio legislature chooses to use in establishing and qualifying a right. . . .

Notes and Questions

1. *The bitter with the sweet.* Since "property" does not exist in the abstract but arises only from statute, contract, or other interest protected by state law, what is wrong with Rehnquist's contention that the state should be allowed to create the procedural as well as the substantive contours of property interests? In other words, why shouldn't the property-holder take "the bitter with the sweet?"

In the portion of the opinion reproduced in § 2.4, *infra,* the Court held that a written, rather than oral, pretermination proceeding is sufficient protection for a discharged employee. Was this a factor in persuading the majority justices to reject the "bitter with the sweet" approach?

2. *Consequences of Loudermill.* Do decisions like *Perry v. Sindermann* (§ 2.2.1, note 6 *supra*) and *Loudermill* go too far in rigidifying public employment so that government must choose between a spoils system and a tenure system which is highly protective of employee job security? Will government be willing or able, practically speaking, to fire incompetent employees if they have entitlements to their jobs protected by due process?

Will these cases encourage government to contract out to private employers such traditional governmental tasks as trash collection, recreation area maintenance, public transportation and the like? Since job security is purely a matter of employer-employee bargaining in the private sector, the private sector may be able to furnish such services more efficiently than government.

3. *Jobs as property—Bishop v. Wood.* How can you tell whether a government job is "property?" Many jobholders have much less protection than a fully tenured college professor but more protection than Mr. Roth. For example, in *Bishop v. Wood*, 426 U.S. 341 (1976), a policeman was classified as a "permanent employee." The ordinance provided that "if a permanent employee fails to perform work up to the standard of the classification held, or continues to be negligent, inefficient, or unfit to perform his duties, he may be dismissed by the City manager. Any discharged employee shall be given written notice of his discharge setting forth the effective date and reasons for his discharge if he shall request such a notice." No North Carolina cases had interpreted this ordinance.

The federal trial judge "who of course sits in North Carolina and practiced law there for many years" concluded that the policeman "held his position at the will and pleasure of the city." The Supreme Court deferred to this construction and held that the job was not "property." Do you agree? Should this sort of determination be left to a case-by-case analysis by trial courts, or should there be a uniform rule which automatically treats a "permanent" job as property? Is *Bishop* consistent with *Loudermill?*

The policeman was fired for reasons that he alleged were both false and professionally harmful. However, the discharge did not deprive him of "liberty" because the city manager did not disclose them to anyone except the policeman himself. Of course, these reasons probably would be disclosed in the future when a potential employer asked about the policeman's employment record. Is this a correct application of *Paul v. Davis*, § 2.2.2 note 6, *supra?*

4. *The new property—beyond Roth.* Besides certain jobs and welfare benefits, what other relationships between persons and government are *entitlements*—and thus treated as *property* for procedural due process purposes? Among the most important are *licenses* to do what cannot be done without governmental permission (for example, to drive

a car or practice medicine). *See e.g. Barry v. Barchi,* 443 U.S. 55 (1979) (suspension of horse trainer's license). Equally important is the right to public *services* such as education. *See e.g. Memphis Light, Gas and Water Div. v. Craft,* 436 U.S. 1 (1978) (right to continued service from municipal utility).

The future will undoubtedly reveal that many forms of status or benefits are "property" which the state cannot adjudicate away without providing due process. Consider, for example, *Logan v. Zimmerman Brush Co.,* 455 U.S. 422 (1982). Illinois law created an agency (FEPA) to investigate and adjudicate claims for employment discrimination based on handicap. Because FEPA inadvertently failed to schedule a conference to determine whether probable cause existed within 120 days after Logan's complaint was filed, as required by state law, FEPA lost jurisdiction over his claim which thus became unenforceable. Logan's right to have his discrimination claim adjudicated by FEPA was *property* according to the Supreme Court. By failing to take action within the 120 day period to determine whether Logan's claim had merit, Illinois had snuffed it out without due process. Consequently, the FEPA had to hear the case, and Zimmerman Brush lost the benefit of the statute of limitation. Did the Supreme Court decision take away Zimmerman Brush's property right without due process?

Similarly, a *contractual* right to discharge an employee for cause is "property." Government cannot require reinstatement of such an employee without providing due process to the employer. *Brock v. Roadway Exp., Inc.,* 107 S.Ct. 1740 (1987).

On the other hand, residents of a nursing home were held to lack any liberty or property entitlement to continue receiving nursing care at government expense in that particular nursing home. As a result, those residents had no right to a hearing before the government decertified the nursing home, even though such action meant they must move to another home. The nursing home had a right to a hearing— but not the residents. The Supreme Court decided that federal law did not confer a right on the residents "to continue residence in the home of one's choice." *O'Bannon v. Town Court Nursing Center,* 447 U.S. 773 (1980). Why not?

5. *Entitlements—principled decision-making?* Does the "entitlement" approach to defining liberty and property interests insure that persons receive procedural protection appropriate for the substantive matters at stake? Does reliance on the entitlement doctrine require a court to engage in sub silentio balancing of the interests of the individual and government, rather than a more accountable, overt balancing of those interests? Is there a better way to match the procedure to the nature of the dispute?

6. *Due process and de minimis deprivations. Goss v. Lopez,* 419 U.S. 565, 576 (1975), held that "as long as a property deprivation is not *de minimis,* its gravity is irrelevant to the question whether account must be taken of the Due Process Clause . . . . the length and severity

of deprivation, while another factor to weigh in determining the appropriate form of hearing, 'is not decisive of the basic right' to a hearing of some kind." Thus a "10–day suspension from school is not *de minimis* in our view and may not be imposed in complete disregard of the Due Process Clause." We discuss the *form* that such a hearing should take in §§ 2.3 and 2.4 *infra*.

Do you agree that due process should be wholly inapplicable to a deprivation of liberty or property merely because the value of the entitlement is so small that its loss may be characterized as *de minimis*? The loss of a $10 welfare benefit to a truly poor person may be of more consequence to that person than the loss of $5000 to a millionaire. *See Gray Panthers v. Schweiker,* 652 F.2d 146 (D.C.Cir. 1980) (Medicare claims under $100—purely written procedures insufficient).

7. *Due process and state tort law.* Suppose a plaintiff who has been deprived of liberty or property could sue the state or the official responsible for the deprivation in state court. Should the state judicial proceeding serve as a substitute for a trial-type hearing?

In *Parratt v. Taylor,* 451 U.S. 527 (1981), prison officials negligently lost a prisoner's hobby kit worth $23. The Court did not hold that a $23 loss was a *de minimis* deprivation; instead, it decided that the availability of a state tort action after such a "random and unauthorized" deprivation of property satisfied the requirements of due process. The same reasoning applied to an *intentional* destruction of a prisoner's property by a prison guard during a search of his cell. *Hudson v. Palmer,* 468 U.S. 517 (1984). Later, overruling *Parratt* on a different issue, the Court held that a merely *negligent* deprivation of property was not a due process violation at all. *Daniels v. Williams,* 474 U.S. 327 (1986).

Similarly, in *Ingraham v. Wright,* 430 U.S. 651 (1977), the issue was whether a school must provide a hearing before a student is paddled. While corporal punishment (like other forms of bodily restraint and punishment) is a deprivation of liberty, the state provided a judicial damage remedy against school officials for excessive punishment. This post-deprivation tort remedy was sufficient in light of the relatively slight incremental benefit of a pre-punishment hearing balanced against the substantial costs of providing such hearings. Note that this approach denies the student any right to a hearing on the issue of whether he committed the violation that led to being paddled.

Do you agree that post-deprivation judicial remedies are an adequate substitute for a pre-deprivation hearing in the case of destruction of a prisoner's property? Corporal punishment of a student? Are the issues to be resolved in the judicial hearing the same as would be resolved in a pre-deprivation agency hearing?

8. *Problem.* Seaside High School hires part-time athletic coaches. The practice is for the principal to enter into contracts with coaches to work not more than 20 hours per week. Coaching contracts provide

that if a coach's work is satisfactory and the coach's services are needed for the next academic year, the contract will be renewed. If a contract is not renewed because of unsatisfactory service, the principal must explain the basis of the decision in writing.

Rex, the principal of Seaside High, hired Doris to coach girls' tennis for the spring semester. The contract called for compensation of $400 per month for four months. Rex's daughter, Ann, was on the team. Ann and Doris did not get along very well and Ann, because of poor attitude, was not allowed to play in several important matches. However, Seaside's team was undefeated, and most of the girls were pleased with Doris.

Rex declined to renew Doris' contract for the following academic year, even though a coach was needed. He stated no reasons and refused to discuss the matter with Doris. What are Doris' rights? *See Vail v. Board of Educ.*, 706 F.2d 1435 (7th Cir.1983), *aff'd by an eq. div. crt.*, 466 U.S. 377 (1984); *S & D Maintenance Co. v. Goldin*, 844 F.2d 962 (2d Cir.1988).

§ 2.3   TIMING OF TRIAL–TYPE HEARINGS

Even if government action has worked a deprivation of liberty or property, the question remains: what process is due? *Goldberg* determined that a trial-type hearing must be held *before* termination of benefits. The timing question is often critical, because a hearing after the event may do little to repair the damage caused by an administrative error. Yet a requirement that a hearing be held before benefits, employment, or some other entitlement can be terminated may impose substantial financial and programmatic costs upon an agency.

Mathews v. Eldridge asks whether trial-type hearings must be provided *before* termination of benefits to *disabled* persons under Title II of the Social Security Act. The complex state-federal system which adjudicates disability claims is described in the *Mathews* opinion. Some additional background on the disability program is helpful in evaluating the decision.

The Social Security Administration (SSA) operates the largest system of administrative adjudication in the Western world. It makes well over 3 million determinations per year on claims for benefits under the Old–Age, Survivors, Disability, and Health Insurance (OASDHI) programs. The portion of the Social Security system considered here, the disability program, is itself massive. Since 1974, initial claims for disability benefits (under both Title II [Disability Insurance] and Title XVI [Supplemental Security Income] of the Social Security Act) have averaged nearly 1,250,000 annually. . . .

There are perhaps 5,600 state agency personnel (supported by 5,000 more) whose sole function is to adjudicate disability claims. Over 625 federal administrative law judges hear administrative appeals from state agency denials. This total of more than 6,000 adjudicators approaches the size of the combined judicial systems of the state and federal governments of the United States. And the claims that these officials adjudicate are not small. The average, present, discounted value of the stream of income from a successful disability application is over $30,000. Disability claims, on the average, thus have a value three times that required by statute for the pursuit of many civil actions in federal district courts. More than 4.3 million disabled workers and their dependents draw annual benefits, which in fiscal year 1982 totaled $21.2 billion. When the Medicaid and Medicare payments for which these beneficiaries are automatically eligible are included, the total figure is $32.4 billion. By any measure the system is massive.

J. Mashaw, BUREAUCRATIC JUSTICE 18–19 (1983).

MATHEWS v. ELDRIDGE
424 U.S. 319 (1976).

[Eldridge's disability benefits were terminated in accordance with all applicable administrative procedures. Those procedures did not give him an opportunity for any kind of trial-type hearing before the termination was effective.]

MR. JUSTICE POWELL delivered the opinion of the Court.

The issue in this case is whether the Due Process Clause of the Fifth Amendment requires that prior to the termination of Social Security disability benefit payments the recipient be afforded an opportunity for an evidentiary hearing. . . . Respondent Eldridge was first awarded benefits in June 1968. In March 1972, he received a questionnaire from the state agency charged with monitoring his medical condition. Eldridge completed the questionnaire, indicating that his condition had not improved and identifying the medical sources, including physicians, from whom he had received treatment recently. The state agency then obtained reports from his physician and a psychiatric consultant. After considering these reports and other information in his file the agency informed Eldridge by letter that it had made a tentative determination that his disability had ceased in May 1972. The letter included a statement of reasons for the proposed termination of benefits, and advised Eldridge that he might request reasonable time in which to obtain and submit additional information pertaining to his condition.

In his written response, Eldridge disputed one characterization of his medical condition and indicated that the agency already had enough evidence to establish his disability. The state agency then made its final determination that he had ceased to be disabled in May 1972. This determination was accepted by the Social Security Administration (SSA), which notified Eldridge in July that his benefits would terminate after that month. The notification also advised him of his right to seek reconsideration by the state agency of this initial determination within six months.

Instead of requesting reconsideration Eldridge commenced this action challenging the constitutional validity of the administrative procedures established by the Secretary of Health, Education, and Welfare for assessing whether there exists a continuing disability. He sought an immediate reinstatement of benefits pending a hearing on the issue of his disability. . . . In support of his contention that due process requires a pretermination hearing, Eldridge relied exclusively upon this Court's decision in *Goldberg v. Kelly*. . . .

A

Procedural due process imposes constraints on governmental decisions which deprive individuals of "liberty" or "property" interests within the meaning of the Due Process Clause of the Fifth or Fourteenth Amendment. The Secretary does not contend that procedural due process is inapplicable to terminations of Social Security disability benefits. He recognizes . . . that the interest of an individual in continued receipt of these benefits is a statutorily created "property" interest protected by the Fifth Amendment. Rather, the Secretary contends that the existing administrative procedures, detailed below, provide all the process that is constitutionally due before a recipient can be deprived of that interest.

This Court consistently has held that some form of hearing is required before an individual is finally deprived of a property interest. The "right to be heard before being condemned to suffer grievous loss of any kind, even though it may not involve the stigma and hardships of a criminal conviction, is a principle basic to our society." *Joint Anti–Fascist Comm. v. McGrath,* 341 U.S. 123 (1951) (Frankfurter, J., concurring). The fundamental requirement of due process is the opportunity to be heard "at a meaningful time and in a meaningful manner." *Armstrong v. Manzo,* 380 U.S. 545 (1965) . . .

In recent years this Court increasingly has had occasion to consider the extent to which due process requires an evidentiary hearing prior to the deprivation of some type of property interest even if such a hearing is provided thereafter. In only one case, *Goldberg v. Kelly,* has the Court held that a hearing closely approximating a judicial trial is necessary. In other cases requiring some type of pretermination hearing as a matter of constitutional right the Court has spoken sparingly about the requisite procedures. . . .

These decisions underscore the truism that " '[d]ue process,' unlike some legal rules, is not a technical conception with a fixed content unrelated to time, place and circumstances." *Cafeteria Workers v. McElroy,* 367 U.S. 886 (1961). "[D]ue process is flexible and calls for such procedural protections as the particular situation demands." *Morrissey v. Brewer,* 408 U.S. 471 (1972).

Accordingly, resolution of the issue whether the administrative procedures provided here are constitutionally sufficient requires analysis of the governmental and private interests that are affected. More precisely, our prior decisions indicate that identification of the specific dictates of due process generally requires consideration of three distinct factors: First, the private interest that will be affected by the official action; second, the risk of an erroneous deprivation of such interest through the procedures used, and the probable value, if any, of additional or substitute procedural safeguards; and finally, the Government's interest, including the function involved and the fiscal and administrative burdens that the additional or substitute procedural requirement would entail.

We turn first to a description of the procedures for the termination of Social Security disability benefits and thereafter consider the factors bearing upon the constitutional adequacy of these procedures.

B

The disability insurance program is administered jointly by state and federal agencies. State agencies make the initial determination whether a disability exists, when it began, and when it ceased. . . .

In order to establish initial and continued entitlement to disability benefits a worker must demonstrate that he is unable

"to engage in any substantial gainful activity by reason of any medically determinable physical or mental impairment which can be expected to result in death or which has lasted or can be expected to last for a continuous period of not less than 12 months. . . ."

To satisfy this test the worker bears a continuing burden of showing, by means of "medically acceptable clinical and laboratory diagnostic techniques," that he has a physical or mental impairment of such severity that

"he is not only unable to do his previous work but cannot, considering his age, education, and work experience, engage in any other kind of substantial gainful work which exists in the national economy, regardless of whether such work exists in the immediate area in which he lives, or whether a specific job vacancy exists for him, or whether he would be hired if he applied for work."

The principal reasons for benefits terminations are that the worker is no longer disabled or has returned to work. As Eldridge's benefits were terminated because he was determined to be no longer disabled, we consider only the sufficiency of the procedures involved in such cases.

The continuing-eligibility investigation is made by a state agency acting through a "team" consisting of a physician and a nonmedical person trained in disability evaluation. The agency periodically communicates with the disabled worker, usually by mail—in which case he is sent a detailed questionnaire—or by telephone, and requests information concerning his present condition, including current medical restrictions and sources of treatment, and any additional information that he considers relevant to his continued entitlement to benefits. Information regarding the recipient's current condition is also obtained from his sources of medical treatment.

If there is a conflict between the information provided by the beneficiary and that obtained from medical sources such as his physician, or between two sources of treatment, the agency may arrange for an examination by an independent consulting physician. Whenever the agency's tentative assessment of the beneficiary's condition differs from his own assessment, the beneficiary is informed that benefits may be terminated, provided a summary of the evidence upon which the proposed determination to terminate is based, and afforded an opportunity to review the medical reports and other evidence in his case file. He also may respond in writing and submit additional evidence. The state agency then makes its final determination, which is reviewed by an examiner in the SSA Bureau of Disability Insurance. If, as is usually the case, the SSA accepts the agency determination it notifies the recipient in writing, informing him of the reasons for the decision, and of his right to seek *de novo* reconsideration by the state agency. Upon acceptance by the SSA, benefits are terminated effective two months after the month in which medical recovery is found to have occurred.

If the recipient seeks reconsideration by the state agency and the determination is adverse, the SSA reviews the reconsideration determination and notifies the recipient of the decision. He then has a right to an evidentiary hearing before an SSA administrative law judge.

The hearing is nonadversary, and the SSA is not represented by counsel. As at all prior and subsequent stages of the administrative process, however, the claimant may be represented by counsel or other spokesmen. If this hearing results in an adverse decision, the claimant is entitled to request discretionary review by the SSA Appeals Council, and finally may obtain judicial review.[21]

Should it be determined at any point after termination of benefits, that the claimant's disability extended beyond the date of cessation initially established, the worker is entitled to retroactive payments. . . . If, on the other hand, a beneficiary receives any payments to which he is later determined not to be entitled, the statute authorizes the Secretary to attempt to recoup these funds in specified circumstances.

C

Despite the elaborate character of the administrative procedures provided by the Secretary, the courts below held them to be constitutionally inadequate, concluding that due process requires an evidentiary hearing prior to termination. In light of the private and governmen-

---

21. Unlike all prior levels of review, which are *de novo,* the district court is required to treat findings of fact as conclusive if supported by substantial evidence.

tal interests at stake here and the nature of the existing procedures, we think this was error.

Since a recipient whose benefits are terminated is awarded full retroactive relief if he ultimately prevails, his sole interest is in the uninterrupted receipt of this source of income pending final administrative decision on his claim. His potential injury is thus similar in nature to that of the welfare recipient in *Goldberg*. . . .

Only in *Goldberg* has the Court held that due process requires an evidentiary hearing prior to a temporary deprivation. It was emphasized there that welfare assistance is given to persons on the very margin of subsistence:

> "The crucial factor in this context—a factor not present in the case of . . . virtually anyone else whose governmental entitlements are ended—is that termination of aid pending resolution of a controversy over eligibility may deprive an *eligible* recipient of the very means by which to live while he waits."

Eligibility for disability benefits, in contrast, is not based upon financial need. Indeed, it is wholly unrelated to the worker's income or support from many other sources, such as earnings of other family members, workmen's compensation awards, tort claims awards, savings, private insurance, public or private pensions, veterans' benefits, food stamps, public assistance, or the "many other important programs, both public and private, which contain provisions for disability payments affecting a substantial portion of the work force. . . ."

As *Goldberg* illustrates, the degree of potential deprivation that may be created by a particular decision is a factor to be considered in assessing the validity of any administrative decisionmaking process. The potential deprivation here is generally likely to be less than in *Goldberg*, although the degree of difference can be overstated. As the District Court emphasized, to remain eligible for benefits a recipient must be "unable to engage in substantial gainful activity." Thus, in contrast to the discharged federal employee in *Arnett*, there is little possibility that the terminated recipient will be able to find even temporary employment to ameliorate the interim loss.

. . . [T]he possible length of wrongful deprivation of . . . benefits [also] is an important factor in assessing the impact of official action on the private interests. The Secretary concedes that the delay between a request for a hearing before an administrative law judge and a decision on the claim is currently between 10 and 11 months. Since a terminated recipient must first obtain a reconsideration decision as a prerequisite to invoking his right to an evidentiary hearing, the delay between the actual cutoff of benefits and final decision after a hearing exceeds one year.

In view of the torpidity of this administrative review process and the typically modest resources of the family unit of the physically disabled worker,[26] the hardship imposed upon the erroneously terminated disability recipient may be significant. Still, the disabled worker's need is likely to be less than that of a welfare recipient. In addition to the possibility of access to private resources, other forms of government assistance will become available where the termination of disability benefits places a worker or his family below the subsistence level.[27]

In view of these potential sources of temporary income, there is less reason here than in *Goldberg* to depart from the ordinary principle, established by our decisions, that something less than an evidentiary hearing is sufficient prior to adverse administrative action.

D

An additional factor to be considered here is the fairness and reliability of the existing pretermination procedures, and the probable value, if any, of additional procedural safeguards. Central to the evaluation of any administrative process is the nature of the relevant inquiry. In order to remain eligible for benefits the disabled worker must demonstrate by means of "medically acceptable clinical and laboratory diagnostic techniques" that he is unable "to engage in any substantial gainful activity by reason of any *medically determinable* physical or mental impairment . . . ." In short, a medical assessment of the worker's physical or mental condition is required. This is a more sharply focused and easily documented decision than the typical determination of welfare entitlement. In the latter case, a wide variety of information may be deemed relevant, and issues of witness credibility and veracity often are critical to the decisionmaking process. *Goldberg* noted that in such circumstances "written submissions are a wholly unsatisfactory basis for decision."

By contrast, the decision whether to discontinue disability benefits will turn, in most cases, upon "routine, standard, and unbiased medical reports by physician specialists" concerning a subject whom they have personally examined.[28] In *Richardson v. Perales,* 402 U.S. 389, 404

26. *Amici* cite statistics compiled by the Secretary which indicate that in 1965 the mean income of the family unit of a disabled worker was $3,803, while the median income for the unit was $2,836. The mean liquid assets—*i.e.,* cash, stocks, bonds—of these family units was $4,862; the median was $940. These statistics do not take into account the family unit's nonliquid assets—*i.e.,* automobile, real estate, and the like.

27. *Amici* emphasize that because an identical definition of disability is employed in both the Title II Social Security Program and in the companion welfare system for the disabled, Supplemental Security Income (SSI), the terminated disability-benefits recipient will be ineligible for the SSI Program. There exist, however, state and local welfare programs which may supplement the worker's income. In addition, the worker's household unit can qualify for food stamps if it meets the financial need requirements. Finally, in 1974, 480,000 of the approximately 2,000,000 disabled workers receiving Social Security benefits also received SSI benefits. Since financial need is a criterion for eligibility under the SSI program, those disabled workers who are most in need will in the majority of cases be receiving SSI benefits when disability insurance aid is terminated. And, under the SSI program, a pretermination evidentiary hearing is provided, if requested.

28. The decision is not purely a question of the accuracy of a medical diagnosis since the ultimate issue which the state agency must resolve is whether in light of the particular worker's "age, education,

(1971), the Court recognized the "reliability and probative worth of written medical reports," emphasizing that while there may be "professional disagreement with the medical conclusions" the "specter of questionable credibility and veracity is not present." To be sure, credibility and veracity may be a factor in the ultimate disability assessment in some cases. But procedural due process rules are shaped by the risk of error inherent in the truthfinding process as applied to the generality of cases, not the rare exceptions. The potential value of an evidentiary hearing, or even oral presentation to the decisionmaker, is substantially less in this context than in *Goldberg*.

The decision in *Goldberg* also was based on the Court's conclusion that written submissions were an inadequate substitute for oral presentation because they did not provide an effective means for the recipient to communicate his case to the decisionmaker. Written submissions were viewed as an unrealistic option, for most recipients lacked the "educational attainment necessary to write effectively" and could not afford professional assistance. In addition, such submissions would not provide the "flexibility of oral presentations" or "permit the recipient to mold his argument to the issues the decision maker appears to regard as important." In the context of the disability-benefits-entitlement assessment the administrative procedures under review here fully answer these objections.

The detailed questionnaire which the state agency periodically sends the recipient identifies with particularity the information relevant to the entitlement decision, and the recipient is invited to obtain assistance from the local SSA office in completing the questionnaire. More important, the information critical to the entitlement decision usually is derived from medical sources, such as the treating physician. Such sources are likely to be able to communicate more effectively through written documents than are welfare recipients or the lay witnesses supporting their cause. The conclusions of physicians often are supported by X–rays and the results of clinical or laboratory tests, information typically more amenable to written than to oral presentation.

A further safeguard against mistake is the policy of allowing the disability recipient's representative full access to all information relied upon by the state agency. In addition, prior to the cutoff of benefits the agency informs the recipient of its tentative assessment, the reasons therefor, and provides a summary of the evidence that it considers most

and work experience" he cannot "engage in any . . . substantial gainful work which exists in the national economy". . . . Yet information concerning each of these worker characteristics is amenable to effective written presentation. The value of an evidentiary hearing, or even a limited oral presentation, to an accurate presentation of those factors to the decisionmaker does not appear substantial. Similarly, resolution of the inquiry as to the types of employment opportunities that exist in the national economy for a physically impaired worker with a particular set of skills would not necessarily be advanced by an evidentiary hearing. The statistical information relevant to this judgment is more amenable to written than to oral presentation.

relevant. Opportunity is then afforded the recipient to submit additional evidence or arguments, enabling him to challenge directly the accuracy of information in his file as well as the correctness of the agency's tentative conclusions. These procedures, again as contrasted with those before the Court in *Goldberg*, enable the recipient to "mold" his argument to respond to the precise issues which the decisionmaker regards as crucial.

Despite these carefully structured procedures, *amici* point to the significant reversal rate for appealed cases as clear evidence that the current process is inadequate. Depending upon the base selected and the line of analysis followed, the relevant reversal rates urged by the contending parties vary from a high of 58.6% for appealed reconsideration decisions to an overall reversal rate of only 3.3%. Bare statistics rarely provide a satisfactory measure of the fairness of a decisionmaking process. Their adequacy is especially suspect here since the administrative review system is operated on an open-file basis. A recipient may always submit new evidence, and such submissions may result in additional medical examinations. Such fresh examinations were held in approximately 30% to 40% of the appealed cases, in fiscal 1973, either at the reconsideration or evidentiary hearing stage of the administrative process. In this context, the value of reversal rate statistics as one means of evaluating the adequacy of the pretermination process is diminished. Thus, although we view such information as relevant, it is certainly not controlling in this case.

E

In striking the appropriate due process balance the final factor to be assessed is the public interest. This includes the administrative burden and other societal costs that would be associated with requiring, as a matter of constitutional right, an evidentiary hearing upon demand in all cases prior to the termination of disability benefits. The most visible burden would be the incremental cost resulting from the increased number of hearings and the expense of providing benefits to ineligible recipients pending decision. No one can predict the extent of the increase, but the fact that full benefits would continue until after such hearings would assure the exhaustion in most cases of this attractive option. Nor would the theoretical right of the Secretary to recover undeserved benefits result, as a practical matter, in any substantial offset to the added outlay of public funds. The parties submit widely varying estimates of the probable additional financial cost. We only need say that experience with the constitutionalizing of government procedures suggests that the ultimate additional cost in terms of money and administrative burden would not be insubstantial.

Financial cost alone is not a controlling weight in determining whether due process requires a particular procedural safeguard prior to some administrative decision. But the Government's interest, and hence that of the public, in conserving scarce fiscal and administrative resources is a factor that must be weighed. At some point the benefit of an additional safeguard to the individual affected by the administrative action and to society in terms of increased assurance that the action is just, may be outweighed by the cost. Significantly, the cost of protecting those whom the preliminary administrative process has identified as likely to be found undeserving may in the end come out of the pockets of the deserving since resources available for any particular program of social welfare are not unlimited.

But more is implicated in cases of this type than ad hoc weighing of fiscal and administrative burdens against the interests of a particular category of claimants. The ultimate balance involves a determination as to when, under our constitutional system, judicial-type procedures must be imposed upon administrative action to assure fairness. We reiterate the wise admonishment of Mr. Justice Frankfurter that differences in the origin and function of administrative agencies "preclude wholesale transplantation of the rules of procedure, trial and review which have evolved from the history and experience of courts." The judicial model of an evidentiary hearing is neither a required, nor even the most effective, method of decisionmaking in all circumstances. The essence of due process is the requirement that "a person in jeopardy of serious loss [be given] notice of the case against him and opportunity to meet it." All that is necessary is that the procedures be tailored, in light of the decision to be made, to "the capacities and circumstances of those who are to be heard," *Goldberg v. Kelly,* to insure that they are given a meaningful opportunity to present their case. In assessing what process is due in this case, substantial weight must be given to the good-faith judgments of the individuals charged by Congress with the administration of social welfare programs that the procedures they have provided assure fair consideration of the entitlement claims of individuals. This is especially so where, as here, the prescribed procedures not only provide the claimant with an effective process for asserting his claim prior to any administrative action, but also assure a right to an evidentiary hearing, as well as to subsequent judicial review, before the denial of his claim becomes final.

We conclude that an evidentiary hearing is not required prior to the termination of disability benefits and that the present administrative procedures fully comport with due process.

The judgment of the Court of Appeals is *Reversed.*

JUSTICES BRENNAN and MARSHALL dissented. They observed: ". . . The Court's consideration that a discontinuance of disability benefits may cause the recipient to suffer only a limited deprivation is no argument. It is speculative. . . . Indeed in the present case, it is indicated that because disability benefits were terminated, there was a foreclosure on the Eldridge home and the family's furniture was repossessed, forcing Eldridge, his wife and children to sleep in one bed. . . ."

Notes and Questions

1. *Exigency and the old property.* The courts have long recognized that in case of emergency the state could deprive an individual of liberty or property without a prior hearing, even if a later remedy is inadequate. *See* note 10 in *Goldberg*. The classic case is *North American Cold Storage Co. v. Chicago,* 211 U.S. 306 (1908), in which the Court upheld a state law providing for the destruction without prior hearing of food held in cold storage which the authorities, after inspection, believed to be rotting and creating a menace to public health. The Court stated that an adequate remedy is provided by a tort action in which the authorities who destroyed the food would have to prove that the food was unfit. However, under present law the officials are likely to be immune from liability; in some states the city may be liable, but plaintiff would have a difficult burden of proof. *See* § 10.2, *infra.*

Was the *North American* case unnecessarily harsh? The city might have protected the public interest by offering the company the option of either destroying the food or impounding it in a safe facility pending a hearing. Should the agency be required by due process to offer such a choice?

In more recent cases involving the exigency problem, the Supreme Court has allowed an agency to act first and provide a hearing later. "An important government interest, accompanied by a substantial assurance that the deprivation is not baseless or unwarranted, may in limited cases demanding prompt action justify postponing the opportunity to be heard until after the initial deprivation." *FDIC v. Mallen,* 108 S.Ct. 1780, 1787 (1988) (suspension of banking executive under indictment for felony involving dishonesty). For example, a mine safety agency closed a mine because an inspection determined that it posed dangers to the health or safety of the public or significant and imminent environmental harm. A hearing on the propriety of the closure was available promptly thereafter. *Hodel v. Virginia Surface Mining Ass'n,* 452 U.S. 264 (1981). Similarly, a state racing board acted properly when it summarily suspended the license of a horse trainer after a drug test showed one of his horses to have been drugged. Here, too, a prompt post-suspension hearing was available. *Barry v. Barchi,* 443 U.S. 55 (1979).

In these cases, did the need for summary action to protect public health, welfare, or safety outweigh the need of the private party for a prior hearing? Can any of these cases be justified on the basis that a neutral test, inspection, or audit that triggered the summary action is an adequate substitute for a pre-deprivation trial-type hearing?

Prior to *Mathews,* however, it was generally held that, absent exigent circumstances, due process required governments to provide a hearing *prior* to depriving a person of liberty or property. *See generally* Freedman, "Summary Action by Administrative Agencies," 40 U.Chi.L. Rev. 1 (1972). Therefore, the statement in *Mathews* to the effect that the *"ordinary* principle, established by our decisions, that something less than an evidentiary hearing is sufficient prior to adverse administrative action" [emphasis added] signalled a significant change in attitude. *Mathews* permitted an agency to take action determining property or liberty interests prior to an evidentiary hearing. The justification for summary action was cost saving to government rather than exigent circumstances. This was a new departure.

2. *Timing and the new property.* *Mathews* represents a very different judicial philosophy from that which underpinned *Goldberg.* The balancing equation laid out in *Mathews* (rather than the more rigid approach taken in *Goldberg*) is the analytical format now used to determine both the *timing* of constitutionally required hearings as well as to determine the *elements* of the hearing. How did Justice Powell distinguish *Goldberg* from *Mathews* on the timing issue? Are his arguments persuasive? Are his factual assumptions well supported?

Between 1983 and 1987, Congress overruled *Mathews* and provided that disability recipients could elect to receive benefits until a hearing was provided. 42 U.S.C. § 423(g). However, this provision expired on Jan. 1, 1988. Why would Congress have overturned *Mathews?* Why did it not make the reversal permanent?

3. *Intuition or multiplication?* Do you agree with Judge Posner's summary of *Mathews:* "[*Mathews* requires] comparing the benefit of the procedural safeguard sought, which is a function of the value of the property interest at stake and the probability of erroneous deprivations if the safeguard is not provided, with the cost of the safeguard. The benefit of the safeguard can be thought of as the product of multiplying the value of the property interest by the probability that the value will be destroyed by a government error if the safeguard is not provided. Quantification will rarely be possible but expressing mathematically the relationship between the value of the interest and probability of its erroneous deprivation may assist in thinking about the tests. . . ." *Sutton v. City of Milwaukee,* 672 F.2d 644, 645 (7th Cir.1982).

4. *Timing and employment decisions.* While *Roth* indicated that a *prior* hearing must be provided before an employee is discharged from a tenured government job, later cases have been more cautious. In recognition of government's interest in immediate removal of an employee to which it objects, the Court has accepted in some contexts pre-termination procedures designed to insure that the government has probable cause for its decision. However, a full-fledged trial-type hearing must be provided promptly after removal.

For example, in *Cleveland Board of Education v. Loudermill,* § 2.2.3 *supra,* the Court held that pre-termination procedure serves as an "initial check against mistaken decisions—essentially, a determination of whether there are reasonable grounds to believe that the charges against the employee are true and support the proposed action." This means that an employee must receive oral or written notice of the charges against him, an explanation of the employer's evidence (although it is not clear how detailed this must be), and an opportunity to present his side of the story—orally or in writing.

How useful is the *Loudermill* pre-termination procedure? Presumably, an official must evaluate the employee's explanation before making the discharge decision. But if the pre-termination procedure is merely to discover whether there are reasonable grounds to believe the charges, why would even the most unbiased of officers not tend to go forward with the discharge and allow the employee's explanation to be evaluated in a post-termination hearing?

The Court also noted that a delay in the post-termination hearing could itself be a constitutional violation, but it held that Loudermill had not alleged sufficient facts to suggest that his wait of about nine months had been unreasonably prolonged. Again in *FDIC v. Mallen, supra,* the Court held that a delay of 90 days before an administrative decision was not an unreasonable delay.

The shoe was on the other foot in *Brock v. Roadway Exp., Inc.,* 107 S.Ct. 1740 (1987) and the balancing was even more complex. The statute allowed the Secretary of Labor to order a trucking company to reinstate an employee who the Secretary determined had been fired for protesting safety conditions. The Court's *Mathews* balancing took account of *three* interests: the employer's (in controlling its workforce), the government's (in improving truck safety), and the employee's (in avoiding unemployment and retaliatory discharge). Before compelling reinstatement, the Secretary must provide the employer with the substance of the evidence against it (apparently including the names of informants), an opportunity to submit a written response, and an opportunity to meet with the investigator and present statements from rebuttal witnesses. Again, the Secretary must provide expeditiously a full-fledged trial-type proceeding after reinstatement.

5. *Suspension or discharge?* In many cases, an agency has the option to suspend (rather than fire) a public employee or to suspend (rather than revoke) a license. A trial-type hearing must be provided after the suspension at which the employee or licensee may challenge the propriety of such action. If the agency then concludes that it has cause to do so, it can discharge the employee or revoke the license. Should an agency with suspension power be required to suspend an employee or license rather than immediately to discharge an employee or revoke a license without providing a prior hearing?

A suspension requirement is often imposed by statute or regulation. For example, § 14(c) of the 1961 MSAPA (on which most state APAs are based) provides: "If the agency finds that the public health, safety, or welfare imperatively requires emergency action, and incorporates a finding to that effect in its order, summary suspension of a license may be ordered pending proceedings for revocation or other action. These proceedings shall be promptly instituted and determined." *See also* 1981 MSAPA § 4–501 and federal APA § 558(c).

6. *Pending criminal proceeding.* Can an agency proceed to revoke a license (or expel a student) on grounds that are also the subject of a pending criminal prosecution? In *Silver v. McCamey,* 221 F.2d 873 (D.C. Cir.1955), a taxicab licensee was charged with rape. While these criminal charges were pending, the taxi licensing agency commenced administrative proceedings against him on the sole ground that he was unfit to hold a license because of the rape incident. The agency then held a hearing at which the licensee was forced either to defend against the charges or lose his license. After the hearing, the agency revoked his license. After being acquitted in the criminal case, he sued to have his license restored.

The court found in favor of the licensee, indicating that "due process is not observed if an accused person is subjected, without his consent, to an administrative hearing on the elements of a serious criminal charge that is pending against him. His necessary defense in the administrative hearing may disclose his evidence long in advance of his criminal trial and prejudice his defense at that trial." *Id.* at 874–75.

Later cases indicate that it is not a due process violation to take administrative action to protect the public while the criminal proceeding is pending. *See, e.g., United States v. Kordel,* 397 U.S. 1 (1970) (simultaneous civil and criminal proceedings for misbranded foods); *Arthurs v. Stern,* 560 F.2d 477 (1st Cir.1977) (physician accused of writing illegal prescriptions—privilege against self incrimination can be claimed in the administrative proceeding); *Savoy Club v. Board of Supervisors,* 91 Cal.Rptr. 198 (Cal.App.1970) (revocation of card club's license while criminal proceeding for illegal gambling is pending).

However, a suggestion in the *Silver* case may have merit: the agency might allow the licensee to choose suspension of the license until the criminal proceeding is completed. This protects the interests of the public as well as those of the licensee. *See SEC v. Dresser Industries,* 628 F.2d 1368, 1376 (D.C.Cir.1980), *cert. denied* 449 U.S. 993 (1980) (court has discretion to defer civil proceeding if public interest would not be jeopardized).

7. *Problem.* Elm City constructed and operated Elm Grove, a large apartment project for low income residents. The relevant statute recites that the problem of low income housing is critical and that poor people have a right to decent housing.

Muriel Miller and her four children are tenants in Elm Grove. Muriel's sole source of income is AFDC and food stamps. When she moved in on January 1, she signed a one-year lease which stated that the lease could be renewed only by agreement between Elm Grove and the tenant. It also stated that tenants could be evicted at any time if they failed to follow the rules of Elm Grove. The rules provided that tenants refrain from damaging apartments or disturbing other tenants. The lease also provided that tenants vacate their apartment within 10 days of receiving an eviction notice. It also stated that Elm Grove would furnish a hearing within two weeks after the apartment is vacated due to eviction if the tenants believe they violated no rules.

Muriel received a notice of eviction on April 19 which stated that she and her children had violated Elm Grove's rules by disturbing other tenants but furnished no specific details. The notice ordered her to move out by April 29 and informed her that a hearing would be held on May 6 if she requested one.

Muriel seeks an injunction in federal district court against her eviction, denying that she or her family had violated the rules and arguing that she has been denied procedural due process. Should the injunction be granted?

Assume Elm Grove loses this case. Could Elm Grove regain the right to discharge tenants without a prior hearing if it replaced the existing one-year leases as they expired with month-to-month tenancies?

See Jeffries v. Georgia Residential Fin. Auth., 678 F.2d 919 (11th Cir.1982); *Lopez v. Henry Phipps Plaza South, Inc.*, 498 F.2d 937 (2d Cir.1974).

§ 2.4 ELEMENTS OF A HEARING

The courts employ the balancing analysis set forth in *Mathews v. Eldridge* to determine *what process* is due as well as *when* it is due. Recall the list in *Goldberg* of precisely what kind of hearing due process requires prior to termination of welfare benefits. Does a *Goldberg* pre-termination hearing differ at all from a normal civil trial before a judge? From a *post*-termination welfare hearing?

We return now to *Hewitt* in which a majority found that Pennsylvania deprived Helms of a liberty interest by confining him to administrative segregation—but only because of discretion-confining language in regulations.

In considering *Hewitt,* it is helpful to review *Wolff v. McDonnell,* 418 U.S. 539 (1974), discussed in the notes following *Hewitt* in § 2.2.2, *supra.* In *Wolff,* the Court held that the state had to provide a prisoner with a hearing before it cancelled "good time credits" and thus lengthened the term of confinement by reason of disciplinary infractions. *Wolff* specified the exact kind of hearing required by due process. Before cancellation of good time credits, inmates are entitled to at least 24 hours written notice of the charges; a written statement by the factfinders as to the evidence relied on and the reason for disciplinary action; and, for illiterate inmates or those whose cases are complex, some advice or help (from the prison staff or a fellow inmate) in presenting their cases. They can call witnesses and present documentary evidence, subject to denial of these rights in the interests of institutional safety or correctional goals. The inmate has no right to confront adverse witnesses because of the danger of retaliation. Finally, there must be "some evidence" in support of the result. *Superinten-dent v. Hill,* 472 U.S. 445 (1985).

Should confinement in administrative segregation trigger the same type of procedures? If not, how much less protection would be appropriate?

HEWITT v. HELMS
459 U.S. 460 (1983).

REHNQUIST, J.:

. . . [We] must . . . decide whether the process afforded respondent satisfied the minimum requirements of the Due Process Clause. We think that it did. The requirements imposed by the Clause are, of course, flexible and variable dependent upon the particular situation being examined. In determining what is "due process" in the prison context, we are reminded that "one cannot automatically apply procedural rules designed for free citizens in an open society . . . to the very different situation presented by a disciplinary proceeding in a state prison." *Wolff v. McDonnell.* "Prison administrators . . . should be accorded wide-ranging deference in the adoption and execution of policies and practices that in their judgment are needed to preserve internal order and discipline and to maintain institutional security." These considerations convince us that petitioners were obligated to engage only in an informal, nonadversary review of the information supporting respondent's administrative confinement, including whatever statement respondent wished to submit, within a reasonable time after confining him to administrative segregation.

Under *Mathews v. Eldridge,* we consider the private interests at stake in a governmental decision, the governmental interests involved, and the value of procedural requirements in determining what process is due under the Fourteenth Amendment. Respondent's private interest is not one of great consequence. He was merely transferred from one extremely restricted environment to an even more confined situation. Unlike disciplinary confinement the stigma of wrongdoing or misconduct does not attach to administrative segregation under Pennsylvania's prison regulations. Finally, there is no indication that administrative segregation will have any significant effect on parole opportunities.

Petitioners had two closely related reasons for confining Helms to administrative segregation prior to conducting a hearing on the disciplinary charges against him. First, they concluded that if housed in the general population, Helms would pose a threat to the safety of other inmates and prison officials and to the security of the institution. Second, the prison officials believed that it was wiser to separate respondent from the general population until completion of state and institutional investigations of his role in the December 3 riot and the hearing on the charges against him. Plainly, these governmental interests are of great importance. The safety of the institution's guards and inmates is perhaps the most fundamental responsibility of the prison administration. Likewise, the isolation of a prisoner pending investigation of misconduct charges against him serves important institutional interests relating to the insulating of possible witnesses from coercion or harm.

Neither of these grounds for confining Helms to administrative segregation involved decisions or judgments that would have been materially assisted by a detailed adversary proceeding. . . . "[A] prison's internal security is peculiarly a matter normally left to the discretion of prison administrators." In assessing the seriousness of a threat to institutional security prison administrators necessarily draw on more than the specific facts surrounding a particular incident; instead, they must consider the character of the inmates confined in the institution, recent and long-standing relations between prisoners and guards, prisoners *inter se,* and the like. In the volatile atmosphere of a prison, an inmate easily may constitute an unacceptable threat to the safety of other prisoners and guards even if he himself has committed no misconduct; rumor, reputation, and even more imponderable factors may suffice to spark potentially disastrous incidents. The judgment of prison officials in this context, like that of those making parole decisions, turns largely on "purely subjective evaluations and on predictions of future behavior;" indeed, the administrators must predict not just one inmate's future actions, as in parole, but those of an entire institution. Owing to the central role of these types of intuitive judgments, a decision that an inmate or group of inmates represents a threat to the institution's security would not be appreciably fostered by the trial-type procedural safeguards suggested by respondent.[7] This, and the balance of public and private interests, leads us to conclude that the Due Process Clause requires only an informal nonadversary review of evidence, discussed more fully below, in order to confine an inmate feared to be a threat to institutional security to administrative segregation.

Likewise, confining respondent to administrative segregation pending completion of the investigation of the disciplinary charges against him is not based on an inquiry requiring any elaborate procedural safeguards. . . .

We think an informal, nonadversary evidentiary review sufficient both for the decision that an inmate represents a security threat and the decision to confine an inmate to administrative segregation pending completion of an investigation into misconduct charges against him. An inmate must merely receive some notice of the charges against him and an opportunity to present his views to the prison official charged with deciding whether to transfer him to administrative segregation. Ordinarily a written statement by the inmate will accomplish this

---

7. Indeed, we think an administrator's judgment probably would be hindered. Prison officials, wary of potential legal liability, might well spend their time mechanically complying with cumbersome, marginally helpful procedural requirements, rather than managing their institution wisely.

purpose, although prison administrators may find it more useful to permit oral presentations in cases where they believe a written statement would be ineffective. So long as this occurs, and the decisionmaker reviews the charges and then-available evidence against the prisoner, the Due Process Clause is satisfied.[8] This informal procedure permits a reasonably accurate assessment of probable cause to believe that misconduct occurred, and the "value [of additional "formalities and safeguards"] would be too slight to justify holding, as a matter of constitutional principle" that they must be adopted.

Measured against these standards we are satisfied that respondent received all the process that was due after being confined to administrative segregation. He received notice of the charges against him the day after his misconduct took place. Only five days after his transfer to administrative segregation a Hearing Committee reviewed the existing evidence against him, including a staff member's statement that "This inmate was a member of an organized plot and did actively involve himself with at least 10 other inmates in the assault upon 5 corrections officers in "C" Block and attempted to break thru the "C" grille to the Control Center to disrupt the normal institutional routine by usurping the authority of institution officials." While the Court of Appeals may have been correct that the record does not clearly demonstrate that a *Wolff* hearing was held, it does show that he had an opportunity to present a statement to the Committee. As noted previously, Helms acknowledged on the misconduct form that he "had the opportunity to have [his] version reported as part of the record;" we see no reason to question the accuracy of his statement. This proceeding plainly satisfied the Due Process requirements for continued confinement of Helms pending the outcome of the investigation.[9]

Accordingly, the judgment of the Court of Appeals is reversed.

JUSTICE STEVENS dissented on this issue, in an opinion in which JUSTICES BRENNAN, MARSHALL and BLACKMUN concurred.

. . . The "touchstone of due process," as we pointed out in *Wolff v. McDonnell,* is "protection of the individual against arbitrary action of government." Pennsylvania may not arbitrarily place a prisoner in administrative segregation. The majority agrees with this general proposition, but I believe its standards guarding against arbitrariness fall short of what the Constitution requires.

8. The proceeding must occur within a reasonable time following an inmate's transfer, taking into account the relatively insubstantial private interest at stake and the traditionally broad discretion of prison officials.

9. Of course, administrative segregation may not be used as a pretext for indefinite confinement of an inmate. Prison officials must engage in some sort of periodic review of the confinement of such inmates. This review will not necessarily require that prison officials permit the submission of any additional evidence or statements. The decision whether a prisoner remains a security risk will be based on facts relating to a particular prisoner—which will have been ascertained when determining to confine the inmate to administrative segregation—and on the officials' general knowledge of prison conditions and tensions, which are singularly unsuited for "proof" in any highly structured manner. . . .

First, the majority declares that the Constitution is satisfied by an initial proceeding with minimal participation by the inmate who is being transferred into administrative custody. . . .

I agree with the Court that the Constitution does not require a hearing with all of the procedural safeguards set forth in *Wolff v. McDonnell* when prison officials initially decide to segregate an inmate to safeguard institutional security or to conduct an investigation of an unresolved misconduct charge. But unlike the majority, I believe that due process does require that the inmate be given the opportunity to present his views in person to the reviewing officials. As many prisoners have little education, limiting an inmate to a written statement is unlikely to provide a "meaningful opportunity to be heard" in accordance with due process principles. See *Goldberg v. Kelly*.[17]

Of greater importance, the majority's due process analysis fails to provide adequate protection against arbitrary continuation of an inmate's solitary confinement.[18] The opinion recognizes that "[p]rison officials must engage in some sort of periodic review of the confinement of such inmates." It thus recognizes that the deprivation of liberty in the prison setting is a continuous process rather than an isolated event. But the Court requires only minimal review procedures; prison officials need not permit the submission of any additional evidence or statements and need not give the inmate a chance to present his position. It is constitutionally sufficient, according to the majority, that administrative segregation not be a pretext for indefinite confinement. In my view, the Due Process Clause requires a more searching review of the justifiability of continued confinement.

[JUSTICE STEVENS urged that there be an opportunity for an oral statement at each periodic review of administrative segregation, at which the prisoner could explain his current attitude toward his past activities and present circumstances and the impact of solitary confinement on his rehabilitation program and training. Further, if segregation is continued, the decision-maker should be required to explain his reasons in a brief written statement which is retained in the file and given to the prisoner.

He observed that neither a right to a personal appearance by the prisoner nor a requirement of written reasons would impose an undue burden on prison officials. Indeed, these very safeguards are provided in regulations governing Pennsylvania's state and federal prison systems. The dissent objected to locating the due process floor at a level below existing procedures.]

17. Indeed, petitioners do not contend that a face-to-face presentation by the inmate would be unduly burdensome. Their brief cites *Goss v. Lopez* as a model of appropriate procedure, noting that there the Court did not require an "elaborate hearing" before a neutral party, "but simply 'an informal give-and-take between student and disciplinarian' which gives the student 'an opportunity to explain his version of the facts.' "

18. Unlike disciplinary custody, which is imposed for a fixed term, in practice administrative custody sometimes continues for lengthy or indefinite periods.

Notes and Questions

1. *Goss v. Lopez: consultative procedure.* In *Goss v. Lopez*, discussed in § 2.2.3, *supra*, the Court held that disciplinary suspension of high school students for ten days or less deprived them of property (because state law created an entitlement to public education) and of liberty (because the suspensions "could seriously damage the students' standing with fellow pupils and teachers as well as interfere with later opportunities for higher education and employment"). The four dissenters argued that suspension did not deprive students of liberty or property and in any event was too trivial to trigger constitutional protection. They voiced concern that the required procedures would have a detrimental effect on the maintenance of discipline in public schools.

The kind of hearing required by the case was markedly different from the adversary trial-type hearing mandated by *Goldberg*. The Court required only "some kind of notice and . . . some kind of hearing." The student must receive "oral or written notice of the charges against him and, if he denies them, an explanation of the evidence the authorities have and an opportunity to present his side of the story." Ordinarily, the discussion with the student could occur minutes after the alleged misconduct occurs and before suspension.

In *Goss* the Court indicated that students did not have the right "to secure counsel, to confront and cross-examine witnesses supporting the charge, or to call his own witnesses to verify his version of the incident." The Court's reason for its conclusion was this:

> Brief disciplinary suspensions are almost countless. To impose in each such case even truncated trial-type procedures might well overwhelm administrative facilities in many places and, by diverting resources, cost more than it would save in educational effectiveness. Moreover, further formalizing the suspension process and escalating its formality and adversary nature may not only make it too costly as a regular disciplinary tool but also destroy its effectiveness as part of the teaching process.

It is fair to conclude that the kind of hearing required in *Goss* was no more than a conversation between the student and the disciplinarian. Should the Court have required school disciplinarians to adhere to the *Goldberg* formula? Would the Court have required the same kind of hearing in *Goss* if a state statute provided that a student suspended from public school three times would automatically be expelled?

2. *Paper hearings.* In *Hewitt* the Court makes clear that in some situations due process does not demand an auditory proceeding—the "hearing" can be on paper. Is it misleading to refer to a paper proceeding as a hearing? Why does the majority in *Hewitt* not require the prison to provide the prisoner a right to an oral hearing of the kind required by *Goss*? Might the reason relate to differences in maintaining order? How much of a burden would a *Goss*-type oral hearing

impose on prison officials? Would you alter the respective balances struck by the Court in these two cases?

3. *Long-term confinement.* The *Hewitt* dissenters were primarily concerned with protecting a prisoner who is held in administrative segregation for a long time. In note 9, the majority states that administrative segregation cannot be a "pretext" for continued confinement. Although it requires "periodic reviews," it does not require the state to permit the prisoner to receive notice of or to participate in these reviews. Thus the level of constitutionally required process is even lower than that required for the initial decision to isolate the prisoner. Is a prisoner likely to have anything useful to contribute to the decision whether administrative confinement should be continued? Is the "periodic review" requirement any protection at all against a mistaken decision to continue confinement in administrative segregation for a lengthy period?

4. *Nature of the issues to be determined.* In *Hewitt,* the Court pointed to the nature of the particular issues involved, noting that they were based on "purely subjective evaluations and predictions of future behavior" and on "intuitive judgments" rather than on specific facts. As a result, an auditory trial-type hearing would not be particularly helpful and, therefore, was not required by due process.

If there are no issues to be resolved that require oral testimony, the agency has discretion to dispense with it. For example, in *FDIC v. Mallen,* 108 S.Ct. 1780, 1791 (1988), the Court held that "there is no inexorable requirement that oral testimony must be heard in every administrative proceeding in which it is tendered." Such testimony might be "merely cumulative to material that was adequately covered by written submissions or . . . otherwise unnecessary or improper." Similarly, in *Codd v. Velger,* 429 U.S. 624 (1977), a policeman was discharged on the basis of a report that he had attempted suicide. The Court decided that even if the discharge deprived him of liberty, he was not entitled to any kind of trial-type hearing because he had not challenged the accuracy of the report. Since the purpose of a hearing would be to clear his name, his failure to challenge the truth of the report entirely removed the need for a hearing.

Do you agree? May a trial-type hearing be useful for determinations other than accurately ascertaining the facts? May it be useful for determinations that are "intuitive judgments" or "subjective evaluations" or "predictions of future behavior" or in cases of discretionary action on uncontested facts, or for purely policy determinations? Recall the various purposes of requiring a hearing set out in § 2.1, note 2.

In *Loudermill,* Justice White wrote: "Even where the facts are clear, the appropriateness or necessity of the discharge may not be; in such cases, the only meaningful opportunity to invoke the discretion of the decisionmaker is likely to be before the termination takes effect." 470 U.S. at 543.

5. *Academic due process.* What sort of hearing should be provided before dismissal of a student for *academic* rather than *disciplinary* reasons? In *Board of Curators, Univ. of Mo. v. Horowitz*, 435 U.S. 78 (1978), the Court held that no process is required in academic dismissal cases.

> The decision to dismiss respondent . . . rested on the academic judgment of school officials that she did not have the necessary clinical ability to perform adequately as a medical doctor . . . Such [an academic] judgment is by its nature more subjective and evaluative than the typical factual questions presented in the average disciplinary decision. Like the decision of an individual professor as to the proper grade for a student in his course, the determination whether to dismiss a student for academic reasons requires an expert evaluation of cumulative information and is not readily adapted to the procedural tools of judicial or administrative decision-making.

Do you agree? Should there be a difference between determinations of what happened and determinations as to whether what happened satisfied the relevant academic standards of competence?

6. *Problem.* New York would like to find a way to cut the cost of hearings in welfare termination cases. In addition, it would like to make the process more convenient and pleasant for all concerned, including recipients who often have to sit around all day or for several days waiting for their hearing to be called. It therefore has proposed new procedural regulations providing that both pre-termination and post-termination hearings may be conducted by telephone conference call in cases where the welfare department wishes to decrease or terminate benefits. You work for a legal service office which frequently provides assistance to welfare claimants. You have been asked to submit comments about these proposed regulations. *See* Note, "Telephonic Hearings in Welfare Appeals," 1984 U.Ill.L.For. 445; *Detroit Base Coalition for Human Rights of Handicapped v. Michigan Dept. of Soc. Serv.,* 405 N.W.2d 136 (Mich.App.1987), app. in Mich.Sup.Ct. pending.

WALTERS v. NATIONAL ASS'N OF RADIATION SURVIVORS

473 U.S. 305 (1985).

Justice Rehnquist delivered the opinion of the Court.

Title 38 U.S.C. § 3404(c) limits to $10 the fee that may be paid an attorney or agent who represents a veteran seeking benefits for service-connected death or disability. The United States District Court for the Northern District of California held that this limit violates the Due Process Clause of the Fifth Amendment, and the First Amendment, because it denies veterans or their survivors the opportunity to retain counsel of their choice in pursuing their claims. . . .

In 1978, . . . approximately 800,000 claims for service-connected disability or death and pensions were decided by the 58 regional offices of the Veterans Administration (VA). . . . Of the 800,000 total claims in 1978, more than 400,000 were allowed, and some 379,000 were denied. Sixty-six thousand of these denials were contested at the regional level; about a quarter of these contests were dropped, 15% prevailed on reconsideration at the local level, and the remaining 36,000 were appealed to the Board of Veterans' Appeals (BVA). At that level some 4,500, or 12%, prevailed, and another 13% won a remand for further proceedings. . . .

As might be expected in a system which processes such a large number of claims each year, the process prescribed by Congress for obtaining disability benefits does not contemplate the adversary mode of dispute resolution utilized by courts in this country. It is commenced by the submission of a claim form to the local veterans agency, which form is provided by the VA either upon request or upon receipt of notice of the death of a veteran. Upon application a claim generally is first reviewed by a three-person "rating board" of the VA regional office—consisting of a medical specialist, a legal specialist, and an "occupational specialist." A claimant is "entitled to a hearing at any time on any issue involved in a claim. . . ." Proceedings in front of the rating board "are ex parte in nature;" no government official appears in opposition. The principal issues are the extent of the claimant's disability and whether it is service-connected. The panel is required by regulation "to assist a claimant in developing the facts pertinent to his claim," and to consider any evidence offered by the claimant. In deciding the claim the panel generally will request the applicant's armed service and medical records, and will order a medical examination by a VA hospital. Moreover, the board is directed by regulation to resolve all reasonable doubts in favor of the claimant.

After reviewing the evidence the board renders a decision either denying the claim or assigning a disability "rating" pursuant to detailed regulations developed for assessing various disabilities. Money benefits are calculated based on the rating. The claimant is notified of the board's decision and its reasons, and the claimant may then initiate an appeal by filing a "notice of disagreement" with the local agency. If the local agency adheres to its original decision it must then provide the claimant with a "statement of the case"—a written description of the facts and applicable law upon which the panel based its determination—so that the claimant may adequately present his appeal to the BVA. Hearings in front of the BVA are subject to the same rules as local agency hearings—they are *ex parte*, there is no formal questioning or cross-examination, and no formal rules of evidence apply. The BVA's decision is not subject to judicial review.

The process is designed to function throughout with a high degree of informality and solicitude for the claimant. There is no statute of limitations, and a denial of benefits has no formal *res judicata* effect; a claimant may resubmit as long as he presents new facts not previously forwarded. . . . **Perhaps more importantly for present purposes, however, various veterans organizations across the country make available trained service agents, free of charge, to assist claimants in developing and presenting their claims.** These service representatives are contemplated by the VA statute, and they are recognized as an important part of the administrative scheme. Appellees' counsel agreed at argument that a representative is available for any claimant who requests one, regardless of the claimant's affiliation with any particular veterans group.[4] . . .

With respect to the merits of appellees' due process claim, the District Court first determined that recipients of service-connected death and disability benefits possess "property" interests protected by the Due Process Clause, see *Mathews v. Eldridge,* and also held that *applicants* for such benefits possess such an interest. Although noting that this Court has never ruled on the latter question, the court relied on several opinions of the Court of Appeals for the Ninth Circuit holding, with respect to similar government benefits, that applicants possess such an interest. . . . Our decisions establish that "due process" is a flexible concept—that the processes required by the Clause with respect to the termination of a protected interest will vary depending upon the importance attached to the interest and the particular circumstances under which the deprivation may occur. See *Mathews.* In defining the process necessary to ensure "fundamental fairness" we have recognized that the Clause does not require that "the procedures used to guard against an erroneous deprivation . . . be so comprehensive as to preclude any possibility of error," and in addition we have emphasized that the marginal gains from affording an additional procedural safeguard often may be outweighed by the societal cost of providing such a safeguard.

These general principles are reflected in the test set out in *Mathews,* which test the District Court purported to follow, and which requires a court to consider the private interest that will be affected by the official action, the risk of an erroneous deprivation of such interest through the procedures used, the probable value of additional or substitute procedural safeguards, and the government's interest in adhering to the existing system. In applying this test we must keep in mind, in addition to the deference owed to Congress, the fact that the very nature of the due process inquiry indicates that the fundamental fairness of a particular procedure does not turn on the result obtained in any individual case; rather, "procedural due process rules are shaped by the risk of error inherent in the truth-finding process as applied to the generality of cases, not the rare exceptions."

---

4. The VA statistics show that 86% of all claimants are represented by service representatives, 12% proceed *pro se,* and 2% are represented by lawyers. App. 190. Counsel agreed at argument that the 12% who proceed *pro se* do so by their own choice.

The government interest, which has been articulated in congressional debates since the fee limitation was first enacted in 1862 during the Civil War, has been this: that the system for administering benefits should be managed in a sufficiently informal way that there should be no need for the employment of an attorney to obtain benefits to which a claimant was entitled, so that the claimant would receive the entirety of the award without having to divide it with a lawyer. This purpose is reinforced by a similar absolute prohibition on compensation of any service organization representative. While Congress has recently considered proposals to modify the fee limitation in some respects . . . the Senate nevertheless concluded that the fee limitation should with a limited exception remain in effect, in order to "protect claimants' benefits" from being unnecessarily diverted to lawyers.

In the face of this congressional commitment to the fee limitation for more than a century, the District Court had only this to say with respect to the governmental interest:

> The government has neither argued nor shown that lifting the fee limit would harm the government in any way, except as the paternalistic protector of claimants' supposed best interests. . . .

It is not for the District Court or any other federal court to invalidate a federal statute by so cavalierly dismissing a long-asserted congressional purpose. . . .

There can be little doubt that invalidation of the fee limitation would seriously frustrate the oft repeated congressional purpose for enacting it. Attorneys would be freely employable by claimants to veterans benefits, and the claimant would as a result end up paying part of the award, or its equivalent, to an attorney. But this would not be the only consequence of striking down the fee limitation that would be deleterious to the congressional plan.

A necessary concomitant of Congress' desire that a veteran not need a representative to assist him in making his claim was that the system should be as informal and nonadversarial as possible. . . . The regular introduction of lawyers into the proceedings would be quite unlikely to further this goal. . . .

> "To be sure, counsel can often perform useful functions even in welfare cases or other instances of mass justice; they may bring out facts ignored by or unknown to the authorities, or help to work out satisfactory compromises. But this is only one side of the coin. Under our adversary system the role of counsel is not to make sure the truth is ascertained but to advance his client's cause by any ethical means. Within the limits of professional propriety, causing delay and sowing confusion not only are his right but may be his duty. The appearance of counsel for the citizen is likely to lead the government to provide one—or at least to cause the government's representative to act like one. The result may be to turn what might have been a short conference leading to an amicable result into a protracted controversy.

. . . .

"These problems concerning counsel and confrontation inevitably bring up the question whether we would not do better to abandon the adversary system in certain areas of mass justice. . . . While such an experiment would be a sharp break with our tradition of adversary process, that tradition, which has come under serious general challenge from a thoughtful and distinguished judge, was not formulated for a situation in which many thousands of hearings must be provided each month." Friendly, "Some Kind of Hearing," 123 U.Pa.L.Rev. 1267, 1287–1290 (1975).

Thus, even apart from the frustration of Congress' principal goal of wanting the veteran to get the entirety of the award, the destruction of the fee limitation would bid fair to complicate a proceeding which Congress wished to keep as simple as possible. . . . And this additional complexity will undoubtedly engender greater administrative costs, with the end result being that less government money reaches its intended beneficiaries.

We accordingly conclude that under the *Mathews v. Eldridge* analysis great weight must be accorded to the government interest at stake here. The flexibility of our approach in due process cases is intended in part to allow room for other forms of dispute resolution; with respect to the individual interests at stake here legislatures are to be allowed considerable leeway to formulate such processes without being forced to conform to a rigid constitutional code of procedural necessities. It would take an extraordinarily strong showing of probability of error under the present system—and the probability that the presence of attorneys would sharply diminish that possibility—to warrant a holding that the fee limitation denies claimants due process of law. We have no hesitation in deciding that no such showing was made out on the record before the District Court.

As indicated by the statistics set out earlier in this opinion, more than half of the 800,000 claims processed annually by the VA result in benefit awards at the regional level. An additional 10,000 claims succeed on request for reconsideration at the regional level, and of those that do not, 36,000 are appealed to the BVA. Of these, approximately 16% succeed before the BVA. . . . If one regards the decision of the BVA as the "correct" result in every case, it follows that the regional determination against the claimant is "wrong" in the 16% of the cases that are reversed by the Board.

Passing the problems with quantifying the likelihood of an erroneous deprivation, however, under *Mathews* we must also ask what value the proposed additional procedure may have in reducing such error. In this case we are fortunate to have statistics that bear directly on this question, which statistics were addressed by the District Court. These unchallenged statistics chronicle the success rates before the BVA depending on the type of representation of the claimant, and are summarized in the following figures taken from the record. App. 568.

ULTIMATE SUCCESS RATES BEFORE THE BOARD OF VETERANS
APPEALS BY MODE OF REPRESENTATION

American Legion	16.2%
American Red Cross	16.8%
Disabled American Veterans	16.6%
Veterans of Foreign Wars	16.7%
Other non-attorney	15.8%
No representation	15.2%
Attorney/Agent	18.3%

The District Court opined that these statistics were not helpful, because in its view lawyers were retained so infrequently that no body of lawyers with an expertise in VA practice had developed, and lawyers who represented veterans regularly might do better than lawyers who represented them only *pro bono* on a sporadic basis. . . .

We think the District Court's analysis of this issue totally unconvincing, and quite lacking in the deference which ought to be shown by any federal court in evaluating the constitutionality of an Act of Congress. We have the most serious doubt whether a competent lawyer taking a veteran's case on a *pro bono* basis would give less than his best effort, and we see no reason why experience in developing facts as to causation in the numerous other areas of the law where it is relevant would not be readily transferable to proceedings before the VA. . . .

The District Court also concluded, apparently independently of its ill-founded analysis of the claim statistics, (1) that the VA processes are procedurally, factually, and legally complex, and (2) that the VA system presently does not work as designed, particularly in terms of the representation afforded by VA personnel and service representatives, and that these representatives are "unable to perform all of the services which might be performed by a claimant's own paid attorney." . . .

The District Court's opinion is similarly short on definition or quantification of "complex" cases. If this term be understood to include all cases in which the claimant asserts injury from exposure to radiation or agent orange, only approximately 3 in 1,000 of the claims at the regional level and 2% of the appeals to the BVA involve such claims. Nor does it appear that all such claims would be complex by any fair definition of that term: at least 25% of all agent orange cases and 30% of the radiation cases, for example, are disposed of because the medical examination reveals no disability. What evidence does appear in the record indicates that the great majority of claims involve simple questions of fact, or medical questions relating to the degree of a claimant's disability; the record also indicates that only the rare case turns on a question of law. There are undoubtedly "complex" cases pending before the VA, and they are undoubtedly a tiny fraction of the total cases pending. Neither the District Court's opinion nor any matter in the record to which our attention has been directed tells us more than this. . . .

This case is further distinguishable from our prior decisions because the process here is not designed to operate adversarially. While counsel may well be needed to respond to opposing counsel or other forms of adversary in a trial-type proceeding, where as here no such adversary appears, and in addition a claimant or recipient is provided with substitute safeguards such as a competent representative, a decision-maker whose duty it is to aid the claimant, and significant concessions with respect to the claimant's burden of proof, the need for counsel is considerably diminished. We have expressed similar concerns in other cases holding that counsel is not required in various proceedings that do not approximate trials, but instead are more informal and nonadversary.

Thus none of our cases dealing with constitutionally required representation by counsel requires the conclusion reached by the District Court. Especially in light of the government interests at stake, the evidence adduced before the District Court as to success rates in claims handled with or without lawyers shows no such great disparity as to warrant the inference that the congressional fee limitation under consideration here violates the Due Process Clause of the Fifth Amendment. What evidence we have been pointed to in the record regarding complex cases falls far short of the kind which would warrant upsetting Congress' judgment that this is the manner in which it wishes claims for veterans benefits adjudicated. The District Court abused its discretion in holding otherwise. . . . *Reversed.*

JUSTICE O'CONNOR, with whom JUSTICE BLACKMUN joins, concurring.

I join the Court's opinion and its judgment. . . .

Nevertheless, it is my understanding that the Court, in reversing the lower court's preliminary injunction, does not determine the merits of the respondents' individual "as applied" claims. . . . As an example, Doris Wilson, a widow who claims her husband's cancer was contracted from exposure to atomic testing, alleges her service representative waived her right to a hearing because he was unprepared to represent her. She contends her claim failed because she was unable without assistance to obtain service records and medical information.

The merits of these claims are difficult to evaluate on the record of affidavits and depositions developed at the preliminary injunction stage. Though the Court concludes that denial of expert representation is not "*per se* unconstitutional," given the availability of service representatives to assist the veteran and the Veterans Administration Board's emphasis on nonadversarial procedures, "[o]n remand, the District Court is free to and should consider any individual claims that [the procedures] did not meet the standards we have described in this opinion."

JUSTICE STEVENS, with whom JUSTICE BRENNAN and JUSTICE MARSHALL join, dissenting.

The Court does not appreciate the value of individual liberty. It may well be true that in the vast majority of cases a veteran does not need to employ a lawyer, and that the system of processing veterans benefit claims, by and large, functions fairly and effectively without the participation of retained counsel. Everyone agrees, however, that there are at least some complicated cases in which the services of a lawyer would be useful to the veteran and, indeed, would simplify the work of the agency by helping to organize the relevant facts and to identify the controlling issues. What is the reason for denying the veteran the right to counsel of his choice in such cases? The Court gives us two answers: First, the paternalistic interest in protecting the veteran from the consequences of his own improvidence; and second, the bureaucratic interest in minimizing the cost of administering the benefit program. I agree that both interests are legitimate, but neither provides an adequate justification for the restraint on liberty imposed by the $10–fee limitation. . . .

I

The first fee limitation—$5 per claim—was enacted in 1862. That limitation was repealed two years later and replaced by the $10–fee limitation, which has survived ever since. The limitation was designed to protect the veteran from extortion or improvident bargains with unscrupulous lawyers. Obviously, it was believed that the number of scoundrels practicing law was large enough to justify a legislative prohibition against charging excessive fees.

At the time the $10–fee limitation was enacted, Congress presumably considered that fee reasonable. The legal work involved in preparing a veteran's claim consisted of little more than filling out an appropriate form, and, in terms of the average serviceman's base pay, a $10 fee then was roughly the equivalent of a $580 fee today. At its inception, therefore, the fee limitation had neither the purpose nor the effect of precluding the employment of reputable counsel by veterans. . . .

II

. . . [T]here is no reason to assume that lawyers would add confusion rather than clarity to the proceedings. As a profession, lawyers are skilled communicators dedicated to the service of their clients. Only if it is assumed that the average lawyer is incompetent or unscrupulous can one rationally conclude that the efficiency of the agency's work would be undermined by allowing counsel to participate whenever a veteran is willing to pay for his services. I categorically reject any such assumption.

The fact that a lawyer's services are unnecessary in most cases, and might even be counter-productive in a few, does not justify a total prohibition on their participation in all pension claim proceedings. . . .

[The] kind of paternalism reflected in this statute as it operates today is irrational. It purports to protect the veteran who has little or no need for protection and it actually denies him assistance in cases in which the help of his own lawyer may be of critical importance.

But the statute is unconstitutional for a reason that is more fundamental than its apparent irrationality. What is at stake is the right of an individual to consult an attorney of his choice in connection with a controversy with the Government. In my opinion that right is firmly protected by the Due Process Clause of the Fifth Amendment and by the First Amendment. . . .

The fundamental error in the Court's analysis is its assumption that the individual's right to employ counsel of his choice in a contest with his sovereign is a kind of second-class interest that can be assigned a material value and balanced on a utilitarian scale of costs and benefits. It is true that the veteran's right to benefits is a property right and that in fashioning the procedures for administering the benefit program, the Government may appropriately weigh the value of additional procedural safeguards against their pecuniary costs. It may, for example, properly decide not to provide free counsel to claimants. But we are not considering a procedural right that would involve any cost to the Government. We are concerned with the individual's right to spend his own money to obtain the advice and assistance of independent counsel in advancing his claim against the Government.

In all criminal proceedings, that right is expressly protected by the Sixth Amendment. As I have indicated, in civil disputes with the Government I believe that right is also protected by the Due Process Clause of the Fifth Amendment and by the First Amendment. If the Government, in the guise of a paternalistic interest in protecting the citizen from his own improvidence, can deny him access to independent counsel of his choice, it can change the character of our free society. Even though a dispute with the sovereign may only involve property rights, or as in this case a statutory entitlement, the citizen's right of access to the independent, private bar is itself an aspect of liberty that is of critical importance in our democracy. . . .

It should not be bargained away on the notion that a totalitarian appraisal of the mass of claims processed by the Veterans' Administration does not identify an especially high probability of error.

Unfortunately, the reason for the Court's mistake today is all too obvious. It does not appreciate the value of individual liberty.

I respectfully dissent.

Notes and Questions

1. *Counting the votes.* What exactly is the holding of *Walters*? Could a veteran who claims that he was given cancer by exposure to a

nuclear test twenty years ago establish that his particular case is sufficiently complex that he is entitled to pay an attorney to press his claim before the VA? If so, can a complex/noncomplex line be drawn reliably?

2. *The right to counsel.* Administrative procedure statutes typically provide a right to retained counsel. *See* APA § 555(b); 1981 MSAPA § 4–203(b). Where no APA is applicable, however, how should a court determine whether the right to counsel exists in a particular context? What are the costs and benefits of a right to retained counsel in administrative proceedings?

Recall that in *Goldberg* the Court said that welfare recipients have a right to retained (but not appointed) counsel in pre-termination hearings. *Wolff v. McDonnell* stated that there is no right to counsel in prison disciplinary proceedings. However, if a disciplinary case is complex, the prisoner has a right to the assistance of a fellow inmate or staff member. And *Goss v. Lopez* stated that a student has no right to counsel during the required consultation with a disciplinarian before a suspension from school of ten days or less.

Lower court cases also indicate that an agency can exclude counsel if administrative proceedings are preliminary, informal, or non-adversary, or if the issues are simple. For example, in *Madora v. Board of Educ. of New York,* 386 F.2d 778 (2d Cir.1967), *cert. denied* 390 U.S. 1028 (1968), the court held that a suspended junior high school student had no right to counsel at a guidance conference called to assess his situation and to consider his potential reassignment to another school. The court thought that a social worker would be a better advocate than a lawyer. *See also Downing v. Lebritton,* 550 F.2d 689 (1st Cir.1977) (mentally retarded state employee has no right to counsel in informal grievance procedure—fellow employee could participate); *Wasson v. Trowbridge,* 382 F.2d 807, 812 (2d Cir.1967) (no right to counsel in dismissal of cadet from Merchant Marine Academy). *See* Blaskey, "University Students' Right to Retain Counsel at Disciplinary Proceedings," 24 Cal.W.L.Rev. 65 (1988).

Should the Supreme Court allow the VA to exclude all attorneys from its proceedings (as distinguished from prohibiting payment of attorney fees)?

3. *Adversary systems.* One fundamental issue posed by *Walters* is whether due process means a trial-type hearing. *Goldberg v. Kelly* was the high-water mark for that point of view. As we have seen, abbreviated procedures are acceptable in prison or in school discipline. *Walters* establishes that Congress can choose a sharply different model for determining qualification for government grants—an informal, investigatory meeting between claimant and panel, with no lawyers representing either side. It agrees with Judge Friendly's contention that lawyers can complicate things, embitter a controversy or delay its resolution.

Could a state decide that lawyers should be barred from license revocation proceedings (or that their fees would be limited to $10)? From AFDC termination hearings? From state university disciplinary hearings? How about the small claims court? Is there a difference between imposing a limit on lawyers' fees and an outright prohibition of representation by counsel?

4. *Outdated statutes.* Professor Calabresi has argued that courts should have power to modify or refuse to follow outdated statutes, thus compelling the legislature to reconsider the statute. Is the $10 attorney fee limitation a good candidate for such treatment? G. Calabresi, A COMMON LAW FOR THE AGE OF STATUTES (1981).

5. *The dissent and due process.* Does the dissent have an absolutist rather than a relativist view of due process, at least as applied to the right to counsel? Does the logic of the dissent suggest that the prisoner in *Hewitt* or the student in *Goss* had a right to retain counsel? Would such a view be defensible?

6. *Variable due process—an assessment.* Is there a danger that application of the *Mathews* balancing test to determine the specific requirements of due process in each context may so water down or trivialize that doctrine as to make it an inadequate protection against unfair or wrong government decisions? Does the *Mathews* formula insure predictable results? Does it facilitate value-laden judicial decision-making under the guise of neutral constitutional adjudication?

Do you agree with this evaluation?

The doctrine of variable due process has been roundly criticized recently because of a fear that it may become unmanageable in application, and that it may water down due process to the point where its protections are nearly meaningless. Nevertheless, it is a reality. . . . Despite its admitted difficulties of application and its practical dangers, the doctrine is bound to endure because the great flexibility it insures is a virtue in constitutional adjudication. . . . [It will] enable the law to avoid [full] trial-type adversary process as the exclusive medium, regardless of cost or efficacy, for resolving all cases to which the due process right to be heard now applies.

Bonfield, "The Definition of Formal Agency Adjudication under the Iowa Administrative Procedure Act," 63 Iowa L.Rev. 285, 343–44 (1977).

§ 2.5 THE RULEMAKING–ADJUDICATION DISTINCTION

This chapter concludes by introducing a fundamental distinction in administrative law. The distinction is between government action which adversely and differentially affects identifiable persons on the basis of facts peculiar to each of them and government action directed in a uniform way against a class of persons. The first kind of action is called "adjudication;" an example is a determination that a person should be denied welfare because he or she does not need it. The second kind of action is called "rulemaking;" an example is the establishment by an agency of a standard for determination of a welfare recipient's need.

The terms "adjudication" and "rulemaking" are useful and are frequently employed in this book. Readers should be forewarned, however, that these terms have sometimes been given slightly different meanings. Federal and state APAs rely on the distinction between rulemaking and adjudication but do not define them precisely in accordance with the traditional usage employed here.

For purposes of procedural due process, the distinction between government action against particular people based on peculiar facts and action against a class is fundamental. The state has normally been required to provide an opportunity for some kind of hearing in the former case but not in the latter.

Our exploration of the distinction begins with two old Supreme Court cases, both of which concerned Denver property tax disputes. Upon this unlikely foundation, much of the structure of procedural due process has been erected. The distinction is then tested in a case involving welfare reductions. Later this book returns to the rulemaking/adjudication distinction and raises the issue of whether an agency has unrestricted power to choose between the two modalities. *See* § 5.4, *infra.*

LONDONER v. DENVER
210 U.S. 373 (1908).

[A Denver ordinance allowed the city council, on recommendation of the board of public works, to establish a special assessment district for the purpose of paving streets. After the paving was completed, the total cost of the job had to be apportioned among the individual property owners in the assessment district. The ordinance provided that the council's determination was binding on the Denver courts.

The board recommended an apportionment to the council. Objecting owners were then permitted to file written complaints with the council. The council considered the complaints and enacted an ordinance assessing each owner an amount the council believed to be appropriate. Nowhere in the process were complainants granted an opportunity for an oral hearing.

Londoner filed a lengthy complaint with the council, making every possible objection. One of the many objections contained in his complaint was an allegation that individual parcels in the district, including his property, were assessed arbitrarily because those with equal assessments had not benefited equally from the paving. Nevertheless, the council's ordinance stated that "no complaint or objection had been filed or made against the apportionment of said assessment."]

. . . Where the legislature of a state, instead of fixing the tax itself, commits to some subordinate body the duty of determining whether, in what amount, and upon whom it shall be levied, and of making the assessment and apportionment, due process of law requires that at some stage of the proceedings before the tax becomes irrevocably fixed, the taxpayer shall have an opportunity to be heard, of which he must have notice . . . It must be remembered that the law of Colorado denies the landowner the right to object in the courts to the assessment, upon the ground that the objections are cognizable only by the [city council].

If it is enough that, under such circumstances, an opportunity is given to submit in writing all objections to and complaints of the tax to the [council], then there was a hearing afforded in the case at bar. But we think that something more than that, even in proceedings for taxation, is required by due process of law. Many requirements essential in strictly judicial proceedings may be dispensed with in proceedings of this nature. But even here a hearing, in its very essence, demands that he who is entitled to it shall have the right to support his allegations by argument however brief, and, if need be, by proof, however informal. . . . It is apparent that such a hearing was denied to [Londoner]. . . . The assessment was therefore void, and [Londoner was] entitled to a decree discharging [his land] from a lien on account of it.

THE CHIEF JUSTICE and JUSTICE HOLMES dissented.

BI–METALLIC INV. CO. v. STATE BOARD OF EQUALIZATION
239 U.S. 441 (1915).

MR. JUSTICE HOLMES delivered the opinion of the court:

This is a suit to enjoin the State Board of Equalization and the Colorado Tax Commission from putting in force and the defendant Pitcher, as assessor of Denver, from obeying, an order of the boards, increasing the valuation of all taxable property in Denver 40 per cent. . . .

The plaintiff is the owner of real estate in Denver, and brings the case here on the ground that it was given no opportunity to be heard, and that therefore its property will be taken without due process of law, contrary to the 14th Amendment of the Constitution of the United States. That is the only question with which we have to deal. . . .

For the purposes of decision we assume that the constitutional question is presented in the baldest way,—that neither the plaintiff nor the assessor of Denver, who presents a brief on the plaintiff's side, nor any representative of the city and county, was given an opportunity to be heard. . . . On this assumption it is obvious that injustice may be suffered if some property in the county already has been valued at its full worth. But if certain property has been valued at a rate different from that generally prevailing in the county, the owner has had his opportunity to protest and appeal as usual in our system of taxation so that it must be assumed that the property owners in the county all stand alike. The question, then, is whether all individuals have a constitutional right to be heard before a matter can be decided in which all are equally concerned,—here, for instance, before a superior board decides that the local taxing officers have adopted a system of underval- uation throughout a county, as notoriously often has been the case. . . .

Where a rule of conduct applies to more than a few people, it is impracticable that everyone should have a direct voice in its adoption. The Constitution does not require all public acts to be done in town meeting or an assembly of the whole. General statutes within the state power are passed that affect the person or property of individuals, sometimes to the point of ruin, without giving them a chance to be heard. Their rights are protected in the only way that they can be in a complex society, by their power, immediate or remote, over those who make the rule. If the result in this case had been reached, as it might have been by the state's doubling the rate of taxation, no one would suggest that the 14th Amendment was violated unless every person affected had been allowed an opportunity to raise his voice against it before the body intrusted by the state Constitution with the power. In considering this case in this court we must assume that the proper state machinery has been used, and the question is whether, if the state Constitution had declared that Denver had been undervalued as com- pared with the rest of the state, and had decreed that for the current year the valuation should be 40 per cent higher, the objection now urged could prevail. It appears to us that to put the question is to answer it. There must be a limit to individual argument in such matters if government is to go on. In Londoner v. Denver a local board had to determine "whether, in what amount, and upon whom" a tax for paving a street should be levied for special benefits. A relatively small number of persons was concerned, who were exceptionally affected, in each case upon individual grounds, and it was held that they had a right to a hearing. But that decision is far from reaching a general determination dealing only with the principle upon which all the assessments in a county had been laid.

Judgment affirmed.

Notes and Questions

1. *An oral hearing.* Londoner was entitled to a trial-type hearing ("the right to support his allegations by argument however brief, and, if need be, by proof, however informal"). He was allowed to complain in writing but that was not enough. If the case came up today, do you think that an oral hearing would still be required?

2. *Londoner and Bi–Metallic.* Mr. Londoner gets a hearing; Bi–Metallic Investment Co. does not. Both are protesting higher property taxes. What's the difference?

An important restatement of the *Londoner–Bi–Metallic* distinction occurs in *United States v. Florida East Coast Ry. Co.,* 410 U.S. 224, 244–46 (1973), a case considered in detail in § 6.3.2. *Florida East Coast* involved the validity of regulations that raised the rates which railroads must pay for the use of freight cars owned by other railroads. The issue was whether a trial-type proceeding was required or whether notice and comment procedures would suffice. The Court observed:

> The basic distinction between rulemaking and adjudication is illustrated by this Court's treatment of two related cases under the Due Process Clause of the Fourteenth Amendment. In *Londoner v. Denver* . . . the Court held that due process had not been accorded a landowner who objected to the amount assessed against his land as its share of the benefit resulting from the paving of a street . . . But in the later case of *Bi–Metallic Investment Co.* . . . the Court held that no hearing at all was constitutionally required prior to a decision by state tax officers in Colorado to increase the valuation of all taxable property by a substantial percentage. The Court distinguished *Londoner* by stating that there a small number of persons "were exceptionally affected, in each case upon individual grounds. . . ."
>
> Later decisions have continued to observe the distinction adverted to in *Bi–Metallic Investment Co., supra.* In *Ohio Bell Telephone Co. v. Public Utilities Commission,* 301 U.S. 292, 304–05 (1937), the Court noted the fact that the administrative proceeding there involved was designed to require the utility to refund previously collected rate charges. The Court held that in such a proceeding the agency could not, consistently with due process, act on the basis of undisclosed evidence which was never made a part of the record before the agency. The case is thus more akin to *Louisville & Nashville R. Co.,* 227 U.S. 88 (1913), holding that due process applied to a decision by the ICC that a specific railroad rate was unreasonable than it is to this case. . . . While the line dividing them may not always be a bright one, these decisions represent a recognized distinction in administrative law between proceedings for the purpose of promulgating policy-type rules or standards, on the one hand, and proceedings designed to adjudicate disputed facts in particular cases on the other.
>
> Here the incentive payments proposed by the Commission in its tentative order, and later adopted in its final order, were applicable across the board to all of the common carriers by railroads subject to the Interstate Commerce Act. No effort was made to single out any particular railroad for special consideration based on its own peculiar circumstances. . . . Though the Commission obviously relied on factual inferences as a basis for its

order, the source of these factual inferences was apparent to anyone who read the order of December 1969. The factual inferences were used in the formulation of a basically legislative-type judgment, for prospective application only, rather than in adjudicating a particular set of disputed facts.

3. *Legislative and adjudicative facts.* In the preceding excerpt, how does Justice Rehnquist distinguish *Londoner* and *Bi–Metallic?*

Is Rehnquist's distinction consistent with that of Davis:

> The crucial difference between the two cases is that in *Londoner* specific facts about the particular property were disputed, but in *Bi–Metallic* no such specific facts were disputed, for the problem was the broad and general problem involving all taxpayers of Denver. The principle emerging from the two cases may be that a dispute about facts that have to be found on "individual grounds" [which Davis calls "adjudicative facts"] must be resolved through trial procedure, but a dispute on a question of policy need not be resolved through trial procedure even if the decision is made in part on the basis of broad and general facts of the kind that contribute to the determination of a question of policy [which Davis calls "legislative facts]. . . .

> Adjudicative facts usually answer the questions of who did what, where, when, how, why, with what motive or intent; adjudicative facts are roughly the kind of facts that go to a jury in a jury case. Legislative facts do not usually concern the immediate parties but are the general facts which help the tribunal decide questions of law and policy and discretion. . . .

> [Adjudicative facts] are intrinsically the kind of facts that ordinarily ought not to be determined without giving the parties a chance to know and to meet any evidence that may be unfavorable to them, that is, without providing the parties an opportunity for trial. The reason is that the parties know more about the facts concerning themselves and their activities than anyone else is likely to know, and the parties are therefore in an especially good position to rebut or explain evidence that bears upon adjudicative facts. Because the parties may often have little or nothing to contribute to the development of legislative facts, the method of trial often is not required for the determination of disputed issues about legislative facts.

2 K. Davis, ADMINISTRATIVE LAW TREATISE 412–13 (2d Ed.1979).

Do you agree with Davis that there is "often" no constitutional right to trial-type procedure in an adjudication where the only dispute concerns legislative facts or the exercise of discretion? Would Rehnquist come to the same conclusion? Is the distinction between legislative and adjudicative facts clear enough for easy application by agencies and courts?

4. *Rulemaking hearings.* Justice Holmes argued in *Bi–Metallic* that no hearing would be required if the state constitution or the state legislature had doubled Denver's tax rate. Therefore, it followed that there was no right to a hearing when the same action was taken by the State Board of Equalization. Does this really follow?

Suppose a state statute required all real property to be assessed at 50% of its value; the State Board of Equalization raised the assessment of all Denver property by 20% because it determined that Denver property was assessed at only 30% of value. Should Denver residents as a class have a right to a trial-type hearing to establish that Denver property was already assessed at 50% of value? Should it matter whether the members of the Equalization Board are elected? Should it matter whether there was a right to judicial review of the Board's action?

Should there be a constitutional right to some kind of a hearing in a case like *Bi–Metallic?* Should there be a statutory right to some kind of hearing? Do you agree that hearings are less useful for determining the legal rights and duties of classes of people, identified by a general description of their group characteristics, rather than the rights and duties of particular individuals? What sort of procedure would be most appropriate to resolve the issues in a case like *Bi–Metallic?*

ATKINS v. PARKER

472 U.S. 115 (1985).

[Prior to 1981, under the food stamp program 20% of a household's earned income was disregarded in computing eligibility. In 1981, Congress reduced this deduction to 18%. This caused a reduction of benefits to many families.

The Massachusetts Department of Public Welfare (DPW) sent the following notice to 16,000 families in English and Spanish:

" * * * *IMPORTANT NOTICE—READ CAREFULLY* * * *

"RECENT CHANGES IN THE FOOD STAMP PROGRAM HAVE BEEN MADE IN ACCORDANCE WITH 1981 FEDERAL LAW. UNDER THIS LAW, THE EARNED INCOME DEDUCTION FOR FOOD STAMP BENEFITS HAS BEEN LOWERED FROM 20 TO 18 PERCENT. THIS REDUCTION MEANS THAT A HIGHER PORTION OF YOUR HOUSEHOLD'S EARNED INCOME WILL BE COUNTED IN DETERMINING YOUR ELIGIBILITY AND BENEFIT AMOUNT FOR FOOD STAMPS. AS A RESULT OF THIS FEDERAL CHANGE, YOUR BENEFITS WILL EITHER BE REDUCED IF YOU REMAIN ELIGIBLE OR YOUR BENEFITS WILL BE TERMINATED. (FOOD STAMP MANUAL CITATION: 106 CMR:364.400).

"*YOUR RIGHT TO A FAIR HEARING:*

"YOU HAVE THE RIGHT TO REQUEST A FAIR HEARING IF YOU DISAGREE WITH THIS ACTION. IF YOU ARE REQUEST-

ING A HEARING, YOUR FOOD STAMP BENEFITS WILL BE REINSTATED . . . IF YOU HAVE QUESTIONS CONCERNING THE CORRECTNESS OF YOUR BENEFITS COMPUTATION OR THE FAIR HEARING PROCESS, CONTACT YOUR LOCAL WELFARE OFFICE. YOU MAY FILE AN APPEAL AT ANY TIME IF YOU FEEL THAT YOU ARE NOT RECEIVING THE CORRECT AMOUNT OF FOOD STAMPS."

For various reasons, DPW made many errors in recomputing the benefit levels of food stamp recipients. Among other problems, there was a substantial data entry backlog in DPW's computerized record system so that its files contained inaccurate earned income information for a number of recipients. The District Court held that DPW was required to add a computerized statement to its general notice to each recipient which included that recipient's old and new benefit amounts and the amount of the recipient's earned income used to compute the change. DPW computer specialists testified that this additional statement for each recipient could be prepared with only minimal reprogramming.

The majority opinion of JUSTICE STEVENS held that DPW's general notice to each recipient satisfied the food stamp statute and federal regulations. He then turned to the due process issue:]

.   .   .

II

[We] must consider petitioners' claim that they had a constitutional right to advance notice of the amendment's specific impact on their entitlement to food stamps before the statutory change could be implemented by reducing or terminating their benefits. They argue that an individualized calculation of the new benefit was necessary in order to avoid the risk of an erroneous reduction or termination.

The record in this case indicates that members of petitioners' class had their benefits reduced or terminated for either or both of two reasons: (1) because Congress reduced the earned-income disregard from 20 percent to 18 percent; or (2) because inadvertent errors were made in calculating benefits. These inadvertent errors, however, did not necessarily result from the statutory change, but rather may have been attributable to a variety of factors that can occur in the administration of any large welfare program. . . . But even if it is assumed that the mass change increased the risk of erroneous reductions in benefits, that assumption does not support the claim that the actual notice used in this case was inadequate. For that notice plainly informed each household of the opportunity to request a fair hearing and the right to have its benefit level frozen if a hearing was requested. . . . Thus, the Department's procedures provided adequate protection against any deprivation based on an unintended mistake. To determine whether the Constitution required a more detailed notice of the mass change, we therefore put the miscellaneous errors to one side and confine our attention to the reductions attributable to the statutory change.

Food-stamp benefits, like the welfare benefits at issue in *Goldberg v. Kelly* "are a matter of statutory entitlement for persons qualified to receive them." Such entitlements are appropriately treated as a form of "property" protected by the Due Process Clause; accordingly, the procedures that are employed in determining whether an individual may continue to participate in the statutory program must comply with the commands of the Constitution.

This case, however, does not concern the procedural fairness of individual eligibility determinations. Rather, it involves a legislatively mandated substantive change in the scope of the entire program. Such a change must, of course, comply with the substantive limitations on the power of Congress, but there is no suggestion in this case that the amendment at issue violated any such constraint. Thus, it must be assumed that Congress had plenary power to define the scope and the duration of the entitlement to food-stamp benefits, and to increase, to decrease, or to terminate those benefits based on its appraisal of the relative importance of the recipients' needs and the resources available to fund the program. The procedural component of the Due Process Clause does not "impose a constitutional limitation on the power of Congress to make substantive changes in the law of entitlement to public benefits."

The congressional decision to lower the earned-income deduction from 20 percent to 18 percent gave many food-stamp households a less valuable entitlement in 1982 than they had received in 1981. But the 1981 entitlement did not include any right to have the program continue indefinitely at the same level, or to phrase it another way, did not include any right to the maintenance of the same level of property entitlement. Before the statutory change became effective, the existing property entitlement did not qualify the legislature's power to substitute a different, less valuable entitlement at a later date. As we have frequently noted: "[A] welfare recipient is not deprived of due process when the legislature adjusts benefit levels. . . . [T]he legislative determination provides all the process that is due."

The participants in the food-stamp program had no greater right to advance notice of the legislative change—in this case, the decision to change the earned-income disregard level—than did any other voters. They do not claim that there was any defect in the legislative process. Because the substantive reduction in the level of petitioners' benefits was the direct consequence of the statutory amendment, they have no basis for challenging the procedure that caused them to receive a different, less valuable property interest after the amendment became effective.

The claim that petitioners had a constitutional right to better notice of the consequences of the statutory amendment is without merit. All citizens are presumptively charged with knowledge of the law. Arguably that presumption may be overcome in cases in which the statute does not allow a sufficient "grace period" to provide the persons affected by a change in the law with an adequate opportunity to become familiar with their obligations under it. In this case, however, not only was there a grace period of over 90 days before the amendment became effective, but in addition, every person affected by the change was given individual notice of the substance of the amendment.

As a matter of constitutional law there can be no doubt concerning the sufficiency of the notice describing the effect of the amendment in general terms. Surely Congress can presume that such a notice relative to a matter as important as a change in a household's food-stamp allotment would prompt an appropriate inquiry if it is not fully understood. The entire structure of our democratic government rests on the premise that the individual citizen is capable of informing himself about the particular policies that affect his destiny. To contend that this notice was constitutionally insufficient is to reject that premise.

The judgment of the Court of Appeals is reversed.

JUSTICE BRENNAN, dissenting.

. . .

[The] Court concludes that the food stamp recipients in this case had no special right to "advance notice of the legislative change" in the earned income deduction in 1981. The recipients, however, have never contended that they had a right to "advance notice" of the enactment of congressional legislation, and I do not intend to argue for that proposition here. "It is plain that sheer impracticality makes it implausible to expect the State *itself* to apprise its citizenry of the enactment of a statute of general applicability."

Instead, this case involves the *implementation* of Congress' decision by its agents, the various State agencies that administer food stamp programs across the country. Owing to factors unique to the State agency and having nothing to do with Congress, implementation of the change in Massachusetts resulted in the *erroneous* reduction of food stamp benefits for a number of households. Because recipients have a constitutionally cognizable property interest in their proper statutory entitlement levels, it is deprivation of those interests by the State agency, and not the passage of legislation by Congress, that requires our constitutional attention in this case. . . .

In my view, the Court's offhand discussion of "inadvertent errors" is fogged by an unspoken conceptual confusion in identifying the constitutional deprivation claimed in this case. In traditional cases arising under the Due Process Clause, a governmental deprivation of property is not difficult to identify: an individual possesses a set amount of property and the government's action either does, or does not, deprive the individual of some or all of it. Where "new" property interests—that is, statutory entitlements—are involved, however, claimants have an interest only in their benefit level as correctly determined under the law, rather than in any particular preordained amount. Thus, while *any* deprivation of tangible property by the State implicates the Due Process Clause, only an *erroneous* governmental reduction of benefits, one resulting in less than the statutorily specified amount, effects a deprivation subject to constitutional constraint. It is the error, and not the reduction *per se,* that is the deprivation.

Keeping this point in mind, it is readily apparent that this Court's application of the Due Process Clause to governmental administrative action has not only encompassed, but indeed has been premised upon, the need for protection of individual property interests against "inadvertent" errors of the State. . . . [When] administrative error—that is, the deprivation—is foreseeable as a general matter and certain to occur in particular cases, constitutional procedures are interposed to ensure correctness insofar as feasible. . . .

[Balancing the intense need of food stamp recipients for their benefits, the high risks of error, the value of a detailed notice, the ease by which DPW could have provided a better notice, the lack of education of most food stamp recipients, the lack of help available to them from welfare workers, and the shortness of the appeal period, Justice Brennan concluded that a detailed notice was constitutionally essential.]

Notes and Questions

1. *Due process and food stamp reductions.* The notice that DPW sent to food stamp recipients stated that they could request a pre-reduction hearing if they disagreed with DPW's recomputation. Are such hearings constitutionally required? Does a recipient's right to a hearing depend on the issue to be raised at the hearing? What if the recipient wanted to challenge the computational method which DPW used for all the recipients in the state?

2. *Adequate notice.* Why does the majority believe that no individualized notice was required—because due process is entirely inapplicable to DPW's action or because DPW's notice met due process standards? Why does the majority not use the *Mathews* balancing test (as the dissent does) to determine the adequacy of the notice? In light of the majority opinion, what notice, if any, must food stamp recipients receive of a change in the applicable law relating to food stamps? Just how detailed does notice in these circumstances have to be to meet due process standards?

In his dissent, Justice Brennan suggested that the ten-day appeal period was too short to allow for an informed decision on whether to appeal. Do you think a food stamp recipient would be precluded from challenging the accuracy of the new computation after the ten-day period had run?

3. *Problem.* A major political issue in Elm City is whether rapid development of residential neighborhoods with high rise apartments

and shopping centers should be slowed down. A newly elected city council is considering a land use plan for the city which provides that no new development (other than single-family dwellings) could occur in large areas of the city, including the Brentwood neighborhood. Ben, who owns an empty lot in Brentwood, seeks a trial-type hearing before the Council before the plan is adopted. He wishes to show that the plan is far too restrictive of development and that the ambiance of Brentwood can be preserved if small shopping centers are permitted. Must the council provide such a hearing?

Assume the council adopted the plan. Ben seeks a zoning variance to allow the construction of a small shopping center on his lot. According to statute, a zoning variance should be granted in cases of "unusual hardship" and only where the requested use "is consistent with the land use plan." He argues that he could make five times as much on his investment if he could build a shopping center. Moreover, it would be a great convenience for the neighborhood because there is no nearby shopping. Finally, he makes the same arguments that he made in originally opposing the land use plan. The council is proposing to deny the request. Is Ben entitled to a trial-type hearing?

Assume instead that the council is proposing to grant the request. Mary, Ben's neighbor, is outraged at the extra noise and traffic that a shopping center would bring to Brentwood. Is Mary entitled to a trial-type hearing? See Neuberger v. City of Portland, 603 P.2d 771 (Or. 1979); R. ELLICKSON & D. TARLOCK, LAND USE CONTROLS 269–94 (1981).

Chapter 3

ADMINISTRATIVE ADJUDICATION: FUNDAMENTAL PROBLEMS

Chapter 2 examined the constitutional right to a trial-type hearing in resolving disputes against government. This chapter continues that theme, but now the source of the right to a hearing is statutory rather than constitutional. In many situations, the rights overlap: both due process and state or federal APAs requires agencies to provide an opportunity for trial-type hearings to specified persons. However, the ingredients of the hearings required by due process and by statute are not the same: the required statutory procedure is likely to be more formal and to contain more protective elements than the proceeding required by due process. In many cases, there is no overlap: a statute may require a hearing even though due process does not or (particularly at the local level) due process may require a hearing even though no statute does so.

This chapter addresses some fundamental problems concerning agency hearings required by statute: When does a statute require an agency to hold a hearing? What is the relationship between statutory and constitutionally required hearings? Can an agency short-circuit a hearing requirement by first adopting a rule that settles the issue? Can an agency adjudicate a case impartially when it first made the rules and then investigated and prosecuted the very case it is about to decide? When is an agency decisionmaker disabled by bias or by having received off-the-record communications?

Chapter 4 takes up many practical procedural problems of agency adjudication. It begins with problems such as investigation and discovery arising in the pre-hearing phase, continues with problems arising at the hearing itself, and concludes with the principles relating to an agency's final decision.

§ 3.1　STATUTORY RIGHTS TO A HEARING IN ADJUDICATION

Administrative procedure statutes have taken two radically different approaches. The federal act and the 1961 MSAPA (on which most state APAs are based) do not require adjudicative hearings. They require a formal hearing, and lay out the ground rules for that hearing, only if *some other statute or the state or federal constitution* requires a hearing. Those ground rules are that the hearing must be a full, formal trial-type proceeding in which the parties have almost all of the rights present in a judicial trial. Such adjudication is called "formal adjudication." If neither another statute nor the constitution requires a hearing, the agency is largely free to choose its own dispute resolution procedure. Such adjudication is called "informal adjudication."

In contrast, the 1981 MSAPA does not leave it to other statutes or the constitution to decide whether a hearing is required. Instead, the 1981 MSAPA itself prescribes when hearings should occur and it provides for different hearing models of varying formality. You should consider whether the 1981 MSAPA approach is better and whether Congress should adopt it.

§ 3.1.1　FEDERAL LAW—RIGHT TO A HEARING UNDER THE APA

Read APA § 554(a). When does this provision require a hearing? If § 554(a) *does* provide for a hearing, what follows from that? *See* §§ 554(b), (c), and (d); 556; 557; 706(2)(E). Note that § 555 applies whether or not § 554(a) was triggered and that the provisions of § 558 are partially but not wholly dependent on § 554.

CITY OF WEST CHICAGO v. UNITED STATES NUCLEAR REGULATORY COMMISSION
701 F.2d 632 (7th Cir.1983).

[Kerr–McGee Corp. (KM) operated a thorium milling plant in West Chicago (City) from 1967 to 1973. A large amount of contaminated radioactive waste material still remains at the plant site; the method of decommissioning the site is in dispute and has been the source of several earlier Nuclear Regulatory Commission (NRC) proceedings.

KM had an NRC "source material" license allowing it to process thorium ore. KM's current application (for Amendment 3) seeks permission to demolish six buildings and to receive and store on-site additional contaminated material. City challenges an NRC order granting the license amendment.]

CUMMINGS, J.:

. . . The Atomic Energy Act of 1954 (AEA), § 189(a), 42 U.S.C. § 2239(a), clearly requires NRC to grant a "hearing" if requested "[i]n any proceeding under this chapter, for the granting, suspending, revoking, or amending of any license or construction permit * * *." [2] The parties in this case are arguing about the kind of "hearing" the NRC is required to conduct when issuing an amendment to a source materials license. The City argues that NRC must hold a formal, adversarial, trial-type hearing as provided by NRC regulations, 10 C.F.R. §§ 2.104 and 2.105. We shall refer to the hearing process outlined in those Sections as a "formal hearing." NRC and intervenor KM argue that the NRC may hold an informal hearing in which it requests and considers written materials without providing for traditional trial-type procedures such as oral testimony and cross-examination. We shall refer to this kind of hearing as an "informal hearing." In the circumstances of this case, we find that an informal hearing suffices. . . .

2. NRC DID NOT VIOLATE THE ATOMIC ENERGY ACT

Our inquiry cannot end with a finding that the NRC acted in conformance with its own regulations, for we must determine whether those regulations as interpreted violate the governing statute. If the AEA requires a formal hearing in the case of a materials license amendment, then the NRC must provide one, despite its interpretation of the regulations.

The City claims that a materials licensing hearing under Section 189(a) of the AEA must be in accordance with Section 5 of the Administrative Procedure Act (APA), 5 U.S.C. § 554. Section 554 does not by its terms dictate the type of hearing to which a party is entitled; rather it triggers the formal hearing provisions of Sections 556 and 557 of the APA if the adjudication in question is required by the agency's governing statute to be "determined on the record after opportunity for an agency hearing. . . ." . . . The City argues that Section 189(a) of the AEA triggers the formal hearing provisions of the APA because it provides that the "Commission shall grant a hearing upon the request of any person whose interest may be affected by the proceeding, and shall admit any such person as a party to such proceeding."

. . . Although Section 554 specifies that the governing statute must satisfy the "on the record" requirement, those three magic words need not appear for a court to determine that formal hearings are required. . . . However, even the City agrees that in the absence of these magic words, Congress must clearly indicate its intent to trigger

2. § 189(a). Hearings and judicial review

(a) In any proceeding under this chapter, for the granting, suspending, revoking, or amending of any license or construction permit, or application to transfer control, and in any proceeding for the issuance or modification of rules and regulations dealing with the activities of licensees, . . .the Commission shall grant a hearing upon the request of any person whose interest may be affected by the proceeding, and shall admit

any such person as a party to such proceeding. The Commission shall hold a hearing after thirty days' notice and publication once in the Federal Register, on each application under section 2133 or 2134(b) of this title for a construction permit for a facility, and on any application under section 2134(c) of this title for a construction permit for a testing facility.

[Sections 2133 and 2134 concern licenses for nuclear reactors.]

the formal, on-the-record hearing provisions of the APA. We find no such clear intention in the legislative history of the AEA, and therefore conclude that formal hearings are not statutorily required for amendments to materials licenses. . . .

While Section 181 of the AEA made the provisions of the APA applicable to all agency actions, it did not specify the "on the record" requirement necessary to trigger Section 554 of the APA. Thus despite the fact that the statute required the Commission to grant a hearing to any materially interested party, there is no indication that Congress meant the hearing to be a formal one. . . .

The AEC continued to hold formal hearings in all contested reactor cases, as well as in materials licensing cases. However, based on the threadbare legislative history concerning materials licenses, we are unable to conclude that the AEC's procedures were mandated by statute. Even if the legislative history indicates that formal procedures are required by statute in reactor licensing cases under the second, third, and fourth sentences of Section 189(a), we do not accept the City's argument that this by necessity indicates that all hearings under the first sentence must be formal as well. While the first sentence of Section 189(a) speaks in terms of "any license or construction permit," it does so in the context of a statute that distinguishes between the licensing of nuclear materials and reactor facilities. . . . In this case, we have no difficulty ascribing different meanings to the word "hearing" even though it appears in succeeding sentences of the same statutory section.

The City argues that under the APA, agency action is classified either as rule-making or adjudication, and since licensing is adjudication, NRC is obliged to provide a formal hearing in this case. The "on the record" requirement of APA Section 554, according to the City has been relevant primarily in cases involving rulemaking, not adjudication. *United States v. Florida East Coast Ry.*, 410 U.S. 224 (1973).

In adjudication, the City claims the absence of the "on the record" requirement is not decisive. For example, Section 402 of the Federal Water Pollution Control Act (FWPCA), 33 U.S.C. § 1342(a)(1), which provides for a "public hearing," has been held by three courts including this one to require a formal hearing pursuant to Section 554. *Seacoast Anti–Pollution League v. Costle*, 572 F.2d 872 (1st Cir.), cert. den. 439 U.S. 824 (1978). The First Circuit relied principally on the adjudicative nature of the decision at issue—issuance of a permit to allow discharge of a pollutant—finding that primarily the rights of the particular applicant would be affected, and that resolution of the issues required specific factual findings by the EPA Administrator.

The court also mentioned the judicial review provision of Section 509 of the FWPCA, which provides for review of a determination required under the FWPCA to be made "on the record.". . . This Court in *United States Steel Corp. v. Train*, 556 F.2d 822, relied principally on the judicial review provision of Section 509, but also found that Section 558(c) of the APA mandated a formal hearing independently of Section 554. . . . After reconsideration, we have decided herein to abandon our position in *Train* insofar as we relied on APA Section 558(c) to order a formal hearing.

We now agree with the First, Fifth and Ninth Circuits that Section 558(c) does not independently provide that formal adjudicatory hearings must be held. "It merely requires any adjudicatory hearings mandated under other provision of law to be set and completed in an expeditious and judicious manner."

All three cases, however, relied at least in part on the presence of the "on the record" requirement in Section 509, indicating that the requirement is indeed relevant to defining the hearing process even in adjudication. . . . Unlike the "on the record" requirement of Section 509 of the FWPCA, ·there is no indication even in the judicial review Section of the AEA, the governing statute, that Congress intended to require formal hearings under the APA. Thus even in adjudication, the "on the record" requirement is significant at least as an indication of congressional intent. We agree with the courts and commentators who recognize that adjudication may be either informal or formal. Formal adjudications are those required by statute to be conducted through on-the-record proceedings. Informal adjudications constitute a residual category including "all agency actions that are not rulemaking and that need not be conducted through 'on the record' hearings." [11] For example, in *United States Lines v. FMC,* 584 F.2d 519 (D.C.Cir. 1978), the court considered the hearing requirement of Section 15 of the Shipping Act of 1916. Under Section 15, the Commission may grant exemptions from the antitrust laws for anticompetitive agreements among ocean carriers when it is in the public interest to do so. *Id.* In analyzing the procedures necessary for a fair hearing, the court found that the case did not involve an adjudication in the constitutional sense, described in *Sangamon Valley Television Corp. v. United States,* 269 F.2d 221, 224 (D.C.Cir.1959), as a "resolution of conflicting private claims to a valuable privilege." Neither did it involve notice and comment rulemaking under APA Section 553. Rather the court characterized the case as involving an issue "quasi-adjudicatory" in nature—an adjudication of the rights of certain named parties to an exemption from the antitrust laws in light of the public interest. This kind of agency action, though quasi-adjudicatory, was not intended by Congress to merit a formal hearing under Section 15 of the Shipping Act. . . .

Despite the fact that licensing is adjudication under the APA, there is no evidence that Congress intended to require formal hearings for all Section 189(a) activities. In light of the above analysis, we conclude

---

11. Of course, if a formal adjudicatory hearing is mandated by the due process clause, the absence of the "on the record" requirement will not preclude application of the APA. *Wong Yang Sung v. McGrath,* 339 U.S. 33.

that NRC did not violate the AEA when it denied the City's request for a formal hearing.[12]

3. NRC Hearing Procedures Satisfy the Requirements of Due Process

The City argues that the NRC proceedings deprived it of liberty or property interests without due process of law. Yet generalized health, safety and environmental concerns do not constitute liberty or property subject to due process protection. Although the City claims that it has presented "specific documented concerns" to the NRC in its petitions such "concerns" do not, without more, require due process protection.

Even if we were to find a protected liberty or property interest in this case, we would hold that Commission procedures constituted sufficient process. The City received a meaningful opportunity to submit statements and data explaining why the amendment should not be granted. . . .

By pressing its request for a formal evidentiary hearing, the City has indicated its belief that written comments and documentation provide an inadequate opportunity to air its concerns. However, we are given no hint by the City of concerns other than the six listed in its November 13 submission to the Commission. Of those six, only two present factual issues, the resolution of which will in large part be based on technical or scientific data that will not necessarily be made more reliable through an oral presentation. *Cf. Mathews v. Eldridge.* In addition, as in a motion for summary judgment, it appears that both the City and KM essentially agreed on the facts but contested their interpretation, thus alleviating the need for an oral hearing.

We find that NRC correctly applied the *Mathews v. Eldridge* analysis in its order. The private interest that would be affected by official action in this case is a generalized one; in fact the health, safety and environmental interests of the City appear to be more "public" than "private." . . . Taking into account the technical, scientific nature of the issues, the absence of credibility questions, and the apparent lack of controverted issues of material fact, the additional value of an oral hearing in this case is minimal. Finally, convening a formal hearing involves a great deal of expense, both for the agency and the parties. According to NRC,

> A three-member licensing board or administrative law judge must be appointed, and with that come all the accouterments that make the proceeding more costly in terms of the time and materials expended: *e.g.,* participation in a pre-hearing conference, preparation of transcripts, discovery, submission of pre-filed testimony, a trial-type hearing at which witnesses are presented and cross-

12. Because we hold that the AEA does not require a formal hearing in this case, we need not address the NRC contention that no hearing is required in the absence of a disputed issue of material fact even when the governing statute by its terms requires an "on the record" hearing. This apparently is the rule in the D.C. Circuit. . . .

examined, and the preparation of findings of fact and conclusions of law.

NRC concluded, and we concur, that in this particular case, the Commission procedures afforded the City all the process that was constitutionally necessary.

The City, however, raises another notice problem. The City contends that NRC regulations provide for only one kind of hearing—a formal one. . . .

NRC seems to admit it has no regulations governing informal hearings, but argues that in this case at least the City had actual notice of the new procedures and an adequate opportunity to conform to them. . . .

A review of the documents in this case indicates that the issue of adequate notice is a close one. . . . [W]e conclude that the City did have adequate notice that the Commission intended to base its decision on written submissions. Other than the mere allegation of prejudice, there is no evidence in the record that the City would have responded differently if it had a more definite idea of the type or scope of the hearing.

The orders under review are affirmed.

Notes and Questions

1. *The real world.* Why did West Chicago want an adjudicatory hearing?

2. *Adjudication required by statute* . . . As *West Chicago* indicates, the elaborate formal hearing requirements set forth in APA §§ 554(b) to (d), as well as §§ 556 and 557, are not applicable in adjudication unless "required by statute to be determined *on the record* after opportunity for an agency hearing . . . ." What does the section mean by the words "on the record"? Is there a "record" whenever someone has written down what happened?

When a statute calls for a "hearing," but does not use the magic words "on the record," does the statute trigger § 554(a)?

In cases of *rulemaking,* the Supreme Court has held that formal procedures are not triggered by a requirement that the ICC act "after hearing." Congress must use the words "on the record" or their equivalent. *United States v. Florida East Coast Ry. Co.,* 410 U.S. 224 (1973), discussed in §§ 2.5 *supra* and 6.3 *infra.*

However, in cases of *adjudication,* several decisions prior to *West Chicago* required formal adjudicatory procedures under statutes (like § 189(a) of the Atomic Energy Act) which call only for a "hearing" or a "public hearing." For example, *see Seacoast Anti–Pollution League,* discussed in *West Chicago. Seacoast* involved a determination by the Environmental Protection Agency of whether to issue a license to a nuclear reactor to discharge hot water into the sea; among the factual issues was the effect of the discharge on sea life.

According to *Seacoast* and similar cases, Congress is *presumed* to intend formal adjudicatory procedures in a statute governing adjudication when it uses the word "hearing." How did *West Chicago* distinguish these cases? Are you convinced? Should formal adjudicatory procedures be required in materials licensing cases before the NRC? How about cases of *nuclear reactor* licensing? Should it matter that the NRC had always granted formal hearings in materials license cases in the past?

Suppose that agency regulations (but not a statute) call for a "hearing" or a "hearing on the record." Should that trigger full APA formal adjudication?

3. *Federal licensing cases.* *West Chicago* is a licensing case. What does § 558(c) require in cases of license *applications?* License *withdrawals?* Is § 558(c) dependent upon another statute that requires a hearing on the record? Do you agree with *West Chicago* that § 558(c) does not, by itself, require formal adjudication? Did NRC comply with the requirements of § 558(c)? Section 14(c) of 1961 MSAPA, applicable in many states, is closely similar to § 558(c).

4. *Informal adjudication.* *West Chicago* holds that NRC initial licensing (except perhaps for nuclear reactor cases) can be conducted as "informal," not "formal" adjudication. Aside from § 558 and § 555, the federal act requires no specific procedures in cases of informal adjudication. Yet § 189 does require NRC to provide a "hearing." Did NRC provide a "hearing" before granting KM the license amendment? Does the requirement of a "hearing" in § 189 mean anything? *See United States Lines, Inc. v. FMC,* 584 F.2d 519 (D.C.Cir.1978) ("hearing" means limits on ex parte contacts with decision-maker). Shouldn't Congress provide for some sort of procedures in case of informal adjudication?

In order to facilitate judicial review, some courts require a system of notice, comment, and explanation, like that required in informal rulemaking, before an agency completes informal adjudication. *American Trading Transp. Co. v. United States,* 841 F.2d 421, 424–25 (D.C.Cir. 1988); *Independent U.S. Tanker Owners Committee v. Lewis,* 690 F.2d 908, 922–26 (D.C.Cir.1982). This requirement might violate the rule in the *Vermont Yankee* case, discussed in § 6.3 *infra,* which precludes courts from demanding rulemaking procedures beyond those set forth in the APA. Is informal adjudication different from rulemaking in this respect—the APA sets forth elaborate procedural requirements for rulemaking but virtually none for informal adjudication?

5. *Issues of technical fact and issues of law or discretion.* City wanted NRC to resolve factual issues concerning harm to its residents from exposure to radiation if KM's license was amended. How useful are adjudicatory, trial-type hearings in cases like *Seacoast* or *West Chicago* anyway? Such technical or scientific questions are quite

different from the sorts of disputes that the agency had to resolve in
Goldberg v. Kelly.

Suppose there had been no factual issues in dispute—only issues of
law, policy, or discretion. If § 189 had required an on-the-record
hearing for material licensing, would NRC have to provide a formal
hearing? We return to this issue in § 3.2.

6. *Is there a better way?* The *West Chicago* court seemed to
believe that formal hearings in all NRC material licensing cases would
be a waste of time and, together with NRC's other burdens, might
paralyze the agency. It believed that the costs of mandatory formal
hearings would outweigh the benefits of providing them. As you read
chapters 3 and 4, ask whether the federal act's requirements for
adjudication are all that onerous, or whether NRC could legally take
shortcuts.

West Chicago assumes that Congress did not want formal adjudication in materials licensing when it provided for a "hearing" in § 189.
In fact, the legislative history was obscure and Congress may never
have squarely considered the question. If the court had held the
opposite, the NRC would, no doubt, have sought a legislative reversal of
the decision. Wouldn't that force Congress to consider the issue on the
merits?

7. *Comparative hearings.* In many situations, several applicants
compete for a single mutually exclusive license. For example, two
radio stations cannot occupy the same frequency or neither could be
heard. Thus if one application for the frequency is approved, a second
application for the same frequency must be rejected. Giving the second
applicant a hearing after granting the first application would be meaningless. In this situation, the Supreme Court held that both applicants
must be considered together in a single comparative hearing or else the
second applicant's statutory right to a hearing would be "an empty
thing." *Ashbacker Radio Corp. v. FCC,* 326 U.S. 327 (1945).

Of course, comparative hearings can become enormously complex
when many applications must be heard at the same time. For that
reason, agencies can establish a cutoff date; applications after that date
need not be consolidated with earlier ones.

The *Ashbacker* principle has frequently been applied in situations
where, for economic or policy reasons, only one of several applications
can be approved, even though it was *physically* possible for both
applicants to operate. See, e.g., *Bio–Medical Applications of Clearwater, Inc. v. Department of Health,* 370 So.2d 19 (Fla.App.1979) (certificates of need for hospital facilities); *Pollack v. Simonson,* 350 F.2d 740
(D.C.Cir.1965) (liquor stores within 300 feet of each other). *But see
Cusano v. Dunn,* 74 A.2d 477 (Conn.1950) (reaching opposite conclusion
on competing liquor licenses).

8. *Constitutionally required hearings.* *West Chicago* holds that
the license amendment did not invade the City's liberty or property

interests. Do you agree? Even if the City were entitled to due process, the Court held that due process had been provided. Do you agree?

Note that the effect of § 554(a) of the federal act is to make §§ 554 and 556–7 applicable only to those adjudications "required by statute to be determined on the record after an opportunity for an agency hearing." Suppose that a trial-type hearing had been required *by due process* in *West Chicago.* Would that trigger APA provisions for formal adjudication? *See* note 11 of *West Chicago,* citing *Wong Yang Sung v. McGrath.*

Wong was a deportation case. The statute did not require the Immigration Service (INS) to provide any kind of hearing, but one was required by due process. The Court held that since a hearing was required by due process before a person could be deported, all of the APA's provisions for formal adjudication would be applicable because the words "required by statute" in § 554(a) were intended to include *constitutional as well as statutory requirements* of a hearing. The court refused to "attribute to Congress a purpose to be less scrupulous about the fairness of a hearing necessitated by the Constitution than one granted as a matter of expediency." 339 U.S. 33, 50.

The Supreme Court's construction of the APA appears to make *all* of the elaborate trial-type requirements contained in §§ 554 and 556–57 applicable in a constitutionally required hearing, even though a *Mathews v. Eldridge* balancing process would require much less formality. The Court indicated, however, that the same is not true with respect to a hearing on the record required only by agency rules. Such a rule, alone, would not trigger formal adjudicatory procedures.

Many lower federal courts have ignored or subverted the apparent holding in *Wong Yang Sung. See* Note, "The Requirement of Formal Adjudication under Section 5 of the Administrative Procedure Act," 12 Harv.J.Leg. 194, 218–41 (1975). For example, despite *Wolff v. McDonnell,* discussed in § 2.2.2 *supra,* which held that the Constitution required a hearing in cases of prison discipline, a court refused to apply the APA adjudication provisions in such a case because they were inappropriately formal. *Clardy v. Levi,* 545 F.2d 1241 (9th Cir.1976). Do you agree with *Clardy?*

In light of *Wong,* would a court be required to apply all of the rights available in formal adjudication under the APA to an elementary student in a federal school suspended for a week, including the right to counsel, right to put on witnesses and to cross examine the school's witnesses? *See* Bonfield, "The Definition of Formal Adjudication under the Iowa Administrative Procedure Act," 63 Iowa L.Rev. 285, 357 (1977).

The *Wong* holding seems inconsistent with the Supreme Court's more recent variable due process decisions, such as *Mathews v. Eldridge* or *Walters v. Radiation Survivors* and it is not at all clear that *Wong* would be followed today, particularly if the private interest invaded was less compelling than that of a deportee. On the other hand, *Wong* construed the intent of Congress. Congress may, after all, confer by statute rights that are greater than those conferred by due process. Do you think Congress intended to require agencies to provide more formal procedure than is required by due process?

§ 3.1.2 RIGHTS TO A HEARING UNDER STATE LAW

Most state APAs follow the 1961 MSAPA and the federal act by requiring a source of law external to the APA to trigger the adjudicatory procedures spelled out by the APA. The 1961 MSAPA defines a "contested case" to which its formal adjudication provisions apply as a "proceeding, including but not restricted to ratemaking and licensing, in which the legal rights, duties, or privileges of a party are required by law to be determined by an agency after an opportunity for hearing." 1961 MSAPA § 1(2).

The "required by law" language in § 1(2)'s definition of "contested case" appears to make the APA's adjudication provisions applicable to hearings required by the constitution (state or federal), by statute, or even by agency rules. If a case like *Wong Yang Sung* arose under state law, what would be the result under § 1(2)? Does the breadth of § 1(2) encourage or discourage agencies to provide for hearings by rule in cases where no statute or constitutional provision requires a hearing? *See* Bonfield, *supra,* 63 Iowa L.Rev. at 308–11.

Most state APAs also follow the 1961 MSAPA and the federal act by providing only one type of adjudication: a full, formal, trial-type proceeding. But if an agency adjudication does not qualify as a "contested case," or there is no external requirement of a hearing, the adjudication is left wholly ungoverned by the APA. Is this rigid statutory scheme better than the flexible due process requirements for adjudication discussed in §§ 2.3 and 2.4, *supra?*

> The primary difficulty with the federal APA scheme for agency adjudication as followed by [the 1961 MSAPA and] most states is its imprecision. Some adjudications are unavoidably governed by all of that act's adjudicative provisions, when it might be more sensible to subject them to only to a few of these provisions. In that respect, the . . . federal act [is] overinclusive. On the other hand, many types of federal agency adjudications are entirely ungoverned by the adjudication provisions of the act, although a few of the adjudication provisions of that statute might properly be applicable . . . In this respect, the federal act [is] also underinclusive . . . Unfortunately, when the states emulated this general concept in their own administrative law, they perpetuated the over- and underinclusiveness of the federal APA adjudication scheme.

Bonfield, "The Federal APA and State Administrative Law," 72 Va.L.Rev. 297, 321–24 (1986).

A number of recent state statutes and the 1981 MSAPA attempt to remedy this problem with an entirely different approach. These statutes create several distinct classes of agency adjudication, each subject to procedural requirements specially tailored to the circumstances. The Florida Act, for example, divides adjudication into "formal proceedings" and "informal proceedings," each with procedural requirements of differing complexity. Similarly, Wisconsin divides its contested case proceedings into three distinct classes, subjecting each class both to a few standard provisions and to others specially tailored to the needs of that particular class. The 1981 MSAPA follows this latter approach in creating several classes of adjudication of descending degrees of formality and complexity. *See* Bonfield, *supra,* 72 Va.L.Rev. at 321–24 (1986) (also citing recent statutes in Delaware, Montana and Virginia).

In reading the following case, consider whether the court would have been as willing to construe the Wisconsin APA in the way it did if the act had not provided for three classes of adjudication of varying degrees of formality rather than only a single class of adjudication of a very formal nature like the federal act and most state APAs.

MILWAUKEE METROPOLITAN SEWERAGE DISTRICT v. WISCONSIN DEPARTMENT OF NATURAL RESOURCES
375 N.W.2d 648 (Wisc.1985).

CALLOW, J. [The issue is whether the Milwaukee Metropolitan Sewerage District (District)] . . . satisfies the requirements for a contested case hearing contained in sec. 227.064(1), Stats. Specifically, we must decide whether sec. 227.064(1) creates an independent right to a contested case hearing; and, if so, whether the District satisfies the qualifying conditions outlined in sec. 227.064(1)(a)–(d).

In 1977, pursuant to court order, the District initiated a massive water pollution abatement program, which initially was expected to cost 1.6 billion dollars. When completed, the system will eliminate the discharge of raw and partially treated sewage into area waterways and ensure compliance with applicable treatment standards.

The District, in 1980, submitted to the [Department of Natural Resources (DNR)] its Master Facilities Plan (MFP), a general, conceptual outline of the major elements of the District's abatement program. The DNR is instructed to approve, approve conditionally, or reject the plan, stating in writing any conditions of approval. After preparing an environmental impact statement and conducting hearings, the DNR conditionally approved the MFP in June, 1981.

This case concerns one element of the MFP—the inline storage system or "deep tunnels." The inline system consists of two large interceptor sewers tunneled in rock between 300 and 400 feet underground. The major purpose of the sewers is to provide storage capacity during periods of peak flow; excess sewage will be contained in the tunnels, thereby preventing an overload of the system during which untreated sewage would flow into Lake Michigan and local rivers.

As generally described in the MFP, the inline system tunnels were to be fully lined with one-foot thick concrete to protect against leaks. In conditionally approving the MFP, however, the DNR instructed the District to conduct further tests regarding the possibility of ground-water or sewage infiltrating into or out of the tunnels. After further study, the District concluded that a concrete lining would not provide added protection against infiltration because the concrete used for lining would be as permeable or more permeable than the rock in which the tunnels would be built. Accordingly, in February of 1982, when the District submitted a more detailed Inline Storage Facilities Plan to the DNR for approval, the plan did not call for concrete lining throughout the tunnels. By omitting the concrete lining, the District expected to save approximately forty-five million dollars.

In August of 1982, the DNR conditionally approved the Inline Storage Facilities Plan. The DNR required, as one of the conditions for approval, that all portions of the deep tunnels be lined with one foot of concrete. The District responded by demanding a contested case hearing under sec. 227.064, Stats., on the requirement that the deep tunnels be lined with concrete. The DNR denied the District's request, believing that sec. 227.064(1) . . . did not authorize a contested case hearing unless the District had a preexisting hearing right under another statute. . . .

In this case we must decide the circumstances in which a party is entitled to a contested hearing under sec. 227.064(1), Stats. The DNR claims that the District is not entitled to a contested case hearing under sec. 227.064(1) because the District lacks a preexisting right to a statutory hearing and does not have a right to a due process hearing. The District contends, however, that to receive a contested hearing under sec. 227.064(1) it does not need to possess a preexisting hearing right, but only needs to satisfy the conditions delineated in sec. 227.064(1)(a)–(d).

Section 227.064(1), Stats., provides:

"In addition to any other right provided by law, any person filing a written request with an agency for hearing shall have the right to a hearing which shall be treated as a contested case if:

"(a) A substantial interest of the person is injured in fact or threatened with injury by agency action or inaction;

"(b) There is no evidence of legislative intent that the interest is not to be protected;

"(c) The injury to the person requesting a hearing is different in kind or degree from injury to the general public caused by the agency action or inaction; and

"(d) There is a dispute of material fact." [2]

---

2. Section 227.064(3), Stats., provides:

"This section does not apply to rule-making proceedings or rehearings, or to actions where hearings at the discretion of the agency are expressly authorized by law."

In denying the District's request for a contested hearing, the DNR relied on *Town of Two Rivers v. DNR*, 315 N.W.2d 378 (Wis.App.1981). The *Two Rivers* court reviewed the first clause of sec. 227.064(1), Stats., and concluded that it established a prerequisite—a person must have a preexisting statutory right to a hearing to be entitled to a contested hearing afforded by sec. 227.064. Because the District did not and could not assert a preexisting statutory hearing right, the DNR denied its request for a contested hearing. . . .

The language of sec. 227.064(1), Stats., is clear and unambiguous. The statute begins with the clause: "In addition to any other right provided by law," and then states that "*any person* filing a written request with an agency for hearing shall have the right to a hearing. . . ." (Emphasis added.) The first clause clearly does not modify *person* in a manner that would restrict who is eligible to file a request for a hearing. The clause is neither an essential clause nor a restrictive clause. It is descriptive. It indicates that a person able to satisfy the conditions outlined in subsections (a) through (d) shall have a right to a hearing under sec. 227.064(1), *even if* the person has other rights provided by law. It does not indicate that a person seeking a contested hearing must have a preexisting hearing right. In its decision, the court of appeals correctly determined that sec. 227.064 creates an independent right to a hearing, conditioned only on the satisfaction of the elements outlined in sec. 227.064(1)(a)–(d). In affirming the court of appeals' decision, we overrule the decisions in *Town of Two Rivers v. DNR, supra,* to the extent that this decision is inconsistent with our holding. . . .

In essence, sec. 227.064(1), Stats., creates a residual hearing right. It serves as a safety net, affording a hearing right to those who are not granted a specific right to a hearing by other statutory provisions or administrative rules. To receive a hearing under sec. 227.064(1), however, a person must satisfy the conditions delineated in subsections (a) through (d). The District shall be entitled to a contested hearing, therefore, only if it fulfills the requirements outlined in subsections (a) through (d). . . .

Subsection (a) commands that the agency action or inaction must injure a substantial interest for a person to receive a contested hearing under sec. 227.064(1), Stats. The DNR's decision to require a concrete lining throughout the tunnels, the court of appeals concluded, threatens injury to the District's substantial interest in avoiding the lining's projected cost of nearly forty-five million dollars and in executing its master plan. The District is the entity statutorily authorized to plan, design, finance, construct, maintain, and operate the sewerage system in the Milwaukee metropolitan area.

It has a substantial interest in carrying out its plans in accordance with its own technical and financial judgments. By requiring the District to alter the master plan to accommodate the installation of concrete linings throughout the tunnels, at a cost of many millions of dollars, the DNR forces the District to incur substantial additional expense. The DNR's requirement threatens injury to the District's substantial interest in fiscal restraint and to the District's substantial interest in executing its statutory duties.

Subsection (b) dictates that a person is not entitled to a contested hearing if there is any evidence of legislative intent to leave the asserted interest unprotected. We find no evidence of legislative intent to leave the District's interest unprotected.

Subsection (c) requires that the person seeking a contested hearing suffer an injury different in degree or kind from the injury to the general public. The concrete lining required by the DNR would cause the District to suffer financial injury different in degree from the injury to the general public. The District finances its sewerage improvements through borrowing and direct tax levies on District residents. Although the state and the federal governments also provide funding for the improvements, the District would bear the greatest share of the additional cost attributable to the lining. The DNR's lining requirement also causes injury to the District's interest in executing its statutory duties. This injury is different in degree and kind from injury to the general public.

Subsection (d) requires a dispute of material fact. The focal point of this entire case is the dispute between the District and the DNR regarding the need for a concrete lining throughout the deep tunnels. Clearly, this is a dispute of material fact.

We have concluded that sec. 227.064(1), Stats., creates an independent right to a hearing conditioned only on the satisfaction of the elements outlined in sec. 227.064(1)(a)–(d). The application of sec. 227.064 is not dependent upon a preexisting hearing right. Because the District satisfies each of the four conditions described in sec. 227.064(1)(a)–(d), we affirm the court of appeals' ruling that the District is entitled to a contested case hearing on the need for a concrete lining throughout the deep tunnels.

Notes and Questions

1. *Federal and state.* How would *Milwaukee Sewerage* have been decided under the federal act? First, is it adjudication at all? (*See* the definitions in federal APA § 551). Second, if it is adjudication, is a formal hearing required under § 554(a)? Third, how about entitlement to a formal adjudicatory hearing under the *Wong Yang Sung* case?

How would *West Chicago* have been decided under the Wisconsin statute and under 1981 MSAPA (*see* §§ 1–102(4)–(5), 4–101, 4–102, and 4–105)?

2. *Wisconsin and 1981 MSAPA.* Compare Wisc. § 227.064(1) to the 1981 MSAPA sections cited above. What differences do you see? Which version do you prefer?

3. *Conference, summary and emergency hearings.* As noted earlier, the federal act requires virtually no adjudicative process unless some other statute or the constitution requires a hearing on the record, and the 1961 MSAPA requires no special adjudicative procedures unless an agency hearing is required by some law external to that act. That leaves a large universe of informal adjudication without any defined procedure.

Examine 1981 MSAPA §§ 4–401 and 4–402. These sections single out certain matters for a "conference adjudicative hearing" if the agency has so designated by rulemaking. What is the criteria for selecting these particular categories? How is a "conference hearing" different from other hearings?

Examine 1981 MSAPA § 4–501 concerning "emergency adjudicative proceedings" and § 4–502 to 4–506 concerning "summary adjudicative proceedings." What due process case does summary procedure remind you of? Again, when can the agency take advantage of emergency and summary procedures? And how are they different from formal adjudication procedure?

Would conference, emergency, or summary procedure apply in some cases in which a hearing is constitutionally required? Would those procedures probably satisfy constitutional demands?

4. *Comparing APAs.* The 1981 MSAPA (and Wisconsin's APA) take a radically different approach from the federal act (and the 1961 MSAPA), because the former creates, on its own, a right to an adjudicative proceeding and provides several distinct classes of proceedings with different degrees of formality. The latter, on the other hand, requires adjudicatory proceedings only if law external to the APA creates such a right and it contains only one quite formal class of adjudication.

Thus the two approaches make different baseline assumptions about what the legislature probably wants. The federal act and the 1961 MSAPA make the baseline assumption that the legislature does not wish to generally require adjudication to be conducted by any defined procedure. If the legislature wants to require such procedure in a given administrative scheme, the legislature (or the agency itself) must say so in the statute or rules creating that scheme. In contrast, the baseline assumption of the 1981 MSAPA is that the legislature ordinarily does want adjudication to be conducted through a defined procedure; if it does not wish to require agencies to follow the usual procedures, the legislature must say so when it enacts a new administrative scheme.

Which approach is superior? In making that determination, consider the extent to which each statute:

(a) adequately protects the individual interests of the private parties involved;

(b) is easy to understand and apply to particular situations;

(c) permits or facilitates the use of procedures proportioned to the importance of the matters at stake; and

(d) promotes the cause of efficient and economic government administration;

(e) is sufficiently flexible to deal with unforeseen or unusual circumstances.

5. *Problem.* Our client Ralph is an employee of Library engaged in classifying new books. His employment contract provides that he cannot be discharged except for good cause. Library's rules for employees prohibit smoking in offices except in designated smoking areas. The rules also provide for disciplinary sanctions in case of rule violations. A supervisor has discretion as to which sanctions should be applied, if any. For a first offense, a supervisor can place a warning letter in an employee's file and can also suspend the employee without pay for a period not to exceed five days.

Martha, Ralph's supervisor, believes that Ralph was smoking at his desk. Ralph denies this (he says the cigarette butts in his trash can were left by a friend who stopped by to visit him). He claims that another employee who hates him told Martha that he had been smoking. Even if he did it, he wants to persuade Martha not to put a letter in his file or suspend him.

Assume that Library is operated by

(i) a county which is not subject to any administrative procedure act,

(ii) a state which has adopted the 1981 MSAPA, or

(iii) the federal government.

Is Ralph entitled to a hearing and, if so, of what sort? What do you advise him to do now?

§ 3.2 CIRCUMVENTING HEARING REQUIREMENTS THROUGH RULEMAKING

A recurring theme in this book is the interplay between agency adjudication and rulemaking. Chapter 2.5 explored the applicability of due process to non-individualized proceedings. Recall *Bi–Metallic* and *Atkins v. Parker.* This section considers the related issue of whether an agency must provide an adjudicatory hearing required by statute when the issue has been resolved by a rule. Chapter 5 will return to the rulemaking/adjudication relationship, taking up in detail the question of whether rulemaking or adjudication is better for the purpose of making new law.

AMERICAN AIRLINES, INC. v. CIVIL AERONAUTICS BOARD

359 F.2d 624 (D.C.Cir.) (en banc), *cert. denied*, 385 U.S. 843 (1966).

[In 1964, the CAB adopted PS–24, a "policy statement" permitting only all-cargo airlines (like Slick) to offer "blocked space" service. Combination airlines (like American) that carry both passengers and freight could not offer blocked space service. Blocked space service allows freight shippers to reserve space in advance, at wholesale rates, by agreeing to pay for a specified amount of space. Accordingly, in adopting PS–24, the CAB amended the licenses of the all-cargo airlines to permit them to offer blocked space and amended the licenses of combination airlines to prohibit them from offering blocked space.

The CAB more than complied with the APA's requirements for rulemaking in adopting PS–24: it gave public notice, invited written comments, and allowed presentation of oral arguments (this is not required by the APA). But it refused American's request for an adjudicatory hearing even though § 401(g) of the Federal Aviation Act, 49 USC § 1371(g), requires a full adjudicatory hearing to modify a license.

In PS–24 the CAB explained that limiting blocked space service to all-cargo carriers would further their role as large volume air-freight transporters. This would facilitate a breakthrough in which more shippers would use air freight rather than surface carriers. This breakthrough would not occur if blocked space service was offered by all carriers—only if it is limited to the all cargo carriers. This would strengthen the all-cargo carriers financially and would tend to shift small volume shipments to combination carriers.

The court first held that PS–24 was substantively permissible; PS 24 drew a rational distinction between different types of carriers. It then turned to the procedural issue.]

LEVENTHAL, J.:

.   .   .

2. Petitioners claim that § 401(g) assures them an "adjudicatory hearing" because the Board action amounts to a modification or suspension of existing rights under their certificates of public convenience and necessity.

In essence, petitioners' argument is the same as the thesis this court accepted ten years ago in the *Storer* case, only to be reversed by the Supreme Court.[10] This court held the multiple ownership rule of the Federal Communications Commission invalid because of the inadequacy of the rule making procedure followed in its adoption, an adjudicatory hearing being expressly guaranteed by statute to applicants for licenses. The Supreme Court, however, held that notwithstanding the

---

10. United States v. Storer Broadcasting Co., 351 U.S. 192.

statutory hearing requirement the Commission retained the power to promulgate rules of general application consistent with the Act, and to deny an adjudicatory hearing to applicants whose applications on their face showed violations of the rule. *Storer's* vitality is attested by its recent application in FPC v. Texaco, 377 U.S. 33 (1964), where the Supreme Court stated:

> [T]he statutory requirement for a hearing under § 7 does not preclude the Commission from particularizing statutory standards through the rule-making process and barring at the threshold those who neither measure up to them nor show reasons why in the public interest the rule should be waived.

Petitioners argue that the *Storer* doctrine is restricted to regulations affecting future applications for new licenses or certificates, whereas here the CAB regulation affected rights under existing certificates. That such a restrictive reading of the *Storer* doctrine is unwarranted, is shown by such decisions as National Broadcasting Co. v. United States, 319 U.S. 190 (1943); Air Line Pilots Ass'n Intern. v. Quesada, 276 F.2d 892 (2d Cir.1960).[13]

The present case is different in particular aspects of the facts or statutory provisions from *Storer* and the other *Storer* doctrine cases. However, the *Storer* doctrine is not to be revised or reshaped by reference to fortuitous circumstances. It rests on a fundamental awareness that rule making is a vital part of the administrative process, particularly adapted to and needful for sound evolution of policy in guiding the future development of industries subject to intensive administrative regulation in the public interest, and that such rule making is not to be shackled, in the absence of clear and specific Congressional requirement, by importation of formalities developed for the adjudicatory process and basically unsuited for policy rule making.

3. The need for and importance of policy rule making made on the basis of a procedure appropriate thereto is clearly identified in the Administrative Procedure Act.

In general, the APA establishes a dichotomy between rule-making and adjudication. For adjudication a formal system is provided.[15]

---

13. The court upheld the promulgation, without adjudicatory hearings, of a Federal Aviation Agency regulation barring individuals sixty years old from serving as pilots, even though that regulation modified rights under all outstanding licenses and effected a termination without hearing of some outstanding licenses. Rejecting a challenge by pilots relying on the statutory provision, 49 U.S.C. § 1371(g), that an adjudicatory hearing must be provided before an airman's license may be revoked or amended, the court stated

The Administrator's action does not lose the character of rule-making because it modifies the plaintiff pilots' claimed property rights in their licenses and their contractual rights under collective bargaining agreements * * *. Administrative regulations often limit in the public interest the use that persons may make of their property without affording each one affected an opportunity to present evidence upon the fairness of the regulation.

15. Section 5 of the APA in substance provides that the officers who receive the evidence shall make an initial decision, or at least a recommended decision, and prohibits any officer engaged in investigating or prosecuting functions from participating in the decision. It protects the right of

Rule making, however, is governed by § 4, which essentially requires only publication of notice of the subject or issues involved, an opportunity for interested persons to participate through submission of written data, and the right of petition in respect of rules. These more limited requirements are geared to the purpose of the rule making proceeding, which is typically concerned with broad policy considerations rather than review of individual conduct. Compare the Attorney General's Manual on the Administrative Procedure Act (1947), pp. 14–15:

> The object of the rule making proceeding is the implementation or prescription of law or policy for the future, rather than the evaluation of a respondent's past conduct. Typically, the issues relate not to the evidentiary facts, as to which the veracity and demeanor of witnesses would often be important, but rather to the policy-making conclusions to be drawn from the facts. Conversely, adjudication is concerned with the determination of past and present rights and liabilities. Normally, there is involved a decision as to whether past conduct was unlawful, so that the proceeding is characterized by an accusatory flavor and may result in disciplinary action. Not only were the draftsmen and proponents of the bill aware of this realistic distinction between rule making and adjudication, but they shaped the entire Act around it.

Rule making has a unique value and importance as an administrative technique for evolution of general policy, notwithstanding, or perhaps indeed because of, the freedom from the procedures carefully prescribed to assure fairness in individual adjudication.

The regulation under discussion, being an "agency statement of general * * * applicability and future effect designed to implement * * * or prescribe law or policy," plainly satisfies the definition of "rule" in § 2(c) of the APA,[17] as well as general understanding. There is therefore a presumptive procedural validity for the rule making procedure prescribed in § 4 of the APA, unless countermanded by a different Congressional mandate.

4. Serious questions have been raised concerning the adjudicatory-type hearings required and held on initial licensing involving specific carriers and routes. It has been suggested that air line certificates are an instance where "functions that are more truly planning than adjudicatory have been forced too rigidly into the latter mould," and that officials engaged in planning functions should be "free to use flexible

cross-examination and the right of presenting oral testimony.

17. 5 U.S.C. § 551(4) defines "rule" as meaning "any agency statement of general or particular applicability and future effect designed to implement, interpret, or prescribe law or policy." Professor Davis points out that the words "or particular" were inserted after Senate passage in order, said the House Committee, to "assure coverage of rule making addressed to named persons," that the words were not intended to change into rule making what was previously considered adjudication but "to make sure that what has traditionally been regarded as a rule will still be a rule even though it has particular instead of general applicability."

procedures in the search for ideas and policies" rather than be "bound either as a matter of routine or law to pursue procedures ill-adapted for the performance of such a function." [18] . . .

The difficulties currently experienced in the administrative process, sometimes referred to as its "malaise," obviously do not warrant departure from procedures mandated by Congress. But they suggest the need for relative certitude before a court concludes that adjudicatory procedures are required. The need for certitude is underscored if the adjudicatory procedure is to be required on the ground that the proceeding involves an amendment of licensing, for under the Administrative Procedure Act that conclusion results in even more rigorous procedural requirements than apply to initial licensing. Thus, the examiner would not even be free to consult with agency technicians, as he is on initial licenses. And the presentation to the agency heads would have to await an examiner's report and proceed on the basis of exceptions thereto, whereas in initial licensing the agency may omit the examiner's report and proceed on the premise that exceptions can be more clearly focused in the light of proposals and views of the senior staff officials. In short, the rigors of the adjudicatory procedure could not even be softened by the exceptions deliberately provided by Congress in the APA in cases of initial licensing (and rule making on the record) in order to provide the flexibility requisite for proceedings principally involving policy determinations.

5. We are not here concerned with a proceeding that in form is couched as rule making, general in scope and prospective in operation, but in substance and effect is individual in impact and condemnatory in purpose. The proceeding before us is rule making both in form and effect. There is no individual action here masquerading as a general rule. We have no basis for supposing that the Board's regulation was based on a sham rather than a genuine classification. The classes of carriers were analyzed both functionally and in terms of capacity for furthering the promotional purposes of the Act. The class of combination carriers is not accorded the same rights as the class of all-cargo carriers, but the difference is in no sense a punishment for sins of commission or omission. They are not, in Judge Washington's phrase, "goats" being separated from favored sheep. . . .

Where the agency is considering an order against a particular carrier or carriers there is protection through the requirement of the adjudicatory procedure appropriate for such individual actions and amendments, . . .

18. Landis, Report on the Regulatory Agencies to the President–Elect, p. 18 (1960).

A leading practitioner before the CAB has even suggested that the breakdown of the administrative process in protracted cases should be overcome by the adoption of a conference-hearing procedure, with virtual elimination of oral testimony, including cross-examination, and hearings confined in substance to conference discussions between lawyers and expert witnesses. Westwood, Administrative Proceedings: Techniques of Presiding, 50 A.B.A.J. 659 (1964).

Where the agency is considering a general regulation, applicable to all carriers, or to all carriers within an appropriate class, then each carrier is protected by the fact that it cannot be disadvantaged except as the Board takes action against an entire class. For any such class regulation there is also protection outside the field of procedure in that the general regulation must be reasonable both as to the classification employed, and as to the nature and extent of the restriction in relation to the evil remedied or other general public purpose furthered.

7. There may be wisdom in providing for oral testimony, at least in legislative-type hearings, in advance of the adoption of controversial regulations governing competitive practices, even though the need for development of overall requirements precluded Congressional requirement of such hearings for rule making generally.

This court has indicated its readiness to lay down procedural requirements deemed inherent in the very concept of fair hearing for certain classes of cases, even though no such requirements had been specified by Congress. However in the present case the CAB did not limit itself to minimum procedures, but rather gave the parties a significantly greater opportunity to persuade and enlighten the Board. It provided not merely for written comment, but in addition for oral argument. The CAB, presumably with the aid of its policy staff, sifted out the dross and delineated key questions on which argument could most helpfully be focused, including the question material to the case at bar.

If additional procedural safeguards are to be imposed as a requirement it would be more salutary to incorporate them into a rule making procedure than to adopt a blanket requirement of an adjudicatory procedure. A rule making setting would better permit confinement of oral hearings to the kind of factual issues which can best be determined in the light of oral hearings, without undue elongation of the proceeding or sacrifice of the expedition and flexibility available in rule making. It would also permit the hearing examiner to confer with experts and the Board concerning "legislative facts" and policy questions.

However, there is no basis on the present record for concluding that additional procedures were requisite for fair hearing. We might view the case differently if we were not confronted solely with a broad conceptual demand for an adjudicatory-type proceeding, which is at least consistent with, though we do not say it is attributable to, a desire for protracted delay. Nowhere in the record is there any specific proffer by petitioners as to the subjects they believed required oral hearings, what kind of facts they proposed to adduce, and by what witnesses, etc. Nor was there any specific proffer as to particular lines of cross-examination which required exploration at an oral hearing.

The particular point most controverted by petitioners is the effect of the CAB regulation on their business. The issue involves what Professor Davis calls "legislative" rather than "adjudicative" facts. It is the kind of issue involving expert opinions and forecasts, which cannot be decisively resolved by testimony. It is the kind of issue where a month of experience will be worth a year of hearings.

It is part of the genius of the administrative process that its flexibility permits adoption of approaches subject to expeditious adjustment in the light of experience. Although the CAB's regulation is not temporary in the sense of being expressly limited in duration, the Board's findings plainly reflect its assumption that the regulation was intended to be subject to re-examination. The Board's regulations provide that "any policy may be amended from time to time as experience or changing conditions may require." In any event, it is the obligation of an agency to make re-examinations and adjustments in the light of experience.

To avoid any possible misapprehension, our affirmance of the Board's action is without prejudice to the right of the combination carriers to reopen the question of their exclusion upon a showing that the Board's assumptions could not reasonably continue to be maintained in the light of actual experience, that their overall cargo business was significantly impaired, or that the air freight market had sufficiently expanded so that the promotion of the air cargo industry through blocked space reduced rates would not be imperiled by their participation. . . .

Meanwhile they have been accorded a hearing conforming to and surpassing the minimum required for rule making. They have not been subject to a denial of procedural rights that undermines the validity of the regulation.

Affirmed.

BURGER, CIRCUIT JUDGE, with whom DANAHER and TAMM, CIRCUIT JUDGES, join (dissenting): . . .

I have trouble seeing how a "regulation" which turns identical certificates into ones which place the licensees in entirely distinct carrier roles, carrying different types of cargo for different types of shippers, can be said to be anything less than an amendment of outstanding certificates. . . . I therefore dissent from the majority's conclusion that an adjudicatory hearing was not required. As I see it this is nothing more than a transparent device to favor some carriers at the expense of others. . . .

The majority opinion cites a number of cases in an effort to sustain its holding that the Board has authority to amend Petitioners' certificates by rulemaking rather than an adjudicatory procedure. Those cases are not in point. . . .

None of the cases relied on by the majority deals with a situation like that before us, where an agency attempts by rulemaking to amend some—but not all—of the outstanding certificates authorizing a particular kind of service so as to deprive the licensees of a significant part of their license authority. . . .

Although it is not necessary to discuss the relative desirability of rulemaking and adjudicatory procedures in a situation where Congress has spoken as clearly as it has here, I note that my conclusion as to congressional meaning is reinforced by a consideration of the types of issues involved here. Rulemaking is normally directed toward the formulation of requirements having a general application to all members of a broadly identifiable class. As pointed out above, however, the CAB's result here is reached by a rule which has different impacts upon members of the same basic category. When the Board makes such a differentiation, the proceedings inescapably become highly adversary in character, especially where the final determination purports to rest upon asserted differences in capabilities and potentialities as between individual carriers. The rulemaking procedure's lack of direct testimony of witnesses, cross-examination, and other features of adjudicatory hearings is totally inadequate for the testing of such competing considerations, both factual and inferential.

While the question whether reduced-rate "blocked-space" service may be offered by *any* carrier might well be appropriate for rulemaking, the selection of particular carriers to provide such service is clearly the sort of question which can be resolved properly and fairly only in an adjudicatory proceeding. Once the Board had decided that it should not allow every freight carrier to offer such service, it was faced with the problem of picking and choosing among competing, mutually exclusive applications. Furthermore, these were not applicants competing for a *new* right which neither had previously held; they were competing to retain a right which their certificates already authorized. The Board's action made some carriers "more equal" than others. . . .

Even if the Board has the power to realign so drastically the competitive positions of carriers holding equal certificates, the Act as I read it requires that the Board first hold an evidentiary hearing, before it may make such a certificate amendment.

Notes and Questions

1. *Rulemaking or adjudication. American Airlines* establishes the validity of "generic rules"—those which determine issues of law, fact and policy all at once so that they need not be redetermined in a string of adjudications. *See also* 1981 MSAPA § 4–105. What are the advantages and disadvantages of settling the issues in a single generic rule as opposed to working them out case by case? The real issue in *American Airlines* is the appropriateness of rulemaking for drawing a distinction between carriers whose licenses had previously been identical. Who has the best of this argument—the majority or dissent?

The court says: "We are not here concerned with a proceeding that in form is couched as rule making, general in scope and prospective in operation, but in substance and effect is individual in impact and condemnatory in purpose." What does this mean? The problem of the use of rulemaking procedure to achieve an individualized result is addressed in § 5.1, *infra.*

2. *Circumventing hearings.* The CAB modified American's license by prohibiting it from offering blocked space. The statute called for an on-the-record adjudicatory hearing before the CAB modified a license. In some circumstances, due process would require a hearing before modification of a license. Why was American not entitled to an adjudicatory hearing? Why did American want such a hearing? If the CAB had lacked the power to make binding rules, how could it have achieved its objective?

3. *Judicial power to prescribe procedure.* Note Judge Leventhal's hint that the court might in the future prescribe rulemaking procedures going beyond those required by the APA (such as oral hearings or the questioning of witnesses). This line of development was cut short by the Supreme Court's decision in the *Vermont Yankee* case, discussed in § 6.3 *infra,* holding that courts had no power to compel agencies to use rulemaking procedures not spelled out in the APA.

4. *Summary judgment.* Another application of the principle of the *American Airlines* case is to "administrative summary judgment." An agency can deny a hearing, otherwise required by statute and the APA, when there are no disputed issues of material fact. This is like a summary judgment in civil litigation. *See* Federal Rul. of Civ.Proc. 56.

The Supreme Court upheld administrative summary judgment in *Weinberger v. Hynson, Westcott & Dunning, Inc.,* 412 U.S. 609 (1973), a case arising out of a massive examination of thousands of existing drugs by the FDA to ascertain whether they were effective for their claimed uses. This process (triggered by a 1962 statute) began with an examination by panels set up by the National Academy of Sciences (NAS). The statute required FDA to withdraw the licenses for such drugs unless their effectiveness was established by "adequate and well-controlled investigations" and it provided for a hearing in case of withdrawal.

FDA regulations spelled out very strict standards for what studies would be acceptable in proving the effectiveness of drugs. For example, anecdotal evidence by physicians was barred. The regulations also provided that a request for hearing must include the studies on which the applicant relied. The request for a hearing would be dismissed when it clearly appeared from the application that there was no "genuine and substantial issue of fact." This would occur if the manufacturer could not introduce any evidence of scientific studies as required by the regulations.

The Supreme Court upheld these regulations. NAS panels had evaluated 16,500 claims made on behalf of 4000 drugs. Seventy percent of these claims were found not to be supported by substantial evidence of effectiveness. The Court said:

We cannot impute to Congress, nor does due process demand, a hearing when it appears conclusively from the applicant's 'pleadings' that the application cannot succeed . . . If FDA were required automatically to hold a hearing for each product whose efficacy was questioned . . . even though many hearings would be an exercise in futility, we have no doubt that it could not fulfill its statutory mandate to remove from the market all those drugs which do not meet the effectiveness requirements of the Act.

The Court also noted that the rules validly placed the *burden* of showing that there is a genuine issue of fact on the applicant (rather than the FDA which in effect is moving for summary judgment). This departs from summary judgment practice in ordinary civil litigation. But the Court also held that summary judgment should not have been granted in the *Hynson* case since there were genuine issues of fact presented about the effectiveness of Lutrexin, the drug in question.

The Court entered one caveat: the application could be dismissed only if it were clear that no factual issues were presented. If the regulation called for discretion or subjective judgment by the FDA, it would not be appropriate to dismiss the application without hearing. 412 U.S. 621, n. 17.

The *American Airlines* and *Hynson* principles are of great importance in administrative law. As *Hynson* shows, if the FDA had to provide full-fledged adjudicatory hearings before withdrawing drug licenses—even though the result was a foregone conclusion because the manufacturers could not meet FDA's evidentiary standards—it might take many decades to remove all the ineffective drugs from the market. For example, Lutrexin was not ultimately withdrawn from the market until 1976—14 years after enactment of the 1962 amendments.

5. *Petitions for waiver of rules foreclosing adjudicatory hearings.* In both the *Storer* and *Texaco* cases, relied on in *American Airlines,* the Court called attention to language in the regulations permitting applicants to seek a waiver of the rules because their situation was different from others affected by the rule. These decisions imply that a waiver provision might be necessary to the validity of the rules. However, there was no waiver provision in the CAB's blocked space rules nor in the CAB's age–60 rule which was upheld in *Airline Pilots v. Quesada* (summarized in n. 13 of *American Airlines*). Note Judge Leventhal's cautionary language about the right of combination carriers to trigger a reexamination of the blocked space rule.

Even without a specific provision in a rule for seeking exceptions, a waiver can always be requested. APA § 555(e). In addition, an agency may simply not bother to enforce a rule in special circumstances. However, a specific and structured provision in a rule entitling affected persons to request waivers is best calculated to ensure a reasoned decision and equal treatment to all affected by the rule. But such provisions can trigger a flood of requests for special treatment; the benefits of using rules instead of case-by-case adjudication can be dissipated.

Should rules affecting across-the-board conduct always contain a provision allowing regulated persons to request a waiver?

6. *Failure to request hearing.* A party to an adjudicative proceeding who has a right to a statutory hearing may also lose that right by failing to comply with reasonable agency procedural requirements. For example, an agency rule might require a party to request a hearing within 60 days, and if the party does not do so, is foreclosed from doing so later. Such a rule will be valid if reasonable under the circumstances and not inconsistent with the agency's enabling act.

7. *Problem.* State A has adopted the 1981 MSAPA. A's Board of Medical Quality Assurance (BMQA) routinely grants a provisional license to practice medicine to any medical school graduate. This allows the graduate to start an internship in a State A hospital prior to passing the usual medical licensing exam. BMQA adopted a rule (after following all procedural requirements) which provides that no graduate of a foreign medical school (except one in certain European countries) can be provisionally licensed to practice in A.

Medical school is four years long; the last year consists entirely of clinical instruction in a hospital. Valerie attended three years of American medical school and passed all courses. As the result of an unfortunate personal encounter with a professor, she wanted to transfer to another school for her fourth year (during which she would be working in a hospital). Thus she enrolled at the Medical College of the Caribbean (MCC) in the Dominican Republic. However, she never took any courses at MCC; it simply gave her a diploma when she finished her clinical work at the hospital in state B with which MCC was affiliated.

Under its rule (which was adopted after Valerie enrolled at MCC), BMQA has refused to grant Valerie a license. Thus she is unable to start an internship in State A. BMQA has declined to grant her a hearing or even a meeting with BMQA personnel. As Valerie's counsel, what do you suggest? (Would your suggestions be different if State A had an APA similar to the federal APA?)

§ 3.3 THE CONFLICT BETWEEN INSTITUTIONAL AND JUDICIALIZED DECISION–MAKING

Students of the administrative process have identified two conflicting models of adjudicative decision-making. Exaggerated statements of the two models follow:

The *judicial* model suggests that an adjudicative decision by an agency is like a decision by a judge, and, therefore, that the administrative process should resemble judicial process as closely as possible. The judge should personally listen to the evidence and argument, have no preconceptions about the case, receive no information about the case except through on-the-record submissions, and be completely independent of investigators and prosecutors. Adherents of the judicial model argue that *fairness* and *acceptability* to private litigants should be primary goals of the agency adjudication process and that the achievement of those goals require no less from agency decisionmakers.

The *institutional* model views an agency as if it were a single unit with the mission of implementing a specific regulatory scheme. A number of agency personnel may take part in deciding a case and all of them should be considered as members of a decisionmaking team who should not be isolated from the rest of the team—the agency staff. The adjudication of cases is one of the techniques for accomplishing regulation—along with rulemaking, advice-giving, and publicity. Adjudication should reach results which are both accurate and consistent with similar cases. To assure results in the decision of individual cases that promote the regulatory scheme, each decisionmaker should be free to consult with any staff member who can be helpful. Adherents of the institutional model stress *accuracy* and *efficiency* as the dominant values to be pursued. As one commentator noted:

> The "institutional method," it has been said, involves "the cooperative effort of a number of officers with the agency head," bringing to bear the "cumulative efforts of specialized officers" and producing "a series of automatic internal checks" by each officer upon the data and ideas the others contribute. In this way a staff of engineers, lawyers, economists, accountants, and other specialists can work together in reaching conclusions. The safeguards to persons who have interests at stake or who are otherwise affected by the decisions an agency reaches in this manner lie in the professional training and responsibility of the officers involved, in cross-checking among them, and in the responsibility of the agency heads who coordinate the entire operation, decide finally upon the result, and must answer for all that transpires.

> Outside of government, the preponderance of human affairs calling for more than individual action is conducted by a consultative method, with or without professional participation. Business decisions are reached, human ailments are diagnosed, and club and church problems are settled in this manner. To only a slight extent are the methods of adjudication applied, as they may be, for example, in the expulsion of an individual from an organization or the dismissal of an employee from his job. In government too, foreign policy, military affairs, and the management of public enterprises and property go forward in the same way. Often vital interests of people are at stake in what transpires, as they are, for instance, in a decision whether to discontinue or move a business or where to locate a park or highway or how much to charge for a service; yet it is rarely suggested that the "hearing" of interested persons be attempted in connection with such matters, or, if it is,

that more than an interview be accorded. Arguably, the same considerations as account for the acceptance of "institutional" methods in these contexts should point to their possible use in licensing, rate fixing, and kindred operations—for which, indeed, they were thought to suffice until relatively recently.

Fuchs, "The Hearing Officer Problem—Symptom and Symbol," 40 Cornell L.Q. 281, 289–90 (1955). © 1955 by Cornell University. All rights reserved.

Although these descriptions are exaggerated and extreme, they can facilitate evaluation of administrative procedures. The administrative process strikes many compromises between these two polar models, sacrificing the virtues of one of them to secure the virtues of the other. Reconsider the chapter on due process in light of the conflict between the two models of administrative adjudication, with *Goldberg v. Kelly* standing as the epitome of the judicial model and cases like *Walters v. Radiation Survivors* representing an institutional approach. What are the advantages and disadvantages of these two forms of adjudicative decisionmaking?

This sub-chapter addresses a number of problems on the borderline between judicial and institutional decisionmaking: personal responsibility of decision-makers, separation of functions, ex parte contacts, bias, and independence of the administrative law judge. As you read this material, try to analyze it as a set of tradeoffs between judicial and institutional methods of adjudication. Has the right compromise been struck in each case—or have we gone too far toward either extreme?

§ 3.3.1 PERSONAL RESPONSIBILITY OF DECISIONMAKERS

In a judicial model, the judge hears all of the evidence and argument and makes a decision based on that input. In an institutional model, one or more persons might hear the evidence and argument but someone else might make the decision. Needless to say, this makes lawyers feel quite uneasy.

During the 1930's and 1940's, in the first of four *Morgan* cases, the Supreme Court indicated a strong preference for the judicial model. *Morgan v. United States*, 298 U.S. 468 (1936). The *Morgan* cases arose out of a ratemaking proceeding begun by the Secretary of Agriculture in 1930. The Secretary fixed the maximum rates of commission which all of the many livestock agents working in a single stockyard in Kansas City could charge. The applicable statute required a "full hearing" and it is not clear whether the decisions articulate constitutional law or whether they only interpret the statute. Would due process have required a trial-type hearing in this case if the statute had not?

In the first *Morgan* case, a large amount of evidence had been taken by a hearing examiner who did not file a report. The Acting Secretary of Agriculture heard oral argument. The parties filed briefs. The plaintiffs asserted that the Secretary of Agriculture, who later made the final decision, had not heard or read any of the evidence or argument or read the briefs. Instead, he rubber-stamped a decision made by someone else. Thus the Court assumed that the Agriculture Department had taken a purely institutional approach to making the rates.

The Court noted that the final decision might have been delegated to the Acting Secretary who heard the argument, but it had not been. The Secretary, who had not heard the case, took responsibility for the final decision.

CHIEF JUSTICE HUGHES continued:

There must be a full hearing. There must be evidence adequate to support pertinent and necessary findings of fact. Nothing can be treated as evidence which is not introduced as such . . .

Facts and circumstances which ought to be considered must not be excluded. Facts and circumstances must not be considered which should not legally influence the conclusion. Findings based on the evidence must embrace the basic facts which are needed to sustain the order. . . .

A proceeding of this sort requiring the taking and weighing of evidence, determinations of fact based upon the consideration of the evidence, and the making of an order supported by such findings, has a quality resembling that of a judicial proceeding. Hence it is frequently described as a proceeding of a quasi-judicial character. The requirement of a "full hearing" has obvious reference to the tradition of judicial proceedings in which evidence is received and weighed by the trier of the facts. The "hearing" is designed to afford the safeguard that the one who decides shall be bound in good conscience to consider the evidence, to be guided by that alone, and to reach his conclusion uninfluenced by extraneous considerations which in other fields might have play in determining purely executive action. The "hearing" is the hearing of evidence and argument. If the one who determines the facts which underlie the order has not considered evidence or argument, it is manifest that the hearing has not been given.

There is thus no basis for the contention that the authority conferred by Section 310 of the Packers and Stockyards Act is given to the Department of Agriculture, as a department in the administrative sense, so that one official may examine evidence, and another official who has not considered the evidence may make the findings and order. In such a view, it would be possible, for example, for one official to hear the evidence and argument and arrive at certain conclusions of fact, and another official who had not heard or considered either evidence or argument to overrule those conclusions and for reasons of policy to announce entirely different ones. It is no answer to say that the question for the court is whether the evidence supports the findings and the findings support the order. For the weight ascribed by the law to the findings—their conclusiveness when made within the sphere of the authority conferred—rests upon the assumption that the officer who makes the findings has addressed himself to the evidence and upon that evidence has conscientiously reached the conclusions which he deems it to justify. That duty cannot be performed by one who has not considered evidence or argument. It is not an impersonal obligation. It is a duty akin to that of a judge. The one who decides must hear.

This necessary rule does not preclude practicable administrative procedure in obtaining the aid of assistants in the department. Assistants may prosecute inquiries. Evidence may be taken by an examiner. Evidence thus taken may be sifted and analyzed by competent subordinates. Argument may be oral or written. The requirements are not technical. But there must be a hearing in a substantial sense. And to give the substance of a hearing, which is for the purpose of making determinations upon evidence, the officer who makes the determinations must consider and appraise the evidence which justifies them. That duty undoubtedly may be an onerous one, but the performance of it in a substantial manner is inseparable from the exercise of the important authority conferred. . . .

Notes and Questions

1. *"The one who decides must hear."* In the first *Morgan* case, the Supreme Court struck a powerful blow for the judicial, rather than the institutional method. Like a judge, an administrator who takes the responsibility for decision must personally have heard the case.

The decision cannot be taken literally. The Secretary was not required to actually "hear" the case or even read all of the evidence. The last paragraph of the quoted excerpt makes clear that an examiner may take the evidence and the evidence "can be sifted and analyzed by competent subordinates." However, the person making the decision "must consider and appraise the evidence" which justifies it. What is the rationale for requiring that the official taking final responsibility for an adjudicative decision "consider and appraise the evidence?"

2. *Getting around Morgan I.* Although the *Morgan I* principle seems reasonable, it is completely unrealistic. The Secretary of Agriculture is not at all like a judge. He has a vast number of administrative and regulatory duties, concerning every aspect of American agriculture, many of them extremely important to the public. He sits as a member of the President's cabinet and must constantly deal with Congress. If he is required to familiarize himself with the voluminous and technical records in all of the ratemaking cases before him, he would have time for little else. Yet this duty is far less important than his other responsibilities. The same thing is true of most federal and many state and local agencies.

In light of that reality, how can an agency comply with *Morgan I?* Consider these options:

i. As suggested by Hughes, an agency head can delegate the power to make final decisions to someone else. In fact, the Department of Agriculture has done exactly that; a "judicial officer" now makes the final decision in all cases in which a trial-type hearing is required. However, there are two problems: First, in some situations such a delegation may not be lawful because the legislature intended that the agency head personally make the decision, particularly in state or local agencies. It is necessary to research the agency enabling legislation and applicable APAs to ascertain whether decisionmaking responsibility can be delegated.

Second, adjudication is often a vehicle for making new law and setting important agency policy. Realistically, this function cannot be carried out by staff below the level of the agency head or heads. The agency head needs to keep the power to decide cases, at least sometimes, in order to maintain control over this important law and policymaking function.

ii. The person who conducts the hearing and hears the evidence could decide the case; that decision would become final unless the agency head, in his discretion, decides to consider an appeal. No party would have a right to appeal the decision to the agency head. Thus the agency head would have discretion to consider appeals only in a few significant, precedent-making situations. Is this authorized by Federal APA § 557(b) or 1981 MSAPA § 4–216(a)?

iii. The decision of the hearing officer could be subject to appeal to an intermediate review board within the agency. The agency head would have discretion to consider appeals from the intermediate review board. Such a scheme would require authorization by the agency's enabling act or other legislation.

iv. The agency head might consider only a highly condensed summary of the evidence and arguments in a case that is prepared by law clerks or other employees. The head would then decide the case solely on the basis of information contained in that summary. *See Jones v. Morris,* 541 F.Supp. 11 (S.D.Ohio 1981), *aff'd mem.,* 455 U.S. 1009 (1982).

Notice how each of these approaches departs from a pure judicial model and approaches an institutional model.

3. *Intermediate reports:* Suppose that a case is heard by a hearing officer but that the agency head makes the final decision. Two issues arise: i) must the hearing officer prepare a recommended decision? ii) if there is a recommended decision, must it be disclosed so that litigants can object to it?

Statutes generally require the hearing officer to prepare a report in order to focus the issues for the benefit of both the parties and the ultimate decisionmaker and require that it be made available to the parties and that they be given an opportunity to object to it before a final decision. *See* § 557(b), (c) of the Federal Act and 1981 MSAPA § 4–215(c), (h).

What happens, however, if no statutes are applicable? In the second *Morgan* case, the Court focussed on the failure of the hearing examiner to prepare a recommended decision. The examiner simply submitted the lengthy record to the Secretary of Agriculture. In the absence of any pleadings or recommendations by the examiner, the issues remained unfocussed and the industry was unable to brief or argue them effectively. This problem was magnified because advocates within the Department prepared recommended findings and discussed them with the Secretary (a problem discussed in § 3.3.2, *infra*).

The Court implied that due process required the preparation of an intermediate report: "Those who are brought into contest with the Government in a quasi-judicial proceeding aimed at the control of their activities are entitled to be fairly advised of what the Government proposes and to be heard upon its proposals before it issues its final command." 304 U.S. 1, 18–19. However, it seems clear that due process does not require an intermediate report in the absence of a showing of substantial prejudice from the failure to prepare one. *See NLRB v. Mackay Radio & Telegraph Co.,* 304 U.S. 333, 350–51 (1938).

Do you agree? Is not demeanor evidence lost if the party who presides does not prepare a report for the person who decides? *Compare Crow v. Industrial Com'n,* 140 P.2d 321, 326 (Utah 1943) (Wolfe, C.J. concurring): "What is required to satisfy the demands of due process, that is, of a full or fair hearing, is that he who observes the witness and listens to the evidence must transmit his observations or conclusions to those others who . . . are to decide . . . ."

If the hearing examiner prepares a recommended decision, do the parties have a right to see and object to it in the absence of a statutory requirement? *Mazza v. Cavicchia,* 105 A.2d 545 (N.J.1954) involved the revocation of a liquor license on the ground that the licensee had permitted "lewd and immoral activity on the premises." A hearing officer (called a "hearer") submitted proposed findings and recommendations to the Alcoholic Beverages Director, but the licensee was not permitted to see the report. The New Jersey Supreme Court held that due process was violated:

> The hearer may have drawn some erroneous conclusions in his report, or he may even have made some factual blunders. Such mistakes are not uncommon in both judicial and administrative proceedings; indeed, the whole process of judicial review in both fields is designed to guard against them. But if a party has no knowledge of the secret report or access to it, how is he to protect himself? . . . That is why it is a fundamental principle of all adjudication, judicial and administrative alike, that the mind of the decider should not be swayed by materials which are not communicated to both parties and which they are not given an opportunity to controvert. In the instant case the hearer can be characterized

as a "witness" giving his evidence to the judge behind the back of the appellant, who has no way of knowing what has been reported to the judge . . . Such conduct not only constitutes a violation of the principle of the exclusiveness of the record in deciding controversies, but it shocks one's sense of fair play on which our fundamental concepts of procedure are based . . .

105 A.2d at 555. Can the hearer be fairly characterized as a " 'witness' giving his evidence to the judge behind the back of the appellant?" Is the holding required by *Morgan I* and *II?* Is the case distinguishable from the *Morgan* decisions? Did the agency procedure in *Mazza* really violate the principle that the decision must be based exclusively on the record? If so, is a party constitutionally entitled to see and object to a memo from a law clerk to a judge that summarizes the record and the applicable law and makes recommendations?

4. *Morgan I in practice.* Because of the practical difficulties that would arise from taking *Morgan I* seriously, most cases brush aside claims that the decision-maker was insufficiently familiar with the record. An occasional case does find a violation. *See* F. Cooper, STATE ADMINISTRATIVE LAW 447–51 (1965); *Halley v. Lavine,* 367 N.Y.S.2d 314 (App.Div.1975) (appellate decision rendered before transcript of welfare fair hearing became available). For example, the Kansas Court of Appeals said:

Because an administrative decision must be based on evidence and not conjecture, on those occasions when the deciding authority chooses not to adopt the findings and recommendations of its hearing officer, it must examine the record independently . . . In the absence of evidence to the contrary, it will be presumed that the deciding officials have so considered the record . . . Here, however, it appears that the three board members who considered the matter were not conversant with the record to the extent required of an informed decision. All three indicated in answers to interrogatories that they had read only "portions" of the transcripts, and only one had read "some" of the exhibits. The duty of the deciding officer to consider and appraise the evidence may on occasion be an onerous one, but its performance in a substantial manner is inseparable from the exercise of the authority conferred. *Morgan v. United States* . . .

Matter of University of Kansas Faculty, 581 P.2d 817 (Kan.App. 1978). How much of a record or of the briefs must a decisionmaker read to understand a case sufficiently to decide it on the merits?

5. *Proving a violation of Morgan I.* In the *Kansas Faculty* case, the court noted the presumption that deciding officials have complied with legal requirements, such as familiarizing themselves with the record. The presumption of regularity is rebuttable, but how can it be rebutted? In the *Kansas Faculty* case, the board members responded to interrogatories about their decision-making process.

However, it is usually not possible to subject decision-makers to discovery or trial about how they made a decision. In fact, such a trial occurred at one point in the *Morgan* saga. In the fourth *Morgan* case, the Court stated:

> [T]he district court authorized the market agencies to take the deposition of the Secretary. The Secretary thereupon appeared in person at the trial. He was questioned at length regarding the process by which he reached the conclusions of his order, including the manner and extent of his study of the record and his consultation with subordinates . . . [T]he short of the business is that the Secretary should never have been subjected to this examination. The proceeding before the Secretary 'has a quality resembling that of a judicial proceeding' [citing *Morgan I*]. Such an examination of a judge would be destructive of judicial responsibility. Just as a judge cannot be subjected to such a scrutiny . . . so the integrity of the administrative process must be equally respected . . . It will bear repeating that although the administrative process has had a different development and pursues somewhat different ways from those of courts, they are to be deemed collaborative instrumentalities of justice and the appropriate independence of each should be respected by the other.

United States v. Morgan, 313 U.S. 409 (1941).

The admonition of *Morgan IV* has generally been respected by both state and federal courts, absent a strong showing of bad faith or improper behavior. As a result, counsel can only rarely raise a plausible *Morgan I* contention. The courts generally rely on the presumption of regularity and take every opportunity to explain how such consideration might have occurred, despite evidence to the contrary. See, e.g., *Altman v. Pace,* 65 P.2d 1164 (Ariz.1937). In *Altman,* the appellant complained that the stenographic notes of a workers' compensation hearing conducted by a hearing officer had not been transcribed so that the commission could not have become familiar with the evidence. The court held that, absent proof to the contrary, it must assume that the commissioners had asked the stenographer to read her notes to them; consequently it was presumed that they were familiar with the evidence.

Should the admonition of *Morgan IV* be applicable to the law clerk or secretary of a decisionmaker thereby barring most efforts to cross-examine them in order to demonstrate that the decisionmaker did not personally "consider and appraise the evidence?"

The Supreme Court approved an exception to *Morgan IV* in *Citizens to Preserve Overton Park, Inc. v. Volpe,* 401 U.S. 402 (1971), an important case discussed in § 9.4, *infra.* In *Overton Park,* the Secretary of Transportation approved a highway project in apparent violation of a statute precluding the building of roads through parks. He made no findings to explain his decision. Over a strong dissent, the

Court approved a remand to the federal district court to obtain an explanation for the Secretary's decision.

The *Overton Park* procedure should occur only where the administrator made no contemporaneous findings or explanation of his decision. If there is an explanation, the court should review the case based on that explanation; if it is unsatisfactory, it should remand to the agency for a better explanation or a new decision. *Camp v. Pitts*, 411 U.S. 138 (1973). Even where there is no explanation at all, it may be preferable to remand the case to the agency to provide an explanation rather than to conduct a trial to find out how the decision was made. See, e.g. *Zions First Nat. Bank, N.A. v. Taylor*, 390 P.2d 854 (Utah 1964). The problem of record exclusivity is considered in detail in § 6.8, *infra*.

6. *Statutory requirements.* The 1946 MSAPA required agency members personally to consider the whole record. Sec. 11 of the 1961 MSAPA omitted this provision but required agency heads to allow a party to examine a proposed decision and to present briefs *and oral argument* to the officials who made the final decision (unless a majority of them had heard the case or read the record). Under the 1981 MSAPA, however, parties must have an opportunity to file briefs upon an appeal to the agency heads but oral argument and preparation of a transcript are optional. § 4–216(e), (f). *See also* Federal APA § 557(b), (c).

If agency heads must listen to oral argument, they will become familiar with the issues in the case, thus insuring compliance with *Morgan I.* Why do you suppose that the 1981 MSAPA, unlike the 1961 MSAPA, does not require agency heads to hear oral argument?

7. *Problem.* The Mountain School District wished to discharge Rex, a tenured junior high school teacher, for drunkenness. No APA is applicable. Under the district's usual procedures, a review committee (consisting of educators) conducted a five-hour hearing on Thursday, December 3 from 9 AM to 3 PM, with one hour for lunch, in order to recommend a decision to the School Board. Rex denied that his drinking problem had ever affected his teaching in any way; he was always sober at school. The hearing was tape recorded. At 6 PM that same day, the review committee issued a brief written recommendation to the Board, stating that Rex had a drinking problem but that it had not affected his teaching. The recommendation was not furnished to Rex.

Two hours later, at 8 PM on Thursday evening, the Mountain School Board decided to fire Rex, finding that he was drunk or hung over at school on many occasions. It provided no opportunity for oral argument or the filing of briefs. The meeting of the Board was over by 9 PM. Should this decision be reversed? *See Bates v. Sponberg*, 547 F.2d 325 (6th Cir.1976).

§ 3.3.2   SEPARATION OF FUNCTIONS AND INTERNAL AGENCY COMMUNICATIONS

Many people have criticized the administrative process because a single agency makes the rules, investigates violations, prosecutes cases, and then decides those very cases. It seems that the agency acts as a legislator, investigator, prosecutor, judge and jury.

Nevertheless, the combination within a single body of all these functions is a hallmark of the administrative process and constitutional challenges to that combination have been unsuccessful. The functions are combined primarily for reasons of efficiency and effectiveness. How would the administrative process look if the various functions were split up between different bodies? *See* § 3.4.3 *infra.*

A more difficult problem is presented by the combination of investigation, prosecution, and judging functions *within a single individual.* An investigator who later decides the same case may consciously or unconsciously rely on evidence not brought into the subsequent hearing or may seek to confirm the results of the prior investigation. A person who finds probable cause to proceed against a party may be predisposed to vindicate that initial finding in the subsequent decision on the merits even though the issues are analytically distinct. Finally, a person charged with prosecuting a case who also takes part in deciding it may be predisposed to decide in favor of his own prior efforts.

A similar problem may be presented if a person engaged in investigation or prosecution or advocacy is a *supervisor* of a person engaged in decisionmaking. This is the problem of "command influence," and there is concern that a decisionmaker might slant a decision in the way that his or her boss would prefer.

Another variation of this problem is presented by internal, off-the-record *communications* between a staff member engaged in investigation or prosecution or advocacy and a person engaged in decisionmaking. While such communications may be helpful to the decisionmaker and thus serve the objective of efficiency and accuracy, such communications would be viewed as unfair by outsiders who are litigating against the agency.

To meet objections of this kind, many agencies are structured to achieve an internal separation of functions. Persons engaged in *adversary* conduct on the agency's behalf—such as investigation, prosecution, or advocacy—cannot participate in the process of making an adjudicative decision or furnish off-the-record advice to the decisionmakers or supervise persons engaged in decisionmaking.

Yet an internal separation of functions can go just so far. If rulemaking, law enforcement, and adjudicating functions are retained within a single body and if the agency heads are ultimately responsible for all of the functions, outsiders will perceive that the desk is stacked against them. Short of splitting up the agency, are there measures that can lessen the potential unfairness of this combination? This chapter discusses provisions in state and federal APAs that are designed to do so.

As background to this material, try to imagine purely judicial and institutional models of separation of functions. The criminal law completely separates its functions: it is unthinkable that a prosecutor could advise a judge, off-the-record, about how to decide the case. Judge and prosecutor are not part of the same team. Participation by prosecutors would violate due process as well as anyone's notion of appropriate procedure. At the opposite extreme, the president of a corporation, deciding whether to produce a new product, is perfectly free to gather evidence, make the case for one side, and to seek confidential advice from anybody in the firm—no holds barred. That is a pure institutional model.

§ 3.3.2a Constitutional Implications of Combination of Functions

The issue of separation of functions in agency adjudication has important due process implications. After considering the constitutional problem, we evaluate the provisions in state and federal APAs.

WITHROW v. LARKIN

421 U.S. 35 (1975).

[The Wisconsin Examining Board enforces statutes concerning medical practice. It has power to suspend or revoke medical licenses and to institute criminal proceedings. Larkin operated an abortion clinic in Milwaukee. The Board suspected Larkin of practicing medicine under another name, of allowing an unlicensed physician to perform abortions, and of illegal fee-splitting.

In June, 1973, it informed Larkin that it would hold an investigatory hearing; he and his attorney could attend but not cross-examine witnesses. The investigatory hearing occurred in July. In September, the Board notified Larkin that it would hold a contested hearing, at which it would decide whether to suspend his license temporarily, revoke it, or institute criminal proceedings against him.

A federal district court issued a preliminary injunction which barred the Board from holding the contested hearing. The Board then issued a statement that there was probable cause to believe that Larkin had committed criminal acts and ordered the District Attorney to initiate criminal proceedings against Larkin.]

WHITE, J.:

Concededly, a "fair trial in a fair tribunal is a basic requirement of due process." This applies to administrative agencies which adjudicate as well as to courts. Not only is a biased decisionmaker constitutionally unacceptable but "our system of law has always endeavored to prevent even the probability of unfairness." [13] In pursuit of this end, various situations have been identified in which experience teaches that the probability of actual bias on the part of the judge or decisionmaker is too high to be constitutionally tolerable. Among these cases are those in which the adjudicator has a pecuniary interest in the outcome and in which he has been the target of personal abuse or criticism from the party before him.

The contention that the combination of investigative and adjudicative functions necessarily creates an unconstitutional risk of bias in administrative adjudication has a much more difficult burden of persuasion to carry. It must overcome a presumption of honesty and integrity in those serving as adjudicators; and it must convince that, under a realistic appraisal of psychological tendencies and human weakness, conferring investigative and adjudicative powers on the same individuals poses such a risk of actual bias or prejudgment that the practice must be forbidden if the guarantee of due process is to be adequately implemented.

Very similarly claims have been squarely rejected in prior decisions of this Court. In FTC v. Cement Institute, 333 U.S. 683 (1948), the Federal Trade Commission had instituted proceedings concerning the respondents' multiple basing-point delivered-price system. It was demanded that the Commission members disqualify themselves because long before the Commission had filed its complaint it had investigated the parties and reported to Congress and to the President, and its members had testified before congressional committees concerning the legality of such a pricing system. At least some of the members had disclosed their opinion that the system was illegal. The issue of bias was brought here and confronted "on the assumption that such an opinion had been formed by the entire membership of the Commission as a result of its prior official investigations."

The Court rejected the claim saying:

"[T]he fact that the Commission had entertained such views as the result of its prior *ex parte* investigations did not necessarily mean that the minds of its members were irrevocably closed on the subject of the respondents' basing point practices. Here, in contrast to the Commission's investigations, members of the cement industry were legally authorized participants in the hearings. They produced evidence—volumes of it. They were free to point out to the Commission by testimony, by cross-examination of witnesses, and by arguments, conditions of the trade practices under attack which they thought kept these practices within the range of legally permissible business activities."

13. After the District Court made its decision, the Board altered its procedures. It now assigns each new case to one of the members for investigation, and the remainder of the Board has no contact with the investigative process. . . .

In specific response to a due process argument, the Court asserted:

"No decision of this Court would require us to hold that it would be a violation of procedural due process for a judge to sit in a case after he had expressed an opinion as to whether certain types of conduct were prohibited by law. In fact, judges frequently try the same case more than once and decide identical issues each time, although these issues involve questions both of law and fact. Certainly, the Federal Trade Commission cannot possibly be under stronger constitutional compulsions in this respect than a court.". . .

More recently we have sustained against due process objection a system in which a Social Security examiner has responsibility for developing the facts and making a decision as to disability claims, and observed that the challenge to this combination of functions "assumes too much and would bring down too many procedures designed, and working well, for a governmental structure of great and growing complexity." Richardson v. Perales, 402 U.S. 389, 410, (1971).

That is not to say that there is nothing to the argument that those who have investigated should not then adjudicate. The issue is substantial, it is not new, and legislators and others concerned with the operations of administrative agencies have given much attention to whether and to what extent distinctive administrative functions should be performed by the same persons. No single answer has been reached. Indeed, the growth, variety, and complexity of the administrative processes have made any one solution highly unlikely. Within the Federal Government itself, Congress has addressed the issue in several different ways, providing for varying degrees of separation from complete separation of functions to virtually none at all. For the generality of agencies, Congress has been content with § 5 of the Administrative Procedure Act, 5 U.S.C. § 554(d), which provides that no employee engaged in investigating or prosecuting may also participate or advise in the adjudicating function, but which also expressly exempts from this prohibition "the agency or a member or members of the body comprising the agency."

It is not surprising, therefore, to find that "[t]he case law, both federal and state, generally rejects the idea that the combination [of] judging [and] investigating functions is a denial of due process. . . . ." 2 K. Davis, Administrative Law Treatise § 13.02, p. 175 (1958). Similarly, our cases, although they reflect the substance of the problem, offer no support for the bald proposition applied in this case by the District Court that agency members who participate in an investigation are disqualified from adjudicating. The incredible variety of administrative mechanisms in this country will not yield to any single organizing principle.

Appellee relies heavily on In re Murchison, 349 U.S. 133 (1955), in which a state judge, empowered under state law to sit as a "one-man grand jury" and to compel witnesses to testify before him in secret about possible crimes, charged two such witnesses with criminal contempt, one for prejury and the other for refusing to answer certain questions, and then himself tried and convicted them. This Court found the procedure to be a denial of due process of law not only because the judge in effect became part of the prosecution and assumed an adversary position, but also because as a judge, passing on guilt or innocence, he very likely relied on "his own personal knowledge and impression of what had occurred in the grand jury room," an impression that "could not be tested by adequate cross-examination."

Plainly enough, *Murchison* has not been understood to stand for the broad rule that the members of an administrative agency may not investigate the facts, institute proceedings, and then make the necessary adjudications. The Court did not purport to question the *Cement Institute* case, *supra*, or the Administrative Procedure Act and did not lay down any general principle that a judge before whom an alleged contempt is committed may not bring and preside over the ensuing contempt proceedings. The accepted rule is to the contrary.

Nor is there anything in this case that comes within the strictures of *Murchison*.[20] When the Board instituted its investigative procedures, it stated only that it would investigate whether proscribed conduct had occurred. Later in noticing the adversary hearing, it asserted only that it would determine if violations had been committed which would warrant suspension of appellee's license. Without doubt, the Board then anticipated that the proceeding would eventuate in an adjudication of the issue; but there was no more evidence of bias or the risk of bias or prejudgment than inhered in the very fact that the Board had investigated and would now adjudicate. Of course, we should be alert to the possibilities of bias that may lurk in the way particular procedures actually work in practice. The processes utilized by the Board, however, do not in themselves contain an unacceptable risk of bias. The investigative proceeding had been closed to the public, but appellee and his counsel were permitted to be present throughout; counsel actually attended the hearings and knew the facts presented to the Board. No specific foundation has been presented for suspecting that the Board had been prejudiced by its investigation or would be disabled from hearing and deciding on the basis of the evidence to be presented at the contested hearing. The mere exposure to evidence presented in nonadversary investigative procedures is insufficient in itself to impugn the fairness of the Board members at a later adversary hearing. Without a showing to the contrary, state administrators "are assumed to be men of conscience and intellectual discipline, capable of

---

20. It is asserted by appellants . . . that an agency employee performed the actual investigation and gathering of evidence in this case and that an assistant attorney general then presented the evidence to the Board at the investigative hearings. While not essential to our decision upholding the constitutionality of the Board's sequence of functions, these facts, if true, show that the Board had organized itself internally to minimize the risks arising from combining investigation and adjudication, including the possibility of Board members relying at later suspension hearings upon evidence not then fully subject to effective confrontation.

judging a particular controversy fairly on the basis of its own circumstances." United States v. Morgan, 313 U.S. 409 (1941).

We are of the view, therefore, that the District Court was in error when it entered the restraining order against the Board's contested hearing and when it granted the preliminary injunction based on the untenable view that it would be unconstitutional for the Board to suspend appellee's license "at its own contested hearing on charges evolving from its own investigation. . . ." The contested hearing should have been permitted to proceed.

Nor do we think the situation substantially different because the Board, when it was prevented from going forward with the contested hearing, proceeded to make and issue formal findings of fact and conclusions of law asserting that there was probable cause to believe that appellee had engaged in various acts prohibited by the Wisconsin statutes. These findings and conclusions were verified and filed with the district attorney for the purpose of initiating revocation and criminal proceedings. Although the District Court did not emphasize this aspect of the case before it, appellee stresses it in attempting to show prejudice and prejudgment. We are not persuaded.

Judges repeatedly issue arrest warrants on the basis that there is probable cause to believe that a crime has been committed and that the person named in the warrant has committed it. Judges also preside at preliminary hearings where they must decide whether the evidence is sufficient to hold a defendant for trial. Neither of these pretrial involvements has been thought to raise any constitutional barrier against the judge's presiding over the criminal trial and, if the trial is without a jury, against making the necessary determination of guilt or innocence. Nor has it been thought that a judge is disqualified from presiding over injunction proceedings because he has initially assessed the facts in issuing or denying a temporary restraining order or a preliminary injunction. It is also very typical for the members of administrative agencies to receive the results of investigations, to approve the filing of charges or formal complaints instituting enforcement proceedings, and then to participate in the ensuing hearings. This mode of procedure does not violate the Administrative Procedure Act, and it does not violate due process of law. We should also remember that it is not contrary to due process to allow judges and administrators who have had their initial decisions reversed on appeal to confront and decide the same questions a second time around. See *Cement Institute.*

Here, the Board stayed within the accepted bounds of due process. Having investigated, it issued findings and conclusions asserting the commission of certain acts and ultimately concluding that there was probable cause to believe that appellee had violated the statutes.

The risk of bias or prejudgment in this sequence of functions has not been considered to be intolerably high or to raise a sufficiently great possibility that the adjudicators would be so psychologically wedded to their complaints that they would consciously or unconsciously avoid the appearance of having erred or changed position. Indeed, just as there is no logical inconsistency between a finding of probable cause and an acquittal in a criminal proceeding, there is no incompatibility between the agency filing a complaint based on probable cause and a subsequent decision, when all the evidence is in, that there has been no violation of the statute. Here, if the Board now proceeded after an adversary hearing to determine that appellee's license to practice should not be temporarily suspended, it would not implicitly be admitting error in its prior finding of probable cause. Its position most probably would merely reflect the benefit of a more complete view of the evidence afforded by an adversary hearing.

The initial charge or determination of probable cause and the ultimate adjudication have different bases and purposes. The fact that the same agency makes them in tandem and that they relate to the same issues does not result in a procedural due process violation. Clearly, if the initial view of the facts based on the evidence derived from non-adversarial processes as a practical or legal matter foreclosed fair and effective consideration at a subsequent adversary hearing leading to ultimate decision, a substantial due process question would be raised. But in our view, that is not this case.[25]

That the combination of investigative and adjudicative functions does not, without more, constitute a due process violation, does not, of course, preclude a court from determining from the special facts and circumstances present in the case before it that the risk of unfairness is intolerably high. Findings of that kind made by judges with special insights into local realities are entitled to respect, but injunctions resting on such factors should be accompanied by at least the minimum findings required by Rules 52(a) and 65(d).

Judgment reversed and case remanded.

Notes and Questions

1. *Due process and separation of functions. Withrow* generally upholds the constitutionality of assigning the roles of investigation, probable cause finding, and adjudication to a single agency and of combining these roles at the level of the agency heads. To that extent, it affirms that the institutional method is as compatible with due process as the judicial method. But was the decision mostly dictum? *See* note 20 of *Withrow.* The *Withrow* decision also contains a useful

---

25. Quite apart from precedents and considerations concerning the constitutionality of a combination of functions in one agency, the District Court rested its decision upon Gagnon v. Scarpelli, 411 U.S. 778 (1973), and Morrissey v. Brewer, 408 U.S. 471 (1972). These decisions, however, pose a very different question. Each held that when review of an initial decision is mandated, the decisionmaker must be oth-er than the one who made the decision under review. . . . [S]ee also Goldberg v. Kelly . . .

Allowing a decisionmaker to review and evaluate his own prior decisions raises problems that are not present here. Under the controlling statutes, the Board is at no point called upon to review its own prior decisions.

discussion of the case law concerning disqualification for bias, an issue addressed in § 3.3.3, *infra.*

2. *Scope of Withrow.* Does *Withrow* hold that a combination of investigating and probable cause finding with decisionmaking in the same person *never* violates due process? If the case does not go that far, when would such a combination of functions be unconstitutional after *Withrow*? Does *Withrow* deal with the combination in one person of the functions of prosecution and decisionmaking? Would such a combination ever be proper? Consider the various cases which the *Withrow* decision distinguishes.

Recall the very end of *Goldberg v. Kelly:* "And, of course, an impartial decision maker is essential. We agree with the District Court that prior involvement in some aspects of a case will not necessarily bar a welfare official from acting as a decision maker. He should not, however, have participated in making the determination under review." *See* note 25 of *Withrow.*

What is the difference between the combination of functions prohibited by *Goldberg* and that upheld in *Withrow?* Wouldn't the Medical Board, at its contested hearing, be reviewing its own prior decision that there was probable cause to believe that Larkin had violated the law?

3. *Involvement of the attorney general.* State agencies often have small staffs and are composed of part-time agency heads. It is not uncommon for the staff of the state attorney general to play the prosecutorial role before such agencies. In such cases, can the attorney general's staff also advise the agency decisionmakers? *Compare Matter of Johnston,* 663 P.2d 457 (Wash.1983) (dictum) *with Hladys v. Commonwealth,* 366 S.E.2d 98 (Va.1988). *Johnston* indicated that the same assistant attorney general could not perform both roles, but *Hladys* held that different assistant attorneys general could prosecute the case and advise an ALJ about procedural issues, provided that they do not discuss the case with each other.

§ 3.3.2b *Statutory Solutions to Combination of Functions*

APA § 554(d) covers a number of issues relating to separation of functions. We emphasize first the language which begins *after* § 554(d) (2): "An employee or agent engaged in the performance of investigative or prosecuting functions . . ." and runs to the end of (C). Also concentrate on 1981 MSAPA § 4–214(a) and (c). *See generally* Asimow, "*When the Curtain Falls: Separation of Functions in the Federal Administrative Agencies,*" 81 Colum.L.Rev. 759, 761–79 (1981).

The purpose of APA § 554(d) was summarized by the Ninth Circuit in *Grolier Inc. v. F.T.C.,* 615 F.2d 1215 (9th Cir.1980), *cert. denied,* 464 U.S. 891 (1983):

In responding to the much criticized union of the investigative, prosecutive, and adjudicative functions within agencies, the report [of the Attorney General's Committee in 1941] suggested the creation of hearing commissioners, now administrative law judges, as a "separate unit in each agency's organization . . . ." Two reasons . . . were given for this recommended separation: "the investigators, if allowed to participate [in adjudication] would be likely to interpolate facts and information discovered by them ex parte and not adduced at the hearing . . ." and "[a] man who has buried himself in one side of an issue is disabled from bringing to its decision that dispassionate judgment which Anglo–American tradition demands of officials who decide questions."

Note the exception from required separation of functions for agency heads in § 554(d)(C). Why did the APA drafters create this exception? Is there a comparable exception in 1981 MSAPA § 4–214?

The Attorney General's Memorandum on the APA explained the (C) exception as follows: "Thus, if a member of the Interstate Commerce Commission actively participates in or directs the investigation of an adjudicatory case, he will not be precluded from participating with his colleagues in the decision of that case." *Id.* at 58. Recall *Withrow* and the discussion of the APA in that case and *see Blinder, Robinson & Co. v. SEC,* 837 F.2d 1099 (D.C.Cir.1988), *pet. for cert. pending* (SEC agency heads can obtain judicial injunction against stockbroker and, at the same time, proceed administratively to suspend his license).

Could the hypothetical member of the ICC both investigate and adjudicate under 1981 MSAPA § 4–214? Should there be a difference between separation of functions provisions in state and federal law? The prohibition against separation of functions in 1981 MSAPA may pose difficult problems for state agencies that often have much smaller staffs than most federal agencies. Because there may be relatively few people to carry out agency functions, it may be difficult to separate functions in such agencies. In such cases, would you recommend that the adjudication function be carried out by some other agency?

§ 3.3.2c   *Internal Agency Communications*

The second *Morgan* case involved a dispute about internal agency communications between counsel representing the agency in the proceeding and the Secretary of Agriculture who was the final decisionmaker in the case. *Morgan v. United States,* 304 U.S. 1 (1938).

After a lengthy but rather diffuse hearing before an examiner on the economics of the stockyards industry, the examiner submitted the record without any preliminary decision to the Secretary for a decision. When it came time for the Secretary to decide, the industry filed briefs and argued orally before the Acting Secretary. However, without any pleadings or initial decision, the issues remained unfocussed. The respondents were never informed precisely what the government wanted or what the issues were. Recall discussion of whether *Morgan II* requires preparation of a recommended decision by the hearing officer in § 3.3.1, n. 3 *supra.*

Agency advocates then prepared and submitted to the Secretary findings of fact which the industry never saw; the advocates also discussed the findings with the Secretary who substantially accepted them. The Court said:

> If in an equity cause, a special master or the trial judge permitted the plaintiff's attorney to formulate the findings upon the evidence, conferred ex parte with the plaintiff's attorney regarding them, and then adopted his proposals without affording an opportunity to his opponent to know their contents and present objections, there would be no hesitation in setting aside the report or decree as having been made without a fair hearing. The requirements of fairness are not exhausted in the taking or consideration of evidence but extend to the concluding parts of the procedure as well as to the beginning and intermediate steps.

As a result, the Court held that the Secretary's order was invalid. Is *Morgan II* consistent with *Withrow*? With *Goldberg v. Kelly?*

Notes and Questions

1. *Some hypotheticals—communications with ALJ's.* Treat each agency as either federal or state. Apply APA § 554(d) for federal agencies and 1981 MSAPA §§ 4–214(a) and (c) and 4–213(b) for state agencies. If the internal communication is permissible under the statute, consider whether it violates due process.

Hypothetical i. The FAA has statutory power to suspend or revoke a pilot's license. It proposed to suspend Mary's license for 20 days because of a failure to file flight plans as required by FAA rules. Len is the FAA investigator who discovered Mary's alleged violation. Although no statute requires FAA to hold a hearing in suspension cases, its rules provides for an informal hearing before an administrative law judge (ALJ). Frank was the ALJ who conducted Mary's hearing. After it was over, Len ran into Frank in the FAA cafeteria. He urged Frank to suspend Mary's license because "we've got to get tough with these private pilots."

Hypothetical ii. In order to discharge pollutants into navigable waters, Trashco must obtain a permit from the EPA. The statute requires a hearing on the record before a permit is denied. Rex is the EPA lawyer assigned to the case and he believes that the permit should not be granted. There is a hearing before Marge, an ALJ. After the hearing is concluded, Rex visits Marge in her office and explains some highly technical evidence in the record which she did not understand.

2. *The agency heads exception.* What is the impact of the agency heads exception in § 554(d)(C) on the rules concerning internal agency communications?

Hypothetical iii: The Federal Trade Commission (FTC) accused Ned of fraudulent practices in the sale of encyclopedias. Gloria was the FTC's prosecutor. The ALJ ruled against Ned and he appeals to the agency heads. While the matter is before them, Gloria discusses the merits of the case with Barbara, one of the agency heads. Is Gloria's action permissible?

No. The exception for "the agency or a member or members of the body comprising the agency" in § 554(d)(C) does *not* cover this discussion by Gloria. Therefore, it violates the APA rules against internal communications. If this were not so, part of § 554(d) would make no sense. Observe that § 554(d) precludes investigators or prosecutors from participating or advising in the "agency review."

See Attorney General's Memorandum on the APA 56 (1947): ". . . on 'agency review' the agency heads, as well as the hearing examiner, will be precluded from consulting or obtaining advice from any officer or employee [who] has participated in the investigation or prosecution."

3. *Discussions at the investigatory stage.* In many agencies, such as the FTC, the agency heads, not the staff, make the decision to issue a complaint. Thus they must consult with staff members who have investigated the case. That discussion exposes the commissioners to factual information about the case—and they hear it from the point of view of the investigators.

Months or years later, the same case returns to the agency heads for a final decision. The same agency heads who took part in the discussion about issuing a complaint then vote on whether a violation of law has occurred. APA § 554(d) does not preclude this particular combination of functions. *See Grolier, Inc. v. FTC, supra.* What result under 1981 MSAPA § 4–214(c)?

> It could be argued that the exposure to adversary presentation inherent in a predecisional conference threatens to contaminate the ultimate decisionmaking. The stock response to this claim is that agency heads do no more than a trial judge who rules on pretrial motions or requests for preliminary injunctions, or who engages in conferences to settle the case . . . and then proceeds to adjudicate the case . . . As a practical matter, the danger of tainting a final administrative decision by predecisional conferences is rather remote; memories fade and there is substantial turnover of both agency heads and advisers during the typically lengthy period between the preliminary conference and ultimate agency-level consideration. More fundamentally, however, the participation of adversaries in predecisional conferences is essential if an agency is to exercise combined functions of investigation, prosecution, and adjudication. By allowing these conferences, despite the fact that they entail off-record exposure to information, the APA strikes a balance between fairness and pragmatism. Separation of functions in administrative agencies is, of necessity, far from the pristine system characteristic of criminal-law enforcement.

Asimow, *supra,* 81 Colum.L.Rev. 759, 767–68.

Do you agree? If you see pre-decisional conferences between adjudicative decisionmakers and adversaries as objectionable, can the problem be avoided by any method short of disqualifying the agency heads from voting? *See* Elman, "A Note on Administrative Adjudication," 74 Yale L.J. 652, 654 (1965) (suggesting delegation of complaint-issuance decision to staff).

4. *Law clerks.* The same rules that apply to agency heads apply to their law clerks. A clerk can take part in a conference about whether to issue a complaint, then advise her boss at the time of the final decision in the case. By the same token, if an agency prosecutor could not discuss the case with an agency head, he would be prohibited from discussing it with the agency head's law clerk. *Grolier, Inc. v. FTC, supra.*

However, *Grolier* also held that a law clerk's exemption lasts only as long as the clerk keeps working for the agency head. A clerk who participates in a discussion about whether to issue a complaint against a respondent cannot then change jobs and serve as an ALJ in a case against that respondent.

5. *Conferences by ALJ's.* Note federal APA § 554(d)(1). That section states that an ALJ "may not (1) consult a person or party on a fact in issue, unless on notice and opportunity for all parties to participate . . ."

Hypothetical iv: Ken is an ALJ in a case before the EPA involving unlawful water pollution. The evidence included a great deal of complex technical material. After the hearing concludes, he realizes that he does not understand some of the equations used by witnesses. He calls Helen, an EPA chemist who has not been involved at all in the case. Helen explains the material that confused Ken. Does this conference violate the APA rule against internal communications? Does it violate § 554(d)(1)? Does it violate 1981 MSAPA § 4–214(a) and 4–213(b)?

The Supreme Court has said of § 554(d)(1): "Nor may a hearing examiner consult any person or party, *including* other agency officials, concerning a fact at issue in the hearing, unless on notice and opportunity for all parties to participate." *Butz v. Economou,* 438 U.S. 478, 514 (1978) (emphasis added). *See generally* Mathias, "The Use of Legal and Technical Assistants by Administrative Law Judges in Administrative Proceedings," 1 Admin.L.J. 107 (1987).

6. *Assistance for decisionmakers.* Agency decisionmakers often need assistance from other agency staff in making their decisions. What off-the-record assistance is permissible to ALJ's? To intermediate appeal boards? To agency heads? Note 1981 MSAPA § 4–213(b) and 1961 MSAPA § 13 ("An agency member (1) may communicate with other members of the agency, and (2) may have the aid and advice of one or more personal assistants.")

§ 3.3.2d *Command Influence*

An additional separation of functions problem arises when an agency decisionmaker is supervised by a person engaged in investigation or prosecution. Obviously, the decisionmaker might be reluctant to render a decision against the wishes of his or her boss.

The federal act addresses this problem in § 554(d)(2) and 1981 MSAPA addresses it in § 4–214(b). Are these provisions likely to be effective?

It appears that command influence over a decisionmaker does not violate due process in the absence of a particularized showing of prejudice. In *Marcello v. Bonds,* 349 U.S. 302 (1955), the Supreme Court indicated that command influence is not a due process violation in a deportation case where there was no showing of prejudice. Such prejudice might be shown in cases where the superior actually engaged in investigation or advocacy in the case or sought to influence the decision. *See also Jonal Corp. v. District of Columbia,* 533 F.2d 1192 (D.C.Cir.1976), cert. denied, 429 U.S. 825 (1976).

Compare *State ex rel. Ellis v. Kelly,* 112 S.E.2d 641 (W.V.Sup.Ct. 1960) overturning a decision revoking a license. "It can hardly be contended that the commissioner, in the making of the investigation and in testifying before the deputy commissioner appointed by him and responsible to him, beyond any reasonable probability, did not become biased and prejudiced in the matter being heard . . . It would seem clear . . . that the deputy commissioner could not have acted with impartiality . . . His actions were for the commissioner, and could not be expected to be free and independent of his influence . . . ." *Id.* at 644.

§ 3.3.2e *The Principle of Necessity*

Under the "principle of necessity," a biased or otherwise disqualified judge can decide a case if there is no legally possible substitute decisionmaker. It is better, in other words, that a possibly unfair decision be made than that no decision be made at all (and a wrongdoer go unpunished or the public unprotected). Does the principle of necessity help to explain cases like *Withrow* and *Cement Institute?* How is it consistent with *Morgan II* and *Goldberg v. Kelly?*

§ 3.3.3 BIAS: PERSONAL INTEREST, PREJUDGMENT, PERSONAL ANIMUS

The previous section considered one kind of bias: a person engaged as a prosecutor, investigator, or advocate may find it difficult to take off the adversary hat and put on an adjudicating hat. This section considers additional problems of decisionmaker impartiality: an adjudicator is disqualified if tainted by personal animus (that is, prejudice or hostility toward a party), prejudgment of the issues, or a personal stake in the decision. As in the previous section, the fundamental question is whether an administrative adjudicator (ALJ or agency head) must be as impartial as a judge. How impartial is that?

Recall the dictum about bias in *Withrow:*

> Concededly, a "fair trial in a fair tribunal is a basic requirement of due process." This applies to administrative agencies which adjudicate as well as to courts. Not only is a biased decisionmaker constitutionally unacceptable but "our system of law has always endeavored to prevent even the probability of unfairness . . ."

> . . . [V]arious situations have been identified in which experience teaches that the probability of actual bias on the part of the judge or decisionmaker is too high to be constitutionally tolerable. Among these cases are those in which the adjudicator has a pecuniary interest in the outcome and in which he has been the target of personal abuse or criticism from the party before him.

Note the relationship between disqualification for bias and the right to a hearing. The purpose of a hearing is to provide a framework within which a decision may be made on the basis of the evidence and arguments introduced at that proceeding. If a decisionmaker renders a decision on the basis of bias rather than on the basis of material in the hearing record, the hearing is superfluous.

ANDREWS v. AGRICULTURAL LABOR RELATIONS BOARD
623 P.2d 151 (Cal.1981).

[The general counsel of ALRB filed a complaint against Andrews alleging unfair labor practices in violation of the California Agricultural Labor Relations Act (ALRA). The charges arose out of a contested election that was lost by the United Farm Workers (UFW). The Board appointed Armando Menocal as a temporary Administrative Law Officer (ALO) to hear the case. Menocal was an attorney in private practice with Public Advocates, a San Francisco public interest law firm. Counsel for Andrews moved to disqualify Menocal on the ground of bias because he and Public Advocates work on racial employment discrimination cases on behalf of Mexican–Americans. Menocal refused to disqualify himself. He found against Andrews. The ALRB affirmed the decision, declaring that it had made an independent review of the entire record.]

MOSK, J:

Petitioners imply that a ground for bias was the ALO's practice of law with a firm which in the past had represented individual farm workers in a suit against the Secretary of Labor and which engaged in employment discrimination suits on behalf of Mexican–Americans. From this, it appears we are to infer that the ALO has some philosophical or political inclination that would make it impossible for him to conduct hearings impartially. Even if the nature of a lawyer's practice could be taken as evidence of his political or social outlook,[3] such evidence, as will appear, is irrelevant to prove bias. Therefore, rather than review the nature of the cases in which the ALO or his firm has participated or attempt to identify what viewpoints those cases might possibly suggest, we will simply reaffirm the general principles that make doing so unnecessary.

The right to an impartial trier of fact is not synonymous with the claimed right to a trier completely indifferent to the general subject matter of the claim before him. . . . The word bias refers " 'to the mental attitude or disposition of the judge towards a party to the litigation, and not to any views that he may entertain regarding the subject matter involved.' " In an administrative context, Professor Davis has written that "Bias in the sense of crystallized point of view about issues of law or policy is almost universally deemed no ground for disqualification." (2 Davis, Administrative Law Treatise (1st ed. 1958) p. 131; also see Morgan IV; *Trade Comm'n. v. Cement Institute* (1948) 333 U.S. 683. This long established, practical rule is merely a recognition of the fact that anyone acting in a judicial role will have attitudes and preconceptions toward some of the legal and social issues that may come before him.

Petitioners revive the same discarded stereotype of bias relative to disqualifying a judicial officer that Judge Jerome Frank addressed many years ago: "Democracy must, indeed, fail unless our courts try cases fairly, and there can be no fair trial before a judge lacking in impartiality and disinterestedness. If, however, 'bias' and 'partiality' be defined to mean the total absence of preconceptions in the mind of the judge, then no one has ever had a fair trial and no one ever will. The human mind, even at infancy, is no blank piece of paper. We are born with predispositions; and the process of education, formal and informal, creates attitudes in all men which affect them in judging situations, attitudes which preceded reasoning in particular instances and which, therefore, by definition, are prejudices. . . . Interests, points of view, preferences, are the essence of living. Only death yields complete dispassionateness, for such dispassionateness signifies utter indifference." . . .

Therefore, even if the viewpoint attributed to an ALO could be inferred from the nature of his legal practice or his clients—which we do not concede—that would be no ground for disqualification. A trier of fact with expressed political or legal views cannot be disqualified on that basis alone even in controversial cases. The more politically or socially sensitive a matter, the more likely it is that the ALO, like most intelligent citizens, will have at some time reached an opinion on the

---

3. Amici assert persuasively that imputing the values of a client to a lawyer is an improper exercise inevitably fraught with dangers of erroneous conclusions. That view is consistent with the American Bar Association Code of Professional Responsibility, E.C. 2–27, which urges every lawyer to accept representation of "unpopular clients and causes . . . [r]egardless of his personal feelings. . . ."

issue. This is an unavoidable feature of a legal system dependent on human beings rather than robots for dispute resolution.

Even assuming, arguendo, the political or legal views of an ALO could result in an appearance of bias, we cannot hold, as requested by petitioners, that a mere appearance of bias is a ground for the disqualification of a judicial officer . . . Appearance, after all, is generally in the eye of the beholder. . . .

Thus, our courts have never required the disqualification of a judge unless the moving party has been able to demonstrate concretely the actual existence of bias.[5] We cannot now exchange this established principle for one as vague, unmanageable and laden with potential mischief as an "appearance of bias" standard, despite our deep concern for the objective and impartial discharge of all judicial duties in this state.

The foregoing considerations, of course, are equally applicable to the disqualification of a judicial officer in the administrative system. Indeed, the appearance of bias standard may be particularly untenable in certain administrative settings. For example, in an unfair labor practice proceeding the Board is the ultimate factfinder, not the ALO. We therefore fail to see how a mere subjective belief in the ALO's appearance of bias, as distinguished from actual bias, can prejudice either party when the Board is responsible for making factual determinations, upon an independent review of the record. In the case at bar the Board declared it did undertake such an independent review of the entire record.

Appellants further contend that the temporary status of the ALO herein should be recognized as a factor in the disqualification analysis because of his increased susceptibility to bias due to the potential influences of a continuing legal practice. However, we know of no case, nor have we been cited to any, that stands for the proposition that a pro tempore judicial officer is peculiarly vulnerable to a disqualification challenge because he is engaged in the practice of law before and after his temporary public service.[6] . . .

5. Of course, there are some situations in which the probability of likelihood of the existence of actual bias is so great that disqualification of a judicial officer is required to preserve the integrity of the legal system, even without proof that the judicial officer is actually biased towards a party. (See e.g., *Tumey v. Ohio* (1927) 273 U.S. 510, in which a judge was disqualified because of his financial stake in the outcome.) In California, these situations are codified in Code of Civil Procedure section 170, subdivisions 1–4. They include cases in which the judicial officer either has a personal or financial interest, has a familial relation to a party or attorney, or has been counsel to a party. The Legislature has demanded disqualification in these special situations regardless of the fact that the judicial officer nevertheless may be able to discharge his duties impartially. The evident and justifiable rationale for mandatory disqualification in all such circumstances is apprehension of an appearance of unfairness or bias. . . .

6. We note that under canon 5F of the Code of Judicial Conduct, a judge, being under a duty to regulate his extrajudicial activities so as to minimize the risk of conflict with his judicial duties, is not allowed to practice law. However, compliance section B(1) of the code specifically exempts judges pro tempore from canon 5F.

Petitioners finally contend that bias appears on the face of the ALO's findings and recommended decision. However, because this contention rests on an erroneous legal foundation, there is no need for us to examine the substance of his report.

It is first asserted that bias may be shown by the fact that some of a hearing officer's findings are not supported by substantial evidence. The fallacy of this assertion is explained in Gellhorn et al., Administrative Law—Cases and Comments (7th ed. 1979) page 767: "If the fact finder has allegedly credited unsubstantial evidence while disregarding utterly irrefutable evidence, the issue before a reviewing court should not be whether the fact finder was biased, but whether his findings of fact are supported by substantial evidence on the whole record." If the challenged findings are not supported by substantial evidence, it is the duty of the reviewing court to overturn those findings and it will do so because of failure of proof, not because the results per se establish bias.

There is no reason to explore the heart and mind of the ALO when effective relief is readily available if the reviewing court concludes a finding is unsupported by substantial evidence. To hold otherwise would encourage a losing party to raise the specter of bias indiscriminately, whenever he could demonstrate that one finding of fact in a large administrative record was not sufficiently supported. We decline to cast that cloud of uncertainty over adjudicative proceedings.

But, petitioners assert, that bias may be established where the record shows the hearing officer uniformly believed evidence introduced by the union and uniformly disbelieved evidence produced by the employer. . . . [Numerous and continuous rulings against a litigant, even when erroneous, form no ground for a charge of bias or prejudice. This rule is tenable in both a judicial and an administrative context. To fulfill his duty, an ALO must make choices when conflicting evidence is offered; thus, his reliance on certain witnesses and rejection of others cannot be evidence of bias no matter how consistently the ALO rejects or doubts the testimony produced by one of the adversaries. . . .

It follows that the ALO did not err in refusing to disqualify himself.

NEWMAN, J., Concurring— . . .

The final paragraph of the 20–page Court of Appeal opinion in this case reads: "Although the ALO could not perceive the justification of petitioners' position, it seems patently clear to us that an attorney, employed by Public Advocates, Inc. in 1975 or 1976, would be perceived as biased against employers generally in disputes against unskilled low paid Spanish-surnamed workers, asserting a community of interests and that he would particularly appear to be biased against an agricultural employer in a dispute with the UFW." . . . My views are outlined briefly in these final paragraphs of the letter to this court filed on March 21, 1980, by California Rural Legal Assistance, Channel Counties Legal Services Association, and the Mexican American Legal Defense and Education Fund:

[T]here is a very troubling aspect of the *Andrews* decision below which requires a sensitive, careful and decisive review by this court. Most of the cases cited by the court as 'politically sensitive' involve clients or groups with hispanic names. Significantly, some of these cases in no way involve employment related issues. . . . The only relationship of these cases to *Andrews* is a common ethnicity among some of the parties. In this context, it is noteworthy that the administrative law officer in *Andrews* also carries an hispanic surname. The court below said that it seemed clear that Menocal 'would be perceived as biased against employers generally in disputes against unskilled low paid *Spanish-surnamed workers*' . . . . It is incumbent upon this Court to ensure that there is no hint of law in this state that an individual cannot serve as a decision-maker in a case involving a class of litigants on one side or the other who share a cultural or racial or sexual identity with the decision-maker or his/her clients. . . .

CLARK, J.—I dissent.

The appearance of bias—those circumstances leading a reasonable person to doubt the impartiality of the trier of fact—is not only a sufficient but a compelling ground for disqualification. Disqualification on the basis that a quasi-judicial officer appears biased is essential to the health and stability of the adjudicative process for two fundamental reasons. 1. The litigant's due process right to a fair hearing is protected. 2. Public confidence in the integrity of our system of justice is sustained.

The United States Supreme Court has long recognized the due process right to a fair trial in a tribunal free from even the appearance of bias. "[E]ven if there is no showing of actual bias in the tribunal, this Court has held that due process is denied by circumstances that create *the likelihood or the appearance of bias.*"

Freedom from the appearance of bias has also been recognized as essential to public respect for, and belief in, the adjudicative process. . . .

By requiring the near impossible—a showing of actual bias—before a quasi-judicial official must disqualify himself, the majority fail to protect due process and public confidence concerns. The "actual bias" standard protects only against the most egregious and flagrant instances of bias. Only in truly rare cases will such blatant displays of bias be openly disclosed. Bias, unlike other deprivations of due process which may be clearly determined on the record, is generally an invisible influence and for that reason must be particularly guarded against.

Under today's ruling, a party appearing before the ALRB will be left without recourse against deprivation of due process by an ALO with an apparently powerful but unprovable predisposition against such party. . . .

Admittedly, use of an "appearance of bias" standard may result in disqualifications both in cases of actual bias and in cases where there is no bias. But when an individual's fundamental right to a fair hearing is at stake, is it not better to err on the side of justice rather than to impose the risk that in an instance of actual but unprovable bias the prejudiced party will be without remedy? . . .

The majority agree that the nature of the ALO's law practice is irrelevant to prove bias, because bias refers to a mental attitude towards a party and not to political or social viewpoints regarding subject matter. However, when an ALO's law firm consistently represents the same limited class of clients, it may be reasonably concluded the ALO is programmed not only to a particular viewpoint on legal and social issues but also to a bias in favor of the particular class he represents and, correspondingly, to a predisposition against those classes generally cast in an opposing role. Bias against a class of which a party is a member is sufficient grounds for disqualification.

The majority argue that because the ALRB may itself engage in factfinding upon its independent review of the record, there exists an adequate remedy when it appears an ALO has been biased. However, after substantial investment of money and other resources in conducting a hearing and producing a decision, the ALRB is naturally reluctant to overturn such decision for any reason other than clear error on the record. Moreover, subtle but nonetheless unfair findings and other influences attributable to a biased ALO cannot be effectively recognized, established or challenged on an administrative record. In the instant case the ALRB adopted essentially all of the ALO's findings and recommendations, not even addressing the issue of the ALO's bias . . .

The record establishes as a matter of law an appearance of bias—denying to petitioners due process of law—when the ALO refused to step aside from this case five years ago. The writ should be granted and the decision set aside.

RICHARDSON, J., concurred.

Notes and Questions

1. *Personal interest.* One well established ground for disqualification of an adjudicator is personal interest—that the decisionmaker or her family has a personal (usually, but not necessarily, a financial) stake in the decision. A personal interest creates such a serious risk of bias that the decisionmaker is automatically disqualified, whether actually biased or not. An easy case of this kind is *Tumey v. Ohio,* discussed in note 5 of *Andrews.*

A more arguable application of the doctrine is *Ward v. City of Monroeville,* 409 U.S. 57 (1972). That case held that a small town mayor must be disqualified from serving as a traffic court judge. The fines went into the city treasury, not the mayor's pocket. However, the fines were a significant part of the town's budget; the more fines the mayor collected as traffic judge, the less taxes he would have to levy on his constituents.

Could a bias for interest argument have been leveled against Menocal in *Andrews* either with respect to future business he might gain or lose in his private practice because of his decision or because of the likelihood of his being rehired by ALRB as a temporary ALO in future cases?

A statute relating to federal *judges* spells out precisely what financial interests are prohibited. The judge must disqualify himself if he "knows that he, individually or as a fiduciary, or his spouse or minor child residing in his household, has a financial interest in the subject matter in controversy or in a party to the proceeding, or any other interest that could be substantially affected by the outcome of the proceeding." 28 U.S.C. § 455(b)(4). The section goes on to define what is or is not a prohibited "financial interest" in painstaking detail. § 455(d)(4). Would this standard require Menocal to be disqualified? See n. 6 in *Andrews*.

As *Andrews* makes clear, the standards for disqualification of judges do not apply to administrative adjudicators. This is particularly true of part-time, unpaid, elected adjudicators who sit on local boards that engage in executive and legislative functions as well as deciding cases involving land use. *See 1000 Friends of Oregon v. Wasco County Court,* 742 P.2d 39 (Or.1987). In the *1000 Friends* case, a county commissioner had sold cattle at an inflated price to persons seeking to incorporate a city. The commissioner later voted in favor of incorporation; he had nothing to gain at the time of the vote. The court rejected the "appearance of bias" standard applicable to judges, holding that this would be inappropriately applied to the board in question.

What if the decision-makers *by profession* have a pecuniary interest adverse to the private party? In a controversial decision, the Supreme Court disqualified an entire licensing agency for this reason. By law, a state agency regulating optometry was composed solely of *independent* optometrists (who operate their own private establishments). The agency determined that optometrists may not work for corporate employers and if they do may lose their license. The Court upheld a lower court's finding that the agency was biased for interest against optometrists who work for corporations. The board members had a personal pecuniary interest in limiting entry into the field to independent optometrists like themselves and keeping corporate chain stores out. *Gibson v. Berryhill,* 411 U.S. 564 (1973). *Gibson* is particularly striking since it ignores the rule of necessity: unless the legislature restructures the agency's membership, there is no agency competent to prohibit corporate optometry practice even if that prohibition is otherwise desirable.

In a later case, the Court considered whether a statute setting up an optometry board consisting of a *majority* of independent optometrists was unconstitutional. It held that the statute was not facially invalid; a bias for interest claim must be based on a particularized analysis of the facts presented; as a result, a board may be properly constituted for most purposes yet potentially disqualified for others because of personal interest. *Friedman v. Rogers,* 440 U.S. 1, 18–19 (1979). Would the board members in the *Friedman* case be disqualified under § 455(b)(4) (defining prohibited financial interests for federal judges)?

2. *Actual bias.* Actual bias may be of two kinds: i) prejudgment of the individualized facts of a case or ii) animus (prejudice) against a particular litigant (or a class which includes that litigant). If a decision-maker's previous statements indicate that either kind of bias is present, due process requires that the decision-maker be disqualified.

However, a prejudgment of the individualized, case-specific facts is not disqualifying where it arises out of a normal agency function. Thus, for example, an ALJ who decides a case against a party is not disqualified from deciding it again after remand by the agency. *NLRB v. Donnelly Garment Co.,* 330 U.S. 219 (1947). Similarly, a school board that conducts negotiations with a teachers' union is not disqualified from discharging teachers who participated in an illegal strike. *Hortonville Joint School District v. Hortonville Educational Ass'n,* 426 U.S. 482 (1976).

In *Hortonville,* there was no dispute about the identity of the striking teachers or about the existence of the strike, the fact that the teachers were on strike and their identities were uncontroverted. The Court rejected claims that the school board was disqualified because of personal interest or prejudice against the teachers. "The teachers did not show . . . that the Board members had the kind of personal or financial stake in the decision that might create a conflict of interest, and there is nothing in the record to support charges of personal animosity . . . Mere familiarity with the facts of a case gained by an agency in the performance of its statutory role does not . . . disqualify a decisionmaker . . . Nor is a decisionmaker disqualified simply because he has taken a position even in public, on a policy issue related to the dispute, in the absence of a showing that he is not 'capable of judging a particular controversy fairly on the basis of its own circumstances . . .' The Board's decision was only incidentally a disciplinary decision; it had significant governmental and public policy dimensions as well." 426 U.S. at 495. The dissenters argued that the discharge decision required the board members to evaluate their own negotiating conduct. As a result, they could not be objective.

On the issue of disqualification because of prior involvement in the dispute, compare *FTC v. Cement Institute,* 333 U.S. 683 (1948) with *American Cyanamid Co. v. FTC,* 363 F.2d 757 (6th Cir.1966), *cert. denied,* 394 U.S. 920 (1969). In *Cement Institute,* the Court upheld a decision by the FTC against the multiple basing-point pricing system used by cement companies. The members of the FTC had previously supervised an investigation of basing-point pricing and testified to

Congress that the system was illegal. Does this indicate that the Commission had prejudged specific factual issues pertaining to the parties that had to be resolved in the cement company case?

In *American Cyanamid*, Dixon, the chair of the FTC, had previously worked as counsel to a Senate committee which investigated the marketing of tetracycline. In that capacity, Dixon had extensively studied the facts, conducted hearings on the subject, and helped write a report which found that certain specific companies had engaged in various illegal activities. He also probably wrote a letter (signed by Senator Kefauver) to the FTC in support of an ALJ decision in the tetracycline case. Then he became FTC chair and voted in favor of a decision which held the same practices illegal. The court of appeals held that he should have been disqualified and the decision was reversed (even though Dixon's vote was not necessary to make a majority).

Can you distinguish *Cement Institute* from *American Cyanamid?* Could both cases be correctly decided?

3. *The appearance of bias.* Is the *Andrews* majority correct that an appearance of bias (without proof of actual bias) does not violate due process? Compare the dictum from *Withrow* at the beginning of this section. See also 28 U.S.C. § 455(a): "Any . . . judge . . . of the United States shall disqualify himself in any proceeding in which his impartiality might reasonably be questioned."

Does the fact that Menocal ruled for the union on every point, believed all of its witnesses and disbelieved the grower's witnesses, establish that he was biased in the union's favor?

If it could be shown that Menocal was philosophically committed to the rights of California farm workers (who are overwhelmingly of Hispanic origin), should he be disqualified from judging in the *Andrews* case? Would the dissent have found Menocal biased if his law firm did tax work for farmers? What if Menocal had strong opinions about how the Agricultural Labor Relations Act should be interpreted?

4. *Raising the bias issue.* Federal APA § 556(b) sets forth the procedure for challenging an ALJ for bias. It does not explain how to challenge the impartiality of an agency member. 1981 MSAPA § 4–202(b)–(f) explains the procedure for challenging a "presiding officer" for bias. As made clear in 1981 MSAPA § 4–216(d), the term "presiding officer" covers both the staff member who hears a case and the persons who decide an appeal (including agency heads).

Notice especially § 4–202(e) and (f). What is the effect of these provisions on the "rule of necessity?" Suppose that an agency is headed by a single person who is biased against a litigant before the agency. Should that person decide the case because of the rule of necessity, or is there a way around the problem? *See International Harvester Co. v. Bowling*, 391 N.E.2d 168 (Ill.App.1979); *Matter of Rollins Environmental Services, Inc.*, 481 So.2d 113 (La.1985). Both cases apply statutes allowing the governor to replace an agency head who is disqualified for bias.

Compare these provisions to the statutes relating to disqualification of federal trial judges: if a party files a "timely and sufficient affidavit that the judge before whom the matter is pending has a personal bias or prejudice either against him or in favor of any adverse party, such judge shall proceed no further therein . . . A party may file only one such affidavit in any case. It shall be accompanied by a certificate of counsel of record stating that it is made in good faith." 28 U.S.C. § 144. 28 U.S.C. § 455 explains the grounds for disqualification. If an affidavit is sufficient on its face (i.e. meets the standards of § 455), the judge must disqualify himself without ruling on the truth of the claims in the affidavit.

In some states, counsel are entitled to one peremptory challenge of a judge. In a portion of the *Andrews* case which was not reproduced, the court ruled that no peremptory challenges were permitted in ALRB cases. Would it be good policy for the ALRB to provide one peremptory challenge of a pro tem hearing officer?

5. *Problem.* A complaint against several toy companies including our client Wham Co. was pending before the FTC. The case had been tried before an ALJ who had not yet rendered her decision. The toy companies engaged in "exclusive dealing." This means that they sold certain popular toys only to chosen toy stores within a given city. Other stores could not obtain the toys. The FTC complaint charged that this practice violated the Federal Trade Commission Act.

Chet, an FTC commissioner, addressed a meeting of the toy retailers trade association. In his speech, he said: "The FTC is keenly aware of the problems of your industry, such as price fixing, price discrimination, exclusive dealing arrangements, inadequate warranties. And we are well aware of the companies—Wham, Slam, and Dunk. You may be sure that the Commission will increase its efforts to promote fair competition in your industry."

Subsequently, the ALJ decided the case against Wham and the other companies who appeal to the Commission. Wham moved to disqualify Chet from considering the appeal. What result? *See Texaco, Inc. v. FTC,* 336 F.2d 754 (D.C.Cir.1964), rev'd on other grds., 381 U.S. 739 (1965).

§ 3.3.4 EX PARTE CONTACTS, DECISION ON THE RECORD, AND LEGISLATIVE PRESSURE

This section addresses additional conflicts between judicial and institutional models. Judges have only one responsibility—to decide cases. In contrast, an agency is a law enforcement body, with substantial responsibilities for rulemaking, research, investigation, and prosecution; an agency must also be acutely sensitive to prevailing political winds because it derives its authority and budget from and is accountable to the legislative and executive branches. These responsibilities require a constant flow of communication between agency personnel and regulated parties, members of the public, legislators, and high-level executive officials. Inevitably, some of this communication touches on matters which the agency is adjudicating. How can the agency heads decide cases fairly when they are exposed to so much off-record communication from outside the agency?

A word of clarification: this section concerns communications between agency decisionmakers and persons who are *not employees* of the agency. The section on separation of functions, § 3.3.2 *supra,* concerned communications between decisionmakers and persons who *are* employees of the agency. Are there reasons why the rules governing these two situations should differ?

PROFESSIONAL AIR TRAFFIC CONTROLLERS ORGANIZATION (PATCO) v. FEDERAL LABOR RELATIONS AUTHORITY (FLRA)

685 F.2d 547 (D.C.Cir.1982).

[The members of PATCO engaged in an illegal strike against the government. Under § 7120(f) of the Civil Service Reform Act, the FLRA "shall revoke the exclusive recognition status" of a union which calls such a strike (in effect, putting the union out of business). After a hearing, the FLRA's ALJ ordered PATCO's exclusive recognition status revoked. This decision was affirmed in a unanimous decision by the three FLRA agency heads (members Applewhaite, Frazier, and Haughton).

This case concerns certain contacts between the agency heads and others while the PATCO case was before FLRA. Concerned by the possible impropriety, the Court of Appeals ordered the FLRA to conduct a hearing with the aid of a specially appointed ALJ from another agency (John Vittone), to determine the extent and effect of these contacts.

The contacts discussed in the excerpted portion of the opinion are as follows:

(i) Secretary of Transportation Andrew Lewis phoned member Frazier. He said he was not calling about the substance of the PATCO case but wanted to tell Frazier that no meaningful efforts to settle the strike were underway. He stated that he would appreciate expeditious handling of the appeal from the ALJ decision to the FLRA agency heads. Lewis also called Applewhaite with the same message and Applewhaite told him that a written motion to expedite the appeal had to be filed. Later, such a motion was filed and FLRA shortened the filing period.

(ii) Albert Shanker, head of the Teachers Union, and a long-time friend of Applewhaite's, met Applewhaite for dinner. Shanker urged Applewhaite not to revoke PATCO's certification.

JUDGE EDWARDS wrote the panel opinion. JUDGE ROBINSON concurred, expressing much stronger condemnation of the incidents.]

C. APPLICABLE LEGAL STANDARDS

1. The Statutory Prohibition of Ex Parte Contacts and the FLRA Rules

The Civil Service Reform Act requires that FLRA unfair labor practice hearings, to the extent practicable, be conducted in accordance with the provisions of the Administrative Procedure Act. Since FLRA unfair labor practice hearings are formal adjudications within the meaning of the APA, *see* 5 U.S.C. § 551(7), section 557(d) governs ex parte communications.

Section 557(d) was enacted by Congress as part of the Government in the Sunshine Act (1976). The section prohibits ex parte communications "relevant to the merits of the proceeding" between an "interested person" and an agency decisionmaker. . . .

Three features of the prohibition on ex parte communications in agency adjudications are particularly relevant to the contacts here at issue. First, by its terms, section 557(d) applies only to ex parte communications to or from an "interested person." Congress did not intend, however, that the prohibition on ex parte communications would therefore have only a limited application. . . .

Second, the Government in the Sunshine Act defines an "ex parte communication" as "an oral or written communication not on the public record to which reasonable prior notice to all parties is not given, but . . . not includ[ing] requests for status reports on any matter or proceeding. . . ." 5 U.S.C. § 551(14) (1976). Requests for status reports are thus allowed under the statute, even when directed to an agency decisionmaker rather than to another agency employee. Nevertheless, the legislative history of the Act cautions:

> A request for a status report or a background discussion may in effect amount to an indirect or subtle effort to influence the substantive outcome of the proceedings. The judgment will have to be made whether a particular communication could affect the agency's decision on the merits. In doubtful cases the agency official should treat the communication as ex parte so as to protect the integrity of the decision making process.

Third, and in direct contrast to status reports, section 557(d) explicitly prohibits communications "relevant to the merits of the proceeding." The congressional reports state that the phrase should "be construed broadly and . . . include more than the phrase 'fact in issue' currently used in [section 554(d)(1) of] the Administrative Procedure Act." While the phrase must be interpreted to effectuate the dual purposes of the Government in the Sunshine Act, i.e., of giving notice of improper contacts and of providing all interested parties an opportunity to respond to illegal communications, the scope of this provision is not unlimited. Congress explicitly noted that the statute does not prohibit procedural inquiries, or other communications "not relevant to the merits."

In sum, Congress sought to establish common-sense guidelines to govern ex parte contacts in administrative hearings, rather than rigidly defined and woodenly applied rules. The disclosure of ex parte communications serves two distinct interests. Disclosure is important in its own right to prevent the appearance of impropriety from secret communications in a proceeding that is required to be decided on the record. Disclosure is also important as an instrument of fair decisionmaking; only if a party knows the arguments presented to a decisionmaker can the party respond effectively and ensure that its position is fairly considered. When these interests of openness and opportunity for response are threatened by an ex parte communication, the communication must be disclosed. It matters not whether the communication comes from someone other than a formal party or if the communication is clothed in the guise of a procedural inquiry. If, however, the communication is truly not relevant to the merits of an adjudication and, therefore, does not threaten the interests of openness and effective response, disclosure is unnecessary. Congress did not intend to erect meaningless procedural barriers to effective agency action. It is thus with these interests in mind that the statutory prohibition on ex parte communications must be applied.

2. Remedies for Ex Parte Communications

Section 557(d) contains two possible administrative remedies for improper ex parte communications. The first is disclosure of the communication and its content. The second requires the violating party to "show cause why his claim or interest in the proceeding should not be dismissed, denied, disregarded, or otherwise adversely affected on account of [the] violation." Congress did not intend, however, that an agency would require a party to "show cause" after every violation or that an agency would dismiss a party's interest more than rarely. Indeed, the statutory language clearly states that a party's interest in the proceeding may be adversely affected only "to the extent consistent with the interests of justice and the policy of the underlying statutes." [30]

The Government in the Sunshine Act contains no specific provisions for judicial remedy of improper ex parte communications. However, we may infer from approving citations in the House and Senate

---

30. By way of example, the Senate Report suggested that:

[T]he interests of justice might dictate that a claimant for an old age benefit not lose his claim even if he violates the ex parte rules. On the other hand, where two parties have applied for a license and the applications are of relatively equal merit, an agency may rule against a party who approached an agency head in an ex parte manner in an effort to win approval of his license.

The legislative history also notes that the dismissal provisions of §§ 556(d) and 557(d)(1)(D) supplement, rather than replace, an agency's authority to censure or dismiss an official who engages in illegal ex parte communications and to prohibit an attorney who violates § 557(d) from practicing before the agency.

Reports that Congress did not intend to alter the existing case law regarding ex parte communications and the legal effect of such contacts on agency decisions.

Under the case law in this Circuit improper ex parte communications, even when undisclosed during agency proceedings, do not necessarily void an agency decision. Rather, agency proceedings that have been blemished by ex parte communications have been held to be *voidable*.

In enforcing this standard, a court must consider whether, as a result of improper ex parte communications, the agency's decisionmaking process was irrevocably tainted so as to make the ultimate judgment of the agency unfair, either to an innocent party or to the public interest that the agency was obliged to protect.[32] In making this determination, a number of considerations may be relevant: the gravity of the ex parte communications; whether the contacts may have influenced the agency's ultimate decision; whether the party making the improper contacts benefited from the agency's ultimate decision; whether the contents of the communications were unknown to opposing parties, who therefore had no opportunity to respond; and whether vacation of the agency's decision and remand for new proceedings would serve a useful purpose. Since the principal concerns of the court are the integrity of the process and the fairness of the result, mechanical rules have little place in a judicial decision whether to vacate a voidable agency proceeding. Instead, any such decision must of necessity be an exercise of equitable discretion.

D. Analysis of the Alleged Ex Parte Communications with FLRA Members

. . . After extensive review of the . . . troubling incidents we believe that they provide insufficient reason to vacate the FLRA Decision or to remand this case for further proceedings before the Authority. . . .

Secretary Lewis' Telephone Calls to Members Frazier and Applewhaite

Transportation Secretary Lewis was undoubtedly an "interested person" within the meaning of section 557(d) and the FLRA Rules when he called Members Frazier and Applewhaite on August 13. Secretary Lewis' call clearly would have been an improper ex parte communication if he had sought to discuss the merits of the PATCO case. The

---

32. We have also considered the effect of ex parte communications on the availability of meaningful judicial review. Where facts and arguments "vital to the agency decision" are only communicated to the agency off the record, the court may at worst be kept in the dark about the agency's actual reasons for its decision. *United States Lines v. FMC*, 584 F.2d 519, 541 (D.C.Cir.1978). At best, the basis for the agency's action may be disclosed for the first time on review. If the off-the-record communications regard critical facts, the court will be particularly ill-equipped to resolve in the first instance any controversy between the parties. *See id.* at 542. Thus, effective judicial review may be hampered if ex parte communications prevent adversarial decision of factual issues by the agency. . . .

Secretary explicitly avoided the merits, however, and mentioned only his view on the possibility of settlement and his desire for a speedy decision. On this basis, Solicitor Freehling and Member Frazier concluded the call was not improper.

We are less certain that Secretary Lewis' call was permissible. Although Secretary Lewis did not in fact discuss the merits of the case, even a procedural inquiry may be a subtle effort to influence an agency decision. We do not doubt that Member Frazier and Solicitor Freehling concluded in good faith that the communications were not improper, but it would have been preferable for them to heed Congress' warning, to assume that close cases like these are improper, and to report them on the public record.

We need not decide, however, whether Secretary Lewis' contacts were in fact improper. Even if they were, the contacts did not taint the proceedings or prejudice PATCO. Secretary Lewis' central concern in his conversations with Member Frazier and Member Applewhaite was that the case be handled expeditiously. Member Applewhaite explicitly told Secretary Lewis that if he wanted the case handled more quickly than the normal course of FLRA business, then the FAA would have to file a written request. If, as A.L.J. Vittone found likely, Member Applewhaite's comments led to the FAA's Motion to Modify Time Limits, *that was exactly the desired result.* Once the FAA filed a motion, PATCO filed its own responsive motions, and the FLRA was able to decide the timing issue based on the pleadings before it. . . .

Finally, PATCO cannot claim that it was prejudiced. The failure of the Authority to notice Secretary Lewis' calls on the public record did not deprive PATCO of an opportunity to comment: PATCO filed responsive motions. (Surely PATCO cannot argue that fairness requires two opportunities to respond rather than one.) Nor has PATCO suggested how it was ultimately injured by the six-day change in the time for filing exceptions. In these circumstances we conclude that Secretary Lewis' telephone calls do not void the FLRA Decision.

Member Applewhaite's Dinner with Albert Shanker

Of course, the most troublesome ex parte communication in this case occurred during the September 21 dinner meeting between Member Applewhaite and American Federation of Teachers President Albert Shanker—the "well-known labor leader" mentioned in Assistant Attorney General McGrath's affidavit. . . .

At the outset, we are faced with the question whether Mr. Shanker was an "interested person" to the proceeding under section 557(d). Mr. Shanker argues that he was not. He suggests that his only connection with the unfair labor practice case was his membership on the Executive Council of the AFL–CIO which, unbeknownst to him, had participated as amicus curiae in the oral argument of the PATCO case before the FLRA. This relationship to the proceeding, Mr. Shanker contends, is too tenuous to qualify him as an "interested person" forbidden to make ex parte communications to the Authority Members.

As noted above, Congress did not intend such a narrow construction of the term "interested person." . . .

The House and Senate Reports agreed that the term covers "any individual or other person with an interest in the agency proceeding that is greater than the general interest the public as a whole may have. The interest need not be monetary, nor need a person be a party to, or intervenor in, the agency proceeding. . . ."

We believe that Mr. Shanker falls within the intended scope of the term "interested person." Mr. Shanker was (and is) the President of a major public-sector labor union. As such, he has a special and well-known interest in the union movement and the developing law of labor relations in the public sector. The PATCO strike, of course, was the subject of extensive media coverage and public comment. Some union leaders undoubtedly felt that the hard line taken against PATCO by the Administration might have an adverse effect on other unions, both in the federal and in state and local government sectors. Mr. Shanker apparently shared this concern. . . .

Even if we were to adopt Mr. Shanker's position that he was not an interested person, we are astonished at his claim that he did nothing wrong. Mr. Shanker frankly concedes that he "desired to have dinner with Member Applewhaite because he felt strongly about the PATCO case and he wished to communicate directly to Member Applewhaite sentiments he had previously expressed in public." While we appreciate Mr. Shanker's forthright admission, we must wonder whether it is a product of candor or a failure to comprehend that his conduct was improper. In case any doubt still lingers, we take the opportunity to make one thing clear: *It is simply unacceptable behavior for any person directly to attempt to influence the decision of a judicial officer in a pending case outside of the formal, public proceedings.* This is true for the general public, for "interested persons," and for the formal parties to the case. This rule applies to administrative adjudications as well as to cases in Article III courts.

We think it a mockery of justice to even suggest that judges or other decisionmakers may be properly approached on the merits of a case during the pendency of an adjudication. Administrative and judicial adjudications are viable only so long as the integrity of the decisionmaking processes remains inviolate. There would be no way to protect the sanctity of adjudicatory processes if we were to condone direct attempts to influence decisionmakers through ex parte contacts.

We do not hold, however, that Member Applewhaite committed an impropriety when he accepted Mr. Shanker's dinner invitation. Member Applewhaite and Mr. Shanker were professional and social friends. We recognize, of course, that a judge "must have neighbors, friends and acquaintances, business and social relations, and be a part of his day and generation." Similarly, Member Applewhaite was not required to renounce his friendships, either personal or professional, when he was appointed to the FLRA. When Mr. Shanker called Member Applewhaite on September 21, Member Applewhaite was unaware of Mr. Shanker's purpose in arranging the dinner. He therefore had no reason to reject the invitation.

The majority of the dinner conversation was unrelated to the PATCO case. Only in the last fifteen minutes of the dinner did the discussion become relevant to the PATCO dispute, apparently when Mr. Shanker raised the topic of local approaches to public employee strikes in New York and Pennsylvania. At this point, and as the conversation turned to the discipline appropriate for a striking union like PATCO, Member Applewhaite should have promptly terminated the discussion. Had Mr. Shanker persisted in discussing his views of the PATCO case, Member Applewhaite should have informed him in no uncertain terms that such behavior was inappropriate. Unfortunately, he did not do so. . . . We do not believe that it is necessary to vacate the FLRA Decision and remand the case. First, while Mr. Shanker's purpose and conduct were improper, and while Member Applewhaite should not have entertained Mr. Shanker's views on the desirability of decertifying a striking union, no threats or promises were made. Though plainly inappropriate, the ex parte communication was limited to a ten or fifteen minute discussion, often couched in general terms, of the appropriate discipline for a striking public employee union. This behavior falls short of the "corrupt tampering with the adjudicatory process" found by this court in *WKAT, Inc. v. FCC*, 296 F.2d 375.

Second, A.L.J. Vittone found that the Applewhaite/Shanker dinner had no effect on the ultimate decision of Member Applewhaite or of the FLRA as a whole in the PATCO case. None of the parties have disputed this finding. Indeed, even Member Frazier, who initiated the FBI investigation of the dinner, testified that "in his opinion the Shanker–Applewhaite dinner did not have an effect on Member Applewhaite ultimate decision in the PATCO case."

Third, no party benefited from the improper contact. The ultimate decision was adverse to PATCO, the party whose interests were most closely aligned with Mr. Shanker's position. The final decision also rejected the position taken by the AFL–CIO as amicus curiae and by Mr. Shanker in his dinner conversation with Member Applewhaite. . . .

Notes and Questions

1. *State law.* For provisions similar to § 557(d), see 1981 MSAPA § 4–213 and 1961 MSAPA § 13 which provides:

". . . members or employees of an agency assigned to render a decision or to make findings of fact and conclusions of law in a contested case shall not communicate, directly or indirectly, in connection with any issue of fact, with any person or party, nor, in connection with any issue of law, with any party or his representative, except upon notice and opportunity for all parties to participate . . ."

One of the few cases arising under 1961 MSAPA involved ex parte contacts between the applicants for a savings and loan charter and the Texas Savings and Loan Commissioner. The Commissioner had already turned down the application in August. During September, the organizers met with him ex parte and furnished new economic information that indicated the need for an additional savings and loan in the town. In October, the organizers then filed a new application that the Commissioner granted.

In an action brought by an existing association in the town, the Texas Court of Civil Appeals reversed the Commissioner's decision because of a violation of 1961 MSAPA § 13. It regarded the first and second application proceedings as "just one ongoing application." Therefore it rejected the argument that the communications were proper because no application was pending at the time they occurred. *First Sav. & Loan Ass'n v. Vandygriff,* 605 S.W.2d 740 (Tex.Civ.App. 1980). It noted: "The statutory prohibition against *ex parte* communications . . . is recognition that such communications discredit the administrative process and undermine public confidence in government."

However, the Texas Supreme Court reversed the decision. *Vandygriff v. First Savings & Loan Ass'n,* 617 S.W.2d 669 (Tex.1981) because it held there was no "contested case" at the time the communications occurred. The first application had been dismissed and the second had not yet been filed. It also held there was no prejudice to opponents of the application because the ex parte communications were fully disclosed at the second hearing and there was opportunity to present contrary evidence. How would this case have been decided under the federal APA? *See* § 557(d)(1)(E). Under 1981 MSAPA? Which of the Texas decisions do you agree with?

2. *Lewis' calls to Frazier and Applewhaite.* Did this call violate APA § 557(d)? Would it violate 1981 MSAPA § 4–213(a) and (c)? Consider the definition of "ex parte communication" in § 551(14). The FLRA's rules permit ex parte contacts concerning settlement. 5 C.F.R. § 2414.6(b), (d). Why is a conversation concerning settlement not a violation of § 557(d)? Could an inquiry about the status of a case or a comment about settlement be a prohibited ex parte communication? See Judge Edwards' comments in part C.1. of the *PATCO* opinion.

Members of Congress often receive requests for assistance from their constituents who are embroiled in controversies with agencies. Typically, the member's staff will call or write to the agency and ask about the status of the matter. These requests are often given priority treatment by agency staff. Congress was anxious to protect its right to make status inquiries (which explains the specific reference to them in APA § 551(14)).

Senator Dirksen once said: "I have been calling agencies for 25 years . . . Are we to be put on the carpet because we represent our constituents, make inquiries, and find out what the status of matters is, and so serve our constituents? . . . I know these people, they are good, reliable operators; they are good solid citizens. I just want to know what the status of the matter is." 105 Cong.Rec. 14057 (1959).

Should we encourage status inquiries about pending adjudication by members of Congress or executive branch officials?

3. *Dinner with Shanker.* Judge Edwards indicates that Shanker's conduct was deplorable and that Applewhaite erred badly by failing to terminate the discussion when it turned to the *PATCO* matter. In his concurring opinion, Judge Robinson indicated that it was inappropriate for Applewhaite to even have dinner with Shanker. Do you agree? Is it likely that Shanker's views came as a surprise to Applewhaite? Should Applewhaite be removed from office?

Do you agree that Shanker is an "interested person?" If you had run into Applewhaite (an old friend of your father's) at the airport and made the same statements that Shanker did, would you have violated § 557(d)?

4. *Remedies for ex parte contact.* What should FLRA have done about the violations of § 557(d) and its own ex parte rules? See § 557(d)(1)(C); 1981 MSAPA § 4–213(e). What additional action could FLRA have taken? See § 557(d)(1)(D) and the fourth sentence of § 556(d); 1981 MSAPA § 4–213(g).

The Court of Appeals was obviously troubled by what it should do aside from laying harsh criticism on all concerned. Certainly, the hearing before ALJ Vittone must have been a humbling experience. Ordinarily, it is improper to "probe the mind" of agency decisionmakers about how they made their decision. *Morgan IV,* discussed in § 3.3.1 *supra.* However, in cases of alleged ex parte contacts, the agency staff and decisionmakers must submit to a grueling inquiry into exactly who said what to whom.

Should the Court have remanded the *PATCO* case for a new FLRA decision, even though it concluded that the ex parte contacts were not prejudicial to any party? In the *Vandygriff* case, discussed in note 1, the lower court remanded the case for a new hearing despite a failure by plaintiff to prove that the Commissioner was persuaded by the ex parte information. Instead the court presumed that such harm occurred—a presumption preferable to probing the mind of the Commissioner in violation of the *Morgan IV* principle. Moreover, the court said that the impropriety was not cured by subsequent disclosure at the second licensing hearing; the opposing party was at a severe disadvantage because it had no effective way to controvert the ex parte evidence until weeks or months after it had been communicated. The Texas Supreme Court disagreed; it said the opportunity to rebut the communications at the second hearing was sufficient and that the Commissioner was presumed to have performed his duties in compliance with the law. Do you agree with the lower court in *Vandygriff* that a case should be automatically remanded for a new hearing if prohibited ex parte communications have occurred?

5. *Who can you talk to?* Notice that § 557(d) prohibits ex parte communications between outsiders and *advisers to decisionmakers.* Thus Shanker's communication would have been equally inappropriate if directed to Applewhaite's attorney-adviser. See also 1981 MSAPA § 4–213(b). And observe also that § 557(d) goes into effect no later than the time a proceeding is noticed for hearing (or, if the outsider knows that it will be noticed, at the time he acquires such knowledge). § 557(d)(1)(E).

There is a clear conflict between the APA provisions that prohibit ex parte contacts and the goals of i) encouraging free communication between the regulated industry and regulatory agencies and ii) making available the largest possible pool of advisers from within the agency for decisionmakers to call on in difficult cases.

For example, suppose Secretary of Transportation Lewis wants to discuss the *PATCO* case with Max. Max is an FLRA attorney who is very experienced in dealing with the problem of public employee strikes. Both Max and Lewis think that Max would be prosecuting the *PATCO* case. Such a conversation (between an agency prosecutor and a person who favors the prosecution) seems entirely appropriate.

Suppose that, after the discussion between Lewis and Max occurs, someone other than Max is selected to prosecute the case. When the time for decision arrives, Member Applewhaite wants to call upon Max for advice. Would Max be disqualified from giving advice because of his earlier and innocent ex parte contact with Lewis? Alternatively, if Max serves as an adviser, would Lewis' ex parte communication violate § 557(d) and therefore must it be placed on the record under § 557(d)(1) (C)? Should it also trigger sanctions against the government under § 557(d)(1)(D) and § 556(d)?

6. *Congressional interference.* As note 2 points out, the law grudgingly tolerates Congressional status inquiries about pending cases. However, the cases sternly condemn Congressional attempts to influence the result in pending cases. The leading decision is *Pillsbury Co. v. FTC,* 354 F.2d 952 (5th Cir.1966).

This case involved review of an FTC order that required Pillsbury to divest itself of baking companies it had earlier acquired. While the matter was before an ALJ (but after the FTC agency heads had rendered a preliminary decision that the acquisitions were not per se violations of the Clayton Act), several members were summoned to testify before the Senate Judiciary Committee. Senators harshly criticized the FTC's earlier decision, mentioning Pillsbury by name more than 100 times.

The Court held that the FTC's decision violated due process. It said:

[W]hen such an investigation focuses directly and substantially upon the mental decisional processes of a Commission in a case which is pending before it, Congress is no longer intervening in the agency's legislative function, but rather in its *judicial* function . . . To subject an administrator to a searching examination as to how and why he reached his decision in a case still pending before him, and to criticize him for reaching the "wrong" decision, as the Senate subcommittee did in this case, sacrifices the appearance of impartiality—the sine qua non of American judicial justice—in favor of some short-run notions regarding the Congressional intent underlying an amendment to a statute, unfettered administration of which was committed by Congress to the FTC . . .

The Court remanded the case to the FTC for a new decision. Because of the passage of time (the case began in 1952, the hearings occurred in 1955, the Court's decision occurred in 1966), the FTC had new commissioners who had not been tainted by Congressional interference. Thus it was possible to avoid the rule of necessity.

7. *The exclusive record for decision.* A due process and APA fundamental is that the record made at a hearing is the exclusive basis for decision. The decisionmaker cannot rely on factual information which is not in the record. See APA § 556(e); 1981 MSAPA § 4–221(b), (c). This concept is explored in detail in § 4.2.3 which considers whether a fact-finder can take *official notice* of factual material. Certainly, one reason for prohibiting ex parte contacts is to prevent off-record factual material from contaminating the mind of the decisionmaker; the requirement that the material be placed on the record at least permits adversaries to rebut it. See *PATCO,* note 32.

8. *Problem.* Decisions concerning zoning are made by the three-person elected board of supervisors of Mountain County. A county ordinance requires that the board provide a "fair hearing" before granting or denying a petition for rezoning. There are no standards in the statute concerning a decision to rezone property.

Martha owned 160 acres of land which was presently zoned for rural use. It was adjacent to Aspen State Park but far from any town. She petitioned to rezone all the land adjacent to the park to permit low-density residential development. She wanted to sell her land to Development Co. which planned to subdivide it into one-half acre lots for a recreational development. Jim, who owned a farm next to Martha's (also adjacent to the park), wanted the area to remain agricultural.

Martha had been a close friend since high school days of Sarah, who is one of the three supervisors. Before filing her petition for rezoning, Martha invited Sarah over for dinner and explained why her land should be rezoned. She stated that the time is right to start developing the property next to Aspen State Park. A development would provide beautiful sites for second homes for city dwellers; and why shouldn't Mountain County residents make some money from the State Park for a change? Sarah encouraged Martha to seek rezoning.

After the petition for rezoning was filed, but before it was heard, Mountain County had an election for county supervisor. Sarah was involved in a hotly contested race. Development Co. contributed $25,000 to Sarah's successful campaign.

At the hearing Jim and 40 other Mountain County residents appeared and opposed rezoning. They argued that development next to the park would permanently and adversely damage the beauty and atmosphere of Aspen Park. They also argued that development was inappropriate because the park was far from any town and there was no demand for housing in the area. Only Martha and representatives of Development Co. appeared in favor of the rezoning.

The Board of Supervisors unanimously granted the petition to rezone the land. Should a reviewing court set this action aside?

What if the Board of Supervisors were bound by 1981 MSAPA § 4–213? By APA § 557(d)? *See E & E Hauling Inc. v. Pollution Control Bd.*, 451 N.E.2d 555, 569–72 (Ill.App.1983), aff'd, 481 N.E.2d 664 (1985); *Woodland Hills Residents Ass'n v. Los Angeles City Council*, 609 P.2d 1029 (Cal.1980).

§ 3.4   ADMINISTRATIVE LAW JUDGES AND DECISIONAL INDEPENDENCE

How should we view the administrative law judge—the individual who conducts the hearing and makes the initial decision in adjudications governed by state and federal APAs? Should the ALJ be treated as a judge, with all that term implies, or should the ALJ be considered as one important member of the agency's team? These questions are rooted in the fundamental and now familiar conflict between the judicial and institutional models.

As explained in the article by Lubbers, *infra*, federal ALJs are employed by, and housed within, a single agency; that agency plays an important role, along with the Office of Personnel Management (OPM), in their selection. Nevertheless, ALJs have considerable de facto and de jure independence from the agency that employs them.

In almost all cases of formal adjudication at the federal level, and in most state cases as well, ALJs render initial decisions and these become final if not appealed. The ALJ who presides at the hearing makes the initial decision unless he or she becomes unavailable to the agency. Thus the agency cannot use one officer to hear the case and another to write the report. *See* APA § 554(d) (first sentence). Under § 556(b), some or all of the agency heads can preside at the taking of evidence instead of an ALJ but this seldom occurs. *See also* 1981 MSAPA 4–202(a). In smaller state agencies, however, the agency heads often preside personally over the hearing and make the final decision themselves. *See* 1981 MSAPA § 4–215(a), (b).

If an ALJ's decision (or the decision of less than a quorum of the agency heads) is appealed, the agency heads (or their designees) have power to reverse the initial decision and make a final decision. APA § 557(b); 1981 MSAPA § 4–216(a). In a few instances, however, Congress departed from this model and took responsibility for making final decisions away from the agency. The most important example is the Occupational Safety and Health Review Commission (OSHRC) which is separated from OSHA and makes the final decisions in cases involving industrial safety issues. Another important example is the Tax Court which independently decides disputes between taxpayers and the IRS.

Most states follow the federal model: agencies hire their own ALJs and retain power to make final adjudicatory decisions. Ten states (California, Colorado, Florida, Iowa, Massachusetts, Minnesota, New Jersey, North Carolina, Tennessee and Washington) have adopted a "central panel" model. ALJs are not hired by or housed within agencies; instead a "central panel" of ALJs are available to agencies that need to conduct hearings. In most of these states, there are some agencies that do not use the central panel and retain their own ALJs. Sections 4–202(a) and 4–301 of 1981 MSAPA adopt the central panel approach. States are offered a choice of adopting § 4–202(a) with or without the bracketed language. What would be the significance of adopting the bracketed material?

Finally, two states (Maine and Missouri) have stripped agencies of the power to make final decisions in at least some cases. Instead, there is a separate "administrative court" which makes these decisions. "Administrative court" decisions can be appealed directly to the state courts.

This subchapter continues with a selection of readings from authors who have considered the issue of decisional independence for ALJs. Please consider these materials in light of three questions:

(i) In light of the article by Lubbers, should there be any changes in the system by which federal ALJs are appointed?

(ii) You are an aide to a state legislator who is chair of a committee considering whether to adopt 1981 MSAPA. Agencies in your state employ their own ALJs. Should you recommend to your boss that the state adopt §§ 4–202(a) and 4–301 and, if so, with or without the bracketed language in § 4–202(a)?

(iii) Another item on your boss' agenda concerns the formation of a new state agency (Toxics Regulatory Board or TRB) to regulate the disposal of toxic wastes and take charge of the cleanup of existing toxic waste dump sites. TRB will adopt regulations and issue permits to disposal facilities. It will investigate and administratively prosecute violations of the regulations. TRB will have power to revoke permits and to punish polluters or disposal facilities that violate the regulations. It will make use of the courts only if it seeks criminal sanctions.

Because of its broad responsibilities, TRB will have many cases to adjudicate. Two problems: a) assuming the state adopts a central panel system for ALJs (as discussed in question (ii) *supra*), should that system apply to the TRB? b) who should have the power to decide appeals from ALJ decisions in TRB cases—the head of TRB or an independent adjudicating agency?

§ 3.4.1 SELECTION AND APPOINTMENT OF ALJs

LUBBERS, "FEDERAL ADMINISTRATIVE LAW JUDGES: A FOCUS ON OUR INVISIBLE JUDICIARY"

33 Admin.L.Rev. 109 (1981).

The administrative law judge (ALJ) is the central figure in formal administrative adjudication. There were 1,146 ALJs employed by twenty-nine federal agencies as of June 1980. One indication of the importance of ALJs as lawmakers and law appliers is suggested by the fact that they outnumber by two to one the corps of United States district court judges who preside over the nation's entire federal civil and criminal trial docket.

Administrative law judges are employed by executive departments and independent agencies to conduct hearings and make decisions in proceedings in which administrative determinations must be based on the records of trial-type hearings. An ALJ's decision may be, and often is, the final decision of the agency without further proceedings if there is no appeal to, or review on the motion of, the agency. . . .

When compared with the role of judges of the federal courts, the role of ALJs in our governmental system is less visible, and, as one would guess, less well understood. The federal judge is, after all, the personification of the judicial branch of the government: a robed authority figure who can demand and receive respect and obeisance even from presidents. Federal judges are guaranteed life tenure by the Constitution; there is little reason to question their independence. The significance of their decisions, which are regularly published and widely accessible, is clearly comprehensible within the context of the familiar three-tier structure of the federal court system (i.e., district courts, courts of appeals, and the Supreme Court). ALJs, on the other hand, in spite of being called judges and functioning as such, are subject to doubts about their independence due in part to their employment status as agency personnel. Furthermore, few agencies systematically publish decisions of their ALJs, and the significance of an ALJ's "decision" as a determinant of his agency's decision or final action varies markedly from agency to agency.

The position of administrative law judge (formerly called "hearing examiner") did not even exist until the APA was enacted in 1946. Prior to the APA, there were no reliable safeguards to ensure the objectivity and judicial capability of presiding officers in formal administrative proceedings. Ordinarily these officers were subordinate employees chosen by the agencies, and the power of the agencies to control and influence such personnel made questionable the contention of any agency that its proceedings assured fundamental fairness. Furthermore, the role of the presiding officer in an agency's decisional process was often unclear; many agencies would ignore the officer's decisions without giving reasons, and enter their own de novo decisions. The APA was designed to correct these conditions. Reshaping the role of the "hearing examiner" was a crucial precondition to both of these basic reforms.

The APA spelled out the powers and duties of these so-called examiners as presiding officers. By giving the Civil Service Commission the authority to determine their qualifications and compensation, the APA attempted to insure their competence, impartiality and independence. The basic structure of the 1946 Act remains unchanged today.

As to the independence issue, the Act lodges in the Office of Personnel Management (OPM, the successor of the Civil Service Commission) exclusive authority for the initial examination and certification for selection of ALJs. In addition, ALJs receive compensation as prescribed only by OPM, independently of agency recommendations or ratings, and they can be removed by the agency which employs them only when good cause is established before the Merit Systems Protection Board after opportunity for hearing. The APA also requires that the ALJs' functions be conducted in an impartial manner and provides that if a disqualification petition is filed against an ALJ in any case, the agency must determine that issue on the record, and as part of the decision in that case. The Act also prescribes that an ALJ may not be responsible to, or subject to supervision by, anyone performing investigative or prosecutorial functions for an agency. This "separation of functions" requirement is designed to prevent the investigative or prosecutorial arm of an agency from controlling a hearing or influencing the ALJ. Finally, to insure that the ALJs are well insulated from improper agency pressure and controls, the APA contains two other provisions designed to make the ALJ at least semi-independent of the employing agency: ALJs are to be assigned to their cases in rotation so far as is practicable; and they may not perform duties inconsistent with their roles as ALJs.

I. SELECTION AND APPOINTMENT OF ALJS

. . . OPM conducts interviews, administers a test of writing ability, evaluates the qualifying experience of all applicants who meet the minimum experience requirements, and scores each of them on a scale of 100 points. Those who score 80 points or above become "eligibles" and are ranked (highest scores at the top) on registers maintained by OPM from which the agencies make their appointments. The office maintains two registers; one at the GS–16 grade level, the other at GS–15. This is done because OPM has created ALJ positions at both of these levels. ALJ positions in a majority of those agencies which employ ALJs (including most of the major agencies engaged in economic regulation) are at the GS–16 level. The positions in the remaining four agencies (including the Social Security Administration which employs over half of all ALJs) are at the GS–15 level. . . .

A. Evaluation by the Office of ALJs . . .

In order to qualify as an ALJ, the applicant must be an attorney and have seven or more years of "qualifying experience . . . ."

Individuals determined eligible for listing on either of the two ALJ registers are ranked in order of their scores with the highest scores at the top of the list, and appointments are made by the individual agencies from these registers. However, the agencies' appointment power is restricted by a statutory requirement known as the "rule of three" which is applicable to all competitive civil service jobs in the federal government. Under this requirement, when an agency requests a list of eligibles, OPM must certify enough names from the top of the register to permit the agency to consider at least three names per appointment to each vacancy. The agency is then obliged to make its selection from those three who have the highest scores and are actually available for appointment. . . .

B. Veterans Preference . . .

The impact of the Veterans Preference Act on register rankings is crucial. . . .

[A] wartime veteran of the armed services is entitled to 5 (10 in the case of a disabled veteran) additional points above his scored rating. Since there is only a 20–point spread on scores among all ALJ eligibles (from 80 to 100), the addition of 5 to 10 veterans preference points to any score can change by many places an eligible's ranking on the register.

[O]f the top 60 eligibles on the GS–15 register, 9 were 10–point veterans, 42 were 5–point veterans, and only 9 had no veteran status. . . .

The impact of veterans preference on the register ranking combined with the "rule of three" has led to criticism of the ALJ selection system as keeping many outstanding candidates, especially women, at the bottom of the register and as discouraging others from even applying. . . .

C. Selective Certification

Many agencies have sought to avoid the restrictions upon their appointment of ALJs through the procedure of "selective certification." Using this process, an agency, upon a showing of necessity and with the prior approval of OPM, is permitted to appoint specially certified eligibles without regard to their ranking in relation to other eligibles on the register who lack the special certification. For example, the

Federal Communications Commission (FCC) has arranged with OPM for special certification of eligibles who can show:

> [t]wo years of experience in the preparation, presentation, or hearing of formal cases, or in making decisions on the basis of the record of such hearings, originating before governmental regulatory bodies at the Federal, state, or local level, *in the field of communications law.*

Suppose that four individuals on the GS–16 register were certified as having these special qualifications and their rankings on the register were 15, 31, 68, and 95, respectively. When the FCC wished to appoint an ALJ, OPM would send it a list containing the names of the top three selectively certified eligibles (numbers 15, 31 and 68). The FCC could then choose from among those three, although the Veterans Preference Act's prohibition against passing over a veteran to select a non-veteran would still apply. . . .

The possible benefits of selective certification to the agencies which have arranged for it are obvious, and those agencies have in fact utilized it extensively. . . . In fiscal years 1975 to 1979, 83 of the 98 appointments from the GS–16 register were selectively certified.

The practice of selective certification has been the subject of criticism on the grounds that it severely limits opportunities for generalist applicants and that it leads to "inbreeding" among an agency's ALJs through biasing the selection process in favor of the agency's own staff attorneys who are most likely to meet the specialized experience criteria. Whether inbreeding actually poses a problem, beyond appearances, is however, debatable. . . .

Selective certification does not apply solely to government attorneys, of course: attorneys in private practice have the same opportunity to be specially certified as do agency staff attorneys. However, it appears that private attorneys who have specialized expertise in law practice within areas of ALJ selective certification have little interest in forsaking their practice to become ALJs. . . . It seems clear that selective certification represents a response by OPM to agencies' complaints about the restrictions upon their power to appoint ALJs with particularized expertise. The policy does strike a sort of balance with the restrictiveness of the applicable provisions of the Veterans Preference Act and the "rule of three," but whether it strikes an optimum balance, whether it enhances the quality or productivity of the ALJs, and whether it unduly discriminates against "generalist" eligibles remain much debated questions. The agencies utilizing selective certification generally favor its continuation, generalist eligibles oppose it, and others have urged its modification.

[ACUS believes] that the objective of selective certification could be achieved without closing the door to highly qualified generalists by changing the process of ALJ certification and selection. Under its recommendation, eligibles would be awarded extra rating points for specialized experience of the kind now recognized for selective certification; a pool of the ten, rather than three, highest ranking eligibles on the register would be certified for agency selection; and, by amendment of the Veterans Preference Act, the agency would be free to select any eligible in the certified pool even if there were a higher-rated veteran in the pool. . . .

§ 3.4.2 ALJs: THE CENTRAL PANEL ISSUE
SEGAL, "THE ADMINISTRATIVE LAW JUDGE"
62 A.B.A.J. 1424 (1976).*

. . . How then do we accelerate the process of attracting the most qualified people to the administrative bench, and how do we improve the system under which they operate? I urge that we begin by completely divorcing administrative law judges from their agencies by the establishment of a unified corps of administrative law judges, centrally located and not regularly assigned to any particular agency. This would not only increase the attractiveness of the office; it would also solidify the mandate that administrative law judges be completely independent and impartial triers of fact.

The most persistent argument against unification is that an administrative law judge must be expert in the substantive law of the agency. I am no more persuaded by this thesis than I am that we need to have specialized judges in our federal court system. I realize that administrative law judges function in very specialized areas of the law, but so do federal district judges, and yet they have demonstrated no ineptitude in making findings and reaching conclusions in the most technical disciplines. . . .

Proponents of the present system cite the fact that specialization has become a way of life among lawyers, and they query, why not among judges? Perhaps one answer is that administrative law judges need not specialize, precisely because the lawyer before them so often does and also because expert witnesses—specialists—may be expected to testify. Our system of adjudicating controversies presumes that the advocate will present his case to an impartial fact finder. It is the advocate who should be the expert on the facts in the courtroom.

Consider . . . the unavoidable appearance of bias when an administrative law judge, attached to an agency, is presiding in litigation by that agency against a private party. One can fill the pages of the United States Code with legislation intended to guarantee the independence of the administrative law judge; but so long as that judge has offices in the same building as the agency staff, so long as the seal of the agency adorns the bench on which that judge sits, so long as that judge's assignment to the case is by the very agency whose actions or contentions that judge is being called on to review, it is extremely difficult, if not impossible, for that judge to convey the image of being an impartial fact finder.

* Reprinted with permission from the *ABA Journal*, The Lawyer's Magazine, published by the American Bar Association (1976).

The permanent assignment of an administrative law judge to a single agency also tends to produce an inbreeding, which in turn contributes even more to the appearance of bias. For example, of the thirteen administrative law judges assigned to the Federal Trade Commission, twelve are former employees of that commission; and of the seven new administrative law judges whose appointment was announced in May by the National Labor Relations Board, every one was either a current or a former member of the board's legal staff. . . .

ABRAMS, "ADMINISTRATIVE LAW JUDGE SYSTEMS: THE CALIFORNIA VIEW"
29 Admin.L.Rev. 487 (1977).

[California has a central panel of ALJs (operating from an independent agency whose director is appointed by the governor). In some cases, where agencies require specialized judges, the central panel assigns a judge to an agency for an extended period. Abrams refers to this as a central panel/specialist approach. Panelists must be used by most state agencies (but not by the Public Utilities Commission or a few others). Panelists are also made available to local government entities which request them.]

A strong argument against adopting a total central panel approach in California is that for [some] agencies it is necessary that hearing officers be real specialists or technical experts and the only way to accomplish this is by attaching them to the agency.

To the extent that special knowledge and information is useful to a hearing officer, can the advantages of expertise and specialization be obtained under a central panel system? If a hearing officer lacks needed technical background, expert witnesses may be called or agency staff may assist at the hearings. Of course, this may involve additional expense and time.

If the concern is that the central panel hearing officer may not be sufficiently familiar with agency policies, that, too, is subject to remedy. Agencies are guided by their governing statutes, formal regulations promulgated by them and by policies, which, whether or not set down in writing, are known generally within the agency. If policy is not written and only known through word of mouth by those actively participating in the agencies' operations, outside hearing officers are not likely to be aware of it. There are two remedies. First, in the context of the particular case, the agency may, consistently with procedural requirements, communicate relevant policies to the hearing officer. A second solution is to require the individual agencies to submit written copies of all pertinent policies to the central panel. This practice, updated frequently enough, should bridge the policy-information gap between the agencies and central panel hearing officers. . . .

Where the agency has a sufficient case load to support a full-time hearing officer, another solution to the expertise problem under a central panel system is to adopt the central panel-specialist approach. This approach assigns a panel hearing officer to the agency for an extended period. By maintaining a base of operations in the central panel (which would retain control over his promotion and related matters), and by not remaining too long with any one agency, the hearing officer should be able to preserve his independence while gaining expert knowledge.

Adoption of a central panel system has implications for the setting of qualifications for hearing officers which, in turn, is related to the expertise-specialization issue. Under an agency staff system, typically no statewide standards for hearing officers are set, and large agencies handling diverse matters may establish several categories of hearing officers with qualifications geared to the various matters within the agency's jurisdiction. Thus in California, the Public Utilities Commission has employed as hearing officers engineering and rate experts as well as attorneys.

It is theoretically possible under a central panel system to establish several categories of hearing officers, each with different qualifications, with the purpose of assigning them to cases which suit their particular qualifications. But such a system would be very complex. Unless the jurisdiction adopted a total central panel system covering all agencies, there would not be enough hearing officers in the panel to justify that degree of specialization. It is worth noting that the California central panel system operates with about twenty hearing officers who handle all APA hearings for the entire state.

The more probable approach to be taken under a central panel system is to set minimal qualifications for all hearing officers. The principal issue in establishing such general minimal qualifications is whether hearing officers should be lawyers. . . . TenBroek argued that hearing officers with a social work background performed better in handling welfare matters than those with legal training. But he was certainly not arguing that *all* hearing officers should be social workers. . . .

CONCLUSION

In the foregoing discussion, I have taken the position that for purposes of maintaining the independence of the hearing officer it is preferable to use structural arrangements that insulate him from agency pressure and influence. That approach seems well-founded in common sense. It assumes: 1) that agency influence in particular matters is undesirable; 2) that either agency officials may want to influence decisions or will be so perceived by hearing officers; and 3) that alternative approaches—informal, internal arrangements or ad hoc inquiry in the individual case—are not sufficient. . . .

Increasing the independence of hearing officers, to be sure, has its costs. The much-praised "institutional method" of arriving at decisions is modified if the hearing officer is less a part of the institution. But the expertise factor is often overrated; the agency and its other functionaries can usually provide the technical information needed. Where more is required for a particular agency as a matter of course, the central panel-specialist system can be utilized.

Judicialization of the hearing officer's role might appear to presage a system in which he makes final decisions rather than initial findings of fact and recommendations to the agency. Such an approach would dramatically change the role of the agency and sharply curtail its responsibilities. Emphasis on the independence of the hearing officer need not carry us that far. Structural arrangements can achieve a large degree of independence for the hearing officer without changing his traditional role in the administrative process.

ZANKEL, "A UNIFIED CORPS OF FEDERAL ADMINISTRATIVE LAW JUDGES IS NOT NEEDED"
6 W.New Eng.L.Rev. 723 (1984).

[Zankel (an NLRB ALJ) criticizes then-pending legislation that would establish a central panel system in the form of a Corps of Federal ALJs. The Corps would consist of seven divisions identified by subject area to preserve the expertise of the present judges. A majority of present ALJs endorse the Corps concept but support is much stronger among Social Security Administration (SSA) ALJs than among other ALJs.]

Many of the affected judges believe that no cogent reasons have been advanced that demonstrate a need to establish such a corps. Principally, the bills are designed to insure administrative law judges' decisional independence. It is asserted, however, that the existing statutes and judicial perception of federal administrative law judges comprise satisfactory and sufficient guarantees of such independence. . . .

A. Judicial Perception . . .

The courts accord administrative law judges and their decisions deference and respect. Congress has consistently pursued a course which is designed to afford maximum assurance of decisional independence and special status to administrative law judges. They have been well-insulated from agency influence by statute. The public appears satisfied with their performance. There simply has been no substantive argument or data presented that requires legislative action to improve perceptions of the administrative judiciary. . . .

B. Decisional Independence

Only one example of possible improper agency interference has been cited. That is, the nascent situation in SSA. In that agency, the judges have complained that they are being subjected to improper pressures to deny disability benefits by the imposition of production quotas, and by the conduct of unauthorized performance appraisals which result in unfounded disciplinary action against them.

The concerns of the SSA judges are clearly legitimate. Their allegations, alone, clearly tend to undermine public confidence in the administrative judiciary. If true, those allegations seriously detract from the critical elements of decisional independence which Congress has taken decades to develop.

However, problems of SSA judges apparently are unique to them. . . . In the absence of empirical information that administrative law judges' independence is threatened in other agencies, it clearly is more efficient and appropriate for Congress to concentrate on methods of solving such problems where they exist than to interrupt a system, developed by careful deliberation and proved successful by experience, where there is no attack upon the judges' independence. . . .

C. Administrative Law Judge Expertise

Clearly, a goal of the legislation is to have a group of administrative law judges who are able to conduct hearings of all types. The bill, however, also recognizes the importance of maintaining expertise in certain areas of the law. The seven enumerated substantive divisions are designed to retain the need for specialization.

The bill's design is flawed.

. . . The subject-matter groupings within the divisions is contrary to the purported aim of expertise preservation. Some of the divisions contain such an amalgam of substantive legal subjects that would require judges expert in one area of the division to undertake extensive training to become competent in another subject.

For example, the Division of General Programs is designed to hear cases currently heard by administrative law judges assigned to the Drug Enforcement Administration and the Merit Systems Protection Board. These areas are plainly unrelated to one another. . . . Separate agencies were established by Congress precisely to assure the development and maintenance of entities imbued with a high level of expertise in specialized legal subjects. A merger of certain areas with others diminishes the congressional intent and operational features which have withstood the tests of time and experience. . . .

D. Cost Effectiveness

It has been urged that a unified corps will result in substantial cost savings and efficiencies. That assertion is undocumented. No cost analysis apparently has been made or presented. Instead, this bare assertion is drawn from recent experience among some states which have adopted central panel systems. . . .

§ 3.4.3 ALJs: THE ADMINISTRATIVE COURT ISSUE

MINOW, LETTER TO PRESIDENT KENNEDY

15 Admin.L.Rev. 146 (1963).

[On resigning as chair of the FCC in 1963, Newton Minow wrote a letter to President Kennedy suggesting that the adjudicatory functions of the FCC (and presumably of the other federal regulatory agencies) be transferred to an independent administrative court. He also suggested that the multi-member FCC be replaced by a single administrator. Minow's suggestions were similar to those made by Louis Hector when he left the chair of the Civil Aeronautics Board a few years before. Similar suggestions had been made by a famous commission on government improvements headed by former president Herbert Hoover.]

There are several advantages to assigning the hearing functions now exercised by the Commission to a new administrative court patterned, for example, after the Tax Court.

First, it is clearly desirable to separate the prosecutory function from the function of judging. An agency should not be called upon to investigate fully whether a violation has occurred, to become steeped in all kinds of investigative reports upon which it determines that a hearing is necessary, and then to judge the merits of the case. . . .

It makes for fair play that an agency with such a mission *not* be charged also with the responsibility of judging the results of its mission.

Second, the establishment of the administrative court would greatly improve the decisional process itself. . . .

FCC Commissioners cannot spend several weeks analyzing the record of a case and drafting their own opinions—the work of the Commission would grind to a stop if they did so. As a result, the Commissioners determine the case largely upon the basis of the staff analysis and oral argument and adopt an institutional decision prepared by the staff.

This may be a necessary process but it is clearly not an optimum one. No one would seriously argue that the present institutional procedure is preferable to an administrative court process where the decision-maker is wholly familiar with the record and pleadings and actually drafts his own opinion.

Finally, the administrative court will lead to better formulation of standards. Not only will the administrator be required to lay down definitive and clear policies, if the administrative court is to follow them, but the court could be expected to apply these policies in a meaningful manner which would build up a body of meaningful precedents.

As a result of these drastic revisions in the decision-making process, the problem of the improper *ex parte* attempt to influence the outcome of hearing cases should largely disappear, as it has in the case of the federal courts. Those who make policy and regulate must necessarily have frequent contact with the industry in order to be well-informed. Under the present system, the possibility of improper influence or at the least of charges of such influence is always present. The administrative court, made up of jurists having *only* judicial functions, would not be a similar breeding ground for the *ex parte* contact. . . .

There is, however, one argument which does have some validity. It may be difficult, in practice, to confine the policy-making function to the administrator. The administrative court, in deciding particular cases, may find itself called upon to make policy or may take action which in the administrator's view is inconsistent with the policies he has established. In a division of responsibility such as this, there is always the possibility of some degree of friction between the administrator and the court.

Taking this argument at face value, I would, on balance, still favor establishment of a single administrator-administrative court for the advantages I have previously discussed. But there are countering considerations to the argument. There is no reason why the administrative court should not make policy if the administrator has failed to do so or, indeed, if the administrator decides that the formulation of policy on some particular matter might better await ascertainment of all the facts in the hearing. Further, if the court does not follow the administrator's policies, it is because the administrator has not set out those policies explicitly and clearly. The administrator thus has a ready remedy and one which greatly serves the public interest—clear formulation of policy. In other words, the relationship of the administrator and court, while admittedly a source of potential friction, has also a salutary aspect of promoting definitive policy making. The court could point up fuzzy areas or policy lucunae or indeed, could call to the administrator's attention countering factors stemming from its considerations which might indicate a need for reevaluation of the policy by the administrator. . . .

My purpose here has not been to present a detailed blueprint but rather to advance the principle of separation of regulatory and hearing functions, in the hope that as more voices declare for the principle, a serious study of it will be undertaken. I do not believe it is possible to be a good judge on Monday and Tuesday, a good legislator on Wednesday and Thursday, and a good administrator on Friday.

AUERBACH, "SOME THOUGHTS ON THE HECTOR MEMORANDUM"

1960 Wisc.L.Rev. 183.

[Auerbach responds to the Hector Memorandum which made suggestions closely parallel to Minow's.]

Mr. Hector charges that the independent regulatory commission performs its adjudicatory functions poorly and unfairly. Specifically, he discloses that the CAB does not decide litigated cases before it "on the basis of general principles and standards known to the parties and applicable to all cases," or "on the basis of the voluminous testimony and arguments advanced by the parties and this alone" and that the Board members do not "personally state the reasons for their decisions."

There are no general administrative principles and standards to guide the decision of particular cases. This lack is, of course, a familiar and in the main justified complaint. But it is not a peculiar failure of the administrative agency. Even the Supreme Court of the United States is being criticized for not developing a coherent and intelligible body of constitutional principles. As we saw, Mr. Hector expects the separation of the "legislative" from the "judicial" functions of the regulatory commission to remedy the situation. The Executive branch of the Government would establish the general policies to be applied by the administrative courts in specific cases. The administrative court would then be "free from policy-making," even when it is deciding contested rate or licensing cases.

The relationship which Mr. Hector envisages between the executive agency and the administrative court fails to take sufficient account of the multiple uses of adjudication—(1) to substitute for rule-making in the development of general principles and standards; (2) to accompany rule-making in the development of policy; (3) to handle situations in which it is difficult to develop general principles and standards because the discretionary element is so important; and (4) to apply pre-established principles and standards to particular cases which do not call for any appreciable exercise of discretion.

If all regulatory situations could be made to fall into category (4), Mr. Hector's proposals would suit them all. For only then would the policy-making element in adjudication, never totally absent in any case, be at a minimum. Yet none of the examples Mr. Hector gives of the CAB's failure to develop consistent standards is likely ever to be made to fall into this category.

It is understandable, for example, why any agency would prefer to use case-by-case adjudication, rather than rule-making, to determine such questions of policy as when (and how much) competitive air service should be permitted between particular cities and when and how new route awards should be used as a means of strengthening the financially weaker carriers. No principles or standards can be promulgated which will do more than set forth criteria to guide the exercise of the decision-maker's discretion in particular cases. And the decision-maker would wish to decide cases for a while before attempting to set down these criteria. Mr. Hector's proposed separation of powers would deprive the rule-maker in such cases of adjudicatory experience and the judge of rule-making experience, with the result that both rule-making and adjudication might be inept. . . .

Legislation turned over to an administrative agency is . . ., "unfinished law" which must be completed by the agency "before it is ready for application." Congress expected the legislation entrusted to the agencies Mr. Hector particularly has in mind—the CAB, the FCC, the ICC—to be completed by agency rule-making or adjudication or both in any combination experience indicated would be best. The agency is already subject to judicial and legislative checks. Will the situation be improved if additional checks are provided by dividing the task of implementing legislative policy in the first instance into two tasks—one labeled "legislative" and entrusted to an executive agency and the other "judicial" and entrusted to an administrative court? Though he thinks that separation will "compel active policy-making" by the Executive branch, Mr. Hector is realist enough to know that this will not always happen. . . . The possibility of conflict between the Executive branch and the administrative court, under Mr. Hector's scheme, would be very real. Whether we should risk it depends, of course, upon how bad we think the present situation is and the feasibility of other alternatives. An evil at hand always seems much worse than an imaginary one. . . .

Contrary to Mr. Hector's assumption, members of regulatory commissions in the past have shown that it is possible for the same men to keep separate their roles as "policy-makers" and as "judges," when separation is called for. But such separation is not always desirable. A commissioner should not drive "from his mind as a judge what he knows as an administrator." Administrative agencies were created so that the commissioner's role as policy-maker might aid him in performing his role as adjudicator and vice versa.

To the extent that policy will continue to be made via adjudication, the creation of administrative courts will not succeed in separating the roles of "policy-maker" and "judge." It will, however, ensure that "the officers of administrative courts" will, as Mr. Hector wishes, "conduct themselves like judges" and make bad policy. They will have no specialized staffs to advise them and no opportunity for day-to-day contact with the individuals and groups that will be affected by their policies. They will tend to think only of the parties appearing before them as adversaries. In short, judicial trial procedures and techniques will be used even more than they are today to solve problems for which they are not suited.

SULLIVAN, "INDEPENDENT ADJUDICATION AND OCCUPATIONAL SAFETY AND HEALTH POLICY: A TEST FOR ADMINISTRATIVE COURT THEORY"
31 Admin.L.Rev. 177, 193, 203–04 (1979).

[Sullivan's article discusses OSHRC—the "Review Commission" which adjudicates cases brought by OSHA (the rulemaking, investigating, and prosecuting agency). The Act left a key point unclear: it required removal of toxic materials from the workplace only "to the extent feasible." OSHA failed to adopt regulations defining feasibility, but its policy was to require industry to remove toxics without regard to cost. OSHRC refused to follow OSHA's policy and held that a cost-benefit analysis was necessary. Several Supreme Court decisions grappled with this difference of opinion. *Industrial Union Dept. v. American Petroleum Inst.,* 448 U.S. 607 (1980) (the "benzene" case); *American Textile Mfgrs. Inst. v. Donovan,* 452 U.S. 490 (1981) (the "cotton dust" case which ultimately decided that cost-benefit analysis was not appropriate).]

If OSHA and the Review Commission are unable to resolve their differences on this issue, then the vigorous enforcement of a health policy which protects workers from potentially catastrophic hazards may be frustrated through the inevitable delay resulting from resolution by the appellate courts. . . . [I]f this technique of independent adjudication is to be used more extensively, Congress should take great care to delineate clearly the appropriate role for each of the agencies that it establishes. The purpose of independent adjudication should be to provide the most fair minded review of facts of a particular case. Neither the theories behind administrative courts nor the OSH Act itself anticipate a policy-making role for the adjudicative body. Accordingly, independent adjudication should serve to provide an incentive for the vigorous employment of rulemaking, thus tying the development of policy to a legislative type of process . . . [W]e can conclude from the experience with OSHA and the Review Commission that significant problems of institutional conflict can arise unless Congress clearly specifies the appropriate relationship among rulemaking, enforcement, and adjudicative functions.

See also Johnson, "The Split Enforcement Model: Some Conclusions from the OSHA and MSHA Experiences," 39 Admin.L.Rev. 315 (1987) (split-enforcement model provides improved perception of fairness in regulated industry but at great cost in terms of conflict between the enforcement and adjudicating arms).

Missouri and Maine have adopted administrative court structures. In Missouri, the Administrative Hearing Commission (AHC) renders final adjudicatory decisions in licensing and tax cases. In licensing cases, if the AHC finds that disciplinary action is warranted, it can recommend but not decide on the appropriate punishment (revocation, suspension, reprimand etc.). Unless both the licensee and the agency agree with AHC's recommendation, the case is returned to the licensing agency for another hearing to determine punishment. For favorable evaluations of the AHC, *see* F. Davis, "Judicialization of Administrative Law: The Trial–Type Hearing and the Changing Status of the Hearing Officer," 1977 Duke L.J. 389, 402–08; Project, "Fair Treatment for the Licensed Professional," 37 Mo.L.Rev. 410, 451–66 (1972).

Chapter 4

THE PROCESS OF ADMINISTRATIVE ADJUDICATION

The previous chapter explored some fundamental and enduring problems of administrative adjudication. This chapter assumes that the formal adjudication process of state or federal APAs is applicable. It explores the elements of adjudication in chronological order: it starts with the pre-hearing phase, exploring issues such as parties, discovery and intervention. It continues with the hearing itself and the decisional process. It concludes with some constraints on the decision (such as res judicata or stare decisis). Thus this chapter might be likened to a civil procedure course—except that we consider procedure before an agency rather than in court.

§ 4.1 THE PRE–HEARING PHASE: PARTIES, INVESTIGATION AND DISCOVERY

§ 4.1.1 PARTIES AND INTERVENTION

Issues concerning parties to administrative adjudication might be of two kinds: i) can a person trigger administrative adjudication? ii) can a person intervene in administrative adjudication?

The first issue arises in cases like *West Chicago* in § 3.1.1. An agency proposes to *grant* permission to an applicant (such as Kerr–McGee in the *West Chicago* case). Neither the applicant nor the agency wants a hearing. However, actions which the permittee will take may cause economic or environmental harm to a third party (such as the residents of the city of West Chicago). Another example: an agency and a regulated party (such as a telephone company) may have agreed on a particular rate. Can a consumer who believes the rate is too high compel the agency to hold a hearing? Or appeal to the agency heads an initial decision in favor of granting a permit or setting the rate?

The second issue arises when a person seeks to force the agency to admit it as a party to ongoing adjudication. The applicant for intervention believes that it has an important interest in the result of that proceeding which is not being properly represented by the agency or the other parties to the adjudication.

i. *Forcing administrative adjudication.* The APA, as we have seen, does not require formal adjudication unless an external source calls for an "on the record" hearing. Therefore, whether a party has a right to compel the agency to hold a hearing depends on the terms of some other statute.

Section 189 of the Atomic Energy Act, at issue in *West Chicago*, requires the Commission to grant a hearing "upon the request of any person whose interest may be affected by the proceeding, and shall admit any such person as a party to such proceeding." Suppose (contrary to *West Chicago*) that § 189 was interpreted to require a hearing on the record but that neither the NRC nor Kerr McGee wanted one. Should the City of West Chicago be treated as a "person whose interest may be affected . . .? If so, the Commission must hold a hearing it does not want to hold. Is that a good result?

Suppose further that a hearing was requested by the Union of Concerned Scientists, an anti-nuclear group which had no members living in the West Chicago area. Should that group be entitled to trigger a hearing?

Now contrast 1981 MSAPA §§ 4–102(b)(4) and 1–102(5). Do these provisions take a different tack from § 189(a)? Imagine the *West Chicago* dispute being adjudicated by a state agency that had jurisdiction to reject Kerr McGee's application but proposed to grant it. Could the City of West Chicago force the agency to hold a hearing? How about the Union of Concerned Scientists?

Which model do you prefer—that of § 189 of the Atomic Energy Act or that of MSAPA § 4–102(b)(4)?

ii. *Intervention.* On intervention in an administrative adjudication involving other parties, contrast §§ 555(b) (third sentence) and 551(3) of the federal act with 1981 MSAPA § 4–209. Does § 555 provide for a right to intervene? What is the effect of § 551(3) and its reference to "limited purposes?" Does § 4–209(a) provide for a right to intervene? What is the difference between § 4–209(a) and (b)? What is the significance of § 4–209(c)?

Why would parties want to intervene in an agency proceeding? Is there some way short of intervention by which they could make their positions known? Why would an agency want to refuse a petition to intervene? *See* Comment, "Licensing of Nuclear Power Plants: Abuse of the Intervention Right," 21 U.S.F.L.Rev. 121 (1986) (in one case, intervenors filed 1600 allegations—all of which were ultimately rejected, greatly prolonged licensing process, delay caused serious increase in cost of nuclear power plant).

Federal cases involving the right to be an intervenor in an adjudicative proceeding have repeatedly linked this issue to a different one: standing to seek judicial review, an issue discussed in § 11.1. In *United Church of Christ (UCC) v. FCC*, 359 F.2d 994 (D.C.Cir.1966), a famous opinion written by former Chief Justice Burger while he sat on the Court of Appeals, the issue was whether TV watchers have a right to initiate and to participate in FCC licensing proceedings. Thus the case involves both the issue of whether a person can force a hearing to occur and whether a person can intervene in an ongoing proceeding.

The Communications Act provided that any "party in interest" could file a petition to deny a license application. Station WLBT, in Jackson, Mississippi, applied for license renewal. On behalf of blacks who lived in Jackson and watched the station, UCC asserted that it was a "party in interest" entitled to file a petition to deny the application and to be a party at the hearing. UCC charged that WLBT engaged in racist programming and gross violations of the fairness doctrine. The FCC refused to allow UCC to be a party because it then allowed only economic competitors of existing stations (or stations that might suffer electrical interference) to be parties, not listeners or viewers.

The Court held that TV viewers were "parties in interest" who had the right to petition for denial of a license, participate or intervene in a licensing hearing, and seek judicial review of an unfavorable FCC decision. Treating the right to participate at the administrative level as equivalent to the right to seek judicial review, the court said:

> Since the concept of standing is a practical and functional one designed to insure that only those with a genuine and legitimate interest can participate in a proceeding, we can see no reason to exclude those with such an obvious and acute concern as the listening audience. This much seems essential to insure that the holders of broadcasting licenses be responsive to the needs of the audience, without which the broadcaster could not exist . . .

> The theory that the Commission can always effectively represent the listener interests in a renewal proceeding without the aid and participation of legitimate listener representatives fulfilling the role of private attorneys general is one of those assumptions we collectively try to work with so long as they are reasonably adequate. When it becomes clear, as it does to us now, that it is no longer a valid assumption which stands up under the realities of actual experience, neither we nor the commission can continue to rely on it . . .

> We cannot believe that the Congressional mandate of public participation . . . was meant to be limited to writing letters to the Commission, to inspection of records, to the Commission's grace in considering listener claims, or to mere non-participating appearance at hearings. We cannot fail to note that the long history of complaints against WLBT beginning in 1955 had left the Commission virtually unmoved in the subsequent renewal proceedings, and

it seems not unlikely that the 1964 renewal application might well have been routinely granted except for the determined and sustained efforts of Appellants at no small expense to themselves. Such beneficial contribution as these Appellants . . . can make must not be left to the grace of the Commission . . .

In order to safeguard the public interest in broadcasting, therefore, we hold that some "audience participation" must be allowed in license renewal proceedings. We recognize this will create problems for the Commission but it does not necessarily follow that "hosts" of protestors must be granted standing to challenge a renewal application or that the Commission need allow the administrative processes to be obstructed or overwhelmed by captious or purely obstructive protests. The Commission can avoid such results by developing appropriate regulations by statutory rulemaking. Although it denied Appellants standing, it employed *ad hoc* criteria in determining that these Appellants were responsible spokesmen for representative groups having significant roots in the listening community. These criteria can afford a basis for developing formalized standards to regulate and limit public intervention to spokesmen who can be helpful . . .

The fears of regulatory agencies that their processes will be inundated by expansion of standing criteria are rarely borne out. Always a restraining factor is the expense of participation in the administrative process, an economic reality which will operate to limit the number of those who will seek participation; legal and related expenses of administrative proceedings are such that even those with large economic interests find the cost burdensome. Moreover, the listening public seeking intervention in a license renewal proceeding cannot attract lawyers to represent their cause by the prospect of lucrative contingent fees, as can be done, for example, in rate cases . . .

The D.C. Circuit continued to link status as a party to the right to seek judicial review in *National Welfare Rights Org. v. Finch*, 429 F.2d 725 (D.C.Cir.1970). NWRO, an organization representing welfare recipients, would have standing to seek judicial review of federal government approval of a state welfare plan. It followed, therefore, that the organization was entitled to intervene in administrative proceedings concerning the legality of that plan. The court noted:

The right of judicial review cannot be taken as fully realized, however, if appellants are excluded from participating in the proceeding to be reviewed . . . [I]ntervention is necessary in order to make the right to review effective . . . [W]ithout participation in the administrative hearing, issues which appellants here might wish to raise about the character of the state's plans may have been foreclosed as a topic for review . . . [T]he Secretary's finding of fact if supported by substantial evidence will be conclusive . . . [T]his limited review underscores the need for appellants' participation in the administrative hearing as a party . . . [B]esides functioning as a means of perfecting the right to review, intervention will serve to foster an important legislative goal. [The Court here quotes material from *Goldberg v. Kelly*] . . .

[I]ncreased participation through intervention creates problems for both the tribunal and other parties; multiple and extended cross-examination may be deleterious to the administrative process. Agencies may fear that "their processes will be inundated by expansion of standing criteria" . . . The threat of hundreds of intervenors in conformity hearings is more apparent than real. The expense of participation, particularly for welfare beneficiaries, is a factor limiting participation; legal and related expenses can be burdensome . . . [A]gencies have some discretion in limiting intervention . . .

[W]e contemplate enlargement of the rights of participation already accorded [appellants] only to the extent of additional right to present live witnesses and to cross-examine witnesses for other parties. We do not hold that this intervenor status creates in appellants a right to participate in any way in the Secretary's informal efforts, before or after the calling of a hearing, to bring a state into conformity, nor do we limit his right to terminate a hearing . . . upon a determination by him that it is no longer necessary because he believes that conformity has been achieved . . .

Although the *NWRO* case holds that a party who has standing to seek judicial review is entitled to intervene, the converse proposition does not hold true. A party who *lacks* standing to seek judicial review need not be *excluded* from administrative proceedings, for standing to sue depends on more restrictive criteria than standing to be a party in administrative proceedings. *Koniag, Inc. v. Andrus,* 580 F.2d 601 (D.C. Cir.1978), *cert. denied,* 439 U.S. 1052 (1978) (party can be both "interested" and "aggrieved" for intervention purposes even though lacking standing to sue because its claim was too speculative). A concurring opinion by Judge Bazelon in the *Koniag* case argues that judicial standing doctrine should be separated from question of party status at the administrative level. Do you agree with Bazelon?

Problem. You are general counsel of a state agency (the Coastal Commission) which grants permits for the development of beachfront property. Without such a permit, owners of beachfront property cannot build on their property or even make changes to existing buildings.

The agency heads are concerned that a large number of persons sometimes ask to be parties to permitting hearings. These are persons who do not live near the beach but are interested in securing access to the beach for the general public or in preventing building projects at the beach. Until now, the Commission allowed anyone who applied to be a party. The result is that a few hearings became quite complicated. Each party wanted to put on its own witnesses, introduce its own documentary and economic analyses, and cross-examine the witnesses of other parties.

What steps are suggested by the *UCC* and *NWRO* decisions? By 1981 MSAPA § 4–209(c)? How about the adoption of rules which circumvent hearing requirements as discussed in § 3.2, *supra?* Or should you tell your bosses that public participation is good and they should not seek to limit it?

§ 4.1.2 INVESTIGATION AND DISCOVERY: AN AGENCY'S POWER TO OBTAIN INFORMATION

In order to enforce the law, an agency must secure massive amounts of information about the regulated industry. The information is needed for a variety of tasks, such as rulemaking, preparation of legislative proposals, or investigating possible violations of the law in preparation for adjudicatory or other law enforcement activity.

Most of the needed information is supplied voluntarily in routinely filed reports or in response to specific requests for information. Occasionally, however, the agency must use more forceful techniques to find out whether the law is being violated or to obtain evidence for an enforcement proceeding. It may do so by requiring private parties to keep *records* and file *reports* or by seeking specific information and documents through a *subpoena duces tecum*. With respect to agency investigation, read APA § 555(c) and (d); 1981 MSAPA § 4–210. Notice the key point: agencies need a statutory basis other than the APA in order to compel the production of information. It is not an inherent power.

Sometimes the necessary information and evidence is obtained through a *physical inspection* of a home (for example to detect housing code violations) or of business records or premises. By the general rule, a search warrant must be obtained before an administrative inspection of a home or the areas of a business that are not open to the public. In *Marshall v. Barlow's Inc.*, 436 U.S. 307 (1978), the Court held that a warrant was required before OSHA could compel a business to submit to inspection of its premises for compliance with employee safety rules.

However, to obtain such a warrant, the inspector need not establish probable cause to believe that a violation had occurred. It is sufficient if the choice of the particular employer to be inspected was based on reasonable and neutral standards, such as a statistical sampling technique approved by the agency or a timetable for inspections based on relevant classifications. The warrant can be obtained ex parte (i.e. without notice to the employer). Although the warrant requirement is thus easy to satisfy, at least it tends to limit the possibility that an inspection is motivated by harassment or other improper purposes.

There are significant exceptions to the rule of the *Barlow's* case. Take, for example, an auto junkyard. State law requires a junk dealer to have and display a license and keep records of purchases and sales. The statute requires him to submit to periodic inspections. Such "pervasively regulated" businesses have a reduced expectation of privacy and warrantless inspections are constitutionally acceptable.

Four criteria must be met to justify warrantless administrative inspections: (i) There must be a substantial government interest in regulating the business, (ii) unannounced inspections must be necessary to further the regulatory scheme, (iii) the statute must advise the owner of the periodic inspection program, and (iv) searches must be limited in time, place and scope. The New York auto junkyard inspection scheme met all of these criteria. *New York v. Burger,* 107 S.Ct. 2636 (1987). On the same basis, warrantless inspections authorized by an agency's enabling act have been upheld for the search of students by public school officials, *New Jersey v. T.L.O.,* 469 U.S. 325 (1985), and on gun and liquor licensees. *United States v. Biswell,* 406 U.S. 311 (1972); *Colonnade Catering Corp. v. United States,* 397 U.S. 72 (1970).

It appears that evidence which has been illegally seized in violation of the Fourth Amendment may nevertheless be admissible in some or all administrative proceedings even if it could not be admitted in a criminal proceeding under the exclusionary rule. The point is not completely settled, however. *See INS v. Lopez–Mendoza,* 468 U.S. 1032 (1984) (exclusionary rule not applicable in deportation proceeding); *United States v. Janis,* 428 U.S. 433 (1976) (evidence obtained by unlawful state search admissible in federal civil tax proceeding).

Are there any limits to an agency's power to compel the production of information through required reports or through a subpoena? Should there be any limits?

APPEAL OF FTC LINE OF BUSINESS REPORT LITIGATION

595 F.2d 685 (D.C.Cir.1978), *cert. denied,* 439 U.S. 958 (1978).

[Sec. 6(b) of the Federal Trade Commission Act empowers the FTC to require the filing of reports regarding a company's "organization, business, conduct, practices, management, and relation to other corporations." In 1975, the FTC ordered 450 of the nation's largest domestic manufacturers to file a Line of Business (LB) form in which it would furnish specific financial information (revenues, profits, assets) for each separate line of business.

The purpose of the LB form was to make statistical studies of various areas of the economy in order to target possible industry-wide antitrust violations or unfair trade practices. This data is not otherwise available because financial statements usually lump together all the lines of business in which a corporation is engaged.

Preparation of the LB form could be costly since the information involved cannot be easily obtained through conventional accounting techniques. The FTC revised the LB form extensively in response to industry criticism and suggestions by the General Accounting Office. The FTC estimated that it might cost an average of $24,000 per corporation to file the form, but it might cost some conglomerates up to $100,000. Dupont claimed that it would cost $350,000 to $700,000 and W.R. Grace estimated it would cost $630,000, but the District Court doubted these figures.

Many corporations refused to file the forms. The FTC obtained federal district court orders requiring the forms to be filed. The Court of Appeals first held that the FTC was not required to employ rulemaking before requiring the forms. The APA distinguishes rulemaking, investigation, and adjudication. Each has independent procedural requirements and the FTC is not required to use either rulemaking or adjudication procedure to conduct investigations. APA § 555(c) makes it clear that investigative acts need only be "authorized by law" and § 6(b) of the FTC Act provides that authority.]

1. THE APPLICABLE STANDARDS OF REVIEW

Section 9 of the Federal Trade Commission Act vests jurisdiction in the district courts to command compliance, by mandamus, with FTC informational report orders issued pursuant to Section 6(b) of the FTC Act. Prior to commanding compliance with the LB . . . orders, the District Court reviewed these FTC programs under the criteria and summary procedures applicable to judicial enforcement of compulsory process by administrative agencies set forth by the Supreme Court in *United States v. Morton Salt Co.,* [89] and by this court in *FTC v. Texaco, Inc.* [90] Appellants contend that a higher standard of review and a plenary review preceding was required on the theory that the LB . . . program [is] "agency action" subject to the arbitrary and capricious standard of Section 706(2) of the Administrative Procedure Act. We reject this argument because in our view the limited scope of review found by the Supreme Court and this court to be appropriate for compulsory process enforcement is applicable to enforcement of the Section 6(b) report orders being enforced in this proceeding.

In *United States v. Morton Salt Co.,* the Supreme Court reviewed Federal Trade Commission orders requiring salt producers to file informational reports designed to determine whether these corporations were complying with a court order to cease and desist certain unfair trade practices. These FTC orders were issued pursuant to Section 6(b) . . . the same authority invoked by the Commission here. Appellants, nevertheless, would have us find *Morton Salt* inapposite because the report orders in *Morton Salt* were part of a focused FTC investigation, whereas the LB order [is] incident to general statistical surveys. The FTC's authority to require reports under Section 6(b) is not limited to pursuing a focused theory of unlawful activity. The Supreme Court in *Morton Salt* discussed the nature and scope of this authority in some detail.

89. 338 U.S. 632 (1950).

90. 555 F.2d 862 (en banc) *cert. denied,* 431 U.S. 974.

The only power that is involved here is the power to get information from those who best can give it and who are most interested in not doing so. Because judicial power is reluctant if not unable to summon evidence until it is shown to be relevant to issues in litigation, it does not follow that an administrative agency charged with seeing that the laws are enforced may not have and exercise powers of original inquiry. It has a power of inquisition, if one chooses to call it that, which is not derived from the judicial function. It is more analogous to the Grand Jury, which does not depend on a case or controversy for power to get evidence but can investigate merely on suspicion that the law is being violated, or even just because it wants assurance that it is not.

The Court went on to state that the purpose of the investigation may be nothing more than to satisfy "official curiosity," because "law enforcing agencies have a legitimate right to satisfy themselves that corporate behavior is consistent with the law and the public interest." Indeed, as we noted in *FTC v. Texaco, Inc.*, the investigative power of the Commission may be used to reveal the need for changes in the law for the purpose of making recommendations to Congress. The Commission's purpose in conducting the LB . . . [survey] falls clearly within the purview of its broad investigative powers under Section 6(b). . . .

The FTC seeks to establish data banks for use in targeting areas for investigating and enforcement efforts.

Although the investigative powers of the regulatory agencies are broad, they are not unlimited, and are subject to judicial review "[t]o protect against mistaken or arbitrary orders." As we stated in *Texaco*, however, "while the court's function is 'neither minor nor ministerial,' *Oklahoma Press Publishing Co. v. Walling*, 327 U.S. at 217 n. 57, the scope of issues which may be litigated in an enforcement proceeding must be narrow, because of the important governmental interest in the expeditious investigation of possible unlawful activity." The agency's investigative order, whether it is a subpoena or an information-report order, must be enforced if it does not transcend the agency's investigatory power, the demand is not unduly burdensome or too indefinite, and the information sought is reasonably relevant.

2. THE RELEVANCE AND BURDENSOMENESS DETERMINATIONS

The corporate appellants argue that if the FTC report orders are summarily enforceable as ordinary compulsory process, as we have concluded they are, the District Court erred in evaluating the relevance and burdensomeness of the Line of Business orders. We understand appellants to make three claims. First, that the District Court failed to determine that the LB data sought was relevant to the agency's general purpose as required by *Texaco*. Second, that it was error for the District Court to decide the question of burdensomeness on the basis of five corporate affidavits and the testimony of two corporate witnesses. And finally, that the Court erred in considering relevance and burdensomeness independently.

As recognized in *Texaco*, relevance is to be measured against the agency's general purpose in gathering the investigative material. The District Court found that "the record in this action provides an ample basis for drawing the limited conclusion, without further evidentiary hearing, that the data sought in the LB program is not totally useless. . . ." If anything, the District Court was too guarded in its assessment of the relevance of the LB data. Indeed, in our view, the record reflects that the Line of Business data sought is reasonably relevant to the Commission's general purpose of collecting corporate financial information in order to assess industry-by-industry performance and market structure. As we are assured that the FTC surveys satisfy this degree of relevance, we need not decide if a lesser standard would suffice.

The next question is whether the District Court abused its discretion in determining that the Line of Business reporting requirements do not impose an undue burden on the respondent corporations. As we indicated in *Texaco*, the onus of demonstrating that a request is unduly burdensome is the corporation's. When the inquiry is conducted pursuant to a lawful purpose and the request is relevant to that objective, its reasonableness will be presumed absent a showing that compliance threatens to disrupt or unduly hinder the normal operations of a business. Concerned that the administrative record was insufficient to permit resolution of the question of burdensomeness, and in view of the corporations' representations that they might lay an adequate evidentiary foundation with financial presentations from a "small number" of their group, the District Court invited the corporate parties to submit five affidavits on the cost of compliance with each of the two reporting programs. In addition, a hearing was held at which all of the affiants were summoned to present oral testimony. The District Court concluded that, assuming the accuracy of the most extravagant cost estimates, the costs of compliance were *de minimis* relative to the overall corporate operating budgets. We think that under the circumstances appellants were extended ample opportunity to establish their claims of burdensomeness, and we are unable to perceive any error in the District Court's assessment of the inadequacy of their showing in that regard.

Finally, appellants have failed to persuade us that the District Court erred in its refusal to disregard the long and consistent line of authority supporting independent consideration of relevance and burdensomeness. . . .

Notes and Questions

1. *Judicial enforcement.* Note that the FTC was required to go to court to enforce the reporting requirement. Why not dispense with this step by giving agencies the contempt power? In *ICC v. Brimson*, 154 U.S. 447 (1894), the Court indicated that an agency could not be given power to enforce its own subpoenas by holding persons who refuse

to comply in contempt. Congress has abided by the *Brimson* decision and assumed that judicial enforcement is needed; thus the issue remains unresolved. A minority view, at the state level, indicates that agencies can be given the contempt power, so that they need not go to court to enforce subpoenas. *See Morton v. Workers Comp. App. Bd.,* 238 Cal.Rptr. 651 (Cal.App.1987). However, the agency given the contempt power in the *Morton* case was created by the state constitution, not a statute, which might give it status equivalent to a court.

Under *Brimson,* an agency may lack power to implement discovery sanctions; if a party ignores a subpoena, the agency must go to court to enforce it and cannot preclude the party from introducing evidence. *See NLRB v. International Medication Systems,* 640 F.2d 1110 (9th Cir. 1981), cert. denied 455 U.S. 1017 (1982). Should an agency be permitted to hold against a party in an adjudication because the party ignores a relevant agency reporting requirement or subpoena?

2. *Defenses to subpoena enforcement.* Like virtually all recent federal cases, the *FTC Line of Business* case defers to broad and burdensome agency demands for information. Cases from the late 1940's like *Morton Salt* (dealing with required reports) and *Oklahoma Press* (dealing with subpoenas) have long since removed the roadblocks. These cases make it clear that such demands are almost always "reasonable" under the Fourth Amendment. The analogy is to a grand jury subpoena, not to a search warrant. Older decisions which condemned agency "fishing expeditions" are not longer followed. *FTC v. American Tobacco Co.,* 264 U.S. 298 (1924), a famous opinion by Justice Holmes to this effect, is now of only historical interest.

The agency need not establish probable cause to believe that a violation of law has occurred, nor that the subpoenaed person is subject to its jurisdiction, nor that the information sought would be relevant evidence in some future adjudication. It is sufficient that the information is gathered for a purpose that the agency is entitled to pursue (e.g. investigating to ascertain whether the antitrust and fair trade practice laws have been violated) and is reasonably relevant to that inquiry. The subpoenaed persons cannot raise defenses relating to the merits (such as that the statute of limitations on filing a complaint has run out). *EEOC v. Tempel Steel Co.,* 814 F.2d 482 (7th Cir.1987).

As the Court said in the leading case on the subject: "Nor was the District Court authorized to decide the question of [whether the statute covered the company] itself. The evidence sought by the subpoena was not plainly incompetent or irrelevant to any lawful purpose of the Secretary in the discharge of her duties under the Act, and it was the duty of the District Court to order its production for the Secretary's consideration . . . The consequence of the action of the District Court [in trying the coverage issue] was to disable the Secretary from rendering a complete decision on the alleged violation as Congress had directed." *Endicott Johnson Corp. v. Perkins,* 317 U.S. 501, 509 (1943). That case also held that the agency need not resolve the issue of coverage before it subpoenaed information concerning violation of the statute. The order in which the agency decided to take up the issues, and to seek information about the issues, was left to agency discretion.

Nevertheless, a few defenses to a subpoena can still be raised: the face of the subpoena might disclose that the information sought concerns a type of matter over which the agency has no jurisdiction and thus no power to investigate. The agency might have violated a procedural requirement in its statute or rules with respect to the issuance of subpoenas. Finally, a trial court might find a request too vague and indefinite or unreasonably broad or burdensome. As the *FTC Line of Business* decision shows, however, these kinds of claims are difficult to sustain. See, e.g., *CAB v. Hermann,* 353 U.S. 322 (1957), upholding a subpoena for all the books, records and documents of an airline and its stockholders for a period of 38 months (the only solace to the company was that inspection would take place at its place of business so that the records did not have to be copied or moved).

In addition, a court may refuse to enforce a subpoena because the subject of the demand sustains the burden of showing that the agency is acting in bad faith for an improper purpose and thus abusing the court's process. Thus it might be found that the agency is trying to harass the demandee or put pressure on him to settle some collateral dispute. In tax cases, for example, the IRS ordinarily has no difficulty enforcing subpoenas. However, the subpoenas must be for the purpose of obtaining information to resolve civil tax disputes; if the IRS has decided to proceed criminally against the taxpayer, it must use a grand jury or district court subpoena to get information. Thus a civil subpoena is no longer enforceable once the IRS has referred (or decided to refer) a case to the Justice Department for prosecution. *United States v. LaSalle Nat. Bank,* 437 U.S. 298 (1978); Int.Rev.Code § 7602(b).

Note that the agency is not required to give notice to the person investigated when it subpoenas materials from a third party—even though it will be too late for the person investigated to raise any of these defenses once the third party turns over the material. *SEC v. Jerry T. O'Brien, Inc.,* 467 U.S. 735 (1984).

3. *State law and investigative subpoenas.* To the authorities discussed in the previous note, compare *Levin v. Murawski,* 449 N.E.2d 730 (N.Y.1983), *cert. denied,* 476 U.S. 1171 (1984), involving an investigative subpoena to a physician for specific patient records issued by the New York Board for Professional Conduct. The Board stated simply that it had received complaints from patients about the doctor. The Court of Appeals held that the Board must meet a minimum threshold foundation before a court can enforce the subpoena. The foundation would resemble the requirement of probable cause in obtaining a search warrant—at least some assurance of the reliability of the complainant. Said the court: "It is ancient law that no agency of government may conduct an unlimited and general inquisition into the affairs of persons within its jurisdiction solely on the prospect of possible

violations of law being discovered, especially with respect to subpoenas duces tecum . . . There must be authority, relevancy, and some basis for inquisitorial action."

The three dissenters in the *Levin* case argued that this requirement would frustrate disciplinary investigations of physicians (which the legislature had been trying to streamline and strengthen). Who is correct? Which authority is more in line with current attitudes about bureaucracy and privacy—carte blanche decisions like *Oklahoma Press* and *Morton Salt* or more restrictive decisions like *Levin?*

4. *Privileges.* The attorney-client privilege and the work product privilege apply to agency investigations. In federal courts there is no accountant-client privilege. *Couch v. United States,* 409 U.S. 322 (1973). At least in the states, other evidentiary privileges apply (spousal, physician-patient etc.). *See* 1981 MSAPA § 4–212(a).

A person who is the subject of administrative investigation (federal, state or local) may assert the constitutional privilege against self incrimination in order to withhold documents or refuse to testify. However, more often than not, the privilege against self incrimination is not applicable and the individual must testify or furnish documents in response to a subpoena.

i. In a criminal case, a defendant can refuse to take the stand. In an administrative case, a witness cannot refuse to take the stand and be sworn (but may assert the privilege to refuse to answer specific questions).

ii. Suppose an administrative proceeding and a criminal case are pending at the same time. For example, the same act might lead to disbarment of an attorney and to conviction of a felony. The attorney would try to defer disbarment proceedings until the criminal case is over, because he might wish to testify in the administrative case but to rely on his privilege in the criminal case. A court has discretion to delay the civil matter but the attorney has no absolute right to a delay. *See SEC v. Dresser Industries, Inc.,* 628 F.2d 1368 (D.C.Cir. en banc 1980), *cert. denied,* 449 U.S. 993 (1980); *Savoy Club v. Board of Supervisors,* 91 Cal.Rptr. 198 (Cal.App.1970).

iii. If authorized by statute, the agency can offer immunity and thus compel disclosure. *See* 18 U.S.C. § 6002(2) (federal agency can compel testimony by granting use immunity to person who refuses to testify or provide other information).

iv. The privilege does not apply to corporations, partnerships or unincorporated entities like unions. Thus the custodian of an entity's records must disclose them and cannot claim any personal privilege relating to the entity's records—even if the materials might incriminate him or her. *Braswell v. United States,* 108 S.Ct. 2284 (1988) (custodian); *Bellis v. United States,* 417 U.S. 85 (1974) (partnership records).

v.   The privilege can be asserted only if the person fearing incrimination (or his attorney, assuming the attorney-client privilege applies) is in possession of the documents subpoenaed. *Couch v. United States, supra* (taxpayer cannot assert privilege with respect to papers in possession of accountant).

vi.   The privilege does not apply to materials seized under a valid search warrant because the person from whom the documents are seized is not compelled to admit anything about them. *Andresen v. Maryland,* 427 U.S. 463 (1976).

vii.   The privilege against disclosure of private papers applies only if the *act* of producing the papers would be incriminatory (because it would admit that the papers existed or were authentic or that the demandee possessed them). The contents of the papers themselves (at least in the case of business records) are not privileged. In effect, this seems to confine the privilege to papers prepared by the individual asserting the privilege (in that case by producing the documents the taxpayer would admit they were authentic). *See United States v. Doe,* 465 U.S. 605 (1984) (act of producing business records would be incriminatory—but it could be compelled under immunity statute); *Fisher v. United States,* 425 U.S. 391 (1976), (taxpayer could not claim the privilege for workpapers prepared by his accountant because the act of producing them is not incriminating).

viii.   The privilege may be inapplicable to the production of records if a statute requires those records to be prepared and maintained. *See Shapiro v. United States,* 335 U.S. 1 (1948), holding that there is no privilege to withhold incriminating business records by a person subject to price controls because the statute required them to be maintained. Similarly, *In re Grand Jury Subpoena Duces Tecum (Underhill),* 781 F.2d 64 (6th Cir.1986), *cert. denied,* 479 U.S. 813 (1986), required an auto dealer to produce odometer records for a grand jury investigation because they were required to be kept under state law. The court held that the *Shapiro* doctrine applies even though the act of producing the records might be incriminating under *United States v. Doe, supra.*

However, at some point the "required records" doctrine runs into the Fifth Amendment privilege, for a person should not be required to maintain records that prove his or her criminality. *See Marchetti v. United States,* 390 U.S. 39 (1968), holding that a statute could not require a gambler to prepare and keep records in order to make the gambler incriminate himself. The *Marchetti* case distinguished *Shapiro* on three grounds: (i) Marchetti was required to supply information unrelated to records he would normally maintain; (ii) there were no "public aspects" to the information demanded from Marchetti; (iii) unlike *Shapiro,* the requirements imposed in *Marchetti* arose in a criminal rather than a regulatory area of inquiry.

This note is intended only to alert you to the existence of common-law and constitutional privileges in administrative investigation; this major subject in constitutional and evidence law cannot be treated in detail here.

5. *Paperwork reduction.* As the *FTC Line of Business* case indicates, under present law courts can do little to inhibit burdensome demands for information. Consider, however, that numerous governmental agencies may all demand that specific records be kept and reports and forms be filed. Viewed individually, these demands may make sense; the regulated party is in the best position to compile the information which an agency needs. In the aggregate, the paperwork burden can be crushing, particularly for a small business.

In 1980, Congress enacted the Paperwork Reduction Act, 44 USC §§ 3501–20. That act gives an office in OMB (the Office of Information and Regulatory Affairs or OIRA) the power to review information-gathering demands of all agencies. Before imposing a new demand, the agency must satisfy OIRA that the information is necessary for the proper performance of the agency's function, including whether the information will have practical utility. OMB has veto power over most agencies; in the case of an independent agency, OMB can be overridden by a majority vote of the agency heads.

OMB has attempted to reduce the total paperwork burden on individuals and business by persuading agencies to cut down on mandatory reporting. It claims that the total burden on the economy of required forms has been considerably decreased since 1980.

6. *Publicity.* Agencies frequently issue press releases to inform the public about a pending investigation, issuance of a complaint, or the conclusion of an adjudication.

> Adverse publicity . . . imposes a deprivation on private . . . firms without the due processes of law normally associated with government action encroaching upon property or persons. Formal orders from administrative agencies are preceded by notice with an opportunity for hearing, and the orders are often supported by a reasoned decision. But usually no protection other than the common sense and good will of the administrator prevents unreasonable use of coercive publicity. Furthermore, judicial review cannot undo the widespread effects of erroneous adverse agency publicity. The result is that the person or industry named may be irretrievably injured by inaccurate, excessive, or premature publicity. Second, agencies sometimes use adverse publicity as an unauthorized sanction . . .

E. Gellhorn, "Adverse Publicity By Administrative Agencies," 86 Harv.L.Rev. 1380, 1419–21 (1973). Gellhorn recommends that agencies adopt published rules of policy and procedure concerning publicity of agency action. The rules should balance the need for adequately serving the public interest and the need for adequately protecting persons affected by adverse publicity. In particular, publicity should be issued only if there is a significant risk that the public health or safety may be impaired or substantial economic harm may occur unless the public is immediately notified. *See* "Adverse Agency Publicity," ACUS Recommendation 73–1, 1 C.F.R. § 305.73–1.

FTC v. Cinderella Career & Finishing Schools, Inc., 404 F.2d 1308 (D.C.Cir.1968), held that the FTC could issue press releases announcing the filing of a complaint because consumers are entitled to know the identity of those who prey upon them. The court also held that a press release announcing that the FTC had "reason to believe" that Cinderella had violated the law did not evidence bias or prejudgment. In a concurring opinion, however, Judge Robinson argued that an agency should not automatically issue adverse publicity. It should balance the damage to private industry against protection of the public.

7. *Discovery.* Once an adjudication has formally commenced (through filing of a complaint or similar document), both the agency and the private party may seek information in the hands of the other or a third party.

Note that neither the federal act nor 1981 MSAPA provides for discovery, although some states do have administrative discovery statutes and some (like Florida) simply apply the ordinary civil discovery rules to administrative cases. In *Shively v. Stewart,* 421 P.2d 65 (Cal. 1966), the California Supreme Court adopted administrative discovery by judicial rule to promote fair adjudication. California then enacted statutes providing for limited discovery such as production of documents and witness lists but not depositions or interrogatories. *See* Cal. Govt.Code §§ 11,507 to 11,507.7 (West, 1988 Supp.).

Many statutes and agency rules provide for the issuance of discovery subpoenas. However, the right to issuance of post-complaint subpoenas may not be as broad as the agency's right to investigate (discussed above). An ALJ may refuse to issue a post-complaint subpoena (either to the agency staff or to the private party) if the information sought would not be relevant to the charges in the complaint (as distinguished from relevant to a much broader investigation) or would be unduly burdensome. *See* APA § 555(d). Compare the bracketed and unbracketed versions of 1981 MSAPA § 4–210(a).

A conflict may arise between the rules for investigative reports or subpoenas (where virtually anything goes) and the rules for post-complaint discovery subpoenas (where the ALJ may exert some control over the process). In the *FTC Line of Business* case, the court refused to halt LB reporting from nine of the parties that were engaged in pending FTC adjudications. Those parties argued that information from the LB reports would find their way "through the back door" into the adjudication despite a failure to meet the more demanding rules for post-complaint discovery. The FTC argued that it could freely use this information in adjudication. The court ruled that the problem can be resolved later if the FTC seeks to introduce evidence obtained through required reports. *See also FTC v. Atlantic Richfield Co.,* 567 F.2d 96 (D.C.Cir.1977) (expressing grave doubts about whether material obtained through investigatory subpoenas can be introduced in evidence without complying with discovery rules).

Another conflict can arise between an individual's right to obtain copies of government documents under state or federal Freedom of Information Acts and the individual's right to discovery of documents from the agency when engaged in litigation before the agency or in court. As further discussed in the chapter on Freedom of Information (§ 8.1 *infra*), the individual can choose either approach.

8. *Compulsory process.* It remains unclear whether an agency is constitutionally required to provide for subpoenas to enable a private party to compel the attendance and testimony of unwilling witnesses. However, compulsory process is usually available and it often requires attendance by witnesses anywhere in the state or (in the case of federal agencies) the entire nation. See, e.g., Cal.Govt.Code § 11,510. What if an agency has no subpoena power and a party to a license revocation proceeding before that agency claims that she cannot present an adequate defense without benefit of a subpoena because witnesses essential to her defense refuse to testify voluntarily?

9. *Confidentiality.* Must an agency keep confidential the information which it obtains through required reports or subpoenas? In the *FTC Line of Business* case, the court refused to enjoin the LB reports on the ground that the FTC might make the information public, particularly in light of safeguards which were built into the program. Instead, the claim of confidentiality must await an actual threat to disclose the information.

In some cases, federal statutes preclude an agency from disclosing information. See, for example, the Privacy Act of 1974, 5 U.S.C. § 552a and the Trade Secrets Act, 18 U.S.C. § 1905. The Privacy Act prohibits disclosure of records about individuals, except in limited circumstances. The Trade Secrets Act makes it a crime for any official of the United States to disclose any trade secret information or confidential financial data "except as provided by law." *See Chrysler Corp. v. Brown,* 441 U.S. 281 (1979) (agency regulation allowing it to disclose confidential material was unauthorized; hence disclosure would violate § 1905). The Privacy Act and Trade Secrets Act are discussed further in §§ 8.1.2 and 8.3, *infra*).

10. *Problem—publicity.* Your client Joan owns La Scala, a gourmet restaurant providing her a net income of $450,000 per year. The Department of Health, a local agency charged by statute with the duty of inspecting and licensing restaurants, inspects La Scala and claims to have found traces of rodents, in violations of the health code. Joan disputes the accuracy of these findings. The Department agrees to hold a hearing on the matter at which time Joan may challenge the findings. The Department also indicates that it will immediately issue a press release indicating its findings and announcing the forthcoming hearing. Joan wants to avoid issuance of the press release. Can she do

anything to prevent it? Would such a press release be lawful even if its effect would be to put Joan out of business?

11. *Problem—subpoenas.* In Madison, it is a crime for an insurance company to engage in "deceptive or manipulative insurance practices." The Madison Insurance Commission (MIC) has power to order any insurance company doing business in Madison to cease and desist from the practice of refusing to pay justified claims. It also has power to order the refund of premiums to persons who were denied payment of clearly proper claims.

Under the Insurance Code, MIC has power to investigate any matter relating to insurance. It can issue a subpoena duces tecum, calling for the production of documents, the answering of written questions, or the testimony of witnesses, if it has reason to believe that any law relating to insurance is being violated. If a subpoena is not complied with, the state Attorney General can seek an order from the Superior Court requiring compliance. Disregard of such an order is punishable as civil contempt. If the Court orders compliance, the demandee must pay the attorneys' fees incurred by the Attorney General.

Your client, Security First Insurance Co., is a large business employing 2700 persons. Its home office is in Madison but it sells insurance in several other states through branch offices. It specializes in selling health insurance to elderly people (who may also be covered by Medicare). The MIC staff believes that Security has a pattern of refusing to pay clearly proper claims so that insured persons are unable to obtain hospital care. Security denies any managerial policy which encourages such tactics or that its record is any worse than that of other companies.

Mr. Warren, a vice president of Security, has received a subpoena duces tecum ordering him to appear in three weeks and bring with him all files and other documents relating to health insurance on persons over the age of 55 years in effect for the years 1982 to 1986. In addition, he was ordered to appear three weeks later to give sworn testimony.

Warren says that there is a record of hostility between Security's management and Bob Jordan, the vigorously pro-consumer Insurance Commissioner. Warren particularly fears adverse publicity; MIC often issues press releases when it begins an investigation but it has not yet done so.

The company is distressed by the breadth of the demand for documents. Literally millions of pieces of paper are covered. Warren thinks they would fill sixty large trucks. There is no staff available to gather them (they are stored in several places and mixed with material on insured persons under 55 and with other kinds of insurance). Some of the older documents are on microfiche and thus difficult to read and easily lost. Many of the records involve currently insured persons and are needed for business. Moreover, management does not trust MIC to take proper care of the documents while they are inspected and copied. Many of the policies cover residents of other states. MIC believes that it has jurisdiction over these employees because Security's home office is in Madison. Security disagrees. What is your strategy?

§ 4.2   THE HEARING PHASE

This subsection addresses some of the issues that arise during the actual process of formal adjudication. That process closely resembles a judicial trial. The parties introduce documentary evidence, call and examine witnesses, cross-examine the witnesses called by their adversaries, make oral arguments and submit briefs. *See* § 556(d) of the federal act; 1981 MSAPA § 4–211(2).

§ 4.2.1   RIGHT TO CLOSED OR OPEN HEARING

Does an individual have the right to an open hearing at which the public and the press can be present when he thinks publicity would be valuable to him? To a closed hearing when the testimony might be embarrassing to him? Why might an agency want a closed or an open hearing? What is the bearing of the right to a public criminal trial under the sixth amendment?

In *Fitzgerald v. Hampton,* 467 F.2d 755 (D.C.Cir.1972), a federal employee claimed that the Air Force fired him because he was a "whistleblower" (he had disclosed information about cost overruns on defense contracts). The Air Force claimed he was fired because of a reduction in staff caused by budget cuts. The court held that the employee had a due process right to an open hearing. However, the case precedes the variable due process era. Can you imagine cases in which a court might strike a different balance?

The federal APA does not address the question of whether a hearing must be open to the public, but 1981 MSAPA § 4–211(6) deals directly with the issue. *See generally* 3 K. Davis, ADMINISTRATIVE LAW TREATISE §§ 14.13, 14.14 (1980).

§ 4.2.2   EVIDENCE AT THE HEARING

TRUJILLO v. EMPLOYMENT SECURITY COMMISSION

610 P.2d 747 (N.M.1980).

Appellant, Jimmie Trujillo, was fired on April 29, 1977, from his job with the Albuquerque–Bernalillo County Economic Opportunity Board. He applied for and was granted unemployment compensation benefits by the Employment Security Commission (E.S.C.), but the E.S.C. Appeals Tribunal reversed the award and demanded the return of amounts already paid to Trujillo. Trujillo sought review in the district court, and the court affirmed the E.S.C.'s final decision, whereupon Trujillo appealed to this Court. We reverse.

Trujillo's employer leveled six charges of employment misconduct against him, any one of which, if substantiated, would have justified his dismissal without unemployment benefits. The only charge which the Appeals Tribunal found meritorious was that Trujillo conspired to align members of an advisory council against his superior, Eric Berg. The only evidence offered in support of that charge was the testimony given by Berg himself. He testified that three members of the council had told him on several occasions prior to official council meetings that Trujillo had told them that Berg was taking actions which violated federal program regulations. As a consequence, Berg testified, council members consistently questioned his decisions and forced him to prove the correctness of his actions.

Trujillo correctly contends that Berg's testimony was based upon hearsay. That testimony, moreover, was controverted by Trujillo. The Appeals Tribunal could not have verified the accuracy of Berg's testimony nor ascertained the impressions of council members as they were never called upon to testify.

This appeal raises one issue: whether the E.S.C.'s decision—that Trujillo was guilty of employment misconduct sufficient to deny him unemployment benefits—is supported by substantial evidence. Related to the resolution of this issue is whether the "legal residuum rule" is applicable to this administrative decision.

"The residuum rule requires a reviewing court to set aside an administrative finding unless the finding is supported by evidence which would be admissible in a jury trial." 2 Davis, Administrative Law Treatise § 14.10, pp. 291–92 (1958). The rule was first enunciated in *Carroll v. Knickerbocker Ice Co.,* 113 N.E. 507 (N.Y.1916). That court set aside the compensation award of an administrative agency because the crucial finding there was based entirely upon the hearsay testimony of witnesses who said that the decedent had told them what caused his injury. The court concluded that "still in the end, there must be a residuum of legal evidence to support the claim before an award can be made."

Since the *Carroll* case, courts have qualified their adherence to the rule. *Altschuller v. Bressler,* 46 N.E.2d 886 (N.Y.1943). Commentators have criticized it. 2 Davis, *supra,* §§ 14.09–14.10 (1958). Professor Davis states that:

> Rejection of the residuum rule does not mean that an agency is compelled to rely upon incompetent evidence; it means only that the agency and the reviewing court are free to rely upon the evidence if in the circumstances they believe that the evidence should be relied upon. Rejection of the residuum rule does not mean that a reviewing court must refuse to set aside a finding based upon incompetent evidence; it means only that the court may set aside the finding or refuse to do so as it sees fit, in accordance with its own determination of the question whether the

evidence supporting the finding should be deemed reliable and substantial in the circumstances.

Id. § 14.10, at p. 293.

This is the proper position regarding evidence in most administrative adjudications. In many circumstances hearsay is reliable and probative, and at times it may be the only evidence available. Nevertheless, we believe that the residuum rule should be retained in those administrative proceedings where a substantial right, such as one's ability to earn a livelihood, is at stake. In those instances, "any action depriving him of that [right or ability] must be based upon such substantial evidence as would support a verdict in a court of law." *Young v. Board of Pharmacy,* 462 P.2d 139, 142 (N.M.1969).

We interpret Section 51–1–3, N.M.S.A.1978, to establish unemployment compensation as a substantial right as a matter of public policy. The benefits in this case may not be denied on the basis of controverted hearsay alone. Controverted hearsay under these facts does not qualify as substantial evidence.

For this reason, we reverse.

Notes and Questions

1. *Admission of evidence.* Separate two issues here: what evidence should be excluded? and to what extent should an agency be able to rely exclusively on evidence which would not be admissible in court?

As to the first issue, read APA § 556(d) (second sentence and last sentence) and 1981 MSAPA § 4–212(a), (d), and (e). Does 1981 MSAPA exclude some items of evidence which would be admissible under the federal act? Can you think of any examples? Would 1981 MSAPA operate differently in states which have (like California) or have not (like New York) codified the rules of evidence?

The records in administrative cases typically contain many items of evidence that would be excluded from a judicial record. While the ALJ should exclude "irrelevant, immaterial, or unduly repetitious evidence," the reality is that most oral or written evidence which a party seeks to introduce is routinely admitted. Although hearsay evidence is excluded in judicial trials (unless covered by one of the many hearsay exceptions), it is admissible in administrative cases. 1981 MSAPA § 4–212(a) is explicit on this point and APA § 556(d) has long been interpreted to permit the admission of hearsay. Do you agree that hearsay evidence should be admissible in administrative cases?

Suppose that a party wishes to introduce evidence (in the form of expert testimony) which is technically material and relevant and is not repetitious but relates only to a minor issue in the case and will not be helpful in making a decision. If the evidence is admitted, other parties will cross examine the expert and the hearing may be prolonged for an extra week. Can the ALJ exclude the evidence?

Some statutes require particular agencies to observe judicial standards of evidence. See, e.g. 29 U.S.C. § 160(b) (NLRB adjudications shall, "so far as practicable," be conducted in accordance with the Federal Rules of Evidence). Other agencies, such as OSHA, have adopted judicial evidence rules by regulation. 29 C.F.R. § 2200.72. ACUS Recommendation 86–2 has criticized such statutes and regulations. "Use of Federal Rules of Evidence in Federal Agency Adjudications," 1 C.F.R. § 305.86–2. Why?

2. *The residuum rule.* Since hearsay (and other evidence barred from judicial proceedings) is generally admitted in administrative proceedings, the second question becomes important: should an agency be able to rely exclusively on evidence that would be excluded in court? See APA § 556(d) (third sentence); 1981 MSAPA § 4–215(d).

The residuum rule is discussed in the *Trujillo* case. In cases where a "substantial right, such as one's ability to earn a livelihood, is at stake," New Mexico retains the residuum rule. Many states have rejected the rule and 1981 MSAPA follows their lead. See 1 J. Wigmore, EVIDENCE 122 (Tillers ed. 1983). Why do you think many states have rejected the residuum rule? Do you think it is a sound rule either in its original form or in the form embraced by *Trujillo*? Suppose New Mexico had rejected the residuum rule. Do you think the court would have upheld the administrative decision in *Trujillo?*

The residuum rule appears not to be followed in the federal courts. *Richardson v. Perales,* 402 U.S. 389 (1971), reviewed a decision by Social Security rejecting a claim for disability benefits. The ALJ, affirmed by the Appeals Council, held that Perales (who complained of disabling back pain) was in fact not disabled. The only evidence in support of this determination was a series of written evaluations by various doctors appointed by Social Security to examine Perales.

The Court of Appeals held that substantial evidence did not support the decision because the written and unsworn medical evidence was hearsay. The Supreme Court reversed, holding that the reports could be substantial evidence for a decision. Although Perales had not cross-examined the doctors who wrote the reports, it was his own fault—his counsel had failed to subpoena them.

It might be argued that this last factor makes *Perales* distinguishable, so that federal courts might continue to follow the residuum rule in cases where the party challenging the hearsay evidence could not have subpoenaed the original declarant.

§ 4.2.3 OFFICIAL NOTICE

A court is permitted to take *judicial* notice—i.e. treat as proven— various facts and propositions which are very likely to be true. This is a great time-saver. For example, under a typical state evidence code, a court takes judicial notice of matters "of such common knowledge . . . that they cannot reasonably be the subject of dispute" or "that are not reasonably subject to dispute and are capable of immediate and accurate determination by resort to sources of reasonably indisputable accuracy." Calif.Evid.Code § 452(g), (h). However, the court must first afford each party reasonable opportunity to present information relevant to the propriety of taking judicial notice and the tenor of the matter to be noticed. Id. § 455(a).

Agencies are permitted to take *official* notice of matters which could be the subject of *judicial* notice—and they can also go further and notice matters which a court could not. Compare federal APA § 556(e) and 1981 MSAPA § 4–212(f) to the California Evidence Code provisions quoted above. Because so much can be the subject of official notice— much of it being the personal knowledge of the fact-finders—it is important that parties have a fair opportunity to "contest and rebut the facts or material so noticed."

There remain several fundamental problems: (i) agency fact-finders (both ALJ's and agency heads) are often experts in the subject matter in dispute. They should and must use that expertise in making factual judgments. *See* 1981 MSAPA § 4–215(d) (last sentence). When they do so, have they taken official notice? If so, they first notify the parties and afford them an opportunity to rebut the agency's conclusion. Or is the use of expertise in making judgments different from taking official notice?

(ii) Agency fact finders sometimes make policy when they decide cases. Necessarily, they must rely on broad factual propositions concerning the nature of the problem to be solved and the effect of proposed solutions. When they do so, have they taken official notice? Must they notify the parties and afford an opportunity for rebuttal before they rely on broad factual propositions relevant to policymaking?

FRANZ v. BOARD OF MEDICAL QUALITY ASSURANCE

642 P.2d 792 (Cal.1982).

[The Board suspended Dr. Franz's license to practice medicine for one year and placed him on ten years' probation after finding him guilty of gross negligence, dishonesty, and falsifying a medical document. The trial court sustained the Board but the Supreme Court reversed on several of the gross negligence charges, holding that substantial evidence did not support the decision.

Wollweber was Dr. Franz's patient. Franz was a general practitioner, not a surgeon. After deciding that Wollweber needed surgery to repair a perforated ulcer, Franz scheduled surgery at Anaheim Doctors' Hospital where he had staff privileges. Anaheim had no intensive care unit (ICU). Because of Wollweber's poor state of health, complications were expected. Franz asked Dr. Olivet, the chief of surgery at Anaheim, to recommend a surgeon. Olivet recommended Dr. Ali. Wollweber signed a consent form that listed Olivet and Franz but not Ali as his surgeons. As the result of various blunders in surgery and in post-operative care, Wollweber suffered a "duodenal blowout" and died ten days after the surgery.]

NEWMAN, J.:

The agency and the court found that Franz' choice of Anaheim was gross negligence because Wollweber was a high-risk patient, Anaheim had no adequate ICU, and Franz made the choice—without regard to his patient's needs—in order to obtain surgical privileges he did not have elsewhere. They also ruled that he committed gross negligence by scheduling surgery before selecting the surgeon. He contends that those findings lack substantial evidence because the Board offered no expert testimony that acts of that kind demonstrate "the want of even scant care or an extreme departure from the ordinary standard of conduct," the definition of gross negligence.

The Board answers that any gap in the record was filled by the panel's expertise in medical matters. Because two of the panel's three members were doctors, the Board urges, it could apply special knowledge in assessing gross negligence by a doctor and needed no expert testimony on the pertinent medical standards. Moreover, as we have seen, four of the seven members of the Division that adopted the panel's decision also were doctors. On mandamus review, the Board argues, courts must defer to this off-the-record agency expertise.

The argument lacks merit. California law provides for judicial review of agency decisions to revoke or suspend medical licenses. Whatever the expertise of certain members of the panel and the Division, we cannot impute similar knowledge to a reviewing judge untrained in medical matters. Yet the trial court is confined to the record of the agency hearing, except in certain cases when evidence was improperly excluded or not previously available with due diligence. Therefore the agency record must provide as complete a basis for judicial review as due diligence makes feasible. It must include any technical matter necessary to enable a lay judge to determine whether the agency's decision has adequate support.

To rule that the agency record must be complete enough to allow judicial review of technical questions imposes no unreasonable burden on the administrative process. The Board did introduce "medical standards" testimony as to most of the gross negligence findings in this case, and inclusion of that kind of testimony appears routine in discipline matters.

We do not, of course, hold that agency adjudicators may not apply their expert opinions to decide issues of legislative fact. (See 3 Davis, Administrative Law Treatise (2d ed. 1980) § 15.2, p. 138.[6]) A unique

---

6. Davis explains the long-recognized distinction between "legislative" and "adjudicative" facts. The latter are "facts concerning immediate parties" and what happened to them; the former are facts "utilized for informing a court's [or agency's] legislative judgment on questions of law and policy." (Id., § 15.1, p. 135.) Community standards of medical practice, and whether particular type of conduct departs grossly from those standards, are "legislative" facts. They inform the agency's judgment about what constitutes a violation of the Medical Practice Act.

efficiency of many agencies is the professional competence they bring to matters delegated to them by the Legislature. We think an agency factfinder may, for example, reject uncontradicted opinion testimony that his own expertise renders unpersuasive. (See *McCarthy v. Industrial Commission,* 215 N.W. 824 (Wis.1927)).

A fortiori, the same expertise may govern even when the record contains no opinion evidence at all.

Yet due process requires, when in an adjudication an agency intends to rely on members' expertise to resolve legislative-fact issues, that it notify the parties and provide an opportunity for rebuttal.

The California Administrative Procedure Act requires notice and opportunity to rebut whenever an agency intends to take "official notice . . . of any generally accepted technical or scientific matter within the agency's special field, [or] of any fact which may be judicially noticed by the courts of this State." (Gov.Code, § 11515; see Evid.Code, § 450 et seq.) [7]

The agency's notification must be complete and specific enough to give an effective opportunity for rebuttal. It must also help build a record adequate for judicial review. If it meets those requirements we can see no prejudice to the parties.[8]

We cannot accept the premise of *Brennan v. State Bd. of Medical Examiners,* 225 P.2d 11 (Cal.App.1950) that it is improper "for the board to decide . . . questions [of violation of professional standards] upon the basis of the opinions held by the several members of the board," and that "*[n]either the board* nor the court could render a just decision except in reliance upon expert testimony." As *Brennan* notes, fairness is satisfied when a party "[is] apprised of the evidence against him so that he may have an opportunity to refute, test and explain it, . . ."

Some questions concerning medical negligence require no expertise. Technical knowledge is not requisite to conclude that complications from a simple injection, a surgical clamp left in the patient's body, or a shoulder injury from an appendectomy indicate negligence. Common sense is enough to make that evaluation. Only where the professional significance of underlying facts seems beyond lay comprehension must the basis for the technical findings be shown and an opportunity for rebuttal given. . . . No expertise is necessary to conclude that

7. Section 11515 provides: "In reaching a decision official notice may be taken, either before or after submission of a case for decision, of any generally accepted technical or scientific matter within the agency's special field, and of any fact which may be judicially noticed by the courts of this State. Parties present at the hearing shall be informed of the matters to be noticed, and those matters shall be noted in the record, referred to therein, or appended thereto. Any such party shall be given a reasonable opportunity on request to refute the officially noticed matters by evidence or by written or oral presentation of authority, the manner of such refutation to be determined by the agency."

8. Arguably the notification should include a brief statement explaining the opinion held by the adjudicative body, the reasons for the opinion, and the members' qualifications to hold it.

Franz' choice of Anaheim for Wollweber's operation was an extreme departure from the acceptable standard of medical care in that county. Accordingly there was no need for the panel to give notice of its own opinion or allow an opportunity for rebuttal. The trial court could resolve the issue on the record presented.

The same is not true, though, of the court's finding that scheduling surgery before choosing a surgeon was grossly negligent. Passaro did testify that the surgeon is responsible for independent diagnosis and evaluation of the need for an operation. Moreover, the Board's brief on appeal explains why premature scheduling involves the vice of interfering with the surgeon's independent role.

However, Ali apparently was retained the same day as surgery was scheduled or within a day or two afterward. There is no evidence he could not have cancelled the operation had he found it unnecessary after independent examination. There was no expert testimony that Franz' conduct in this instance was an extreme departure from community medical standards. Common knowledge does not supply the link between premature scheduling and independent surgical evaluation. The record does not disclose the basis of either the panel's or the Division's expert opinion on the issue, and Franz had no opportunity to refute that opinion. Hence the record was inadequate for a trial court finding that the scheduling of surgery before a surgeon was selected constituted gross negligence. The finding cannot be sustained. . . .

If an agency has imposed a single discipline for multiple charges, some of which are found not sustained by evidence, and if there is "real doubt" whether the same action would have been taken on proper findings, the matter will be returned to the agency for redetermination of penalty.

The findings held improper in this opinion imply serious dereliction of a doctor's duty to his patient. We cannot say they had no influence in setting the discipline. On the other hand, major charges have been sustained and some discipline clearly is warranted. Franz should not practice free of restrictions while the penalty is being reconsidered. The conditions imposed by the stay order therefore should apply in the interim.

The judgment is reversed and the superior court is directed to issue a peremptory writ of mandate requiring the Board to reconsider petitioner Franz' discipline in light of our conclusions. . . .

Notes and Questions

1. *Taking official notice.* In a medical malpractice case in court, a plaintiff would be required to offer expert testimony about medical standards in the community (and defendant's departure from those standards) unless the negligence would be obvious even to a lay jury. Does a medical licensing board consisting of physicians have to summon

experts and hear their testimony before disciplining a licensee for malpractice?

What is the difference between taking official notice of medical standards in the community and calling expert witnesses to establish the standards? Why did the Court uphold the Board's finding that Franz's choice of Anaheim Hospital was gross negligence but reject its finding that the scheduling of surgery before finding a surgeon was gross negligence? What's the difference? Suppose the California Supreme Court had affirmed the Board and Franz had appealed to the U.S. Supreme Court. Would that Court have reversed the Board's decision?

2. *Official notice or evaluation of the evidence*? When the Board decided that Franz had been grossly negligent, was it (i) using its experience as a substitute for further evidence on community standards, as the court assumed, or (ii) was it using its experience to draw conclusions from the evidence?

When an agency relies on background knowledge and experience to evaluate evidence, it is not taking official notice of anything and need not specially notify the parties and afford an opportunity to contest the evaluation. *See* the last sentence of 1981 MSAPA § 4–215(d). For example, an experienced and expert agency is allowed to make predictions about the future without first taking official notice of all the underlying facts. *Market St. Ry. Co. v. Railroad Com'n*, 324 U.S. 548 (1945) (prediction that lowering fares would increase the number of passengers carried).

Often an agency seeks to use its expertise to evaluate the testimony of expert witnesses. Suppose that Franz offers expert testimony that it was not gross negligence to perform ulcer surgery in a hospital without an ICU, even if complications were expected. Without introducing any contrary testimony, the Board holds that it was gross negligence. Is this reversible error? *See* the dictum in *Franz* citing *McCarthy v. Industrial Commission*.

With *Franz*, compare *Davis & Randall, Inc. v. United States*, 219 F.Supp. 673 (W.D.N.Y.1963), an opinion of a three-judge court written by Judge Friendly of the Second Circuit. In *Davis & Randall*, the ICC had rejected the testimony of an expert who predicted that a trucker would make a profit if it charged a certain rate. The ICC substituted its own view that the rate would not be profitable. Friendly wrote:

> Without wishing to be held to the letter, we suggest that a rejection of unopposed testimony by a qualified and disinterested expert on a matter susceptible of reasonably precise measurement, without the agency's developing its objections at a hearing, ought to be upheld only when the agency's uncommunicated criticisms appear to the reviewing court to be both so compelling and so deeply held that the court can be fairly sure the agency would not have been affected by anything the witness could have said had he known of them, *and* the court would have been bound to affirm, despite the

expert's hypothetical rebuttal, out of deference to the agency's judgment on so technical a matter.

3. *Policy-making facts.* Suppose that in a medical licensing case, the Board decides that, in this and future cases, it will suspend for at least one year the license of any physician who is found to have prescribed a "controlled substance" (such as amphetamines) in amounts which exceed medical needs. This decision is based on the determination that there is a serious problem of physicians whose prescription books are for sale to drug abusers and that no lesser sanction would provide an adequate deterrent to such doctors. Must the Board follow the official notice statute in each case in which it assesses this penalty? In the first such case?

4. *Problem.* An Elm City ordinance establishes rent control in mobile home parks. An elected three-person Rent Control Board (consisting of residents of Elm City) sets the rents, can order rents to be decreased, and must approve rent increases. According to statute, rents must "provide a fair return on the owner's investment." The Board is required to follow 1981 MSAPA. It also administers several rent control ordinances relating to apartments and other dwellings.

Your client, Red's Mobile Home Park sought a rent increase. There was a lengthy hearing conducted before the full Board. Red testified that the cost of the park, with all improvements, was $2,000,000. His books and records were introduced into evidence to prove this figure. Max, a tenant in the park, testified that he knew Gloria, Red's mother, and Gloria had recently told Max that Red had told her that he actually had only $1,400,000 invested in the park and had falsified his records. Red denied that he had ever had any such conversation with Gloria and affirmed the accuracy of his records.

Red presented the testimony of Beth, an appraiser who was an expert in the mobile home park industry, that 12% per year would be a reasonable rate of return on investment. This figure was based on an analysis of the risks of the business, the possibility of appreciation in the underlying real property, an analysis of sale prices of such parks, and similar factors. Beth was not cross examined and there was no other testimony on rate of return.

The Board found that Red's investment in the park was $1,400,000 (based on Max's testimony). It also determined that a reasonable rate of return would be 9% per year. The Board simply noted that it did not agree with Beth's analysis and it was basing its conclusion on its experience in rent control. It noted that the land underlying the Park was probably appreciating greatly in value and that 9% was more than Red could get from investing in a long-term bank account. It was also the figure the Board had been using in all of its rent control cases. As a result of these findings, the Board ordered a 15% cut in rents rather than an increase.

On judicial review, should this decision be upheld? *See Whispering Pines Mobile Home Park, Ltd. v. City of Scotts Valley,* 225 Cal.Rptr. 364 (Cal.App.1986).

§ 4.3 THE DECISION PHASE: FINDING FACTS AND STATING REASONS

Fundamental to any system of adjudicatory procedure is a requirement that the decisionmaker state findings of fact and reasons for the decision. Recall the elements of a constitutionally required adjudicative hearing in *Goldberg v. Kelly* ("the decision maker should state the reasons for his determination and indicate the evidence he relied on, though his statement need not amount to a full opinion or even formal findings of fact and conclusions of law"). All APA's include such requirements. *See* § 556(c) of the federal act and the even more exacting requirements in 1981 MSAPA § 4–215(c). Indeed, § 555(e) requires a statement of reasons in certain cases of informal adjudication—one of the very few federal act provisions applicable to informal adjudication.

What are the rationales for requiring an agency decision-maker to state findings and reasons in adjudication? How detailed must they be? As detailed, in every case, as required by 1981 MSAPA § 4–215(c)?

Can a reviewing court require an agency to make findings and provide reasons in an adjudication if no statute calls for them? And what should a reviewing court do when it is dissatisfied with an agency's statement of findings and reasons (or the absence thereof)?

MATLOVICH v. SECRETARY OF THE AIR FORCE
591 F.2d 852 (D.C.Cir.1978).

[After twelve years of excellent service, Matlovich was discharged from the Air Force on the ground that he was a homosexual. Although the issue was presented, the court did not decide whether private consensual homosexual acts were constitutionally protected. Subsequently, it was held that such acts can be criminalized and can also be the basis for discharge from the Service. *Bowers v. Hardwick,* 478 U.S. 186 (1986); *Dronenburg v. Zech,* 741 F.2d 1388 (D.C.Cir.1984), reh'ng den. 746 F.2d 1579 (1984).]

We do not reach these questions because a narrower problem looming before us requires remand of this case to the Air Force, and after further action by that Service renewed consideration by the District Court. The Air Force regulation expressly contemplates that exceptions can be made to the general policy of separating homosexuals and the record shows that the Air Force has in the past retained members on active duty who had engaged in homosexual activity. With respect to Matlovich the Air Force said that it had considered whether to make an exception in his case but had decided against it. But what disturbs us is that it is impossible to tell on what grounds the

Service refused to make an exception or how it distinguished this case from the ones in which homosexuals have been retained. The regulation gives only the most general of guidance when it limits exceptions to those "where the most unusual circumstances exist and provided that the airman's ability to perform military service has not been compromised." Also, "an exception is not warranted *simply* because the airman has extensive service" (emphasis added) or because of intoxication. No other pertinent standards are laid down. . . .

What we have, then, is a serviceman with an admittedly outstanding record of considerable duration, with minimal sexual involvement with Air Force personnel and none with those with whom he worked and with substantial testimony that the Air Force community would be able to accept his homosexuality. Neither the Correction Board nor the Secretary (in confirming that board) suggested that his ability to perform military service had been compromised, and we do not understand the Administrative Discharge Board to have made such a finding either. What is missing, the Air Force says, are the "unusual circumstances" which have to exist to warrant retention even if the other conditions are satisfied. But what are "unusual circumstances," or what they have been in past cases, is left uncertain and unknown.

We are at sea as to the circumstances—aside from the exception for youths—in which the Air Force makes exceptions to its policy of eliminating homosexuals and when it refuses to make an exception. The absence of articulated standards, policies, or considerations—plus the absence of any reasoned explanation in this particular case—makes it impossible to decide whether or not there has been an abuse of discretion in this instance or whether improper factors have played a material role. We suppose that everyone would admit that the Air Force could not decide, under its all-inclusive but unarticulated rubric, to retain only black homosexuals or only white ones, or homosexuals of one religion but not of others, or homosexuals of one ethnic background but not of others, or only homosexuals who were proteges of senior officers. We do not suppose that such blatantly improper distinctions entered into the decision in this case, but the almost-total lack of specificity in the Air Force's determinations leads one to consider the possibility, for instance, whether Matlovich's failure of retention may have been affected by his "going public" with his homosexuality and the publicity surrounding his case, and that if his homosexuality had been discovered and handled by the Air Force, without public notice, the result might have been different. If that factor entered into the refusal to retain, both appellant and the reviewing court are entitled to know it—so that appellant can challenge the propriety of reliance on that consideration and, if he does, the court can pass upon that contention.

We do not say at this stage, because we do not know, that the Air Force cannot justify appellant's discharge. What we say is that the Air Force should explicate more fully its reasons for refusing to retain appellant—As its regulation provides that it may do and its practice shows that it has done in other cases—so that the court can decide if it was arbitrary, capricious, or unlawful in exercising its discretion whether or not to retain Matlovich.

III

The normal rule where a discretionary administrative decision is to be reviewed by a court (other than on a *de novo* basis) is that the agency must give sufficient indication of the grounds for its exercise of discretion that the reviewing tribunal can appraise that determination under the appropriate standards of review (and the applicant for relief can challenge it). This basic concept has been reiterated time and again—in differing formulations and contexts but always centering on the need for the court, and the complaining party, to be given some helpful insight into the agency's reasoning. *See, e.g., United States v. Chicago, M., St. P. & P. R.R.,* 294 U.S. 499 (1935) ("We must know what a decision means before the duty becomes ours to say whether it is right or wrong"); *SEC v. Chenery Corp.,* 332 U.S. 194, 196–97. ("It will not do for a court to be compelled to guess at the theory underlying the agency's action * * *): [11] . . .

The fundamental principle of reasoned explanation embodied in these (and comparable) decisions serves at least three interrelated purposes: enabling the court to give proper review to the administrative determination; helping to keep the administrative agency within proper authority and discretion, as well as helping to avoid and prevent arbitrary, discriminatory, and irrational action by the agency; and informing the aggrieved person of the grounds of the administrative action so that he can plan his course of action (including the seeking of judicial review).

We know of no reason why this umbrella principle should be inapplicable to the Air Force's decision not to retain appellant—as its regulation expressly contemplated that it could do. The explicit provision for exceptions to the overall policy of separating homosexuals is binding on the Air Firce, *Service v. Dulles,* 354 U.S. 363 (1957) . . . just as much as the general directive calling for discharge of homosexuals. And the procedure established for processing these contested cases shows that the Service was expected to support its determinations of separation by some reasoned explanation.

The general Defense Department Regulations on enlisted administrative separations of all types—applicable to each of the armed services—describes an administrative discharge board (such as acted in this case) as "appointed to render findings based on facts obtaining, or believed to obtain, in a case and to recommend retention in the Service

---

11. In the same general class are those rulings invalidating administrative action because the agency had no articulated standards governing its discretionary determinations, or requiring the adoption of such standards. *See Hornsby v. Allen,* 326 F.2d 605 (5th Cir.1964); *Holmes v. New York City Housing Authority,* 398 F.2d 262 (2d Cir.1968); *White v. Roughton,* 530 F.2d 750 (7th Cir.1976).

or discharge, with reason for and the type of separation or discharge certificate to be furnished." . . .

These Defense Department directives are implemented and pointed up by Air Force regulations—including those contained in the portion of the Air Force Manual governing separation of enlisted personnel for unsuitability, unfitness or misconduct—which consistently stress the need for reasoned explanations and determinations in these circumstances. . . .

In the light of these Defense Department and Air Force directives, we cannot escape the conclusion that the military has itself provided that in cases of this type a reasoned explanation should be made for any detrimental action ordered. The whole system of regulations is infused with this concept. And since the Air Force regulation on homosexuality expressly contemplates that retention in the service is an alternative in proper cases, the procedural regulations we have just summarized demand some reasoned explanation why that alternative is rejected in the case at hand. The history of this matter within the Air Force shows that it considered itself bound to give such reasons because it purported to do so, all along the line. The problem, as we have pointed out, is that no such reasoned explanation was given in a form which is intelligible to this court or permits any meaningful judicial review. . . .

Appellees seem to suggest that, in the nature of things, these principles cannot be used for the retention exception at issue here—that it is impossible for the service to specify "where the most unusual circumstances exist" and what constitutes a compromise of the airman's "ability to perform military service." We cannot accept such a contention. This problem is no more difficult than that presented in the conscientious objector cases, and there is no valid reason why a statement cannot be given which will show the reviewing court that improper considerations were not taken into account, that the particular airman was not treated differently from others in the same position, and that there is a rational basis for the refusal to retain this serviceman. The mere conclusion, tracking the terms of the regulation, that sufficient "unusual circumstances" do not exist in the particular case is inadequate compliance with the reasons requirement. Undoubtedly the Air Force was much more specific and precise in its thinking when it passed upon Sgt. Matlovich's case—and there is no good ground why he and the court should be screened off from that reasoning.[20] That is

20. Appellees' brief states (at 28) that the exception policy was designed to benefit the military, not the servicemen, and then goes on to say that the discretionary determination involves a weighing of the need of the service for the specific attributes and talents of the particular airman "and the affect [sic] on the military of the loss of the services of that individual, against the actual or probably [sic] detriment that retention of the individual would have upon the military in general, and the effectiveness of the serviceman in particular."

We find neither of these statements in any of the Air Force's determinations in this case—and it is understood by now that counsel's post hoc rationalizations cannot substitute for the agency's own failure.

true whatever the scope of judicial review of the service's exercise of its discretion, a separate issue which we do not now touch.

There are two means by which an administrative entity can develop standards for rational action in an area of formal or informal adjudication. The first is by advance promulgation of written rules, directives or formulated criteria; the other is through case-by-case decision making. . . . There are advantages to the former method— in Judge Leventhal's words "rulemaking assures that any modification in position will represent a generalized approach to a general problem, avoiding the uneasiness that results from the greater possibility of discrimination in a case-by-case approach"—but . . . we leave to the Air Force the choice of the path it will pursue to clarify its policy on retention of homosexuals and the application of those standards to this case. In either event, the Secretary of the Air Force may do so through such permissible means as he considers appropriate.

Accordingly, the decision granting summary judgment to the Government is vacated and remanded with instructions to remand to the Air Force for further proceedings consistent with this opinion. Appellant can of course seek judicial relief from any adverse determination made on this remand.

Notes and Questions

1. *Legal authority.* What is the legal basis for the Court of Appeals to require the Air Force to make findings in *Matlovich?* Due process? APA § 557(c)? APA § 555(e)? The Defense Department and the Air Force's own regulations? The underlying statutes relating to Air Force personnel practices? Administrative common law? *See* Shapiro & Levy, "Heightened Scrutiny of the Fourth Branch: Separation of Powers and the Requirement of Adequate Reasons for Agency Decisions," 1987 Duke L.J. 387 (requirement of findings and reasons is common law technique to promote rational administrative decisionmaking and facilitate judicial review).

If the latter, the decision might be in conflict with *Vermont Yankee Nuclear Power Corp. v. NRDC,* § 6.3, *infra. Vermont Yankee* held that a court could not impose procedural requirements beyond those specified in the APA. Although it involves rulemaking rather than adjudication, *Vermont Yankee* indicates that a court can seldom impose procedures on an agency simply because they would improve decisionmaking or facilitate judicial review.

2. *MSAPA and informal hearings.* Note the detailed requirements of 1981 MSAPA § 4–215(c). Would those requirements be applicable in the case of a conference adjudicative hearing? *See* § 4–402. A summary proceeding? *See* §§ 4–201(2) and § 4–503(b)(2) and (d). An emergency proceeding? *See* §§ 4–201(3) and 4–501(c).

Moreover, even if the general standard outlined by counsel were adopted by the service, we would expect some more specific spelling out of the reasons why the balance went against Sgt. Matlovich.

3. *Rationale for requiring findings and reasons.* What reasons does the opinion give for requiring findings and reasons? Which of them are convincing rationales for the result in *Matlovich?* Is the court trying to send the Air Force a message? What message? Will the Air Force have any difficulty getting its decision to terminate Matlovich affirmed on appeal if it does a better job of finding facts and stating reasons? In fact, the Air Force settled with Matlovich, giving him an honorable discharge and $160,000 in cash. TIME, July 4, 1988, p. 53.

4. *Explanation and discretion.* A requirement that an agency state findings and reasons is particularly valuable when the agency adjudicative action in question is discretionary. For example, suppose the decision in question is to approve a company's request to pollute water or to deny a stay of deportation. In most such cases, there is no formal procedure such as a hearing and no applicable APA provision.

If there is a requirement that the decision-maker explain his action, it is more likely that the decision will be carefully considered and thus less likely that discretion will be abused. Moreover, judicial review would be meaningless without a contemporaneous agency explanation of that action.

But what authority would support a holding that an agency must explain discretionary decisions (if APA §§ 555(e) or 557(c) are inapplicable)? Sometimes, a court will interpret the underlying statute to require an explanation. The leading case is *Dunlop v. Bachowski,* 421 U.S. 560 (1975). *Dunlop* involved a statute allowing the Secretary of Labor to sue in District Court to set aside a union election tainted by fraud.

The Secretary refused to bring suit to set aside a particular election. The Court held his action judicially reviewable and interpreted the underlying statute to require the Secretary to state reasons for his refusal and the essential facts on which the decision was based. Such a statement would permit intelligent judicial review, would inform a complaining union member why his request had been denied, and would promote careful consideration. The Secretary had furnished a brief letter to the complainant; the Court stated that it might satisfy APA § 555(e) but not the more exacting requirement of explanation that it had discovered in the statute.

A good example of such judicial creativity at the state level is *Ship Creek Hydraulic Syndicate v. State of Alaska,* 685 P.2d 715 (Alaska 1984). The statute required the state to balance public good and private harm when it seized land to build a highway. The court held that the state must prepare a "decisional document" before doing so. The document would contain fact findings and an explanation of how the balance had been struck. The court implied the requirement into the underlying statute and also seemed to require it as a matter of common law since such a document was needed to facilitate judicial review. It held that the rationale of the United States Supreme Court's *Vermont Yankee* opinion did not preclude it from doing so.

However, in *Citizens to Preserve Overton Park, Inc. v. Volpe,* 401 U.S. 402 (1971), the United States Supreme Court declined to imply a requirement of an explanation into a statute. (This important case is further discussed in §§ 9.4 and 10.4) Pursuant to statute, the Secretary of Transportation granted funds to build an interstate highway through Overton Park in Memphis. The statute provided that a road should not be built through a park unless there is no feasible and prudent alternative. The Secretary did not explain why there was no such alternative and the Supreme Court held that no such explanation was required by the statute.

But without any explanation or administrative record, how could the Court review the Secretary's decision? The Supreme Court remanded the case to the District Court to conduct a de novo trial at which the decision would be reviewed on the full administrative record. At the trial, the court could require the Secretary to provide an explanation if that were necessary. Two justices dissented on this latter point. They believed that the case should first be remanded to the Secretary to provide the necessary explanation. Later cases generally follow the route suggested by the dissenters. They require a remand to the decisionmaker to supply an explanation, rather than a trial at which that explanation is adduced. *See Camp v. Pitts,* 411 U.S. 138 (1973). This issue is discussed in greater detail in § 3.3.1, *supra.*

Is there any significant difference between the failure of an agency to provide findings and an explanation in cases like *Matlovich, Dunlop,* and *Ship Creek,* where a statute expressly or impliedly requires them, and such a failure in cases like *Overton Park* and *Camp,* where there is no such statutory requirement? Should there be a significant difference between these two situations?

5. *Choice between rulemaking and adjudication.* As the court in *Matlovich* observes near the end of its opinion, an agency generally can choose between resolving a problem by rulemaking and case-by-case adjudication. See § 5.4 *infra.* If you were advising the Air Force, would you suggest it adopt rules spelling out more precisely the grounds on which homosexuals could be retained in the service? Does note 11 suggest that the Air Force might be required to adopt such rules?

6. *Post-hoc rationalizations.* Note 20 indicates that if an agency has failed to make findings or to state reasons, the deficiency cannot be repaired by agency counsel in its brief. *Overton Park* is also a strong authority for this proposition. However, agency lawyers represent the agency; they consult with agency decisionmakers in preparing their briefs. At the time of judicial review, why shouldn't agency lawyers be allowed to supply any findings or reasons missing in the agency decision so long as they are supported by the administrative record? Isn't it a meaningless ritual for a court to remand a case to an agency

rather than allow agency lawyers to supply the missing findings or reasons in light of the fact that on remand to the agency, those same agency lawyers will probably compose the missing findings and reasons for the agency head to sign?

Note that if an agency's findings or reasons are not supported by the administrative record or are otherwise unacceptable or improper, a court cannot supply additional findings or reasons to uphold the decision. So, for example, if an agency gave improper reasons for its action, the reviewing court must reverse and remand to the agency even though other proper reasons for that action existed and could be supported in the record of the agency proceeding. The United States Supreme Court has noted in this connection that "a reviewing court, in dealing with a determination or judgment that an administrative agency alone is authorized to make, must judge the propriety of such action solely by the grounds invoked by the agency. If those grounds are inadequate or improper, the court is powerless to affirm the administrative action by substituting what it considers to be a more adequate or proper basis." *SEC v. Chenery Corp.*, 332 U.S. 194, 196 (1947).

7. *Problem.* Gambling is legal in Nevada. A statute permits the Gaming Board, in its discretion, to exclude a person from the premises of all licensed gambling casinos if he is found to have been convicted of various crimes or if has an "unsavory reputation which would adversely affect public confidence that the gaming industry is free from corruptive elements." The Gaming Board has never adopted any rules which clarify this statute but it has entered about a dozen exclusion orders in the past.

Sally, who lives in Pennsylvania, enjoys gambling and often visits Nevada casinos. After conducting a hearing, the Board entered an order excluding Sally from all Nevada casinos. Evidence presented at the hearing indicated that Sally had a long-term romantic relationship with Max. Max is generally considered to be an important figure in organized crime in Pennsylvania. Neither Max nor Sally has ever been convicted of a crime. At the hearing both Max and Sally denied any connection with organized crime. However, there was evidence that Sally often carried messages and did other chores for the members of Max's crime "family."

The Board's only finding was that Sally had an unsavory reputation which would adversely affect public confidence that the gaming industry is free from corruptive elements. On judicial review, should the Board's order be reversed if a) no APA applies? b) 1981 MSAPA applies? *See Spilotro v. State ex rel. Nevada Gaming Com'n*, 661 P.2d 467 (Nev.1983).

§ 4.4   EFFECT OF DECISION: RES JUDICATA, STARE DECISIS, ESTOPPEL

This subchapter considers a range of problems which center on the subsequent effect of an agency adjudicatory decision.

First, it addresses the preclusive effect of a decision upon later adjudication—the doctrines of res judicata and collateral estoppel. Should these familiar principles operate differently in the administrative than in the judicial context? Next, it takes up stare decisis—the extent to which an agency should or must follow its own prior decision. Should an agency be more free than a court to reconsider its precedents? Finally, it considers the extent to which an agency is bound to respect reliance interests created by its actions—whether those actions are adjudicatory or arise out of other agency functions such as advice-giving. Should an agency be bound by the doctrines of equitable estoppel and apparent authority?

§ 4.4.1   RES JUDICATA

Under the rule of res judicata (sometimes called "claim preclusion"), a valid and final personal judgment is conclusive of a claim. If the judgment is for the plaintiff, the claim is extinguished and merged in the judgment; if the judgment is for the defendant, plaintiff is barred from reasserting the claim. RESTATEMENT OF JUDGMENTS 2d § 17.

Under the related doctrine of collateral estoppel (or "issue preclusion"), when an issue of fact or law is actually litigated and determined by a valid and final judgment, and the determination is essential to the judgment, the determination is conclusive in a subsequent action between the parties, even on a different claim. Id. § 27.

In recent years, collateral estoppel has frequently been applied despite a lack of mutuality: i.e. a person precluded from relitigating an issue against the opposing party is also precluded from doing so against a third person. However, if the person lacked a full and fair opportunity to litigate the issue in the first action or other circumstances justify affording an opportunity to relitigate the issue, preclusion would be improper. Id. § 29.

Do these principles apply with full force to subsequent adjudications when the first adjudication was administrative rather than judicial?

UNIVERSITY OF TENNESSEE v. ELLIOTT
478 U.S. 788 (1986).

JUSTICE WHITE delivered the opinion of the Court.

A state Administrative Law Judge determined that petitioner was not motivated by racial prejudice in seeking to discharge respondent. The question presented is whether this finding is entitled to preclusive effect in federal court, where respondent has raised discrimination claims under various civil rights laws, including Title VII of the Civil Rights Act of 1964 and 42 U.S.C. § 1983.

I

In 1981, petitioner University of Tennessee informed respondent, a black employee of the University's Agricultural Extension Service, that he would be discharged for inadequate work performance and misconduct on the job. Respondent requested a hearing under the Tennessee Uniform Administrative Procedures Act to contest his proposed termination. Prior to the start of the hearing, respondent also filed suit in the United States District Court for the Western District of Tennessee, alleging that his proposed discharge was racially motivated and seeking relief under Title VII and other civil rights statutes, including 42 U.S.C. § 1983. The relief sought included damages, an injunction prohibiting respondent's discharge, and classwide relief from alleged patterns of discrimination by petitioner.

There followed a hearing at which an administrative assistant to the University's Vice President for Agriculture presided as an Administrative Law Judge (ALJ). The focus of the hearing was on 10 particular charges that the University gave as grounds for respondent's discharge. Respondent denied these charges, which he contended were motivated by racial prejudice, and also argued that the University's subjecting him to the charges violated his rights under the Constitution, Title VII, and other federal statutes. The ALJ held that he lacked jurisdiction to adjudicate respondent's federal civil rights claims, but did allow respondent to present, as an affirmative defense, evidence that the charges against him were actually motivated by racial prejudice and hence not a proper basis for his proposed discharge.

After hearing extensive evidence,[2] the ALJ found that the University had proved some but not all of the charges against respondent, and that the charges were not racially motivated. Concluding that the proposed discharge of respondent was too severe a penalty, the ALJ ordered him transferred to a new assignment with supervisors other than those with whom he had experienced conflicts. Respondent appealed to the University's Vice President for Agriculture, who affirmed the ALJ's ruling. The Vice President stated that his review of the record persuaded him that the proposed discharge of respondent had not been racially motivated.

Respondent did not seek review of these administrative proceedings in the Tennessee courts; instead, he returned to federal court to pursue his civil rights claims. There, petitioner moved for summary judgment on the ground that respondent's suit was an improper collateral attack on the ALJ's ruling, which petitioner contended was entitled to preclusive effect. The District Court agreed, holding that the civil rights

2. The hearing continued intermittently for more than five months, involved more than 100 witnesses and 150 exhibits, and generated over 5,000 pages of transcript.

statutes on which respondent relied "were not intended to afford the plaintiff a means of relitigating what plaintiff has heretofore litigated over a five-month period." . . .

We granted certiorari to consider petitioner's contention that the Sixth Circuit erred in holding that state administrative factfinding is never entitled to preclusive effect in actions under Title VII or the Reconstruction civil rights statutes. . . . [We] will consider whether a rule of preclusion is appropriate, first with respect to respondent's Title VII claim, and next with respect to his claims under the Constitution.

III

Under 42 U.S.C. § 2000e–5(b), the Equal Employment Opportunity Commission (EEOC), in investigating discrimination charges, must give "substantial weight to final findings and orders made by State or local authorities in proceedings commenced under State or local [employment discrimination] law." As we noted in *Kremer v. Chem. Constr. Co.*, 456 U.S. 461 (1982), it would make little sense for Congress to write such a provision if state agency findings were entitled to preclusive effect in Title VII actions in federal court.

Moreover, our decision in *Chandler v. Roudebush*, 425 U.S. 840, strongly supports respondent's contention that Congress intended one in his position to have a trial *de novo* on his Title VII claim. In *Chandler*, we held that a federal employee whose discrimination claim was rejected by her employing agency after an administrative hearing was entitled to a trial *de novo* in federal court on her Title VII claim. After reviewing in considerable detail the language of Title VII and the history of the 1972 amendments to the statute, we concluded:

> The legislative history of the 1972 amendments reinforces the plain meaning of the statute and confirms that Congress intended to accord federal employees the same right to a trial *de novo* [following administrative proceedings] as is enjoyed by private-sector employees and employees of state governments and political subdivisions under the amended Civil Rights Act of 1964. . . .

IV

We see no reason to suppose that Congress, in enacting the Reconstruction civil rights statutes, wished to foreclose the adaptation of traditional principles of preclusion to such subsequent developments as the burgeoning use of administrative adjudication in the 20th century.

We have previously recognized that it is sound policy to apply principles of issue preclusion to the factfinding of administrative bodies acting in a judicial capacity. In a unanimous decision in *United States v. Utah Construction & Mining Co.*, 384 U.S. 394 (1966), we held that the factfinding of the Advisory Board of Contract Appeals was binding in a subsequent action in the Court of Claims involving a contract dispute between the same parties. We explained:

. . . the result we reach is harmonious with general principles of collateral estoppel. Occasionally courts have used language to the effect that *res judicata* principles do not apply to administrative proceedings, but such language is certainly too broad. . . . When an administrative agency is acting in a judicial capacity and resolves disputed issues of fact properly before it which the parties have had an adequate opportunity to litigate, the courts have not hesitated to apply *res judicata* to enforce repose.

Thus, *Utah Construction* teaches that giving preclusive effect to administrative factfinding serves the value underlying general principles of collateral estoppel: enforcing repose.[6] This value, which encompasses both the parties' interest in avoiding the cost and vexation of repetitive litigation and the public's interest in conserving judicial resources is equally implicated whether factfinding is done by a federal or state agency.

Having federal courts give preclusive effect to the factfinding of state administrative tribunals also serves the value of federalism. . . . Perhaps the major purpose of the Full Faith and Credit Clause is to act as a nationally unifying force, and this purpose is served by giving preclusive effect to state administrative factfinding rather than leaving the courts of a second forum, state or federal, free to reach conflicting results.[7] Accordingly, we hold that when a state agency "acting in a judicial capacity . . . resolves disputed issues of fact properly before it which the parties have had an adequate opportunity to litigate," *Utah Construction & Mining Co.,* federal courts must give the agency's factfinding the same preclusive effect to which it would be entitled in the State's courts.[8]

---

6. As one respected authority on administrative law has observed:

"The law of res judicata, much more than most other segments of law, has rhyme, reason, and rhythm—something in common with good poetry. Its inner logic is rather satisfying. It consists entirely of an elaboration of the obvious principle that a controversy should be resolved once, not more than once. The principle is as much needed for administrative decisions as for judicial decisions. To the extent that administrative adjudications resemble courts' decisions—a very great extent—the law worked out for courts does and should apply to agencies." 4 K. Davis, Administrative Law Treatise § 21.9, (2d ed. 1983).

The Restatement (Second) of Judgments § 83, p. 269 (1982), reaches a similar conclusion:

"Where an administrative forum has the essential procedural characteristics of a court, . . . its determinations should be accorded the same finality that is accorded the judgment of a court. The importance of bringing a legal controversy to conclusion is generally no less when the tribunal is an administrative tribunal than when it is a court."

7. Congress of course may decide, as it did in enacting Title VII, that other values outweigh the policy of according finality to state administrative factfinding. See Part III, *supra.*

8. Respondent argues against preclusion on the grounds that the administrative hearing in this case did not satisfy the standard set out in *Utah Construction & Mining Co.,* and that the ALJ's factfinding would not be given preclusive effect in the Tennessee courts. These contentions were not passed upon below, and we leave them for resolution on remand.

The judgment of the Court of Appeals is affirmed in part and reversed in part, and the case remanded for further proceedings consistent with this opinion.

JUSTICE MARSHALL took no part in the consideration or decision of this case.

JUSTICE STEVENS, with whom JUSTICE BRENNAN and JUSTICE BLACKMUN join, concurring in part and dissenting in part.

. . . Preclusion of claims brought under the post-Civil War Acts does not advance the objectives typically associated with finality or federalism. In the employment setting which concerns us here, precluding civil rights claims based on the Reconstruction-era statutes fails to conserve the resources of either the litigants or the courts, because the complainant's companion Title VII claim will still go to federal court under today's decision. Nor does preclusion show respect for state administrative determinations, because litigants apprised of this decision will presumably forgo state administrative determinations for the same reason they currently forgo state judicial review of those determinations—to protect their entitlement to a federal forum. . . .

The relevant federal statute in this case is the 1871 Civil Rights Act. . . . Needless to say, there is nothing in the legislative history of the post-Civil War legislation remotely suggesting that Congress intended to give binding effect to unreviewed rulings by state administrators in litigation arising under that statute. Quite the contrary, as we explained in *Monroe v. Pape,* 365 U.S. 167;

> It is abundantly clear that one reason the legislation was passed was to afford a federal right in federal courts because, by reason of prejudice, passion, neglect, intolerance or otherwise, state laws might not be enforced and the claims of citizens to the enjoyment of rights, privileges, and immunities guaranteed by the Fourteenth Amendment might be denied by the state agencies.

Due respect for the intent of the Congress that enacted the Civil Rights Act of 1871, as revealed in the voluminous legislative history of that Act, should preclude the Court from creating a judge-made rule that bars access to the express legislative remedy enacted by Congress.

Notes and Questions

1. *Res judicata in administrative law.* In *Elliott* the Court holds that an unreviewed state administrative decision has preclusive effect on a § 1983 action in federal court but not on a Title VII action in federal court. Why the difference?

Many states also apply res judicata principles to administrative adjudications. See, e.g., *Ryan v. New York Telephone Co.,* 467 N.E.2d 487 (N.Y.Ct.App.1984). In that case, Ryan was fired for theft of company property. He sought unemployment compensation benefits but they were denied because, after a hearing at which he chose to appear with a union representative, the Labor Department upheld the theft charge. Later criminal proceedings were dismissed "in the interests of justice." Ryan sued the company for false arrest, wrongful discharge, and slander. The court held that collateral estoppel applied. The issues resolved in the administrative proceeding were dispositive of his tort claims and he had a full and fair opportunity to litigate them before the agency. It was his choice to appear without counsel.

2. *Preclusion against the government.* In *United States v. Stauffer Chemical Co.,* 464 U.S. 165 (1984), the Court held that the federal government could be barred from relitigating a *legal* issue it had lost in an action involving the same party. Stauffer had won a Tenth Circuit decision that it could exclude certain inspectors from its plant. The identical issue arose in the Sixth Circuit where Stauffer had another plant. The government was precluded from relitigating the issue in the Sixth Circuit (which had not previously decided the issue). The Court did not decide what would happen if the issue arose in another circuit which had previously ruled in favor of the government.

On the same day, the Court decided that *non-mutual* collateral estoppel does not lie against the government. *United States v. Mendoza,* 464 U.S. 154 (1984). In *Mendoza,* an earlier *trial court* decision (in the Ninth Circuit) held that certain Philippine nationals were entitled to U.S. citizenship. The government did not appeal. The present case (which also arose in the Ninth Circuit) involved the same issue but with different plaintiffs. They argued that the government was precluded from relitigating the issue.

The Court held that non-mutual collateral estoppel is not applicable against the United States (although it would be applicable against private parties). The government should be allowed (or even encouraged) to relitigate the issue, in hope of creating a conflict between the circuits, so that the issue might "percolate" to the Supreme Court. Also, the Court was concerned with the realities of government litigation: the U.S. should not be forced to appeal every case it loses in a trial court, no matter how unimportant, in order to guard against preclusion in later (and perhaps far more important) litigation. Moreover, a new administration should be able to change the policy of a prior one (which had decided to accept a defeat and not appeal).

Should the government be less vulnerable to res judicata than other litigants? *See* Note, "Collateral Estoppel and Non–Acquiescence: Precluding Government Relitigation," 99 Harv.L.Rev. 847 (1986).

3. *Non–Acquiescence.* Pushing its advantage, the federal government argues that it can freely relitigate an issue, despite having lost an *appellate* decision on the identical point in the *same circuit.* The courts have rejected the government's position in rather strong language. *See, e.g., Lopez v. Heckler,* 713 F.2d 1432 (9th Cir.1983) (preliminary injunction granted); 464 U.S. 879 (1984) (5–4 vote to stay the injunction); 725 F.2d 1489 (9th Cir.1984) (narrower injunction issued).

The background of the *Lopez* case was a policy of the Department of Health and Human Services (HHS). HHS terminated large numbers of persons receiving federal disability payments without any new evidence that their conditions had improved. Earlier Ninth Circuit cases had held that this was improper. But HHS went right on terminating recipients, even though they lived in the Ninth Circuit. As a result the recipients (mostly poor and quite sick) had to go to the expense of litigating the issue; because of the prior cases, they were certain to win—if they could survive long enough. In *Lopez* (a class action brought by persons whose benefits had been terminated), the court affirmed a preliminary injunction against HHS' non-acquiescence policy.

A concurring opinion said:

> The Secretary's ill-advised policy of refusing to obey the decisional law of this circuit is akin to the repudiated pre-Civil War doctrine of nullification whereby rebellious states refused to recognize certain federal laws within their boundaries. The Secretary's non-acquiescence not only scoffs at the law of this circuit, but flouts some very important principles basic to our American system of government—the rule of law, the doctrine of separation of powers embedded in the constitution, and the tenet of judicial supremacy laid down in *Marbury v. Madison* . . . The government expects its citizens to abide by the law—no less is expected of those charged with the duty to faithfully administer the law.

713 F.2d at 1441. The first *Lopez* decision preceded *Mendoza;* the second *Lopez* opinion said that *Mendoza* was not applicable. 725 F.2d at 1497, n. 5. Is *Lopez* distinguishable from *Mendoza?* Congress eventually resolved the legal issue involved in *Lopez* without deciding the propriety of governmental non-acquiescence. P.L. 98–460.

Can you make an argument in favor of allowing the government to continue to litigate an issue before a circuit court despite having already lost on that identical issue before a panel of that same circuit? *See* Draft Report of the ACUS Committee on Judicial Review, 53 Fed. Reg. 12444 (April 14, 1988).

4. *Abbreviated hearings.* Suppose a prisoner in a state penal institution is disciplined by that institution because of an alleged attack on a guard. The prison supplied a hearing that fully satisfied the due process requirements of *Wolff v. McDonnell,* discussed in chapter 2.2.2 *supra.* Such a hearing need not and did not give the prisoner all of the rights to confront and cross-examine opposing witnesses that would be available in a hearing held in court. Assume the prisoner is sued by the guard for battery. Is the prisoner bound by findings of fact made in the disciplinary proceeding?

5. *Criminal cases.* Suppose a welfare recipient is criminally prosecuted for welfare fraud. She is convicted. The state sues her to recover the illegal payments. Can she relitigate the issue of whether she was entitled to the payments?

Suppose she was acquitted in the criminal case. Can the state relitigate the issue of whether she was entitled to the payments?

Suppose a civil or administrative action precedes the criminal case and the recipient wins. Can the state relitigate the issue in the criminal case? *See People v. Sims,* 186 Cal.Rptr. 77 (Cal.1982) (welfare hearing finds no fraud; issue precluded in subsequent criminal welfare fraud case). Suppose the recipient loses the civil proceeding. Can she relitigate the issue in the criminal case?

6. *Problem.* The Monroe Corporations Commission (MCC) engages in licensing security brokers in the state of Monroe. Following a full adjudicatory hearing, MCC can impose penalties (such as license revocation) against brokers who engage in misconduct (such as insider trading).

Your client, Jed, is a stock broker in Monroe. MCC suspects that directors of Z Corp. gave Jed inside information about Z Corp. mergers. It further suspects that Jed used this information to buy Z Corp. stock, thus making large profits for himself and for clients. Jed denies that he engaged in insider trading (he says he received no tips and instead developed the information by his own shrewd analysis).

Jed has very large potential liability in civil litigation that might be brought in federal court under SEC rules by persons who sold Z Corp. while Jed and his clients were buying it.

MCC has told you that they are willing to negotiate a one-year suspension of Jed's license. Jed wants to fight the case before MCC. Do you advise him to take the deal? *See Kerr & Stillman, "Collateral Estoppel Implications of SEC Adjudications,"* 42 Bus.Lwyr. 441 (1987).

§ 4.4.2 CONSISTENT DECISIONMAKING: STARE DECISIS

Under the principle of stare decisis, courts generally follow their own precedents and lower courts must adhere to precedents established by higher courts. Stare decisis assures a reasonable degree of consistency and predictability in the law; by minimizing litigation it also serves the purpose of judicial economy. Yet courts occasionally reconsider and depart from prior precedents; they do not always admit they are doing so. Do the reasons for stare decisis apply with equal force to agency adjudicatory decisions? Greater or less force? To all agency decisions?

INTERNATIONAL UNION, UNITED AUTOMOBILE WORKERS OF AMERICA v. NLRB
802 F.2d 969 (7th Cir.1986).

[A collective bargaining agreement provided that National Lock Co. would "discuss" any relocation of its plant with the Union. Applicable labor law provides that a company must negotiate a plant relocation with the union if it is motivated by concern over labor costs. However, this statutory protection can be waived. The Board held that the agreement to "discuss" relocation was a waiver of the Union's right to "negotiate" over the issue. Prior Board decisions hold that a waiver of a statutory right must be clear and unmistakable. The Board did not discuss or cite any of those prior decisions in this case.]

POSNER, J.:

We grant that despite the strong judicial endorsement of the rule, the Board—which knows more about the dynamics of collective bargaining than the courts—might be able to dilute or abandon it, since the rule is a nonobvious gloss on the statute. And there are two bits of evidence that a desire to abandon or dilute, rather than mere oversight, does indeed lie behind the Board's failure to mention the rule. The first is that the administrative law judge had relied heavily on the presumption against inferring the waiver of a statutory right and that the union had argued the presumption vigorously throughout the case. So the Board could not just have forgotten about the rule; and if it didn't mention the rule just because it did not want to weaken the force of its opinion, this would be the equivalent of wanting to dilute or abandon the rule. Second, in support of the conclusion that the union had waived its statutory right the Board cited only *Consolidated Foods Corp.*, one of the few decisions that does not say that the waiver of a statutory right must be clear and unmistakable—though whether the omission to say this in *Consolidated* was deliberate or not is unclear.

All this is rather bootless conjecture, though. For it makes no difference what the Board may have had in mind but failed to express; an administrative agency is not allowed to change direction without some explanation of what it is doing and why. This general principle of administrative law, see, e.g., *Motor Vehicle Mfrs. Ass'n v. State Farm Mutual Automobile Ins. Co.*, 463 U.S. 29 [*infra* § 9.4] has been applied to the Labor Board. . . . [T]he principle is applicable to adjudication as well as to explicit "notice and comment" rulemaking. The fact that the Board has such broad discretion in deciding which route to follow, *NLRB v. Bell Aerospace Co.*, [*infra* § 5.4] shows that the Board cannot be allowed to escape the obligation of justifying changes in its policies merely by following the common law route; the fact that common law rulemaking is retroactive buttresses this conclusion. So while not bound by *stare decisis,* the Board can jettison its precedents only if it has "adequately explicated the basis of its [new] interpretation." . . .

The citation to a previous decision of the Board that may have departed (but without explanation) from the traditional standard does not satisfy the duty to explicate; a previous violation of the duty cannot validate the subsequent one.

Forcing an administrative agency to 'fess up to its changes of position may seem productive merely of paper shuffling, and also inconsistent with the genius of the common law, which allows new doctrines to be created implicitly and even surreptitiously by judges who deny all the while that they are changing the law. Yet agencies often are forced to explicate decisions that judges and juries, not to mention legislative and executive branch officials, are allowed to make without explanation. The reason may be that agencies unlike courts are not constrained to make policy by the common law route, but can use explicit rulemaking procedures. Indeed, agencies are often criticized (none more so than the Labor Board) for not making greater use of their rulemaking powers, see, e.g., *NLRB v. Wyman–Gordon Co.,* [*infra* § 5.4] although *NLRB v. Bell Aerospace Co., supra,* suggests that the criticism cuts little ice with the Supreme Court. Another consideration may be that independent agencies, such as the Labor Board, in combining legislative, executive, and judicial functions, seem somehow to elude the constitutional system of checks and balances. But these agencies are checked by other organs of government (as a legislature with executive and judicial functions, or an executive with legislative and judicial functions, would not be), even if they lack internal checks and balances—and the Administrative Procedure Act creates some. Moreover, the rule that the agency must explain its about-faces is not limited to the independent agencies; it extends to administrative agencies within the executive branch, as the *State Farm* decision shows. In any event, the Board violated the rule in this case. . . .

The decision reversing the administrative law judge does not contain a reasoned analysis of the law and the evidence, and we therefore set aside the decision and return the case to the Board.

Notes and Questions

1. *UAW and waiver.* Why do you think the NLRB failed to " 'fess up to its changes in position?" And if courts can and often do avoid unwelcome prior precedents by ignoring them or confining them "to their facts," why can an agency not do so?

Is it a waste of time for a court to reverse an agency decision which makes an unexplained shift in position even though the decision is otherwise legally correct (i.e. both the old and the new positions are consistent with the underlying statute) and supported by substantial evidence? Will the agency not just reach the same result over again?

The *UAW* case observes that agencies can change course through rulemaking as well as through case-by-case adjudication, although traditionally the NLRB has eschewed rulemaking (see § 5.4 *infra*). Is the requirement that an agency identify and justify a change in position more important in adjudication than in rulemaking? Or less important?

2. *Traditional rule.* Traditionally agencies were considered to be free of the constraints of consistency; if a second decision was itself consistent with statute, it was upheld. See F. Cooper, STATE ADMINISTRATIVE LAW 530–34 (1965). The recognition that agencies must explain and justify changes in position is a relatively recent development which is followed by both state and federal courts. See, e.g., *Matter of Charles A. Field Delivery Serv., Inc.,* 488 N.E.2d 1223 (N.Y.Ct.

App.1985). What accounts for the traditional rule? What accounts for the change?

Note that the requirement of explanation of a change in position is simply one example of the broader requirement that an agency state findings and reasons for its action, discussed in § 4.3, *supra*.

3. *Problem.* The Internal Revenue Service (IRS) issues private letter rulings about the tax consequences of proposed transactions. These letters (about 30,000 per year) are published (without identifying details). The IRS cautions that taxpayers cannot rely on a letter ruling issued to someone else. By statute, private letter rulings cannot be used or cited as precedent. IRC § 6110(j)(3).

Generally the cost of attending law school is not deductible as a business expense because it qualifies a student to enter a new profession—even if a legal education would help the student in her existing profession. In the past, the IRS ruled privately several times that a taxpayer who would be professionally helped by legal training can deduct the cost of a correspondence law school because its graduates are not entitled to take the Bar Exam.

Gloria, a Michigan police officer who was not aware of the prior rulings, pays $2500 tuition to Learn by Mail Law School. The IRS denies the deduction because there are two states (not including Michigan) where a graduate of a correspondence law school can take the Bar. Thereafter, IRS issues rulings allowing real estate brokers to deduct the cost of correspondence law schools. Should a court compel the IRS to allow Gloria the deduction? *See* Zelenak, "Should Courts Require the IRS to Be Consistent?" 40 Tax.L.Rev. 411 (1985).

§ 4.4.3 ESTOPPEL

The principle of equitable estoppel has been applied countless times in nearly every area of law. Under that principle, if A's statement or conduct reasonably induces B's detrimental reliance, A will not be permitted to act inconsistently with its statement or conduct. Under another commonly applied private law rule, a principal is bound by the actions of its agent under either actual or apparent authority. Apparent authority arises if the principal has caused third parties reasonably to believe that the agent has authority to act—even if the agent has no such authority.

Should the government be bound by equitable estoppel and apparent authority when the action of its agent misleads a person to his detriment?

FOOTE'S DIXIE DANDY, INC. v. MCHENRY

607 S.W.2d 323 (Ark.1980).

[This case concerns the tax levied on employers to support the system of unemployment compensation for employees. Foote's operated two grocery stores (Hamburg and Crossett) within a single corporate entity. In 1971, it separately incorporated the Crossett store. Foote's had a good unemployment record which resulted in a low employment tax. If Foote's had filed a request for a transfer of that record, the new Crossett corporation would also have a low tax rate.

In 1971, Foote's CPA asked Mr. Yates, a field auditor for the Employment Security Division, about the procedures the new corporation should use in complying with the employment tax law. Foote's had always dealt exclusively with Yates about such questions. Yates said to do nothing special. In 1976, Yates retired and the new auditor discovered that a request for transfer had not been filed in 1971. As a result, the state claimed that an additional $20,000 in taxes were due for the 1971–76 period.]

The State's claim is simply that it cannot be estopped regardless of the facts. Its position is based on a series of cases which announce the principle that the State cannot be estopped by the actions of its agent. . . .

We do not overrule those cases but we do abandon the principle stated in those cases that the state can *never* be estopped by the actions of its agents. Estoppel is not a defense that should be readily available against the state, but neither is it a defense that should never be available. Estoppel of the state is a principle of law recognized in more and more jurisdictions.

The United States Court of Appeals, Eighth Circuit, has found that:

The equitable claims of the state or of the United States are no stronger than those of an individual under like circumstances, and a state or the United States may waive a claim and be estopped from the assertion of a claim under circumstances that would estop an individual from the assertion of a similar claim. *United States v. Denver & R.G.W.R. Co.,* 16 F.2d 374 (8th Cir.1926).

Estoppel is governed by fairness, as the court said in *United States v. Lazy FC Ranch,* 481 F.2d 985 (9th Cir.1973):

We think the estoppel doctrine is applicable to the United States where justice and fair play require it. . . . This court has also followed this rationale and permitted the estoppel defense against the government in cases where basic notions of fairness required us to do so.

In *Gestuvo v. District Director of the United States Immigration and Naturalization Service,* 337 F.Supp. 1093 (C.D.Cal.1971), the court recognized estoppel when certain essential elements were present. As the court stated:

Four elements are necessary: (1) the party to be estopped must know the facts; (2) he must intend that his conduct shall be acted on or must so act that the party asserting the estoppel had a right to believe it is so intended; (3) the latter must be ignorant of the true facts; and (4) he must rely on the former's conduct to his injury.

In explaining the application of estoppel, the court, in *Gestuvo,* continued:

> [T]he requirements of morals and justice demand that our administrative agencies be accountable for their mistakes. Detrimental reliance on their misrepresentations or mere unconscientiousness should create an estoppel, at least in cases where no serious damage to national policy would result . . . The contrary conclusion sacrifices 'to form too much of the American spirit of fair play in both our judicial and administrative processes.'

Other jurisdictions have come to the same conclusion. These states include: Alabama . . . California . . . New York . . . and Pennsylvania . . .

The decisions of the federal and state courts favoring estoppel of the government are closely aligned with the abandonment of the doctrine of sovereign immunity. This trend was recognized by Kenneth Culp Davis in his *Administrative Law Treatise* where he said:

> Because of the erosion of the doctrine of sovereign immunity the cases estopping the government may largely represent the law of the future, even though they are still exceptional. § 17.03 at 504.

Arkansas has not abandoned the doctrine of sovereign immunity which is in our constitution. . . .

Estoppel will protect the citizen only to the extent that he relied upon actions or statements by an agent. In the present case there was good faith reliance by Foote's C.P.A. on the advice of the Employment Security Division's field agent. There was no reason for the C.P.A. to question the agent's credibility since he had dealt with him frequently on Employment Security Division matters and no problems had arisen. Fairness has to be a two edged sword. People who deal with the state must be fair and the same principle should apply to the state. Justice Holmes made the remark many years ago that "Men must turn square corners when they deal with the government." Years later, two commentators added the logical corollary to Holmes' remark: "It is hard to see why the government should not be held to a like standard of rectangular rectitude when dealing with its citizens." We agree with both ideas.

We are satisfied that all the circumstances of this case warrant applying the doctrine of equitable estoppel. The facts are that *only* a form was not filed which would have been routinely approved if it had been filed; that there was not a scintilla of evidence of bad faith; and that an important agent of the State of Arkansas, clothed with considerable authority, had told Foote's that it did not have to file any further documentation. . . .

The State had all the necessary information in the present case—the name of the new corporation, the record of the older corporation and timely filed reports. The Footes were ignorant of the true facts. These factors, as well as others, satisfy us that estoppel should be applied in this case.

We are not unmindful of the wisdom of those decisions denying estoppel. In most instances estoppel would not have been a justifiable defense. But in this case, except for a routine application not filed, there would have been no attempt by the State to collect the contributions. . . .

Because the State was entitled to rely upon a principle of law that we now abandon, it should be allowed to offer proof as to whether its auditor Yates did in fact make the statements attributed to him. Therefore, the cause is remanded for the sole purpose of permitting the State the opportunity of calling Yates as a witness on this fact issue. If Yates agrees that he did so advise the C.P.A., then the chancellor will enter a decree for the appellant; if Yates disagrees, or if it appears the facts are in dispute, the chancellor will make a finding and enter a decree consistent with this opinion.

Reversed and remanded.

Notes and Questions

1. *Federal law.* The *Foote's* case gives the impression that federal cases support its holding that the government can be estopped. While there are numerous lower court cases like *Georgia–Pacific* or *Gestuvo,* the Supreme Court has never accepted an estoppel claim and has rejected them on numerous occasions. The *Foote's* case ignores these Supreme Court decisions, including several that decline to estop the government in tax cases.

The leading Supreme Court case is *Federal Crop Ins. Corp. v. Merrill,* 332 U.S. 380 (1947). In *Merrill,* an FCIC agent advised a farmer that a crop was insurable. In reliance on the advice, the farmer planted the crop. The advice was contrary to a regulation and FCIC refused to pay when the crop was destroyed. By a 5–4 vote, the Court held that the government was not bound by the mistaken advice because the principle of apparent authority did not apply to the government.

The Court said: "[I]t is too late in the day to urge that the Government is just another private litigant . . . [A]nyone entering into an arrangement with the Government takes the risk of having accurately ascertained that he who purports to act for the Government stays within the bounds of his authority . . . And this is so even though, as here, the agent himself may have been unaware of the limitations upon his authority . . . Men must turn square corners when they deal with the Government . . . ."

Similarly, *see Schweiker v. Hansen,* 450 U.S. 785 (1981), a decision which seems contrary to *Foote's.* In *Schweiker,* an applicant for social security was wrongly told by a Social Security Administration (SSA) representative in 1974 that she was ineligible for benefits. In addition, she was not advised to file a written claim for benefits, even though the Claims Manual states that SSA representatives should advise claimants to file written claims in all doubtful situations. Later she discovered she was eligible for benefits. If she had filed a written claim in 1974, she would have received benefits back to 1973. It was held that the Government was not estopped by the mistaken advice nor by the failure to follow the Claims Manual.

More recently, however, the Court hinted that the government might be bound by estoppel if the facts were strong enough. *Heckler v. Community Health Services*, 467 U.S. 51 (1984), involved a hospital which had applied for and received government reimbursements to which it was not legally entitled. It had been orally advised on several occasions by Travelers' Insurance (a private company which handled claims for the government) that it was entitled to the grants and, in reliance thereon, incurred much larger expenditures for CETA personnel who provided home visits to patients.

The Court held that the government was not estopped to recover the grants because plaintiff's showing of detrimental reliance was insufficient. However, the Court's language was more receptive to estoppel claims than in earlier cases. It said: "[W]e are hesitant . . . to say that there are *no cases* in which the public interest in ensuring that the government can enforce the law free from estoppel might be outweighed by the countervailing interest of citizens in some minimum standard of decency, honor, and reliability in their dealings with their Government."

The Court stated that the government could be estopped only by "affirmative misconduct." It warned that it would not be reasonable to rely on oral (as opposed to written) advice and that a plaintiff should obtain advice from the highest possible level of the agency itself, not from an intermediary like Travelers'. Moreover, the plaintiff's detriment was unpersuasive—it had received government funds to which it was not legally entitled in the first place and thus had not suffered the loss of a legal right or any adverse change in status.

2. *Rationale.*

It is no longer realistic or just, if it ever was, to hold every person dealing with the government to knowledge of everything in the statute books and the Federal Register. As a matter of practice, most agencies consider themselves bound by erroneous advice . . . Thus it may well be that the legal doctrines to the contrary serve no useful purpose. It no longer seems credible that the government will be ruined by a judicious application of estoppel . . . The application of estoppel hardly means the repeal of a statute; it would simply preclude the retroactive correction as to particular individuals of a particular mistake, spreading the loss over all the taxpayers rather than the unfortunate individuals who relied to their detriment upon a governmental error or misrepresentation.

M. Asimow, ADVICE TO THE PUBLIC FROM FEDERAL ADMIN-ISTRATIVE AGENCIES 60–61 (1973). Do you agree? Why is the Supreme Court so reluctant to accept claims of estoppel against the government? Why are the courts of many states (such as Arkansas) willing to go the other way? Should the government be subject to estoppel and apparent authority principles in the same way as a private entity or are there some differences? Might there be a reason to draw a distinction between claims that would estop an agency from relying upon or enforcing a statute and claims that would estop an agency from relying upon or enforcing one of its own rules or its own case precedents?

3. *Detrimental reliance.* The *Foote's* case indicates that the state can be estopped by erroneous oral advice. *Schweiker v. Hansen* suggests the contrary. Should someone who seeks to rely on erroneous governmental advice always get it in writing? Compare the reliance interests claimed in the *Foote's* case and in the cases discussed in note 1, *supra.* Are some of the interests more compelling than others?

4. *Advice-giving.* Every government agency furnishes advice to the public on how to comply with the agency's law. Every day agencies advise taxpayers about whether a transaction is taxable, whether an issuance of stock must be registered, whether an alien might jeopardize her immigration status by leaving the country, or whether action taken by a professional licensee might jeopardize the license. *See generally* M. Asimow, *supra* at 11–13, 142–193.

Advice-giving is an extraordinarily valuable service to the public (and, since it diminishes inadvertent violations of law, to the agency as well). The advice is usually correct and, when it is incorrect, the government usually protects reliance interests created by the mistake even though it is probably not legally required to do so. As the cases discussed above illustrate, however, this is not always true. If the government could be estopped by mistaken advice, would that discourage agencies from giving the advice? If it did, the public as a whole might be worse off even though some individuals who had detrimentally relied on the advice would be better off.

5. *Declaratory rulings.* Both the federal APA and 1981 MSAPA expressly authorize agencies to issue declaratory rulings. *See* federal APA § 554(e), 1981 MSAPA § 2–103. The acts of many states are based on § 8 of 1961 MSAPA which provides: "Each agency shall provide by rule for the filing and prompt disposition of petitions for declaratory rulings as to the applicability of any statutory provision or rule of the agency. Rulings disposing of petitions have the same status as agency orders or decisions in contested cases." For discussion of cases arising under this provision, *see* Bonfield, "The Iowa Administrative Procedure Act," 60 Iowa L.Rev. 731, 805–23 (1975).

How do declaratory rulings differ from agency advice-giving? From ordinary contested adjudications? When would you recommend a client seek a declaratory ruling? On what basis may an agency properly refuse to issue such a ruling?

The comment to 1981 MSAPA § 2–103 explains the utility and operation of that provision as follows:

The purpose of that proceeding is to provide an inexpensive and generally available means by which persons may obtain fully reliable information as to the applicability of agency administered law to their particular circumstances. . . .

As subsection (b) indicates, each agency is required to issue rules specifying all of the details surrounding the declaratory order process . . . . [A]n agency may include in its rules reasonable standing, ripeness, and other requirements for obtaining a declaratory order. . . . Note that there are no contested issues of fact in declaratory order proceedings because their function is to declare the applicability of the law in question to unproven facts furnished by petitioner. The actual existence of the facts upon which such an order is based will usually become an issue only in a later proceeding in which a party to the declaratory order proceeding seeks to use the order as a justification for that party's conduct. Note also that the party requesting a declaratory order has the choice of refraining from filing such a petition and awaiting the ordinary agency adjudicative process governed by Article IV. Declaratory orders are, of course, subject to the provisions of this Act for judicial review of agency orders and for public inspection and indexing of agency orders. . . . When the agency declines to issue a declaratory order it must also include therein a statement of the precise grounds for that disposition. This statement of reasons will help to assure that the propriety of the denial of such a declaratory order in the circumstances will be carefully considered by the agency. Since an agency's refusal to issue a declaratory order is "agency action" which is judicially reviewable, the required statement of reasons for an agency's refusal to issue such an order will also assure that the courts will have an opportunity for meaningful review of all negative agency responses to such a petition. . . .

Is the MSAPA declaratory ruling provision superior to the federal act's provision on that subject?

6. *Problem.* Recall the problem at § 4.4.2 note 3, *supra.* The IRS issued numerous private letter rulings that allow taxpayers to deduct the cost of a correspondence law school. The Learn By Mail Law School advertised these rulings in its advertising brochure. Ted received such a ruling and told his friend Gloria about it. In reliance on the ruling, both Ted and Gloria enrolled in Learn by Mail and paid and deducted $12,000 tuition during her four years of correspondence study. At that point, the IRS revoked all the prior letter rulings. It billed Ted and Gloria for $3700 (the tax saved by deducting $12,000). Should the IRS be estopped? *See Automobile Club of Michigan v. Commissioner,* 353 U.S. 180 (1957); *Bookwalter v. Brecklein,* 357 F.2d 78 (8th Cir.1966).

Chapter 5

THE RELATIONSHIP BETWEEN RULEMAKING AND ADJUDICATION

§ 5.1 DEFINITION OF "RULE"

Statutes and case law divide the administrative process into two principal processes, each governed by separate procedures. The first resembles the judicial process and is called "adjudication." Its product is an "order." Adjudication was the subject of the prior three chapters. The second process resembles the legislative process and is called "rulemaking." Its product is a "rule." Rulemaking is the subject of the next chapter. Recall § 2.5, *supra,* which traced the constitutional roots of the rulemaking-adjudication distinction. This chapter contrasts the two processes.

All APAs define the term "rule" to which their rulemaking procedures apply. Read § 551(4) of the federal APA and consider the following analysis.

ACUS, A GUIDE TO FEDERAL AGENCY RULEMAKING
17–19 (1983).

Standing alone, the APA's definition of "rule" is not very helpful. For example, an agency order directing Company X to cease and desist from engaging in a certain unlawful practice would fall within the literal terms of this definition. Yet it is clear [according to the Attorney General's Manual on the APA] that . . . a proceeding leading to the issuance of a cease-and-desist order is adjudication and not rulemaking. The APA definition of "adjudication" sheds little additional light, for "adjudication" is defined as the agency process for formulating an "order," and "order" is defined as "a final disposition whether affirmative, negative, injunctive, or declaratory in form of an agency in a matter other than rule making but including licensing."

244

Thus, the definition of adjudication is largely residual; it is agency process in "a matter other than rule making."

To understand the thrust of the APA's distinction between rulemaking and adjudication, one should turn to the discussion in the Attorney General's Manual on the APA:

> [T]he entire Act is based upon a dichotomy between rule making and adjudication. Examination of the legislative history of the definitions and of the differences in the required procedures for rule making and for adjudication discloses highly practical concepts of rule making and adjudication. Rule making is agency action which regulates the future conduct of either groups of persons or a single person; it is essentially legislative in nature, not only because it operates in the future but also because it is primarily concerned with policy considerations. The object of the rule making proceeding is the implementation or prescription of law or policy for the future, rather than the evaluation of a respondent's past conduct. Typically, the issues relate not to the evidentiary facts, as to which the veracity and demeanor of witnesses would often be important, but rather to the policy-making conclusions to be drawn from the facts. . . .

Given the breadth of the definitions of rulemaking and adjudication in the APA, it is not surprising that some confusion has existed with respect to the proper classification of certain agency proceedings.

The inclusion in the APA's definition of rule [of] agency statements of "particular applicability" probably creates the most difficulty, for most people think of rules as addressed to general situations and adjudication as addressed to particular situations. While it is true that the great majority of rules have some general application and adjudication is nearly always particularized in its immediate application, the drafters of the APA wished certain actions of a particular nature, such as the setting of future rates or the approval of corporate reorganizations, to be carried out under the relatively flexible procedures governing rulemaking. Consequently, the words "or particular" were included in the definition.

In 1970 the American Bar Association recommended revising the definition of "rule" to delete the words "or particular." The Administrative Conference endorsed the ABA proposal with the understanding that "[a] matter may be considered of 'general applicability' even though it is directly applicable to a class which consists of only one or a few persons if the class is open in the sense that in the future the number of members of the class may be increased." Courts have upheld classification of agency action as a "rule" even though it applied to the activities of a single entity. Probably no great change would occur if the words "or particular" were deleted from the definition of rule in section 551 of the APA. . . .

———

Read the definition of "rule" in 1981 MSAPA § 1–102(10). Note that this definition is similar to the definition contained in § 1(7) of the 1961 MSAPA which defines a "rule" as "each agency statement of general applicability that implements, interprets, or prescribes law or policy, or describes the organization, procedure, or practice requirements of any agency. The term includes the amendment or repeal of a prior rule. . . ."

The phrase "the whole or a part of an agency statement of *general applicability*" is probably the most important part of the definition of "rule" in 1981 MSAPA § 1–102(10). Every statement implementing, interpreting, or prescribing law or policy that is directed at a class by description, that is, directed at all persons similarly situated, rather than at named individuals, is within the ambit of the definition. Contrast the definition of "order" in § 1–102(5) of 1981 MSAPA. An "order" is "agency action of *particular applicability* that determines the legal rights, duties, privileges, immunities or other legal interests of one or more specific persons."

How are ratemaking and licensing treated under 1981 MSAPA? If the ratemaking or licensing determination is of particular applicability, addressed to named or specified parties such as a certain utility company or a particular licensee, it is an "order" subject to the adjudication provisions of the statute. On the other hand, ratemaking and licensing actions of general applicability, that is, addressed to all members of a described class of providers or licensees, are "rules" under the statute. The 1961 MSAPA treated ratemaking and licensing similarly. *See* 1961 MSAPA § 1(2), (7).

Contrast federal APA § 551(4), which defines ratemaking as rulemaking for all purposes. However, many federal enabling acts require a hearing on the record before ratemaking of particular applicability; this triggers the process of "formal rulemaking," discussed in § 6.3.2, *infra,* which involves most of the APA's adjudication provisions. *See* APA §§ 551(4), 553(c). Would due process permit individualized ratemaking for a telephone company or a cable television franchise without a trial-type hearing?

In addition to the general-particular dichotomy, there are other ways to distinguish rulemaking from adjudication. A rule is usually prospective, an order is usually retroactive. A rule usually requires a further proceeding (an adjudication) to make it concretely effective against a particular individual, while an order needs no further proceeding to make it effective. A rule is usually directed at and binds a described class that may open to admit new members, while an order is directed at and binds only those who were parties to the adjudicative proceeding. A rule ordinarily is based on findings of fact that are legislative or general in nature and is often based on predictions about the future; an adjudication is ordinarily based, at least in part, on facts specific to the parties and on findings of past events.

Should classification of a statement as a rule depend on the terminology used by the agency? May a statement denominated as an "order," "memorandum," "notice," "bulletin," or "guideline" be a "rule" and thus subject to APA rulemaking procedure? *See* A. Bonfield, STATE ADMINISTRATIVE RULE MAKING 74–75 (1986).

Notes and Questions

1. *Concrete applicability of rules.* It has been suggested that a rule "affects the rights of individuals in the abstract and must be applied in a further proceeding before the legal position of any particular individual will be definitely touched by it; while adjudication operates concretely upon individuals in their individual capacity." J. Dickinson, ADMINISTRATIVE JUSTICE AND THE SUPREMACY OF LAW IN THE UNITED STATES 21 (1927). Is this distinction reliable? Are some rules obeyed without further proceedings? Are some orders ignored until further enforcement proceedings are concluded?

2. *Future effect.* Rules normally establish law or policy for the future, while orders generally determine individual rights based on past events and with retroactive effect. The federal APA and the APAs of a number of states explicitly provide that a rule must be a statement of "future effect." *See* federal APA § 551(4); 1 F. Cooper, STATE ADMINISTRATIVE LAW 108 (1965). Note, however, that both § 1(7) of 1961 MSAPA and § 1–102(10) of 1981 MSAPA omit the "future effect" language from their definitions of "rule." Is this omission significant? Does it blur the distinction between rules and orders?

Georgetown Univ. Hospital v. Bowen, 821 F.2d 750 (D.C.Cir.1987), cert. granted, 108 S.Ct. 1073 (1988), involved a challenge to a 1984 rule of the Department of Health and Human Services that purported to have retroactive as well as prospective effect. In holding the retroactive application of the rule to be invalid, the court stated:

> The instant case does not in any way involve a new agency policy articulated in the course of adjudication. Rather, it involves a *legislative rule* adopted by the Secretary pursuant to the notice and comment procedures of the APA, 5 U.S.C. § 553. As recognized in [*Retail, Wholesale and Department Store Union v. NLRB*, 466 F.2d 380 (D.C.Cir.1972),] the APA requires that legislative rules be given future effect only. Because of this clear statutory command, equitable considerations are irrelevant to the determination of whether the Secretary's rule may be applied retroactively; such retroactive application is foreclosed by the express terms of the APA.

> In his final rulemaking notice, the Secretary suggested that a retroactive rule was warranted under the circumstances of this case to correct what was simply a "procedural defect" in his previous rule. It is clear, however, that this proffered exception to the requirement that legislative rules be prospective in effect only is completely at odds with basic tenets of administrative law. . . .

The Secretary's suggestion that retroactive rulemaking is permissible to remedy a procedural defect in a rule would, if accepted, make a mockery of the provisions of the APA. Obviously, agencies would be free to violate the rulemaking requirements of the APA with impunity if, upon invalidation of a rule, they were free to "reissue" that rule on a retroactive basis. If an agency rule is invalidated on procedural grounds, the agency must, of course, be given an opportunity to correct the procedural defect and promulgate a new rule. However, both the express terms of the APA and the integrity of the rulemaking process demand that the corrected rule, like all other legislative rules, be prospective in effect only.

Do you think the holding of the *Georgetown Univ. Hospital* case is sound? Could you argue that the rule in that case was necessarily of "future effect" because, at the time it was adopted, it was effective in the future even if it has consequences that are retroactive? After all, a rule does not actually alter legal relations until the time that it is effective and that time is normally required by statute to be a specified time after the date of the adoption of the rule. Should the result in the *Georgetown* case be the same under the 1961 and 1981 MSAPAs in light of the fact that they do not contain the "future effect" language found in § 551(4) of the federal act?

Suppose a federal agency issues a rule that purports to protect persons who had previously relied in good faith on an earlier rule that had subsequently been declared invalid. Would such a rule be invalid because it would not be of "future effect?" *See* Auerbach, "Administrative Rulemaking in Minnesota," 63 Minn.L.Rev. 151, 157 (1979).

What are the policy reasons for and against permitting agencies to treat as rules some legal statements of general applicability that have retroactive effects? Note that civil *statutes* sometimes apply retroactively and courts often uphold them if the legislative purpose is sufficient and can only be achieved through retroactivity. L. Tribe, AMERICAN CONSTITUTIONAL LAW, § 9.8.–.11 (2nd ed. 1988). Does the existence in the federal APA and in most state APAs of a delayed effective date provision for newly adopted rules mute or eliminate any of the arguments against permitting agencies to treat as rules legal statements of general applicability that have retroactive effects? *See* federal APA § 553(d); 1981 MSAPA § 3–115. Both provisions are discussed in § 6.9, *infra*. Or do those deferred effective date provisions further establish the invalidity of retroactive rules?

What is the real effect of the *Georgetown Univ. Hospital* case? Does it ensure that agency actions with retroactive consequences must be executed through orders utilizing adjudication procedures, rather than through rules utilizing rulemaking procedures? Is *that* a desirable result? Section 5.3, *infra,* deals with the comparative advantages and disadvantages of using adjudication rather than rulemaking as a means of agency lawmaking.

3. *Implement, interpret, or prescribe, law or policy.* Is a statement that only *describes* rather than prescribes or interprets or implements law or policy a rule under the federal act or either of the MSAPAs? Why is a statement that only interprets law or policy classified as a rule? Should it matter whether the statement is directed, by its terms, at agency staff rather than at members of the public? *See* A. Bonfield, STATE ADMINISTRATIVE RULE MAKING § 3.3.4 (1986).

Should there be a distinction between statements of policy and statements of law for purposes of determining whether an agency statement is a rule? Do any of these APAs draw such a distinction? What is the difference between statements of policy and statements of law? *See* § 6.11.5, *infra.*

④ *Legal effect of rules.* Legislative rules are rules issued by an agency pursuant to an express or implied grant of authority to issue rules with the binding force of law. Nonlegislative rules, often called interpretive rules or statements of policy, are agency rules that do not have the force of law because they are not based upon any delegated authority to issue such rules. *See* 2 K. Davis, ADMINISTRATIVE LAW TREATISE §§ 7:9–:14 (2d. ed. 1979). The distinction between legislative and nonlegislative rules is explored in § 6.11.5, *infra.*

Valid *legislative* rules are binding and enforceable in the same way as other species of effective law. So, for example, the United States Supreme Court has noted that a "regulation . . . made by . . . [a] commission in pursuance of constitutional statutory authority . . . has the same force as though prescribed in terms by the statute." *Atchison, T. & S.F. Ry. Co. v. Scarlett,* 300 U.S. 471, 474 (1937). Furthermore, a state agency legislative rule has been treated as the "law of the state" under a federal statute that made it illegal for a person to deliver fish for interstate transportation when such transportation was prohibited by the "law of the state" where the fish originated. *United States v. Howard,* 352 U.S. 212 (1957). Violation of a valid legislative rule, therefore, may generally be used as a basis for imposing civil and criminal sanctions. *See* B. Schwartz, ADMINISTRATIVE LAW § 4.7 (2nd ed. 1984).

It is clear that valid legislative rules bind the issuing agency as well as the persons subject to their terms. *United States v. Nixon,* 418 U.S. 683, 694–96 (1974); *Tew v. City of Topeka Police & Fire Civil Service Com'n,* 697 P.2d 1279, 1282–83 (Kan.1985). Consequently, an agency may not violate its own legislative rules, although it may be able to waive them in appropriate cases for the benefit of individual members of the public, at least if the rights of third parties are not prejudiced thereby. *See American Airlines v. C.A.B.,* § 3.2, *supra.* "The idea that legislative rules are binding on the issuing agency is deeply embedded." 2 K. Davis at 98. Nevertheless, this conclusion does not appear to be required by due process; instead, it appears to be a product of federal and state administrative law. *Board of Curators of Univ. of Mo. v. Horowitz,* 435 U.S. 78, 92 n. 8 (1978); 1981 MSAPA § 5–

116(c)(8)(ii). Procedural rules are often legislative rules, having the force of law, and, therefore, bind the issuing agency. *See Service v. Dulles,* 354 U.S. 363, 388 (1957) and *Vitarelli v. Seaton,* 359 U.S. 535 (1959) (holding agencies bound by procedural rules they had previously adopted.)

On the other hand, nonlegislative rules might not be binding on the agency that adopted them. A recent decision stated that "the agency remains free in any particular case to diverge from whatever outcome . . . [a] policy statement or interpretive rule might suggest." *Vietnam Veterans of America v. Secretary of the Navy,* 843 F.2d 528, 537 (D.C.Cir.1988). However, the issue is not yet settled and the cases and commentators present mixed views. *Compare* 2 K. Davis, ADMINISTRATIVE LAW TREATISE 100 (2nd. ed. 1979) (interpretive rules may often be assumed not to be binding on agency) with B. Schwartz, ADMINISTRATIVE LAW 165–66 (2nd ed. 1984) and *Realty Group, Inc. v. Department of Revenue,* 702 P.2d 1075, 1079 n. 3 (Or.1985) (agency bound to follow an interpretive rule until it amends or recinds that rule). Do you think that an agency should ever be bound by its nonlegislative rules? Suppose the elements of an estoppel are present? See § 4.4.3, *supra.* In some states, nonlegislative rules appear to be binding on the issuing agency because the state APA explicitly provides that an agency may not violate its own rules and the APA's definition of "rule" includes nonlegislative rules. *See, e.g.,* 1981 MSAPA §§ 5–116(c)(8)(ii), 1–102(10).

Of course, an agency may always amend a rule that binds the agency in a way it believes is undesirable. Note 2, *supra,* deals with agency authority to give such an amendment to its rules retroactive effect.

5. *Problem.* Are the following agency statements rules under the federal APA or the MSAPAs? Should they be treated as rules?

(a) A policy bulletin issued by a state commissioner of public welfare requiring a county to provide medical assistance to welfare recipients for elective, nontherapeutic abortions. *See McKee v. Likins,* 261 N.W.2d 566 (Minn.1977).

(b) A policy of an agency requiring certain standard contract specifications to be inserted in all highway construction contracts. *See Greenfield Constr. Co. v. Michigan Dept. of State Highways,* 261 N.W.2d 718 (Mich.1978).

(c) A statement that only explains the meaning of an earlier rule.

(d) A statement by an agency to the effect that no further permits would be issued for a specified period even to applicants who had admittedly complied with all conditions for such permits contained in current rules. *See In re Application of Orr,* 396 N.W. 2d 657 (Minn.1986); *Balsam v. Department of Health and Rehabilitative Services,* 452 So.2d 976 (Fla.App.1984).

(e) An agency statement of law prohibiting all trucks over a certain weight from driving over a named bridge. *See* A. Bonfield, STATE ADMINISTRATIVE RULE MAKING 79–80 (1986).

(f) An agency statement establishing a particular statistical methodology for collecting certain data when a statute specifies that the resulting data is to be used as the basis for determining the allocation of certain public monies to qualified recipients. *See Batterton v. Marshall,* 648 F.2d 694 (D.C.Cir.1980).

ANACONDA CO. v. RUCKELSHAUS

482 F.2d 1301 (10th Cir.1973).

[The question presented is] whether the Environmental Protection Agency [EPA] is obligated to grant to Anaconda an adjudicatory hearing with the right to subpoena and cross-examine witnesses before promulgating or indeed holding further hearings on its proposed regulation under § 110(c) of the Clean Air Act Amendments. The crucial aspect of the case is then the validity of the *proposed* EPA regulation for the control of sulfur oxide emissions in Deer Lodge County, Montana where Anaconda operates its smelter. The company is the only significant source of sulfur oxide pollution in the county and so concededly the proposed regulation, although general in form, would apply to Anaconda alone. . . .

Anaconda immediately demanded an adjudicatory hearing on EPA's proposed regulation, but EPA's reply was that the public hearings were to be legislative or informational and not adjudicatory. Subsequently, it was further explained that the hearing would not be conducted in the nature of a trial. Instead, any interested persons or corporations could make a statement and all relevant testimony would be received. Also, the hearing record would remain open until October 7, 1972, for written statements or other submissions. After that there would be a further hearing to allow further public statements.

Anaconda's position expressed at the hearing was that it was spending large sums of money on its own initiative in an effort to control sulfur oxide emissions; that it was preparing to restrict them from the current rate of 64,000 pounds per hour to 50,000 pounds per hour. Its position was further expressed that the 7,040 pounds per hour would be technologically and economically unfeasible and would create a significant water pollution problem. . . .

[The] question is whether there was sufficient substance to Anaconda's contention so that it would appear that it has been deprived of procedural due process by EPA's refusal to grant a trial-type adjudicatory hearing. Assuming that a showing of real deprivation would justify a threshold injunctive hearing, we must determine that the showing here was grossly insufficient to justify the action taken. The trial court saw as a result of denial of an adjudicatory hearing a violation of procedural due process together with a violation of the Clean Air Act and the Administrative Procedure Act. We must disagree. The Administrative Procedure Act requires that there be an adjudicatory hearing only if the agency statute specifies that the particular rule-making hearings be "on the record after opportunity for an agency hearing." No such requirement is set forth in the Clean Air Act. Notwithstanding that these words are used in other sections of the Act, omission of them in § 110(c) is therefore significant. . . .

By requiring that the hearing under § 110(c) be public Congress sought to bring about broad and flexible participation from all interested groups subject always to a review by the court of appeals. The fact that the proceedings are transcribed does not, of course, mean that the hearing is "on the record."

The fact that Anaconda alone is involved is not conclusive on the question as to whether the hearing should be adjudicatory, for there are many other interested parties and groups who are affected and are entitled to be heard. So the guidelines enunciated by Mr. Justice Holmes in Bi–Metallic Investment Co. v. State Board of Equalization, 239 U.S. 441 (1915) are not applicable.

We have also examined the early decision in Londoner v. Denver, 210 U.S. 373 (1908), and nothing therein imposes the adjudicatory requirement. There it was said by Justice Moody:

Many requirements essential in strictly judicial proceedings may be dispensed with in proceedings of this nature. But even here a hearing, in its very essence, demands that he who is entitled to it shall have the right to support his allegations by argument, however brief; and, if need be, by proof, however informal.

From our examination of the Act and the related case law and statutes, it would appear that the congressional requirement of a public hearing has been satisfied. Notice has been given and the proposed regulation has been issued. Anaconda appeared at that hearing and submitted material and was given an opportunity to submit more material and information for a period of 75 days following the public hearing. We perceive no violation of Anaconda's right to procedural due process. . . .

Unending procedure could be produced by an adjudicatory hearing. This could bring about unending delay which would not only impede but completely stifle congressional policy. We do not, of course, condemn the trial court's concern for the rights of Anaconda. Those rights are important and the court should be sensitive to them, but those rights are not of such magnitude as to overcome congressional policy and the rights of the remainder of the community. . . .

Notes and Questions

1. *The Anaconda case.* The District Court in *Anaconda* treated the agency action at issue in that case as an adjudication of Anaconda's rights, subject to adjudication procedures, rather than as a rulemaking, subject to rulemaking procedures. The reason for the court's decision

was that the agency action was based, in part, on data solicited from and specific to Anaconda, that company was the only source of such emissions in the county, and it was very unlikely that there would be any other source of such emissions in the county in the future. *See* 352 F.Supp. 697, 700 (D.Colo.1972).

Which court reached a more defensible result, the District Court or the Court of Appeals? Should the EPA's action in this case have been treated as a rule or as an order?

If it is treated as a rule, what is the appropriate procedure under the federal APA and 1981 MSAPA? If it is treated as an order, what is the appropriate procedure under the federal APA and under the 1981 MSAPA? Does due process require any particular procedure in these circumstances? If so, did the procedure used by EPA provide due process?

Were legislative-type procedures or judicial-type procedures more appropriate for issuing the emission standard? Was Anaconda the only entity or person affected by EPA's action? Was it the only entity or person with something to contribute to the agency determination at issue?

The Court of Appeals held that Anaconda did not have a right to a trial-type adjudicatory hearing before the EPA prior to the time the agency issued the emission standard. Is the Court of Appeals decision inconsistent with a right of Anaconda to a hearing before *a court* to determine the lawfulness of that standard, including its reasonableness in light of all relevant facts? Would Anaconda have a right to a hearing before the EPA prior to the time it is sanctioned by that agency for violation of the emission standard?

2. *Orders disguised as rules.* Schwartz maintains that

[i]f the administrative process is directed at particular persons— even if it be termed rulemaking [because it is on its face of general applicability]—those affected should be given the same hearing rights as in proceedings which are clearly judicial in nature: "if the resulting administrative action, whether regarded as rulemaking or otherwise, *is individual in impact . . .*, a hearing preceding any final administrative action is appropriate."

B. Schwartz, ADMINISTRATIVE LAW § 5.8, at 217 (2d ed. 1984). Do you agree with Schwartz? Should an agency statement that is of general applicability in form be treated as a rule even though, at present, it is only applicable to a single person whose identity and circumstances were known to the issuing agency at the time the statement was formulated and adopted? The 1961 MSAPA § 1(7) Comment states: "Attention should be called to the fact that rules, like statutory provisions, may be of 'general applicability' even though they may be of immediate concern to only a single person or corporation, provided the form is general and others who may qualify in the future will fall within its provisions." Note also that the Wisconsin Supreme

Court stated that "[e]ven though an action applies only to persons within a small class, the action is of general application if that class is described in general terms and new members can be added to the class." *Citizens for Sensible Zoning, Inc. v. Department of Natural Resources,* 280 N.W.2d 702, 707–08 (Wis.1979).

Suppose the class described in an agency statement of law or policy is defined in a way that makes it *impossible* for the statement to be applicable to new members? May an agency couch action that is in fact of particular applicability in the form of a rule to avoid adjudicatory procedures? Is the following a satisfactory test for identifying statements of agency law or policy that appear, facially, to be rules because they are of general applicability, but that should be treated as orders because they are in fact of particular applicability?

A four-part test may be posited for identifying those situations where an agency statement of law that is on its face of general applicability should be treated as an "order" subject to adjudicatory procedures rather than as a "rule" subject to rule-making procedures despite its external form. Such an agency statement of law should be treated as an "order" rather than a "rule" only where it can be demonstrated that: (1) in effect, the impact of the statement falls exclusively on one identifiable individual or entity; *and* (2) it can be demonstrated that, on the basis of current information, no other individual or entity could ever join the described class; *and* (3) the statement is based wholly on specific facts pertaining to the circumstances or conduct of that particular individual; *and* (4) as a matter of subjective agency intention, the statement is directed only at the particular individual or entity in question.

A. Bonfield, STATE ADMINISTRATIVE RULE MAKING 85 (1986).

3. *Classification by appropriate procedure.* In close cases should a court determine whether a particular proceeding is rulemaking or adjudication by determining whether rulemaking or adjudication procedures are most appropriate for its efficient, effective, and expeditious operation? The next section deals with many of these issues.

§ 5.2   RULE–ORDER DICHOTOMY: JUSTIFICATION

Due process often requires personal notice and some kind of a hearing prior to the issuance of an order; but neither appear to be required by due process prior to the issuance of a rule. *See* discussion of *Londoner, Bi–Metallic,* and *Atkins* in § 2.5., *supra.* Similarly, federal and state APAs divide formal agency action into rulemaking and adjudication, and impose very different procedures on each of them. Challenges to the classification of an agency action as a rule or an order, therefore, are primarily the result of disagreements over the appropriateness of the procedures used by the agency in taking that action.

In recent years, the rulemaking-adjudication dichotomy as a basis for imposing procedural requirements upon agency action has been criticized. Professor Robinson notes:

It is time to ask whether the approach of the [APA] in classifying all administrative procedures as either adjudication or rulemaking, and in attempting to prescribe procedures in accordance with this classification, is not a hindrance to adapting administrative procedures more closely tailored to the needs of different agencies and distinctive agency functions. It is true, of course, that in setting down certain basic, procedural standards for rulemaking and adjudication, the APA does not mandate detailed procedures. It does not necessarily preclude reasonable flexibility by an agency in adapting rulemaking or adjudicatory procedures to the variable needs of the agency and the interests of affected private parties. For example, the prescription of an adjudicatory hearing does not preclude an agency from allowing widespread industry and public participation through intervention and presentation of testimony in written affidavits. By the same token, the use of nonhearing rulemaking procedures clearly permits appropriate use of facets of adjudicatory procedure, such as cross-examination, oral arguments, and the like.

Having acknowledged that reasonable flexibility is possible within the adjudication-versus-rulemaking dichotomy, the fact remains that the present approach of the APA and the individual regulatory statutes fosters a general tendency to adopt doctrinal distinctions which are not conducive to a pragmatic use of either rulemaking or adjudicative techniques. Moreover, the arbitrary distinction between modes of proceeding does not provide useful criteria for determining what are the appropriate procedures in any particular kind of case. The same can be said for the "adjudicative fact" versus "legislative fact" distinction. These highly elastic concepts tend to obscure the varied needs of different agencies and varied demands of different regulatory functions.

Future efforts in the direction of administrative procedure reform should steer away from prescription of uniform procedures for the entire administrative system and focus instead on specific procedures tailored to the distinctive functions of each individual agency. . . .

This is not to suggest that there would not be certain uniform procedures appropriate to all, or most, of these varied functions. But such uniformity would not be imposed on the proceedings because they are "adjudicative" or "legislative" in character, but would emerge only out of basic similarities in agency functions and in the private interests affected, where they were shown in fact to exist.

Candor requires an admission that this approach does not provide any simple solution to the problem of prescribing appropriate administrative procedures. It will not always be possible to break down an agency's business into distinctive "functions," each with its own distinctive procedures. There must be great room for flexibility in the "mix" of various procedural methods in any given type of case. However, by focusing on particular functions, on the kinds of issues normally confronted, and on the parties normally involved and interested in that function, it should be possible to deal with the problem of procedure in a more pragmatic and useful way than by simply attaching the labels "adjudication" or "rulemaking" to particular cases or issues:

Robinson, "The Making of Administrative Policy: Another Look at Rulemaking and Adjudication and Administrative Procedure Reform," 118 U.Pa.L.Rev. 485, 536–38 (1970).

Davis also argues that procedures should not be imposed upon agency action entirely on the basis of its classification as rulemaking or adjudication. Instead, he would identify the appropriate procedures for each type of agency task and require agencies to follow those procedures whenever they perform that task—whether they do so in rulemaking or in adjudication. He believes that either in rulemaking or in adjudication, the following are appropriate:

(1) procedure of briefs and arguments to resolve nonfactual issues of law or policy, (2) procedure of notice and comment for making new law or new policy on a nonfactual basis, (3) procedure of notice and comment for resolving issues of broad legislative fact, (4) trial procedure to find most disputed adjudicative facts, and, especially, (5) nonuse of trial procedure to perform functions other than finding adjudicative facts (or, rarely, specific legislative facts).

3 K. Davis, ADMINISTRATIVE LAW TREATISE § 14.4 at 23 (2d ed. 1980). Verkuil has also proposed that the rule-order distinction be discarded as a basis for imposing procedural requirements on agencies and that, instead, a unitary minimum administrative procedure, which may be expanded to include additional elements in the discretion of the agencies, should be established for all formal agency action. *See* Verkuil, "The Emerging Concept of Administrative Procedure," 78 Colum.L.Rev. 258, 322 (1978).

Despite criticisms of the rulemaking-adjudication dichotomy as a basis for assigning procedures to govern agency action, and alternative proposals for more functional procedural schemes, the dichotomy has survived as a major feature of contemporary administrative law. The drafters of the recent 1981 MSAPA, for instance, calculatedly chose to perpetuate the rule-order dichotomy contained in the federal act and the many state acts. They believed that the alternative of

[c]hoosing procedures based on a distinction between legislative facts and adjudicative facts could involve substantial costs. The conclusion that trial-type procedures may only be desirable for the

determination of adjudicative facts does not solve the more difficult question of how to identify such facts. The distinction between adjudicative facts and legislative facts is generally more difficult to draw in practice than the distinction between rulemaking and adjudication although, admittedly, the latter distinction is also sometimes difficult to draw. Nevertheless, established procedures for broad, fairly clearly defined classes of agency activities such as rulemaking and adjudication normally enable administrators to ascertain easily and accurately the method by which they should proceed when they perform their duties. Without this facility, the costs of deciding which procedures to use in any particular circumstances, including the costs of invalidating the agency decision because the wrong procedures were employed by competent administrators acting in good faith, will be excessive.

Consequently, as long as the procedures used as a result of the rule-order dichotomy *generally* provide a good fit between their specific requirements and the precise function performed and are normally fair, that dichotomy seems defensible. Because rulemaking rarely involves facts so specific that fairness under the circumstances would require them to be established by the trial-type procedures mandated in adjudications, notice and comment procedures of the type required in rulemaking will ordinarily be appropriate for the issuance of a rule.

Bonfield, "The Federal APA and State Administrative Law," 72 Va.L. Rev. 297, 311 (1986).

Do you believe the rulemaking-adjudication distinction should be discarded as a means of determining, even initially, the types of procedures applicable to agency proceedings? Would the costs of administering properly a scheme of the kind proposed by Robinson, Davis, or Verkuil outweigh the benefits of discarding the rule-order dichotomy for this purpose?

Are the proposals of Robinson and Davis wholly incompatible with the current classification of agency action as rulemaking or adjudication? Recall that Robinson admitted that "reasonable flexibility is possible within the adjudication-versus-rulemaking dichotomy. . . ." Similarly, Davis insists that "nothing in the APA prevents complete adoption of our principal proposition that the specific task, not the characterization of a whole proceeding as rulemaking or adjudication, should determine the basic procedure." 3 K. Davis, ADMINISTRATIVE LAW TREATISE § 14.4 at 21 (2d ed. 1980).

Is the argument that the rulemaking and adjudication requirements of the various APAs are only minimum requirements and that agencies are free, under current APAs, to impose *additional* procedures when they believe such procedures are appropriate, a fully satisfactory answer to critics of the rule-order dichotomy?

AGENCY LAWMAKING: ADVANTAGES ND DISADVANTAGES OF RULEMAKING AND ADJUDICATION

all the *American Airlines* case in § 3.2, *supra.* The decision ized the advantages of rulemaking over adjudication. This takes a closer look at the relative advantages and disadvantages of each process. Which of these supposed distinctions are significant and realistic in practice? Which are illusory?

Some advantages of rulemaking:

a. Participation by all affected parties: Only those persons who are parties to a particular dispute normally have a right to participate in an adjudicatory proceeding to resolve it. Yet the decision in such a proceeding serves as precedent for similar cases involving different parties who may find it difficult to persuade the agency to distinguish or overrule the prior case. In contrast, anyone who wishes to do so can participate in rulemaking. Notice is given to all concerned and anyone can submit comments.

b. Appropriate procedure: When an agency makes new law or policy, the procedures of rulemaking (which resemble legislation) are superior to those of adjudication (which resemble trials). Trials and trial records are good for establishing individualized facts but not particularly suitable for determining broad questions of legislative fact and for ventilating important issues of policy. In adjudication, the law relating to official notice, separation of functions, and internal and external communications with decisionmakers, may insulate the decisionmakers from important factual and policy data needed to make new agency law or policy.

c. Retroactivity: When an agency adopts a new principle in an adjudication, it applies retroactively to the parties to the proceeding. As a result, the agency may upset important reliance interests. Rules, in contrast, apply prospectively and thus furnish fair warning to those whose conduct is affected.

d. Uniformity: Agency law made by rule affects all persons subject to its terms at the same time and in the same way. The same is not true of agency law made in the course of adjudication because an agency precedent technically binds only the specific parties to that adjudication, leaving other similarly situated persons free of any binding order. In addition, lawmaking by adjudication facilitates the drawing of distinctions between otherwise similarly situated individuals on the basis of differences that may not be significant enough to justify those distinctions.

e. Politicking: Lawmaking is a highly political process. Rulemaking provides a regularized opportunity for politically active persons and groups to participate in the process and to mobilize political pressures for or against a proposed agency policy. The procedures utilized in adjudication are unsuited for the making of essentially political decisions.

f. Agency agenda setting: When agencies make law through adjudications, their agenda is controlled by the happenstance of whatever cases come before them. As a result, they may be forced to spend time on relatively trivial problems and fail to address more important ones. When an agency decides to make law through rulemaking, it controls its own agenda, and is free to attack its highest priority problems first. In rulemaking, the agency also avoids becoming distracted by the particular facts of each case or the particular problems of litigants; it can focus exclusively on the central policy issue.

g. Agency efficiency: Although rulemaking can be time consuming, it is ordinarily more efficient for the agency to settle an issue definitively through a rule than to litigate the same issue in numerous proceedings in order to accomplish that result.

h. Availability of law: It is easier for affected persons to locate and research applicable law issued in the form of rules than agency case law. This is so because rules are published and, therefore, are widely available, while agency case law is often unpublished and available for inspection only at agency offices.

i. Difficulty of research: By the same token, it is often difficult to distill agency law from a mass of case precedents even when they can be found. Agency cases are often inconsistent, and there are conflicting lines of authority. Significant statements of law may be buried amid massive fact-findings or may take the form of dictum. Cases that make new law often do not clearly say they are doing so. When law is set forth in rules, it is easier to ascertain and understand.

j. Oversight: For the reasons just stated, it is far easier for the executive and legislative branches to exercise oversight over the merits and legality of agency-made law when the law is made through rulemaking rather than adjudication. In addition, most state APAs and the 1981 MSAPA provide formal schemes for the legislative and executive review of rules; these schemes may be entirely circumvented if agencies make law through adjudication, because there are no formal schemes for the legislative and executive review of agency law embodied in individual cases. Legislative and executive oversight is discussed in § 7.6, *infra*.

Nevertheless, there are some advantages to adjudication:

a. Flexibility: Rules are often over- or under-inclusive; and they may operate inflexibly because they usually do not take into account individual differences in the circumstances of those subject to their terms. On the other hand, adjudication allows a response that is tailored to the special facts of each case, thereby allowing maximum flexibility and avoiding over- or under-inclusiveness.

b. Abstraction: Adjudication requires the agency to make its law on a step by step basis in concrete situations in which it can observe the actual operation of that law. Rulemaking requires the agency to create a principle divorced from the specific facts of a particular case. Because it operates abstractly, therefore, rulemaking may produce cruder, less sensitive law, than adjudication.

c. The new and unexpected: A case-by-case approach may be better where the agency is not yet in a position to make generally applicable law due to lack of sufficient expertise or because the distinctions in the area are likely to be so numerous or complex that they resist generalized treatment in a rule.

Moreover, especially in the case of newer statutes, an agency may discover a pattern of harmful behavior that has already occurred and which should be addressed through enforcement action. If the problem was unanticipated, the agency could not have adopted a prospective rule to deal with it. Only retroactively effective adjudication can solve the problem.

d. Residual adjudication: Regardless of how many rules an agency makes, it can never dispense entirely with adjudication. There will always be ambiguities in rules that need to be answered in individual cases, thereby inevitably creating new precedents.

For a more complete catalog of the advantages and disadvantages of rulemaking and adjudication, *see* Bonfield, "Mandating State Agency Lawmaking by Rule," 2 B.Y.U.J. of Pub.L. 161, 168–80 (1988).

Notes and Questions

1. *Costs and benefits; political accountability.* Are the advantages of agency lawmaking by rule as compared to lawmaking by adjudication overstated by the preceding material? May some of the supposed disadvantages of using adjudication be reduced or eliminated? How could that result be accomplished? In short, are the differences between rulemaking and adjudication as a means for making agency law really as great as suggested? *See* Robinson, "The Making of Administrative Policy: Another Look at Rulemaking and Adjudication and Administrative Procedure Reform," 118 U.Pa.L.Rev. 485, 514–28 (1970).

Recall the discussion of agency legitimacy and the role of administrative law in § 1.7, *supra*. Which means of administrative lawmaking, rulemaking or adjudication, is more likely to ensure that its product is consistent with the political will of the community at large? Or is it impossible to generalize on this subject? Even if one means of administrative lawmaking is more likely than the other to ensure that its product reflects the political will of the community at large, is this advantage sufficient to justify a preference for that form of lawmaking in all situations? Or must the advantages of one form of agency lawmaking in securing the consistency of its product with the political will of the community be balanced against its disadvantages in other respects?

2. *Making the choice.* Considering the need for accuracy, efficiency, economy, effectiveness, and public satisfaction, when should agencies make law by order rather than by rule? When by rule rather than by order? What specific factors should be considered to determine the most appropriate agency lawmaking modality in particular situations?

3. *Problem.* Auto insurance companies in the state of Madison typically rate customers by the ZIP Code in which they reside. Insurance in some neighborhoods is much more expensive, and much less available, than in other neighborhoods. The Madison Insurance Commission has authority to deal with "unfair insurance practices." It has power to adopt legislative rules, but has never used that power. It also has power to enter cease-and desist orders on a case by case basis, a power it has often used. If it finds that an "unfair insurance practice" has occurred, it can order refunds of premiums or provide other appropriate relief to consumers.

You are the law clerk for one of the commissioners. At this morning's meeting between the commissioners and the enforcement staff, the staff presented data it has gathered on the practices of Ranchers Insurance Co. Ranchers is one of the larger auto insurance companies in Madison and it utilizes ZIP Code pricing. The staff seeks authorization to issue an administrative complaint against Ranchers in the hopes that this will produce a good test case on ZIP Code pricing.

What is your advice to your boss? Should he vote to authorize issuance of the complaint in this case or should he insist that the Commission commence a rulemaking proceeding to deal with the ZIP Code pricing problem? What other facts might be relevant to his decision?

§ 5.4 DISCRETION TO CHOOSE
RULEMAKING OR ADJUDICATION

Section 5.3, *supra,* suggested some advantages and disadvantages of adjudication and rulemaking as agency lawmaking modalities. Although the decision to make law by rule rather than by order or vice versa has significant consequences, courts have generally been reluctant to interfere with an agency's choice of lawmaking procedures.

NLRB v. BELL AEROSPACE CO., DIVISION OF
TEXTRON, INC.
416 U.S. 267 (1974).

MR. JUSTICE POWELL delivered the opinion of the Court.

[The second issue in this case is] whether the Board must proceed by rulemaking rather than by adjudication in determining whether certain buyers are "managerial employees." . . .

Respondent Bell Aerospace Co., Division of Textron, Inc. (company), operates a plant in Wheatfield, New York. . . . [T]he United Automobile, Aerospace and Agricultural Implement Workers of America (union) petitioned the National Labor Relations Board (Board) for a representation election to determine whether the union would be certified as the bargaining representative of the buyers in the purchasing and procurement department at the company's plant. The company opposed the petition on the ground that the buyers were "managerial employees" and thus were not covered by the Act. . . .

[The Supreme Court affirmed the Court of Appeals decision that the Board applied the wrong legal standard when it determined whether these buyers were covered by the Act. As a result, the Supreme Court remanded the case to the NLRB.]

[T]he present question is whether on remand the Board must invoke its rulemaking procedures if it determines, in light of our opinion, that these buyers are not "managerial employees" under the Act. The Court of Appeals thought that rulemaking was required because *any* Board finding that the company's buyers are not "managerial" would be contrary to its prior decisions and would presumably be in the nature of a general rule designed "to fit all cases at all times."

A similar issue was presented to this Court in its second decision in *SEC v. Chenery Corp.,* 332 U.S. 194 (1947) (*Chenery II*). There, the respondent corporation argued that in an adjudicative proceeding the Commission could not apply a general standard that it had formulated for the first time in that proceeding. Rather, the Commission was required to resort instead to its rulemaking procedures if it desired to promulgate a new standard that would govern future conduct. In rejecting this contention, the Court first noted that the Commission had a statutory duty to decide the issue at hand in light of the proper standards and that this duty remained "regardless of whether those standards previously had been spelled out in a general rule or regulation." The Court continued:

"The function of filling in the interstices of the [Securities] Act should be performed, as much as possible, through this quasi-legislative promulgation of rules to be applied in the future. But any rigid requirement to that effect would make the administrative process inflexible and incapable of dealing with many of the specialized problems which arise. . . . Not every principle essential to the effective administration of a statute can or should be cast immediately into the mold of a general rule. Some principles must await their own development, while others must be adjusted to meet particular, unforeseeable situations. *In performing its important functions in these respects, therefore, an administrative agency must be equipped to act either by general rule or by individual order. To insist upon one form of action to the exclusion of the other is to exalt form over necessity.*

"In other words, problems may arise in a case which the administrative agency could not reasonably foresee, problems which must be solved despite the absence of a relevant general rule. Or the agency may not have had sufficient experience with a particular problem to warrant rigidifying its tentative judgment into a hard and fast rule. *Or the problem may be so specialized and varying in nature as to be impossible of capture within the boundaries of a general rule.* In those situations, the agency must retain power to deal with the problems on a case-to-case basis if the administrative process is to be effective. There is thus a very definite place for the case-by-case evolution of statutory standards." *Id.*, at 202–203. (Emphasis added.)

The Court concluded that "the choice made between proceeding by general rule or by individual, *ad hoc* litigation is one that lies primarily in the informed discretion of the administrative agency."

The views expressed in *Chenery II* make plain that the Board is not precluded from announcing new principles in an adjudicative proceeding and that the choice between rulemaking and adjudication lies in the first instance within the Board's discretion. Although there may be situations where the Board's reliance on adjudication would amount to an abuse of discretion or a violation of the Act, nothing in the present case would justify such a conclusion. Indeed, there is ample indication that adjudication is especially appropriate in the instant context. As the Court of Appeals noted, "[t]here must be tens of thousands of manufacturing, wholesale and retail units which employ buyers, and hundreds of thousands of the latter." Moreover, duties of buyers vary widely depending on the company or industry. It is doubtful whether any generalized standard could be framed which would have more than marginal utility. The Board thus has reason to proceed with caution, developing its standards in a case-by-case manner with attention to the specific character of the buyers' authority and duties in each company. The Board's judgment that adjudication best serves this purpose is entitled to great weight.

The possible reliance of industry on the Board's past decisions with respect to buyers does not require a different result. It has not been shown that the adverse consequences ensuing from such reliance are so substantial that the Board should be precluded from reconsidering the issue in an adjudicative proceeding. Furthermore, this is not a case in which some new liability is sought to be imposed on individuals for past actions which were taken in good-faith reliance on Board pronouncements. Nor are fines or damages involved here. In any event, concern about such consequences is largely speculative, for the Board has not yet finally determined whether these buyers are "managerial."

It is true, of course, that rulemaking would provide the Board with a forum for soliciting the informed views of those affected in industry and labor before embarking on a new course. But surely the Board has discretion to decide that the adjudicative procedures in this case may also produce the relevant information necessary to mature and fair consideration of the issues. Those most immediately affected, the buyers and the company in the particular case, are accorded a full opportunity to be heard before the Board makes its determination. . . .

Notes and Questions

1. *Bell Aerospace.* According to *Bell Aerospace,* agencies are generally free to use their own judgment in determining whether to make new law by rule or by order. Their discretion in choosing a lawmaking modality is limited only by any special statutory requirement or agency rule to the contrary and by the APA prohibition on agency action that is an "abuse of discretion." *See* federal APA § 706(2)(A), discussed in § 9.4, *infra.* The cases prior and subsequent to *Bell Aerospace* also indicate that the federal courts rarely find an abuse of discretion with respect to an agency's choice of lawmaking modality. *See generally* Weaver, "*Chenery II* : A Forty-year Retrospective," 40 Admin.L.Rev. 161 (1988).

Is this agency freedom of choice too broad? Should it be further limited in some way? If so, how? Does *Bell Aerospace* suggest any situations where a choice to make new law by order rather than by rule would be an abuse of discretion?

In deciding whether an abuse of discretion occurred when an agency makes new law by ad hoc order to determine the result in a particular case, some lower federal courts consider: 1) whether the particular case is one of first impression (or whether it overturns a prior case); 2) whether the new law represents an abrupt departure from well established practice or merely attempts to fill a void in an unsettled area of the law; 3) the extent to which the party against whom the new law is applied relied on the prior law; 4) the degree of the burden which a retroactive order imposes on a party; and 5) the statutory interest in applying the new law to the case at hand despite the reliance of a party on the old standard. *Retail, Wholesale and Dept. Store Clerks Union v. NLRB,* 466 F.2d 380, 390 (D.C.Cir.1972). In the case, the NLRB relied on one of its recent cases that had overruled one of its prior cases. As a result, the NLRB decided that the conduct by the employer involved was an unfair labor practice even though it had been permissible at the time it occurred. The NLRB also required the employer to give back pay to employees who were victims of this unfair labor practice. Applying the above factors to the particular circumstances, the court decided that the NLRB order was an abuse of discretion and, therefore, should be set aside.

2. *Other limits on discretion.* Ford Motor Co. v. Federal Trade Commission, 673 F.2d 1008 (9th Cir.1981), *cert. denied,* 459 U.S. 999 (1982), is an atypical federal court decision. In that case the Federal Trade Commission (FTC) instituted an adjudicatory proceeding against Francis Ford, a retail automobile dealer. The Commission found the repossession practices used by Francis Ford against its defaulting purchasers to be a violation of Section 5 of the FTC Act and issued a cease and desist order. The Court of Appeals vacated the order stating:

In the present case, the FTC, by its order, has established a rule that would require a secured creditor to credit the debtor with the "best possible" value of the repossessed vehicle, and forbid the creditor from charging the debtor with overhead and lost profits. . . . [T]he precise issue therefore is whether this adjudication changes existing law, and has widespread application. It does, and the matter should be addressed by rulemaking.

The FTC admits that industry practice has been to do what Francis Ford does—credit the debtor with the wholesale value and charge the debtor for indirect expenses. . . .

By all accounts this adjudication is the first agency action against a dealer for violating ORS 79.5040 by doing what Francis Ford does. Although the U.C.C. counterpart of ORS 79.5040 is enacted in 49 states, nearly word for word, we have been cited to no case which has interpreted the provision to require a secured creditor to credit the debtor for the "best possible price" and not charge him for overhead and lost profits. It may well be that Oregon courts will interpret U.C.C. § 9–504 in the manner advocated by the FTC if the question is put to them. But it is speculation to contend, as does the FTC here, that Francis Ford is in violation of *existing* Oregon law.

Ultimately, however, we are persuaded to set aside this order because the rule of the case made below will have general application. It will not apply just to Francis Ford. Credit practices similar to those of Francis Ford are widespread in the car dealership industry; and the U.C.C. section the FTC wishes us to interpret exists in 49 states. . . .

673 F.2d 1008, 1009–10 (9th Cir.1981).

Does *Ford Motor Co.* suggest that an agency may not proceed by ad hoc order and must proceed by rule when it makes a change in existing law that will necessarily have wide-spread application? Is this an illustration of a situation where an agency's choice to proceed by adjudication is an abuse of discretion? Or is the case simply inconsistent with *Bell Aerospace?* Does it correctly balance the factors set forth in *Retail Clerks Union?*

The *Ford Motor Co.* case was the subject of a study conducted by the ABA Section of Administrative Law. The Section prepared the following resolution, which was adopted by the ABA's House of Delegates.

RESOLVED, That the American Bar Association approves the following principles respecting the choice between rulemaking and adjudication in administrative agency proceedings:

1. An agency is generally free to announce new policy through an adjudicative proceeding.

2. When rulemaking is feasible and practicable, an agency which has been granted broad rulemaking authority ordinarily

should use rulemaking rather than adjudication for large-scale changes, such as proscribing established industry-wide practices not previously thought to be unlawful.

3.   An agency should not be empowered to treat its adjudicatory decisions precisely as if they were rules. In particular, it is inappropriate to empower an agency or court to treat third-party departures from holdings in agency adjudications as, *ipso facto*, violations of law. Where the precedent of a prior adjudication is sought to be applied in a subsequent adjudication, a party should have a meaningful opportunity to persuade the agency that the principle involved should be modified or held inapplicable to his situation.

Does the ABA approve or disapprove of the principle announced in *Ford Motor Co.?* Is the resolution simply a restatement of current federal law? Or does it go beyond current federal law in certain respects? If so, how? Does the resolution satisfactorily resolve the tension between agency discretion to choose the means by which to make law and the desire to avoid retroactive agency lawmaking? For an explanation of the study and resolution see Berg, "Re-examining Policy Procedures: The Choice Between Rulemaking and Adjudication," 38 Admin.L.Rev. 149 (1986).

3.   *Required rulemaking.* In the absence of a statute explicitly requiring that result, a few other federal cases hold that an agency must execute specified lawmaking by rule rather than by order. The most important such case is *Morton v. Ruiz,* 415 U.S. 199, 231–35 (1974), involving the issue of whether welfare benefits should be paid to those Indians who live near as well as those who live on reservations. According to *Morton,* if the agency did not have sufficient funds to pay all eligible beneficiaries, "it would be incumbent upon [it] to develop an eligibility standard to deal with this problem. . . .   But in such a case the agency must, at a minimum, let the standard be generally known so as to assure that it is being applied consistently and so as to avoid both the reality and the appearance of arbitrary denial of benefits to potential beneficiaries. . . .   No matter how rational or consistent with congressional intent a particular decision might be, the determination of eligibility cannot be made on an ad hoc basis by the dispenser of the funds."

As a result, the agency in *Morton* was required to issue a legislative rule specifying the eligibility requirements for the benefits in question. Although the agency had set forth its policy in a staff manual, this did not suffice as a rule because it was not published in the Federal Register, as required both by the APA and by the agency's own procedural rules.

The opinion in *Morton* does not make clear whether the rulemaking obligation it imposes is drawn from the underlying benefits statute, from the abuse of discretion prohibition in the APA, from its failure to follow its own procedural rules, or from administrative common law. It does not appear to be based on due process. The requirements of due process in this regard are discussed in note 1 after the *Megdal* case which follows.

Most states appear to follow the principle that agencies generally have discretion to make their law either by order or by rule. This discretion appears to be limited only by a specific statute or agency rule to the contrary, and by a general unreasonableness or abuse of discretion standard. *See* Bonfield, "Mandating State Agency Lawmaking by Rule," 2 B.Y.U.J. of Pub.L. 161, 166–67 (1988).

A number of states, however, appear to be in the vanguard of a developing movement in the contrary direction. Several state courts have relied upon a principle of statutory construction as a means of requiring agencies to elaborate their law by rule rather than by order. A few additional state courts have relied upon the demands of due process or an abuse of discretion standard for this purpose. And other states have resorted to the enactment of specific statutes to impose such a requirement. So far, however, only a little more than half a dozen states have used these mechanisms to impose on their agencies a general requirement that they make their law primarily by rules. *See* Bonfield, *supra,* at 180–205.

MEGDAL v. OREGON STATE BOARD OF DENTAL EXAMINERS
605 P.2d 273 (Or.1980).

LINDE, JUSTICE.

Petitioner, a dentist licensed both in Oregon and in California and maintaining offices in both states, seeks review of an order of the State Board of Dental Examiners which revoked his Oregon license on the ground of "unprofessional conduct."

The conduct which the board found unprofessional under the statute was that petitioner obtained malpractice insurance coverage for other dentists employed by him in his California practice by a misrepresentation that they were employed in Oregon. . . . The issue, in sum, is whether the board may revoke a dentist's license under an unparticularized rubric of "unprofessional conduct" upon an administrative finding that he practiced a fraud on an insurance company.

Petitioner objects that before revoking a license for unprofessional conduct other than the kinds specified in the statute itself the board must first adopt rules indicating the forbidden conduct, because the phrase "unprofessional conduct" alone is too vague a standard to be applied directly from case to case. . . . We allowed review in order to reexamine the role of broadly stated standards in laws governing disciplinary actions against occupational licensees. For the reasons that follow, we conclude that the board's order must be reversed. . . .

There is no lack of suggestion that a prior specification of grounds should be a prerequisite of due process in administrative as well as penal deprivations. *See, e.g.,* Davis, Administrative Law of the Seventies 28, 224 (1976); Note, Due Process Limitations on Occupational Licensing, 59 Va.L.Rev. 1097, 1104–1106 (1973). At least one modern court has held that the grounds to revoke a pharmacist's license for "grossly unprofessional conduct" must be limited to those further spelled out in the statute or in rules, because "revocation of licenses and permits for conduct not specifically defined or prohibited by the statute, would render the statute unconstitutional on grounds of vagueness in violation of the Due Process Clause of the Fourteenth Amendment." *Pennsylvania State Board of Pharmacy v. Cohen,* 292 A.2d 277, 282 (1972). To support this conclusion the court took the step of tacking together the two propositions that an individual's exclusion from an occupation requires due process and that penal statutes must give adequate notice of the forbidden or required conduct. . . .

Perhaps federal "due process" law will move toward the step anticipated by the Pennsylvania court. But, there has been no clear signal from the United States Supreme Court that the standards for occupational licensing decisions must meet those for penal laws. The Court's later holdings sustaining the adequacy of phrases such as "conduct unbecoming an officer and a gentleman" for military punishment, *Parker v. Levy,* 417 U.S. 733 (1974), and a string of epithets for disciplinary discharge of civil service employees, *Arnett v. Kennedy,* 416 U.S. 134 (1974), can be distinguished as dealing with special relationships. Nonetheless, the gravity of the losses there permitted to be inflicted under vague standards leaves the crucial step assumed by the Pennsylvania court in doubt. Again, the factors from which *Mathews v. Eldridge,* 424 U.S. 319 (1976), directs us to derive the requirements of due process—the private interest affected, the chances of error and of its reduction by better procedures, and the countervailing governmental interests—clearly affirm a licensee's right to the kind of adjudicatory procedures of notice, hearing, and findings based on evidence that, in this state, are provided him under the administrative procedure act; but nothing indicates whether this due process calculus extends also to restricting adverse action to the enforcement of previously specified norms. For the moment, at least, support for finding such a requirement in federal due process appears primarily in *Soglin v. Kauffman,* 418 F.2d 163 (7th Cir.1969), which applied the requirement to standards for expelling university students for "misconduct," and in decisions involving criteria for the bestowing of benefits.

In sum, the most that can be said about "due process" as a possible premise for petitioner's constitutional attack on the phrase "unprofessional conduct" is that the state of the federal law is inconclusive and the attack perhaps only premature. . . .

Since 1939 the statute has authorized the board to "make and enforce rules . . . for regulating the practice of dentistry." The statute does not expressly state that the expanded grounds for disciplinary action under the rubric "unprofessional conduct" were to be created by board rules. But there are reasons to believe that this is the legislative policy. One is that the legislature should not be assumed to be insensitive to the importance of fair notice of grounds that may lead to loss of one's profession or occupation, whether or not this is a constitutional requirement. More concretely, the legislature made this policy explicit in many similar licensing statutes even if not in this one. Repeatedly the legislature has specified that the several boards are to exercise their control over professional standards by adopting codes or rules. . . .

Sometimes such differences in statutory drafting represent deliberate differences in policy. We see no reason to believe that this was the case here. The difference of the potential impact, when one occupation is given fair notice of obligatory standards of propriety by prior rulemaking and another occupation is given no such prior notice, is too pronounced to be attributed to the legislature without some showing that it was intended. Thus we doubt that the stylistic differences among 30–odd statutes separately enacted over many years mean that some of the boards are to develop professional standards by rulemaking and others by ad hoc determinations, insofar as they are authorized to add to the express statutory grounds for discipline at all. Rather, we infer from statutes such as those cited above that when a licensing statute contains both a broad standard of "unprofessional conduct" that is not fully defined in the statute itself and also authority to make rules for the conduct of the regulated occupation, the legislative purpose is to provide for the further specification of the standard by rules, unless a different understanding is shown. . . .

When a board lays down a new rule of proscribed or required conduct under delegated authority to do so, this is reviewable to determine whether the rule remains within the intended scope and purpose of the delegated authority. . . .

Doubts are sometimes expressed whether rules can encompass the variety of acts that should be recognized as "unprofessional," or "unethical," or "unbecoming," or otherwise improper. An attempt to "catalogue all the types of professional misconduct" might well seem infeasible. . . . But rules need not imitate a detailed criminal code to serve the two purposes of giving notice of censurable conduct and confining disciplinary administration to the announced standards. Nor is the only alternative to include some form of catchall clause that is as general as the standard it purports to elucidate. The resources of rulemaking are not so limited.

For instance, as this case illustrates, an important question is what relationships are covered by the term "unprofessional conduct" and thus within the range of professional discipline. It might be agreed that the term covers conduct in the course of rendering the professional service on the one hand, and on the other that it excludes the licensee's purely private affairs unrelated to any relevant professional qualification or performance. But between these two poles, there may be questions how far "unprofessional conduct" extends to financial arrangements or to mixing professional with other relationships. There may be disagreement whether the term should extend beyond conduct toward the patient or other recipient of the regulated service so as to cover relationships with employees or suppliers, with other professionals, or perhaps with the regulating agency itself. As stated above, in many licensing statutes the legislature does not itself provide explicit or implicit answers to these and similar questions; it delegates this task, within the limits of each statute's objectives, to the licensing agencies. . . . Thus, when the statute itself offers no further definition, the legislative delegation to the agency calls for such questions to be resolved in principle by rules rather than being confronted and disputed for the first time in charging a particular respondent directly under a conclusory term such as "unprofessional conduct." . . .

We conclude that petitioner is entitled to relief. His license has been revoked under a statutory standard of "unprofessional conduct," that was broadened beyond its original list of specifications, which the statute means the board to particularize by rules. Although his original attack was couched in constitutional terms, its target was the same lack of comprehensible and channeling criteria that the rules are meant to provide. No such rule having been made to proscribe the kind of conduct charged against petitioner, there was no legal ground on which to revoke his license. . . .

Notes and Questions

1. *Due process.* A number of federal and state cases hold that in some circumstances due process requires agencies to structure their discretionary powers with agency-created standards. *See e.g., Holmes v. New York City Housing Authority,* 398 F.2d 262, 265 (2d Cir.1968) (distribution of public housing units), discussed in note 3 after the *Industrial Union Department* case, § 7.3, *infra; Hornsby v. Allen,* 326 F.2d 605, 610 (5th Cir.1964) (issuance of liquor licenses). While these cases require agencies to create such standards in order to ensure that they do not exercise their discretionary powers in a wholly arbitrary manner, they do not appear to require those standards to be created by rule rather than by a system of precedents created in individual cases.

Do you agree with the conclusion of the court in *Megdal* that due process does not limit the discretion of agencies exercising authority in a nonpenal context to make law by retrospective order rather than by prospective rule? The *Pennsylvania State Board of Pharmacy* case discussed in *Megdal,* and a few other cases, have come to the opposite conclusion. For example, *Elizondo v. State Department of Revenue, Motor Vehicle Div.,* 570 P.2d 518 (Colo.1977), held that due process required the issuance of rules "to guide hearing officers in their decisions regarding requests for probationary [driver's] licenses" in order to assure advanced notice to the public and to avoid arbitrary agency decisionmaking. The court apparently assumed that case-by-case decisionmaking would not adequately secure those results.

Similarly, *White v. Roughton,* 530 F.2d 750 (7th Cir.1976), held invalid the denial or termination of benefits under a local general relief welfare program. No written standards governed the eligibility for such aid, which appeared to be determined wholly on the basis of the "unwritten personal standards" of administrators. In these circumstances the court held that the lack of "written standards and *regulations*" was a denial of due process. Id. at 754. (Emphasis supplied).

Note that *Soglin v. Kauffman,* 418 F.2d 163, 168 (7th Cir.1969), discussed in *Megdal,* also appeared to require the agency to create discretion-limiting standards by *rule.* But *Soglin* may be distinguished from *Elizondo* and *White* on the ground that the student disciplinary proceedings involved in *Soglin* were viewed as *penal,* thereby justifying a due process requirement of rulemaking in that case on a ground not available on the facts of the other two cases.

2. *Megdal principle.* Does *Megdal* preclude all adjudicative lawmaking for the purpose of refining the term "unprofessional conduct," or does it only require the agency to elaborate by rule the general contours of that term? Could all interstitial lawmaking by ad hoc order for the purpose of giving content to the term "unprofessional conduct" be sensibly or successfully prohibited?

Was the court in *Megdal* justified in construing the agency's enabling act to require the agency to elaborate by rule the meaning of the term "unprofessional conduct" in light of the fact that the enabling act involved did not explicitly indicate any such intention and the enabling acts of some other agencies did? It is possible that the willingness of the court in *Megdal* to construe this unclear enabling act to require elaboration of the statutory standard by rule was primarily a product of the court's belief that rulemaking was a fairer means for the agency to make this law than ad hoc adjudication. Was rulemaking a fairer means of lawmaking than adjudication in this context? If the advantages of rulemaking in this particular situation are so clear, why do you suppose the agency in this case chose to proceed by ad hoc order rather than by rule?

At a fairly high level of generalization, the *Megdal* principle appears to be that when a regulatory agency is vested with broad discretion by a statute containing a vague standard, and the statute also expressly authorizes the agency to issue rules to implement that delegation, the legislature intends the agency to elaborate the major contours of that standard by rule rather than by ad hoc order, in the absence of any clear statutory indication to the contrary. Is it likely that the *Megdal* principle will be adopted by the courts of other states? Is the *Megdal* rulemaking requirement more attractive than a rulemaking requirement based upon the due process clause because the *Megdal* theory for such a requirement allows the legislature to alter the result by statute if it disagrees with the principle?

3. *Subsequent developments in Oregon.* In *Trebesch v. Employment Division,* 710 P.2d 136, 139–40 (Or.1985), the Oregon Supreme Court read the *Megdal* principle narrowly. It construed *Megdal* to mean that in situations where the legislature has not expressly indicated its specific intentions with respect to mandatory agency rulemaking, courts must determine those intentions by analyzing a number of factors. These factors include the character of the statutory term, the particular authority delegated and the specific breadth and type of tasks assigned to the agency, and the structure used by the agency to execute its tasks. While the court did not explain exactly how to apply these factors, it indicated clearly that they must all be considered in order to determine the extent to which the legislature intended to require rulemaking under each particular statute.

It has been argued that the approach of *Trebesch* appears to "substitute a full-scale, particularized inquiry producing unpredictable and inconsistent results, for a broad rule of construction based on *Megdal* that would be easier to apply and that would yield relatively predictable and consistent results . . . [, and that the *Megdal* approach to statutory construction] is more reasonable, functional, and practical than a multi-factored, in-depth analysis of probable legislative intent on this question of the kind adopted by the recent *Trebesch* case." Bonfield, "Mandating State Agency Lawmaking By Rule," 2 B.Y.U.J. of Pub.L. 161, 192 (1988). Do you agree with this criticism of the *Trebesch* approach? Is a broad rule of construction based on *Megdal* justified and superior to the *Trebesch* approach in light of the significant advantages of state agency lawmaking by rule, and the fact that the legislature may always alter the application of a broad *Megdal* principle to any situation where it believes the principle to be inappropriate?

4. *Other state cases.* Other state cases have reached the same conclusion as *Megdal,* and have required agencies, in the absence of an express statutory requirement, to elaborate the major contours of their law by rule. *See* Bonfield, *supra,* 2 B.Y.U.J. of Pub.L. 161, 183–92 (1988). However, in reading state cases invalidating agency decisions because they were not grounded on a properly adopted rule, you must be careful to distinguish between two different kinds of cases. Some state cases hold particular agency action invalid because that action was a rule *de facto* but not *de jure,* that is, was in substance a legal statement of general applicability issued without observance of required rulemaking procedures. Other state cases hold particular agency adjudicatory action invalid because it made law that was required to be issued by *rule* in advance of that agency decision. Only the latter class of cases deal with the issue addressed in this subsection; but it is often difficult to distinguish cases in the former class from cases in the latter class. *See* Bonfield, *supra,* at 180–82.

5. *1981 MSAPA.* Section 2–104(3) of the 1981 MSAPA provides that "as soon as feasible, and to the extent practicable, [each agency must] adopt rules, in addition to those otherwise required . . . embodying appropriate standards, principles, and procedural safeguards, that the agency will apply to the law it administers." The Comment to that section explains that "to the extent an agency can feasibly and practicably further structure its discretion by rule to avoid arbitrary action, and to give fair notice to the public of the precise content of the law it administers, the agency should be required to do so." Section 2–104(4) of the 1981 MSAPA also requires agencies, "as soon as feasible and to the extent practicable, [to] adopt rules to supersede principles of law or policy lawfully declared by the agency as the basis for its decisions in particular cases."

Are these provisions desirable? Are they enforceable? Which one of them is more likely to be successful? Could it be argued that both of these MSAPA provisions are excessively vague and impractical, and that they would create more problems for agencies than they would provide solutions to problems for the public? *See* Bonfield, *supra*, 2 B.Y.U.J. of Pub.L. 161, 205–16 (1988).

6. *Difference between state and federal law.* Why are some states apparently more willing than the national government to require their agencies to develop the major contours of agency law by rules, rather than by orders? Consider the following explanation for the developing difference between state and federal law on this subject.

[T]he advantages of rulemaking over adjudication for administrative lawmaking are greater, in a number of important respects, for state agencies than for federal agencies. First, state agency decisions in particular adjudications are virtually never published while the decisions of many federal agencies are published. This makes public access to state agency case law much more difficult, in general, than public access to federal agency case law, or public access to state agency rules which are virtually always published. Second, the legislatures of most states have established comprehensive and effective means for the gubernatorial and legislative review of state agency lawmaking by rule, [discussed § 7.5, *infra,*] while Congress has not established any similar scheme with which to review the rules of federal agencies. For this reason, there is a special need to ensure that state agencies (but not federal agencies) make their law primarily by rules which are subject to these elaborate review mechanisms rather than by orders which are not. Third, persons affected by state agency proceedings are far less likely to be represented by lawyers than persons affected by federal agency proceedings. As a result, there is a greater need for state agencies than for federal agencies to make agency law through rulemaking proceedings that do not usually require the use of the special skills of lawyers, than through adjudicatory proceedings where the use of the special skills of lawyers are often essential.

Finally, the procedural advantages of rulemaking over adjudication for most agency lawmaking are greater for state agencies than for federal agencies because virtually all state rulemaking is still of the simple notice and comment variety, while a great deal of the federal rulemaking authorized in recent years is of a hybrid variety [, *see* § 6.3.1, *infra,*] and, therefore, is more complicated and expensive. All of these reasons suggest that a [mandatory] preference for agency lawmaking by rule is more justified for state agencies than for federal agencies.

Bonfield, "Mandating State Agency Lawmaking by Rule," 2 B.Y.U.J. of Pub.L., 161, 178 (1988).

7. *Special requirements for ad hoc lawmaking.* While Florida cases do not generally *require* state agencies to prefer rulemaking for their lawmaking, they do require an agency elaborating its law by adjudication to observe specified procedures. These cases hold that a Florida agency may make law by adjudication only if the record of the adjudicatory proceeding contains fully adequate reasons and factual support for the ad hoc law it creates, and the parties to the proceeding are given a trial-type opportunity to challenge the foundation for the new caselaw principle created in that proceeding. *See McDonald v. Department of Banking and Finance,* 346 So.2d 569, 582–83 (Fla.App. 1977); *Florida Cities Water Co. v. Florida Pub. Serv. Com'n,* 384 So.2d 1280, 1281 (Fla.1980).

Is this requirement likely to induce Florida agencies to make their law primarily by rule rather than by order? As you will see in Chapter 6, *infra,* in most state agency rulemaking proceedings agencies are not *required* to include in the agency rulemaking record any factual support for the proposed rule in question; and agencies are not *required* to provide a trial-type opportunity for opponents of a proposed rule to challenge any reasons or factual support for the rule that may be proffered by the agency or other persons in the rulemaking proceeding. According to these Florida cases, however, the situation is reversed when the agency chooses to make its law ad hoc in the course of an adjudication.

Is the approach of the Florida courts a fair and adequate compromise between complete agency freedom to choose the means by which it makes law and a mandatory preference for rulemaking of the kind that would be imposed by the 1981 MSAPA provisions discussed in note 5, *supra?*

NATIONAL LABOR RELATIONS BOARD v. WYMAN–GORDON CO.
394 U.S. 759 (1969).

JUSTICE FORTAS announced the judgment of the Court and delivered an opinion in which THE CHIEF JUSTICE, JUSTICE STEWART, and JUSTICE WHITE join.

[The NLRB ordered Wyman–Gordon Co. to furnish contesting unions a list of the names and addresses of its employees who could vote in an election to choose an exclusive bargaining representative or to choose not to be represented by a union at all. In issuing that order in this case the NLRB cited its earlier adjudicatory decision in *Excelsior Underwear, Inc.* In that earlier decision, the Board] purported to establish the general rule that such a list must be provided, but it declined to apply its new rule to the companies involved in the *Excelsior* case. Instead, it held that the rule would apply "only in those elections that are directed, or consented to, subsequent to 30 days from the date of [the] Decision." . . . The Board asks us to hold that it has discretion to promulgate new rules in adjudicatory proceedings, without complying with the requirements of the Administrative Procedure Act.

The rule-making provisions of that Act, which the Board would avoid, were designed to assure fairness and mature consideration of rules of general application. They may not be avoided by the process of making rules in the course of adjudicatory proceedings. There is no warrant in law for the Board to replace the statutory scheme with a rule-making procedure of its own invention. Apart from the fact that the device fashioned by the Board does not comply with statutory command, it obviously falls short of the substance of the requirements of the Administrative Procedure Act. The "rule" created in *Excelsior* was not published in the Federal Register, which is the statutory and accepted means of giving notice of a rule as adopted; only selected organizations were given notice of the "hearing," whereas notice in the Federal Register would have been general in character; under the Administrative Procedure Act, the terms or substance of the rule would have to be stated in the notice of hearing, and all interested parties would have an opportunity to participate in the rule making.

The Solicitor General . . . [admits that the Board did not use rulemaking procedures [3] in *Excelsior* but] appears to argue that *Excelsior's* command is a valid substantive regulation, binding upon this respondent as such, because the Board promulgated it in the *Excelsior* proceeding, in which the requirements for valid adjudication had been met. This argument misses the point. There is no question that, in an adjudicatory hearing, the Board could validly decide the issue whether the employer must furnish a list of employees to the union. But that is not what the Board did in *Excelsior*. The Board did not even apply the rule it made to the parties in the adjudicatory proceeding, the only entities that could properly be subject to the order in that case. Instead, the Board purported to make a rule: *i.e.,* to exercise its quasi-legislative power.

Adjudicated cases may and do, of course, serve as vehicles for the formulation of agency policies, which are applied and announced there-

---

3. The Board has never utilized the Act's rule-making procedures. It has been criticized for contravening the Act in this manner. See, *e.g.*, 1 K. Davis, Administrative Law Treatise § 6.13 (Supp.1965); Peck, The Atrophied Rule–Making Powers of the National Labor Relations Board, 70 Yale L.J. 729 (1961).

in. . . . They generally provide a guide to action that the agency may be expected to take in future cases. Subject to the qualified role of *stare decisis* in the administrative process, they may serve as precedents. But this is far from saying, as the Solicitor General suggests, that commands, decisions, or policies announced in adjudication are "rules" in the sense that they must, without more, be obeyed by the affected public.

In the present case, however, the respondent itself was specifically directed by the Board to submit a list of the names and addresses of its employees for use by the unions in connection with the election. This direction, which was part of the order directing that an election be held, is unquestionably valid. Even though the direction to furnish the list was followed by citation to "*Excelsior Underwear Inc.,* 156 NLRB No. 111," it is an order in the present case that the respondent was required to obey. Absent this direction by the Board, the respondent was under no compulsion to furnish the list because no statute and no validly adopted rule required it to do so.

Because the Board in an adjudicatory proceeding directed the respondent itself to furnish the list, the decision of the Court of Appeals for the First Circuit must be reversed. . . .

MR. JUSTICE BLACK, with whom MR. JUSTICE BRENNAN and MR. JUSTICE MARSHALL join, concurring in the result. . . .

Most administrative agencies, like the Labor Board here, are granted two functions by the legislation creating them: (1) the power under certain conditions to make rules having the effect of laws, that is, generally speaking, quasi-legislative power; and (2) the power to hear and adjudicate particular controversies, that is quasi-judicial power. The line between these two functions is not always a clear one and in fact the two functions merge at many points. For example, in exercising its quasi-judicial function an agency must frequently decide controversies on the basis of new doctrines, not theretofore applied to a specific problem, though drawn to be sure from broader principles reflecting the purposes of the statutes involved and from the rules invoked in dealing with related problems. If the agency decision reached under the adjudicatory power becomes a precedent, it guides future conduct in much the same way as though it were a new rule promulgated under the rule-making power, and both an adjudicatory order and a formal "rule" are alike subject to judicial review. Congress gave the Labor Board both of these separate but almost inseparably related powers. No language in the National Labor Relations Act requires that the grant or the exercise of one power was intended to exclude the Board's use of the other.

Nor does any language in the Administrative Procedure Act require such a conclusion. . . .

Thus, although it is true that the adjudicatory approach frees an administrative agency from the procedural requirements specified for rule making, the Act permits this to be done whenever the action involved can satisfy the definition of "adjudication" and then imposes separate procedural requirements that must be met in adjudication. Under these circumstances, so long as the matter involved can be dealt with in a way satisfying the definition of either "rule making" or "adjudication" under the Administrative Procedure Act, that Act should be read as conferring upon the Board the authority to decide, within its informed discretion, whether to proceed by rule making or adjudication. . . .

In the present case there is no dispute that all the procedural safeguards required for "adjudication" were fully satisfied in connection with the Board's *Excelsior* decision, and it seems plain to me that that decision did constitute "adjudication" within the meaning of the Administrative Procedure Act, even though the requirement was to be prospectively applied. See *Great Northern R. Co. v. Sunburst Co.,* 287 U.S. 358 (1932). The Board did not abstractly decide out of the blue to announce a brand new rule of law to govern labor activities in the future, but rather established the procedure as a direct consequence of the proper exercise of its adjudicatory powers. . . .

A controversy arose between the Excelsior Company and its employees as to the bargaining agent the employees desired to act for them. The Board's power to provide the procedures for the election was invoked. Undoubtedly the Board proceeding for determination of whether to confirm or set aside that election was "agency process for the formulation of an order" and thus was "adjudication" within the meaning of the Administrative Procedure Act. . . .

Apart from the fact that the decisions whether to accept a "new" requirement urged by one party and, if so, whether to apply it retroactively to the other party are inherent parts of the adjudicatory process, I think the opposing theory accepted by the Court of Appeals and by the prevailing opinion today is a highly impractical one. In effect, it would require an agency like the Labor Board to proceed by adjudication only when it could decide, *prior* to adjudicating a particular case, that any new practice to be adopted would be applied retroactively. Obviously, this decision cannot properly be made until all the issues relevant to adoption of the practice are fully considered in connection with the final decision of that case. If the Board were to decide, after careful evaluation of all the arguments presented to it in the adjudicatory proceeding, that it might be fairer to apply the practice only prospectively, it would be faced with the unpleasant choice of either starting all over again to evaluate the merits of the question, this time in a "rule-making" proceeding, or overriding the considerations of fairness and applying its order retroactively anyway, in order to preserve the validity of the new practice and avoid duplication of effort. I see no good reason to impose any such inflexible requirement on the administrative agencies.

For all of the foregoing reasons I would hold that the Board acted well within its discretion in choosing to proceed as it did.

JUSTICE DOUGLAS, dissenting.

I am willing to assume that, if the Board decided to treat each case on its special facts and perform its adjudicatory function in the conventional way, we should have no difficulty in affirming its action. The difficulty is that it chose a different course in the *Excelsior* case and, having done so, it should be bound to follow the [rule-making] procedures prescribed in the Act as my Brother HARLAN has outlined them. . . .

The Committee reports make plain that the Act "provides quite different procedures for the 'legislative' and 'judicial' functions of administrative agencies." . . .

The rule-making procedure performs important functions. It gives notice to an entire segment of society of those controls or regimentation that is forthcoming. It gives an opportunity for persons affected to be heard. . . . Failure to make full use of rule-making power is attributable at least in part "to administrative inertia and reluctance to take a clear stand."

Rule making is no cure-all; but it does force important issues into full public display and in that sense makes for more responsible administrative action.

I would hold the agencies governed by the rule-making procedure strictly to its requirements and not allow them to play fast and loose as the National Labor Relations Board apparently likes to do.

As stated by the Court of Appeals, the procedure used in the *Excelsior* case plainly flouted the Act:

"Recognizing the problem to be one affecting more than just the parties before it, the Board chose to solicit the assistance of selected amici curiae, and, ultimately, to establish a rule which not only did not apply to the parties before it, but did not take effect for thirty days. In so doing we consider that the Board, to put it bluntly, designed its own rulemaking procedure, adopting such part of the Congressional mandate as it chose, and rejecting the rest." . . .

JUSTICE HARLAN, dissenting.

The language of the Administrative Procedure Act does not support the Government's claim that an agency is "adjudicating" when it announces a rule which it refuses to apply in the dispute before it. The Act makes it clear that an agency "adjudicates" only when its procedures result in the "formulation of an *order.*" 5 U.S.C. § 551(7). (Emphasis supplied.) An "order" is defined to include "the whole or a *part* of a final disposition . . . of an agency *in a matter other than rule making.* . . ." 5 U.S.C. § 551(6). (Emphasis supplied.) This definition makes it apparent that an agency is not adjudicating when it is making a rule, which the Act defines as "an agency statement of general or particular applicability and *future effect.* . . ." 5 U.S.C. § 551(4). (Emphasis supplied.) Since the Labor Board's *Excelsior* rule was to be effective only 30 days after its promulgation, it clearly falls within the rule-making requirements of the Act.

Nor can I agree that the natural interpretation of the statute should be rejected because it requires the agency to choose between giving its rules immediate effect or initiating a separate rule-making proceeding. An agency chooses to apply a rule prospectively only because it represents such a departure from pre-existing understandings that it would be unfair to impose the rule upon the parties in pending matters. But it is precisely in these situations, in which established patterns of conduct are revolutionized, that rule-making procedures perform the vital functions that my Brother Douglas describes so well in a dissenting opinion with which I basically agree.

Given the fact that the Labor Board has promulgated a rule in violation of the governing statute, I believe that there is no alternative but to affirm the judgment of the Court of Appeals in this case. . . .

Notes and Questions

1. *Wyman–Gordon.* Which opinion in *Wyman–Gordon* do you find most persuasive?

Justice Fortas decided that the NLRB should prevail in *Wyman–Gordon* despite the fact that he believed it had issued a rule in *Excelsior* without following the required rulemaking procedures, and despite the fact that it had cited *Excelsior* in this case as a basis for its decision. Could it be argued that the Fortas opinion, in the end, gave effect to an invalid rule? Did the NLRB suffer in any way because of its failure to follow rulemaking proceedings when it issued the wholly prospective statement of law in *Excelsior?* Does the Fortas opinion do any more than suggest to agencies that they should not make principles enunciated in adjudications wholly prospective? How does Fortas justify his conclusion that the NLRB adjudicated anew in this case the invalid principle of *Excelsior,* rather than applied the invalid rule issued in *Excelsior* to this case?

In his dissent Justice Harlan stated that the requirement enunciated in *Excelsior* was an invalid rule, the Board relied upon that invalid rule in this case and, therefore, its action was based upon an improper reason. The first *Chenery* case requires a court to reverse an agency decision based on an improper ground even though that decision would be sustainable on some other ground. *SEC v. Chenery Corp.,* 318 U.S. 80 (1943). As a result, he would affirm the judgment of the Court of Appeals or, at least, remand the case for the Board's determination as to whether it would reach the same result without relying upon the invalidly adopted rule. Do you agree with Justice Harlan's alternative disposition? Is it likely that on remand the Board would come to a different result?

Does the opinion of Justice Black suggest that an agency may utilize adjudicatory procedures to issue a statement of general applicability and future effect, implementing, interpreting, or prescribing law or policy? If so, are agencies completely free to issue rules in adjudications, so long as proper adjudicatory procedures are used? Would the distinction between rules and orders be irrelevant if agencies could issue either rules or orders in adjudications?

2. *Agency reliance upon reasoning behind invalid rules.* May an agency rely upon the reasoning behind an invalid rule or behind a proposed rule as the basis for an adjudicatory decision so long as it does not treat the invalid rule or proposed rule as binding upon the agency when it makes its decision? Justice Fortas' opinion in *Wyman–Gordon* appeared to answer this question in the affirmative.

A state case recently came to the same result but suggested that it might not have done so on the facts of *Wyman–Gordon.* In *Young Plumbing and Heating Co. v. Iowa N.R.C.,* 276 N.W.2d 377, 382–83 (Iowa 1979), an agency denied an application to construct a building on a flood plain. It relied on the contents of a proposed but unadopted rule prohibiting such construction. The court upheld the agency's decision, because the agency had relied on the proposed rule merely as an aid in the resolution of a case before it, and did not treat the proposed rule as if it were binding. The court noted:

> There is no indication in the record that the statutory procedure for contested cases was not complied with or that the Council attempted to promulgate a rule through the proceeding. We hold that a consideration relevant to the merits of an issue in a contested case proceeding before an administrative body is not precluded from being a basis for the agency decision because it is also the subject matter of a proposed rule, so long as it is applied in an adjudicative manner dependent upon and limited to a particular factual situation, and not simply as a valid rule. The existence of alternative means for the formulation of agency policy indicates that the procedures facilitating such means must be strictly adhered to. If an agency relies upon a rule as such to support its action, the rule must have been promulgated in accord with the procedure in effect at that time. Until such time as the rule becomes effective, its subject matter is not precluded from being considered in a contested case when relevant and being applied to only the facts at hand. . . .

> Thus where, as here, the proposed rule is not applied as a matter of law, but is found to be relevant to the factual situation of the contested case and is applied only to those facts as a basis for decision, [the decision of the agency must be upheld].

In *Young Plumbing* the court also indicated that it might have reached the opposite result in *Wyman–Gordon,* apparently because it concluded that the NLRB had treated the invalid rule issued in the *Excelsior* case as if it were binding in the subsequent *Wyman–Gordon* case.

Is the effort of the court in *Young Plumbing* to distinguish the result in *Wyman–Gordon* from the result in *Young Plumbing* persuasive? How did the court in *Young Plumbing* know that the agency in that case had not treated the proposed rule as binding? How did it know that the NLRB in *Wyman–Gordon* had treated the invalid rule issued in the *Excelsior* case as binding?

If an agency says it adjudicated the principle involved in such a case entirely anew in that case, will a reviewing court always believe the agency's assertion? Should the citation by the NLRB in *Wyman–Gordon* of the *Excelsior* case when it issued its order have been enough to demonstrate that, in fact, no matter what the NLRB said at the time of judicial review, it really did apply the requirement of *Excelsior* as a binding rule?

3. *Significance of rule-order dichotomy.* Do the results in the *Wyman–Gordon* and *Young Plumbing* cases suggest that the rule-order dichotomy and its accompanying two track system of procedures is in fact illusory or in fact involves only questions of form rather than substance and, therefore, is not of great practical significance?

4. *Problem.* Madison University (MU) student disciplinary rules (adopted after appropriate notice and comment procedures) provide that a student can be suspended or expelled for "conduct inappropriate for a student." A Student Discipline Board (SDB), consisting of both faculty and students, administers the student disciplinary rules.

Mark, an MU student, received 185 tickets for illegal parking in MU parking lots. After providing notice and a trial-type hearing, the SDB suspended Mark from school for six months, holding that such flagrant disregard of the MU parking rules was "conduct inappropriate for a student." SDB had never before treated a parking or traffic violation as a violation of the student disciplinary rules.

(a) Should the SDB's decision be reversed? Assume that MU is (i) a federal government institution and (ii) a state university in a state that has adopted the 1981 MSAPA.

(b) Suppose that six months before the SDB hearing in Mark's case, the President of MU issued a statement to the effect that flagrant disregard of parking rules would be treated under the student disciplinary rules as "conduct inappropriate for a student." In its decision, SDB stated that it was required to follow the President's statement and it was doing so in Mark's case. Should SDB's decision in Mark's case be reversed?

Chapter 6

RULEMAKING PROCEDURES

§ 6.1 THE OBJECTIVES OF RULEMAKING PROCEDURE

BONFIELD, STATE ADMINISTRATIVE RULE MAKING
143–53 (1986).

The soundness of [the 1981 MSAPA] . . . rule-making scheme should be measured, in part, on the basis of the adequacy and desirability of the objectives it seeks, and the extent to which the scheme provided is likely to achieve those objectives in practice. . . .

[1] LAWFUL RULES

[T]he procedures provided in Article III of the 1981 MSAPA seek to ensure that rule-making determinations made by agencies are . . . within the bounds of their legislative authorizations. . . .

The desirability of procedures calculated to assure lawful agency rule making in advance of judicial review is clear. Agencies may only exercise those powers expressly or impliedly delegated to them [and] . . . the exercise of those powers must be consistent with any procedural or substantive limits placed upon the agencies by various species of law up to and including the state and federal constitutions. Since judicial review of the legality of agency rule making is expensive, often inaccessible, and inherently retrospective because it is only designed to void illegal agency rule making *after* it occurs, agency procedures calculated to avoid or discourage such rule making before it takes place are especially desirable. . . .

[2] TECHNICALLY SOUND RULES

[T]he rule-making procedures provided in the 1981 MSAPA seek to facilitate the making of rules that are as technically sound as is possible under the circumstances of everyday government operation. That is, the procedure seeks to assure that agencies making rules do so in light of all relevant information, that the rules are based upon accurate assessments by the agencies of all relevant data and opinions, and that the rules issued are in fact calculated to accomplish their objectives in the most sensible way possible. . . .

In the long run, government cannot maintain the support of its people if government decision making is technically unsound. After all, decision making that is not based on a consideration of all relevant information, or not calculated to accomplish its purpose, or not calculated to accomplish that purpose in the most sensible way possible under the circumstances is irrational and inconsistent with the basic function of government. . . .

[3] POLITICALLY RESPONSIBLE RULES

[T]he procedures . . . of the 1981 MSAPA also seek to assure that agency rule-making determinations are, in the end, political rather than technocratic—that the body politic may effectively prevent the adoption of lawful and technically sound rules by agencies that are unacceptable to the current wishes of the community at large. This is a clear recognition that agencies work for the people, and that the current views of the community at large, rather than the views of technocrats, should ultimately prevail when the question is whether agencies should adopt particular policies that will have the effect of law. Therefore, the procedures for rule adoption established by the 1981 MSAPA intentionally provide opportunities for concerned members of the community to organize and to direct effectively at agencies day-to-day political pressures. The theory of those procedures is that if agencies making rules are subjected to the same kinds of interest group political pressures as are focused on the legislature when it enacts statutes, the agencies will find themselves unable, as a practical matter, to adopt rules that the legislature would not have adopted because of similar considerations. . . .

[S]uch a system [is] "an essential part of the democratic process." It is essential because, in our society, the current popular will and not the views of technocrats, however defensible their views may be from a purely analytical point of view, should ultimately prevail on the desirability of government-imposed policies. The reason for this is that, in our society, sovereignty ultimately resides in the community at large— that is, in the people as a body politic—and not in its administrative agents. Consequently, an everyday, "politically sensitive" scheme of rule making "seems infinitely preferable to the regime of 'public policy by analysis.' " . . . [*See also* McCubbins, Noll, and Weingast, § 1.7, *supra*, and Scalia, "Two Wrongs Make a Right," § 6.6.1, *infra*.]

[4] ADEQUATE NOTICE OF RULES

[T]he procedures provided in [the 1981 MSAPA] also seek to assure affected members of the public adequate notice of, and time to adjust to, the requirements of new rules before they take effect. It is obviously desirable to assure that those subject to rules can easily ascertain their content. After all, the purpose of rules is to secure compliance with the legal norms they establish, and individuals cannot observe those norms if they do not know such norms exist or cannot easily discover their precise content. It is clear that adequate notice of rules helps secure compliance with their terms and reduces the costs of enforcing them. There is also a consensus in this society that it is unfair to sanction people for violating rules if those people had no reasonable means by which to ascertain the contents of the rules. Furthermore, insofar as possible, it is desirable to give people a reasonable time to prepare for new law embodied in rules before it takes effect. . . .

[5] PREVENTION OF OVERREGULATION

[T]hese procedures are also designed to ensure that, at any given point in time, agencies maintain as effective law only those particular rules that are desirable because, on balance, they advance the public interest. We have all come to recognize that overregulation is as harmful to the welfare of our society as underregulation and, therefore, should be avoided. It is important, therefore, to provide mechanisms that will induce in an effective way the elimination of unnecessary, unsound, or otherwise undesirable rules that have, at some time in the past, been adopted by agencies and that are continued in force only because of inertia or bureaucratic paralysis.

[6] [FAIRNESS, PUBLIC SATISFACTION, AND EFFICIENCY]

The procedures required by the MSAPA also seek to ensure a general objective in the rule-making process—fairness, which is ultimately a political and philosophical judgment. . . .

Fairness certainly requires rule-making procedures to achieve the five specific objectives noted earlier. . . .

Fairness must also be measured in terms of public satisfaction with the procedures by which agencies make their rules, independent of the extent to which those procedures achieve the particular objectives for which they were instituted. Aside from the utility of good rule-making procedures in achieving the particular objectives for which they were initially devised—their "instrumental" value—good rule-making procedures should provide user satisfaction and enhanced public confidence in government—their "intrinsic" value. Intrinsic value includes, therefore, incidental by-products of rule-making procedures in the form of feelings by users that, without regard to the result, they had an adequate opportunity to defend their interests and that the process treated them equitably. The presence or absence of such satisfaction is not necessarily a function of any particular set of procedures; rather, it is a function of the overall impression a particular procedural system leaves with its users. Intrinsic value also includes the extent to which the procedures, as by-products of their specific purposes, instill public confidence in government because they secure a regularization of governmental action that is perceived to make it worthy of deference and respect. The benefits of agency rule-making procedures, therefore, include the extent to which those procedures advance instrumental values by achieving the particular objectives for which they were devised, and also the extent to which they advance intrinsic values by providing user satisfaction and enhancing public confidence in government. Fairness demands that rule-making procedures seek to maximize both kinds of values.

However, fairness demands even more. The instrumental and intrinsic values that may be served by procedures governing agency rule making must be balanced against the equally important need for agency decision making that is workable, effective, efficient, and economical. After all, in addition to creating benefits, mandatory rule-making procedures calculated to achieve these objectives will also impose costs. The fairness of rule-making procedures must be judged, therefore, not only on the extent to which they accomplish the objectives noted earlier, but also on the extent to which they accommodate those important competing values in the administrative process that dictate fewer rather than greater procedural impositions on agencies in the performance of their decision-making functions.

Mandatory procedures do impose a significant social cost—they are expensive and time-consuming. Resources diverted to the execution of required procedures will not be available for the implementation of substantive social and economic programs. Legislatures, therefore, must seek a sound balance between the need for workable, efficient, effective, and economical rule making and the need to provide persons with adequate and acceptable procedural protections when agencies take actions affecting them. The procedures of the 1981 MSAPA seek to achieve that balance. . . .

Notes and Questions

1. *Political or technocratic rulemaking.* Do you agree that rulemaking should, in the end, be political rather than technocratic? Is a political system of administrative rulemaking inconsistent with the legislative decision to create agencies staffed with experts to administer law in specified areas? In thinking about the answers to these questions reconsider the discussion of various theories for administrative law in § 1.7, *supra.*

2. *Conflicting objectives.* Do any of the objectives of rulemaking procedure described above conflict with other such objectives? If so, how should those conflicts be resolved?

3. *Directional note.* In this chapter, consider each of the aspects of rulemaking procedure against the background of the objectives noted above. Examine how each procedural element or issue in that process is consistent or inconsistent with those objectives. Note also how conflicts between the different objectives have been resolved with respect to each element or issue.

§ 6.2 INITIATING RULEMAKING PROCEEDINGS

§ 6.2.1 FORMULATION OF PROPOSED RULES

Proposed rules are usually formulated entirely on the basis of intra-agency consultations and reflect agency judgment and expertness. The reason for this is that the public does not normally have notice of an agency's intention to make rules on a particular subject, or an opportunity to participate in the rulemaking process, prior to the time that the agency formally commences a rulemaking proceeding by publishing a proposed rule in a formal notice of proposed rulemaking. However, as § 6.2.2, note 5, *infra,* indicates, federal agencies are required by an Executive Order to publish a semi-annual agenda of *major* rules under development. Furthermore, prior to the initial formulation of proposed rules, some agencies have published informational notices indicating the particular subject matter with respect to which they were contemplating future rulemaking and soliciting public comment thereon. In formulating the text of proposed rules, other agencies have sought to incorporate prior efforts of the private sector by relying upon standards originally created and adopted by trade associations or other private standard setting organizations. Some agencies have also consulted standing advisory committees or potentially affected individuals or organizations prior to the formulation of particular proposed rules. The Federal Advisory Committee Act is discussed in § 8.2.2, *infra.*

Section 3–101 of the 1981 MSAPA explicitly provides that agencies "may," prior to publishing a notice of proposed rule adoption, "solicit comments from the public on a subject matter of possible rulemaking . . . by causing notice to be published in the [administrative bulletin]. . . ." It also explicitly authorizes agencies to appoint standing committees to comment on such subjects prior to the proposal of rules. In what types of situations do you think such notices and consultations might be desirable and useful prior to agency formulation of the text of proposed rules? *See* 1981 MSAPA § 3–101, Comment; ACUS, A GUIDE TO FEDERAL AGENCY RULEMAKING 95 (1983).

Agencies have recently attempted to utilize another technique to formulate the contents of some proposed rules. That technique is called *regulatory negotiation* or *negotiated rulemaking* and is an effort to avoid "the polarization of viewpoints that often occurs in complex rulemaking proceedings," and the extensive costs associated with prolonged rulemaking proceedings involving controversial matters.

Regulatory negotiation involves the convening of a group representing all the interests that would be affected by an agency rule on a particular subject. The group is asked to attempt to negotiate issues, with the goal of adopting a consensus proposal that will be published as the agency's notice of proposed rulemaking. Thus, regulatory negotiation is not an alternative to notice and comment rulemaking, but rather is [a preliminary] . . . step in that process.

In Recommendation 82–4, . . . [ACUS] urged Congress to expressly authorize agency use of regulatory negotiation procedure, but only on an experimental basis. The recommendation recognizes that regulatory negotiation will not be appropriate for many, or even most, rulemakings, and the factors bearing on the decision to use the procedure are set out in the recommendation. Although Congress has not yet enacted legislation, a few agencies have decided to try regulatory negotiation in selected rulemakings.

ACUS, A GUIDE TO FEDERAL AGENCY RULEMAKING 97 (1983).

In 1985 ACUS acted again on the subject of regulatory negotiation. Recommendation 85–5: "Procedures for Negotiating Proposed Regulations," 1 C.F.R. § 305.85–5, noted:

Since Recommendation 82–4 was adopted, its recommended procedures have been followed four times by federal agencies. The Federal Aviation Administration used negotiated rulemaking to develop a new flight and duty time regulation for pilots. The Environmental Protection Agency used negotiated rulemaking to develop proposed rules on nonconformance penalties for vehicle emissions and on emergency exemptions from pesticide regulations. The Occupational Safety and Health Administration encouraged labor, public interest, and industry representatives to negotiate a standard for occupational exposure to benzene. The benzene negotiations did not result in agreement among the parties on a proposed rule, but the other three negotiations did lead to substantial agreement resulting in two final rules (which have thus far not been challenged) and one draft rule which, after public comment, is pending before the agency.

The experience of these four cases has shown that the original recommendation was basically sound, and has provided a basis for the Administrative Conference to use in supplementing Recommendation 82–4.

Among the specific recommendations of ACUS to facilitate negotiated rulemaking were the following:

1. An agency sponsoring a negotiated rulemaking proceeding should take part in the negotiations. Agency participation can occur in various ways. The range of possibilities extends from full participation as a negotiator to acting as an observer and commenting on possible agency reactions and concerns. . . .

2. Negotiations are unlikely to succeed unless all participants (including the agency) are motivated throughout the process by the view that a negotiated agreement will provide a better alternative than a rule developed under traditional processes. The agency, accordingly, should be sensitive to each participant's need to have a

reasonably clear expectation of the consequences of not reaching a consensus. . . .

3. The agency should recognize that negotiations can be useful at several stages of rulemaking proceedings. For example, negotiating the terms of a final rule could be a useful procedure even after publication of a proposed rule. Usually, however, negotiations should be used to help develop a notice of proposed rulemaking, with negotiations to be resumed after comments on the notice are received. . . .

5. The agency should select a person skilled in techniques of dispute resolution to assist the negotiating group in reaching an agreement. . . .

There may be specific proceedings, however, where party incentives to reach voluntary agreement are so strong that a mediator or facilitator is not necessary. . . .

7. The agency, the mediator or facilitator, and, where appropriate, other participants in negotiated rulemaking should be prepared to address internal disagreements within a particular constituency. . . .

8. Where appropriate, the agency, the mediator or facilitator, or the negotiating group should consider appointing a neutral outside individual who could receive confidential data, evaluate it, and report to the negotiators. . . .

PERRITT, "NEGOTIATED RULEMAKING AND ADMINISTRATIVE LAW"
38 Admin.L.Rev. 471, 471–74 (1986).

Negotiated rulemaking is a realistic alternative to adversarial administrative procedures. The technique permits affected interests to retain greater control over the content of agency rules, while ensuring fairness and balance. It also permits agencies to obtain a more accurate perception of the costs and benefits of policy alternatives than can be obtained from digesting voluminous records of testimonial and documentary evidence presented in adversarial hearings. . . .

It is important to view both the 1982 and the 1985 ACUS recommendations as a conceptual framework for negotiated rulemaking and not as a formula for success. Negotiations cannot be designed in advance like an engineering project. Accordingly, whether negotiations will succeed in a particular case depends on the substantive issues, the perception of the agency's position by affected parties, past relationships among the parties, the authority of party representatives in the negotiations, the negotiating style of the representatives, the number and divergence of views among individual units within each constituency represented, and the skill of agency personnel and mediators. Some of these variables, or particular configurations of variables, existing when negotiations commence almost certainly will change several times before negotiations conclude. An agency cannot expect that the pattern followed successfully by another agency, or even by itself on another issue, can be transplanted automatically to another negotiation without modification.

The APA need not be amended to provide for negotiated rulemaking. Indeed, amending the APA now could destroy the flexibility to adapt the negotiation process to the needs of different regulatory situations. Also, the four agency experiences do not show that the Federal Advisory Committee Act (FACA), as interpreted by the sponsoring agencies and participants, was a serious impediment to effective negotiations. There is no reason to believe, under current judicial and agency interpretation of the Act, that caucuses and other working group meetings may not be held in private, where this is necessary to promote an effective exchange of views.

Perhaps the most important insight to be gained from an assessment of the four completed negotiated rulemaking efforts is that an agency sponsoring a negotiated rulemaking should take part in negotiations, recognizing that negotiations are unlikely to succeed unless all parties are motivated throughout the negotiations by a perception that a negotiated rule would be preferable to a rule developed under traditional processes. To foster this belief, as an incentive to negotiating an agreement, the agency should help create realistic expectations of the consequences of not reaching a consensus. Agencies must be mindful, from the beginning to the end of negotiations, of the impact that agency conduct and statements have on party expectations. The agency may need to communicate with other participants—perhaps with the assistance of a mediator or facilitator—to ensure that each one has realistic expectations about the outcome of agency action in the absence of a negotiated agreement. Parties will agree only on something they perceive as preferable to what the agency will do unilaterally through traditional administrative procedures. . . .

A final comment is appropriate on the use of negotiated rulemaking at the state level. Most states have far fewer resources for the administrative process than the federal government. Accordingly, administrative litigation before state agencies has not reached the level of complexity that it has before federal agencies. Rather, a measure of informal negotiation between affected interests is a regular feature of the state process. Such negotiations are not very visible though. In addition, a number of states have adopted various procedures to permit legislative . . . advice on specific proposed agency rules. Participation by the legislative branch in the rulemaking process also facilitates negotiation among affected interests of the kind commonly conducted in the legislative arena.

W. FUNK, "WHEN SMOKE GETS IN YOUR EYES: REGULATORY NEGOTIATION AND THE PUBLIC INTEREST—EPA's WOODSTOVE STANDARDS"

18 Envtl. L. 55, 56–57, 93–97 (1987).

To avoid the necessity of substantial amendment of the Administrative Procedure Act . . . a scheme for negotiating regulations [has been suggested] which . . . would not run afoul of current administrative law concepts. . . . [T]his involve[s] the negotiation of a proposed rule, which the agency would then publish as its proposed rule and thereafter treat pretty much as it would any proposed rule. In this way possible [legal] complications . . . are minimized. . . .

[However, it] is the thesis of this Article that . . . the nature of regulatory negotiation has the tendency to obscure, if not pervert, the public interest to the benefit of private interests, and that the regulatory negotiation of the [EPA] woodstove emission [rule] is a case study of such a perversion. . . .

[While the agency in negotiated rulemaking] technically has the final decision, this power becomes theoretical at best where the agency has already agreed beforehand along with all the other participants to seek consensus in good faith, to support the consensus result, and in particular to publish as a proposed rule the rule developed by that consensus. . . .

That the agency plays no special role in the negotiation is made clear by certain other recommendations of the Administrative Conference. . . .

This fundamental change in the role of the agency in the rulemaking process is mirrored by the fundamental change in the underlying theoretical justification for the eventual rule. . . . "[U]nder the traditional . . . process, the legitimacy of the rule rests on a resolution of complex factual materials and rational extrapolation from those facts, guided by the criteria of the statute. Under regulatory negotiation, however, the regulation's legitimacy would lie in the overall agreement of the parties." . . .

To say that regulatory negotiation turns the traditional concept of administrative rulemaking on its head does not, however, compel the conclusion that it is necessarily unlawful. The Administrative Conference recommendations are carefully crafted in an attempt to comply with all the procedural requirements attendant to rulemaking. . . .

Reliance on the absence of disagreement as evidence of legitimacy for a regulation puts a premium on assuring that the negotiating group adequately represents all affected interests. There are, however, both practical and theoretical limitations on the number of interests that may be represented and the quality of representation each interest may obtain. . . .

However, it is not the purpose of this Article to conclude that regulatory negotiation is necessarily bad and should be shot dead in its tracks. To the contrary, the practical benefits of regulatory negotiation cannot be gainsaid, and if they have not received much attention here, it is only because there are ample other sources. . . . Rather, it is the purpose of this Article to demonstrate that regulatory negotiation, despite the fact that it can probably be accomplished without violating existing procedural requirements, fundamentally alters the dynamics of traditional administrative rulemaking from a search for the public interest, however imperfect that search may be, to a search for a consensus among private parties representing particular interests.

Only after one recognizes this fundamental change can one fully assess the advantages and disadvantages of regulatory negotiation as an alternative to traditional administrative rulemaking. Up to now, the debate over regulatory negotiation has revolved around its feasibility and methods to improve its "success" rate. Now, however, the debate should include the appropriateness of private interests determining the public values at stake in the rulemaking. In some cases the issues to be decided in the negotiation may be so bounded that any threat to public values disappears. In other cases the negotiation may claim as its subject matter issues which properly should be decided only by an agency.

Notes and Questions

1. *Feasibility of process.* Under what circumstances is negotiated rulemaking likely to work or to fail? Is the process as suitable for state agencies as federal agencies? Is it clear that agencies have authority to use negotiated rulemaking to formulate the contents of a proposed rule in the absence of express statutory language to that effect?

2. *Advantages and disadvantages.* What are the specific advantages and disadvantages of negotiated rulemaking? Whose interests are served and whose are disserved by the process? Could the negotiated rulemaking process undercut the public participation provisions of the federal APA or state APAs because it effectively makes the form of the proposed rule produced by such regulatory negotiation the final rule ultimately adopted by the agency? Is negotiated rulemaking a desirable means for formulating the contents of a proposed rule? In all or some situations?

§ 6.2.2 NOTICE OF PROPOSED RULEMAKING

ACUS, A GUIDE TO FEDERAL AGENCY RULEMAKING
115–18 (1983).

Section 553(b) of the APA requires publication of a notice of proposed rulemaking (NPRM) in the Federal Register. This constitutes what is legally referred to as "constructive notice," and it is deemed sufficient to give affected persons notice of the NPRM's contents. Failure to publish a Federal Register notice of rulemaking, or failure to include mention of a significant subject covered in a final rule, may result in a court setting aside the rule and remanding it to the agency for further proceedings. . . .

Section 553 of APA states that the NPRM must state the "time, place, and nature" of the public proceedings. . . . In the context of informal rulemaking, this language requires the agency to specify the type of rule involved, the time during which the agency will receive written comments on the proposal, as well as instructions regarding the manner of filing comments.

The APA does not specify a minimum period for comment. A common misconception is that the APA prescribes a 30–day minimum comment period—a belief that probably derives from the APA's requirement that final rules be published 30 days prior to their effective date. A reasonable time should be allowed for comment, with "reasonableness" judged in relation to the particular facts of each rulemaking. . . .

Pending in both houses of Congress in 1982 were comprehensive regulatory reform bills that would have established a minimum 60–day comment period. The Administrative Conference, in a statement of views on those bills, stated that it has "no objection to enactment . . . [of the minimum comment period provision] . . . provided that the 'good cause' exception in section 553(b) is retained." . . .

The section 553 notice must also contain a "reference to the legal authority under which the rule is proposed." Though this requirement is fairly straightforward, it occasionally has been an issue in proceedings for the review of rules, and courts have invalidated rules for failure to comply with it.

Finally, section 553 requires that the rulemaking notice contain "either the terms or substance of the proposed rule or a description of the subjects and issues involved." The Attorney General's Manual on the APA recommended that agencies only include a description of the subjects and issues, rather than the terms of a proposed rule, if "publication . . . in full would unduly burden the Federal Register or would in fact be less informative to the public." Today most agencies publish a specific rulemaking proposal when commencing rulemaking. Requirements of additional analysis and the heightened scrutiny given agency rules are incentives for prior agency . . . publication of specific proposals. Specific proposals help focus public comment, and that, in turn, assists reviewing courts in deciding whether interested persons were given a meaningful opportunity to participate in the rulemaking.

Notes and Questions

1. *Reasonable time.* If a federal agency publishes notice of a proposed rule in the *Federal Register* on May 1 and adopts the rule on

May 5, has it violated the federal APA? How should an agency or a court determine what is a reasonable time for public comment on a proposed rule? *See Connecticut Light and Power Co. v. NRC*, 673 F.2d 525 (D.C.Cir.1982) (30 day period not unreasonable in light of industry familarity with problem—but no period shorter than 30 days is allowed); *Florida Power & Light Co. v. United States*, 846 F.2d 765, 772 (D.C.Cir.1988) (15 day period not unreasonable in light of 90 day statutory reporting requirement and additional 45 day statutory deadline for issuance of final rule, agency's receipt of 61 comments on proposed rule, fact comments had an effect on content of final rule, and fact no additional criticisms beyond those originally contained in comments were raised during period after publication of final rule.)

2. *State provisions.* The notice provisions of the typical state APA are similar to those contained in the federal APA. Most state acts, however, require notice of proposed rulemaking to be published within a specified minimum time period, such as 30 days, prior to adoption of a proposed rule. States typically have an official publication like the *Federal Register* in which such notices are required to be published.

In addition to specifying a minimum time period for the publication of notices of proposed rulemaking, § 3–103 of the 1981 MSAPA ordinarily requires publication of the full text of a proposed rule. By requiring inclusion of the full text in the notice, the new Model Act avoids a debate over the content of the notice that may occur when the agency publishes only the "substance of the proposed rule or a description of the subjects and issues involved." Under the federal APA and most state APAs, only such a fair notice summary of the contents need be published.

Are these features of the 1981 MSAPA improvements over the federal act? Are they any less practical at the federal level than at the state level?

3. *Variance between proposed rule and final rule.* Suppose an agency publishes the full text of a proposed rule in the notice of proposed rulemaking and then, as a result of information learned during the course of the rulemaking, changes the text of the rule at the time of its adoption. What test should apply to determine the validity of such a rule? Consider the following analysis of this question under the federal APA in *BASF Wyandotte Corp. v. Castle*, 598 F.2d 637, 642 (1979):

> "The requirement of submission of a proposed rule for comment does not automatically generate a new opportunity for comment merely because the rule promulgated by the agency differs from the rule it proposed, partly at least in response to submissions."
> . . . Even substantial changes in the original plan may be made so long as they are "in character with the original scheme" and "a logical outgrowth" of the notice and comment already given. . . .

The essential inquiry is whether the commenters have had a fair opportunity to present their views on the contents of the final plan. We must be satisfied, in other words, that given a new opportunity to comment, commenters would not have their first occasion to offer new and different criticisms which the Agency might find convincing.

American Bankers, Etc. v. Division of Consumer Counsel, 263 S.E.2d 867, 875–76 (Va.1980), explains the rationale for the "logical outgrowth" test as followed in Virginia:

[The purpose of notice and comment rulemaking provisions is] "to apprise interested parties of the pendency of the action and afford them an opportunity to present their objections." . . . Such notice and comment provisions clearly contemplate that an agency may wish to alter its proposal after receiving public comment. Since possible change in the regulation is the very reason for the public comment, a party is not denied due process merely because the proposed regulation was not "an accurate forecast of the precise action which [the agency] will take upon the subjects mentioned in the notice of hearing." . . .

Requiring an agency to provide an additional notice and comment period when it decides to change any provisions in a proposed rule would change the purpose of these notice provisions. Knowing that changes would trigger an additional round of notice and comment, agencies might be reluctant to change an original proposal even though the arguments for change offered at a hearing are persuasive. *Bassett v. State Fish and Wildlife Commission,* 556 P.2d 1382, 1384 (Or.1976). Parties desiring to delay regulation would be inclined to point to potential weaknesses in a proposed plan without offering alternatives, knowing that an agency would be required to undertake an additional round of notice and comment before making any change. Such a process might lead to an endless round of notices and hearings before a regulation could be implemented.

Nevertheless, the changes in a promulgated rule may occasionally be so significant that their adoption without an additional period for notice and comment would deny interested parties their rights guaranteed by . . . [such notice and comment provisions. An agency] is not required, however, to provide additional notice and opportunity for comment where the changes in the promulgated rule, even if substantial, do not enlarge the proposed rule's subject matter, *Schenley Affiliated Brands Corp. v. Kirby,* 98 Cal. Rptr. 609, 622 (1971); *Bassett v. State Fish and Wildlife Commission,* 556 P.2d 1382, 1384 (Or.1976); *East Greenwich Fire District v. Penn Central Co.,* 302 A.2d 304, 310–11 (R.I.1973), and are a logical outgrowth of the public comments received. *South Terminal Corp. v. Environmental Protection Agency,* 504 F.2d 646, 658–59 (1st Cir. 1974).

Read § 3–107 of the 1981 MSAPA. Is this provision creating a "substantially different" test more helpful or desirable than the "logical outgrowth test" developed by the federal courts under the federal APA? What are the differences between the "logical outgrowth" test and the "substantially different" test? *See* Beck, Bakken, and Muck, MINNESOTA ADMINISTRATIVE PROCEDURE § 23.5 (1987), discussing Minnesota's "substantially different" test in relation to the federal "logical outgrowth" test. Under the "logical outgrowth" test, may an agency adopt a rule that is "substantially different" from the proposed rule contained in the notice of proposed rule adoption?

An alternative approach is to require agencies to publish a new notice of proposed rulemaking if they intend to make *any changes* in the text of the proposed rule. Is this approach impractical because it could result in an endless series of rulemaking notices, further delaying the issuance of rules or subtly inducing agencies to resist even desirable changes in the text of proposed rules? Or is this approach desirable because it is the only practical way by which the public can have a fair chance to protect itself against unwise or unwanted rules?

4. *Actual notice.* Suppose that a notice of proposed rulemaking fails to furnish adequate notice of the contents of the final rule. However, some interested persons had *actual* notice of its contents prior to the close of the comment period. Is the rule valid? Section 553(b) of the federal APA expressly states that published notice of proposed rulemaking is unnecessary if "persons subject [to the rule] are named and either personally served or otherwise have actual notice." In *AFL–CIO v. Donovan,* 757 F.2d 330 (D.C.Cir.1985), the court invalidated a rule on the ground that it was not a logical outgrowth of the proposed rule. It was claimed that the final rule should be upheld because the material changes made in the proposed rule were suggested in one of the 1,600 comments submitted in the rulemaking proceeding. The court said that this comment was insufficient to furnish actual notice to other interested persons.

State laws do not generally excuse the failure to publish notice of proposed rulemaking when persons subject to the rule have actual notice that the agency was contemplating its adoption. *See, e.g., H.F. Wilcox Oil & Gas Co. v. Walker,* 32 P.2d 1044, 1051 (Okl.1934). In that case, plaintiff had actual knowledge of an agency's contemplated action, yet was allowed to challenge an adopted rule on the ground that the agency failed to publish advance notice of a proposed rule. The court reasoned that although the plaintiff had actual notice, other persons may have participated in the rulemaking if notice had been provided in the required manner.

5. *Other notice requirements.* Congress has enacted statutes requiring some agencies to use additional notice procedures not required by the APA. *See, e.g.,* 42 U.S.C. § 7410(c)(2)(E) (EPA must hold at least one additional notice and comment round if the agency is contemplating substantial changes in the final rule.)

Recent Presidents have also sought to require further notice of proposed rulemaking. For example, President Reagan's Executive Order 12,291 requires agencies to publish a semi-annual agenda of major regulations under development. *See* Exec. Order No. 12,291, 46 Fed. Reg. 13,193 (1981). This agenda would indicate the current direction of an agency's program and provides notice of forthcoming agency rulemaking activities prior to the actual publication of particular proposed rules. E.O. 12,291 is discussed in §§ 6.5 and 7.5.6(b), *infra.*

6. *Statement of purpose.* Further requirements for the notice of proposed rulemaking have been imposed by the Office of the Federal Register. A notice that does not comply with *Federal Register* publication requirements may be returned to the agency. 1 C.F.R. § 2.4(b). One of the general requirements for publication of a rulemaking notice is that it must include "a preamble which will inform the reader, who is not an expert in the subject area, of the basis and purpose for the rule or proposal." 1 C.F.R. § 18.12(a). Section 3–103(a)(1) of the 1981 MSAPA also provides that a notice of proposed rule adoption must include "a short explanation of the purpose of the proposed rule." Such a preamble helps interested persons to ascertain whether the proposal is reasonable in light of its stated purposes and to determine the likelihood that the proposal will actually accomplish those purposes. Note that the federal APA requires that rules shall incorporate "a concise general statement of their basis and purpose." APA § 553(c). However, the basis and purpose statement need not accompany a *proposed* rule, only the final rule.

7. *Information that forms basis of rule.* Should the notice of rulemaking be required to include a summary of information or ideas upon which the agency relied in formulating its proposal? Should it be required to include any scientific data or methodology on which the agency relied? Consider, in this connection, the following excerpt from *Portland Cement Association v. Ruckelshaus,* 486 F.2d 375, 377–78, 392–94 (D.C.Cir.1973), *cert. denied,* 417 U.S. 921 (1974):

> Portland Cement Association seeks review of the action of the Administrator of the Environmental Protection Agency (EPA) in promulgating stationary source standards for new or modified portland cement plants. . . .

> We find a critical defect in the decision-making process in arriving at the standard under review in the initial inability of petitioners to obtain—in timely fashion—the test results and procedures used on existing plants which formed a partial basis for the emission control level adopted, and in the subsequent seeming refusal of the agency to respond to what seem to be legitimate problems with the methodology of these tests.

> The regulations under review were first proposed on August 3, 1971 and then adopted on December 16, 1971. Both the proposed and adopted rule cited certain portland cement testing as forming a basis for the standards. . . .

[T]he proposed standard was accompanied by a Background Document which disclosed some information about the tests, but did not identify the location or methodology used in the one successful test conducted on a dry-process kiln. . . .

[T]he details, aside from a summary of test results, were not made available to petitioners until mid-April 1972. . . . The full disclosure of the methodology followed in these tests raised certain problems, in the view of petitioners, on which they had not yet had the opportunity to comment. Their original comments in the period between the proposal and promulgation of the regulation could only respond to the brief summary of the results of the tests that had been disclosed at that time. . . .

It is not consonant with the purpose of a rule-making proceeding to promulgate rules on the basis of inadequate data, or on data that, [to a] critical degree, is known only to the agency. . . .

In order that rule-making proceedings to determine standards be conducted in orderly fashion, information should generally be disclosed as to the basis of a proposed rule at the time of issuance. If this is not feasible, as in case of statutory time constraints, information that is material to the subject at hand should be disclosed as it becomes available.

Similarly, in *Connecticut Light and Power Co. v. NRC,* 673 F.2d 525, 530–31 (D.C.Cir.1982), the court said, in referring to the NRC's failure to disclose technical studies about fire prevention in nuclear power plants:

The purpose of the comment period is to allow interested members of the public to communicate information, concerns, and criticisms to the agency during the rule making process. If the notice of proposed rule making fails to provide an accurate picture of the reasoning that has led the agency to the proposed rule, interested parties will not be able to comment meaningfully upon the agency's proposals. As a result, the agency may operate with a one-sided or mistaken picture of the issues at stake in a rule making. In order to allow for useful criticism, it is especially important for the agency to identify and make available technical studies and data that it has employed in reaching the decisions to propose particular rules. To allow an agency to play hunt the peanut with technical information, hiding or disguising the information that it employs, is to condone a practice in which the agency treats what should be a genuine interchange as mere bureaucratic sport. An agency commits serious procedural error when it fails to reveal portions of the technical basis for a proposed rule in time to allow for meaningful commentary.

Is it sufficient if the agency simply describes the factual basis for its proposed rule in the notice of proposed rulemaking, or do *Portland Cement* and *Connecticut Power* require it to disclose all of the specific information upon which it relies to support that proposal?

B.F. Goodrich Co. v. Department of Transportation, 541 F.2d 1178, 1184 (6th Cir.1976) suggests that the APA does not require that every bit of background information used by an administrative agency be published for public comment. It is enough that "[t]he basic data upon which the agency relied in formulating the regulation was available to petitioners for comment." Is this a fair reading of § 553 of the federal APA?

The traditional complaint is that the information made available by the agency at the time it publishes notice of proposed rulemaking is inadequate to provide sufficient notice. Could an oversupply of information be equally detrimental? The Administrative Conference studied FTC rulemaking under the Magnuson–Moss Act and reported:

> Several factors tended to cause an expansion in the volume of paper in the rulemaking proceedings. . . . This expansion of volume had two important consequences. First, it took time for the staff to collect the material and transmit it to the rulemaking record. Much material was made public too late to be used by participants submitting written comments or proposing disputed issues of fact for consideration at the oral hearings. Second, the records generated were too massive and poorly organized to be used effectively. . . . The net result was that in many situations it became virtually impossible for a participant to determine with any confidence which material was relevant to or significant for any particular point raised by a proposed rule. This seriously undermined the concept that the basis of a rule should be tested.

44 Fed.Reg. 38,817, 88,820–21 (1979). What procedures could be adopted to prevent this problem? *See* ACUS, Recommendation 79–1, "Hybrid Rulemaking Procedures of the Federal Trade Commission," 1 C.F.R. § 305.79–1.

8. *Problem.* Biologists at High Tech Corp. have developed a genetically engineered bacteria that, they hope, will lower the freezing point of citrus fruit, thus protecting the fruit from frost damage. The biologists now wish to test the bacteria on orange trees. However, considerable opposition to the tests has developed; many people are concerned that the bacteria, once released into the environment, might have dangerous effects.

The State Health Department proposed to adopt rules relating to tests of genetically engineered organisms. The proposed rules would allow such tests upon twenty days notice if an environmental impact statement is filed at the time of notice disclosing to the public all information relevant to the test that was in the possession of the individual or organization conducting the test. On behalf of your client, High Tech Corp., you filed a comment on the proposed regulation approving its contents.

The final rules prohibited all tests of genetically engineered organisms outside the laboratory. You have also discovered that Health Department scientists produced several extensive analyses of the problem during the comment period. These reports, which opposed any open-air testing, were never disclosed to persons commenting on the proposed rule.

What are the prospects for judicial challenge of the final rules under the federal APA and the 1981 MSAPA?

§ 6.3   PUBLIC PARTICIPATION

§ 6.3.1   INFORMAL AND HYBRID RULEMAKING

The federal APA provides for two kinds of rulemaking—"formal" and "informal." *Formal rulemaking* involves an opportunity for a trial-type hearing including the right to present evidence, conduct cross examination, and submit rebuttal evidence, conducted according to most of the adjudication provisions of the federal act. Formal rulemaking procedures are applicable only "[w]hen rules are required by statute to be made on the record after opportunity for an agency hearing." APA § 553(c). *Informal rulemaking,* often called notice and comment rulemaking, is governed by far less rigorous procedural requirements. After the required notice of proposed rulemaking, the federal APA requires only that "the agency shall give interested persons an opportunity to participate in the rule making through submission of written data, views, or arguments with or without opportunity for oral presentation." APA § 553(c). Informal rulemaking is the norm; formal rulemaking the exception. However, in particular classes of informal rulemaking, Congress may and often has inserted additional or alternate procedural requirements in the particular agency enabling act. When it does so, the resulting rulemaking is often called *hybrid rulemaking.* State APAs explicitly recognize only one type of rulemaking—informal rulemaking of the notice and comment variety.

Notes and Questions

1. *Written or oral comment.* In informal rulemaking under the federal APA the agency is free to limit public participation to written submissions unless the agency determines otherwise or some other species of law requires more. Nevertheless, federal agencies frequently exercise their discretion to conduct oral hearings on proposed rules.

The typical state APA follows 1961 MSAPA § 3(a)(2) and requires an opportunity to make written submissions to the agency concerning a proposed rule and also, if properly demanded, an opportunity for an "oral hearing." An oral hearing is construed to be an argument or legislative style hearing rather than a trial-type hearing. It must be demanded by 25 persons, a government subdivision, another agency, or an association with 25 or more members. Section 3–104(b)(1) of the 1981 MSAPA also requires an "oral proceeding" as well as an opportunity to make written submissions in its informal rulemaking scheme after a proper demand of the kind specified in the typical state APA.

Should an opportunity for interested persons to make oral presentations be required in every rulemaking? Should it be available only in situations where the invocation of a triggering mechanism, like that found in most state acts, demonstrates a sufficient demand? What are the relative advantages and disadvantages of oral proceedings in rulemaking? What, if anything, is wrong with limiting public participation to written submissions in rulemaking, since a rule only settles issues of law and policy in the abstract and does not determine the rights, duties, or privileges of particular persons based on their particular facts?

Consider the following justification for some kind of oral proceedings in rulemaking:

It must be admitted that in some situations oral presentations will be more effective than written submissions to communicate to an agency relevant information or arguments, and also to enable the agency to resolve any questions it may have through the oral questioning process. In some situations, oral presentations in rule making may be more effective simply because they are delivered in person, they allow a direct and instantaneous interplay of information and argument between members of the public and the agency, and they are better than written presentations to express depth of feeling or emotion. In addition, oral proceedings may be more effective than proceedings limited entirely to written submissions for provoking broad-based public opposition to a proposed rule. Oral presentations are also likely to be more effective than written submissions for persons who lack the ability to engage in effective written communication.

Bonfield, STATE ADMINISTRATIVE RULE MAKING 194 (1986).

In addition, an opportunity for members of the public to make oral submissions in rulemaking may ensure greater public satisfaction with the process. An opportunity to submit only written comment may seem less effective and very remote, and thus may engender little personal satisfaction in the individual submitting such comments. On the other hand, an opportunity for oral communication in rulemaking may enhance the communicator's sense of meaningful participation in a significant way. One commentator noted that "[u]nless the individual commenting is filing views as part of an organization known to have significant strength before the agency, the filing of a [written] comment is much akin to dropping a feather into the Grand Canyon and trying to hear the impact." Williams, "Securing Fairness and Regularity in Administrative Proceedings," 29 Admin.L.Rev. 1, 16 (1977).

2. *Interested persons.* The federal APA and the typical state APA rulemaking provision which is based on § 3(a)(2) of the 1961 MSAPA, give "*interested*" persons the right to make written submissions in rulemaking. The 1981 MSAPA omits the word "interested" in its similar provision, § 3–104. Does this mean that the agency could refuse to accept submissions from certain persons on the grounds they

lack a sufficient "legal interest?" Agencies appear to allow anyone who wishes to do so to participate in a rulemaking proceeding. The question as to whether a person has a "legal interest" as opposed to a merely political interest does not arise in practice.

3. *Participation by the disadvantaged.* The general theories for administrative law discussed in § 1.7, *supra,* and the specific purposes of rulemaking procedures discussed in § 6.1, *supra,* suggest that one of the major functions of rulemaking procedures is to ensure that agency rules are consistent with the political will of the community at large. Another major function of rulemaking procedures is to ensure that agency rulemakers possess all of the information necessary to make technically sound rules. These objectives can be successfully achieved, however, only if all affected interests have a realistic opportunity to participate in the rulemaking process. The fact is that they do not. Despite the opportunities created by rulemaking procedures for all interested persons to participate fully in the process by which rules are made, some sectors of our society are unable to do so because they lack the necessary economic, educational, or organizational resources. After all, it does take significant resources for a particular interest group to monitor and to participate in the rulemaking process in order to ensure that relevant officials are fully informed about its concerns, and that the outcome of the process takes account of its actual or potential political influence in the community.

The problem created by the practical inability of the poor to participate in rulemaking proceedings affecting them has been characterized as follows:

> An agency promulgating rules affecting the poor cannot assume that it automatically knows what is best for such people. Government administrators are usually persons with middle-class backgrounds, experiences, and associations; therefore, they tend to have middle-class viewpoints, orientations, and understandings. . . . Consequently, there is a special reason for concern when . . . the interests of poor people are inadequately represented in the rulemaking process.

> The administration of government [also] suffers as a whole from the inability of the economically underprivileged segment of our society to represent adequately its group interests in the rulemaking process . . . because . . . [that inability] sometimes results in the formulation and promulgation of [unsound or politically unacceptable] policy.

Bonfield, "Representation For the Poor In Federal Rulemaking," 67 Mich.L.Rev. 511 (1969).

Do you think there should be a special concern for the inability in practice of poor persons to represent their views adequately in the rulemaking process? Note that outcomes in many aspects of our governance directly or indirectly reflect inequalities of private resources. For example, the more affluent may be able to exercise greater influence in the legislative process than the less affluent by virtue of the ability of the former to make campaign contributions and to lobby legislators more effectively than the latter. Does that mean we should be no more concerned about inequalities of private resources when they affect outcomes in the agency rulemaking process than when they affect outcomes in the legislative process? Note that the enactment of several statutes relating to election campaign contributions and lobbying activities demonstrate some public concern about the effects of the inequality of private resources in the legislative process. Furthermore, agency rulemakers are less visible than legislators; and federal agency heads and most state agency heads are appointed while legislators are directly elected. In addition, the successful administration of many government programs requires agency rulemakers to have access to information in the possession of the disadvantaged before rules relating to those programs are adopted. These factors might suggest a special need to ensure that the more disadvantaged sectors of our society have a realistic opportunity to utilize in the agency rulemaking process the mechanisms provided for the participation of all interested persons.

As a result, ACUS recommended that "agencies should engage more extensively in affirmative, self-initiated efforts to ascertain directly from the poor their views with respect to rulemaking that may affect them substantially." It suggested that "[f]or this purpose, agencies should make strong efforts, by use of existing as well as newly devised procedures, to obtain information and opinion from those whose circumstances may not permit conventional participation in rulemaking proceedings." In addition, the Administrative Conference urged the creation of an independent People's Counsel, financed with federal funds and authorized to represent the interests of the poor in federal agency rulemaking that substantially affects their interests. *See* Recommendation 68–5, "Representation of the Poor in Agency Rulemaking of Direct Consequence to Them," 1 C.F.R. § 305.68–5; Bonfield, *supra,* 67 Mich.L.Rev. 511 (1969).

Should representation for the interests of the poor be of any more concern in this connection than representation for the interests of other groups in our society whose views, in practice, may not be adequately represented in rulemaking proceedings? What mechanisms might an agency use to ensure that the views of poor persons substantially affected by proposed rules are adequately represented in rulemaking proceedings? Consider also whether agency use of those same mechanisms would be equally effective and desirable to secure adequate representation in rulemaking proceedings for the interests of other groups in our society whose views, in practice, are unrepresented? Is the People's Counsel proposal desirable? Consider, in this connection, whether a better system for representing the interests of the poor or other unrepresented groups in such proceedings might be to authorize the payment of legal fees to private lawyers for the representation of those interests in particular rulemaking proceedings. The availability of lawyers fees for participation in agency proceedings is discussed in § 10.3, *infra*.

4. *Trial-type proceedings.* When, if ever, are trial-type proceedings in rulemaking desirable? The 1981 MSAPA uses the words "oral proceeding" rather than the word "hearing" used in most state APAs to describe the nature of the oral process triggered in rulemaking on proper demand. The term "proceeding" was used to make clear that an adjudicative or trial-type process is not required by that provision; it only requires an argument style or legislative-type proceeding. A trial-type proceeding is held only if the agency chooses to have such a proceeding. *See* 1981 MSAPA § 3–104 Comment.

In its recommendation for "Procedures for the Adoption of Rules of General Applicability" ACUS states:

[1] In future grants of rulemaking authority to administrative agencies, Congress ordinarily should not impose mandatory procedural requirements other than those required by 5 U.S.C. § 553, except that when it has special reason to do so, it may appropriately require opportunity for oral argument . . . or trial-type hearings on issues of specific fact.

[2] Congress should never require trial-type procedures for resolving questions of policy or of broad or general fact. Ordinarily it should not require such procedures for making rules of general applicability, except that it may sometimes appropriately require such procedures for resolving issues of specific fact. . . .

[3] Each agency should decide in the light of the circumstances of particular proceedings whether or not to provide procedural protections going beyond those of section 553, such as opportunity for oral argument, . . . opportunity for parties to comment on each other's written or oral submissions, a public-meeting type of hearing, or trial-type hearing for issues of specific fact.

ACUS, Recommendation 72–5, "Procedures for the Adoption of Rules of General Applicability," 1 C.F.R. § 305.72–5.

Are cross-examination, rebuttal, and other rights normally associated with adjudicative hearings useful in the rulemaking context? Do the cost of such trial-type rights in this context outweigh their benefits?

One reason for the opposition to trial-type hearings in rulemaking is based on efficiency concerns. The classic example is a Food and Drug Administration formal rulemaking that began in 1959 and ended in 1968, generating 7,736 pages of transcript. The issue was whether peanut butter should be required to have 87 or 90 percent peanuts. *Corn Products Co. v. FDA,* 427 F.2d 511 (3d Cir.1970), *cert. denied,* 400 U.S. 957 (1970).

In upholding the Federal Power Commission's use of notice and comment procedures rather than trial-type procedures to issue a rule fixing a nationwide rate for natural gas sales a United States Court of Appeals stated:

> Were the Commission to have allowed all interested parties to submit oral testimony and conduct oral cross-examination on an undertaking so massive and novel as setting a national rate for new gas, the proceeding would have taken years, and the Commission's power to effectively regulate the industry would have been destroyed.

Shell Oil Company v. F.P.C., 520 F.2d 1061, 1076 (5th Cir.1975).

ACUS did a study of cross-examination in rulemaking under the Federal Trade Commission Improvements Act. That statute included an express right to conduct cross-examination and present rebuttal evidence with respect to disputed issues of fact in certain FTC rulemaking. According to ACUS:

> [T]he delay in FTC rulemaking cannot be attributed solely to cross-examination. The amount of time consumed by cross-examination at oral hearings was not great when compared to the total length of the proceedings. The study also documented instances in which cross-examination revealed flaws in studies or surveys introduced in the proceedings. Unquestionably, some benefit was produced by the cross-examination.

> On the other hand, the FTC study showed that injecting cross-examination into rulemaking may produce negative—albeit hard-to-measure—effects. Cross-examination is just one element of adversary procedure, and once a right of cross-examination is created, participants are likely to argue that the right will be meaningful only if other elements of adversary procedure are provided. For example, participants in FTC rulemaking proceedings were unhappy when presiding officers attempted to limit, or refused to allow, "re-direct" examination of witnesses who had been cross-examined by representatives of other interests. Participants also complained that they were not given adequate time to prepare for cross-examination and that discovery was inadequate. Introducing cross-examination in rulemaking also may lead to demands for an impartial decisionmaker to preside at the hearing and for a prohibition on ex parte communications with the presiding officer.

> The FTC's chief presiding officer during the period covered by the Conference's study has argued that adversary behavior can be successfully controlled by the presiding officer in the rulemaking, and that cross-examination need not disrupt or delay rulemaking. In his view, cross-examination is a "non-problem," and opposition to its use stems from "irrational emotions" and "a basic, philosophic aversion to the process." The Conference's position, however, is not that cross-examination can never be useful in rulemaking. Rather, the Conference opposes a statutory requirement of cross-examination because, unless it is strictly controlled, it could go a long way toward converting rulemaking into an adversary process

much like agency or court litigation. A key attribute of litigation is that the parties are given a degree of control over the agenda and the pace of the proceeding, through exercise of their rights to present evidence, to cross-examine witnesses, to obtain discovery, etc. Where such procedures are employed in agency rulemaking involving multiple issues of fact and policy and the participation of representatives of many diverse interests, the difficulties in controlling the course and maintaining the focus of the proceeding are multiplied.

Though opposing a requirement of cross-examination in agency rulemaking, the Conference has recognized that cross-examination is a device that agencies may find useful [in their discretion] for developing specific issues or information. . . .

See ACUS, A GUIDE TO FEDERAL AGENCY RULEMAKING, 135–36 (1983).

A second concern is that the use of trial-type hearings in rulemaking tends to obstruct agency action and frustrate agency regulatory goals. Hamilton noted in a report to the Administrative Conference:

[T]he primary impact of . . . [trial-type] procedural requirements [in rule making] is often not, as one might otherwise have expected, the testing of agency assumption by cross-examination, or the testing of agency conclusions by courts on the basis of substantial evidence of record. Rather these procedures either cause the *abandonment* of the program . . ., the development of techniques to reach the same regulatory goal but without a hearing . . ., or the promulgation of noncontroversial regulations by a process of negotiation and compromise. . . . In practice, therefore, the principal effect of imposing [formal requirements on] rule making . . . has often been the *dilution of the regulatory process rather than the protection of persons from arbitrary action.*

Hamilton, "Procedures for the Adoption of Rules of General Applicability: The Need for Procedural Innovation in Administrative Rulemaking," 2 Recommendations and Reports of the ACUS 834, 870–71 (1970–1972) (emphasis added).

A third reason for the opposition to trial-type proceedings in rulemaking is their unsuitability for determining most issues presented in rulemaking proceedings. Trial-type procedures, which include the right to present evidence, cross-examine witnesses, and present rebuttal evidence, are usually considered to be most helpful in settling disputed facts of a specific nature about particular persons and circumstances. Rulemaking procedures, on the other hand, are designed to formulate general policy. The formation of such policy may be based in part on general legislative facts, but only rarely on specific facts, and in the end is based upon value judgments. The *desirability* of a certain policy cannot be proven through trial-type procedures although, admittedly, the resolution of some subsidiary specific factual premises of such a policy may, in at least some situations, be aided by their use. Do you agree?

5. *Additional procedures.* The 1981 MSAPA does not require any trial-type procedures in rulemaking except "[t]o the extent another statute *expressly* requires a particular class of rulemaking to be conducted pursuant to the adjudicative procedures provided in Article IV, Section 4–101(b)." 1981 MSAPA § 3–104 Comment. It does, however, permit agencies to provide such procedures in their discretion, where they find them to be useful and feasible.

At the federal level, a variety of additional procedures are required by specific statutes. As noted, the resulting procedure is often called "hybrid rulemaking."

> Though the [federal] APA does not contain an oral hearing requirement for informal rulemaking, numerous laws enacted in the last decade contain a requirement that the agency hold a "public hearing" or provide interested persons "an opportunity for the oral presentation of data, views, or arguments" in rulemaking. Statutes calling for a legislative-type hearing include the Federal Coal Mine Health and Safety Act (1969); the Occupational Safety and Health Act (1970); the Consumer Product Safety Act (1972); the Safe Drinking Water Act (1974); the Energy Policy and Conservation Act (1975); the Clean Water Act (1977); the Clean Air Act Amendments (1977), and the Endangered Species Act Amendments (1978).
>
> A few hybrid rulemaking statutes require not only a legislative-type hearing, but also an opportunity for interested persons to question or cross-examine opposing witnesses. These include the Federal Trade Commission Improvements Act (1975); the Securities Act Amendments (1976), and the Toxic Substances Control Act (1976).
>
> The large number of statutes requiring an oral hearing probably reflects a strong belief among legislators in the value of oral communication between regulators and the regulated.

ACUS, A GUIDE TO FEDERAL AGENCY RULEMAKING, 131 (1983).

Are statutes calling for hybrid rulemaking a good idea? Why did Congress enact them? Are they justified on the merits?

6. *Political implications.* In most cases, would hybrid or formal rulemaking be promoted by pro-regulation or anti-regulation forces? Could it be argued that members of Congress often vote to require additional rulemaking procedures for implementing particular statutes because it will be harder for agencies to execute those laws? Members of Congress could then claim to have served the interests of both pro- and anti-regulation forces and, therefore, to be entitled to support from both of them. Or is this view excessively cynical, disregarding the actual benefits and justification on the merits for these additional procedures?

Is hybrid or formal rulemaking any more or less consistent with the theory for administrative law espoused by McCubbins, Noll, and Weingast, § 1.7, *supra,* than informal rulemaking? Any more or less consistent with the "expertise" theory for administrative law discussed in § 1.7, *supra,* than informal rulemaking? These issues are revisited in §§ 6.5, 6.6, and 6.8, *infra.*

§ 6.3.2 FORMAL RULEMAKING REQUIREMENTS

When must an agency use formal rulemaking procedures to issue rules because of the federal APA § 553(c) requirement that "[w]hen rules are required by statute to be made on the record after opportunity for an agency hearing, sections 556 and 557 of this title" are applicable? Sections 556 and 557 require trial-type hearings which include the right to present evidence, cross-examine witnesses, and submit rebuttal evidence. Furthermore, in such formal rulemaking proceedings, the record made before the agency in that proceeding is the exclusive basis for agency action. In formal rulemaking, ex parte communications, as defined by § 557(d), are also prohibited; however the separation of functions provisions of § 554(d) are inapplicable to such proceedings. Since the rights of private parties are much more detailed and extensive in formal rulemaking than in informal or even hybrid rulemaking, it is a matter of great importance to identify adequately the mechanism by which the normal informal rulemaking procedures are displaced by the extraordinary formal rulemaking procedures.

UNITED STATES v. FLORIDA EAST COAST RAILWAY CO.

410 U.S. 224 (1973).

[The Interstate Commerce Commission (ICC) adopted rules that fixed the daily charge that a railroad must pay another railroad for the use of the latter's freight-cars during peak use periods. The ICC had been directed by statute to increase the charge in order to create an incentive for railroads to return the cars quickly or to purchase their own cars. Apparently the previous charges were so low that they encouraged railroads to keep the cars owned by other railroads. This, in turn, caused underinvestment in freight-cars and resulted in a chronic shortage.

The ICC refused to grant protesting railroads an oral hearing. The lower court held that failure to provide an oral hearing violated § 1(14) (a) of the Interstate Commerce Act which provides that the ICC "after hearing" can establish rules with respect to car service.]

REHNQUIST, J.:

In *United States v. Allegheny–Ludlum Steel Corp.,* 406 U.S. 742 (1972), . . . we held that the language of § 1(14)(a) of the Interstate Commerce Act authorizing the Commission to act "after hearing" was not the equivalent of a requirement that a rule be made "on the record after opportunity for an agency hearing" as the latter term is used in

§ 553(c) of the Administrative Procedure Act. Since the 1966 amendment to § 1(14)(a), under which the Commission was here proceeding, does not by its terms add to the hearing requirement contained in the earlier language, the same result should obtain here unless that amendment contains language that is tantamount to such a requirement. Appellees contend that such language is found in the provisions of that Act requiring that:

> "[T]he Commission shall give consideration to the national level of ownership of such type of freight car and to other factors affecting the adequacy of the national freight car supply, and shall, on the basis of such consideration, determine whether compensation should be computed. . . ."

While this language is undoubtedly a mandate to the Commission to consider the factors there set forth in reaching any conclusion as to imposition of per diem incentive charges, it adds to the hearing requirements of the section neither expressly nor by implication. We know of no reason to think that an administrative agency in reaching a decision cannot accord consideration to factors such as those set forth in the 1966 amendment by means other than a trial-type hearing or the presentation of oral argument by the affected parties. Congress by that amendment specified necessary components of the ultimate decision, but it did not specify the method by which the Commission should acquire information about those components. . . .

Inextricably intertwined with the hearing requirement of the Administrative Procedure Act in this case is the meaning to be given to the language "after hearing" in § 1(14)(a) of the Interstate Commerce Act. Appellees . . . contend that the Commission procedure here fell short of that mandated by the "hearing" requirement of § 1(14)(a), even though it may have satisfied § 553 of the Administrative Procedure Act. The Administrative Procedure Act states that none of its provisions "limit or repeal additional requirements imposed by statute or otherwise recognized by law." 5 U.S.C. § 559. Thus, even though the Commission was not required [in this rulemaking] to comply with §§ 556 and 557 of that Act, it was required to accord the "hearing" specified in § 1(14)(a) of the Interstate Commerce Act. . . .

The term "hearing" in its legal context undoubtedly has a host of meanings. Its meaning undoubtedly will vary, depending on whether it is used in the context of a rulemaking-type proceeding or in the context of a proceeding devoted to the adjudication of particular disputed facts. It is by no means apparent what the drafters of . . . the first part of § 1(14)(a) of the Interstate Commerce Act, meant by the term. . . . What is apparent, though, is that the term was used in granting authority to the Commission to make rules and regulations of a prospective nature. . . . [C]onfronted with a grant of substantive authority made after the Administrative Procedure Act was enacted, we think that reference to that Act, in which Congress devoted itself exclusively to questions such as the nature and scope of hearings, is a satisfactory basis for determining what is meant by the term "hearing" used in another statute. Turning to that Act, we are convinced that the term "hearing" as used therein does not necessarily embrace either the right to present evidence orally and to cross-examine opposing witnesses, or the right to present oral argument to the agency's decisionmaker. . . .

We think this treatment of the term "hearing" in the Administrative Procedure Act affords a sufficient basis for concluding that the requirement of a "hearing" contained in § 1(14)(a), in a situation where the Commission was acting under the 1966 statutory rulemaking authority that Congress had conferred upon it, did not by its own force require the Commission either to hear oral testimony, to permit cross-examination of Commission witnesses, or to hear oral argument. Here, the Commission promulgated a tentative draft of an order, and accorded all interested parties 60 days in which to file statements of position, submissions of evidence, and other relevant observations. The parties had fair notice of exactly what the Commission proposed to do, and were given an opportunity to comment, to object, or to make some other form of written submission. The final order of the Commission indicates that it gave consideration to the statements of the two appellees here. Given the "open-ended" nature of the proceedings, and the Commission's announced willingness to consider proposals for modification after operating experience had been acquired, we think the hearing requirement of § 1(14)(a) of the Act was met. . . .

The basic distinction between rulemaking and adjudication is illustrated by this Court's treatment of two related cases under the Due Process Clause of the Fourteenth Amendment. In *Londoner v. Denver*, [§ 2.5, *supra*,] the Court held that due process had not been accorded a landowner who objected to the amount assessed against his land as its share of the benefit resulting from the paving of a street. Local procedure had accorded him the right to file a written complaint and objection, but not to be heard orally. This Court held that due process of law required that he "have the right to support his allegations by argument however brief, and, if need be, by proof, however informal." But in the later case of *Bi–Metallic Investment Co. v. State Board of Equalization* [§ 2.5, *supra*,] the Court held that no hearing at all was constitutionally required prior to a decision by state tax officers in Colorado to increase the valuation of all taxable property in Denver by a substantial percentage. The Court distinguished *Londoner* by stating that there a small number of persons "were exceptionally affected, in each case upon individual grounds."

. . . While the line dividing them may not always be a bright one, these decisions represent a recognized distinction in administrative law between proceedings for the purpose of promulgating policy-type rules or standards, on the one hand, and proceedings designed to adjudicate disputed facts in particular cases on the other.

Here, the incentive payments proposed by the Commission in its tentative order, and later adopted in its final order, were applicable across the board to all of the common carriers by railroad subject to the Interstate Commerce Act. No effort was made to single out any particular railroad for special consideration based on its own peculiar circumstances. Indeed, one of the objections of appellee Florida East Coast was that it and other terminating carriers should have been treated differently from the generality of the railroads. But the fact that the order may in its effects have been thought more disadvantageous by some railroads than by others does not change its generalized nature. Though the Commission obviously relied on factual inferences as a basis for its order, the source of these factual inferences was apparent to anyone who read the order of December 1969. The factual inferences were used in the formulation of a basically legislative-type judgment, for prospective application only, rather than in adjudicating a particular set of disputed facts.

Notes and Questions

1. *The meaning of "hearing."* According to the *Florida East Coast* case, in the context of rulemaking, written submissions may satisfy a statutory requirement of a "hearing," or an "opportunity to be heard." Hence, only when a statute prescribing procedures for rulemaking of general applicability explicitly provides that the rule be made after a hearing on the record, will the agency be required to go beyond the informal procedures of § 553 and apply §§ 556 and 557.

Does the *Florida East Coast* case mean that a statute triggering formal rulemaking must actually repeat the exact words of § 553(c)— "on the record after opportunity for an agency hearing?" If not, how far from that language may a triggering statute stray?

Could the Court in the *Florida East Coast* case have just as easily construed the terms "after hearing" in the statute involved to mean that formal rulemaking *was* required? Is its failure to do so evidence that the court believed trial-type procedures are ordinarily inappropriate for rulemaking of general applicability? Does this case suggest a predilection of courts to construe the ambiguous word "hearing" in a statute to mean a trial-type hearing when specific facts about particular persons are in dispute, but not when more generalized, legislative type facts are in dispute?

Can you distinguish *Florida East Coast* from *Morgan I* and *Morgan II* in § 3.3, *supra?* Recall that the *Morgan* cases, calling for judicial methods, were based on a statute requiring a "full hearing" before an agency set the rates that brokers could charge.

2. *The rulemaking—adjudication distinction.* Recall the conflicting cases of *City of West Chicago* and *Seacoast Anti–Pollution League* in § 3.1, *supra.* Those cases involved the issue of whether a statute calling for a "hearing" triggered trial-type procedures under the federal APA. In light of *Florida East Coast,* is *West Chicago* clearly right and

Seacoast clearly wrong? Or do those cases involve a different problem from that involved in *Florida East Coast?*

Davis contends that *Florida East Coast* contains language indicating that the Court's construction of the term "hearing" is applicable only to statutes prescribing procedures for rulemaking of general applicability, and, therefore, does not apply to the use of that term in statutes prescribing procedures for adjudication or rulemaking of particular applicability. Is this a correct reading of the case? *See* 1 K. Davis, ADMINISTRATIVE LAW TREATISE, § 6:23 (2d ed. 1978).

3. *Dissenting views.* Justice Douglas states in his dissent that he considers the *Florida East Coast* decision to be a "sharp break" with traditional concepts of procedural due process.

> I do not believe it is within our traditional concepts of due process to allow an administrative agency to saddle anyone with a new rate, charge, or fee without a full hearing that includes the right to present oral testimony, cross-examine witnesses, and present oral argument.

410 U.S. 224, 247 (1973).

Is the majority's approach in that case as inconsistent with the traditional concepts of due process as Douglas portrays it? Does due process require different procedures for ratemaking of particular applicability than it requires for ratemaking of general applicability? Does Justice Douglas confuse the two?

The requirements of due process in rulemaking have been summarized in the following way: "When not bounded by statutory procedural requirements the Supreme Court has consistently been willing to assume that due process does not require any hearing or participation in 'legislative' decisionmaking other than that afforded by judicial review after rule promulgation." *Pickus v. United States Bd. of Parole,* 543 F.2d 240, 244 (D.C.Cir.1976). Does the *Florida East Coast* majority opinion support this assertion?

4. *Problem.* A statute provides that the Cable Television Commission (CTC), after providing "a fair hearing," shall set the rates that may be charged for cable television service at a level which assures the cable operator will earn a reasonable return on its investment. Acme Cable Co. provides the exclusive cable service to Madison County. At a hearing called by CTC to fix Acme's rates, CTC introduced into the record a written report by Mary, one of its staff members. The report indicated that Acme's proposed rates were about 30% higher than needed to assure a reasonable return. Acme seeks to cross-examine Mary. Is it entitled to do so if CTC is subject to i) the federal APA, ii) the 1981 MSAPA, iii) no APA?

§ 6.3.3 JUDICIAL IMPOSITION OF ADDITIONAL PROCEDURES IN RULEMAKING

When may a reviewing court impose procedural requirements in informal rulemaking beyond those required by the APA or the issuing agency's own enabling act? In a number of cases, the Court of Appeals for the District of Columbia Circuit imposed such additional procedures on certain classes of informal rulemaking. Recall the dictum to that effect in the *American Airlines* case, § 3.2, *supra*.

VERMONT YANKEE NUCLEAR POWER CORP. v. NATURAL RESOURCES DEFENSE COUNCIL, INC. [NRDC]

435 U.S. 519 (1978).

[The Atomic Energy Commission (AEC, now the Nuclear Regulatory Commission) has regulatory authority over nuclear energy. Before a utility can start constructing a nuclear power plant, it must obtain a construction permit from the AEC. Applications for construction permits undergo extensive safety and environmental review by the AEC staff and a public adjudicatory hearing occurs before the permit can be granted.

At issue in Vermont Yankee's application was the environmental effect of the disposal and storage of highly toxic nuclear waste produced by operating the plant. Because this is a recurring issue, the AEC conducted a rulemaking proceeding to determine how the nuclear waste storage issue should be resolved in each licensing proceeding. The objective was to settle the issue so it would not have to be relitigated in every single license application.

The proposed and final AEC rule specified numerical values for the environmental impact of waste disposal; these values would be part of an overall cost-benefit analysis of whether the permit should be granted. The practical effect of the values assigned would be that the AEC would essentially ignore the waste disposal problem. This approach was based on the AEC's determination that in the future methods of storage of nuclear waste would be developed that would render the wastes non-hazardous.

The only support in the record for this conclusion was a 20–page report by Dr. Pittman of the AEC staff. According to the D.C. Circuit opinion, Pittman's report offered reassurances but little detailed backup on precisely how the wastes could be safely handled in the future. 547 F.2d 633, 646–52. NRDC and others sought to cross-examine Dr. Pittman but AEC refused to allow cross-examination.]

REHNQUIST, J.:

In 1946, Congress enacted the Administrative Procedure Act, which as we have noted elsewhere was not only "a new, basic and comprehensive regulation of procedures in many agencies," but was also a legislative enactment which settled "long-continued and hard-fought contentions, and enacts a formula upon which opposing social and political forces have come to rest." Section 553 dealing with rulemaking, requires in subsection (b) that "notice of proposed rule making shall be published in the Federal Register . . .," describes the contents of that notice, and goes on to require in subsection (c) that after the notice the agency "shall give interested persons an opportunity to participate in the rule making through submission of written data, views, or arguments with or without opportunity for oral presentation. After consideration of the relevant matter presented, the agency shall incorporate in the rules adopted a concise general statement of their basis and purpose." Interpreting this provision of the Act in *United States v. Allegheny–Ludlum Steel Corp.*, 406 U.S. 742 (1972), and *United States v. Florida East Coast R. Co.*, 410 U.S. 224 (1973), we held that generally speaking this section of the Act established the maximum procedural requirements which Congress was willing to have the courts impose upon agencies in conducting rulemaking procedures. Agencies are free to grant additional procedural rights in the exercise of their discretion, but reviewing courts are generally not free to impose them if the agencies have not chosen to grant them. This is not to say necessarily that there are no circumstances which would ever justify a court in overturning agency action because of a failure to employ procedures beyond those required by the statute. But such circumstances, if they exist, are extremely rare. . . .

It is in the light of this background of statutory and decisional law that we granted certiorari to review . . . [this] judgment of the Court of Appeals for the District of Columbia Circuit because of our concern that they had seriously misread or misapplied this statutory and decisional law cautioning reviewing courts against engrafting their own notions of proper procedures upon agencies entrusted with substantive functions by Congress. . . .

Respondents appealed from both the [Atomic Energy] Commission's adoption of the rule [dealing with the environmental effects of the uranium fuel cycle] and its decision to grant Vermont Yankee's license [to operate a nuclear power plant] to the Court of Appeals for the District of Columbia Circuit. . . .

With respect to the challenge of Vermont Yankee's license, the court [of appeals] first [held] that in the absence of effective rulemaking proceedings, the Commission must deal with the environmental impact of fuel reprocessing and disposal in individual licensing proceedings. . . . The court then examined the rulemaking proceedings and despite the fact that it appeared that the agency employed all the procedures required by 5 U.S.C. § 553 and more, the court determined the proceedings to be inadequate and overturned the rule. Accordingly, the Commission's determination with respect to Vermont Yankee's license was also remanded for further proceedings. . . .

After a thorough examination of the opinion itself, we conclude that . . . the majority of the Court of Appeals struck down the rule because of the perceived inadequacies of the procedures employed in the rulemaking proceedings. . . . The court conceded that absent extraordinary circumstances it is improper for a reviewing court to prescribe the procedural format an agency must follow, but it likewise clearly thought it entirely appropriate to "scrutinize the record as a whole to insure that genuine opportunities to participate in a meaningful way were provided. . . ." The court also refrained from actually ordering the agency to follow any specific procedures, . . . but there is little doubt in our minds that the ineluctable mandate of the court's decision is that the procedures afforded during the hearings were inadequate. . . .

In prior opinions we have intimated that even in a rulemaking proceeding when an agency is making a " 'quasi-judicial' " determination by which a very small number of persons are " 'exceptionally affected, in each case upon individual grounds,' " in some circumstances additional procedures may be required in order to afford the aggrieved individuals due process. *United States v. Florida East Coast R. Co.*, 410 U.S., at 242, 245, quoting from *Bi–Metallic Investment Co. v. State Board of Equalization*, 239 U.S. 441, 446 (1915). It might also be true, although we do not think the issue is presented in this case and accordingly do not decide it, that a totally unjustified departure from well-settled agency procedures of long standing might require judicial correction.

But this much is absolutely clear. Absent constitutional constraints or extremely compelling circumstances the "administrative agencies 'should be free to fashion their own rules of procedure and to pursue methods of inquiry capable of permitting them to discharge their multitudinous duties.' " . . . Respondent NRDC argues that . . . 5 U.S.C. § 553 . . . merely establishes lower procedural bounds and that a court may routinely require more than the minimum when an agency's proposed rule addresses complex or technical factual issues or "Issues of Great Public Import." . . . We have, however, previously shown that our decisions reject this view. We also think the legislative history does not bear out its contention. . . . In short, all of this leaves little doubt that Congress intended that the discretion of the *agencies* and not that of the courts be exercised in determining when extra procedural devices should be employed.

There are compelling reasons for construing . . . [the APA] in this manner. In the first place, if courts continually review agency proceedings to determine whether the agency employed procedures which were, in the court's opinion, perfectly tailored to reach what the court perceives to be the "best" or "correct" result, judicial review would be totally unpredictable. And the agencies, operating under this vague injunction to employ the "best" procedures and facing the threat of reversal if they did not, would undoubtedly adopt full adjudicatory procedures in every instance. Not only would this totally disrupt the statutory scheme, through which Congress enacted "a formula upon which opposing social and political forces have come to rest," but all the inherent advantages of informal rulemaking would be totally lost.

Secondly, it is obvious that the court in these cases reviewed the agency's choice of procedures on the basis of the record actually produced at the hearing, and not on the basis of the information available to the agency when it made the decision to structure the proceedings in a certain way. This sort of Monday morning quarterbacking not only encourages but almost compels the agency to conduct all rulemaking proceedings with the full panoply of procedural devices normally associated only with adjudicatory hearings.

Finally, and perhaps most importantly, this sort of review fundamentally misconceives the nature of the standard for judicial review of an agency rule. The court below uncritically assumed that additional procedures will automatically result in a more adequate record because it will give interested parties more of an opportunity to participate in and contribute to the proceedings. But informal rulemaking need not be based solely on the transcript of a hearing held before an agency. Indeed, the agency need not even hold a formal hearing. Thus, the adequacy of the "record" in this type of proceeding is not correlated directly to the type of procedural devices employed, but rather turns on whether the agency has followed the statutory mandate of the Administrative Procedure Act or other relevant statutes. If the agency is compelled to support the rule which it ultimately adopts with the type of record produced only after a full adjudicatory hearing, it simply will have no choice but to conduct a full adjudicatory hearing prior to promulgating every rule. In sum, this sort of unwarranted judicial examination of perceived procedural shortcomings of a rulemaking proceeding can do nothing but seriously interfere with that process prescribed by Congress.

Respondent NRDC also argues that the fact that the Commission's inquiry was undertaken in the context of [the National Environmental Policy Act] NEPA somehow permits a court to require procedures beyond those specified in . . . the APA when investigating factual issues through rulemaking. . . . But we search in vain for something in NEPA which would mandate such a result. . . .

In short, nothing in the APA, NEPA, the circumstances of this case, the nature of the issues being considered, past agency practice, or the statutory mandate under which the Commission operates permitted the court to review and overturn the rulemaking proceeding on the basis of the procedural devices employed (or not employed) by the Commission so long as the Commission employed at least the statutory *minima*, a matter about which there is no doubt in this case. . . . We have made it abundantly clear before that when there is a contemporaneous explanation of the agency decision, the validity of that action must "stand or fall on the propriety of that finding, judged, of course, by the appropriate standard of review. If that finding is not sustainable on the administrative record made, then the Comptroller's decision must be vacated and the matter remanded to him for further consideration." *Camp v. Pitts,* 411 U.S. 138, 143 (1973). The court should engage in this kind of review and not stray beyond the judicial province to explore the procedural format [beyond that required by the APA] or to impose upon the agency its own notion of which procedures are "best" or most likely to further some vague, undefined public good. . . .

Reversed and remanded.

Notes and Questions

1. *Administrative common law.* Davis has suggested that court-created administrative common law is necessary to ensure an acceptable administrative law system. He contends that *Vermont Yankee* is in error to the extent it precludes judicially created common law rulemaking requirements that are in addition to those provided in federal APA § 553. The argument is that the Supreme Court improperly ignored APA § 559 which provides that this Act does "not limit or repeal additional requirements imposed by statute or otherwise *recognized by law.*" (Emphasis added).

Section 559 makes clear, Davis argues, that the APA imposes only minimum not maximum procedural requirements and the "recognized by law" language permits judge-made common law to supplement APA requirements. Davis also concludes that the Supreme Court's statement about the procedures of § 553 being the maximum Congress intended to be imposed on agencies in rulemaking is only dictum, is inconsistent with many other decisions of the Supreme Court, and violates both the words and legislative history of the APA. He predicts that courts will continue to insist on additional procedures in particular instances of rulemaking where they believe those procedures are necessary to ensure fairness under the circumstances, and that to do so the courts will rely on the exception noted in *Vermont Yankee* for "extremely rare" circumstances, or will find a violation of due process, or will act as if the procedural infirmity they detect is in fact substantive. *See* K. Davis, "Administrative Common Law and the *Vermont Yankee* Opinion," 1980 Utah L.Rev. 3. Do you agree with Davis? Or do the courts lack power, independent of statute or the constitution, to compel a government agency to do anything? *See* R. Pierce, S. Shapiro, and P. Verkuil, ADMINISTRATIVE LAW AND PROCESS, § 6.4, 333 (1985).

2. *"Extremely rare" circumstances.* What is an "extremely rare" circumstance within the meaning of the *Vermont Yankee* case justifying a reviewing court in imposing procedures on an agency in rulemaking that are in addition to those required by § 553 of the APA and other statutes? In thinking about the criteria that might define an "extremely rare" circumstance, note that § 706(2)(A) of the federal APA prohibits agency action that is "arbitrary, capricious or an abuse of discretion or otherwise not in accordance with law." Is this provision very

helpful in giving content to the criteria that might define an "extremely rare" circumstance?

3. *Complex issues in rulemaking.* Where complex scientific and technical issues are involved in a rulemaking, and they must be resolved in part on the basis of conflicting data, should agencies be able to limit themselves to the use of § 553 notice and comment procedures? Should the APA be amended in some respect to deal with that situation? Or, instead, should we rely on Congress to provide hybrid rulemaking procedures in agency enabling acts where that is appropriate? Should Congress overrule the conclusion of *Vermont Yankee* on this issue, leaving judges to fashion on a common law basis additional procedural requirements where fairness under the circumstances warrants them?

4. *Judicial review—procedure or substance.* Before the *Vermont Yankee* case, there was an extended debate in the Court of Appeals for the District of Columbia Circuit over the issue of whether procedure rather than substance should be emphasized in the judicial review of rulemaking. Judge Bazelon, who penned one of the Court of Appeals decisions that were heavily criticized in *Vermont Yankee,* said in that earlier case that the courts should not "scrutinize the technical merits of each decision" but should "establish a decision-making process which assures a reasoned decision . . . ." *International Harvester Co. v. Ruckelshaus,* 478 F.2d 615, 652 (D.C.Cir.1973). This approach has been criticized on the ground that the APA "has clearly provided for a substantive as well as a procedural check on administrative action." K. Davis, ADMINISTRATIVE LAW OF SEVENTIES, 668 (1976). Was the Supreme Court's decision in *Vermont Yankee* a rejection of Bazelon's approach?

In the *Vermont Yankee* case, the Supreme Court remanded the case for substantive review of the question of whether the agency finding was "sustainable on the administrative record made." Should a rule be considered substantively arbitrary if it is based on an arbitrary procedure? *See Aqua Slide 'N' Dive Corp. v. Consumer Product Safety Commission,* 569 F.2d 831, 842 (5th Cir.1978) (rule held substantively invalid because only evidence on crucial finding not produced until comment period closed).

5. *Sequel to Vermont Yankee.* In a later decision, the Supreme Court upheld the rule assigning virtually zero impact to the waste disposal problem. It held that the agency had wisely attempted to deal with the problem on a generic basis (rather than case-by-case) and noted that additional evidence on the issue could be presented in subsequent adjudications. Additionally, it held that the agency had carefully balanced environmental and economic factors and that a court must give great deference to agency predictions, within the area of its expertise, at the frontier of science. *Baltimore Gas and Elec. Co. v. NRDC,* 462 U.S. 87 (1983), reversing a Court of Appeals decision that

had found the rule arbitrary and capricious, 685 F.2d 459 (D.C.Cir. 1982).

6. *Effect of Vermont Yankee.* What is the effect of *Vermont Yankee* on the court's power to remand cases where the original notice of proposed rulemaking is insufficient? On the "logical outgrowth" test? On the *Portland Cement* case, § 6.2, *supra?* On the *Bell Aerospace* case, § 5.4, *supra?* On cases discussed in § 3.1.1, note 4, *supra,* requiring agencies to provide minimal procedures in informal adjudication? On *Matlovich,* § 4.3, *supra?*

To what extent does *Vermont Yankee* undermine prior creative judicial interpretations of the notice and comment provisions of the federal APA or of hybrid rulemaking statutes?

The *Vermont Yankee* holding (as opposed to its sweeping generalizations about judicial review) does not necessarily undermine judicial interpretations of the notice and comment or statement of basis and purpose requirements in section 553. Yet clearly some of these interpretations go beyond what was contemplated by the drafters of the APA. It is noteworthy that the court cited with approval one such interpretation in *Vermont Yankee.*

The reason some of the judicial interpretations of section 553's requirements may survive *Vermont Yankee* is that they were made in response to major changes that occurred in administrative law and federal regulation after 1946. One change was the tremendous increase in the volume and scope of federal regulation. In the late 1960's and throughout the 1970's, Congress established a number of major regulatory schemes designed to address health and safety or environmental problems. Not only did this new legislation produce more agency rulemaking, it led to rulemaking in which the issues were often very complex and the stakes very high.

Another change was in the context and timing of judicial review of agency rules. When the APA was written, it was expected that judicial review of the validity of rules would take place in a proceeding to enforce or enjoin enforcement of rules. Therefore, a record for review would be developed either by the agency or *de novo* in the reviewing court when the rule was challenged. However, accompanying the increased use of informal rulemaking was a trend toward pre-enforcement review of agency rules; typically (as required by statute) in the federal courts of appeal. The law relating to standing to sue also changed, so that it became easier for a wider range of interested persons to challenge rules prior to their enforcement in specific cases.

These changes combined to make it easier for interested persons to get into court to challenge rules with the potential for major impact on persons or society as a whole, but the procedures required for rulemaking did not ensure development of a record that would be adequate for courts to perform their review function. The Court's analysis in *Vermont Yankee* does not discuss these changes, and there remains much uncertainty about the limits of procedural and substantive review of agency rulemaking [in light of these changes.]

ACUS, A GUIDE TO FEDERAL AGENCY RULEMAKING, 4–6 (1983).

§ 6.4   GOOD CAUSE EXEMPTIONS

Federal and state APAs contain good cause exemptions providing that notice and comment proceedings may be omitted in particular circumstances. These exemptions provide some flexibility so that the need to observe usual rulemaking procedures can, in appropriate situations, be accommodated with the equally important need to conduct government administration in an expeditious, effective, efficient, and economical manner.

Read federal APA § 553(b)(B) and the almost identical provision contained in 1981 MSAPA § 3–108. They exempt rules from usual notice and comment procedures when it would be "unnecessary, impracticable, or contrary to the public interest" for the agency to follow them. Contrast those provisions with Section 3(b) of the 1961 MSAPA, adopted in many states, which provides:

> If an agency finds that an imminent peril to the public health, safety, or welfare requires adoption of a rule upon fewer than 20 days' notice and states in writing its reasons for that finding, it may proceed without prior notice or hearing or upon any abbreviated notice and hearing that it finds practicable, to adopt an emergency rule.

ACUS, A GUIDE TO FEDERAL AGENCY RULEMAKING
39–43 (1983).

[Good cause] exceptions give agencies flexibility by allowing them to dispense with procedures in promulgating rules not otherwise exempted, but like other exemptions, they are to be construed narrowly. Moreover, an agency must give supporting reasons for invoking the "good cause" exemptions. The agency's findings of "good cause" are judicially reviewable on the same basis as any other findings committed to the agency's judgment. Though the language of the exemption from the delayed effective date requirement is more general than the standard for dispensing with notice and comment, several commentators have expressed the view that "good cause" under both sections must be predicated on similar findings.

The terms "impracticable," "unnecessary" or "contrary to the public interest" used in section 553(b)(B) indicate the circumstances in which the good cause exceptions may be employed. The APA's legislative history defines the terms this way:

> "Impracticable" means a situation in which the due and required execution of the agency functions would be unavoidably prevented

by its undertaking public rule-making proceedings. "Unnecessary" means unnecessary so far as the public is concerned, as would be the case if a minor or merely technical amendment in which the public is not particularly interested were involved. "Public interest" supplements the terms "impracticable" or "unnecessary"; it requires that public rulemaking procedures shall not prevent an agency from operating and that, on the other hand, lack of public interest in rulemaking warrants an agency to dispense with public procedure.

Ordinarily, covered situations are those in which advance notice would defeat the agency's regulatory objective; immediate action is necessary to reduce or avoid health hazards or other imminent harm to persons or property; or inaction will lead to serious dislocation in government programs or the marketplace.

Reviewing courts generally have applied the section 553(b)(B) good cause exemption to prevent agencies using it as an "escape clause" from notice and comment requirements. Several patterns emerge from the caselaw interpreting the APA's grounds for invoking the exemption. Courts applying the "contrary to the public interest" ground for exemption are inclined to err on the side of the public safety. They tend to defer to the agency if the challenged action was taken to avoid imminent or direct physical harm to the public; they carefully scrutinize agency action that might increase public exposure to the risk of harm. Courts generally apply the "unnecessary" ground for exemption to minor rules or merely technical amendments that involve little exercise of agency discretion. The "impracticable" ground for exemption often is asserted with the "contrary to the public interest" ground. One area that has generated conflicting caselaw involving these grounds is the Environmental Protection Agency's invocation of the good cause exemption to comply with a statutory deadline in the Clean Air Act for approving state lists of areas "attaining" and "not attaining" national air quality standards. As a general proposition, courts are skeptical of agency reliance on statutory deadlines to justify use of the exemption.

A factor that often surfaces in the judicial decisions applying the good cause exemption is whether or not the agency has made a good faith attempt to comply with the APA's requirements. Courts are more inclined to uphold the agency's action if the agency responded to circumstances beyond its control; adopted an emergency rule of limited scope or duration, and initiated follow-up proceedings allowing for public participation.

Courts have had difficulty deciding the appropriate remedy for erroneous use of the good cause exemption from notice and comment. Section 706 of the APA states that "reviewing courts shall . . . hold unlawful and set aside agency action . . . found to be . . . without observance of procedure required by law." However, courts often are reluctant to invalidate otherwise valid rules if it will disrupt on-going programs, and some courts have used their equitable powers to fashion relief that balances the need to uphold procedural values with the need for agencies to carry out important programs. Sometimes courts allow the emergency rules to remain in effect pending completion of new proceedings in accordance with the APA. In one case, the court held the agency's rule was valid, but only as an interim measure. One thing courts have been unwilling to do is excuse wrongful or erroneous use of the good cause exemption because the agency "cured" the procedural defect with an opportunity for public comment after promulgation. Most courts have concluded that post-promulgation comment is not a substitute for comment before rule adoption.

Notes and Questions

1. *"Unnecessary."* When are usual rulemaking procedures "unnecessary" within the meaning of the federal APA and the 1981 MSAPA good cause exemptions? Are usual notice and comment procedures "unnecessary" for the issuance of:

(a) rules announcing the exact penalty rates to be imposed as sanctions for certain actions, when the enabling statutes specify that the exact penalty rates imposed are to be a certain percentage of an indisputable and easily ascertainable figure?

(b) a rule requiring natural gas companies to pay a compound interest rate, for the first time, on all amounts refunded to their customers because of overcharges resulting from new rates subsequently found to be unjustified?

(c) a rule requiring monthly billing by hospitals in connection with a public financed medical care plan, but allowing a three month grace period for such billing?

(d) a rule whose substance might have been adopted by the agency as the basis for a decision in one of its adjudications?

(e) rules that have only a small impact on a limited segment of the public?

See A. Bonfield, STATE ADMINISTRATIVE RULE MAKING § 6.8.2 (1986).

2. *"Impracticable."* When are usual rulemaking procedures "impracticable" within the meaning of the federal APA and the 1981 MSAPA good cause exemptions? Are usual procedures "impracticable" for safety rules applicable to trucks or airplanes and for health rules applicable to drug manufacturers or food producers, where any delay in their adoption and implementation might result in injuries to the public? Is your conclusion altered by the fact that the costs imposed on regulated parties by the implementation of the rules would be very large, or the fact that the rules are based on controversial assumptions about whether they are needed or would be effective, or whether less costly alternatives are available?

Note that if usual procedures may be omitted on the grounds of "impracticability" for *all* health and safety rules because someone may be injured during the time necessary to complete the rulemaking proceedings, that would change the exemption from a special circumstances-good cause exemption to a categorical flat exemption for all health and safety rules. One might think the legislature would have explicitly said so if that was its intention. Do you think that usual procedures should be inapplicable to *all* health and safety rules because of the danger that persons may be injured during the time necessary to complete normal rulemaking proceedings?

When, if ever, should a statutory deadline for the issuance of rules justify the omission of usual rulemaking procedures for those rules? Should the answer depend upon the extent to which the agency diligently attempted to issue the rules in time to satisfy the deadline? Should time constraints caused by the issuing agency's own negligence or avoidable delay be a basis for omitting usual procedures on the ground they are "impracticable" in the circumstances?

3. *"Contrary to the public interest."* When are usual rulemaking procedures "contrary to the public interest" within the meaning of the federal APA and the 1981 MSAPA good cause exemptions? Are notice and comment procedures "contrary to the public interest" for rules regulating financial institutions where the delay involved in their utilization would prevent the rules from becoming effective in time to deal with current economic exigencies or might permit individuals to reap unfair profits or to interfere with the efficacy of the agency's rules? (Note that the "impracticable" exemptive standard and this standard overlap to a large extent.) Could the "contrary to the public interest" standard apply to the issuance of a rule instituting a moratorium on new applications for a licence because of the inability of the agency to process the huge backlog of existing applications?

Could this standard be used as a proper basis for an agency's refusal to follow rulemaking procedures when, and to the extent that, they would occasion delay or expense disproportionate to the public interest? For instance, should there be an exemption under the "contrary to the public interest" standard when an agency is required to issue so many different rules of a particular type during a limited time period and on a recurrent basis that observance of those procedures would cause excessive delay, expense, and frustration of the program's objectives?

4. *Comparing standards.* Which exemptive standard for dispensing with usual notice and comment rulemaking procedures is superior, the "impracticable, unnecessary, or contrary to the public interest" standard contained in § 553(b)(B) of the federal act and § 3–108 of the 1981 MSAPA, or the "imminent peril to the public health, safety, or welfare" standard contained in § 3(b) of the 1961 MSAPA? What is the practical difference between these two standards? Which one is

harder to satisfy? *See* A. Bonfield STATE ADMINISTRATIVE RULE MAKING § 6.8.8 (1986).

Is the meaning of "good cause" in § 553(b)(B) the same as "good cause" in § 553(d)(3), even though the former exemption governing notice and comment procedures contains the additional "impracticable, unnecessary or contrary to the public interest" language while the latter governing delayed effectiveness of rules does not?

Note that the 1981 MSAPA uses the "unnecessary, impracticable, or contrary to the public interest" standard for waiving the notice and comment provisions, and the "imminent peril to the public health, safety, or welfare" standard for waiving the delayed effective date provisions. *See* 1981 MSAPA §§ 3–108(a), 3–115(b)(2)(iv). Which rulemaking requirements should be easier to waive for good cause, those dealing with advance notice and public opportunity to comment, or those prescribing a delayed effective date? Should the good cause standard for these purposes be identical?

5. *Class exemptions.* Do the good cause exemptions contained in the federal act and the 1981 MSAPA permit agencies to exempt *an entire class* of rules from usual procedures with a single finding for the whole class? Or is the purpose of good cause exemptions to require a particularized assessment of the circumstances surrounding each individual rulemaking for which such an exemption is claimed? If class exemptions should be permitted under these good cause exemptions, what criteria should be employed to assess the propriety of any such class exemption?

6. *Burden of persuasion.* On whom should the burden of persuasion rest with respect to the propriety of an agency's issuance of rules on the basis of the good cause exemption? Note that the federal APA is silent on this issue. Does that mean the ordinary presumption of regularity answers the question? On whom does § 3–108(b) of the 1981 MSAPA place the burden of persuasion with respect to this issue? Practically speaking, does the placement of the burden of persuasion on this issue make much difference? Should a court use the balancing analysis of *Mathews v. Eldridge,* § 2.3, *supra,* to decide whether notice and comment should have been provided? Or is the purpose of the good cause exemptions different from that of due process? *See* Jordan, "The Administrative Procedure Act's 'Good Cause' Exemption," 36 Admin.L.Rev. 113, 163 (1984).

7. *Partial or complete exemption.* If an opportunity for public comment on a proposed rule is "impracticable" or "contrary to the public interest," but prior publication of notice of an intention to adopt the rule is not, may the agency omit the published notice as well as the opportunity for public comment? Is the language of the federal act as clear as the language of the 1981 MSAPA on this point? Should agencies be exempted from *all* usual procedural requirements just because *some* of those requirements should be waived for good cause?

8. *Post hoc rulemaking proceedings.* The permanence of rules issued under the federal good cause exemptions without usual procedural protections has been a subject of complaint. As a result, the Administrative Conference recommended that whenever an agency properly relies upon the good cause exemption because prior notice and comment were "impracticable" or "contrary to the public interest," it should provide the public an opportunity for post-promulgation comment to explore errors or oversights in the contents of the rule. *See* ACUS, "The 'Good Cause' Exemption from APA Rulemaking Requirements," Recommendation 83–2, 1 C.F.R. § 305.83–2. Was this recommendation necessary in light of the right to petition created by § 553(e)? Was the Administrative Conference right in urging such post hoc rulemaking proceedings in *every* situation where the "impracticable" or "contrary to the public interest" standard is utilized? Should a triggering device in the form of some required showing be necessary before an agency is required to hold such a post hoc proceeding?

The new MSAPA adopts a different solution to this problem. Read 1981 MSAPA § 3–108(c). Is the 1981 MSAPA solution superior to the post hoc rulemaking proceedings advocated by the Administrative Conference? Is the new MSAPA approach unsound because the public officials who have the authority to force post hoc rulemaking proceedings on an agency may not be sufficiently responsive to the needs of politically powerless individuals or groups?

Unlike the federal act and 1981 MSAPA, which allow permanent rules to be issued on the basis of their good cause exemptions, § 3(b) of the 1961 MSAPA provides that rules issued on the basis of its good cause exemption "may be effective for a period of not longer than 120 days [renewable once for a period not exceeding _____ days], but the adoption of an identical rule" through usual procedures during that period is not precluded. Is this solution to the permanence of rules issued without usual procedures on the basis of the good cause exemption sound?

Which approach to this problem is best, that found in the federal act, the 1981 MSAPA, or the 1961 MSAPA? Is there another approach which is better than any of them? *See* A. Bonfield, STATE ADMINISTRATIVE RULE MAKING § 6.8.9 (1986).

9. *Remedy.* Assume an agency, in reliance on the good cause exceptions, adopted rules without notice and comment and without a deferred effective date. A person adversely affected by the rule seeks judicial review and persuades a court that good cause was not present. However, the rule is substantively valid and has been relied upon by many persons. The agency is certain to readopt it. Should the court invalidate the rules? Should the invalidation take effect at the time of the court's decision, or thirty days later, or should it apply retroactively? Should invalidation be for the benefit of the plaintiff or for everyone similarly situated? *See* Jordan, "The Administrative Proce-

dure Act's 'Good Cause' Exemption," 36 Admin.L.Rev. 113, 166–68 (1984).

10. *Problem.* The Fair Labor Standards Act prohibits child labor but allows the Secretary of Labor to grant applications by farmers to employ children in short-season agricultural harvesting. The Secretary validly adopted a rule providing that children could not enter berry fields that had been treated with Captan (a pesticide) within three days of spraying. Under that rule, the Secretary granted an application by Smith Farms to employ children to pick berries on fields sprayed with Captan one week before harvesting.

Two days later, the Secretary received a study that concluded that Captan residues were dangerous to children regardless of when spraying had occurred. Without any prior notice and comment (but after informal communication with both farmer and farmworker organizations), the Secretary amended the rule. Under the amendment, children could not be employed on fields that had been sprayed with Captan within the preceding year. This rule was effective immediately. Under authority of the amended rule, the Secretary revoked Smith Farms' permit. As a result, Smith Farms is unable to obtain a substitute labor supply in time to harvest the berries and fears the loss of its entire crop. Smith Farms vehemently disputes the correctness of the Captan study.

It seeks an immediate court order restoring its permit. How should the court rule? *See Washington State Farm Bureau v. Marshall,* 625 F.2d 296, 307 (9th Cir.1980); *National Ass'n of Farmworkers Org. v. Marshall,* 628 F.2d 604, 620–22 (D.C.Cir.1980).

§ 6.5 REGULATORY ANALYSIS

A regulatory analysis is a procedural device calculated to ensure that agency rulemaking is well-reasoned and results in a product whose benefits outweighs its costs. Such an analysis aids the careful consideration of the desirability of particular rules by structuring agency consideration of their costs and benefits, their advantages and disadvantages, and the various alternatives available. Regulatory analyses also help to focus public attention on, and public discussion of, proposed rules in a manner that should improve the ultimate agency decision-making process.

Read 1981 MSAPA § 3–105. Compare the following Executive Order adopted by President Reagan shortly after he took office.

EXECUTIVE ORDER 12,291
46 Fed.Reg. 13,193 (1981).

Section 1. Definitions. For the purposes of this Order: . . .

(b) "Major rule" means any regulation that is likely to result in:

(1) An annual effect on the economy of $100 million or more;

(2) A major increase in costs or prices for consumers, individual industries, Federal, State, or local government agencies, or geographic regions; or

(3) Significant adverse effects on competition, employment, investment, productivity, innovation, or on the ability of United States-based enterprises to compete with foreign-based enterprises in domestic or export markets. . . .

Section 2. General Requirements. In promulgating new regulations, reviewing existing regulations, and developing legislative proposals concerning regulation, all agencies, to the extent permitted by law, shall adhere to the following requirements:

(a) Administrative decisions shall be based on adequate information concerning the need for and consequences of proposed government action;

(b) Regulatory action shall not be undertaken unless the potential benefits to society for the regulation outweigh the potential costs to society;

(c) Regulatory objectives shall be chosen to maximize the net benefits to society;

(d) Among alternative approaches to any given regulatory objective, the alternative involving the least net cost to society shall be chosen; and

(e) Agencies shall set regulatory priorities with the aim of maximizing the aggregate net benefits to society, taking into account the condition of the particular industries affected by regulations, the condition of the national economy, and other regulatory actions contemplated for the future.

Section 3. Regulatory Impact Analysis and Review.

(a) In order to implement Section 2 of this Order, each agency shall, in connection with every major rule, prepare, and to the extent permitted by law consider, a Regulatory Impact Analysis. . . .

(d) To permit each proposed major rule to be analyzed in light of the requirements stated in Section 2 of this Order, each preliminary and final Regulatory Impact Analysis shall contain the following information:

(1) A description of the potential benefits of the rule, including any beneficial effects that cannot be quantified in monetary terms, and the identification of those likely to receive the benefits;

(2) A description of the potential costs of the rule, including any adverse effects that cannot be quantified in monetary terms, and the identification of those likely to bear the costs;

(3) A determination of the potential net benefits of the rule, including an evaluation of effects that cannot be quantified in monetary terms;

(4) A description of alternative approaches that could substantially achieve the same regulatory goal at lower cost, together with an analysis of this potential benefit and costs and a brief explanation of the legal reasons why such alternatives, if proposed, could not be adopted; and

(5) Unless covered by the description required under paragraph (4) of this subsection, an explanation of any legal reasons why the rule cannot be based on the requirements set forth in Section 2 of this Order. . . .

Section 4. Regulatory Review. Before approving any final major rule, each agency shall:

(a) Make a determination that the regulation is clearly within the authority delegated by law and consistent with congressional intent, and include in the Federal Register at the time of promulgation a memorandum of law supporting that determination.

(b) Make a determination that the factual conclusions upon which the rule is based have substantial support in the agency record, viewed as a whole, with full attention to public comments in general and the comments of persons directly affected by the rule in particular. . . .

Section 9. Judicial Review. This Order is intended only to improve the internal management of the Federal government, and is not intended to create any right or benefit, substantive or procedural, enforceable at law by a party against the United States, its agencies, its officers or any person. The determinations made by agencies under Section 4 of this Order, and any Regulatory Impact Analyses for any rule, shall be made part of the whole record of agency action in connection with the rule. . . .

Notes and Questions

1. *Purposes of regulatory analysis.* The analyses required by Executive Order 12,291 and the 1981 MSAPA ensure explicit consideration of several issues in relation to proposed rules. Should these issues have already been addressed in an agency's initial determination of whether to propose a rule for adoption? Or is it unrealistic to expect agencies to have carefully and systematically considered all such issues prior to the time they propose rules for adoption? Is there a difference between the typical federal agency when compared to the typical state agency in this regard?

Specification of the costs and benefits of proposed rules to affected classes enables both interested persons outside the agency and agency staff to ascertain whether any groups will be unfairly burdened or benefited. The evaluation of alternatives also facilitates such a fairness determination, because it may reveal that there are less instrusive and less costly procedures available to accomplish the desired objectives. On the other hand, the lack of any practical alternatives may suggest that the proposed rules are desirable. The evaluation of alternatives also promotes public satisfaction by helping to demonstrate to the citizens at large that, in light of the circumstances, the course of action proposed is justifiable.

An evaluation of the costs and benefits of proposed rules in comparison to the costs and benefits of *inaction* promotes efficiency and facilitates rational consideration of the desirability of such proposals. The objectives of proposed rules may be desirable, but the costs in achieving them may outweigh their benefits. There also may be situations in which the costs of proposed rules seem, when viewed in isolation, to be exceptionally large, but a comparison of the costs of those proposals as compared to the costs of agency inaction may reveal that the costs of inaction would be even greater.

2. *Statutory requirements.* The federal APA does not require a regulatory analysis in rulemaking. The same is true of most state APAs. However, in recent years a substantial number of states have amended their APAs to require such analyses, sometimes called impact statements, in specified circumstances. *See* A. Bonfield, STATE ADMINISTRATIVE RULE MAKING, 212 n. 22–26 (1986).

Congress has also provided for limited forms of such analyses in specified situations. The National Environmental Policy Act requires all agencies to include in proposals for "major Federal actions significantly affecting the quality of the human environment" a detailed environmental impact statement addressing that subject and applying the particular substantive criteria set forth in that Act. *See* 42 U.S.C. §§ 4321–4361. The Regulatory Flexibility Act requires agencies to consider and to embody in an analysis the impact of proposed rules on "small entities," including "small businesses," "small (not-for-profit) organizations," and "small governmental jurisdictions." *See* 5 U.S.C. §§ 601–612. President Reagan also has ordered agencies to prepare a Federalism Assessment that considers the impact of agency action on state authority. Exec.Order 12,612, 3 C.F.R. 252 (1988).

3. *Triggering regulatory analysis.* The execution of regulatory analyses with any degree of care or technical proficiency can be burdensome and expensive. In 1982 the Comptroller General estimated that each required analysis under Executive Order 12,291 cost an average of $212,000. *See* R. Pierce, S. Shapiro, and P. Verkuil, ADMINISTRATIVE LAW AND PROCESS § 9.6, 521 n. 131, (citing General Accounting Office, IMPROVED QUALITY, ADEQUATE RESOURCES, AND CONSISTENT OVERSIGHT NEEDED IF REGULATORY ANALYSIS IS TO HELP CONTROL COSTS OF REGULATION 3 (1982)).

Executive Order 12,291 contains a rough, built-in cost-benefit determination for invoking the regulatory analysis mechanism. In § 3 it requires a regulatory analysis only for "major rules." Is this a satisfactory filtering device to ensure such analyses are employed only where their benefits are likely to exceed their costs? Is the "major rule" definition in § 1(b) sufficiently clear so that the agencies will know when such analyses are required?

Section 3–105(a) of the 1981 MSAPA contains a different filtering mechanism. Is that mechanism preferable to the "major rule" filtering device found in the Executive Order? Should any 300 persons be able to trigger the regulatory analysis requirement? Is it sounder to rely on triggers by the administrative rules review committee, the governor, a political subdivision, or an agency, because they are politically responsible?

By not requiring a regulatory analysis in every rulemaking proceeding, the 1981 MSAPA attempts to balance the benefits of mandatory analysis against the need for agencies to act efficiently. The assumption is that in most instances of state agency rulemaking, the costs of preparing such a formal, detailed regulatory analysis will far exceed the benefits of such an analysis. Do you agree?

Reasons other than monetary cost have been urged as a basis for limiting the circumstances under which a regulatory analysis may be requested:

> A further justification for requiring agencies to prepare a regulatory analysis only under select circumstances is that there is a "large potential for disagreement about the accuracy of its contents." If the regulatory analysis requirement were not limited, opponents of proposed rules could request the issuance of these time-consuming and expensive statements simply to harass agencies, or to delay their rule making without any compensating public benefit. Moreover, if agencies were required to issue such an analysis [upon request] in every instance of rule making, . . . agencies would be likely to compile those statements in a haphazard way, to divert resources to that task from more essential functions, or to de-emphasize policy making by rule in favor of increased law making by ad hoc adjudicatory orders that could subsequently be relied upon as precedent.

A. Bonfield, STATE ADMINISTRATIVE RULE MAKING 214 (1986). Do you agree?

4. *Use of regulatory analyses.* 1981 MSAPA § 3–105(d) ensures public access to regulatory analyses *before* the period of public participation expires. Consequently, the analysis can be used by the public when it files comments on a proposed rule and it may significantly improve the ability of committees to prepare pointed meaningful comments. The regulatory analyses required by the Executive Order, on the other hand, seem intended wholly for the use of the Office of Management and Budget. That Office reviews all proposed rules on behalf of the President in an effort to ensure compliance with the provisions of the Order. Would regulatory analyses be most effective if they were used by members of the public *and* by extra-agency executive authorities prior to the adoption of rules? Note that under 1981 MSAPA § 3–105(a) either the governor or the legislature's administrative rules review committee may require the issuance of such an analysis for a specified proposed rule.

5. *Judicial review of analyses.* On both the federal and state levels, judicial review of regulatory analyses is usually quite limited. As McGowan noted in 1981, "[i]t seems fairly clear that the current mood . . . is to keep the courts out of controversies over the way an agency has gone about performing its regulatory analysis responsibilities." McGowan, "Regulatory Analysis and Judicial Review," 42 Ohio St.L.J. 627, 634 (1981).

There are two principal reasons for limiting judicial review of such analyses. First, since predictions of the type required by such analyses cannot be precise, there will often be arguments over the accuracy of the analysis. Second, judicial review of such analyses can easily be used to harass an agency and to delay agency action. This is particularly true in light of the first point.

Section 9 of Executive Order 12,291 states that its regulatory analysis provisions are not intended to provide new grounds for judicial review, although such an analysis will be part of the whole record available to a court when the merits of a rule are subject to judicial review. *See State of Michigan v. Thomas,* 805 F.2d 176, 187 (6th Cir. 1986) (non-compliance with Executive Order not judicially reviewable); *Center for Auto Safety v. Peck,* 751 F.2d 1336, 1342 (D.C.Cir.1985) (thorough analysis helpful in upholding rule on the merits).

The analysis required by the Regulatory Flexibility Act is also not subject to independent judicial review although that analysis is also part of the whole agency rulemaking record before the court on judicial review of the merits of the rule to which it pertains. 5 U.S.C. § 611 (1982). This means that the analysis will be relevant to the substantive merits of the rule on judicial review, but deficiencies in its contents will not be independent grounds with which to invalidate the rule. *See Small Refiner Lead Phase–Down Task Force v. E.P.A.,* 705 F.2d 506, 537–39 (D.C.Cir.1983) (court cannot review compliance with Regulatory Flexibility Act but can consider material in the analysis in reviewing a rule under the arbitrary and capricious test). Compare the National Environmental Policy Act, note 2, *supra,* where compliance with the environmental impact report requirement is frequently litigated. Total failure to issue a Regulatory Flexibility Analysis in circumstances where such an analysis is required, however, may justify invalidation of the relevant rule by a reviewing court on that basis alone. *See* 126 Cong.Rec. 24,582–84 (Statements of Cong. Broomfield and McDade), 24,579 (statements of Cong. Kastenmeier and Levitas), 24,592–93 (statement of Cong. Butler).

Although § 3–105(f) of the 1981 MSAPA attempts to limit judicial review of regulatory analyses, it does so in a more restricted way. It allows courts to determine whether the agency made a "good faith effort to comply" with regulatory analysis requirements. The Comment to this provision of the 1981 MSAPA explains the meaning of "good faith" in this way:

Since subsection (f) provides that a "good faith effort to comply with the requirements of subsections (a)-(c)" entirely precludes invalidation of the rule "on the ground that the contents of the regulatory analysis are insufficient or inaccurate," "good faith" must be ascertained for this purpose without any judicial evaluation of the actual sufficiency or accuracy of the contents of that regulatory analysis. To ascertain "good faith" for this purpose, therefore, a court should only determine if the analysis was actually issued, and if on its face it actually addresses in some manner all of the points specified in subsections (b)-(c). If so, the sufficiency or accuracy of its contents are not subject to judicial review.

Is the 1981 MSAPA provision limiting judicial review of regulatory analyses superior or inferior to a provision that would simply declare that "the adequacy of the contents of a regulatory analysis are not subject to judicial review?" Does the 1981 MSAPA provision open the door to repetitive litigation over whether the issuing agency actually engaged in a "good faith" effort to comply with the regulatory analysis requirements?

In a number of states with regulatory analysis requirements in their APAs, the statute is silent with respect to the judicial reviewability of the contents of those analyses. This silence may mean that in these states the contents of such analyses are subject to judicial review and that if they are found to be "arbitrary, capricious, or unreasonable" in any respect, the rules to which they pertain may be held to be invalid even though they may be lawful in all other respects. Should those states adopt a provision like § 9 of Executive Order 12,291? Like § 3–105(f) of the 1981 MSAPA?

6. *Required cost-benefit analysis.* Does Executive Order 12,291 go beyond § 3–105 of the 1981 MSAPA because the former seeks to *require* federal agencies subject to the Order to abide by the conclusions of a cost-benefit analysis while the Model Act does not? What is the effect in this regard of the "to the extent permitted by law" language of § 2 of the Executive Order? *See American Textile Mfrs. Inst., Inc. v. Donovan,* 452 U.S. 490, 509 (1981) (Occupational, Safety, and Health Administration may not base rule on cost-benefit analysis). Should agencies be prevented from issuing rules whose costs exceed their benefits as measured by formal cost-benefit analyses? Or should such analyses be used only as tools to aid decisionmaking rather than as formulas that specify required results? Do the answers to these questions depend upon how much confidence you have in the theory and practice of cost-benefit analysis? Do they depend on whether you support a political rather than a technocratic approach to rulemaking?

KELMAN, "COST–BENEFIT ANALYSIS: AN ETHICAL CRITIQUE"

Regulation, Jan.–Feb. 1981, at 33, 33–40.

[T]he answer given by cost-benefit analysis, that actions should be undertaken so as to maximize net benefits, represents one of the classic answers given by moral philosophers—that given by utilitarians. To determine whether an action is right or wrong, utilitarians tote up all the positive consequences of the action in terms of human satisfaction. The act that maximizes attainment of satisfaction under the circumstances is the right act. . . . [However,] some acts whose costs are greater than their benefits may be morally right and, contrariwise, some acts whose benefits are greater than their costs may be morally wrong.

This does not mean that the question whether benefits are greater than costs is morally irrelevant. Few would claim such. Indeed, for a broad range of individual and social decisions, whether an act's benefits outweigh its costs is a sufficient question to ask. But not for all such decisions. These may involve situations where certain duties—duties not to lie, break promises, or kill, for example—make an act wrong, even if it would result in an excess of benefits over costs. Or they may involve instances where people's rights are at stake. . . .

We do not do cost-benefit analyses of freedom of speech or trial by jury. . . . The notion of human rights involves the idea that people may make certain claims to be allowed to act in certain ways or to be treated in certain ways, even if the sum of benefits achieved thereby does not outweigh the sum of costs. . . .

In addition to questions involving duties and rights, there is a final sort of question where, in my view, the issue of whether benefits outweigh costs should not govern moral judgment. I noted earlier that, for the common run of questions facing individuals and societies, it is possible to begin and end our judgment simply by finding out if the benefits of the contemplated act outweigh the costs. This very fact means that one way to show the great importance, or value, attached to an area is to say that decisions involving the area should not be determined by cost-benefit calculations. This applies, I think, to the view many environmentalists have of decisions involving our natural environment. When officials are deciding what level of pollution will harm certain vulnerable people—such as asthmatics or the elderly—while not harming others, one issue involved may be the right of those people not to be sacrificed on the altar of somewhat higher living standards for the rest of us. But more broadly than this, many environmentalists fear that subjecting decisions about clean air or water to the cost-benefit tests that determine the general run of decisions removes those matters from the realm of specially valued things. In order for cost-benefit calculations to be performed the way they are supposed to be, all costs and benefits must be expressed in a common measure, typically dollars, including things not normally bought and sold on markets, and to which dollar prices are therefore not attached. The most dramatic example of such things is human life itself; but many of the other benefits achieved or preserved by environmental policy—such as peace and quiet, fresh-smelling air, swimmable rivers, spectacular vistas—are not traded on markets either. . . .

A second problem is that the attempts of economists to measure people's willingness to pay for non-marketed things assume that there is no difference between the price a person would require for *giving up* something to which he has a preexisting right and the price he would pay to *gain* something to which he enjoys no right. . . .

Available evidence suggests that most people would insist on being paid far more to assent to a worsening of their situation than they would be willing to pay to improve their situation. . . .

Third, the efforts of economists to impute willingness to pay invariably involve bundled goods exchanged in *private* transactions. Those who use figures garnered from such analysis to provide guidance for *public* decisions assume no difference between how people value certain things in private individual transactions and how they would wish those same things to be valued in public collective decisions. . . . [However] public, social decisions provide an opportunity to give certain things a higher valuation than we choose, for one reason or another, to give them in our private activities. . . .

Finally, one may oppose the effort to place prices on a non-market thing and hence in effect incorporate it into the market system out of a fear that the very act of doing so will reduce the thing's perceived value. To place a price on the benefit may, in other words, reduce the value of that benefit. Cost-benefit analysis thus may be like the thermometer that, when placed in a liquid to be measured, itself changes the liquid's temperature. . . .

My own judgment is that modest efforts to assess levels of benefits and costs are justified, although I do not believe that government agencies ought to sponsor efforts to put dollar prices on non-market things. I also do not believe that the cry for more cost-benefit analysis in regulation is, on the whole, justified.

Notes and Questions

1. *In praise of cost-benefit analysis.* Kelman presents a number of ethical problems with cost-benefit analyses. Would a decisionmaking process that did not include such analyses more thoroughly protect the interest of the public? Kelman has been criticized for proposing a system of analysis that has more difficulties than the system he criticized.

Kelman's proposal is to adopt an ethical system that balances conflicts between certain unspecified "duties" and "rights" according to "deliberate reflection." But who is to do the reflecting, and on whose behalf? His guide places no clear limits on the actions of regulatory agencies. Rather than enhancing the connections between individual values and state decisions, such a vague guideline threatens to sever them. Is there a common moral standard that every regulator will magically and independently arrive at through "deliberate reflection"? We doubt it. Far more likely is a system in which bureaucratic decisions reflect the preferences, not of the citizens, but of those in a peculiar position to influence decisions. What concessions to special interests cannot be disguised by claiming that it is degrading to make explicit the trade-offs reflected in the decision? What individual crusade cannot be rationalized by an appeal to "public values" that "rise above" values revealed by individual choices?

Butters, Calfee & Ippolito, "Defending Cost–Benefit Analysis," Regulation, Mar.–Apr. 1981, at 41, 42.

2. *Purpose of analysis.* Executive Order 12,291 states that its purpose, and accordingly the purpose of the regulatory analyses it requires, is to "reduce the burdens of existing and future regulations, increase agency accountability for regulatory actions . . . and insure well-reasoned regulations." Does this support Kelman's premise that the aim of cost-benefit analysis is to maximize the attainment of human satisfaction? DeLong states:

> The decision to use cost-benefit analysis by no means implies adoption of the reductionist utilitarianism described by Kelman. It is based instead on the pragmatic conclusion that any value system one adopts is more likely to be promoted if one knows something about the consequences of the choices to be made. The effort to put dollar values on noneconomic benefits is nothing more than an effort to find some common measure for things that are not easily comparable when, in the real world, choice must be made. Its object is not to write a computer program but to improve the quality of difficult social choices under conditions of uncertainty, and no sensible analyst lets himself become the prisoner of the numbers.

DeLong, "Defending Cost–Benefit Analysis," Regulation, Mar.–Apr. 1981, at 39. The Comment to § 3–105 of the 1981 MSAPA supports the approach taken by DeLong. It states that one of the purposes of regulatory analysis is to "assure sound agency consideration of the desirability of a rule."

3. *Non-monetary factors.* Throughout his critique of cost-benefit analyses, Kelman suggests that cost-benefit analyses exclude consideration of those things specially valued and focus solely on monetary analysis. Is this an accurate interpretation of the regulatory analyses authorized by Executive Order 12,291 and § 3–105 of the 1981 MSAPA? Section 3(d) of the Executive Order specifically provides for consideration of beneficial and adverse effects "that cannot be quantified in monetary terms." The 1981 MSAPA also makes specific provision for

including in such analyses impacts of proposed rules, "economic *or otherwise.*" *See* § 3–105(b)(2); *see also* Solow, "Defending Cost–Benefit Analysis," Regulation, Mar.–Apr. 1981, at 40, 41 (cost-benefit analysis as it is applied today invariably captures the ethical and moral principles that Kelman values).

4. *Criticisms of analysis.* Cost-benefit analysis requirements have been criticized on the ground they exceed the practical capacity of the administrative process.

> [C]ost-benefit analysis generates a number of . . . doubts. As is often asked, is it really possible to determine in advance all of the material consequences of all possible alternative means to all reasonable intermediate goals that would further some given ultimate end, and to assess these various consequences in terms of some common standards of "costs" and "benefits"? The theory of cost-benefit analysis, taken to its extreme, would require such a herculean undertaking in order to arrive at a truly rational result. However, it commonly is noted that, at least as a practical matter, cost-benefit analysis must take for granted some reasonably limited set of preconceived ends and means, and their selection will depend on choices that themselves are not founded on any cost-benefit analysis.
>
> Moreover, assuming a limited range of preconceived ends and means, will it actually be possible to measure with accuracy the benefits as well as the costs of the consequences of different possible agency actions? One must establish some common denominator in terms of which to assess or assign weights to various outcomes. However, the outcomes may have significantly differing characteristics and thus may not be readily susceptible to reduction to a common standard of measurement. Also, it frequently is observed that cost-benefit analysis may be systematically skewed by the particular difficulties of predicting and assigning values to the benefits, as opposed to the costs, of rules. Benefits, such as cleaner air or water, may be more difficult to predict and measure simply because of limits in our scientific understanding, for instance of the effects on human health and the environment of varying degrees of improvement in air or water quality. Also, benefits are especially difficult to state in quantifiable terms since they commonly are diffuse and long-term.

Sargentich, "The Reform of the American Administrative Process: The Contemporary Debate," 1984 Wis.L.Rev. 385, 416–17. *See also* McGarity, "Regulatory Analysis and Regulatory Reform," 65 Tex.L.Rev. 1243, 1271–1317 (1987).

Do these criticisms suggest that regulatory analyses requirements should be abandoned? In light of the moral and practical critiques by Kelman and Sargentich, and the large burdens associated with such analyses, do their costs outweigh their benefits?

Does Weidenbaum provide a specially good reason for the selective use of regulatory analyses in administrative rulemaking?

The motive for incorporating benefit-cost analysis into public decision making is to lead to a more efficient allocation of government resources by subjecting the public sector to the same type of quantitative constraints as those in the private sector. In making an investment decision business executives compare the total costs to be incurred with the total revenues expected to accrue. If the expected costs exceed the revenues, the investment is usually not considered worthwhile.

The government agency decision maker, however, usually does not face such constraints. If the costs to society of an action by an agency exceed the benefits, that situation has no immediate adverse impact on the agency, as would be the case if the private business executive makes a decision error. In requiring agencies to perform benefit-cost analysis, the aim is to make the government's decision-making process more effective, presumably eliminating those regulatory actions whose net benefits are negative. This result is not ensured by benefit-cost analysis, since political and other important but non-quantifiable considerations may dominate and result in actions which are not economically efficient, but which are desired on grounds of equity or income distribution. Yet benefit-cost analysis can provide valuable information for government decision makers.

M. Weidenbaum, BUSINESS, GOVERNMENT, AND THE PUBLIC 217 (3d ed. 1986).

5. *Effectiveness of Executive Order 12,291.* Opinions vary on whether the Order significantly improved the regulatory process (by producing more efficient rules) or lightened the load of regulation (by producing less onerous and fewer rules).

Studies of the Order in practice are inconclusive. They indicate that there was relatively little overt conflict between the agencies and the Office of Management and Budget (OMB). Very few rules were disapproved by OMB. Thus by the end of 1982, there had been 5,436 submissions to OMB of which only 2% were rejected, 1% were withdrawn, and 8% were approved after minor changes. About 2% of the rules were "major" and OMB allowed agencies to dispense with the preparation of regulatory impact analyses in a number of those cases. Weidenbaum, "Regulatory Reform under the Reagan Administration," in G. Eads & M. Fix, eds., THE REAGAN REGULATORY STRATEGY 25 (1984).

What accounts for the relatively small number of rejections by OMB? One reason is that OMB had inadequate resources to do much full-scale regulatory analysis. By necessity, it could target very few rules. In addition, President Reagan's agency heads were sympathetic with his point of view; they sought to produce regulations consistent with the Order. There were, however, a couple of well-publicized confrontations between agencies and OMB—and the agencies ultimately prevailed. *See* G. Eads and M. Fix, RELIEF OR REFORM? REAGAN'S REGULATORY DILEMMA, 133–35 (1984).

The real question—impossible to answer definitively—is whether, and to what extent, the review process made a difference. Did the rules differ from the form they would have taken if there had been no process? Because OMB did not communicate its objections or suggestions in writing, it left no tracks; it is difficult to know what OMB's input was and whether the agencies paid attention to it. Certainly, no agency sought a conflict with OMB; undoubtedly they tried to draw their proposed and final rules in ways that would tend to minimize any chance of conflict. It seems reasonable to suppose that a good many rules would have been different (i.e., more costly, more protective) if the Order had not been in place. Moreover, it is likely that some rules never saw the light of day at all after OMB criticized them before they were ever publicly proposed.

In any event, the Reagan administration claimed that initiatives of its Task Force on Regulatory Relief, plus the Executive Order review process, resulted in savings to industry of nine to eleven billion dollars in initial investment costs and ten billion dollars in annually recurring costs and an annual savings of three hundred million hours on paperwork. Weidenbaum, *supra.* Eads and Fix are skeptical of these estimates, however. According to Eads and Fix there were some serious problems with the Order in practice. Several have already been mentioned. One was that OMB lacked the resources to do much economic analysis on its own or to clarify the many uncertainties (for example in defining a "major rule" or in setting uniform figures for the value of saving a life). Another was the uneven quality of economic analysis performed by the agencies and the extreme subjectivity of the analyses; it is difficult indeed to place a dollar figure on the value of a single life, on recreational benefits, on cleaner air, or on preserving wildlife. Still another was OMB's refusal to communicate its objections or suggestions in writing, thus making assessment of the process very difficult.

The General Accounting Office criticized the quality of economic analysis submitted to OMB and the quality of OMB's scrutiny of the material submitted. *See* General Accounting Office, IMPROVED QUALITY, ADEQUATE RESOURCES, AND CONSISTENT OVERSIGHT NEEDED IF REGULATORY ANALYSIS IS TO HELP CONTROL COST OF REGULATIONS (1982).

A particularly serious objection to the Order in practice is that it undercut the APA notice and comment procedure. As it has evolved, the notice and comment procedure entails an open exchange of views between private parties and agency staff. But OMB's vitally important submissions were not on the record so nobody could respond to them and they could not be considered by a court upon judicial review of the rule. In addition, private parties who wished to have influence on the form of the rule were able to communicate ex parte with OMB. That meant that OMB might serve as a conduit through which the views and factual submissions of outsiders were brought to the agencies without going on the public record—or at least, so it seemed. OMB sent a memo to the agencies to the effect that any factual material coming from outsiders to OMB would be submitted to the agencies to appear in public files, but it is not clear whether this policy was enforced.

§ 6.6 AGENCY DECISIONMAKERS, EX PARTE COMMUNICATIONS, BIAS, AND PERSONAL INVOLVEMENT

This section focuses on the process of decision in rulemaking proceedings and on objections that interested persons outside the agency might lodge against those proceedings. It considers ex parte contacts by outsiders with the agency, bias of the agency heads, and a requirement that the agency head be personally familiar with the record before deciding. Section 3.3, *supra,* focused on similar problems as they arise in *adjudication*; the solution to these problems required tradeoffs between the judicial and institutional approaches to decisionmaking. Is rulemaking different from adjudication for this purpose? Should rulemaking be purely an institutional product? Or should the decisionmaking process in rulemaking borrow from both the institutional and judicial models?

§ 6.6.1 EX PARTE COMMUNICATIONS AND POLITICAL INFLUENCE IN RULEMAKING

During the course of every rulemaking proceeding, an agency acquires a voluminous amount of material concerning the proposed rule. The compilation of this material is known as the rulemaking record. The record serves three basic functions: it aids public participation, it provides materials helpful to the agency in making a decision, and it facilitates judicial review of the agency decision. Although the rulemaking record serves these important functions, the federal APA, the 1961 MSAPA and the many state acts based on that Model Act, are silent with respect to the creation and maintenance of any official agency record in rulemaking. Section 3–112(b) of the 1981 MSAPA, on the other hand, specifically provides for a rulemaking record and specifies the materials it must include.

To what extent may persons outside an agency engage in off-the-record, ex parte communications with an agency about a proposed rule? In *formal* rulemaking the answer is clear. Since such rulemaking must be conducted according to the requirements of §§ 556–57 of the federal APA, ex parte communications are forbidden in that kind of rulemaking. *See* federal APA § 557(d). On the other hand, in *informal* rulemaking, the assumption was that the federal APA neither banned ex parte communications nor required the inclusion of such communications in the agency rulemaking record. Drafters of the APA apparently believed that any general prohibition on ex parte communications in informal rulemaking would be inappropriate because they had decided that agency decisions in such proceedings need not be based on any official evidentiary record. It has been noted that the APA does not

> require the formulation of rules upon the exclusive basis of any "record" made in informal rulemaking proceedings . . . . Accordingly, . . . an agency is free to formulate rules [in informal notice and comment rulemaking] upon the basis of materials in its files and the knowledge and experience of the agency, in addition to the materials adduced in public rulemaking proceedings.

U.S. Dept. of Justice, ATTORNEY GENERAL'S MANUAL ON THE ADMINISTRATIVE PROCEDURE ACT 31–32 (1947).

HOME BOX OFFICE, INC. v. FCC
567 F.2d 9 (D.C.Cir.1977), *cert. denied,* 434 U.S. 829 (1977).

Before WRIGHT and MACKINNON, CIRCUIT JUDGES, and WEIGEL, DISTRICT JUDGE.

PER CURIAM:

[This case involved a challenge to FCC rules that limited the types of programming and advertising that cable television and subscription television could run in order to prevent those types of television from luring away popular program material from free broadcast television.]

We have recently had occasion to review at length our obligation to set aside agency [rulemaking] action which is "arbitrary, capricious, an abuse of discretion, or otherwise not in accordance with law", 5 U.S.C. § 706(2)(A). . . .

From this survey of the case law emerge two dominant principles. First, an agency proposing informal rulemaking has an obligation to make its views known to the public in a concrete and focused form so as to make criticism or formulation of alternatives possible. Second, . . . [The record must] enable us to see what major issues of policy were ventilated by the informal proceedings and why the agency reacted to them as it did. . . .

It is apparently uncontested that a number of participants before the Commission sought out individual commissioners or Commission employees for the purpose of discussing *ex parte* and in confidence the merits of the rules under review here. In fact, the Commission itself solicited such communications in its notices of proposed rulemaking. . . .

. . . It is important to note that many contacts occurred in the crucial period between the close of oral argument . . . and the adoption of the *First Report and Order* . . . when the rulemaking record should have been closed while the Commission was deciding what rules to promulgate. The information submitted to this court by the Commission indicates that during this period broadcast interests met some 18 times with Commission personnel, cable interests some nine times, motion picture and sports interests five times each, and "public interest" intervenors not at all.

Although it is impossible to draw any firm conclusions about the effect of *ex parte* presentations upon the ultimate shape of the pay cable rules, the evidence is certainly consistent with often-voiced claims of undue industry influence over Commission proceedings, and we are particularly concerned that the final shaping of the rules we are reviewing here may have been by compromise among the contending industry forces, rather than by exercise of the independent discretion in the public interest the Communications Act vests in individual commissioners. . . .

Even the possibility that there is here one administrative record for the public and this court and another for the Commission and those "in the know" is intolerable. Whatever the law may have been in the past, there can now be no doubt that implicit in the decision to treat the promulgation of rules as a "final" event in an ongoing process of administration is an assumption that an act of reasoned judgment has occurred, an assumption which further contemplates the existence of a body of material—documents, comments, transcripts, and statements in various forms declaring agency expertise or policy—with reference to which such judgment was exercised. Against this material, "the full administrative record that was before [an agency official] at the time he made his decision," *Citizens to Preserve Overton Park, Inc. v. Volpe, supra,* 401 U.S. at 420, it is the obligation of this court to test the actions of the Commission for arbitrariness or inconsistency with delegated authority. Yet here agency secrecy stands between us and fulfillment of our obligation. As a practical matter, *Overton Park's* mandate means that the public record must reflect what representations were made to an agency so that relevant information supporting or refuting those representations may be brought to the attention of the reviewing courts by persons participating in agency proceedings. This course is obviously foreclosed if communications are made to the agency in secret and the agency itself does not disclose the information presented. Moreover, where, as here, an agency justifies its actions by reference only to information in the public file while failing to disclose the substance of other relevant information that has been presented to it, a reviewing court cannot presume that the agency has acted properly, *Citizens to Preserve Overton Park, Inc. v. Volpe, supra,* 401 U.S. at 415, 419–420, but must treat the agency's justifications as a fictional account of the actual decisionmaking process and must perforce find its actions arbitrary.

The failure of the public record in this proceeding to disclose all the information made available to the Commission is not the only inadequacy we find here. Even if the Commission had disclosed to this court the substance of what was said to it *ex parte,* it would still be difficult to judge the truth of what the Commission asserted it knew about the television industry because we would not have the benefit of an adversarial discussion among the parties. The importance of such discussion to the proper functioning of the agency decisionmaking and judicial review processes is evident in our cases. We have insisted, for example, that information in agency files or consultants' reports which the agency has identified as relevant to the proceeding be disclosed to the parties for adversarial comment. Similarly, we have required agencies to set out their thinking in notices of proposed rulemaking. This requirement not only allows adversarial critique of the agency but is perhaps one of the few ways that the public may be apprised of what the agency thinks it knows in its capacity as a repository of expert opinion. From a functional standpoint, we see no difference between assertions of fact and expert opinion tendered by the public, as here, and that generated internally in an agency: each may be biased, inaccurate, or incomplete—failings which adversary comment may illuminate. Indeed, the potential for bias in private presentations in rulemakings which resolve "conflicting private claims to a valuable privilege," *Sangamon Valley Television Corp. v. United States*, 269 F.2d 211, 224, seems to us greater than in cases where we have reversed agencies for failure to disclose internal studies. We do not understand the rulemaking procedures adopted by the Commission to be inconsistent with these views since those procedures provide for a dialogue among interested parties through provisions for comment, reply-comment, and subsequent oral argument. What we do find baffling is why the Commission, which apparently recognizes that ready availability of private contacts saps the efficacy of the public proceedings, nonetheless continues the practice of allowing public and private comments to exist side by side.

Equally important is the inconsistency of secrecy with fundamental notions of fairness implicit in due process and with the ideal of reasoned decisionmaking on the merits which undergirds all of our administrative law. . . .

From what has been said above, it should be clear that information gathered *ex parte* from the public which becomes relevant to a rulemaking will have to be disclosed at some time. On the other hand, we recognize that informal contacts between agencies and the public are the "bread and butter" of the process of administration and are completely appropriate so long as they do not frustrate judicial review or raise serious questions of fairness. Reconciliation of these considerations in a manner which will reduce procedural uncertainty leads us to conclude that communications which are received prior to issuance of a formal notice of rulemaking do not, in general, have to be put in a public file. Of course, if the information contained in such a communication forms the basis for agency action, then, under well established principles, that information must be disclosed to the public in some form. Once a notice of proposed rulemaking has been issued, however, any agency official or employee who is or may reasonably be expected to be involved in the decisional process of the rulemaking proceeding, should "refus[e] to discuss matters relating to the disposition of a [rulemaking proceeding] with any interested private party, or an attorney or agent for any such party, prior to the [agency's] decision . . . ." If *ex parte* contacts nonetheless occur, we think that any written document or a summary of any oral communication must be placed in the public file established for each rulemaking docket immediately after the communication is received so that interested parties may comment thereon. . . .

MACKINNON, CIRCUIT JUDGE, concurring specially:

This particular rulemaking proceeding began with a number of petitions by broadcast interests for reconsideration of earlier Docket orders and requested that certain existing rules of a highly restrictive nature be applied to all cablecasting programming. . . .

I agree that this [ban on ex parte communications] is the proper rule to apply in this case because the rulemaking undeniably involved competitive interests of great monetary value and conferred preferential advantages on vast segments of the broadcast industry to the detriment of other competing business interests. The rule as issued was in effect an adjudication of the respective rights of the parties vis-a-vis each other. And since that is the nature of the case and controversy that we are deciding and to which our opinion is limited, I would make it clear that that is all we are deciding. I would not make an excessively broad statement to include *dictum* that could be interpreted to cover the entire universe of informal rulemaking. There are so many situations where the application of such a broad rule would be inappropriate that we should not paint with such a broad brush.

Notes and Questions

1. *Rulemaking or adjudication.* Recall the treatment of ex parte contacts in § 3.3, *supra.* Even before they were banned by federal APA § 557(d), the federal courts strictly prohibited ex parte contacts by outsiders with agency adjudicatory decisionmakers. Several of those cases involved the FCC. *WKAT, Inc. v. FCC,* 296 F.2d 375 (D.C.Cir. 1961), cert. denied 368 U.S. 841 (1961). Do the reasons for prohibiting ex parte contacts in adjudication apply with the same force to rulemaking? Are there significant reasons to permit ex parte contacts in rulemaking that do not apply to adjudication?

Both the majority and concurring opinions in *Home Box Office* refer to *Sangamon Valley Television Corp. v. United States,* 269 F.2d 221 (D.C.Cir.1959). *Sangamon* was an FCC rulemaking proceeding that involved the allocation of television channels between two communities. Thus it involved a struggle between the competing interests of two potential licensees. Judge MacKinnon's concurrence suggests that *Home Box Office* involves a quasi-adjudicatory dispute similar to *Sangamon.* Is *Sangamon* distinguishable from *Home Box Office?*

Both *Sangamon* and *Home Box Office* involve ex parte contacts made after the public comment period closed. Does it matter whether the comments are made before or after the closing of the comment period?

2. *Vermont Yankee.* Does *Vermont Yankee,* § 6.3, *supra,* overrule *Home Box Office?* Does it undercut some but not all of the rationales of *Home Box Office? See* ACUS, A GUIDE TO FEDERAL AGENCY RULEMAKING, 163 (1983). Is a prohibition on ex parte contacts in rulemaking necessary so that on judicial review a court can examine the "full administrative record" as required by *Citizens to Preserve Overton Park, Inc. v. Volpe,* 401 U.S. 402, 420 (1971)? Even if *Vermont Yankee* does overrule *Home Box Office,* should agencies follow the admonitions of that case as a matter of sound administrative policy?

3. *Ulterior motives.* The court in *Home Box Office* seems to be concerned that the rulemaking record on judicial review will not reflect an agency's actual basis of decision unless it contains all ex parte communications to the agency. Is this concern limited to the problem of ex parte communications or is it a problem inherent in all administrative decisionmaking processes?

Nathanson notes:

So far as judicial review is concerned, if the formulation given is an appropriate one under the governing statute, that should be sufficient to sustain the administrative action. It might be that administrative action was also motivated by some other policy considerations which could not be so easily articulated or which had no relation to the acknowledged purposes of the statute or the agency. Such ulterior purposes might or might not be suggested by disclosure of ex parte communications. Even so it is hard to see why the existence of such ulterior motives should be the proper concern of a reviewing court, any more than it would be if the court were reviewing the reasonableness of legislation.

Nathanson, "Report to the Select Committee on Ex Parte Communications in Informal Rulemaking Proceedings," 30 Admin.L.Rev. 377, 395 (1978). Do you agree with Nathanson?

4. *Adversarial discussion and fairness.* The *Home Box Office* majority opinion was also concerned about ex parte communications depriving parties of a fair opportunity for an adversarial discussion in rulemaking. Do the benefits of an opportunity to make ex parte communications in rulemaking outweigh the risks of depriving parties of the ability to respond to ex parte communications? Are there less drastic measures than a general ban on ex parte communications that would preserve the function of rulemaking proceedings as an informal means of gathering as much relevant information from as many sources as possible, yet assure that affected parties are treated fairly in the circumstances?

5. *Political rulemaking.* Recall the various theories for administrative law discussed in § 1.7, *supra.* How are they relevant to the
Home Box Office decision? Note that *Home Box Office* squarely raises
the question of whether we should prefer a political or technocratic
scheme of rulemaking. In evaluating the court's reasoning in *Home
Box Office,* United States Supreme Court Justice Scalia, when he was a
law school professor, urged that oral ex parte communications be
allowed in rulemaking and that they be excluded from the official
agency rulemaking record. Scalia's argument was based on the desirability of a political rather than a technocratic rulemaking process.

I take it to be axiomatic that, in a democratic government,
agency rulemaking is meant to reflect the will of the elected
assembly. This goal can intelligently be pursued in one of two
ways. First, the delegation of legislative, rulemaking authority
may be made with such precise instructions concerning the end to
be achieved that logic and technological competence (which are
qualities reviewable by the courts) will dictate a relatively narrow
range of results. Or, second, the manner of exercising an imprecise
delegation may be designed to reflect the same forces that work
upon the legislature itself, and thus to produce approximately the
same results.

Until the 1930s the federal government had, formally at least,
chosen the first of these courses. "Congress," said the Supreme
Court (and seemed to mean it), "cannot delegate any part of its
legislative power except under the limitation of a prescribed standard." This was the principle of unconstitutional delegation of
legislative authority—which, if it was ever really followed, has in
any case not been applied since 1935. Modern delegations include
standards no more precise (and no more limiting) than the injunction to adopt rules "in the public interest." The system has
functioned reasonably well, however, because—either consciously
or through that instinctive capacity for fashioning workable arrangements that characterizes Anglo–American politics—the second method for achieving rough compliance with the legislative
will has in fact been adopted.

It is unquestionably true that the regulated industries have
had—to use the censorious phrase adopted by the *Home Box Office*
case—"undue" influence in the rulemaking decisions of their governing agencies. The court might have added that Ralph Nader,
Common Cause, and the Sierra Club have also had "undue" influence—in the sense that their positions, like those of the proximately affected industries, have been given greater weight than positions espoused by, let us say, private citizens such as you and me.
The rulemaking process has assuredly not been an open forum
producing an ultimate decision which values each presentation on
the basis of its intrinsic intellectual worth, with no regard to the
political power of its proponent. To be sure, the initial stage of

agency action has consisted of inquiries and investigations designed to elicit all the facts and to disclose, where possible, the most rational solution; but the final rules have been undeniably political—not (hopefully) in the partisan sense, but in the sense that the sometimes irrational desires of the public and of interest groups within the public have affected the outcome. This would be grave criticism of a court, but is it so clear that it is proper ground for censure of the agencies? Is it so clear that it produces a result that contradicts, rather than parallels, the result that would obtain in that best of all possible worlds, where the legislature itself does all the rulemaking? I suggest that the answer is quite clearly no. If the views of the airlines (and of the Airline Passengers Association) are given greater weight by the CAB than the views of John Doe, one would expect them to be given "undue" weight by the Congress as well, with respect to legislation vitally affecting their selfish interests. This process of accommodating public desires, including the ardent support or vehement opposition of interest groups most proximately affected, is an essential part of the democratic process, however untidy and unanalytic it may be. To prohibit rulemaking agencies from seeking such accommodation, and at the same time to give those agencies no more specific legislative charge than to act "in the public interest," is to convert a large segment of our legal system into a technocracy. It may indeed be true that the present system of what I might term "politically sensitive" agency rulemaking does not mirror, or mimic, congressional action with sufficient accuracy; in my view congressional specification of intelligible and enforceable standards to be applied in the rules is a much more effective means of ensuring compliance with the popular will. But where such standards to guide the agency have not been imposed, the existing system seems infinitely preferable to the regime of "public policy by analysis" which the *Home Box Office* court evidently favors. . . . An agency will be operating politically blind if it is not permitted to have frank and informal discussions with members of Congress and the vitally concerned interest groups; and it will often be unable to fashion a politically acceptable (and therefore enduring) resolution of regulatory problems without some process of negotiation off the record.

Scalia, "Two Wrongs Make a Right: The Judicialization of Standardless Rulemaking," Regulation, July–Aug. 1977, at 38, 40–41.

Scalia concluded that a prohibition of ex parte communications would increase the likelihood that agency rulemaking would be politically unacceptable to the legislature and the people. This, in turn, would lead to three undesirable consequences. First, since it will be more difficult for an agency to gauge the political acceptability of its rules, the legislature will be required to intervene into agency rulemaking to avoid an increased number of unacceptable rules. Second, this increased need for intervention will generate tension between the agencies and Congress, making it increasingly difficult for them to get along on a day-to-day basis. Third, substantial and unnecessary costs would be imposed on regulated persons and agencies when rules turn out in the end to be politically unacceptable and, therefore, are reversed by action of the legislature.

It has also been argued that several other consequences would result from the *Home Box Office* ban on off-the-record communications in rulemaking. More specifically:

> Some of its probable effects will be (1) to reduce substantially the voice of the regulated industry in rulemaking, particularly in one-industry agencies such as the FCC where staff and the commissioners have frequent informal contacts with industry representatives; (2) to reduce the influence of the congressional committees with substantive jurisdiction over the agencies, whose chairmen and members are often consulted (or volunteer their views) informally; (3) to increase substantially the power of agency staff members who draft proposed rules, since they alone among all the participants in the proceedings will have informal access to the decision-makers; (4) to impede, to some extent, agency acquisition of the expertise that comes from constant informal discussion with the regulated industry—since even the most generalized issues (for instance, in the present case, the anticipated growth rate of cable) may be relevant to a pending rulemaking and thus not a proper subject of discussion; and (5) to cause agencies to examine proposed rules more carefully *before* issuing them for comment (since it is only upon issuance that the ex parte prohibition attaches), with the result that the task of persuading a regulatory commission to change a proposed rule will be harder than it is now.

"Perspectives on Current Developments: On Cable T.V. and 'Lobbying' before the Agencies," Regulation, July–Aug. 1977 at 4, 4–5.

Do you agree with these predictions? Even if they are accurate, are they undesirable?

6. *Public disclosure.* Following *Home Box Office,* ACUS issued a recommendation on the subject of ex parte communications in informal rulemaking.

> In rulemaking proceedings subject only to the procedural requirements of section 553 of the APA:

> 1. A general prohibition applicable to all agencies against the receipt of private oral or written communications is undesirable, because it would deprive agencies of the flexibility needed to fashion rulemaking procedures appropriate to the issues involved, and would introduce a degree of formality that would, at least in most instances, result in procedures that are unduly complicated, slow and expensive, and, at the same time, perhaps not conducive to developing all relevant information.

> 2. All written communications addressed to the merits, received after notice of proposed rulemaking and in its course, from

outside the agency by an agency or its personnel participating in the decision should be placed promptly in a file available for public inspection.

3. Agencies should experiment in appropriate situations with procedures designed to disclose oral communications from outside the agency of significant information or argument respecting the merits of proposed rules, made to agency personnel participating in the decision on the proposed rule, by means of summaries promptly placed in the public file, meetings which the public may attend, or other techniques appropriate to their circumstances. To the extent that summaries are utilized they ordinarily should identify the source of the communications, but need not do so when the information or argument is cumulative. Except to the extent the agencies expressly provide, the provisions of this paragraph and the preceding paragraph should not be construed to create new rights to oral proceedings or to extensions of the periods for comment on proposed rules.

ACUS, Recommendation 77–3, "Ex parte Communications in Informal Rulemaking Proceedings," 1 C.F.R. § 305.77–3.

This recommendation encourages, but does not require, significant oral ex parte communications relating to the merits of informal rulemaking to be reduced to writing and to be included in the rulemaking record. While the 1981 MSAPA requires all *written* materials received or considered by an agency to be included in the record, it does not require *oral* ex parte communications to be included in the rulemaking record. MSAPA § 3–112(b)(3). Thus it purposefully leaves open one channel—oral ex parte communications—whereby persons can communicate freely with agencies without worrying that if they do so their messages will be made part of the official record. *See* 1981 MSAPA § 3–112(b)(3) Comment.

Do the approaches proposed by ACUS and the 1981 MSAPA strike a fair balance between the need for interested persons to reply effectively to information or argument presented to agencies ex parte during the course of their rulemakings, and the need to facilitate the flow to agencies in such proceedings of all information relevant to their decisions? Is there a possible compromise between requiring *all* oral ex parte contacts to be summarized and placed in the rulemaking record or requiring *none* of them to be placed in the record? One compromise was considered and rejected in the drafting of the 1981 MSAPA. That compromise would have allowed oral ex parte communications, but required all factual material relevant to the merits of a proposed rule that are contained in such oral ex parte communications to be summarized in writing and to be included in the agency rulemaking record. Would this compromise be desirable? Workable? The new Model Act rejected this solution for the following practical reasons.

First, it would be almost impossible to enforce such a requirement. That is so because it would be virtually impossible to demonstrate, in any situation, that factual matter relevant to the technical merits of a rule, rather than opinion or political information, was the substance of an oral ex parte conversation whose content was omitted from the agency rule-making record. Nevertheless, the possibility of success, no matter how remote, and the facial legitimacy of attempts to demonstrate a violation of such a requirement, may induce, and will facilitate, lawsuits whose only purpose is to delay the rule-making process. . . .

Second, it would be very difficult for agencies and courts to draw a clear line between factual information relevant to the technical merits of a proposed rule contained in oral ex parte communications, which must be reduced to writing and included in the agency rule-making record, and material of an opinion or political nature not relevant to the technical merits of a proposal, which therefore need not be included in the agency rule-making record. Finally, it is unlikely that significant or dispositive factual information relevant to the technical merits of a proposed rule will often be communicated to an agency through *oral* ex parte communications; when such information is communicated to an agency in that manner, its general substance is also unlikely to remain unknown to opposing parties in the rule-making proceeding. Even if opposing parties initially discover agency reliance on such information that was communicated orally and ex parte only in the required reasons statement issued at the time the rule was adopted, they have a partial remedy. At the time they discover that information those persons can petition the agency . . . for a reconsideration of its action, and include in that petition material rebutting the previously unknown factual data on which the agency relied. In addition, all of that rebuttal material will be in the record before the court when it judicially reviews the substantive validity of the rule.

A. Bonfield, STATE ADMINISTRATIVE RULE MAKING, 340–41 (1986).

7. *Application of Home Box Office.* The Court of Appeals for the District of Columbia Circuit has refused to apply the rationale of the *Home Box Office* case, generally, that is, to all informal rulemaking. *See Action for Children's Television v. FCC,* 564 F.2d 458 (D.C.Cir.1977); *Hercules, Inc. v. EPA,* 598 F.2d 91 (D.C.Cir.1978); *United Steelworkers of America v. Marshall,* 647 F.2d 1189 (D.C.Cir.1980). A case that may have definitively limited *Home Box Office* follows.

SIERRA CLUB v. COSTLE

657 F.2d 298 (D.C.Cir.1981).

[The Environmental Protection Agency (EPA) adopted rules governing the emissions of sulfur dioxide by new coal-fired electric generators. Extremely high stakes were involved. In part, the process degenerated into a struggle between states that produce high and low sulfur coal. The

White House tried to influence EPA to adopt a less costly solution. One issue was whether the rule issued by EPA was invalid because it was a result of an "ex parte blitz" that began after the close of the comment period and included meetings between the agency and private persons, executive branch officials, and elected officials. In its evaluation of the post-comment period meetings held with individuals outside of the EPA, the court stated, in an opinion by WALD, J.:]

Oral face-to-face discussions are not prohibited anywhere, anytime, in the [APA]. The absence of such prohibition may have arisen from the nature of the informal rulemaking procedures Congress had in mind. Where agency action resembles judicial action, where it involves formal rulemaking, adjudication, or quasi-adjudication among "conflicting private claims to a valuable privilege," the insulation of the decisionmaker from ex parte contacts is justified by basic notions of due process to the parties involved. But where agency action involves informal rulemaking of a policymaking sort, the concept of ex parte contacts is of more questionable utility.

Under our system of government, the very legitimacy of general policymaking performed by unelected administrators depends in no small part upon the openness, accessibility, and amenability of these officials to the needs and ideas of the public from whom their ultimate authority derives, and upon whom their commands must fall. As judges we are insulated from these pressures because of the nature of the judicial process in which we participate; but we must refrain from the easy temptation to look askance at all face-to-face lobbying efforts, regardless of the forum in which they occur, merely because we see them as inappropriate in the judicial context. Furthermore, the importance to effective regulation of continuing contact with a regulated industry, other affected groups, and the public cannot be underestimated. Informal contacts may enable the agency to win needed support for its program, reduce future enforcement requirements by helping those regulated to anticipate and shape their plans for the future, and spur the provision of information which the agency needs. The possibility of course exists that in permitting ex parte communications with rulemakers we create the danger of "one administrative record for the public and this court and another for the Commission." Under the Clean Air Act procedures, however, "[t]he promulgated rule may not be based (in part or whole) on any information or data which has not been placed in the docket. . . . Thus EPA must justify its rulemaking solely on the basis of the record it compiles and makes public.

Regardless of this court's views on the need to restrict all post-comment contacts in the informal rulemaking context, however, it is clear to us that Congress has decided not to do so in the statute which controls this case. As we have previously noted:

> Where Congress wanted to prohibit *ex parte* contacts it clearly did so. Thus [the] APA . . . forbids *ex parte* contacts when an "adjudication" is underway. . . .

If Congress wanted to forbid or limit *ex parte* contact in every case of informal rulemaking, it certainly had a perfect opportunity of doing so when it enacted the Government in the Sunshine Act.

That it did not extend the ex parte contact provisions of the amended section 557 to section 553—even though such an extension was urged upon it during the hearing—is a sound indication that Congress still does not favor a per se prohibition or even a "logging" requirement in all such proceedings.

Lacking a statutory basis for its position, [Environmental Defense Fund] EDF would have us extend our decision in *Home Box Office, Inc. v. FCC* to cover all meetings with individuals outside EPA during the post-comment period.   Later decisions of this court, however, have declined to apply *Home Box Office* to informal rulemaking of the general policymaking sort involved here, and there is no precedent for applying it to the procedures found in the Clean Air Act Amendments of 1977.   It still can be argued, however, that if oral communications are to be freely permitted after the close of the comment period, then at least some adequate summary of them must be made in order to preserve the integrity of the rulemaking docket, which under the [Clean Air Act] must be the sole repository of material upon which EPA intends to rely.   The statute does not require the docketing of all post-comment period conversations and meetings, but we believe that a fair inference can be drawn that in some instances such docketing may be needed in order to give practical effect to section 307(d)(4)(B)(i) [of that Act] which provides that all *documents* "of central relevance to the rulemaking" shall be placed in the docket as soon as possible after their availability.   This is so because unless *oral* communications of central relevance to the rulemaking are also docketed in some fashion or other, information central to the justification of the rule could be obtained without ever appearing on the docket, simply by communicating it by voice rather than by pen, thereby frustrating the command of section 307 that the final rule not be "based (in part or whole) on any information or data which has not been placed in the docket. . . ."

EDF is understandably wary of a rule which permits the agency to decide for itself when oral communications are of such central relevance that a docket entry for them is required.   Yet the statute itself vests EPA with discretion to decide whether "documents" are of central relevance and therefore must be placed in the docket; surely EPA can be given no less discretion in docketing oral communications, concerning which the statute has no explicit requirements whatsoever.   Furthermore, this court has already recognized that the relative significance of various communications to the outcome of the rule is a factor in determining whether their disclosure is required.   A judicially imposed blanket requirement that all post-comment period oral communications be docketed would, on the other hand, contravene our limited powers of review, would stifle desirable experimentation in the area by Congress and the agencies, and is unnecessary for achieving the goal of an established, procedure-defined docket, *viz.,* to enable reviewing courts to fully evaluate the stated justification given by the agency for its final rule. . . .

We have already held that a blanket prohibition against meetings during the post-comment period with individuals outside EPA is unwarranted, and this perforce applies to meetings with White House officials. . . .

[I]t is hard to believe Congress was unaware that intra-executive meetings and oral comments would occur throughout the rulemaking process. We assume, therefore, that unless expressly forbidden by Congress, such intra-executive contacts may take place, both during and after the public comment period; the only real issue is whether they must be noted and summarized in the docket. The court recognizes the basic need of the President and his White House staff to monitor the consistency of executive agency regulations with Administration policy. He and his White House advisers surely must be briefed fully and frequently about rules in the making, and their contributions to policymaking considered. The executive power under our Constitution, after all, is not shared—it rests exclusively with the President. . . . To ensure the President's control and supervision over the Executive Branch, the Constitution—and its judicial gloss—vests him with the powers of appointment and removal, the power to demand written opinions from executive officers, and the right to invoke executive privilege to protect consultative privacy. In the particular case of EPA, Presidential authority is clear since it has never been considered an "independent agency," but always part of the Executive Branch.

The authority of the President to control and supervise executive policymaking is derived from the Constitution; the desirability of such control is demonstrable from the practical realities of administrative rulemaking. Regulations such as those involved here demand a careful weighing of cost, environmental, and energy considerations. They also have broad implications for national economic policy. Our form of government simply could not function effectively or rationally if key executive policymakers were isolated from each other and from the Chief Executive. Single mission agencies do not always have the answers to complex regulatory problems. An over-worked administrator exposed on a 24–hour basis to a dedicated but zealous staff needs to know the arguments and ideas of policymakers in other agencies as well as in the White House.

We recognize, however, that there may be instances where the docketing of conversations between the President or his staff and other Executive Branch officers or rulemakers may be necessary to ensure due process. This may be true, for example, . . . in some circumstances where a statute like this one *specifically requires* that essential "information or data" upon which a rule is based be docketed. But in the absence of any further Congressional requirements, we hold that it was not unlawful in this case for EPA not to docket a face-to-face policy session involving the President and EPA officials during the post-comment period, since EPA makes no effort to base the rule on any "information or data" arising from that meeting. Where the President himself is directly involved in oral communications with Executive Branch officials, Article II considerations—combined with the strictures of *Vermont Yankee*—require that courts tread with extraordinary caution in mandating disclosure beyond that already required by statute.

The purposes of full-record review which underlie the need for disclosing ex parte conversations in some settings do not require that courts know the details of every White House contact, including a Presidential one, in this informal rulemaking setting. After all, any rule issued here with or without White House assistance must have the requisite *factual support* in the rulemaking record, and under this particular statute the Administrator may not base the rule in whole or in part on any *"information or data"* which is not in the record, no matter what the source. The courts will monitor all this, but they need not be omniscient to perform their role effectively. Of course, it is always possible that undisclosed Presidential prodding may direct an outcome that *is* factually based on the record, but different from the outcome that would have obtained in the absence of Presidential involvement. In such a case, it would be true that the political process did affect the outcome in a way the courts could not police. But we do not believe that Congress intended that the courts convert informal rulemaking into a rarified technocratic process, unaffected by political considerations or the presence of Presidential power. In sum, we find that the existence of intra-Executive Branch meetings during the post-comment period, and the failure to docket one such meeting involving the President, violated neither the procedures mandated by the Clean Air Act nor due process.

Finally, EDF challenges the rulemaking on the basis of alleged Congressional pressure, citing principally two meetings with Senator Byrd. EDF asserts that under the controlling case law the political interference demonstrated in this case represents a separate and independent ground for invalidating this rulemaking. . . .

[T]wo conditions [must] be met before an administrative rulemaking may be overturned simply on the grounds of Congressional pressure. First, the content of the pressure upon the Secretary is designed to force him to decide upon factors not made relevant by Congress in the applicable statute. . . .

Second, the Secretary's determination must be affected by those extraneous considerations. In the case before us, there is no persuasive evidence that either criterion is satisfied. . . . We believe it entirely proper for Congressional representatives vigorously to represent the interests of their constituents before administrative agencies engaged in informal, general policy rulemaking, so long as individual Congressmen do not frustrate the intent of Congress as a whole as expressed in statute, nor undermine applicable rules of procedure. Where Congress-

men keep their comments focused on the substance of the proposed rule
. . . administrative agencies are expected to balance Congressional
pressure with the pressures emanating from all other sources. To hold
otherwise would deprive the agencies of legitimate sources of information and call into question the validity of nearly every controversial
rulemaking.

Notes and Questions

1. *Contrasting views.* *Home Box Office* and *Sierra Club* present
polar views on the subject of ex parte communications in informal
rulemaking. How do these cases compare in balancing the objectives of
efficiency, public satisfaction, and fairness? In their visions about
rulemaking as a political or a technocratic process? In their consistency with the various theories for administrative rulemaking discussed in
§ 1.7, *supra?* Is the view of the *Home Box Office* case or the *Sierra
Club* case more defensible?

2. *Written summary of ex parte communications.* Relying upon a
specific provision in the Clean Air Act, the *Sierra Club* case requires a
summary in the agency rulemaking record of oral and written ex parte
communications which are "of central relevance to rulemaking." Such
disclosure of ex parte communications is necessary under this Clean Air
Act provision only when the communications are of "relative significance" to the outcome of the rule. Would this be a good compromise
position for informal rulemaking under statutes other than the Clean
Air Act?

3. *Political interference generally.* According to *Sierra Club,* when
is political pressure a sufficient basis for judicial invalidation of a rule?
Recall the material on political interference in adjudication in § 3.3.4,
supra, particularly the *Pillsbury* case. Are the principles applicable to
political interference in rulemaking the same? Should they be?

4. *Executive branch interference in rulemaking.* The President (or
the Governor) frequently has an intense interest in pending agency
rulemaking because such rules may either obstruct or promote the
political agenda of the chief executive. For example, the President
may be concerned that a rule would be too costly to business or that it
may not be protective enough. Whether you think the President (or
the Governor) should be permitted to intervene in pending rulemaking
may depend, in part, on whether you view rulemaking as a political or
a technocratic process.

Sierra Club is the leading decision on the propriety of Presidential
interference in rulemaking. Is there a constitutional basis for protecting the power of the chief executive to intervene in pending rulemaking
proceedings?

Does the court in *Sierra Club* view the President as part of the
agency team? If the President is considered part of the agency team,
and separation of functions requirements and internal agency commu-

nications limitations do not apply to rulemaking, ex parte Presidential communications to rulemakers are perfectly appropriate and need not be placed in the record. Nevertheless, are there circumstances in which the special provision of the Clean Air Act would require that Presidential communications be placed in the record?

Or should the President be viewed as an *outsider,* subject to whatever limits the court (or a statute) places on outsider ex parte communications?

The EPA is not an independent agency (meaning that the President can discharge the agency head for any reason). *See* discussion of independent agencies in § 7.5.6b, *infra.* If EPA were independent, would that have changed the court's analysis?

ACUS, Recommendation 80–6, "Intragovernmental Communications in Informal Rulemaking Proceedings," 1 C.F.R. § 305.80–6, provides:

> When the rulemaking agency receives communications from the President, advisers to the President, the Executive office of the President, or other administrative bodies which contain material factual information (as distinct from indications of governmental policy) pertaining to or affecting a proposed rule, the agency should promptly place copies of the documents or summaries of any oral communications, in the public file of the rulemaking proceeding.

Is this a fair compromise? Is it workable? *See generally* Verkuil, "Jawboning Administrative Agencies: Ex Parte Contacts by the White House," 80 Colum.L.Rev. 943 (1980). *See* also note 6, *supra,* after *Home Box Office,* for the reasons why the 1981 MSAPA rejected such a compromise.

Recall that in Executive Order 12,291, discussed in § 6.5, *supra,* the President entrusted the Office of Management and Budget (OMB) with a supervisory role over agency rulemaking in an effort to ensure that agencies covered by that order did not undertake regulatory rulemaking unless its potential benefits exceeded its potential costs. In exercising this role OMB acts as the President's watchdog. Political and policy factors, as well as purely technical factors, may influence OMB when it decides whether the benefits of a proposed agency rule outweigh the costs of the proposed rule in light of the regulatory analysis submitted to OMB by the agency. As a result, should some or all ex parte communications to OMB officials that are relevant to a rule being reviewed by them under the Executive Order be prohibited? To the extent they are permissible, should some or all of these communications be required to be summarized and to be placed in the rulemaking record? Are ex parte communications to officials acting for the President in the performance of an extra-agency review function over proposed rules any more or less desirable or dangerous than ex parte communications to the agency officials who will actually issue the rules? *See* Comment, "Ex Parte Contacts and Institutional Roles: Lessons from the OMB Experience," 55 U.Chic.L.Rev. 591 (1988).

5. *Congressional interference in rulemaking.* In *Sierra Club,* the court rejected claims that Congressional interference tainted the final rule. Assuming there are limitations on ex parte contacts in rulemaking (either under a specific statute like the Clean Air Act or under *Home Box Office*), should members of Congress be required to submit their comments for the record during the comment period just like any other interested person? Or is there something special about their status as members of Congress that should exempt them from such a requirement?

In *Sierra Club* the court had to distinguish an earlier case on Congressional interference, *D.C. Federation of Civic Associations v. Volpe,* 459 F.2d 1231 (D.C.Cir.1971), cert. denied, 405 U.S. 1030 (1972). In that case, the Department of Transportation was prodded into approving a bridge that it did not want to build. A Congressman made clear that the Secretary would not get funding to build the D.C. subway unless he approved the bridge. The court indicated that the decision to build the bridge would be invalid if based on Congressional pressure on a matter extraneous to the bridge decision.

Is the *D.C. Federation* case distinguishable from *Sierra Club?* Should members of Congress be permitted to put pressure on rulemakers?

6. *Ex parte communications and extra-agency political checks.* Should all ex parte communications be prohibited in informal rulemaking, leaving a veto power over all rules in the legislature and chief executive to ensure that each instance of agency rulemaking is in fact responsible to the popular will? Would such a solution be consistent with the theory for administrative law espoused by McCubbins, Noll, and Weingast, § 1.7, *supra?*

The drafters of the 1981 MSAPA rejected this compromise, believing that it would provide an unsatisfactory accommodation between the technocratic and political models of administrative rulemaking. They were convinced that such a scheme would repeatedly cause a substantial waste of public resources because it would enable agencies to adopt rules, after expensive agency proceedings, that would subsequently have to be vetoed by the governor and legislature because the agency could not effectively discover beforehand that they were politically unacceptable. A scheme of this kind would also impose on the governor and legislature a significantly increased work load that they could not practically perform. Finally, such a scheme would continuously cause great friction between agencies and the governor and the legislature because the latter two would be deemed responsible in the public's mind for the agencies' repeated actions in adopting rules that later had to be vetoed because they were unacceptable to the community at large. *See* A. Bonfield, STATE ADMINISTRATIVE RULE MAKING 341–43 (1986). Do you agree with these conclusions?

7. *Problem.* Recall the rule concerning waste disposal in nuclear power plant licensing that was the subject of *Vermont Yankee.* The AEC (now the NRC) is an independent federal agency.

Assume that the AEC agency heads received numerous oral and written communications from the nuclear industry about proposed solutions to the nuclear waste problem and about the importance of adopting a rule that would allow nuclear power plant construction to continue. The President contacted several of the agency heads by telephone with a similar message. Finally, several members of Congress communicated with the agency heads to argue that the AEC should adopt a stringent rule about nuclear waste because of the enormous environmental dangers posed by storage of that material. None of these communications were placed in the record by the AEC agency heads. Should a court set aside the resulting rule?

§ 6.6.2 ROLE OF AGENCY HEADS

Recall the discussion of *Morgan I*, § 3.3.1, *supra.* That case obligates the person who takes responsibility for an agency decision to have at least some personal familiarity with the record. *Morgan I* involved ratemaking for a large number of individuals, but the Court treated the proceeding as quasi-judicial. Should the *Morgan I* principle apply to informal rulemaking?

The federal APA and both the 1961 and 1981 MSAPAs specifically provide that agency decisionmakers must actually consider the written and oral submissions received in the course of the rulemaking proceeding. *See* federal APA § 553(c), 1961 MSAPA § 3(a)(2), 1981 MSAPA § 3–106(c). However, this requirement does not necessarily mean that the agency head must personally preside at an oral proceeding or personally read all written submissions. In practice, it is seldom feasible for an agency head to perform these functions personally, although in the end it is the agency head who must personally make the determination whether to adopt proposed rules and in what form.

Should state agency heads be expected to be more personally involved in such proceedings than federal agency heads? Such personal participation on the part of agency heads has been a tradition in the states to a far greater extent than in the federal government. *See* A. Bonfield, STATE ADMINISTRATIVE RULE MAKING 229 (1986).

Section 3–104(b)(3) of the 1981 MSAPA explicitly provides that others may preside at oral rulemaking proceedings and prepare summaries for subsequent personal consideration by the agency head. Both the federal APA and state APAs have been construed in the same manner. An agency head need not read all of the written submissions, transcripts and summaries, but must understand their contents so that he or she can make a fully informed decision.

Can persons who wish to challenge a rule examine an agency head in court to ascertain whether he or she understood the record assembled during the rulemaking proceeding? Recall *Morgan IV,* discussed in § 3.3.1, *supra,* holding that such examination is improper. Should *Morgan IV* be limited to judicial review of adjudication or does it apply equally to judicial review of rulemaking? Would such review be as destructive to the agency's legislative process as an examination of an administrator's knowledge of the record in a particular case would be destructive of the judicial process?

§ 6.6.3   BIAS OF AGENCY HEADS

Recall the material in § 3.3.3, *supra,* on the various forms of bias that disqualify an adjudicatory decisionmaker. Which, if any, of those forms should disqualify a rulemaker? What would be the statutory or constitutional basis for such disqualification?

ASSOCIATION OF NATIONAL ADVERTISERS v. FTC

627 F.2d 1151 (D.C.Cir.1979), cert. denied, 447 U.S. 921 (1980).

[TAMM, J. The Association sought to prohibit Michael Pertschuk, Chairman of the FTC, from participating in a rulemaking proceeding concerning children's television.

In 1978, the FTC issued a notice of proposed rulemaking that suggested restrictions regarding television advertising directed toward children. The rule would have banned televised advertising for any product that is directed to children too young to understand the selling purpose of the ad. It also would ban ads for sugared food products directed to children.

Before the notice was issued, Pertschuk wrote several articles and gave several speeches on the subject of children's television. For example, he referred to the "moral myopia of children's television advertising" and stated that "advertisers seize on the child's trust and exploit it as a weakness for their gain . . . . Why shouldn't established legal precedents embodying this public policy be applied to protect children from this form of exploitation? In short, why isn't such advertising unfair within the meaning of the Federal Trade Commission Act and, hence, unlawful?"]

The district court, citing this court's decision in Cinderella Career & Finishing Schools, Inc. v. FTC, 425 F.2d 583 (D.C.Cir.1970), found that Chairman Pertschuk had prejudged issues involved in the rulemaking and ordered him disqualified. We hold that the *Cinderella* standard is not applicable to the Commission's rulemaking proceeding. An agency member may be disqualified from such a proceeding only when there is a clear and convincing showing that he has an unalterably closed mind on matters critical to the disposition of the rulemaking. Because we find that the appellees have failed to demonstrate the requisite prejudgment, the order of the district court is reversed. . . .

In *Cinderella,* we held that the standard for disqualifying an administrator in an adjudicatory proceeding because of prejudgment is whether "a disinterested observer may conclude that [the decisionmaker] has in some measure adjudged the facts as well as the law of a particular case in advance of hearing it." 425 F.2d at 591. This standard guarantees that the adjudicative hearing of a person facing administrative prosecution for past behavior is before a decisionmaker who has not prejudged facts concerning the events under review. . . .

The district court in the case now before us held that "the standard of conduct delineated in *Cinderella*" governs agency decisionmakers participating in a . . . proceeding . . . to promulgate rules designed to "define with specificity acts or practices which are unfair or deceptive." . . .

Congress chose, however, to delegate its power to proscribe unfair or deceptive acts or practices to the Commission because "there were too many unfair practices for it to define."

In determining the due process standards applicable in [such a] proceeding, we are guided by its nature as rulemaking. When a proceeding is classified as rulemaking, due process ordinarily does not demand procedures more rigorous than those provided by Congress. See Vermont Yankee Nuclear Power Corp. v. NRDC. . . .

We never intended the *Cinderella* rule to apply to a rulemaking procedure such as the one under review [here]. . . .

The legitimate functions of a policymaker, unlike an adjudicator, demand interchange and discussion about important issues. We must not impose judicial roles upon administrators when they perform functions very different from those of judges. . . .

The *Cinderella* view of a neutral and detached adjudicator is simply an inapposite role model for an administrator who must translate broad statutory commands into concrete social policies. If an agency official is to be effective he must engage in debate and discussion about the policy matters before him. As this court has recognized before, "informal contacts between agencies and the public are the 'bread and butter' of the process of administration." . . .

The appellees have a right to a fair and open proceeding; that right includes access to an impartial decisionmaker. Impartial, however, does not mean uninformed, unthinking, or inarticulate. The requirements of due process clearly recognize the necessity for rulemakers to formulate policy in a manner similar to legislative action. The standard enunciated today will protect the purposes of a section 18 [rulemaking] proceeding, and, in so doing, will guarantee the appellees a fair hearing.

We would eviscerate the proper evolution of policymaking were we to disqualify every administrator who has opinions on the correct course of his agency's future action. . . . The importance and legitimacy of rulemaking procedures are too well established to deny administrators such a fundamental tool.

Finally, we eschew formulation of a disqualification standard that impinges upon the political process. . . . We are concerned that implementation of the *Cinderella* standard in the rulemaking context would plunge courts into the midst of political battles concerning the proper formulation of administrative policy. We serve as guarantors of statutory and constitutional rights, but not as arbiters of the political process. Accordingly, we will not order the disqualification of a rulemaker absent the most compelling proof that he is unable to carry out his duties in a constitutionally permissible manner.

Reversed.

Notes and Questions

1. *Formal rulemaking requirements.* If a statute required the FTC to engage in formal rulemaking procedure to adopt a trade regulation rule, would the result in the *Association of National Advertisers* case have been the same? Which bias standard would apply—the *Cinderella* standard or the *Association of National Advertisers* standard?

In fact, the Magnuson–Moss Act did incorporate some formal rulemaking ingredients. However, the Court in *Association of National Advertisers* stated:

The district court ruled that a section 18 proceeding, notwithstanding the appellation rulemaking, "is neither wholly legislative nor wholly adjudicative." According to the district court, the "adjudicative aspects" of the proceeding render *Cinderella* applicable.

The appellees . . . emphasize two allegedly "adjudicatory aspects" of a section 18 proceeding: (1) interested persons are entitled [by statute] to limited cross-examination of those who testify to disputed issues of material fact, and (2) [according to statute] a reviewing court must set aside any rule not supported by substantial evidence in the rulemaking record taken as a whole.

The district court's characterization of section 18 rulemaking as a . . . quasi-adjudicative proceeding ignores the clear scheme of the APA. Administrative action pursuant to the APA is either adjudication or rulemaking. The two processes differ fundamentally in purpose and focus. . . .

Congress has, in the Magnuson–Moss Warranty—Federal Trade Commission Improvement Act and elsewhere, enacted specific statutory rulemaking provisions that require more procedures than those of section 553 but less than the full procedures required under sections 556 and 557. The presence of procedures not mandated by section 553, however, does not, as the appellees urge, convert rulemaking into quasi-adjudication. The appellees err by focusing on the details of administrative process rather than the nature of administrative action.

627 F.2d at 1159–61.

2. *The "unalterably closed mind" standard.* Does the *Association of National Advertisers (ANA)* standard make it nearly impossible to disqualify an agency official on the basis of prejudgment? If so, should the standard be abandoned in order to discourage costly but futile litigation? ACUS supports disqualification if there is "at least a preponderant showing that an agency member or decisonal employee has a closed mind regarding those facts." ACUS, Recommendation 80–4, "Decisional Officials' Participation in Rulemaking Proceedings," 1 C.F.R. § 305.80–4. But one commentator proposes a "duty to act fairly" standard in lieu of the "unalterably closed mind" standard of the *ANA* case. *See* Neely, "The Duty to Act Fairly: An Alternative to the 'Unalterably Closed Mind' Standard for Disqualification of Administrators in Rulemaking," 16 New Eng.L.Rev. 733, 780–87 (1981). Of the various approaches suggested in this note (no disqualification, the *ANA* test, the ACUS test, Neely's test, or the *Cinderella* test), which do you prefer in the context of FTC trade regulation rulemaking? In the context of informal rulemaking generally?

3. *Inherent bias of agency head.* Agency heads are likely to be biased in favor of policies they believe will advance the objectives sought by their agencies. Furthermore, to be effective leaders, agency heads must have some general idea about the direction in which the lawmaking of their agency should move well in advance of that lawmaking. They are also likely to have at least some preconceptions about which specific policies will be effective and in the public interest. In addition, when an agency publishes a proposed rule for public comment, that indicates at least some degree of commitment to the contents of that proposal on the part of the agency decisionmakers.

In light of these circumstances, would any attempt to ensure that rulemakers be neutral about proposed agency rules be both unrealistic and counter-productive? Would neutrality of agency rulemakers on the merits of proposed rules be consistent with a political or technocratic model of administrative lawmaking? In light of the competing purposes of agency rulemaking procedure, is the *ANA* standard for decisionmaker disqualification for bias a sound compromise?

§ 6.7 FINDINGS AND REASONS

CALIFORNIA HOTEL & MOTEL ASS'N v. INDUSTRIAL WELFARE COM'N

599 P.2d 31 (Cal.1979).

[The Association appeals from Order 5–76, a rule adopted by the Commission raising the wages and fixing the hours and working conditions of hotel employees. Labor Code § 1177 provided: "Each order [rule] of the commission shall include a statement as to the basis upon which the order is predicated, and shall be concurred in by a majority of the commissioners."]

An effective statement of basis fulfills several functions. First, the statement satisfies the legislative mandate of section 1177. Second, the statement facilitates meaningful judicial review of agency action. . . . Third, the exposition requirement subjects the agency, its decisionmaking processes, and its decisions to more informed scrutiny by the Legislature, the regulated public, lobbying and public interest groups, the media, and the citizenry at large. Fourth, requiring an administrative agency to articulate publicly its reasons for adopting a particular order, rule, regulation, or policy induces agency action that is reasonable, rather than arbitrary, capricious, or lacking in evidentiary support. Fifth, by publicizing the policies, considerations and facts that the agency finds significant, the agency introduces an element of predictability into the administrative process. This enables the regulated public to anticipate agency action and to shape its conduct accordingly. Sixth, requiring an agency to publicly justify its orders, rules, regulations, and policies stimulates public confidence in agency action by promoting both the reality and the appearance of rational decisionmaking in government. . . .

The commission . . . exercised a legislative function in promulgating Order 5–76. The courts exercise limited review of legislative acts by administrative bodies out of deference to the separation of powers between the Legislature and the judiciary, to the legislative delegation of administrative authority to the agency, and to the presumed expertise of the agency within its scope of authority. Although administrative actions enjoy a presumption of regularity, this presumption does not immunize agency action from effective judicial review. A reviewing court will ask three questions: first, did the agency act within the scope of its delegated authority; second, did the agency employ fair procedures; and third, was the agency action reasonable. Under the third inquiry, a reviewing court will . . . uphold the agency action unless the action is arbitrary, capricious, or lacking in evidentiary support. A court must ensure that an agency has adequately considered all relevant factors, and has demonstrated a rational connection between those factors, the choice made, and the purposes of the enabling statute. . . .

In light of these considerations, we define the standard to evaluate the statement of basis required by section 1177. . . . A statement of basis will necessarily vary depending on the material supporting an order and the terms of the order. The statement should reflect the factual, legal, and policy foundations for the action taken. The statement of basis must show that the order adopted is reasonably supported by the material gathered by or presented to the commission—through its own investigations, the wage board proceedings, and the public hearings—and is reasonably related to the purposes of the enabling statute. The statement of basis is not the equivalent of the findings of fact that a court may be required to make. A statement of basis is an explanation of how and why the commission did what it did. If terms of the order turn on factual issues, the statement must demonstrate reasonable support in the administrative record for the factual determinations. If, on the other hand, the terms of the order turn on policy choices, an assessment of risks or alternatives, or predictions of economic or social consequences, the statement of basis must show how the commission resolved conflicting interests and how that resolution led to the order chosen. If an order differentiates among classes of industries, employers, or employees, the statement of basis must show that the distinctions drawn are reasonably supported by the administrative record and are reasonably related to the purposes of the enabling statute. A statement meeting these standards will facilitate review by the judiciary, the Legislature, and the regulated public by presenting a reasoned response to or resolution of the salient comments, criticisms, issues, and alternatives developed during the commission's proceedings.

The "To Whom It May Concern" provision of Order 5–76 does not satisfy this standard. The provision is simply a recitation of the commission's authority and of the procedures outlined in sections 1171 through 1204. This purported statement of basis does not fulfill any of the functions of an effective statement outlined above.

The commission argues that even if the "To Whom It May Concern" provision does not satisfy the statement of basis requirement of section 1177, the document entitled "Statement of Findings" included in the administrative record does satisfy section 1177. The commission adopted the Statement of Findings and Order 5–76 at the same meeting. The Statement of Findings does not satisfy the statement of basis requirement for several reasons.

First, section 1177 states that each order shall include a statement of basis. Sections 1182 and 1183 require that an order be published and mailed to employers. Order 5–76 does not include or even mention the Statement of Findings, and the statement was not published or mailed to employers. The statement simply remained in the administrative record. The Statement of Findings therefore does not satisfy the requirements of sections 1177, 1182, and 1183.

Second, the Statement of Findings does not address salient comments and alternatives presented during the public hearings on proposed Order 5–76. For example, the commission exempted a number of industries from its regulations covering hours and days of work, because the commission concluded that collective bargaining agreements "adequately" protected employees in those industries. However, the commission did not exempt the public housekeeping industry from coverage, even though the association presented evidence that collective bargaining in the industry was "adequate" rather than "weak." The commission did not explain how it distinguished adequate from inadequate collective bargaining agreements. The commission did not explain why it exempted other industries, but not the public housekeeping industry. Similarly, the commission reduced the workweek in the public housekeeping industry from 48 to 40 hours, without responding to the association's argument that the industry practice of having a longer workweek benefited both employers and employees because of the peak-load demand for employment peculiar to the industry. The Statement of Findings thus does not satisfy the standard of an adequate statement of basis under section 1177 outlined above.

In conclusion, the commission failed to include an adequate statement of basis in Order 5–76 as required by sections 1177, 1182, and 1184. Order 5–76 is therefore invalid as promulgated. However, the order has been in effect since 1976. The minimum wage order is of critical importance to significant numbers of employees. Those employees bear no responsibility for the deficiencies of Order 5–76. This court has inherent power to make an order appropriate to preserve the status quo pending correction of deficiencies. Order 5–76 is to remain operative pending further proceedings to be taken promptly by the commission.

The judgment is reversed with directions to issue a writ of mandate to compel the commission to take further action in a manner consistent with this opinion within 120 days of the finality of the opinion.

NEWMAN, J.—I dissent. I believe that experienced observers of how government agencies work will be astonished to learn that, when a statute requires a statement "as to the basis" on which rules are predicated, administrative rulemaking in California is now to be encumbered as [*described in the majority opinion*]. . . .

That much-too-detailed set of instructions to agency rulemakers should be contrasted with this introductory paragraph in § 6.01–2 of Davis, Administrative Law of the Seventies (1976): "The [Federal] Administrative Procedure Act provides in § 553 that the agency, after receiving written comments, 'shall incorporate in the rules adopted a concise general statement of their basis and purposes.' The APA does not require a statement of findings of fact. See Att'y Gen. Manual on the APA 32 (1947): 'Except as required by statutes providing for "formal" rule making procedure, findings of fact and conclusions of law are not necessary. Nor is there required an elaborate analysis of the rules or of the considerations upon which the rules were issued. Rather, the statement is intended to advise the public of the general basis and purpose of the rules.' "

Unlike the federal APA, the California statute that governs here does not require a "statement of . . . basis and purpose." It does not even require a "statement of basis" (though that phrase appears more than 25 times in the majority opinion here). Our Legislature's sole command is that there be a "statement *as to* the basis" (italics added).

By no means is the To–Whom–It–May–Concern provision of Order 5–76 a model or prototype statement. It hardly merits inclusion in any formbook. In my view, though, its arguable defects have not caused prejudicial error. (Cf. Gov.Code, § 11440 ("any regulation . . . *may be* declared to be invalid for a *substantial* failure to comply"). (Italics added.) The following observations by Kenneth Culp Davis seem to me to evidence more insight as to overall fairness in governing than does the majority ("By the Court") opinion here: "[A] statement that 'findings' and 'reasons' are required for informal rulemaking would be inaccurate, for such a statement would be an oversimplification. The focus of discerning judges is not on such words as 'findings' and 'reasons' but is on the total picture in each case of the reasonableness of the support for the rules in the rulemaking record and the adequacy of the agency's explanation for its determination. In most cases in which the question has been important, the adequacy of the explanation is mixed in with other facets of the challenge of the rules, so that *a focus on the explanation, without taking into account the interrelated complexities, is somewhat artificial.*"

CHRISTIAN, J., Concurring.

It is not clear what the dissent means when it asserts that "experienced observers of how government agencies work will be astonished to learn" that this court has adopted this standard. Presumably, experienced observers of how agencies work will be familiar with developments in administrative law over the last decade. For example, students of administrative law will be familiar with the long line of cases from the federal appellate courts interpreting [federal APA] section 553(c) which contains a statement of basis requirement similar to the requirement of Labor Code section 1177. . . .

The standard adopted in the majority opinion represents a distillation of the standards articulated in these cases and commentaries. Students of administrative law familiar with these materials will not be astonished to learn that the California Supreme Court has adopted a position in line with the contemporary trend of authority.

Notes and Questions

1. *Adjudication v. rulemaking.* Note the discussion in the *California Hotel* case about the purposes of requiring a statement of reasons in rulemaking. Recall the discussion in *Matlovich*, § 4.3, *supra*, about the purposes of requiring such a statement in adjudication. These purposes include facilitating judicial review, helping to secure a decision within an agency's authority and discretion, preventing arbitrary conduct, and informing aggrieved persons of the grounds for agency action so that they can effectively plan their future course of action, including judicial review. Are these purposes equally persuasive in the rulemaking context? Are they even more persuasive?

2. *Concise and general.* Federal APA § 553(c) provides that "[a]fter consideration of the relevant matter presented [through informal notice and comment procedures] the agency shall incorporate in the rules adopted a concise general statement of their basis and purpose." Contrast this to the requirements imposed on *formal* rulemaking and adjudication in § 557(c).

Section 3–110(a) of the 1981 MSAPA also requires, for each rule, a "concise explanatory statement" of the reasons for adopting the rule and "an indication of any change between the text of the proposed rule contained in the published notice of adoption and the text of the rule as finally adopted, with the reasons for any change." On the other hand, § 3(a)(2) of the 1961 MSAPA (incorporated in the acts of many states) requires the issuance of such a statement only if the agency is "requested to do so by an interested person either prior to adoption or within 30 days thereafter." The 1961 MSAPA provision also is more specific than the federal act or the 1981 MSAPA provisions because it requires the statement to include "the principal reasons for and against . . . [the rule's] adoption, incorporating therein . . . [the agency's] reasons for overruling the considerations urged against its adoption."

The federal APA requirement that an agency issue for each rule made by informal procedures a "concise general statement" has been summarized in the following manner.

> The statement is to be "concise" and "general." Except as required by statutes providing for "formal" rule making procedure, findings of fact and conclusions of law are not necessary. Nor is there required an elaborate analysis of the rules or of the considerations upon which the rules were issued. Rather, the statement is intended to advise the public of the general basis and purpose of the rules.

U.S. Dept. of Justice, ATTORNEY GENERAL'S MANUAL ON THE ADMINISTRATIVE PROCEDURE ACT 32 (1947).

3. *Modern developments.* During the 1970's Congress increasingly enacted provisions in statutes that specially required findings, reasons, or both in particular classes of notice and comment rulemaking. *See, e.g.,* The Occupational Safety and Health Act of 1970, 29 U.S.C. § 655(e), providing that the Secretary of Labor must include a statement of reasons for any rule issued to implement the Act, and publish that statement in the *Federal Register.* In addition, the federal courts, during that period, imposed requirements under the "concise general statement . . . of basis and purpose" provision that went well beyond a literal reading of its language. As the court in *Automotive Parts & Accessories Ass'n v. Boyd,* 407 F.2d 330, 338 (D.C.Cir.1968) stated:

> [I]t is appropriate for us to . . . caution against an overly literal reading of the statutory terms 'concise' and 'general.' These adjectives must be accommodated to the realities of judicial scrutiny, which do not contemplate that the court itself will, by a laborious examination of the record, formulate in the first instance the significant issues faced by the agency and articulate the rationale of their resolution. We do not expect the agency to discuss every item of fact or opinion included in the submissions made to it in informal rule making. We do expect that, if the judicial review which Congress has thought it important to provide is to be meaningful, the "concise general statement of . . . basis and

purpose" mandated by Section . . . [553] will enable us to see what major issues of policy were ventilated by the informal proceedings and why the agency reacted to them as it did.

Is *California Hotel* consistent with these federal cases? Does it go even further?

4. *Responding to comments.* Modern federal cases have made it clear that the agency must explain how and why it reacted to important comments it received during the course of the rulemaking proceeding. As the court stated in *Rodway v. USDA,* 514 F.2d 809, 817 (D.C. Cir.1975):

> The basis and purpose statement is not intended to be an abstract explanation addressed to imaginary complaints. Rather, its purpose is, at least in part, to respond in a reasoned manner to the comments received, to explain how the agency resolved any significant problems raised by the comments, and to show how that resolution led the agency to the ultimate rule. . . . The basis and purpose statement is inextricably intertwined with the receipt of comments.

However, this does not mean that an agency must respond to each comment received during the course of the proceeding. The required statement is, after all, to be "concise" and "general." As a result, the statement need not respond to each and every issue raised in the comments—only to those that are both significant and material. *See* 1 C. Koch, ADMINISTRATIVE LAW AND PRACTICE 301 (1985). Is *California Hotel* consistent with these federal cases? Does it go even further?

Note that the failure to submit comments on a proposed rule in a timely fashion and in a fashion that indicates why or how the comments are relevant to the proceeding, may sometimes relieve the agency of any responsibility for considering them or for responding to them. *See Northside Sanitary Landfill, Inc. v. Thomas,* 849 F.2d 1516 (D.C.Cir.1988) (where relevance of 420 pages of submitted documents was facially unclear, failure of petitioner to be specific as to why and how it thought the documents were relevant to the rulemaking proceeding relieved the agency of the responsibility for considering them and responding to them).

5. *Justification for modern cases.* In light of the terms "concise" and "general" in § 553(c) are the above expansive constructions of this provision by the courts justified? Are they overruled by *Vermont Yankee,* § 6.3, *supra?* In light of the above constructions, how "concise" and how "general" can a statement of basis and purpose be in practice?

6. *Post hoc rationalizations.* Can the agency supply the necessary explanatory statements *after* adopting the rule? In *Motor Vehicle Manufacturers Ass'n of U.S., Inc. v. State Farm Mutual Auto Ins. Co.,* 463 U.S. 29, 50 (1983), the Supreme Court stated: "[T]he courts may not

accept appellate counsel's *post hoc* rationalizations for agency action. *Burlington Truck Lines, Inc. v. United States,* 371 U.S. [156,] 168. It is well-established that an agency's action must be upheld, if at all, on the basis articulated by the agency itself. . . . *SEC v. Chenery Corp.,* 332 U.S. [194,] 196 (1945). . . ." In other words, where there is a "contemporaneous explanation of the agency decision . . ., [t]he validity of the . . . action must . . . stand or fall on the propriety of that finding. . . ." *Camp v. Pitts,* 411 U.S. 138, 143 (1973). *See also Vermont Yankee Nuclear Power Corp. v. N.R.D.C.,* 435 U.S. 519, 549 (1978). As a result, both federal and state agencies must be cautious in drafting their explanatory statements for rules. As suggested by the *Motor Vehicles* case, which is treated more fully in § 9.4, *infra,* federal and state common law holds that the contemporaneous reasons for agency action contained in such an explanatory statement become the *exclusive* basis upon which the agency may defend the legality of a rule in subsequent judicial review proceedings.

This principle was codified in § 3–110(b) of the 1981 MSAPA which provides that "[o]nly the reasons contained in the concise explanatory statement may be used by any party as justifications for the adoption of the rule in any proceeding in which its validity is at issue." Therefore, post hoc rationalizations offered by an agency for its rulemaking action may not be relied upon as a basis to uphold a rule. If an agency fails to state *all* of the reasons for a rule in its required statement and any of the omitted reasons are necessary to support the rule's validity, the rule will be invalidated. This means that a rule for which there are adequate reasons at the time of its adoption may be held invalid merely because the issuing agency was negligent or incompetent in drafting its explanatory statement.

What alternatives does an agency have in such a situation? Must it initiate an entirely new rulemaking proceeding to readopt the rule? *Tabor v. Joint Bd. for Enrollment of Actuaries,* 566 F.2d 705, 711–12 (D.C.Cir.1977), suggests that under the federal APA an agency may readopt the rule with a sufficient statement without engaging in an entirely new notice and comment proceeding. Do you agree? Would the *Tabor* conclusion be proper under § 3–110(b) of the 1981 MSAPA? Is the result suggested in *Tabor* desirable? *Compare* A. Bonfield, STATE ADMINISTRATIVE RULE MAKING 318–19 (1986) with Auerbach, "Bonfield on State Administrative Rulemaking: A Critique," 71 Minn.L.Rev. 543, 581–84 (1987). Do you agree with the remedy decreed in the *California Hotel* case?

7. *Justification for principle.* Significant costs are involved in invalidating a rule solely because the particular reasons contained in its explanatory statement are inadequate, when other adequate reasons for the rule exist. There are also significant benefits which may justify such action. The Comment to § 3–110 of the 1981 MSAPA lists some of these benefits.

There are several reasons why agencies and other parties seeking to justify agency action should not be permitted to use *post hoc* reasons to rescue agency action which was unsupportable on the basis of the specific formal reasons given when it was originally taken. If agencies had the right to rely on *post hoc* reasons they would be encouraged to offer at a later time false, but convenient, rationalizations for their earlier otherwise unsupportable action. Such a right would also allow agencies to make rules in a way that would entirely remove from the scrutiny of the rule-making process those later justifications which ultimately become the basis for upholding the rule. In addition, it would undesirably protect agencies from any adverse consequences for their improper failure to consider carefully, *prior to the time they take rule-making action,* all of the reasons why they should or should not take that action.

Do you agree that these benefits outweigh the costs to the public of invalidating a rule solely because the reasons contained in its explanatory statement are inadequate? Is the principle that prohibits agencies from using post hoc reasons to defend their rules necessary to preserve the function of rulemaking proceedings? To ensure that agencies consider fully the lawfulness and desirability of their proposed rules *at the time of those proceedings?*

8. *Arguments for and against the rule.* Although § 3–110 of the 1981 MSAPA goes beyond the language contained in the federal act and the 1961 MSAPA, it has been criticized for not going far enough because it omits the requirement that the explanatory statement contain all of "the arguments for and against the rule considered by the agency," as well as "its reasons for rejecting the arguments against adoption of the rule." This language was in an earlier draft of the 1981 Model Act as prepared by the Reporter and also appears in § 3(a)(2) of the 1961 Model State APA and in the acts of many states. Nevertheless, the Commissioners purposely deleted this language when they adopted the new Model Act.

> The omitted [language is] very desirable for a number of reasons. Most importantly, forcing an agency to articulate all of the arguments raised in the proceeding for and against the rule would effectively require the agency to structure its consideration of the rule in a useful manner. This requirement would also help assure that the agency in fact considers all submissions made to it in that rule-making proceeding. . . . After all, . . . if a concise agency statement overlooks a significant argument made against a rule, it does so [with] peril. Those opposed to the rule will be able to use any such omission to prove that the agency violated its statutory duty to consider fully *all* submitted views. So, too, the requirement that the agency formally and clearly articulate all of the grounds for overruling the arguments made against a rule will force the agency to do that which it is supposed to do in any event: directly confront all objections to a proposed rule and determine

whether they are sufficient to prevent its adoption. Requiring the agency to articulate in the concise statement the precise reasons why it rejected those arguments against the proposed rule will also facilitate public and judicial scrutiny of the rationality of the agency's action.

Bonfield, "Rule Making Under the 1981 Model State Administrative Procedure Act: An Opportunity Well Used," 35 Admin.L.Rev. 77, 92 (1983).

Do you agree that the benefits of requiring the explanatory statement to include a brief summary of the arguments for and against the rule and the reasons for rejecting the arguments against its adoption outweigh the costs of doing so? Is the language of the 1981 MSAPA requiring that the explanatory statement include the agency's "reasons for adopting the rule" an adequate substitute for the omitted language? Does the judicial gloss that has been placed on the federal act's requirement of a statement of basis and purpose, *see* notes 3–4, *supra,* functionally impose on federal agencies the requirements contained in the 1961 MSAPA language that was omitted from the 1981 MSAPA?

9. *Changes from proposed rule.* Section 3–110(a)(2) of the 1981 MSAPA requires an agency to indicate in its concise statement any textual changes between the proposed rule and the adopted rule, and the reasons for those changes. Should federal APA § 553(c) be amended to include such a requirement, or is such an amendment unnecessary because the judicial gloss put on that provision of the federal act already requires such an explanation? If so, have the courts gone too far in "creatively" interpreting § 553(c)?

10. *Necessity of statement when terminating proceedings.* Should an agency be required to issue an explanatory statement when it entirely withdraws a proposed rule, terminating all rulemaking proceedings thereon? *See* Mo.Rev.Stat. § 536.021(5)(3) (Supp.1984).

11. *Improper reasons.* Does the explanatory statement requirement really thwart an agency that desires to make a rule for reasons that are improper? May an agency successfully draft a statement of reasons solely for its cosmetic effect and thereby create an adequate basis for the validity of the rule that is wholly disingenuous? Is there any solution for this problem?

12. *Statutory interpretation or judge-made law.* In fleshing out the details of the statement of basis and purpose requirement, most courts have justified their actions as statutory interpretation of § 553(c) or corresponding provisions of state law. At least one court, however, has acknowledged that it was making common law when it elaborated the details of such a requirement. *See Kennecott Copper Corp. v. EPA,* 462 F.2d 846 (D.C.Cir.1972). The court noted that "fairness may require more than the APA minimum." Even without any statutory requirement to rely upon, some courts have demanded, as a matter of judge-made common law, that an agency provide a contemporaneous statement containing the principal reasons for its adoption of a rule,

and have then held the agency to that statement. *See Tri–State Generation and Transmission Ass'n, Inc. v. Environmental Quality Council,* 590 P.2d 1324 (Wyo.1979). Compare *Borden, Inc. v. Commissioner of Public Health,* 448 N.E.2d 367, 378 n. 9 (Mass.1983), § 9.4, *infra,* ("an agency is not, barring a specific statutory mandate, obliged to provide a statement of reasons which support its adoption of a regulation.") Does *California Hotel* engage in statutory interpretation or does it make administrative common law?

IOWA BANKERS ASS'N v. IOWA CREDIT UNION DEPT.

335 N.W.2d 439 (Iowa 1983).

[Following § 3(a)(2) of the 1961 MSAPA, Iowa Code § 17A.4(1)(B) provides: "If requested to do so by an interested person, either prior to adoption or within thirty days thereafter, the agency shall issue a concise statement of the principal reasons for and against the rule it adopted, incorporating therein the reasons for overruling considerations urged against the rule."

The Department adopted rules broadening the authority of credit unions to provide banking services. After the rules were proposed but before they were adopted, the Association filed a request for a concise statement under § 17A.4(1)(B). The Department failed to issue the statement until *after* the association filed its petition for judicial review, which was almost six months after the request was filed. The lower court held that § 17A.4(1)(B) requires the agency to supply the concise statement at the time the rule is adopted when it is requested prior to adoption.

The state Supreme Court held that the agency could supply the statement after the rule was adopted, regardless of when it was requested. Because the statute in question did not specify when the agency must *issue* the requested statement, the court refused to read a specified time limit for agency compliance into the statute. It did, however, have to decide whether the agency had substantially complied with the requirement that it issue such a statement.]

REYNOLDSON, C.J.:

Our prior decisions have noted the requirement a petitioner show prejudice as a condition precedent to judicial relief from agency action. . . . Iowa Code section 17A.4(3), however, contains a more specific standard on agency rule-making:

> No rule adopted after July 1, 1975, is valid unless adopted in substantial compliance with the above requirements of . . . section [17A.4].

The purpose of section 17A.4(3) is to enforce strict compliance with statutory rule-making procedures, in view of the tendency by some administrators to skirt the requirements. The provision effectuates the general IAPA purposes of increasing public accountability of agencies, fostering public participation in rule-making, and assuring agency adherence to a uniform minimum procedure. We are instructed to broadly construe the IAPA in furtherance of these purposes.

. . . We think department's argument the association was required to show personal prejudice contravenes the legislature's purpose in enacting section 17A.4(3). An agency aware that its rules will withstand procedural invalidation absent prejudice to the complaining party will be more apt to violate IAPA rule-making provisions. Conversely, enforcement of the substantial compliance standard will encourage agency adherence to the statutory procedure, and further the IAPA purpose of increasing agency accountability to the public. Finally, requiring petitioner in a rule-making review to show prejudice in order to invalidate an agency rule on the basis of improper procedure would render section 17A.4(3) a nullity. . . .

Our inquiry under the substantial compliance standard must include not only harm suffered by the parties, but harm to persons not parties, and the interest in strict compliance with the IAPA. Probative will be the magnitude of the deviation, whether it was purposeful, and whether interested parties were prevented from participating in, or reacting to, the rule-making process.

Here the agency's deviation from statutory procedure was flagrant, not merely technical. Despite the association's expressed continuing interest in the expansion of credit union authority, the agency failed to produce a concise statement of its reasons for adopting the share-draft rules until after a judicial review petition was filed—almost six months after the association's request. Countenancing such agency inaction ultimately will degrade the value of and discourage public involvement in the rule-making process. Further, concise statements tendered as late as those at issue here are of limited value. Notwithstanding the IAPA's noninclusion of a specific time requirement, a concise statement should be issued close enough in time to the rule adoption and to the request that it accurately capsulizes the agency decision process, rather than merely rationalizing a past act.

District court properly held the department's share-draft rules, 295 Iowa Administrative Code chapter 7, invalid for lack of substantial compliance with section 17A.4(1)(b).

Notes and Questions

1. *Triggering.* Should an explanatory statement be required in *all* cases, as provided in federal APA § 553(c) and 1981 MSAPA § 3–110(a), or only if requested, as provided in the Iowa APA and § 3(a)(2) of the 1961 MSAPA?

2. *Time of issuance.* When should the explanatory statement be issued? At the time the rule is adopted? Would its issuance thirty days, ninety days, six months, or even a year later be satisfactory? When does the statement start being a post hoc litigation affidavit

instead of an agency explanatory statement? Are there any practical or strategic reasons why agencies might want some flexibility on this matter? When must such statements be issued under the federal act? Under the 1981 MSAPA?

3. *Substantial compliance.* The "substantial compliance" provision of the Iowa APA discussed in the prior case is based upon § 3(c) of the 1961 MSAPA and is replicated in the acts of many states. Do you agree with the Iowa Supreme Court's construction of that provision? What does "substantial compliance" with statutory rulemaking requirements mean? Did the Labor Commission "substantially comply" with § 1177 in the *California Hotel* case? Should a person be entitled to have a rule set aside merely for technical noncompliance with statutory requirements? Should a person who was not personally prejudiced by an agency's failure to comply with statutory rulemaking requirements be able to have the rule set aside by a court? Are the interests of the public at large effectively protected only by dispensing with a requirement of personal prejudice by petitioner in this context?

§ 6.8 EXCLUSIVITY OF THE AGENCY RULEMAKING RECORD

An important and unsettled issue in informal rulemaking is whether an agency adopting a rule may consider only the materials actually before the agency during the rulemaking process or whether it may take account of other materials that were not before the agency during that process. A related issue is whether a court in conducting review of a rule is limited to examining the materials actually before the agency during the rulemaking process or whether additional evidence and argument may be introduced in court by either the challenger or the agency.

In *formal* rulemaking it is clear that agencies must make and courts must review such rules wholly on the basis of the formal agency rulemaking record. *See* federal APA §§ 553(c), 556(e); 1981 MSAPA §§ 4–101(b) and –215(d); 3–112 Comment. In *informal* rulemaking, the exclusivity or nonexclusivity of the agency rulemaking record as a basis for agency action or judicial review is less clear. It might be supposed that one of the principal distinctions between formal and informal rulemaking is that the former embodies an exclusive record requirement while the latter does not. Nevertheless, this distinction is not as clear as one might suppose; and the courts have had great difficulty in dealing with agency rulemaking records when they review rules.

Section 3–112(c) of the 1981 MSAPA explicitly deals with the exclusivity of the agency rulemaking record by stating that the official agency rulemaking record need not be the "exclusive basis for agency action" on a rule nor the "exclusive basis . . . for judicial review thereof." However, there is no provision in the federal APA similar to § 3–112(c) of the 1981 MSAPA. Nor is there a similar provision in the

1961 MSAPA or the many state acts modeled thereon. Indeed, those acts are totally silent on the subject of an official agency rulemaking record. Nevertheless, the federal APA and these state acts probably intend the same result as that achieved by § 3–112(c) of the 1981 MSAPA. Auerbach notes, in this connection:

> Just as the [federal] APA does not require the agency to issue a rule on the exclusive basis of any "record" made in an informal rule-making proceeding, so it does not require the courts to review the validity of such an agency rule on the exclusive basis of any such record. . . .

> This conclusion is not negated by section 706's directive to the reviewing court to review the "whole record." This requirement means only that "courts may not look only to the case presented by one party, since other evidence may weaken or even indisputably destroy that case." The reports of the Senate and House Judiciary Committees did not in any way imply that the "whole record" would always be an administrative record. It was understood that it might be a judicial record. Congressman Walter explained that "[w]hether a court is proceeding upon an administrative or a judicial record, the requirement of review upon the whole record means that courts may not look only to the case presented by one of the parties but must decide upon all of the proofs submitted."
> . . .

> [Despite this federal APA legislative history] there is a strong tendency in recent statutes and judicial decisions to make the Section 553 rule-making record exclusive in the . . . sense that . . . (1) the agency must itself base its rule exclusively on that record; (2) the reviewing court must take that record as the exclusive basis on which to inquire into the factual predicates of the rule; (3) no objection to the rule may be considered by the reviewing court if it was not presented during the course of the rule-making proceeding unless there was reasonable ground for failure to do so; and (4) if the taking of additional evidence is warranted for any reason, the reviewing court may not itself do so . . . but must remand to the agency.

Auerbach, "Informal Rule Making: A Proposed Relationship Between Administrative Procedures and Judicial Review," 72 Nw.U.L.Rev. 15, 22–30 (1977). What accounts for the statutes and decisions referred to by Auerbach? In part, they stem from a desire to strike a fair balance between the need to protect the public from arbitrary agency rulemaking and the need to retain an efficient and flexible rulemaking process.

Another factor that encouraged federal courts to confine the review of federal agency rules to the rulemaking record was a line of important judicial review cases. In *Citizens to Preserve Overton Park, Inc. v. Volpe,* 401 U.S. 402 (1971), a case involving review of informal agency action, the Court indicated that it would review the action "on the full administrative record that was before the Secretary at the time he made that decision." This important case is considered further in § 9.4, *infra.* Subsequently, in *Camp v. Pitts,* 411 U.S. 138 (1973), which involved review of informal agency adjudication, the Court stated that judicial review must be based on the agency record already in existence and not on some new record made especially for that purpose. *Vermont Yankee,* § 6.3, *supra,* appeared to approve *Overton Park* and *Camp* in the rulemaking context. 435 U.S. 519, 549 (1978). However, it seems doubtful that these cases intended to disturb the traditional distinction between formal and informal rulemaking with respect to the question of exclusivity of the record. That distinction is explicitly maintained in 1981 MSAPA § 3–112(c).

One commentator criticizes the MSAPA provision, arguing that in rulemaking an agency should be limited to considering only material in the agency rulemaking record at the time a rule is adopted; and judicial review of a rule should occur exclusively on the basis of that agency rulemaking record. Rago, "Rulemaking under the Model State Administrative Procedure Act: An Opportunity Missed," 34 Admin.L. Rev. 445, 459 (1982). What is the justification for this criticism? Does this criticism fail to take into account the explanatory statement requirement of § 3–110 and the rule against post hoc rationalization discussed in § 6.7, *supra?* Note the relationship between §§ 3–110 and 3–112(c) of the 1981 MSAPA discussed in the Comment to the former provision:

> Section 3–112(c) of this Act and its Comments regarding the *non*-exclusivity of the agency rule-making record [should be compared] with the requirement in subsection (b) of this section of the exclusivity of an agency's contemporaneous formal *reasons* for a rule. The cumulative effect of these two provisions is as follows. In a proceeding in which the validity of a rule is at issue, the agency may rely *only* on the particular factual, legal, and policy reasons for its adoption contained in the concise explanatory statement. In that proceeding, however, the agency may supplement the agency rule-making record with further evidence and argument to justify or to demonstrate the propriety of those particular reasons contained in the concise explanatory statement.

Note also that § 3–112(b)(3) requires all written materials considered by the agency in adopting a rule (but not oral ex parte contacts) be part of the record on judicial review. Does that provision meet Rago's concerns?

There are strong arguments against a *general* requirement that all informal rulemaking and judicial review of rules be based on the agency rulemaking record. "Conventional wisdom and substantial experience dictate that neither the making of usual rules by an agency nor judicial review of their validity should be *required* to be based wholly on any official agency rulemaking record." 1981 MSAPA § 3–112 Comment. In support of that "conventional wisdom" Auerbach states:

[R]equiring judicial review [of rule making] to proceed exclusively on the basis of the "hearing record" would have unfortunate consequences. Once it is understood that all persons and groups that may be affected by a proposed rule will be limited to the "hearing record" in any judicial proceeding challenging the validity of the rule, the parties participating in the public hearing would multiply—and so would the issues. Only by participation would they be able to affect the contents of the record and preserve the issues they may wish to present to a reviewing court.

The agency's "affirmative presentation" at the public hearing "of facts establishing the need for and reasonableness" of the proposed rule would have to include a presentation of all the significant data, inferences, and conclusions upon which it relies to support the rule. Representatives of the affected interests participating in the public hearing would have to be given an opportunity to challenge the agency presentations and produce rebuttal or countervailing data. . . .

Because a reviewing court would refuse to hear any objection to a rule not made during the public hearing, participants opposing the proposed rule would voice all possible objections and introduce data to support them. Since it could not know which of these objections might eventually become the basis of a challenge to the rule's validity, the agency would have no choice but to respond—for the "hearing record"—to each objection with its own data and arguments.

All these factors would operate to produce large and diffuse records that the agencies and reviewing courts would find cumbersome to manage. Finally, the agency would be required to conduct such an on-the-record rulemaking proceeding before issuing any rule, regardless of its importance and even though it is probable that only a small percentage of any agency's rules will be subjected to judicial review.

Auerbach, "Administrative Rulemaking in Minnesota," 63 Minn.L.Rev. 151, 221–22 (1979) (footnote omitted).

The desirability of a *general* requirement that rules be made and judicially reviewed entirely on the basis of the agency rulemaking record is also questioned by the Comment to § 3–112 of the 1981 MSAPA, which states:

The burden imposed on agencies by a duty in every case to assemble their entire factual and argumentative justification for a rule prior to its adoption, and to enter that entire justification in the official agency record of the rule-making proceeding, is far too great to justify such a requirement.

In addition, a requirement that the validity of a rule, on judicial review, be based wholly on an official record made before the agency in the rule-making proceeding, could be inconsistent with the policy of Section 5–107(1). That provision states that a petitioner for judicial review of a rule "need not have participated in the rule-making proceeding on which that rule is based." It may be unfair to bind persons with an agency rule-making record as the only basis for judicial review of a rule if they did not participate in the rule-making proceeding. . . . [As Auerbach has noted,] an APA should distinguish "between the administrative proceedings on the basis of which an agency promulgates an informal rule and the record on the basis of which the courts determine the rule's validity. The record for judicial review should not be the product of the informal rule-making proceedings, but a record especially made for the purpose." The reason for this is that the purpose of rule-making proceedings should be " 'not to try a case' but to contribute to the dual objectives of informing the agency and safeguarding private interests."

Notes and Questions

1. *Disciplining agency proceeding.* One commentator argues that confining judicial review of a rule made by notice and comment procedures to the agency rulemaking record would have the effect of disciplining the agency proceeding and the record it creates in a way that would be very helpful to both the agency and a reviewing court. *See* Pedersen, "Formal Records and Informal Rulemaking," 85 Yale L.J. 38, 73 (1975). Is this argument sound? Could the same result be achieved by rigorously enforcing the exclusivity of the statement of basis and purpose so that an agency would be barred from using any post hoc rationalizations to support a rule?

2. *Materials examined on judicial review.* According to ACUS, Recommendation 74–4, "Preenforcement Judicial Review of Rules of General Applicability," 1 C.F.R. § 305.74–4, the following administrative materials should be before a court in instances of pre-enforcement judicial review of rules made by § 553 procedures:

(1) The notice of proposed rulemaking and any documents referred to therein;

(2) comments and other documents submitted by interested persons;

(3) any transcripts of oral presentations made in the course of the rulemaking;

(4) factual information not included in the foregoing that was considered by the authority responsible for promulgation of the rule or that is proffered by the agency as pertinent to the rule;

(5) reports of any advisory committees; and

(6) the agency's concise general statement or final order and any documents referred to therein.

What does this recommendation suggest with respect to the exclusivity of the agency rulemaking record on judicial review of rules made by notice and comment procedures?

As noted earlier, the federal APA is silent on the precise contents of the agency rulemaking record, leading to confusion about its contents. The ACUS recommendation was intended to clarify the contents of that record and thereby to eliminate that confusion. How does this recommendation differ from 1981 MSAPA § 3–112?

3. *MSAPA provision and deliberative materials.* Is § 3–112(b)(3) of the 1981 MSAPA sound insofar as it requires inclusion in the agency rulemaking record of "*all* . . . written materials considered by the agency in connection with the formulation, proposal, or adoption of the rule or the proceeding upon which the rule is based?" (Emphasis supplied). Does this provision require inclusion in the rulemaking record of material that an agency may ordinarily claim is privileged, such as opinions by agency staff members who are called upon to give advice to agency decisionmakers? Will staff members be reluctant to give advice frankly if it is all included in the rulemaking record? To the extent staff members may be called upon to summarize the record for decisionmakers, will the inclusion of those summaries in the rulemaking record be obvious targets for challenge in the courts on the grounds they are inadequate, inaccurate, or biased in some way? Is the problem of disclosure here similar to that of disclosure of staff help and advice in administrative adjudication discussed earlier in relation to *Morgan IV,* § 3.3.1, *supra.* In light of that discussion, should the 1981 MSAPA § 3–112(b)(3) be amended? The availability of agency deliberative materials to members of the public under freedom of information legislation is discussed in § 8.1.1, *infra.*

4. *Exclusivity of record in practice.* Despite the *Overton Park* and *Camp v. Pitts* decisions, and their apparent approval in the *Vermont Yankee* case, the United States Courts of Appeals still admit evidence to supplement the agency rulemaking record on review of federal rules made by informal notice and comment procedures. Those courts accomplish that result by recognizing exceptions to the *Overton Park* and *Camp v. Pitts* principles.

> An examination of these exceptions reveals that they are now so far-reaching that they can be applied in almost any case. Furthermore, when a court is faced with an argument from a challenging party that relevant evidence was withheld from the record, it usually must look at the evidence first to determine whether the claim is true. Therefore, even in cases where challengers lose their arguments to submit extra-record evidence, they almost always force a court to examine the evidence anyway.

> Briefly, the exceptions which have developed to allow extra-record evidence are the following: (1) when agency action is not adequately explained in the record before the court; (2) when the agency failed to consider factors which are relevant to its final

decision; (3) when an agency considered evidence which it failed to include in the record; (4) when a case is so complex that a court needs more evidence to enable it to understand the issues clearly; (5) in cases where evidence arising after the agency action shows whether the decision was correct or not; (6) in cases where agencies are sued for a failure to take action; (7) in cases arising under the National Environmental Policy Act; and (8) in cases where relief is at issue, especially at the preliminary injunction stage.

Stark & Wald, "Setting No Records: The Failed Attempts to Limit the Record in Review of Administrative Action," 36 Admin.L.Rev. 333, 343–44 (1984).

What factors do the courts appear to be balancing in allowing these exceptions? In light of these exceptions, do you think the following statement is accurate: "[T]he trend in the courts is clearly in favor of a requirement that the agency defend its rule in court on the record assembled during the course of the rulemaking proceeding." ACUS, A GUIDE TO FEDERAL AGENCY RULEMAKING 237–38 (1983).

5. *Disclosure of agency files or knowledge.* Auerbach notes with respect to the federal APA:

> It is clear beyond question that the APA "does not require the formulation of rules upon the exclusive basis of any 'record' made in informal rule making proceedings." The agency is "free to formulate rules upon the basis of materials in its files and the knowledge and experience of the agency, in addition to the materials adduced in public rule making proceedings." It is not required to disclose the materials in its files or the knowledge and experience on which it based the rule, either prior to its promulgation or in the concise general statement of its basis and purpose.

Auerbach, "Informal Rule Making: A Proposed Relationship Between Administrative Procedures and Judicial Review," 72 Nw.U.L.Rev. 15, 23 (1977).

Should an agency be able to take official notice of legislative facts within its expert knowledge and rely upon them without assembling in the agency rulemaking record, prior to its taking final action on that rule, the actual data to support those facts? *See* Levin, "Scope-of-Review Doctrine Restated: An Administrative Law Section Report," 38 Admin.L.Rev. 239, 279–82 (1986).

Is Auerbach's last point about the required contents of the "concise statement of basis and purpose" correct in light of the judicial gloss on that provision in recent years? Is there a difference between that which must be disclosed in a statement of basis and purpose and that which Auerbach insists need not be disclosed prior to or at the time an agency makes a rule—the materials in its files and the agency knowledge and experience upon which it based the rule?

6. *Supplementation of record by challenging parties.* If, on the basis of *Overton Park* and *Camp v. Pitts,* the agency record in informal

rulemaking is to be the exclusive basis for *agency* action so that on judicial review the agency may not supplement that record in support of the rule, may those who challenge such a rule supplement the agency record at the time of judicial review to demonstrate that the rule is substantively *in*valid? If they may not do so, would that mean, in effect, that persons could not obtain a fair opportunity to challenge the validity of a rule unless they had participated in the rulemaking proceeding on which it is based? Should persons who desire to challenge a rule be directly or indirectly required to have participated in the agency rulemaking proceeding on which it is based as a prerequisite to such a plenary challenge? *See* discussion of exhaustion of remedies in § 11.2.4, *infra*. What if the persons in question did not know at the time of the rulemaking proceeding that their interests would later be affected by the rule they now desire to challenge in court, and the data upon which they would like to rely in making their challenge are not contained in the agency rulemaking record?

7. *State courts.* Most state courts appear to permit both the agency issuing a rule and persons challenging a rule to submit to the reviewing court information and argument relating to the validity of the rule that were not incorporated in the agency rulemaking record at the time the rule was adopted, although the agency is normally deemed bound by any reasons it gave for the rule in its explanatory statement. So, as noted earlier, most states appear to follow the 1981 MSAPA in this respect. *Borden, Inc. v. Commissioner of Public Health,* 448 N.E.2d 367, 380–82 (Mass.1983), § 9.4, *infra,* is instructive in this regard. In that case the court clearly indicated that in determining the validity of a rule it was free to consider evidence that was before the agency, "as well as any other relevant information;" the court also held that in light of evidence presented initially before the trial court in that case, the agency rule being challenged was reasonable and valid.

§ 6.9 PUBLICATION OF RULES AND DEFERRED EFFECTIVE DATE

Publication of agency rules is important because it facilitates easy public access to their contents. That access allows affected parties to ascertain the relevant law and to adjust their conduct accordingly. Limited availability of agency rules creates a risk that individuals may be adversely affected by rules that were not only unknown to them, but that could not have been easily discovered. Because most people obey rules they know about, publication of rules also facilitates compliance with the law, thereby reducing the enforcement workload of agencies. Furthermore, the publication of rules communicates to the general public the standards by which agencies must operate, and the standards by which agencies may be measured. Publication of rules therefore helps to ensure that agencies as well as regulated parties follow the law. For all of these reasons rules are required to be published and normally may not be effective until a specified period after their publication.

The publication requirements for federal agency rules are contained in APA § 552.

[It] requires agencies to publish certain items in the Federal Register for the "guidance of the public." The items include "rules of procedure" and "substantive rules of general applicability adopted as authorized by law, and statements of general policy or interpretations of general applicability formulated and adopted by the agency." [§ 552(a)(1)(D)]. The section also requires publication of "descriptions of [agency] organization" and "statements of the general course and method by which [the agency's] functions are channeled and determined," [§ 552(a)(1)(A)–(B)], which may be rules as defined in 5 U.S.C. § 551(4). Finally, section 552 specifically directs agencies to publish changes in, or repeals of, their rules and policies.

While the phraseology of section 552 is different from that used in the section 551 definition of rule, it appears to encompass almost all of the rules included in section 551. The one exception is "rules of particular applicability," which need not be published in the Federal Register. Failure to comply with section 552's publication requirements means that "a person may not in any manner be required to resort to, or be adversely affected by, a matter required to be published in the Federal Register and not so published," unless the person has actual and timely notice of the matter.

ACUS, A GUIDE TO FEDERAL AGENCY RULEMAKING 20–21 (1983).

A general principle at both the federal and state level is that, absent good cause, a final rule may not become effective immediately upon publication or filing. Section 553(d) of the federal APA states that a final agency rule becomes effective no sooner than 30 days following publication of that final rule in the *Federal Register;* § 4(b) of the 1961 MSAPA, which has been adopted in many states, provides that a rule will become effective 20 days after its filing; and § 3–115(a) of the 1981 MSAPA states that a rule will become effective 30 days after the latest of its filing, publication, and indexing.

An important function of the delayed effectiveness provision is to give persons subject to a new rule an adequate opportunity to learn of its existence and its contents. A contemporaneous claim was that the objective of the delayed effective date "is to 'afford persons affected a reasonable time to prepare for the effective date of a rule or rules or to take any other action which the issuance of rules may prompt.' " U.S. Dept. of Justice, ATTORNEY GENERAL'S MANUAL ON THE ADMINISTRATIVE PROCEDURE ACT 36 (1947), *quoting,* Sen.Rep. 15; H.R.Rep. 25 (Sen.Doc. 201, 259). The delay in effect has also proved to be of value to agencies because it gives them time to detect and correct purely technical errors or omissions in newly adopted rules. In addition, the delayed effectiveness time period gives agencies an opportunity to reevaluate and revise their procedures and to revise the rules in light of public reaction and unanticipated enforcement problems that surface during the pre-effective period.

UNITED STATES v. GAVRILOVIC
551 F.2d 1099 (8th Cir.1977).

[The Administrator of the Drug Enforcement Agency issued a regulation adding mecloqualone to the schedule of controlled substances—Schedule I.] [U]nless he could show "good cause" the Administrator was required to give the public 30 days notice before the regulation became effective. *See* 5 U.S.C. § 553(d). . . . [T]he effective date for the addition of mecloqualone was July 10, 1975, just two days after publication in the Federal Register.

In order to justify the July 10 effective date the Administrator made the following finding of "good cause":

> *Effective dates.* Based on investigations conducted by the Drug Enforcement Administration, the Acting Administrator hereby finds that mecloqualone, in the past, has been clandestinely manufactured for purposes of distribution and diversion outside legitimate drug channels. A most recent investigation has revealed that this clandestine manufacturing activity continues. . . .

> Considering the danger inherent in mecloqualone as a drug meeting the criteria for inclusion into Schedule I, and considering that Congress intended that controls apply to drugs in a preventative manner, the Acting Administrator hereby finds, based upon the above, that the public health, as well as safety, necessitate the placement of Schedule I controls upon mecloqualone at a date earlier than thirty days from the date of publication of this order in the Federal Register.

On July 31, 1975, the defendants were arrested, and charged with manufacturing a controlled substance and conspiracy from April 1975 to July 31, 1975.

On appeal the defendants do not challenge the placement of mecloqualone on Schedule I, but assert that the Administrator's finding of good cause was arbitrary, since he failed to demonstrate a public necessity for the early effective date.

The government, on the other hand, contends that the Administrator's finding that the continuing manufacturing of mecloqualone, an inherently dangerous drug, constituted an immediate danger to public health and safety, was sufficient to justify the July 10 effective date. The government also contends that the defendants were given adequate notice of the proposed placement of mecloqualone on Schedule I by the May 29, 1975, notice in the Federal Register. Furthermore, the government urges that the clandestine nature of defendants' operations demonstrated that they had actual knowledge that their activities were illegal.

It is a fundamental principle of law that "[n]o one can be criminally punished . . . except according to a law prescribed . . . by the sovereign authority before the imputed offense was committed, and which existed as a law at that time." Thus the basic issue, as perceived by this court, is whether the criminal prohibition against the manufacture of mecloqualone was in effect before the defendants' manufacture of the drug.

The general rule is that in the absence of an express provision, an act of Congress takes effect on the date of its enactment. Here, however, because the rule making authority has been delegated to the DEA, § 553(d) of the Administrative Procedure Act requires publication in the Federal Register at least 30 days prior to the rule's effective date unless good cause is shown to forego the full notice period. Thus, if good cause is lacking here, the defendants' conduct which occurred within 23 days of publication would not be unlawful. . . .

The legislative history . . . indicates the APA was not intended to unduly hamper agencies from making a rule effective immediately or at some time earlier than 30 days. However, proponents of the bill make clear that the good cause exception was not to be an "escape clause which may be arbitrarily exercised but requires legitimate grounds supported in law and fact by the required finding." Legitimate grounds were defined as an "urgency of conditions coupled with demonstrated and unavoidable limitations of time," and that the primary consideration was to be the "convenience or necessity of the people affected."

In keeping with the legislative history the DEA has defined good cause in terms of whether "the conditions of public health or safety *necessitate* an earlier effective date."

We think it clear that Congress intended to impose upon an administrative agency the burden of showing a public necessity for an early effective date and that an agency cannot arbitrarily find good cause. In determining whether the good cause exception is to be invoked, an administrative agency is required to balance the necessity for immediate implementation against principles of fundamental fairness which require that all affected persons be afforded a reasonable time to prepare for the effective date of its ruling. When the consequence of agency rule making is to make previously lawful conduct unlawful and to impose criminal sanctions, the balance of these competing policies imposes a heavy burden upon the agency to show public necessity. . . .

The government concedes that the defendants' operation was a substantial factor in the Administrator's finding of good cause, but at the same time it contends that overall considerations of "public health, as well as safety" necessitated immediate controls. The government relies upon the Administrator's finding that "Congress intended that the Attorney General '. . . . should not be required to wait until a number of lives have been destroyed or substantial problems have already arisen before designating a drug as subject to the controls of the [Act] . . . .' "

The House Report discussed the term "potential for abuse" as a key criterion for placement of a drug on the schedules. However, whether a drug has met the criteria for placement on the schedules of controlled substances is a separate question from whether a public necessity exists for an early effective date. This is not to say that general considerations of public health and safety cannot outweigh the public policy of giving adequate notice. As the degree of risk and the potential for harm increase the need to provide immediate controls increases accordingly. The issue is whether the need is so great and the emergency so defined that it justifies administrative rule making without according the public the ordinary notice required by law.

A review of the record reveals that the Administrator's finding of good cause was not based on an acute and immediate threat to public health and safety posed by general use of the drug, but rather on the specific threat posed by defendants' operation. . . .

The record further reveals that mecloqualone and the thiophene analog of phencyclidine posed the same general threat to public health and safety, yet only the placement of mecloqualone on Schedule I was given an early effective date. . . .

The conclusion by the Administrator that the defendants' operation "necessitated" immediate control presupposes that the only effective means of preventing the distribution of mecloqualone by the defendants was to place it on Schedule I without further notice. Yet, it must be acknowledged that the defendants' operations could have been enjoined immediately, since the defendants were not registered as a drug manufacturer as required by 21 U.S.C. § 360. The "immediacy" argument for control of defendants' operation loses additional persuasion upon the government's concession that the DEA did not attempt to shut down defendants' operations until 21 days after the effective date.

We find no public necessity for the advancement of the effective date of the placement of mecloqualone on Schedule I. The record established that the Administrator possessed effective means of closing down the defendants' operation without placing the defendants in jeopardy of a felony conviction under § 841(a)(1). Under the circumstances, we find the justification for the administrative decision to waive the statutory waiting period under § 553(d) inadequate. Although the agency must be given broad leeway in exercising its administrative expertise, we think Congress intended it to carry a heavy burden to justify waiving the 30–day period. This burden is necessarily an exacting one where the exercise of administrative rule making creates harsh criminal sanctions (possession with intent to distribute) where none existed before. . . .

The judgments of conviction are ordered vacated.

Notes and Questions

1. *Which publication?* *Rowell v. Andrus,* 631 F.2d 699 (10th Cir. 1980) makes clear that the required publication for purposes of § 553(d) is *not* the publication of the notice of proposed rulemaking specified in § 553(b); instead, § 553(d) refers to a separate publication of the final rule after its adoption.

2. *Federal Register Act.* In addition to meeting the publication requirements of the federal APA, federal agencies must also abide by the Federal Register Act (FRA), 44 U.S.C. §§ 1501–1511 (1982). The FRA requires the *Federal Register* to be published each federal working day. That publication includes all rules of "general applicability and legal effect" and notices of proposed rulemaking. In addition, FRA requires the publication of a complete codification of all documents having "general applicability and legal effect" that were published in the *Federal Register.* This publication is entitled the *Code of Federal Regulations* (C.F.R.) and consists of 50 titles that are arranged by subject matter similar to the U.S.Code. It is kept up to date by a process of continuous revision.

The C.F.R., with its many volumes, can be difficult to use effectively. Does the public have a right to an index of the C.F.R.? *Cervase v. Office of Federal Register,* 580 F.2d 1166, 1169 (3d Cir.1978), held that the Office of Federal Register is under a statutory duty to publish such an index. The court stated, "[t]he Federal Register Act was enacted because of widespread dissatisfaction with the unsystematic manner in which executive orders, agency regulations, and similar materials were being made available to the public. . . . We think that the indexing obligation is a central and essential feature of this congressional plan. Without that obligation the periodic codification of regulations cannot serve the congressional purpose of providing public access to what has been published in the *Federal Register.*"

3. *State publication requirements.* Section 2–101(c)–(d) of the 1981 MSAPA also requires the periodic publication and indexing of all proposed and recently adopted state agency rules in a frequently issued publication similar to the *Federal Register,* and the compilation and indexing of all such rules in a publication similar to the C.F.R. Today, the overwhelming number of states have both types of publications. A survey completed in early 1983 revealed that published administrative rules compilations are available in thirty-three states, and codification projects were underway in at least five other states. *See* Tseng & Pedersen, "Acquisition of Administrative Rules and Regulations—Update 1983," 35 Admin.L.Rev. 349 (1983).

In an effort to balance the costs and benefits of publication, § 2–101(e) of the 1981 MSAPA authorizes omission from the state register or code of any rules whose publication would be "unduly cumbersome, expensive, or otherwise inexpedient," but only if three conditions are met. Read § 2–101(e). Does this provision fairly balance the interests of the general public with the need for economy and efficiency of government?

4. *Consequences of non-publication.* The consequences of non-publication of a rule were spelled out in *Morton v. Ruiz,* 415 U.S. 199 (1974), discussed in § 5.4, *supra.* The issue in that case was whether the Bureau of Indian Affairs (BIA) must pay welfare benefits to those Indians who live near as well as on reservations. BIA adopted a rule that precluded such payments to Indians living near reservations, but published it only in a manual intended for guidance of the agency staff. BIA regulations required "directives that relate to the public" to be published in the *Federal Register* and codified in C.F.R.

The Supreme Court said:

Where the rights of individuals are affected, it is incumbent upon agencies to follow their own procedures. This is so even where the internal procedures are possibly more rigorous than otherwise would be required. . . . Before the BIA may extinguish the entitlement of these otherwise eligible beneficiaries, it must comply, at a minimum, with its own internal procedures.

The Secretary has presented no reason why the requirement of the [APA] could not or should not have been met . . . [The rule is] ineffective as far as extinguishing rights of those otherwise within the class of beneficiaries contemplated by Congress is concerned . . . .

[I]t is essential that the legitimate expectation of these needy Indians not be extinguished by what amounts to an unpublished ad hoc determination of the agency that was not promulgated in accordance with its own procedures, to say nothing of those of the [APA.]

Would an individual be bound by an unpublished rule if he or she had actual knowledge of the rule? *See* federal APA § 552(a)(1), concluding paragraph; 1981 MSAPA §§ 3–115(a), 2–101(g)(2).

What if an unpublished rule does not require a person to do or refrain from doing anything? In other words, it is an interpretive rule or a policy statement. (These categories are discussed in § 6.11.5, *infra*). Should a court invalidate the rule? In *Zaharakis v. Heckler,* 744 F.2d 711, 714 (9th Cir.1984), the court noted:

[A]ppellant has failed to make an initial showing that he was adversely affected by the lack of publication. "The requirement for publication attaches only to matters which if not published would adversely affect a member of the public. The appellant does not allege that he was adversely affected by a lack of publication or that he would have been able to pursue an alternative course of conduct had the . . . [rule] . . . been published. Under these circumstances, we cannot conclude that the . . . [rule] is invalid."

However, in some situations an interpretive rule or a policy statement may have a substantial practical impact on a person. In such situations, some courts have held the rule to be invalid if it was not published. *See Lewis v. Weinberger*, 415 F.Supp. 652 (D.N.M.1976); Comment, "Publication Under the Freedom of Information Act of Statements of General Policy and Interpretations of General Applicability," 47 U.Chi.L.Rev. 351 (1980).

5. *Filing of rules.* The 1961 and 1981 MSAPAs and virtually all state APAs provide for the filing of rules in a designated centrally located depository open to the public that is independent of the issuing agency. *See* 1961 MSAPA § 4(a); 1981 MSAPA § 3–114(a). The MSAPAs and state statutes typically provide that an unfiled rule is wholly ineffective. *See, e.g., People v. Cull*, 176 N.E.2d 495 (N.Y.1961). What is the virtue of such a requirement? As a norm, should rules be effective prior to their publication *and* indexing *and* filing? What is the argument for requiring all three as a condition for a rule's effectiveness?

6. *Burden of persuasion.* Is *Gavrilovic* correct that the burden is on the agency under § 553(d) to demonstrate "good cause" for dispensing with the period of delayed effectiveness? Contrast your response here with your response to the questions in note 6, § 6.4, *supra*. Note that 1981 MSAPA § 3–115(b)(2) expressly places the burden on the agency for demonstrating grounds for dispensing with the usual period of delayed effectiveness while § 553(d) of the federal act is silent on this subject.

7. *Good cause exceptions.* Section 3–115(b)(2)(iv) of the 1981 MSAPA contains a catch-all emergency provision stating that a rule may be made effective after filing at an earlier date than usual if that earlier date is "*necessary* because of *imminent peril* to the public health, safety, or welfare." (Emphasis supplied). This phrase comes from § 4(b)(2) of the 1961 MSAPA and is found in APAs of many states.

Various kinds of emergency rules may become effective immediately under 1981 MSAPA § 3–115(b)(2)(iv). For example, rules ordering the termination of health or safety hazards that are likely to cause injury during the delayed effectiveness period may be made effective immediately upon filing. Consequently, if an agency finds that certain automobile tires are subject to sudden blowouts, and the agency has the authority to prohibit the use of such tires, it is clear that it may do so immediately on the ground that the lives of drivers would be jeopardized by the use of those tires during any waiting period. The delayed effectiveness period also may be waived on the grounds of imminent peril to the public welfare with respect to matters not involving health or safety. For example, an agency regulating securities fraud may discover that its rules do not bar the sale of a certain type of fraudulent security that it is authorized to prohibit. The agency may adopt rules prohibiting such sales that are effective immediately because the sale of securities of this type consummated during any period of delayed effectiveness would cause imminent injury to the unprotected buyers.

See generally A. Bonfield, STATE ADMINISTRATIVE RULE MAKING 385–87 (1986).

8. *Comparing standards.* Which exemptive standard for dispensing with the usual delayed effectiveness requirement is superior, that contained in § 553(d) of the federal act, "good cause," or that contained in § 3–115(b)(2)(iv) of the 1981 MSAPA, and § 4(b)(2) of the 1961 MSAPA, "imminent peril to the public health, safety, or welfare"? Contrast your answer to this question with your response to the questions in note 4, § 6.4, *supra*.

9. *No opposition.* The court in the *Gavrilovic* case quoted from the legislative history of the federal APA to the effect that the primary concern of this good cause exception was the "convenience or necessity of the people affected." Does this mean that if there is no opposition to the immediate effectiveness of a new rule by those who are subject to its provisions, the issuing agency may lawfully disregard the usual thirty day delayed effectiveness period?

10. *Rules conferring benefits.* Both the federal APA, § 553(d)(1), and the 1981 MSAPA, § 3–115(b)(2)(ii), provide that an agency need not delay the effective date of newly adopted rules if they grant an exemption or relieve a restriction. Since such rules confer benefits rather than impose burdens on regulated persons, those persons usually do not need and do not want a delayed effective date. They want the rules to be effective as soon as possible.

Is this exemption from usual delayed effective date requirements justifiable? What about the collateral effects of rules granting an exemption or relieving a restriction on persons other than those who are the direct beneficiaries of such rules? For example, when an agency relieves a restriction on a class of businesses by deregulating their activities, the direct beneficiaries (the regulated businesses) will want the rule to be effective immediately. But members of the general public who are protected by the regulation of these businesses may be harmed if such a deregulatory rule is effective immediately. Should those persons be given time to prepare for the impact of such rules? Is the language of the 1981 MSAPA provision superior, in this respect, to the language contained in the federal act, because the former allows immediate effectiveness of a rule if "the rule *only* confers a benefit or removes a restriction on the public or some segment thereof" (emphasis added), while the latter allows immediate effectiveness of a rule if it "grants or recognizes an exemption or relieves a restriction?"

11. *Other exemptions.* The 1981 MSAPA allows an additional exception to delayed effectiveness requirements when a rule "only delays the effective date of another rule that is not yet effective." § 3–115(b)(2)(iii). This allows an agency to issue a rule that would immediately delay the effectiveness of another newly adopted rule, which had been found to have defects only after the final text of that rule had been published.

The federal APA also allows interpretive rules and general statements of policy to be immediately effective. This provision will be discussed later when the categorical exemptions from rulemaking procedures are examined. *See* § 6.11, *infra.*

§ 6.10 PETITION FOR ADOPTION, AMENDMENT, OR REPEAL OF RULES

Section 553(e) of the federal APA, § 6 of the 1961 MSAPA, and § 3–117 of the 1981 MSAPA, all authorize members of the public to petition an agency for the issuance, amendment, or repeal of a rule. The worthwhile objectives of these provisions have resulted in their widespread incorporation in state APAs.

Perhaps the most important purpose of the petition for rulemaking is to force an agency to re-examine the status quo, either by requesting that the agency undertake additional regulation or that it repeal or modify existing rules that are not working properly or have become obsolete. Such petitions bring to the agency's attention situations requiring prompt action and thus help to insure more responsive government.

Another important purpose of petitions for rulemaking is to supply a means for focused public input when an agency has adopted a rule without advance notice and comment, either under the categorical exceptions, § 6.11, *infra,* or under the good cause exceptions, § 6.4, *supra. See Guardian Federal Savings and Loan Ass'n v. FSLIC,* 589 F.2d 658, 668 (D.C.Cir.1978). Similarly, even when an agency has provided advance notice and comment, some members of the public who did not know about the proposed rule, or who did not participate in the process, may be dissatisfied with the final rule and wish to persuade the agency to modify it. The right to file a rulemaking petition may help them.

Note that 1981 MSAPA § 3–117 requires an agency to adopt rules prescribing the form of petitions and the procedure for their submission, consideration, and disposition. Federal APA § 553(e) contains no such requirement. As a result, "[p]ersistence and a knowledge of the workings of the [federal] agency to which the petition is addressed are essential elements of success in the [federal] petition process, since explicit statutory support for the petition [other than the bare language of § 553(e)] is usually shallow or lacking." J. O'Reilly, ADMINISTRATIVE RULEMAKING 329 (1983).

Section 3–117 of the 1981 MSAPA requires that the agency act on a petition within sixty days either to deny the petition, to initiate rulemaking proceedings, or to adopt a rule. The 1961 MSAPA provision, adopted by many states, requires such an agency response within thirty days. Federal act § 553(e) contains no time limit provision. As a result, petitions are often filed with a federal agency and never heard of again. Nevertheless, federal agencies may not "abuse their discretion" or act "arbitrarily" or "capriciously" in delaying a response to such a petition. Federal act § 706(2)(A).

Both MSAPAs require a statement of reasons upon denial of a rulemaking petition. Federal APA § 553(e) does not require any such statement, but federal act § 555(e) requires a brief statement of the grounds for denial of any application or petition filed with an agency. The requirement for a statement of reasons is important because it forces agencies to consider carefully their precise reasons for any such denial, thereby discouraging automatic or impulsive dismissals of rulemaking petitions. The required written statement also facilitates judicial review (assuming such review is available). If the agency gives an improper reason for denial of a petition, the court must remand the denial to the agency for reconsideration, even if there would have been appropriate reasons for the agency action. *SEC v. Chenery Corp.*, 318 U.S. 80 (1943); *Bargmann v. Helms*, 715 F.2d 638 (D.C.Cir.1983) (agency dismissed petition on erroneous ground that it lacked jurisdiction to adopt the suggested rule).

Notes and Questions

1. *Adequacy of APA provisions.* Are the federal and MSAPA provisions for rulemaking petitions defective because they do not require a hearing—an oral proceeding—upon receipt of a petition for rulemaking? Should an informal notice and comment proceeding be required upon receipt of such a petition? *See Wisconsin Elec. Power Co. v. Costle*, 715 F.2d 323 (7th Cir.1983) (refusing to order such procedure). May an agency provide such a hearing or begin an informal rulemaking proceeding upon receipt of a petition if it chooses to do so?

Is the federal act defective because it does not provide that an agency must respond to such a petition within a specified number of days? Is § 555(e) providing for "prompt notice . . . of the denial . . . of a . . . petition" really much help? What does "prompt" mean? In any case, is a duty to give prompt notice of *the denial* of a petition the same as a duty to give a prompt response to a petition? Under the 1961 or 1981 MSAPA, what practical remedy does a petitioner have if an agency does not respond to a petition within the number of days specified in those acts? Would it be wise to provide by statute that an agency failing to comply with the requirements pertaining to such a petition is barred from acting in a way that would prejudice the particular petitioner if that prejudicial action would not have been possible had the agency taken the requested rulemaking action? *See* A. Bonfield, STATE ADMINISTRATIVE RULE MAKING § 6.18.2 (1986).

2. *Exemptions.* The § 553(e) right to petition for rulemaking under the federal APA is limited by the categorical exemptions from rulemaking procedures discussed in § 6.11, *infra*. This means that there is no right to petition for the issuance, amendment, or repeal of rules involving military or foreign affairs functions, or rules relating to agency management or personnel, or to public property, loans, grants,

benefits, or contracts. *See* § 553(a). As a practical matter, does the inapplicability of § 553(e) make any difference?

On the other hand, 1981 MSAPA § 3–117 confers a right to petition for the issuance, amendment, or repeal of rules that are entirely excluded from other usual rulemaking and rule-effectiveness requirements by the unqualified categorical exemptions of § 3–116, discussed in § 6.11, *infra*. Is the position of the federal act or the 1981 MSAPA best on this issue?

3. *Agency procedures for dealing with petitions.* In light of the sparseness of federal and state statutory provisions governing rulemaking petitions, the effectiveness of the current process is largely a function of the procedures used by agencies to handle such petitions. What kind of procedures should an agency adopt for dealing with rulemaking petitions? For a discussion of this and other issues concerning rulemaking petitions under the federal APA see Luneburg, "Petitioning Federal Agencies for Rulemaking: An Overview of Administrative and Judicial Practice and some Recommendations for Improvement," 1988 Wis.L.Rev. 1.

4. *Problem.* Assume that a valid agency rule requires a permit before a piece of undeveloped land is subdivided into more than four lots. No permit is issued without proof that the subdividers have provided for roads, sewers, and other improvements. The agency is bound by the 1981 MSAPA.

Your client Mary owns a large parcel that she would like to split up for sale into eight lots but she does not want to build sewers because the land is in the desert, far from available sewer hookups. She believes she can avoid the permit requirement by giving half of her land to her brother Bill. Then Mary and Bill could each split up their parcels into four lots without obtaining a permit. However, they are uncertain whether the rule would prohibit them from doing so. What are their options?

One option, of course, is to ignore the rule and proceed, taking the risk that they will not be detected, or that the rule would be found inapplicable to their plan. Do you recommend this course of action? What are the risks of doing so?

A second option is to ask the agency for advice as to whether the rule, as properly interpreted, would apply to the plan. If the agency replied favorably, could it later change its mind and seek to apply its rule to prevent sale of the lots? Is this likely? Should the request be oral or written? In a certain form? *See* discussion of estoppel against the government in § 4.4.3, *supra*. If the agency replied negatively, would this make it more likely that the client would be the subject of enforcement action if she goes ahead with her plan anyway?

A third option is to ask the agency for a waiver of the rule, arguing that the rule should not be applied in her case. She would argue that the requirement of building sewers makes no sense when the land is so remote. Thus she concedes that the rule is generally valid and applicable to her plan, but contends that her situation is different from that contemplated by the agency when it made the rule. *See* discussion of waivers in § 3.2, *supra.* Assuming the rule made no provision for waiver requests, can such an application be filed anyway?

A fourth option is to petition for an amendment of the rule so that it would be made inapplicable to remote sites or to land owned by several related family members. What if the agency has never adopted rules concerning the procedure for petitions for the amendment of rules? What happens if the agency ignores the petition? What happens if it rejects the petition but gives no reasons? What happens if it rejects the petition for reasons that, in your opinion, are legally wrong, for example, because the agency states that it has no legal authority to make exceptions for remote parcels? Is judicial review possible in any of these rulemaking petition situations? Is judicial review of agency action in relation to such a rulemaking petition practical for this client? If your client seeks judicial review in any of the above situations relating to a rulemaking petition and is successful, what remedy is the court likely to order?

WWHT, INC. v. F.C.C.

656 F.2d 807 (D.C.Cir.1981).

EDWARDS, J.:

This case raises the questions of whether, and under what circumstances, a reviewing court may require an agency to institute rulemaking proceedings after the agency has denied a petition for rulemaking. . . .

Section 4 of the [federal APA] § 553, sets out the procedures to be followed by administrative agencies in informal rulemaking. . . . Although the legislative history accompanying section 4(d) [§ 553(e)] makes it plain that an agency must receive and respond to petitions for rulemaking, it is equally clear from the legislative history that Congress did not intend to compel an agency to undertake rulemaking merely because a petition has been filed. When petitions for rulemaking are filed, section 4(d) requires the agency to

> fully and promptly consider them, take such action as may be required, and . . . notify the petitioner in case the request is denied. The agency may either grant the petition, undertake public rule making proceedings . . . or deny the petition.

S.Rep. No. 752, 79th Cong., 1st Sess. (1945).

In its report on the APA, the Senate Judiciary Committee emphasized that

> [t]he mere filing of a petition does not require an agency to grant it, or to hold a hearing, or engage in any other public rule making proceedings. The refusal of an agency to grant the petition or to hold rule making proceedings, therefore, would not per se be

subject to judicial reversal. However, the facts or considerations brought to the attention of an agency by such a petition might be such as to require the agency to act to prevent the rule from continuing or becoming vulnerable upon judicial review. . . .

Id. at 201–02.

The *Attorney General's Manual* on the APA confirms these interpretations of the APA. The *Manual* parallels the language of the Senate Report, indicating that an agency is not required to grant a petition for rulemaking merely because it is filed, and that prompt notice should be given when a petition is denied. With respect to the particular procedures followed by each agency in receiving and disposing of petitions for rulemaking, the *Manual* refers to the rules promulgated by each agency pursuant to 5 U.S.C. § 553.

Under existing rules of the FCC, any interested party may petition the Commission for "the issuance, amendment or repeal" of a rule or regulation. When a petition is filed, the Commission is to determine whether the petition "discloses sufficient reasons in support of the action requested to justify the institution of a rulemaking proceeding." In cases where the Commission determines that rulemaking is not warranted, the "petition for rule making will be denied and the petitioner will be notified of the Commission's action with the grounds therefor." . . .

Under 5 U.S.C. § 702, any person adversely affected by agency action is entitled to judicial review, except where the statute under which the action was taken precludes judicial review, or where the action is committed to agency discretion by law. 5 U.S.C. § 701(a). While there is no claim in this case that judicial review is barred by some statutory preclusion, there is a question as to whether the Commission's denial of the petition for rulemaking was an "agency action committed to agency discretion by law."

The 1947 *Attorney General's Manual* interpreted section 4(d), of the APA to preclude judicial review of the denial of a petition to promulgate a rule or amendment, or of an agency's refusal to institute rulemaking proceedings.

While we agree that judicial intrusion into an agency's exercise of discretion in the discharge of its essentially legislative rulemaking functions should be severely circumscribed, we reject the suggestion that agency denials of requests for rulemaking are exempt from judicial review. . . .

In *Natural Resources Defense Council,* this court stated that 5 U.S.C. § 701(a) "creates a strong presumption of reviewability that can be rebutted only by a clear showing that judicial review would be inappropriate." 606 F.2d at 1043. The court referred to language in Senate Committee Report No. 752, *reprinted in* Legislative History, at 185, 201, noting that "[t]he refusal of an agency to grant the petition or to hold rule making proceedings . . . would not per se be subject to judicial *reversal,"* and concluded that the language implied that judicial review *would* sometimes be available when agencies refuse to institute rulemaking proceedings.

The *NRDC* court also noted that, notwithstanding the role played by the Justice Department in drafting the APA, the *Attorney General's Manual* was not entitled to particular deference, "to the extent that it is inconsistent with the Senate Report." . . .

In the context of the instant case, petitioners have alleged that the FCC abused its discretion when it denied the request for rulemaking. This contention presents an issue that is plainly cognizable under 5 U.S.C. § 706(2)(A) of the APA. Although we believe that the *scope* of review must of necessity be narrow, we nevertheless hold that this court has jurisdiction to review the issue posed by petitioners. . . .

In determining the scope of review in this case, we follow the lead of *NRDC.* In particular, we adhere to Judge McGowan's suggestion that, where the proposed rule pertains to a matter of policy within the agency's expertise and discretion, the scope of review should "perforce be a narrow one, limited to ensuring that the Commission has adequately explained the facts and policy concerns it relied on and to satisfy ourselves that those facts have some basis in the record."

We also recognize that where the agency decides not to proceed with rulemaking, the "record" for purposes of review need only include the petition for rulemaking, comments pro and con where deemed appropriate, and the agency's explanation of its decision to reject the petition. . . .

Because of the broad discretionary powers possessed by administrative agencies to promulgate (or not promulgate) rules, and the narrow scope of review to which the exercise of that discretion is subjected, there are very few cases in which courts have forced agencies to institute rulemaking proceedings on a particular issue after it has declined to do so. As was recognized in *Action for Children's Television:*

> As a corollary of [the agency's] broad general discretion, the Commission has considerable latitude in responding to requests to institute proceedings or to promulgate rules, even though it possesses the authority to do so should it see fit. . . .

It is only in the rarest and most compelling of circumstances that this court has acted to overturn an agency judgment not to institute rulemaking.

In *Geller v. FCC,* 610 F.2d 973 (D.C.Cir.1979) . . . the court reversed the Commission's order, finding the Commission's exercise of discretion *not* to institute rulemaking proceedings to be "plainly misguided." 610 F.2d at 979. The court in *Geller* ruled that an agency "cannot sidestep a re-examination of particular regulations when abnormal circumstances make that course imperative." The rule that emerges from *Geller,* then, is a limited one: that an agency may be forced by a reviewing court to institute rulemaking proceedings if a significant factual predicate of a prior decision on the subject (either to promulgate or not to promulgate specific rules) has been removed. . . .

It is significant that in [no case] did the court compel the agency to actually institute rulemaking proceedings. Rather, each agency was required on remand to *reconsider* its denial of the petition, in light of the correct interpretation of the law as enunciated by the court. . . .

Our review of the record indicates that no procedural infirmity mars the actions of the agency below.

We are left then, with a challenge to the factual and policy determinations of the Commission. . . .

For us to seriously indulge petitioners' claims in this case would be to ignore the institutional disruption that would be visited on the Commission by our second-guessing its "expert" determination not to pursue a particular program or policy at a given time. It would also require us to ignore the plain fact that the policy determinations made by the Commission in this case raise issues that are not well-suited for determination by this court. These considerations lead us to conclude that our review of the Commission's actions should be *extremely narrow,* consistent with the views heretofore expressed. The Commission's substantive determinations are essentially legislative in this case and are thus committed to the discretion of the agency.

Nevertheless, as we have already held, the Commission is required to give some explanation for its actions. Such an explanation enables a reviewing court to satisfy itself that the agency's action was neither arbitrary, nor capricious, nor an abuse of discretion, nor otherwise contrary to statutory, procedural or constitutional requirements.

Having considered the record in this case, we are satisfied that the orders of the Commission must be affirmed. The Commission adequately explained the facts and policy concerns it relied on, and there is nothing to indicate that the opinions of the Commission are unlawful, arbitrary, capricious or wholly irrational. Therefore, the judgment of the Commission not to proceed with rulemaking at this time must be left undisturbed.

NOTES AND QUESTIONS

1. *Is WWHT good law?* Even the very limited form of review permitted in *WWHT* may be contrary to the Supreme Court's decision in *Chaney v. Heckler,* § 10.5, *infra,* which held that an agency refusal to take enforcement action is presumptively unreviewable. Be sure to reconsider whether *WWHT* is correct and whether it states sound policy after you read *Chaney v. Heckler,* which was decided after the *WWHT* case.

2. *State case. Community Action Research Group v. Iowa State Commerce Com'n,* 275 N.W.2d 217 (Iowa 1979), involved a petition for

rulemaking under a state APA and came to a similar result as the *WWHT* case. In *Community Action Research Group* the claim was that the agency's reason 'for denial of the petition was improper. The court responded that the right to petition for adoption of a rule "requires only that an agency give fair consideration to the propriety of issuing the proposed rule." If there are good reasons for the refusal of the agency to take the particular rulemaking action requested, the court must uphold the agency action, whether the reasons relate to the merits of the proposed rule itself or to the inability of the agency at that time "to take a stand on the substantive issues that might prompt the proposal of a rule." The court insisted that "[i]t is not for the courts to question the wisdom of such a position. It is enough to hold it was one the [*agency*] was legally entitled to take" because the agency complied with all the requirements of the statute and acted reasonably.

In this state case the court noted explicitly that on judicial review of the denial of the petition for rulemaking, the reviewing court "is free to receive and consider such additional evidence as it feels is appropriate. Such additional evidence, of course, is to be considered in addition to that offered before the agency. [So] . . . the record for our review on appeal consists of evidence presented both to the Commission and to the district court."

Was the "record" before the state court the same as the "record" before the federal court in the *WWHT* case? Note the comments of the court in the *WWHT* case on that point. What should a court consider when it makes the determination as to whether an agency denying a petition for rulemaking acted lawfully?

If the agency acted improperly on a procedural basis, the court may presumably remand to the agency to follow proper procedures. What remedy is appropriate if the agency acted in a substantively unlawful manner because its denial rested on an improper reason or was otherwise an abuse of discretion?

§ 6.11   CATEGORICAL EXEMPTIONS TO RULEMAKING REQUIREMENTS

Section 6.1 noted the purposes of rulemaking procedures. For some classes of rulemaking, however, the legislature considers the costs of these procedural requirements to outweigh their benefits. Both federal and state APA's provide categorical exemptions from the usual requirements for certain types of rules and for rules relating to certain governmental functions. Commentators disagree on whether these exemptions are appropriate and needed. There is a general consensus, however, that the exemptions should be "narrowly construed and only reluctantly countenanced." *American Fed. Govt. Employees v. Block,* 655 F.2d 1153, 1156 (D.C.Cir.1981). Furthermore, these exemptions are inapplicable to the extent other law requires an agency to follow usual rulemaking procedures for any of the rules within these excepted categories.

Unlike the good cause exemptions, discussed in §§ 6.4 and 6.9, *supra*, the categorical exemptions are not based upon an evaluation of the particular circumstances surrounding each individual rulemaking. Instead they represent a generalized judgment that *all* rules falling into the defined categories should be exempt, regardless of individual circumstances.

As to each categorical exemption, consider:

  (i) whether the costs of requiring the usual procedures clearly outweigh the benefits of those procedures;

  (ii) whether the exemptions might be narrowed or otherwise modified;

  (iii) whether the good cause exemptions might be sufficient to accomplish the objectives of the categorical exemption;

  (iv) whether some categorical exemptions appropriate at the federal level are inappropriate at the state level, or vice versa;

  (v) whether the categorical exceptions should apply to the right to petition for the issuance, amendment, or repeal of a rule.

§ 6.11.1 PROPRIETARY MATTERS

Federal APA § 553(a)(2) excludes rules relating to "public property, loans, grants, benefits, or contracts" from *all* of the requirements of § 553 including the provisions for deferred effective date and the right to petition. This broad exemption covers rulemaking involving hundreds of billions of dollars each year and affects a vast number of business concerns as well as recipients of government benefits.

The "public property" exemption includes rules relating to the public domain such as the sale or lease of public lands or of mineral, timber, or grazing rights in such lands. It covers rules relating to the use of public buildings and surplus federal property (including farm surpluses) and to the use of national forests and national parks.

The "loans" exemption applies to rules relating to a very great variety of federal loan programs. The exempted rules concern loans to local government for urban mass transportation systems, small business loans, disaster loans, student loans, and many others.

The "grants" exemption covers rules relating to a range of federal subsidy and grants-in-aid programs that provide assistance to state and local government as well as to individuals. The "benefits" exemption covers rules relating to pensions, social security old age and disability payments, and such welfare programs as Aid to Families with Dependent Children.

Finally, the "contracts" exemption covers rules relating to government contracts for the procurement of land, goods, or services, and for construction of any kind. It also exempts from usual procedures rules relating to the issuance of government securities and to research conducted under federal contract.

On the proprietary matters exemptions *see generally* Bonfield, "Public Participation in Federal Rulemaking Relating to Public Property, Loans, Grants, Benefits, or Contracts," 118 U.Pa.L.Rev. 540 (1970) (discussing whether § 553 adequately accommodates the need for "public participation in the rule making process" with the need for "exemptions . . . absolutely necessary to preserve other values").

HUMANA OF SOUTH CAROLINA v. CALIFANO
590 F.2d 1070 (D.C.Cir.1978).

SPOTTSWOOD W. ROBINSON, III, CIRCUIT JUDGE:

Humana of South Carolina, Inc., a proprietary hospital, asserts procedural, statutory and constitutional challenges to a regulation promulgated by the Secretary of Health, Education and Welfare limiting the rate of return on equity capital recoverable as a cost item by providers of services under the Medicare Act. . . .

Humana contends, and the Secretary appears to concede, that the challenged return-on-equity regulation was not promulgated compliantly with the notice-and-comment requirements delineated in the Administrative Procedure Act. The controversy, rather, is whether the rulemaking in question was exempt from the strictures of the Act by virtue of the "benefits" exception in Section 553(a)(2). . . . The District Court agreed with the Secretary that this provision is broad enough to embrace the reimbursement rule that Humana seeks to nullify, and we are of the same view.

The salutary effect of the Act's public comment procedures cannot be gainsaid, so only reluctantly should courts recognize exemptions therefrom. But even construed narrowly, Section 553(a)(2) cuts a wide swath through the safeguards generally imposed on agency action. Its literal reach is circumscribed somewhat by relevant legislative history, but nonetheless a broad domain is preserved for its operation. More specifically, "to the extent that" any one of the enumerated categories is "clearly and directly" involved in the regulatory effort at issue, the Act's procedural compulsions are suspended. That the governmental function is not strictly "proprietary," or the regulation's character is not "mechanical," does not curtail Section 553(a)(2)'s permissive effect. Public policy may be sorely affected, and the wisdom of public input manifest, but the statutory exemption still prevails when "grants," "benefits" or other named subjects are "clearly and directly" implicated. . . .

The Medicare program has as an essential objective alleviation of the financial burdens associated with medical needs borne by the aged and the disabled. . . . The [most common] method of subsidy is extension of Medicare funds directly to providers of services on behalf of patients participating in the program.

Regulations governing the amount of reimbursement allocable to providers, then, plainly implicate administration of Medicare funds. The extent to which providers incidentally benefit from participation in the program may be somewhat uncertain. But, as the District Court observed, rules "establishing a reimbursement formula for payments to organizations in order that they actually deliver . . . benefits [to subscribing patients] can only be viewed as 'relating to' those benefits." To this we might add our own conviction that the nexus is "clear and direct."

Humana contends, however, that the situation of a provider is closer to that of firms in regulated industries, which generally are afforded an opportunity to participate in rulemaking, than to aid-beneficiaries, who indisputably are affected by the benefits exemption. Humana makes much of the fact that providers themselves are not recipients of gratuitous benefits, but of compensation for services performed. And though participation in the Medicare hospitalization-insurance program must be initiated by the hospital, Humana maintains that as a practical matter such organizations have little choice but to seek certification as a "provider of services."

That providers are not afforded governmental assistance in the strict sense has little bearing on the applicability of Section 553(a)(2). Certainly a provider's interest in reimbursement is of no greater magnitude than a beneficiary's concern for program funding, and the citizenry is affected no more substantially by rules implicating one rather than the other. Nor does the record indicate that providers participate significantly less willingly in the Medicare program than do beneficiaries. "Realistically, the conditions imposed on [all] recipients of . . . grants, benefits, or public contracts . . . frequently cannot be avoided" for "in the world as it actually is, most people are in no position to refuse the 'privilege' to which the strings are attached." Thus neither the impact of the reimbursement regulation on Humana nor the public interest more generally implicated by its promulgation distinguishes the present regulation from others concededly encompassed by Section 553(a)(2). In all cases in which the excepted subject matter is "clearly and directly" involved, the congressional aim was to afford agencies procedural latitude regardless of the interest of affected parties and the public generally in contributing to formulation of the exempted rule.

Cognizant of the prudence, however, of allowing public input in the wide variety of rulemaking covered by Section 553(a)(2), the Secretary in 1971 elected to waive the exemption and to submit to the normal requirements of the Administrative Procedure Act, and regulations promulgated since that time are subject to mandatory rulemaking procedures. But the regulation challenged in the instant case was issued in 1966, and consequently was not dependent for its effectiveness upon the Secretary's adherence to the Act's commands. Humana's procedural challenge therefore cannot prevail.

Notes and Questions

1. *Desirability of proprietary matters exemption.* The rules described in federal APA § 553(a)(2) have a significant impact on the daily lives of millions of people. Nevertheless, they are all exempt from federal notice and comment rulemaking procedures. This means that affected people do not have any opportunity to influence the contents of these rules. It also means that agencies covered by the exemption may become out of touch with public needs and desires.

What justification can be offered for a proprietary matters exemption of such vast scope? Do you detect a vestige of the right-privilege distinction discussed in § 2.2, *supra.* Even if such rules should be exempt from notice and comment procedures, why should they be exempt from the delayed effectiveness and right to petition requirements?

2. *State law.* Neither the MSAPAs nor the state APAs contain exemptions of the scope of those found in federal APA § 553(a)(2). Is there some reason why the exemption is appropriate at the federal but not the state level?

Based on a number of similar provisions found in state acts, the new MSAPA exempts certain categories of rules from all rulemaking requirements except the right to petition. Read 1981 MSAPA § 3–116(3)–(5). Are these categorical exemptions justified? Does the narrowness of these MSAPA exemptions suggest that the federal exemption is overbroad? Could an agency omit rulemaking procedures under the good cause exemptions as "unnecessary" for all rules specified in § 3–116(3)–(5)?

3. *Waiver of exemptions.* The *Humana* decision observed that the agency had waived the federal act's § 553(a)(2) exemptions. Numerous agencies did so in response to an ACUS recommendation that called on Congress to repeal § 553(a)(2) and on agencies to utilize rulemaking procedures without awaiting a legislative command to do so. ACUS, Recommendation 69–8, "Elimination of Certain Exemptions from the APA Rulemaking Requirements," 1 C.F.R. § 305.69–8; Bonfield, "Public Participation in Federal Rulemaking Relating to Public Property, Loans, Grants, Benefits, or Contracts," 118 U.Pa.L.Rev. 540 (1970).

If an agency adopts a procedural rule that commits it to follow § 553 procedure, despite a statutory exemption, it will be required to conform to its own rule. *See Rodway v. USDA,* 514 F.2d 809 (D.C.Cir. 1975). *See also* n. 4, § 5.1, *supra.* Absent such a procedural rule, however, occasional compliance with § 553 would not commit the agency to follow rulemaking procedure in other situations. *Malek-Marzban v. INS,* 653 F.2d 113, 116 (4th Cir.1981); ACUS, A GUIDE TO FEDERAL AGENCY RULEMAKING 27 (1983).

§ 6.11.2   MILITARY AND FOREIGN AFFAIRS FUNCTIONS

Federal APA § 553(a)(1) exempts a rule from all rulemaking procedures "to the extent there is involved . . . a military or foreign affairs function of the United States." This exemption is motivated largely by international, rather than domestic concerns, and applies to a rule adopted by any agency that "clearly and directly" involves either of these functions.

As in the case of the proprietary matters exception discussed in § 6.11.1, *supra*, it seems clear that the military and foreign affairs exception is broader than required by legitimate national security concerns. Should this exemption be narrowed? If so, how? *See generally* ACUS, Recommendation 73–5, "Elimination of the 'Military or Foreign Affairs Function' Exemption from APA Rulemaking Requirements," 1 C.F.R. § 305.73–5; Bonfield, "Military and Foreign Affairs Function Rulemaking Under the APA," 71 Mich.L.Rev. 221 (1972).

The Department of Defense has established a general policy favoring notice and comment procedures in the development of rules having a substantial and direct effect on the public, unless a "significant and legitimate interest" of the DOD or the public requires the omission of those procedures. *See* 32 C.F.R. § 296.3. Since 1974, the Department of State has also normally provided for notice and comment procedures in its rulemaking. ACUS, A GUIDE TO FEDERAL AGENCY RULEMAKING 31 (1983).

§ 6.11.3   AGENCY MANAGEMENT AND PERSONNEL

Under federal APA § 553(a)(2), rules "relating to agency management or personnel" are excepted from all rulemaking requirements. The exemption has been deemed inapplicable to rules that have a substantial effect on persons outside of the national government. ACUS, A GUIDE TO FEDERAL AGENCY RULEMAKING 28 (1983).

Section 3–116(1) of the 1981 MSAPA is quite explicit on this point: it excepts from usual rulemaking procedures rules "concerning only the internal management of an agency which [do] . . . not directly and substantially affect the procedural or substantive rights or duties of any segment of the public." A similar exemption is found in § 1(7)(A) of the 1961 MSAPA and in the acts of many states. Is the language of the new MSAPA exemption better drafted than the language of the federal agency management and personnel exemption?

Under the federal APA or the 1981 MSAPA, would a rule describing the performance criteria for agency employees engaged in law enforcement be exempt from the usual rulemaking procedures? How about a rule prescribing the office hours of an agency? Or a rule prescribing the standards applicable to the hiring of government employees?

In practice, the effect of the federal APA personnel exemption has been reduced somewhat by other statutes. The Federal Civil Service

Reform Act of 1978, for example, requires the Office of Personnel Management to follow notice and comment procedures in formulating government-wide personnel rules unless they are "temporary in nature and . . . necessary to be implemented expeditiously as the result of an emergency." 5 U.S.C. §§ 1103(b)(3), 1105.

In the 1961 MSAPA and most state acts the internal agency management exemption and other categorical exemptions from usual requirements applicable to rules are effectuated by defining the term "rule" to exclude agency statements of law or policy within that category. *See* 1961 MSAPA § 1(7). In the 1981 MSAPA and the federal act, however, statements within such categorical exemptions are "rules," but they are specifically exempted from all requirements applicable to rules. 1981 MSAPA § 3–116; federal APA § 553(a), (b) (A), d(2). Which is the better drafting approach? *See* A. Bonfield, STATE ADMINISTRATIVE RULE MAKING 396–97 (1986).

§ 6.11.4 PROCEDURAL RULES

"Rules of agency organization, procedure, or practice" are exempted from usual notice and comment procedures by federal APA § 553(b) (A). They are not, however, excluded from the delayed effectiveness and right to petition requirements of § 553. There is no similar exemption for such rules in the MSAPAs or in state APAs. A constant problem in the law is to distinguish "procedure" from "substance." Nevertheless, such a distinction must be drawn under this exemption.

UNITED STATES DEPARTMENT OF LABOR v. KAST METALS CORP.

744 F.2d 1145 (5th Cir.1984).

[Before inspecting a factory for unsafe working conditions, OSHA must secure a warrant. Recall *Marshall v. Barlow's Inc.*, discussed in § 4.1.2, *supra.* Under prior practice, OSHA selected businesses for inspection by a random method. Without notice and comment, OSHA adopted a new instruction to staff to select businesses with the highest accident rates. Instruction CPL 2.25B. Applying that formula, OSHA selected Kast Metals for inspection. OSHA secured a warrant, but Kast denied entry to the inspectors and moved to quash the warrant, arguing that CPL 2.25B was invalidly adopted. The District Court agreed because it found that CPL 2.25B had a substantial impact on regulated persons.

The Court of Appeals (Goldberg, J.) first held that CPL 2.25B was a rule as defined in APA § 551(4), rather than an investigatory action that was outside the definition of a "rule."]

The APA expressly exempts "rules of agency organization, procedure, or practice" from the requirements of notice and comment rulemaking. 5 U.S.C. § 553(b)(A). This exemption, as well as others specified proximately in the Act, is a consequence of Congress's belief that "certain administrative pronouncements [do] not require public participation in their formulation." In exempting procedural rules, Congress has placed a premium on efficiency by avoiding the often cumbersome and time-consuming mechanisms of public input. This judgment prevailed despite the widely-shared recognition that administrative agencies need direct lines to the public voice because of their distance from the elective process.

It is beyond dispute that CPL 2.25B is, on the surface, a procedural rule. . . . Whereas substantive or "legislative" rules affect individual rights and obligations and are binding on the courts, nonlegislative rules do not have the force of law.

At least initially, courts "will honor [an agency's] characterization if it reasonably describes what the agency in fact has done."

The plan's stated purpose was to "describe[ ] the steps to be followed and the criteria to be applied in selecting workplace establishments for programmed inspection" pursuant to the OSH Act. Moreover, the plan does not purport or seem to create new law; instead, it contained an OSHA policy of "simplified . . . scheduling procedures in order to ease the administrative burden." The Secretary used CPL 2.25B to concentrate OSHA's inspection resources in industries with the highest potential for safety and health violations. The plan is procedural on its face.

This conclusion, however, does not end our inquiry. As noted earlier, the distinction between a rule of procedure and one of substance is not black and white. . . as we must look beyond the label in determining whether agency action is a "rule," we must make a similar probe in categorizing the type of rule for purposes of APA notice and comment under section 553.

Inevitably, in determining whether the APA requires notice and comment rulemaking, the interests of agency efficiency and public input are in tension. The exemption from informal rulemaking requirements for procedural rules reflects the congressional judgment that such rules, because they do not directly guide public conduct, do not merit the administrative burdens of public input proceedings. In applying this exemption, then, courts have been less concerned with the formal appellation of a rule—whether it is "procedural" or "substantive"—than with its effect on those within its regulatory scope.

In *Brown Express* [*Inc. v. U.S.*, 607 F.2d 695] we recognized that a seemingly procedural rule does not have its apparent nature cast in stone for purposes of APA rulemaking requirements:

"[W]hen a proposed regulation of general applicability has a *substantial impact* on the regulated industry, or an important class of the members or the products of that industry, notice and opportunity for comment should first be provided." The exemption of section 553(b)(A) from the duty to provide notice by publication [and a forum for public comment] does not extend to those procedural rules that depart from existing practice and have a substantial impact on those regulated.

In essence, the substantial impact test is the primary means by which courts look beyond the label "procedural" to determine whether a rule is of the type Congress thought appropriate for public participation. An agency rule that modifies substantive rights and interests can only be nominally procedural and the exemption for such rules of agency procedure cannot apply. Kast urges that, having found CPL 2.25B to be a procedural rule, we should nevertheless not give effect to the APA's procedural rules exemption from informal rulemaking requirements because the rule has substantial impact on those regulated. We disagree.

OSHA's inspection plan casts not the stone of substantial impact. . . . CPL 2.25B has no cognizable impact, substantial or otherwise, on any right or interest of Kast. While the company has an "interest . . . in being free from *unreasonable* intrusions onto its property by agents of the government," this interest does not extend to freedom from *any* OSHA inspection. The government still must satisfy a federal magistrate, as it did in this case, "that the inspection is reasonable under the Constitution, is authorized by statute, and is pursuant to an administrative plan containing specific neutral criteria." *Marshall v. Barlow's, Inc.*

Moreover, the rights and obligations of an employer within OSHA's jurisdiction exist independently of a plan whose sole purpose is the funnelling of agency inspection resources. If Kast's argument is that another directive might have spared it an inspection, or given rise to one at another time, we find no merit therein. Adherence to the safety and health standards promulgated by OSHA under 29 U.S.C. § 655, should not turn on the agency's ability or inclination to play watchdog. No inspection plan creates in an employer the right to be free of citation; the relevant standards of employer conduct originate not in CPL 2.25B but elsewhere. . . .

In our case . . . appellee asserts no defeated expectations as a result of CPL 2.25B . . . . Although the plan departed from a previous inspection formula, change alone is insufficient to satisfy the twin prongs of departure and substantial impact found in *Brown Express*. . . .

The substantive effect of CPL 2.25B is purely derivative: the source of the employers' woes is the OSH Act itself as well as in the legislative rules promulgated in its shadow, which alone are responsible for having shaped employer conduct. . . . Because the district court should have honored the inspection warrant, we reverse the judgment below and remand with instructions to dismiss appellee's motion to quash.

Notes and Questions

1. *Substance and procedure—rationale.* The agency rule in the *Kast Metals* case was held to be procedural since it told agency staff how to proceed. In other cases, rules telling regulated parties how to proceed (e.g. rules describing how and when they may present their cases to the agency) have also been considered procedural. Why are procedural rules exempted from notice and comment procedures? If such an exemption is justified, why do state APAs not include a similar exemption?

2. *Substance v. procedure—the substantial impact test.* In the *Kast Metals* case, the court acknowledged that the rule "on the surface" was "procedural" since it told agency staff how to select businesses for inspection and did not tell the businesses to do anything. Why did not the opinion stop there? Would *any* rule that tells staff what to do be "procedural" rather than "substantive?" What if the rule told agency inspectors to cite all factories as unsafe which used two-prong rather than three-prong electrical outlets, and there was no other rule relating to electrical outlets?

In *Kast Metals* the court claims it is following the holding in the *Brown Express* case that a rule is not "procedural" if it "departs from existing practice" and has a "substantial impact on the regulated industry . . . ." Did not CPL 2.25B clearly "depart from existing practice" and have a "substantial impact?" CPL 2.25B meant that dangerous factories, like those of Kast Metals Corporation, were more likely to be inspected and to become subject to penalties than under the prior practice of random selection. That seems quite "substantial." Or did the court mean something different by its "substantial impact" test?

3. *Substantial impact test and Vermont Yankee.* The court would have held the rule "substantive" rather than "procedural" if it had a "substantial impact" on "any right or interest" of the Kast Metals Corporation. Thus it would have required notice and comment even though the rule was procedural on its face. Does this approach violate *Vermont Yankee,* § 6.3, *supra.*

4. *What is a rule?* The *Kast Metals* case holds that CPL 2.25B was a rule according to the federal APA rather than an investigation. That means, for example, that it must be published, § 552(a)(1)(D), and that it is "agency action" potentially subject to judicial review. §§ 551(13), 702. It may be argued that despite the breadth of the federal APA's definition of a "rule" in § 551(4), some agency action of general applicability may not qualify as a rule because it does not have sufficient impact.

For example, in *National Ornament & Elec. Light Christmas Ass'n v. Consumer Product Safety Commission,* 526 F.2d 1368 (2d Cir.1975), the CPSC organized a group of "consumer deputies" to visit stores, to look for dangerous Christmas tree lights, and to demonstrate to retailers how to test for dangerous lights. The Association was concerned that this program would coerce retailers to drop certain lights from their stock or return them to manufacturers. The court indicated that CPSC's conduct was not a "rule." Similarly, *see Industrial Safety Equipment Ass'n v. EPA,* 837 F.2d 1115 (D.C.Cir.1988) (report encouraging the use of only two of eleven approved safety devices is a recommendation, not a rule). Are there reasons other than a lack of substantial impact why these agency activities did not qualify as a rule? *See* § 5.1, *supra.*

§ 6.11.5   INTERPRETIVE RULES AND POLICY STATEMENTS

Federal APA §§ 553(b)(A) and 553(d)(2) exempt "interpretive rules" and "general statements of policy" from the usual notice and comment and delayed effectiveness procedures. These rules may be described as "non-legislative;" they were not issued pursuant to any delegation of authority to make rules with the force of law. *See* note 4, § 5.1, *supra.* This categorical exemption is extremely important because every agency adopts large numbers of non-legislative rules, many of which are of great practical importance to regulated parties.

If an agency lacks delegated rulemaking power, its rules cannot be legislative. However, if the agency has such power, it is necessary to decide which of its rules are legislative and which are non-legislative. That has proven to be an extremely difficult task in practice. (Note that some of the case law uses the term "substantive" rather than "legislative" rules.)

§ 6.11.5a   *Interpretive Rules*

Interpretive rules (or *interpretative* rules—both words are in common usage) are designed to *interpret* words. The words might be in a statute, in a legislative rule, or in a prior agency or judicial adjudicatory decision. Because words are never self-defining, every agency needs constantly to furnish interpretive guidance both to agency staff and to the public. Thus many agencies build up a vast bulk of interpretive material.

Under federal APA §§ 553(b)(A) and 553(d)(2), interpretive rules are exempt from notice and comment procedures as well as deferred effectiveness requirements. But how can you tell whether a rule is interpretive in situations where an agency has also been delegated authority to issue *legislative* rules that interpret words in a statute? In cases of doubt, the court must decide whether the agency "intended" to use its delegated legislative rulemaking powers or "intended" only to supply interpretive guidance to its staff and the public.

CHAMBER OF COMMERCE v. OSHA

636 F.2d 464 (D.C.Cir.1980).

[The Occupational Safety Health Act provides that employers must allow employees to accompany OSHA inspectors who examine the workplace environment and prohibits employer "discrimination" against employees who do so. 29 U.S.C. § 657(e). The question is whether the employees must be paid for this "walk-around time." A proper answer requires an interpretation of the word "discrimination." At first, OSHA ruled that employees need not be paid for that time. It did not employ notice and comment procedure in adopting this rule, which was upheld on substantive grounds by the D.C. Circuit. *Leone v. Mobil Oil Corp.*, 523 F.2d 1153 (D.C.Cir.1975).

President Carter appointed a new OSHA head who reversed the earlier rule; the new rule required that employees be paid. She first announced the turnabout in a speech. OSHA did not employ notice and comment procedure for the new rule, labelling it as an "interpretive rule and general statement of policy" and declaring it was retroactive to the date of the speech.]

TAMM, J.:

A rule is interpretive, rather than legislative, if it is not "issued pursuant to legislatively-delegated power to make rules having the force of law" or if the agency intends the rule to be no more than an expression of its construction of a statute or rule. Because the Administration [OSHA] possesses legislatively delegated power to make legislative rules and because it is apparent to us that the Administration must have intended this regulation to be an exercise of that power, we hold that the walkaround pay regulation is a legislative rule.

There is little room for doubt that Congress authorized the Secretary of Labor to issue legislative rules regarding workplace inspections. Section 8(g)(2) of the Act empowers the Secretary to prescribe "such rules and regulations as he may deem necessary to carry out [his] responsibilities under this chapter, including rules and regulations dealing with the inspection of an employer's establishment." This provision allows the Secretary to promulgate legislative as well as interpretive rules, and the Secretary has already employed quasi-legislative power with respect to workplace inspections. . . .

Ascertaining that an agency intended to engage in legislative rulemaking presents a far more difficult inquiry. Divining agency intent is rarely a simple matter, for bureaucratic boilerplate often obscures the true purpose. The administrative agency's own label is indicative but not dispositive; we do not classify a rule as interpretive just because the agency says it is. Instead, "it is the substance of what the [*agency*] has purported to do and has done which is decisive."

Despite the Administration's averments, we cannot conclude that it intended its new regulation to be interpretive. In *Leone* we held that neither the terms of the Act nor the Act's legislative history nor the policies underlying the employee walkaround right require employers to compensate employees for walkaround time. We would prefer to believe that the Administration acts in good faith; we therefore believe the Administration would not issue an interpretation in flagrant defiance of this court's *Leone* decision. In any event, we are certain the

Administration realized that statutory interpretation by an agency is not necessarily controlling, and thus it knew that although "courts often defer to an agency's interpretive rule they are always free to choose otherwise."

After this court's ruling in *Leone* that the Act, its legislative history, and its policies do not mandate walkaround pay, an Administration issuance of a differing view solely as a matter of its own interpretation would be inconceivable. Such a rule would be a mere phasm of agency action, "full of sound and fury, Signifying nothing," W. Shakespeare, *Macbeth,* act V, sc. v, lines 27–28.

Moreover, the effect of the new regulation exposes the Administration's true intent. Interpretive rules " 'are statements as to what the administrative officer thinks the statute or regulation means.' " Such rules only provide a "clarification of statutory language; " the interpreting agency only " 'reminds' affected parties of existing duties."

The Administration could not be explaining or clarifying the Act's language, for, as we concluded in *Leone,* the Act neither prohibits nor compels pay for walkaround time. There was no "existing duty" to serve as the subject of an Administration reminder. Congress has not "legislated and indicated its will" on the question of walkaround pay, therefore the Administration must have done more than exercise its " 'power to fill up the details.' "

Though the walkaround pay regulation does not merely *explain* the statute, the effect of an interpretive rule, the regulation certainly endeavors to *implement* the statute, the effect of a legislative rule.

The Administration found walkaround pay essential because "the failure [of an employer] to pay for [an employee's] walkaround is inherently destructive . . . of the entire enforcement scheme of the Act." By making this determination, the Administration provided the policy decision Congress omitted—namely, that without walkaround pay there is no walkaround right. It is clear to us that the Administration has attempted through this regulation to supplement the Act, not simply to construe it, and therefore the regulation must be treated as a legislative rule.

Because the Administration's rule is an attempted exercise of legislative power, it must be vacated for failure to comply with the procedures specified by the Administrative Procedure Act, 5 U.S.C. § 553. . . .

In holding that this regulation is legislative in nature but improperly promulgated, we intimate no view on whether the Assistant Secretary could reissue the same rule after satisfying the requirements of 5 U.S.C. § 553. Only after the full notice-and-comment procedures have run their course will we have a record enabling us to judge whether ordering pay for walkaround time is indeed a statutorily authorized, rational, nonarbitrary, and noncapricious method of supplementing the Act's provisions. . . .

Notes and Questions

1. *Legislative v. interpretive.* Why did OSHA not employ notice and comment procedure in changing its position on walk-around-pay? What would be the advantages and disadvantages to OSHA of employing these procedures?

There is an important theoretical difference between treating the walk-around-pay rule as legislative or interpretive. If it is legislative, it states an obligation that binds employers, unless a court should invalidate it as ultra vires or arbitrary and capricious on judicial review. However, if it is interpretive, it is not binding on employers. It merely represents OSHA's view of an employer's obligation. OSHA would have to proceed against employers in a subsequent adjudication to penalize them for non-payment of wages—and it would apply the statute in that case, not the rule. On judicial review, the employer would try to persuade a court that OSHA's interpretation of § 657(e) was erroneous.

If you represented an employer, would you put much weight on this distinction? You might well advise the employer to pay employees for walkarounds for two reasons. First, the rule would probably be upheld by the courts, no matter what it was called, because of the deference often paid to agency legal interpretations. *See* § 9.2, *infra.* Second, litigating the issue would probably cost more that just paying for walkarounds.

2. *Intended legal effect test.* In *Chamber of Commerce,* the majority first ascertained that OSHA had legislative rulemaking power. Then it decided that the walkaround-pay rule was legislative, not interpretive. Note that it disregarded the label that the agency had placed on its rule. The great majority of cases defer to the agency's label, absent an unusual situation in which the rule has a self-executing legal effect.

The court held that the agency must have intended legislative effect because the new rule was contrary to the court's previous *Leone* decision. But why does that follow? There might be two reasonable interpretations of § 657(e)—the prior one, upheld in *Leone,* and the current one. It is possible that a court might uphold both of them. *See Chevron, U.S.A., Inc. v. Natural Resources Defense Council, Inc.,* § 9.2, *infra.* Even if the new interpretation is not legally supportable, why would that suggest that OSHA did not intend it as an interpretive rule? In other words, what difference does the *Leone* case make to determining the agency's intent?

3. *Substantial impact test.* Judge Bazelon concurred in the result in *Chamber of Commerce.* He found the rule to be legislative because "although it serves as an interpretation of existing law, it also effectively enunciates a new requirement heretofore nonexistent for compliance with the law. . . . This agency action would wield a significant change in the practices which private employers must follow and in the

enforcement steps the agency must take." Is Bazelon using a test based on practical impact rather than ascertaining the agency intent or measuring the rule's legal effect?

Most cases hold that the substantial impact test is inappropriate for distinguishing interpretive from legislative rules. For example, the United States Court of Appeals for the District of Columbia Circuit stated:

> Although the substantial impact test may be useful in determining whether agency action is a general statement of policy . . . or whether agency action is exempt for good cause, this circuit has declined to use the test for distinguishing between substantive and interpretative rules. . . .[4] Merely because a rule has a wide ranging effect does not mean that it is legislative rather than interpretative. . . .

> Interpretative and substantive rules may both vitally affect private interests,[6] thus, the substantial impact test has no utility in distinguishing between the two. . . .

Cabais v. Egger, 690 F.2d 234, 237–38 (D.C.Cir.1982).

On the other hand, ACUS recommends that as a matter of practice, but not as a matter of law, agencies should provide for notice and comment procedures in the case of nonlegislative rules that would have a substantial impact. ACUS, Recommendation 76–5, "Interpretive Rules of General Applicability and Statements of General Policy," 1 C.F.R. § 305.76–5. What is wrong with using a substantial impact test as the basis for determining whether a rule is interpretive or legislative?

4. *Authority to make legislative rules.* Agencies are often delegated authority in specific terms to make rules with the binding force of law. For example, a statute may explicitly prohibit conduct to be described by agency rules. Such a statute clearly provides the agency with authority to adopt legislative rules. Note that in the *Chamber of Commerce* case, OSHA acted under authority of a *general* rulemaking power. Section 8(g)(2) generally authorized the Secretary to make rules necessary to carry out his responsibilities, including rules dealing with inspection. This provision does not make clear whether it empowers the agency to make legislative, as opposed to merely interpretive rules. Whether a general rulemaking power in fact authorizes adoption of legislative rules is an issue of statutory interpretation.

4. Another possible application of the "substantial impact test" is to determine whether agency action should be invalidated where the action did not comport with APA procedures. This use of the test is similar to the concept of harmless error. . . .

6. A failure to require rulemaking procedures for interpretative rules with substantial impact may not seem fair but strict adherence to the letter of the APA without reference to "elementary fairness" . . . is not so harsh as it seems. Affected parties may seek redress in the courts and courts are not strictly bound by an agency's interpretative rules.

Most courts construe such statutes to authorize the issuance of legislative rules, recognizing that legislative rulemaking is an essential tool in carrying out a regulatory program. *See* § 5.3, *supra.* A leading case is *National Petroleum Refiners Ass'n v. FTC,* 482 F.2d 672 (D.C.Cir. 1973), cert. denied, 415 U.S. 951 (1974), which upheld the FTC's rule requiring gas stations to post octane ratings. Although the FTC had and continually exercised adjudicative authority to make law on a case-by-case basis, the FTC had never before sought to use its general rulemaking power to adopt legislative rules defining unfair trade practices; and many people believed that it lacked such power. The Court of Appeals decision reading the agency enabling act to authorize the FTC to issue such legislative rules emphasized the enormous advantages of rulemaking over case-by-case adjudication in implementing a program of consumer protection. *Id.* at 681. It was an important case in modern administrative law. *See United Air Lines v. CAB,* 766 F.2d 1107, 1112 (1985).

5. *State law.* The 1961 MSAPA contained no exception for interpretive rules, but most state agencies seem to have ignored the requirement that they employ notice and comment procedures before adopting such rules. Section 3–109 of the 1981 MSAPA contains an exception for interpretive rules that is much narrower than federal APA § 553(b) (A). In the first place, the new MSAPA provision only exempts such rules from usual notice and comment procedures while the federal act also exempts them from its delayed effectiveness provisions. Is this distinction of any practical significance?

Note also that § 3–109 of the 1981 MSAPA requires an initial determination of whether the agency has been delegated authority to bind the courts with any interpretation embodied in its rule. If the agency has that authority, the agency *must* follow the MSAPA rulemaking procedures, even though the agency intends the rule to be wholly interpretive rather than legislative. Only if the agency does not have such delegated power, is it free to omit notice and comment for that rule. As a result, in every situation where an agency omits usual procedures for a rule because it is interpretive, § 3–109 of the 1981 MSAPA appears to require the courts to resolve this often obscure question of whether the agency had authority to issue the rule *with the binding force of law.* On the other hand, so long as a federal agency rule is intended to be wholly interpretive, a reviewing court need not determine whether the agency had authority to issue it as a binding legislative rule when it decides whether that rule was subject to usual notice and comment procedures.

Is there a justification for the refusal of the MSAPA to allow an agency to avoid usual notice and comment procedures for rules that an agency says it intends to be wholly interpretive when the agency also has authority to issue them as legislative rules with the binding force of law? In practical terms, may the effect of the former rules be similar to the effect of the latter? It could be argued that the ability of a federal agency possessing legislative rulemaking authority to avoid usual rulemaking procedures when it issues rules that it says it intends to be wholly interpretive might allow such an agency to accomplish, without using rulemaking procedures, some of the objectives that it is otherwise required to accomplish by legislative rules issued after notice and comment proceedings. Do you agree? *See Chevron, U.S.A. Inc. v. Natural Resources Defense Council,* § 9.2, *infra.*

Assume a state agency lacking delegated power to issue an interpretive rule with the binding force of law chooses to adopt a wholly interpretive rule without notice and comment as permitted by § 3–109(a). Note the price-tag: a reviewing court must determine wholly de novo the validity of that interpretive rule adopted without notice and comment. 1981 MSAPA § 3–109(b). Generally, a court may, and often must, pay deference to agency interpretations. *See* § 9.2, *infra.* Section 3–109(b) prohibits the court from doing so when an interpretive rule was issued without benefit of usual notice and comment procedures. Is this wise? *See* A. Bonfield, STATE ADMINISTRATIVE RULE MAKING § 6.9.2(d) (1986).

Which approach to interpretive rulemaking is best—federal APA § 553(b)(A) or 1981 MSAPA § 3–109? Which approach best encourages agencies to adopt interpretive rules? Which approach is most likely to minimize costly litigation about procedure? Which approach provides the best resolution of the conflict between the need for procedures to protect adequately private interests against unsound, unpopular, or improper interpretive rules, and the need for effective, efficient, and economical governmental administration? *See* Asimow, "Nonlegislative Rulemaking and Regulatory Reform," 1985 Duke L.J. 381, 410–15; A. Bonfield, STATE ADMINISTRATIVE RULE MAKING § 6.9.2 (1986).

§ 6.11.5b *Policy Statements*

MADA–LUNA v. FITZPATRICK

813 F.2d 1006 (9th Cir.1987).

[Petitioner Mada–Luna was a Mexican national who had been a legal permanent resident of the U.S. He was subject to deportation because of a narcotics conviction. He applied for "deferred action" status that would delay his deportation. He had served as an undercover agent for the federal government, his wife and children were U.S. citizens, and he had been kidnapped and threatened with death by Mexican drug traffickers.

The Immigration and Naturalization Service (INS) adopted an Operations Instruction to its staff in 1978 that instructed INS personnel to consider humanitarian factors in recommending deferred action. In 1981, INS adopted a new version of the Instruction that focused on factors relating to the management and public image of the INS. It did not employ notice and comment procedures in 1978 or 1981 and did not publish either version in the *Federal Register*.

The District Director denied deferred status under the 1981 Instruction. Mada–Luna would have had a better chance under the 1978 version, so he contends that the 1981 version was invalidly adopted. The INS contends that both versions were "general statements of policy."]

FLETCHER, J.: The APA does not define the term "general statements of policy" as it is used in § 553. However, it is defined in the Attorney General's Memorandum on the APA, which was issued in 1947, just after the APA's enactment, as "statements issued by an agency to advise the public prospectively of the manner in which the agency proposes to exercise a discretionary power." When agencies have been delegated discretionary authority over a given area, such as the Attorney General and the INS in the field of immigration, such policy statements serve a dual purpose. Besides informing the public concerning the agency's future plans and priorities for exercising its discretionary power, they serve to "educate" and provide direction to the agency's personnel in the field, who are required to implement its policies and exercise its discretionary power in specific cases. Bonfield, Some Tentative Thoughts on Public Participation in the Making of Interpretative Rules and General Statements of Policy Under the APA, 23 Admin.L.Rev. 101, 115 (1970–71) ("It may be that 'general statements of policy' are rules directed primarily at the staff of an agency describing how it will conduct agency discretionary functions, while other rules are directed primarily at the public in an effort to impose obligations on them.").

When a federal agency issues a directive concerning the future exercise of its discretionary power, for purposes of APA section 553, its directive will constitute either a substantive rule, for which notice-and-comment procedures are required, or a general statement of policy, for which they are not. The critical factor to determine whether a directive announcing a new policy constitutes a rule or a general statement of policy is "the extent to which the challenged [directive] leaves the agency, or its implementing official, free to exercise discretion to follow, or not to follow, the [announced] policy in an individual case." To the extent that the directive merely provides *guidance* to agency officials in exercising their discretionary powers while preserving their flexibility and their opportunity to make "individualized determination[s]," it constitutes a general statement of policy.

In such cases, Congress has determined that notice-and-comment rulemaking would be of limited utility, *see* 5 U.S.C. §§ 553(b)(A), 553(d) (2), and parties can challenge the policy determinations made by the agency only if and when the directive has been applied specifically to them. In contrast, to the extent that the directive "narrowly limits administrative discretion" or establishes a *"binding norm"* that "so fills out the statutory scheme that upon application one need only determine whether a given case is within the rule's criterion," it effectively replaces agency discretion with a new "binding rule of substantive law." In these cases, notice-and-comment rulemaking proceedings are required, as they would be for any other substantive rule, and they will represent the only opportunity for parties to challenge the policy determinations upon which the new rule is based.

Thus, for the 1978 and 1981 Operating Instructions to qualify under section 553's "general statement of policy" exception, they must satisfy two requirements. First, they must operate only prospectively. Second, they must not establish a "binding norm" or be "finally determinative of the issues or rights to which [they are] addressed," but must instead leave INS officials "free to consider the individual facts in the various cases that arise." . . .

We note that two considerations that Mada relies upon to establish that the 1978 and 1981 Operating Instructions do not constitute general statements of policy are not determinative of the issue. First, Mada appears to assume that if an agency's decisions applying a particular regulation are reviewable by courts, then the regulation must automatically be a substantive rule for which notice-and-comment rulemaking procedures are required. . . .

The determinations of whether an agency's decisions implementing a particular directive are subject to judicial review and whether the directive itself constitutes a general statement of policy exempt from section 553's notice-and-comment requirements are not necessarily interdependent. The two issues involve different statutory provisions, are analyzed under different standards, and arise at different chronological stages of a directive's history.

To qualify as a general statement of policy under section 553, a directive must not establish a "binding norm" and must leave agency officials "free to consider the individual facts in the various cases that arise" and to exercise discretion. In contrast, for an agency's action pursuant to a particular directive to be unreviewable by the courts under APA section 701(a)(2), it is not alone sufficient that the action involves agency discretion; courts must also have "no meaningful standard against which to judge the agency's exercise of discretion. . . . [or] to evaluate [it] for 'abuse of discretion.'" *Heckler v. Chaney,* [§ 10.5, *infra.*][11] Furthermore, several courts have suggested that agency decisions made pursuant to general statements of policy may be judicially reviewable at least for abuse of discretion. . . .

Second, Mada apparently assumes that the 1978 Instruction cannot constitute a general statement of policy under section 553 because the

---

11. Because many general statements of policy have a substantial impact, *see Jean,* 711 F.2d at 1480, broad application of the "substantial impact" test could well obliterate much of the "general statement of policy" exception to the APA's notice-and-comment procedures. We conclude that Congress could not have intended such a result, given the structure of section 553 and its use of classifications like "general statement of policy," which focus upon the effect a directive has upon agency decision-making, rather than the effect on the public at large.

INS's replacement of the 1978 Operating Instruction with the 1981 Instruction diminishes the likelihood that he and other similarly situated aliens will be granted deferred action status, and eliminates their opportunity to obtain judicial review. In essence, Mada suggests that if the repeal of an agency directive will cause a "substantial impact" to the rights of a specific class it cannot be exempt from section 553's notice-and-comment requirements. However, we have expressly "rejected the argument that, for the purposes of imposing notice-and-comment requirements on [an] agency for a particular rule, [courts should] look to the 'substantial impact' of the rule."

We have concluded that " '[s]imply because agency action has substantial impact does not mean it is subject to notice and comment if it is otherwise expressly exempt under the APA.' " Rivera v. Becerra, 714 F.2d 887 (citing the Supreme Court's admonition in *Vermont Yankee* that courts should not impose procedural requirements upon agencies beyond those expressly provided in the APA. . . .)

In determining whether particular regulations or directives qualify for one of section 553's exemptions from notice-and-comment requirements, we have focused upon the effect of the regulation or directive upon *agency decisionmaking,* not the public at large. . . .

We conclude that the 1981 Operating Instruction presents even a clearer case of a general statement of policy. Like the 1978 Operating Instruction, it operates only prospectively. Moreover, the wording and structure of the amended Instruction emphasizes the broad and unfettered discretion of the district director in making deferred action determinations. None of the factors listed in the 1981 Instruction establishes a "binding norm": they require the district director to evaluate the "sympathetic" appeal of the deferred action applicant and to surmise the possible internal agency reaction and publicity that would result from his deportation and exclusion. The Instruction leaves the district director "free to consider the individual facts" in each case.

Notes and Questions

1. *Procedural rules.* Since the 1978 and 1981 Instructions told the INS staff how to process applications for deferred status, why did INS not claim that they were exempt from notice and comment as procedural rules?

2. *Policy statements v. legislative rules.* INS could have adopted the 1978 and 1981 Instructions as legislative rules instead of as statements of policy. Why did it not do so?

Note the standard by which the court distinguishes between legislative rules that constrain agency discretion and policy statements. Is it really possible to distinguish rules that "establish a binding norm" from those that leave officials "free to consider the individual facts in the various cases that arise?" Why should it matter whether a rule is "prospective" in determining whether it is a policy statement? Are not legislative rules prospective too?

The rationale for the standard used in the *Mada–Luna* case might be as follows: when an agency makes a discretionary decision that is guided by a policy statement (i.e. a rule that leaves the agency free to consider particular facts), an individual can argue that the agency should disregard the policy statement and treat his case differently. However, if a discretionary decision is dictated by a legislative rule, the agency has not left itself free to consider individual circumstances. In the latter situation, therefore, the individual should have a chance to influence the rule at the time it is adopted since it will be binding at the time it is applied. Are you convinced?

3. *State law.* The MSAPAs contain no exception for policy statements. Note, however, that 1981 MSAPA § 3–116(2) excludes from all usual rulemaking and rule-effectiveness requirements many rules that would also be policy statements under federal APA § 553(b)(A). Would the INS Operations Instructions in *Mada–Luna* be exempt from notice and comment under MSAPA § 3–116(2)?

Even if a rule comes within 1981 MSAPA § 3–116(2) because it embodies "criteria or guidelines to be used by the staff of an agency" in performing the listed functions, it is still not exempt from usual rulemaking and rule-effectiveness requirements unless disclosure would be contrary to the public interest in the ways described in § 3–116(2)(i)-(iii). For example, disclosure of the rules might frustrate law enforcement by disseminating information that would facilitate the disregard of requirements imposed by law, enable law violators to avoid detection, or might give persons contracting with the state an unfair competitive advantage. Note that rules exempted by § 3–116(2) are exempt from all rulemaking and rule-effectiveness requirements and all requirements applicable to the publication of rules; and they need not be made available for public inspection. Section 2–101(g)(1).

What is the precise scope of § 3–116(2)? Is that exemption justified? *See* A. Bonfield, STATE ADMINISTRATIVE RULE MAKING 404–06 (1986). How would the problems with which § 3–116(2) deals be handled under the federal APA? Is every rule within the scope of that MSAPA provision an exempted statement of policy under the federal act?

Because of the narrowness of § 3–116(2), state agencies must follow usual notice and comment procedures before adopting a great number of rules that might qualify as policy statements exempted from usual procedures by the federal act. So, the drafters of 1981 MSAPA § 3–116(2) struck a vastly different balance from the drafters of the federal APA § 553(b)(A). Which balance best encourages agencies to adopt policy statements of the kind exempted from usual rulemaking procedures by the federal act? Which one is best designed to minimize costly litigation of the kind involved in the *Mada–Luna* case? Which balance provides the best resolution of the conflict between the need for procedures to protect adequately private interests against unsound, unpopular, or improper policy statements, substantially affecting them, and the need for effective, efficient, and economical governmental administration?

4. *Rationale for non-legislative rule exemptions.* Several justifications for the non-legislative rule exemptions have been suggested. It has been noted that "[n]onlegislative rules are enormously important to members of the public who must live with regulation. Any significant diminution in the flow of interpretive rules or policy statements disserves the public interest. . . . In 1946, the drafters of the APA concluded that the benefits of mandatory public procedure were outweighed by the issuance of fewer rules and by reduced effectiveness, increased cost, and undue delay. . . . [T]heir call was close but right. Mandatory pre-adoption procedure would be a significant disincentive to nonlegislative rulemaking. The public would lose more than it would gain. The loss of a large quantity of relatively unimportant nonlegislative material outweighs the benefits of providing a relatively small number of people additional opportunities to influence the content of a relatively small number of important rules." Asimow, "Nonlegislative Rulemaking and Regulatory Reform," 1985 Duke L.J. 381, 408–09.

In addition, an exemption for interpretive rules is deemed warranted on the grounds that the "practical effectiveness of any available remedy for a procedurally improper agency issuance of an interpretative rule is in doubt. For even if a court voided an improperly issued interpretative rule, the agency could still *ad hoc* construe the law interpreted by the void rule and apply that *ad hoc* construction of the law to the particular case at hand. Furthermore, courts may, although they do not in practice always choose to do so, judicially review an interpretative rule wholly *de novo,* that is, without any deference to the adopting agency. So, the adverse consequences of such a rule on the affected persons are normally less than the consequences of a legislative rule." 1981 MSAPA § 3–109 Comment.

It has also been noted that without an exemption for nonlegislative rules, "agencies will be forced to greatly increase their reliance on the much more limited . . . 'good cause' exemptions. . . . The specific circumstances under which these sorts of rules fit within such qualified exemptions is much more unclear than the categorical exclusion of all interpretative rules and general statements of policy. [T]his . . . uncertainty would probably cause much litigation and/or encourage the use of usual rulemaking procedures in situations where they would be unwise." Bonfield, "Some Tentative Thoughts on Public Participation in the Making of Interpretive Rules and General Statements of Policy Under the A.P.A.," 23 Admin.L.Rev. 101, 119 (1971).

Are the above justifications for an interpretative rule and general statement of policy exemption sound? Consider the relevance to your answer of the fact that judicial review of federal agency interpretive rules often involves substantial deference to the agency interpretation. *See Chevron, U.S.A., Inc. v. Natural Resources Defense Council,* § 9.2, *infra.* Should the 1981 MSAPA be amended to include a broad and unqualified exemption for nonlegislative rules similar to federal APA § 553(b)(A)? Or should state nonlegislative rulemaking be treated differently than federal?

5. *Post hoc procedure.* The Administrative Conference recommends that federal agencies adopting nonlegislative rules without notice and comment invite the public to submit comments within a 30–day period after the rule is published. Within 60 days, the agency would be required to reconsider the rule in light of any comment received. ACUS, Recommendation 76–5, "Interpretive Rules of General Applicability and Statements of General Policy," 1 C.F.R. § 305.76–5. Is post-hoc procedure effective in causing an agency to consider public comments? Would such a procedure be better than nothing—or worse? *See* Asimow, "Public Participation in the Adoption of Interpretive Rules and Policy Statements," 75 Mich.L.Rev. 520, 573–84 (1977).

Is the ACUS recommendation excessive for the purpose of assuring adequate protection of private rights in nonlegislative rulemaking? Is the right to petition for the amendment or repeal of a nonlegislative rule issued without the benefit of pre-promulgation notice and comment procedures an adequate protection for private rights? Note that the right to petition created by 1981 MSAPA § 3–117 differs in a number of respects from the similar right created by § 553(e) of the federal act and, therefore, the answer to the latter question might be different under each of these two acts. *See* A. Bonfield, STATE ADMINISTRATIVE RULE MAKING 304–06 (1986).

6. *Rules governing certain institutions.* Section 3–116(6) of the 1981 MSAPA is based on the unusually large burden of subjecting to normal rulemaking and rule-effectiveness requirements the thousands of rules concerning the details of the daily relationship of penal, educational, and hospital institutions, with their inmates, students, and patients. It has been suggested that for rules concerning *only* inmates of a correctional or detention facility, students enrolled in an educational institution, or patients admitted to a hospital, if adopted by that facility, institution, or hospital, "internal agency procedures devised specially to elicit and facilitate their input on institutional policies would be more appropriate and effective than the rulemaking procedures of the MSAPA because the latter are designed to elicit and process input from the public at large." A. Bonfield, STATE ADMINISTRATIVE RULE MAKING 416 (1986). Do you agree? *See* Auerbach, "Administrative Rulemaking in Minnesota," 63 Minn.L.Rev. 151, 245 (1979).

Based on the language of § 3–116(6), are rules specifying the substantive grounds for which an inmate of a correctional institution may have his or her parole revoked subject to usual rulemaking procedures? *See Airhart v. Iowa Department of Social Services,* 248

N.W.2d 83 (Iowa 1976). Would a rule specifying the hours during which prisoners could receive visitors be exempt under this provision of the 1981 MSAPA? *See* A. Bonfield, STATE ADMINISTRATIVE RULE MAKING 414 (1986).

7. *Recommended provision.* As noted, § 3–116 of the MSAPA entirely exempts certain specified classes of rules from all rulemaking and rule-effectiveness requirements. The Comment to the section recommends that the following language be added to that section: "To the extent that it is practicable an agency shall, before adopting a rule [exempt from usual rulemaking and rule-effectiveness requirements] under this section, give advance notice in some suitable manner of the contents of the contemplated rule to persons who would be affected by it, and solicit their views thereon." Would the addition of this provision create a better balance between the competing interests involved in the creation of these categorical exemptions?

8. *Problem—interpretive rules.* Recall *Megdal v. Oregon State Board of Dental Examiners,* § 5.4, *supra.* Assume that after that decision, the Board adopted, without prior notice and comment, an entirely new rule providing that misrepresentation in an application for malpractice insurance would be considered "unprofessional conduct." Assume that the Board has been delegated legislative rulemaking power to define "unprofessional conduct," but it clearly labelled the new rule as an interpretive rule. In a subsequent case, the Board suspended from practice Susan, a dentist who failed to disclose in her malpractice insurance application several prior malpractice cases she had lost. The Board decision simply cited the new rule as authority for its decision. Susan appeals, contending that the new rule was invalidly adopted. Who wins, assuming that (i) federal APA § 553(b)(A) is applicable; (ii) 1981 MSAPA § 3–109 is applicable? Assume that the new rule was a validly adopted interpretive rule. Does this satisfy the rulemaking requirement set forth in the *Megdal* case?

9. *Problem—policy statements.* A statute allows the Food and Drug Administration (FDA) to adopt rules limiting the amount of poisonous substances in food. With or without such rules, FDA is authorized to seek an injunction against shipments of food containing poisonous substances.

Without notice and comment, FDA adopted an "action level" concerning aflatoxins in corn. Under the "action level," FDA stated that it would take no enforcement action against a producer whose corn contained less than 100 parts per million (ppm) of aflatoxins (a potent carcinogen that occurs naturally in corn). However, it stated that it would take enforcement action against corn containing 100 or more ppm.

Consumer groups, who believe that 100 ppm far exceeds a safe level, seek judicial review, asserting that the action level was invalidly adopted. Assume that (i) federal APA § 553(b)(A) is applicable; (ii) 1981 MSAPA § 3–116(2) is applicable. Should they prevail?

Part II

NONJUDICIAL CONTROL OF AGENCY ACTION

In this Part we examine mechanisms, other than agency procedures and judicial review, for ensuring that administrative action is consistent with legal requirements and with the current political will of the community. The primary focus, therefore, will be on mechanisms calculated to ensure that the political branches of government—the legislature and the chief executive—control agency action. Because effective control of administrative action by the political process in the community requires widespread access to information about the policies and activities of agencies, this Part also examines the right of the public to obtain such information.

Chapter 7

CONTROL OF AGENCIES BY THE POLITICAL BRANCHES OF GOVERNMENT

---

§ 7.1 INTRODUCTION

Administrative agencies typically possess delegated authority to make rules, to adjudicate individual cases, to engage in law enforcement, and to conduct various kinds of other activities related to those functions. The legitimacy of such delegations has been a great concern especially because most agency heads in this country are appointed rather than elected and, therefore, are not directly responsible to the body politic. Various theories for the legitimacy of agency activities and the role of administrative law were suggested in § 1.7, *supra,* and were pursued subsequently, especially in chapters 5 and 6. This chapter continues the inquiry into the legitimacy of agencies in our governmental structure and the role of administrative law in assuring agency responsibility to the wishes of our political community. More specifically, this chapter will focus on the control of agencies by the political branches of government through means other than agency procedures which were discussed earlier. So, this chapter will examine the substantive and procedural powers of the political branches of our government in relation to their administrative bodies.

An examination of the role of administrative law in legitimating agency activities also requires us to consider two very fundamental constitutional principles of government in this country: the principle of separation of powers and the principle of checks and balances. These two principles are especially important here because they raise certain fundamental questions about the position and role of agencies. They also create certain problems that need to be solved by administrative law in order to ensure that agencies function in a manner that is consistent with our constitutional form of government and the day-to-day political will of the community at large.

The drafters of our federal and state constitutions believed that concentration of power created grave dangers to the liberties of the people that would be significantly ameliorated by the creation of three distinct branches of government, each authorized to exercise only its own specialized powers. Nevertheless, most people today concede that a joinder of rulemaking, adjudication, and law enforcement, within a single administrative unit, is legitimate, and a practical necessity in modern government, even though it appears to involve a combination rather than a separation of powers. *See* Strauss, "The Place of Agencies in Government: Separation of Powers and the Fourth Branch," 84 Colum.L.Rev. 573 (1984). As a result, in considering agency legitimacy, we must examine the theories justifying such a combination of disparate functions in one body despite the separation of powers notion embedded in our federal and state constitutions.

The founders of our federal and state governments also believed that it was not enough to create three separate governmental branches; each branch must be protected against encroachment by the other branches and each must be in a position to check and balance the others. As a result, we must examine the extent to which legislative and judicial power may be vested in agencies that are more or less located in, or subject to the authority of, the executive branch. And we must examine the checks on agency authority that are necessary to assure the legality of agency action and its consistency with the wishes of the people.

Because this chapter continues the inquiry into the techniques of assuring agency political accountability in relation to the role of administrative law, it is also an appropriate place to make another point: the problem of political accountability for some state agencies may be different and more complicated than the similar problem for federal agencies. Some state agencies are directly created by their state constitutions while all federal agencies (and most state agencies) are created by statute or executive order. As a result, the political accountability of the former state agencies may present special problems. The fact that they are directly created by their state constitutions may give those state agencies a status equivalent to the legislature and governor and make some or all of the normal legislative and gubernatorial mechanisms to review and control agency action partially or wholly inapplicable to them as a matter of state constitutional law.

On the other hand, note that the problem of political accountability of some state agencies might be easier than the similar problem for federal agencies. Unlike federal agencies (and most state agencies), the heads of some state agencies are directly elected because a state constitutional provision or statute so provides. The political accountability of those state agencies is clear and direct. However, direct election will make those agency heads less responsible to the governor and legislature. This may cause managerial and policy difficulties in state government, and potential political dissonance without any obvious solution. In addition, by dividing political accountability of state agencies so that a few of them are directly responsible to the people at the polls while most of them are directly responsible to the legislature and governor, the result may be less political accountability of the state administrative process as a whole than would be the case if all state agencies were directly responsible to the elected representatives of the people.

In this chapter, we first consider the authority of the legislature to define the scope and limits of agency authority. Then we ask how far the legislature may go in vesting agencies with legislative power. That inquiry is followed by a consideration of the extent to which a legislature may delegate adjudicatory power to agencies. To the extent such delegations are permissible, we then inquire about the various means by which the legislature and chief executive may control the exercises of agency authority implementing those delegations to ensure that they are lawful and consistent with the wishes of the body politic.

§ 7.2 DEFINING THE SCOPE AND LIMITS OF AGENCY AUTHORITY

The most direct means by which the political branches of government may control administrative action is by the enactment of legislation defining the scope and limits of agency authority. It is clear that the elected political branches of government are the principal, and the administrative bodies are the agents. Administrative bodies do not have inherent authority. As a general proposition, the only authority they may legitimately exercise is that delegated to them by their respective enabling acts or by other legislation. The basic principle has been stated this way:

Administrative agencies derive their power and authority from other sources. They are agents of those principals and cannot act beyond the intended grant of authority. Generally the authority comes from a delegation by the legislative branch or from a delegation by the executive to perform some duty assigned to it by the legislature. From this we derive a basic concept that an agency cannot act outside its delegated authority.

C. Koch, Jr., 1 ADMINISTRATIVE LAW AND PRACTICE, § 1.22, at 39 (1985). As a result, an authority superior to the agency, typically the elected legislature, defines the scope of agency power and may check, modify, or remove it whenever that authority believes such action is desirable.

In every instance of agency action, therefore, the doctrine of ultra vires applies: agency action is illegal if it is not expressly or impliedly authorized by the legislature (or by the executive authority or state constitution creating the particular agency in question). So, in every instance of agency action, adversely affected persons may appropriately question whether the action involved was expressly or impliedly authorized by the principal—usually the legislature. Because of the normal presumption of regularity or validity of agency action, (*see* C. Koch, Jr., ADMINISTRATIVE LAW AND PRACTICE, § 1.28 (1985)), the courts usually place the burden of persuasion on the person challenging agency action to demonstrate that it is procedurally or substantively ultra vires—beyond the scope of agency authority. In practice, however, an agency will rarely wait until the person challenging its action in a court overcomes that presumption of regularity to submit to the court information supporting the agency's claim that the action in question was expressly or impliedly authorized by its enabling legislation. The agency is more likely to proffer that information early in the judicial review process rather than waiting until the last possible moment to meet a shifted burden of persuasion resulting from an effective presentation by plaintiff of his or her case.

The determination as to whether particular agency action is intra vires or ultra vires involves a process of statutory construction in which a reviewing court may give varying amounts of deference to the agency's interpretation of its enabling legislation. *See* § 9.2, *infra*. In determining whether particular agency action is intra vires or ultra vires, however, the reviewing court may have to decide: whether the agency enabling act should be construed broadly or narrowly; whether the actual language used in the agency enabling act appears to authorize the action at issue; whether the particular action of the agency in question is consistent with the general or specific intention of the legislature at the time it enacted the enabling act; whether the express grant of certain authority to the agency negatively implies the absence of other authority not expressly granted; whether certain agency powers can be implied from the express grant to the agency of other powers; whether legislative inaction during a long period when the agency purported to exercise certain authority constitutes legislative ratification of that authority even though the agency enabling act is unclear; whether the failure of an agency to exercise certain powers, over a long period of time, that were plausibly delegated to the agency in its enabling act, have been lost through desuetude because the act should be read in light of the agency's own conduct during that period; and whether a particular construction of an agency's enabling act may make that act unconstitutional.

Do you think one may sensibly generalize about the relevance of these issues to the courts' construction of the scope of agency authority in particular situations? Or are judicial determinations concerning the intra vires or ultra vires nature of particular agency action context specific so that general principles of statutory construction in that process are not really very useful or reliable?

KENT v. DULLES
357 U.S. 116 (1958).

[The Secretary of State refused to issue a passport to Rockwell Kent on the basis of § 51.135 of the Department of State regulations which provided that passports would not be issued to members of the

Communist party or to persons who engage in activities which support the Communist movement. A statute enacted in 1856 and codified in 1926 authorized the Secretary to grant and issue passports "under such rules as the President shall designate." Another statute, adopted in 1952, prohibits a citizen from entering or leaving the U.S. unless he or she bears a valid passport.]

DOUGLAS, J.:

Freedom to travel is, indeed, an important aspect of the citizen's "liberty." We need not decide the extent to which it can be curtailed. We are first concerned with the extent, if any, to which Congress has authorized its curtailment.

The difficulty is that while the power of the Secretary of State over the issuance of passports is expressed in broad terms, it was apparently long exercised quite narrowly. So far as material here, the cases of refusal of passports generally fell into two categories. First, questions pertinent to the citizenship of the applicant and his allegiance to the United States had to be resolved by the Secretary, for the command of Congress was that "No passport shall be granted or issued to or verified for any other persons than those owing allegiance, whether citizens or not, to the United States." Second, was the question whether the applicant was participating in illegal conduct, trying to escape the toils of the law, promoting passport frauds, or otherwise engaging in conduct which would violate the laws of the United States. . . .

The grounds for refusal asserted here do not relate to citizenship or allegiance on the one hand or to criminal or unlawful conduct on the other. Yet, so far as relevant here, those two are the only ones which it could fairly be argued were adopted by Congress in light of prior administrative practice. . . .

Since we start with an exercise by an American citizen of an activity included in constitutional protection, we will not readily infer that Congress gave the Secretary of State unbridled discretion to grant or withhold it. If we were dealing with political questions entrusted to the Chief Executive by the Constitution we would have a different case. But there is more involved here. In part, of course, the issuance of the passport carries some implication of intention to extend the bearer diplomatic protection, though it does no more than "request all whom it may concern to permit safely and freely to pass, and in case of need to give all lawful aid and protection" to this citizen of the United States. But that function of the passport is subordinate. Its crucial function today is control over exit. And, as we have seen, the right of exit is a personal right included within the word "liberty" as used in the Fifth Amendment. If that "liberty" is to be regulated, it must be pursuant to the law-making functions of the Congress. And if that power is delegated, the standards must be adequate to pass scrutiny by the accepted tests. Where activities or enjoyment, natural and often necessary to the well-being of an American citizen, such as travel, are involved, we will construe narrowly all delegated powers that curtail or dilute them. . . .

Thus we do not reach the question of constitutionality. We only conclude that [*the Act of 1856 does*] not delegate . . . the . . . authority exercised here.

Notes and Questions

1. *The dissent.* Four justices dissented, arguing that the legislative history of the relevant statutes and prior administrative practice suggested that the Secretary did have authority to prohibit travel for reasons relating to national security. They furnished numerous examples of this practice. Why did the majority not respond to these arguments?

2. *Avoiding constitutional questions. Kent v. Dulles* is one of many cases that construe statutory delegations narrowly to avoid serious constitutional questions. What are the advantages and disadvantages of construing an agency enabling act narrowly to avoid serious constitutional questions, rather than deciding those constitutional questions directly? Of invalidating an agency enabling act as an undue delegation of legislative power rather than determining through a narrow construction of that act that particular agency action was ultra vires? Are there good reasons other than the avoidance of constitutional questions that might lead courts to construe agency enabling acts narrowly to the extent they arguably authorize the regulation of fundamental rights or the use of suspect classifications?

Note that in order to avoid deciding constitutional questions, courts will usually adjudicate ultra vires challenges before they adjudicate constitutional challenges. *See, e.g., Commodity Futures Trading Com'n v. Schor,* 478 U.S. 833, 841–47 (1986).

BOREALI v. AXELROD
517 N.E.2d 1350 (N.Y.1987).

TITONE, JUDGE.

We hold that the Public Health Council overstepped the boundaries of its lawfully delegated authority when it promulgated a comprehensive code to govern tobacco smoking in areas that are open to the public. . . .

More than two decades ago, the Surgeon General of the United States began warning the American public that tobacco smoking poses a serious health hazard. Within the past five years, there has been mounting evidence that even nonsmokers face a risk of lung cancer as a result of their exposure to tobacco smoke in the environment. As a consequence, smoking in the workplace and other indoor settings has become a cause for serious concern among health professionals.

This growing concern about the deleterious effects of tobacco smoking led our State Legislature to enact a bill in 1975 restricting smoking in certain designated areas, specifically, libraries, museums, theaters and public transportation facilities. [Subsequent efforts] . . . to adopt more expansive restrictions on smoking in public places were, however, unsuccessful. In fact, it is undisputed that while some 40 bills on the subject have been introduced in the Legislature since 1975, none have passed both houses.

In late 1986 the Public Health Council (PHC) took action of its own. Purportedly acting pursuant to the broad grant of authority contained in its enabling statute, the PHC published proposed rules, held public hearings and, in February of 1987, promulgated the final set of regulations prohibiting smoking in a wide variety of indoor areas that are open to the public, including schools, hospitals, auditoriums, food markets, stores, banks, taxicabs and limousines. Under these rules, restaurants with seating capacities of more than 50 people are required to provide contiguous nonsmoking areas sufficient to meet customer demand. Further, employers are required to provide smoke-free work areas for nonsmoking employees and to keep common areas free of smoke, with certain limited exceptions for cafeterias and lounges. Affected businesses are permitted to prohibit all smoking on the premises if they so choose. Expressly excluded from the regulations' coverage are restaurants with seating capacities of less than 50, conventions, trade shows, bars, private homes, private automobiles, private social functions, hotel and motel rooms and retail tobacco stores. Additional "waivers" of the regulations' restrictions may be obtained from the Commissioner upon a showing of financial hardship. Implementation of these regulations, which were to become effective May 7, 1987, has been suspended during the pendency of this litigation. . . .

Section 225(5)(a) of the Public Health Law authorizes the PHC to "deal with any matters affecting the . . . public health". At the heart of the present case is the question whether, . . . assuming the propriety of the Legislature's grant of authority, the agency exceeded the permissible scope of its mandate by using it as a basis for engaging in inherently legislative activities. While the separation of powers doctrine gives the Legislature considerable leeway in delegating its regulatory powers, enactments conferring authority on administrative agencies in broad or general terms must be interpreted in light of the limitations that the Constitution imposes (N.Y. Const., art. III, § 1).

However facially broad, a legislative grant of authority must be construed, whenever possible, so that it is no broader than that which the separation of powers doctrine permits. . . . Here, we cannot say that the broad enabling statute in issue is itself an unconstitutional delegation of legislative authority. However, we do conclude that the agency stretched that statute beyond its constitutionally valid reach when it used the statute as a basis for drafting a code embodying its own assessment of what public policy ought to be. . . .

A number of coalescing circumstances that are present in this case persuade us that the difficult-to-define line between administrative rule-making and legislative policy-making has been transgressed. While none of these circumstances, standing alone, is sufficient to warrant the conclusion that the PHC has usurped the Legislature's prerogative, all of these circumstances, when viewed in combination, paint a portrait of an agency that has improperly assumed for itself "[t]he open-ended discretion to choose ends" which characterizes the elected Legislature's role in our system of government.

First, while generally acting to further the laudable goal of protecting nonsmokers from the harmful effects of "passive smoking," the PHC has, in reality, constructed a regulatory scheme laden with exceptions based solely upon economic and social concerns. The exemptions the PHC has carved out for bars, convention centers, small restaurants, and the like, as well as the provision it has made for "waivers" based on financial hardship, have no foundation in considerations of public health. Rather, they demonstrate the agency's own effort to weigh the goal of promoting health against its social cost and to reach a suitable compromise. . . .

Striking the proper balance among health concerns, cost and privacy interests, however, is a uniquely legislative function. While it is true that many regulatory decisions involve weighing economic and social concerns against the specific values that the regulatory agency is mandated to promote, the agency in this case has not been authorized to structure its decision making in a "cost-benefit" model and, in fact, has not been given any legislative guidelines at all for determining how the competing concerns of public health and economic cost are to be weighed. Thus, to the extent that the agency has built a regulatory scheme on its own conclusions about the appropriate balance of trade-offs between health and cost to particular industries in the private sector, it was "acting solely on [its] own ideas of sound public policy" and was therefore operating outside of its proper sphere of authority. This conclusion is particularly compelling here, where the focus is on administratively created exemptions rather than on rules that promote the legislatively expressed goals, since exemptions ordinarily run counter to such goals and, consequently, cannot be justified as simple implementations of legislative values. . . .

The second, and related, consideration is that in adopting the antismoking regulations challenged here the PHC did not merely fill in the details of broad legislation describing the over-all policies to be implemented. Instead, the PHC wrote on a clean slate, creating its own comprehensive set of rules without benefit of legislative guidance. Viewed in that light, the agency's actions were a far cry from the "interstitial" rule making that typifies administrative regulatory activity. . . .

A third indicator that the PHC exceeded the scope of the authority properly delegated to it by the Legislature is the fact that the agency acted in an area in which the Legislature had repeatedly tried—and failed—to reach agreement in the face of substantial public debate and vigorous lobbying by a variety of interested factions. While we have often been reluctant to ascribe persuasive significance to legislative inaction, our usual hesitancy in this area has no place here. Unlike the cases in which we have been asked to consider the Legislature's failure to act as some indirect proof of its actual intentions in this case it is appropriate for us to consider the significance of legislative inaction as evidence that the Legislature has so far been unable to reach agreement on the goals and methods that should govern in resolving a society-wide health problem. Here, the repeated failures by the Legislature to arrive at such an agreement do not automatically entitle an administrative agency to take it upon itself to fill the vacuum and impose a solution of its own. Manifestly, it is the province of the people's elected representatives, rather than appointed administrators, to resolve difficult social problems by making choices among competing ends.

Finally, although indoor smoking is unquestionably a health issue, no special expertise or technical competence in the field of health was involved in the development of the antismoking regulations challenged here. Faced with mounting evidence about the hazards to bystanders of indoor smoking, the PHC drafted a simple code describing the locales in which smoking would be prohibited and providing exemptions for various special interest groups. . . .

In summary, we conclude that while Public Health Law § 225(5)(a) is a valid delegation of regulatory authority, it cannot be construed to encompass the policy-making activity at issue here without running afoul of the constitutional separation of powers doctrine. . . .

BELLACOSA, JUDGE (dissenting).

I would reverse and uphold the Public Health Council (PHC) regulation, adopted to preserve and improve the public health, prohibiting smoking indoors in some public places and in designated portions of workplaces.

The Legislature declared its intent that there be a PHC in this State and empowered it to adopt a Sanitary Code for the preservation and improvement of the public health. The Legislature also wisely refrained from enacting a rigid formula for the exercise of the PHC's critical agenda of concerns because that calls for expert attention. That legislative forbearance represents both a sound administrative law principle and, at the threshold, a constitutional one as well. . . . It was prescient and sound governance as well to grant flexibility to the objective expert entity so it could in these exceptional instances prescribe demonstrably needed administrative regulation for the public health, free from the sometimes paralyzing polemics associated with the legislative process. . . .

It is painfully ironic that the PHC, as the legislatively designated body of experts for a vast litany of public health concerns is declared for the first time and against a long line of precedents to lack expertise in this instance. . . .

Along the way to its decision, the majority somewhat hesitantly deals with a legislative history aspect of the case. It concludes that the law passed by the Legislature and on the books for 75 years is nullified or neutralized by the inability of the Legislature to broaden its existing narrow ban. The functional consequence of the negatively implied repeal of the broader authorization, imputed by the majority to these recent failed legislative efforts, will be welcomed by opponents of all kinds of existing laws from now on, because the majority's rule dramatically changes the use of legislative history and of the principles of ordinary statutory construction. . . .

No decision of this court and no relevant administrative law principle have been found where general rule-making power was nullified by a court because exceptions to the rule were also promulgated by the regulating entity in response to ancillary social, economic or even policy factors. The majority argument in this respect seems to assert that the PHC was too reasonable and too forthright, and that what it perhaps should have done was create an absolute ban on indoor smoking expressly and pristinely premised on public health concerns. Life and government are not so neatly categorized. Surely, if the greater power exists, the lesser, as responsibly exercised here, should not be forbidden! . . .

Finally, there should be great concern about another and broader precedential regression lurking behind the diaphanous analysis of the majority's holding. . . . The majority's invocation of the nondelegation doctrine sounds a discordant note which can summon no good in future administrative law disputes. This doctrine was last used to invalidate an act of Congress in 1935.

Notes and Questions

1. *Comparing Boreali and Kent.* Note that in the *Kent* case the United States Supreme Court construed a federal agency enabling act narrowly because of concerns that a broader construction might, in the case before it, violate civil liberties provisions (the first and fifth amendments) of the federal constitution, while the Court of Appeals of New York in *Boreali* construed a state agency enabling act narrowly because of concerns that a broader construction might, in the case before it, violate structural provisions (separation of powers requirements) of the New York constitution. Is there any greater justification for such narrow constructions of agency enabling acts when the first kind of constitutional provision rather than the second kind is involved? Was the narrow construction of the agency enabling act in *Boreali* more or less justified than the similar construction in *Kent?* Or is there no discernible difference between them in this respect?

2. *Lawyering skills or predictable results?* Would you have advised the parties who challenged these rules that there was a good chance that the highest court of the state would declare them ultra vires? Was the majority opinion in *Boreali* a tribute to the great skill

of the lawyers for the parties challenging these rules, or do the relevant legal materials and arguments discussed in the opinions demonstrate that the result in this case was inevitable?

Consider, for example, the use of legislative history by the majority opinion. Was it persuasive? Were the objections of the dissent sound? Note that the use of legislative history to draw inferences of the kind drawn by the majority in this case *could* be used as a mask for hidden judicial agendas. Of course, that does not necessarily mean that was so in this case. What do *you* think? Contrast the use of legislative history in the *Boreali* majority opinion and the dissent's view on that question, with the use of administrative practice in the *Kent* majority opinion and the objections of the dissent in *Kent* to the conclusions of the majority in that regard. May any useful generalizations concerning the construction of agency enabling acts be drawn from the use of such materials as legislative history and administrative practice in these two cases?

If you were the Judge required to decide the *Boreali* case, would you have come to the same result? Why? Which of the arguments made by the majority opinion would you find most persuasive? Which by the dissent?

3. *Undue delegation.* Note the distinction drawn by the majority opinion between legislative-type decisions that may be made only by the legislature itself, and administrative-type decisions that may be delegated by the legislature to an agency. Is this distinction clear, defensible, or utilitarian? Think about the answer to this question as you consider the propriety of delegations of legislative authority to administrative agencies in the next subsection.

4. *Problem.* Since 1870 State University has operated under the following enabling act:

(1) The objectives of State University shall be to facilitate and secure quality higher education in the liberal arts and sciences, applied sciences, and learned professions, and to foster worthwhile research in these subjects.

(2) State University is authorized to exercise those powers reasonably suitable and necessary to accomplish these purposes including, but not limited to, the power to acquire and hold title to real and personal property, to enter into contracts, to employ staff and admit students, to make rules for the governance of its staff and students, to determine the nature and scope of its programs, to impose fees, and to receive monies for its support from any appropriate and lawful source.

This statute has been amended only three times. In 1900 a section 3 was added providing that "State University may establish a program of hotel administration and a hotel for the training of its students." This amendment resulted from the refusal of the President of State University at that time to establish such a program on the articulated ground that the University did not have the authority to do so. In 1940, a section 4 was added providing that "State University is authorized to own and operate one or more radio stations in this state." This amendment resulted from a dictum in a State Supreme Court opinion dealing with the authority of another state agency to the effect that "we doubt whether the authority of State University, for example, would extend to its ownership and operation of a radio station, because that would be unrelated to its statutorily mandated objectives." In 1958 a section 5 was added providing that "State University may enter into joint or cooperative ventures for the economic development of this state." This amendment was a direct response to a State Supreme Court decision holding invalid an agreement between State University and a manufacturer whereby the manufacturer would establish a plant in the state if State University gave it an exclusive license to manufacture all new drugs developed in State University research laboratories that had commercial potential.

You are counsel to State University. What would you advise the University about its authority to engage in the following actions?

(a) The creation of a University computer store to sell computers and related equipment and service to students, faculty, and alumni, at cut-rate prices. This store would be in direct competition with private vendors of such equipment and services.

(b) The issuance of a rule prohibiting all State University faculty and students from smoking or drinking alcoholic beverages at any place on University property (including University dormitories and University apartments rented to students and faculty) and at any event sponsored by the University or any of its recognized organizations, regardless of its location.

(c) A rule imposing civil fines on all persons who improperly park on University property, and providing for the forfeiture to the University of any vehicle improperly left on University property for more than a week.

§ 7.3　DELEGATION OF LEGISLATIVE POWER TO AGENCIES

§ 7.3.1　THE NONDELEGATION DOCTRINE AND FEDERAL AGENCIES

Article I of the federal Constitution vests legislative power in Congress. To what extent may Congress delegate its legislative power to administrative agencies? It has always been clear that some legislative power may be and, for government to function, must be delegated.

The general source of Congress' power to delegate legislative authority to agencies is clear. The Constitution expressly authorizes Congress to enact laws that are necessary and proper means of implementing its delegated powers. Therefore, unless otherwise constitutionally prohibited, Congress should be able to delegate to agencies as much of its legislative power as it believes necessary or appropriate to execute any of its powers. Nevertheless, courts have maintained that Congress' power to delegate its legislative authority is limited. The source of this limitation is the non-delegation doctrine.

This non-delegation doctrine invokes both separation of powers and checks and balances arguments. The separation of powers argument is that the Constitution assigned all legislative power to the legislature; therefore it cannot give any part of that power to agencies that are part of the executive branch. The checks and balances argument recognizes that delegation may be inevitable, but insists that the legislature impose adequate limits on the discretion of the agent carrying out the delegation. It remains a source of continuing controversy whether there really is a delegation doctrine today and, if there is, whether courts can and should enforce it through invalidation of improper delegations.

§ 7.3.1a From Field to the New Deal

Field v. Clark, 143 U.S. 649 (1892), sounded themes of both separation of powers and checks and balances. A statute empowered the President to raise tariffs and suspend trade with foreign countries "for such time as he shall deem just." The President was to take this action if he deemed the tariffs imposed by such countries on American goods to be unequal and unreasonable. Of course, Congress ordinarily reserves to itself decisions on the imposition of import tariffs. Why would Congress have delegated such an important power to the President?

The Supreme Court stated the nondelegation doctrine broadly. "That Congress cannot delegate legislative power to the President is a principle universally recognized as vital to the integrity and maintenance of the system of government ordained by the constitution." What makes this "principle" so "vital?"

Nevertheless, the Court upheld the delegation to the President to establish tariffs.

As the suspension was absolutely required when the President ascertained the existence of a particular fact, it cannot be said that in ascertaining that fact and in issuing his proclamation, in obedience to the legislative will, he exercised the function of making laws. Legislative power was exercised when Congress declared that the suspension should take effect upon a named contingency. What the President was required to do was simply in execution of the act of Congress. It was not the making of law. He was the mere agent of the law-making department to ascertain and declare the event upon which its expressed will was to take effect. It was a part of the law itself as it left the hands of Congress that [favorable tariff provisions] should be suspended, in a given contingency, and in [such cases] certain duties should be imposed.

143 U.S. at 693.

Of course, the power given to the President in the *Field* case was far more significant than a mere power to "ascertain the fact" of whether a "given contingency" had occurred. It was indeed "the making of law." A decision about whether foreign tariffs are unequal and unreasonable, and thus justify retaliation, calls for considerable analysis and subtle judgment and entails deeply political as well as economic calculations.

From the time of the *Field* case until the early 1930's, the Supreme Court continued to assert that there was a non-delegation doctrine, while consistently upholding every delegation that came before it. In those cases, which involved steadily more sweeping delegations of lawmaking power to administrative agencies, the Supreme Court looked to see whether Congress had established an "intelligible principle" or a "primary standard" to guide the delegate in making the decision. *See, e.g., J.W. Hampton & Co. v. United States,* 276 U.S. 394 (1928) ("if Congress shall lay down by legislative act an intelligible principle to which the person or body authorized to [regulate] is directed to conform, such legislative action is not a forbidden delegation of legislative power"). During this period the Court upheld delegations to the Federal Trade Commission to prohibit "unfair methods of competition" and to the predecessor of the Federal Communications Commission to regulate the airwaves as the "public convenience, interest or necessity requires." *FTC v. Gratz,* 253 U.S. 421 (1920); *Federal Radio Com'n v. Nelson Bros. Bond & Mortgage Co.,* 289 U.S. 266 (1933).

In each case, the Court found that an intelligible principle or a primary standard was in fact present. What purposes might the standards requirement serve? Do general and vague standards like "unfair methods of competition" and "public interest, convenience and necessity" really furnish any guidance to anyone? Why should the presence in a statute of an intelligible principle or a primary standard validate a statute under attack on delegation grounds?

Who should have the burden of persuasion in a suit to challenge the lawfulness of a delegation of power—the agency or the person challenging the delegation? Of what relevance is the usual presumption of constitutionality that attaches to legislative action?

In 1935, the Supreme Court twice held statutes unconstitutional under the delegation doctrine. Both provisions were contained in the National Industrial Recovery Act (NIRA) of 1933, an early New Deal measure passed in the depths of the Great Depression. These cases were the first and the last Supreme Court decisions to overturn statutes as invalid legislative delegations to administrative agencies. They must be viewed in light of the extreme judicial activism of the early 1930's, an attitude which also resulted in the invalidation of many New

Deal laws on other grounds, including a lack of Congressional power to act under the commerce and the spending clauses of Article I.

The NIRA contained various legislative findings about the economic emergency and declared Congressional policy that there should be cooperation among trade groups, including labor and management, to revive the economy, relieve unemployment, increase production and consumption, and conserve natural resources. Thus the Act apparently contained a wealth of "standards" and "intelligible principles" to guide the delegate.

The first delegation case arose under § 9 of the NIRA allowing the President to ban the shipment of oil in interstate commerce that had been produced in violation of an order of a state agency (so called "hot oil"). The background of this provision was that new oil discoveries in Texas had led to massive overproduction. Each producer pumped as much oil as fast as possible lest other producers deplete the pool first. The result was a drastic fall in the price of oil, a massive waste of a non-renewable resource, and complete disorganization of the oil industry.

Texas set up a state agency to control the amount that each producer could pump; but the interstate nature of the oil business meant that state regulation could not be effective without national help. The language and legislative history of § 9 indicated that it was intended to provide that help by making interstate shipment of "hot oil" a federal crime when the President deemed such a ban desirable to eliminate those evils.

In *Panama Refining Co. v. Ryan,* 293 U.S. 388 (1935), the Supreme Court invalidated the delegation to the President of the power to decide whether and when to ban the shipment of "hot oil." It declared:

> In every case in which the question has been raised, the Court has recognized that there are limits of delegation which there is no constitutional authority to transcend. We think that section 9(c) goes beyond those limits. As to the transportation of oil production in excess of state permission, the Congress has declared no policy, has established no standard, has laid down no rule. There is no requirement, no definition of circumstances and conditions in which the transportation is to be allowed or prohibited.

293 U.S. at 430. Only Justice Cardozo dissented, pointing out that the statute defined the precise act which the President was to perform and, in context, made abundantly clear the circumstances in which it should be performed. Was *Panama* consistent with *Field v. Clark?*

The second decision invalidated a much more important and vastly more sweeping delegation of authority to the President contained in the NIRA. The background of § 3 was the catastrophic depression engulfing the American economy. Unemployment exceeded 25%, wages and prices plummeted, banks and businesses of every sort failed. The NIRA was an attempt to reverse the terrifying downward spiral of the depression and start the economy moving upward again. Section 3 of the NIRA empowered the President to adopt "codes of fair competition" for any industry. The codes would prescribe maximum and minimum prices to be charged, wages, hours and working conditions of labor, levels of production, and many other competitive practices which previously had been left solely to the market. The Act also provided that violations of a code were a criminal offense.

In *A.L.A. Schechter Poultry Corp. v. United States,* 295 U.S. 495 (1935), the Supreme Court invalidated § 3 under the delegation doctrine (and also because Congress had exceeded the scope of its power to regulate interstate commerce, a rationale not explored here but one that was totally repudiated by later decisions). *Schechter* arose under the poultry code. In addition to setting poultry prices, the code required retailers to take all the chickens offered to them by wholesalers; they could no longer pick and choose. Schechter Poultry, a wholesaler in New York, was convicted because it permitted retailers to reject chickens.

The Supreme Court held unanimously that the delegation to the President to adopt "codes of fair competition" was invalid because the NIRA lacked an adequate standard to govern the drafting of codes. The Court objected to the lack of any procedure for adopting the codes, and questioned the involvement of dominant private producers in proposing and writing a code that would bind their competitors. It distinguished the earlier cases which had upheld delegations to various agencies, including the Federal Trade Commission, to prevent "unfair methods of competition" or to act in the "public interest." In these situations, unlike the NIRA, Congress created agencies to enforce the law in accordance with defined and fair procedures.

Moreover, as Justice Cardozo pointed out in his concurring opinion, the statutes involved in the earlier precedents were different from the NIRA because they focused on practices which generally would be considered oppressive or unfair, or upon economically unsound practices in specific industries. The NIRA went much further. It extended to the entire economy and entailed a "roving commission" to achieve positive reform of industrial practice. "The extension becomes as wide as the field of industrial regulation. If that conception shall prevail, anything that Congress may do within the limits of the commerce clause for the betterment of business may be done by the President upon the recommendation of a trade association by calling it a code. This is delegation running riot. No such plenitude of power is susceptible of transfer. The statute, however, aims at nothing less, as one can learn both from its terms and from the administrative practice under it." 295 U.S. at 553.

Was the problem in *Schechter* the lack of adequate standards, the excessively broad scope of the delegation, the lack of procedural safeguards, the delegation to private groups, or the cumulative effect of all of them?   How can one explain Justice Cardozo's dissent in *Panama* in light of his concurrence in *Schechter?*

§ 7.3.1b   From the New Deal to the Present

Following the *Schechter* and *Panama* decisions, the Supreme Court returned to its pre–1930's practice of giving lip service to the delegation doctrine, while upholding ever more sweeping and vague delegations of legislative authority to administrative agencies.   For example, in *Yakus v. United States,* 321 U.S. 414 (1944), the Court upheld (with a single dissent) a delegation in the Emergency Price Control Act of 1942 to the Price Administrator to fix maximum prices.   Like the NIRA, the 1942 Act was designed to deal comprehensively with an economic emergency—in this case, the inflationary spiral generated by World War II.   The standard for fixing prices was that such prices had to be "generally fair and equitable."   The Administrator had to ascertain and give due consideration to the prices prevailing in October, 1941, and was required to furnish a statement of the considerations involved in setting particular prices.   Did that statute furnish an "intelligible principle" or a "primary standard" to guide the delegate?

Yakus was convicted of selling beef for a price in excess of a ceiling set by the Administrator.   In responding to the claim that the statute was an unlawful delegation, the Supreme Court stated:

> The Constitution as a continuously operative charter of government does not demand the impossible or the impracticable . . . .
> The essentials of the legislative function are the determination of the legislative policy and its formulation and promulgation as a defined and binding rule of conduct—here the rule, with penal sanctions, that prices shall not be greater than those fixed by maximum price regulations which conform to standards and will tend to further the policy which Congress has established . . . .
> It is no objection that the determination of facts and the inferences to be drawn from them in the light of the statutory standards and declaration of policy call for the exercise of judgment, and for the formulation of subsidiary administrative policy within the prescribed statutory framework . . . .
>
>   Congress is not confined to that method of executing its policy which involves the least possible delegation of discretion to administrative officers . . . . It is free to avoid the rigidity of such a system, which might well result in serious hardship, and to choose instead the flexibility attainable by the use of less restrictive standards . . . . Only if we could say that there is an absence of standards for the guidance of the Administrator's action, so that it would be impossible in a proper proceeding to ascertain whether the will of Congress has been obeyed, would we be justified in overriding its choice of means for effecting its declared purpose of preventing inflation.

321 U.S. at 424–26.

The Court quickly distinguished *Schechter* on the ground that the NIRA had failed to provide standards for the codes of fair competition and because the delegation to write the codes was to individuals in the industries to be regulated. *Panama Refining* was not mentioned. Although cases like *Yakus* (and there have been many) suggest that the Supreme Court is unwilling to invalidate a statute on the grounds of unlawful delegation, the *Schechter* and *Panama* cases have never been overruled.

Do you agree with Professor Davis?

Congress may and does lawfully delegate legislative power to administrative agencies. The Supreme Court has *said* many times—more than a hundred—that standards are required, but it has often *held* that standards are not required. The Supreme Court throughout the twentieth century has upheld congressional delegations without standards, and except for two 1935 decisions, it has never held unconstitutional any delegation to an administrative agency. Since 1935, the nondelegation doctrine has had no reality in the holdings, although remnants of the doctrine persist in judicial verbiage.

The law allowing delegation of rulemaking power to administrative agencies is clear law, sound law, and necessary law. It is sure to continue for the kind of government we have developed could not operate without it.

1 K. Davis, ADMINISTRATIVE LAW TREATISE § 3.1, at 150 (2d ed. 1978).

§ 7.3.1c　Revival of the Delegation Doctrine

Is the delegation doctrine as dead as Davis claims? Consider the two cases excerpted below. The first, *Amalgamated Meat Cutters,* is an often-cited opinion by Judge Leventhal for a special three-judge court. The second, *Industrial Union Department,* is a dissenting opinion by Justice Rehnquist.

AMALGAMATED MEAT CUTTERS AND BUTCHER WORKMEN v. CONNALLY
337 F.Supp. 737 (D.C.D.C.1971).

[Plaintiff Union challenged the Economic Stabilization Act of 1970 (Act) under the delegation doctrine. That Act empowered the President "to issue such orders and regulations as he may deem appropriate to stabilize prices, rents, wages, and salaries." To restrain inflation during the Vietnam conflict, President Nixon used his authority under the Act to freeze prices, rents, wages, and salaries for a ninety-day period. He also put in place a system of wage and price controls for the period after the freeze expired. Violators were subject to a fine of $5000 per violation. The Union argued that the Act "vests unbridled legislative power in the President."]

The Government cites numerous authorities but relies most heavily on *Yakus v. United States, supra,* sustaining the grant in the Emergency Price Control Act of 1942 of broad price-fixing authority. . . . We may usefully begin with the modest observation that the Constitution does not forbid every delegation of "legislative" power. . . . The *Yakus* ruling . . . carries forward the doctrine [of the *J.W. Hampton* case, *supra,*] . . . that there is no forbidden delegation of legislative power "if Congress shall lay down by legislative act an intelligible principle" to which the official or agency must conform.

Concepts of control and accountability define the constitutional requirement. The principle permitting a delegation of legislative power, if there has been a sufficient demarcation of the field to permit a judgment whether the agency has kept within the legislative will, establishes a principle of accountability under which compatibility with the legislative design may be ascertained not only by Congress but by the courts and the public. That principle was conjoined in *Yakus* with a recognition that the burden is on the party who assails the legislature's choice of means for effecting its purpose, a burden that is met "only if we could say that there is an absence of standards for the guidance of the Administrator's action, so that it would be impossible in a proper proceeding to ascertain whether the will of Congress has been obeyed. . . ."

[The Court held that sufficient standards had been supplied. The Act did not permit the President to set prices and wages below their level on May 25, 1970. The statute precluded the President from singling out a particular sector of the economy in which to impose controls, absent a finding that wages or prices in that sector had increased disproportionately. Moreover, the legislative history set forth the legislative purpose plainly. That purpose was the same as the purpose of the 1942 act sustained in *Yakus.* There is no requirement that standards be set forth in express language of the statute as distinguished from its legislative history.] . . .

We see no merit in the contention that the Act is constitutionally defective because the timing of the imposition of controls was delegated to the President. . . . Viewing the President as a physician in charge, Congress could advise but not mandate his diagnosis. It sought in the national interest to have the right remedy available on a standby basis, if the President should wish to adopt that prescription, following his further reflection and taking into account future developments and experience. . . .

[The court emphasized the connection between domestic inflation and international trade.] The consequence for international trade, liquidity and monetary relationships enhances the range of power Congress can permissibly delegate to the President. *United States v. Curtiss–Wright Export Corp.,* 299 U.S. 304 (1936); *Zemel v. Rusk,* 381 U.S. 1 (1965). . . .

It is also material, though not dispositive, to note the limited time frame established by Congress for the stabilization authority delegated to the President. [The 1970 Act had a six month lifespan.] Two subsequent extensions provided even shorter durations.

[The court then turned to the issue of whether Congress had provided sufficient standards for wage-price controls after the freeze expired. It concluded that Congress provided a standard of broad fairness and the removal of "gross inequities." These standards were sufficient to meet any constitutional objections.] . . .

Another feature that blunts the "blank check" rhetoric is the requirement that any action taken by the Executive under the law, subsequent to the freeze, must be in accordance with further standards as developed by the Executive. This requirement, inherent in the Rule of Law and implicit in the Act, means that however broad the discretion of the Executive at the outset, the standards once developed limit the latitude of subsequent executive action. . . . [T]here is an on-going requirement of intelligible administrative policy that is corollary to and implementing of the legislature's ultimate standard and objective. . . .

The claim of undue delegation of legislative power broadly raises the challenge of undue power in the Executive and thus naturally involves consideration of the interrelated questions of the availability of appropriate restraints through provisions for administrative procedure and judicial review. . . .

The safeguarding of meaningful judicial review is one of the primary functions of the doctrine prohibiting undue delegation of legislative powers. . . . The Government concedes and we agree that the Executive's actions under the 1970 Act are not immune from judicial review . . . . Challenges may be made under the provisions for judicial review in the [APA, §§ 701–706]. . . .

By the same token actions under this 1970 Act are subject to the administrative procedure provisions of the APA. [However, the court noted that the rulemaking provisions would likely be unavailable because the President could utilize the good-cause exemptions. The adjudication provisions are applicable only when an on-the-record hearing is required by statute or "compulsion of general law" (citing *Wong Yang Sung v. McGrath,* 339 U.S. 33 (1950)). *Yakus* upheld the validity of the failure to provide for such hearings in the 1942 Act. The court also suggested that the on-going administration of the program could be challenged for failure to provide reasonable and meaningful opportunity for interested persons to present objections or for courts to discharge their judicial review function.]

We end this section of the opinion with broad closing references to precedent. . . . We do not understand *Yakus* to rest in a crucial sense on the exercise of the war power. . . . [T]here have not been any Supreme Court rulings holding statutes unconstitutional for excessive delegation of legislative power since *Panama Refining* and *Schecht-*

er. . . . These cases express a principle that has validity—reserved for the extreme instance. . . . Both cited cases dealt with delegation of a power to make federal crimes of acts that never had been such before and to devise novel rules of law in a field in which there had been no settled law or custom. They are without vigor in a case like [this] where the delegation is in a context of historical experience with anti-inflation legislation.

The particular application of the delegation principle in *Panama Refining* was colored . . . by the circumstance that the regulation in that case was not generally available and had been inadvertently amended out of effect—a circumstance that led to the creation of the Federal Register. . . .

Schechter has fairly been described as a ruling that administered "the hemlock of excessive delegation" in a case of "delegation run riot." We think the extremist pattern then before the Court cannot fairly be analogized to the anti-inflation statute, limited in life and passed in a context of experiences with similar legislation, that is before us for consideration.

INDUSTRIAL UNION DEPARTMENT, AFL–CIO V. AMERICAN PETROLEUM INSTITUTE

448 U.S. 607 (1980).

[The Occupational Safety and Health Act delegates authority to the Secretary of Labor to adopt safety and health standards for the workplace. Under § 3(8) of the Act, the standards must be "reasonably necessary or appropriate to provide safe or healthful . . . places of employment." In setting standards for toxic materials, § 6(b)(5) of the Act directs the Secretary "to set the standard which most adequately assures, to the extent feasible . . . that no employee will suffer material impairment of health. . . ."

The Occupational Safety and Health Administration (OSHA), which discharges the Secretary's responsibilities under this Act, construed the statute to require it to set standards at the safest possible level which is technologically feasible and which would not cause material economic impairment of the industry.

This case involves the standard for benzene, an industrial chemical which in high concentration causes leukemia and other illnesses. OSHA set the standard for benzene at 1 part per million, although OSHA did not find, and research did not establish, that there is danger to the health of workers at levels of concentration below 10 parts per million.

In the enabling act Congress never made it clear whether it wanted OSHA to balance costs to industry against benefits to workers or whether it wanted OSHA to set standards at the safest possible level without consideration of costs. The majority of the Court overturned the benzene standard, holding that OSHA must find, before promulgating a standard, that it is necessary and appropriate to remedy a significant risk of material health impairment. One justice thought that a cost-benefit balancing was required. The dissent vigorously disagreed, arguing that Congress intended precisely what OSHA had done. Justice Rehnquist concurred in the judgment, but for an entirely different reason. He first pointed to the sharp split among the other justices about what Congress had intended. He then asserted that § 6(b)(5) was invalid under the delegation doctrine.]

In my opinion decisions such as *Panama Refining Co. v. Ryan,* [*supra,*] suffer from none of the excesses of judicial policymaking that plagued some of the other decisions of that era. The many later decisions that have upheld congressional delegations of authority to the Executive Branch have done so largely on the theory that Congress may wish to exercise its authority in a particular field, but because the field is sufficiently technical, the ground to be covered sufficiently large, and the Members of Congress themselves not necessarily expert in the area in which they choose to legislate, the most that may be asked under the separation-of-powers doctrine is that Congress lay down the general policy and standards that animate the law, leaving the agency to refine those standards, "fill in the blanks," or apply the standards to particular cases. These decisions, to my mind, simply illustrate the above-quoted principle stated more than 50 years ago by Mr. Chief Justice Taft that delegations of legislative authority must be judged "according to common sense and the inherent necessities of the governmental co-ordination."

Viewing the legislation at issue here in light of these principles, I believe that it fails to pass muster. Read literally, the relevant portion of § 6(b)(5) is completely precatory, admonishing the Secretary to adopt the most protective standard if he can, but excusing him from that duty if he cannot. In the case of a hazardous substance for which a "safe" level is either unknown or impractical, the language of § 6(b)(5) gives the Secretary absolutely no indication where on the continuum of relative safety he should draw his line. Especially in light of the importance of the interests at stake, I have no doubt that the provision at issue, standing alone, would violate the doctrine against uncanalized delegations of legislative power. For me the remaining question, then, is whether additional standards are ascertainable from the legislative history or statutory context of § 6(b)(5) or, if not, whether such a standardless delegation was justifiable in light of the "inherent necessities" of the situation.

One of the primary sources looked to by this Court in adding gloss to an otherwise broad grant of legislative authority is the legislative history of the statute in question. The opinions of Mr. Justice Stevens and Mr. Justice Marshall, however, give little more than a tip of the hat to the legislative origins of § 6(b)(5). Such treatment is perhaps understandable, since the legislative history of that section, far from shedding light on what important policy choices Congress was making in the statute, gives one the feeling of viewing the congressional purpose "by the dawn's early light."

I believe that the legislative history demonstrates that the feasibility requirement, as employed in § 6(b)(5), is a legislative mirage, appearing to some Members but not to others, and assuming any form desired by the beholder. . . .

In prior cases this Court has looked to sources other than the legislative history to breathe life into otherwise vague delegations of legislative power. In *American Power & Light Co. v. SEC,* 329 U.S. 90 (1946), for example, this Court concluded that certain seemingly vague delegations "derive[d] much meaningful content from the purpose of the Act, its factual background and the statutory context in which they appear." Here, however, there is little or nothing in the remaining provisions of the Occupational Safety and Health Act to provide specificity to the feasibility criterion in § 6(b)(5). . . .

In some cases where broad delegations of power have been examined, this Court has upheld those delegations because of the delegatee's residual authority over particular subjects of regulation. In *United States v. Curtiss–Wright Export Corp.,* 299 U.S. 304, 307 (1936), this Court upheld a statute authorizing the President to prohibit the sale of arms to certain countries if he found that such a prohibition would "contribute to the reestablishment of peace." This Court reasoned that, in the area of foreign affairs, Congress "must often accord to the President a degree of discretion and freedom from statutory restriction which would not be admissible were domestic affairs alone involved." . . . In the present cases, however, neither the Executive Branch in general nor the Secretary in particular enjoys any independent authority over the subject matter at issue.

Finally, as indicated earlier, in some cases this Court has abided by a rule of necessity, upholding broad delegations of authority where it would be "unreasonable and impracticable to compel Congress to prescribe detailed rules" regarding a particular policy or situation. But no need for such an evasive standard as "feasibility" is apparent in the present cases. In drafting § 6(b)(5), Congress was faced with a clear, if difficult, choice between balancing statistical lives and industrial resources or authorizing the Secretary to elevate human life above all concerns save massive dislocation in an affected industry. . . . That Congress chose, intentionally or unintentionally, to pass this difficult choice on to the Secretary is evident from the spectral quality of the standard it selected and is capsulized in Senator Saxbe's unfulfilled promise that "the terms that we are passing back and forth are going to have to be identified."

As formulated and enforced by this Court, the nondelegation doctrine serves three important functions. First, and most abstractly, it ensures to the extent consistent with orderly governmental administration that important choices of social policy are made by Congress, the branch of our Government most responsive to the popular will. . . .

Second, the doctrine guarantees that, to the extent Congress finds it necessary to delegate authority, it provides the recipient of that authority with an "intelligible principle" to guide the exercise of the delegated discretion. . . . Third, and derivative of the second, the doctrine ensures that courts charged with reviewing the exercise of delegated legislative discretion will be able to test that exercise against ascertainable standards.

I believe the legislation at issue here fails on all three counts. The decision whether the law of diminishing returns should have any place in the regulation of toxic substances is quintessentially one of legislative policy. For Congress to pass that decision on to the Secretary in the manner it did violates, in my mind, John Locke's caveat—reflected in the cases cited earlier in this opinion—that legislatures are to make laws. Nor, as I think the prior discussion amply demonstrates, do the provisions at issue or their legislative history provide the Secretary with any guidance that might lead him to his somewhat tentative conclusion that he must eliminate exposure to benzene as far as technologically and economically possible. Finally, I would suggest that the standard of "feasibility" renders meaningful judicial review impossible.

We ought not to shy away from our judicial duty to invalidate unconstitutional delegations of legislative authority solely out of concern that we should thereby reinvigorate discredited constitutional doctrines of the pre-New Deal era. If the nondelegation doctrine has fallen into the same desuetude as have substantive due process and restrictive interpretations of the Commerce Clause, it is, as one writer has phrased it, "a case of death by association." J. Ely, Democracy and Distrust, A Theory of Judicial Review 133 (1980).

If we are ever to reshoulder the burden of ensuring that Congress itself make the critical policy decisions, these are surely the cases in which to do it. It is difficult to imagine a more obvious example of Congress simply avoiding a choice which was both fundamental for purposes of the statute and yet politically so divisive that the necessary decision or compromise was difficult, if not impossible, to hammer out in the legislative forge. Far from detracting from the substantive authority of Congress, a declaration that the first sentence of § 6(b)(5) of the Occupational Safety and Health Act constitutes an invalid delegation to the Secretary of Labor would preserve the authority of Congress. If Congress wishes to legislate in an area which it has not previously sought to enter, it will in today's political world undoubtedly run into opposition no matter how the legislation is formulated. But that is the very essence of legislative authority under our system. It is the hard choices, and not the filling in of the blanks, which must be made by the elected representatives of the people. When fundamental policy decisions underlying important legislation about to be enacted are to be made, the buck stops with Congress and the President insofar as he exercises his constitutional role in the legislative process.

Notes and Questions

1. *Subsequent case.* In a subsequent case involving the same issue, the Supreme Court held that OSHA did not have to balance costs and benefits when it set standards. This time Justice Rehnquist dissented on delegation grounds and was joined by Chief Justice Burger. *American Textile Mfrs. Inst., Inc. v. Donovan,* 452 U.S. 490 (1981).

2. *Standards.* What are the purposes of the standards requirement according to Justice Rehnquist in *Industrial Union?* If standards are needed to validate a delegation of legislative authority, where (aside from the language of the statute) may they be found? What sources are identified in *Amalgamated Meatcutters?* In *Industrial Union? In Kent v. Dulles,* § 7.2, *supra? See also* Merrill, "Standards—A Safeguard for the Exercise of Delegated Power," 47 Neb.L.Rev. 469 (1968). Should the courts require more precise standards in a legislative delegation when the statute threatens a fundamental right such as freedom of speech? *See Shuttlesworth v. Birmingham,* 394 U.S. 147 (1969), holding unconstitutional a delegation to issue a parade permit "unless in its judgment the public welfare, peace, safety, health, decency, good order, morals or convenience require that it be refused." Note that vague standards like this have often been upheld by federal courts in cases involving economic interests. The *Shuttlesworth* court insisted, however, that "narrow, objective, and definite standards [are necessary] to guide the licensing authority" in the first amendment area.

3. *Safeguards.* Note the reliance of the *Amalgamated Meatcutters* opinion on the safeguards provided by an agency's adoption of its own discretion-limiting standards, by administrative procedure, and by judicial review. What is the relevance of these safeguards to the delegation issue? May safeguards be a substitute for legislative standards? Recall the importance of "checks and balances" in our constitutional system. Can the presence of safeguards serve a "check and balance" function?

Do you agree with the following proposal by Professor Davis?

> Five principal steps should be taken to alter the non-delegation doctrine and to move toward a system of judicial protection against unnecessary and uncontrolled discretionary power: (a) the purpose of the non-delegation doctrine should no longer be either to prevent delegation or to require meaningful statutory standards; the purpose should be the much deeper one of protecting against unnecessary and uncontrolled discretionary power; (b) the exclusive focus on standards should be shifted to an emphasis more on safeguards than on standards; (c) when legislative bodies have failed to provide standards, the courts should not hold the delegation unlawful but should require that the administrators must as rapidly as feasible supply the standards; (d) the non-delegation doctrine should gradually grow into a broad requirement extending beyond the subject of delegation—that officers with discretionary power

must do about as much as feasible to structure their discretion through appropriate safeguards and to confine and guide their discretion through standards, principles, and rules; (e) the protection should reach not merely delegated power but also such undelegated power as that of selective enforcement. . . .

Safeguards are usually more important than standards, although both may be important. The criterion for determining the validity of a delegation should be the totality of the protection against arbitrariness, not just the one strand having to do with statutory standards.

For instance, a delegation *without standards* of power to make rules in accordance with proper rule-making procedure and a delegation *without standards* of power to work out policy through case-to-case adjudication based on trial-type hearings should normally be sustained, whenever the general legislative purpose is discernible. The risk of arbitrary or unjust action is much greater from informal discretionary action, but even there the protection from safeguards is likely to be more effective than protection from standards. For instance, if one administrator in exercising discretionary power without hearings uses a system of open findings, open reasons, and open precedents, but another who is also acting without hearings never states findings or reasons and never uses precedents as a guide, the delegation to the first administrator is much more deserving of judicial support than the delegation to the second. . . . What is needed is not simply a substitution of a requirement of safeguards for a requirement of standards but a consideration of both safeguards and standards in order to determine whether the total protection against arbitrary power is adequate. . . .

When an administrator is making a discretionary determination affecting a private party, standards which have been adopted through administrative rule-making are just as effective in confining and guiding the discretionary determination as would be standards stated in the statute. They are not only as effective but in one important aspect they are better. The weakness of a judicial requirement of *statutory* standards is that legislators are often unable or unwilling to supply them. The strength of a judicial requirement of *administrative* standards is that, with the right kind of judicial prodding, the administrators can be expected to supply them. To the extent that the objective is to require standards to guide discretionary determinations in cases affecting particular parties, that objective can be better attained through judicial insistence that administrators create the standards through rule-making than by judicial insistence upon statutory standards. Legislative bodies should clarify their purposes to the extent that they are able and willing to do so, but when they choose to delegate without standards, the courts should uphold the delegation whenever the needed standards to guide particular determinations have been supplied through administrative rules or policy statements. . . .

As the courts shift the non-delegation doctrine from a requirement of statutory standards to a requirement of administrative standards and safeguards, then shift further to a broad requirement that administrators do what they reasonably can do to structure and confine their discretionary powers through safeguards, standards, principles, and rules, . . . [t]he non-delegation doctrine will merge with the concept of due process and may perhaps move from a constitutional base to a common-law base. . . .

Let us examine [an] illustrative case, *Holmes v. New York City Housing Authority,* [398 F.2d 262 (2d Cir.1968)]. . . . The Authority received 90,000 applications annually but could admit only 10,000 families to public housing. Except for some preference candidates, "Applications . . . are not processed chronologically, or in accordance with ascertainable standards, or in any other reasonable and systematic manner.' Each application expired after two years, a renewed application stood no better than a first application of the same date, no open waiting list was used, determinations of ineligibility were not made known to applicants, and many applications were never considered by the Authority. The complaint charged that "these procedural defects increase the likelihood of favoritism, partiality, and arbitrariness." The court held that "due process requires that selections among applicants be made in accordance with 'ascertainable standards,' . . . and, in cases where many candidates are equally qualified under these standards, that further selections be made in some reasonable manner such as 'by lot or on the basis of the chronological order of application.' "

Although the *Holmes* opinion was quite properly written in terms of due process, it could also have been properly written in terms of a non-delegation doctrine. Either way, the key factor is not the failure of the statute to control or guide the determination of which applications to grant or deny; the key factor is the *administrative* failure to control or guide that determination. The court's assumption was entirely sound that absence of either a substantive or a procedural system in the statutory framework would be permissible if the administrators provided such a system. So the court might properly have held that the delegation was unlawful unless or until the requisite procedural and substantive system was worked out through administrative action.

Davis, "A New Approach to Delegation," 36 U.Chi.L.Rev. 713, 725–32 (1969). Does Davis present a solution to the problem of undue delegation or only a solution to the ultra vires problem?

4. *Arguments against reviving delegation doctrine.* What arguments can you make against reviving the delegation doctrine? Professor Stewart opposes any effort to revive the delegation doctrine for the following reasons:

> [A]ny large-scale enforcement of the nondelegation doctrine would clearly be unwise. Detailed legislative specification of policy under contemporary conditions would be neither feasible nor desirable in many cases and the judges are ill-equipped to distinguish contrary cases . . . .
>
> Administration is an exercise in experiment. If the subject is politically and economically volatile—such as wage and price regulation—constant changes in the basic parameters of the problem may preclude the development of a detailed policy that can consistently be pursued for any length of time . . . .
>
> There appear to be serious institutional constraints on Congress' ability to specify regulatory policy in meaningful detail. Legislative majorities typically represent coalitions of interests that must not only compromise among themselves but also with opponents. Individual politicians often find far more to be lost than gained in taking a readily identifiable stand on a controversial issue of social or economic policy. Detailed legislative specification of policy would require intensive and continuous investigation, decision, and revision of specialized and complex issues. Such a task would require resources that Congress has in most instances, been unable or unwilling to muster . . . .
>
> Finally there are serious problems in relying upon the judiciary to enforce the nondelegation doctrine. A court may not properly insist on a greater legislative specification of policy than the subject matter admits of. But how is the judge to decide the degree of policy specification that is possible? . . . Such judgments are necessarily quite subjective, and a doctrine that made them determinative of an administrative program's legitimacy could cripple the program by exposing it to continuing threats of invalidation and encouraging the utmost recalcitrance by those opposed to its effectuation. Given such subjective standards, and the controversial character of decisions on whether to invalidate legislative delegations, such decisions will almost inevitably appear partisan, and might often be so.

Stewart, "The Reformation of American Administrative Law," 88 Harv. L.Rev. 1667, 1695–97 (1975).

Professor Koch agrees that the delegation doctrine should not be revived. He suggests that Congress does not spend the time necessary to write clear, detailed instructions for agencies in its legislation because its members and the public prefer that those officials devote their energies to "serving their constituents" rather than to legislating; because "vague statutes" delegating authority to agencies allow members of Congress to "duck political responsibility;" and because broad delegations often result from a lack of legislative expertise. Koch also states that there is no evidence that specific statutes delegating authority to agencies are "more successful or satisfactory" than vague, general statutes. Finally, he concludes that efforts to require more specific delegation statutes "would only result in more power in the Congressional staff. Not only are they just as much bureaucrats, but they are much less expert and visible than the agencies. Hence the net result of a strong nondelegation doctrine might be to shift decisions from one bureaucracy to another and the second bureaucracy seems much less capable." 1 C. Koch, Jr., ADMINISTRATIVE LAW AND PRACTICE § 1.22, at 41–42 (1985).

5. *Arguments for reviving delegation doctrine.* Are you persuaded by the reasons for revival of the delegation doctrine offered by Justice Rehnquist in *Industrial Union?* Are those reasons persuasive as applied to the facts of *Industrial Union?* Of *Amalgamated Meatcutters?* Should delegations be upheld or overturned if political considerations make Congress institutionally incapable of legislating except by delegating the tough decisions to agencies? Could revival of the delegation doctrine effectively force Congress to shoulder its proper decisionmaking responsibilities?

There is a body of academic opinion in favor of reviving the delegation doctrine. *See, e.g.,* Aranson, Gellhorn, & Robinson, "A Theory of Legislative Delegation," 68 Cornell L.R. 1 (1982) (delegation doctrine helpful in preventing enactment of laws dictated by special interests); Schoenbrod, "The Delegation Doctrine: Could the Court give it Substance?" 83 Mich.L.Rev. 1223 (1985) (doctrine should be applied when legislature only states goals rather than rules).

Consider also the following analysis of the Rehnquist *Industrial Union* opinion written by United States Supreme Court Justice Scalia when Scalia was a law school professor:

There are several problems with revivification of the unconstitutional delegation doctrine. First, it does not square very easily (to put it mildly) with the case law that has developed in the forty-five years since the Supreme Court last used it as a basis of decision. . . .

But one might say, presumably, that bygones will be bygones—that the Court will leave the questionable legislation of the past in place, while holding new legislation to a stricter test, now that the danger of government by bureaucracy supplanting government by the people has become alarmingly apparent. That is hardly the traditional judicial manner of proceeding, but to engage in such innovation (explicitly or *sub silentio*) is not beyond the present Court. That would still leave, however, the second problem, which is actually the root cause of the first: the difficulty of enunciating how much delegation is too much. The relevant factors are simply too multifarious: How significant is the power in question? . . . How technical are the judgments left for executive determination?

. . . What degree of social consensus exists with respect to those nontechnical judgments committed to the executive? And—most imponderable of all—how great is the need for immediate action? Rehnquist's opinion . . . distinguishes some of the earlier cases, but provides no solution to this second problem of establishing a workable test. It does little more than recite Chief Justice Taft's conclusion that delegations of legislative authority must be judged "according to common sense and the inherent necessities of the governmental coordination." And one can probably not intelligently say much more than that.

A doctrine so vague, it may be said, is no doctrine at all, but merely an invitation to judicial policy making in the guise of constitutional law. This fear is indeed the reason for the alleged demise of the doctrine—because its use in 1935 paralleled the Court's now discredited use of the due process clause to impose its own notions of acceptable social legislation. But surely vague constitutional doctrines are not automatically unacceptable. . . . And the risk of vagueness here is much less than elsewhere. Decisions under the due process clause . . ., for example, are an absolute impediment to governmental action. A decision based on the unconstitutional delegation doctrine is not; it merely requires the action to be taken in a different fashion. . . .

In fact, the argument may be made that in modern circumstances the unconstitutional delegation doctrine, far from permitting an increase in judicial power, actually reduces it. For now that judicial review of agency action is virtually routine, it is the courts, rather than the agencies, that can ultimately determine the content of standardless legislation. In other words, to a large extent judicial invocation of the unconstitutional delegation doctrine is a self-denying ordinance—forbidding the transfer of legislative power not to the agencies, but to the courts themselves. The benzene case itself is illustrative. In giving content to a law which in fact says no more than that OSHA should ensure "safe places of employment" (whatever that means) and should maximize protection against toxic materials "to the extent feasible" (whatever that means), it was the plurality of the Court, rather than OHSA, that ended up doing legislator's work.

So even with all its Frankenstein-like warts, knobs, and (concededly) dangers, the unconstitutional delegation doctrine is worth hewing from the ice. The alternative appears to be continuation of the widely felt trend toward government by bureaucracy or (what is no better) government by courts. In truth, of course, no one has ever thought that the unconstitutional delegation doctrine did not exist as a principle of our government. If it did not, the Congress could presumably vote all powers to the President and adjourn. The only issue has been whether adherence to this fundamental principle is properly enforceable by the courts, or rather should be left (except perhaps in extreme cases of the sort just mentioned) to the wisdom of the Congress. As an original matter, there is much to be said for the latter view. The sorts of judgments alluded to above—how great is the need for prompt action, how extensive is the social consensus on the vague legislated objective, and so forth—are much more appropriate for a representative assembly than for a hermetically sealed committee of nine lawyers. In earlier times heated constitutional debate did take place at the congressional level.

Recently, however, the notion seems to have taken root that if a constitutional prohibition is not enforceable through the courts it does not exist. Where that mind set obtains, the congressional barrier to unconstitutional action disappears unless reinforced by judicial affirmation. So even those who do not relish the prospect of regular judicial enforcement of the unconstitutional delegation doctrine might well support the Court's making an example of one—just one—of the many enactments that appear to violate the principle. The educational effect on Congress might well be substantial.

Scalia, "A Note on the Benzine Case," Regulation, July/August 1980 at 27–28.

6. *Delegation and foreign affairs.* Note that Justice Rehnquist suggested in the *Industrial Union* case, and the court suggested in the *Amalgamated Meat Cutters* case, that Congress has broader authority to delegate uncabined authority to the President with respect to matters affecting foreign affairs than with respect to matters concerning only domestic affairs. Both opinions cited *United States v. Curtis–Wright Export Corp.,* 299 U.S. 304 (1936), for this proposition. Why should standardless delegations of authority over the actions of persons inside the United States be more supportable if they affect the foreign affairs of this nation than if they affect only our domestic affairs? Can the line between wholly domestic affairs and our nation's foreign affairs be easily drawn today—even assuming that it could be easily drawn fifty years ago at the time of *Curtis–Wright?* Note that in *Curtis–Wright* the issue was the lawfulness of an embargo, imposed by the President pursuant to an act of Congress authorizing such action, on the shipment of arms to a foreign country by persons who intended to ship those arms from inside this country. 299 U.S. at 311 (1936). If the President in such a situation really is exercising wholly independent constitutional authority, is not the delegation doctrine irrelevant?

7. *Problem.* Public hysteria about the uncontrolled spread of AIDS caused Congress to enact a statute giving the Director of the Public Health Service the power to adopt rules to contain the epidemic. The rules are to be "appropriate and necessary" in light of the AIDS public health emergency. The statute provides that violation of the rules is a criminal offense.

The Director adopted a rule requiring every federal government employee, and every applicant for a federal government job, to take a blood test. If the test detects the presence of AIDS antibodies, the individual must be discharged from government employment (or the person's application for employment must be rejected).

Before adopting the rule, the Director gave public notice of the proposal and invited comments. Research studies, on which the Director relied, indicate that at least one million Americans have been exposed to AIDS and thus have the antibodies in their blood. It is not known what fraction of them will develop the disease. The research study indicates that AIDS can be spread through sexual contact and through contact with contaminated blood or needles, but not through other forms of contact.

A union of government employees opposed to the rule has consulted you. Assuming that the rule is judicially reviewable, what arguments can you make that would invalidate the rule and what are the prospects that these arguments will be accepted?

§ 7.3.2 THE NON–DELEGATION DOCTRINE AND STATE AGENCIES

Although the delegation doctrine appears to retain little vitality on the federal level, the doctrine is still of great practical significance in the states. A sampling of state materials follows. Consider why many state courts have not given up on the delegation doctrine; the extent to which the delegation doctrine is any more likely to achieve its objectives at the state level than the federal level; and whether federal courts should emulate state courts.

THYGESEN v. CALLAHAN
385 N.E.2d 699 (Ill.1979).

MORAN, J.:

[This case involved a challenge, on grounds of undue delegation, to § 19.3 of the Illinois currency exchange act, which provided:]

> "The Director [of Financial Institutions] shall, by rules adopted in accordance with the Illinois Administrative Procedure Act, formulate and issue, within 120 days from the effective date of this amendatory Act, schedules of maximum rates which can be charged for check cashing and writing of money orders by community currency exchanges and ambulatory currency exchanges. Such rates may vary according to such circumstances and conditions as the Director determines to be appropriate. The schedule so established may be modified by the Director from time to time by the same procedure.". . .

For this court's most recent and comprehensive pronouncement on the delegation of power to administrative agencies, we defer to *Stofer v. Motor Vehicle Casualty Co.* (1977), 369 N.E.2d 875. In *Stofer,* the court reaffirmed its adherence to the guiding principle that intelligible standards or guidelines must accompany legislative delegations of power. This court, thus, implicitly recognized both the constitutional dimensions of the principle (Ill. Const.1970, art. IV, sec. 1) and the practical functions which standards continue to serve. Intelligible standards help guide the administrative agency in the application of the statutes involved and, thereby, safeguard against the unwarranted or unintended extension of legislative delegation. They tend to insure that the legislature does not abdicate to the agency the legislature's primary responsibility to determine, from among the policy alternatives, those objectives the legislation is meant to achieve. Moreover, intelligible standards are indispensable to a meaningful judicial review of any action ultimately taken by the administrative agency. . . .

In an attempt to endow the requisite of intelligible standards with a conceptual foundation, the *Stofer* court declared that a legislative delegation is valid if it sufficiently identifies:

"(1) The *persons* and *activities* potentially subject to regulations;

(2) the *harm* sought to be prevented; and

(3) the general *means* intended to be available to the administrator to prevent the identified harm."

In *Stofer,* the legislature had delegated to the Director of Insurance the power to promulgate a standard policy as a means of ensuring uniformity in the insurance of identical risks. The legislation clearly satisfied the first prong of the test by specifying that the regulation was to apply to fire and lightning insurance issued in Illinois. As to the second prong, the court noted that the legislature had articulated its intention to prevent a chaotic proliferation of disparate fire insurance policies. In discussing the general *means* intended to be available to the Director to prevent the identified harm (the third prong), the court cautioned:

"[H]ad the legislature left the Director completely free to promulgate a 'reasonable' uniform fire insurance policy, we would have serious doubts as to the constitutionality of such uncabined discretion. We find, however, that the legislature has provided substantial additional standards defining the harm sought to be prevented and thereby limit[ed] the Director's discretion." (*Stofer v. Motor Vehicle Casualty Co.* (1977), 369 N.E.2d 875, 879.)

The court then referred to a related statutory provision which delegated to the Director the power to order the discontinuation of any policy which contained "inconsistent, ambiguous or misleading clauses, or [any] exceptions or conditions that will unreasonably or deceptively affect the risks that are purported to be assumed by the policy . . . . ." The court, reasoning that the delegated authority to promulgate a reasonable uniform policy necessarily incorporated the above-quoted limitation, held that the Director's discretion was limited sufficiently to withstand constitutional scrutiny.

Here, as in *Stofer,* the legislature clearly satisfied the first prong of the test. Those subject to regulation under section 19.3 of the currency exchange act are community and ambulatory currency exchanges, and the regulation is limited to the activities of cashing checks and issuing money orders. In contrast to *Stofer,* the legislature made no attempt to identify the "harm sought to be prevented" in delegating to defendant the power to set maximum rates and did not sufficiently identify the "means . . . intended to be available . . . to prevent the identified harm." Section 19.3 is devoid of any reference to the harm to be remedied. The currency exchange act contains no other provision which indicates, explicitly or implicitly, general purposes which the legislature might have intended to foster with respect to setting rates for cashing checks and issuing money orders.

The legislature's failure to convey, within the Act, the harm which it sought to remedy by the setting of maximum rates, is compounded by its failure to set forth any meaningful standards to guide defendant in setting the maximum rates. The only provision cited by defendant which in any way guides defendant's discretion in setting maximum rates is an omnibus provision which states:

> "The Director may make and enforce such *reasonable,* relevant regulations, directions, orders, decisions and findings as may be necessary for the execution and enforcement of this Act *and the purposes sought to be attained herein.*"

As we have already discussed, the Act fails to identify any purposes which the legislature might have sought to attain by providing for the establishment of maximum check-cashing and money-order rates. Defendant refers to various provisions in the Act that, he contends, limit his discretion to the promulgation of maximum rates which promote economic benefit and stability to both the currency exchange and the public. The provisions cited by defendant, however, apply to regulatory matters, such as the issuance of licenses and the appointment of advisory board members, which are totally unrelated to the promulgation of maximum check-cashing and money-order rates. We find that the only statutory limitation on defendant's discretion in establishing maximum rates is that the rates be *reasonable.* This court, in *Stofer,* rightfully expressed serious doubt as to the constitutionality of such "uncabined discretion." Here, where the legislature has not only failed to provide any additional standards to guide defendant's discretion, but has failed to communicate to defendant the harm it intended to prevent, it is clear that the legislature has unlawfully delegated its power to set such maximum rates.

Notes and Questions

1. *Inconsistent application of standards requirement.* Many state supreme courts still insist that a legislative delegation of authority to an agency may not be upheld in the absence of adequate statutory standards. *See* B. Schwartz, ADMINISTRATIVE LAW § 2.12, at 54 (2d

ed. 1984). For example, *Fitanides v. Crowley,* 467 A.2d 168 (Me.1983), held invalid, as an undue delegation of legislative authority, a statute authorizing an agency to issue exceptions from a zoning ordinance if the exceptions would promote the "public health, safety, or general welfare." In doing so, the court noted that in "delegating power to an administrative agency, the legislative body must spell out its policies in sufficient detail to furnish a guide which will enable those to whom the law is to be applied to reasonably determine their rights thereunder, and so the determination of those rights will not be left to the purely arbitrary discretion of the administrator." 467 A.2d at 172. *See also Askew v. Cross Keys Waterways,* 372 So.2d 913 (Fla.1978); *Commissioner of Agriculture v. Plaquemines Parish Commission Council,* 439 So.2d 348 (La.1983).

The Illinois Supreme Court noted in *Thygesen* that the standards requirement in that state had been rigidly applied in some cases and permissively applied in others without adequate explanation. That is a fair summary of the application of the standards requirement by many other state supreme courts. Does this indicate the practical futility of the standards requirement or does it indicate a lack of judicial resolve?

2. *Lawfulness of state delegations: factors considered.* One commentator concluded that many factors play a part in state judicial decisions about the validity of legislative delegations to agencies. These factors include the presence or absence of established legal concepts that may limit agency discretion; the tradition in the particular subject area; whether or not substantial property interests are involved; the availability of judicial review; the availability of fair agency procedures; the need for administrative expertness; the extent to which there is a threat to the public health or safety that requires such a delegation; and the need to preserve the independence of the three separate branches of government. 1 F. Cooper, STATE ADMINISTRATIVE LAW 73–91 (1965).

3. *Relevance of procedural safeguards:* The Illinois statute involved in *Thygesen* provided that the rulemaking procedures of the state APA would apply when the agency exercised its delegated power. Procedural requirements ensuring public involvement in agency rulemaking may make unsound or improper agency action less likely. Should this procedural safeguard have been taken into account in deciding whether the statute in *Thygesen* was an unlawful delegation?

WARREN v. MARION COUNTY
353 P.2d 257 (Or.1960).

[This case involved a challenge to a building code on the ground that the statute authorizing its issuance was an undue delegation of legislative powers to the governmental body involved.

O'Connell, J.:]

There is no constitutional requirement that all delegation of legislative power must be accompanied by a statement of standards circumscribing its exercise. It is true that a contrary view has frequently been expressed in the adjudicated cases, particularly the earlier ones, but the position taken in such cases is not defensible. It is now apparent that the requirement of expressed standards has, in most instances, been little more than a judicial fetish for legislative language, the recitation of which provides no additional safeguards to persons affected by the exercise of the delegated authority. Thus, we have learned that it is of little or no significance in the administration of a delegated power that the statute which generated it stated the permissible limits of its exercise in terms of such abstractions as "public convenience, interest or necessity" or "unjust or unreasonable," or "for the public health, safety, and morals" and similar phrases accepted as satisfying the standards requirement.

As pointed out in Davis on Administrative Law, the important consideration is not whether the statute delegating the power expresses *standards,* but whether the procedure established for the exercise of the power furnishes adequate *safeguards* to those who are affected by the administrative action. 1 Davis, Administrative Law Treatise, §§ 2.10, 2.15, 7.20.

In testing the statute for the adequacy of such safeguards it is important to consider the character of administrative action which the statute authorizes. The statute here authorizes the establishment of building codes, including the adoption by reference of published codes such as the Uniform Building Code which the defendant adopted in modified form. Such codes are in themselves a statement of specific standards for the construction of buildings. The administrative official charged with the duty of enforcing a building code ordinance is called upon to decide whether the specifications set out in the code have been met in the construction of a particular building. His action can, therefore, be tested against the specific description of adequate construction set out in the building code. The statute then requires that the county set up appeal procedures so that persons dissatisfied with the building inspector's action in ruling upon the suitability of materials or construction may have that action reviewed by a separate administrative body. What further safeguards are needed to protect persons subjected to regulation under such a code?

We believe that the appeals procedure provided a sufficient safeguard to persons wishing to contest administrative action in the enforcement of the code. Plaintiff has not mentioned the standards which he thinks would satisfy the requirement for an adequate statute. We doubt that any standards which he could suggest for inclusion in the statute would make any clearer the scope of the delegated power or contribute materially to the protection of a citizen against unwarranted administrative action. We hold that ORS 215.108 constitutes a valid delegation of legislative power.

Notes and Questions

1. *Procedural protections without substantive standards.* Do you agree that a delegation should be upheld *wholly* on the basis of the presence of adequate procedural protections? How may a court determine whether agency action is ultra vires in situations where the legislature does not even explain the purpose of its delegation? Note that when the legislature has adopted no standards to guide an agency in the exercise of its delegated authority, the legislature effectively delegates to the courts, rather than to the agencies, authority to determine the actual scope of the delegation. Is delegation of such authority to courts rather than to agencies more defensible? Does the fact that state judges are often elected while federal judges are not make this result more acceptable on the state than on the federal level?

2. *Comparative importance of safeguards and standards.* While not going as far as Oregon, Iowa has emphasized procedural safeguards and deemphasized standards. In 1964, the Iowa Supreme Court invalidated a delegation because of the absence of standards. The absence of standards was illustrated by the fact that the administrator applied the standards he developed under the delegation in some cases, waived them in others, and deferred their application in still others. The court stated that "where standards . . . are readily possible we think the legislature may not abandon them altogether and say in effect to the administrative body: 'you may do anything you think will further the purpose of the law'. . . ." *Lewis Consol. School Dist. v. Johnston,* 127 N.W.2d 118 (Iowa 1964).

Four years later, the court stated: "We have always held to the adequate standards test in determining the propriety of delegation of legislative power to administrative bodies, but we agree the presence or absence of procedural safeguards is important in determining whether this delegation is reasonable. With such safeguards interested parties are protected against arbitrary and capricious conduct on the part of administrative officials." *Elk Run Telephone Co. v. General Telephone Co.,* 160 N.W.2d 311 (Iowa 1968).

Finally, in 1971, the same court noted: "On the question of power delegation we recently held the important consideration is not whether the statute delegating the power expresses precise standards but whether the procedure established for the exercise of power furnishes adequate safeguards for those affected by the administrative action." *Iron Workers Local No. 67 v. Hart,* 191 N.W.2d 758 (Iowa 1971). *See* generally Note, "Safeguards, Standards, and Necessity: Permissible Parameters for Legislative Delegations in Iowa," 58 Iowa L.Rev. 974, 996–97 (1973).

3. *State APA.* A good state APA may save an otherwise improper rulemaking delegation in a state like Iowa or Oregon because it provides significant procedural safeguards against unfair or unwise

agency action. Is this likely to make the agencies champions of such legislation?

4. *Federal Constitution and state delegation.* Does the United States Constitution impose any limits on the authority of a state legislature to delegate rulemaking authority to a state agency? Compare 1 K. Davis ADMINISTRATIVE LAW TREATISE § 3.14 and *Gold v. Lomenzo,* 304 F.Supp. 3 (S.D.N.Y.1969) with *Shuttlesworth v. Birmingham,* 394 U.S. 147 (1969). Consider the possible relevance of U.S. Const. art. IV, § 4: "The United States shall guarantee to every state a republican form of government."

5. *Incorporation by reference of future standards.* All states operate major state programs that are funded, at least in part, by the national government on condition that the state programs follow changing federal guidelines embodied in federal statutes or federal agency rules. As a result, many state statutes incorporate federal law by reference or authorize state agencies to adopt federal law by reference in their rules. Where such a state statute or agency rule incorporates *future* changes in federal law, is the statute or rule an unlawful delegation of power to the federal government?

This issue arose in *Hutchins v. Mayo,* 197 So. 495 (Fla.1940). The Florida Supreme Court invalidated a state statute purporting to incorporate *future* federal law by reference on the ground that such a statute was an undue delegation of state legislative authority to the federal government. The court held that such future changes in federal law could not automatically become part of state law, but would have to be adopted or rejected by the state agency as they occurred. *See also Wallace v. Commissioner of Taxation,* 184 N.W.2d 588 (Minn.1971); Rochvarg, "State Adoption of Federal Law—Legislative Abdication or Reasoned Policymaking," 36 Admin.L.Rev. 277 (1984).

Rochvarg suggests a compromise position:

The state adoption of federal law issue should be addressed in terms of the governmental policies being sought, and the substantive area being regulated. In matters where uniform regulation among the states and the federal government is desirable in order to implement a consistent national and local policy, to further identical state and federal goals, and to combat one "evil" which impacts on both the national and local level equally, and where the area being regulated involves matters which are highly technical, requires a level of expertise beyond that available to the states, requires a commitment of resources greater than what can be allocated by the states, and requires constant revision and quick response to new developments, state adoption of federal law should be encouraged. This is especially true if the state adoption of federal law would not create additional significant burdens on regulated persons, and if the efficiency of the regulatory process would be improved by state adoption. On the other hand, in those matters where local interests differ from national policy goals, where the federal law being adopted is premised on policy goals unrelated to the state regulatory scheme, where the states do have the expertise and resources to develop their own policy without a significant loss in regulatory efficiency, or where the burden on regulated persons is vastly increased with no concomitant increase in policy achievement, automatic state adoption of federal law should be discouraged.

Under this approach, the legislature's function is to determine, based on its own independent evaluation, whether the factors discussed above indicate that adoption of federal law is desirable. The legislature in order to fulfill its legislative duty must consider and evaluate these factors to determine whether state policy goals can be best served by laws not dependent upon the federal government. Additionally, to ensure that the state legislature's decision to delegate legislative power to the federal government does not amount to an abdication of its legislative responsibility, it is submitted that the legislature should not only be required to make findings on each factor, but also to include in such findings an explanation why state adoption of federal law best serves local needs. This findings requirement should be seen as satisfying the requirement of the delegation doctrine that basic policy choices be made by politically responsible officials.

In its determination whether state adoption of federal law is appropriate, the state legislature also might consider modified adoption approaches. For example, a state statute could be drafted which adopts federal law, but it could also require periodic review of the federal law by the state. In matters where the balance of factors leans toward but does not compel state adoption, the statute perhaps should be drafted so that the federal law does not become effective as state law until the federal law is *accepted* by either the legislature or a state agency after public procedures. Alternatively, instead of a statute which requires the state to accept the federal law, the statute could be drafted so that the federal law becomes effective as state law unless the legislature or state agency after public procedure *rejects* it. A legislature's decision to enact an "accepting-adoption" or "rejecting-adoption" statute should be based on the balancing of factors discussed in this article. A "rejecting-adoption" scheme would be preferable in cases where there is a close issue as to whether adoption of federal law is appropriate. An "accepting-adoption" statute may be preferable in matters where the balance of factors makes a more persuasive showing in favor of adoption. Clear cases in favor of adoption could lead to an automatic adoption mechanism. In all cases, legislative findings and explanations would be required.

The judicial function under the proposed approach is to ensure that the appropriate findings have been made by the legislature, and that these findings have rational support in the legislative record. The judicial role is necessarily limited in order that it not usurp the legislature's role of determining state policy. The court's inquiry should end once it is satisfied that the appropriate factors have been considered, and that the legislature's analysis of these factors and consequent conclusions are reasonable.

Id. at 297–99.

6. *Delegation of authority to private persons.* A legislative body may sometimes delegate governmental authority to private persons or entities. Private persons or entities are even more removed from direct political controls over their actions than are public agencies, and such persons or entities are more likely than agencies to have a self-interest in the use of that authority that is inconsistent with the public interest. As a result, serious delegation problems may arise when governmental authority is vested in private persons or entities.

On a number of occasions, in the early part of this century, the United States Supreme Court held delegations of governmental authority to private persons or entities to be improper. *See, e.g., Washington ex rel. Seattle Title Trust Co. v. Roberge,* 278 U.S. 116, 122 (1928) (law prohibiting location of home for aged in zoning district unless consent of specified portion of neighbors obtained was improper delegation); *Eubank v. City of Richmond,* 226 U.S. 137, 144 (1912) (law authorizing two thirds of specified property owners to decide the distance buildings must be set back from street was improper delegation). These cases cited the due process clause as the basis for their holdings.

However, since 1936 no delegation of governmental authority to a private person or entity has been invalidated by the United States Supreme Court because it was an improper delegation. In that year the Supreme Court held void a federal statute providing that maximum hours and minimum wages agreed upon by a majority of affected miners and mine-operators would be binding upon the rest of them. *Carter v. Carter Coal Co.,* 298 U.S. 238 (1936). The Court in *Carter* stressed the peculiar dangers inherent in a delegation of governmental authority to private parties: Such a delegation "is not even delegation to an official or an official body, presumptively disinterested, but to private persons whose interests may be and often are adverse to the interests of others in the same business." *Id.* at 311. The decision in *Carter,* like the decisions in the earlier cases, was apparently based on due process grounds, rather than separation of powers notions. As a result, its holding is potentially applicable to delegations of state governmental authority to private persons or entities as well as to delegations of federal governmental authority to such persons or entities.

Since 1936 the federal courts have virtually ignored the earlier cases, and have upheld a number of delegations of governmental authority to private persons or entities. *See* Robbins, "The Impact of the Delegation Doctrine on Prison Privatization," 35 U.C.L.A.L.Rev. 911 at 919 n. 44, 922–25 (1988). For instance, two United States Court of

Appeals cases upheld, against an undue delegation challenge, a federal statute authorizing a private securities dealer association to issue rules prescribing the conduct of its members and to engage in disciplinary proceedings against its members for violation of those rules. The rules issued by the association were subject to Securities and Exchange Commission (SEC) approval or disapproval, and all disciplinary proceedings before the association were subject to plenary review by the SEC according to fixed statutory standards. *See R.H. Johnson & Co. v. SEC,* 198 F.2d 690, 695 (2d Cir.1952); *Todd & Co. Inc. v. SEC,* 557 F.2d 1008, 1012 (3d Cir.1977). These cases appear to suggest that the validity of the delegation to this private entity was lawful in large part because the SEC, a public body, retained authority to approve or disapprove the rules of the association in question and to review effectively the association's disciplinary actions.

Although federal cases since 1936 have not placed significant hurdles in the path of efforts by Congress to vest federal lawmaking authority in private persons or entities, a significant number of state cases have voided efforts by state governments to vest their lawmaking authority in private persons or entities. The activist role of some state courts in checking delegations of state lawmaking authority to private persons or entities parallels their efforts to limit effectively delegations of such state governmental authority to public agencies.

For example, most state courts appear to hold invalid state statutes delegating final rulemaking authority to private parties. The rationale for these state cases is that private parties might "make rules that placed personal gain ahead of the public welfare . . . [and] the absence of neutral [and independent] administrative agency review of the private parties' determination would encourage self serving policies. This latter aspect was particularly troublesome . . . because the private parties themselves were not subject to any political control. . . . [However], . . . a rule that a private party proposes is not constitutionally suspect if it is adopted by an administrative agency that has power to accept, reject, or modify the rule." Robbins, *supra,* at 941.

Is the lesson of these cases that delegations of governmental rulemaking authority to private persons or entities are not improper so long as they occur in contexts adequate to ensure that the rules adopted actually serve the public interest rather than only the interests of the private persons or entities formulating them? So long as there are, in total, adequate safeguards to ensure that the authority vested in such persons or entities is not used in an arbitrary or capricious way?

Could the legislature by statute adopt an electrical code of a private organization of electricians, including future amendments to the code by that organization, and make violations of that code unlawful? *See Hillman v. Northern Wasco County People's Utility District,* 323 P.2d 664 (Or.1958); *Agnew v. City of Culver City,* 304 P.2d 788, 797 (Cal.1956). Could the legislature by statute, or an agency authorized by statute to do so, allow only those persons to obtain a license to practice dentistry who have graduated from a school that is now or in the future approved by a specified private association accrediting dental schools? *See Garces v. Dept. of Registration and Education,* 254 N.E.2d 622 (Ill. 1969); *Gumbhir v. Kansas State Bd. of Pharmacy,* 618 P.2d 837 (Kan. 1980).

May a state or the federal government delegate the authority to run a penal institution to a private entity? Is there a distinction that is relevant here between a delegation to such an entity of purely management functions as opposed to a delegation of lawmaking or law-applying functions? Between delegations of authority to private entities over property rights as opposed to delegations of authority over liberty rights? *See* Robbins, *supra,* at 929–52.

§ 7.4   DELEGATION OF ADJUDICATORY POWER TO AGENCIES

§ 7.4.1   GENERALLY

This section examines the legitimacy of legislative delegations of adjudicatory power to agencies—the power to determine the rights or duties of particular persons based on their individual circumstances. The materials pertaining to legislative delegations are equally applicable here. The presence of standards and safeguards seems relevant to the propriety of adjudicatory as well as legislative delegations. Indeed, many of the cases considered in the prior section involve delegations of both rulemaking *and* adjudicatory authority.

The federal judicial power was vested in Article III judges—judges with life tenure and protection against salary reduction—to ensure unbiased consideration of cases and to ensure that the other branches could not overwhelm the judiciary or deprive it of its essential functions. A delegation of adjudicatory power to agencies transfers to them authority that appears to belong exclusively to the judicial branch. This section considers whether such delegations run afoul of the requirements of Article III of the United States Constitution or comparable provisions in state constitutions. Before considering the principal case, it will be helpful to summarize two of the leading federal cases on adjudicatory delegation.

In *Northern Pipeline Const. Co. v. Marathon Pipe Line Co.,* 458 U.S. 50 (1982), the Supreme Court invalidated a statute that assigned the trial of all the issues in a bankruptcy case, including disputes arising out of breaches of contract, to bankruptcy judges who were not appointed according to the requirements of Article III and, therefore, lacked life tenure and salary protection. Writing for a plurality of four, Justice Brennan held that such contract cases involve "private rights" and, consequently, must be decided by Article III judges. Justices Rehnquist and O'Connor concurred in the result but on the narrower ground that issues arising out of state law contract disputes must be decided by Article III judges.

Crowell v. Benson, 285 U.S. 22 (1932), was decided during the brief period in which a majority of the Supreme Court was hostile to administrative delegations. Recall the *Schechter* and *Panama Refining* cases, § 7.3.1, *supra. Crowell* concerned a federal workers' compensation statute that provided benefits based on strict liability if an "employee" was injured while working on "navigable waters." An administrative agency was authorized to conduct the necessary adjudications under this statute. Despite the fact that the statute at issue in *Crowell* had displaced a common law cause of action and had affected a preexisting relationship based on a common law employment contract, the Supreme Court upheld the delegation to the agency to try such cases.

However, because "private rights" were involved (i.e. tort liability of employer to employee), the Court held that on review of the agency's decision in such a case, Article III judges must have *independent power* to decide all issues of law and "jurisdictional fact." Jurisdictional facts were those on which the agency's constitutional jurisdiction depended— in *Crowell*, whether an employment relationship existed and whether the injury occurred on navigable waters.

COMMODITY FUTURES TRADING COMMISSION v. SCHOR
478 U.S. 833 (1986).

[The Commodity Exchange Act (CEA) created the Commodity Futures Trading Commission (CFTC) as an independent agency to regulate trading in commodity futures. CEA empowered CFTC to award reparations (damages) to disgruntled customers from their brokers for violations of the Act or regulations. CFTC regulations provided that in such cases brokers could submit counterclaims against their customers. The brokers could also choose to assert their counterclaims in court.

Schor incurred heavy commodity trading losses in his account with ContiCommodity Services (Conti). His account reflected a large debit balance (i.e. an amount owed to Conti). Schor commenced a reparation proceeding against Conti before CFTC and Conti counterclaimed for the amount of the debit balance (essentially a simple claim for contract damages). CFTC held for Conti on both claim and counterclaim. Schor contends that the delegation to CFTC to try the counterclaim violates Article III.]

JUSTICE O'CONNOR delivered the opinion of the Court.

Article III, § 1 directs that the "judicial Power of the United States shall be vested in one supreme Court and in such inferior Courts as the Congress may from time to time ordain and establish," and provides that these federal courts shall be staffed by judges who hold office during good behavior, and whose compensation shall not be diminished during tenure in office. Schor claims that these provisions prohibit

Congress from authorizing the initial adjudication of common law counterclaims by the CFTC, an administrative agency whose adjudicatory officers do not enjoy the tenure and salary protections embodied in Article III.

Although our precedents in this area do not admit of easy synthesis, they do establish that the resolution of claims such as Schor's cannot turn on conclusory reference to the language of Article III. Rather, the constitutionality of a given congressional delegation of adjudicative functions to a non-Article III body must be assessed by reference to the purposes underlying the requirements of Article III. This inquiry, in turn, is guided by the principle that "practical attention to substance rather than doctrinaire reliance on formal categories should inform application of Article III."

Article III, § 1 serves both to protect the role of the independent judiciary within the constitutional scheme of tripartite government, and to safeguard litigants' right to have claims decided before judges who are free from potential domination by other branches of government. . . . Article III, § 1 safeguards the role of the Judicial Branch in our tripartite system by barring congressional attempts to transfer jurisdiction [to non-Article III tribunals] for the purpose of emasculating" constitutional courts, and thereby preventing the encroachment or aggrandizement of one branch at the expense of the other. . . .

In determining the extent to which a given congressional decision to authorize the adjudication of Article III business in a non-Article III tribunal impermissibly threatens the institutional integrity of the Judicial Branch, the Court has declined to adopt formalistic and unbending rules.

Although such rules might lend a greater degree of coherence to this area of the law, they might also unduly constrict Congress' ability to take needed and innovative action pursuant to its Article I powers. Thus, in reviewing Article III challenges, we have weighed a number of factors, none of which has been deemed determinative, with an eye to the practical effect that the congressional action will have on the constitutionally assigned role of the federal judiciary.

Among the factors upon which we have focused are the extent to which the "essential attributes of judicial power" are reserved to Article III courts, and, conversely, the extent to which the non-Article III forum exercises the range of jurisdiction and powers normally vested only in Article III courts, the origins and importance of the right to be adjudicated, and the concerns that drove Congress to depart from the requirements of Article III.

An examination of the relative allocation of powers between the CFTC and Article III courts in light of the considerations given prominence in our precedents demonstrates that the congressional scheme does not impermissibly intrude on the province of the judiciary. The CFTC's adjudicatory powers depart from the traditional agency model in just one respect: the CFTC's jurisdiction over common law counterclaims. While wholesale importation of concepts of pendent or ancillary jurisdiction into the agency context may create greater constitutional difficulties, we decline to endorse an absolute prohibition on such jurisdiction out of fear of where some hypothetical "slippery slope" may deposit us. . . .

[T]here is little practical reason to find that this single deviation from the agency model is fatal to the congressional scheme. Aside from its authorization of counterclaim jurisdiction, the CEA leaves far more of the "essential attributes of judicial power" to Article III courts than did that portion of the Bankruptcy Act found unconstitutional in *Northern Pipeline* [, *supra.*]

The CEA scheme in fact hews closely to the agency model approved by the Court in *Crowell v. Benson* [, *supra.*]

The CFTC, like the agency in *Crowell,* deals only with a "particularized area of law," whereas the jurisdiction of the bankruptcy courts found unconstitutional in *Northern Pipeline* extended to broadly "all civil proceedings arising under title 11 or arising in or *related to* cases under title 11."

CFTC orders, like those of the agency in *Crowell,* but unlike those of the bankruptcy courts under the 1978 Act, are enforceable only by order of the District Court. CFTC orders are also reviewed under the same "weight of the evidence" standard sustained in *Crowell,* rather than the more deferential standard found lacking in *Northern Pipeline.* The legal rulings of the CFTC, like the legal determinations of the agency in *Crowell,* are subject to *de novo* review. Finally, the CFTC, unlike the bankruptcy courts under the 1978 Act, does not exercise "all ordinary powers of district courts," and thus may not, for instance, preside over jury trials or issue writs of habeas corpus.

Of course, the nature of the claim has significance in our Article III analysis quite apart from the method prescribed for its adjudication. The counterclaim asserted in this case is a "private" right for which state law provides the rule of decision. It is therefore a claim of the kind assumed to be at the "core" of matters normally reserved to Article III courts. Yet this conclusion does not end our inquiry; just as this Court has rejected any attempt to make determinative for Article III purposes the distinction between public rights and private rights, there is no reason inherent in separation of powers principles to accord the state law character of a claim talismanic power in Article III inquiries.

We have explained that "the public rights doctrine reflects simply a pragmatic understanding that when Congress selects a quasi-judicial method of resolving matters that 'could be conclusively determined by the Executive and Legislative Branches,' the danger of encroaching on the judicial powers" is less than when private rights, which are normally within the purview of the judiciary, are relegated as an initial matter to administrative adjudication.

Similarly, the state law character of a claim is significant for purposes of determining the effect that an initial adjudication of those claims by a non-Article III tribunal will have on the separation of powers for the simple reason that private, common law rights were historically the types of matters subject to resolution by Article III courts. The risk that Congress may improperly have encroached on the federal judiciary is obviously magnified when Congress "withdraw[s] from judicial cognizance any matter which, from its nature, is the subject of a suit at the common law, or in equity, or admiralty" and which therefore has traditionally been tried in Article III courts, and allocates the decision of those matters to a non-Article III forum of its own creation. Accordingly, where private, common law rights are at stake, our examination of the congressional attempt to control the manner in which those rights are adjudicated has been searching. See, e.g., *Northern Pipeline.*

In this case, however, "[l]ooking beyond form to the substance of what" Congress has done, we are persuaded that the congressional authorization of limited CFTC jurisdiction over a narrow class of common law claims as an incident to the CFTC's primary, and unchallenged, adjudicative function does not create a substantial threat to the separation of powers. . . .

When Congress authorized the CFTC to adjudicate counterclaims, its primary focus was on making effective a specific and limited federal regulatory scheme, not on allocating jurisdiction among federal tribunals. Congress intended to create an inexpensive and expeditious alternative forum through which customers could enforce the provisions of the CEA against professional brokers. Its decision to endow the CFTC with jurisdiction over such reparations claims is readily understandable given the perception that the CFTC was relatively immune from political pressures, and the obvious expertise that the Commission possesses in applying the CEA and its own regulations. This reparations scheme itself is of unquestioned constitutional validity. *Crowell v. Benson.*

It was only to ensure the effectiveness of this scheme that Congress authorized the CFTC to assert jurisdiction over common law counterclaims. . . . [T]he CFTC's assertion of counterclaim jurisdiction is limited to that which is necessary to make the reparations procedure workable. The CFTC adjudication of common law counterclaims is incidental to, and completely dependent upon, adjudication of reparations claims created by federal law, and in actual fact is limited to claims arising out of the same transaction or occurrence as the reparations claim.

In such circumstances, the magnitude of any intrusion on the Judicial Branch can only be termed *de minimis.* Conversely, were we to hold that the Legislative Branch may not permit such limited cognizance of common law counterclaims at the election of the parties, it is clear that we would "defeat the obvious purpose of the legislation to furnish a prompt, continuous, expert and inexpensive method for dealing with a class of questions of fact which are peculiarly suited to examination and determination by an administrative agency specially assigned to that task." *Crowell v. Benson*. . . . [T]he separation of powers question presented in this case is whether Congress impermissibly undermined, without appreciable expansion of its own power, the role of the Judicial Branch. In any case, we have looked to a number of factors in evaluating the extent to which the congressional scheme endangers separation of powers principles under the circumstances presented, but have found no genuine threat to those principles to be present in this case.

In so doing, we have also been faithful to our Article III precedents, which counsel that bright line rules cannot effectively be employed to yield broad principles applicable in all Article III inquiries. Rather, due regard must be given in each case to the unique aspects of the congressional plan at issue and its practical consequences in light of the larger concerns that underlie Article III. We conclude that the limited jurisdiction that the CFTC asserts over state law claims as a necessary incident to the adjudication of federal claims willingly submitted by the parties for initial agency adjudication does not contravene separation of powers principles or Article III. . . .

[JUSTICES BRENNAN and MARSHALL dissented, arguing that the delegation to CFTC to adjudicate state-law counterclaims offends both the system of checks and balances and the right of litigants to impartial adjudication by life-tenured judges. They found the case indistinguishable from *Northern Pipeline*.]

Notes and Questions

1. *Public and private rights.* The opinions in *Northern Pipeline* and *Crowell* rested heavily on the distinction between "public rights" and "private rights." In *Northern Pipeline*, the court defined "public rights" as matters arising between the government and persons subject to its authority in connection with the performance of the constitutional functions of the legislative or executive departments. "Private rights" were defined as the liability of one individual to another. According to the plurality opinion in *Northern Pipeline*, Congress could not delegate authority to a non-Article III tribunal to decide questions of private right. According to the concurring opinion in *Northern Pipeline*, Congress could not delegate authority to decide typical state law contract issues.

In the *CFTC* case the Court noted that it "has rejected any attempt to make determinative for Article III purposes the distinction between public rights and private rights." While that distinction is not "determinative," however, the Court was clear that it is relevant. Recall, however, that *Crowell v. Benson* upheld a delegation to an agency of authority to adjudicate what had been a common law tort action before it was embedded in a modified form in a statutory scheme. Is the distinction between public and private rights, in the end, only a distinction between rights embodied in common law precedent and rights embodied in statute? Or is the distinction, instead, between law that settles disputes involving the government and individual members of the public on the one hand, and law that settles disputes involving two or more private persons on the other?

Does the public rights/private rights distinction make any sense? Is not the purpose of common law principles that settle private rights the same as the purpose of statutory principles that settle public rights—the maximization of the welfare of the community at large? Even if the public rights-private rights dichotomy is viable, why should it be relevant to the authority of the legislature to vest adjudicatory power in agencies, given the purposes of Article III to ensure an unbiased consideration of cases and an adequate system of checks and balances between the three branches of government? Should not judicial independence be a *greater* concern in cases involving public rights where government is one of the litigants, than in cases involving private rights where the government is not involved? If adequate judicial review by an Article III court is provided, why should there be any concern with a delegation of adjudicatory power to an agency? *See* Fallon, "Of Legislative Courts, Administrative Agencies, and Article III," 101 Harv.L.Rev. 915 (1988).

2. *After Schor.* After *CFTC v. Schor,* when, if ever, would a delegation of adjudicatory power to a federal agency violate the mandate of the Constitution that the judicial power be vested in Article III courts? What are the relevant factors set forth in *Schor?* Note the reliance in *Schor* on Congress' reasons for making the delegation and on safeguards such as judicial review. Is there any fundamental difference, after *Schor,* between federal law concerning the delegation of legislative powers and federal law concerning the delegation of adjudicatory powers?

3. *Crowell v. Benson today.* Both *Northern Pipeline* and *Schor* rely on *Crowell v. Benson,* discussed above. As noted, *Crowell* upheld a delegation to an agency of authority to adjudicate a workers' compensation claim arising under a federal statute. However, *Crowell* also required a de novo judicial trial of the issues of "jurisdictional fact" arising in the case. This requirement appears to have been a condition of the Court's willingness to uphold the delegation.

Although never formally overruled, the holding of *Crowell* with respect to the scope of judicial review of "jurisdictional fact" is considered to be a relic of a bygone era. *See, e.g., Estep v. United States,* 327 U.S. 114, 142 (1946) (Frankfurter, J. concurring) (in view of the criticism of *Crowell* and "the attritions of that case through later decisions, one had supposed that the [jurisdictional fact] doctrine had earned a deserved repose"). In *Northern Pipeline,* Justice Brennan noted that *Crowell's* precise holding, with respect to de novo trials of "jurisdictional" or "constitutional" facts, had been undermined by later cases.

4. *State cases and adjudication of private rights.* A number of state decisions have insisted that adjudication of private rights cannot be vested in administrative agencies. Is the multi-factor analysis of *CFTC v. Schor* preferable to the exclusive focus in state cases on the public rights/private rights dichotomy?

In the course of the only state supreme court opinion invalidating a workers' compensation law providing for the administrative adjudication of claims, the New Mexico Supreme Court stated:

> The attack on the [Workmen's Compensation] Act is multiple but the main question is whether it confers an unlawful delegation of judicial power on the commission. We think it does . . . .

> This is not to say that the legislature, in the exercise of its police powers, may not confer 'quasi-judicial' power on administrative boards for the protection of the rights and interest of the public in general whose orders are not to be overruled if supported by substantial evidence. For instance, boards regulating common carriers, transportation, telephone rates, Barber Boards, Medical Boards, Boards of Registration, Tax Boards, Division of Liquor Control, etc. . . . But nowhere does this power extend to a determination of rights and liabilities between individuals.

State ex rel. Hovey Concrete Products Co. v. Mechem, 316 P.2d 1069 (N.M.1957).

Similarly, in *Wright v. Central DuPage Hospital Association,* 347 N.E.2d 736 (Ill.1976), the court invalidated a scheme for adjudication of medical malpractice disputes by a panel of a judge, a doctor, and an attorney. The court stated that the scheme violated the Illinois Constitution because it vested essentially judicial functions in nonjudicial personnel, and because it impaired plaintiff's constitutionally protected interests in trial by jury. Finally, *In re Opinion of the Justices,* 179 A. 344 (N.H.1935), advised that the adjudication of negligence cases arising out of auto accidents could not be transferred to an agency. The court concluded that "the function of trying and deciding litigation is strictly and exclusively for the judiciary when it is between private parties, neither of whom seeks to come under the protection of a public interest and to have it upheld and maintained for his benefit. The function cannot be executive unless executive activity may embrace litigation in general. If the proposed jurisdiction might be bestowed, the limits of executive authority would be almost without bounds and indefinite encroachment on judicial power would be possible."

Do you agree with *Mechem, Wright,* and *Opinion of the Justices?* Since workers' compensation schemes have been upheld in all states except New Mexico, why would agency-administered medical malpractice or auto accident cases be treated differently? Is there a distinction that would justify a difference in result?

Suppose Congress, rather than a state legislature, enacted adjudicatory delegations like those discussed in *Mechem, Wright,* or *Opinion of the Justices.* Would they be valid?

5. *State cases and vesting of other kinds of judicial power in agencies.* A Missouri case, *State Tax Com'n v. Administrative Hearing Com'n,* 641 S.W.2d 69, 73–77 (Mo.1982), suggests that in some states there are other kinds of limits on the types of issues that may be delegated to an agency for adjudicative decisionmaking. That case holds invalid a statutory delegation to the Administrative Hearing Commission of authority to issue a declaratory order with respect to the validity of an agency rule on the ground that such a delegation violates the separation of powers principle embedded in the state constitution. The Administrative Hearing Commission was an independent agency empowered to conduct hearings and make findings of fact and conclusions of law for many different licensing agencies. The court "recognized that executive agencies may exercise 'quasi judicial powers' that are 'incidental and necessary to the proper discharge' of their administrative functions, even though by doing so they at times determine questions of a 'purely legal nature'." However, its opinion stressed that the legislature could not vest "purely judicial functions" in an administrative agency, and that agency adjudicative power could extend "only to the ascertainment of facts and the application of existing law thereto in order to resolve issues within the given area of agency expertise." The court was convinced that the "declaration of the validity or invalidity of statutes and administrative rules . . . is purely a judicial function." By authorizing the Administrative Hearing Commission to render declaratory orders regarding the validity of agency rules, the legislature had unconstitutionally "attempted to elevate the . . . Commission to the status of a court."

In the *Administrative Hearing Com'n* case the court stressed that unlike Congress, which is authorized by Article III, § 1 of the federal Constitution to create such inferior courts as it deems proper, the legislature of that state could not create a new species of court because the Missouri Constitution expressly provided for all state courts. Consequently, the legislature "has no authority to create any other tribunal and invest it with judicial power," and "cannot turn an administrative agency into a court by granting it power that has been constitutionally reserved to the judiciary." Since the statute at issue unambiguously vested in the Commission "a power equal to the power of the courts to render declaratory judgments declaring the validity or invalidity of agency rules," the court held it to be a violation of the state constitution. The fact that judicial review of any such commission determination was available did not alter the conclusion that the vesting of this power in that administrative body usurped the judicial function. The court stated:

> That argument, carried to its logical conclusion, would mean that the legislative and executive branches could exercise powers consti-

tutionally reserved to the judiciary as long as judicial review was available. Yet "[i]t is emphatically the province and duty of the judicial department to say what the law is." *Marbury v. Madison,* . . . 5 U.S. 137, 177 (1803). The doctrine of separation of powers, which the people unequivocally embraced in adopting Article II, § 1 of the Missouri Constitution, would be reduced to a mere shibboleth were this attempted grant of power sustained.

Is the reasoning and result in the *Administrative Hearing Comm'n* case sound? Why is a legislative delegation to an agency to determine the validity of a statute or agency rule a usurpation of a judicial function if adequate review of that determination is available in the courts? Why is there a difference between the "application of existing law" to facts "to resolve issues within the given area of agency expertise," which the court says is properly delegated to an agency, and an adjudicative determination of the validity of an agency rule, which the court says may not be delegated to an agency? In both cases, must not *the agency* determine *what* the law is and apply it to the facts?

Of course, legislatures usually do not wish to delegate to agencies authority to determine, even initially, the validity of *statutes* on the ground that it is unseemly for an agent to determine the validity of the action of its principal. As a result, courts ordinarily deny agencies such authority on the ground that it was not delegated to them. *See* § 11.2.4, *infra.* But what is wrong with the legislature delegating to a body in the executive branch authority to issue a determination concerning the validity of agency rules, subject to an opportunity for subsequent judicial review? Does not every agency necessarily have to determine, initially, the validity of any rule it proposes to adopt? The Missouri *Administrative Hearing Comm'n* case appears to be unusual insofar as it holds that an agency may not be delegated adjudicative authority to issue an order determining the validity of an agency rule, subject to subsequent plenary judicial review. Note, in this connection, that Florida has a special statute authorizing a hearing officer employed by an independent central hearing panel to determine, subject to judicial review, the validity of an agency rule upon petition by an appropriate person. *See* Fla.Stat.Ann. § 120.56 (1982).

6. *Jury trials.* The Seventh Amendment to the United States Constitution provides: "In Suits at common law, where the value in controversy shall exceed twenty dollars, the right of trial by jury shall be preserved. . . ." May Congress avoid the Seventh Amendment by removing certain kinds of adjudications from courts to agencies?

The answer is clearly "yes" for certain types of cases. *Atlas Roofing Co. v. Occupational Safety and Health Rev. Comm'n,* 430 U.S. 442 (1977), involved the validity of a statute authorizing an administrative agency (the Occupational Safety and Health Review Commission) to impose penalties, which could range up to $10,000 per violation, on employers who maintained an unsafe workplace. If an employer did not pay a penalty, the government could collect it by an action in federal district court.

In *Atlas,* the Supreme Court rejected a Seventh Amendment attack on the enabling statute, holding that the imposition of the penalty was a means of enforcing a "public right" rather than a "private right." The Court stated that "Congress is not required by the Seventh Amendment to choke the already crowded federal courts with new types of litigation or prevented from committing some new types of litigation to administrative agencies with special competence in the relevant field. This is the case even if the Seventh Amendment would have required a jury where the adjudication of those rights is assigned to a federal court of law instead of an administrative agency." The Court was clear that Congress could "create new public rights and remedies by statute and commit their enforcement, if it chose, to a tribunal other than a court of law—such as an administrative agency—in which facts are not found by juries."

In a footnote, the Court pointed out that decisions of the Commission were reviewable by the United States Court of Appeals (both as to legal questions and as to whether there was substantial evidence to support its fact findings). "Thus these cases do not present the question whether Congress may commit the adjudication of fines for [the] violation [of these public rights] to an administrative agency without any sort of intervention by a court at any stage of the proceedings."

Is the public-private rights dichotomy any more helpful in determining the applicability of the Seventh Amendment than the limitations imposed by Article III? Assuming a delegation of adjudicatory power is otherwise valid, should the Seventh Amendment be inapplicable on the ground that it was intended to be relevant only to cases tried in courts of law?

Compare *Tull v. United States,* 481 U.S. 412 (1987), to the *Atlas Roofing* case. In *Tull,* a court awarded both injunctive relief and monetary penalties to the government in a suit under the Clean Water Act. It was held that the defendant had a right to a jury trial on the question of whether civil penalties should be imposed (but not on the issue of the amount of the penalties). Thus the right to a jury trial may turn on whether the agency sets the penalty (*Atlas Roofing*) or whether a court sets the penalty (*Tull*).

§ 7.4.2 DELEGATION OF AUTHORITY TO PENALIZE OR FINE

§ 7.4.2a Authority to Decide Whether Conduct Is Criminal

UNITED STATES v. GRIMAUD
220 U.S. 506 (1911).

MR. JUSTICE LAMAR, delivered the opinion of the court.

The defendants were indicted for grazing sheep on the Sierra Forest Reserve without having obtained the permission required by the regulations adopted by the Secretary of Agriculture. They demurred on the ground that the Forest Reserve Act of 1891 was unconstitutional, in so far as it delegated to the Secretary of Agriculture power to make rules and regulations and made a violation thereof a penal offense.

From the various acts relating to the establishment and management of forest reservations it appears that . . . the Secretary "may make such rules and regulations and establish such service as will insure the objects of such reservation, namely, to regulate their occupancy and use and to preserve the forests thereon from destruction; *and any violation of the provisions of this act or such rules and regulations shall be punished* " as is provided in § 5388 of the Revised Statutes. . . .

A violation of reasonable rules regulating the use and occupancy of the property is made a crime, not by the Secretary, but by Congress. The statute, not the Secretary, fixes the penalty. . . . The Secretary did not exercise the legislative power of declaring the penalty or fixing the punishment for grazing sheep without a permit, but the punishment is imposed by the act itself. The offense is not against the Secretary, but, as the indictment properly concludes, "contrary to the laws of the United States and the peace and dignity thereof." The demurrers should have been overruled. . . .

Notes and Questions

1. *Who defines crimes?* Legislatures often authorize an agency to make rules on a particular subject and include in the enabling legislation a provision stating that violation of those rules is a crime. Do you agree with *Grimaud* that in such circumstances it is the *legislature* that determines the criminal offense?

Most state courts agree with *Grimaud*. See, e.g., *People v. Turmon*, 340 N.W.2d 620 (Mich.1983); *New York v. Kantrowitz*, 173 N.Y.S.2d 213 (1958); *State v. Lambert*, 229 N.W.2d 622 (Wis.1975). However, some states hold that the legislature may delegate authority to determine which acts are criminal only to *elected* officials. See, e.g., *Casey v. People*, 336 P.2d 308 (Colo.1959); *State v. Maitrejean*, 192 So. 361 (La. 1939).

2. *Nebraska cases.* In *Lincoln Dairy Co. v. Finigan*, 104 N.W.2d 227, 232 (Neb.1960), the court noted that the legislature may not avoid the performance of its exclusive function to define and provide punishment for crimes by delegating such authority to an agency. "For this court to hold that administrative or executive officers, or departments, could make rules and regulations from time to time according to judgment or whim, which would have the effect of law and the violation of which would be punishable as crimes, would be to deprive the people of the protection of the personal rights for which constitutions were devised to protect."

In a subsequent decision, the Nebraska court retreated from *Lincoln Dairy*. *State v. Cutright,* 226 N.W.2d 771 (Neb.1975), involved the validity of a delegation to the state Game and Parks Commission of the power "to promulgate rules . . . prohibiting swimming and other water activities in the lakes in state parks, . . . except where the Commission shall have given permission for such activity in the specified area." The statute in question also provided that a violation of any of these Commission rules would be a criminal offense. The court distinguished the statutory delegation in *Cutright* from the statutory delegation in *Lincoln Dairy.*

[The statute in *Lincoln Dairy* provided:] "The director is hereby authorized to adopt, by regulation, minimum standards for the sanitary quality, production, processing, distribution, and sale of Grade A milk and Grade A milk products, and for labeling of the same. Such regulations shall comply generally with the Milk Ordinance and Code—1953 recommendations of the Public Health Service, of the Department of Health, Education and Welfare of the United States." It was further provided in another part of the act that any person or persons violating the rules or regulations issued therein shall be guilty of a misdemeanor. . . . [I]n the statute involved in the instant case, the Legislature itself actually established the crime and the penalty for violation of the statute. . . . The only thing that is left to the decision or discretion of the commission is the designation of the appropriate areas where swimming may be permitted, and the posting of the proper notices for such areas. Obviously the filling in of the minor details relative to the implementation of the statute would have to be delegated by the Legislature, as it is not to be expected and, in fact, would be a physical impossibility for the Legislature to visit all the state lakes personally, and make its own determination of where swimming should be permitted.

On the other hand, the act involved in Lincoln Dairy Co. v. Finigan, *supra,* did not contain a legislative definition of the crime itself, as did the statute in this case. It merely provided that the Director should have the power to make rules and regulations, and if he did so, the Legislature provided that a violation of such regulations would be a misdemeanor, and punishable as such. In other words, the Director, under that act, was given the absolute power to determine what conduct would be punishable under the regulations that *he* drew. This clearly would be an unconstitutional delegation of its power by the Legislature to an administrative agency or an executive of the government; and this court so held. The statute involved in this case is totally unlike the act involved in the Lincoln Dairy Co. case for the reasons previously stated; and we conclude that there is no unconstitutional delegation of legislative power involved in the statute in this case. . . .

226 N.W.2d at 773–774.

Is the court's effort in *Cutright* to distinguish *Lincoln Dairy* satisfactory? *See* Gellhorn, "Administrative Prescription and Imposition of Penalties," 1970 Wash.U.L.Q. 265, 266, noting that "the 'act' held in Grimaud's case to be criminal was disregarding the Secretary of Agriculture's regulation. Congress, not the Secretary, had declared that a crime."

§ 7.4.2b Power of Agencies to Adjudicate Penalties

The United States Constitution provides many procedural protections for persons charged with a crime. May an agency be authorized to determine whether a person has violated an agency rule and to punish that person by imprisonment or criminal fine if it finds such a violation?

Only the judiciary may impose a sentence of imprisonment. *Wong Wing v. United States*, 163 U.S. 228 (1896), indicated that a person may be temporarily detained by an agency pending proceedings to decide whether exclusion or expulsion as an illegal alien is appropriate, and that an alien may be administratively excluded or expelled from the country. However, an illegal alien may not be sentenced to prison without the protection of a judicial trial.

On the other hand, both federal and state courts permit agencies to impose monetary penalties. At the federal level, recall *Atlas Roofing*, § 7.4.1, *supra*.

WAUKEGAN v. POLLUTION CONTROL BOARD
311 N.E.2d 146 (1974).

WARD, JUSTICE.

In October, 1971, the Illinois Environmental Protection Agency filed a complaint with the Pollution Control Board (hereafter, the Board) against the City of Waukegan, Zion State Bank and Trust Company, T–K City Disposal, Inc., and Tewes Co., Inc., charging various violations of the Environmental Protection Act. . . . After a hearing, the Board imposed a fine of $1000 against the City of Waukegan, and fines of $250 against the T–K Disposal, Inc., and Tewes Co., Inc.. . .

[O]ne question is before us: Was the authority given the Board to impose monetary penalties under the Environmental Protection Act a delegation of judicial power in violation of the separation-of-powers provision of the Constitution of Illinois or in violation of the Constitution of the United States?

The challenged section of the Act confers authority on the board to impose a penalty of not to exceed $10,000 for a violation of the Act, or of a Board regulation or order, and to impose an additional penalty not to exceed $1,000 for each day of continuing violation. . . .

The Supreme Court of the United States has never . . . expressed alarm or undue concern about conferring a power to impose monetary penalties on an administrative body. As early as 1909 the court upheld the grant of power to the Secretary of Commerce and Labor to impose monetary penalties for violations of an immigration statute. In Oceanic Steam Navigation Co. v. Stranahan, 214 U.S. 320, 339, it was said:

"In accord with this settled judicial construction the legislation of Congress from the beginning, not only as to tariff, but as to internal revenue, taxation, and other subjects, has proceeded on the conception that it was within the competency of Congress, when legislating as to matters exclusively within its control, to impose appropriate obligations, and sanction their enforcement by reasonable money penalties, giving to executive officers the power to enforce such penalties without the necessity of invoking the judicial power." . . .

Partly as a consequence of the court's decisions, many Federal agencies have been empowered by the Congress to impose monetary penalties directly, that is, on the agency's 'own action and authority.

The Administrative Conference of the United States in a recommendation to the Congress made on December 14, 1972 (Recommendation 72–6, entitled "Civil Money Penalties as a Sanction") observed: "Federal administrative agencies enforce many statutory provisions and administrative regulations for violation of which fixed or variable civil money penalties may be imposed. . . . Increased use of civil money penalties is an important and salutary trend. . . . In many areas of increased concern (e.g., health and safety, the environment, consumer protection) availibility of civil money penalties might significantly enhance an agency's ability to achieve its statutory goals." 2 Administrative Conference 67–68. . . .

State courts as well have approved grants of power to administrative agencies to impose monetary penalties.

New York's insurance law providing for monetary penalties for violations after notice and hearing by the superintendent of insurance has been upheld. (Old Republic Life Insurance Co. v. Thacher (1962), 186 N.E.2d 554.) In Jackson v. Concord Co. (1969), 253 A.2d 793, the Supreme Court of New Jersey observed that there could not be any valid constitutional objection to the grant of authority to award money damages "at this advanced date in the development of administrative law" (253 A.2d at 800) and in view of a provision in the statute for judicial review. . . .

It is clear that the trend in State decisions is to allow administrative agencies to impose discretionary civil penalties. See W. Gellhorn, Administrative Prescription and Imposition of Penalties, 1970 Wash. U.L.Q. 265. . . .

Turning to the Environmental Protection Act, we consider that the authority given the Board to impose monetary penalties does not violate the constitutional separation of powers. The interpretations given the separation doctrine by this court and by the Supreme Court of the United States, the decisions approving delegations of authority to impose civil penalties, the detailed hearing and related provisions of the statute, the Act's providing for adequate judicial review, and the statute's establishment of protective guidelines that the Board must follow in imposing penalties, direct this conclusion. . . .

The Environmental Protection Act obviously contemplates a specialized statewide and uniform program of environmental control and enforcement. The legislature considered this could be more readily brought about if the responsibility of imposing penalties was placed on the same authority that conducted hearings and determined violations.

The Board is to conduct hearings and, if violations are found, appropriately it is to impose penalties. The legislature may confer those powers upon an administrative agency that are reasonably necessary to accomplish the legislative purpose of the agency, and we consider that it was appropriate to give the Board the authority to impose monetary penalties.

There are adequate standards provided and safeguards imposed on the power given the Board to impose these penalties. The granting of this authority does not constitute an unconstitutional delegation of judicial power.

Notes and Questions

1. *Other cases.* Some states permit the legislature to delegate authority to impose fixed penalties but not variable penalties. *See, e.g., County Council for Montgomery County v. Investors Funding Corp.,* 312 A.2d 225, 246 (Md.1973); *Tite v. State Tax Commission,* 57 P.2d 734, 740 (Utah 1936).

Is there a possibility that an agency with authority to determine the level of a monetary penalty will abuse that discretion? Is that any more of a problem than giving an agency authority to suspend or revoke a license?

Is the *Waukegan* case consistent with the other Illinois cases in this chapter—*Thygesen v. Callahan,* § 7.3.2, *supra,* and *Wright v. Central DuPage Hospital Association,* § 7.4.1, *supra?*

2. *Agency imposition of damage awards and other remedies.* A number of cases uphold legislative delegations to agencies of authority to award damages to a non-governmental litigant. For instance, in *Jackson v. Concord Co.,* 253 A.2d 793, 800 (N.J.1969), a state civil rights agency ordered reimbursement for out-of-pocket loss suffered in a racial discrimination case. The New Jersey Supreme Court stated that "at this advanced date in the development of administrative law, we see no constitutional objection to legislative authorization to an administrative agency to award, as incidental relief in connection with a subject delegable to it, money damages, ultimate judicial review thereof being available."

On the other hand, *Iron Workers Local No. 67 v. Hart,* 191 N.W.2d 758 (Iowa 1971), held that a state Civil Rights Commission had acted beyond its statutory authority in attempting to award damages in a collateral matter for a business which had not itself been discriminated against in violation of state law. The Commission had sought to award the business compensatory damages based on losses to the company through its increased expenses because of a dispute with a labor union over the business' hiring of minority employees. In rejecting the agency's authority to make such a damage award, the court stated: "The right granted to the Commission to allow back pay for employees ordered hired, reinstated, or upgraded is only incidental to affirmative action equitably decreed and cannot by analogy generate a power to enter judgment for other common law damages. If the legislature had intended to constitute [the] Commission as an additional court for adjudicating damages it would have so stated." 191 N.W.2d at 767. Does *Iron Workers* suggest a predisposition on the part of the courts to construe narrowly delegations to agencies of authority to make damage awards? Would such a predisposition be defensible?

Is *Jackson* consistent with *CFTC v. Schor,* § 7.4.1, *supra?*

Both the *Jackson* case and the *Iron Workers* case held that the legislature could delegate to an agency authority to issue cease and desist orders (the administrative equivalent of a prohibitory injunction) or to issue orders directing respondents to take affirmative action such as the hiring or reinstatement of employees (the administrative equivalent to an affirmative injunction).

3. *Enforcement of agency orders.* Typically agencies must go to court to enforce their orders. A failure to obey an enforcement order issued by a court is punishable as contempt. Historically, only courts, not agencies, were given contempt powers. *See ICC v. Brimson,* 154 U.S. 447, 485 (1894); *Wright v. Plaza Ford,* 395 A.2d 1259, 1265 (N.J. 1978). It was generally believed that such powers could not be conferred upon agencies. However, there is a minority view that agencies can be given contempt powers by statute. *See Morton v. Workers Comp. App. Bd.,* 238 Cal.Rptr. 651, 653 (Cal.1987). Should agencies have the power to hold in contempt persons who disobey their orders?

Would you favor a statute which made it a crime to violate a lawful agency order? If criminalizing the violation of agency orders is a more desirable and efficient method for their enforcement, why do you suppose that statutes do not ordinarily provide criminal sanctions for the violation of lawful agency orders?

4. *Problem.* A recent state statute transferred adjudication of all moving traffic violations and parking tickets to a newly formed Traffic Agency. The purpose of the statute was to lessen congestion in the criminal courts and to assure expedited treatment of such offenses.

If the Traffic Agency finds that a violation has been proved by a preponderance of the evidence, it may impose penalties of up to $1000 per violation. Your client Ralph is charged with speeding. Can he object to trial of his case before the Traffic Agency? *See Rosenthal v. Hartnett,* 326 N.E.2d 811 (N.Y.1975). What if the Traffic Agency were a federal agency created to adjudicate cases involving alleged moving traffic violations and parking tickets on federal lands?

§ 7.5 LEGISLATIVE AND EXECUTIVE CONTROLS OF AGENCY ACTION

§ 7.5.1 DESIRABILITY OF LEGISLATIVE AND EXECUTIVE REVIEW OF AGENCY ACTION

BONFIELD, STATE ADMINISTRATIVE RULE MAKING
456–60 (1986).

Through judicial review of agency rules courts can help to ensure that [rules] are legal in all respects. . . . But courts are not the proper bodies to protect us against legal agency rules that are simply unwise or unpopular, because courts are not broadly representative institutions that are directly responsible to the people. . . . On the other hand, gubernatorial and legislative review of agency rules can provide a direct and effective check on unwise or unpopular agency rules. The governor and the legislature are directly elected, have broad constituencies, and therefore have great legitimacy to decide finally, on behalf of all the people, issues of everyday public policy. . . .

Judicial review of agency rule making should also be supplemented by an effective scheme of gubernatorial and legislative review of rule making because such a scheme will make that agency law-making process more realistically approximate the representative legislative process it was intended to replace. . . .

A related reason to supplement judicial review of agency rules with an effective scheme of external review directly involving the governor and legislature has to do with the right of those institutions to preserve the effectiveness of their law-making function. Agencies should be directly accountable to those authorizing their rule-making actions. Ordinarily, both the governor and the legislature approve laws delegating rule-making authority to agencies. Consequently, both the governor and the legislature should be able to satisfy themselves that their will is being executed in a manner consistent with their wishes and, if it is not, should be able to take suitable action to ensure conformity with their wishes. . . .

Furthermore, . . . [o]nly institutions with direct political legitimacy like the governor and the legislature can coordinate potentially divergent, conflicting, or inconsistent rules of several agencies purely on policy grounds. The courts cannot perform that function because their intervention is limited entirely to resolving matters of legality rather than matters of policy. . . .

Gubernatorial and legislative review of rules can also check unlawful agency rule making. While the courts can perform that function, as will be seen, they can often do so only in an untimely fashion, at an unacceptable cost, or in a relatively ineffective way. . . .

Another reason why judicial review of agency rule making should be supplemented by a scheme for gubernatorial and legislative review of that agency function is that the agencies themselves will often benefit from systematic review of their rules by the governor and legislature. In practice, that external review will provide them with an additional means by which to discover deficiencies in their rules before they become effective or are invalidated by the courts.

§ 7.5.2 LEGISLATIVE VETO: INTRODUCTION

In § 7.2, *supra,* we noted that the most direct means by which a legislature may control agency action is by specifying its desires in the agency's enabling act thereby initially limiting the agency to specified actions deemed acceptable to the elected representatives of the people. However, for reasons noted in § 7.3, *supra,* legislatures have been unable or unwilling to be very specific in their statutes delegating authority to agencies. Instead, they have, in general, initially vested agencies with broad discretion under vague, open-ended, statutory delegations of authority. The most obvious means by which the legislature may directly overturn agency action it finds unacceptable after that action has occurred under such a vague, open-ended, statutory delegation is by amending the agency's enabling act to contract its power or to overturn the specific agency action deemed objectionable.

However, the practical difficulties encountered in efforts to amend a statute makes that remedy for redress of an objection to specific agency action one that is rarely used in practice. Enactment of a statute to overcome agency action is difficult, in part, because it requires the concurrence of both houses of the legislature and the chief executive, or if the latter vetoes the legislature's action, an override of such a veto by a super-majority of both houses of the legislature. That is why many legislatures have turned to the "legislative veto."

The term "legislative veto" describes a mechanism that allows the legislature to invalidate or suspend agency action by less authoritative means than the enactment of a statute. For example, if the legislature can veto an agency rule solely by a resolution of one or two of its houses, or solely by action of one of its committees, without any participation by the chief executive, this would be a legislative veto. It authorizes all or part of the legislative process to affect the validity of an otherwise valid agency rule without resort to the usual statute-making process which requires participation by the chief executive.

LEVINSON, "THE DECLINE OF THE LEGISLATIVE VETO: FEDERAL/STATE COMPARISONS AND INTERACTIONS"

17 Publius: The Journal of Federalism 115, 115–20 (1987).

The era of the legislative veto started when Congress enacted the Reorganization Act of 1932. That statute authorized the President to adopt reorganization plans, but empowered either house of the Congress to nullify any plan adopted by the President. The first state legislative veto system was enacted in Kansas in 1939. The Kansas system was "generic," that is, it empowered the legislature, by concurrent resolution, to nullify any regulation adopted by any administrative agency in the implementation of any enabling act. The 1932 congressional Reorganization Act and the 1939 Kansas statute shared one essential feature—each system provided for the nullification of the actions of an administrative agency by some type of legislative action other than a statute. . . .

The earliest versions of the legislative veto, such as the statutes mentioned above, provided for the *nullification* of the actions of administrative agencies. A variant approach soon emerged, providing for the *suspension* of the actions of administrative agencies by some type of legislative action other than a statute. Since suspension is a provisional or temporary version of nullification, . . . both suspension and nullification [are] . . . two distinct categories within the legislative veto concept. . . .

Congress has never created a generic legislative veto system. A bill to establish such a system passed the Senate in 1982 but failed to win House approval. Starting with the Reorganization Act of 1932, the Congress included specific legislative veto systems in numerous enabling statutes, each empowering one or both houses of Congress to nullify an agency's action. By 1983, the number of federal programs that were subject to one- or two-house nullification had risen to approximately 200, despite recurring criticisms by presidents during that fifty-year period. In addition, starting in the 1950s, Congress inserted committee suspension provisions in a number of appropriations acts. . . .

[G]eneric provisions for one- or two-house nullification existed in only one state (Kansas) at the end of 1939. The number of states with such systems gradually increased to eleven by the end of 1979. During the next six years, new systems were added in six states while existing systems were discontinued in eight states, leaving nine states with nullification systems at the end of 1985. Generic provisions for suspension by a legislative committee, subject to final legislative action by statute, did not exist in any state at the end of 1939. By the end of 1979, eight states had such systems. During the next six years, three more states adopted committee suspension systems but four states discontinued theirs, leaving seven states with committee suspension systems (subject to final legislative action by statute) at the end of 1985. In some states, various enabling statutes include specific provisions for one- or two-house nullification, or for committee suspension, of the agencies' actions in implementing these statutes.

———

The policy reasons urged in support of legislative vetoes focus on their utility in securing agency accountability under vague legislative delegations of power. Opponents of the legislative veto agree that the legislature should be able to check agency action that it deems undesirable; however, they object to the means by which that check is exercised. They argue that a legislative veto of agency rules might induce agencies to make more of their law by ad hoc orders rather than by rules, a result which would be undesirable.

By providing that the legislature may overcome or suspend an agency rule *only* by the enactment of a statute, the 1981 MSAPA rejected the legislative veto. The Comment to § 3–204 states the reasons for the rejection of this device:

> There are many reasons why legislative vetoes or suspensions of administrative rules by means other than statute should be avoided. In the first place, schemes of this sort may unduly aggrandize the legislature's authority at the expense of the executive branch's countervailing independence. By cutting out the veto power of the governor present in the usual legislative process, such mechanisms weaken the state chief executive's bargaining power with the legislature and disable him from checking legislative action he deems unsound. They also may facilitate over-involvement of the legislative branch in the day-to-day administration of programs it creates by statute and induce an unhealthy split in perceived authority over purely administrative matters.
>
> Furthermore, a legislative mechanism for veto or suspension of state agency rules will be useful primarily as a check against unwise rules that are otherwise clearly lawful. An effective check against most *unlawful* rules is provided by judicial review. . . . Therefore, legislative veto or suspension of particular state agency rules will have its primary practical impact on *lawful* rules and, in effect, would constitute a *pro tanto* narrowing of the authorizing legislation under which they were otherwise properly issued. Such a narrowing of the authorizing legislation should be executed in the same manner as the legislation was initially adopted. Otherwise, a committee, one house, or two houses of the state legislature, would continually be in a position to subvert proper authorizing action of a more representative and authoritative lawmaking process with built-in checks and balances. A part of the usual statute-making process should not be able to nullify action of the *more* representative and *more* authoritative whole, with its built-in checks and balances, lest the very virtues of the whole process be lost. Therefore, all efforts to nullify otherwise lawful agency rules should be

executed by joint legislative action, subject to the veto of the governor.

In addition, legislative committee veto or suspension of rules, or one house or two house veto or suspension of rules, may be more susceptible to undue influence by special interest groups acting contrary to the public interest than is veto or suspension by the usual legislative process of statutory enactment. This is another policy reason against veto or suspension of state agency rules by any means other than joint legislative action submitted to the governor. It should also be noted that in some cases the existence of a legislative mechanism to veto or suspend rules by a means that is easier to invoke than the usual statute-making process may have the following undesirable consequence. That mechanism may encourage people to reduce their participation in the rule-making proceeding before the agency and, instead, concentrate their efforts on the alternative legislative veto or suspension mechanism.

As you read the next subsection dealing with *constitutional* issues, consider the following questions: Do you think a one or two house legislative veto or a legislative committee veto of agency action is desirable? Is there a difference between the desirability of one-house vetoes and two-house vetoes, or between the desirability of those kinds of vetoes and legislative committee vetoes? Is there a difference between the desirability of legislative vetoes that invalidate agency action and legislative vetoes that only suspend agency action? Is there a difference between the desirability of legislative vetoes of agency rulemaking and such vetoes of agency adjudication?

§ 7.5.3 LEGISLATIVE VETO: CONSTITUTIONAL PROBLEMS

IMMIGRATION AND NATURALIZATION SERVICE [INS] v. CHADHA

462 U.S. 919 (1983).

[Section 244(a)(1) of the Immigration and Nationality Act provides that the Attorney General may in his discretion "suspend" the deportation of an otherwise deportable alien who meets certain statutory standards including a finding that deportation would cause "extreme hardship." The Attorney General delegated this power to the INS.

Chadha was an East Indian who had been born in Kenya and held a British passport; he had been admitted on a student visa but had overstayed the expiration date. Following an on-the-record hearing, an immigration judge held that Chadha was deportable but ordered that deportation be suspended because Chadha met the "extreme hardship" requirements of the statute.

Section 244(c)(1) provides that the Attorney General must report all suspensions of deportation to Congress; and § 244(c)(2) provides that Congress may "veto" the suspension by a resolution passed by either house during the legislative session in which the suspension is reported or the next session.

Chadha's suspension was reported to Congress and remained outstanding for a year and a half. At almost the last possible moment, a resolution was introduced in the House to veto deportation suspensions of six aliens, including that of Chadha, on the ground that those aliens had not met the statutory requirements of undue hardship. Because the resolution passed, Chadha was ordered to be deported. He questions the constitutionality of the legislative veto provision in § 244(c)(2).

The Court held that the provision for legislative veto was "severable" from the provision for suspension of deportation. Consequently, if the veto were invalidated, the INS decision suspending Chadha's deportation remained in effect.

BURGER, C.J.:]

We turn now to the question whether action of one House of Congress under § 244(c)(2) violates strictures of the Constitution. We begin, of course, with the presumption that the challenged statute is valid. . . .

By the same token, the fact that a given law or procedure is efficient, convenient, and useful in facilitating functions of government, standing alone, will not save it if it is contrary to the Constitution. Convenience and efficiency are not the primary objectives—or the hallmarks—of democratic government and our inquiry is sharpened rather than blunted by the fact that Congressional veto provisions are appearing with increasing frequency in statutes which delegate authority to executive and independent agencies. . . .

JUSTICE WHITE undertakes to make a case for the proposition that the one-House veto is a useful "political invention," and we need not challenge that assertion. We can even concede this utilitarian argument although the long range political wisdom of this "invention" is arguable. . . . But policy arguments supporting even useful "political inventions" are subject to the demands of the Constitution which defines powers and, with respect to this subject, sets out just how those powers are to be exercised.

Explicit and unambiguous provisions of the Constitution prescribe and define the respective functions of the Congress and of the Executive in the legislative process. Since the precise terms of those familiar provisions are critical to the resolution of this case, we set them out verbatim. Art. I provides:

"All legislative Powers herein granted shall be vested in a Congress of the United States, which shall consist of a Senate *and* a House of Representatives." Art. I, § 1.

"Every Bill which shall have passed the House of Representatives and the Senate, *shall*, before it becomes a Law, be presented to the President of the United States; . . . ." Art. I, § 7, cl. 2.

"Every Order, Resolution, or Vote to which the Concurrence of the Senate and House of Representatives may be necessary (except on a question of Adjournment) *shall be* presented to the President of the United States; and before the Same shall take Effect, *shall be* approved by him, or being disapproved by him, shall be repassed by two thirds of the Senate and House of Representatives, according to the Rules and Limitations prescribed in the Case of a Bill." Art. I, § 7, cl. 3.

These provisions of Art. I are integral parts of the constitutional design for the separation of powers. . . .

Just as we relied on the textual provision of Art. II, § 2, cl. 2, to vindicate the principle of separation of powers in *Buckley v. Valeo*, 424 U.S. 1 (1976) we find that the purposes underlying the Presentment Clauses, Art. I, § 7, cls. 2, 3, and the bicameral requirement of Art. I, § 1 and § 7, cl. 2, guide our resolution of the important question presented in this case. . . .

The records of the Constitutional Convention reveal that the requirement that all legislation be presented to the President before becoming law was uniformly accepted by the Framers. Presentment to the President and the Presidential veto were considered so imperative that the draftsmen took special pains to assure that these requirements could not be circumvented. During the final debate on Art. I, § 7, cl. 2, James Madison expressed concern that it might easily be evaded by the simple expedient of calling a proposed law a "resolution" or "vote" rather than a "bill." As a consequence, Art. I, § 7, cl. 3, was added.

The decision to provide the President with a limited and qualified power to nullify proposed legislation by veto was based on the profound conviction of the Framers that the powers conferred on Congress were the powers to be most carefully circumscribed. It is beyond doubt that lawmaking was a power to be shared by both Houses and the President. In The Federalist No. 73 (H. Lodge ed. 1888), Hamilton focused on the President's role in making laws:

"If even no propensity had ever discovered itself in the legislative body to invade the rights of the Executive, the rules of just reasoning and theoretic propriety would of themselves teach us that the one ought not to be left to the mercy of the other, but ought to possess a constitutional and effectual power of self-defense." *Id.,* at 457–458. . . .

The President's role in the lawmaking process also reflects the Framers' careful efforts to check whatever propensity a particular Congress might have to enact oppressive, improvident, or ill-considered measures. . . .

The bicameral requirement of Art. I, §§ 1, 7 was of scarcely less concern to the Framers than was the Presidential veto and indeed the two concepts are interdependent. By providing that no law could take effect without the concurrence of the prescribed majority of the Members of both Houses, the Framers reemphasized their belief, already remarked upon in connection with the Presentment Clauses, that legislation should not be enacted unless it has been carefully and fully considered by the Nation's elected officials. . . .

We see therefore that the Framers were acutely conscious that the bicameral requirement and the Presentment Clauses would serve essential constitutional functions. The President's participation in the legislative process was to protect the Executive Branch from Congress and to protect the whole people from improvident laws. The division of the Congress into two distinctive bodies assures that the legislative power would be exercised only after opportunity for full study and debate in separate settings. The President's unilateral veto power, in turn, was limited by the power of two thirds of both Houses of Congress to overrule a veto thereby precluding final arbitrary action of one person. It emerges clearly that the prescription for legislative action in Art. I, §§ 1, 7 represents the Framers' decision that the legislative power of the Federal government be exercised in accord with a single, finely wrought and exhaustively considered, procedure. . . .

When any Branch acts, it is presumptively exercising the power the Constitution has delegated to it. See *Hampton & Co. v. United States*, 276 U.S. 394, 406 (1928). When the Executive acts, it presumptively acts in an executive or administrative capacity as defined in Art. II. And when, as here, one House of Congress purports to act, it is presumptively acting within its assigned sphere.

Beginning with this presumption, we must nevertheless establish that the challenged action under § 244(c)(2) is of the kind to which the procedural requirements of Art. I, § 7 apply. Not every action taken by either House is subject to the bicameralism and presentment requirements of Art. I. Whether actions taken by either House are, in law and fact, an exercise of legislative power depends not on their form but upon "whether they contain matter which is properly to be regarded as legislative in its character and effect."

Examination of the action taken here by one House pursuant to § 244(c)(2) reveals that it was essentially legislative in purpose and effect. In purporting to exercise power defined in Art. I, § 8, cl. 4 to "establish an uniform Rule of Naturalization," the House took action that had the purpose and effect of altering the legal rights, duties and relations of persons, including the Attorney General, Executive Branch officials and Chadha, all outside the legislative branch. Section 244(c)(2) purports to authorize one House of Congress to require the Attorney General to deport an individual alien whose deportation otherwise would be cancelled under § 244. The one-House veto operated in this case to overrule the Attorney General and mandate Chadha's deportation; absent the House action, Chadha would remain in the United States. Congress has *acted* and its action has altered Chadha's status.

The legislative character of the one-House veto in this case is confirmed by the character of the Congressional action it supplants.

Neither the House of Representatives nor the Senate contends that, absent the veto provision in § 244(c)(2), either of them, or both of them acting together, could effectively require the Attorney General to deport an alien once the Attorney General, in the exercise of legislatively delegated authority,[16] had determined the alien should remain in the United States. Without the challenged provision in § 244(c)(2), this could have been achieved, if at all, only by legislation requiring deportation. Similarly, a veto by one House of Congress under § 244(c)(2) cannot be justified as an attempt at amending the standards set out in § 244(a)(1), or as a repeal of § 244 as applied to Chadha. Amendment and repeal of statutes, no less than enactment, must conform with Art. I.

The nature of the decision implemented by the one-House veto in this case further manifests its legislative character. After long experience with the clumsy, time consuming private bill procedure, Congress made a deliberate choice to delegate to the Executive Branch, and specifically to the Attorney General, the authority to allow deportable aliens to remain in this country in certain specified circumstances. It is not disputed that this choice to delegate authority is precisely the kind of decision that can be implemented only in accordance with the procedures set out in Art. I. Disagreement with the Attorney General's decision on Chadha's deportation—that is, Congress' decision to deport Chadha—no less than Congress' original choice to delegate to the

---

16. Congress protests that affirming the Court of Appeals in these cases will sanction "lawmaking by the Attorney General. . . . Why is the Attorney General exempt from submitting his proposed changes in the law to the full bicameral process?"

To be sure, some administrative agency action—rulemaking, for example—may resemble "lawmaking." See 5 U.S.C. § 551(4), which defines an agency's "rule" as "the whole or part of an agency statement of general or particular applicability and future effect designed to implement, interpret, or prescribe *law* or policy. . . ." . . . Clearly, however, "[i]n the framework of our Constitution, the President's power to see that the laws are faithfully executed refutes the idea that he is to be a lawmaker."

When the Attorney General performs his duties pursuant to § 244, he does not exercise "legislative" power. . . . The bicameral process is not necessary as a check on the Executive's administration of the laws because his administrative activity cannot reach beyond the limits of the statute that created it—a statute duly enacted pursuant to Art. I, §§ 1, 7. The constitutionality of the Attorney General's execution of the authority delegated to him by § 244 involves only a question of delegation doctrine. The courts, when a case or controversy arises, can always "ascertain whether the will of Congress has been obeyed," and can enforce adherence to statutory standards.

It is clear, therefore, that the Attorney General acts in his presumptively Art. II capacity when he administers the Immigration and Nationality Act. Executive action under legislatively delegated authority that might resemble "legislative" action in some respects is not subject to the approval of both Houses of Congress and the President for the reason that the Constitution does not so require. That kind of Executive action is always subject to check by the terms of the legislation that authorized it; and if that authority is exceeded it is open to judicial review as well as the power of Congress to modify or revoke the authority entirely. A one-House veto is clearly legislative in both character and effect and is not so checked; the need for the check provided by Art. I, §§ 1, 7, is therefore clear. Congress' authority to delegate portions of its power to administrative agencies provides no support for the argument that Congress can constitutionally control administration of the laws by way of a congressional veto.

Attorney General the authority to make that decision, involves determinations of policy that Congress can implement in only one way; bicameral passage followed by presentment to the President. Congress must abide by its delegation of authority until that delegation is legislatively altered or revoked. . . .

Since it is clear that the action by the House under § 244(c)(2) was not within any of the express constitutional exceptions authorizing one House to act alone, and equally clear that it was an exercise of legislative power, that action was subject to the standards prescribed in Article I. The bicameral requirement, the Presentment Clauses, the President's veto, and Congress' power to override a veto were intended to erect enduring checks on each Branch and to protect the people from the improvident exercise of power by mandating certain prescribed steps. To preserve those checks, and maintain the separation of powers, the carefully defined limits on the power of each Branch must not be eroded. To accomplish what has been attempted by one House of Congress in this case requires action in conformity with the express procedures of the Constitution's prescription for legislative action: passage by a majority of both Houses and presentment to the President.

The veto authorized by § 244(c)(2) doubtless has been in many respects a convenient shortcut; the "sharing" with the Executive by Congress of its authority over aliens in this manner is, on its face, an appealing compromise. In purely practical terms, it is obviously easier for action to be taken by one House without submission to the President; but it is crystal clear from the records of the Convention, contemporaneous writings and debates, that the Framers ranked other values higher than efficiency. The records of the Convention and debates in the States preceding ratification underscore the common desire to define and limit the exercise of the newly created federal powers affecting the states and the people. There is unmistakable expression of a determination that legislation by the national Congress be a step-by-step, deliberate and deliberative process.

The choices we discern as having been made in the Constitutional Convention impose burdens on governmental processes that often seem clumsy, inefficient, even unworkable, but those hard choices were consciously made by men who had lived under a form of government that permitted arbitrary governmental acts to go unchecked. There is no support in the Constitution or decisions of this Court for the proposition that the cumbersomeness and delays often encountered in complying with explicit Constitutional standards may be avoided, either by the Congress or by the President. . . .

We hold that the Congressional veto provision in § 244(c)(2) is severable from the Act and that it is unconstitutional.

JUSTICE POWELL, concurring in the judgment.

The Court's decision, based on the Presentment Clauses, Art. I, § 7, cls. 2 and 3, apparently will invalidate every use of the legislative veto. The breadth of this holding gives one pause. Congress has included the veto in literally hundreds of statutes, dating back to the 1930s. Congress clearly views this procedure as essential to controlling the delegation of power to administrative agencies. One reasonably may disagree with Congress' assessment of the veto's utility, but the respect due its judgment as a coordinate branch of Government cautions that our holding should be no more extensive than necessary to decide this case. In my view, the case may be decided on a narrower ground. When Congress finds that a particular person does not satisfy the statutory criteria for permanent residence in this country it has assumed a judicial function in violation of the principle of separation of powers. Accordingly, I concur only in the judgment. . . .

On its face, the House's action appears clearly adjudicatory. The House did not enact a general rule; rather it made its own determination that six specific persons did not comply with certain statutory criteria. It thus undertook the type of decision that traditionally has been left to other branches. Even if the House did not make a *de novo* determination, but simply reviewed the Immigration and Naturalization Service's findings, it still assumed a function ordinarily entrusted to the federal courts. See 5 U.S.C. § 704 (providing generally for judicial review of final agency action);

Where, as here, Congress has exercised a power "that cannot possibly be regarded as merely in aid of the legislative function of Congress, the decisions of this Court have held that Congress impermissibly assumed a function that the Constitution entrusted to another branch.

The impropriety of the House's assumption of this function is confirmed by the fact that its action raises the very danger the Framers sought to avoid—the exercise of unchecked power. In deciding whether Chadha deserves to be deported, Congress is not subject to any internal constraints that prevent it from arbitrarily depriving him of the right to remain in this country. Unlike the judiciary or an administrative agency, Congress is not bound by established substantive rules. Nor is it subject to the procedural safeguards, such as the right to counsel and a hearing before an impartial tribunal, that are present when a court or an agency adjudicates individual rights. The only effective constraint on Congress' power is political, but Congress is most accountable politically when it prescribes rules of general applicability. When it decides rights of specific persons, those rights are subject to "the tyranny of a shifting majority."

. . . In my view, when Congress undertook to apply its rules to Chadha, it exceeded the scope of its constitutionally prescribed authority. I would not reach the broader question whether legislative vetoes are invalid under the Presentment Clauses.

JUSTICE WHITE, dissenting.

Today the Court not only invalidates § 244(c)(2) of the Immigration and Nationality Act, but also sounds the death knell for nearly 200 other statutory provisions in which Congress has reserved a "legislative veto." For this reason, the Court's decision is of surpassing importance. And it is for this reason that the Court would have been well-advised to decide the case, if possible, on the narrower grounds of separation of powers, leaving for full consideration the constitutionality of other congressional review statutes operating on such varied matters as war powers and agency rulemaking, some of which concern the independent regulatory agencies.

The prominence of the legislative veto mechanism in our contemporary political system and its importance to Congress can hardly be overstated. It has·become a central means by which Congress secures the accountability of executive and independent agencies. Without the legislative veto, Congress is faced with a Hobson's choice: either to refrain from delegating the necessary authority, leaving itself with a hopeless task of writing laws with the requisite specificity to cover endless special circumstances across the entire policy landscape, or in the alternative, to abdicate its lawmaking function to the executive branch and independent agencies. To choose the former leaves major national problems unresolved; to opt for the latter risks unaccountable policymaking by those not elected to fill that role. Accordingly, over the past five decades, the legislative veto has been placed in nearly 200 statutes. The device is known in every field of governmental concern: reorganization, budgets, foreign affairs, war powers, and regulation of trade, safety, energy, the environment and the economy. . . .

Even this brief review suffices to demonstrate that the legislative veto is more than "efficient, convenient, and useful." It is an important if not indispensable political invention that allows the President and Congress to resolve major constitutional and policy differences, assures the accountability of independent regulatory agencies, and preserves Congress' control over lawmaking. Perhaps there are other means of accommodation and accountability, but the increasing reliance of Congress upon the legislative veto suggests that the alternatives to which Congress must now turn are not entirely satisfactory.

The history of the legislative veto also makes clear that it has not been a sword with which Congress has struck out to aggrandize itself at the expense of the other branches—the concerns of Madison and Hamilton. Rather, the veto has been a means of defense, a reservation of ultimate authority necessary if Congress is to fulfill its designated role under Article I as the nation's lawmaker. While the President has often objected to particular legislative vetoes, generally those left in the hands of congressional committees, the Executive has more often agreed to legislative review as the price for a broad delegation of authority. To be sure, the President may have preferred unrestricted power, but that could be precisely why Congress thought it essential to retain a check on the exercise of delegated authority. . . .

The Court holds that the disapproval of a suspension of deportation by the resolution of one House of Congress is an exercise of legislative power without compliance with the prerequisites for lawmaking set forth in Art. I of the Constitution. Specifically, the Court maintains that the provisions of § 244(c)(2) are inconsistent with the requirement of bicameral approval, implicit in Art. I, § 1, and the requirement that all bills and resolutions that require the concurrence of both Houses be presented to the President, Art. I, § 7, cl. 2 and 3.

I do not dispute the Court's truismatic exposition of these clauses. There is no question that a bill does not become a law until it is approved by both the House and the Senate, and presented to the President. Similarly, I would not hesitate to strike an action of Congress in the form of a concurrent resolution which constituted an exercise of original lawmaking authority. I agree with the Court that the President's qualified veto power is a critical element in the distribution of powers under the Constitution, widely endorsed among the Framers, and intended to serve the President as a defense against legislative encroachment and to check the "passing of bad laws through haste, inadvertence, or design." The Federalist No. 73, at 458 (A. Hamilton). The records of the Convention reveal that it is the first purpose which figured most prominently but I acknowledge the vitality of the second. *Id.,* at 443. I also agree that the bicameral approval required by Art. I, §§ 1, 7 "was of scarcely less concern to the Framers than was the Presidential veto," and that the need to divide and disperse legislative power figures significantly in our scheme of Government. All of this, the Third Part of the Court's opinion, is entirely unexceptionable.

It does not, however, answer the constitutional question before us. The power to exercise a legislative veto is not the power to write new law without bicameral approval or presidential consideration. The veto must be authorized by statute and may only negative what an Executive department or independent agency has proposed. On its face, the legislative veto no more allows one House of Congress to make law than does the presidential veto confer such power upon the President. Accordingly, the Court properly recognizes that it "must establish that the challenged action under § 244(c)(2) is of the kind to which the procedural requirements of Art. I, § 7 apply" and admits that "not every action taken by either House is subject to the bicameralism and presentation requirements of Art. I." . . .

It is long-settled that Congress may "exercise its best judgment in the selection of measures, to carry into execution the constitutional powers of the government," and "avail itself of experience, to exercise its reason, and to accommodate its legislation to circumstances." *McCulloch v. Maryland,* 4 Wheat. 316, 415–416, 420 (1819).

The Court heeded this counsel in approving the modern administrative state. The Court's holding today that all legislative-type action must be enacted through the lawmaking process ignores that legislative authority is routinely delegated to the Executive branch, to the independent regulatory agencies, and to private individuals and groups. . . .

This Court's decisions sanctioning such delegations make clear that Article I does not require all action with the effect of legislation to be passed as a law.

Theoretically, agencies and officials were asked only to "fill up the details," and the rule was that "Congress cannot delegate any part of its legislative power except under a limitation of a prescribed standard." . . .

If Congress may delegate lawmaking power to independent and executive agencies, it is most difficult to understand Article I as forbidding Congress from also reserving a check on legislative power for itself. Absent the veto, the agencies receiving delegations of legislative or quasi-legislative power may issue regulations having the force of law without bicameral approval and without the President's signature. It is thus not apparent why the reservation of a veto over the exercise of that legislative power must be subject to a more exacting test. In both cases, it is enough that the initial statutory authorizations comply with the Article I requirements.

Nor are there strict limits on the agents that may receive such delegations of legislative authority so that it might be said that the legislature can delegate authority to others but not to itself. While most authority to issue rules and regulations is given to the executive branch and the independent regulatory agencies, statutory delegations to private persons have also passed this Court's scrutiny. . . . [T]he Court's decision today suggests that Congress may place a "veto" power over suspensions of deportation in private hands or in the hands of an independent agency, but is forbidden from reserving such authority for itself. Perhaps this odd result could be justified on other constitutional grounds, such as the separation of powers, but certainly it cannot be defended as consistent with the Court's view of the Article I presentment and bicameralism commands. . . .

The Court also takes no account of perhaps the most relevant consideration: However resolutions of disapproval under § 244(c)(2) are formally characterized, in reality, a departure from the status quo occurs only upon the concurrence of opinion among the House, Senate, and President. Reservations of legislative authority to be exercised by Congress should be upheld if the exercise of such reserved authority is consistent with the distribution of and limits upon legislative power that Article I provides. . . .

The history of the Immigration Act makes clear that § 244(c)(2) did not alter the division of actual authority between Congress and the Executive. At all times, whether through private bills, or through affirmative concurrent resolutions, or through the present one-House veto, a permanent change in a deportable alien's status could be accomplished only with the agreement of the Attorney General, the House, and the Senate.

The central concern of the presentation and bicameralism requirements of Article I is that when a departure from the legal status quo is undertaken, it is done with the approval of the President and both Houses of Congress—or, in the event of a presidential veto, a two-thirds majority in both Houses. This interest is fully satisfied by the operation of § 244(c)(2). The President's approval is found in the Attorney General's action in recommending to Congress that the deportation order for a given alien be suspended. The House and the Senate indicate their approval of the Executive's action by not passing a resolution of disapproval within the statutory period. Thus, a change in the legal status quo—the deportability of the alien—is consummated only with the approval of each of the three relevant actors. The disagreement of any one of the three maintains the alien's pre-existing status: the Executive may choose not to recommend suspension; the House and Senate may each veto the recommendation. The effect on the rights and obligations of the affected individuals and upon the legislative system is precisely the same as if a private bill were introduced but failed to receive the necessary approval. . . .

It is true that the purpose of separating the authority of government is to prevent unnecessary and dangerous concentration of power in one branch. For that reason, the Framers saw fit to divide and balance the powers of government so that each branch would be checked by the others. Virtually every part of our constitutional system bears the mark of this judgment.

But the history of the separation of powers doctrine is also a history of accommodation and practicality. . . . The legislative veto provision does not "prevent the Executive Branch from accomplishing its constitutionally assigned functions." . . .

A legislative check on an inherently executive function, for example that of initiating prosecutions, poses an entirely different question. But the legislative veto device here—and in many other settings—is far from an instance of legislative tyranny over the Executive. It is a necessary check on the unavoidably expanding power of the agencies, both executive and independent, as they engage in exercising authority delegated by Congress.

I regret that I am in disagreement with my colleagues on the fundamental questions that this case presents. But even more I regret the destructive scope of the Court's holding. It reflects a profoundly different conception of the Constitution than that held by the Courts which sanctioned the modern administrative state. Today's decision strikes down in one fell swoop provisions in more laws enacted by Congress than the Court has cumulatively invalidated in its history. I fear it will now be more difficult "to insure that the fundamental policy decisions in our society will be made not by an appointed official but by the body immediately responsible to the people."

[Justice Rehnquist dissented, arguing that the suspension and veto provisions were not severable. Justice White agreed.]

Notes and Questions

1. *Use of the legislative veto.* As Justice White pointed out, Congress has used the legislative veto device in a wide variety of settings. The veto provision involved in *Chadha* was designed to provide a Congressional check on discretionary *adjudicative* action by the executive branch which favored deportable aliens. Justice Powell's opinion was limited to this form of legislative veto. Why would Congress insert a legislative veto in a provision granting such an adjudicative suspension power to the Attorney General?

Congress has frequently granted *rulemaking* power to an agency but retained a one- or two-house veto power over the resulting rules. For example, Congress empowered the Federal Trade Commission to adopt consumer protection rules but required that such rules be submitted to Congress. Such rules would become effective unless both Houses of Congress adopted a concurrent resolution (a resolution that is not submitted to the President for his approval or veto) disapproving the rule. In 1981 the FTC adopted a rule covering used car warranties, but Congress vetoed it. The Court of Appeals held that the legislative veto provision was invalid and a few weeks after deciding *Chadha* the Supreme Court summarily affirmed. *Consumers Union of United States v. FTC,* 691 F.2d 575 (D.C.Cir.1982), *aff'd,* 463 U.S. 1216 (1983). Accord: *Consumers Energy Council of America v. FERC,* 673 F.2d 425 (D.C.Cir.1982), *aff'd,* 463 U.S. 1216 (1983) (invalidating a statute which provided that rule would take effect only if, within 30 days, neither house of Congress adopted a resolution disapproving it).

Why would Congress insert legislative vetoes into rulemaking statutes? Do you agree with Justice White that the legislative veto is "an important if not indispensable political invention that allows the President and Congress to resolve major constitutional and policy differences, assures the accountability of independent regulatory agencies, and preserves Congress' control over lawmaking?"

In addition, Congress has used the legislative veto device in statutes which directly constrain Presidential action. For example, the War Powers Resolution of 1973 provides that the President must remove armed forces from hostilities outside the United States if Congress so directs by concurrent resolution. Pub.L. 93–148 § 5(c), 50 U.S.C. § 1544(c) (approved over Presidential veto). Similarly, a statute adopted in 1974 deals with Presidential refusals to spend appropriated funds. If the President proposes to defer the expenditure, either house may disapprove the deferral by adopting a simple resolution. Congressional Budget and Impoundment Control Act of 1974, Pub.L. 93–344 § 1013(b), 31 U.S.C. § 1403(b). Why would Congress seek to retain the power to veto Presidential warmaking or impoundment action?

2. *Distinguishing types of legislative vetoes.* Should the Supreme Court draw distinctions between the validity of different types of legislative veto statutes? For example, should a distinction be drawn

between the validity of statutes authorizing a legislative veto over agency adjudications and those authorizing such a veto over agency rules or over Presidential actions? Between statutes authorizing a one-house legislative veto and those authorizing a two-house veto? Between statutes authorizing a legislative committee veto and those authorizing a one- or two-house veto? Or between statutes authorizing a legislative veto whose only effect is to suspend agency action for a specified period, and those authorizing such a veto that would finally set aside or invalidate agency action?

3. *Rulemaking and the legislative veto.* *Chadha* holds that a legislative veto of the Attorney General's decision to suspend deportation is "legislation"—and invalid because of a failure to satisfy the bicameralism and presentment provisions of the United States Constitution. How does the Chief Justice define "legislation?" According to that definition, is administrative rulemaking also legislation and, therefore, invalid for the same reasons? How does the Chief Justice distinguish rulemaking from a legislative veto? Is the distinction convincing?

4. *Rulemaking and delegation.* Section 7.3, *supra,* discussed the problem of broad, standardless delegations of legislative power to agencies. Did the legislative veto solve this problem? Could the legislative veto be viewed as a means by which to legitimate such delegations because it provided a substitute for more specific legislative standards in the agency's enabling act? Or did the legislative veto simply encourage the enactment of statutes without adequate standards?

5. *After Chadha.* What sorts of controls may Congress retain over administrative rules? A statutory requirement would be constitutional if it only provided that an agency must notify Congress, or a specific committee of Congress, before or immediately after proposing a new rule, or before the effective date of a newly adopted rule. Such a notice procedure would enable members of Congress to take part in the notice and comment proceedings on the adoption of the rule by the agency, to take whatever informal actions they thought wise to influence the agency's action, or to prevent, alter, or cancel a new rule before it becomes effective by enacting a statute to that effect.

Would the Supreme Court uphold a statute providing that agency rules would not become effective until after they were presented to Congress and sustained by a concurrent resolution approved by both houses of Congress? Would the absence of presentment to the President of such a resolution create the same constitutional defect the Court found in *Chadha?* Would you favor such a provision as applied to all agencies or as applied to a particular agency, such as the Federal Trade Commission? Would such a provision be practicable? *See* Note, "*Chadha* and the Nondelegation Doctrine: Defining a Restricted Legislative Veto," 94 Yale L.J. 1493 (1985).

6. *Reverse legislation.* Congress may override a Presidential veto by a two-thirds vote. Would a scheme authorizing Congress to veto

agency action by a two-thirds vote of each house, without presentment to the President, be constitutional?

Recall that in *Chadha,* the alien was made deportable by a statute passed by both houses of Congress and signed by the President, and executed by the Immigration and Naturalization Service. When the Attorney General suspended that deportation, he altered the legal status quo initially established by the statute, *Chadha's* deportability; the House then vetoed the suspension—vetoed the alteration of the legal status quo by the Attorney General. Should the veto of the House have been upheld because it demonstrated that all three constituencies necessary to alter the legal status quo (the House, Senate, and President) did not concur in its alteration and, therefore, it was impermissible?

7. *Problem.* A statute allowed the President to reorganize executive branch functions by transferring them from one agency or department to another. The statute also provided that either house of Congress could veto reorganization plans by adopting a resolution to that effect. Under this power, the President, in 1978, transferred the power to enforce the Age Discrimination in Employment Act (ADEA) from the Department of Labor to the Equal Employment Opportunity Commission (EEOC). Congress carefully considered the merits of this transfer but did not veto it.

In 1985, the EEOC began investigating claims that Ojos Optical Co. had violated ADEA by refusing to hire persons because of their age. In pursuit of its investigation, the EEOC sought judicial enforcement of a subpoena against Ojos. Ojos argues that the court should not enforce the subpoena because the EEOC is not empowered to enforce ADEA. Spell out Ojos' argument. Should the court enforce the subpoena? *See Muller Optical Co. v. EEOC,* 743 F.2d 380 (6th Cir.1984).

A. BONFIELD, STATE ADMINISTRATIVE RULE MAKING
498–501 (1986)

[*Constitutionality of State Legislative Vetoes.*] [I]n two states some form of committee suspension device is clearly constitutional. Michigan and South Dakota are both unusual because those states have constitutional provisions expressly authorizing the suspension, by a designated legislative committee, of agency rules that the committee finds objectionable. It is also true that in Iowa [and Connecticut] legislative vetos of agency rules by means less than statutory are lawful. The constitution[s of these states] . . . expressly authorize . . . [their legislatures] to overcome an agency rule by a joint resolution. However, in the absence of a constitutional provision expressly authorizing such action, nonstatutory legislative vetoes or suspensions of particular agency rules are probably impermissible under most state constitutions. . . .

For instance, an Alaska statute authorizing the two houses of that state's legislature, acting on their own, to nullify an agency rule was declared invalid by the Alaska Supreme Court. [*State v. A.L.I.V.E. Voluntary*, 606 P.2d 769 (Alaska 1980).] The opinion of the court was based upon the provisions of the state constitution prescribing the mechanics of legislation. . . . Evident in the opinion was a concern that the nonstatutory mechanism for nullifying agency rules would denigrate the governor's constitutionally conferred veto power over legislation. The majority also rejected the argument that the legislature could condition its delegation of rule-making authority to agencies by reserving such a veto to itself. If the legislature sought to veto a particular agency rule by nonstatutory means, the legislature would be attempting to exercise executive power in violation of the separation of powers concept embedded in the Alaska Constitution.

Similarly, the Supreme Court of New Jersey . . . declared invalid a statute authorizing the state legislature, with certain narrow exceptions, to veto by a concurrent resolution of both houses "every rule hereafter proposed by a state agency." [*General Assembly of N.J. v. Byrne*, 448 A.2d 438, (N.J.1982). *See also State ex rel. Stephen v. Kansas House of Rep.*, 687 P.2d 622 (Kan.1984)]. The court held that such a "broad and absolute legislative veto" of state agency rules violated the separation of powers principle embedded in that state's constitution "by excessively interfering with the functions of the executive branch . . ., by impeding the Executive in its constitutional mandate to faithfully execute the law . . ., and by allowing the Legislature to effectively amend or repeal existing laws without participation by the Governor." In addition, the . . . court stated that such a two-house legislative veto of agency rules violated the state constitution's presentment clause. . . . The court emphasized, however, "that not every action by the Legislature requires a majority vote of both houses and presentment to the Governor." Therefore, in a companion case, the Supreme Court of New Jersey upheld a statute authorizing two houses of the legislature to veto certain actions of the New Jersey Building Authority "that require continuing budget appropriations by the Legislature." [*Enourato v. N.J. Bldg. Auth.*, 448 A.2d 449 (N.J.1982)]. The court stated that "[w]here legislative action is necessary to further a statutory scheme requiring cooperation between the two branches, and such action offers no substantial potential to interfere with exclusive executive functions or alter the statute's purposes, legislative veto power can pass [state] constitutional muster."

The West Virginia Supreme Court also voided a scheme purportedly authorizing the rules review committee of its legislature to invalidate, by its own action, otherwise lawful agency rules. [*State ex rel. Barker v. Manchin*, 279 S.E.2d 622 (W.Va.1981)]. Its decision rested on the separation of powers provisions of the West Virginia Constitution. Like the Alaska court, the West Virginia court stressed the fact that the legislature may take action having the effect of law only by the enactment of a statute. When the legislature purports to take action with the effect of law by nonstatutory means, the legislature acts as an administrative agency and improperly assumes powers entrusted exclusively to the executive branch of the government.

In an advisory opinion, the New Hampshire Supreme Court came to a similar conclusion. [*Opinion of the Justices,* 431 A.2d 783 (N.H.1981)]. It held that neither committees of the state's two legislative houses nor the president of the senate and speaker of the house could be authorized to veto permanently an agency rule. The court suggested, however, that the legislature could constitutionally authorize one of its committees to suspend a proposed agency rule during the period when the legislature was not in session, but only until a specified time after the legislature reconvened. It reasoned that the legislature may properly provide a mechanism to assure a reasonable opportunity to veto a newly adopted agency rule by statute before the rule actually takes effect.

On the other hand, the Supreme Court of Kentucky held invalid a provision of the statutes of that state authorizing a joint legislative committee to delay the effectiveness of any rule to which it objected for a period of up to 21 months. [*Legislative Research Com'n v. Brown,* 664 S.W.2d 907 (Ky.1984)]. The Kentucky court decided that this provision violated the state constitution for three reasons: It authorized a legislative body to encroach upon executive authority, it authorized action that was inconsistent with the separation of powers principle, and it was an undue delegation of legislative law-making authority to the committee.

Notes and Questions

1. *State courts and legislative vetoes.* Since each state supreme court is free to determine under its state constitution whether all or some types of legislative vetoes are unconstitutional, one cannot safely make blanket statements about the legality of all such devices in the states. As the prior excerpt indicates, however, the dominant movement in the states was clear, even before *Chadha.* In these state cases do you detect any theories, in addition to those relied upon in *Chadha,* to justify a holding that various types of legislative vetos are unconstitutional? If so, are these additional theories stronger or weaker than the theories relied upon in *Chadha* to reach that result? Do these state cases suggest any additional theories that might be used to support the constitutionality of some types of legislative vetos?

2. *State legislative committee vetoes.* Are there greater constitutional justifications for permitting state legislatures to authorize one of their committees to suspend an agency rule during the period in which the legislature is not in session than for permitting Congress to do so? What additional arguments may be made for the unconstitutionality of legislative vetoes exercised by legislative committees rather than by one or two houses of the legislature?

3. *State legislative vetoes and United States Constitution.* Does the federal Constitution contain any impediment to the adoption by the states of various kinds of legislative vetoes?

§ 7.5.4 OTHER LEGISLATIVE CONTROLS

Aside from amendment or repeal of substantive legislation or the legislative veto, what other techniques are available to Congress or a state legislature to control administrative agencies?

a. *Administrative Rules Review Committee.* Read 1981 MSAPA §§ 3–203, 3–204, establishing an Administrative Rules Review Committee (ARRC) to review state agency rules. During the last twenty or thirty years, most states have adopted formal continuing legislative oversight mechanisms to review the legality and desirability of agency rules. *See generally* A. Bonfield, STATE ADMINISTRATIVE RULE MAKING § 8.3.1 (1986); Levinson, "Legislative and Executive Veto of Rules of Administrative Agencies: Models and Alternatives," 24 Wm. & Mary L.Rev. 79 (1982).

These oversight functions are normally performed by special standing joint legislative committees whose sole function is to review the legality and desirability of the proposed and adopted rules of the many agencies of those states. Committees of this kind are typically authorized to hold public hearings on proposed or adopted agency rules, to advise agencies with respect to the committee's view of such rules, and to submit bills to the legislature to overcome by statute rules deemed by the committee to be unsound. These arrangements seem clearly to be constitutional under the relevant state constitutions.

As noted in the previous subsection, a few state legislatures have also authorized their ARRC to suspend, for a specified period, the effectiveness of proposed or adopted rules to which they object. In most of these states subsequent legislative action may extend the effect of the review committee's action or end its effect prematurely. Some states also control review committee discretion by limiting rule suspensions to that period during which the legislature is not in session, while others allow such committee suspensions at any time. Similarly, some states do not specify the particular grounds upon which a committee may suspend a rule, while others expressly enumerate specific criteria that must be met to justify a suspension. These provisions authorizing committee suspensions (or even vetoes) of agency rules have raised serious constitutional questions in the states.

Section 3–204(d) of the 1981 MSAPA contains a provision for legislative review of agency rules that is a compromise between the views of proponents and opponents of the legislative veto. Read § 3–204(d). On what grounds may the ARRC object to a rule under that provision? What is the legal effect of such an objection? Does the objection device present the same policy problems and constitutional questions as a legislative veto device?

Five states—Iowa, Montana, New Hampshire, North Dakota, and Vermont—have provisions similar to 1981 MSAPA § 3–204(d). The Comment to § 3–204(d) stresses that this device is not a legislative veto because it only authorizes the ARRC to "alter one aspect of the procedure by which *the legality of the rule will be finally determined by the courts.*" In light of the fact that the legislature has authority to allocate the burden of persuasion in civil litigation, the Comment argues that the shift in the burden of persuasion authorized by that provision is constitutional. Furthermore, the claim is made that it is "logical to shift to the agency the burden of demonstrating the validity of a rule in subsequent litigation when a more politically accountable and independent body [like the ARRC] objects thereto." The Comment also argues that the mere existence of § 3–204(d) will make agencies act more responsibly than otherwise, and that the actual use of that provision by the ARRC will induce agencies to withdraw or modify rules of "doubtful or clear illegality," thereby saving members of the public "the cost of complying with those rules or contesting them in the courts." This is said to be so because the shift in burden of persuasion that occurs after the filing of an objection under this provision will result in the invalidation of many rules of doubtful legality. *See, e.g., Schmitt v. Iowa Dept. of Soc. Ser.,* 263 N.W.2d 739 (Iowa 1978).

Do you agree with the above analysis of § 3–204(d)? *See generally* A. Bonfield, STATE ADMINISTRATIVE RULE MAKING § 8.3.3 (1986); Note "Legislative Review of Agency Rule–Making: Vermont's Antlerless Deer Hunting Regulation," 11 Vt.L.Rev. 105 (1986) (discussing whether Vermont's Legislative Committee on Administrative Rules properly objected to a rule issued by a board chosen by the governor).

Section 3–204(e) of the 1981 MSAPA authorizes the ARRC "to *require* an agency to publish notice of . . . [a] rule change recommended by [that] . . . committee as a proposed rule of the agency, and to conduct public proceedings thereon according to the [rule-making] provisions of [the 1981 MSAPA]." The Comment to that provision goes on to indicate its objectives:

> The purpose of this provision is to assure fully informed agency decision making on the subject of a committee recommendation. It also is geared to assure increased agency accountability to the public by focusing some of the same political pressures on the agency with respect to the subject at issue as are focused on the legislative process. Authorizing this legislative committee, on its own say so, to *require* an agency to initiate such rule making does not seem an undue legislative encroachment on lawful agency administrative initiatives in light of the express reservation in the last sentence of ultimate authority in the agency over whether it will finally adopt a proposed rule based upon a committee recommendation.

Is § 3–204(e) desirable?   Constitutional?

b. *Investigations and hearings.* The standing committees of Congress and of state legislatures engage in extensive oversight of agency activities. In the states with an ARRC, however, the oversight role of standing committees tends to be less important than the oversight role of the ARRC.

The many standing committees of Congress and state legislatures constantly investigate the manner in which agencies spend money as well as discharge their responsibilities. Thus they hold hearings, request agencies to furnish written reports or studies, and write committee reports. Inadequate legislative staffing and less professionalism in some state legislatures appears to make this form of oversight less effective in some states than at the federal level.

Why do you suppose Congress has not followed most state legislatures and created a *single* joint committee to review the proposed and adopted rules of *all* federal agencies? Is the present congressional system of parcelling out that function to the various subject matter committees a better approach?

It is helpful to separate the different functions of committees which may become involved in the oversight of agencies. The legislative committees of Congress are responsible for considering legislation in a particular area—such as commerce or energy or labor. These committees also supervise the administration of previously enacted legislation in those particular areas and the agencies which perform that administration. Thus a legislative committee engages in oversight of an agency's work in a variety of settings. The Government Affairs Committees (investigative committees) of both houses of Congress investigate a variety of government business. This sometimes includes examination of issues which involve administrative agencies.

Each year, an agency's budget request is scrutinized in hearings conducted by the Appropriations Committees of each house. Specialized subcommittees of the Appropriations Committees are expert in the work of each agency, and occasionally investigate the manner in which the agency is spending money, an inquiry which covers everything the agency does. Appropriation Committee hearings may well be the most potent and consistently effective form of oversight.

Finally, hearings conducted in connection with legislative confirmation of politically appointed personnel (such as agency heads) sometimes focus on policy issues and involve scrutiny of an agency's performance. This would be especially likely to occur if the individual is seeking reappointment to the job or is being promoted from the staff level to the agency head level.

In addition to committee investigations, legislative investigative agencies may be employed for oversight purposes. The federal General Accounting Office (GAO), headed by the Comptroller General, is an example of such a legislative agency. The GAO is concerned primarily with the efficiency of federal government operation and with the manner in which government funds are used. Much of its time is spent

in studying executive branch activities and evaluating particular programs. The GAO can launch an investigation on its own initiative or
at the request of a member of Congress or a committee. It has an
excellent reputation for objectivity and independence and its studies
are given careful attention.

Several states, including Hawaii, Iowa, and Nebraska, have also
created an office of ombudsman that is authorized to receive and
investigate citizen complaints about any state agency or aspect of the
state administrative process, and to make a report and recommendation
to the legislature and/or governor on such complaints. The office of
ombudsman may have various names, such as Ombudsman, Citizens'
Aide, or Public Counsel, and is usually located in the legislative branch.
See, e.g., Hawaii Rev.Stat. ch. 96 (1985) (Ombudsman); Code of Iowa ch.
601G (1987) (Citizens' Aide); Rev.Stat.Neb. § 81–8, 240–254 (1987) (Public Counsel). *See also* Gnaizda, "Californians Need an Ombudsman," 2
Calif. Lawyer 21 (1982). The most potent oversight weapon of this body
is usually publicity for its investigations and recommendations. In
some circumstances the office of ombudsman may be very effective in
securing individual justice and political accountability in the state
administrative process.

In connection with a legislative investigation, an agency may be
requested to furnish information or documents; if these are not forthcoming, the legislative committee or investigative agency sometimes
exercises its subpoena power to obtain documents which the agency
prefers not to disclose. The extent to which an agency can withhold
documents from the legislature, upon a claim of executive privilege,
remains unsettled.

Some legislative committee hearings draw the attention of print or
broadcast media and generate a great deal of publicity. Although most
hearings are conducted in a dignified manner, there are occasions in
which proceedings become quite adversary. At times, agency witnesses
are treated harshly and committee members seem more interested in
scoring political points than in obtaining information. Preparing for
legislative committee hearings, and actually testifying, often consumes
a substantial portion of the time of an agency head—sometimes to the
detriment of his or her other responsibilities.

c. *Funding.* Congress and state legislatures appropriate funds for
every unit of government—usually every year, although in some states
it occurs every other year. Consequently, the appropriation mechanism provides a convenient way to achieve legislative objectives without
altering the statutes which furnish authority to agencies. For example,
measures appropriating money to an agency sometimes contain provisions cutting the amount spent on one agency function while increasing
another—thus altering an agency's priorities. Similarly, an activity
can be deliberately underfunded, thus preventing effective enforcement.

Indeed, appropriation measures sometimes bar an agency from spending any money in carrying out a particular program or enforcing a particular regulation. Is this a good way for a legislature to make law? Is it an appropriate way to control agency action? *See* Kaiser, "Congressional Action to Overturn Agency Rules: Alternatives to the 'Legislative Veto'," 32 Admin.L.Rev. 667, 687–89 (1980).

Often, legislative action in the appropriation process falls short of the enactment of binding legislation. Instead, a committee report (or even a statement in committee or on the floor) will contain an admonition to the agency about how it should conduct its business. While not binding, such statements are likely to influence the persons responsible for spending the appropriated funds.

d. *Direct contacts.* Individual members of Congress and state legislatures consider that their responsibilities include making direct contacts with units of government that are causing problems for their constituents. For example, at the federal level, legislative staff members frequently contact the Veterans Administration or the Social Security Administration on behalf of constituents. For the most part, these contacts are relatively harmless requests by staff for "status reports" about pending matters or attempts to cut through red tape for a constituent who is inexperienced in dealing with bureaucracy. Responding to such requests, however, can consume a considerable portion of agency resources.

Legislators or members of their staff occasionally take part in pending rulemaking proceedings (either through submitting formal comments or by off-the-record contacts with the agency). Indeed, a legislator or staff member sometimes seeks to influence a pending matter such as an adjudication or a grantmaking decision. At that point, and especially if the participation is off-the-record, serious questions emerge concerning the propriety of such interference. *See* § 3.3.4, *supra.*

e. *Problem.* You are an administrative assistant to a newly elected state senator who belongs to the majority party. During the campaign, your boss promised to try to increase the regulation of insurance. She secured a position (as the most junior member) on the Banking Committee, which oversees the state Insurance Commissioner.

Although the Senator favors legislation which would prohibit auto insurance companies from charging premiums based on the auto owner's ZIP code, she lacks the votes to pass such legislation, much less to override a likely gubernatorial veto. She asks you what other legislative techniques are available by which this issue can be pressed.

§ 7.5.5 EXECUTIVE CONTROL OF AGENCY ACTION

Political control over agency action may also be exercised through oversight by the elected chief executive. Like legislative oversight, presidential and gubernatorial oversight can check discretionary activities of unelected agency heads so that the popular will prevails in the administrative process. Moreover, control by the chief executive of all agencies of government can minimize inconsistent administrative policies and facilitate the coordination of agency policies.

Executive control over agency action takes many forms. The President and Governor participate in the legislative process, including the approval of all agency enabling legislation and appropriations. Their vetoes are powerful tools with which to help shape legislation defining agency authority and priorities. The availability in many states of an item veto over appropriations gives the governor in those states an especially important role in limiting agency actions through control over their spending. The authority of the chief executive to appoint and discharge agency officials is also a potent power with which the President and Governor can control agency activities. In addition, various formal mechanisms for direct superintendance of agencies are vested in the chief executive by constitution and statute. For example, Article II, § 2 of the United States Constitution provides that the President "may require the Opinion, in writing, of the principal Officer in each of the executive Departments, upon any Subject relating to the Duties of their respective Offices." Similar provisions exist in many state constitutions.

This subsection discusses various formal mechanisms for extra-agency, executive oversight of agency rulemaking. There are no such mechanisms for control of agency policy made through case-by-case adjudication. What is the reason for that? Should such mechanisms be created? If so, in what form?

a. *Executive veto of rules.* The Governors of Hawaii, Nebraska, and Indiana are authorized by statute to veto agency rules. These provisions are silent with respect to the reasons that would justify such disapproval. Wyoming law allows the Governor to veto agency rules that are not within the legislative purpose or not adopted in compliance with applicable rulemaking procedure. Three additional states, Iowa, Louisiana, and Missouri, authorize their Governors to rescind or suspend agency rules after they become effective. *See* A. Bonfield, STATE ADMINISTRATIVE RULE MAKING 466–67 (1986).

1981 MSAPA § 3–202 follows the lead of these states by empowering the Governor to rescind or suspend a rule or to terminate any pending rulemaking proceeding, to the extent the agency involved would itself have had that authority. Before rescinding or suspending a rule, the Governor must follow MSAPA rulemaking procedures, but he or she may rescind or suspend a rule at any time and for any reason. Should § 3–202 have specified the particular grounds on which the Governor could act? Should it have limited the time within which he or she could rescind or suspend a rule to a specified period after its adoption? Does it make sense to require *the Governor* to employ usual rulemaking procedures to rescind or suspend a rule?

Would § 3–202 be constitutional as applied to a state agency explicitly created by the state constitution itself? Would it be valid with respect to a state agency which the legislature has made "independent?"

b. *Imposing a new vision.* Section 3–202 does not give the Governor any affirmative authority to adopt a new agency rule. It gives the Governor only a negative political check against unwise agency action. Is that a defect?

Every President and Governor attempts to assert control over the agencies of government in order to assure that they act in accordance with the policy views of the chief executive. After all, election of a new chief executive is presumably a mandate for that official to implement his or her executive policies after the election. Historically, this has proved difficult. There is great inertia in government and a President or Governor must often expend considerable resources to alter the course of agency administration and to change regulatory policy in a fundamental way. Remember that most of the work of government agencies is done by civil servants who are protected by civil service laws against discharge except for "good cause" which tends to be construed narrowly.

Career government employees tend to have strong opinions about how their agency should function. As you might expect, they are often personally committed to the agency's programs and, therefore, have a vested interest in maintaining the status quo. These career people have been doing their work a long time and they will be there doing it long after the current President or Governor has departed. Career civil servants tend to resist attempts to change regulatory policy in ways with which they fundamentally disagree.

In light of this, is a negative veto over proposed new rules of agencies, or even a power to rescind or suspend existing rules, enough to give the President and Governors the leverage they need to implement their policies? Should the chief executive also have authority to force agencies to adopt specified new rules?

c. *Executive review in California.* In California, the Office of Administrative Law (OAL), an executive-branch agency, is authorized to veto newly proposed or adopted agency rules and to rescind existing rules. A veto or rescission may occur if the rule was adopted without proper procedure or because it is ultra vires, unclear, inconsistent, duplicative of other rules, or unnecessary. An agency whose rule is vetoed or rescinded by the OAL may appeal to the Governor who has authority to override the OAL's action. Cal.Govt.Code §§ 11340.1–.3, 11349.1–.7 (West Supp.1985). *See* Starr, "California's New Office of Administrative Law and Other Amendments to the California APA: A Bureau to Curb Bureaucracy and Judicial Review, Too," 32 Admin.L. Rev. 713 (1980).

In light of the fact that OAL has a small staff and many rules to review, how can it determine whether an agency rule is "necessary?" Might the public interest be poorly served by having OAL second-guess an expert agency's decision that a rule is "necessary?" *See* Cohen,

"Regulatory Reform: Assessing the California Plan," 1983 Duke L.J. 231. Which approach to executive control of agency rulemaking do you prefer—1981 MSAPA § 3–202 or the California OAL scheme?

The latter has been criticized in relation to the former on five grounds. First, when it is compared to the new Model Act scheme, the California scheme appears to be too complex. Second, the California scheme, unlike that created by the MSAPA, vests review authority over agency rules in a body that is itself likely to become bureaucratic and is not sufficiently accountable to the people because it is not directly elected; the OAL, unlike the Governor, will also probably remain a low-visibility institution whose activities are not easily monitored by the general public. Third, by providing specific standards for executive review of agency rulemaking, the California statute, unlike the MSAPA provision, prevents an exercise of such authority for sound practical reasons other than those enumerated. Fourth, by allowing an agency authority to modify an adopted rule without resort to the entire rulemaking process, as a means of curing objections made by the OAL, the California statute may, in some instances, render the earlier process by which that rule was initially adopted by the agency entirely superfluous. Finally, in practice, the California scheme for executive review of rules is likely to be far more expensive than the MSAPA scheme. *See* A. Bonfield, STATE ADMINISTRATIVE RULE MAKING 475–76 (1986). Do you agree with these criticisms?

Note that the California OAL scheme also contains another feature that appears to be an inexpensive and useful mechanism with which citizens may seek to secure, through extra-agency executive review, agency compliance with applicable rulemaking procedures. Cal.Govt. Code § 11347.5 (West 1988 Supp.) authorizes the OAL to issue, in response to a request or on its own motion, a determination as to whether an agency "guideline, criterion, bulletin, manual, instruction, order, standard of general application, or other rule which has not been adopted as a regulation and filed with the Secretary of State pursuant to this chapter, is a regulation" subject to usual rulemaking procedures and, therefore, is invalid. Such a determination is to be widely publicized and is subject to judicial review. With some qualifications, the OAL determination is apparently to be considered by a court in any case where the court must determine the validity of that agency statement. The precise effect a court would give an OAL determination is unclear. However, courts may be inclined to give such a determination great weight in light of the special role of that office as defined by the legislature.

Note also that in Florida a hearing officer in the Division of Administrative Hearings is authorized to issue an order determining the validity of a rule in response to a complaint by an adversely affected party. Such an order is subject to judicial review in the same manner as other agency orders. Fla.Stat. § 120.54(4), .56 (1987). The constitutionality of such devices was considered in note 5, § 7.4, *supra*.

Are devices of this kind by which a person may seek a determination of the validity of a rule from an independent executive branch body outside of the issuing agency a desirable form of check on agency rulemaking? What are the limitations of these devices as a means of securing responsible agency rulemaking?

d. *Executive review in Arizona.* A scheme of review was created in Arizona wholly on the basis of the authority of the Governor. An Executive Order created a five member council to review the proposed rules issued by all agencies whose heads are appointed by the Governor. The Order requires these agencies to submit an analysis of all proposed rules, including a cost-benefit analysis and an economic impact statement, to the Council prior to the usual notice and comment period. The Council then reviews the rules and determines if their benefits outweigh their costs, if the rules are clearly and understandably written, and if they serve the public interest. The Council is authorized by the Executive Order to approve the rules or to return them to the agency for "revision or reconsideration." *See* Rose, "Executive Oversight of Rulemaking in Arizona: The Governor's Regulatory Review Council—The First Three Years," 1985 Ariz.St.L.J. 425, Appendix I at 469–70. Do you see any advantages or disadvantages in the Arizona scheme of executive review of agency rules as compared to the California OAL scheme or the 1981 MSAPA scheme?

e. *Federal Executive Order 12,291.* No statute vests in the President, or in any other federal executive official, general review authority over agency rules. Executive review of federal agency rules, therefore, is based entirely upon the constitutional authority of the President. The current federal scheme is based on Executive Order 12,291, issued by President Reagan early in his first term. This Order replaces a somewhat similar system of review created by an earlier Executive Order issued by President Carter.

Executive Order 12,291 was considered in § 6.5, *supra.* That section analyzed the Order as an essential step in rulemaking because it required agencies to engage in regulatory analysis (a form of cost-benefit calculation) before adopting certain rules. You should reconsider the Order now as a technique for executive control over the rulemaking process. Reread Executive Order 12,291.

Note that the legal basis for Executive Order 12,291 has never been squarely addressed by the courts. The preamble to the Order does little to clarify its legal status. Although Congress has considered the matter several times, no statute clearly permits or clearly prohibits the procedures or the substantive results prescribed in the Order.

What is the legal status of the Order? First, suppose that an environmental rule is based on a cost-benefit analysis, as required by the Order, and as permitted but not required by the underlying statute. However, it can be shown that the agency would have adopted a much more costly, but more protective, rule if OMB had not compelled a different result. Should a court set aside the rule?

Secondly, assume the converse situation. Suppose an agency head decides to flout the order by refusing to prepare a Regulatory Impact Analysis, or refusing to submit rules to OMB, before proposing or adopting a "major rule." Is the rule invalid?

In considering these issues, take into account the provisions of Article II of the United States Constitution. The "executive power shall be vested" in the President who "shall take care that the laws be faithfully executed." He "may require the Opinion, in writing, of the principal Officer in each of the executive Departments, upon any Subject relating to the Duties of their respective Offices."

Consider also *Youngstown Sheet & Tube Co. v. Sawyer,* 343 U.S. 579 (1952). *Youngstown* involved the legality of President Truman's seizure of the steel mills by an Executive Order for the purpose of preventing a strike during the Korean War. The Supreme Court held that this action was invalid.

The opinion for the Court by Justice Black took a straightforward approach to the separation of powers issue. He decided that the President's seizure was not authorized by statute and could not be justified by his independent constitutional powers as commander-in-chief or as chief executive. As a result, he concluded that the President's action was a legislative act (apparently because it created new legal rights and obligations) which exceeded his powers. 343 U.S. at 587–88. Under the Black approach, what would be your view of the legality of Executive Order 12,291?

The concurring opinion of Justice Jackson in the *Youngstown* case takes a more flexible view of the President's power and has received much subsequent support. Justice Jackson sketched three situations. In the first, the President acts pursuant to an express or implied authorization from Congress. As a result, his authority is at its maximum because his action is based on all the authority that he possesses in his own right plus all that Congress can delegate to him. In the second, the President acts in the absence of statutes supporting or prohibiting his action. Here the President can only rely on his own independent constitutional powers and, therefore, he has less authority than in the first situation. In the third, the President takes action that is inconsistent with express or implied will of Congress. In this situation his power is at its lowest ebb, for then he can rely only upon his own constitutional powers *minus* any constitutional power of Congress over the matter. 343 U.S. at 634–38.

The *Youngstown* case fit in Justice Jackson's third category because the President's action in that case was deemed to be inconsistent with a statute properly enacted by Congress pursuant to its constitutionally delegated powers. So even if the President might have had authority, in the circumstances, to seize the steel mills under his independent constitutional powers, the fact that Congress, pursuant to a constitutional grant of authority authorizing it to act on the same subject, prohibited him from doing so, was controlling. The Court apparently was of the view that when there is a conflict between Congress and the President with respect to matters over which they each have independent constitutional competence to act, the conflict should be resolved in favor of Congress. (The reason for this conclusion may be that Congress is more broadly representative than the President and the Constitution expressly provides that Congress may overcome a presidential veto.) A majority of the Court in *Youngstown* appears to have accepted this principle as the basis for its decision. 343 U.S. at 602 (Frankfurter), at 633 (Douglas), at 640 (Jackson), at 660 (Burton), and at 662 (Clark). Using Justice Jackson's approach, what is your conclusion about the legality of Executive Order 12,291?

Note that the federal Constitution contains clear separation of powers notions and that *The President* is vested with the authority to "take care that the laws are faithfully executed." Most state constitutions have separation of powers provisions that are even more explicit than that found in the United States Constitution, and many state constitutions expressly provide that the "*supreme* executive power of this state shall be vested in . . . the governor. . . ." (Emphasis supplied.)

In light of these federal and state constitutional provisions, may the President or the Governor veto proposed rules of their agencies or rescind or suspend their adopted rules, even if no statute authorizes them to take such action? May they do so even if a statute purports to vest final rulemaking authority in the agency issuing the rule? In other words, to what extent may the legislature effectively insulate, by statute, agency lawmaking from a veto, rescission, or suspension by the chief executive? Is the *Youngstown* case relevant to this question? May governors be given statutory authority to veto proposed rules or rescind adopted rules of state agencies that are directly created by the state constitution?

f. *Problem.* You are a member of the White House staff of a newly elected President. This President ran on a platform of reducing the burdens of regulation, making regulation more efficient, and generally getting the government "off the backs of the people" by getting rid of intrusive, costly, or unnecessary rules. In particular, he believes that various environmental, health, safety, and consumer protection rules have imposed costs on industry and consumers which considerably exceed their benefits. Short of seeking repeal or modification of the underlying statutes (for which he lacks the votes in Congress), what steps can the President take to carry out his campaign promises? Be sure to consider presidential control over appointments and personnel, the budget, and reorganization, as well as other presidential powers.

§ 7.5.6 EXECUTIVE OVERSIGHT AND THE APPOINTMENTS POWER

The President and governors indirectly control agency action and ensure that it is politically responsive by exercising their authority to appoint and discharge officials who execute the laws. This subsection considers the extent to which the chief executive is authorized to appoint and remove administrative officers, and the extent to which Congress or a state legislature may limit the exercise of that authority.

§ 7.5.6a *The Chief Executive's Appointment Power*

Article II, Section 2, Clause 2 of the United States Constitution provides that the President "shall nominate, and by and with the Advice and Consent of the Senate, shall appoint . . . Officers of the United States, whose Appointments are not herein otherwise provided for, and which shall be established by Law: but the Congress may by Law vest the Appointment of such inferior Officers, as they think proper, in the President alone, in the Courts of Law, or in the Heads of Departments."

State governors appoint most executive branch officers, some with and some without legislative confirmation. *See* Council of State Governments, 27 THE BOOK OF THE STATES 53–57 (1988). Other state executive branch officials are elected rather than appointed. The source of the governor's appointment power varies from state to state. Apparently, "most [state] constitutions allocate to the governor the power, in whole or in part, to appoint state officers." *See* T. Marks and J. Cooper, STATE CONSTITUTIONAL LAW § 28 at 62 (1988). In states where that is not the case, the appointment authority is usually vested in the chief executive by statute. However, when a state constitution does not expressly vest the appointment power in the governor, it is not always clear as a matter of state constitutional law whether that power impliedly resides in the governor or the legislature. *See* Dawley, "The Governors' Constitutional Power of Appointment and Removal," 22 Minn.L.Rev. 451, 452–454 (1938); *Leek v. Theis,* 539 P.2d 304, 315–320 (Kan.1975).

The chief executive's power to appoint administrative officials may be limited by the authority of the legislature to impose reasonable qualifications for such appointees. Congress and the state legislatures have often imposed such qualifications, and they have ordinarily been upheld. *See, e.g., Friedman v. Rogers,* 440 U.S. 1 (1979), (upholding a Texas statute requiring four members of a six-member state optometry board to be members of the Texas Optometric Association); *Humane Society v. State Fish and Game Council,* 362 A.2d 20 (N.J.1976), (upholding a statute requiring three members of the Council to be farmers, six to be sportsmen recommended for appointed by state federation of sportsmen's clubs, and two to be commercial fishermen). *See also Leek v. Theis, supra,* at 323, (stating that legislature has plenary authority to determine the qualifications for appointment to state offices).

On the other hand, in *Buckley v. Valeo,* 424 U.S. 1, 140–41 (1976), the United States Supreme Court held that the Federal Election Commission was invalidly constituted because its enabling act required four of its six members to be appointed by Congress (two by the Senate, two by the House). If the Commission had been engaged exclusively in performing functions such as investigation that facilitated legislation, its members could be appointed by Congress. But since the Commission was engaged in "the performance of a significant governmental duty exercised pursuant to a public law," that is, the administrative functions of rulemaking, adjudication, and law enforcement, its members were "Officers of the United States" who could be appointed only by the President according to the Appointments Clause of Article II, Section 2. Consequently, the Commission could not perform these administrative functions unless Congress restructured that body by providing for exclusively presidential appointments. The Court's opinion appears to suggest that separation of powers notions are embedded in the Appointments Clause and that the Clause was intended to ensure that officials engaged in administrative functions would be appointed by the chief executive rather than by the legislature.

More recently, *Morrison v. Olson,* 108 S.Ct. 2597 (1988), upheld a statute creating a special court that was authorized, in specified circumstances, to appoint an independent counsel to investigate and prosecute potential violations of federal law by certain high ranking government officials. The opinion of the Supreme Court, joined by seven Justices, noted that the appointments clause divides "Officers of the United States" into two categories—principal officers that must be selected by the President with the advise and consent of the Senate, and inferior officers which Congress may allow to be appointed by "the President alone, [by] the Courts of Law, or [by] . . . the Heads of Departments." The Court admitted that the line between principal and inferior officers was far from clear. Nevertheless, the Court concluded that the status of the independent counsel was clear: that official was an inferior officer because she was subject to removal by a higher executive branch officer, she was empowered to perform only limited duties and had limited jurisdiction, and her position was temporary. Furthermore, in light of the explicit language of the Appointments Clause authorizing Congress to vest appointments of inferior officers in the "Courts of Law," nothing in the Clause prevented Congress from authorizing the *courts* to appoint inferior *executive* officers.

The opinion of the Court in *Morrison* stressed, however, that the power of Congress to provide for judicial appointments of inferior executive officers was not unlimited. It was clear that " 'incongruous' interbranch appointments" by the courts were prohibited by the Constitution. But there was nothing incongruous about the appointment of the independent counsel by a special court in light of the fact that the special court was ineligible to participate in matters relating to the subsequent work of that counsel, and the purpose of the counsel was to avoid "the conflicts of interest that could arise in situations where the Executive Branch is called upon to investigate its own high ranking officers." As a result, the Supreme Court held that the statute authorizing appointment by a special court of an independent counsel exercising limited executive functions for the specified purpose was not inconsistent with the Appointments Clause.

Justice Scalia dissented on the ground that the independent counsel was not an inferior officer and, therefore, had to be appointed by the President. He found the justifications advanced in the majority opinion for classifying the independent counsel as an inferior officer wholly inadequate. On the basis of an analysis of the status and powers of that officer Scalia concluded that she could not be an inferior officer because she was "*independent* of, not *subordinate* to, the President and the Attorney General." (Other aspects of the *Morrison* case are addressed in § 7.5.6b, *infra.*)

Could the Court in *Morrison* have read the language of the appointments clause in a way that would have *denied* Congress authority to vest the power to appoint inferior *executive* officers in the courts? Should the court have read the Appointments Clause in that way if it was possible to do so? Is the power of Congress to authorize courts to appoint executive officers a greater or lesser threat to executive authority than a power of Congress to appoint or require the appointment of legislators as executive officers? As noted earlier, *Buckley v. Valeo* held that the latter was impermissible under the federal Constitution.

Most state cases appear to agree with *Buckley v. Valeo* and hold that the separation of powers provision of their state constitution prohibits the legislature from appointing or requiring the appointment of legislators to state administrative bodies. For example, in *State ex rel. Wallace v. Bone,* 286 S.E.2d 79 (N.C.1982), the North Carolina Supreme Court held unconstitutional a state statute providing that two members of the State Environmental Management Commission would be appointed by the Speaker of the House from among its membership and two members would be appointed by the President of the Senate from among its membership. The Court noted that the duties of the Commission were administrative or executive in character and had no relation to the function of the legislative branch. The Court was clear that the legislature could not enact a law and then retain some control over the implementation of that law by appointing legislators to the agency charged with its administration. *Accord: Book v. State Office Building Com'n,* 149 N.E.2d 273 (Ind.1958); *Greer v. State of Georgia,* 212 S.E.2d 836 (Ga.1975).

On the other hand, in *State ex rel. Schneider v. Bennett,* 547 P.2d 786 (Kan.1976), the court concluded that the separation of powers doctrine does not, in all cases, bar members of the legislature from serving on administrative bodies. Legislators may serve on administrative bodies "where such service falls in the realm of cooperation on the part of the legislature and there is no attempt to usurp functions of the executive department." Legislative participation on such bodies violates the separation of powers doctrine only when that participation causes a "significant interference" with the operations of the executive branch. Four factors should be considered in determining whether the service of legislators on an agency governing body is invalid on that basis: 1) the nature of the powers being exercised by the agency; 2) the degree of control the appointed legislators may exercise over those powers; 3) the nature and importance of the objectives sought by the appointment of legislators to the position in question; and 4) the practical results of this blending of legislative and administrative powers. 547 P.2d at 792.

However, in *Bennett* the court held that the legislature could not authorize the State Finance Council, which had several legislator members, to supervise the day-to-day operations of the Department of Administration. The presence of legislators on a body with such authority amounted to a legislative usurpation of executive power. This was so because the Finance Council could approve, modify, or reject rules of the Department of Administration (a super-agency that coordinated and supervised the activities of other state agencies), thereby giving the legislature coercive control over the operations of the executive branch. 547 P.2d 797–98. But another state case concluded that legislators could be appointed to an administrative body in a situation where the designated legislators constituted only a minority of the membership of the administrative body, and their membership could be viewed as cooperation with the executive on matters related to legislative functions rather than as a legislative attempt to usurp functions belonging only to the executive department. *State ex rel. McLeod v. Edwards,* 236 S.E.2d 406 (S.C.1977).

The *Bennett* case suggests that legislative action causing a significant interference with the operations of the executive branch violates the separation of powers provision of the state constitution. Consider the four part *Bennett* test for determining significant interference in relation to the constitutionality of various state schemes for the legislative review of rules. On the basis of that test, which state schemes for the legislative review of agency rules violate the separation of powers provisions of state constitutions, and which do not?

§ 7.5.6b *The Chief Executive's Discharge Power*

The language of the federal Constitution does not expressly indicate whether Congress may impose a limit on the President's power to discharge his appointees. The subject was debated in the first Congress, in the context of legislation which created the position of Secretary of State. Apparently, the sense of Congress in 1789 was that the President could remove the Secretary of State whether Congress gave him removal power or not.

The view that Congress could not prevent the President from removing at will the principal officers of government was challenged by the 1867 Tenure of Office Act. This statute forbade presidential removal of designated cabinet members without the consent of the Senate. President Andrew Johnson dismissed the Secretary of War, in violation of the Tenure of Office Act. That action led to the President's impeachment by the House; but the Senate failed to convict him by a single vote.

The Supreme Court was not called upon to decide whether the Tenure of Office Act was constitutional until *Myers v. United States,* 272 U.S. 52 (1926). The issue arose in connection with a suit for backpay by a postmaster in Oregon whom President Wilson had discharged without cause. The discharge violated a statute (passed a few years after the Tenure of Office Act) which required the consent of the Senate for the appointment and also for the suspension or removal of a postmaster.

Chief Justice Taft (who had earlier been President) indicated that Congress could not limit the President's removal power over any officer of the United States. Consequently, both the Tenure of Office Act (which had long since been repealed) and the statute relating to postmasters were invalid. In part, this holding was grounded on a reading of the appointments clause. Because that clause explicitly gave the Senate a role in appointments, the Court concluded that it was intended to negative any role for Congress in removals. More significantly, the holding was based on the President's duty to ensure that the laws "be faithfully executed." Since that duty was vested in *the President* by the Constitution, and he needed the help of other officials to secure its performance, the President necessarily must be authorized to fire at will any of those officials so that his power would be commensurate with his responsibility. 272 U.S. at 117, 163–64.

MORRISON v. OLSON
108 S.Ct. 2597 (1988).

[The 1978 Ethics in Government Act created a special court (the Special Division) that was authorized, in specified circumstances, to appoint an independent counsel to investigate and prosecute potential violations of federal law by certain high ranking government officials. The Act provided that the Attorney General could remove the independent counsel, but only for "good cause." Following all of the procedures outlined in the Act, Morrison was appointed independent counsel. A motion was made to quash certain subpoenas issued by a grand jury at the request of Morrison on the ground that the Act creating the office of independent counsel was unconstitutional and, therefore, that she had no authority to proceed. The District Court held the Act constitutional. The Court of Appeals reversed, holding that it violated the Appointments Clause and the principle of separation of powers. The Appointments Clause aspects of this case were discussed in § 7.5.6a, *supra.* Seven members of the Supreme Court joined in an opinion by REHNQUIST, C.J.:]

We now turn to consider whether the Act is invalid under the constitutional principle of separation of powers. [The question] is whether the provision of the Act restricting the Attorney General's power to remove the independent counsel to only those instances in which he can show "good cause," taken by itself, impermissibly inter-feres with the President's exercise of his constitutionally appointed functions. . . .

Two Terms ago we had occasion to consider whether it was consis-tent with the separation of powers for Congress to pass a statute that authorized a government official who is removable only by Congress to participate in what we found to be "executive powers." *Bowsher v. Synar,* 478 U.S. 714, 730 (1986). We held in *Bowsher* that "Congress cannot reserve for itself the power of removal of an officer charged with the execution of the laws except by impeachment." A primary antece-dent for this ruling was our 1925 decision in *Myers v. United States,* 272 U.S. 52 (1926). *Myers* had considered the propriety of a federal statute by which certain postmasters of the United States could be removed by the President only "by and with the advice and consent of the Senate." There too, Congress' attempt to involve itself in the removal of an executive official was found to be sufficient grounds to render the statute invalid. As we observed in *Bowsher,* the essence of the decision in *Myers* was the judgment that the Constitution prevents Congress from "draw[ing] to itself . . . the power to remove or the right to participate in the exercise of that power. To do this would be to go beyond the words and implications of the [Appointments Clause] and to infringe the constitutional principle of the separation of governmental powers."

Unlike both *Bowsher* and *Myers,* this case does not involve an attempt by Congress itself to gain a role in the removal of executive officials other than its established powers of impeachment and convic-tion. The Act instead puts the removal power squarely in the hands of the Executive Branch; an independent counsel may be removed from office "only by the personal action of the Attorney General, and only for good cause."]There is no requirement of congressional approval of the Attorney General's removal decision, though the decision is subject to judicial review.7 In our view, the removal provisions of the Act make this case more analogous to *Humphrey's Executor v. United States,* 295 U.S. 602 (1935), and *Wiener v. United States,* 357 U.S. 349 (1958), than to *Myers* or *Bowsher.*

In *Humphrey's Executor,* the issue was whether a statute restrict-ing the President's power to remove the commissioners of the Federal Trade Commission only for "inefficiency, neglect of duty, or malfea-sance in office" was consistent with the Constitution. We stated that whether Congress can "condition the [President's power of removal] by fixing a definite term and precluding a removal except for cause, will depend upon the character of the office." Contrary to the implication of some dicta in *Myers,* the President's power to remove government officials simply was not "all-inclusive in respect of civil officers with the exception of the judiciary provided for by the Constitution." At least in regard to "quasi-legislative" and "quasi-judicial" agencies such as the FTC, "[t]he authority of Congress, in creating [such] agencies, to require them to act in discharge of their duties independently of executive control . . . includes, as an appropriate incident, power to fix the period during which they shall continue in office, and to forbid their removal except for cause in the meantime." In *Humphrey's Executor,* we found it "plain" that the Constitution did not give the President "illimitable power of removal" over the officers of independent agencies. Were the President to have the power to remove FTC commissioners at will, the "coercive influence" of the removal power would "threate[n] the independence of [the] commission."

Similarly, in *Wiener* we considered whether the President had unfettered discretion to remove a member of the War Claims Commission, which had been established by Congress in the War Claims Act of 1948. The Commission's function was to receive and adjudicate certain claims for compensation from those who had suffered personal injury or property damage at the hands of the enemy during World War II. Commissioners were appointed by the President, with the advice and consent of the Senate, but the statute made no provision for the removal of officers, perhaps because the Commission itself was to have a limited existence. As in *Humphrey's Executor,* however, the Commissioners were entrusted by Congress with adjudicatory powers that were to be exercised free from executive control. In this context, "Congress did not wish to have hang over the Commission the Damocles' sword of removal by the President for no reason other than that he preferred to have on that Commission men of his own choosing." Accordingly, we rejected the President's attempt to remove a Commissioner "merely because he wanted his own appointees on [the] Commission," stating that "no such power is given to the President directly by the Constitution, and none is impliedly conferred upon him by statute."

Appellees contend that *Humphrey's Executor* and *Wiener* are distinguishable from this case because they did not involve officials who performed a "core executive function." They argue that our decision in *Humphrey's Executor* rests on a distinction between "purely executive" officials and officials who exercise "quasi-legislative" and "quasi-judicial" powers. In their view, when a "purely executive" official is involved, the governing precedent is *Myers,* not *Humphrey's Executor.* And, under *Myers,* the President must have absolute discretion to discharge "purely" executive officials at will.

We undoubtedly did rely on the terms "quasi-legislative" and "quasi-judicial" to distinguish the officials involved in *Humphrey's Executor* and *Wiener* from those in *Myers,* but our present considered view is that the determination of whether the Constitution allows Congress to impose a "good cause"-type restriction on the President's power to remove an official cannot be made to turn on whether or not that official is classified as "purely executive." The analysis contained in our removal cases is designed not to define rigid categories of those officials who may or may not be removed at will by the President, but to ensure that Congress does not interfere with the President's exercise of the "executive power" and his constitutionally appointed duty to "take care that the laws be faithfully executed" under Article II. *Myers* was undoubtedly correct in its holding, and in its broader suggestion that there are some "purely executive" officials who must be removable by the President at will if he is to be able to accomplish his constitutional role. But as the Court noted in *Wiener,*

> "The assumption was short-lived that the *Myers* case recognized the President's inherent constitutional power to remove officials no matter what the relation of the executive to the discharge of their duties and no matter what restrictions Congress may have imposed regarding the nature of their tenure."

At the other end of the spectrum from *Myers,* the characterization of the agencies in *Humphrey's Executor* and *Wiener* as "quasi-legislative" or "quasi-judicial" in large part reflected our judgment that it was not essential to the President's proper execution of his Article II powers that these agencies be headed up by individuals who were removable at will. We do not mean to suggest that an analysis of the functions served by the officials at issue is irrelevant. But the real question is whether the removal restrictions are of such a nature that they impede the President's ability to perform his constitutional duty, and the functions of the officials in question must be analyzed in that light.

Considering for the moment the "good cause" removal provision in isolation from the other parts of the Act at issue in this case, we cannot say that the imposition of a "good cause" standard for removal by itself unduly trammels on executive authority. There is no real dispute that the functions performed by the independent counsel are "executive" in the sense that they are law enforcement functions that typically have been undertaken by officials within the Executive Branch. As we noted above, however, the independent counsel is an inferior officer under the Appointments Clause, with limited jurisdiction and tenure and lacking policymaking or significant administrative authority. Although the counsel exercises no small amount of discretion and judgment in deciding how to carry out her duties under the Act, we simply do not see how the President's need to control the exercise of that discretion is so central to the functioning of the Executive Branch as to require as a matter of constitutional law that the counsel be terminable at will by the President.[31]

Nor do we think that the "good cause" removal provision at issue here impermissibly burdens the President's power to control or supervise the independent counsel, as an executive official, in the execution of her duties under the Act. This is not a case in which the power to

---

31. We note by way of comparison that various federal agencies whose officers are covered by "good cause" removal restrictions exercise civil enforcement powers that are analogous to the prosecutorial powers wielded by an independent counsel. See, *e.g.,* 15 U.S.C. § 45(m) (giving the FTC the authority to bring civil actions to recover civil penalties for the violations of rules respecting unfair competition); 15 U.S.C. §§ 2061, 2071, 2076(b)(7)(A) (giving the Consumer Product Safety Commission the authority to obtain injunctions and apply for seizure of hazardous products).

remove an executive official has been completely stripped from the President, thus providing no means for the President to ensure the "faithful execution" of the laws. Rather, because the independent counsel may be terminated for "good cause," the Executive, through the Attorney General, retains ample authority to assure that the counsel is competently performing her statutory responsibilities in a manner that comports with the provisions of the Act.[32] Although we need not decide in this case exactly what is encompassed within the term "good cause" under the Act, the legislative history of the removal provision also makes clear that the Attorney General may remove an independent counsel for "misconduct." Here, as with the provision of the Act conferring the appointment authority of the independent counsel on the special court, the congressional determination to limit the removal power of the Attorney General was essential, in the view of Congress, to establish the necessary independence of the office. We do not think that this limitation as it presently stands sufficiently deprives the President of control over the independent counsel to interfere impermissibly with his constitutional obligation to ensure the faithful execution of the laws.

The final question to be addressed is whether the Act, taken as a whole, violates the principle of separation of powers by unduly interfering with the role of the Executive Branch. Time and again we have reaffirmed the importance in our constitutional scheme of the separation of governmental powers into the three coordinate branches. . . . As we stated in *Buckley v. Valeo,* 424 U.S. 1 (1976), the system of separated powers and checks and balances established in the Constitution was regarded by the Framers as "a self-executing safeguard against the encroachment or aggrandizement of one branch at the expense of the other." We have not hesitated to invalidate provisions of law which violate this principle. On the other hand, we have never held that the Constitution requires that the three Branches of Government "operate with absolute independence." *United States v. Nixon,* 418 U.S., at 707. . . . In the often-quoted words of Justice Jackson,

> "While the Constitution diffuses power the better to secure liberty, it also contemplates that practice will integrate the dispersed powers into a workable government. It enjoins upon its branches separateness but interdependence, autonomy but reciprocity." *Youngstown Sheet & Tube Co. v. Sawyer,* 343 U.S. 579, 635 (1952) (concurring opinion).

We observe first that this case does not involve an attempt by Congress to increase its own powers at the expense of the Executive

---

32. Indeed, during the hearings on the 1982 amendments to the Act, a Justice Department official testified that the "good cause" standard contained in the amendments "would make the special prosecutor no more independent than officers of the many so-called independent agencies in the executive branch." Ethics in Government Act Amendments of 1982, Hearing before the Subcommittee on Oversight of Government Management of the Senate Committee on Governmental Affairs, 97th Cong., 2d Sess., 7 (1981) (Associate Attorney General Giuliani).

Branch. Cf. *Commodity Futures Trading Comm'n v. Schor,* 478 U.S., at 856. Unlike some of our previous cases, most recently *Bowsher v. Synar,* this case simply does not pose a "dange[r] of congressional usurpation of Executive Branch functions." Indeed, with the exception of the power of impeachment—which applies to all officers of the United States—Congress retained for itself no powers of control or supervision over an independent counsel. The Act does empower certain members of Congress to request the Attorney General to apply for the appointment of an independent counsel, but the Attorney General has no duty to comply with the request, although he must respond within a certain time limit. Other than that, Congress' role under the Act is limited to receiving reports or other information and oversight of the independent counsel's activities, § 595(a), functions that we have recognized generally as being incidental to the legislative function of Congress.

Similarly, we do not think that the Act works any *judicial* usurpation of properly executive functions. As should be apparent from our discussion of the Appointments Clause above, the power to appoint inferior officers such as independent counsels is not in itself an "executive" function in the constitutional sense, at least when Congress has exercised its power to vest the appointment of an inferior office in the "courts of Law." We note nonetheless that under the Act the Special Division has no power to appoint an independent counsel *sua sponte*; it may only do so upon the specific request of the Attorney General, and the courts are specifically prevented from reviewing the Attorney General's decision not to seek appointment. In addition, once the court has appointed a counsel and defined her jurisdiction, it has no power to supervise or control the activities of the counsel. . . . The Act does give a federal court the power to review the Attorney General's decision to remove an independent counsel, but in our view this is a function that is well within the traditional power of the judiciary.

Finally, we do not think that the Act "impermissibly undermine[s]" the powers of the Executive Branch, or "disrupts the proper balance between the coordinate branches [by] prevent[ing] the Executive Branch from accomplishing its constitutionally assigned functions." It is undeniable that the Act reduces the amount of control or supervision that the Attorney General and, through him, the President exercises over the investigation and prosecution of a certain class of alleged criminal activity. The Attorney General is not allowed to appoint the individual of his choice; he does not determine the counsel's jurisdiction; and his power to remove a counsel is limited. Nonetheless, the Act does give the Attorney General several means of supervising or controlling the prosecutorial powers that may be wielded by an independent counsel. Most importantly, the Attorney General retains the power to remove the counsel for "good cause," a power that we have already concluded provides the Executive with substantial ability to ensure that the laws are "faithfully executed" by an independent counsel. No independent counsel may be appointed without a specific request by the Attorney General, and the Attorney General's decision not to request appointment if he finds "no reasonable grounds to believe that further investigation is warranted" is committed to his unreviewable discretion. The Act thus gives the Executive a degree of control over the power to initiate an investigation by the independent counsel. In addition, the jurisdiction of the independent counsel is defined with reference to the facts submitted by the Attorney General, and once a counsel is appointed, the Act requires that the counsel abide by Justice Department policy unless it is not "possible" to do so. Notwithstanding the fact that the counsel is to some degree "independent" and free from Executive supervision to a greater extent than other federal prosecutors, in our view these features of the Act give the Executive Branch sufficient control over the independent counsel to ensure that the President is able to perform his constitutionally assigned duties.

In sum, we conclude today that . . . the Act does not violate the separation of powers principle by impermissibly interfering with the functions of the Executive Branch. The decision of the Court of Appeals is therefore

Reversed.

JUSTICE SCALIA, dissenting.

[Justice Scalia emphasized that in separation of powers disputes between Congress and the President, neither can be presumed to be correct. Then he stressed that Article II, § 1, Cl. 1 of the Constitution vests the executive power in *the President*. His dissent continued:]

As I described at the outset of this opinion, this does not mean *some of* the executive power, but *all of* the executive power. It seems to me, therefore, that the decision of the Court of Appeals invalidating the present statute must be upheld on fundamental separation-of-powers principles if the following two questions are answered affirmatively: (1) Is the conduct of a criminal prosecution (and of an investigation to decide whether to prosecute) the exercise of purely executive power? (2) Does the statute deprive the President of the United States of exclusive control over the exercise of that power? Surprising to say, the Court appears to concede an affirmative answer to both questions, but seeks to avoid the inevitable conclusion that since the statute vests some purely executive power in a person who is not the President of the United States it is void.

The Court concedes that "[t]here is no real dispute that the functions performed by the independent counsel are 'executive'." . . . There is no possible doubt that the independent counsel's functions fit this description. She is vested with the "full power and independent authority to exercise all *investigative and prosecutorial* functions and powers of the Department of Justice [and] the Attorney General." Governmental investigation and prosecution of crimes is a quintessentially executive function.

As for the second question, whether the statute before us deprives the President of exclusive control over that quintessentially executive activity: The Court does not, and could not possibly, assert that it does not. That is indeed the whole object of the statute. Instead, the Court points out that the President, through his Attorney General, has at least *some* control. That concession is alone enough to invalidate the statute, but I cannot refrain from pointing out that the Court greatly exaggerates the extent of that "some" presidential control. "Most importan[t]" among these controls, the Court asserts, is the Attorney General's "power to remove the counsel for 'good cause.'" This is somewhat like referring to shackles as an effective means of locomotion. As we recognized in *Humphrey's Executor v. United States,* 295 U.S. 602 (1935)—indeed, what *Humphrey's Executor* was all about— limiting removal power to "good cause" is an impediment to, not an effective grant of, presidential control. We said that limitation was necessary with respect to members of the Federal Trade Commission, which we found to be "an agency of the legislative and judicial departments," and "wholly disconnected from the executive department," because "it is quite evident that one who holds his office only during the pleasure of another, cannot be depended upon to maintain an attitude of independence against the latter's will." What we in *Humphrey's Executor* found to be a means of eliminating presidential control, the Court today considers the "most importan[t]" means of assuring presidential control. Congress, of course, operated under no such illusion when it enacted this statute, describing the "good cause" limitation as "protecting the independent counsel's ability to act independently of the President's direct control" since it permits removal only for "misconduct."

Moving on to the presumably "less important" controls that the President retains, the Court notes that no independent counsel may be appointed without a specific request from the Attorney General. As I have discussed above, the condition that renders such a request mandatory (inability to find "no reasonable grounds to believe" that further investigation is warranted) is so insubstantial that the Attorney General's discretion is severely confined. And once the referral is made, it is for the Special Division to determine the scope and duration of the investigation. And in any event, the limited power over referral is irrelevant to the question whether, *once appointed,* the independent counsel exercises executive power free from the President's control. Finally, the Court points out that the Act directs the independent counsel to abide by general Justice Department policy, except when not "possible." The exception alone shows this to be an empty promise. . . . Almost all investigative and prosecutorial decisions—including the ultimate decision whether, after a technical violation of the law has been found, prosecution is warranted—involve the balancing of innumerable legal and practical considerations. Indeed, even political considerations (in the nonpartisan sense) must be considered, as exemplified by the recent decision of an independent counsel to subpoena the former Ambassador of Canada, producing considerable tension in our relations with that country. . . . In sum, the balancing of various legal, practical and political considerations, none of which is absolute, is the very essence of prosecutorial discretion. To take this away is to remove the core of the prosecutorial function, and not merely "some" presidential control.

As I have said, however, it is ultimately irrelevant *how much* the statute reduces presidential control. The case is over when the Court acknowledges, as it must, that "[i]t is undeniable that the Act reduces the amount of control or supervision that the Attorney General and, through him, the President exercises over the investigation and prosecution of a certain class of alleged criminal activity." It effects a revolution in our constitutional jurisprudence for the Court, once it has determined that (1) purely executive functions are at issue here, and (2) those functions have been given to a person whose actions are not fully within the supervision and control of the President, nonetheless to proceed further to sit in judgment of whether "the President's need to control the exercise of [the independent counsel's] discretion is *so central* to the functioning of the Executive Branch" as to require complete control (emphasis added), whether the conferral of his powers upon someone else "*sufficiently* deprives the President of control over the independent counsel to interfere impermissibly with [his] constitutional obligation to ensure the faithful execution of the laws," (emphasis added), and whether "the Act give[s] the Executive Branch *sufficient* control over the independent counsel to ensure that the President is able to perform his constitutionally assigned duties," (emphasis added). It is not for us to determine, and we have never presumed to determine, how much of the purely executive powers of government must be within the full control of the President. The Constitution prescribes that they *all* are. . . . We should say here that the President's constitutionally assigned duties include *complete* control over investigation and prosecution of violations of the law, and that the inexorable command of Article II is clear and definite: the executive power must be vested in the President of the United States. . . .

The Court has, nonetheless, replaced the clear constitutional prescription that the executive power belongs to the President with a "balancing test." What are the standards to determine how the balance is to be struck, that is, how much removal of presidential power is too much? . . . Having abandoned as the basis for our decisionmaking the text of Article II that "the executive Power" must be vested in the President, the Court does not even attempt to craft a *substitute* criterion—a "justiciable standard," however remote from the Constitution—that today governs, and in the future will govern, the decision of such questions. . . .

There is of course no provision in the Constitution stating who may remove executive officers, except the provisions for removal by impeachment. Before the present decision it was established, however, (1) that the President's power to remove principal officers who exercise purely executive powers could not be restricted, see *Myers v. United States,* and (2) that his power to remove inferior officers who exercise purely executive powers, and whose appointment Congress had removed from the usual procedure of presidential appointment with Senate consent, could be restricted, at least where the appointment had been made by an officer of the Executive Branch, see *ibid.* . . .

The Court could have resolved the removal power issue in this case by simply relying upon its erroneous conclusion that the independent counsel was an inferior officer, and then extending our holding that the removal of inferior officers appointed by the Executive can be restricted, to a new holding that even the removal of inferior officers appointed by the courts can be restricted. That would in my view be a considerable and unjustified extension, giving the Executive full discretion in *neither* the selection *nor* the removal of a purely executive officer. The course the Court has chosen, however, is even worse.

Since our 1935 decision in *Humphrey's Executor v. United States,* . . . it has been established that the line of permissible restriction upon removal of principal officers lies at the point at which the powers exercised by those officers are no longer purely executive. Thus, removal restrictions have been generally regarded as lawful for so-called "independent regulatory agencies," such as the Federal Trade Commission, the Interstate Commerce Commission, and the Consumer Products Safety Commission, which engage substantially in what has been called the "quasi-legislative activity" of rulemaking, and for members of Article I courts, such as the Court of Military Appeals, who engage in the "quasi-judicial" function of adjudication. It has often been observed, correctly in my view, that the line between "purely executive" functions and "quasi-legislative" or "quasi-judicial" functions is not a clear one or even a rational one. But at least it permitted the identification of certain officers, and certain agencies, whose functions were entirely within the control of the President. Congress had to be aware of that restriction in its legislation. Today, however, *Humphrey's Executor* is swept into the dustbin of repudiated constitutional principles. "[O]ur present considered view," the Court says, "is that the determination of whether the Constitution allows Congress to impose a 'good cause'-type restriction on the President's power to remove an official cannot be made to turn on whether or not that official is classified as 'purely executive.'" What *Humphrey's Executor* (and presumably *Myers*) really means, we are now told, is not that there are any "rigid categories of those officials who may or may not be removed at will by the President," but simply that Congress cannot "interfere with the President's exercise of the 'executive power' and his constitutionally appointed duty to 'take care that the laws be faithfully executed.'"

. . . The President is directly dependent on the people, and since there is only *one* President, *he* is responsible. The people know whom to blame, whereas "one of the weightiest objections to a plurality in the executive . . . is that it tends to conceal faults and destroy responsibility." . . .

Today's decision on the basic issue of fragmentation of executive power is ungoverned by rule, and hence ungoverned by law. It extends into the very heart of our most significant constitutional function the "totality of the circumstances" mode of analysis that this Court has in recent years become fond of. Taking all things into account, we conclude that the power taken away from the President here is not really too much. The next time executive power is assigned to someone other than the President we may conclude, taking all things into account, that it is too much. That opinion, like this one, will not be confined by any rule. We will describe, as we have today (though I hope more accurately) the effects of the provision in question, and will authoritatively announce: "The President's need to control the exercise of the [subject officer's] discretion is so central to the functioning of the Executive Branch as to require complete control." This is not analysis; it is ad hoc judgment. And it fails to explain why it is not true that— as the text of the Constitution seems to require, as the Founders seemed to expect, and as our past cases have uniformly assumed—all purely executive power must be under the control of the President.

Notes and Questions

1. *Before and after Morrison.* You should pay careful attention to the *Humphrey's Executor* and *Wiener* cases discussed in *Morrison* because those cases, along with the *Myers* case discussed earlier and the *Bowsher* case discussed in note 7, *infra,* were the principal precedents in this area before *Morrison.* They seemed to draw a distinction between officials exercising purely executive functions and officials exercising other functions. The power of the President to fire the former at will appeared to be plenary while the power of the President to fire the later appeared to be limited by the authority of Congress to impose restrictions on such action. *Morrison* appears to reject this distinction between officials exercising purely executive powers and those exercising other powers and, instead, indicates that the validity of any limitation on the President's removal power depends upon an analysis of the particular functions of the official involved and a determination as to "whether the removal restrictions are of such a nature that they impede the President's ability to perform his constitutional duty."

2. *Drawing lines.* How can you tell whether Congress may properly limit the President's authority to fire the head of a particular agency at will? That is, when is the removal power of the President protected on the basis of the *Myers* holding rather than subject to the authority of Congress to restrict it on the basis of the *Humphrey's Executor, Wiener,* or *Morrison* holdings?

In the words of the *Morrison* majority, when does a limitation on the President's authority to remove an officer performing executive functions "interfere *impermissibly* with [his] constitutional obligation to ensure the faithful execution of the laws?" When is the "President's need to control the exercise of [executive] discretion . . . so *central* to the function of the Executive Branch" that he must be able to fire at will the officials initially exercising that discretion? Justice Scalia maintains that the majority does not furnish a justiciable standard that is adequate to answer these questions. Do you agree?

Do you agree with Scalia that the line between those officials exercising purely executive powers and those exercising other powers is a better line for distinguishing between officials that must be subject to a plenary presidential authority to fire and those that may be subject only to a limited presidential authority to fire? How easily can purely executive functions be distinguished from other functions? How should we characterize administrative rulemaking? Administrative adjudication? Administrative prosecution? Do any of the cases in this section satisfactorily answer these questions?

3. *Independent agencies. Humphrey's Executor, Wiener,* and *Morrison,* upheld limitations on the authority of the President to fire officials exercising executive functions. Consequently, those cases suggest that Congress may create some agencies that are independent of plenary presidential authority. While a majority of agencies are located within the executive branch of government, quite a few are considered independent. For example, agencies such as the Federal Trade Commission, the Nuclear Regulatory Commission, the Securities and Exchange Commission, and the Interstate Commerce Commission, are said to be independent, in the sense that their respective heads may be removed only for "good cause," and their respective governing statutes place them outside of any of the three branches of government. As a result, these agencies are deemed not to be subject to direct controls by the President and the Executive Branch. Generally, Congress creates an independent agency in the hope of lessening political influence over its decisions; the idea is that free of direct executive control, the agency can perform its administrative functions impartially and regulate purely in the public interest.

4. *Removal power, independence, and political control of agencies.* Consider the question of the removal power of the President and agency independence in light of the several theories for administrative law discussed in § 1.7, *supra.* Is the power of the President to remove at will the head of every agency exercising executive functions necessary to ensure adequate political controls over the day-to-day decisionmaking of agencies? That is, must the *elected* President have such authority to ensure that the daily operations of unelected administrative bodies are consistent with the political will of the community at large? Is such a power also necessary to ensure the coordination and rationalization of all executive functions? Scalia's dissent in *Morrison* certainly

suggests that a unitary executive authority empowered to remove at will all officials exercising executive functions is necessary for these purposes, and that the holding of that case endangers the ability of the President to secure these results. Do you think Scalia's arguments in this regard are overdrawn?

Aside from the removal issue, is it a good idea to insulate some agencies from direct political control over their decisions by placing them outside of the Executive Branch? Would a proper response vary depending upon the precise nature of the function being performed by the agency and the subject matter involved? In particular, should an agency engaged in law enforcement, rulemaking, and adjudication, concerning important matters of economic policy, like the Federal Trade Commission or the Federal Communications Commission, be made wholly independent of the chief executive?

If the heads of such agencies are not elected, may not be removed by the President at will, *and* their decisionmaking is not subject to direct control by the chief executive because they are placed outside of the Executive Branch, how can we ensure that their day-to-day decisions are consistent with the will of the body politic? That is, how can we ensure that independent agencies are as politically responsible as executive agencies which are subject to the direct authority of the elected chief executive? Are the other checks on independent agencies, such as the checks provided by administrative procedure acts and legislative review of agency action, sufficient to provide adequate political accountability for independent agencies? Of course, in deciding whether to create any particular independent agency, we might balance any loss of political accountability that would result from the creation of such a body against any special benefits that might accrue from its independent status. While such a calculus might help to ensure that independent agencies are created only when the benefits of their independence outweighs the costs of that independence, it would not ensure, in the end, that such agencies are in fact politically accountable in some effective way. What can be done to ensure *that* result?

5. *Further implications of independence.* As noted above, the *Humphrey's Executor, Wiener,* and *Morrison* cases establish that Congress may limit the President's authority to fire the heads of certain agencies. In *Morrison,* seven members of the Supreme Court agreed that purely executive powers could be vested in an official who was removable by the Attorney General only for "good cause." Is the constitutionality of a congressional limitation on the President's removal power a sufficiently different question from the constitutionality of such a limitation on the President's substantive authority to control finally all executive functions, that a decision on the former does not necessarily settle the latter? Is the peculiar role of an independent counsel so distinct from the role of most independent agencies as to make the *Morrison* case inapposite to the validity of the usual independent agency?

(B. & A.) State & Fed'l Admin.Law ACB—19

The assumption has been that the *Humphrey's Executor, Wiener,* and *Morrison* cases also establish that Congress may insulate such agencies from presidential interference on policy matters relating to the execution of laws entrusted to them. In light of these cases, is that assumption justified? Is a system in which the chief executive is not supreme on all executive matters constitutional? Is it desirable? Consider in this connection the Scalia dissent as well as the majority opinion in *Morrison,* and the discussion of *Youngstown Sheet and Tube v. Sawyer,* § 7.5.5, *supra.* Consider also whether Congress' authority to insulate agencies from interference by the chief executive is or should be any different with respect to agency rulemaking as compared to agency adjudication or law enforcement.

Is the answer to any of these inquiries clearer under those state constitutions specifying that the Governor is the "*supreme* executive power" than under constitutions that do not contain such a provision?

Note that § 1(d) of Executive Order 12,291 exempts from its requirements all agencies specified in 44 U.S.C. § 3502(10). The agencies listed in this section are those considered to be independent of the executive branch because statutes appear to insulate them from direct presidential control of their operations. However, Vice President Bush (who headed the Task Force on Regulatory Relief), asked the so called independent agencies to comply voluntarily with the Order. Although several independent agencies voiced support for the Order, none of them agreed to comply fully. Why do you think that the President exempted the independent agencies from this Executive Order? Could the President make the Executive Order applicable to the independent agencies? Should the President do so if he has the authority?

6. *How independent are independent agencies?* In most cases, when an agency is independent of the executive branch, the statute explicitly protects agency heads against removal without cause. However, the statutes creating some independent agencies (such as the Federal Communications Commission) say nothing about removal. Does that mean that the President could remove the members of the FCC without cause?

In addition to protection of the agency heads from removal without cause, independent agencies appear to have somewhat more autonomy than Executive Branch agencies because they are deemed to be located outside that Branch. Typically, the heads of independent agencies appoint the agency staff wholly on their own authority; in executive agencies, the White House often plays a much larger role in the ultimate staffing decisions. Moreover, independent agencies tend to have somewhat greater authority to conduct their own litigation than Executive Branch agencies. Finally, independent agencies tend to be somewhat more free of executive control in rulemaking, (*see* discussion of Executive Order 12,291, note 5, *supra,*) and in matters relating to communication with Congress such as advance submission of draft statutes or testimony. *See* Strauss, "The Place of Agencies in Government: Separation of Powers and the Fourth Branch," 84 Colum.L.Rev. 573, 589–90 (1984).

Professor Strauss contends that, as a practical matter, not very much of importance turns on whether an agency is independent. All agencies function in about the same way (carrying out rulemaking, adjudication, and law enforcement) and are subject identically to the APA, judicial review, and congressional oversight. All agencies are staffed (below the top levels) by civil service employees who are protected against discharge except for cause and who often resist new initiatives.

As a practical matter, both independent and executive agencies usually work closely with the President and his staff in formulating policy and in mediating inter-agency disputes. All agencies submit budgetary requests each year to the Office of Management and Budget and all are treated alike in the President's budget as submitted to Congress. Moreover, the President usually has power to choose which of the several agency heads of multi-member independent agencies will be the chair. The chair is likely to be a person with whom the President has a good working relationship, and the chair makes a great many important practical decisions for the agency. In short, Strauss concludes that the de facto independence of an agency from presidential control depends much more on political factors than on whether the agency is formally independent. Id. at 583–596. Nevertheless, the fact remains that independence seems to count for a lot in determining congressional attitudes toward agencies and presidential attempts to control them.

7. *Congressional removal power.* While *Humphrey's Executor, Wiener,* and *Morrison,* affirm that Congress may limit the President's power to remove some agency officials, they do not mean that Congress may retain for itself the power to remove officials engaged in administrative functions. In *Bowsher v. Synar,* 478 U.S. 714 (1986), discussed in *Morrison,* the Supreme Court held unconstitutional a part of the Gramm–Rudman Act, a budget-balancing measure enacted in 1985. That Act provided that if the projected federal budget deficit for a particular year exceeds a certain level, and Congress cannot cut the budget to bring the deficit within the limits set by the Act, an across-the-board percentage slash in the appropriation for almost all programs will occur.

But who determines how big the projected deficit will be? This is anything but a bookkeeping chore. It requires forecasts about projected federal revenues and expenditures, employment rates, interest rates, inflation, and many other economic factors. The Gramm–Rudman Act left this determination to the Comptroller General. Under the 1921 law which created that post, the Comptroller may be removed only by a joint Congressional resolution (which the President could veto) for inefficiency, neglect of duty, or malfeasance. However, this power had never been exercised; as a practical matter, Congress had never sought to control, much less to remove, the Comptroller.

The Court held that the Comptroller's duties were clearly "executive" because the Gramm–Rudman Act required him to interpret and carry out its provisions. His duties involved an enormous amount of judgment and discretion concerning the facts affecting application of the Act, and his budgetary determination binds the President, triggering a process that leads to budget cuts. Since Congress could remove the Comptroller, and the Comptroller performed executive functions under this Act, Congress improperly retained control over the execution of the law. And the *Chadha* case made clear that Congress could not participate in executing laws.

In a concurring opinion, Justice Stevens, joined by Justice Marshall, argued that the flaw in the Gramm–Rudman Act was that the Comptroller is an agent of Congress; when Congress seeks to make policy that will bind the nation, it must do so by following Article I legislative procedures. The Comptroller is part of the legislative branch not only because the authority to remove that official is vested in Congress, but also, and much more importantly, because his other duties are intended to aid Congress in the process of passing laws and appropriating money. Moreover, the Comptroller's functions under the Gramm–Rudman Act are primarily legislative, not executive, in the same sense that agency rulemaking is legislative.

But, said the concurrence, when Congress delegates power (whether executive or legislative in nature) to make fundamental and binding policy decisions, it may delegate only to the executive or to an independent agency—not to its own agent. Otherwise, it could evade the Article I requirements for legislation—passage by both houses of Congress and approval by the President.

Justice White's dissent argued that the carefully limited and never used congressional power to remove the Comptroller was of no practical significance. There is no genuine likelihood that the Comptroller would be subservient to Congress. Moreover, vesting the deficit determination power in the Comptroller made good sense because he is nonpartisan and independent of the President and his political agenda. Justice Blackmun's dissent argued that the Court should strike down the removal power by stating that it would refuse to uphold a removal and save the Gramm–Rudman Act.

Recall the distinction in § 7.1, *supra*, between separation of powers and checks and balances. If the Gramm–Rudman Act is considered from a checks and balances point of view, is there merit in Justice White's dissenting analysis in *Bowsher?* Did not Gramm–Rudman strike a fair compromise between congressional and presidential control over the painful process of budget-cutting? Or did the Gramm–Rudman Act represent a congressional attempt to interfere with functions that are properly executive?

8. *More on discharges.* Suppose that the President stated that there was good cause, such as corruption or inefficiency, to remove a visible, high level executive official whose position is protected by a good cause standard. Would that official be entitled to a hearing on this issue? By whom? Do you think most such highly visible, important officials are likely to resist a presidential request that they resign? If they do resist, is the President likely to press the point by firing them?

9. *Authority of governor to remove administrative officials.* "State constitutional provisions relating to the power of the governor to remove public officials vary dramatically from state to state." T. Marks & J. Cooper, STATE CONSTITUTIONAL LAW § 28, at 65 (1988). When the state constitution is silent with respect to the removal authority of the governor, there is disagreement about whether the authority to remove administrative officials is vested in the governor by the general delegation of executive powers to the chief executive, or resides in the legislature. *See,* Dawley, "The Governors' Constitutional Powers of Appointment and Removal," 22 Minn.L.Rev. 451, 452–56, 477–78 (1938); *Ahearn v. Bailey,* 451 P.2d 30, 33 (Ariz.1969), (power to remove public officers is an executive function); *State ex rel. Thompson v. Morton,* 84 S.E.2d 791, 797 (W.Va.1954), (power to remove public officers is inherently vested in the legislature).

Most states appear to vest in the governor express or implied authority to remove administrative officials as an incident to the constitutional or statutory power of the chief executive to appoint those officials. But in most states the governor is not authorized to remove all agency officials at will, either because the language of the state constitution limits the governor's removal power, or because it permits the legislature to enact statutes that limit the governor's authority in this regard and the legislature has done so. *See, e.g., State ex rel. Pearson v. Hansen,* 401 P.2d 954, 956 (Wyo.1965), (governor's power of removal can be limited either by constitution or by statute). So, governors often cannot remove administrative officers at will; with respect to many administrative officers, such a removal may be proper only for good cause.

At least one state constitution authorizes the governor to remove some elected officers. Pa.Const. Art. VI, § 7. Absent an explicit constitutional or statutory authorization may a governor remove, for good cause, an administrative officer who is directly elected by the people?

As noted, when a governor is authorized by the state constitution to remove administrative officers, that power is often limited. Similarly, when authority to remove administrative officers is granted to the governor by statute, it often limits that power. In addition to providing explicitly that removal may only be for good cause, a common method used by state legislatures to restrain the governor's removal power is to provide specified terms for officers that the governor is authorized to appoint. *See, e.g., State ex rel. Todd v. Essling,* 128 N.W.2d 307, 311 (Minn.1964) and *Watson v. Pennsylvania Turnpike Com'n,* 125 A.2d 354, 357 (Pa.1956), (where a statute fixes the term of an officer, the authority of the governor to remove at will is no longer an implied incident to the power to appoint). In such a situation, "[i]t is presumed that the creators of the office intended the occupant to serve out the term unless good cause could be shown as to why he should be removed." T. Marks & J. Cooper, *supra,* at 66. On the other hand, if the legislature does not specify the term of an administrative officer the governor is authorized to appoint, and does not otherwise explicitly limit the governor's power to remove that officer, the power to remove the officer at will may be assumed to be delegated to the governor.

Suppose the legislature established an administrative office with a specified term and also expressly authorized the governor to remove that official. Should this statute be construed to support a delegation to the governor of authority to remove the official at will or only for good cause? *Collison v. State ex rel. Green,* 2 A.2d 97, 106 (Del.1938), held that such a statute should be construed to provide unrestrained gubernatorial removal powers. Is the result in that case sound?

In the end, it is difficult to generalize about the removal power of governors over administrative officers because of the great variations in that power among the states. Consequently, the constitution and statutes of each state must be examined to determine the exact scope of gubernatorial power in this regard.

10. *Problem.* A federal statute provides that claims against employers by workers injured on navigable waters are to be first considered by Deputy Commissioners of the Department of Labor. In the event that the Deputy Commissioners cannot settle a dispute, the case is heard by an Administrative Law Judge (ALJ). Appeals from the ALJ's decision are heard by a Review Board. Decisions by the Review Board may be appealed to the United States Court of Appeals. The Court must reverse the decision below if it is not supported by substantial evidence.

The statute also provides that the Review Board members are appointed by the Secretary of Labor but says nothing about their term of office or about their removal. The statute clearly places the Review Board within the Department of Labor which is not an independent agency.

The Secretary of Labor fired Mr. Smith, a member of the Review Board, without stating any cause. Does the Secretary have the power to do so? What arguments should Smith make in an action seeking payment of his salary, and how should they be resolved?

§ 7.6 POLITICAL CONTROL: APPRAISING MEANS

McCUBBINS, NOLL, WEINGAST, "ADMINISTRATIVE PROCEDURES AS INSTRUMENTS OF POLITICAL CONTROL"

3 Journal of Law, Economics, & Organization 243, 248–253 (1987).*

REWARDS, SANCTIONS, AND MONITORING AS CONTROL STRATEGIES

The literature on political control of the bureaucracy describes a variety of control strategies [other than the imposition of administrative procedures] available to political actors that exemplify traditional solutions to the principal-agent problem. For the most part, the scholarly literature emphasizes the use of "reactive" strategies which elected politicians adopt after some blunder or radical departure [by an agency] from their intended policy has occurred. . . .

[The authors indicate that there are many means by which the elected legislature and chief executive may reward or sanction agencies in order to ensure that agencies follow the policy preferences of their principals who are elected to represent the political will of the community at large. These means of imposing rewards and sanctions require extensive monitoring to ensure administrative compliance with the political will, and include the use of appropriations bills, public hearings and investigations, legislation and executive orders to alter agency authority, and the removal of administrators from office or even, in rare cases, their prosecution for breaking the law.

However, the authors conclude that an effective system of rewards and sanctions is unlikely to be a wholly effective solution to the political control problem. This is so because of the high cost of monitoring agency activities, the limited range of rewards and sanctions available to the legislature and chief executive, and the cost to those principals of implementing the most important types of rewards and sanctions.]

Monitoring. By themselves, rewards and punishments do not deal directly with the problem of asymmetric information. If agencies have better information, they have a range of discretion that is undetectable to political overseers, and so, in the absence of monitoring, some noncomplying decisions will not be subject to retribution. Thus, if noncompliance is a serious problem, one would expect political actors to invest substantial resources in monitoring; indeed, this appears to be the case. . . .

Policy monitoring in Congress takes two forms. The more apparent, but probably less important, is ongoing oversight and evaluation by congressional subcommittees and agencies that are arms of Congress, such as the Congressional Budget Office (CBO) and the General Accounting Office (GAO). Less apparent, but probably more important (judging from how members of Congress allocate their time and staff), is "fire-alarm" monitoring. This form of monitoring consists of disappointed constituents pulling a member's fire alarm whenever an agency harms them. Oversight is then a form of constituency service for members. Constituency service has become an increasingly important activity of members of Congress in the postwar era, to the point where it now accounts for more than half of the staff effort in Congress and is a critical factor in assuring the reelection success of members.

Policy monitoring in the Executive Branch is concentrated in the evaluation process. The Executive Office of the President is comprised of numerous organizations, most notably the Office of Management and Budget (OMB), that scrutinize budgets, programs, and operations of agencies. Furthermore, cabinet officials—the people most politically responsive to the President—also have their own independent evaluation staffs.

To facilitate the monitoring process, political actors impose information collection and reporting requirements on agencies. Both Congress and the OMB receive oceans of data and reports from offices within agencies about ongoing programs. And, through GAO and the General Services Administration (GSA), political actors impose rigid accounting and record-keeping requirements on agencies that can be used subsequently as the basis for sanctions.

Though monitoring is probably far more pervasive and effective than was once thought, it imposes costs on political actors. First, resources devoted to monitoring have an opportunity cost, for they presumably could be devoted to delivering more government services to constituents or shrinking the burden of the public sector. Second, the time used by political principals in acquiring information, assessing the degree of noncompliance, and deciding what punishment strategy, if any, to undertake also has an opportunity cost. Easy and quick compliance is preferred, for it enables political actors to provide more service to constituents in a given amount of time.

In addition to imposing significant costs, monitoring is likely to be only an imperfect mechanism for detecting noncompliance. First, cause-effect relations in human affairs often are subject to an important degree of irreducible uncertainty, so that no matter how carefully the consequences of an agency's actions are monitored, political actors will be unsure about the extent to which an agency undertook best efforts to comply with its principals' wishes. Second, monitoring consists primarily of information received after an action is taken. One form of noncompliance is for an agency to make a decision that creates a new political interest which is antithetical to the existing political structure. In this case, sanctions against an agency generate political costs that would not have to be faced had the policy decision been anticipated and prevented. . . .

The final difficulty of any monitoring system pertains primarily to the more traditional oversight function, as practiced in OMB and in congressional hearings. It is the ultimate dependence of external monitors on information supplied by agencies. In a sense, the agency both keeps the books and performs the audit. If agencies have important private information, not all of which can be obtained by external monitors, they can use this information to hide noncompliance. This problem cannot be solved by increasing the intensity of external monitoring, but must be solved by giving the agency an incentive to make all of its information public.

We have already observed that noncompliance must be perceived as a serious problem because so much effort is devoted to monitoring. Now we conclude that direct monitoring by elected representatives is likely to be an imperfect mechanism for detecting noncompliance. If so, there is a good chance that some shirking by bureaucrats goes undetected. This can be offset only if penalties are sufficiently high and sanctions, when applied, are not commensurately costly to political principals.

Limits to sanctions. A key result in principal-agent theory is that in some circumstances—and especially when noncompliance is difficult to detect—the magnitude of the sanctions necessary to effect compliance must be very large (indeed, often much larger than the potential rewards to the principal from compliance). In the case of policy implementation through administrative agencies, the maximal stakes of bureaucrats are criminal penalties, and these are available only when noncompliance takes the form of willful violation of the letter of the law. In cases where noncompliance is not criminal, the range of sanctions is more limited and of comparable magnitude to the costs an agency can impose on political actors. Specifically, each can undermine the career objectives of the other, and each can thwart the other from achieving preferred policy actions. Thus, absent illegal activities by agencies, the sanctions available to political actors are roughly comparable to the costs agencies can impose on politicians.

If this is the case, two logical consequences follow. First, monitoring effort should be intensive so that the limits to sanctions can be offset to some degree by higher detection probabilities. Hence, limits to sanctions of public officials provide an explanation for the elaborate monitoring system of the public sector. Second, if sanctions are based primarily on monitoring, then imperfect monitoring implies that substantial noncomplying behavior will go undetected.

Political costs of sanctions. Not only is the magnitude of sanctions for noncompliance limited, but most of the methods for imposing meaningful sanctions also create costs for political principals. Some forms of sanctions require legislation, which demands the coordinated effort of both houses of Congress and the President. The introduction of legislation creates the additional problem that it can reopen longsettled, but still contentious, aspects of a policy that are unrelated to the compliance problem. To impose legislative sanctions, therefore, requires running the risk of other undesirable legislative outcomes from the perspective of any given elected official.

Another potential cost of sanctions is the response of the electorate to new information about government wrongdoing. Citizens have a principal-agent relationship with elected political officials that is broadly similar to the relationship between elected officials and bureaus. Specifically, in the face of imperfect and costly information of considerable complexity, constituents must assess the extent to which elected officials, not agencies, are guilty of noncompliance with wishes of the electorate. Hence, a publicly visible investigation and punishment of an agency may raise doubts in the minds of the electorate about the attentiveness to business of their elected officials. They may conclude that Congress or the White House, not the agency, was the Washington branch of Club Med. Or, if citizens vote retrospectively, they may respond to information about government malfeasance of any sort by simply voting against incumbents.

Finally, the act of imposing sanctions distracts agencies from the delivery of public services, focusing their attention on minimizing the damage they will suffer as a result of detected malfeasance. Investigations, "midnight massacres" of key officials, and reorganizations are disruptive of the business of the agency. To the extent the agency is delivering some politically relevant services, this disruption, too, is costly to elected politicians.

Of course, if imposing significant sanctions is costly to political actors as well as to bureaucrats, the ardor for them among politicians will be proportionately dampened. Specifically, not all acts of noncompliance, once detected, will be punished significantly, giving agencies an additional incentive to pursue their own preferences at the expense of political principals.

The thrust of these arguments is not that rewards, punishment, and monitoring are unimportant in the public sector. Indeed, monitoring is intense only if it is useful to political principals, and its utility arises in part from the ability of political actors to punish or reward agencies on the basis of detected compliance patterns. Extensive monitoring makes detection of noncompliance more likely and sharpens the incentive effects of sanctions by allowing political actors to impose them in more exact proportion to the probability and magnitude of noncompliance. Consequently, shirking and malfeasance are going to be less attractive to agencies than they would be in the absence of monitoring and sanctions.

Nevertheless, by themselves, monitoring and sanctions do not comprise a perfect solution to the problem of bureaucratic compliance because they are costly, inexact, and subject to fundamental limitations. Thus, one would expect politicians to welcome other measures that may be available for altering the incentive structure of agencies, especially if these alternatives have relatively low cost. An optimal mix of the measures, where each measure complements the strengths of the other and substitutes for the other's weaknesses, will establish less costly and more effective control of the bureaucracy by political principals. Hence, the stage is set for analyzing administrative law as such a mechanism. . . .

Notes and Questions

1. *Role of administrative procedure and theories for administrative law.* The authors of the above analysis go on to explain why administrative procedures surrounding agency decisionmaking processes can ensure "more effective control of the bureaucracy by political principals" than rewards, sanctions, and monitoring, and that most of administrative law is an effort to solve the political control problem through procedural means. This further explanation is contained in § 1.7, *supra.* Reread that subsection in light of the materials in all of the subsequent chapters, including this chapter.

How would you now evaluate the various theories for administrative law discussed in § 1.7, *supra*? Is the theory proposed by McCubbins, Noll, and Weingast consistent with what you think you now know about administrative agencies and administrative law? Is their theory consistent with the other theories for administrative law discussed in § 1.7, *supra* ? More or less useful than those other theories?

2. *Insufficiency of direct, substantive political checks.* Administrative procedures are an *indirect, nonsubstantive* means of solving the political control problem; yet, McCubbins, Noll, and Weingast consider administrative procedures to be the most practical and effective (but not only) solution to that problem. *See* § 1.7, *supra.* Why are *direct, substantive* legislative and executive checks, such as the incorporation of detailed standards in legislation delegating authority to agencies, or a veto of particular agency action by the legislature and/or chief executive, not the best means by which to assure that agency action is consistent with the preferences of elected officials? Why are *procedures* that structure agency decisionmaking processes essential for that purpose?

3. *Combination of checks best.* It should be obvious that, in the end, a combination of various means of securing politically responsible agency action is necessary to accomplish the desired result. For this purpose we must use means that are direct *and* indirect, substantive *and* procedural, including legislative specifications of agency authority, the use of rewards, sanctions, and monitoring, and the imposition of administrative procedures to structure agency decisionmaking processes. Given the realities in which the agencies, the legislature, and the chief executive operate, however, McCubbins, Noll, and Weingast may well be right: Administrative *procedures* may be the single most potent and continuing means of securing politically responsible agency action. But procedures cannot wholly substitute for direct substantive action by political principals, both before and after the fact, to ensure that the administrative process delivers the outcomes desired by the community at large.

Chapter 8

FREEDOM OF INFORMATION
AND OTHER OPEN
GOVERNMENT LAWS

This chapter addresses statutes that relate in various ways to the issue of governmental openness. It asks the question of whether, and to what extent, government functions and documents should be open to public scrutiny. What are the legitimate bases for governmental secrecy? Should governmental openness to public scrutiny be viewed as a political control, a check on agency action, like the legislative and executive controls discussed in chapter 7?

The chapter concentrates on the federal Freedom of Information Act—a charter of government openness that remains virtually unique in the world. The chapter also summarizes two statutes designed to achieve open government: the federal Sunshine Act, which requires agency meetings to be public, and the Federal Advisory Committee Act, which opens advisory committees to scrutiny. The chapter concludes with a brief treatment of the federal Privacy Act, which is intended both to permit individuals to correct government files concerning them and to safeguard the confidentiality of those files.

§ 8.1 FREEDOM OF INFORMATION

The federal Freedom of Information Act (often referred to as FOIA) was passed in 1966. It was amended and vastly strengthened in 1974 at a time when mistrust of government was rampant.

The Act consists of three parts, all found in § 552 of the APA. (i) Under APA § 552(a)(1) (parts of which were in the original 1946 APA), an agency must *publish* certain important information, including a statement of its organization and procedure and substantive rules of general applicability (including statements of general policy and interpretations of general applicability). A person without actual timely knowledge of such material cannot be adversely affected by it. The Supreme Court held that rules relating to Indian welfare payments could not be applied because they had not been published in accordance with this section. *Morton v. Ruiz,* 415 U.S. 199 (1974). For a similar provision, see 1981 MSAPA § 2–101.

(ii) Under APA § 552(a)(2), agencies must *make available* (but not necessarily publish) specified additional material. This includes final opinions, staff manuals, instructions to staff that affect the public, and policy statements and interpretations of particular (rather than general) applicability. This material must also be indexed. Material covered by this provision may not be used adversely to a person unless these requirements are met or the person had actual, timely knowledge of its contents. This requirement is discussed in the *Sears, Roebuck* case which follows. For a similar provision, see 1981 MSAPA § 2–102.

(iii) Most important, under APA § 552(a)(3), an agency must furnish *any reasonably described record requested by any person for any reason.* If the agency refuses (or fails to act within the very short time frame described in § 552(a)(6)), the requester is entitled to go to federal district court to compel disclosure and, if he substantially prevails, in many cases can recover attorney's fees. The agency has the burden to justify non-disclosure on the basis of one of the nine exemptions to the Act's disclosure requirements contained in § 552(b). To do so, the agency must claim and justify exemptions for each document (or part of a document) through a detailed index and itemization. The court decides the matter de novo (i.e. without deferring to the agency's judgment). This truly revolutionary provision is what people generally mean when they discuss the Freedom of Information Act.

Comparable provisions have been adopted in every state (Mississippi was the last to join the fold in 1983). *See* Braverman & Heppler, "A Practical Review of State Open Records Laws," 49 Geo.Wash.L.Rev. 720 (1981); Tseng & Pederson, "Acquisition of State Administrative Rules and Regulations—Update 1983," 35 Admin.L.Rev. 349 (1983). Many states also recognize a common law right to inspect state and local documents. Traditionally, this right was really a form of civil discovery; it was available only to persons who needed the document for litigation purposes, and it covered only records that were legally required to be kept. *See* Note, 45 Fordham L.Rev. 1105, 1107–11 (1977). But in some states any public purpose would be a sufficient interest to demand documents. And in some states the common law right of inspection survives the adoption of a Freedom of Information law. *See Irval Realty Inc. v. Board of Public Util. Com'rs,* 294 A.2d 425 (N.J.1972) (common law right applies to information exempt under state information law).

What are the benefits and costs of laws like FOIA or similar state acts?

A broad right of public access to governmental information confirms the idea that the people are sovereign and facilitates control by the principals (the people) over their agent (the government). Easily accessible information about government operations enables members of the general public to discover the actual norms guiding governmental behavior, to monitor the government's compliance with law, to evaluate the quality of its performance, and to object in a more effective way to improper or unacceptable governmental behavior . . . . Broad public access to information about government operations also deters official misconduct and induces greater care by officials in their dealings with the general public and in their handling of its affairs . . . . [T]he sunlight of public access to information about governmental operations kills or retards the growth of mould in government . . . .

On the other hand . . . a broad public right of access to governmental information must have limits and can be overdone . . . [As noted] mould does not grow where there is light . . . but too much sunlight causes sunburn . . . . At some point, the costs of such a right exceed its benefits . . . . As a result, any broad public right of access must be limited to accommodate in a reasonable way other important public interests that, at some point, compete and conflict with that right. Of course a completely fair balance between the important public right of access and the other potentially conflicting important public interests in effective, efficient, and economical government administration, and personal privacy, is hard to achieve. Nevertheless, an acceptable and workable balance among these interests is necessary and is one of the more important tasks of federal and state freedom of information legislation . . . . We may always be reevaluating the fairness of that balance in light of new experiences, current societal problems, and changing public values.

Bonfield, "Chairman's Message," 40 Admin.L.Rev. iii (Win.1988).

At the federal level, the costs of disclosure on the scale required by FOIA have proved to be far in excess of what FOIA's drafters ever imagined. The federal government is estimated to receive more than 300,000 requests for information under FOIA each year, of which about 90% are granted administratively. Most requests appear to involve efforts by one business to obtain information about another business for private gain. Many agencies are hopelessly backlogged with FOIA requests and cannot possibly comply with the time requirements of § 552(a)(6). A single request can be enormously time consuming; one company's request to the Navy was estimated to include several million documents which would span 10,000 linear feet. Susman, "Introduction to the Issues, Problems, and Relevant Law," 34 Admin.L.Rev. 117, 118 (1982).

It is difficult to estimate the cost to government but estimates range between about $50 million and $250 million per year or more. A large number of agency employees, who would otherwise be engaged in carrying out agency programs, are instead employed to respond to FOIA requests—searching for documents, redacting (deleting) material from records that should not become public (sometimes word-by-word review is needed), duplicating them, or reviewing disclosure decisions by other employees. This work is laborious and unpopular. Several thousand FOIA cases have been filed in the already swamped federal courts; the cases often receive priority (28 U.S.C. § 1657) and require the judge to conduct in camera review of a mass of documents. The Supreme Court had decided nineteen FOIA cases by 1985.

> FOIA . . . is the Taj Mahal of the Doctrine of Unanticipated Consequences, the Sistine Chapel of Cost Benefit Analysis Ignored . . . The foregoing defects [of excessive costs and burdens on government and the courts] . . . might not be defects in the best of all possible worlds. They are foolish extravagances only because we do not have an unlimited amount of federal money to spend, an unlimited number of agency employees to assign, an unlimited number of judges to hear and decide cases. We must, alas, set some priorities—and unless the world is mad the usual FOIA request should not be high on the list.

Scalia, "The Freedom of Information Act Has No Clothes," Regulation 15, 17–18 (March/April 1982). Do you think the benefits of FOIA are worth the costs? If not, would you repeal FOIA?

In evaluating FOIA, it is necessary to take account of its nine exemptions. If FOIA is too costly, one policy alternative is to broaden the existing exemptions or create new ones. Or are these exemptions already too broad?

§ 8.1.1　FOIA EXEMPTIONS

There is now a vast body of caselaw struggling with each of the nine exceptions set forth in § 552(b) and with other issues arising under FOIA (such as entitlement to attorney's fees). The following discussion considers in detail two of the exceptions: § 552(b)(5), discussed in *Sears, Roebuck,* and § 552(b)(4), discussed in *Chrysler.*

NATIONAL LABOR RELATIONS BOARD v. SEARS, ROEBUCK & CO.

421 U.S. 132 (1975).

WHITE, J.:

The National Labor Relations Board (the Board) and its General Counsel seek to set aside an order of the United States District Court directing disclosure to respondent, Sears, Roebuck & Co. (Sears), pursuant to the Freedom of Information Act, 5 U.S.C. § 552 (Act), of certain memoranda, known as "Advice Memoranda" and "Appeals Memoranda," and related documents generated by the Office of the General Counsel in the course of deciding whether or not to permit the filing with the Board of unfair labor practice complaints. . . .

As the Act is structured, virtually every document generated by an agency is available to the public in one form or another, unless it falls within one of the Act's nine exemptions. Certain documents described in 5 U.S.C. § 552(a)(1) such as "rules of procedure" must be published in the Federal Register; others, including "final opinions . . . made in the adjudication of cases," "statements of policy and interpretations which have been adopted by the agency," and "instructions to staff that affect a member of the public," described in 5 U.S.C. § 552(a)(2), must be indexed and made available to a member of the public on demand. Finally, and more comprehensively, all "identifiable records" must be made available to a member of the public on demand. 5 U.S.C. § 552(a) (3). The Act expressly states, however, that the disclosure obligation "does not apply" to those documents described in the nine enumerated exempt categories listed in § 552(b).

Sears claims, and the courts below ruled, that the memoranda sought are expressions of legal and policy decisions already adopted by the agency and constitute "final opinions" and "instructions to staff that affect a member of the public," both categories being expressly disclosable under § 552(a)(2) of the Act, pursuant to its purposes to prevent the creation of "secret law." In any event, Sears claims, the memoranda are nonexempt "identifiable records" which must be disclosed under § 552(a)(3). The General Counsel, on the other hand, claims that the memoranda sought here are not final opinions under § 552(a)(2) and that even if they are "identifiable records" otherwise disclosable under § 552(a)(3), they are exempt under § 552(b), principally as "intra-agency" communications under § 552(b)(5) (Exemption 5), made in the course of formulating agency decisions on legal and policy matters. . . .

It is clear, and the General Counsel concedes, that Appeals and Advice Memoranda are at the least "identifiable records" which must be disclosed on demand, unless they fall within one of the Act's exempt categories. It is also clear that, if the memoranda do fall within one of the Act's exempt categories, our inquiry is at an end, for the Act "does not apply" to such documents. Thus our inquiry, strictly speaking, must be into the scope of the exemptions which the General Counsel claims to be applicable—principally Exemption 5 relating to "intra-agency memorandums." The General Counsel also concedes, however, and we hold for the reasons set forth below, that Exemption 5 does not apply to any document which falls within the meaning of the phrase "final opinion . . . made in the adjudication of cases." 5 U.S.C. § 522(a)(2)(A). The General Counsel argues, therefore, as he must, that no Advice or Appeals Memorandum is a final opinion made in the adjudication of a case and that all are "intra-agency" memoranda within the coverage of Exemption 5. . . .

A

The parties are in apparent agreement that Exemption 5 withholds from a member of the public documents which a private party could not discover in litigation with the agency. Since virtually any document not privileged may be discovered by the appropriate litigant, if it is relevant to his litigation, and since the Act clearly intended to give any member of the public as much right to disclosure as one with a special interest therein, it is reasonable to construe Exemption 5 to exempt those documents, and only those documents, normally privileged in the civil discovery context. The privileges claimed by petitioners to be relevant to this case are (i) the "generally . . . recognized" privilege for "confidential intra-agency advisory opinions. . . .," disclosure of which "would be 'injurious to the consultative functions of government . . .'" (sometimes referred to as "executive privilege"), and (ii) the attorney-client and attorney work-product privileges generally available to all litigants.

(I)

That Congress had the Government's executive privilege specifically in mind in adopting Exemption 5 is clear. . . . The cases uniformly rest the privilege on the policy of protecting the "decision making processes of government agencies," and focus on documents "reflecting advisory opinions, recommendations and deliberations comprising part of a process by which governmental decisions and policies are formulated." . . . [T]he "frank discussion of legal or policy matters" in writing might be inhibited if the discussion were made public; and that the "decisions" and "policies formulated" would be the poorer as a result "there are enough incentives as it is for playing it safe and listing with the wind," and as we have said in an analogous context, "[h]uman experience teaches that those who expect public dissemination of their remarks may well temper candor with a concern for appearances . . . to the *detriment of the decisionmaking process.*" United States v. Nixon, 418 U.S. 683, 705 (1974).

Manifestly, the ultimate purpose of this long-recognized privilege is to prevent injury to the quality of agency decisions. The quality of a particular agency decision will clearly be affected by the communications received by the decisionmaker on the subject of the decision prior to the time the decision is made. However, it is difficult to see how the quality of a decision will be affected by communications with respect to the decision occurring after the decision is finally reached; and therefore equally difficult to see how the quality of the decision will be affected by forced disclosure of such communications, as long as prior communications and the ingredients of the decisionmaking process are not disclosed. Accordingly, the lower courts have uniformly drawn a distinction between predecisional communications, which are privileged, and communications made after the decision and designed to explain it, which are not.[19] This distinction is supported not only by

---

19. We are aware that the line between predecisional documents and postdecisional documents may not always be a bright one. Indeed, even the prototype of the postdecisional document—the "final opinion"—serves the dual function of explaining the decision just made and providing guides for decisions of similar or analogous cases arising in the future. In its latter function, the opinion is predecisional; and the manner in which it is written may, therefore, affect decisions in later cases. For present purposes it is sufficient to note that final opinions are *primarily* postdecisional—looking back on and explaining, as they do, a decision already reached or a policy already adopted—and that their disclosure poses a negligible risk of denying to agency decisionmakers the uninhibited advice which is so important to agency decisions.

the lesser injury to the decisionmaking process flowing from disclosure of postdecisional communications, but also, in the case of those communications which explain the decision, by the increased public interest in knowing the basis for agency policy already adopted. The public is only marginally concerned with reasons supporting a policy which an agency has rejected, or with reasons which might have supplied, but did not supply, the basis for a policy which was actually adopted on a different ground. In contrast, the public is vitally concerned with the reasons which did supply the basis for an agency policy actually adopted. These reasons, if expressed within the agency, constitute the "working law" of the agency and have been held by the lower courts to be outside the protection of Exemption 5. Exemption 5, properly construed, calls for "disclosure of all 'opinions and interpretations' which embody the agency's effective law and policy, and the withholding of all papers which reflect the agency's group thinking in the process of working out its policy and determining what its law shall be."

This conclusion is powerfully supported by the other provisions of the Act. The affirmative portion of the Act, expressly requiring indexing of "final opinions," "statements of policy and interpretations which have been adopted by the agency," and "instructions to staff that affect a member of the public," 5 U.S.C. § 552(a)(2), represents a strong congressional aversion to "secret [agency] law," and represents an affirmative congressional purpose to require disclosure of documents which have "the force and effect of law." We should be reluctant, therefore, to construe Exemption 5 to apply to the documents described in 5 U.S.C. § 552(a)(2); and with respect at least to "final opinions," which not only invariably explain agency action already taken or an agency decision already made, but also constitute "final dispositions" of matters by an agency, Exemption 5 can never apply.

(II)

It is equally clear that Congress had the attorney's work-product privilege specifically in mind when it adopted Exemption 5 and that such a privilege had been recognized in the civil discovery context by the prior case law. The case law clearly makes the attorney's work-product rule of Hickman v. Taylor, 329 U.S. 495 (1947), applicable to Government attorneys in litigation. Whatever the outer boundaries of the attorney's work-product rule are, the rule clearly applies to memoranda prepared by an attorney in contemplation of litigation which set forth the attorney's theory of the case and his litigation strategy.

B

Applying these principles to the memoranda sought by Sears, it becomes clear that Exemption 5 does not apply to those Appeals and Advice Memoranda which conclude that no complaint should be filed and which have the effect of finally denying relief to the charging party; but that Exemption 5 does protect from disclosure those Appeals and Advice Memoranda which direct the filing of a complaint and the commencement of litigation before the Board.

(I)

Under the procedures employed by the General Counsel, Advice and Appeals Memoranda are communicated to the Regional Director *after* the General Counsel, through his Advice and Appeals Branches, has decided whether or not to issue a complaint; and represent an explanation to the Regional Director of a legal or policy decision already adopted by the General Counsel. In the case of decisions *not* to file a complaint, the memoranda effect as "final" a "disposition," as an administrative decision can—representing, as it does, an unreviewable rejection of the charge filed by the private party. Disclosure of these memoranda would not intrude on predecisional processes, and protecting them would not improve the quality of agency decisions, since when the memoranda are communicated to the Regional Director, the General Counsel has already reached his decision and the Regional Director who receives them has no decision to make—he is bound to dismiss the charge. Moreover, the General Counsel's decisions not to file complaints together with the Advice and Appeals Memoranda explaining them, are precisely the kind of agency law in which the public is so vitally interested and which Congress sought to prevent the agency from keeping secret.

For essentially the same reasons, these memoranda are "final opinions" made in the "adjudication of cases" which must be indexed pursuant to 5 U.S.C. § 552(a)(2)(A). The decision to dismiss a charge is a decision in a "case" and constitutes an "adjudication": an "adjudication" is defined under the Administrative Procedure Act, of which 5 U.S.C. § 552 is a part, as "agency process for the formulation of an order," 5 U.S.C. § 551(7); an "order" is defined as "the whole or a part of a *final disposition,* whether affirmative [or] negative . . . of an agency in a matter . . .," 5 U.S.C. § 551(6) and the dismissal of a charge, as noted above, is a "final disposition." Since an Advice or Appeals Memorandum explains the reasons for the "final disposition" it plainly qualifies as an "opinion"; and falls within 5 U.S.C. § 552(a)(2) (A). . . .

(II)

Advice and Appeals Memoranda which direct the filing of a complaint, on the other hand, fall within the coverage of Exemption 5. The filing of a complaint does not finally dispose even of the General Counsel's responsibility with respect to the case. The case will be litigated before and decided by the Board; and the General Counsel will have the responsibility of advocating the position of the charging party before the Board. The Memoranda will inexorably contain the General Counsel's theory of the case and may communicate to the Regional Director some litigation strategy or settlement advice. Since the Memoranda will also have been prepared in contemplation of the upcoming litigation, they fall squarely within Exemption 5's protection of an attorney's work product. At the same time, the public's interest in disclosure is substantially reduced by the fact that the basis for the General Counsel's legal decision will come out in the course of litigation before the Board; and that the "law" with respect to these cases will ultimately be made not by the General Counsel but by the Board or the courts.

We recognize that an Advice or Appeals Memorandum directing the filing of a complaint—although representing only a decision that a legal issue is sufficiently in doubt to warrant determination by another body—has many of the characteristics of the documents described in 5 U.S.C. § 552(a)(2). Although not a "final opinion" in the "adjudication" of a "case" because it does not effect a "final disposition," the memorandum does explain a decision already reached by the General Counsel which has real operative effect—it permits litigation before the Board; and we have indicated a reluctance to construe Exemption 5 to protect such documents. We do so in this case only because the decisionmaker—the General Counsel—must become a litigating party to the case with respect to which he has made his decision. The attorney's work-product policies which Congress clearly incorporated into Exemption 5 thus come into play and lead us to hold that the Advice and Appeals Memoranda directing the filing of a complaint are exempt whether or not they are, as the District Court held, "instructions to staff that affect a member of the public."

C

Petitioners assert that the District Court erred in holding that documents incorporated by reference in nonexempt Advice and Appeals Memoranda lose any exemption they might previously have held as "intra-agency" memoranda. We disagree.

The probability that an agency employee will be inhibited from freely advising a decisionmaker for fear that his advice *if adopted,* will become public is slight. First, when adopted, the reasoning becomes that of the agency and becomes *its* responsibility to defend. Second, agency employees will generally be encouraged rather than discouraged by public knowledge that their policy suggestions have been adopted by the agency. Moreover, the public interest in knowing the reasons for a policy actually adopted by an agency supports the District Court's decision below. Thus, we hold that, if an agency chooses *expressly* to adopt or incorporate by reference an intra-agency memorandum previously covered by Exemption 5 in what would otherwise be a final opinion, that memorandum may be withheld only on the ground that it falls within the coverage of some exemption other than Exemption 5.

Petitioners also assert that the District Court's order erroneously requires it to produce or create explanatory material in those instances in which an Appeals Memorandum refers to the "circumstances of the case." We agree. The Act does not compel agencies to write opinions in cases in which they would not otherwise be required to do so. It only requires disclosure of certain documents which the law requires the agency to prepare or which the agency has decided for its own reasons to create. Thus, insofar as the order of the court below requires the agency to create explanatory material, it is baseless. Nor is the agency required to identify, after the fact, those pre-existing documents which contain the "circumstances of the case" to which the opinion may have referred, and which are not identified by the party seeking disclosure. . . .

Notes and Questions

1. *Exemption 5 and § 552(a)(2).* As explained by *Sears, Roebuck,* under Exemption 5 a document that would be normally privileged from discovery in civil litigation is exempt from FOIA disclosure. The most important such privilege, for FOIA purposes, is the government's right to withhold records that would expose its deliberative processes. What is the rationale for the deliberative process privilege? Do you agree with it? Does the privilege diminish the value of FOIA as a political check on agencies?

A comparable exemption exists in about one-third of state open records laws. Braverman & Heppler, *supra* at 743–45. However, in many states these exemptions are significantly narrower than FOIA Exemption 5. For example, the California exemption applies only to material that is not retained by the agency in the ordinary course of business and also requires a showing that the public interest in withholding the records clearly outweighs the public interest in disclosure. *See Citizens for a Better Environment v. California Dept. of Food and Agriculture,* 217 Cal.Rptr. 504 (Cal.App.1985). Similarly, the Michigan statute requires a showing that the public interest in encouraging frank communications within agencies outweighs the public interest in disclosure. *See Milford v. Gilb,* 384 N.W.2d 786 (Mich.App.1985). Do these narrower exemptions better serve the objective of using FOIA as a political check on agency action?

2. *The Sears holdings.* In *Sears, Roebuck* certain of the NLRB general counsel's appeals or advice memos were found to be exempt from disclosure. Others were not exempt from disclosure and were treated as "final opinions." This means that they must be routinely made available (as distinguished from being furnished on specific request) and indexed under § 552(a)(2). How did the Court distinguish between exempt and non-exempt memoranda? Does the distinction make sense?

Sears, Roebuck holds that Exemption 5 does not apply to the documents described in § 552(a)(2)—documents which embody the agency's effective law and policy. Is there something especially odious about "secret law?" Does that suggest a greater justification for § 552(a)(1) and (2) than for § 552(a)(3)?

Note that § 552(a)(2) also requires disclosure and indexing of statements of policy and interpretations adopted by the agency. See discussion of interpretive rules and policy statements in § 6.11.5 *supra.* These do not have to be "final." Should the general counsel's memoranda have been disclosed under this provision?

Courts often distinguish in applying Exemption 5 between factual and non-factual material. The notion is that disclosure of factual material in agency memoranda would not impact negatively on the decision-making process. Is this always true? The New York statute explicitly provides that its deliberative process exemption neither applies to "statistical or factual tabulations or data" nor to "instructions to staff that affect the public." Public Officers Law § 87(g).

3. *FOIA as discovery.* Why did Sears want the documents? Why did the NLRB want to keep them confidential?

In material edited out of the case, the Court explained that Sears had requested all advice and appeals memoranda issued within the preceding five years on the subject of the propriety of withdrawals by employers or unions from multi-employer bargaining units. The regional director (after receiving advice from the general counsel) had refused to issue a complaint requested by Sears. Sears was in the process of preparing an appeal to the general counsel of that refusal. The Court observed:

> Sears' rights under the Act are neither increased nor decreased by reason of the fact that it claims an interest in the Advice and Appeals Memoranda greater than that shared by the average member of the public. The Act is fundamentally designed to inform the public about agency action and not to benefit private litigants.

421 U.S. at 143, n. 10. Thus, for example, an agency proceeding against a party would not ordinarily be delayed because the parties are also litigating the party's FOIA demand. *Renegotiation Board v. Bannercraft Clothing Co.,* 415 U.S. 1 (1974).

The *Sears* case is a good example of one of the most important functions of FOIA—and one of its most controversial. It is used as a technique for discovery in pending administrative or judicial litigation. *See generally* Tomlinson, "Use of the Freedom of Information Act for Discovery Purposes," 43 Md.L.Rev. 119 (1984).

Why would a litigator prefer to conduct discovery through a FOIA request (in addition to conventional discovery processes)? Agency rules may not provide for any discovery or only for very limited discovery. *See* § 4.1.2 *supra.* Discovery may not be available in connection with judicial review in appellate courts of agency rules. When discovery is available, it is provided only at defined times (i.e. after a complaint is filed) and is controlled by an adjudicator (an ALJ or a judge if the case is in court). Under conventional discovery rules, a party can resist production of irrelevant or excessively burdensome materials. But when documents are demanded under FOIA, there are no such limits.

Unless an exemption applies, all of the requested documents must be promptly disclosed.

The regular discovery process has some advantages over FOIA. For example, a person making a FOIA request must ordinarily pay the costs of search and duplication. APA § 552(a)(4)(A) sets forth detailed ground rules on the subject of fees. No such costs are imposed in discovery. Discovery offers processes such as depositions and interrogatories that are unavailable under FOIA. Finally, discovery privileges might be less protective to the government than the FOIA exemptions. For example, although the deliberative process privilege involved in *Sears, Roebuck* is also applicable to a request for documents in discovery, a court may require disclosure of the documents upon a showing of special need. *See, e.g., United States v. Nixon,* 418 U.S. 683 (1974) (documents and tapes protected by executive privilege must be disclosed because needed in prosecution of criminal case).

Should FOIA be amended to preclude requests by persons engaged in litigation with the agency, thus remitting such persons to conventional discovery? Or is such a litigant the person with the strongest claim for FOIA disclosure? ACUS recommended that a party to litigation with the government be required to notify government counsel of any FOIA requests relevant to the proceeding. But it did not recommend closing the FOIA to parties in litigation. *See* Recommendation 83–4, "The Use of the Freedom of Information Act for Discovery Purposes," 1 C.F.R. § 305.83–4.

4. *Related exemptions.* The deliberative process privilege is a component of "executive privilege;" another component is the privilege to withhold state secrets. The state secret exemption is spelled out in exemption (1) of FOIA. Exemption (1) leaves substantial discretion to the executive branch in making classification decisions and, under President Reagan, many more documents were classified as secret. Nevertheless, exemption (1) does permit the court to conduct an in camera review of the propriety of the decision to classify a document.

FOIA Exemption (7) protects the government's interest in the confidentiality of law enforcement files and manuals. For example, a document that could reasonably be expected to disclose the identity of a confidential source is protected. Similarly, material that would disclose law enforcement techniques or guidelines is exempt if disclosure might facilitate circumvention of the law. *See also* 1981 MSAPA §§ 3–116(2) and 2–101(g)(1) and discussion in § 6.11.5b, note 3, *supra.*

§ 8.1.2 CONFIDENTIAL PRIVATE INFORMATION: § 552(b)(4)

CHRYSLER CORPORATION v. BROWN
441 U.S. 281 (1979).

[Chrysler is required to comply with Executive Orders 11246 and 11275 which prohibit government contractors from engaging in employment discrimination on the basis of race or sex. Under regulations adopted by the Office of Federal Contract Compliance (OFCCP), Chrysler must file with the Defense Logistics Agency (DLA) detailed reports on its affirmative action plans and composition of its workforce.

OFCCP regulations provide that such reports shall be made available for public inspection and copying "if it is determined that the requested inspection or copying furthers the public interest and does not impede any of the functions of OFCCP or the Compliance Agencies except in the case of records disclosure of which is prohibited by law." OFCCP proposed to furnish Chrysler's affirmative action plan to someone who requested it. Chrysler sought to enjoin this release in the District Court, asserting that exemption (4) of FOIA *prevented* DLA from disclosing the material (a so-called "reverse FOIA" suit). That court granted the injunction but the Court of Appeals reversed, holding that Chrysler could not prevent the release.]

REHNQUIST, J.:

The expanding range of federal regulatory activity and growth in the Government sector of the economy have increased federal agencies' demands for information about the activities of private individuals and corporations. These developments have paralleled a related concern about secrecy in Government and abuse of power. The Freedom of Information Act (hereinafter FOIA) was a response to this concern, but it has also had a largely unforeseen tendency to exacerbate the uneasiness of those who comply with governmental demands for information. For under the FOIA third parties have been able to obtain Government files containing information submitted by corporations and individuals who thought that the information would be held in confidence. . . .

II

Chrysler contends that the nine exemptions in general, and Exemption 4 in particular, reflect a sensitivity to the privacy interests of private individuals and nongovernmental entities. That contention may be conceded without inexorably requiring the conclusion that the exemptions impose affirmative duties on an agency to withhold information sought. . . .

That the FOIA is exclusively a disclosure statute is, perhaps, demonstrated most convincingly by examining its provision for judicial relief. Subsection (a)(4)(B) gives federal district courts "jurisdiction to enjoin the agency from withholding agency records and to order the production of any agency records improperly withheld from the complainant." That provision does not give the authority to bar disclosure, and thus fortifies our belief that Chrysler, and courts which have shared its view, have incorrectly interpreted the exemption provisions of the FOIA. The Act is an attempt to meet the demand for open government while preserving workable confidentiality in governmental decisionmaking. Congress appreciated that, with the expanding sphere of governmental regulation and enterprise, much of the information within Government files has been submitted by private entities seeking

Government contracts or responding to unconditional reporting obligations imposed by law. There was sentiment that Government agencies should have the latitude, in certain circumstances, to afford the confidentiality desired by these submitters. But the congressional concern was with the *agency's* need or preference for confidentiality; the FOIA by itself protects the submitters' interest in confidentiality only to the extent that this interest is endorsed by the agency collecting the information.

Enlarged access to governmental information undoubtedly cuts against the privacy concerns of nongovernmental entities, and as a matter of policy some balancing and accommodation may well be desirable. We simply hold here that Congress did not design the FOIA exemptions to be mandatory bars to disclosure. . . .

III

Chrysler contends, however, that even if its suit for injunctive relief cannot be based on the FOIA, such an action can be premised on the Trade Secrets Act, 18 U.S.C. § 1905. The Act provides:

> Whoever, being an officer or employee of the United States . . . makes known in any manner or to any extent not authorized by law any information coming to him in the course of his employment or official duties or by reason of any examination or investigation made by, or return, report or record made to or filed with, such department or agency or officer or employee thereof, which information concerns or relates to the trade secrets, processes, operations, style of work, or apparatus, or to the identity, confidential statistical data, amount or source of any income, profits, losses, or expenditures of any person, firm, partnership, corporation, or association; or permits any income return or copy thereof or any book containing any abstract or particulars thereof to be seen or examined by any person except as provided by law; shall be fined not more than $1,000, or imprisoned not more than one year, or both; and shall be removed from office or employment.

There are necessarily two parts to Chrysler's argument: that § 1905 is applicable to the type of disclosure threatened in this case, and that it affords Chrysler a private right of action to obtain injunctive relief.

A

The Court of Appeals held that § 1905 was not applicable to the agency disclosure at issue here because such disclosure was "authorized by law" within the meaning of the Act. The court found the source of that authorization to be the OFCCP regulations that DLA relied on in deciding to disclose information on the Hamtramck and Newark plants. Chrysler contends here that these agency regulations are not "law" within the meaning of § 1905.

It has been established in a variety of contexts that properly promulgated, substantive agency regulations have the "force and effect of law." This doctrine is so well established that agency regulations implementing federal statutes have been held to pre-empt state law under the Supremacy Clause. It would therefore take a clear showing of contrary legislative intent before the phrase "authorized by law" in § 1905 could be held to have a narrower ambit than the traditional understanding. . . . But in order for such regulations to have the "force and effect of law," it is necessary to establish a nexus between the regulations and some delegation of the requisite legislative authority by Congress. . . . The pertinent inquiry is whether under any of the arguable *statutory* grants of authority the OFCCP disclosure regulations relied on by the respondents are reasonably within the contemplation of that grant of authority. We think that it is clear that when it enacted these statutes, Congress was not concerned with public disclosure of trade secrets or confidential business information. . . .

There is also a procedural defect in the OFCCP disclosure regulations which precludes courts from affording them the force and effect of law. That defect is a lack of strict compliance with the APA. . . .

Certainly regulations subject to the APA cannot be afforded the "force and effect of law" if not promulgated pursuant to the statutory procedural minimum found in that Act. . . .

B

We reject, however, Chrysler's contention that the Trade Secrets Act affords a private right of action to enjoin disclosure in violation of the statute. In *Cort v. Ash,* 422 U.S. 66 (1975), we noted that this Court has rarely implied a private right of action under a criminal statute, and where it has done so "there was at least a statutory basis for inferring that a civil cause of action of some sort lay in favor of someone." Nothing in § 1905 prompts such an inference. Nor are other pertinent circumstances outlined in *Cort* present here. As our review of the legislative history of § 1905—or lack of same—might suggest, there is no indication of legislative intent to create a private right of action. Most importantly, a private right of action under § 1905 is not "necessary to make effective the congressional purpose," for we find that review of DLA's decision to disclose Chrysler's employment data is available under the APA.

IV

While Chrysler may not avail itself of any violations of the provisions of § 1905 in a separate cause of action, any such violations may have a dispositive effect on the outcome of judicial review of agency action pursuant to the APA. . . .

[O]ur discussion in Part III demonstrates that § 1905 and any "authoriz[ation] by law" contemplated by that section place substantive limits on agency action. Therefore, we conclude that DLA's decision to disclose the Chrysler reports is reviewable agency action and Chrysler is a person "adversely affected or aggrieved". . . . For the reasons previously stated, we believe any disclosure that violates § 1905 is "not in accordance with law" within the meaning of 5 U.S.C. § 706(2)

(A). . . . The District Court in this case concluded that disclosure of some of Chrysler's documents was barred by § 1905, but the Court of Appeals did not reach the issue. We shall therefore vacate the Court of Appeals' judgment and remand for further proceedings consistent with this opinion in order that the Court of Appeals may consider whether the contemplated disclosures would violate the prohibition of § 1905.[49]

Vacated and remanded.

MARSHALL, J. concurred, pointing out that the Court had not ruled on the validity of the executive orders.

Notes and Questions

1. *The (4) exemption.* Unlike the *Chrysler* situation, in many cases an agency *refuses* to furnish information previously submitted to it because it is "trade secrets and commercial or financial information obtained from a person and privileged or confidential." The difficult problem is to decide what information should be treated as "confidential," given that the submitters of the material would like none of it disclosed.

The courts have applied an objective standard in interpreting the word "confidential." Regardless of the subjective expectations of the submitter and regardless of any pledge of confidentiality by the agency, the information would be considered confidential only in two situations: i) disclosure is likely to impair the government's ability to obtain necessary information in the future (this is applicable only to voluntarily submitted information, not information the government has power to compel); or ii) disclosure is likely to cause substantial harm to the competitive position of the outside party. *National Parks and Conservation Ass'n v. Morton,* 498 F.2d 765 (D.C.Cir.1974). Needless to say, this standard is difficult for courts to apply (can a court reliably distinguish "substantial" from "insubstantial" competitive harm?) Approximately one-third of the states have a comparable exemption in their information statutes (and most of the others protect confidential information under other statutes). Braverman & Heppler, *supra* at 741–43.

2. *Reverse FOIA suits.* *Chrysler* held that FOIA is purely a disclosure statute. It does not empower submitters to prevent the government from disclosing information which the government might have kept secret under exemption (4) but wishes to disclose. However,

---

49. Since the Court of Appeals assumed for purposes of argument that the material in question was within an exemption to the FOIA, that court found it unnecessary expressly to decide that issue and it is open on remand. We, of course, do not here attempt to determine the relative ambits of Exemption 4 and § 1905, or to determine whether § 1905 is an exempting statute within the terms of the amended Exemption 3, 5 U.S.C. § 552(b)(3). Although there is a theoretical possibility that material might be outside Exemption 4 yet within the substantive provisions of § 1905, and that therefore the FOIA might provide the necessary "authoriz[ation] by law" for purposes of § 1905, that possibility is at most of limited practical significance in view of the similarity of language between Exemption 4 and the substantive provisions of § 1905.

the Court held that § 1905, the Trade Secrets Act, prohibits such disclosures, unless a statute or a validly adopted legislative regulation permits it. Moreover, it held that a proposed agency disclosure of information was agency action, reviewable under the APA for compliance with § 1905. This supplied the remedy which submitters like Chrysler had been looking for.

The issues left open in note 49 of *Chrysler* were resolved in *CNA Financial Corp. v. Donovan,* 830 F.2d 1132 (D.C.Cir.1987). *CNA* held that § 1905 is not a statute forbidding disclosure within the meaning of exemption (3) (since it allows an agency to adopt rules that permit disclosure of any of the items mentioned in § 1905). The *CNA* decision also held that § 1905 and exemption (4) cover the same ground. As a result, if no rule permits disclosure of information that would be "confidential" within the meaning of exemption (4), the agency cannot disclose it. *CNA* involved the same type of employment records that were at issue in *Chrysler.* The agency had ruled that disclosure would not cause the submitter any competitive injury within the meaning of exemption (4), and the court upheld this determination.

3. *Disclosure of confidential material.* Agency disclosure of materials submitted to it by outsiders poses severe practical problems. There is a vast amount of technical or financial information which government obtains through its regulatory, procurement, licensing, and law enforcement activity. The submitters of much of that material have a vital stake in keeping it confidential. And there is no doubt that a high percentage of FOIA requesters are actually commercial firms trying to find out information about their competitors.

Although the *Chrysler* decision might seem to provide adequate protection, a submitter might not be informed that the agency proposed to disclose the information in time to prevent it (many agencies do notify submitters as a matter of course when their material has been requested). Apparently some information that might be covered by both exemption (4) and § 1905 has been released inadvertently by low-level personnel who did not appreciate its confidentiality. (Many submitters stamp their material "confidential" to alert agency personnel to such claims.) Or an agency like OFCCP that wants to release the information might adopt a rule having the force of law that would allow it to do so under § 1905. One commentator recently noted:

> Suzuki Motor Company has been an effective collector of Toyota's submissions to the U.S. government in 1981, though neither firm would enjoy access to the other's data in Japan. A food processor which saves tens of thousands of dollars of its filtration costs because of its innovations may never enjoy the . . . advantages, because its blueprints were photocopied last week at a regional office of the EPA and mailed to its larger competitor for ten cents per copy. And the small inventor with the archetypal better mousetrap finds that contracting or proposing to contract with the government opens detailed design data to larger competi-

tors, who can enter the market more quickly and dispose of both mice and the innovator.

> The FOIA was meant by all its sponsors to keep agencies accountable for their workings and official conduct. By 1982, the quarter of a billion dollar cost of the Act was subsidizing Swedish ball bearing makers in their searches at [the] FTC, French aviation firms at [the] DOT, and competitive searches throughout the government.

O'Reilly, "Regaining a Confidence: Protection of Business Confidential Data through Reform of the Freedom of Information Act," 34 Admin.L. Rev. 263, 263–64 (1982) (arguing for a significant broadening of exemption (4) so that any possibility of competitive harm would prevent disclosure).

Should FOIA be amended to preclude its use by business to obtain information about competitors? To charge requestors a much higher fee in such situations so that the process is not subsidized by the taxpayers?

Another commentator concluded:

> Even if, as appears from the admittedly less than comprehensive survey performed in the course of this study, the instances of disclosure of business secrets through the operation of FOIA are relatively rare and insignificant, the perceptual problem *is* real and appears to be generating unnecessary friction in the relations between government and business . . . There is, therefore, a need to improve the procedures used by agencies in handling FOIA requests for business information in order to alter the perception prevailing in the private sector that business secrets are not safe from disclosure once they come into the hands of the federal government.

Stevenson, "Protecting Business Secrets Under the Freedom of Information Act: Managing Exemption 4," 34 Admin.L.Rev. 207, 222 (1982) (arguing only for modest procedural changes and an upgrading in the quality of personnel doing FOIA work, not for expansion of exemption (4)).

4. *Related exemption.* Consider also FOIA exemption (6) which prevents disclosure of material (such as personnel or medical files) that would constitute a clearly unwarranted invasion of personal privacy. Note that this exemption requires a court to balance the public interest in disclosure against the private interest in preserving privacy. See *Department of Air Force v. Rose,* 425 U.S. 352 (1976) (summaries of Air Force Academy disciplinary cases, with names and other identifying details removed, are not exempt).

5. *Problem.* Gloria is a psychology professor at Madison State Univ. (MSU) who is doing research on the effect on parents of having been subjected to physical abuse in childhood. The work has no commercial application, but it requires substantial outside funding. As

a result Gloria applied to the National Institute of Mental Health (NIMH), a federal agency that makes research grants to scholars, and received a $400,000 grant for the current year.

Gloria's application set forth the experiments that she intended to perform and the results she hoped to achieve. NIMH always performs a lengthy evaluation of each application. That process includes a committee of professors that writes candid appraisals of each application. The committee recommends which applications should be granted (and in which priority if the funds are not sufficient for all of them) and which should be denied. However, the decision is up to John, the director of NIMH. John writes a detailed report on his reasons for having selected particular applications and turned down others. NIMH promised its applicants that all of the above material would remain confidential.

Bob, a psychology professor at Adams State University, filed a FOIA request to receive Gloria's application, the minutes of the committee's deliberation, and John's report.

(a) Assume that NIMH refuses to disclose any of the information and Bob brings a FOIA action to compel its disclosure. What part of the material, if any, is exempt from disclosure?

(b) Assume that NIMH proposes to disclose all of the information. Gloria seeks judicial review of this decision. Can she prevent the disclosure? *See Washington Research Project v. H.E.W.,* 504 F.2d 238 (D.C.Cir.1974), *cert. denied,* 421 U.S. 963 (1975).

§ 8.2 THE SUNSHINE AND ADVISORY COMMITTEE ACTS

§ 8.2.1 SUNSHINE ACT

All fifty states have statutes requiring that most agency meetings (as well as meetings of the legislature) be held in public. *See* Fossey & Roston, "Invalidation as a Remedy for Violation of Open Meeting Statutes: Is the Cure Worse than the Disease?" 20 U.S.F.L.Rev. 163 (1986) (note 2 cites all state statutes). Finally, in 1976, the federal government followed suit by enacting the Sunshine Act, 5 U.S.C. § 552b. The Sunshine Act requires the meetings of agency heads to be held in public unless the meeting falls under one of ten exemptions in the statute. It requires advance public notice of such meetings, certification by the chief legal officer of the agency that a meeting can be closed to the public, and the making of a transcript of all closed meetings.

Like FOIA, the Sunshine Act allows any person to seek judicial enforcement and allows the award of attorney's fees to a substantially prevailing party. Under the Sunshine Act, a court cannot invalidate agency action simply because a closed meeting should have been open. However, a majority of state laws do permit invalidation of the action.

Fossey & Roston, *supra*, criticize invalidation as a sanction because it leaves the finality of government action in limbo, perhaps for many years, while litigation wends its way through the courts.   Moreover, invalidation might be extremely detrimental to the public interest if the result is to abrogate agency rules protective of health or safety. Some states also provide for civil money penalties against members of an agency that violate open meeting laws. *See Merz v. Leitch*, 342 N.W.2d 141 (Minn.1984).

Are open meeting statutes a significant political check on agency action? The purposes of the federal Act were recently summarized:

> Congress enacted the Sunshine Act to open the deliberations of multi-member federal agencies to public view. It believed that increased openness would enhance citizen confidence in government, encourage higher quality work by government officials, stimulate well-informed public debate about government programs and policies, and promote cooperation between citizens and government. In short, it sought to make government more fully accountable to the people.

Common Cause v. NRC, 674 F.2d 921, 928 (D.C.Cir.1982).

In interpreting the law, the main difficulties center on the definition of "meeting," the requirement that agencies publish agendas of their meetings in advance, and the application of the exemptions.

a. *Definition of meeting*. If "meeting" is defined too broadly, the Act would prevent informal discussions between members of the agency, but if it is defined too narrowly, the members can easily circumvent it by making collegial decisions in secret, then rubberstamping them in brief public sessions.

In *Moberg v. Indep. School Dist. No. 281*, 336 N.W.2d 510 (Minn. 1983), the Court considered a series of informal discussions between members of a school board who were seeking to break a deadlock over an important policy issue. It said:

> We therefore hold that "meetings" subject to the requirements of the Open Meeting Law are those gatherings of a quorum or more members of the governing body, or a quorum of a committee . . . at which members discuss, decide, or receive information as a group on issues relating to the official business of that governing body. Although "chance or social gatherings" are exempt from the requirements of the statute . . . a quorum may not, as a group, discuss or receive information on official business in any setting under the guise of a private social gathering. The statute does not apply to letters or telephone conversations between fewer than a quorum.

> Appellants correctly point out that this rule may be circumvented by serial face-to-face or telephone conversations between board members to marshall their votes on an issue before it is initially raised at a public hearing. It does not follow that two- or three-

person conversations should be prohibited, however, because officials who are determined to act furtively will hold such discussions anyway, or might simply use an outsider as an intermediary. There is a way to illegally circumvent any rule the court might fashion, and therefore it is important that the rule not be so restrictive as to lose the public benefit of personal discussion between public officials while gaining little assurance of openness. Of course, serial meetings in groups of less than a quorum for the purposes of avoiding public hearings or fashioning agreement on an issue may also be found to be a violation of the statute depending upon the facts of the individual case.

Id. at 517–18. However, in *FCC v. ITT World Communications, Inc.,* 466 U.S. 463 (1984), the Supreme Court defined "meeting" more narrowly under the Sunshine Act to exclude gatherings of an agency to receive information. The *ITT* case involved a committee of FCC members who engaged in consultation with their foreign counterparts. The FCC committee was itself treated as an "agency" because it had power to approve certain applications. But its consultations were not "meetings" because they did not concern such approvals. According to the Court, a "meeting" occurs only when the agency deliberates on matters within its formal delegated authority, whereas the meetings in question were background discussions and exchanges of views with non-agency members. "Informal background discussions that clarify issues and expose varying views" are not "meetings" because Congress thought that keeping such discussions private was necessary for the effective conduct of agency business.

Which definition of "meeting" better serves the objective of using open meeting statutes as a political check on agencies?

b. *Advance publication of agendas.* In order for open meeting statutes to be a meaningful political check on government, members of the public must be able to attend the meetings. This requires reasonable advance publication of the time and place of the meeting and the agenda. Yet an overly rigid application of this rule would prevent agencies from dealing with important new business that demands immediate attention. Thus the Texas Supreme Court held that a Board of Education violated the act when it merely notified the public that it would consider "personnel" and "litigation" matters. The public was entitled to a more specific agenda, in this case that the Board was going to consider the appointment of a new school superintendent and a major desegregation lawsuit—even though it was legally entitled to go into closed session on these matters. *Cox Enterprises v. Board of Trustees of Austin Independent School Dist.,* 706 S.W.2d 956 (Tex.1986).

c. *Exemptions.* The exemptions to the federal act closely parallel the FOIA exemptions. Where a meeting or part of a meeting falls within an exemption, it can be closed—but the rest of the meeting, dealing with non-exempt matters, must be kept open. Generally speaking, if an agency could resist a FOIA demand (for example, a request for a confidential private financial document under exemption (4)), it could close a meeting which considers the same sort of information.

However, there are several additional exemptions in the Sunshine Act. One is for information, premature disclosure of which would "be likely to significantly frustrate implementation of a proposed agency action." § 552b(c)(9)(B). This exemption has been held to be very narrow—relating only to matters like a pending embargo. Premature disclosure of an embargo would cause the goods to be exported before the agency had time to act. *Common Cause v. NRC, supra* (discussions about agency budget must be public).

Another Sunshine exception not found in FOIA concerns discussions of the agency's participation in pending civil litigation or its discussions concerning the initiation, conduct, or disposition of formal, on-the-record agency adjudication. Thus the agency can close a meeting where it discusses how to decide an appeal from an ALJ adjudicatory decision. But it must hold open meetings at which it makes decisions about rulemaking.

For treatment of exemptions to state open meeting laws, *see* Note, 10 Nova L.J. 106, 110–14 (1985). In some states, there is a much broader exemption. In Nebraska, for example, a meeting can be closed if "clearly necessary for the protection of the public interest or for the prevention of needless injury to the reputation of an individual." For a strict construction, see *Grein v. Board of Educ.*, 343 N.W.2d 718 (Neb. 1984).

The most important difference between the Sunshine and FOIA exceptions is that Sunshine contains no exemption parallel to FOIA exemption (5). As a result, pre-decisional communications between agency members, occurring in meetings, must be open to the public. The absence of a pre-decisional exemption has significant consequences. There is a natural tendency for agency heads and staff to prefer that their tentative discussions about politically sensitive matters be kept out of the public eye. *See generally* D. Welborn, W. Lyon, L. Thomas, IMPLEMENTATION AND EFFECTS OF THE FEDERAL GOVERNMENT IN THE SUNSHINE ACT (1984). Many observers of the federal bureaucracy believe that the result is fewer meetings of agency heads, decisions made through seriatim written approvals instead of collegially, or one-on-one meetings between agency heads and other members or with the staff. Do the laudable goals of the Sunshine Act (summarized above in the *Common Cause* case) justify the very real costs of the Act?

§ 8.2.2   FEDERAL ADVISORY COMMITTEE ACT (FACA)

FACA was enacted in 1972. P.L. 92–463, 5 U.S.C.App. I, 5 U.S.C.A. App. II. Congress was concerned by the proliferation of advisory committees to federal agencies.

Viewed in its worst light, the federal advisory committee can be a convenient nesting place for special interests seeking to change and preserve a federal policy for their own ends. Such committees stacked with giants in their respective fields can overwhelm a federal decision maker, or at least make him wary of upsetting the status quo.

NRDC v. Herrington, 637 F.Supp. 116, 120 (D.D.C.1986) (quoting FACA legislative history). The solution was to limit the number of such committees and open up the remaining ones to public scrutiny and input.

FACA requires that a detailed charter of each advisory committee to a federal agency be filed with the agency. Notice of committee meetings must be published in advance in the Federal Register, and the meetings must be open to the public (except under the same exemptions that apply to the Sunshine Act). All of its records and documents are also open to the public (except under the same exceptions that apply to FOIA). Detailed minutes must be kept. A designated agency employee must be present at every such meeting and must approve the agenda. There are detailed record-keeping requirements.

FACA causes a good deal of uncertainty when it is applied to ad hoc groups that seek or are invited to furnish input to an agency. For example, consider the Securities Law Committee of the American Bar Association (ABA). It is asked by the SEC to meet with its staff once or a few times to help frame some new regulations. Does the Securities Law Committee fall under FACA? If so, the FACA requirements are so onerous that the committee cannot realistically comply with them and therefore cannot give the requested advice. Moreover, the SEC's ability to obtain advice from experts in its field would be drastically circumscribed. *See* Vandegrift & Rosenblat, "The Federal Advisory Committee Act: Its Impact on Informal Contacts with the Staffs of Administrative Agencies," 41 Bus.Law. 1281 (1986).

An "advisory committee" covered by FACA includes every "committee . . . or other similar group . . . utilized" by an agency to obtain advice. This definition is broad enough to cover any meeting of two or more persons with agency staff. However, the courts have not interpreted the provision strictly. For example, it did not cover a panel of six nuclear physicists asked by the Secretary of Energy to evaluate the safety of a nuclear reactor after the Chernobyl incident. The court noted that the experts were asked to give individual, not collective advice, and had no selfish advantage to gain from giving such advice. *NRDC v. Herrington, supra.*

In an earlier decision, the court declined to apply FACA to ad hoc groups of business leaders invited to meet in the White House with executive branch officials in single, unstructured sessions. Only groups having an established structure and defined purpose, giving advice on an identified government policy, would qualify. *Nader v. Baroody,* 396 F.Supp. 1231 (D.D.C.1975). The court observed that Congress did not intend to intrude on the day-to-day functioning of government or impede casual, informal contacts with the public. Indeed, regulation of such meetings would raise serious separation of powers issues as to congressional power to restrict the discharge of the president's business.

After considering the *NRDC* and *Nader* cases, what is your advice to the ABA Securities Law Committee?

§ 8.3   PRIVACY ACT

The federal Privacy Act was enacted in 1974. Pub.L. 93–579; 5 U.S.C. § 552a. Numerous states followed the federal lead. *See generally* Gemberling & Weissman, "Data Privacy: Everything You Wanted to Know about the Minnesota Government Data Practices Act," 8 Wm. Mitchell L.Rev. 573 (1982); Feldman & Gordin, "Privacy and Personal Information Reporting: The Legislative Boom," 35 Bus.Law. 1259 (1980).

Unlike FOIA, open meeting, and advisory committee acts previously discussed in this chapter, the privacy acts cannot be viewed as techniques for politically checking agency behavior. Instead, they represent an important civil liberty—protection of individuals from harmful or unnecessary governmental information-keeping and reporting practices.

The federal and state acts are designed to limit the extent of government record-keeping about individuals and to assure that the records which are maintained are accurate. Thus an agency may maintain only such information about an individual as is relevant and necessary to accomplish a legitimate agency purpose. § 552a(e)(1). The federal act precludes an agency from maintaining a record describing how an individual exercises first amendment rights unless pertinent to and within the scope of an authorized law enforcement activity. § 552a(e)(7).

The acts afford individuals a right to have access to records concerning them and to correct those records. An individual can seek such access under either FOIA or the Privacy Act, whichever is most favorable. § 552a(q). The acts limit the extent to which information about an individual can be disclosed and call for reporting of most such instances of disclosure. *See Hinderliter v. Humphries,* 297 S.E.2d 684 (Va.1982) (unlawful dissemination of personnel report). Like FOIA, the acts provide for judicial enforcement and for award of attorney's fees to prevailing parties. The federal act provides for damage awards in case of intentional or wilful violations of the Act. *See Tijerina v. Walters,* 821 F.2d 789 (D.C.Cir.1987).

In an era of expanding surveillance and computer technology and increasing use of computer matching techniques to carry out government functions, the rights secured by federal and state privacy acts are of great importance. However, in comparison to FOIA, the federal act has had a relatively small impact. As one commentator noted:

> The weaknesses [of the Privacy Act] have been apparent since its inception. The product of hurried congressional consideration in

the closing days of the 93rd Congress, the Act displays its compromises in the form of broad exemptions and qualifications. As one commentator has noted, the Act is "its own worst enemy." Individuals seeking to enforce its provisions must contend with an ineffective remedial scheme, and substantive provisions that are subject to numerous exceptions and broad interpretations. The weaknesses of the Act have been illuminated by case law that, on the whole, has not been kind to aggrieved persons seeking relief under the Act.

Ehlke, "The Privacy Act After a Decade," 18 J. Marshall L.Rev. 829 (1985). An example of the weaknesses to which Ehlke refers is the definition of "records" and "system of records" on which the entire Act depends. A "record" is an item of information about an individual that contains his name or other identifying information; a "system of records" is a group of such records "under the control of any agency" from which information "is retrieved by the name of the individual" or some other identifying particular. § 552a(a)(4), (5).

These definitions render the Act inapplicable to a large amount of information about individuals. For example, the Act does not apply to personal notes made by agency employees about other employees (unless incorporated in an agency file), nor to information disclosed to an outsider if drawn from the speaker's independent knowledge rather than from a record, nor to files kept by the agency in which information cannot be retrieved by the names of individuals. *See Chapman v. NASA,* 682 F.2d 526 (5th Cir.1982), *cert. denied,* 469 U.S. 1038 (1984) (supervisor's personal notes covered by Act when added to employee's file); *Savarese v. U.S. Dept. of Health,* 479 F.Supp. 304 (N.D.Ga.1979), *aff'd,* 620 F.2d 298 (5th Cir.1980), *cert. denied,* 449 U.S. 1078 (1981) (disclosure of information about an employee not covered by Act because based on speaker's own knowledge and conversation with others, not on records; correspondence file not covered by Act since not indexed by names of persons, only by date of letter).

For thorough treatment of both the Privacy Act and FOIA, see Braverman & Chetwynd, INFORMATION LAW (1985).

Part III

JUDICIAL REVIEW

In this Part we examine judicial review of agency action—the role of the courts as a check upon improper administration. After examining the scope and availability of judicial review, this Part will examine the various limitations on its exercise.

Courts are authorized to review agency action in order to ensure that it is *lawful* because agency procedures and nonjudicial means of controlling agency action alone are insufficient to ensure the legality of agency action. However, courts are not empowered to review agency action in order to ensure that it is *desirable*. This is so because the method by which we typically select judges and retain them in office is calculated to mute the popular will on such policy matters rather than to focus it, and because courts do not have the necessary expertness to determine the desirability (as opposed to legality) of agency action.

Chapter 9

SCOPE OF JUDICIAL REVIEW

§ 9.1 SCOPE OF REVIEW OF AGENCY FINDINGS OF BASIC FACT

In adjudicating a dispute, an agency must make findings of basic fact. These are determinations of what happened and why, or who did what to whom, with what state of mind. Many formulas describe the scope of a reviewing court's power to overturn an agency's findings of basic fact. These formulas might be arrayed as follows, starting with those that provide for the largest judicial powers and finishing with the smallest:

i. *Trial de novo.* The court rehears the evidence and redecides the case. See federal APA § 706(2)(F). There are a number of examples in state and federal administrative law of de novo judicial trials on specific issues of fact determined initially by an agency. They will be discussed in § 9.1.2.

ii. *Independent judgment on the evidence.* The court decides the case on the record made by the agency but need not give any deference to agency fact findings. This formula is infrequently employed in federal administrative law (except with reference to a few constitutionally sensitive issues) but is sometimes employed in the states, especially in California.

iii. *Clearly erroneous.* The court reverses if it "is left with the definite and firm conviction that a mistake has been committed." *United States v. U.S. Gypsum Co.,* 333 U.S. 364, 395 (1948). Sometimes this test is referred to as the "manifest weight of the evidence" test. It is the standard used by a federal court of appeal to review the decision of a trial judge when there is no jury. Fed.R.Civ.P. 52(a). It was used in the 1961 Model State APA, § 15(g)(5), and is used in a substantial number of states. See *DeFries, infra.*

iv. *Substantial evidence.* The court cannot reverse if a reasonable person could have reached the same conclusion as the agency. This is the standard used by a federal court of appeals in reviewing the findings of a jury (or for a trial court in taking a matter from the jury).

It is the prevailing standard of federal administrative law, APA § 706(2)(E), and is discussed in *Universal Camera, infra*. It is used in many states and is the standard set forth under 1981 MSAPA, § 5–116(c)(7).

The substantial evidence test of APA § 706(2)(E) is applicable only to judicial review of agency factfinding occurring in formal adjudication or formal rulemaking. Agency factfinding in informal adjudication is reviewed under § 706(2)(A), which authorizes a reviewing court to reverse the agency only if its findings are arbitrary, capricious, or an abuse of discretion. Because that test also boils down to an assessment of the reasonableness of agency action, the scrutiny it calls for probably does not differ significantly from the substantial evidence test. That issue will be discussed in § 9.4, *infra*.

v. *No basis in fact.* The court cannot reverse if there is any evidence in support of the agency's conclusion. Sometimes this is called the "scintilla" test. It was employed in judicial review of the determinations of selective service boards. *Estep v. United States*, 327 U.S. 114 (1946).

vi. *Facts not reviewable at all.* A statute may preclude any judicial review of an agency's factual determinations but not of its procedures or of questions of law. The issue of preclusion of review is treated in § 10.4, *infra*. At common law, review by writ of certiorari did not permit review of factual issues. *See* § 10.1.2c, *infra*.

You should ask whether these gradations make any practical difference: isn't a reviewing court likely to reverse agency fact findings which it strongly believes are wrong regardless of what formula is employed?

Consider also the relationship between judicial scope of review and the scope of authority delegated to the agency by the legislature. This relationship is the most important factor in understanding the appropriate scope of review. After all, a legislative delegation of discretion to an agency suggests that the agency has primary responsibility for resolution of matters falling within the scope of that discretion; within that zone a court ought not to substitute its judgment for that of the agency. Instead, it should defer to the agency's judgment unless that judgment is unreasonable. On the other hand, when the legislature settles a matter by a statutory provision, thereby withholding discretion from the agency, the court ought to feel free to substitute its judgment for the agency's.

Of course, that leaves the initial question to be determined: did the legislature delegate discretion to decide a particular matter? The resolution of that question is virtually never delegated to the agency's discretion, and courts are free to substitute their judgment for that of the agency on the resolution of this threshold issue.

§ 9.1.1   THE SUBSTANTIAL EVIDENCE AND CLEARLY ERRO-NEOUS TESTS

UNIVERSAL CAMERA CORP. v. NLRB

340 U.S. 474 (1951).

[The NLRB decided that Universal discharged an employee (Chairman) in reprisal for his testimony at a previous NLRB hearing. Universal contended that Chairman was discharged for insubordination which occurred about two months after he gave the testimony. The NLRB's hearing examiner believed the company's witnesses, but the NLRB reversed and reinstated Chairman with back pay.

In an opinion by Judge Learned Hand, the Second Circuit affirmed the Board, finding that its reversal of the hearing examiner's findings did not detract from the substantiality of evidence in support of its conclusions and that there was substantial evidence in support of the Board's findings. Frankfurter, J.:]

The essential issue raised by this case . . . is the effect of the Administrative Procedure Act and . . . the Taft–Hartley Act on the duty of Courts of Appeals when called upon to review orders of the National Labor Relations Board.

*I.   . . .

The Wagner Act provided: "The findings of the Board as to the facts, if supported by evidence, shall be conclusive." This Court read "evidence" to mean "substantial evidence," and we said that "[s]ubstantial evidence is more than a mere scintilla. It means such relevant evidence as a reasonable mind might accept as adequate to support a conclusion." Accordingly, it "must do more than create a suspicion of the existence of the fact to be established. . . . [I]t must be enough to justify, if the trial were to a jury, a refusal to direct a verdict when the conclusion sought to be drawn from it is one of fact for the jury."

The very smoothness of the "substantial evidence" formula as the standard for reviewing the evidentiary validity of the Board's findings established its currency. But the inevitably variant applications of the standard to conflicting evidence soon brought contrariety of views and in due course bred criticism. Even though the whole record may have been canvassed in order to determine whether the evidentiary foundation of a determination by the Board was "substantial," the phrasing of this Court's process of review readily lent itself to the notion that it was enough that the evidence supporting the Board's result was "substantial" when considered by itself. . . .

Criticism of so contracted a reviewing power reinforced dissatisfaction felt in various quarters with the Board's administration of the Wagner Act in the years preceding the war. . . .

. . . [T]he legislative history of [the APA] hardly speaks with that clarity of purpose which Congress supposedly furnishes courts in order to enable them to enforce its true will. On the one hand, the sponsors of the legislation indicated that they were reaffirming the prevailing "substantial evidence" test. But with equal clarity they expressed disapproval of the manner in which the courts were applying their own standard. The committee reports of both houses refer to the practice of agencies to rely upon "suspicion, surmise, implications, or plainly incredible evidence," and indicate that courts are to exact higher standards "in the exercise of their independent judgment" and on consideration of "the whole record."

Similar dissatisfaction with too restricted application of the "substantial evidence" test is reflected in the legislative history of the Taft–Hartley Act. The bill as reported to the House provided that the "findings of the Board as to the facts shall be conclusive unless it is made to appear to the satisfaction of the court either (1) that the findings of fact are against the manifest weight of the evidence, or (2) the findings of fact are not supported by substantial evidence." The bill left the House with this provision. Early committee prints in the Senate provided for review by "weight of the evidence" or "clearly erroneous" standards. But, as the Senate Committee Report relates, "it was finally decided to conform the statute to the corresponding section of the Administrative Procedure Act where the substantial evidence test prevails. In order to clarify any ambiguity in that statute, however, the committee inserted the words 'questions of fact, if supported by substantial evidence *on the record considered as a whole.* . . .' " . . .

It is fair to say that in all this Congress expressed a mood. And it expressed its mood not merely by oratory but by legislation. As legislation that mood must be respected, even though it can only serve as a standard for judgment and not as a body of rigid rules assuring sameness of application. . . .

Whether or not it was ever permissible for courts to determine the substantiality of evidence supporting a Labor Board decision merely on the basis of evidence which in and of itself justified it, without taking into account contradictory evidence or evidence from which conflicting inferences could be drawn, the new legislation definitely precludes such a theory of review and bars its practice. The substantiality of evidence must take into account whatever in the record fairly detracts from its weight. This is clearly the significance of the requirement in both statutes that courts consider the whole record. Committee reports and the adoption in the Administrative Procedure Act of the minority views of the Attorney General's Committee demonstrate that to enjoin such a duty on the reviewing court was one of the important purposes of the movement which eventuated in that enactment.

To be sure, the requirement for canvassing "the whole record" in order to ascertain substantiality does not furnish a calculus of value by which a reviewing court can assess the evidence. Nor was it intended to negative the function of the Labor Board as one of those agencies

presumably equipped or informed by experience to deal with a specialized field of knowledge, whose findings within that field carry the
authority of an expertness which courts do not possess and therefore
must respect. Nor does it mean that even as to matters not requiring
expertise a court may displace the Board's choice between two fairly
conflicting views, even though the court would justifiably have made a
different choice had the matter been before it de novo. Congress has
merely made it clear that a reviewing court is not barred from setting
aside a Board decision when it cannot conscientiously find that the
evidence supporting that decision is substantial, when viewed in the
light that the record in its entirety furnishes, including the body of
evidence opposed to the Board's view.

There remains then the question whether enactment of these two
statutes has altered the scope of review other than to require that
substantiality be determined in the light of all that the record relevant-
ly presents. A formula for judicial review of administrative action may
afford grounds for certitude but cannot assure certainty of application.
Some scope for judicial discretion in applying the formula can be
avoided only by falsifying the actual process of judging or by using the
formula as an instrument of futile casuistry. . . . To find the change
so elusive that it cannot be precisely defined does not mean it may be
ignored. We should fail in our duty to effectuate the will of Congress if
we denied recognition to expressed Congressional disapproval of the
finality accorded to Labor Board findings by some decisions of this and
lower courts, or even of the atmosphere which may have favored those
decisions.

We conclude, therefore, that the Administrative Procedure Act and
the Taft–Hartley Act direct that courts must now assume more responsibility for the reasonableness and fairness of Labor Board decisions
than some courts have shown in the past. Reviewing courts must be
influenced by a feeling that they are not to abdicate the conventional
judicial function. Congress has imposed on them responsibility for
assuring that the Board keeps within reasonable grounds. That responsibility is not less real because it is limited to enforcing the
requirement that evidence appear substantial when viewed, on the
record as a whole, by courts invested with the authority and enjoying
the prestige of the Courts of Appeals. The Board's findings are entitled
to respect; but they must nonetheless be set aside when the record
before a Court of Appeals clearly precludes the Board's decision from
being justified by a fair estimate of the worth of the testimony of
witnesses or its informed judgment on matters within its special competence or both. . . .

Our power to review the correctness of application of the present
standard ought seldom to be called into action. Whether on the record
as a whole there is substantial evidence to support agency findings is a
question which Congress has placed in the keeping of the Courts of
Appeals. This Court will intervene only in what ought to be the rare

instance when the standard appears to have been misapprehended or grossly misapplied.

II. . . .

The decision of the Court of Appeals is assailed on two grounds. It is said (1) that the court erred in holding that it was barred from taking into account the report of the examiner on questions of fact insofar as that report was rejected by the Board, and (2) that the Board's order was not supported by substantial evidence on the record considered as a whole, even apart from the validity of the court's refusal to consider the rejected portions of the examiner's report.

The latter contention is easily met. . . . [I]t is clear from the court's opinion in this case that it in fact did consider the "record as a whole," and did not deem itself merely the judicial echo of the Board's conclusion. The testimony of the company's witnesses was inconsistent, and there was clear evidence that the complaining employee had been discharged by an officer who was at one time influenced against him because of his appearance at the Board hearing. On such a record we could not say that it would be error to grant enforcement.

The first contention, however, raises serious questions to which we now turn.

III.

The Court of Appeals deemed itself bound by the Board's rejection of the examiner's findings because the court considered these findings not "as unassailable as a master's." They are not. Section 10(c) of the Labor Management Relations Act provides that "If upon the preponderance of the testimony taken the Board shall be of the opinion that any person named in the complaint has engaged in or is engaging in any such unfair labor practice, then the Board shall state its findings of fact. . . ." The responsibility for decision thus placed on the Board is wholly inconsistent with the notion that it has power to reverse an examiner's findings only when they are "clearly erroneous." Such a limitation would make so drastic a departure from prior administrative practice that explicitness would be required. . . .

We are aware that to give the examiner's findings less finality than a master's and yet entitle them to consideration in striking the account, is to introduce another and an unruly factor into the judgmatical process of review. But we ought not to fashion an exclusionary rule merely to reduce the number of imponderables to be considered by reviewing courts.

The Taft–Hartley Act provides that "The findings of the Board with respect to questions of fact if supported by substantial evidence on the record considered as a whole shall be conclusive." Surely an examiner's report is as much a part of the record as the complaint or the testimony. According to the Administrative Procedure Act, "All decisions (including initial, recommended, or tentative decisions) shall become a part of the record. . . ." [§ 557(c)]. . . .

It is therefore difficult to escape the conclusion that the plain language of the statutes directs a reviewing court to determine the substantiality of evidence on the record including the examiner's report. . . . Nothing in the statutes suggests that the Labor Board should not be influenced by the examiner's opportunity to observe the witnesses he hears and sees and the Board does not. Nothing suggests that reviewing courts should not give to the examiner's report such probative force as it intrinsically commands. To the contrary, § 11 of the Administrative Procedure Act contains detailed provisions designed to maintain high standards of independence and competence in examiners. Section 10(c) of the Labor Management Relations Act requires that examiners "shall issue . . . a proposed report, together with a recommended order." Both statutes thus evince a purpose to increase the importance of the role of examiners in the administrative process. High standards of public administration counsel that we attribute to the Labor Board's examiners both due regard for the responsibility which Congress imposes on them and the competence to discharge it. . . .

We do not require that the examiner's findings be given more weight than in reason and in the light of judicial experience they deserve. The "substantial evidence" standard is not modified in any way when the Board and its examiner disagree. We intend only to recognize that evidence supporting a conclusion may be less substantial when an impartial, experienced examiner who has observed the witnesses and lived with the case has drawn conclusions different from the Board's than when he has reached the same conclusion. The findings of the examiner are to be considered along with the consistency and inherent probability of testimony. The significance of his report, of course, depends largely on the importance of credibility in the particular case. To give it this significance does not seem to us materially more difficult than to heed the other factors which in sum determine whether evidence is "substantial." . . .

We therefore remand the cause to the Court of Appeals. On reconsideration of the record it should accord the findings of the trial examiner the relevance that they reasonably command in answering the comprehensive question whether the evidence supporting the Board's order is substantial. But the court need not limit its reexamination of the case to the effect of that report on its decision. We leave it free to grant or deny enforcement as it thinks the principles expressed in this opinion dictate.

Judgment vacated and cause remanded.

BLACK and DOUGLAS, JJ., concur with parts I and II of this opinion but as to part III agree with the opinion of the court below.

DEFRIES v. ASSOCIATION OF OWNERS, 999 WILDER

555 P.2d 855 (Hawaii 1976).

RICHARDSON, C.J.

Claimant-appellant appeals from an order of the Labor and Industrial Relations Appeals Board denying workers' compensation benefits for a partially disabled right knee.

It is undisputed that claimant stumbled and fractured the big toe of his right foot on August 30, 1970, in the course of his employment as a security guard. The factual issue presently in dispute is whether or not the same stumble also aggravated or accelerated an osteoarthritic condition in claimant's right knee.

At the appeals board hearing, claimant testified that, while running after a suspicious person, he failed to notice a step up to a higher floor level so that he struck his foot against the face of the step, fracturing his toe and also striking his knees on the floor, although his hands helped break the impact of the fall. The employer does not dispute that claimant stumbled and fractured his toe, but does question whether claimant's knees struck the ground. It is undisputed that claimant then weighed approximately 285 pounds and was 63 years old.

The Employer's Report of Industrial Injury and two Physician's Reports to the Division of Workmen's Compensation, all filed during the latter months of 1970, refer only to the fracture of the right big toe and make no mention of impact or injury to the right knee. However, one of the physician's reports does make reference to "[claimant's] fall."

At the appeals board hearing, claimant stated that his right knee did not hurt until about a week after the accident; that the pain then felt "very minor"; that he couldn't remember whether or not he mentioned such pain to the doctor then treating the fractured toe; that the knee thereafter bothered him off and on, perhaps once a month; and that he treated it at home with a heating pad and ointment. He further testified that on July 21, 1972, approximately two years later, while in the continued employ of appellee, his right knee seemed to lock as he was stepping down from his work stool and he was forced to limp because of the pain. It is undisputed that on the next day, July 22, 1972, claimant obtained treatment for the knee from Dr. Shimamura, the same doctor who had treated the broken toe. At the hearing claimant stated that, at this July 22, 1972 office visit, as far as he could remember, he did not mention the 1970 accident to the doctor. He explained that he assumed Dr. Shimamura already knew that he had struck his knees in the 1970 stumble and fall. In a letter in evidence at the hearing, Dr. Shimamura wrote that the first time claimant told him that the injury to the right knee was related to the 1970 stumble was on September 8, 1972. . . .

Dr. Richard Dodge, who had been treating claimant since October 1972, was called as an expert witness for the employer. With respect to claimant's testimony that he had not noticed pain in the right knee until about a week after the stumble, Dr. Dodge testified that it was "not the usual case" for pain to be so slow in manifesting itself; that the week's delay before pain was noticed "raises questions in my mind"; that it "would be possible, but it would be very strange for him to go a week after a fall" without any pain or mention of pain to his doctor. However, other testimony by Dr. Dodge is more favorable:

"Q [Chairman of Appeals Board] I know anything's possible but based on medical probability, what is your opinion? Probability, now.

"A [Dr. Dodge] . . . My opinion is that it [injury to the knee in the 1970 stumble] couldn't have been very severe, but it could have happened. If he did have a fall it could have happened and he could have gone on and treated it at home until it became severe enough to seek medical help in 1972. . . ."

Even though claimant did see Dr. Shimamura a number of times during 1970–1972 for other ailments, Dr. Dodge still saw nothing unusual about failure to mention minor knee pain to Dr. Shimamura during that period. . . .

A letter from the employer's medical expert, Dr. Luke, concludes on the basis of a single examination:

"Based on the facts known about this case as rendered by the patient and based on this examination, it is my opinion that the patient's right knee problem has nothing to do either by way of injury or by way of aggravation in so far as the accident of 1970 is concerned. It is only by retrospect and hindsight that the patient is trying to establish a causal relationship for purposes of putting in an industrial claim. . . ."

THE APPEALS BOARD DECISION

Although the Director of the Department of Labor and Industrial Relations had determined after an administrative hearing that claimant's right knee injury was compensable, the appeals board reversed: It is clear from the board's written decision that its primary reason for reversing the director was its conclusion that claimant's testimony was not credible.

In its decision, the board noted that claimant had limped decidedly at the hearing and had testified that his limp had been even worse on the day he first consulted Dr. Dodge in 1972; and yet, the board noted, Dr. Dodge had not recorded claimant's limping in his 1972 medical records, even though Dr. Dodge testified that he thought he "surely would have" made a note in 1972 of limping so obvious as the limping at the hearing. No one disputes that claimant was suffering from objectively manifested osteoarthritis by the time of his first consultation with Dr. Dodge in 1972, but the board evidently believed that claimant's testimony, by reason of deliberate exaggeration or confused memory, inaccurately described the extent of the 1972 limp. From this the board apparently drew the inference that claimant's testimony on material issues was less credible.

The board's decision also noted that claimant had emphatically, and inaccurately, denied having filed any workers' compensation claim prior to 1970; yet the board found the record to show that claimant had filed a claim for his left knee in 1962. The board found it difficult to believe that the claimant, after prior experience with a claim involving a knee, would fail to claim or mention an injury to his other knee in 1970, "particularly in light of his testimony that his right knee bothered him to the extent that he subjected himself to heat treatments at home."

The board found that, in general, conflicts between claimant's testimony and evidence in the record "cast a very dark shadow on his credibility." The board concluded that in light of claimant's "general course of conduct" and the "evident lack of credibility" in his testimony, no connection existed between the 1970 stumble and claimant's right knee injury.

STANDARD OF REVIEW ON APPEAL

. . . . [A]ppeals from the Labor and Industrial Relations Appeals Board are governed by Hawaii's Administrative Procedure Act, which provides in pertinent part that:

"[T]he court may . . . reverse . . . the decision and order [of an administrative body] if . . . the administrative findings, conclusions, . . . or orders are: . . . (5) *Clearly erroneous* in view of the reliable, probative, and substantial evidence on the whole record. . . ."

Under the clearly erroneous standard, this court will reverse findings by the appeals board if this court is left with the definite and firm conviction that a mistake has been made.

The clearly erroneous standard gives the reviewing court greater leeway to reverse a lower court's findings than the substantial evidence test applicable to review of jury verdicts (including jury verdicts in criminal cases) and administrative fact-finding under the *federal* Administrative Procedures Act. Under the clearly erroneous standard, the reviewing court *will reverse*

"[i]f the findings [by the lower court] . . . are against the clear weight of the evidence or [if] the appellate court otherwise reaches a definite and firm conviction that a mistake has been made, . . . *even though there is evidence* [supporting the findings] *that, by itself, would be substantial.*" 9 Wright & Miller, Federal Practice and Procedure: Civil § 2585 (emphasis added)

BURDEN OF PROOF

In reviewing the decision by the appeals board, this court must also take into consideration the burden of proof imposed upon the employer by HRS § 386–85:

> "Presumptions. In any proceeding for the enforcement of a claim for compensation . . . it shall be presumed, in the absence of substantial evidence to the contrary;

> "(1) That the claim is for a covered work injury."

This section has been construed in numerous Hawaii cases. The cases have liberally construed the statutory language in order to effectuate the humanitarian purposes of the workers' compensation act. In general, it has been found that the workers' compensation act "cast[s] a heavy burden on the employer". The "substantial evidence" burden imposed on employers by § 386–85 entails not only a burden of going forward with the evidence but also a burden of ultimate persuasion. . . . "Substantial evidence" as used in § 386–85 means a high quantum of evidence. This is evident from *Akamine v. Hawaiian Packing,* in which this court, after rigorously examining the extensive testimony offered by two medical experts on behalf of the employer, concluded that the experts' testimony was insufficiently relevant and probative in "net weight" to qualify as "substantial evidence" under the statute. However, the court in *Akamine* did not rely solely on the "substantial evidence" requirement of § 386–85 in reaching its results. *Akamine* further holds that the broad humanitarian purpose of the workers' compensation statute *read as a whole* requires that all reasonable doubts be resolved in favor of the claimant:

> "[I]f there is *reasonable doubt* as to whether an injury is work-connected, the humanitarian nature of the statute demands that doubt be *resolved in favor of the claimant.*" . . .

APPLICATION OF LEGAL STANDARDS TO THE FACTS OF THIS CASE

✳ This court concludes that the decision of the appeals board was clearly erroneous. We hold that, taking the evidence as a whole and giving due consideration to the opportunity of the appeals board to judge the demeanor and credibility of witnesses, there was insufficient evidence, giving the claimant the benefit of every reasonable doubt, including the factual, for the board to conclude that the 1970 stumble neither aggravated nor accelerated the arthritic condition in claimant's right knee.

The board's conclusion that claimant's testimony lacked credibility is of course entitled to weight on appeal. If this had been a case where there existed no objective corroboration of claimant's story, then the board's finding of a lack of credibility, coupled with expert medical testimony favoring the employer, would permit the board to conclude that the claim was invalid. In this case, however, even assuming arguendo that portions of claimant's testimony were confused or fabricated, there is objective corroboration of the claim itself. . . .

Given the undisputed facts in this case and the opinion by two medical experts that injury to the knee may have been caused by the stumble, the rule that reasonable doubts be resolved in claimant's favor forces the conclusion that the claim in this case is valid.

The judgment of the appeals board is reversed, and the case is remanded to the board for determination of the amount of compensation to be awarded.

KIDWELL, J., dissenting, with whom KOBAYASHI, J., joins.

I respectfully dissent.

This case presents the troublesome question of the weight which should be given to a finding of the Labor and Industrial Relations Appeals Board that a claimant's testimony as to the occurrence of an injury is incredible in light of the attendant circumstantial evidence. The majority imposes on the board the obligation to resolve all reasonable doubts in the claimant's favor and concludes that the circumstantial evidence indicating fabrication of the claim was insufficient to overcome the claimant's testimony. I agree that this court may review the sufficiency of the evidence upon which the board relied in rejecting the claimant's testimony. However, I cannot concur in the majority's conclusion that the decision of the board was "clearly erroneous". . . .

Notes and Questions

1. *Substantial evidence v. clearly erroneous.* If Hawaii used the standard of substantial evidence on the whole record rather than the clearly erroneous test, do you think the court would have reversed the appeals board? How about substantial evidence with a mood of more rigorous review described by Justice Frankfurter in *Universal Camera?*

2. *Rationale for substantial evidence test.* The substantial evidence test is designed to limit an appellate court's power to reverse agency fact findings. The court's power is the same when it reviews factual determinations made by a jury. Should an administrative agency's findings be treated like those of a jury, or is a jury entitled to greater latitude than an agency?

Why shouldn't a court which believes that agency findings are clearly erroneous (but supported by substantial evidence) be permitted to overturn the agency decision? Some possible explanations might be:

   i. Agencies specialize and develop expertise in the areas they regulate. Their fact-finding process reflects that expertise, and thus their findings should receive only limited judicial scrutiny.

   ii. When it creates a regulatory program, the legislature usually delegates to an agency the responsibility for executing the legislative scheme. The legislature also delegates all powers necessary to discharge the legislative mandate, including the power to find facts in the course of adjudication. In such situations, the legislature vests primary responsibility for factfinding with the agency. It intends a court to respect those findings, even if it disagrees with them, absent a very serious error by the agency.

iii. The narrowness of the reviewing power discourages disappointed litigants from appealing. Fewer appeals conserves the resources of both courts and agencies and facilitates the administration of the law.

iv. Courts are likely to have a different political orientation than administrative agencies. An agency is expected to carry out the political objective set by the legislature and to reflect the political views of the executive who appointed its members. A reasonableness scope of review limits the ability of a court to impose its values on the administrative process.

3. *Is there a difference between the tests?* Compare these views:

a. Cooper, "Administrative Law: The 'Substantial Evidence' Rule," 44 A.B.A.J. 945, 947 (1958)* (Cooper was a draftsman of the 1961 Model State APA which adopted the clearly erroneous test):

> Many judges find it most difficult to distinguish between the "substantial evidence" and "clear error" tests. Attempts to differentiate between the two tests produce confusion for Bench and Bar alike. . . . The cases studied [188 federal court of appeals cases between 1951 and 1958] vindicate the rule-of-thumb test commonly employed by practicing attorneys, *viz.* if the appellant can convince the appellate court that the administrative finding of facts is obviously just plain wrong, and if the appellant can at the same time arouse the court with a zealous desire to correct the error, the court can always find means to do so, whatever labels must be applied.

Cooper's study indicated that the Fifth Circuit reversed 16 of 30 NLRB cases (53%) while the Second Circuit reversed 3 out of 24 (12%). What might account for this divergence?

b. L. Jaffe, JUDICIAL CONTROL OF ADMINISTRATIVE ACTION 603 (1965):

> But the abuse of the "whole record" test is not a sufficient reason for disowning it. If the distinction between substantial evidence and weight of evidence is subtle and difficult, it is nevertheless an old one, long used in jury trials. It has never been easy to verbalize or to apply. Its sound administration has depended on the intelligence and self-discipline of the judges, and the answer must be the same for review of administrative findings.

4. *Burden of proof and scope of review.* Evidence law distinguishes between the burden of producing evidence and the burden of persuasion. The burden of producing evidence allocates to one party the obligation to come forward with evidence on a particular point.

* Reprinted with permission from the *ABA Journal*, The Lawyer's Magazine, published by the American Bar Association (1958).

The burden of persuasion indicates how strong a party's evidence on an issue must be to avoid losing on that issue.

Depending on the situation, the burden of persuasion may be much heavier than usual. For example, in a criminal case, the prosecution must prove guilt "beyond a reasonable doubt." In a contract case, a plaintiff must prove fraud by "clear and convincing evidence." In general, however, a plaintiff must prove its case by a "preponderance of the evidence."

Which burden of persuasion test do the federal and state APA's employ? *See* APA § 556(d); 1981 MSAPA § 4–215(d). The federal APA employs the common law "preponderance of the evidence" test. *Steadman v. SEC,* 450 U.S. 91 (1981). *Steadman* was a case which imposed disciplinary sanctions on a broker for securities fraud; nevertheless, the Court held, the agency need not satisfy the common law "clear and convincing" test that is ordinarily used in fraud cases.

In other cases, however, the Supreme Court has manipulated burdens of persuasion in order to achieve a desired result or provide a high degree of protection against error. For example, in *Woodby v. INS,* 385 U.S. 276 (1966), the Court interpreted a statute very much like APA § 556(d) to require the government to prove a deportation case by "clear, unequivocal and convincing evidence." Similarly, in *Ettinger v. Board of Medical Quality Assurance,* 185 Cal.Rptr. 601 (Cal.App.1982), the court held that the state had to prove its case by "clear and convincing proof to a reasonable certainty" before revoking a physician's license.

Consider the relationship between burden of persuasion at the hearing and scope of judicial review and note that *these need not be the same.* In a criminal case tried to a jury, for example, the prosecution must prove its case beyond a reasonable doubt; but the court of appeals must affirm if a reasonable juror could have found the defendant guilty beyond a reasonable doubt. That is not at all the same as allowing the appellate court to reverse if its examination of the record indicates to it that the prosecution failed to prove guilt beyond a reasonable doubt.

How did the burden of persuasion affect the result in *DeFries?*

5. *Disagreement between agency and ALJ.* In *Universal Camera,* the NLRB overturned fact findings made by its hearing examiner (hearing examiners are now called ALJs). The dispute concerned the credibility of witnesses which the examiner had heard and the Board had not.

Both the Second Circuit and the Supreme Court rejected the analogy between a hearing officer and a master appointed by a trial court to take testimony. A trial court cannot reverse a master's findings unless it finds them clearly erroneous. Fed.R.Civ.P. 53(e)(2). Why is the relationship between a court and a master different from that between an agency and its ALJ? Consider the relevance of APA § 557(b) (third sentence) and 1981 MSAPA § 4–216(d).

Judge Hand's first opinion in *Universal Camera* stated that a reviewing court has no middle ground between disregarding an agency's reversal of its examiner and making the examiner's findings as unassailable as those of a master. 179 F.2d 749, 753 (2d Cir.1950). Did the Supreme Court identify a middle ground? Where is that ground located?

On remand, Judge Hand went to the opposite extreme: he ruled "an examiner's findings on veracity must not be overruled without a very substantial preponderance in the testimony as recorded." 190 F.2d 429, 430 (2d Cir.1951). The Supreme Court later disapproved this approach since it appeared to treat ALJs the same as masters. *FCC v. Allentown Broadcasting Corp.*, 349 U.S. 358 (1955).

How much weight should a court give to an ALJ's findings when the agency heads disagree with them?

Note that in *DeFries* the Appeals Board reversed the findings of the Director of the Department who had determined after a hearing that the injury was compensable. Why didn't the Hawaii Supreme Court cite that reversal as a factor in its decision?

Not all states follow *Universal Camera* on this point. For example, in Florida, an agency cannot reject or modify an ALJ's findings of fact "unless the agency first determines from a review of the complete record, and states with particularity in the order, that the [ALJ's] findings of fact were not based upon competent substantial evidence . . . ." Fla.Stats. ch. 120.57(1)(b)10 (West, 1988). *See* 2 A. England & H. Levinson, FLORIDA ADMINISTRATIVE PRACTICE MANUAL § 13.09 (1979). Is this a sounder approach to the problem than taken in *Universal Camera?* Does it appropriately enhance the status of the ALJ in the adjudicatory process? Does it enhance the status of the ALJ too much?

6. *The record for judicial review.* What is the record that a court reviews when it applies the substantial evidence test? May it take additional evidence? See APA §§ 556(e), 706(2)(E), 706(2) last paragraph; 1981 MSAPA §§ 5–113, 5–114. *Compare* § 9.4, notes 2–3 *infra*, § 6.8, *supra*.

7. *Supreme Court review of Court of Appeals.* What standard of review did the Supreme Court indicate that it would use in subsequent cases when it reviews a court of appeals decision that reviewed the sufficiency of evidence supporting an agency factfinding? The highest courts of some states review decisions of lower courts that reviewed the sufficiency of agency factfindings with the same scrutiny that the lower court gives to the agency findings. *See, e.g., Jackson County Public Hospital v. Public Employment Rel. Bd.*, 280 N.W.2d 426, 429 (Iowa 1979). Is this an appropriate use of the scarce resources of a state supreme court? Does it provide a strong incentive for losing parties to keep appealing?

8. *Problem.* Minnesota law prohibits discrimination by any business establishment on the basis of race, religion, gender, or "affectional preference." Some of the members of City Health Club in Minneapolis were homosexuals and a number of heterosexual members complained to the management about it or resigned. The Club had asked members to refrain from any conduct which might cause embarrassment or discomfort to other members or to the staff. It ignored the conduct of heterosexual members (such as telling jokes in the locker room or arranging dates) while threatening homosexual members with termination for comparable conduct.

On April 2, Joe (a staff member) overheard Ted (a homosexual Club member) arranging to meet another male Club member for a beer after their workout. As Ted was leaving the Club, Mark (the manager) asked Ted to come into the office and discuss his conduct. Ted told him to drop dead and left the Club. That day, Mark terminated Ted's membership; Mark's letter stated that termination occurred because Ted's conduct had caused embarrassment or discomfort to a member of the staff and because he had refused to discuss the matter with management.

Ted complained to the Civil Rights Commission (CRC) which enforces the antidiscrimination law. Gloria, the CRC's ALJ, found that Ted had been terminated because his conduct had offended a staff member and because of his refusal to discuss it, not because of his affectional preference. Consequently, she denied relief.

Ted appealed the decision to the full CRC which reversed. Its opinion stated that Ted had been terminated because he was a homosexual, not because of his conduct. It found that the Club was trying to rid itself of homosexual members. It also found that Joe had not been offended, and that Ted's conduct could not be the basis for terminating him, whether Joe was offended or not. Thus it awarded Ted compensatory and punitive damages, as well as attorney's fees, as permitted by the statute.

Should a court reverse this decision assuming (i) the state subscribes to the substantial evidence on the whole record test? (ii) To the clearly erroneous test?

Suppose the CRC had agreed with Gloria, and Ted sought judicial review. What result? *See Blanding v. Sports & Health Club, Inc.,* 373 N.W.2d 784 (Minn.App.1985).

§ 9.1.2 INDEPENDENT JUDGMENT AND DE NOVO REVIEW

§ 9.1.2a *Federal Decisions*

As just discussed, the prevailing test for judicial review of basic facts in both federal and state courts is a reasonableness test (substantial evidence on the whole record) although many states use the clearly erroneous test. This subchapter explores instances in which a much broader scope of basic fact review is employed. An odd collection of

Supreme Court decisions of the 1920's and 1930's call for the substitution of judicial judgment for agency judgment on the basis of the record made before the agency or even for a judicial trial de novo.

   i. *Constitutional facts.* The earliest such case is *Ohio Valley Water Co. v. Ben Avon Borough,* 253 U.S. 287 (1920), involving the judicial review of a state agency's valuation of the property of a utility company. That value was critical since the company was constitutionally entitled to rates which yield a fair return on its assets. The Supreme Court held that due process entitled a utility to a judicial trial de novo on the valuation issue.

   In *St. Joseph Stock Yards Co. v. United States,* 298 U.S. 38 (1936), a decision involving ratemaking for a stockyard, the Court reaffirmed the *Ben Avon* decision. It held that a stockyard was entitled to a trial de novo on the valuation issue and implied that the right might extend to alleged administrative denial of any constitutional right. However, the *St. Joseph* case modified *Ben Avon* in several significant respects. First, it required that a reviewing court give presumptive weight to the fact findings of the agency; these findings should be sustained unless a complaining party makes a convincing showing that they are wrong. The Court also precluded the company from introducing evidence in court that could have been introduced at the agency hearing.

   These cases have never been overruled and they are still followed in a minority of the states. *See* Glick, "Independent Judicial Review of Administrative Rate–Making: The Rise and Demise of the Ben Avon Doctrine," 40 Ford.L.Rev. 305, 313 (1971). However, the Supreme Court has never extended the *Ben Avon* and *St. Joseph* cases and has failed to apply them even in cases which raised the issue of whether administrative orders had confiscated a plaintiff's property. *See, e.g., Railroad Com'n v. Rowan & Nichols Oil Co.,* 310 U.S. 573 (1940), 311 U.S. 570 (1941) (rejecting claims that a court should independently examine a state oil proration order).

   Moreover, the very issue on which the *Ben Avon* and *St. Joseph* cases turned—valuation of a utility's property by a ratemaking agency—need no longer be judicially reviewed in detail. Any method of valuation is permitted, provided that the final result of the ratemaking process is reasonable in the sense that the rates cover the utility's costs. *FPC v. Hope Natural Gas Co.,* 320 U.S. 591 (1944).

   ii. *Jurisdictional facts.* Traditionally, a person claiming to be a citizen and seeking *admission* to the United States has no right to judicial review of an administrative finding of non-citizenship. *United States v. Ju Toy,* 198 U.S. 253 (1905). Thus it was surprising when, shortly after the *Ben Avon* case, the Supreme Court held that individuals in the United States whose *deportation* had been ordered, but who maintained they were citizens, were entitled to a judicial trial de novo on the citizenship issue. *Ng Fung Ho v. White,* 259 U.S. 276 (1922). Citizenship was stated to be an essential "jurisdictional fact," and deportation of a citizen based on agency action "deprives him of liberty

. . . It may result also in loss of both property and life; or of all that makes life worth living. Against the danger of such deprivation without the sanction afforded by judicial proceedings, the Fifth Amendment affords protection in its guarantee of due process of law." *Id.* at 284–85. The *Ng Fung Ho* case is still followed today; persons facing deportation (but not persons seeking admission) are entitled (both by the Constitution and by statute) to a de novo judicial trial on the citizenship issue. *Agosto v. INS,* 436 U.S. 748 (1978), interpreting 8 U.S.C. § 1105a(a)(5)(B).

The other major "jurisdictional fact" case is *Crowell v. Benson,* 285 U.S. 22 (1932). *Crowell* involved judicial review of a commissioner's decision awarding compensation under the Longshoremen's and Harbor Workers' Act (a federal statute providing benefits for persons injured in the course of employment on navigable waters). That Act provided for judicial review of such decisions in district court.

The Court upheld the administrative scheme against most constitutional objections. It drew a distinction between "public rights" and "private rights." Public rights, roughly speaking, are disputes between the government and private individuals arising out of the performance of legislative or executive functions; "private rights" are disputes between individuals, like the employee-employer dispute at issue in *Crowell.* In matters of public right, article III allows Congress to provide for settlement of disputes in legislative courts or in agencies.

Even in disputes concerning private rights, the Court noted, Congress could provide for hearings before an agency rather than a court with appropriate provision for judicial review. It found that the judicial review provisions in the Longshoremen's Act were, for the most part, acceptable; the Act was construed to allow a reviewing court to re-determine questions of law and fact (but if a fact finding was "supported by evidence" it would be final).

However, the Court drew a distinction between most factual disputes (such as whether an injury occurred) and those that are "jurisdictional" in the sense that their existence is a condition precedent to the operation of the statutory scheme. In *Crowell,* the issues of "jurisdictional fact" were whether an employment relationship existed and whether the injury occurred on navigable waters. The Court held that, under article III of the Constitution, an employer was entitled to a judicial trial de novo at which a court would independently determine jurisdictional facts on a new record. Note that the distinction between jurisdictional and other facts necessary to support an agency decision may be illusory because the existence of every fact necessary to support such a decision may be deemed to be a prerequisite to the agency action and therefore jurisdictional.

Crowell has never been squarely overruled, but the courts have never extended it to any other "jurisdictional" facts under the Longshoremen's Act or any other statute. Indeed, it is now largely ignored even in cases arising under that Act. *Associated Indem. Corp. v. Shea,*

455 F.2d 913, 914 n. 2 (5th Cir.1972). *Crowell's* jurisdictional fact doctrine has seldom been followed in state courts. Although *Crowell's* distinction between public rights and private rights was endorsed by the plurality opinion of the United States Supreme Court in *Northern Pipeline Const. Co. v. Marathon Pipe Line Co.,* 458 U.S. 50 (1982) (discussed in § 7.4, *supra*) the Court observed in a footnote that *Crowell's* jurisdictional/nonjurisdictional fact distinction is no longer followed. *Id.* at 82 n. 34.

iii. *Summary.* It is interesting to note that the Court has never extended *Ben Avon* or *St. Joseph*—but also has not overruled them. Similarly, it allowed *Crowell v. Benson* to continue in limbo, never following it but never overruling it, until its public right-private right distinction (but not its jurisdictional-nonjurisdictional fact distinction) was employed in *Northern Pipeline.*

One explanation for the shadowy existence of these cases might be that they can prove useful in the event the Supreme Court wishes to protect federal court jurisdiction against Congressional incursion. For example, suppose Congress seeks to make administrative fact-findings final or to prevent judicial review in sensitive constitutional cases such as school prayer or abortion. Consider the relevance of the dictum in *Crowell v. Benson:*

> . . . [T]he question [is] whether . . . Congress may substitute for constitutional courts, in which the judicial power of the United States is vested, an administrative agency . . . for the final determination of the existence of the facts upon which the enforcement of the constitutional rights of the citizen depend . . . [Allowing Congress] . . . [to] completely oust the courts of all determinations of fact . . . would be to sap the judicial power as it exists under the Federal Constitution, and to establish a government of a bureaucratic character alien to our system, wherever fundamental rights depend, as not infrequently they do depend, upon the facts and finality as to facts becomes in effect finality in law. . . . In cases brought to enforce constitutional rights, the judicial power of the United States necessarily extends to the independent determination of all questions, both of fact and law, necessary to the performance of that supreme function.

285 U.S. at 56–57, 60.

It is also worth noting that the Court has historically employed independent judgment in judicially reviewing the findings of lower courts in certain sensitive constitutional areas. The *Ng Fung Ho* case (concerning citizenship in deportation cases) is still followed. Moreover, the Court undertakes an independent examination of facts in the record when the issue is whether a confession was coerced or whether publications are "obscene." *See Miller v. Fenton,* 474 U.S. 104 (1985) (habeas review of confession issue); *Miller v. California,* 413 U.S. 15, 25 (1973) (obscenity); *Bekiaris v. Board of Educ.,* 493 P.2d 480 (Cal.1972) (whether probationary teacher was dismissed because of exercising First Amendment rights).

It seems clear that the precise holdings of *Ben Avon, St. Joseph,* and *Crowell* are discredited, but the idea that, in cases requiring enhanced judicial protection, a court should engage in independent judgment of the facts is by no means dead. And, as we shall see, that idea remains very much alive in some state courts.

§ 9.1.2b *State Decisions*

State statutes requiring de novo trials for review of administrative decisions are not uncommon. *See, e.g., Weeks v. Personnel Bd. of Review,* 373 A.2d 176 (R.I.1977) (review of decision to discharge police officer) which cites cases from other states.

However, Texas provides the best example of de novo judicial review. Apparently Texas legislators distrust administrative agencies, because de novo trials of matters already determined by administrative decisions are extremely common. At such trials, the previous agency decision is treated as a complete nullity. *See* Note, "The Future of Judicial Review Under the Administrative Procedure and Texas Register Act," 57 Tex.L.Rev. 253, 271–73 (1979) (listing thirty statutes which grant de novo review, sometimes including jury trials, including "brake fluid marketing regulations" and "public surveyor registration revocation" along with revocation of the licenses of attorneys, physicians, dentists and barbers). Until recently in Texas, even statutes calling for substantial evidence review required a de novo judicial trial (on a wholly new record) to determine whether substantial evidence supported the agency's findings!

Under siege from all this unwelcome business, the Texas courts have held it unconstitutional to vest certain "legislative functions" in the courts through the requirement of a de novo trial. *Id.* at 259, n. 44. For example, the Texas Supreme Court held that the legislature could not leave to the de novo determination of the courts the decisions of whether to award a license to open a new savings and loan association or whether a neighborhood was a "slum" subject to urban renewal. *See Gerst v. Nixon,* 411 S.W.2d 350 (1966); *Davis v. City of Lubbock,* 326 S.W.2d 699 (Tex.1959). *See also American Beauty Homes Corp. v. Louisville and Jefferson County Planning Com'n,* 379 S.W.2d 450 (Ky. 1964) (zoning decisions).

The federal courts, apparently, are also precluded from undertaking such review. *See Federal Radio Com'n v. General Electric Co.,* 281 U.S. 464 (1930). In the *General Electric* case, a statute vested a federal agency with power to grant and revoke radio licenses and gave the Court of Appeals for the District of Columbia the power to "alter or revise the decision appealed from and enter such judgment as to it seems just." The Court held that Congress could vest such power in the lower court (because the District courts were then considered legislative courts) but that "the proceeding in [the Court of Appeals] was not a case or controversy in the sense of the judiciary article, but was an administrative proceeding, and therefore the decision therein is not reviewable by [the Supreme Court]." *Id.* at 470.

Do you agree that the separation of powers provisions in state and federal constitutions prohibit the legislature from assigning to courts the obligation to conduct de novo trials of administrative licensing or zoning determinations? What is wrong with such delegations?

California provides the leading example of judicial review of agency fact-findings without trial de novo but under an independent judgment standard. Cal.Code of Civ.Proc. § 1094.5 (West 1988) provides for judicial review (through mandamus in the Superior Court) of agency decisions resulting from a trial-type agency hearing. However, the writ actually resembles certiorari rather than mandamus, since it calls for the court to review the evidence in the trial record. *See* § 10.1.2, *infra*.

In general, § 1094.5 provides that the agency has abused its discretion if its fact findings are not supported by "substantial evidence in the light of the whole record." However, "in cases in which the court is authorized by law to exercise its independent judgment on the evidence, abuse of discretion is established if the court determines that the findings are not supported by the weight of the evidence." When the independent judgment test is employed, the court can permit introduction of evidence which could not reasonably have been produced before the agency or evidence which was improperly excluded. Thus independent judgment review can turn into a partial trial de novo.

The independent judgment test of § 1094.5 was originally (but is no longer) grounded in state constitutional law; it has been maintained and steadily expanded through judicial discretion. It applies to decisions of local and state agencies (other than those created by the California constitution). It applies only if the decision "substantially affects a vested, fundamental right." Note the ambiguity in this phrase: does it mean "vested *and* fundamental" or "vested *or* fundamental?" And how does one distinguish vested from non-vested rights, not to mention fundamental from non-fundamental ones?

In *Bixby v. Pierno,* 481 P.2d 242 (Cal.1971), the California Supreme Court announced its continued adherence to the independent judgment test. It reviewed the tortured history of the standard, making clear its close kinship with *Ben Avon, St. Joseph,* and *Crowell,* and offered an articulate defense of the test:

> Since the 1930's the courts have redefined their role in the protection of individual and minority rights. The courts have realized that in the area of economic due process the will of the majority as expressed by the Legislature and its delegated administrative agencies must be permitted to meet contemporary crucial problems. . . . Courts have explained that powerful economic forces can obtain substantial representation in the halls of the Legislature and in the departments of the executive branch and thus do not impel the same kind of judicial protection as do the

minorities: the unpopular religions, the racial subgroups, the criminal defendants, the politically weak and underrepresented.

By carefully scrutinizing administrative decisions which substantially affect vested, fundamental rights, the courts of California have undertaken to protect such rights, and particularly the right to practice one's trade or profession, from untoward intrusions by the massive apparatus of government. If the decision of an administrative agency will substantially affect such a right, the trial court not only examines the administrative record for errors of law but also exercises its independent judgment upon the evidence disclosed in a limited trial de novo. . . .

Although we recognize that the California rule yields no fixed formula and guarantees no predictably exact ruling in each case, it performs a precious function in the protection of the rights of the individual. Too often the independent thinker or crusader is subjected to the retaliation of the professional or trade group; the centripetal pressure toward conformity will often destroy the advocate of reform. The unpopular protestant may well provoke an aroused zeal of scrutiny by the licensing body that finds trivial grounds for license revocation. Restricted to the narrow ground of review of the evidence and denied the power of an independent analysis, the court might well be unable to save the unpopular professional or practitioner. Before his license is revoked, such an individual, who walks in the shadow of the governmental monoliths, deserves the protection of a full and independent judicial hearing.

481 P.2d at 250–51, 254.

Is this rhetoric convincing? Could the court achieve the same result under the substantial evidence test or the arbitrary-capricious test? What are the reasons for and against judicial substitution of judgment with respect to issues of fact? Issues of law? Issues of discretion? Are there some issues that are simply too important to entrust to agency discretion? If so what are they and how may they be identified?

FRINK v. PROD

643 P.2d 476 (Cal.1982).

BROUSSARD, J.—Helene Frink petitioned for writ of mandate to vacate an administrative decision denying benefits under the aid to the totally disabled program (ATD). The superior court judgment states that while "the weight of the evidence was in petitioner's favor, there was substantial evidence in the administrative record to support the respondent's decision." Relief was denied. On this appeal, petitioner contends that the trial court should have exercised its independent judgment on the evidence rather than apply the substantial evidence rule. . . .

In administrative mandamus actions to review decisions *terminating* welfare assistance, the trial court exercises its independent judgment on the evidence. However, administrative determinations of *applications* for welfare benefits traditionally have been reviewed under the substantial evidence rule. . . . [It] is apparent that in accordance with section 1094.5, subdivision (c), it is for the courts to establish the appropriate standard of review in determining whether there has been an abuse of discretion. . . .

In *Bixby v. Pierno,* it was concluded that the "courts must decide on a case-by-case basis whether an administrative decision or class of decisions substantially affects fundamental vested rights and thus requires independent judgment review . . . In determining whether the right is fundamental the courts do not alone weigh the economic aspect of it, but the effect of it in human terms and the importance of it to the individual in the life situation. This approach finds its application in such an instance as the opportunity to continue the practice of one's trade or profession—a right which induced this court's statement in 1939: 'it necessarily follows that the court to which the application for mandate is made to secure the restoration of a professional license must exercise an independent judgment on the facts. . . .' "

The court also pointed out that "in determining whether the right is sufficiently basic and fundamental to justify independent judgment review, the courts have considered the degree to which that right is 'vested,' that is, already possessed by the individual." In cases involving applications for a license, the courts have largely deferred to the administrative expertise of the agency. Courts are relatively ill-equipped to determine whether an individual would be qualified, for example, to practice a particular profession or trade. In a case involving the agency's initial determination whether an individual qualifies to enter a profession or trade the courts uphold the agency decision unless it lacks substantial evidentiary support or infringes upon the applicant's statutory or constitutional rights. Once the agency has initially exercised its expertise and determined that an individual fulfills the requirements to practice his profession, the agency's subsequent revocation of the license calls for an independent judgment review of the facts underlying any such administrative decision. . . .

Weighing the importance and effect of the right and the degree to which it is possessed, it is apparent that the right of the needy disabled to public assistance is of such significance as to require independent judgment review. . . .

The right of the needy applicant to welfare benefits is as fundamental as the right of a recipient to continued benefits. Because need is a condition of benefits, erroneous denial of aid in either case deprives the eligible person "of the very means for his survival and his situation becomes immediately desperate."

The decisions subsequent to *Bixby* denying independent review to decisions on applications for welfare benefits were not based on the theory that there was no fundamental right but reasoned that the right of the applicant was not vested. Although *Bixby* distinguished between possessed and vested rights and rights "merely sought" it immediately pointed out the reason for substantial evidence review in the latter situation: "[S]ince the administrative agency must engage in the delicate task of determining whether the individual qualifies for the sought right, the courts have deferred to the administrative expertise of the agency." (*Id.*) When the court, discussing licensing cases, returned to the vested issue, it again pointed out that courts "are relatively ill-equipped to determine whether an individual would be qualified, for example, to practice a particular profession or trade. [Citation.] . . . Once the agency has initially exercised its expertise and determined that an individual fulfills the requirements to practice his profession, the agency's subsequent revocation of the license calls for an independent judgment review.". . .

Evaluating the degree to which the right is vested, it is apparent that the right to welfare benefits is not based on expertise, competence, learning, or purchase or ownership claim. Determination of qualification for public assistance does not involve the "delicate task" of evaluating competence to engage in a broad field of endeavor as is true in most licensing cases.

Rather, the qualification for public assistance primarily is based on need, the absence of income or other source of funds. The applicant for public assistance is seeking aid because of deterioration of his life situation in economic terms. Unlike the applicant for a license, he is not seeking advancement of his earlier life situation. The statutory public assistance programs provide protection to citizens who through economic adversity are in need and as such should be viewed as residual rights possessed by all of the citizenry to be exercised when circumstances require.

While the degree to which the right is vested may not be overwhelming, the degree of fundamentalness is. Weighing them together as required by *Bixby,* we conclude the independent judgment standard should be applied to decisions denying applications for welfare benefits. . . .

The judgment is reversed with directions to enter judgment for petitioner.

NEWMAN, J., joined by RICHARDSON and KAUS, JJ., dissented. The dissent was based on the language of Welf. & Inst.Code § 10,962 which provided for review "under the provisions of § 1094.5 . . . upon questions of law involved in the case." Both majority and dissent agreed that this section permitted the court to review whether the agency decision was factually supported. The majority stated that the legislature left it to the court to decide the scope of review. The dissent argued that the statute mandated substantial evidence rather than independent judgment review. The dissent concluded:

Three little words in a statute ("questions of law") surely are to be preferred over the incessant litigants' parade to this court . . . [contending] that (1) each right-privilege borderline be confronted judicially (with demonstrable frequency in this court), and "intrusion" by the Legislature be strictly scrutinized. Section 1094.5 law differs greatly from equal protection law, and I believe we should respond to arguably ambiguous commands of the Legislature as allies, not as strict-scrutiny antagonists.

Notes and Questions

1. *California's independent judgment test.* Is the independent judgment test needed in a case like *Frink* to protect the petitioner's interests? Are these the sort of interests identified in *Bixby*? Is the court as well or not as well qualified as the welfare department to find the facts? Do you agree with the majority's construction of § 10,962? The dissent's construction?

2. *Vested, fundamental rights.* After *Frink,* when should a trial court use the substantial evidence test and when should it use the independent judgment test? Is the vagueness of the California test acceptable? Does a California litigant have the same right to independent judgment review as to a trial-type agency hearing under due process? What did Justice Newman mean at the end of his dissent by equating independent judgment review with strict scrutiny under equal protection?

3. *Problem.* Recall the problem about Ted's membership termination by City Health Club in § 9.1.1, note § 8. Suppose it arose in California. Would the court have power to exercise independent judgment if the CRC had found in Ted's favor? The Club's favor? Suppose the case was before a health club licensing board which revoked City's license because of repeated incidents of affectional discrimination?

§ 9.2 SCOPE OF REVIEW OF ISSUES OF LEGAL INTERPRETATION

In the course of its work, an agency constantly interprets and reinterprets the meaning of the words in legal materials like statutes or its own prior rules or decisions. For example, an agency might engage in the process of legal interpretation in rendering an adjudicative decision, in engaging in legislative or interpretive rulemaking, or in giving advice to the public.

There are two approaches which a court might take to the review of such interpretations. Under the traditional view (sometimes called "rightness" or "independent judgment" or "substitution of judgment") a court decides the interpretive issue for itself. Both federal and state APAs permit reviewing courts to substitute judgment on questions of legal interpretation. *See* APA § 706 (first paragraph and (2)(B), (C)) and 1981 MSAPA § 5–116(c)(2), (4). When substituting judgment on questions of law, the courts usually grant at least some "weight" (sometimes referred to as "deference" or "weak deference") to the agency's interpretation. The *Madison* case which follows illustrates the "rightness" approach.

In another group of decisions (sometimes referred to as the "reasonableness" or "strong deference" approach), courts treat interpretive issues the same as they treat agency findings of basic fact under the substantial evidence test. Under this approach, a court must accept the agency's interpretation if it is "reasonable;" it cannot substitute its own preferred interpretation for that of the agency. The *Chevron* case illustrates the "reasonableness" approach.

As you might expect, these two approaches shade into one another. A court which purports to employ the "rightness" approach, but which grants "great deference" to the agency's interpretation, may really be using the "reasonableness" approach. If a court employing the "reasonableness" approach conducts an intensive examination of the statute's history and policy to assess "reasonableness," it may really be using the "rightness" approach.

Note the important link between the scope of review issue and the various sorts of checks and balances addressed in chapters 7 and 8. When a court substitutes its judgment for that of an agency, it plays an intrusive checking role. When a court takes a reasonableness approach, it plays a much less intrusive role. Indeed, this entire chapter on scope of review really asks again and again the fundamental question of the extent to which agencies should be checked by the judicial branch.

MADISON v. ALASKA DEPT. OF FISH AND GAME

696 P.2d 168 (Alaska 1985).

[For many years, Madison has fished for salmon in the Cook Inlet. Pursuant to a Board of Fisheries regulation, he was denied a permit for subsistence fishing. He challenged the regulation as inconsistent with a statute.

The statute provides that the Board can issue permits for subsistence fishing, which means "customary and traditional uses," but the statute did not define those terms. The statute required the Board to adopt regulations permitting subsistence fishing absent a showing that such use would jeopardize the sustained yield of the fishery. The regulations define "customary and traditional" by reference to ten criteria. Using these criteria, the Board allows subsistence permits at only three communities in the Cook Inlet because only those communities had traditionally engaged in subsistence fishing. Madison does not live in one of those communities.]

MOORE, J.: . . .

In *Kelly v. Zamarello*, 486 P.2d 906, 917 (Alaska 1971), we stated that the "reasonable basis approach should be used for the most part in cases concerning administrative expertise as to either complex subject matter or fundamental policy formulations." However, the issues in this case concern statutory interpretation of the words "customary and traditional" and the question whether the board has acted within the scope of its statutory authority. Such issues "fall into the realm of special competency of the courts."

In this instance, we are dealing with a question of statutory interpretation and will apply the substitution of judgment standard.

> The substitution of judgment standard is applied when the questions of law presented do not involve agency expertise, and, thus, a court need not take the deferential stance embodied in the rational basis test. . . . The standard is appropriate where the knowledge and experience of the agency is of little guidance to the court or where the case concerns *statutory interpretation* or other analysis of legal relationships about which courts have specialized knowledge and experience."

. . . Application of this standard allows the reviewing court to substitute its judgment about a statute's meaning for the board's interpretation, even if the board's interpretation had a reasonable basis in law. In this case, [the] trial court erred by applying the reasonable basis standard to the board's statutory interpretation.

Before 1978, subsistence fishing was defined as fishing for "personal use and not for sale or barter." The 1978 subsistence law redefined subsistence fishing as fishing for "subsistence uses." . . . The board argues that the legislature intended to narrow the scope of subsistence fishing to mean fishing by individuals residing in those rural communities that have historically depended on subsistence hunting and fishing. Under this interpretation, the board asserts that its criteria are consistent with the legislature's intent.

The board's argument reveals a fundamental misconception about the structure of the 1978 subsistence law. There are potentially two tiers of subsistence users. The first tier includes *all* subsistence users. Under the statute, all subsistence uses have priority over sport and commercial uses "whenever it is necessary to restrict the taking of fish to assure the maintenance of fish stocks on a sustained-yield basis, or to assure the continuation of subsistence uses of such resources. . . ." If the statutory priority given all subsistence users over commercial and sport users still results in too few fish for all subsistence uses, then the board is authorized to establish a second tier of preferred subsistence users based on the legislative criteria, namely, customary and direct dependence on the resource, local residency, and availability of alternative resources. . . .

The legislative history indicates that the legislature intended to protect subsistence use, not limit it. The words "customary and traditional" serve as a guideline to recognize historical subsistence use by individuals, both native and non-native Alaskans. In addition, subsistence use is not strictly limited to rural communities. For these reasons, the board's interpretation of "customary and traditional" as a restrictive term conflicts squarely with the legislative intent.

The board's regulation is inconsistent with the legislative intent to provide guidelines for the protection of subsistence fishing. The regulation exceeds the authority delegated to the board because it operates too restrictively in its initial differentiation between subsistence and non-subsistence uses. Under a statute designed to protect subsistence uses, the board has devised a regulation to disenfranchise many subsistence users whose interests the statute was designed to protect.

The decision of the trial court is REVERSED.

CHEVRON U.S.A., INC. v. NATURAL RESOURCES DEFENSE COUNCIL

467 U.S. 837 (1984).

[The Clean Air Act required states that had not met EPA's air quality standards to prohibit the construction of a "new or modified major stationary source" of air pollution without obtaining a permit. No such permit can be issued without meeting several stringent conditions.

An EPA legislative regulation allows states to treat an entire plant as a single "stationary source." Under this approach, if a plant contains several pollution-emitting devices, it may install or modify one piece of equipment without meeting the permit requirements if the alteration will not increase the total emissions from the plant. For example, a plant might install a new process which increases pollution if, at the same time, it alters or abandons other equipment which produces an equal or greater amount of pollution. This approach is often referred to as the "bubble" concept, since it treats a single plant as if it was encased in a "bubble."

The issue is whether the statutory term "stationary source" means each major source of pollution within a plant or whether it can refer to an entire plant (the view EPA took in the "bubble" regulation). The Court of Appeals found that the statute and legislative history were inconclusive, but it decided that EPA's interpretation was contrary to Congressional purpose in improving air quality in non-attainment areas. Thus it invalidated the "bubble" regulation. Stevens, J. delivered an opinion for a unanimous court (Rehnquist, O'Connor and Marshall, JJ. did not participate):]

.   .   .

When a court reviews an agency's construction of the statute which it administers, it is confronted with two questions. First, always, is the question whether Congress has directly spoken to the precise question at issue. If the intent of Congress is clear, that is the end of the matter; for the court, as well as the agency, must give effect to the unambiguously expressed intent of Congress.[9] If, however, the court determines Congress has not directly addressed the precise question at issue, the court does not simply impose its own construction on the statute, as would be necessary in the absence of an administrative interpretation.   Rather, if the statute is silent or ambiguous with respect to the specific issue, the question for the court is whether the agency's answer is based on a permissible construction of the statute.[11]

"The power of an administrative agency to administer a congressionally created . . . program necessarily requires the formulation of policy and the making of rules to fill any gap left, implicitly or explicitly, by Congress." If Congress has explicitly left a gap for the agency to fill, there is an express delegation of authority to the agency to elucidate a specific provision of the statute by regulation. Such legislative regulations are given controlling weight unless they are arbitrary, capricious, or manifestly contrary to the statute. Sometimes the legislative delegation to an agency on a particular question is implicit rather than explicit. In such a case, a court may not substitute its own construction of a statutory provision for a reasonable interpretation made by the administrator of an agency.

We have long recognized that considerable weight should be accorded to an executive department's construction of a statutory scheme it is entrusted to administer, and the principle of deference to administrative interpretations "has been consistently followed by this Court whenever decision as to the meaning or reach of a statute has involved reconciling conflicting policies, and a full understanding of the force of the statutory policy in the given situation has depended upon more than ordinary knowledge respecting the matters subjected to agency regulations.

". . . If this choice represents a reasonable accommodation of conflicting policies that were committed to the agency's care by the statute, we should not disturb it unless it appears from the statute or its legislative history that the accommodation is not one that Congress would have sanctioned."

In light of these well-settled principles it is clear that the Court of Appeals misconceived the nature of its role in reviewing the regulations at issue. Once it determined, after its own examination of the legislation, that Congress did not actually have an intent regarding the applicability of the bubble concept to the permit program, the question before it was not whether in its view the concept is "inappropriate" in the general context of a program designed to improve air quality, but

---

9. The judiciary is the final authority on issues of statutory construction and must reject administrative constructions which are contrary to clear congressional intent. If a court, employing traditional tools of statutory construction, ascertains that Congress had an intention on the precise question at issue, that intention is the law and must be given effect.

11. The court need not conclude that the agency construction was the only one it permissibly could have adopted to uphold the construction, or even the reading the court would have reached if the question initially had arisen in a judicial proceeding.

whether the Administrator's view that it is appropriate in the context of this particular program is a reasonable one. Based on the examination of the legislation and its history which follows, we agree with the Court of Appeals that Congress did not have a specific intention on the applicability of the bubble concept in these cases, and conclude that the EPA's use of that concept here is a reasonable policy choice for the agency to make. . . .

In this case, the Administrator's interpretation represents a reasonable accommodation of manifestly competing interests and is entitled to deference: the regulatory scheme is technical and complex, the agency considered the matter in a detailed and reasoned fashion, and the decision involves reconciling conflicting policies. Congress intended to accommodate both interests, but did not do so itself on the level of specificity presented by this case. Perhaps that body consciously desired the Administrator to strike the balance at this level, thinking that those with great expertise and charged with responsibility for administering the provision would be in a better position to do so; perhaps it simply did not consider the question at this level; and perhaps Congress was unable to forge a coalition on either side of the question, and those on each side decided to take their chances with the scheme devised by the agency. For judicial purposes, it matters not which of these things occurred.

Judges are not experts in the field, and are not part of either political branch of the Government. Courts must, in some cases, reconcile competing political interests, but not on the basis of the judges' personal policy preferences. In contrast, an agency to which Congress has delegated policy-making responsibilities may, within the limits of that delegation, properly rely upon the incumbent administration's views of wise policy to inform its judgments. While agencies are not directly accountable to the people, the Chief Executive is, and it is entirely appropriate for this political branch of the Government to make such policy choices—resolving the competing interests which Congress itself either inadvertently did not resolve, or intentionally left to be resolved by the agency charged with the administration of the statute in light of everyday realities.

When a challenge to an agency construction of a statutory provision, fairly conceptualized, really centers on the wisdom of the agency's policy, rather than whether it is a reasonable choice within a gap left open by Congress, the challenge must fail. In such a case, federal judges—who have no constituency—have a duty to respect legitimate policy choices made by those who do. The responsibilities for assessing the wisdom of such policy choices and resolving the struggle between competing views of the public interest are not judicial ones: "Our Constitution vests such responsibilities in the political branches." *TVA v. Hill*, 437 U.S. 153.

We hold that the EPA's definition of the term "source" is a permissible construction of the statute which seeks to accommodate progress in reducing air pollution with economic growth. "The Regulations which the Administrator has adopted provide what the agency could allowably view as . . . [an] effective reconciliation of these twofold ends. . . ."

The judgment of the Court of Appeals is reversed.

Notes and Questions

1. *Reasonableness or rightness?* The *Madison* decision probably represents the dominant view among state courts. However, many state courts would grant greater deference to the agency's interpretation than does *Madison*, and others take a "reasonableness" approach. *See, e.g., Springfield Educ. Ass'n v. Springfield School Dist. No. 19,* 621 P.2d 547 (Or.1980).

Nor does *Chevron* represent the approach always taken by federal courts. Often the courts simply interpret the statute themselves without referring to *Chevron*. Consider, for example, *Bureau of Alcohol, Tobacco and Firearms (BATF) v. Federal Labor Relations Authority (FLRA),* 464 U.S. 89 (1983), a decision handed down a few months before *Chevron*. *BATF* considered an interpretive rule of FLRA requiring the government to pay travel expenses for union negotiators who bargain with it. The statute required the government to pay its employees while they engage in bargaining, but neither the statute nor legislative history was clear on the issue of travel reimbursement. The Court analyzed the statutory text and legislative history for itself, made its own assessment of Congressional policy, and came to the conclusion that reimbursement was not required. The Court declared:

> . . . [T]he "deference owed to an expert tribunal cannot be allowed to slip into a judicial inertia which results in the unauthorized assumption by an agency of major policy decisions properly made by Congress". Accordingly, while reviewing courts should uphold reasonable and defensible constructions of an agency's enabling act . . . they must not "rubber-stamp . . . administrative decisions that they deem inconsistent with a statutory mandate or that frustrate the Congressional policy underlying a statute."

Id. at 97. In a footnote, the court elaborated the extent to which a court should defer to an agency's legal interpretation.

> . . . When an agency's decision is premised on its understanding of a specific congressional intent . . . it engages in the quintessential judicial function of deciding what a statute means. In that case, the agency's interpretation, particularly to the extent it rests on factual premises within its expertise, may be influential but it cannot bind a court. For the reasons set out below, we conclude that the FLRA's decision in this case neither rests on specific congressional intent nor is consistent with the policies underlying the Act.

Id. at 98 n. 8. *Chevron* did not mention *BATF.* Is *BATF* over-ruled? Whether *BATF* is still good law, the jurisprudential view it articulates is shared by many judges and legal scholars.

2. *Is the reasonableness test appropriate?* "Many decisions of this Court . . . have unequivocally reaffirmed the holding of *Marbury v. Madison* that '[i]t is emphatically the province and duty of the judicial department to say what the law is.'" *United States v. Nixon,* 418 U.S. 683, 703 (1974). Given that tradition, and given state and federal APAs which empower courts to substitute judgment on questions of law, and given the "mood" of stronger judicial review articulated in *Universal Camera,* is *Chevron* correct? Does a court abdicate its responsibility by upholding an administrative interpretation different from one the court would prefer?

3. *The Bumpers Amendment.* Senator Bumpers has repeatedly sponsored legislation which would prevent courts from deferring to agency interpretations. One version of the Bumpers Amendment required de novo judicial review on all questions of law and required that the validity of a rule be shown clearly and convincingly. A milder version of the Bumpers Amendment passed the Senate (but not the House); it required "independent judgment" on issues of law and abolished the presumption that agency action is valid. It also allowed courts to "take into account the discretionary authority provided to the agency by law." S. 1080, 97th Cong., 2d Sess. § 5.

Would adoption of the latter version of the Bumpers Amendment change the reasoning or the result in *Chevron?* How? Do you favor the Bumpers Amendment?

4. *The Chevron two-step.* The *Chevron* opinion appears to require a two-step process. In the first step, the court decides whether the statute (or other legal text such as a prior regulation) has a plain meaning, as illustrated by its text and legislative history. If the first step does not yield a plain answer, the court proceeds to the second step. In that step, the court must accept the agency's interpretation if it is reasonable, which it ordinarily is. In a high percentage of difficult cases, a conscientious judge will find that the statute does not yield a plain meaning, often because the legislature simply never considered the issue at all. Under one reading of *Chevron,* that conclusion alone triggers the second step. That method of analysis will require the courts to accept an agency's interpretation in most cases.

However, there is another reading of *Chevron.* Under that approach, there are three steps instead of two. After taking the first step (and finding no plain meaning), the court must take an intermediate step by deciding whether the legislature *delegated to the agency* the power to make the legal interpretation in question. The court makes this decision without deferring to the agency's view of whether a delegation occurred.

If no such delegation was intended, the court retains the dominant interpretive role, even though the text in question does not have a plain meaning. The court might, of course, still give weak deference to the agency's view if it finds that the legislature did not delegate law-interpretive power to the agency. If interpretive delegation was intended, the court then proceeds to the third step and must affirm the agency's interpretation if it is reasonable.

Judge Easterbrook recently articulated this view in a case which involved the appropriate scope of judicial review of an agency's interpretation of its own regulation:

> An ambiguous legal rule does not have a single "right" meaning; there is a range of possible meanings; the selection from the range is an act of policymaking. The person who fleshes out the meaning of the rule is the true law-giver in the circumstances.

> When the legal rule binds the agency—for example, when it appears in the Constitution—courts do not adhere to the agency's views, because the agency lacks discretion to set policy. When the legal rule appears in a statute, the first question in determining the deference appropriate to the agency's construction is whether Congress has transferred discretion to the agency. If the legislation either calls for the agency's decision or contains no disposition of the subject, then the agency has been deputized to make a rule, and its decision should be respected. When Congress tries to settle the subject on its own, however, the agency is not the policy-maker, and its opinion is entitled to correspondingly little force. . . . Different statutes transfer different sorts of implementing authority to agencies, and therefore there is not one but many standards of deference when agencies interpret statutory language. When a court deals with the interpretation of regulations, however, it can be sure that the agency possesses the full power of implementation.

Homemakers North Shore, Inc. v. Bowen, 832 F.2d 408, 411–12 (7th Cir.1987).

5. *Indicia of interpretive delegation.* If Easterbrook's reading of *Chevron* is accepted, how does one decide whether the legislature has implicitly delegated the law-interpretive power to an agency? A court might take account of these factors, among others:

　　i. *Comparative competence.* Is a court or an agency more competent to make a correct interpretation? In comparing institutional competence, an agency might be better suited than a court to interpret a statute which deals with technically complex matters (such as air pollution, nuclear power, or banking). Also relevant in assessing competence is the agency's expertise and experience in dealing with the area. On the other hand, a court might be better suited for interpretive jobs that require facility in dealing with common law or constitutional concepts or other traditional legal materials.

　　ii. *Policy-making delegation.* The legislature probably delegated law-interpreting authority to an agency if it also delegated authority to make policy through legislative rules. If an agency has adjudicating but not rulemaking power, it seems less likely that the legislature delegated it interpretive power and still less so if the agency has only law enforcement but not adjudicating or rulemaking power.

iii. *Broad standards.* When the statute assigns the agency responsibility to implement a broad and relatively standardless criterion (such as "the public interest"), it seems likely that Congress intended to delegate law-interpreting authority relevant to that responsibility.

iv. *Reconciliation of clashing policies.* It is likely that the legislature delegated authority to interpret law which requires reconciliation of clashing policies embodied in the statute.

v. *Difficult interpretive problems.* It is more likely that the legislature delegated power to answer questions which are difficult to interpret through conventional tools of statutory interpretation—for example, statutory provisions which directly conflict with each other.

vi. *Practical problems.* The legislature is likely to have delegated interpretive power if the answer to the particular question will significantly impact on the agency's operation—for example, its enforcement program or its allocation of budgetary resources. Similarly, if the question is one which is best answered and refined by practical experience in administering the statute, it is more likely that the agency has delegated interpretive power.

vii. *Court's attitude toward agency.* A court is more likely to find an interpretive delegation to an agency in whose fairness and competence it has confidence. It is less likely to entrust interpretive power to an agency which it views as "captured" by the regulated industry or one which is subject to undue political pressure from the legislature or executive to decide an issue a particular way.

6. *Affirming a reasonable interpretation.* Is it likely that a judge will affirm a reasonable agency interpretation if the judge thinks it is wrong? Judge Breyer of the U.S. Court of Appeals for the First Circuit writes:

[The *Chevron* formula] asks judges to develop a cast of mind that often is psychologically difficult to maintain. It is difficult, after having examined a legal question in depth with the object of deciding it correctly, to believe both that the agency's interpretation is legally wrong, *and* that its interpretation is reasonable. More often one concludes that there is a "better" view of the statute for example, and that the "better" view is "correct," and that the alternative view is "erroneous." There is not much room in this kind of thinking for the notion of "both this view and its contrary are reasonable," a notion with which one is more "at home" when, for example, juries apply standards to facts or agencies promulgate rules under a general delegation of authority.

Breyer, "Judicial Review of Questions of Law and Policy," 38 Admin.L. Rev. 363, 379 (1986).

7. *The weight of an agency's interpretation.* Under a "rightness" approach, courts give weight ("weak deference") to the agency's interpretation. A number of factors are traditionally employed in determining how much. These factors can best be thought of as principles of statutory construction. Note that if a court employed the "reasonableness" approach, it might still employ the same factors in deciding whether a particular interpretation is reasonable.

i. *Procedures and thoroughness.* The procedures employed in adopting the interpretation and the thoroughness of its consideration are important. For example, an interpretation contained in a rule adopted by the agency head after full-fledged notice and comment procedure should be entitled to greater weight than one adopted by a single staff member without any public input or without review by superior levels within the agency. Similarly, an interpretation adopted in the course of adjudication should be entitled to greater weight if the case was vigorously litigated and thoroughly considered by the agency head than if it was weakly litigated and the final decision was by an ALJ.

ii. *Contemporaneous construction.* Greater deference is due to an interpretation made contemporaneously with enactment of the statute, particularly if the agency members or staff participated in drafting the legislation.

iii. *Long-standing construction.* An interpretation maintained for a long time is entitled to more deference than one recently adopted (and much more than one adopted while the case is pending).

iv. *Consistency.* Greater deference is owed to a consistently maintained interpretation, less to one that contradicts an earlier view.

v. *Reliance.* Greater deference is owed to an interpretation on which the public has relied.

vi. *Reenactment.* Greater deference is owed to an interpretation if it can be shown that the legislature endorsed it. If the legislature reenacted a statute, knowing about a prior agency interpretation, this is strong evidence in favor of that interpretation. Usually, however, it cannot be shown that legislators knew about the interpretation so that the mere fact of statutory reenactment is uninformative.

vii. *Interpretation of rules.* Greater deference is owed to an agency's interpretation to its own rules than to its interpretation of a statute.

viii. *Comparative competence.* Many of the factors mentioned in note 5 are relevant here as well. Clearly a court gives greater weight to an interpretation which the agency is unusually competent to make (because the issue is technical or is informed by practical experience) and less to interpretations by agencies it distrusts.

How do these factors point in *Madison?* In *Chevron?* In *BATF?*

8. *Deference and rulemaking procedure.* Consider 1981 MSAPA § 3–109(a). Under this provision, an agency may dispense with notice and comment procedure in adopting interpretive rules only if the agency does not possess delegated authority to bind the courts with its definition. Suppose *Chevron* is followed in a state which adopts this provision; will an agency know whether it can dispense with notice and comment?

Consider also § 3–109(b). If an agency takes advantage of the exemption in § 3–109(a) in adopting an interpretive rule, a reviewing court must determine "wholly de novo" the validity of the resulting rule. Is this wise?

9. *Problem.* § 320 of the Welfare Code provides that a recipient of welfare who has suffered the loss of clothing or furniture "as the result of a fire, flood or other like catastrophe" is entitled to a special grant to replace the lost possessions. § 320 was added to the Welfare Code in 1975. According to the legislative committee report accompanying the bill, the purpose of the revision was to abandon a discretionary program of special grants to welfare recipients. This discretionary program was objectionable because the discretion was often abused by social workers. Also, it was considered demeaning for recipients to have to ask for the grants. Instead, the Code provided, insofar as possible, for entitlements to special grants for emergency situations. There was no further explanation of § 320.

The State Welfare Department has authority "to make such rules and regulations as are needed to carry out the provisions of this Code." The Department did not adopt a regulation interpreting § 320, but it did adopt a provision in the Welfare Manual which states that the loss must arise from natural (i.e. non-human) causes. The Manual was adopted in 1975 soon after adoption of the new Code.

Arthur is a welfare recipient. He is a single parent who lives in a slum neighborhood. As the result of a burglary, he lost all of his clothing and furniture, worth $2000. He applied for a special grant which the Department rejected. He requested a "fair hearing" but the officer who conducted it rejected his claim in reliance on the Manual.

On judicial review, what result? *See Howard v. Wyman,* 319 N.Y.S.2d 754 (App.Div.1971), *rev'd,* 322 N.Y.S.2d 683 (N.Y.1971).

§ 9.3 SCOPE OF REVIEW OF APPLICATION OF LAW TO FACTS

Once an agency has found the basic facts (§ 9.1) and interpreted the governing law (§ 9.2), it must *apply* that law to the facts. Sometimes the application of law to facts is referred to as a "mixed question of law and fact," an "ultimate fact," or an "inference" from the facts. Should the court use a "reasonableness" or a "rightness" standard in reviewing the agency's application of law to facts?

McPHERSON v. EMPLOYMENT DIVISION

591 P.2d 1381 (Or.1979).

LINDE, J.

Petitioner, Marlynn McPherson, seeks review of a decision of the Employment Division denying her unemployment compensation on the ground that she left her employment voluntarily and without good cause. After the "Administrator's Decision," [1] the claimant requested a hearing. A referee denied her claim upon findings of fact and conclusions of law that will be discussed below. The Employment Appeals Board affirmed the referee's decision.

The issue is whether the Division misconstrued the unemployment compensation law in concluding that McPherson did not have "good cause" to leave her employment. That question in turn involves a question of the scope of judicial review of the Division's determinations of "good cause." This court has not previously had occasion to address these questions. For the reasons that follow, we reverse and remand petitioner's claim to the Division.

The statute and the facts. Since its initial enactment in 1935, the unemployment law has been a program designed to provide a source of substitute income from a public fund for any eligible unemployed person unless the person is disqualified for one of the reasons provided in the statute. In one phrasing or another, the disqualifying reasons essentially have been loss of employment due to the employee's own misconduct, giving up one's job voluntarily without good cause, and failure to apply for or to accept suitable employment. At present, ORS 657.176 provides: ...

> (2) If the authorized representative designated by the assistant director finds:
>
> . . .

---

1. The "administrator" to which this heading of the decision refers is the Assistant Director of Employment, who heads the Employment Division within the De-partment of Human Resources and "administer[s] the provisions" of the unemployment compensation law. . . .

(c) The individual voluntarily left work without good cause the individual shall be disqualified from the receipt of benefits. . . .

Briefly, it appears from the findings and the undisputed evidence on which they are based that claimant was employed by the City of Salem . . . . Throughout her employment two male coworkers with whom she was required to work complained to her and to others that they did not approve of a female worker in the maintenance position, and that she lacked the strength to do the job. They did not give McPherson information or other assistance that she needed to develop her job skills. She filed a union grievance over additional difficulties with one of the men after she declined to date him, which was later settled by an apology. McPherson repeatedly brought the matter to the attention of her supervisor and the employer's affirmative action officer. The supervisor told her to ignore the men's remarks; he also said that he was satisfied with her work and progress and recommended her periodically for pay raises. However, claimant decided that she would not be able to obtain technical work experience on the job beyond attending courses or seminars and reading manuals. She gave notice in February, 1977, and quit the following month.

In summary, it is undisputed that claimant left work voluntarily and that she did so because of the "sexist" behavior of male employees with whom she was assigned to work and who objected to her doing "men's work." The issue before us is not whether we would reach the same decision on the facts that the Employment Division did. The purpose of our review is to determine whether the Division reached its conclusion denying claimant unemployment benefits under a misapprehension of the scope of "good cause." Before examining that question, we must clarify the appropriate scope of review.

Scope of review. At the outset, it should be recalled that the scope of judicial review of an administrative decision does not follow simply from the nature of the decision and of the disputed issue. The rules governing judicial review can be and generally are provided by law. In [this case the APA provides]:

(8) The court may affirm, reverse or remand the order. The court shall reverse or remand the order only if it finds:

(a) The order to be unlawful in substance or procedure, but error in procedure shall not be cause for reversal or remand unless the court shall find that substantial rights of the petitioner were prejudiced thereby; or

. . .

(d) The order is not supported by substantial evidence in the whole record.

The statute thus requires a party challenging an agency determination to specify, and the court to decide, whether the asserted agency error is one of fact, lacking support in the evidence, or a misapplication of the relevant substantive or procedural law. Of course the challenge may involve several grounds, but it remains necessary to identify which is which. . . .

The identification of errors of fact and errors of law for scope of review [purposes], when an agency applies a broad statutory term to a particular situation, is one of the most problematic issues in administrative law. *See, e.g.,* 4 K.C. Davis, Administrative Law Treatise §§ 30.01, 30.02 (1958) and later supplements; Jaffe, Judicial Control of Administrative Action 556–564 (1965); B. Schwartz, Administrative Law 642–662 (1976). Agency decisions interpreting a legal term in applying it to particular facts are sometimes said to pose a "mixed question of law and fact."

The Court of Appeals has so characterized determinations of "good cause" under the unemployment compensation law. When such a determination is reviewed, [the APA] calls for separating the elements of the mixture that are "facts" from those that interpret the law. . . .

"Facts," it has been said, are those elements entering into the decision that describe phenomena and events without reference to their significance under the law in question, or to put it another way, as they might be described by a lay person unaware of the disputed legal issue.[3] In that sense, the claimant's reasons for quitting her employment and the events that led up to them are questions of fact. The meaning of the words "good cause" . . . on the other hand, is plainly a question of law. But that is not the end of the inquiry into the scope of judicial review, for this question of law in turn leads to the question how far ORS 657.176 entrusts to the agency the determination of what kind of reasons are "good cause" to leave employment and what kind of reasons are not.

In prior cases under the unemployment compensation law, this court has faced the problem of reviewing agency determinations whether various relationships between providers of services and those who pay for them constituted employment within the coverage of the act. *Baker v. Cameron,* 401 P.2d 691 (1965), concluded that "if the facts are not disputed, the question of whether one is an 'employee' or the contractor of another is a question of law," although the views of the agency on the issue "should be given some consideration." This stops well short of the position taken in *NLRB v. Hearst Publications,* 322 U.S. 111, (1944), that a specialized agency's view of an employment relationship within the meaning of its governing statute should be accepted if it has "a reasonable basis in law." Judicial respect for an agency's interpretation of a legal term, though it is a question of law, is often explained on a theory of agency "expertise." That may apply where statutory terms are drawn from a technical vocabulary which takes its meaning from a particular science, industry, trade, or occupa-

---

3. In *NLRB v. Marcus Trucking Co.,* 286 F.2d 583 (1961), Judge Henry Friendly cited this quotation of O.W. Holmes, Jr., from Jaffe, *Judicial Review: Questions of Law,* 69 Harv.L.Rev. 239, 241 (1955): "A finding of fact is the assertion that a phenomenon has happened or is or will be happening independent of or anterior to its legal effect." 286 F.2d at 590.

tion in which the agency has genuine expertise, but an agency's administration of a specialized program does not mean that its political head or changing personnel either need or acquire expertise in that sense. As this court said about applying the *Hearst Publications* formula to the Public Utility Commissioner's interpretation of a term in a highway use tax law, the agency's special experience calls for deference to "the degree to which the problem involves knowledge peculiar to the industry, business, etc.," knowledge which was not shown to be involved in interpreting the term at issue.

Distinct from such agency "expertise" in giving meaning to a technical or specialized terminology is the question how far the statutory term entrusts to the agency some range of choice in carrying out the legislative policy. We do not regard the Employment Division as the kind of "expert agency" that has special knowledge of the meaning of such statutory terms as "employment," "direction or control," "independently established business," and the like. In those phrases, the legislature refers to relationships that meet certain definable legal tests, though applying the tests to the facts of any given arrangement may sometimes be a close question. But the phrase "good cause" is not that kind of a statutory term. Like standards such as "fair" or "unfair," "undue" or "unreasonable," or "public convenience and necessity," "good cause" in its own terms calls for completing a value judgment that the legislature itself has only indicated: evaluating what are "good" reasons for giving up one's employment and what are not. Judicial review of such evaluations, though a "question of law," requires a court to determine how much the legislature has itself decided and how much it has left to be resolved by the agency. For an agency decision is not "unlawful in substance," if the agency's elaboration of a standard like "good cause" is within the range of its responsibility for effectuating a broadly stated statutory policy.

Review under ORS 657.176. The history of Oregon's unemployment compensation law shows that some range of agency responsibility for defining "good cause" was intended. . . . [T]he responsibility to which we refer has been placed in the administrator, now the Assistant Director of Employment. . . . He is directed to "determine all questions of general policy and promulgate rules and regulations and be responsible for the administration of this chapter." If, for instance, the Division were to issue interpretative rules describing one or more characteristics of "good cause" independently of the decision of a concrete case, the assistant director is the "agency" authorized to do so. . . .

Application to the present case. We . . . turn to the agency's decision to examine on what view of the governing law it was based. [The referee] concluded that the claimant voluntarily left work without good cause.

[T]he referee . . . apparently assumed that his conclusions were not merely permitted but compelled as a matter of law. As stated above, this assumption takes an improperly narrow view of the Division's own responsibility to define "good cause" within the overall policy and provisions of the Unemployment Compensation Law. But there is little in the record or briefs to show what criteria of "good cause" the Division might develop in the absence of that misconception. . . . The law does not extend its benefits to a worker who has a job and voluntarily gives it up without "good cause." But it also does not impose upon the employee the one-dimensional motivation of Adam Smith's "economic man." The workplace is the setting of much of the worker's daily life. The statute does not demand as a matter of law that he or she sacrifice all other than economic objectives and, for instance, endure racial, ethnic, or sexual slurs or personal abuse, for fear that abandoning an oppressive situation will disqualify the worker from unemployment benefits. . . .

How far "good cause" encompasses such non-economic values also is left to the agency in the first instance.

Conclusion. As stated above, there are implications in the referee's "Conclusions and Reasons," adopted by the Employment Appeals Board, that the agency assumed its decision to be compelled as a matter of law by the statute. . . . We cannot discern what criteria of "good cause" the agency might have applied on its own in the absence of that assumption. This does not mean that on the present record the Court of Appeals or this court might not have reached the same result. That, however, is not our assignment but the Division's, subject only to review whether its assessment of the kind of reasons that are "good cause" to leave employment is "unlawful in substance." For these reasons, the case must be remanded to the Division for reconsideration by the assistant director's authorized representative in the light of this opinion.

Reversed and remanded.

TONGUE, J., dissenting [dissent omitted].

Notes and Questions

1. *Fact or law?* Is an application of law to facts (such as whether Ms. McPherson had "good cause" to quit) a question of *fact* or a question of *law?* In considering whether the "voluntariness" of a confession was a question of fact or law, the Supreme Court said:

   . . . [T]he appropriate methodology for distinguishing questions of fact from questions of law has been, to say the least, elusive. . . . [T]he Court has yet to arrive at "a rule or principle that will unerringly distinguish a factual finding from a legal conclusion." Perhaps much of the difficulty in this area stems from the practical truth that the decision to label an issue a "question of law," a "question of fact," or a "mixed question of law and fact" is sometimes as much a matter of allocation as it is of analysis. At least in those instances in which Congress has not spoken and in which the issue falls somewhere between a pristine legal standard and a simple historical fact, the fact/law distinction at times has turned on a determination that, as a matter of the sound administration of justice, one judicial actor is better positioned than another to decide the issue in question.

Miller v. Fenton, 474 U.S. 104, 113–14 (1985).

Courts often denominate issues of application of law to fact as questions of law or of fact depending on their unexplained conclusion about the proper scope of review. If a court decides to substitute judgment, it often identifies the issue as one of law, while if it decides that reasonableness is the appropriate standard, it identifies the issue as one of fact. Of course, application issues involve both law and fact— which is the reason they are often referred to as "mixed questions of law and fact."

2. *Reasonableness or rightness?* State and federal decisions relating to the scope of judicial review of an agency's application of law to fact appear to be in hopeless conflict. There are countless cases which subject application issues to rightness review and probably just as many which employ reasonableness review. These cases can be reconciled, if at all, only on the basis of differential legislative delegations of discretion to apply law to facts. *McPherson* is a useful treatment because it expressly relates the scope of review to the scope of agency discretion. Most decisions simply employ one approach or the other without explaining why.

The apparent conflict can be illustrated by cases which concern judicial review of agency findings that an individual is an "employee" for purposes of various labor law or social benefit statutes. *McPherson* contrasts an Oregon case, *Baker v. Cameron,* 401 P.2d 691 (1965) with the Supreme Court case of *NLRB v. Hearst Publications Inc.,* 322 U.S. 111 (1944).

Baker concerned the issue of whether aluminum siding salesmen were "employees" or "independent contractors" for purposes of the unemployment compensation law. The Oregon statute defined a person as an "employee" unless "such individual [is] . . . free from control or direction over the performance of such services . . ." In other words, the statute used the traditional common law test for distinguishing employees from independent contractors for purposes of determining vicarious liability in tort. The Court treated the issue as one of law and engaged in rightness review, although it gave "some consideration" to the agency's decision because of its "expertise," and ultimately affirmed the agency's determination.

Hearst is the leading federal case calling for reasonableness review of application questions. In *Hearst,* the issue was whether newsboys were "employees" (rather than independent contractors). If the newsboys were "employees" (as the NLRB held they were), the newspaper was required by the National Labor Relations Act to bargain with their union. The Supreme Court first decided (using "rightness" review) that the NLRB correctly held that the definition of "employee" used in common-law tort cases should not be used because it would defeat the purposes of the Act. Instead, the proper legal test was whether the conditions of the relationship (such as inequality of bargaining power) required the protection of a union.

However, when it came to applying this definition to the actual facts of the case, the Court switched to "reasonableness" review and upheld the Board's determination. The Court justified its use of a reasonableness standard to the application issue on the following basis:

> That task has been assigned primarily to the agency created by Congress to administer the Act. Determination of "where all the conditions of the relation require protection" involves inquiries for the Board charged with this duty. Everyday experience in the administration of the statute gives it familiarity with the circumstances and backgrounds of employment relationships in various industries, with the abilities and needs of the workers for self-organization and collective action, and with the adaptability of collective bargaining for the peaceful settlement of their disputes with their employers. The experience thus acquired must be brought frequently to bear on the question who is an employee under the Act. Resolving that question, like determining whether unfair labor practices have been committed, "belongs to the usual administrative routine" of the Board . . . [W]here the question is one of specific application of a broad statutory term in a proceeding in which the agency administering the statute must determine it initially, the reviewing court's function is limited. . . . [T]he Board's determination that specified persons are "employees" under this Act is to be accepted if it has "warrant in the record" and a reasonable basis in law.

322 U.S. at 130–31.

3. *Employees and managerial employees.* With *Hearst,* compare *NLRB v. Yeshiva Univ.,* 444 U.S. 672 (1980). *Yeshiva* involved an attempt by professors to organize and form a union. Although the Act provides that "professional employees" have a right to unionize, the courts have held that "managerial employees" do not. "Managerial employees" are those who are "aligned with management" in the sense that they take or recommend discretionary actions that effectively control or implement employer policy. Yeshiva contended that professors were managerial because of their great authority over admissions and other academic matters (such as curriculum and grading).

Following numerous previous decisions involving private universities, the Board held that professors were not "managerial employees," because their participation in governance of the University was an exercise of their own professional judgment, rather than in support of management policies. Consequently, there was no danger of divided loyalty and no need for the managerial exclusion. The Court of Appeals reversed.

The Supreme Court affirmed the Court of Appeals, independently deciding that the professors were "managerial employees." The professors are aligned with the institution's interests because their participation in governance made the interests of professors and the institution inseparable. In its concluding paragraph, the Court stated:

> Finally, the Board contends that the deference due its expertise in these matters requires us to reverse the decision of the Court of Appeals. The question we decide today is a mixed one of fact and law. But the Board's opinion may be searched in vain for relevant findings of fact. The absence of factual analysis apparently reflects the Board's view that the managerial status of particular faculties may be decided on the basis of conclusory rationales rather than examination of the facts of each case. The Court of Appeals took a different view, and determined that the faculty of Yeshiva University, "in effect, substantially and pervasively operat[e] the enterprise." We find no reason to reject this conclusion. As our decisions consistently show, we accord great respect to the expertise of the Board when its conclusions are rationally based on articulated facts and consistent with the Act. . . . In this case, we hold that the Board's decision satisfies neither criterion.

Id. at 672. The four dissenters in *Yeshiva* argued that:

> [P]rimary authority to resolve these conflicts [between inclusion of professional employees and exclusion of managerial employees] and to adapt the Act to the changing patterns of industrial relations was entrusted to the Board, not to the judiciary. . . . Accordingly, the judicial role is limited; a court may not substitute its own judgment for that of the Board. The Board's decision may be reviewed for its rationality and its consistency with the Act, but once these criteria are satisfied, the order must be enforced.
>
> [After arguing that the Board's decision was correct, the dissent concluded:] [E]ven were I to have reservations about the specific result reached by the Board on the facts of this case, I would certainly have to conclude that the Board applied a proper mode of analysis to arrive at a decision well within the zone of reasonableness.

Id. at 692–94, 706. Can *Hearst* be reconciled with *Yeshiva?*

4. *Delegation to apply the law.* McPherson employs analysis similar to that in *Chevron:* a legislature may implicitly delegate authority to an agency to apply the law to facts. If it has done so, the court can review the application only for reasonableness, not for rightness. Recall the factors which might be considered by a court in identifying an implicit interpretive delegation (note 5 after *Chevron*). Could these factors help to reconcile *Baker, Hearst,* and *Yeshiva?*

What result in a state adopting 1981 MSAPA? See § 5–116(c)(4). The comment to that provision states:

Paragraph (c)(4) includes two distinct matters—interpretation and application of the law. With regard to the agency's *interpretation* of the law, courts generally give little deference to the agency . . . By contrast, with regard to the agency's *application* of the law to specific situations, the enabling statute normally confers some discretion upon the agency. Accordingly, a court should find reversible error in the agency's application of the law only if the agency has improperly exercised its discretion, within the frame-work of paragraph (c)(8).

5. *Remand to the Division.* In *McPherson,* the Court remanded the case to the Employment Division—not to the Employment Appeals Board (whose decision it was reviewing). Why? Suppose the Division adopts a regulation that sexual harassment by co-workers is not good cause to quit. It then refuses a claim similar to Ms. McPherson's, and the Board affirms denial of the claim. Would the court affirm?

6. *Prejudicial error.* Note that the Oregon APA provision in-volved in *McPherson* states: "error in procedure shall not be cause for reversal or remand unless the court shall find that substantial rights of the petitioner were prejudiced thereby." How about an error of sub-stance rather than procedure?

This rule that an agency decision will not be reversed for a non-prejudicial error is also set forth in the federal APA § 706 (last sentence) and 1981 MSAPA § 5–116(c) and is part of the common law as well. The non-prejudicial error rule requires a reviewing court to ascertain whether the agency would have reached the same result even if it had not made the error in question.

Suppose in *McPherson* that the Employment Division denied com-pensation because the claimant had quit her job because the salary was too low, and that substantial evidence supported this conclusion. The Employment Division also stated that even if she had resigned only because of sexual harassment, she would still have been denied compen-sation because such harassment is not "good cause" to quit as a matter of law. Would the court reverse this decision?

7. *Problem.* Dr. Sherman specialized in the treatment of obesity. He believed that the best treatment for obesity was the use of a combination of amphetamine and barbiturate drugs in conjunction with diet. He routinely prescribed the same drugs for every patient. Pa-tients were told to call if they had any adverse reaction to the drugs and to return in two weeks.

Dr. Sherman testified that he had studied the problem of obesity extensively, had served 48,000 patients, and had never been sued for malpractice. He testified that none of the drugs he prescribed could adversely affect any medical condition.

Several other doctors testified that the method of treatment used by Dr. Sherman was a fraud, that it could not help patients, was likely to produce addiction, and could adversely affect other medical conditions.

The State Medical Board revoked Dr. Sherman's license to practice medicine on the ground that this method of treatment was a "fraud and deceit in the practice of medicine" (one of the statutory grounds for discipline of physicians). What is the scope of judicial review of the Board's finding that Dr. Sherman's method of treatment was a "fraud and deceit in the practice of medicine?" *See Sherman v. Board of Regents,* 266 N.Y.S.2d 39 (App.Div.1966).

§ 9.4 JUDICIAL REVIEW UNDER THE ARBITRARY AND CAPRICIOUS STANDARD

A great variety of administrative action is judicially reviewed under § 706(2)(A) of the APA and corresponding provisions in state law: "arbitrary, capricious, an abuse of discretion, or otherwise not in accordance with law." This review standard is referred to as the "arbitrary and capricious" test.

Courts use the arbitrary and capricious test in reviewing the discretionary element of administrative rules, as in the *State Farm* case which follows, and many other forms of discretionary action, such as grantmaking (as in *Overton Park,* note 1, *infra*). In addition, that test applies to review of discretionary elements in formal adjudication, such as an agency's choice of remedy. *Butz v. Glover Livestock Commission Co.,* 411 U.S. 182 (1973). Finally, as noted at the beginning of § 9.1, *supra,* it applies to review of factfinding in adjudications in which the agency is not required to conduct a formal hearing.

MOTOR VEHICLE MANUFACTURERS ASS'N v. STATE FARM MUTUAL AUTOMOBILE INS. CO.

463 U.S. 29 (1983).

[The National Highway Traffic Safety Administration (NHTSA) rescinded a prior rule known as Motor Vehicle Safety Standard 208. Standard 208, adopted in 1977, required cars produced after September, 1982 to be equipped with "passive restraints" (either airbags or automatic seatbelts).

The standard was the subject of 60 rulemaking notices; it was imposed, amended, rescinded, reimposed, and finally rescinded again. The first version of the standard required installation of non-automatic seatbelts, but the level of use was too low to reduce traffic injuries much (passive restraints could prevent about 12,000 deaths and over 100,000 serious injuries each year). At one point, NHTSA required an "ignition interlock" which prevented the car from starting until seatbelts were attached; this was unpopular and was banned by statute. In 1981, pursuant to a deregulatory initiative of the Reagan administration, NHTSA delayed the effective date of the 1977 standard.

After a notice and comment proceeding, NHTSA rescinded the standard.

NHTSA explained that it could not find that the standard would produce significant safety benefits. Virtually all cars would be produced with *automatic detachable belts* (rather than airbags). Once this type of belt is unbuckled, it loses its automatic feature until it is rebuckled. Thus, Standard 208 might not significantly increase usage of restraints at all.

Since the standard would cost $1 billion to implement, NHTSA did not believe it reasonable to impose such costs on manufacturers and consumers without more adequate assurance of sufficient safety benefits. In addition, NHTSA concluded that automatic restraints might have an adverse effect on the public's attitude toward safety, "poisoning popular sentiment toward efforts to improve occupant restraint systems in the future." Insurance companies challenged the rescission which the D.C. Circuit held arbitrary and capricious.]

WHITE, J.:

. . .

III

Unlike the Court of Appeals, we do not find the appropriate scope of judicial review to be the "most troublesome question" in the case. Both the Motor Vehicle Safety Act and the 1974 Amendments concerning occupant crash protection standards indicate that motor vehicle safety standards are to be promulgated under the informal rulemaking procedures of § 553 of the Administrative Procedure Act. The agency's action in promulgating such standards therefore may be set aside if found to be "arbitrary, capricious, an abuse of discretion, or otherwise not in accordance with law." § 706(2)(A). *Citizens to Preserve Overton Park v. Volpe,* 401 U.S. 402. We believe that the rescission or modification of an occupant protection standard is subject to the same test. . . .

Petitioner Motor Vehicle Manufacturers Association (MVMA) disagrees, contending that the rescission of an agency rule should be judged by the same standard a court would use to judge an agency's refusal to promulgate a rule in the first place—a standard Petitioner believes considerably narrower than the traditional arbitrary and capricious test. We reject this view. The Motor Vehicle Safety Act expressly equates orders "revoking" and "establishing" safety standards; neither that Act nor the APA suggests that revocations are to be treated as refusals to promulgate standards. Petitioner's view would render meaningless Congress' authorization for judicial review of orders revoking safety rules. Moreover, the revocation of an extant regulation is substantially different than a failure to act. Revocation constitutes a reversal of the agency's former views as to the proper course. A "settled course of behavior embodies the agency's informed judgment that, by pursuing that course, it will carry out the policies committed to it by Congress. There is, then, at least a presumption that those policies will be carried out best if the settled rule is adhered to." Accordingly, an agency changing its course by rescinding a rule is obligated to supply a reasoned analysis for the change beyond that which may be required when an agency does not act in the first instance. . . . In so holding, we fully recognize that "regulatory agencies do not establish rules of conduct to last forever," and that an agency must be given ample latitude to "adapt their rules and policies to the demands of changing circumstances."

But the forces of change do not always or necessarily point in the direction of deregulation. In the abstract, there is no more reason to presume that changing circumstances require the rescission of prior action, instead of a revision in or even the extension of current regulation. If Congress established a presumption from which judicial review should start, that presumption—contrary to petitioners' views—is not *against* safety regulation, but *against* changes in current policy that are not justified by the rulemaking record. While the removal of a regulation may not entail the monetary expenditures and other costs of enacting a new standard, and accordingly, it may be easier for an agency to justify a deregulatory action, the direction in which an agency chooses to move does not alter the standard of judicial review established by law. . . .

[U]nder [the arbitrary and capricious] standard, a reviewing court may not set aside an agency rule that is rational, based on consideration of the relevant factors and within the scope of the authority delegated to the agency by the statute. We do not disagree with this formulation.[9] The scope of review under the "arbitrary and capricious" standard is narrow and a court is not to substitute its judgment for that of the agency. Nevertheless, the agency must examine the relevant data and articulate a satisfactory explanation for its action including a "rational connection between the facts found and the choice made." *Burlington Truck Lines v. United States*, 371 U.S. 156. In reviewing that explanation, we must "consider whether the decision was based on a consideration of the relevant factors and whether there has been a clear error of judgment." *Citizens to Preserve Overton Park v. Volpe,* *supra.*

Normally, an agency rule would be arbitrary and capricious if the agency has relied on factors which Congress has not intended it to consider, entirely failed to consider an important aspect of the problem, offered an explanation for its decision that runs counter to the evidence before the agency, or is so implausible that it could not be ascribed to a difference in view or the product of agency expertise. The reviewing

9. The Department of Transportation suggests that the arbitrary and capricious standard requires no more than the minimum rationality a statute must bear in order to withstand analysis under the Due Process Clause. We do not view as equivalent the presumption of constitutionality afforded legislation drafted by Congress and the presumption of regularity afforded an agency in fulfilling its statutory mandate.

court should not attempt itself to make up for such deficiencies: "We may not supply a reasoned basis for the agency's action that the agency itself has not given." *SEC v. Chenery Corp.,* 332 U.S. 194. We will, however, "uphold a decision of less than ideal clarity if the agency's path may reasonably be discerned." For purposes of this case, it is also relevant that Congress required a record of the rulemaking proceedings to be compiled and submitted to a reviewing court, 15 U.S.C. § 1394, and intended that agency findings under the Motor Vehicle Safety Act would be supported by "substantial evidence on the record considered as a whole." S.Rep. No. 1301, 89th Cong., 2d Sess. p. 8 (1966). . . .

V

The ultimate question before us is whether NHTSA's rescission of the passive restraint requirement of Standard 208 was arbitrary and capricious. We conclude, as did the Court of Appeals, that it was. We also conclude, but for somewhat different reasons, that further consideration of the issue by the agency is therefore required. We deal separately with the rescission as it applies to airbags and as it applies to seatbelts.

A

The first and most obvious reason for finding the rescission arbitrary and capricious is that NHTSA apparently gave no consideration whatever to modifying the Standard to require that airbag technology be utilized. Standard 208 sought to achieve automatic crash protection by requiring automobile manufacturers to install either of two passive restraint devices: airbags or automatic seatbelts. . . . The agency has now determined that the detachable automatic belts will not attain anticipated safety benefits because so many individuals will detach the mechanism. . . . Given the effectiveness ascribed to airbag technology by the agency, the mandate of the Safety Act to achieve traffic safety would suggest that the logical response to the faults of detachable seatbelts would be to require the installation of airbags. At the very least this alternative way of achieving the objectives of the Act should have been addressed and adequate reasons given for its abandonment. But the agency not only did not require compliance through airbags, it did not even consider the possibility in its 1981 rulemaking. Not one sentence of its rulemaking statement discusses the airbags-only option. Because, as the Court of Appeals stated, "NHTSA's . . . analysis of airbags was nonexistent," what we said in *Burlington Truck Lines v. United States,* is apropos here:

> There are no findings and no analysis here to justify the choice made, no indication of the basis on which the [agency] exercised its expert discretion. We are not prepared to and the Administrative Procedure Act will not permit us to accept such . . . practice. . . . Expert discretion is the lifeblood of the administrative process, but 'unless we make the requirements for administrative action strict and demanding, *expertise*, the strength of modern

government, can become a monster which rules with no practical
limits on its discretion.'

We have frequently reiterated that an agency must cogently explain
why it has exercised its discretion in a given manner, and we reaffirm
this principle again today.

The automobile industry has opted for the passive belt over the
airbag, but surely it is not enough that the regulated industry has
eschewed a given safety device. For nearly a decade, the automobile
industry waged the regulatory equivalent of war against the airbag and
lost—the inflatable restraint was proven sufficiently effective. Now
the automobile industry has decided to employ a seatbelt system which
will not meet the safety objectives of Standard 208. This hardly
constitutes cause to revoke the standard itself. Indeed, the Motor
Vehicle Safety Act was necessary because the industry was not sufficiently responsive to safety concerns. The Act intended that safety
standards not depend on current technology and could be "technology-
forcing" in the sense of inducing the development of superior safety
design.

Although the agency did not address the mandatory airbags option
and the Court of Appeals noted that "airbags seem to have none of the
problems that NHTSA identified in passive seatbelts," petitioners recite
a number of difficulties that they believe would be posed by a mandatory airbag standard. These range from questions concerning the installation of airbags in small cars to that of adverse public reaction. But
these are not the agency's reasons for rejecting a mandatory airbag
standard. Not having discussed the possibility, the agency submitted
no reasons at all. The short—and sufficient—answer to petitioners'
submission is that the courts may not accept appellate counsel's *post
hoc* rationalizations for agency action. It is well-established that an
agency's action must be upheld, if at all, on the basis articulated by the
agency itself. *Ibid.; SEC v. Chenery.*

Petitioners also invoke our decision in *Vermont Yankee Nuclear
Power Corp. v. NRDC,* as though it were a talisman under which any
agency decision is by definition unimpeachable. Specifically, it is
submitted that to require an agency to consider an airbags-only alternative is, in essence, to dictate to the agency the procedures it is to follow.
Petitioners both misread *Vermont Yankee* and misconstrue the nature
of the remand that is in order. In *Vermont Yankee,* we held that a
court may not impose additional procedural requirements upon an
agency. We do not require today any specific procedures which NHT-
SA must follow. Nor do we broadly require an agency to consider all
policy alternatives in reaching decision. It is true that a rulemaking
"cannot be found wanting simply because the agency failed to include
every alternative device and thought conceivable by the mind of man
. . . regardless of how uncommon or unknown that alternative may
have been. . . ." But the airbag is more than a policy alternative to
the passive restraint standard; it is a technological alternative within

the ambit of the existing standard. We hold only that given the judgment made in 1977 that airbags are an effective and cost-beneficial life-saving technology, the mandatory passive-restraint rule may not be abandoned without any consideration whatsoever of an airbags-only requirement.

B

Although the issue is closer, we also find that the agency was too quick to dismiss the safety benefits of automatic seatbelts. NHTSA's critical finding was that, in light of the industry's plans to install readily detachable passive belts, it could not reliably predict "even a 5 percentage point increase as the minimum level of expected usage increase." The Court of Appeals rejected this finding because there is "not one iota" of evidence that Modified Standard 208 will fail to increase nationwide seatbelt use by at least 13 percentage points, the level of increased usage necessary for the standard to justify its cost. Given the lack of probative evidence, the court held that "only a well-justified refusal to seek more evidence could render rescission non-arbitrary."

Petitioners object to this conclusion. In their view, "substantial uncertainty" that a regulation will accomplish its intended purpose is sufficient reason, without more, to rescind a regulation. We agree with petitioners that just as an agency reasonably may decline to issue a safety standard if it is uncertain about its efficacy, an agency may also revoke a standard on the basis of serious uncertainties if supported by the record and reasonably explained. Rescission of the passive restraint requirement would not be arbitrary and capricious simply because there was no evidence in direct support of the agency's conclusion. It is not infrequent that the available data does not settle a regulatory issue and the agency must then exercise its judgment in moving from the facts and probabilities on the record to a policy conclusion. Recognizing that policymaking in a complex society must account for uncertainty, however, does not imply that it is sufficient for an agency to merely recite the terms "substantial uncertainty" as a justification for its actions. The agency must explain the evidence which is available, and must offer a "rational connection between the facts found and the choice made." Generally, one aspect of that explanation would be a justification for rescinding the regulation before engaging in a search for further evidence.

In this case, the agency's explanation for rescission of the passive restraint requirement is *not* sufficient to enable us to conclude that the rescission was the product of reasoned decisionmaking. To reach this conclusion, we do not upset the agency's view of the facts, but we do appreciate the limitations of this record in supporting the agency's decision. We start with the accepted ground that if used, seatbelts unquestionably would save many thousands of lives and would prevent tens of thousands of crippling injuries. Unlike recent regulatory decisions we have reviewed, *Industrial Union Department v. American*

Petroleum Institute, 448 U.S. 607, the safety benefits of wearing seatbelts are not in doubt and it is not challenged that were those benefits to accrue, the monetary costs of implementing the standard would be easily justified. We move next to the fact that there is no direct evidence in support of the agency's finding that detachable automatic belts cannot be predicted to yield a substantial increase in usage. The empirical evidence on the record, consisting of surveys of drivers of automobiles equipped with passive belts, reveals more than a doubling of the usage rate experienced with manual belts. Much of the agency's rulemaking statement—and much of the controversy in this case—centers on the conclusions that should be drawn from these studies. The agency maintained that the doubling of seatbelt usage in these studies could not be extrapolated to an across-the-board mandatory standard because the passive seatbelts were guarded by ignition interlocks and purchasers of the tested cars are somewhat atypical. Respondents insist these studies demonstrate that Modified Standard 208 will substantially increase seatbelt usage. We believe that it is within the agency's discretion to pass upon the generalizability of these field studies. This is precisely the type of issue which rests within the expertise of NHTSA, and upon which a reviewing court must be most hesitant to intrude.

But accepting the agency's view of the field tests on passive restraints indicates only that there is no reliable real-world experience that usage rates will substantially increase. To be sure, NHTSA opines that "it cannot reliably predict even a 5 percentage point increase as the minimum level of increased usage." But this and other statements that passive belts will not yield substantial increases in seatbelt usage apparently take no account of the critical difference between detachable automatic belts and current manual belts. A detached passive belt does require an affirmative act to reconnect it, but—unlike a manual seat belt—the passive belt, once reattached, will continue to function automatically unless again disconnected. Thus, inertia—a factor which the agency's own studies have found significant in explaining the current low usage rates for seatbelts—works in *favor* of, not *against,* use of the protective device. Since 20 to 50% of motorists currently wear seatbelts on some occasions, there would seem to be grounds to believe that seatbelt use by occasional users will be substantially increased by the detachable passive belts. Whether this is in fact the case is a matter for the agency to decide, but it must bring its expertise to bear on the question.

The agency is correct to look at the costs as well as the benefits of Standard 208. The agency's conclusion that the incremental costs of the requirements were no longer reasonable was predicated on its prediction that the safety benefits of the regulation might be minimal. Specifically, the agency's fears that the public may resent paying more for the automatic belt systems is expressly dependent on the assumption that detachable automatic belts will not produce more than "negligible safety benefits." When the agency reexamines its findings as to the likely increase in seatbelt usage, it must also reconsider its judgment of the reasonableness of the monetary and other costs associated with the Standard. In reaching its judgment, NHTSA should bear in mind that Congress intended safety to be the preeminent factor under the Motor Vehicle Safety Act. . . .

The agency also failed to articulate a basis for not requiring nondetachable belts under Standard 208. It is argued that the concern of the agency with the easy detachability of the currently favored design would be readily solved by a continuous passive belt, which allows the occupant to "spool out" the belt and create the necessary slack for easy extrication from the vehicle. The agency did not separately consider the continuous belt option, but treated it together with the ignition interlock device in a category it titled "option of use-compelling features." The agency was concerned that use-compelling devices would "complicate extrication of [a]n occupant from his or her car." . . . In addition, based on the experience with the ignition interlock, the agency feared that use-compelling features might trigger adverse public reaction.

By failing to analyze the continuous seatbelts in its own right, the agency has failed to offer the rational connection between facts and judgment required to pass muster under the arbitrary and capricious standard. We agree with the Court of Appeals that NHTSA did not suggest that the emergency release mechanisms used in nondetachable belts are any less effective for emergency egress than the buckle release system used in detachable belts. . . . While the agency is entitled to change its view on the acceptability of continuous passive belts, it is obligated to explain its reasons for doing so.

The agency also failed to offer any explanation why a continuous passive belt would engender the same adverse public reaction as the ignition interlock, and, as the Court of Appeals concluded, "every indication in the record points the other way." We see no basis for equating the two devices: the continuous belt, unlike the ignition interlock, does not interfere with the operation of the vehicle. More importantly, it is the agency's responsibility, not this Court's, to explain its decision.

VI

"An agency's view of what is in the public interest may change, either with or without a change in circumstances. But an agency changing its course must supply a reasoned analysis. . . ." *Greater Boston Television Corp. v. FCC,* 444 F.2d 841, 852 (CADC). . . . [W]e do conclude that the agency has failed to supply the requisite "reasoned analysis" in this case. Accordingly, we vacate the judgment of the Court of Appeals and remand the case to that court with directions to remand the matter to the NHTSA for further consideration consistent with this opinion.

[Rehnquist, J., joined by Burger, C.J. and Powell and O'Connor, JJ., concurred in part and dissented in part. They argued that NHTSA had adequately explained its decision to reject the automatic seatbelt alternative. It was reasonable for NHTSA to accept studies indicating that such belts would not save enough lives to be worth the cost.]

The agency's changed view of the standard seems to be related to the election of a new President of a different political party. It is readily apparent that the responsible members of one administration may consider public resistance and uncertainties to be more important than do their counterparts in a previous administration. A change in administration brought about by the people casting their votes is a perfectly reasonable basis for an executive agency's reappraisal of the costs and benefits of its programs and regulations. As long as the agency remains within the bounds established by Congress, it is entitled to assess administrative records and evaluate priorities in light of the philosophy of the administration.

BORDEN, INC. v. COMMISSIONER OF PUBLIC HEALTH

448 N.E.2d 367 (Mass.1983), *appeal dism'd*, 464 U.S. 936 (1983).

[General Laws c. 94B provides that the Commissioner of Public Health can ban any hazardous substance if public health cannot be protected through adequate labelling. After notice and comment procedure, the Commissioner banned urea-formaldehyde foamed-in-place insulation (UFFI), finding that it emitted gasses hazardous to particularly sensitive people (such as asthmatics). Manufacturers of UFFI challenged the regulation in the trial court, which held an evidentiary hearing at which both sides presented evidence about the toxicity of formaldehyde insulation. The trial court invalidated the regulation.]

NOLAN, J.:

. . . We take this opportunity to set forth, once again, the guiding principles for judicial review of agency regulations. We begin by noting that an agency's power to make regulations is delegated by the Legislature. Acting upon this delegation, an agency may, unless specifically prohibited, properly base its regulatory decisions on the same kinds of "legislative facts" on which the Legislature could rely in its enactment of a statute. A regulation is essentially an expression of public policy. The issue on review is not whether the regulation was supported by substantial evidence in the record before the agency. Indeed, "[f]acts represented in material submitted to an agency, unless stipulated as admitted, may not be relied on in a judicial challenge to an administrative regulation." Rather, the person challenging the regulation must prove in the judicial proceeding that the regulation is illegal, arbitrary, or capricious.[8] Because the agency proceeding is not

8. The plaintiffs contend that the court's function is "to determine whether there is any rational basis upon which the regulation can be sustained." We agree. However, we do not agree with the plaintiffs' contentions that in making this deter-

an adjudicatory one, a plaintiff may not meet its burden "by arguing that the record does not affirmatively show facts which support the regulation." "If the question is fairly debatable, courts cannot substitute their judgment for that of the Legislature."

A plaintiff must prove "the absence of any conceivable ground upon which [the rule] may be upheld."[9] This is so because a properly promulgated regulation has the force of law and must be accorded all the deference due to a statute. "Thus, [a court] must apply all rational presumptions in favor of the validity of the administrative action and not declare it void unless its provisions cannot by any reasonable construction be interpreted in harmony with the legislative mandate." This deference is necessary to maintain the separation between the powers of the Legislature and administrative agencies and the powers of the judiciary. "A court may not substitute its judgment for that of the Legislature if the regulation comports with the power delegated." This deference also precludes the possibility that a plaintiff may frustrate administrative policy merely by amassing facts, statistics, and testimony before a judge, all of which may have little or nothing to do with the legislative facts which the administrative agency relied upon in making its regulation. "[R]espect for the legislative process means that it is not the province of the court to sit and weigh conflicting evidence supporting or opposing a legislative enactment." . . . There are no requirements in G.L. c. 94B that the commissioner conduct any specific tests or determine that any specific number of people are or will be affected by a particular substance in making his finding concerning [whether it is a "hazardous substance."]. Nor is there any indication that the commissioner must hold an adjudicatory hearing before making his finding. The commissioner may act only with respect to those substances concerning which he makes certain findings, but his power to make those findings is limited only in that he must not exercise it illegally, arbitrarily, or capriciously.

The judge found that "[f]ormaldehyde, . . . at some level of concentration, becomes an irritant. . . . [F]urther . . . as this abrasive level of exposure is increased, the exposure level becomes toxic." We accept this finding. Since formaldehyde meets the definition of hazardous substance, we conclude that formaldehyde is properly regulated under G.L. c. 94B. The crux of the issue before us, then, is—

mination the court must view the regulations in light of the factors and standards required or deemed relevant under the Federal Administrative Procedure Act. While some of these factors are helpful, others are neither necessary nor appropriate under this State's Administrative Procedure Act. Cf. *Grocery Mfrs. of America, Inc. v. Department of Pub. Health,* 393 N.E.2d 881 (1979) (State agency need not make findings of legislative facts in the record of regulatory proceeding although Federal agency would be so required). The

United States Supreme Court itself did not rely on these factors when it recently upheld the validity of State legislation banning the use of plastic, nonrefillable milk containers. *Minnesota v. Clover Leaf Creamery Co.,* 449 U.S. 456 (1981). . . .

9. This is consistent with the fact that an agency is not, barring a specific statutory mandate, obliged to provide a statement of the reasons which support its adoption of a regulation.

as it was before the judge—whether the presence of formaldehyde in UFFI justifies the ban of the latter product. The ban would be justified if the commissioner could rationally find that UFFI could not "be labeled adequately to protect the public health and safety, or [that UFFI] present[ed] an imminent danger to the public health and safety."

We have in the past sustained regulations on the ground that there was a conceivable basis for the agency decision. . . . In this case, we need not go so far.[13] We have examined relevant portions of the trial transcript, and we conclude that there was evidence presented there which warranted the commissioner's action.

We briefly summarize portions of that evidence. At trial, Dr. Richard Gammage, a chemist, testified that tests conducted at the Oak Ridge National Laboratory on panels of wood foamed internally with UFFI and maintained under conditions which would approximate those of a corner room in a normal house indicated that UFFI emitted formaldehyde into the "room" in levels of concentration which ranged from .03 to about .25 or .3 parts per million. There was also testimony from Dr. George Allen, a professor of fiber and polymer science at the University of Washington, called by the plaintiffs, that a greater amount of formaldehyde is released from UFFI with increases in heat and humidity. The judge found that improper mixing or installation of UFFI could increase the rate of formaldehyde emission. Dr. Murray Cohn, a biochemist at the Consumer Product Safety Commission (CPSC), testified that he conducted statistical tests to compare the average level of formaldehyde in houses that were insulated with UFFI with the average level found in houses not insulated with UFFI. His results indicated that the average level in houses insulated with UFFI was .12 parts per million whereas the average level in noninsulated houses was .03 parts per million. . . . Dr. Andrew Ulsamer, Director of the Division of Health Effects at the CPSC, testified that his opinion, based on his review of the National Academy of Sciences report, was that "there are health effects of formaldehyde at relatively low levels, and if one considers the various sensitive populations that may be involved, that there may indeed not be a population threshold at any measurable level of formaldehyde within the general population." He further testified that persons who suffer from asthma, chronic obstructive pulmonary diseases such as emphysema or chronic bronchitis, and persons who are allergic to formaldehyde, would suffer health effects at exposure to levels less than .1 parts per million. He estimated these groups to compose about ten per cent of the population. . . . Thus, there was evidence before the judge indicating that UFFI would potentially in some conditions emit formaldehyde into houses at levels above which at least a significant portion of the population would experience adverse health effects. In light of this evidence, we cannot say that the

13. "We note that we are, of course, free to consider the evidence before the Commissioner, as well as any other relevant information, including that provided in the briefs in determining whether there was a rational basis for the Commissioner's regulations."

commissioner acted arbitrarily or capriciously in banning UFFI. That the commissioner was unable to determine the amount of formaldehyde that UFFI contributed to the indoor environment, that he did not know how many people in the Commonwealth had been affected by UFFI, that he had not compared the levels of formaldehyde in UFFI and non-UFFI houses, that he had not caused epidemiological studies to be made to determine the incidence of symptoms allegedly caused by UFFI, that experts called by the plaintiff at trial offered evidence contrary to the commissioner's, and that the commissioner's experts significantly qualified their testimony on cross-examination [20] does not obviate the fact that he had a rational and certainly conceivable basis for his decision. . . .

Conclusion. We conclude that the judge erred in holding that the commissioner's regulations were illegal, arbitrary, and capricious. Accordingly, we reverse the judgments of the Superior Court and remand the case with directions to grant declaratory relief consistent with this decision.

Notes and Questions

1. *Overton Park.* Before *State Farm*, the leading federal case on review of discretion was *Citizens to Preserve Overton Park v. Volpe,* 401 U.S. 402 (1971). *Overton Park* involved review of a decision by the Secretary of Transportation to grant funds to build an interstate highway through a park. A statute prohibited the use of parks for highways unless "there is no feasible and prudent alternative." The Secretary did not explain why there were no feasible and prudent alternatives.

The Court construed the word "feasible" to mean that an alternative route must be infeasible from an engineering point of view. It defined "prudent" to mean that any alternative route would present "unique problems." The scope of review was provided by § 706(2)(A) of the APA: "arbitrary, capricious, an abuse of discretion. . . ."

The "substantial evidence" standard was not applicable since it applies only to formal rulemaking or formal adjudication and the decision here was neither. Although a hearing was required, it was merely a public hearing for the purpose of informing the community about the project and eliciting its views. Such a hearing "is not designed to produce a record that is to be the basis of agency action—the basic requirement for substantial-evidence review."

Under the arbitrary and capricious test

. . . [T]he reviewing court [must] engage in a substantial inquiry. Certainly, the Secretary's decision is entitled to a presumption of regularity. But that presumption is not to shield his action from a thorough, probing, in-depth review.

---

20. We can conceive of circumstances where scientific evidence could be so severely impeached as to render any reliance upon it unreasonable. This is not the case here, especially given the inherently tentative nature of most scientific inquiry.

The court is first required to decide whether the Secretary acted within the scope of his authority. This determination naturally begins with a delineation of the scope of the Secretary's authority and discretion. As has been shown, Congress has specified only a small range of choices that the Secretary can make. Also involved in this initial inquiry is a determination of whether on the facts the Secretary's decision can reasonably be said to be within that range . . . [i.e. that he] could have reasonably believed that in this case there are no feasible alternatives or that alternatives do involve unique problems.

Scrutiny of the facts does not end, however, with the determination that the Secretary has acted within the scope of his statutory authority. Section 706(2)(A) requires a finding that the actual choice made was not "arbitrary, capricious, an abuse of discretion. . . ." To make this finding the court must consider whether the decision was based on a consideration of the relevant factors and whether there has been a clear error of judgment. Although this inquiry into the facts is to be searching and careful, the ultimate standard of review is a narrow one. The court is not empowered to substitute its judgment for that of the agency.

Id. at 415–16.

2. *The record for judicial review of rules.* In the *State Farm* case, the record considered by the courts consisted of the published documents (notice of proposed rulemaking, final rule, statement of basis and purpose), public comments, and various studies and other materials considered by NHTSA. This is the customary record for pre-enforcement review of legislative rules. (*See* further discussion in § 6.8, *supra*).

Such records can be massive and disorganized and evaluating them can impose enormous burdens. At the end of a 120 page opinion (with numerous charts and 540 footnotes) which reviewed air pollution standards for coal-fired power plants, Judge Wald wrote:

We reach our decision after interminable record searching (and considerable soul searching). We have read the record with as hard a look as mortal judges can probably give its thousands of pages. We have adopted a simple and straight-forward standard of review, probed the agency's rationale, studied its references (and those of appellants), endeavored to understand them where they were intelligible (parts were simply impenetrable), and on close questions given the agency the benefit of the doubt out of deference for the terrible complexity of its job. We are not engineers, computer modelers, economists or statisticians, although many of the documents in this record require such expertise—and more.

Cases like this highlight the critical responsibilities Congress has entrusted to the courts in proceedings of such length, complexity and disorder. Conflicting interests play fiercely for enormous stakes, advocates are prolific and agile, obfuscation runs high, common sense correspondingly low, the public interest is often obscured.

Sierra Club v. Costle, 657 F.2d 298, 410 (D.C.Cir.1981).

Is it realistic to expect judges to review such records in the way mandated by the *State Farm* case? What was the record for decision in the *Borden* case? Does the approach taken in that decision simplify the task of reviewing courts?

3. *Findings, reasons, and the record for review of informal action.* In *Overton Park,* judicial review was hampered by the lack of any findings or statement of reasons by the Secretary and also by the lack of any record containing the materials he had considered. The lack of findings and reasons was not, in itself, a reversible procedural error, since no statute required them. There were some "litigation affadavits" purporting to state the Secretary's reasons, but the Court found them unacceptable "post hoc rationalizations."

Since APA § 706 requires review to be on the "whole record," the Court faced a dilemma: how could the Secretary's conclusion that the highway was the only "feasible and prudent" alternative be reviewed without any findings or reasons and without access to materials considered by the decisionmaker?

The Court remanded to the district court for a trial on the merits, based on the full administrative record that was before the Secretary when he made the decision. In addition, if necessary, the trial court could require the officials who made the decision to give testimony explaining their action. Justices Black and Brennan dissented on this point, arguing that the case should be remanded to the Secretary, not to the trial court. Was the dissent correct on the question of remand?

In subsequent decisions, the Court has favored the route urged by the *Overton Park* dissenters—a remand to the agency for proper findings and reconsideration. *Camp v. Pitts,* 411 U.S. 138 (1973). *Camp* held that judicial review of a decision denying a license for a new bank had to be on the record considered by the agency—not a record created by a new trial. The agency had explained its reasons for denial in brief letters to the applicant. Its action must be judged on the basis of these "contemporaneous explanations." If the letters failed to explain the action sufficiently to permit effective review, the court should remand to the agency for further consideration, not hold a new trial. For further discussion, see § 3.3.1, *supra.*

There is a significant difference between an agency's failure to make findings required by law (*see* §§ 4.3 and 6.7, supra) and its failure to make findings in other situations. A failure to make findings required by law is an independent basis for judicial invalidation of the agency action in question (assuming the court finds that the error was prejudicial). In other situations, an agency's failure to make findings is not a ground for reversal of agency action but may require a remand to the agency for an explanation of its action to facilitate judicial review on the merits.

Was the Supreme Court in *Overton Park* and *Camp v. Pitts* correct in concluding that judicial review of informal adjudication must be on the basis of the record originally considered by the agency rather than on the basis of a record created at a new trial? At the time of judicial review, should an agency be permitted to supplement the materials it originally considered? May opposing parties supplement that record? In answering these questions, reconsider the discussion of the exclusivity of the record of informal rulemaking discussed in § 6.8, *supra*.

4. *Chalking in the boundary lines.* In reviewing agency action under the arbitrary and capricious standard, the inquiry begins with issues of legal *interpretation:* what are the boundaries of the agency's discretionary power? In this step, the court may use either "reasonableness" review, as in *Chevron,* or "rightness" review as in *Overton Park.* *See* 1981 MSAPA § 5–116(c)(8)(i).

In *Overton Park*, the Court independently determined the meaning of the words "feasible and prudent" in a way which left very little room for the Secretary to exercise judgment. In this phase of the inquiry, a reviewing court often determines the relevant factors which a statute requires the agency to consider or not consider. If the agency failed to consider a relevant factor, or took account of a factor it was forbidden to consider, its action should be set aside.

5. *Hard look review.* Traditionally, judicial review of regulations in federal courts under the "arbitrary, capricious" standard was extremely deferential, perhaps close to the "minimum rationality" test for the validity of *statutes* under substantive due process. "[W]here the regulation is within the scope of authority legally delegated, the presumption of the existence of facts justifying its specific exercise attaches alike to statutes, to municipal ordinances, and to orders of administrative bodies." *Pacific States Box & Basket Co. v. White,* 296 U.S. 176, 186 (1935). *Borden* is an example of a state court decision that employs minimum rationality analysis in reviewing rules. For state cases, *see generally* 2 F. Cooper, STATE ADMINISTRATIVE LAW 791–96 (1965). As note 9 of *State Farm* points out, federal courts no longer use this approach.

Today, the phrase "hard look" often is used to describe the review function, particularly in federal courts. *State Farm* is the leading but certainly not the only example. "Hard look" review is composed of two distinct elements:

First, the court insures that *the agency* has taken a "hard look" at the problem. This might be referred to as the *quasi-procedural* element. It requires the agency to furnish a sufficient explanation of its factual findings and conclusions, to establish that it has sought out the necessary information, and to show that it actually took into account the appropriate factors and seriously considered the available data and alternative solutions. Are these procedural demands consistent with *Vermont Yankee?*

Second, the court takes a "hard look" at the substance of the decision under review—familiarizing itself, if necessary, with the economic or technical material in the record. This is *quasi-substantive* review. The court's scrutiny is more exacting if it detects "danger signals" that something may be amiss: for example, if the court suspects undue bias toward a private interest, the agency has a history of ad hoc and inconsistent judgments on the question, or the agency's result departs without explanation from its long-standing precedents. *Natural Resources Defense Council v. SEC,* 606 F.2d 1031, 1049 (D.C.Cir. 1979).

The grounds for reversal under quasi-substantive review have been "restated" by the ABA Section on Administrative Law:

> i.   The action rests upon a policy judgment that is so unacceptable as to render the action arbitrary.
>
> ii.   The action rests upon reasoning that is so illogical as to render the action arbitrary.
>
> iii.   The asserted or necessary factual premises of the action do not withstand scrutiny . . .
>
> iv.   The action is, without good reason, inconsistent with prior agency policies or precedents.
>
> v.   The agency arbitrarily failed to adopt an alternative solution to the problem addressed in the action.
>
> vi.   The action fails in other respects to rest upon reasoned decisionmaking.

38 Admin.L.Rev. 235 (1986). *See* Levin, "Scope-of-Review Doctrine Restated: An Administrative Law Section Report," 38 Admin.L.Rev. 239 (1986). In the end, however, arbitrary and capricious review is for reasonableness, not rightness. As *Overton Park* put it, the "inquiry into the facts is to be searching and careful, [but] the ultimate standard of review is a narrow one. The court is not empowered to substitute its judgment for that of the agency."

Does the *State Farm* case engage in a quasi-procedural or quasi-substantive "hard look"—or both? Using the above "restatement," what was wrong with the rescission of Standard 208?

Do you think that quasi-substantive hard-look review is appropriate? Does it allow unelected and inexpert judges to substitute their own judgments and values for those of an expert agency, even though the agency was legislatively designated to make the choice? Or is it a necessary corrective to bureaucratic tendencies to build empires, be captured by the regulated industry, or act unreasonably, maliciously, politically, carelessly, or inconsistently? In short, what are the costs and benefits of hard look review? What are the costs and benefits of the minimum rationality approach taken in *Borden?* Is hard look review consistent with the "strong deference" to agency interpretations mandated by *Chevron?* *See* Breyer, "Judicial Review of Questions of Law and Policy," 38 Admin.L.Rev. 363 (1986).

6. *Hard look and predictive facts.* When it rescinded Standard 208, NHTSA concluded that seat belt usage would not increase much even if automatic seat belts were mandatory. This was a prediction— nobody could know for sure. NHTSA argued that courts must accept an agency's prediction, particularly when it relied on agency expertise. Similarly, in *Borden,* the Commissioner predicted that UFFI emissions would cause health problems for sensitive individuals.

This is an important issue in administrative law, because most health, safety, and environmental regulations rely on predictions, computer modeling, extrapolations, and other techniques by which government tries to minimize risks in the face of economic or scientific uncertainty. For example, suppose high dosage of a chemical induces cancer in rats. Can an agency conclude that much lower doses will induce cancer in some humans and thus ban or restrict exposure to the chemical?

In *Baltimore Gas & Elec. Co. v. NRDC,* 462 U.S. 87 (1983), the Supreme Court upheld a rule adopted by the Nuclear Regulatory Commission which was premised on a conclusion that permanent storage of nuclear waste would have no significant environmental impact. This was a newer version of the rule considered in the *Vermont Yankee* case. As in *Vermont Yankee,* the Court of Appeals had invalidated the rule. The Supreme Court said:

> . . . [A] reviewing court must remember that the Commission is making predictions, within its area of special expertise, at the frontiers of science. When examining this kind of scientific determination, as opposed to simple findings of fact, a reviewing court must generally be at its most deferential.

Id. at 103. How deferential is that? As deferential as *Borden?* Has the agency made a "simple finding of fact" or has it exercised discretion? How did the majority in *State Farm* respond to NHTSA's argument that the Court must defer to its predictions of seatbelt usage?

7. *The hard look and the 1981 MSAPA.* The 1961 MSAPA, § 15(g)(6), allowed a court to reverse if administrative decisions were "arbitrary or capricious or characterized by abuse of discretion or clearly unwarranted exercise of discretion." This section, especially the last clause, appeared to call for a fairly hard look. *See* Cooper, *supra* at 756, 771–72. However, it applied only to review of "contested cases"—essentially adjudication.

The 1981 MSAPA covers judicial review of all "agency action." Sec. 5–116(c) reflects serious misgivings on the part of its drafters toward hard look review of discretionary action. It provides some specific bases for judicial reversal (*see* §§ (c)(7) and (c)(8)(i), (ii), (iii)). It then *brackets* the language "otherwise unreasonable, arbitrary or capricious." The effect of bracketing the language is to offer states the option of omitting the language. The drafters explain:

> Without the bracketed language, this paragraph provides a more limited judicial role than the 1961 Model Act. The intent of this limitation is to discourage reviewing courts from substituting their judgment for that of the agency as to the wisdom or desirability of the agency action under review.

See Brodie & Linde, "State Court Review of Administrative Action: Prescribing the Scope of Review," 1977 Ariz.St.L.J. 537, 553–60 (describing omission of "accordion-like" epithets arbitrary, capricious and abuse from Florida APA). Did the drafters of 1981 MSAPA opt for the *State Farm* model, the *Borden* model, or something in between?

8. *Deregulation: the battle continues.* Both before and after the *State Farm* case, the courts have reviewed numerous rule rescissions. Not all the cases take as skeptical a view as *State Farm.* For example, *Center for Auto Safety v. Peck,* 751 F.2d 1336 (D.C.Cir.1985) upheld NHTSA's decision to require auto bumpers to withstand a 2.5 mph crash instead of 5 mph as previously required. NHTSA decided there was no acceptable evidence that the 5.0 standard significantly promoted safety (by protecting lights, etc.) and thus that the much less costly 2.5 mph standard yielded greater net benefits to consumers.

> Compare these statements in the majority and dissenting opinions:

> Majority (by Judge Scalia): The burden was on the agency . . . to justify the change from the status quo, *see State Farm.* But that justification need not consist of affirmative demonstrations that the status quo is wrong; it may also consist of demonstration, on the basis of careful study, that there is no cause to believe that the status quo is right, so that the existing rule has no rational basis to support it. . . . The position in effect espoused by the dissent— that obviously small but precisely unknowable risks of injury must be presumed to be significant once they have been treated as such by the agency—is a formula for rendering an erroneously adopted standard, *itself unsupported by any scientific analysis,* essentially irremediable.

Id. at 1349.

> Dissent (by Judge J. Skelly Wright): In my judgment, NHTSA's actions in this rulemaking were clearly arbitrary and capricious and not in accordance with its statutory mandates. NHTSA first dealt in a wholly inadequate manner with the safety concerns which prompted promulgation of the bumper standard originally. Then, having dismissed these concerns, NHTSA proceeded to perform a cost-benefit analysis that appears, given the contortions that the agency went through to reach its final conclusion, to have been solely a formalistic exercise aimed at justifying a preordained result. The majority's approval of these actions in the name of deference to agency expertise is, I believe, an unacceptable retreat

from our judicial responsibility to carefully review agency decision-making and an unsupportable condonation of agency failure to act in accordance with explicit instructions from the legislative branch.

Id. at 1371. Does it all depend on who is taking the "hard look?" Note that both *State Farm* and *Chevron* reviewed deregulatory rules adopted early in the Reagan administration. Are the two cases consistent?

9. *Substantial evidence v. arbitrary and capricious.* Recall that the legislative history of the Motor Vehicle Safety Act (construed in *State Farm*) said that the findings of the agency must be supported by "substantial evidence on the record considered as a whole." However, the statute itself called only for arbitrary and capricious review and the Court makes nothing of the difference. In a number of other statutes, Congress explicitly called for substantial evidence judicial review of legislative rules. For example, occupational safety and health standards adopted by OSHA must be supported by substantial evidence. 29 U.S.C. § 655(f). Does this make a difference in the judicial review function?

The substantial evidence test ordinarily applies to formal adjudication or rulemaking—proceedings at which evidence is taken in a trial-type setting and the decision-maker considers only material in the record. This is not true of many decisions reviewed under the arbitrary and capricious test; often there has been no hearing (formal or informal) or any opportunity to examine and rebut materials considered by the decision-maker. As explained in note 2, those materials constitute the record for purposes of judicial review.

The prevailing view is that judicial review of rules under a substantial evidence standard is no different than under an arbitrary and capricious standard. Both standards call for reasonableness review and both require that there be a sufficient factual basis in the record (however that record is assembled) for the result reached by the agency. *See Association of Data Processing Service Orgs. v. Board of Governors, Fed. Reserve Sys.,* 745 F.2d 677, 680–86 (D.C.Cir.1984); Note, "Convergence of the Substantial Evidence and Arbitrary and Capricious Standards of Review During Informal Rulemaking," 54 Geo.Wash.L.Rev. 541 (1986).

Some authority, including Supreme Court dictum, indicates that the substantial evidence test may somehow impose a *greater* burden on the reviewing court; it should take a "harder look" than it would otherwise. *American Paper Inst. v. American Elec. Power Serv. Corp.,* 461 U.S. 402, 412 n. 7 (1983); Koch, "Confining Judicial Authority over Administrative Action," 49 Mo.L.Rev. 183, 198, 231–32 (1984). It may be that when Congress deliberately uses the substantial evidence test, rather than the arbitrary-capricious test, it wants more rigorous review. *Aqua Slide 'n' Dive Corp. v. CPSC,* 569 F.2d 831 (5th Cir.1978). Still it is hard to imagine how the *State Farm* decision could have taken a "harder look" at the facts if it had been using the substantial evidence rather than the arbitrary and capricious test.

10. *Problem—Discretion in adjudication.* A local school board discharged two tenured high school teachers for misconduct. Both had taught in the district for thirty years.

At Alice's hearing, testimony by her ex-husband revealed that Alice had, over a period of years, taken home for her own use $35 of school supplies (paper, pens, tape, etc.). She admitted that it was true.

Bob was discharged for insubordination. The evidence showed that parents had complained to the principal and the school board about Bob's use of the book "Catcher in the Rye" in English class in 1984. They objected to the "explicit street language" used in the book. After a discussion with the principal, Bob agreed not to use the book again. However, in 1986, Bob assigned "Catcher in the Rye." When summoned to a conference with the principal to discuss this, Bob walked out and refused to discuss it any further.

Alice and Bob seek judicial review. They question only the Board's choice to discharge them instead of imposing some lesser sanction such as a reprimand in their file or a brief suspension. How should the court rule? *See Pell v. Board of Educ.*, 313 N.E.2d 321 (N.Y.1974); *Harris v. Mechanicville Central Sch. Dist.*, 380 N.E.2d 213 (N.Y.1978).

11. *Problem—Discretion in rulemaking.* By statute, OSHA must set reasonably necessary and feasible standards for exposure of workers to toxic chemicals at a level that assures that no employee will suffer material impairment of health. The statute also provides that OSHA standards must be sustained if supported by substantial evidence in the record considered as a whole.

Ethylene oxide (EtO) is a hazardous chemical used to sterilize hospital instruments. In 1971, OSHA adopted a standard that workers must not be exposed to more than 50 parts per million (ppm) of EtO averaged over a workday. Since 1971, there has been increasing (though inconclusive) evidence that EtO causes cancer and spontaneous abortion. Last year, after a lengthy notice and comment proceeding, OSHA found that any exposure to EtO presented a significant health risk; it set an exposure limit of 1 ppm averaged over a workday. Compliance with this standard will cost hospitals many millions of dollars over the next few years. A standard of 5 ppm would save the industry 85% of those costs.

OSHA relied on several studies in support of the standard. According to the Hogstedt study, there were 3 deaths from leukemia at a Swedish hospital out of 230 workers (all exposed to significant EtO) when only 0.2 deaths would normally be expected in a similar group. The Bushy Run study indicated that rats exposed to 100 ppm of EtO every day for a year developed various cancers; rats exposed to 60 ppm developed fewer cancers. However, the rats also developed a severe viral ailment during the study. The Hemminki study indicated that nurses exposed to EtO while pregnant reported on questionnaires that they had a higher rate of spontaneous abortion than a control group. However, the nurses studied knew the purpose of the questionnaire was to test the effects of EtO on pregnant women.

The level of 1 ppm was set by extrapolating the results of the Bushy Run study to humans by making a series of mathematical assumptions. OSHA found that there would be between 12 and 23 additional cancer deaths even at a level of 1 ppm, but it found that it was not technically or economically feasible to set a zero tolerance.

At the same time it originally proposed the 1 ppm limit for exposure to EtO averaged over a workday, OSHA also proposed a short-term exposure limit (STEL)—that no single exposure to EtO could exceed 10 ppm, no matter how brief. The Office of Management and Budget objected to the STEL (on the grounds of excessive cost and lack of benefit) and OSHA decided not to adopt any STEL. Its stated reason was that the 1 ppm limit offered sufficient protection, especially because it would induce hospitals to lower short-term exposures so as to meet the eight-hour average.

Industry groups seek review of the 1 ppm standard. Public interest groups seek review of the decision not to adopt a STEL. What should the court decide? *See Public Citizen Health Research Group v. Tyson,* 796 F.2d 1479 (D.C.Cir.1986).

Chapter 10

REMEDIES AND REVIEWABILITY OF AGENCY DECISIONS

The previous chapter made clear the indispensable role of judicial review in controlling illegal or unwarranted agency action—but it also demonstrated that limitations on the scope of review restrain courts from substituting their judgment for that of agencies.

The next group of chapters concern additional limitations on judicial review. Chapter 10 begins with a treatment of judicial procedure: jurisdiction to review agency action and the availability of and limitations on judicial remedies. It then considers two additional remedies: damage actions against an official or against an agency and recovery of attorney fees from an agency. It concludes with doctrines which make agency action unreviewable by anyone: preclusion of review and commitment to agency discretion. Chapter 11 considers problems of standing—whether a particular plaintiff can challenge agency action—and timing—is judicial review premature?

Of course, quite apart from these legalistic limits on review, judicial review may be useless for practical reasons. Judicial review means hiring lawyers and a great deal must be at stake to justify the costs of paying counsel in what may well be a losing enterprise. Moreover, obtaining judicial relief is likely to take a long time; litigants must take their turn in an ever-lengthening queue. Besides, the harm from the agency's action may already be done and it may be irremediable. Once a person is out of business or a product has been banned, it may be impossible ever to start up again, regardless of what a court might say. Even if review is successful, the remedy may be a remand to the agency which may take the same action for different reasons, thus starting the process anew. Also, quite often, it may be imprudent to antagonize an agency with which a litigant must continue to live and be regulated by. In short, it is often better to accept an unfavorable result and move on than undergo years of costly struggle and uncertainty.

As you consider judicial review from the point of view of a private client who feels wronged by agency action, the many limitations on review may seem frustratingly technical. However, there is another side to this coin, for judicial interference with agencies has significant systemic costs as well as benefits. Judicial review, particularly of complex agency action or of legislative rules, can consume enormous resources, particularly the time and energy of judges that could be used for other matters. It can greatly congest appellate dockets, thus exacerbating an already serious problem. And the public interest is not always served by the substitution of a less-informed judicial view for a better-informed agency view.

Consider also the balance of resources: we often think of an ordinary person (say a taxpayer, welfare recipient, or professional licensee) up against a huge, unfeeling bureaucracy. But sometimes the balance is quite different. The private party may be a Fortune 500 corporation with virtually unlimited resources that can be deployed to prevent or at least delay unfavorable agency action. Judicial review can be a very costly process for the agency as well as its opponent and it can take a long time; during that time, the private litigant may be able to continue polluting or selling a product which harms the public. Or, during the review process, plans to build a highway, a dam, a shopping mall or a nuclear power plant can be sidetracked indefinitely or even killed by delays and rising construction costs during the appeal period. Perhaps the projects should not be built, but the decision should not be a function of whether tenacious opponents can litigate them to death.

Indeed, an agency may be hopelessly overloaded with regulatory chores and operating under severe budget constraints which prevent it from hiring sufficient staff, or sufficiently skillful and experienced staff, to discharge its responsibilities. Thus, rather than defend a completely justified action in court, it may feel compelled to settle the case unfavorably or give up entirely. Beware of accepting claims that more judicial review is always a good thing and should be encouraged without reservation.

§ 10.1 JUDICIAL REMEDIES

In order to seek the assistance of a court in reviewing agency action, counsel must confront the basics:

(i) the chosen court must have jurisdiction to hear the case, and

(ii) plaintiff must plead a recognized cause of action and seek a recognized remedy that provides the needed relief.

We consider these hurdles in turn.

§ 10.1.1 JUDICIAL JURISDICTION

a. *Explicit statutory review procedure.* The statute that creates an agency often explicitly lays out the road to judicial review of its actions—what court has jurisdiction, who can seek review, time limits for seeking review, and so on. Ordinarily, when a statute prescribes a review procedure, that procedure is exclusive, and no other route can be pursued. Some state APAs and 1981 MSAPA § 5–101 expressly provide that the APA review procedure is exclusive.

The clear trend at the federal level is to lodge responsibility for statutory review of rules and final orders in appellate, not in trial courts. In most states, however, judicial review begins at the trial court level. *See* 1961 MSAPA § 7, 15(b). The 1981 MSAPA, § 5–104, gives states a choice in this regard—Alternative A provides for venue in a trial court while Alternative B provides for venue in an appellate court. Unfortunately, statutes are not always clear about where a particular agency action should be reviewed, and the courts have had to struggle with numerous disputes about whether an appeal was filed in the proper court. In construing ambiguous review statutes, courts often prefer appellate court, not trial court, review unless there is a need for additional evidence to be taken in which case a trial court is preferred.

There are some persuasive reasons for preferring appellate court review. Judicial review is, after all, an appellate function; appellate judges may be better at it than trial judges who are accustomed to deciding matters de novo. In general, appellate judges are likely to be more experienced and, on the whole, better qualified than trial judges, to decide issues with important public policy dimensions. The waiting line may be shorter at the appellate than at the trial court level. More important, the matter may well be appealed anyway; why not save the cost and delay of an unnecessary trial court proceeding?

On the other hand, if the class of matters produces a great many appeals, involving relatively small amounts of money and seldom raising significant legal questions, it may be better to place them in trial, rather than appellate courts. This conserves the scarce time of appellate court judges, and it may be more convenient for litigants to go to court in their home town. Thus social security disability and retirement cases are reviewed in federal district court. There are a vast number of these cases and the decision to place them in trial courts seems sensible.

If the particular review function requires a court to receive testimony, a trial court is more appropriate than an appellate court. For example, § 9.1 noted that some action is reviewed de novo; if that entails a retrial, a trial court is the best place to do it. Also, review of administrative rules or orders sometimes occurs in the context of a judicial enforcement action against a private party who has violated the rule or order; enforcement actions typically occur in a trial court.

Sometimes, in the course of reviewing a case, an appellate court finds that the record is inadequate and that additional evidence must be taken. In some circumstances, the appellate court can take the evidence itself. *See* 1981 MSAPA § 5–114(a). That provision allows an appellate court to take evidence, assisted by a referee, master or trial court judge, with respect to facts not entrusted to agency discretion (such as improper qualification, bias or motives of the decisionmakers or unlawfulness of the agency procedure or decisionmaking process) or with respect to facts that the agency was not required to determine exclusively on the basis of an agency record that was suitable for review by the courts.

More often, however, an appellate court will not receive the additional evidence itself but will remand to the agency (or in some circumstances to a trial court) to amplify the record. *See, e.g.,* 28 U.S.C. § 2347(b) and (c) (applicable to review of orders of the FCC, FMC, ICC, NRC and several other agencies); 1981 MSAPA § 5–114(b). Thus, the possibility that additional evidence might be needed does not, in itself, require that a trial court conduct judicial review.

b. *Administrative procedure statutes.* Many states have adopted statutes specifically conferring jurisdiction on particular courts to review some or all agency actions. For example, New York law (Civil Practice Law and Rules Art. 78) provides for a proceeding against a body or officer to take the place of certiorari, mandamus, and prohibition; it is commenced in a trial court and, if it entails review of formal adjudication, is transferred to an appellate court. California Code of Civ.Proc. § 1094.5, considered in § 9.1 *supra,* also lodges responsibility for review of all adjudication in trial courts.

The 1961 MSAPA provided for judicial review of "contested cases" by filing a petition in a trial court. It also provided for review of the validity or applicability of a rule by an action for declaratory judgment in a trial court. However, it provided no guidance on review of other kinds of agency action (such as informal adjudication) and it did not cover local agencies. The 1981 MSAPA is more comprehensive. It states: "This Act establishes the exclusive means of judicial review of agency action . . ." § 5–101. Review is obtained by filing a petition in the trial court. § 5–104. However, the 1981 MSAPA covers only state, not local agencies. § 1–102(1). Thus even where the 1961 or 1981 MSAPA has been adopted, counsel must still resort to other law to obtain judicial review of local action.

c. *No explicit statutory review procedure.* If there is no explicit statute concerning judicial review of particular agency action or of agency action in general, a private litigant must file a civil action against the agency or the official who invaded the person's legal rights. The ordinary rules about jurisdiction and venue are applicable to such cases.

Federal district courts have jurisdiction to conduct judicial review of agency action under:

i. 28 U.S.C. § 1331, which covers actions "arising under the Constitution, laws, or treaties of the United States." For most purposes, this section is adequate to provide for jurisdiction to review the actions of any federal agency or official in a federal district court.

    ii. 28 U.S.C. 1361, which gives district courts jurisdiction of "any action in the nature of mandamus to compel an officer or employee of the United States or any agency thereof to perform a duty owed to the plaintiff."

    iii. 28 U.S.C. § 1343(3) which provides jurisdiction to hear cases under 42 U.S.C. § 1983 and other federal civil rights statutes. Section 1983 actions provide a remedy against *state* officials who have subjected persons to deprivation of constitutional rights. We consider section 1983 actions in § 10.2.

In years past, section 1331 was unavailable unless the "amount in controversy" exceeded $10,000; sometimes it was difficult to decide whether various kinds of intangible claims met that test. The $10,000 limit was deleted in 1976 with respect to judicial review of federal agency action; it was deleted with respect to all federal question cases in 1980. Whether plaintiff should proceed under § 1361 for mandamus is a distinct question postponed to later discussion.

In prior years, the doctrine of sovereign immunity sometimes barred the courthouse door. This doctrine immunized the United States from being sued without its consent. Consequently, a litigant seeking non-statutory judicial review of agency action had to sue a federal official instead of the agency itself. Such actions were permitted only if the official acted under an unconstitutional statute or was acting outside the powers conferred by statute. *See, e.g., Larson v. Domestic & Foreign Commerce Corp.,* 337 U.S. 682 (1949).

The confusion and serious injustices resulting from the doctrine of sovereign immunity led Congress to abolish it in 1976. *See* APA §§ 702 (all material after the first sentence) and 703 (middle sentence). Note, however, that the 1976 waiver of sovereign immunity applies only to actions "seeking relief other than money damages." We consider the narrower waiver of immunity in suits for money damages in § 10.2.

In an action seeking judicial review of federal agency action under section 1331, the plaintiff may choose to sue in any judicial district where a defendant resides, or the cause of action arose, or any real property involved in the action is situated, or the plaintiff resides (if no real property is involved). 28 U.S.C. § 1391(e). The defendant is the United States, the agency by its official title, or the appropriate officer. APA § 703; Fed.R.Civ.Proc. 25(d)(2).

Once federal jurisdiction under section 1331 is established, the federal APA comes into play. Sections 701 to 706 establish the parameters for judicial review: what action is reviewable, who can seek review, when can it be sought, what are the court's powers, what is the scope of review. The APA does not itself provide for federal jurisdiction; it provides the ground rules for review once jurisdiction is otherwise established. *Califano v. Sanders,* 430 U.S. 99 (1977).

§ 10.1.2 CAUSE OF ACTION AND REMEDY

If the party seeking review proceeds under a statute specific to the agency, that statute establishes the ground rules for judicial review and may set forth some or all of the available remedies. If an administrative procedure statute is applicable, that statute too will set forth at least some of the parameters of judicial review. Generally, such statutes are vague about available remedies and they must be understood in light of existing procedural and remedial law. *See* APA § 703; 1981 MSAPA § 5–117(b).

If there is no statute specific to the agency or no applicable administrative procedure statute, a plaintiff must state a claim for relief in a trial court under other state or federal law. This subchapter is concerned largely with non-monetary relief—an order that an agency should do something, or not do something, as opposed to an order for the payment of money. The problems of seeking monetary damages are addressed in § 10.2.

As so often occurs in the law, the problem of cause of action and remedy are inextricably mixed. Therefore, it is convenient to consider substance and procedure together by examining the remedies which a plaintiff might seek in an action for judicial review.

§ 10.1.2a *Injunction and Declaratory Judgment*

Generally the most useful remedies, and those least encumbered by technicalities, are injunction and declaratory judgment. For all practical purposes, these are the same—it does not matter whether plaintiff seeks a *declaration* that agency action is illegal or an *injunction* ordering the agency to take action or refrain from taking action. One caution, however: if the plaintiff seeks a mandatory injunction (*i.e.* ordering the agency to do something as opposed to stop doing something), the court may treat the action as one for *mandamus*—which brings in its wake a series of complexities that are treated below.

Injunction as an administrative remedy has long been recognized in federal court. For example, in the famous case of *American School of Magnetic Healing v. McAnnulty,* 187 U.S. 94 (1902), the plaintiff sought relief from an order by the post office cutting off its mail because of fraud. It had previously been held that common law writs like mandamus and certiorari were not available in federal court (see below). No problem: the Supreme Court held that plaintiff could obtain an injunction requiring the post office to deliver its mail, assuming that plaintiff sufficiently established that the fraud order was erroneous.

Both injunction and declaratory judgment are equitable remedies and thus *discretionary.* If a court believes that an injunction or declaration against the government would cause harm to the public that outweighs the benefit to the plaintiff, or the remedies are for some other reason inappropriate, it can refuse to grant relief.

In many states, a plaintiff must pursue other remedies at law if they are available, such as the "extraordinary" or "prerogative" writs of mandamus, certiorari or prohibition (discussed below). In those states, injunction and declaratory judgment are unavailable whenever the prerogative writs might be used. This sometimes results in "Catch 22" situations in which cases are dismissed because litigants sought the wrong remedy. The better approach, of course, is to freely permit amendment of the pleadings so that a plaintiff is not penalized for selecting the wrong cause of action.

In federal courts, the extraordinary writs (perhaps fortunately) were generally unavailable; thus injunction and declaratory judgment became the remedies of choice, as they remain today. Thus the flexible "equity" tradition prevailed, not the typically inflexible traditions associated with prerogative writs.

§ 10.1.2b *Mandamus*

American courts inherited the prerogative writs from English jurisprudence; each writ developed separately in the English courts to enable the judges to look into and correct a peculiar injustice and each had its own peculiar limitations. The writs became generally available in the United States to review administrative action, but courts often preserved the rigid body of rules relating to each writ. Sometimes they have done so even though a statute purports to dispense with the writs in favor of a new administrative review petition.

The various rules relating to prerogative writs became the subject of extensive litigation in every state. As a result, each state has its own body of statutes and confusing case law relating to these writs; precedents from one state, or from the federal system, are largely worthless elsewhere.

The usual use of mandamus in administrative law is to compel action which an agency refuses to take—for example, to issue a license, grant a zoning variance, pay a claim, hold a hearing. However, in some states the writ is used much more broadly. In California, for instance, mandamus is used to review rules and formal adjudication as well.

In many states, a mandamus plaintiff must show that the defendant owes a "clear legal duty" to plaintiff and that the desired action is "ministerial" rather than "discretionary." The law of mandamus is haunted by the need to distinguish ministerial and discretionary acts. In addition, mandamus is available only if a plaintiff has no other adequate remedy. In some states, as in Illinois, the writ will correct abuse of discretion. Even if the other requirements are met, a court can decline to issue the writ in its discretion (if, for example, the harm to government outweighs the benefit to plaintiff).

A court which wants to dispel rather than create confusion should not jump to the conclusion that a duty is "discretionary" or that it is "unclear" and thus dismiss the case out of hand. Instead, the court should interpret the relevant law—whether it is clear or unclear—to establish the precise scope of agency discretion. *See, e.g., 13th Regional Corp. v. U.S. Dept. of Interior,* 654 F.2d 758 (D.C.Cir.1980) (construing statute to find the duty to make a study was ministerial—but denying mandamus on the equitable ground of plaintiff's laches). In § 9.4, this process was called "chalking in the boundary line" of discretion. This process may reveal that the action taken is not within the scope of delegated authority or that the agency took account of an improper factor (or failed to consider an appropriate factor). If discretionary action thus turns out to be legally improper, plaintiff should be entitled to mandamus.

After deciding that action is within the scope of discretion, the court should then ask whether there has been an abuse of discretion. In other words, it should apply the arbitrary and capricious analysis discussed in § 9.4. However, many states refuse to review for abuse of discretion in mandamus cases.

A typical mandamus case comes to court without a formal evidentiary record. The court has discretion to receive additional evidence from either side in order to assemble an adequate record for its decision (or, in many states, a jury's decision). Often, the court must reconsider agency findings of fact (as well as conclusions of law or discretion). State law varies as to whether the courts simply accept agency factual conclusions, apply the substantial evidence test, or retry the facts for themselves.

Mandamus in the federal courts began auspiciously with *Marbury v. Madison,* 5 U.S. (1 Cranch) 137 (1803). In *Marbury,* the Supreme Court held that mandamus would lie to require Madison to issue Marbury his judicial commission (but only in an inferior court—not by an original action in the Supreme Court). Soon thereafter, the Court held that federal courts outside the District of Columbia could not issue mandamus. *McIntire v. Wood,* 11 U.S. (7 Cranch) 504 (1813); *Kendall v. United States ex rel. Stokes,* 37 U.S. (12 Pet.) 524 (1838).

Federal courts outside the District evaded this limitation by issuing injunctions which were prohibitory in form but mandatory in effect, as in *American School of Magnetic Healing v. McAnnulty,* discussed above (enjoining local postmaster from refusing to deliver plaintiff's mail). The equity tradition made it possible to provide flexible and adequate relief, even if it was affirmative in character. However, other courts held that the mandamus tradition prevailed even though plaintiff sought an injunction instead of mandamus.

The inability of federal courts outside the District to issue mandamus changed in 1962 with the enactment of 28 U.S.C. § 1361, which provides: "The district courts shall have original jurisdiction of any action in the nature of mandamus to compel an officer or employee of the United States or any agency thereof to perform a duty owed to the plaintiff." Thus plaintiffs often seek mandamus in federal district court. Unfortunately, many courts still feel compelled to wander into the ministerial/discretionary swamp or to search for a "clear duty". Sometimes, the federal courts in § 1361 cases have refused to decide questions of law about the scope of discretion.

So far, the Supreme Court has not had occasion to decide whether mandamus under § 1361 (or, for that matter, mandatory injunctions) are still inhibited by restrictive mandamus tradition. See, however, *American Cetacean Soc. v. Baldridge*, 768 F.2d 426, 433–34 (D.C.Cir. 1985), *rev'd on other grds*, 478 U.S. 221 (1986), treating an action for mandamus the same as one for injunction and declaratory judgment and reviewing the decision under the APA.

Generally, counsel are well advised not to sue under § 1361 but to seek an injunction and declaratory judgment under § 1331 instead. It should not matter whether the desired relief is affirmative or negative. After all, § 706(1) of the APA clearly provides that a court can "compel agency action unlawfully withheld." Under these circumstances, there seems little to be gained by suing under § 1361—and quite a bit to be lost.

§ 10.1.2c *Certiorari*

At common law, certiorari was a writ directed to an inferior tribunal (which could be a court or an administrative body) which required that the latter certify a copy of the record and convey it to the reviewing court. Review lay only for absence of jurisdiction or for an error of law that appeared on the face of the record.

Certiorari is designed to provide judicial review of action of a *judicial* character based upon a hearing on the record. Indeed certiorari was the model for judicial review of adjudication spelled out in the 1961 and 1981 MSAPA's. Despite a proliferation of state statutes providing for judicial review, certiorari remains important in many states, particularly in reviewing decisions of local agencies or school boards.

Traditionally, certiorari could be used to review only "judicial" action, meaning functions that had been historically performed by judges (or at least action taken after a trial-type hearing). It was not available to review action of a "legislative" or "administrative" nature. Needless to say, these categories are difficult to distinguish and the lawbooks contain a large body of formalistic decisions struggling with the distinction. *See* 3 K. Davis, ADMINISTRATIVE LAW TREATISE § 24.02 (1958) (the current edition of Davis' treatise does not pursue the subject); L. Jaffe, JUDICIAL CONTROL OF ADMINISTRATIVE ACTION 169–73 (1965).

The scope of review available in a certiorari action varies from state to state. Generally, the court reviews the case strictly on the record; it does not receive additional evidence. In Illinois, certiorari is indistinguishable from ordinary statutory review—courts can reverse a decision for errors of law or procedure, arbitrary and capricious action, or a lack of substantial evidence. *See Odell v. Village of Hoffman*

Estates, 443 N.E.2d 247 (Ill.App.1982) (discharge of police employee for cause). At the other extreme, some states cling to the historically narrow scope of review: lack of jurisdiction or errors of law on the face of the record and no review of factual determinations. Most states are probably in between: in addition to errors of law, a court considers whether the agency action was arbitrary and capricious or completely lacking in factual support in the record. *See Yerardi's Moody Street Restaurant v. Board of Selectmen,* 473 N.E.2d 1154 (Mass.App.1985).

In an early decision, the Supreme Court held that *federal* courts could not grant certiorari to review a fraud order by the post office. *Degge v. Hitchcock,* 229 U.S. 162 (1913). As a result, injunction and declaratory judgment emerged to fill the gap—remedies happily free of the ancient restrictions on certiorari.

§ 10.1.2d *Other Writs*

A few other common law writs have utility as forms of judicial review of administrative action. Prohibition lies to prevent an inferior judicial body (including an agency) from initiating a case because it lacks jurisdiction to proceed. Quo warranto is used to test the right to an office. Habeas corpus has been used to review orders relating to the confinement of aliens or mentally ill persons. It has also been used to review decisions which interfere with the liberty of a member of the military (such as a refusal to discharge the member).

§ 10.2 DAMAGE ACTIONS AS A FORM OF JUDICIAL REVIEW

The discussion of remedies in § 10.1 concentrated on non-monetary remedies, such as statutory forms of judicial review and non-statutory writs such as mandamus, injunction or declaratory judgment, as vehicles for judicial review of agency action. This subchapter, which considers damage actions against officials or against government as a form of relief, could be entitled "public torts."

Tort actions are an important administrative law remedy. It may be that a private individual has already been harmed by a government official; damages are the only remedy that would make any difference. In addition, there are certain kinds of illegal government action (such as negligent infliction of economic or physical harm) that are inevitable byproducts of government activity but could not be prevented by any form of prospective relief. Again, money damages are the only effective remedy. In other situations, damages are a plausible alternative to trial-type hearings required by procedural due process: perhaps it is better to pay damages to the victims of government errors than to require government always to provide hearings before it acts. Finally, the existence of a tort remedy may serve as a potent deterrent against illegal government action.

The subject of common law and constitutional torts committed by government officials has grown enormously in recent years. Complex statutes govern many aspects of the problem. Courses in torts and civil rights cover much of the ground. Therefore, this chapter is intended largely as a survey which will omit many important details. It will, however, highlight some particularly contentious issues, focussing on damage remedies as a form of review of agency action.

§ 10.2.1 TORT LIABILITY OF GOVERNMENT

To what extent is government itself liable for actions committed by its agents? Recall the doctrine of sovereign immunity (discussed in § 10.1, *supra*): government is immune from suit unless it consents to be sued. Absent a statute or a change in the common law, it is not vicariously liable in tort, at least for peculiarly governmental activity. We are concerned here with the terms on which government has given its consent.

§ 10.2.1a *The Federal Tort Claims Act*

In 1946 Congress abolished the federal government's traditional immunity from suit for torts committed by its agents. Under the Federal Tort Claims Act, 28 U.S.C. §§ 1346(b) and 2671–80 (FTCA), the government is liable for the wrongful acts of its employees committed within the scope of their employment. Broadly speaking, the federal government is vicariously liable in tort if a private employer would be liable under state law.

However, some special rules distinguish the government from other employers.

i. *Strict liability torts.* The United States is not strictly liable where plaintiff claims injury from extra-hazardous activity carried on by government employees, unless negligence can be shown. *Laird v. Nelms*, 406 U.S. 797 (1972) (damage from sonic boom).

ii. *Intentional torts.* Under a 1974 amendment to the FTCA, the government is liable for injuries arising out of assault, battery, false imprisonment, false arrest, abuse of process, or malicious prosecution committed by federal investigative or law enforcement officers. 28 USC § 2680(h). But the government is not liable for these intentional torts when committed by persons other than investigative or law enforcement officers and never liable for torts such as defamation, misrepresentation, or interference with contract rights. It is liable for other intentional torts such as trespass or conversion.

iii. *Execution of statute or regulation.* The government is not liable for a claim based on an act or omission of a government employee, exercising due care, in the execution of a statute or regulation, whether or not such statute or regulation be valid. § 2680(a).

iv. *Discretionary functions.* The most important FTCA exemption immunizes the government from damages for any claim "based upon the exercise or performance or the failure to exercise or perform a discretionary function or duty on the part of a federal agency or an employee of the Government, whether or not the discretion involved be abused." Id. Although the Supreme Court has addressed the discretionary function exception on several occasions, it remains difficult to apply to concrete situations.

Clearly, high-level policy judgments about how to implement a regulatory program are within the discretionary function exception. In *United States v. Varig Airlines,* 467 U.S. 797 (1984), the victims of an air crash sued the government on the theory that the FAA had negligently approved the design of the towel disposal container in Boeing 707 aircraft. The container did not meet FAA's fire protection standards, but the design defect had been overlooked in FAA's inspection process. That process consisted of spot-checking the design of new aircraft. The high-level decision to spot-check designs of new aircraft, rather than to approve every detail of the design, was a policy judgment that was covered by the discretionary function exception.

The more difficult problem is whether actions taken in carrying out regulatory programs are discretionary functions. The key issue is whether the action in question involves the "permissible exercise of policy judgment." *Berkovitz v. United States,* 108 S.Ct. 1954, 1960 (1988). If the action in question is not permissible under a statute or regulation, obviously it involved no choice and could not be a discretionary function. Even if the action did involve some judgment, it would not be a discretionary function unless the judgment involved the application of policy. The *Berkovitz* case makes clear that government can be liable even though the action in question arises out of a regulatory program (in that case, the licensing of polio vaccines).

In *Berkovitz,* plaintiff was injured by faulty vaccine. He first alleged that the FDA should not have licensed the vaccine in the first place. Thus, he claimed that FDA had approved it without requiring submission of test data required by law. Since this action violated the regulations, it could not be a discretionary function. Plaintiff also claimed that FDA had incorrectly determined that the vaccine met regulatory standards. The Court remanded for further consideration of this claim. If the determination in question was based on objective scientific standards, it would not be protected by the discretionary function exception, but if the determination involved policy judgment, it would fall within the exception.

Secondly plaintiff alleged that FDA negligently approved for use the particular batch of vaccine that injured him. Again, this claim was remanded for further consideration. If FDA policy allowed no room for policy judgment by its inspectors, its approval would not be a discretionary function. However, if FDA policy did allow inspectors to make independent policy judgments, the approval would be a discretionary function. On the latter point, *see also Varig Airlines, supra,* which held that the actual process of spot-checking the design of a new aircraft involved independent policy judgment by the inspectors and was thus a discretionary function.

§ 10.2.1b *State and Local Government Liability*

In considering the liability of state and local government for damages, it is necessary to separate the question of liability in state court from the question of liability in federal court.

Looking first to state courts: Traditionally, state government was completely immune from tort liability. Local government was immune from actions for damages arising out of "governmental" functions but liable for claims arising out of "proprietary" functions. Sometimes the governmental/proprietary distinction was changed into a discretionary/ministerial distinction (similar to that in the FTCA, *supra*). Although it is easy to classify many functions as either "governmental" or "proprietary" (it is "governmental" to fight fires, "proprietary" to operate a bus company), the distinction gave rise to a vast and confusing body of case law. The governmental/proprietary distinction was rejected by the United States Supreme Court in construing the discretionary function exception of the FTCA. *Indian Towing Co. v. United States,* 350 U.S. 61 (1955).

For the most part, state legislatures refused to consent to suit, despite the enormous injustice caused by governmental tort immunity. Finally, as a result of judicial reconsideration of immunity doctrine, the logjam began to break up. Pioneering state supreme court decisions abolished governmental immunity in many states. *See Muskopf v. Corning Hospital Dist.,* 359 P.2d 457 (Cal.1961). This forced legislatures to act. In the great majority of states (around 40), state and local government is now vicariously liable for most torts committed by government employees. In some states, there is a cap on liability (apparently to limit exposure of the state to judgments in excess of insurance policies) and there may be exemptions (such as one for discretionary functions) comparable to those in FTCA. As under the FTCA, courts and legislatures struggle to define the circumstances in which government is different from the private sector and thus to carve out some remaining sphere of immunity.

COMMONWEALTH OF KENTUCKY, DEPARTMENT OF BANKING AND SECURITIES v. BROWN
605 S.W.2d 497 (Ky.1980).

This action arose in the Board of Claims pursuant to KRS 44.070. It is bottomed upon the alleged malfeasance of the Commonwealth, acting through its Department of Banking and Securities in the regulation of the American Building and Loan Association and Prudential Building and Loan Association under the provisions of KRS 289.710. The Board of Claims found the examiners . . . were derelict in not ascertaining and not reporting the true condition of the records of the Associations. We agree.

Both lower courts held . . . that in Kentucky when the state government takes upon itself a regulatory function and negligently performs that function the Board of Claims Act waives both constitutional and common law immunity; and, as a result the state is liable as any other individual or corporation. . . . It is now incumbent upon us to define the duty and liability of state government to those persons injured by such performance.

Section 231 of the Constitution of Kentucky accords the Commonwealth absolute immunity from suit until such time as the General Assembly elects to subject the Commonwealth to claims against it. In 1946, the General Assembly enacted the first Board of Claims Act, limiting its application to personal injury or property damage due to negligence in the construction, reconstruction, maintenance and policing of highways by the Department of Highways. In 1950, the General Assembly extended the jurisdiction of the Board of Claims to negligence on the part of the Commonwealth, any of its departments or agencies, or any of its agents or employees while acting within the scope of their employment.

Prior to 1946, there was no body of law defining the obligation or duty of the Commonwealth in situations such as the matter at bar. There was, however, a body of law which established the parameters of the application of tort liability to municipalities. This body of law was predicated upon the fact that municipalities are governmental bodies which have never been protected by constitutional immunity under Section 231 of the Constitution. Hence, the liability vis-a-vis non-liability of municipalities for injuries resulting from malfeasance in the execution of certain of their functions, was based upon the public policy of this Commonwealth as developed by the courts.

This was the state of the law at the time of the enactment of the Board of Claims Act by the General Assembly. By such act, the General Assembly concluded to waive—at least in part—the constitutional immunity which had theretofore been enjoyed by the Commonwealth and to allow it to be answerable before the Board of Claims for the negligence of its officers and agents. However, we perceive that the extent of the waiver of such constitutional immunity was limited by KRS 44.120, which provides:

> "An award shall be made only after consideration of the facts surrounding the matter in controversy, and no award shall be made unless the Board is of the opinion that the damage claimed was caused by such negligence on the part of the Commonwealth or its agents *as would entitle claimant to a judgment in an action at law if the state were amenable to such action* ". (Emphasis ours.)

The phrase: ". . . as would entitle claimant to a judgment in an action at law if the state were amenable to such action" has been relied upon by both parties to this appeal in support of diametrically opposed propositions. This forces us to interpret its impact upon the Commonwealth. . . . [B]y use of this phraseology, we perceive that the

General Assembly intended the Board of Claims Act to be a limited waiver, placing the Commonwealth in the same posture in actions under such Act as municipalities enjoy under the common law as it has been developed and applied to them in this state. The Board of Claims Act did not create new causes of action. . . . It appears that the Legislature did not intend to assess any duty or obligation upon the Commonwealth otherwise not applicable to other governmental entities under the common law. It follows that the intent of the General Assembly in the enactment of the Board of Claims Act was a waiver of the constitutional immunity of the Commonwealth to allow it to be treated in the same manner the common law treats municipalities.

The arguments and authorities advanced by Appellees that the Commonwealth was intended to be treated as an individual requires the straining of the language of KRS 44.120. The argument primarily rests upon the Federal Torts Claim Act and the Florida Torts Claim Act and is inapposite. Both of these statutes, by express terms, provide that the government is to be treated as if it were a private individual. Our statute mandates no such treatment of the Commonwealth.

Given the foregoing, we hold that the Commonwealth of Kentucky, under the Board of Claims Act, enjoys the same status as municipalities under the common law of this state. . . . [G]overnmental bodies "simply are not the same animals" as individuals and private corporations. As a result, the traditional "duty" analysis applied in actions for negligence against individuals is not appropriate in suits against governmental bodies. There is no public policy requiring government to guarantee the success of its efforts. When the governmental entity is performing a self-imposed protective function as it was in the case at hand, the individual citizen has no right to demand recourse against it though he is injured by its failure to efficiently perform such function. Any ruling to the contrary would tend to constitute the Commonwealth an insurer of the quality of services its many agents perform and serve only to stifle government's attempts to provide needed services to the public which could not otherwise be effectively supplied.

We, of course, concede that the state may act imperfectly at times; but such is the risk which this Court believes is the natural concomitant of our form of government. We perceive that the public interest is better served by a government which can aggressively seek to identify and meet the current needs of the citizenry, uninhibited by the threat of financial loss should its good faith efforts provide less than optimal— or even desirable—results. Thus, we here accord the Commonwealth that unique consideration which it deserves when it acts in a capacity which has no comparable counterpart in the private sector. "[A] city's relationship to individuals and to the public is not the same as if the city itself were a private individual or corporation and its duties are not the same". We hold that the rule is the same as to the Commonwealth. We will not here indulge in the niceties of academic analysis to define whether there is a duty upon the Commonwealth, the liability for which is shielded by common law immunity, or whether no duty exists for actions by the Commonwealth in its unique role. We leave such niceties to the academicians. The pragmatic effect of our holding is that under the Board of Claims Act, the Commonwealth has no common law liability for the malfeasance of its agents in the performance of obligations running to the public as a whole. It follows that in the matter at bar, the Commonwealth is not liable for the derelictions of its bank examiners in the performance of their regulatory function.

We, of course, recognize that Section 231 of the Constitution of this Commonwealth grants the General Assembly the exclusive authority to decide when and under what conditions the Commonwealth will allow itself to be subjected to suit. If we have here misinterpreted its intent we are sure that it will clarify its position in future legislation.

The judgment is reversed.

Notes and Questions

1. *Board of claims.* Instead of leaving tort claims against the state to the courts, Kentucky, like a number of other states, established an administrative agency to resolve the claims. The Kentucky board's decisions are judicially reviewable. The state is not liable for more than $50,000 for any single claim.

2. *State immunity for governmental functions.* The Kentucky statute appeared to make the state vicariously liable for its agents' torts to the same extent as a private employer. It contained no exception for discretionary or governmental functions. Thus in *Brown* the question might simply have been whether an accounting firm is liable to persons who relied on negligently prepared financial statements. If so, the state would also be liable. Should the state be liable to depositors of a bank who are injured because state bank inspectors negligently fail to discover that a bank is failing?

However, the court shied away from a pure vicarious liability approach. There must be some sphere of immunity for uniquely governmental functions, for it should not be a tort for government to govern (by planning, adopting laws and regulations, adjudicating, etc.), even if it does so negligently. How did the Kentucky court define the area of immunity? How else could the problem have been resolved?

3. *The eleventh amendment.* There is another important dimension to the issue of tort liability of state and local government. Suppose a government entity is sued *in federal court* for damages arising out of a constitutional violation. Can the entity claim sovereign immunity? In one respect, state sovereign immunity has a constitutional root. The eleventh amendment deprives *federal courts* of jurisdiction over suits against a state by citizens of a different state. By judicial interpretation, the eleventh amendment also prohibits suits in federal court against a state by citizens of that state. The eleventh amendment was enacted after the Supreme Court held that a state could be sued for its debts in federal court. *Chisholm v. Georgia,* 2 U.S. (Dall.) 419 (1793).

However, it does not apply to actions against local government—only against states. *Mt. Healthy City School Dist. v. Doyle,* 429 U.S. 274 (1977).

While the eleventh amendment prohibits federal court actions directly against states, it primarily applies to *damage* actions. Thus it does not preclude *injunctive* relief against a state official whose authority is based upon an unconstitutional statute (or whose action is otherwise contrary to federal law), even though the effect is to prevent the official from carrying out state law. *Ex parte Young,* 209 U.S. 123 (1908). While the eleventh amendment does not bar damage actions against officials in their *individual* capacity (discussed below), it does preclude actions against individuals for past violations of law if, as a practical matter, the state would have to pay. *See Edelman v. Jordan,* 415 U.S. 651 (1974). *Edelman* was an action against a state officer for retroactive welfare benefits denied by the state under an unlawful regulation. Since liability ultimately would fall on the state treasury, the action was barred by the eleventh amendment.

The eleventh amendment can be overridden by later constitutional amendments. Thus, a statute passed under the authority of the fourteenth amendment can impose damage liability on states if Congress explicitly makes states liable. *Atascadero State Hospital v. Scanlon,* 473 U.S. 234 (1985) (state not liable for damages under Rehabilitation Act of 1973, authorizing suits by handicapped victims of discrimination, because Congress did not explicitly authorize actions against states). The *Atascadero* case also held that a state does not waive the protection of the eleventh amendment by consenting to actions against itself in state court or by accepting funds under a federal statute that imposes obligations on states.

The eleventh amendment does not bar *prospective* relief against a state because of a violation of the Constitution or federal law by means of an injunction against a state official—even if compliance will be expensive. See, e.g., *Edelman v. Jordan, supra* (approving order that increased future welfare payments). Nor does it preclude an award of attorneys' fees against a state, provided that the state is otherwise liable for damages or other relief. *Kentucky v. Graham,* 473 U.S. 159 (1985).

§ 10.2.2 TORT LIABILITY OF OFFICIALS

Officials may be liable either for common law torts or for violation of constitutional rights. However, in either case, they may be able to claim immunity from liability, but the scope of immunity is not necessarily the same in an action for common law tort as in an action for constitutional tort.

§ 10.2.2a *Bases of Liability*

Before considering the question of immunities, it is necessary to consider the bases on which officers can become liable for constitutional torts in federal court. 42 U.S.C. § 1983 (which was part of the Civil Rights Act of 1871) provides:

> Every person who, under color of any statute, ordinance, regulation, custom, or usage, of any State or Territory, subjects, or causes to be subjected, any citizen of the United States or other person within the jurisdiction thereof to the deprivation of any rights, privileges, or immunities secured by the Constitution and laws, shall be liable to the party injured in an action at law, suit in equity, or other proper proceeding for redress.

In recent years, an enormous number of § 1983 actions have been brought in federal court against persons operating under color of state law and against local governments. A great deal of the Court's procedural due process jurisprudence has arisen from this source. Although precise figures on § 1983 are unavailable, civil rights cases (not counting prisoner petitions or cases brought under anti-discrimination laws) filed in federal district court increased from 280 in 1960 to over 10,000 in 1984. *See* Eisenberg & Schwab, "The Reality of Constitutional Tort Litigation," 72 Cornell L.Rev. 641, 666 (1987).

Section 1983 liability runs against individuals operating under color of state law and local government (if it is the moving force behind a deprivation of civil rights), but not against state government. *See City of St. Louis v. Praprotnik*, 108 S.Ct. 915 (1988) (city not liable unless individual who ordered illegal action had final decisionmaking authority under local law). A prevailing party under § 1983 is entitled in an appropriate case to compensatory damages, to injunctive relief, to punitive damages from individual (but not governmental) defendants, and to reasonable attorneys fees. 42 U.S.C. § 1988.

The relationship between § 1983 and state tort law is unclear. In an increasing number of cases, the Court has held that § 1983 does not apply to actions for which there is an adequate state tort remedy. *See Hudson v. Palmer*, 468 U.S. 517 (1984) (no § 1983 action for intentional misconduct by prison guard where adequate state remedy exists). Section 1983 covers *intentional* and probably reckless actions by officials but not cover *negligent* actions regardless of whether state tort law provides an adequate remedy. *Daniels v. Williams*, 474 U.S. 327 (1986) (prison guard negligently caused prisoner to slip and fall—prisoner may have action against guard or the state under state law but no § 1983 action).

Congress has never enacted a statute like § 1983 which makes *federal officials* personally liable for constitutional or statutory violations, but the Supreme Court has filled the gap. In *Bivens v. Six Unknown Agents of the Federal Bureau of Narcotics*, 403 U.S. 388 (1971), the Court held that a right of action for damages from an unlawful search and seizure arises from the fourth amendment. The process of spelling out which provisions of the Constitution give rise to implied rights of action has continued since that time. About 800 *Bivens* actions were filed in federal court in 1983.

§ 10.2.2b *Immunity From Liability*

The most difficult problems arising in damage actions against officials concern *immunity*. At common law an official carrying out a statute was subject to strict liability if he made a mistake. *Miller v. Horton,* 26 N.E. 100 (Mass.1891) (official who mistakenly destroyed a horse suspected of disease is liable in tort without regard to good faith or reasonableness). This view has long been rejected since it inhibits officials from carrying out their responsibilities, to the detriment of the public.

Until 1978, the leading federal authority on individual immunity from tort liability for government officials was *Barr v. Matteo,* 360 U.S. 564 (1959). In *Barr,* the Court considered whether the head of a federal agency was liable in tort for issuing a press release which defamed agency employees. The Court held that he was absolutely immune from liability (even if he acted "maliciously") because the issuance of press releases was within the "outer perimeter of his line of duty" and was an "appropriate exercise of the discretion which an officer of that rank must possess if the public service is to function effectively." This decision implied that if issuance of press releases had not been within the defendant's authority, his conduct would not have been privileged. However, only three justices joined Justice Harlan's plurality opinion in *Barr;* Justice Black concurred in the judgment and four justices dissented.

Barr does not apply if the conduct involved is non-discretionary. An official is not immune from liability in tort for non-discretionary actions. *See Westfall v. Erwin,* 108 S.Ct. 580 (1988) (negligently failing to warn plaintiff that he was working with dangerous chemical). Thus the same problem of distinguishing discretionary from non-discretionary action arises in cases involving individual liability as under the Federal Tort Claims Act, § 10.2.1, *supra.*

State law generally follows *Barr.* It typically immunizes government officials from liability for negligent or intentional torts in the discharge of authorized discretionary functions but leaves them liable for action clearly outside the scope of their authority (so called ultra vires action) or for tortious discharge of ministerial functions. Unlike *Barr,* some state cases withdraw immunity if the action was "malicious." *See generally Carter v. Carlson,* 447 F.2d 358, 361–62 (D.C.Cir. 1971), *rev'd on other grds.,* 409 U.S. 418 (1973); L. Jaffe, JUDICIAL CONTROL OF ADMINISTRATIVE ACTION 240–47 (1965); RESTATEMENT OF TORTS 2d § 895D (especially comments e. and f.).

Of course, the ministerial/discretionary distinction is as difficult to apply here as under the "discretionary function" exception to the FTCA, discussed *supra.* Virtually every task involves at least some ministerial elements along with some discretion (in the sense that an employee must use some judgment to do it). As a practical matter, the discretionary-ministerial test made government employees liable for negligent driving. It left police officers and possibly other "street level bureaucrats" liable for misconduct, such as arresting suspects without probable cause, even though police have great discretion in how they carry out their work. Thus the official who mistakenly destroyed the horse in *Miller v. Horton* might be liable even today, but only if plaintiff proved he acted *unreasonably* in believing the horse was diseased. However, relatively few other torts committed by officials were covered.

The following decision distinguishes (but does not overrule) *Barr* and is now the leading federal statement on immunities from constitutional torts:

BUTZ v. ECONOMOU
438 U.S. 478 (1978).

[Respondent Economou conducted a commodity futures business. He had sharply criticized the regulatory program of the Agriculture Department (USDA). USDA issued an administrative complaint against him based on a failure to maintain minimum capital. The Chief Hearing Officer sustained the complaint and the Judicial Officer (to whom the Secretary of Agriculture delegated his decisional authority) affirmed. However, the Court of Appeals reversed because USDA had failed to issue its customary warning letter before starting proceedings.

Economou had sought unsuccessfully to enjoin the complaint and agency proceedings against him and now sues for damages. The defendants are the Secretary and Assistant Secretary of Agriculture; the Judicial Officer and Chief Hearing Examiner; several officials of the Commodities Exchange Authority who made the decision to prosecute Economou; the USDA attorney who prosecuted the enforcement proceeding; and several auditors who had investigated respondent or were witnesses against him.

Economou's complaint presented causes of action arising from the Constitution: denial of due process because of failure to give proper notice before starting agency proceedings against him and deprivation of rights under the first amendment because the proceedings were in retaliation for his criticism of USDA. Relying on *Barr v. Matteo,* the district court dismissed the action because the defendants showed that their acts were within the scope of their authority and discretion. However the Court of Appeals reversed, contending that *Barr* had been undermined by later decisions giving only qualified, not absolute, immunity to state defendants in § 1983 cases.]

WHITE, J.:

. . .

Barr does not control this case. It did not address the liability of the acting director had his conduct not been within the outer limits of his duties, but from the care with which the Court inquired into the scope of his authority, it may be inferred that had the [press] release [in that case] been unauthorized, and surely if the issuance of press releases had been expressly forbidden by statute, the claim of absolute immunity would not have been upheld. . . . It is apparent also that a quite different question would have been presented had the officer ignored an express statutory or constitutional limitation on his authority. . . .

In *Scheuer v. Rhodes,* 416 U.S. 232 (1974), the issue was whether "higher officers of the executive branch" of state governments were immune from liability under § 1983 for violations of constitutionally protected rights. . . . We explained that the doctrine of official immunity from § 1983 liability, although not constitutionally grounded and essentially a matter of statutory construction, was based on two mutually dependent rationales:

> "(1) the injustice, particularly in the absence of bad faith, of subjecting to liability an officer who is required, by the legal obligations of his position, to exercise discretion; (2) the danger that the threat of such liability would deter his willingness to execute his office with the decisiveness and the judgment required by the public good."

The opinion also recognized that executive branch officers must often act swiftly and on the basis of factual information supplied by others. . . . [But] we did not believe that there was a need for absolute immunity from § 1983 liability for high-ranking state officials. Rather the considerations discussed above indicated:

> "[I]n varying scope, a qualified immunity is available to officers of the executive branch of government, the variation being dependent upon the scope of discretion and responsibilities of the office and all the circumstances as they reasonably appeared at the time of the action on which liability is sought to be based. . . .

. . . In the absence of congressional direction to the contrary, there is no basis for according to federal officials a higher degree of immunity from liability when sued for a constitutional infringement as authorized by *Bivens* than is accorded state officials when sued for the identical violation under § 1983. The constitutional injuries made actionable by § 1983 are of no greater magnitude than those for which federal officials may be responsible. The pressures and uncertainties facing decisionmakers in state government are little if at all different from those affecting federal officials. We see no sense in holding a state governor liable but immunizing the head of a federal department. . . . Surely, *federal* officials should enjoy no greater zone of protection when they violate *federal* constitutional rules than do *state* officers.

The Government argues that the cases involving state officials are distinguishable because they reflect the need to preserve the effectiveness of the right of action authorized by § 1983. But as we discuss more fully below, the cause of action recognized in *Bivens* would similarly be "drained of meaning" if federal officials were entitled to absolute immunity for their constitutional transgressions. Moreover, the Government's analysis would place undue emphasis on the congressional origins of the cause of action in determining the level of immunity. It has been observed more than once that the law of privilege as a defense to damages actions against officers of Government has "in large part been of judicial making." . . . The federal courts are equally competent to determine the appropriate level of immunity where the suit is a direct claim under the Federal Constitution against a federal officer, [as in cases brought against state officers].

Accordingly, without congressional directions to the contrary, we deem it untenable to draw a distinction for purposes of immunity law between suits brought against state officials under § 1983 and suits brought directly under the Constitution against federal officials. The § 1983 action was provided to vindicate federal constitutional rights. That Congress decided, after the passage of the Fourteenth Amendment, to enact legislation specifically requiring state officials to respond in federal court for their failures to observe the constitutional limitations on their powers is hardly a reason for excusing their federal counterparts for the identical constitutional transgressions. To create a system in which the Bill of Rights monitors more closely the conduct of state officials than it does that of federal officials is to stand the constitutional design on its head.

IV

As we have said, the decision in *Bivens* established that a citizen suffering a compensable injury to a constitutionally protected interest could invoke the general federal-question jurisdiction of the district courts to obtain an award of monetary damages against the responsible federal official. . . . [T]he action for damages recognized in *Bivens* could be a vital means of providing redress for persons whose constitutional rights have been violated. The barrier of sovereign immunity is frequently impenetrable.[31] Injunctive or declaratory relief is useless to a person who has already been injured. "For people in Bivens' shoes, it is damages or nothing."

Our opinion in *Bivens* put aside the immunity question; but we could not have contemplated that immunity would be absolute. If, as the Government argues, all officials exercising discretion were exempt from personal liability, a suit under the Constitution could provide no redress to the injured citizen, nor would it in any degree deter federal officials from committing constitutional wrongs. Moreover, no compensation would be available from the Government, for the Tort Claims

---

31. At the time of the *Bivens* decision, the Federal Tort Claims Act prohibited recovery against the Government for

"Any claim arising out of assault, battery, false imprisonment, false arrest, malicious prosecution, abuse of process, libel, slander, misrepresentation, deceit, or interference with contract rights." 28 U.S.C. § 2680(h).

The statute was subsequently amended in light of *Bivens* to lift the bar against some of these claims when arising from the act of federal law enforcement officers.

Act prohibits recovery for injuries stemming from discretionary acts, even when that discretion has been abused.

The extension of absolute immunity from damages liability to all federal executive officials would seriously erode the protection provided by basic constitutional guarantees. The broad authority possessed by these officials enables them to direct their subordinates to undertake a wide range of projects—including some which may infringe such important personal interests as liberty, property, and free speech. It makes little sense to hold that a Government agent is liable for warrantless and forcible entry into a citizen's house in pursuit of evidence, but that an official of higher rank who actually orders such a burglary is immune simply because of his greater authority. Indeed, the greater power of such officials affords a greater potential for a regime of lawless conduct. Extensive Government operations offer opportunities for unconstitutional action on a massive scale. In situations of abuse, an action for damages against the responsible official can be an important means of vindicating constitutional guarantees. . . . We therefore hold that, in a suit for damages arising from unconstitutional action, federal executive officials exercising discretion are entitled only to the qualified immunity specified in *Scheuer*, subject to those exceptional situations where it is demonstrated that absolute immunity is essential for the conduct of the public business.

The *Scheuer* principle of only qualified immunity for constitutional violations is consistent with *Barr v. Matteo*. Federal officials will not be liable for mere mistakes in judgment, whether the mistake is one of fact or one of law. But we see no substantial basis for holding, as the United States would have us do, that executive officers generally may with impunity discharge their duties in a way that is known to them to violate the United States Constitution or in a manner that they should know transgresses a clearly established constitutional rule. The principle should prove as workable in suits against federal officials as it has in the context of suits against state officials. Insubstantial lawsuits can be quickly terminated by federal courts alert to the possibilities of artful pleading. Unless the complaint states a compensable claim for relief under the Federal Constitution, it should not survive a motion to dismiss. Moreover, the Court recognized in *Scheuer* that damages suits concerning constitutional violations need not proceed to trial, but can be terminated on a properly supported motion for summary judgment based on the defense of immunity. . . .

V

Although a qualified immunity from damages liability should be the general rule for executive officials charged with constitutional violations, our decisions recognize that there are some officials whose special functions require a full exemption from liability.

In *Bradley v. Fisher*, the Court analyzed the need for absolute immunity to protect judges from lawsuits claiming that their decisions had been tainted by improper motives. . . . If a civil action could be maintained against a judge by virtue of an allegation of malice, judges would lose "that independence without which no judiciary can either be respectable or useful." Thus, judges were held to be immune from civil suit "for malice or corruption in their action whilst exercising their judicial functions within the general scope of their jurisdiction."

The principle of *Bradley* was extended to federal [and] state prosecutor[s] . . .

Despite these precedents, the Court of Appeals concluded that all of the defendants in this case—including the Chief Hearing Examiner, Judicial Officer, and prosecuting attorney—were entitled to only a qualified immunity. . . .

We think that adjudication within a federal administrative agency shares enough of the characteristics of the judicial process that those who participate in such adjudication should also be immune from suits for damages. The conflicts which federal hearing examiners seek to resolve are every bit as fractious as those which come to court. . . . Moreover, federal administrative law requires that agency adjudication contain many of the same safeguards as are available in the judicial process. The proceedings are adversary in nature. They are conducted before a trier of fact insulated from political influence. A party is entitled to present his case by oral or documentary evidence, and the transcript of testimony and exhibits together with the pleadings constitute the exclusive record for decision. The parties are entitled to know the findings and conclusions on all of the issues of fact, law, or discretion presented on the record.

There can be little doubt that the role of the modern federal hearing examiner or administrative law judge within this framework is "functionally comparable" to that of a judge. His powers are often, if not generally, comparable to those of a trial judge: He may issue subpoenas, rule on proffers of evidence, regulate the course of the hearing, and make or recommend decisions. More importantly, the process of agency adjudication is currently structured so as to assure that the hearing examiner exercises his independent judgment on the evidence before him, free from pressures by the parties or other officials within the agency. . . .

In light of these safeguards, we think that the risk of an unconstitutional act by one presiding at an agency hearing is clearly outweighed by the importance of preserving the independent judgment of these men and women. We therefore hold that persons subject to these restraints and performing adjudicatory functions within a federal agency are entitled to absolute immunity from damages liability for their judicial acts. Those who complain of error in such proceedings must seek agency or judicial review.

We also believe that agency officials performing certain functions analogous to those of a prosecutor should be able to claim absolute immunity with respect to such acts. The decision to initiate administrative proceedings against an individual or corporation is very much like the prosecutor's decision to initiate or move forward with a criminal prosecution. An agency official, like a prosecutor, may have broad discretion in deciding whether a proceeding should be brought and what sanctions should be sought. . . .

The discretion which executive officials exercise with respect to the initiation of administrative proceedings might be distorted if their immunity from damages arising from that decision was less than complete. While there is not likely to be anyone willing and legally able to seek damages from the officials if they do *not* authorize the administrative proceeding, there is a serious danger that the decision to authorize proceedings will provoke a retaliatory response. An individual targeted by an administrative proceeding will react angrily and may seek vengeance in the courts. A corporation will muster all of its financial and legal resources in an effort to prevent administrative sanctions. "When millions may turn on regulatory decisions, there is a strong incentive to counter-attack."

The defendant in an enforcement proceeding has ample opportunity to challenge the legality of the proceeding. An administrator's decision to proceed with a case is subject to scrutiny in the proceeding itself. The respondent may present his evidence to an impartial trier of fact and obtain an independent judgment as to whether the prosecution is justified. His claims that the proceeding is unconstitutional may also be heard by the courts.

We believe that agency officials must make the decision to move forward with an administrative proceeding free from intimidation or harassment. Because the legal remedies already available to the defendant in such a proceeding provide sufficient checks on agency zeal, we hold that those officials who are responsible for the decision to initiate or continue a proceeding subject to agency adjudication are entitled to absolute immunity from damages liability for their parts in that decision. We turn finally to the role of an agency attorney in conducting a trial and presenting evidence on the record to the trier of fact. We can see no substantial difference between the function of the agency attorney in presenting evidence in an agency hearing and the function of the prosecutor who brings evidence before a court. In either case, the evidence will be subject to attack through cross-examination, rebuttal, or reinterpretation by opposing counsel. . . . We therefore hold that an agency attorney who arranges for the presentation of evidence on the record in the course of an adjudication is absolutely immune from suits based on the introduction of such evidence.

VI

There remains the task of applying the foregoing principles to the claims against the particular petitioner-defendants involved in this case. Rather than attempt this here in the first instance, we vacate the judgment of the Court of Appeals and remand the case to that court with instructions to remand the case to the District Court for further proceedings consistent with this opinion.

REHNQUIST, J., joined by BURGER, C.J. and STEWART and STEVENS, JJ., dissented:

. . . [I]f we allow a mere allegation of unconstitutionality, obviously unproved at the time made, to require a Cabinet-level official, charged with the enforcement of the responsibilities to which the complaint pertains, to lay aside his duties and defend such an action on the merits, the defense of official immunity will have been abolished in fact if not in form. The ease with which a constitutional claim may be pleaded in a case such as this, where a violation of statutory or judicial limits on agency action may be readily converted by any legal neophyte into a claim of denial of procedural due process under the Fifth Amendment, will assure that. The fact that the claim fails when put to trial will not prevent the consumption of time, effort, and money on the part of the defendant official in defending his actions on the merits. The result can only be damage to the "interests of the people," which "require[s] that due protection be accorded to [Cabinet officials] in respect of their official acts."

It likewise cannot seriously be argued that an official will be less deterred by the threat of liability for unconstitutional conduct than for activities which might constitute a common-law tort. The fear that inhibits is that of a long, involved lawsuit and a significant money judgment, not the fear of liability for a certain type of claim. Thus, even viewing the question functionally—indeed, *especially* viewing the question functionally—the basis for a distinction between constitutional and common-law torts . . . in this context is open to serious question. . . .

The Court purports to find support for this distinction, and therefore this result, in the principles supposedly underlying *Marbury v. Madison* and *Bivens v. Six Unknown Fed. Narcotics Agents,* and the fact that cognate state officials are not afforded absolute immunity for actions brought under 42 U.S.C. § 1983. Undoubtedly these rationales have some superficial appeal, but none withstands careful analysis.

Marbury, like numerous other [cases] which followed, involved equitable-type relief by way of mandamus or injunction. In the present case, respondent sought damages in the amount of $32 million. . . . [T]here is at least as much force to the argument that the threat of injunctive relief without the possibility of damages in the case of a Cabinet official is a better tailoring of the competing need to vindicate individual rights, on the one hand, and the equally vital need, on the other, that federal officials exercising discretion will be unafraid to take vigorous action to protect the public interest.

The Court also suggests in sweeping terms that the cause of action recognized in *Bivens* would be " 'drained of meaning' if federal officials were entitled to absolute immunity for their constitutional transgressions." But *Bivens* is a slender reed on which to rely when abrogating official immunity for Cabinet-level officials. In the first place, those officials [such as police officers] most susceptible to claims under *Bivens* have historically been given only a qualified immunity. . . . But even more importantly, on the federal side, when Congress thinks redress of grievances is appropriate, it can and generally does waive sovereign immunity, allowing an action directly against the United States. This allows redress for deprivations of rights, while at the same time limiting the outside influences which might inhibit an official in the free and considered exercise of his official powers. In fact, Congress, making just these sorts of judgments with respect to the very causes of action which the Court suggests require abrogation of absolute immunity, has amended the Federal Tort Claims Act, to allow suits against the United States on the basis of certain intentional torts if committed by federal "investigative or law enforcement officers."

The Court also looks to the question of immunity of state officials for causes arising under § 1983. . . . [E]ven a moment's reflection on the nature of the *Bivens*-type action and the purposes of § 1983 . . . supplies a compelling reason for distinguishing between the two different situations. [Congress has allowed direct action against the government in many *Bivens*-type situations. In addition, the] Federal Government can internally supervise and check its own officers. The Federal Government is not so situated that it can control state officials or strike this same balance, however. Hence the necessity of § 1983 and the differing standards of immunity. . . .

My biggest concern, however, is not with the illogic or impracticality of today's decision, but rather with the potential for disruption of Government that it invites. The steady increase in litigation, much of it directed against governmental officials and virtually all of which could be framed in constitutional terms, cannot escape the notice of even the most casual observer. From 1961 to 1977, the number of cases brought in the federal courts under civil rights statutes increased from 296 to 13,113. . . . It simply defies logic and common experience to suggest that officials will not have this in the back of their minds when considering what official course to pursue. . . .

The Court, of course, recognizes this problem and suggests two solutions. First, judges, ever alert to the artful pleader, supposedly will weed out insubstantial claims. That, I fear, shows more optimism than prescience.

The second solution offered by the Court is even less satisfactory. The Court holds that in those special circumstances "where it is demonstrated that absolute immunity is essential for the conduct of the public business," absolute immunity will be extended. But this is a form of "absolute immunity" which in truth exists in name only. If, for example, the Secretary of Agriculture may never know until inquiry by a trial court whether there is a possibility that vexatious constitutional litigation will interfere with his decisionmaking process, the Secretary will obviously think not only twice but thrice about whether to prosecute a litigious commodities merchant [who has a] reputation for using litigation as a defense weapon . . .

[While] I believe that history will look approvingly on the motives of the Court in reaching the result it does today, I do not believe that history will be charitable in its judgment of the all but inevitable result of the doctrine espoused by the Court in this case.* That doctrine seeks to gain and hold a middle ground which, with all deference, I believe the teachings of those who were at least our equals suggest cannot long be held. That part of the Court's present opinion from which I dissent will, I fear, result in one of two evils, either one of which is markedly worse than the effect of according absolute immunity to the Secretary and the Assistant Secretary in this case. The first of these evils would be a significant impairment of the ability of responsible public officials to carry out the duties imposed upon them by law. If that evil is to be avoided after today, it can be avoided only by a necessarily unprincipled and erratic judicial "screening" of claims such as those made in this case, an adherence to the form of the law while departing from its substance. Either one of these evils is far worse than the occasional failure to award damages caused by official wrongdoing . . . As Judge Learned Hand said in *Gregoire v. Biddle,* 177 F.2d, at 581:

> The justification for doing so is that it is impossible to know whether the claim is well founded until the case has been tried, and that to submit all officials, the innocent as well as the guilty, to the burden of a trial and to the inevitable danger of its outcome, would dampen the ardor of all but the most resolute, or the most irresponsible, in the unflinching discharge of their duties. Again and again the public interest calls for action which may turn out to be founded on a mistake, in the face of which an official may later find himself hard put to it to satisfy a jury of his good faith. There must indeed be means of punishing public officers who have been truant to their duties; but that is quite another matter from exposing such as have been honestly mistaken to suit by anyone who has suffered from their errors. As is so often the case, the answer must be found in a balance between the evils inevitable in either alternative. In this instance it has been thought in the end better to leave unredressed the wrongs done by dishonest officers

* The ultimate irony of today's decision is that in the area of common-law official immunity, a body of law fashioned and applied by judges, absolute immunity within the federal system is extended only to judges and prosecutors functioning in the judicial system.

If one were to hazard an informed guess as to why such a distinction in treatment between judges and prosecutors, on the one hand, and other public officials on the other, obtains, mine would be that those who decide the common law know through personal experience the sort of pressures that might exist for such decisionmakers in the absence of absolute immunity, but may not know or may have forgotten that similar pressures exist in the case of nonjudicial public officials to whom difficult decisions are committed. But the cynical among us might not unreasonably feel that this is simply another unfortunate example of judges treating those who are not part of the judicial machinery as "lesser breeds without the law."

than to subject those who try to do their duty to the constant dread of retaliation.

Notes and Questions

1. *Barr and Butz.* *Butz* is important for at least four different reasons:

(i) it establishes a sharp distinction between tort actions against federal officials who act within their statutory powers and without violating the constitution (who are not liable under *Barr*) and those who act outside their statutory powers or who violate constitutional principles (who are liable under *Butz*);

(ii) it confirms that agency adjudicators and prosecutors are entitled to absolute immunity from damage suits, like judges and criminal prosecutors;

(iii) it holds that other law enforcement officials (including the heads of agencies) have only qualified immunity;

(iv) it unifies immunity law in cases of constitutional tort, so that federal officials have no greater immunity than state officials, despite the differing history of § 1983 and *Bivens* actions and despite the provisions of the Federal Tort Claims Act.

This was a large amount to bite off in one case and it remains to be seen whether shifts in personnel of the Court will bring Justice Rehnquist's sharply contrasting views into the majority. On the other hand, perhaps the absolute immunity rule of *Barr* for common law torts will crumble in favor of the qualified immunity of *Butz* for constitutional torts. The two cases do not fit together very comfortably.

2. *Constitutional torts.* *Bivens* established a right of action arising from the fourth amendment against federal law enforcement officials for an unlawful search and seizure. Note that *Butz* assumes without deciding that plaintiffs have a right of action arising from both the first and fifth amendments (the latter for violation of procedural due process). It appears that rights of action also arise from the cruel and unusual punishment provision of the eighth amendment and from the implied equal protection component of the fifth amendment. *Carlson v. Green,* 446 U.S. 14 (1980); *Davis v. Passman,* 442 U.S. 228 (1979) (sex discrimination by a member of Congress).

Note that amendments to the Federal Tort Claims Act after *Bivens* was decided make it possible to sue the government for many intentional torts committed by law enforcement officials. Why would a plaintiff prefer to sue the officials rather than (or in addition to) the federal government?

3. *Absolute immunity.* The charmed circle of officials who are absolutely immune from damage actions for constitutional torts includes judges, including administrative judges. However, to gain absolute immunity an administrative law judge must be independent of control by other agency officials; thus the members of prison disciplina-

ry committees who conduct misconduct hearings do not have absolute immunity. They are not really neutral and detached adjudicators, are not independent of the warden or of the jail employees who lodge the charges, and utilize informal procedures. *Cleavinger v. Saxner,* 474 U.S. 193 (1985).

Prosecutors are within the circle but not public defenders. *Tower v. Glover,* 467 U.S. 914 (1984). What is a "prosecutor" under *Butz* and why were the Secretary and Assistant Secretary of Agriculture not treated as prosecutors? The distinction, apparently, is this: an agency official who is preparing to present the agency's case in an adjudicatory proceeding is a "prosecutor" and is absolutely immune, but an agency official who is engaged in the regulatory process (apart from preparing or presenting an adjudication) is not a "prosecutor" and has only qualified immunity. *Schlegel v. Bebout,* 841 F.2d 937 (9th Cir.1988).

Absolute immunity covers the President (*Nixon v. Fitzgerald,* 457 U.S. 731 (1982)) and presidential aides, but only to the extent the latter are engaged in highly sensitive activity. *Harlow v. Fitzgerald,* 457 U.S. 800 (1982). Members of Congress have immunity for actions in a legislative capacity under the Speech and Debate Clause (Art. I, § 6) and state legislators enjoy comparable immunity. *Tenney v. Brandhove,* 341 U.S. 367 (1951). Legislative immunity extends to agency officials engaged in rulemaking. *Supreme Court of Virginia v. Consumers Union,* 446 U.S. 719 (1980) (rules governing the practice of law); *Jayvee Brand, Inc. v. United States,* 721 F.2d 385, 394–95 (D.C.Cir. 1983) (rulemaking by Consumer Product Safety Commissioners which violated mandatory procedures).

4. *Qualified immunity.* Officials who cannot claim absolute immunity are entitled only to qualified immunity. This covers law enforcement officials all the way from the top of an agency (*e.g.* the Secretary of Agriculture in *Butz* or a state governor as in *Scheuer*) to the cop on the beat. Qualified immunity is a compromise between conflicting and irreconcilable policies: i) providing effective redress to injured persons, ii) deterring officials from abusing their power, iii) avoiding over-deterrence (i.e. limiting the extent to which fear of liability will distract officials from their duties, inhibit vigorous decision-making, and deter able people from public service).

A defendant with qualified immunity is liable only if his conduct is not "objectively reasonable." The standard against which the conduct is measured is whether it violated "clearly established" constitutional limitations of which the official reasonably should have been aware. Thus the qualified immunity test is objective; it does not matter whether the official actually was aware of the limitation or acted "maliciously." *Harlow v. Fitzgerald, supra; Davis v. Scherer,* 468 U.S. 183 (1984). An objective test makes it easier to resolve cases quickly on summary judgment since the defendant's "malice" or knowledge of constitutional law is not in issue.

Local government entities, which are liable under § 1983 if they are the "moving force" behind a violation, are not entitled to any immunities at all. *Owen v. City of Independence*, 445 U.S. 622 (1980) (city liable for denial of procedural due process even though the right in question emerged in court decisions only after the violations occurred).

Is there any persuasive justification for treating the personal liability of judges, prosecutors, legislators and the President differently from top administrative officials or state governors? From street-level bureaucrats like police, teachers, welfare workers, or prison guards? *See* footnote * in Justice Rehnquist's *Butz* dissent.

5. *Shifting the burden to government.* Usually, but not always, federal, state and local government provide free legal representation to officials who are sued for misconduct within the scope of their employment. However, the federal government refuses to provide such service if the individual will be criminally indicted, where the acts sued on were not within the scope of federal employment, or where representation "is not in the interests of the United States." P. Schuck, SUING GOVERNMENT 84 (1983).

As to actual liability, public officials generally do not have and cannot obtain insurance against liability. When an official is liable and the federal government is not liable under the Federal Tort Claims Act, it does not indemnify the official against liability. (For example, this would occur if the Secretary of Agriculture were ultimately found to be liable in the *Butz* case). At the state and local level, indemnity either through law or collective bargaining is common, but there are many exceptions and loopholes (for example for actions taken with malice or actions subjecting the individual to disciplinary action). *Id.* at 85–88. Where government provides legal defense and indemnity against liability, the actual result is governmental, not official, liability.

6. *Who should be the defendant?* ACUS has proposed that federal officials should be immune from liability in actions brought against them for violation of constitutional rights. All such actions would instead be brought directly against the federal government which could then claim benefit of any qualified or absolute immunity which the official would have enjoyed. The officials might be the subject of disciplinary proceedings brought against them by the agency that employs them, but they would not be subject to monetary liability. ACUS Recommendation 82–6, "Federal Officials' Liability for Constitutional Violations," 1 C.F.R. § 305.82–6.

Do you favor this recommendation? How about holding government liable for officials' torts (constitutional or common law) and abolishing or limiting immunities?

7. *Problem.* The Commission on Pornography was appointed to study the impact of pornography on society and to recommend legal means by which the spread of pornography could be contained. The Commission concluded that erotic photographs in nationally circulated magazines provoke assaults against women. Since such photographs

are not "obscene" and thus are protected by the first amendment, they cannot legally be suppressed. The Commission singled out several magazines, including *Penthouse*, for special criticism. Its report recommended that local citizens institute boycotts against "pornographers" who sell these magazines and it named several retail chains as "pornographers" and thus possible boycott targets.

Mercury Stores was on the list of possible targets. It ignored the report and continued to sell *Penthouse*. As a result it was subjected to picketing and boycotts in several states which caused it considerable damage. Mercury has asked for advice about suing for damages either the government or the Commission members. Analyze the prospects for litigation if

(a) The Commission was appointed by the President of the United States;

(b) The Commission was appointed by a state governor.

Cf. Playboy Enterprises, Inc. v. Meese, 639 F.Supp. 581 (D.D.C.1986).

§ 10.3 RECOVERY OF FEES

Like all litigation, administrative adjudication is time consuming and costly. A client must take account of those costs in deciding whether it is worthwhile to challenge an adverse agency decision; many times, even though the client has a strong position, the costs of litigation simply make it impracticable to proceed.

The cost of litigation is a particularly severe problem for public interest plaintiffs. Typically, public interest groups (such as environmental, civil rights, or consumer protection organizations) are underfunded. Even if great numbers of citizens agree with them, the free rider effect makes it difficult and costly to obtain voluntary contributions (a free rider refuses to contribute since he can receive the benefits provided by the group whether he contributes or not). Yet to challenge agency action, such a group must be prepared for long and costly years of litigation against skilled, determined and well-funded adversaries.

For these reasons, a vitally important remedial issue is whether a prevailing party can obtain an award of attorney's fees (as well as other costs such as the fees charged by expert witnesses). There are now a large number of statutory provisions which authorize a court to require the losing party to pay the winner's fees. If such a statute is applicable, it may be feasible to pursue litigation which otherwise would simply be too costly. This subchapter explores a range of issues arising under fee shifting statutes.

PENNSYLVANIA v. DELAWARE VALLEY CITIZENS' COUNCIL FOR CLEAN AIR
478 U.S. 546 (1986).

[Both Delaware Valley Citizens' Council (Delaware Valley) and the United States sued Pennsylvania in 1977 to require it to implement a vehicle emission inspection and maintenance program as required by the Clean Air Act. A consent decree ordered Pennsylvania to adopt a program but the state legislature refused to cooperate. There followed years of struggle and delays, proceeding through nine distinct phases in which legal work was done. Sec. 304(d) of the Clean Air Act provides that a court issuing a final order in a citizen's suit under the Act can award costs of litigation (including reasonable attorney's fees) to any party "whenever the court determines such award is appropriate." Delaware Valley sought $209,813 in attorneys' fees. The District Court awarded $205,433 in fees.]

WHITE, J.:

[Although the proceedings involved in Phases II (submission of comments in rulemaking proceeding and monitoring of the consent decree) and IX (adjudication before EPA)] were not "judicial" in the sense that they did not occur in a courtroom or involve "traditional" legal work such as examination of witnesses or selection of jurors for trial, the work done by counsel in these two phases was as necessary to the attainment of adequate relief for their client as was all of their earlier work in the courtroom which secured Delaware Valley's initial success in obtaining the consent decree. . . .

Several courts have held that, in the context of the Civil Rights Attorney's Fees Awards Act of 1976, 42 U.S.C. § 1988, post-judgment monitoring of a consent decree is a compensable activity for which counsel is entitled to a reasonable fee. . . . [T]he purposes behind both § 304 and § 1988 are nearly identical, which lends credence to the idea that they should be interpreted in a similar manner. Section 1988 was enacted to insure that private citizens have a meaningful opportunity to vindicate their rights protected by the Civil Rights Laws. "The effective enforcement of Federal civil rights statutes depends largely on the efforts of private citizens," and unless reasonable attorney's fees could be awarded for bringing these actions, Congress found that many legitimate claims would not be redressed.

Similarly, § 304 authorizes private citizens to sue any person violating the Clean Air Act, and provides for reasonable attorney's fees whenever appropriate. Congress enacted this provision specifically to encourage "citizen participation in the enforcement of standards and regulations established under this Act," and intended for the Section "to afford . . . citizens . . . very broad opportunities to participate in the effort to prevent and abate air pollution[.]" Congress found that "Government initiative in seeking enforcement under the Clean Air Act has been restrained," and urged the courts to "recognize that in bringing legitimate actions under this section citizens would be performing a public service and in such instances the courts should award costs of litigation to such party."

Given the common purpose of both § 304 and § 1988 to promote citizen enforcement of important federal policies, we find no reason not to interpret both provisions governing attorney's fees in the same manner. We hold, therefore, that the fact that the work done by counsel in Phases II and IX did not occur in the context of traditional judicial litigation does not preclude an award of reasonable attorney's fees under § 304 for the work done during these portions of present action. . . . .

III

A

It is well-established that, under the "American Rule," "the prevailing litigant is ordinarily not entitled to collect a reasonable attorneys' fee from the loser." *Alyeska Pipeline Service Co. v. Wilderness Society*, 421 U.S. 240 (1975). There are exceptions to this principle, the major one being Congressional authorization for the courts to require one party to award attorney's fees to the other.[6] There are over 100 separate statutes providing for the award of attorney's fees; and although these provisions cover a wide variety of contexts and causes of action, the benchmark for the awards under nearly all of these statutes is that the attorney's fee must be "reasonable."

Courts have struggled to formulate the proper measure for determining the "reasonableness" of a particular fee award. One method, first employed by the Fifth Circuit in *Johnson v. Georgia Highway Express, Inc.*, 488 F.2d 714 (1974), involved consideration of 12 factors. *Johnson* was widely followed by other courts, and was cited with approval by both the House and the Senate when § 1988 was enacted into law.

This approach required trial courts to consider the elements that go into determining the propriety of legal fees and was intended to provide appellate courts with more substantial and objective records on which to review trial court determinations. This mode of analysis, however, was not without its shortcomings. Its major fault was that it gave very little actual guidance to District Courts. Setting attorney's fees by reference to a series of sometimes subjective factors placed unlimited discretion in trial judges and produced disparate results.

For this reason, the Third Circuit developed another method of calculating "reasonable" attorney's fees. This method, known as the "lodestar" approach, involved two steps. First, the court was to calculate the "lodestar," determined by multiplying the hours spent on a case by a reasonable hourly rate of compensation for each attorney involved. Second, using the lodestar figure as a starting point, the

---

6. In addition to this statutory exception, courts traditionally have recognized three other exceptions to the "American Rule." First, courts can enforce their own orders by assessing attorneys' fees for the wilfull violation of a court order. *Alyeska*, 421 U.S., at 258.

Second, courts are empowered to award fees against a losing party that has acted in bad faith, vexatiously, wantonly, or for oppressive reasons. And finally, a court's equitable powers allow it to award fees in commercial litigation to plaintiffs who recovered a "common fund" for themselves and others through securities or antitrust litigation. None of these situations are involved in the present case.

court could then make adjustments to this figure, in light of "(1) the contingent nature of the case, reflecting the likelihood that hours were invested and expenses incurred without assurance of compensation; and (2) the quality of the work performed as evidenced by the work observed, the complexity of the issues and the recovery obtained." . . . This formulation emphasized the amount of time expended by the attorneys, and provided a more analytical framework for lower courts to follow than the unguided "factors" approach provided by *Johnson.* On the other hand, allowing the courts to adjust the lodestar amount based on considerations of the "riskiness" of the lawsuit and the quality of the attorney's work could still produce inconsistent and arbitrary fee awards. . . .

We further refined our views in *Blum v. Stenson,* 465 U.S. 886 (1984). *Blum* restated that the proper first step in determining a reasonable attorney's fee is to multiply "the number of hours reasonably expended on the litigation times a reasonable hourly rate." We emphasized, however, that the figure resulting from this calculation is more than a mere "rough guess" or initial approximation of the final award to be made. Instead, we found that "[w]hen . . . the applicant for a fee has carried his burden of showing that the claimed rate and number of hours are reasonable, the resulting product *is presumed* to be the reasonable fee" to which counsel is entitled.

Blum also limited the factors which a district court may consider in determining whether to make adjustments to the lodestar amount. . . . [The] "novelty [and] complexity of the issues," "the special skill and experience of counsel," the "quality of representation," and the "results obtained" from the litigation are presumably fully reflected in the lodestar amount, and thus cannot serve as independent bases for increasing the basic fee award. Although upward adjustments of the lodestar figure are still permissible, such modifications are proper only in certain "rare" and "exceptional" cases, supported by both "specific evidence" on the record and detailed findings by the lower courts.

A strong presumption that the lodestar figure—the product of reasonable hours times a reasonable rate—represents a "reasonable" fee is wholly consistent with the rationale behind the usual fee-shifting statute, including the one in the present case. These statutes were not designed as a form of economic relief to improve the financial lot of attorneys, nor were they intended to replicate exactly the fee an attorney could earn through a private fee arrangement with his client. Instead, the aim of such statutes was to enable private parties to obtain legal help in seeking redress for injuries resulting from the actual or threatened violation of specific federal laws. Hence, if plaintiffs, such as Delaware Valley, find it possible to engage a lawyer based on the statutory assurance that he will be paid a "reasonable fee," the purpose behind the fee-shifting statute has been satisfied.

Moreover, when an attorney first accepts a case and agrees to represent the client, he obligates himself to perform to the best of his ability and to produce the best possible results commensurate with his skill and his client's interests. Calculating the fee award in a manner that accounts for these factors, either in determining the reasonable number of hours expended on the litigation or in setting the reasonable hourly rate, thus adequately compensates the attorney, and leaves very little room for enhancing the award based on his post-engagement performance. In short, the lodestar figure includes most, if not all, of the relevant factors comprising a "reasonable" attorney's fee, and it is unnecessary to enhance the fee for superior performance in order to serve the statutory purpose of enabling plaintiffs to secure legal assistance.

Dissenting opinion of BLACKMUN, J. (with which BRENNAN and MARSHALL, JJ. concurred) is omitted.

Notes and Questions

1. *The American rule.* In *Wilderness Society v. Morton,* 495 F.2d 1026 (D.C.Cir.1974), the Court held that public interest environmental groups were entitled to an award of attorney's fees for their efforts (4500 hours of lawyers' time) in halting the trans-Alaska pipeline. The rationale was that they had served as a private attorney general in vindicating important Congressional policies protective of the environment.

This decision was reversed by the Supreme Court in the *Alyeska Pipeline* case cited in *Delaware Valley.* Under the "American rule" each party in litigation bears its own attorneys' fees, absent a statute providing for fees or one of the exceptions mentioned in note 6 of *Delaware Valley.* There is no exception for suits brought by a private attorney general vindicating an important public interest.

However, not all states follow the *Alyeska* case. *See Serrano v. Priest,* 569 P.2d 1303 (Cal.1977) (public interest law firms win $800,000 attorney fee award under private attorney general theory in case relating to constitutionality of public school financing). *Serrano* was codified by Cal.Code of Civ.Proc. § 1021.5:

Upon motion, a court may award attorneys' fees to a successful party against one or more opposing parties in any action which has resulted in the enforcement of an important right affecting the public interest if: (a) a significant benefit, whether pecuniary or nonpecuniary, has been conferred on the general public or a large class of persons, (b) the necessity and financial burden of private enforcement are such as to make the award appropriate, and (c) such fees should not in the interest of justice be paid out of the recovery, if any . . .

2. *Statutes providing for fees. Delaware Valley* discusses two of the many federal statutes that authorize a court to require one side to pay the other's fees—the Clean Air Act and the Civil Rights Attorney's Fees Act. Under the latter provision, 42 U.S.C. § 1988, a prevailing

civil rights plaintiff (including one asserting rights of procedural due process) should ordinarily recover attorneys' fees unless special circumstances render an award unjust, but a prevailing defendant gets a fee award only if the plaintiff's action was frivolous. *Newman v. Piggie Park Enterprises, Inc.,* 390 U.S. 400, 402 (1968); *Hughes v. Rowe,* 449 U.S. 5, 14 (1980).

Like a number of other environmental statutes, § 304 of the Clean Air Act provides for attorneys' fees if the trial court determines that an award is "appropriate." How should the court decide when it is "appropriate" to make the loser pay the winner's fees? *See Carson–Truckee Water Cons. Dist. v. Secretary of the Interior,* 748 F.2d 523 (9th Cir.1984), *cert. denied,* 471 U.S. 1065 (1985), which construes a "when appropriate" fee provision under the Endangered Species Act. The court held that a fee award is "appropriate" if a plaintiff "substantially contributes to the goals of the Act," for example by assisting in its interpretation and implementation. In *Carson–Truckee,* the court found that an award of fees to an Indian tribe would not be "appropriate"—other parties had raised the same issues first, the issues were narrow, and the tribe raised defenses inconsistent with assisting in the implementation of the Act.

3. *Reasonable attorneys' fees.* Counsel should maintain meticulous time records and be prepared to itemize exactly how the time was spent. In addition, an attorney should be prepared to justify as high a lodestar hourly rate as possible since it is unlikely that the court will approve a higher rate.

Good record keeping pays off. *See City of Riverside v. Rivera,* 477 U.S. 561 (1986), arising under § 1988. On the merits, the *Riverside* case involved an action by Hispanics against the police who broke up a party and arrested them without a warrant. The jury awarded them damages of $33,350. After a lengthy struggle over the fee issue, the Supreme Court upheld attorneys' fees of $245,456 (based on 1,946.75 hours spent by attorneys at $125 per hour and 84.5 hours spent by law clerks at $25 per hour). This was more than seven times the damages in the case! However, the decision was 5–4 and Justice Powell's concurrence in the judgment was reluctant.

Note that the $245,456 figure covers only the cost of litigating the merits—not the cost of litigating the fee issue. Considering that the fee issue went to the Supreme Court twice (and also included two Ninth Circuit and one district court decision), the attorneys' fees arising out of the attorney fee issue may well exceed the fees arising from the merits.

On rehearing, *Delaware Valley* decided an additional important issue. 107 S.Ct. 3078 (1987). It held that ordinarily the lodestar cannot be adjusted upward to take account of the contingency that an attorney gets nothing if the plaintiff loses (even though the lodestar is an hourly rate which attorneys charge when they expect to be paid whether they win or lose.) Yet the Court held that enhancement for the risk of loss (by not more than one-third of the lodestar) can be justified in exceptional cases upon a showing of substantial difficulties in finding counsel to work for the unadjusted rate.

4. *Equal Access to Justice Act.* Under the Equal Access to Justice Act (EAJA), enacted in 1980 and expanded in 1985, Congress departed substantially from the American rule. In litigation at the agency level or in court, EAJA provides that a prevailing party (other than the United States) is entitled to attorneys' fees and other expenses unless the government's position was "substantially justified" or special circumstances make an award unjust.

EAJA consists of two related statutes: Under 5 U.S.C. § 504, an agency shall award fees and expenses to a prevailing party unless an ALJ finds that the agency's position was substantially justified. The person seeking fees can appeal the ALJ decision but the government cannot. Section 504 covers the costs of a formal agency adjudication (other than ratemaking or granting a license) in which the government is represented by counsel. This excludes social security cases because the government does not appear by counsel in such cases.

Under 28 U.S.C. § 2412(d) a court shall award to a prevailing party fees and expenses incurred in any civil action (except a tort action) brought by or against the United States, *including judicial review of agency action,* unless the court finds that the government's position was substantially justified. Section 2412(d) permits an award of costs incurred at both the agency and judicial levels.

Both §§ 504 and 2412(d) permit awards only to parties whom Congress thought needed assistance in litigating against the government: broadly speaking, awards can be made only to an individual whose net worth did not exceed $2 million or to a business whose net worth did not exceed $7 million and which had not more than 500 employees. However, tax exempt charitable organizations (such as most public interest law firms) qualify regardless of their net worth. Small local government units also qualify.

The amount which can be paid under these sections include the cost of expert witnesses, the costs of necessary studies or tests, and reasonable attorney fees. However, attorney fees cannot exceed $75 per hour unless it is determined that an increase in the cost of living or a special factor (such as limited availability of qualified attorneys for the proceedings involved) justifies a higher fee. The $75 per hour figure is far below the amount currently charged by big city law firms. However, the exception for "limited availability" only applies to attorneys having some distinctive knowledge or specialized skill needed for the litigation in question, such as an identifiable specialty like patent law or knowledge of foreign law or language—not simply general legal competence. *Pierce v. Underwood,* 108 S.Ct. 2541 (1988).

Recent amendments to EAJA make clear that the government's "position" covers not only its litigating position but also the original action, or failure to act, on which the adjudication was based. Under both sections, the government has the burden to show that its position was substantially justified. Congress intended EAJA as a compromise between always shifting and never shifting a prevailing party's fees to the government. "Substantially justified" means that the government's position is "justified to a degree that could satisfy a reasonable person." Thus it closely resembles the test for "substantial evidence on the whole record" discussed in § 9.1. *Pierce v. Underwood, supra.* Could the government's position be "substantially justified" if it lost the case because its action was found to be arbitrary and capricious? *See FEC v. Rose,* 806 F.2d 1081 (D.C.Cir.1986).

A number of states have adopted provisions similar to EAJA. *See* Comment, 71 Iowa L.Rev. 1553 (1986). Another similar provision applies to fees incurred in tax litigation by or against the IRS (limiting recovery of fees to $25,000) if the government's position was "unreasonable." Int.Rev.Code § 7430.

5. *Problem.* Assume the state of Monroe adopts provisions identical to EAJA and to Calif.Code of Civ.Proc. § 1021.5 (quoted in note 1 supra). The Monroe Corporations Commission (MCC) has power to prevent the public issue of any security unless the issuing corporation first files a prospectus fully and accurately disclosing financial information about itself and the stock issue. MCC adopted a regulation allowing it to disapprove a stock sale, even if disclosure in the prospectus is complete and accurate, if the terms of the sale are not fair to investors.

Accuchip Inc. is a privately owned high-tech company which wants to sell $3 million of stock to investors living in Monroe. It has 85 employees and a net worth of $2 million. It files a prospectus with MCC disclosing its plans to sell stock for $42 per share.

The MCC staff believes that Accuchip failed adequately to disclose the highly risky nature of Accuchip's business (it is competing against some very large companies). It also believes that even if this were fully disclosed, the offering is not fair because $42 is too high a price. In the staff's opinion, $12 a share would be more appropriate. Therefore MCC entered a stop order against any sale of the shares.

Accuchip received an immediate hearing before an ALJ which agreed with the staff's position. On appeal, the MCC agency head upheld the ALJ's decision. On judicial review, a trial court held that i) Accuchip's disclosure of risk was inadequate but ii) the regulation which allows MCC to disapprove a stock sale found to contain unfair terms is invalid because it is contrary to statute. Both parties appealed to the Monroe Supreme Court which affirmed the trial court's decision.

Judy, Accuchip's lawyer, is a member of a major big city law firm and she charges $250 per hour for her time. Her fees are broken down as follows: (i) supervision of prospectus preparation—20 hours; (ii) negotiating with MCC staff before the stop order was issued—10 hours; (iii) preparation for and hearing before ALJ—50 hours; (iv) MCC appeal—30 hours; (v) judicial review in trial court—120 hours; (vi) appeal to Monroe Supreme Court—100 hours. Thus Judy's bill for 330 hours of time was $82,500. How much, if any, of those fees can MCC be compelled to pay?

§ 10.4 PRECLUSION OF JUDICIAL REVIEW

Although there is a presumption that administrative action is subject to judicial review, that presumption can be rebutted. The legislature can preclude judicial review, thus rendering administrative action partially or completely unreviewable. *See* APA § 701(a)(1): "This chapter applies . . . except to the extent that—(1) statutes preclude judicial review . . . ." Compare 1981 MSAPA 5–102(a) and 1–103(b) (to diminish any right created by MSAPA, another statute must expressly so provide). What happens if judicial review seems inconsistent with the statutory scheme but the legislature did not explicitly preclude it?

BOWEN v. MICHIGAN ACADEMY OF FAMILY PHYSICIANS

476 U.S. 667 (1986).

[A rule adopted by the Secretary of Health and Human Services, under Part B of the Medicare program, provides for lower payments to allopathic family physicians than other physicians. The issue is whether statutes preclude judicial review of regulations adopted under Part B.]

STEVENS, J.:

. . . We begin with the strong presumption that Congress intends judicial review of administrative action. From the beginning "our cases [have established] that judicial review of a final agency action by an aggrieved person will not be cut off unless there is persuasive reason to believe that such was the purpose of Congress." *Abbott Laboratories v. Gardner,* 387 U.S. 136 (1967). In *Marbury v. Madison,* 5 U.S. 137, (1803), a case itself involving review of executive action, Chief Justice Marshall insisted that "[t]he very essence of civil liberty certainly consists in the right of every individual to claim the protection of the laws." . . .

Committees of both Houses of Congress have endorsed this view in undertaking the comprehensive rethinking of the place of administrative agencies in a regime of separate and divided powers that culminated in the passage of the Administrative Procedure Act (APA) . . . The Committee on the Judiciary of the House of Representatives agreed that Congress ordinarily intends that there be judicial review, and emphasized the clarity with which a contrary intent must be expressed:

"The statutes of Congress are not merely advisory when they relate to administrative agencies, any more than in other cases. To preclude judicial review under this bill a statute, if not specific in withholding such review, must upon its face give clear and convincing evidence of an intent to withhold it. The mere failure to provide specially by statute for judicial review is certainly no evidence of intent to withhold review." *Ibid.* . . .

This standard has been invoked time and again when considering whether the Secretary has discharged "the heavy burden of overcoming the strong presumption that Congress did not mean to prohibit all judicial review of his decision," *Dunlop v. Bachowski,* 421 U.S. 560 (1975).[3]

Subject to constitutional constraints, Congress can, of course, make exceptions to the historic practice whereby courts review agency action. The presumption of judicial review is, after all, a presumption, and "like all presumptions used in interpreting statutes, may be overcome by," *inter alia,* "specific language or specific legislative history that is a reliable indicator of congressional intent," or a specific congressional intent to preclude judicial review that is " 'fairly discernible' in the detail of the legislative scheme." *Block v. Community Nutrition Institute,* 467 U.S. 340 (1984).

In this case, the Government asserts that [a] statutory provision remove[s] the Secretary's regulation from review under the grant of general federal-question jurisdiction found in 28 U.S.C. § 1331. The Government contends that 42 U.S.C. § 1395ff(b) which authorizes "Appeal by individuals," impliedly forecloses administrative or judicial review of any action taken under Part B of the Medicare program by failing to authorize such review while simultaneously authorizing administrative and judicial review of "any determination . . . as to . . . the amount of benefits under part A." . . . Section 1395ff on its face is an explicit authorization of judicial review, not a bar. As a general matter, " '[t]he mere fact that some acts are made reviewable should not suffice to support an implication of exclusion as to others. The right to review is too important to be excluded on such slender and indeterminate evidence of legislative intent.' " *Abbott Laboratories v. Gardner,*

In the Medicare program, however, the situation is somewhat more complex. Under Part B of that program, which is at issue here, the Secretary contracts with private health insurance carriers to provide benefits for which individuals voluntarily remit premiums. This optional coverage, which is federally subsidized, supplements the

---

3. . . . Of course, this Court has "never applied the 'clear and convincing evidence' standard in the strict evidentiary sense"; nevertheless, the standard serves as "a useful reminder to courts that, where substantial doubt about the congressional intent exists, the general presumption favoring judicial review of administrative action is controlling."

A strong presumption finds support in a wealth of scholarly literature. See, *e.g.,* 2 K. Davis, Administrative Law § 9:6, p. 240 (1979) (praising "the case law since 1974" for being "strongly on the side of review-ability"); L. Jaffe, Judicial Control of Administrative Action 327 (1965) ("An agency is not an island entire of itself. It is one of the many rooms in the magnificent mansion of the law. The very subordination of the agency to judicial jurisdiction is intended to proclaim the premise that each agency is to be brought into harmony with the totality of the law, the law as it is found in the statute at hand, the statute book at large, the principles and conceptions of the 'common law,' and the ultimate guarantees associated with the Constitution"): . . .

mandatory institutional health benefits (such as coverage for hospital expenses) provided by Part A. Subject to an amount in controversy requirement, individuals aggrieved by delayed or insufficient payment with respect to benefits payable under Part B are afforded an "opportunity for a fair hearing by the *carrier*." In comparison, and subject to a like amount in controversy requirement, a similarly aggrieved individual under Part A is entitled "to a hearing thereon by the *Secretary* . . . and to judicial review."

"In the context of the statute's precisely drawn provisions," we held in *United States v. Erika, Inc.*, 456 U.S. 201, that the failure "to authorize further review for determinations of the amount of Part B awards . . . provides persuasive evidence that Congress deliberately intended to foreclose further review of such claims." Not limiting our consideration to the statutory text, we investigated the legislative history which "confirm[ed] this view," and disclosed a purpose to "'avoid overloading the courts'" with "'trivial matters,'" a consequence which would "'unduly ta[x]'" the federal court system with "'little real value'" to be derived by participants in the program.

Respondents' federal-court challenge to the validity of the Secretary's regulation is not foreclosed by § 1395ff as we construed that provision in *Erika*. The reticulated statutory scheme, which carefully details the forum and limits of review of "any determination . . . of . . . the amount of benefits under part A." and of the "amount of . . . payment" of benefits under Part B simply does not speak to challenges mounted against the *method* by which such amounts are to be determined rather than the *determinations* themselves. As the Secretary has made clear, "the legality, constitutional or otherwise, of any provision of the Act or regulations relevant to the Medicare Program" is not considered in a "fair hearing" held by a carrier to resolve a grievance related to a determination of the amount of a Part B award. As a result, an attack on the validity of a regulation is not the kind of administrative action that we described in *Erika* as an "amount determination" which decides "the amount of the Medicare payment to be made on a particular claim" and with respect to which the Act impliedly denies judicial review. . . .

In light of Congress' express provision for carrier review of millions of what it characterized as "trivial" claims, it is implausible to think it intended that there be *no* forum to adjudicate statutory and constitutional challenges to regulations promulgated by the Secretary. The Government nevertheless maintains that this is precisely what Congress intended to accomplish. . . . [W]e will not indulge the Government's assumption that Congress contemplated review by carriers of "trivial" monetary claims, but intended no review at all of substantial statutory and constitutional challenges to the Secretary's administration of Part B of the Medicare program. This is an extreme position, and one we would be most reluctant to adopt without a showing of "clear and convincing evidence," to overcome the "strong presumption that Congress did not mean to prohibit all judicial review" of executive action. We ordinarily presume that Congress intends the executive to obey its statutory commands and, accordingly, that it expects the courts to grant relief when an executive agency violates such a command. That presumption has not been surmounted here.[12]

Notes and Questions

1. *The APA and the presumption of reviewability.* In *Michigan Academy,* the Court relied on legislative history for the proposition that the APA broadened the right to judicial review. However, other legislative history indicates that Congress intended no change in the pre–1946 law of judicial review. *See* ATTORNEY GENERAL'S MANUAL ON THE APA 94 (1947). Regardless of Congressional intent in 1946, the APA has dramatically broadened the right to judicial review—not only as to reviewability but also as to standing and ripeness.

In *United States v. Erika, Inc.,* 456 U.S. 201 (1982), the Court interpreted the provisions at issue in the excerpted portion of *Michigan Academy.* It held that Congress had completely precluded judicial review of a determination by Social Security that it would pay only a certain amount for kidney dialysis supplies used in Medicare Part B. Why did the Court reach a different result in *Michigan Academy?*

2. *Preclusion of review of decisions concerning veterans' benefits.* Congress has explicitly precluded judicial review of decisions relating to claims for veterans' benefits in 38 U.S.C. § 211(a):

> [T]he decisions of the Administrator on any question of law or fact under any law administered by the Veterans' Administration providing benefits for veterans and their dependents or survivors shall be final and conclusive and no other official or any court of the United States shall have power or jurisdiction to review any such decision by an action in the nature of mandamus or otherwise.

Section 211(a) came before the Supreme Court in a case brought by draftees who had rendered alternative service as conscientious objectors (CO's). The statute provided for veterans' benefits only to veterans of military service, but plaintiff asserted that the statutory distinction between CO's and other draftees violated the first and fifth amendments. The Court held that § 211(a) did not apply and it decided the constitutional claims on the merits (it rejected them). *Johnson v. Robison,* 415 U.S. 361 (1974). Why did § 211(a) not preclude judicial review of the constitutional claims?

---

12. Our disposition avoids the "serious constitutional question" that would arise if we construed § 1395(ff) to deny a judicial forum for constitutional claims arising under Part B of the Medicare program. *Johnson v. Robison,* 415 U.S. 361 (1974). *See Yakus v. United States,* 321 U.S. 414 (1944); *St. Joseph Stock Yards Co. v. United States,* 298 U.S. 38, 84 (1936) (Brandeis, J., concurring); Gunther, Congressional Power to Curtail Federal Court Jurisdiction: An Opinionated Guide to the Ongoing Debate, 36 Stanford L.Rev. 895, 921, n. 113 (1984) ("[A]ll agree that Congress cannot bar all remedies for enforcing federal constitutional rights"). Cf. Hart, The Power of Congress to Limit the Jurisdiction of Federal Courts: An Exercise in Dialectic. 66 Harv.L.Rev. 1362, 1378–1379 (1953).

In a split decision, the Court of Appeals held that § 211(a) precludes judicial review where the only issue was the procedural validity of a regulation adopted by the VA concerning veterans' benefits. *Gott v. Walters*, 756 F.2d 902 (D.C.Cir.1985), rehearing en banc granted, vacated and dismissed, 791 F.2d 172 (D.C.Cir.1985) (Scalia, J.). *Gott* considered the validity of a VA rule (adopted without notice and comment under the APA) that servicemen exposed to radiation at Hiroshima and in nuclear bomb tests did not suffer service-connected injury. Is *Gott* consistent with *Michigan Academy?* With *Johnson v. Robison?* And recall *Walters v. Radiation Survivors* in § 2.4, *supra* (right to counsel in complex VA benefit adjudications).

3. *Finality statutes.* As cases like *Johnson v. Robison* show, the courts frequently construe apparently preclusive statutory language to permit some form of review. Thus a statute providing that certain agency action "shall be final" is often read to permit review of the action on some grounds or by some means. See, e.g., *Shaughnessy v. Pedreiro*, 349 U.S. 48 (1955) ("shall be final" means final in administrative branch and is not intended to preclude judicial review); *Harmon v. Brucker*, 355 U.S. 579 (1958) (findings "shall be final subject only to review by the Secretary of the Army" permits review where Board exceeded statutory powers by taking illegal factor into account); *Estep v. United States*, 327 U.S. 114 (1946) ("shall be final" allows court to determine if draft board acted within its jurisdiction when issue is raised in defense of criminal prosecution for refusal to be inducted).

4. *Constitutionality of preclusion of review.* Perhaps the most important part of *Michigan Academy* is the final footnote. This dictum speaks to one of the great unresolved controversies of constitutional law: the power of Congress to deprive federal courts of jurisdiction over constitutional issues (such as abortion or school prayer). As in *Michigan Academy* and *Johnson v. Robison*, the Court generally construes preclusion statutes to permit review of constitutional issues, thus avoiding the problem. Again, in *Webster v. Doe*, 108 S.Ct. 2047 (1988), the Court indicated that Congress had precluded review of the merits of certain employment decisions by the CIA but had not chosen to preclude review of constitutional claims. "Where Congress intends to preclude judicial review of constitutional claims its intent to do so must be clear." However, Justice Scalia in dissent argued strongly that Congress constitutionally could have and did preclude review of both statutory and constitutional claims.

We cannot do justice to this debate here. See, e.g., Tribe, AMERICAN CONSTITUTIONAL LAW §§ 3–5 (2d ed. 1988). The consensus is that Congress can probably deprive the federal courts of the power to review some disputes (such as claims for veterans' or Medicare benefits), but cannot deny litigants a federal forum for the assertion of constitutional claims (Scalia's dissent in *Webster v. Doe, supra*, takes strong issue with the latter assertion).

Most authorities argue that Congress must permit judicial review of prior administrative action (even for nonconstitutional errors) in the context of a civil or criminal enforcement action. A good example is *United States v. Mendoza–Lopez,* 481 U.S. 828 (1987). This case involved a criminal prosecution of an alien for illegal entry into the country following an earlier deportation for a prior illegal entry. A second illegal entry, after a prior deportation, is a felony; thus the earlier deportation was an element of the crime. The Court held that due process requires that the prior deportation be judicially reviewable, *either* at the time it occurred or in the criminal trial relating to the second illegal entry.

Does the *Mendoza–Lopez* decision mean that Congress can always validly preclude review, at the time of an enforcement proceeding, if review was available at the time of the earlier administrative action? Suppose that the subject of the enforcement action did not even know about the earlier agency action in time to seek review of it?

Yakus v. United States, 321 U.S. 414 (1944), involved regulations setting maximum prices for goods during wartime. The only time the regulations could be challenged was by an action brought in the Emergency Court of Appeals within 60 days after the regulation was promulgated. The statute provided that persons who were criminally prosecuted for violating a price regulation could not question its validity.

Yakus was criminally charged with violating a regulation which set a ceiling price for meat. He had not challenged the regulation within 60 days of its adoption. Over a strong dissent by Justice Rutledge, the Court held that he could not challenge the regulation in his criminal trial. However, the majority reserved the question of whether Congress could preclude a *constitutional* challenge to the regulation.

Is *Yakus* still good law? Or should it be treated as a precedent applicable only in a wartime emergency? *Yakus* has served as the prototype for a number of modern environmental statutes which permit pre-enforcement review of rules—and preclude review of the rules in subsequent enforcement actions against polluters who violate the rules. *See* Verkuil, "Congressional Limitations on Judicial Review of Rules," 57 Tul.L.Rev. 733 (1983). Considerable doubt was cast on *Yakus* in *Adamo Wrecking Co. v. United States,* 434 U.S. 275 (1978), in which the court construed an environmental statute to avoid the issue.

5. *State law.* The states vary considerably in their approach to preclusion of judicial review. The majority seem to follow federal law: subject to due process constraints, the legislature can preclude judicial review but statutes that do so are narrowly construed. See, e.g., *Guardian Life Ins. Co. v. Bohlinger,* 124 N.E.2d 110 (N.Y.1954) (despite preclusion statute judicial review available if action is ultra vires); *City Council of Watertown v. Carbone,* 389 N.Y.S.2d 678 (App.Div.1976) (finality statute allows review if decision is "purely arbitrary"). Other

states appear to allow preclusion without any exceptions. *See Neyland v. Board of Educ.,* 487 A.2d 181 (Conn.1985); *Mason v. Thetford School Bd.,* 457 A.2d 647 (Vt.1983).

At the other extreme, some states do not permit any preclusion of review. *See Salk v. Weinraub,* 390 N.E.2d 995 (Ind.1979) (statute cannot preclude review of local decision to approve urban renewal). In some states, constitutional provisions guarantee a right of judicial review of all quasijudicial agency action affecting private rights; such provisions would invalidate a preclusion statute. *See State ex rel. Missouri Power & Light Co. v. Riley,* 546 S.W.2d 792 (Mo.App.1977); *McAvoy v. H.B. Sherman Co.,* 258 N.W.2d 414 (Mich.1977).

6. *Problem.* Veterans are entitled to educational assistance ("The G.I. Bill of Rights") for ten years following their military service. According to the statute, the ten year period can be extended if a veteran is prevented from using the benefits earlier by a "physical or mental disorder which was not the result of willful misconduct." Ted sought to claim educational benefits twelve years after his service ended; he was prevented from using them earlier because he had been an alcoholic. However, he now claims to be completely cured of alcoholism. VA regulations state that alcoholism is "willful misconduct."

Ted claims that this regulation is ultra vires and also that it is contrary to the federal Rehabilitation Act which prohibits discrimination in federal programs on the basis of handicap. He sues in federal district court to invalidate the regulation. The VA argues that judicial review is precluded under § 211(a), quoted in note 2, *supra.* Should the court dismiss the case? *See Traynor v. Turnage,* 108 S.Ct. 1372 (1988).

§ 10.5 COMMITMENT TO AGENCY DISCRETION

Chapter 9.4 *supra* considered the scope of judicial review of discretionary action. You should review that material now. This subchapter considers agency action which is unreviewable because it is "committed to agency discretion by law." APA § 701(a)(2). Thus the federal APA contemplates two kinds of agency discretion—that which is reviewable under APA § 706(2)(A) ("arbitrary, capricious, an abuse of discretion, or otherwise not in accordance with law") and that which is not reviewable at all. Note that § 701(a)(2) provides for judicial review "except to the extent that— . . ." Thus a decision may be partly unreviewable, because committed to agency discretion, but partly reviewable.

HECKLER v. CHANEY
470 U.S. 821 (1985).

[Chaney is a prisoner sentenced to death by lethal injection under Texas law. He petitioned the Food and Drug Administration (FDA), alleging that the use of drugs for capital punishment violated the food and drug law (because it was an unapproved use) and petitioned FDA to take enforcement action to prevent the violation. The FDA Commissioner refused to do so, disagreeing with Chaney's construction of the law and also concluding that he had discretion not to enforce the law where there is no serious danger to the public health or a blatant scheme to defraud. The lower court held that FDA's refusal to take enforcement action was reviewable and an abuse of discretion.]

REHNQUIST, J.:

. . . In reaching our conclusion that the Court of Appeals was wrong we need not and do not address the thorny question of the FDA's jurisdiction. For us, this case turns on the important question of the extent to which determinations by the FDA *not to exercise* its enforcement authority over the use of drugs in interstate commerce may be judicially reviewed. That decision in turn involves the construction of two separate but necessarily interrelated statutes, the APA and the FDCA.

The APA's comprehensive provisions for judicial review of "agency actions" are contained in 5 U.S.C. §§ 701–706. Any person "adversely affected or aggrieved" by agency action, see § 702, including a "failure to act," is entitled to "judicial review thereof," as long as the action is a "final agency action for which there is no other adequate remedy in a court," see § 704. The standards to be applied on review are governed by the provisions of § 706. But before any review at all may be had, a party must first clear the hurdle of § 701(a). That section provides that the chapter on judicial review "applies, according to the provisions thereof, except to the extent that—(1) statutes preclude judicial review; or (2) agency action is committed to agency discretion by law." Petitioner urges that the decision of the FDA to refuse enforcement is an action "committed to agency discretion by law" under § 701(a)(2).[2]

This Court has not had occasion to interpret this second exception in § 701(a) in any great detail. On its face, the section does not obviously lend itself to any particular construction; indeed, one might wonder what difference exists between § 701(a)(1) and § 701(a)(2). The former section seems easy in application; it requires construction of the substantive statute involved to determine whether Congress intended to preclude judicial review of certain decisions. That is the approach taken with respect to § (a)(1) . . . But one could read the language "committed to agency discretion *by law*" in § (a)(2) to require a similar inquiry. In addition, commentators have pointed out that construction of § (a)(2) is further complicated by the tension between a literal reading of § (a)(2), which exempts from judicial review those decisions committed to agency "discretion," and the primary scope of review prescribed by § 706(2)(A)—whether the agency's action was "arbitrary, capricious, or an *abuse of discretion*." How is it, they ask, that an

2. . . . Respondents have not challenged the statement that all they sought were certain enforcement actions, and this case therefore does not involve the question of agency discretion not to invoke rulemaking proceedings.

action committed to agency discretion can be unreviewable and yet courts still can review agency actions for abuse of that discretion? . . . [W]e think there is a proper construction of § (a)(2) which satisfies each of these concerns.

This Court first discussed § (a)(2) in *Citizens to Preserve Overton Park v. Volpe.* That case dealt with the Secretary of Transportation's approval of the building of an interstate highway through a park in Memphis, Tennessee. The relevant federal statute provided that the Secretary "shall not approve" any program or project using public parkland unless the Secretary first determined that no feasible alternatives were available. . . . After setting out the language of § 701(a), the Court stated:

> Similarly, the Secretary's decision here does not fall within the exception for action 'committed to agency discretion.' This is a very narrow exception. . . . The legislative history of the Administrative Procedure Act indicates that it is applicable in those rare instances where 'statutes are drawn in such broad terms that in a given case there is no law to apply.' . . .

The above quote answers several of the questions raised by the language of § 701(a), although it raises others. First, it clearly separates the exception provided by § (a)(1) from the § (a)(2) exception. The former applies when Congress has expressed an intent to preclude judicial review. The latter applies in different circumstances; even where Congress has not affirmatively precluded review, review is not to be had if the statute is drawn so that a court would have no meaningful standard against which to judge the agency's exercise of discretion. In such a case, the statute ("law") can be taken to have "committed" the decisionmaking to the agency's judgment absolutely. This construction avoids conflict with the "abuse of discretion" standard of review in § 706—if no judicially manageable standards are available for judging how and when an agency should exercise its discretion then it is impossible to evaluate agency action for "abuse of discretion." In addition, this construction satisfies the principle of statutory construction mentioned earlier, by identifying a separate class of cases to which § 701(a)(2) applies.

To this point our analysis does not differ significantly from that of the Court of Appeals. That court purported to apply the "no law to apply" standard of *Overton Park.* We disagree, however, with that court's insistence that the "narrow construction" of § (a)(2) required application of a presumption of reviewability even to an agency's decision not to undertake certain enforcement actions. Here we think the Court of Appeals broke with tradition, case law, and sound reasoning.

Overton Park did not involve an agency's refusal to take requested enforcement action. It involved an affirmative act of approval under a statute that set clear guidelines for determining when such approval should be given. Refusals to take enforcement steps generally involve precisely the opposite situation, and in that situation we think the presumption is that judicial review is not available. This Court has recognized on several occasions over many years that an agency's decision not to prosecute or enforce, whether through civil or criminal process, is a decision generally committed to an agency's absolute discretion. This recognition of the existence of discretion is attributable in no small part to the general unsuitability for judicial review of agency decisions to refuse enforcement.

The reasons for this general unsuitability are many. First, an agency decision not to enforce often involves a complicated balancing of a number of factors which are peculiarly within its expertise. Thus, the agency must not only assess whether a violation has occurred, but whether agency resources are best spent on this violation or another, whether the agency is likely to succeed if it acts, whether the particular enforcement action requested best fits the agency's overall policies, and indeed, whether the agency has enough resources to undertake the action at all. An agency generally cannot act against each technical violation of the statute it is charged with enforcing. The agency is far better equipped than the courts to deal with the many variables involved in the proper ordering of its priorities. Similar concerns animate the principles of administrative law that courts generally will defer to an agency's construction of the statute it is charged with implementing, and to the procedures it adopts for implementing that statute.

In addition to these administrative concerns, we note that when an agency refuses to act it generally does not exercise its *coercive* power over an individual's liberty or property rights, and thus does not infringe upon areas that courts often are called upon to protect. Similarly, when an agency *does* act to enforce, that action itself provides a focus for judicial review, inasmuch as the agency must have exercised its power in some manner. The action at least can be reviewed to determine whether the agency exceeded its statutory powers. Finally, we recognize that an agency's refusal to institute proceedings shares to some extent the characteristics of the decision of a prosecutor in the Executive Branch not to indict—a decision which has long been regarded as the special province of the Executive Branch, inasmuch as it is the executive who is charged by the Constitution to "take care that the Laws be faithfully executed." U.S. Const., Art. II, § 3.

We of course only list the above concerns to facilitate understanding of our conclusion that an agency's decision not to take enforcement action should be presumed immune from judicial review under § 701(a)(2). For good reasons, such a decision has traditionally been "committed to agency discretion," and we believe that the Congress enacting the APA did not intend to alter that tradition. Cf. Davis, § 28.5 (APA did not significantly alter the "common law" of judicial review of agency action). In so stating, we emphasize that the decision is only presumptively unreviewable; the presumption may be rebutted where the substantive statute has provided guidelines for the agency to follow in exercising its enforcement powers.[4] Thus, in establishing this presumption in the APA, Congress did not set agencies free to disregard legislative direction in the statutory scheme that the agency administers. Congress may limit an agency's exercise of enforcement power if it wishes, either by setting substantive priorities, or by otherwise circumscribing an agency's power to discriminate among issues or cases it will pursue. How to determine when Congress has done so is the question left open by *Overton Park.*

Dunlop v. Bachowski, 421 U.S. 560, relied upon heavily by respondents and the majority in the Court of Appeals, presents an example of statutory language which supplied sufficient standards to rebut the presumption of unreviewability. *Dunlop* involved a suit by a union employee, under the Labor–Management Reporting and Disclosure Act, (LMRDA), asking the National Labor Relations Board to investigate and file suit to set aside a union election. Section 482 provided that, upon filing of a complaint by a union member, "[t]he Secretary shall investigate such complaint and, if he finds probable cause to believe that a violation . . . has occurred . . . he shall . . . bring a civil action. . . ." After investigating the plaintiff's claims the Secretary of Labor declined to file suit, and the plaintiff sought judicial review under the APA. This Court held that review was available. . . . It [relied] on the Court of Appeals' opinion to hold that the § (a)(2) exception did not apply. The Court of Appeals, in turn, had found the "principle of absolute prosecutorial discretion" inapplicable, because the language of the LMRDA indicated that the Secretary was required to file suit if certain "clearly defined" factors were present. The decision therefore was not " 'beyond the judicial capacity to supervise.' "

Dunlop is thus consistent with a general presumption of unreviewability of decisions not to enforce. The statute being administered quite clearly withdrew discretion from the agency and provided guidelines for exercise of its enforcement power. Our decision that review was available was not based on "pragmatic considerations," such as those cited by the Court of Appeals that amount to an assessment of whether the interests at stake are important enough to justify intervention in the agencies' decisionmaking. The danger that agencies may not carry out their delegated powers with sufficient vigor does not necessarily lead to the conclusion that courts are the most appropriate

---

4. We do not have in this case a refusal by the agency to institute proceedings based solely on the belief that it lacks jurisdiction. Nor do we have a situation where it could justifiably be found that the agency has "consciously and expressly adopted a general policy" that is so extreme as to amount to an abdication of its statutory responsibilities. See, *e.g., Adams v. Richardson,* 480 F.2d 1159 (1973) (en banc). Although we express no opinion on whether such decisions would be unreviewable under § 701(a)(2), we note that in those situations the statute conferring authority on the agency might indicate that such decisions were not "committed to agency discretion."

body to police this aspect of their performance. That decision is in the first instance for Congress, and we therefore turn to the FDCA to determine whether in this case Congress has provided us with "law to apply." If it has indicated an intent to circumscribe agency enforcement discretion, and has provided meaningful standards for defining the limits of that discretion, there is "law to apply" under § 701(a)(2), and courts may require that the agency follow that law; if it has not, then an agency refusal to institute proceedings is a decision "committed to agency discretion by law" within the meaning of that section. . . . The Act's enforcement provisions thus commit complete discretion to the Secretary to decide how and when they should be exercised. . . .

The Court of Appeals placed considerable weight on an FDA policy statement that seemed to constrain enforcement discretion. However, the statement was attached to a rule that was never adopted. Whatever force such a statement might have, and leaving to one side the problem of whether an agency's rules might under certain circumstances provide courts with adequate guidelines for informed judicial review of decisions not to enforce, we do not think the language of the agency's "policy statement" can plausibly be read to override the agency's express assertion of unreviewable discretion contained in the above rule.

IV

. . . The FDA's decision not to take the enforcement actions requested by respondents is therefore not subject to judicial review under the APA. The general exception to reviewability provided by § 701(a)(2) for action "committed to agency discretion" remains a narrow one, see *Overton Park,* but within that exception are included agency refusals to institute investigative or enforcement proceedings, unless Congress has indicated otherwise. In so holding, we essentially leave to Congress, and not to the courts, the decision as to whether an agency's refusal to institute proceedings should be judicially reviewable. No colorable claim is made in this case that the agency's refusal to institute proceedings violated any constitutional rights of respondents, and we do not address the issue that would be raised in such a case. Cf. *Johnson v. Robison,* 415 U.S. 361; *Yick Wo v. Hopkins,* 118 U.S. 356.

The fact that the drugs involved in this case are ultimately to be used in imposing the death penalty must not lead this Court or other courts to import profound differences of opinion over the meaning of the Eighth Amendment to the United States Constitution into the domain of administrative law.

The judgment of the Court of Appeals is

Reversed.

JUSTICE MARSHALL, concurring in the judgment.

I write separately to argue for a different basis of decision: that refusals to enforce, like other agency actions, are reviewable in the absence of a "clear and convincing" congressional intent to the contrary, but that such refusals warrant deference when, as in this case, there is nothing to suggest that an agency with enforcement discretion has abused that discretion. . . . [Justice Brennan concurred in the majority opinion but wrote briefly to point out the numerous issues left open in that opinion.]

Notes and Questions

1. *No law to apply.* Recall *Webster v. Doe,* 108 S.Ct. 2047 (1988), discussed in § 10.4, *supra. Webster* involved termination without giving any reasons of "Doe," a CIA employee who had voluntarily informed the agency that he was a homosexual. The CIA director acted under § 102(c) of the National Security Act which provides that "The [CIA] Director may, in his discretion, terminate the employment of any officer or employee of the Agency whenever he shall deem such termination necessary or advisable in the interests of the United States . . ." Doe argued that the decision was arbitrary and capricious and an abuse of discretion, in part because of the lack of any statement of reasons.

After reviewing *Overton Park* and *Chaney v. Heckler,* Justice Rehnquist's opinion held that the decision was not judicially reviewable on these grounds. He emphasized the word "deem" in the statute. "This standard fairly exudes deference to the Director, and appears to us to foreclose the application of any meaningful judicial standard of review. Short of permitting cross-examination of the Director concerning his views of the Nation's security and whether the discharged employee was inimical to those interests, we see no basis on which a reviewing court could properly assess an Agency termination decision." He also relied on the entire structure of the Act and the peculiar need for protecting intelligence sources and assuring the reliability and trustworthiness of CIA employees. Recall, however, that the Court also held that the CIA's decision was reviewable on *constitutional* grounds and it remanded to the lower court for that purpose.

Justice Scalia concurred that CIA employment decisions under § 102(c) are committed by law to agency discretion under APA § 701(a)(2) but he criticized the majority opinion for inferring that the only basis for applying § 701(a)(2) was in cases where there is "no law to apply." He wrote:

> The key to understanding the "committed to agency discretion *by law*" provision of § 701(a)(2) lies in contrasting it with the "*statutes* preclude judicial review" provision of § 701(a)(1). Why "statutes" for preclusion, but the much more general term "law" for commission to agency discretion? The answer is, as we implied in *Chaney,* that the latter was intended to refer to "the 'common law' of judicial review of agency action," . . .—a body of jurisprudence that had marked out, with more or less precision, certain issues and certain areas that were beyond the range of judicial review. That jurisprudence included principles ranging from the "political

question" doctrine, to sovereign immunity . . . to official immunity, to prudential limitations upon the courts' equitable powers, to what can be described no more precisely than a traditional respect for the functions of the other branches . . .

All this law, shaped over the course of centuries and still developing in its application to new contexts, cannot possibly be contained within the phrase "no law to apply." It is not surprising, then, that although the Court recites the test it does not really apply it . . . It is not really true "that a court would have no meaningful standard against which to judge the agency's exercise of discretion . . ." The standard set forth in § 102(c) . . . "necessary or advisable in the interests of the United States," at least excludes dismissal out of personal vindictiveness, or because the Director wants to give the job to his cousin. Why, on the Court's theory, is respondent not entitled to assert the presence of such excesses, under the "abuse of discretion" standard of § 706?

2. *Affirmative v. negative.* While the *Chaney* decision agreed with *Overton Park* that the exception in § 701(a)(2) was "very narrow" in cases of affirmative agency action, it held that an agency decision *not* to enforce the law is presumed to be unreviewable. What reasons does Justice Rehnquist give for this presumption? Are they persuasive?

The majority opinion mentions numerous possible exceptions to the presumption. How many can you list? Why did Justice Rehnquist take such care to mention the issues he was not deciding?

Is it feasible to review agency non-enforcement decisions? Prior to *Chaney,* the leading Supreme Court case on the review of agency inaction was *Dunlop v. Bachowski,* 421 U.S. 560 (1975), summarized in *Chaney.* In *Dunlop,* the Secretary of Labor had refused to file an action at plaintiff's request to set aside a union election.

The Court did not require the Secretary to file suit but it did require him to provide a statement of reasons supporting his refusal to do so. Then a reviewing court could decide from the statement of reasons whether the Secretary's decision was arbitrary and capricious. However, the court could not go behind the statement of reasons. Justice Rehnquist dissented, on the ground that the Secretary's action was not reviewable under APA § 701(a)(2). How does Rehnquist distinguish *Dunlop* in his *Chaney* opinion? Could the Court have applied the *Dunlop* principle in *Webster v. Doe,* note 1, *supra?*

In *Chaney,* the Court holds that Congress imposed no limits on the FDA's enforcement discretion. Is this an invalid delegation of power? How would Rehnquist reconcile his concurring opinion in the *Benzene* case, *supra* § 7.3, with his conclusion in *Chaney* that there was no law to apply and, therefore, the agency's inaction was unreviewable?

3. *Agency inaction and rights of initiation.* Note that plaintiffs who complain of agency *inaction* are likely to be the persons who are beneficiaries of the statutory scheme. Suppose your clients ask FDA or

EPA to take action against a particular health hazard, but the agency does nothing. Will a court compel the agency to take action if it finds the agency's inaction to be arbitrary and capricious? What other remedies should your clients consider?

How about:

(i) considering the various loopholes left by the *Chaney* decision? For example, did the legislature really give the agency discretion to refuse to regulate? *See Farmworker Justice Fund v. Brock*, 811 F.2d 613 (D.C.Cir.1987) (court can review question of whether Congress gave OSHA discretion to refuse to adopt any standard guaranteeing farmworkers access to potable drinking water and toilets), vacated as moot, 817 F.2d 890 (D.C.Cir.1987).

(ii) construing the statute to provide a private right of action against the person creating the health hazard? The implication of such private rights is discussed in § 11.2.5 *infra*.

(iii) petitioning the agency to adopt a legislative rule on the subject or a policy statement that would structure its discretion?

(iv) engaging in political action—either through grass roots activism or lobbying the legislature to take corrective action?

4. *Refusal to make a rule.* Recall the *State Farm* case (§ 9.4 *supra*) in which the Court invalidated NHTSA's rescission of its safety standard. What if NHTSA had refused to adopt any standard relating to seatbelts in the first place? Could a court review that decision? *See* note 2 in *Chaney.*

In decisions both prior to and after *Chaney,* courts tentatively asserted power to review an agency decision refusing to adopt a rule after conducting a rulemaking proceeding. *Natural Resources Defense Council v. SEC,* 606 F.2d 1031 (D.C.Cir.1979); *Farmworkers Justice Fund v. Brock, supra.* In the *NRDC* case, the SEC invited comments on whether it should adopt rules requiring corporations to make greater disclosure of environmental problems in proxy solicitations. Ultimately, the SEC decided not to adopt any rule at all.

In applying § 701(a)(2), the Court of Appeals held that it should balance i) the need for judicial supervision to safeguard the plaintiff's interests, ii) the impact of review on the effectiveness of the agency in carrying out its role, iii) and the appropriateness of the issues for judicial review. The first factor pointed away from reviewability but because the SEC had actually conducted a lengthy notice and comment proceeding, the second two factors pointed toward reviewability. It was this sort of pragmatic balance that the Supreme Court rejected in *Chaney.*

Ultimately, the Court held the SEC's decision was not arbitrary and capricious, but it reviewed the SEC's explanation for its decision, found the explanation rational, and ascertained that there was factual support in the record for that explanation.

In *WWHT v. FCC,* 656 F.2d 807 (D.C.Cir.1981), the court reviewed an agency's decision not to start rulemaking proceedings after receiving a petition to make a rule under APA § 553(e). Again, the court was quite deferential. It required only an explanation of the policy concerns that led the agency to refuse to act and some factual support for these conclusions in the record.

Which is better—absolute preclusion of review of non-enforcement decisions, as in *Chaney,* or cautious and deferential review as in *NRDC* and *WWHT?*

5. *State law.* How would *Chaney* be decided under the 1981 MSAPA? *See* §§ 1–102(2), 5–102(a), 5–116(c)(8). In an action for mandamus?

6. *Problem.* The Farmers Home Administration (FmHA) is a federal agency that makes loans to farmers. Section 19 of FmHA's statute provides: "At the request of the borrower, the Secretary of Agriculture may permit the deferral of principal and interest payments on any outstanding loan, and may forego foreclosure of any such loan, for such period as the Secretary deems necessary upon a showing by the borrower that due to circumstances beyond the borrower's control, the borrower is temporarily unable to continue making such payments when due without impairing the standard of living of the borrower."

The House Report accompanying the bill which contained § 19 said: "The purpose of this legislation is to broaden FmHA's authority to cope with today's problems and be of greater service to farmers and the rural community."

Mary failed to make payments of principal or interest on her $250,000 FmHA loan because of a disastrous drought which wiped out her crop. The FmHA foreclosed the loan and sold her farm; Mary appeals from the judgment of foreclosure. Mary did not request FmHA to defer payments or to forego foreclosure because she did not know about § 19 until after foreclosure was completed.

FmHA has never used its authority under § 19 to defer payments or forego foreclosure because it believes that the program is permissive, not mandatory. It has never notified any borrowers about its authority under § 19.

Should the court affirm the judgment of foreclosure and, if not, what relief should it grant?

Suppose FmHA did occasionally exercise its § 19 authority—but declined to do so in Mary's case. Would that decision be reviewable? *See United States v. Markgraf,* 736 F.2d 1179 (7th Cir.1984), *cert. dismisd.,* 469 U.S. 1199 (1985).

Chapter 11

STANDING TO SEEK JUDICIAL REVIEW AND THE TIMING OF JUDICIAL REVIEW

This chapter considers several important obstacles to seeking judicial review. First, it addresses the issue of standing—can a particular plaintiff seek review? Second, it considers timing issues—has the plaintiff sought review prematurely?

§ 11.1 STANDING TO SEEK REVIEW

In the history of administrative law, few issues have remained as contentious and as unsettled as the question of whether a particular individual or entity can seek the aid of a court to review the legality of government action.

In part, standing to sue in federal court is a constitutional doctrine, one of several access restrictions encompassed under the nebulous term "justiciability." Under Article III, a federal court can only entertain "cases" or "controversies." The "case or controversy" requirement is not satisfied unless a plaintiff or appellant has a sufficient stake in the dispute to justify judicial intervention. In part, the standing doctrine is also statutory; statutes (including the APA) often provide the basis for standing to seek review or preclude review which otherwise would be available. Finally, standing has a "prudential" component, meaning that in some circumstances the federal courts will deny standing to someone who otherwise would be entitled to it. In reading the materials which follow, try to separate these three strands of standing doctrine.

What are the reasons for restricting standing to seek judicial review? Why should anyone who is willing to file suit to challenge agency action not be permitted to do so? Another important question is when (if ever) standing should be allowed to plaintiffs representing third persons or the public interest, as they see it, as opposed to their own private interest. To take an extreme example, should an individual be allowed to go to court to enjoin government action which would destroy an endangered species of animal or plant life?

Consider this situation: John owns a bar. His license to operate it is revoked because he served liquor to minors. John, of course, can challenge the revocation on substantive or procedural grounds, but who else should be allowed to do so? His family (supported by John out of the profits from the bar)? His employees or customers? Other bar owners who fear that the same thing could happen to them? Does it matter that John himself refuses to challenge the revocation?

In evaluating these materials, be sure to ask also whether standing serves as a surrogate for a decision on the substantive issues: are judges voting to grant or deny standing because they wish to decide, or to avoid, the underlying legal questions in the case?

Federal standing doctrine has evolved over time and continues to evolve today. Consequently, the doctrine cannot be understood without a brief historical introduction.

§ 11.1.1 STANDING TO SEEK REVIEW IN THE FEDERAL COURTS: HISTORICAL INTRODUCTION

When a person seeking judicial review has been ordered to do something or stop doing something (whether through rulemaking or adjudication), that person's standing to seek review is unquestioned. Thus a person ordered to pay money, to charge a specific rate, or to cease and desist from a business practice, or whose license was revoked or whose property was seized, is an appropriate person to seek judicial review of the government action in question.

Historically, however, standing is very much in issue when an individual is harmed indirectly by government action that directly involves someone else. As an example of indirect harm, consider the plight of a business which is the subject of unwanted competition, either by the government itself or by a government licensee. Suppose that the afflicted business person has a plausible argument that the competition is unlawful; is judicial review available?

For many decades, the answer to this question was no. This result flowed logically from the "legal wrong" approach to standing. This test requires an analysis of whether a plaintiff has a *common law* right to prevent a *private* defendant from engaging in the same activity in which the government is engaged. If, but only if, there is such a common law right in tort, property, or contract law, the plaintiff has standing to seek judicial review of the government action.

Under the legal wrong test, a person subjected to allegedly illegal competition from the government or from a government licensee had no standing. Thus, in *Tennessee Electric Power Co. v. TVA*, 306 U.S. 118 (1939), private power companies sought to enjoin the federal government, in the guise of the Tennessee Valley Authority (TVA), from competing with them on the ground that the Constitution does not allow the federal government to enter the electric power business.

Since there is no common law right to enjoin competition in our free market system, it followed that the power companies had no standing to raise this claim against the government. Does the "legal wrong" test seem an appropriate technique to assess whether a plaintiff should have standing to challenge agency action in court?

The courts recognized one major exception to the "legal wrong" test. A statute might confer standing on a particular plaintiff to seek review even when no common law "legal wrong" had occurred. Statutory standing might be inferred from a provision which evidenced a legislative intention to benefit the plaintiff's class. *See Hardin v. Kentucky Utilities Co.,* 390 U.S. 1 (1968) (competitor of TVA has standing to challenge its actions because Congress enacted a statute protecting certain TVA competitors). Alternatively, standing might flow from a provision allowing members of the plaintiff's class to seek judicial review. *See FCC v. Sanders Brothers Radio Station,* 309 U.S. 470 (1940).

In *Sanders Brothers,* the FCC granted a license to a radio station which would compete with another operated by Sanders. The *TVA* case had established that unwelcome competition by a government licensee cannot be the basis for standing. However, a statute provided that anyone "aggrieved or whose interests were adversely affected" by a licensing decision of the FCC could seek review. The Supreme Court held that the FCC should concern itself only with the public interest when it made a licensing decision. Economic harm to a competitor is not, in itself, an appropriate reason to deny a license (although it is relevant if the competition would be harmful to the public interest).

Nevertheless, under the statute, Sanders was "aggrieved" and thus had standing to question the legality of the Commission's order as a surrogate for the public interest (even though Sanders really wished only to vindicate its own interest, not that of the public). In effect, the statute had deputized Sanders to serve as a "private attorney general," litigating solely to vindicate the right of the public to a correct interpretation and application of a federal law.

As finally enacted in 1946, § 10(a) of the federal APA (now the first sentence of § 702) provided: "A person suffering legal wrong because of agency action, or adversely affected or aggrieved by agency action within the meaning of a relevant statute, is entitled to judicial review thereof." Given the pre–1946 case law discussed above, did § 10(a) change the law? Did it overrule cases like *Tennessee Elec. Power v. TVA?* In his authoritative Manual on the APA, the Attorney General argued that § 10(a) did not change the law. P. 96 (1947).

Between 1946 and 1970, the issue of whether § 10(a) changed or merely restated prior law remained unresolved. Nevertheless, the lower courts pushed the available precedents to the limit. For example, under the same statute construed in *Sanders Brothers,* the Court of Appeals held that television viewers had standing to challenge a renewal of a TV license.

United Church of Christ v. FCC, 359 F.2d 994 (D.C.Cir.1966), involved a challenge by television viewers to renewal of the license of WLBT, Jackson, Mississippi. The basis of the challenge was that WLBT failed to serve the interests of black viewers and that it was guilty of overt racism in its programming. The Court of Appeals (in a famous decision written by Warren Burger) held that the viewers had standing both to intervene as a party before the FCC and to seek judicial review to "vindicate the broad public interest relating to a licensee's performance of the public trust inherent in every license." In the past, the Court noted, it relied on the agency to protect the interest of viewers, but it could no longer indulge in that comfortable assumption. The *Church of Christ* case was also discussed and quoted from at length in § 4.1.1 on the issue of intervention in administrative adjudication.

§ 11.1.2   INJURY IN FACT AND ZONE OF INTEREST TESTS

ASSOCIATION OF DATA PROCESSING SERVICE ORGS. v. CAMP

397 U.S. 150 (1970).

[Petitioners sell data processing services to businesses. They challenge a ruling by the Comptroller of the Currency that national banks may provide such service to their customers. The lower courts dismissed for lack of standing. The Court surveyed prior law and disapproved cases such as *Tennessee Elec. Power.*]

DOUGLAS, J.:

. . . Generalizations about standing to sue are largely worthless as such. One generalization is, however, necessary and that is that the question of standing in the federal courts is to be considered in the framework of Article III which restricts judicial power to "cases" and "controversies." As we recently stated in *Flast v. Cohen*, 392 U.S. 83: "[I]n terms of Article III limitations on federal court jurisdiction, the question of standing is related only to whether the dispute sought to be adjudicated will be presented in an adversary context and in a form historically viewed as capable of judicial resolution." *Flast* was a *taxpayer's* suit. The present is a *competitor's* suit. And while the two have the same Article III starting point, they do not necessarily track one another.

The first question is whether the plaintiff alleges that the challenged action has caused him injury in fact, economic or otherwise. There can be no doubt but that petitioners have satisfied this test. The petitioners not only allege that competition by national banks in the business of providing data processing services might entail some future loss of profits for the petitioners, they also allege that respondent American National Bank & Trust Company was performing or preparing to perform such services for two customers for whom petitioner Data Systems, Inc., had previously agreed or negotiated to perform such services. . . . [The second] question [is] whether the interest sought to be protected by the complainant is arguably within the zone of interests to be protected or regulated by the statute or constitutional guarantee in question. Thus the Administrative Procedure Act grants standing to a person "aggrieved by agency action within the meaning of a relevant statute." § 702. That interest, at times, may reflect "aesthetic, conservational, and recreational" as well as economic values. *Scenic Hudson Preservation Conference v. FPC*, 2 Cir., 354 F.2d 608, 616; *United Church of Christ v. FCC*, . . . A person or a family may have a spiritual stake in First Amendment values sufficient to give standing to raise issues concerning the Establishment Clause and the Free Exercise Clause. We mention these noneconomic values to emphasize that standing may stem from them as well as from the economic injury on which petitioners rely here. Certainly he who is "likely to be financially" injured, *FCC v. Sanders Bros. Radio Station*, may be a reliable private attorney general to litigate the issues of the public interest in the present case. . . .

§ 4 of the Bank Service Corporation Act of 1962 . . . provides: "No bank service corporation may engage in any activity other than the performance of bank services for banks." . . . We think . . . that § 4 arguably brings a competitor within the zone of interests protected by it.

That leaves the remaining question, whether judicial review of the Comptroller's action has been precluded. We do not think it has been. . . . We find no evidence that Congress in either the Bank Service Corporation Act or the National Bank Act sought to preclude judicial review of administrative rulings by the Comptroller as to the legitimate scope of activities available to national banks under those statutes. Both Acts are clearly "relevant" statutes within the meaning of § 702. The Acts do not in terms protect a specified group. But their general policy is apparent; and those whose interests are directly affected by a broad or narrow interpretation of the Acts are easily identifiable. It is clear that petitioners, as competitors of national banks which are engaging in data processing services, are within that class of "aggrieved" persons who, under § 702, are entitled to judicial review of "agency action."

Whether anything in the Bank Service Corporation Act or the National Bank Act gives petitioners a "legal interest" that protects them against violations of those Acts, and whether the actions of respondents did in fact violate either of those Acts, are questions which go to the merits and remain to be decided below.

We hold that petitioners have standing to sue and that the case should be remanded for a hearing on the merits.

[In a case decided the same day as *Data Processing*, the Court held that tenant cotton farmers had standing to challenge a regulation which would allow them, for the first time, to pledge federal subsidy payments to their landlords as security for the payment of rent. The farmers met the "injury in fact" test by alleging that the regulation would allow landlords to demand such assignments, thus increasing their dependency on the landlords. The "zone of interests" test was met because the statute provides that "the Secretary shall provide adequate safeguards to protect the interests of tenants . . ." *Barlow v. Collins,* 397 U.S. 159 (1970).]

JUSTICE BRENNAN, joined by JUSTICE WHITE, concurred in the result of both cases, but disagreed with their reasoning:

. . . My view is that the inquiry in the Court's first step [injury in fact] is the only one that need be made to determine standing. I had thought we discarded the notion of any additional requirement when we discussed standing solely in terms of its constitutional content in *Flast v. Cohen.* By requiring a second, non-constitutional step [zone of interest] the Court comes very close to perpetuating the discredited requirement that conditioned standing on a showing by the plaintiff that the challenged governmental action invaded one of his legally protected interests. . . .

Before the plaintiff is allowed to argue the merits, it is true that a canvass of relevant statutory materials must be made in cases challenging agency action. But the canvass is made, not to determine *standing,* but to determine an aspect of *reviewability;* that is, whether Congress meant to deny or to allow judicial review of the agency action at the instance of the plaintiff. The Court in the present cases examines the statutory materials for just this purpose but only after making the same examination during the second step of its standing inquiry. Thus in *Data Processing* the Court determines that the petitioners have standing because they alleged injury in fact and because "§ 4 [of the Bank Service Corporation Act of 1962] arguably brings a competitor within the zone of interests protected by it." . . .

I submit that in making such examination of statutory materials an element in the determination of standing, the Court not only performs a useless and unnecessary exercise but also encourages badly reasoned decisions, which may well deny justice in this complex field. When agency action is challenged, standing, reviewability, and the merits pose discrete, and often complicated, issues which can best be resolved by recognizing and treating them as such. . . . More fundamentally, an approach that treats separately the distinct issues of standing, reviewability, and the merits, and decides each on the basis of its own criteria, assures that these often complex questions will be squarely faced, thus contributing to better reasoned decisions and to greater confidence that justice has in fact been done. The Court's approach does too little to guard against the possibility that judges will use standing to slam the courthouse door against plaintiffs who are entitled to full consideration of their claims on the merits. The Court's approach must trouble all concerned with the function of the judicial process in today's world.

IOWA BANKERS ASS'N v. IOWA CREDIT UNION DEPT.

335 N.W.2d 439 (Iowa 1983).

[The Credit Union Department adopted rules (pursuant to a revised statute) allowing credit unions to have checking accounts (share-drafts), to make loans secured by real estate, and to open branch offices. The Bankers Association challenged the procedural validity of the rules. The Department challenged the Association's standing.]

. . .

Section 17A.19(1) of the Iowa Administrative Procedure Act (IAPA) provides in relevant part:

A person or party who has exhausted all adequate administrative remedies and who is *aggrieved or adversely affected* by any final agency action is entitled to judicial review under this chapter.

We have utilized a two-part test to determine whether a litigant is "aggrieved or adversely affected." A party must demonstrate a specific, personal, and legal interest in the subject matter of the agency decision, and show that interest has been specially and injuriously affected.

The corresponding provision of the federal Administrative Procedure Act (APA) renders judicial review of agency action available to persons

suffering legal wrong because of agency action, or adversely affected or aggrieved by agency action, within the meaning of a relevant statute.

§ 702. The zone of interest test has been identified by federal courts as arising from the language "within the meaning of a relevant statute." . . . Our statutory requirement on standing to seek judicial review of agency action does not contain the qualifying language present in the federal APA. . . . We decline to read into the statute an intent or meaning not expressed therein. Although ordinarily the primary purpose of an act is easily identified, and the objects of that purpose obviously possess standing, other purposes underlying an act often are uncertain. Agency action may have impact on persons other than those who are the immediate object of the act. We believe the legislature intended to make a judicial remedy available to any person or party who can demonstrate the requisite injury. Our holding finds support in decisions of other state courts that have addressed the issue. . . . The department also contends the association failed to show a specially and injuriously affected, specific, personal, and legal interest in the agency action. . . . Unrebutted testimony supported district court's finding that credit unions compete with banks in providing similar services. The association's competitor status distinguishes its interest from that of the community as a whole, and demonstrates the requisite specific, personal, and legal interest in the agency's rule-making. The only evidence presented regarding a special, injurious effect to the association's interest, however, was unrebutted testimony some banks have lost business as a result of credit union share-draft business. The association failed to show injury, or potential injury, as a result of the rules regarding loans secured by real estate, insolvency, small employee groups, or branch offices. This failure precludes assertion of jurisdiction with regard to these rules. The association's showing of past lost business due to credit union share-draft business is sufficient, however, to demonstrate a special, injurious effect to its competitive interest. Only a likelihood or possibility of injury need be shown. A party need not demonstrate injury will accrue with certainty, or already has accrued.

It may be true, as the department alleges, that the gravamen of the association's complaint is the legislative enactment, rather than the department's rules promulgated pursuant to those statutes. This contention goes to the merits of the association's challenge to the rules, and not to its standing to bring the challenge.

The association contends the legislature has "preselected trade associations with twenty-five or more members as persons always having standing" to challenge agency action. It bases this argument on Iowa Code section 17A.2(6), which defines "person" to include associations for purposes of the IAPA, and section 17A.4, which provides in relevant part:

> 1. Prior to the adoption, amendment, or repeal of any rule an agency shall: . . .

> b. Afford all interested persons not less than twenty days to submit data, views or arguments in writing. If timely requested . . . by an association having not less than twenty-five members, the agency must give interested persons an opportunity to make oral presentation.

Including association within the definition of "person" statutorily recognizes an organization's capacity to represent its members' views. It does not, however, alter the necessity to show adverse effect or aggrievement. Iowa Code section 17A.19 renders these requirements separate and distinct. Neither does the automatic right to make oral presentations during the rule-making process exempt associations from demonstrating adverse effect or aggrievement. Section 17A.4(1)(b) merely grants the opportunity to be heard to "literally anyone who cares enough to do so." The adverse effect or aggrievement requirement is applicable to every party to agency action.

We hold the association has standing to challenge [the rule relating to share draft accounts], but failed to show standing to challenge the remaining rules at issue. . . .

Notes and Questions

1. *Standing and the APA.* Did the Court in *Data Processing* rely on APA § 702 in discarding the legal wrong test? In adopting the zone of interest test? Based on *Data Processing,* how should each phrase in the first sentence of § 702 be construed? Is the injury in fact test the same as the injury test set forth in the *Iowa Bankers* case? Which test is more generous to the plaintiff?

Read 1981 MSAPA § 5–106(a). Does this provision adopt the zone of interest test? Does it come closer to the federal injury test or the Iowa test?

Under § 7 of 1961 MSAPA, which is the law of many states, "the validity or applicability of a rule may be determined in an action for declaratory judgment . . . if it is alleged that the rule, or its threatened application, interferes with or impairs . . . the legal rights or privileges of the plaintiff." How would *Data Processing* and *Iowa Credit Union* have been decided if § 7 applied?

2. *The injury in fact test: non-economic injuries.* Justice Douglas makes clear that article III requires, at a minimum, that a plaintiff must allege that the government action in dispute caused her "injury in fact." In addition to economic injuries, "noneconomic values" such as "aesthetic, conservational, and recreational" claims meet the constitutional test.

For example, in *Duke Power Co. v. Carolina Environmental Study Group, Inc.,* 438 U.S. 59 (1978), plaintiffs asserted that a nuclear power plant to be built in their vicinity would emit radiation into their environment (with potential health and genetic consequences) and would increase the temperature of several lakes used for recreation purposes (with negative aesthetic and environmental consequences). The Court held these harms satisfied the injury in fact test. Similarly, whale watchers have standing to attack governmental decisions that fail to enforce treaties that limit the killing of whales. *Japan Whaling Ass'n v. American Cetacean Soc.,* 478 U.S. 221, 227 n. 4 (1986).

3. *The zone of interests test.* The Supreme Court never took the zone of interests test articulated in *Data Processing* too seriously, but lower courts struggled endlessly with it and commentators unanimously denounced it. Cases like *Iowa Bankers Ass'n.* rejected it under state law. However, other states appear to accept it. *See, e.g., Fox v. Wisconsin Dept. of Health & Soc. Serv.,* 334 N.W.2d 532 (Wis.1983) (plaintiff suffering psychological injury is not within zone of interests protected by statute requiring environmental impact statement); *In re Application of El Rancho Grande, Inc.,* 437 A.2d 1150 (Pa.1981); *Dairylea Coop., Inc. v. Walkley,* 377 N.Y.S.2d 451 (N.Y.1975).

Finally, after seventeen years, the Supreme Court devitalized (but did not completely abandon) the test in *Clarke v. Securities Industry Ass'n,* 479 U.S. 388 (1987). In *Clarke,* the plaintiffs were stock brokers.

They sought review of an agency decision allowing banks to open stock brokerage offices on the theory that such offices would violate a federal statute limiting branch banking.   The Court held that the brokers satisfied the zone test because Congress had expressed concern that branching might give big banks control over money and credit.   The plaintiff's interest (to prevent competition by banks) was plausibly related to this policy (since both banks and stock brokers supply credit).

In explaining the "zone" test, the Court said:

> In cases where the plaintiff is not itself the subject of the contested regulatory action, the test denies a right of review if the plaintiff's interests are so marginally related to or inconsistent with the purposes implicit in the statute that it cannot reasonably be assumed that Congress intended to permit the suit.   The test is not meant to be especially demanding; in particular, there need be no indication of congressional purpose to benefit the would-be plaintiff.

Id. at 757.

In *Clarke,* the Court indicated that the zone of interests test applied only under § 702—not in other contexts where standing is drawn into question.   The Court also made clear that the "relevant statute" in § 702 need not be the one under which the agency acted; a later statute indicating Congressional intention to protect plaintiff would suffice.   Why did the Court not completely abandon the zone of interests test instead of watering it down?

4.   *Standing of agencies.*   Can a government official or an agency that is displeased with the decision of another agency seek judicial review of that decision?   In general, if the plaintiff agency is viewed as a subordinate to the decision-maker, it cannot seek review.   *See, e.g., Mortensen v. Pyramid Sav. & Loan Ass'n,* 191 N.W.2d 730 (Wis.1971) (savings and loan commissioner cannot appeal decision of savings and loan review board).   However, if the plaintiff is a separate agency or governmental unit whose legal mission is jeopardized by the decision, it can seek judicial review.   *See, e.g., Bradford Cen. School Dist. v. Ambach,* 451 N.Y.S.2d 654 (N.Y.1982) (school board can seek review of decision by state education commissioner certifying a teacher).   *See generally* Davis, "Standing of a Public Official to Challenge Agency Decisions: A Unique Problem of State Administrative Law," 16 Admin. L.Rev. 163 (1964).

When a statute creates a separate administrative court, both the government and the private litigant can seek judicial review of such court's decisions.   For example, the Commissioner of Internal Revenue can obtain judicial review of decisions of the United States Tax Court, and OSHA can seek review of decisions by the Occupational Safety and Health Review Commission.

What is the objection to allowing government officials who disagree with agency decisions to appeal them?   Would this not be a valuable check on the tendency of agencies to be captured by the interests they regulate? Or does it entangle a court excessively in conflicts within the executive branch of government?

5. *Problem.* The Legal Services Corp. (a federal agency) established a new office in Florida to provide free legal services to persons in poverty who need representation in family law matters (such as divorce, child custody, or collection of support). The Miami Family Law Bar Association (MFLBA), whose members now represents such persons, challenges LSC's action in federal court. It contends that, properly interpreted, the statute requires each office to provide services to all comers, thus prohibiting specialized offices. Does MFLBA have standing to raise this claim?

Assume that § 8 of the statute creating LSC provides: "The Director of LSC shall consult local bar associations in the community to be served by any proposed project and shall provide an opportunity for them to submit comments and recommendations before the project is funded." Officials of LSC did consult MFLBA before funding the new office but decided to ignore its objections. Does § 8 give MFLBA standing? *See Troutman v. Shriver,* 417 F.2d 171 (5th Cir.1969), *cert. denied,* 397 U.S. 923 (1970).

§ 11.1.3 CAUSAL CONNECTION AND PUBLIC ACTIONS

ALLEN v. WRIGHT

468 U.S. 737 (1984).

[This class action brought by parents of black public school children alleges that the Internal Revenue Service (IRS) has failed to enforce its own policies to deny tax-exempt status to racially discriminatory private schools in school districts that are subject to court-ordered desegregation. This pattern of conduct violated not only the Internal Revenue Code but also federal anti-discrimination laws and the constitution. Last term, in *Bob Jones Univ. v. United States,* 461 U.S. 574 (1984), the Court held that discriminatory schools are not entitled to a tax exemption.

The tax exemption allows the schools to be supported through tax-deductible charitable contributions. The private schools drain white students from the public schools, thus thwarting integration of those schools. The plaintiffs' children do not seek admission to the private schools; they want integrated public schools. The Court of Appeals held they had standing.]

O'CONNOR, J.:

A

. . . Article III of the Constitution confines the federal courts to adjudicating actual "cases" and "controversies." As the Court explained in *Valley Forge Christian College v. Americans United for Separation of Church and State, Inc.,* 454 U.S. 464 (1982), the "case or controversy" requirement defines with respect to the Judicial Branch the idea of separation of powers on which the Federal Government is founded. The several doctrines that have grown up to elaborate that requirement are "founded in concern about the proper—and properly limited—role of the courts in a democratic society." *Warth v. Seldin,* 422 U.S. 490 (1975). "All of the doctrines that cluster about Article III—not only standing but mootness, ripeness, political question, and the like—relate in part, and in different though overlapping ways, to an idea, which is more than an intuition but less than a rigorous and explicit theory, about the constitutional and prudential limits to the powers of an unelected, unrepresentative judiciary in our kind of government." *Vander Jagt v. O'Neill,* 699 F.2d 1166, 1178–1179 (1983) (Bork, J., concurring). The case-or-controversy doctrines state fundamental limits on federal judicial power in our system of government.

The Art. III doctrine that requires a litigant to have "standing" to invoke the power of a federal court is perhaps the most important of these doctrines. "In essence the question of standing is whether the litigant is entitled to have the court decide the merits of the dispute or of particular issues." Standing doctrine embraces several judicially self-imposed limits on the exercise of federal jurisdiction, such as the general prohibition on a litigant's raising another person's legal rights, the rule barring adjudication of generalized grievances more appropriately addressed in the representative branches, and the requirement that a plaintiff's complaint fall within the zone of interests protected by the law invoked. See *Valley Forge, supra.* The requirement of standing, however, has a core component derived directly from the Constitution. A plaintiff must allege personal injury fairly traceable to the defendant's allegedly unlawful conduct and likely to be redressed by the requested relief.

Like the prudential component, the constitutional component of standing doctrine incorporates concepts concededly not susceptible of precise definition. The injury alleged must be, for example, " 'distinct and palpable,' " and not "abstract" or "conjectural" or "hypothetical." The injury must be "fairly" traceable to the challenged action, and relief from the injury must be "likely" to follow from a favorable decision. See *Simon v. Eastern Kentucky Welfare Rights Org.,* 426 U.S. 26 (1976). These terms cannot be defined so as to make application of the constitutional standing requirement a mechanical exercise. . . .

Determining standing in a particular case may be facilitated by clarifying principles or even clean rules developed in prior cases. Typically, however, the standing inquiry requires careful judicial examination of a complaint's allegations to ascertain whether the particular plaintiff is entitled to an adjudication of the particular claims asserted. Is the injury too abstract, or otherwise not appropriate, to be considered judicially cognizable? Is the line of causation between the illegal conduct and injury too attenuated? Is the prospect of obtaining relief from the injury as a result of a favorable ruling too speculative? These questions and any others relevant to the standing inquiry must be answered by reference to the Art. III notion that federal courts may exercise power only "in the last resort, and as a necessity," and only when adjudication is "consistent with a system of separated powers and [the dispute is one] traditionally thought to be capable of resolution through the judicial process." *Flast v. Cohen,* 392 U.S. 83, 97.

B

Respondents allege two injuries in their complaint to support their standing to bring this lawsuit. First, they say that they are harmed directly by the mere fact of Government financial aid to discriminatory private schools. Second, they say that the federal tax exemptions to racially discriminatory private schools in their communities impair their ability to have their public schools desegregated. . . .

1

Respondents' first claim of injury can be interpreted in two ways. It might be a claim simply to have the Government avoid the violation of law alleged in respondents' complaint. Alternatively, it might be a claim of stigmatic injury, or denigration, suffered by all members of a racial group when the Government discriminates on the basis of race. Under neither interpretation is this claim of injury judicially cognizable.

This Court has repeatedly held that an asserted right to have the Government act in accordance with law is not sufficient, standing alone, to confer jurisdiction on a federal court. In *Schlesinger v. Reservists Committee to Stop the War,* 418 U.S. 208 (1974), for example, the Court rejected a claim of citizen standing to challenge Armed Forces Reserve commissions held by Members of Congress as violating the Incompatibility Clause of Art. I, § 6, cl. 2, of the Constitution. As citizens, the Court held, plaintiffs alleged nothing but "the abstract injury in nonobservance of the Constitution". . . . Respondents here have no standing to complain simply that their Government is violating the law.

Neither do they have standing to litigate their claims based on the stigmatizing injury often caused by racial discrimination. There can be no doubt that this sort of noneconomic injury is one of the most serious consequences of discriminatory government action and is sufficient in some circumstances to support standing.

Our cases make clear, however, that such injury accords a basis for standing only to "those persons who are personally denied equal treatment" by the challenged discriminatory conduct. . . . In *O'Shea v. Littleton,* 414 U.S. 488 (1974), the Court held that the plaintiffs had no standing to challenge racial discrimination in the administration of their city's criminal justice system because they had not alleged that they had been or would likely be subject to the challenged practices. . . . In each of those cases, the plaintiffs alleged official racial discrimination comparable to that alleged by respondents here. Yet standing was denied in each case because the plaintiffs were not personally subject to the challenged discrimination. Insofar as their first claim of injury is concerned, respondents are in exactly the same position. . . . [T]hey do not allege a stigmatic injury suffered as a direct result of having personally been denied equal treatment.

The consequences of recognizing respondents' standing on the basis of their first claim of injury illustrate why our cases plainly hold that such injury is not judicially cognizable. If the abstract stigmatic injury were cognizable, standing would extend nationwide to all members of the particular racial groups against which the Government was alleged to be discriminating by its grant of a tax exemption to a racially discriminatory school, regardless of the location of that school. All such persons could claim the same sort of abstract stigmatic injury respondents assert in their first claim of injury. A black person in Hawaii could challenge the grant of a tax exemption to a racially discriminatory school in Maine. Recognition of standing in such circumstances would transform the federal courts into "no more than a vehicle for the vindication of the value interests of concerned bystanders." . . .

2

It is in their second claim of injury that respondents allege harm to a concrete, personal interest that can support standing in some circumstances. The injury they identify—their children's diminished ability to receive an education in a racially integrated school—is, beyond any doubt, not only judicially cognizable but, as shown by cases from *Brown v. Board of Education*, 347 U.S. 483 (1954), to *Bob Jones Univ.*, one of the most serious injuries recognized in our legal system. Despite the constitutional importance of curing the injury alleged by respondents, however, the federal judiciary may not redress it unless standing requirements are met. In this case, respondents' second claim of injury cannot support standing because the injury alleged is not fairly traceable to the Government conduct respondents challenge as unlawful.

The illegal conduct challenged by respondents is the IRS's grant of tax exemptions to some racially discriminatory schools. The line of causation between that conduct and desegregation of respondents' schools is attenuated at best. From the perspective of the IRS, the injury to respondents is highly indirect and "results from the independent action of some third party not before the court." . . .

The diminished ability of respondents' children to receive a desegregated education would be fairly traceable to unlawful IRS grants of tax exemptions only if there were enough racially discriminatory private schools receiving tax exemptions in respondents' communities for withdrawal of those exemptions to make an appreciable difference in public-school integration. Respondents have made no such allegation. It is, first, uncertain how many racially discriminatory private schools are in fact receiving tax exemptions. Moreover, it is entirely speculative . . . whether withdrawal of a tax exemption from any particular school would lead the school to change its policies. It is just as speculative whether any given parent of a child attending such a private school would decide to transfer the child to public school as a result of any changes in educational or financial policy made by the private school once it was threatened with loss of tax-exempt status. It is also pure speculation whether, in a particular community, a large enough number of the numerous relevant school officials and parents would reach decisions that collectively would have a significant impact on the racial composition of the public schools.

The links in the chain of causation between the challenged Government conduct and the asserted injury are far too weak for the chain as a whole to sustain respondents' standing. . . .   The chain of causation . . . involves numerous third parties (officials of racially discriminatory schools receiving tax exemptions and the parents of children attending such schools) who may not even exist in respondents' communities and whose independent decisions may not collectively have a significant effect on the ability of public-school students to receive a desegregated education.

The idea of separation of powers that underlies standing doctrine explains why our cases preclude the conclusion that respondents' alleged injury "fairly can be traced to the challenged action" of the IRS. That conclusion would pave the way generally for suits challenging, not specifically identifiable Government violations of law, but the particular programs agencies establish to carry out their legal obligations. Such suits, even when premised on allegations of several instances of violations of law, are rarely if ever appropriate for federal-court adjudication . . . .   When transported into the Art. III context, that principle, [that the Government has traditionally been granted the widest latitude in the dispatch of its own internal affairs,] grounded as it is in the idea of separation of powers, counsels against recognizing standing in a case brought, not to enforce specific legal obligations whose violation works a direct harm, but to seek a restructuring of the apparatus established by the Executive Branch to fulfill its legal duties. The Constitution, after all, assigns to the Executive Branch, and not to the Judicial Branch, the duty to "take Care that the Laws be faithfully executed." U.S. Const., Art. II, § 3. We could not recognize respondents' standing in this case without running afoul of that structural principle. . . .   The judgment of the Court of Appeals is accordingly reversed, and the injunction issued by that court is vacated.

JUSTICE STEVENS, with whom JUSTICE BLACKMUN joins, dissenting. . . .

In final analysis, the wrong the respondents allege that the Government has committed is to subsidize the exodus of white children from schools that would otherwise be racially integrated. The critical question in this case, therefore, is whether respondents have alleged that the Government has created that kind of subsidy.

In answering that question, we must of course assume that respondents can prove what they have alleged . . . .

"Both tax exemptions and tax-deductability are a form of subsidy that is administered through the tax system. A tax exemption has much the same effect as a cash grant to the organization of the amount of tax it would have to pay on its income. Deductable contributions are similar to cash grants of the amount of a portion of the individual's contributions."

This causation analysis is nothing more than a restatement of elementary economics: when something becomes more expensive, less of it will be purchased. Sections 170 and 501(c)(3) are premised on that recognition. If racially discriminatory private schools lose the "cash grants" that flow from the operation of the statutes, the education they provide will become more expensive and hence less of their services will be purchased. Conversely, maintenance of these tax benefits makes an education in segregated private schools relatively more attractive, by decreasing its cost. Accordingly, without tax exempt status, private schools will either not be competitive in terms of cost, or have to change their admissions policies, hence reducing their competitiveness for parents seeking "a racially segregated alternative" to public schools, which is what respondents have alleged many white parents in desegregating school districts seek . . . .

Considerations of tax policy, economics, and pure logic all confirm the conclusion that respondents' injury in fact is fairly traceable to the Government's allegedly wrongful conduct. The Court therefore is forced to introduce the concept of "separation of powers" into its analysis . . . . [T]he Court could be saying that it will require a more direct causal connection when it is troubled by the separation of powers implications of the case before it. That approach confuses the standing doctrine with the justiciability of the issues that respondents seek to raise . . . . The strength of the plaintiff's interest in the outcome has nothing to do with whether the relief it seeks would intrude upon the prerogatives of other branches of government; the possibility that the relief might be inappropriate does not lessen the plaintiff's stake in obtaining that relief. If a plaintiff presents a nonjusticiable issue, or seeks relief that a court may not award, then its complaint should be dismissed for those reasons, and not because the plaintiff lacks a stake in obtaining that relief and hence has no standing. Imposing an undefined but clearly more rigorous standard for redressability for reasons unrelated to the causal nexus between the injury and the challenged conduct can only encourage undisciplined, *ad hoc* litigation, a result that would be avoided if the Court straightforwardly considered the justiciability of the issues respondents seek to raise, rather than using those issues to obfuscate standing analysis.

[Or] the Court could be saying that it will not treat as legally cognizable injuries that stem from an administrative decision concerning how enforcement resources will be allocated. This surely is an important point. Respondents do seek to restructure the IRS' mechanisms for enforcing the legal requirement that discriminatory institutions not receive tax-exempt status. Such restructuring would dramatically affect the way in which the IRS exercises its prosecutorial discretion. The Executive requires latitude to decide how best to enforce the law, and in general the Court may well be correct that the exercise of that discretion, especially in the tax context, is unchallengeable.

However, as the Court also recognizes, this principle does not apply when suit is brought "to enforce specific legal obligations whose violation works a direct harm." . . .

Respondents contend that these cases limit the enforcement discretion enjoyed by the IRS. They establish, respondents argue, that the IRS cannot provide "cash grants" to discriminatory schools through preferential tax treatment without running afoul of a constitutional duty to refrain from "giving significant aid" to these institutions. Similarly, respondents claim that the Internal Revenue Code itself, as construed in *Bob Jones,* constrains enforcement discretion. It has been clear since *Marbury v. Madison,* that "[i]t is emphatically the province and duty of the judicial department to say what the law is." Deciding whether the Treasury has violated a specific legal limitation on its enforcement discretion does not intrude upon the prerogatives of the Executive, for in so deciding we are merely saying "what the law is."

. . .

[BRENNAN, J. also dissented. MARSHALL, J. did not participate]

Notes and Questions

1. *The public action.* The plaintiffs in *Allen* asserted two theories in support of their standing. The first claim was based on their disagreement with government assistance to discriminating private schools and the stigma imposed on them by this assistance. How did the inaction of the IRS stigmatize the plaintiffs and why did plaintiffs lack standing under this theory? Is the problem that the injury is too abstract? Or too generalized? Was their claimed injury different from that found acceptable in *United Church of Christ* or *Duke Power Co. v. North Carolina Envtl. Study Group?*

This branch of *Allen* raises the question of whether the federal courts should grant standing to "ideological" plaintiffs: persons outraged (but not otherwise harmed) by allegedly illegal government action. The leading authority for denying standing in such cases is *Sierra Club v. Morton,* 405 U.S. 727 (1972). In that case the Sierra Club sought to enjoin a ski development in Mineral King, a pristine area of the Sierras. It based its standing solely on its historic interest in the conservation of the Sierras and other wilderness areas. The Court held that Sierra Club lacked standing because it had failed to allege that it or its members had suffered any injury. A historic commitment to conservation is not enough.

In dissent, Justice Douglas argued that standing should be granted to an "inanimate object about to be despoiled, defaced, or invaded by roads and bulldozers and where injury is the subject of public outrage." *Id.* at 741. Sierra Club then amended its complaint to allege that its members camped in Mineral King. The defendants' motion to dismiss the amended complaint was denied. Ultimately the developer abandoned the project.

Does it make sense to deny standing to the Sierra Club, a well-funded conservation group, but grant it to a single camper at Mineral King? What is wrong with granting standing to "ideological" plaintiffs? Is the problem that ideological plaintiffs may do a poor job of presenting their case, thus depriving the federal courts of the sharp adversary clash necessary to decide difficult issues? Or would the federal courts be flooded with cases if it allowed outraged citizens to sue? Or is the concern that such cases inevitably present difficult remedial problems? Or do the majority of the justices simply oppose the claim on substantive grounds and use standing doctrine to avoid dealing with the merits? Or is the real explanation drawn from separation of powers doctrine? Can you articulate the separation of powers argument more precisely than the *Allen* majority opinion?

2. *Taxpayer actions.* In almost every state, taxpayers have standing to challenge the legality of action taken by the legislature or the executive branch (at either the state or local level) which they allege involves an unlawful expenditure of public funds. See, e.g., *Dodge v. Department of Social Serv.*, 600 P.2d 70 (Colo.1979) (taxpayer has standing to question legality of expenditures for non-therapeutic abortions); *Regents of Univ. of Cal. v. Superior Court*, 476 P.2d 457 (Cal. 1970) (based on trifling expenditure, taxpayer has standing to question rule denying employment to Communists). Many states even allow taxpayer challenges to action which does not involve the spending of public money. Typically the remedy sought is injunctive, and in some states a prevailing plaintiff is entitled to attorney's fees. Apparently the result has not been an unmanageable flood of litigation. *See generally* Comment, "Taxpayers' Suits: Standing Barriers and Pecuniary Restraints," 59 Temp.L.Q. 951 (1986).

In contrast to experience at the state level, at the federal level recognition of taxpayer actions has been extremely grudging. A federal taxpayer ordinarily lacks standing to challenge the expenditure of federal funds unless it can be demonstrated that a victory on the merits will reduce the amount of taxes the taxpayer is required to pay. However, in *Flast v. Cohen*, 392 U.S. 83 (1968), the Court allowed a taxpayer standing to challenge as facially unconstitutional a government expenditure program benefiting religious schools. Breaking with prior cases that had refused standing to taxpayers, the Court fashioned a "double nexus" test for federal taxpayers seeking to challenge expenditures. Under this test, a taxpayer has standing to enjoin an expenditure program only if:

(i) the program attacked is a legislative decision to spend tax dollars, so that plaintiff's status as taxpayer is logically connected to his claim of unlawful spending; and

(ii) the expenditure is allegedly prohibited by a specific, rather than a general, constitutional provision. The establishment clause of the first amendment was held sufficiently specific.

The *Flast* case was later expanded to allow an "as applied" establishment clause challenge to a federal spending program, *Bowen v. Kendrick*, 108 S.Ct. 2562 (1988). Although *Flast* was originally hailed as opening the door to all sorts of public actions by citizens or taxpayers, all attempts to expand it to other sorts of claims have failed.

Why couldn't the *Allen* plaintiffs assert standing as taxpayers under *Flast* to question the IRS' conduct? After all, they alleged that lax enforcement by the IRS promoted unconstitutional racial discrimination in public education and also that it was costing the government tax dollars (through undeserved charitable contribution deductions and tax exemptions for the schools)?

Do you prefer the state or the federal approach to taxpayer actions?

3. *The causation and remediability requirements.* The *Allen* plaintiffs contended that they had standing on a second theory: lax enforcement by the IRS amounted to a subsidy which encouraged the formation and expansion of segregated private schools, thus interfering with federal court desegregation orders in the plaintiffs' school districts. Clearly, federal and state government cannot provide funding or other encouragement for segregated education nor otherwise undermine court-ordered desegregation. Why then does the Court hold that this allegation of harm is an insufficient foundation for standing to sue?

Cases like *Allen* emphasize that injury in fact is not enough: plaintiffs must establish that the injury is "fairly traceable" to defendants' conduct (the causation requirement) and that the judicial remedy plaintiffs seek is likely to redress that injury (the remediability requirement). For example, *Warth v. Seldin*, 422 U.S. 490 (1975) held that various plaintiffs, including poor people who wanted to live in Penfield, N.Y., had no standing to challenge Penfield's zoning laws which prohibited the construction of low-income housing. The Court held that even if the zoning laws were struck down, builders still might not construct housing which the plaintiffs could afford. The zoning laws did not necessarily cause the injury; striking them down would not necessarily redress that injury. Causation requirements have emerged in state standing cases as well. *See, e.g., Fox v. Wisconsin Dept. of Health & Soc. Serv.*, 334 N.W.2d 532 (Wis.1983).

Yet the causation and remediability barriers can be overcome. In *Village of Arlington Heights v. Metropolitan Housing Dev. Corp.*, 429 U.S. 252 (1977), a builder and a buyer of low income housing were granted standing to attack exclusionary zoning laws. They demonstrated that the challenged law had prevented construction of a specific low income housing project which the builder was prepared to build and in which the buyer could have afforded to purchase a home.

Why couldn't the plaintiffs in *Allen* make a comparable showing? Should they have been permitted to conduct discovery in order to establish that a sufficient causal connection existed between the actions of the IRS and the harm to desegregated public schools, and that the remedy they sought was likely to rectify that harm?

A taxpayer has no difficulty challenging an IRS decision that tax is owed. But *Allen* and other cases indicate that the Court is extremely reluctant to second-guess an IRS decision that *favors* a taxpayer. Should the federal courts entertain such claims? *Compare* Stephan, "Nontaxpayer Litigation of Income Tax Disputes," 3 Yale L. & Pol'y Rev. 73 (1984) (no) *with* Asimow, "Standing to Challenge Lenient Tax Rules: A Statutory Solution," 57 Taxes 483 (1979) (yes).

Did 1981 MSAPA § 5–106(a)(5)(iii) adopt the causation and remediability tests? If so, do you agree with the decision to incorporate those doctrines into state law?

4. *Third party standing.* An important prudential limitation on standing is the rule that a plaintiff cannot assert the rights of third parties—only its own rights. This is often referred to as the *jus tertii* rule. Recall the hypothetical in § 11.1 about whether John's customers have standing to protest revocation of his license for serving minors. *See* 1981 MSAPA § 5–106(a)(5)(i). For that reason, the *Allen* plaintiffs could not sue on behalf of black children who wanted to attend the private schools but were denied admission on racial grounds.

The courts have frequently made exceptions to the *jus tertii* rule. For example, a plaintiff can assert the rights of third parties when the latter are legally or practically disabled from suing or when there is a protected relationship (such as doctor-patient or vendor-purchaser) between the plaintiff and the third party. *See generally* Tribe, AMERICAN CONSTITUTIONAL LAW 134–42 (2d ed. 1987).

5. *Overcoming prudential standing limits by statute.* Note that several of the limitations on standing discussed in this chapter are prudential rather than constitutional: the zone of interest test, the requirement that injury be particularized rather than generalized, and the *jus tertii* rule. Congress can overcome these limitations by granting statutory standing and has frequently done so. But the legislature cannot override constitutional barriers to standing (such as the requirement of injury in fact, the requirement that the injury be concrete rather than abstract, and the causation and remediability requirements).

The Clean Air Act gives standing to "any person" to seek injunctions against polluters or against the EPA. 42 U.S.C. § 7604. To use Justice O'Connor's example from *Allen,* the Act allows an environmentalist in Hawaii to sue a polluter in Maine. A similar example:

the Endangered Species Act allows "any person" to sue to prevent federal action that might destroy an endangered species. 16 U.S.C. § 1540(g). Are these provisions constitutional? Could Congress enact a constitutional statute that would provide standing for the assertion of both sets of claims made by the *Allen* plaintiffs?

6. *Problem.* The Madison Arts Fund (MAF) makes grants to an array of local arts organizations. According to MAF's regulations, between 15% and 25% of the annual grants should go to theatrical organizations, and the grants should be distributed equitably throughout the state. The regulations also provide that MAF grants should be used primarily, though not exclusively, to help new organizations get started as opposed to providing an annual subsidy.

For each of the last four years, MAF granted $200,000 to City Theater Company to offset City's annual deficit. City stages musicals and light comedy in a dinner theater format. Mort, the director of MAF, used to be a donor to and director of City.

For several years, Ellen has been trying to start another theater company in the same city—the Elm Actors Theater (EAT)—to produce new plays. EAT has not raised enough funds to produce any plays. Her troupe of actors are willing to work for free or for very low salaries. Ellen has applied three times for an MAF grant which would be used to match contributions from the community. Each time, MAF rejected her application, stating that the city cannot support two theater companies.

Ellen believes that the grants to City are an abuse of MAF's discretion. She points to Mort's pre-existing relationship to City and to the fact that City has been treated with undue favoritism; its three grants were to offset operating expenses rather than to aid in development, and its cultural contribution is minimal.

As a lover of avant garde theater, you have volunteered to litigate pro bono on EAT's behalf. Should the plaintiff be you or EAT? What are the prospects for this lawsuit?

§ 11.2 TIMING OF JUDICIAL REVIEW

§ 11.2.1 INTRODUCTION

This subchapter addresses issues of timing: when can a litigant engage a court in a dispute which involves an administrative agency? Often, the question of whether judicial review can be obtained immediately—or only after protracted administrative proceedings—is critically important.

The four parts of the subchapter concern four different timing doctrines. Each of them can be viewed as a separate hurdle over which a litigant must pass before securing judicial involvement. The four doctrines are closely related and sometimes overlap. They are often confused with one another in discussion and in judicial decisions.

Nevertheless, each of the four doctrines serves different functions, draws upon different bodies of precedent, and should be carefully distinguished. Thus a preliminary sketch of the doctrines, and how they differ from each other, may be helpful.

a. *The final order rule.* Litigants are sometimes dissatisfied with decisions taken by the agency during the administrative process. For example, an agency might exclude certain evidence at a hearing or refuse to take immediate action to remove a dangerous pesticide from the market. However, as a general rule, courts review only "final orders." This means that ordinarily—but not always—a litigant must complete the entire administrative process before a court will review decisions which the agency took along the way.

b. *Ripeness.* A private party may be threatened by agency action which has not yet occurred. For example, an agency might adopt a new rule or policy—but not yet actually have enforced or otherwise applied it against the plaintiff. In many cases, but by no means always, the dispute is not yet "ripe" for review. This means that a court will await a concrete application of the agency action to the plaintiff before reviewing its legality.

c. *Exhaustion of remedies.* A private party may have an administrative remedy available which has not yet been employed. It is possible that this remedy might be successful; the party's position might prevail and the problem would be solved. Nevertheless, the party wants to skip the administrative remedy and go immediately to court. By the general rule—but not always—a court will not hear the case until the party has first exhausted all administrative remedies whereby the point at issue might be resolved in the party's favor.

Alternatively, a party may have failed to take advantage of an administrative remedy until it is too late to do so. For example, an ALJ may have ruled against a party who failed to appeal the ALJ's decision to the agency head. Now, when the time for administrative appeal has run out, the party wishes to obtain judicial review, but it would ordinarily be denied because of the failure to exhaust remedies.

d. *Primary jurisdiction.* In many situations, a statute confers jurisdiction on an agency to resolve a particular dispute or enforce a statute. However, the courts also have jurisdiction to deal with the same problem. Under the doctrine of "primary jurisdiction," the courts reject jurisdiction, allowing the matter to be tried before the agency instead. Thus judicial involvement occurs only in the form of judicial review of the agency decision, as opposed to conducting the original trial in court. In other cases, the court may reject jurisdiction in favor of agency jurisdiction over only a single issue; after the agency adjudicates that issue, the remaining issues are litigated in court.

For example, a carrier and a shipper might disagree over the cost of transporting a particular cargo. The dispute concerns the interpretation of the carrier's tariff. This could be viewed as a typical contractual dispute which would be heard in court. But an agency which regulates the carrier might also have jurisdiction to resolve such disputes. If the doctrine of primary jurisdiction applies to all the issues, the court must refuse to hear the case and instead transfer it to the agency. The only way to get the dispute to court is through judicial review of the agency's decision.

Primary jurisdiction differs significantly from the three timing doctrines mentioned above. These doctrines (final order, ripeness, exhaustion) all concern the issue of when a court may review agency action. The primary jurisdiction doctrine concerns the issue of whether a court will be involved in the dispute at the trial stage or only at the judicial review stage.

This introduction has crudely sketched the four timing doctrines as if they were simple, absolute rules. Nothing could be further from the truth. Each of the four doctrines is riddled with exceptions and qualifications. Many cases are judicially reviewed in the absence of a final order, or before an administrative policy has been applied to the plaintiff, or despite a plaintiff's failure to exhaust administrative remedies. Similarly, the courts frequently retain jurisdiction, holding the doctrine of primary jurisdiction inapplicable.

As you study the material which follows, try to identify the policy reasons for denying someone immediate judicial review (or judicial trial). Then identify the circumstances in which exceptions are appropriate: when those policy reasons are inapplicable or are outweighed by considerations of hardship.

§ 11.2.2 THE FINAL ORDER RULE

FEDERAL TRADE COMMISSION v. STANDARD OIL CO. OF CALIFORNIA

449 U.S. 232 (1980).

[In 1973, the FTC issued a complaint against major oil companies (including Socal) averring that it had "reason to believe" that they were engaging in unfair methods of competition. Socal moved to dismiss the complaint on the ground that the FTC did not have "reason to believe" that it had violated the Act, but the FTC denied the motion. Adjudication of the charges before an ALJ began and is still pending. In 1975, Socal filed a complaint in the District Court seeking review of whether the FTC had "reason to believe" it was violating the Act. Socal argues that political pressure arising from gasoline shortages in 1973 induced the FTC to issue a complaint against the major oil companies despite insufficient investigation.

The issue is whether issuance of the complaint before administrative adjudication concludes is "final agency action" subject to judicial review. The District Court dismissed the complaint but the Ninth Circuit reversed. It held that the District Court could inquire whether the Commission *in fact* had made the determination that it had "reason to believe" Socal was violating the Act.

The Supreme Court held that issuance of the complaint was review-able only if it was "final agency action" or otherwise was "directly reviewable" under § 704 of the APA. It concluded that it was neither.]

POWELL, J.:

. . .

A

The Commission's issuance of its complaint was not "final agency action." The Court observed in *Abbott Laboratories v. Gardner,* 387 U.S. 136, 149 (1967), that "[t]he cases dealing with judicial review of administrative actions have interpreted the 'finality' element in a pragmatic way." In *Abbott Laboratories,* for example, the publication of certain regulations by the Commissioner of Food and Drugs was held to be final agency action subject to judicial review in an action for declaratory judgment brought prior to any Government action for enforcement. . . .

By its terms, the Commission's averment of "reason to believe" that Socal was violating the Act is not a definitive statement of position. It represents a threshold determination that further inquiry is warranted and that a complaint should initiate proceedings. To be sure, the issuance of the complaint is definitive on the question whether the Commission avers reason to believe that the respondent to the complaint is violating the Act. But the extent to which the respondent may challenge the complaint and its charges proves that the averment of reason to believe is not "definitive" in a comparable manner to the regulations in *Abbott Laboratories* and the cases it discussed. . . .

Serving only to initiate the proceedings, the issuance of the complaint averring reason to believe has no legal force comparable to that of the regulation at issue in *Abbott Laboratories,* nor any comparable effect upon Socal's daily business. The regulations in *Abbott Laboratories* forced manufacturers to "risk serious criminal and civil penalties" for noncompliance, or "change all their labels, advertisements, and promotional materials; . . . destroy stocks of printed matter; and . . . invest heavily in new printing type and new supplies." Socal does not contend that the issuance of the complaint had any such legal or practical effect, except to impose upon Socal the burden of respond-ing to the charges made against it. Although this burden certainly is substantial, it is different in kind and legal effect from the burdens attending what heretofore has been considered to be final agency action.

In contrast to the complaint's lack of legal or practical effect upon Socal, the effect of the judicial review sought by Socal is likely to be interference with the proper functioning of the agency and a burden for the courts. Judicial intervention into the agency process denies the agency an opportunity to correct its own mistakes and to apply its expertise. *Weinberger v. Salfi,* 422 U.S. 749, 765 (1975). Intervention also leads to piecemeal review which at the least is inefficient and upon completion of the agency process might prove to have been unnecessary. *McGee v. United States,* 402 U.S. 479, 484 (1971); *McKart v. United States,* 395 U.S. 185, 195 (1969). Furthermore, unlike the review in *Abbott Laboratories,* judicial review to determine whether the Commission decided that it had the requisite reason to believe would delay resolution of the ultimate question whether the Act was violated. Finally, every respondent to a Commission complaint could make the claim that Socal had made. Judicial review of the averments in the Commission's complaints should not be a means of turning prosecutor into defendant before adjudication concludes.

In sum, the Commission's issuance of a complaint averring reason to believe that Socal was violating the Act is not a definitive ruling or regulation. It had no legal force or practical effect upon Socal's daily business other than the disruptions that accompany any major litigation. And immediate judicial review would serve neither efficiency nor enforcement of the Act. These pragmatic considerations counsel against the conclusion that the issuance of the complaint was "final agency action."

B

Socal relies, however, upon different considerations than these in contending that the issuance of the complaint is "final agency action."

Socal first contends that it exhausted its administrative remedies by moving in the adjudicatory proceedings for dismissal of the complaint. By thus affording the Commission an opportunity to decide upon the matter, Socal contends that it has satisfied the interests underlying the doctrine of administrative exhaustion. The Court of Appeals agreed. 596 F.2d, at 1387. We think, however, that Socal and the Court of Appeals have mistaken exhaustion for finality. By requesting the Commission to withdraw its complaint and by awaiting the Commission's refusal to do so, Socal may well have exhausted its administrative remedy as to the averment of reason to believe. But the Commission's refusal to reconsider its issuance of the complaint does not render the complaint a "definitive" action. The Commission's refusal does not augment the complaint's legal force or practical effect upon Socal. Nor does the refusal diminish the concerns for efficiency and enforcement of the Act.

Socal also contends that it will be irreparably harmed unless the issuance of the complaint is judicially reviewed immediately. Socal argues that the expense and disruption of defending itself in protracted adjudicatory proceedings constitutes irreparable harm. As indicated above, we do not doubt that the burden of defending this proceeding will be substantial. But "the expense and annoyance of litigation is 'part of the social burden of living under government.'" . . .

Socal further contends that its challenge to the Commission's averment of reason to believe can never be reviewed unless it is reviewed before the Commission's adjudication concludes. As stated by the Court of Appeals, the alleged unlawfulness in the issuance of the complaint "is likely to become insulated from any review" if deferred until appellate review of a cease-and-desist order. Socal also suggests that the unlawfulness will be "insulated" because the reviewing court will lack an adequate record and it will address only the question whether substantial evidence supported the cease-and-desist order.[11]

We are not persuaded by this speculation. The Act expressly authorizes a court of appeals to order that the Commission take additional evidence. 15 U.S.C. § 45(c). Thus, a record which would be inadequate for review of alleged unlawfulness in the issuance of a complaint can be made adequate. We also note that the APA specifically provides that a "preliminary, procedural, or intermediate agency action or ruling not directly reviewable is subject to review on the review of the final agency action," 5 U.S.C. § 704, and that the APA also empowers a court of appeals to "hold unlawful and set aside agency action . . . found to be . . . without observance of procedure required by law." 5 U.S.C. § 706. Thus, assuming that the issuance of the complaint is not "committed to agency discretion by law," a court of appeals reviewing a cease-and-desist order has the power to review alleged unlawfulness in the issuance of a complaint. We need not decide what action a court of appeals should take if it finds a cease-and-desist order to be supported by substantial evidence but the complaint to have been issued without the requisite reason to believe. It suffices to hold that the possibility does not affect the application of the finality rule. . . .

Because the Commission's issuance of a complaint averring reason to believe that Socal has violated the Act is not "final agency action" under § [704] of the APA, it is not judicially reviewable before administrative adjudication concludes.[14] . . .

JUSTICE STEVENS concurred in the judgment.

11.   The Court of Appeals additionally suggested that the complaint would be "insulated" from review because the alleged unlawfulness would be moot if Socal prevailed in the adjudication. These concerns do not support a conclusion that the issuance of a complaint averring reason to believe is "final agency action." To the contrary, one of the principal reasons to await the termination of agency proceedings is "to obviate all occasion for judicial review." Thus, the possibility that Socal's challenge may be mooted in adjudication warrants the requirement that Socal pursue adjudication, not shortcut it.

14.   By this holding, we do not encourage the issuance of complaints by the Commission without a conscientious compliance with the "reason to believe" obligation in 15 U.S.C. § 45(b). The adjudicatory proceedings which follow the issuance of a complaint may last for months or years. They result in substantial expense to the respondent and may divert management personnel from their administrative and productive duties to the corporation. Without a well-grounded reason to believe that unlawful conduct has occurred, the Commission does not serve the public interest by subjecting business enterprises to these burdens.

Notes and Questions

1. *The final order rule in statutes.* Judicial review statutes frequently authorize the courts to review only "final orders." Even when the adjective "final" does not appear, the statute is construed as if it did. *See, e.g., Rosenthal & Co. v. CFTC,* 614 F.2d 1121 (7th Cir.1980) (statute providing for review of "any order" means "any final order").

The final order doctrine is embodied in both federal and state APA's. Read and compare § 704 of the federal APA and §§ 5–102 and 5–103 of 1981 MSAPA. § 5–103 of 1981 MSAPA explicitly permits an exception to the final order rule. Does *Socal* suggest that the first sentence of § 704 contains a similar (but implicit) exception? Does the second sentence of § 704 suggest that there are exceptions to the final order rule of the first sentence?

2. *Socal and final orders.* Was the FTC's determination that it had "reason to believe" that Socal was violating the law a "final order" as defined in MSAPA § 5–102(b)? If not, should the determination still have been subject to immediate judicial review? *See* MSAPA § 5–103(2). What is the "public benefit derived from postponement" to which § 5–103(2) refers? Is § 5–103(2) consistent with the reasoning in the *Socal* case?

3. *Remand orders.* Suppose that state law prohibits employment discrimination on various grounds, including marital status, but it allows a defense of "business necessity." X Co.'s policy is to refuse to hire any close relative of an existing employee. An ALJ of the Human Relations Commission held that X Co.'s policy was not discrimination on the basis of marriage. On appeal, the Commission reversed, holding that X Co.'s policy did violate the statute. It remanded to the ALJ to consider whether the policy could be defended on the basis of business necessity. Should X Co. be able to obtain immediate judicial review of this order?

See Maryland Com'n on Human Relations v. Baltimore Gas & Elec., 459 A.2d 205 (Md.1983), holding that this is not an appealable final order. The court stated: ". . . ordinarily the action of an administrative agency, like the order of a court, is final if it determines or concludes the rights of the parties, or if it denies the parties means of further prosecuting or defending their rights and interests in the subject matter proceedings before the agency, thus leaving nothing further for the agency to do." *Id.* at 211.

The court distinguished the case of a lower court decision remanding a case to an agency; such a court decision is immediately appealable to a higher court. Are these cases distinguishable?

4. *Exhaustion, finality, and ripeness.* Did Socal exhaust its remedies? What is the difference between the rule that the courts review only "final orders" and that a litigant must "exhaust its administrative

remedies?" Between the "final order" rule and the "ripeness" doctrine?

5. *Witchhunts and judicial review.* Socal claimed that the FTC's decision to prosecute was politically motivated (it occurred during a period of extreme public resentment of big oil companies) and was not based upon an adequate investigation. This claim was not at all implausible. What can a victim do if an agency prosecutes it for reasons relating to politics or public relations? Is judicial review of the agency's decision to issue a complaint a good remedy? If so, when should review occur? Do you think that footnote 14 of the *Socal* opinion will help?

6. *The final order rule and administrative delay.* Despite the final order rule, a court can review an agency's failure to act on a matter before it. *See* APA §§ 555(b), 706(1). The 1981 MSAPA is quite specific in setting deadline dates for agency action. *See* §§ 3–106(b), 3–117, 4–104(a), 4–215(g), 4–216(h).

However, a court asked to remedy agency footdragging faces a dilemma: an order to expedite one matter may delay other matters or force the agency to decide a matter before it is properly prepared to do so. After all, an agency has broad discretion with respect to the deployment of its limited resources in carrying out all of its assigned tasks. Thus a court should hesitate before imposing its own timing priorities.

See Heckler v. Day, 467 U.S. 104 (1984). In the *Day* case, a group of Vermont applicants for Social Security disability benefits brought a class action to force a speed-up in claims processing. In fact, administration of the disability program is characterized by agonizing delays. Recall *Mathews v. Eldridge* in § 2.3.

The trial court ordered that the state agency complete its reconsideration of negative initial decisions within 90 days and that Social Security schedule hearings before ALJ's within 90 days. In a 5–4 decision, the Supreme Court set the decision aside. While Congress was concerned about sluggish administration of the disability program, it had repeatedly rejected mandatory deadline schemes because of concern that deadlines might jeopardize the quality and uniformity of decisions. The Supreme Court deferred to that Congressional judgment. Moreover, the Court observed, it made no sense to have rigid deadlines in Vermont but not in other states (since Social Security might simply shift resources from other states to Vermont).

7. *Exceptions to the final order rule.* What kind of a showing must a litigant make to persuade a court to review a non-final order? Most courts require the litigant to show that if review is denied until the issuance of a final order, the litigant or the public would suffer irreparable harm. Would heavy litigation costs in the agency proceeding be enough to demonstrate irreparable harm? If not, what kinds of harm might be sufficient?

One important example of review of non-final orders arises in health and safety cases, as illustrated in several cases involving the banning of the pesticide DDT. By statute, EPA must cancel the registration of a pesticide (and thus prevent its sale) if it is unsafe. After EPA issues a "notice of cancellation," a lengthy administrative investigatory and adjudicatory process ensues before the pesticide is finally banned. In the case of an "imminent hazard to health and safety," however, EPA can suspend registration and thereby remove the product from the market immediately. The Court of Appeals has jurisdiction only to review EPA "final orders."

Despite having information suggesting that DDT posed an imminent health hazard, EPA took no action on a request to suspend DDT's registration. Instead, it issued a notice of cancellation for some uses of DDT while continuing to study other uses. The Court of Appeals held that EPA's failure to take action on the petition to suspend was immediately reviewable. If DDT poses an "imminent" health hazard, the public suffers irreparable injury during the lengthy cancellation process because DDT remains on the market. On two different occasions, the court remanded the matter to EPA to suspend DDT's registration or explain why it had not done so. *Environmental Defense Fund, Inc. v. Hardin,* 428 F.2d 1093 (D.C.Cir.1970); *Environmental Defense Fund, Inc. v. Ruckelshaus,* 439 F.2d 584 (D.C.Cir.1971).

8. *Problem.* Madison has adopted 1981 MSAPA. The Madison Aviation Agency (MAA) has authority to suspend for safety reasons the certificate of any airline operating solely within Madison's borders. A suspension order grounds an airline's aircraft without any prior hearing. Yesterday, MAA suspended the certificate of our client Commuter Helicopter Service, claiming serious safety defects. MAA has also begun proceedings to revoke Commuter's license because of these safety defects and will supply a hearing (in about two months) in connection with that revocation proceeding. Our client does not believe that MAA had probable cause to suspend its license. Can it get immediate judicial review of the suspension decision? *See Nevada Airlines, Inc. v. Bond,* 622 F.2d 1017 (9th Cir.1980).

§ 11.2.3 RIPENESS

ABBOTT LABORATORIES v. GARDNER
387 U.S. 136 (1967).

[This case involves the labelling of prescription drugs which are sold under both a trade (or "proprietary" name) and at a lower price under a generic (or "established") name. In 1962, Congress amended the Federal Food, Drug and Cosmetic Act to require makers of drugs with trade names to print the generic names on labels and other printed material. The purpose of the law was to bring to the attention of doctors and patients the fact that many drugs sold under familiar trade names are identical to drugs sold under generic names at lower prices.

The Food and Drug Administration (FDA), exercising legislative rulemaking authority, adopted a rule requiring that the generic name appear on labels and other material *every time* the trade name is used. This is a class action by manufacturers of 90% of prescription drugs for declaratory and injunctive relief. They argue that the "every time" rule exceeded FDA's authority. The Court of Appeals held that i) pre-enforcement review of FDA rules was precluded, and ii) the regulation was not ripe for review. The Supreme Court first held that Congress had not precluded pre-enforcement review of FDA regulations.]

HARLAN, J.:

. . .

A further inquiry must, however, be made. The injunctive and declaratory judgment remedies are discretionary, and courts traditionally have been reluctant to apply them to administrative determinations unless these arise in the context of a controversy "ripe" for judicial resolution. Without undertaking to survey the intricacies of the ripeness doctrine it is fair to say that its basic rationale is to prevent the courts, through avoidance of premature adjudication, from entangling themselves in abstract disagreements over administrative policies, and also to protect the agencies from judicial interference until an administrative decision has been formalized and its effects felt in a concrete way by the challenging parties. The problem is best seen in a twofold aspect, requiring us to evaluate both the fitness of the issues for judicial decision and the hardship to the parties of withholding court consideration.

As to the former factor, we believe the issues presented are appropriate for judicial resolution at this time. First, all parties agree that the issue tendered is a purely legal one: whether the statute was properly construed by the Commissioner to require the established name of the drug to be used *every time* the proprietary name is employed. Both sides moved for summary judgment in the District Court, and no claim is made here that further administrative proceedings are contemplated. It is suggested that the justification for this rule might vary with different circumstances, and that the expertise of the Commissioner is relevant to passing upon the validity of the regulation. This of course is true, but the suggestion overlooks the fact that both sides have approached this case as one purely of congressional intent, and that the Government made no effort to justify the regulation in factual terms.

Second, the regulations in issue we find to be "final agency action" within the meaning of § [704 of the APA], as construed in judicial decisions. . . .

The regulation challenged here, promulgated in a formal manner after announcement in the Federal Register and consideration of comments by interested parties is quite clearly definitive. There is no hint that this regulation is informal, see *Helco Products Co. v. McNutt*, 137 F.2d 681, or only the ruling of a subordinate official, or tentative. It was made effective upon publication, and the Assistant General Counsel for Food and Drugs stated in the District Court that compliance was expected. . . .

[The regulations] have the status of law and violations of them carry heavy criminal and civil sanctions. . . . Moreover, the agency does have direct authority to enforce this regulation in the context of passing upon applications for clearance of new drugs, or certification of certain antibiotics.

This is also a case in which the impact of the regulations upon the petitioners is sufficiently direct and immediate as to render the issue appropriate for judicial review at this stage. These regulations purport to give an authoritative interpretation of a statutory provision that has a direct effect on the day-to-day business of all prescription drug companies; its promulgation puts petitioners in a dilemma that it was the very purpose of the Declaratory Judgment Act to ameliorate. As the District Court found on the basis of uncontested allegations, "Either they must comply with the every time requirement and incur the costs of changing over their promotional material and labeling or they must follow their present course and risk prosecution." The regulations are clear-cut, and were made effective immediately upon publication; as noted earlier the agency's counsel represented to the District Court that immediate compliance with their terms was expected. If petitioners wish to comply they must change all their labels, advertisements, and promotional materials; they must destroy stocks of printed matter; and they must invest heavily in new printing type and new supplies. The alternative to compliance—continued use of material which they believe in good faith meets the statutory requirements, but which clearly does not meet the regulation of the Commissioner—may be even more costly. That course would risk serious criminal and civil penalties for the unlawful distribution of "misbranded" drugs.

It is relevant at this juncture to recognize that petitioners deal in a sensitive industry, in which public confidence in their drug products is especially important. To require them to challenge these regulations only as a defense to an action brought by the Government might harm them severely and unnecessarily. Where the legal issue presented is fit for judicial resolution, and where a regulation requires an immediate and significant change in the plaintiffs' conduct of their affairs with serious penalties attached to noncompliance, access to the courts under the Administrative Procedure Act and the Declaratory Judgment Act must be permitted, absent a statutory bar or some other unusual circumstance, neither of which appears here. . . .

The Government further contends that the threat of criminal sanctions for noncompliance with a judicially untested regulation is unrealistic; the Solicitor General has represented that if court enforcement becomes necessary, "the Department of Justice will proceed only civilly for an injunction . . . or by condemnation." We cannot accept this argument as a sufficient answer to petitioners' petition. This action at its inception was properly brought and this subsequent representation of the Department of Justice should not suffice to defeat it.

Finally, the Government urges that to permit resort to the courts in this type of case may delay or impede effective enforcement of the Act. We fully recognize the important public interest served by assuring prompt and unimpeded administration of the Pure Food, Drug, and Cosmetic Act, but we do not find the Government's argument convincing. First, in this particular case, a pre-enforcement challenge by nearly all prescription drug manufacturers is calculated to speed enforcement. If the Government prevails, a large part of the industry is bound by the decree; if the Government loses, it can more quickly revise its regulation.

The Government contends, however, that if the Court allows this consolidated suit, then nothing will prevent a multiplicity of suits in various jurisdictions challenging other regulations. The short answer to this contention is that the courts are well equipped to deal with such eventualities. The venue transfer provision, 28 U.S.C. § 1404(a), may be invoked by the Government to consolidate separate actions. Or, actions in all but one jurisdiction might be stayed pending the conclusion of one proceeding. A court may even in its discretion dismiss a declaratory judgment or injunctive suit if the same issue is pending in litigation elsewhere.

Further, the declaratory judgment and injunctive remedies are equitable in nature, and other equitable defenses may be interposed. If a multiplicity of suits are undertaken in order to harass the Government or to delay enforcement, relief can be denied on this ground alone. . . .

In addition to all these safeguards against what the Government fears, it is important to note that the institution of this type of action does not by itself stay the effectiveness of the challenged regulation. There is nothing in the record to indicate that petitioners have sought to stay enforcement of the "every time" regulation pending judicial review. See 5 U.S.C. § 705. If the agency believes that a suit of this type will significantly impede enforcement or will harm the public interest, it need not postpone enforcement of the regulation and may oppose any motion for a judicial stay on the part of those challenging the regulation. Ibid. It is scarcely to be doubted that a court would refuse to postpone the effective date of an agency action if the Government could show, as it made no effort to do here, that delay would be detrimental to the public health or safety. . . .

Reversed and remanded.

[On the same day as the *Abbott Laboratories* decision, the Court decided *Gardner v. Toilet Goods Ass'n,* 387 U.S. 167 (1967), holding that another FDA rule was not ripe for pre-enforcement review. The rule in *Toilet Goods* provided that if a maker of color additives refused to permit FDA inspectors free access to its facility and formulae, FDA may immediately suspend certification service to the maker. Without FDA certification the additives could not be sold.

Although the regulation was "final" and its validity presented a strictly legal issue, the Court held that the case was not ripe for immediate review. The rule provided that the FDA "may" order an inspection and, if it is refused, "may" suspend certification. Thus it would help the Court to know about FDA's enforcement problems and the adequacy of safeguards to protect trade secrets. "We believe that judicial appraisal of these factors is likely to stand on a much surer footing in the context of a specific application of this regulation than could be the case in the framework of the generalized challenge made here."

Moreover, the Court was not impressed by the degree of hardship encountered by the additive makers. It was not comparable to that in the *Abbott* case

> where the impact of the administrative action could be said to be felt immediately by those subject to it in conducting their day to day affairs . . . This is not a situation in which primary conduct is affected—when contracts must be negotiated, ingredients tested or substituted, or special records compiled . . . Moreover, no irremediable adverse consequences flow from requiring a later challenge to this regulation by a manufacturer who refuses to allow this type of inspection . . . [R]efusal to allow an inspector here would at most lead only to suspension of certification services to the particular party, a determination that can then be promptly challenged through an administrative procedure, which in turn is reviewable by a court. Such review will provide an adequate forum for testing the regulation on a concrete situation.

JUSTICE FORTAS dissented from *Abbott Laboratories* and concurred in *Toilet Goods*. He contended that both cases were not ripe for review "at this stage, under these facts and in this gross, shotgun fashion."]

The Court, by today's decisions has opened Pandora's box. Federal injunctions will now threaten programs of vast importance to the public welfare. The Court's holding here strikes at programs for the public health. The dangerous precedent goes even further. It is cold comfort—it is little more than delusion—to read in the Court's opinion that "It is scarcely to be doubted that a court would refuse to postpone the effective date of an agency action if the Government could show . . . that delay would be detrimental to the public health or safety." Experience dictates, on the contrary, that it can hardly be hoped that some federal judge somewhere will not be moved as the Court is here, by the cries of anguish and distress of those regulated, to grant a disruptive injunction. . . . I believe that this approach improperly and unwisely gives individual federal district judges a roving commission to halt the regulatory process, and to do so on the basis of abstractions and generalities instead of concrete fact situations, and that it impermissibly broadens the license of the courts to intervene in administrative action by means of a threshold suit for injunction rather than by the method provided by statute. . . .

As to the "every time" rule, the Court says that this confronts the manufacturer with a "real dilemma." But the fact of the matter is that the dilemma is no more than citizens face in connection with countless statutes and with the rules of the SEC, FTC, FCC, ICC, and other regulatory agencies. This has not heretofore been regarded as a basis for injunctive relief unless Congress has so provided. The overriding fact here is—or should be—that the public interest in avoiding the delay in implementing Congress' program far outweighs the private interest; and that the private interest which has so impressed the Court is no more than that which exists in respect of most regulatory statutes or agency rules. Somehow, the Court has concluded that the damage to petitioners if they have to engage in the required redesign and reprint of their labels and printed materials without threshold review outweighs the damage to the public of deferring during the tedious months and years of litigation a cure for the possible danger and asserted deceit of peddling plain medicine under fancy trademarks and for fancy prices which, rightly or wrongly, impelled the Congress to enact this legislation. I submit that a much stronger showing is necessary than the expense and trouble of compliance and the risk of defiance. Actually, if the Court refused to permit this shotgun assault, experience and reasonably sophisticated common sense show that there would be orderly compliance without the disaster so dramatically predicted by the industry, reasonable adjustments by the agency in real hardship cases, and where extreme intransigence involving substantial violations occurred, enforcement actions in which legality of the regulation would be tested in specific, concrete situations. I respectfully submit that this would be the correct and appropriate result. Our refusal to respond to the vastly overdrawn cries of distress would reflect not only healthy skepticism, but our regard for a proper relationship between the courts on the one hand and Congress and the administrative agencies on the other. It would represent a reasonable solicitude for the purposes and programs of the Congress. And it would reflect appropriate modesty as to the competence of the courts. The courts cannot properly—and should not—attempt to judge in the abstract and generally whether this regulation is within the statutory scheme. Judgment as to the "every time" regulation should be made only in light of specific situations, and it may differ depending upon whether the FDA seeks to enforce it as to doctors' circulars, pamphlets for patients, labels, etc. . . . .

Notes and Questions

1. *The Abbott Labs equation.* Justice Harlan's opinion in *Abbott Labs* dominates the law of ripeness. Its statement of the rationale for the ripeness doctrine and its balancing test have been repeated and applied in countless federal and state decisions. What is balanced

against what under the *Abbott Labs* test? How does the ripeness doctrine relate to the final order rule? Do you agree that *Abbott Labs* and *Toilet Goods* should have been decided differently?

The *Abbott Labs* equation has been summarized as follows:

> Pursuant to the "fitness of the issues" prong, we first must decide whether the disputed claims raise purely legal questions and would, therefore, be presumptively suitable for judicial review. Second, we determine whether the court or the agency would benefit from the postponement of review until the agency action or policy in question has assumed either a final or more concrete form. Finally, we examine the appellants' interest in immediate review. In order to outweigh any institutional interests in the deferral of review, appellants must demonstrate "hardship," *i.e.,* that the "impact of the administrative action could be said to be felt immediately by those subject to it in conducting their day-to-day affairs."

Better Government Ass'n v. Department of State, 780 F.2d 86 (D.C.Cir. 1986).

2. *Justice Fortas and predictions of doom.* Before Justice Fortas was appointed to the Supreme Court, he had been a partner of a leading Washington D.C. law firm. He had ample experience in challenging administrative regulations and in using the courts to obstruct enforcement of unwelcome rules. Thus his dissenting remarks about the risks of broadening pre-enforcement review of rules are worth careful consideration. However, decades of experience with the *Abbott Labs* test have not borne out his dire predictions. Pre-enforcement review of regulations appears to have functioned well in clearing away legal doubts about the validity of regulations, thus allowing administration to proceed, or in immediately exposing legal problems with regulations, thus allowing Congress or the agency to correct the problems promptly.

3. *Ripeness and non-legislative rules.* As *Abbott Labs* and *Toilet Goods* show, most (but not all) legislative regulations are ripe for pre-enforcement review. How about interpretive rules and policy statements? Why are non-legislative rules less likely to be treated as ripe for immediate review than legislative rules? *See, e.g., Pacific Legal Foundation v. California Coastal Com'n,* 655 P.2d 306 (Cal.1982) (guidelines not ripe for review because they would be clarified by application in particular cases and because they imposed no great hardship except uncertainty in planning).

In a number of instances, interpretive rules and policy statements have been held ripe for review. In these cases, top decisionmakers in the agency have approved the rule without any indication that the matter is tentative or subject to reconsideration. The agency expects the rule to immediately alter the behavior of the persons to whom it is addressed. See *Better Government Ass'n v. Department of State, supra,* involving guidelines adopted by the Justice Department which listed factors that agencies should consider in granting fee waivers to document requesters under the Freedom of Information Act, discussed in § 8.1 *supra*. Upon a showing of hardship by the plaintiffs (public interest groups who constantly requested documents), the court held that the guidelines were ripe for immediate review.

4. *Ripeness under state law.* Read 1981 MSAPA §§ 5–102, 5–103. If *Abbott Labs* and *Toilet Goods* arose under state law, would the rules be subject to pre-enforcement judicial review? How about the Justice Department guidelines in *Better Government Ass'n?* *See* Auerbach, "Bonfield on State Administrative Law: A Critique," 71 Minn.L.Rev. 543, 571–73 (1987) (criticizing Act for vagueness on issue of whether non-legislative rules are immediately reviewable).

5. *Judicial stays.* An appellate court has discretion to grant a stay of the agency action under review. See APA § 705; 1981 MSAPA § 5–111. Whether a stay is granted may be the most critical timing issue of all. If the court refuses a stay, the damage to the petitioner may be irreparable; even if the petitioner ultimately wins on the merits, it may be too late. However, if the court does stay the agency action, a law enforcement program may be sidetracked for years, with great damage to the public interest.

MSAPA § 5–111 sets forth the factors that should be considered in deciding whether to grant a stay over the objection of the agency. Federal law is similar. See *Cuomo v. NRC,* 772 F.2d 972 (D.C.Cir.1985), refusing to grant a stay of NRC's decision to permit low power testing of the Shoreham Nuclear Power Station.

Note the discussion of judicial stays in both the Harlan and Fortas opinions in *Abbott Labs*. Harlan argues that pre-enforcement review of regulations won't harm the public interest because courts would refuse to grant a stay. Fortas counters that some court, somewhere, undoubtedly would grant a stay despite harm to the public interest.

Should a court grant a stay of the "every time" regulation in *Abbott Labs?* Of the Justice Department guidelines in *Better Government Ass'n?*

6. *Problem.* The "Superfund" Act provides for cleaning up toxic waste dumps. Without notice and comment, EPA adopted a policy statement called the Hazardous Ranking System (HRS). EPA intended HRS to serve as a guideline (to itself and to the public) in setting toxic waste cleanup priorities, but it was not to be binding on anyone. HRS is a methodology for setting priorities as to which sites are most dangerous and should be cleaned up first. HRS took account of many factors, such as the toxicity of the particular hazardous substance that might be released, the likelihood of release into the environment, and the threatened population or other sensitive environment. While HRS enabled the calculation of a danger "score" for a particular site, it did not set any cleanup priorities or single out any sites.

Is HRS ripe for immediate review in an action brought by Zolt Chemicals—a manufacturer that anticipated that the HRS methodology would place its toxic waste dump high on a cleanup priority list? *See Eagle–Picher Industries v. U.S. EPA,* 759 F.2d 905 (D.C.Cir.1985).

§ 11.2.4 EXHAUSTION OF ADMINISTRATIVE REMEDIES

MYERS v. BETHLEHEM SHIPBUILDING CORP.

303 U.S. 41 (1938).

[The NLRB filed a complaint against Bethlehem Shipbuilding, asserting that it violated the National Labor Relations Act by maintaining a company union. The employer argued that its business was not in interstate commerce, hence the NLRB had no jurisdiction under the Act. It sought to enjoin the Board from holding a hearing on its complaint. The lower court granted the injunction.]

BRANDEIS, J.:

.　.　.

We are of opinion that the District Court was without power to enjoin the Board from holding the hearings.

First. There is no claim by the corporation that the statutory provisions and the rules of procedure prescribed for such hearings are illegal; or that the corporation was not accorded ample opportunity to answer the complaint of the Board; or that opportunity to introduce evidence on the allegations made will be denied. The claim is that the provisions of the act are not applicable to the corporation's business at the Fore River Plant, because the operations conducted there are not carried on, and the products manufactured are not sold, in interstate or foreign commerce; that, therefore, the corporation's relations with its employees at the plant cannot burden or interfere with such commerce; that hearings would, at best, be futile; and that the holding of them would result in irreparable damage to the corporation, not only by reason of their direct cost and the loss of time of its officials and employees, but also because the hearings would cause serious impairment of the good will and harmonious relations existing between the corporation and its employees, and thus seriously impair the efficiency of its operations.[4]. . .

Second. The District Court is without jurisdiction to enjoin hearings because the power "to prevent any person from engaging in any unfair practice affecting commerce" has been vested by Congress in the Board and the Circuit Court of Appeals, and Congress has declared: "This power shall be exclusive, and shall not be affected by any other means of adjustment or prevention that has been or may be established by agreement, code, law, or otherwise."　. . .　No power to enforce an

---

4. It is alleged that in 1934 and 1935 the predecessor of the present National Labor Relations Board instituted somewhat similar action against the corporation. Although the proceedings were eventually dismissed, the hearings consumed a total of some 2,500 hours of working time of officials and employees and cost the corporation more than $15,000, none of which could be recovered.

order is conferred upon the Board. To secure enforcement, the Board must apply to a Circuit Court of Appeals for its affirmance. And, until the Board's order has been affirmed by the appropriate Circuit Court of Appeals, no penalty accrues for disobeying it. The independent right to apply to a Circuit Court of Appeals to have an order set aside is conferred upon any party aggrieved by the proceeding before the Board.

. . .

It is true that the Board has jurisdiction only if the complaint concerns interstate or foreign commerce. Unless the Board finds that it does, the complaint must be dismissed. And, if it finds that interstate or foreign commerce is involved, but the Circuit Court of Appeals concludes that such finding was without adequate evidence to support it, or otherwise contrary to law, the Board's petition to enforce it will be dismissed, or the employer's petition to have it set aside will be granted. Since the procedure before the Board is appropriate and the judicial review so provided is adequate, Congress had power to vest exclusive jurisdiction in the Board and the Circuit Court of Appeals.

Third. The corporation contends that, since it denies that interstate or foreign commerce is involved and claims that a hearing would subject it to irreparable damage, rights guaranteed by the Federal Constitution will be denied unless it be held that the District Court has jurisdiction to enjoin the holding of a hearing by the Board. So to hold would, as the government insists, in effect substitute the District Court for the Board as the tribunal to hear and determine what Congress declared the Board exclusively should hear and determine in the first instance. The contention is at war with the long-settled rule of judicial administration that no one is entitled to judicial relief for a supposed or threatened injury until the prescribed administrative remedy has been exhausted. That rule has been repeatedly acted on in cases where, as here, the contention is made that the administrative body lacked power over the subject matter. Obviously, the rule requiring exhaustion of the administrative remedy cannot be circumvented by asserting that the charge on which the complaint rests is groundless and that the mere holding of the prescribed administrative hearing would result in irreparable damage. Lawsuits also often prove to have been groundless; but no way has been discovered of relieving a defendant from the necessity of a trial to establish the fact. . . .

Decrees for preliminary injunction reversed, with direction to dismiss the bills.

NEW JERSEY CIVIL SERVICE ASS'N (NJCSA) v. STATE

443 A.2d 1070 (N.J.1982).

SCHREIBER, J.

At issue in this case is whether state employees who formerly functioned as hearing officers in the Division of Motor Vehicles are entitled to appointment as administrative law judges under the act creating the Office of Administrative Law. Appellants are certain individuals, who before the implementation of N.J.S.A. 52:14F–1 were hearing officers in the Division of Motor Vehicles, and the New Jersey Civil Service Association and the New Jersey State Employees Association who brought this action on behalf of their respective members.

Prior to 1978 many contested cases before state agencies were initially heard by a hearing officer or an examiner who was an employee of the agency responsible for rendering a decision. Some hearing officers were part-time employees who were paid on a per diem basis; others were full-time state employees who performed other duties for their agencies in addition to holding hearings. The use of agency employees to adjudicate claims against an agency encouraged an institutional bias that undermined the fairness and impartiality desired in administrative adjudication. *Mazza v. Cavicchia*, 105 A.2d 545 (1954) (Jacobs, J., dissenting).

To rectify this condition the Legislature amended the Administrative Procedure Act in 1978 to create an independent Office of Administrative Law, staffed by a corps of independent examiners known as administrative law judges. The major purpose of this legislation was "to bring impartiality and objectivity to agency hearings and ultimately to achieve higher levels of fairness in administrative adjudications." Except for the State Board of Parole, the Public Employment Relations Commission, the Division of Workers' Compensation, and the Department of Defense, state agencies can no longer use their own employees to preside over contested cases. Instead, that function is performed by administrative law judges, who are directly responsible to the Director of the Office of Administrative Law.

It is the duty of the Director to "[a]ssign an administrative law judge to any agency empowered to conduct contested cases to preside over . . . proceedings in contested cases. . . ." . . .

The Act provides that it is subject to the provisions of the State Agency Transfer Act. Under the terms of the State Agency Transfer Act, whenever the functions, powers and duties of one agency of the state government are transferred to another, the employees of the agency are transferred as well. In view of the explicit reference to the State Agency Transfer Act, the Director of the Office of Administrative Law inquired of the Attorney General whether the then-employed hearing officers were entitled to appointment as administrative law judges. In an opinion of March 1, 1979, the Attorney General expressed the view that "the functions and responsibilities of Hearing Officers–Examiners in the respective state agencies, insofar as they pertain to presiding over contested cases as are required by the Administrative Procedure Act, have now been abolished and placed exclusively by the Legislature in the Office of Administrative Law." He found that the State Agency Transfer Act did not apply to hearing officers in the several state agencies. . . .

Although the Director of the Office of Administrative Law did not announce that he had followed the Attorney General's advice, or adopted his opinion, hearing officers were not automatically transferred to the Office of Administrative Law. Rather, they were invited to apply for appointment as administrative law judges. Of the forty-five individuals now acting as administrative law judges, approximately half were formerly hearing officers. None of the individual appellants has been appointed an administrative law judge. . . .

After issuance of the Attorney General's opinion, appellants filed a complaint in lieu of prerogative writ and for a declaratory judgment in the Law Division, and also filed a notice of appeal from the Attorney General's opinion to the Appellate Division. The gist of their complaint in both proceedings was that persons holding the title of Hearing Officer/Examiner in the various state agencies were entitled under the provisions of N.J.S.A. 52:14F–9 to appointment as administrative law judges. . . .

I . . .

We have declined to review mere "opinions" or "conclusions" of administrative officers on which no official action was based.

Certainly the Attorney General's Opinion expressing the view that hearing officers are not entitled to appointment as administrative law judges was not a final agency action subject to review. However, the Director of the Office of Administrative Law has followed the Attorney General's advice and has not appointed any of the individual appellants as administrative law judges. The appellants' action may thus fairly be considered an appeal from the implicit refusal of the Director to appoint them as administrative law judges.

Such a construction does not conflict with the Court's reluctance to render opinions in the abstract. Our principal aim in avoiding premature review of administrative determinations has been to protect the Court from becoming entangled in abstract disagreements over administrative policies, and also to refrain from judicial interference until an administrative decision has been formed and its effects felt in a concrete way by the challenging parties. In this case, although administrative policy has not been formally expressed, three years have passed since the Director of the Office of Administrative Law received the Attorney General's opinion. The Director's failure to appoint any of the individual appellants as an administrative law judge is tantamount to final agency action. The effect of that action is directly felt by appellants. In considering their claim we do not intrude into agency policymaking.

Similar considerations prompt us to excuse the failure to exhaust available administrative remedies. Rather than pursue their rights as classified civil service employees to present their claim to the Civil Service Commission, the individual appellants went directly to the Appellate Division in apparent violation of R. 2:2–3(a). The rule provides that "[u]nless the interest of justice requires otherwise, review . . . shall not be maintainable so long as there is available a right of review before any administrative agency or office."

The exhaustion of administrative remedies is not an absolute prerequisite to seeking appellate review, however. Exceptions are made when the administrative remedies would be futile, when irreparable harm would result, when jurisdiction of the agency is doubtful, or when an overriding public interest calls for a prompt judicial decision. We have frequently held that in a case involving only legal questions, the doctrine of exhaustion of administrative remedies does not apply. As Justice Jacobs has explained, in determining when the exhaustion requirement may be waived,

> we are not particularly concerned with the label or description placed on the issue but are concerned with underlying considerations such as the relative delay and expense, the necessity for taking evidence and making factual determinations thereon, the nature of the agency and the extent of judgment, discretion and expertise involved, and such other pertinent factors . . . as may fairly serve to aid in determining whether, on balance, the interests of justice dictate the extraordinary course of bypassing the administrative remedies made available by the Legislature. [*Roadway Express, Inc. v. Kingsley,* 179 A.2d 729 (1962)]

In this case, there are no facts in dispute. We need consider only the law and legislative history. Nor does resolution of the disputed issue call for the exercise of special administrative expertise. In these circumstances, putting appellants to the additional expense and delay of bringing their case in the appropriate administrative forum is unjustified. . . .

II

In support of their contention that former hearing officers are entitled to appointment as administrative law judges, appellants rely on the provision of the Act establishing the Office of Administrative Law that provides that that Act shall be subject to the State Agency Transfer Act. . . .

An analysis of the plain terms of the Office of Administrative Law act reveals a legislative intent inconsistent with appellants' interpretation. . . .

The . . . elements of the statutory scheme indicate that the Legislature intended to create a corps of independent professionals, who were not simply hearing officers under a different title, but had greatly expanded duties. There is nothing in the Office of Administrative Law act that suggests that former hearing officers were to be imported en masse into the new office. This is not to say that no former hearing officer may be made an administrative judge. Some have been. However, the Act vests the power of appointment in the Governor. It is within the Governor's prerogative to determine initially whether a former hearing officer is to become an administrative law judge. . . .

Notes and Questions

1. *The Myers case.* *Myers* is the leading federal case on exhaustion of administrative remedies. Justice Brandeis' statement is often quoted: "The contention is at war with the long-settled rule of judicial administration that no one is entitled to judicial relief for a supposed or threatened injury until the prescribed administrative remedy has been exhausted." Consider whether that "long-settled rule" is as absolute as Brandeis suggests.

Note that the NLRB had not definitively ruled that it had jurisdiction because Bethlehem's business sufficiently affected interstate commerce. It had merely issued a complaint. Should the case have been dismissed under the final order rule as well as the exhaustion of remedies rule?

2. *New Jersey Law.* New Jersey law differs sharply from federal law and from the law of most states. *See, e.g., County of Contra Costa v. State,* 222 Cal.Rptr. 750 (Cal.App.1986) (exhaustion required although issues were both legal and constitutional). Do you agree that "the interests of justice" excuse the hearing officers from pursuing their remedy before the Civil Service Commission? That the courts should decide issues of law without requiring exhaustion? That the court was reviewing a final order?

3. *Statutory bases for the exhaustion rule.* 1961 MSAPA § 15(a) provides: "A person who has exhausted all administrative remedies available within the agency and who is aggrieved by a final decision in a contested case is entitled to judicial review." Study carefully the two provisions on exhaustion in the 1981 MSAPA: §§ 5–107, 5–112. Is § 5–107 consistent with *Myers?* With *NJCSA?*

Does § 704 of the federal APA excuse litigants from exhausting the remedy of appeal to superior agency authority (i.e. to the agency heads), unless the agency otherwise requires such appeal by rule and provides that the action meanwhile is inoperative? Or is there a different way to read § 704?

Should courts have greater discretion to ignore a litigant's failure to exhaust adequate administrative remedies when the exhaustion doctrine is wholly a product of court-created equitable doctrine (as it is in many federal court cases) than when the doctrine is a product of a statutory mandate as under the 1961 and 1981 MSAPAs?

4. *Social Security and exhaustion.* Many federal statutes relating to particular agencies impose specific exhaustion requirements. In such cases, courts have less discretion about excusing exhaustion. One frequently litigated example is 42 USC § 405(g) of the Social Security Act, which provides for judicial review of determinations under the old age, disability, and Medicare programs. Sec. 405(g) states: "Any indi-

vidual, after any final decision of the Secretary made after a hearing to which he was a party . . . may obtain a review of such decision" by a civil action in federal district court. This provision generally requires a litigant to file a claim, exhaust state and federal remedies (including a hearing before an ALJ), and appeal a negative decision to the Appeals Council (which stands in for the "Secretary"). However, the Supreme Court has allowed some, but not all, litigants to proceed despite a failure to exhaust remedies.

Recall *Mathews v. Eldridge,* § 2.3 *supra,* involving the issue of whether a recipient of disability payments has a right to a pre-termination hearing. The Court allowed Eldridge to sue without waiting for a hearing and without an appeal. Why? Similarly, in *Bowen v. City of New York,* 476 U.S. 467 (1986), the Court excused exhaustion. *Bowen* was a class action which contended that the agency had an unpublished policy that required it to refuse applications for psychiatric disability, even though published rules required individualized considerations of such claims. The Court held that claimants could be members of the class (thus qualifying for a rehearing of their claim) even if they had failed to exhaust remedies. Why?

In *Heckler v. Ringer,* 466 U.S. 602 (1984), the Court required exhaustion of the appeal remedy and dismissed the complaint. The claimants wished to have Medicare pay for a certain surgery (bilateral carotid body resection), but the Secretary had ruled that it was not "reasonable and necessary" so she would not pay for it. The claimants argued that the ruling was invalid because it was arbitrary and capricious, because it prevented ALJ's from exercising their discretion in individual cases, and because the Secretary had failed to comply with APA rulemaking requirements. Since at bottom these were claims to be paid for surgery, the Court held that administrative remedies must be exhausted. Unlike *Mathews v. Eldridge* and *Bowen v. City of NY* (where the procedural issues were collateral to the question of whether plaintiff was entitled to benefits), the issues could be raised and decided in an administrative appeal without undue hardship.

5. *When is an administrative remedy "adequate?"* Parties need only exhaust *adequate* administrative remedies; failure to exhaust an inadequate remedy is excusable. When is a remedy inadequate? Is the fact that a litigant wants to skip the remedy evidence that it is inadequate? Is a remedy inadequate because it would be very expensive to exhaust? *See* note 4 in *Myers.*

6. *Factors in the judicial balance.* In considering the cases in the next two notes, try to list the factors which, together or separately, might influence a court to exercise its discretion to excuse a failure to exhaust remedies. Consider also whether 1981 MSAPA § 5–107 fairly summarizes federal law. Some factors which might appear on your list include:

　　　i. The nature and severity of harm to plaintiff from delayed review;

ii.   The need for agency expertise in resolving the issue;

iii.   The nature of the issue involved (issues of law, constitutional issue, jurisdictional issue, application of law to fact);

iv.   The adequacy of the remedy in light of plaintiff's particular claim;

v.   The extent to which the claim appears to be serious rather than a tactic for delaying the agency process;

vi.   The apparent clarity or doubt as to the resolution of the merits of plaintiff's claim;

vii.   The extent to which exhaustion would be futile because an adverse decision is certain.

viii.   The extent to which petitioner had a valid excuse for its failure to exhaust.

a. *Andrade v. Lauer,* 729 F.2d 1475 (D.C.Cir.1984). Andrade, an employee of agency A, was laid off as part of a federal government "reduction in force" (RIF). She complains that this was unlawful for two reasons: i) Agencies A and B had been unlawfully combined in the RIF (if they had been kept separate, employees of A would have kept their jobs); ii) the official who conducted the RIF had been illegally appointed by the President without the advice and consent of the Senate. Recall § 7.5.6, *supra.*

A collective bargaining agreement gave Andrade a series of remedies. She could protest her layoff by filing a grievance with a person in management; protest that person's decision to the head of the agency; refer the matter to arbitration—if her union was willing to do so; and appeal the arbitrator's award to the Federal Labor Relations Authority.

In discussing exhaustion, the court stated that "when the reasons supporting the doctrine are found inapplicable, the doctrine should not be blindly applied."

The exhaustion requirement serves four primary purposes. First, it carries out the congressional purpose in granting authority to the agency by discouraging the "frequent and deliberate flouting of administrative processes [that] could . . . encourag[e] people to ignore its procedures." . . . Second, it protects agency autonomy by allowing the agency the opportunity in the first instance to apply its expertise, exercise whatever discretion it may have been granted, and correct its own errors. Third, it aids judicial review by allowing the parties and the agency to develop the facts of the case in the administrative proceeding. Fourth, it promotes judicial economy by avoiding needless repetition of administrative and judicial factfinding, and by perhaps avoiding the necessity of any judicial involvement at all if the parties successfully vindicate their claims before the agency.

The court held that Andrade had to exhaust remedies with respect to her first claim but not the second. What is the difference? Is the holding on the first claim (an issue of statutory construction) consistent with *NJCSA?*

Was there a meaningful administrative remedy with respect to the constitutional issue? The general rule is that an agency lacks authority to determine the constitutionality of statutes. *See* Comment, "When Constitutional Issues Arise in Agency Adjudications: A Suggested Approach," 65 Or.L.Rev. 413 (1986). The same may not be true with respect to the constitutionality of the application of statutes or of the agency's own action. See *id.* at 420 n. 31, 443–49; B. Schwartz, ADMINISTRATIVE LAW § 8.37 at 519 (2d ed. 1984). What is the reason for distinguishing between a challenge to the constitutionality of the agency's enabling act and a challenge to the application of the statute to a particular situation? Even though an agency lacks power to decide a facial constitutional attack on a statute, many cases require exhaustion of the non-constitutional issues before reviewing the constitutional issues. Why?

b. *Athlone Industries, Inc. v. Consumer Product Safety Com'n* (CPSC), 707 F.2d 1485 (D.C.Cir.1983). CPSC asserts that Athlone and Advance failed to notify buyers of their automatic baseball pitching machines of safety hazards in using the machines. CPSC also asserts that it has power to assess civil penalties against both companies for failing to notify buyers, and it started proceedings to assess them. Athlone argues that only a court, not CPSC, has power to impose penalties. Advance had already secured a decision from a different court of appeals that CPSC had no authority to assess penalties.

The court excused Athlone's failure to exhaust remedies and to obtain a final order and took up the substantive issue. It held that CPSC lacked power to assert penalties.

Why did the court excuse the failure to exhaust remedies and secure a final order? Is the case consistent with *Andrade?*

c. *Andrade* and *Athlone* illustrate the indeterminacy of exhaustion doctrine. Because the issue is decided through an ad hoc application of the factors which might excuse exhaustion, the results are difficult to predict, courts must constantly confront the issue, and litigants are encouraged to try for premature review. Would you favor a more determinate rule? If so, what would it be? Always require exhaustion? Never require it?

7. *Too late to exhaust—exhaustion as preclusion.* Suppose a party has failed to exhaust a remedy relating to an issue in the case *and the remedy is no longer available.* For example, a party might have failed to raise an issue like exclusion of evidence before the agency. Courts generally refuse to consider that particular issue on appeal. See *United States v. L.A. Tucker Truck Lines,* 344 U.S. 33, 37 (1952): "Simple fairness to those who are engaged in the tasks of administration, and to litigants, requires as a general rule that courts should not topple over administrative decisions unless the administrative body not only has erred but has erred against objection made at the time

appropriate under its practice." Yet this rule is not absolute. Courts may consider the issue to "prevent a miscarriage of justice or to preserve the integrity of the judicial process." *See California Dept. of Educ. v. Bennett,* 843 F.2d 333, 339 (9th Cir.1988). 1981 MSAPA § 5–112 also provides for exceptions to this principle.

An even more serious problem arises when the appellant has failed to pursue an administrative remedy that is no longer available, such as appealing an ALJ's decision to the agency heads, which involves all of the issues in the case. If a court requires exhaustion of the administrative remedy in such cases, it has precluded judicial review of the entire case. Two Supreme Court cases illustrate preclusive exhaustion in a particularly harsh setting.

The only means by which a registrant could obtain judicial review of the classification decision of his draft board was to refuse induction into the armed forces. Refusal to be inducted was a federal crime. At his criminal trial, a registrant could raise the defense that there was "no basis in fact" for his classification. This meager form of judicial review, which was unique to Selective Service cases, had been rather boldly fashioned by the Supreme Court in the teeth of a statute which provided that decisions of Selective Service boards were "final." *See* § 10.4, *supra. Estep v. United States,* 327 U.S. 114 (1946). In *McKart* and *McGee,* the issue was whether a registrant must have pursued remedies within Selective Service (appearing before the local board and appealing to the state appeal board) in order to question a classification at trial.

a. *McKart v. United States,* 395 U.S. 185 (1969). McKart argued that he should be exempt from the draft as a "sole surviving son," since his father had been killed in World War II. After his mother died, McKart's local board denied this classification (on the advice of the National Director), since both of the registrant's parents were dead. McKart made his claim to the local board in writing but made no personal appearance before the board and failed to appeal to the state appeal board. The Court did not require exhaustion and held that McKart was entitled to the claimed exemption.

b. *McGee v. United States,* 402 U.S. 479 (1971). McGee argued that his local Board erred in denying his claim as a conscientious objector (CO). While still in school (and exempt as a student), he submitted the CO application form to the Board. Later, after mailing the charred remains of his draft card to the President, he adopted a policy of non-cooperation with Selective Service. He returned the Board's questionnaire unopened and made no personal appearance before the board. He did not appeal the denial of CO status to the state appeal board. The Court held that the defense of improper classification could not be raised at his criminal trial because of the failure to exhaust remedies. Can you reconcile the holdings in these cases?

c. The APA and appeals: The APA was, by statute, inapplicable to Selective Service. However, suppose it were applicable; what would be the effect of the last clause of the third sentence of § 704 on *McKart* and *McGee?*

8. *Actions under § 1983.* In *Patsy v. Florida Board of Regents,* 457 U.S. 496 (1982), the Court considered whether exhaustion of state remedies was required before bringing a civil rights suit in federal court under § 1983. Ms. Patsy was employed by a public university in Florida and alleged that she had been discriminated against in promotions because of her age and sex. Patsy did not take advantage of the remedies provided by Florida for race and sex discrimination (a grievance procedure within the university). The Supreme Court held that a § 1983 plaintiff is never required to exhaust state remedies, no matter how adequate or easily exhausted those remedies might be. Does this mean that Ms. Patsy was not even required to complain to her boss about the alleged discrimination before filing suit? Is this wise policy? Why might Patsy prefer to avoid the state remedies and go directly to court?

9. *Problem.* After proper notice and comment, a state Water Quality Board adopted a regulation concerning the dumping of mining debris into lakes and rivers. The regulation provides that suspended solids in the debris must not exceed 30 milligrams per liter. Under a variance procedure in the regulation, a miner who believes that the limitation should not apply to it can apply for permission to exceed it.

Taconite Mining Co. dumps tailings which contain 14,000 milligrams of solids per liter into Inspiration Lake. It did not submit comments during the rulemaking proceeding (although it knew it was going on) and did not apply for a variance. It contends that the regulation is arbitrary and capricious, as applied to it, because its tailings are so heavy that they sink directly to the bottom of Inspiration Lake (which is extremely deep) and stay there. If it is compelled to alter its disposal practices so that its emissions contain only 30 milligrams per liter, the solid material will float and thus cause a more serious pollution problem. Nobody raised this issue during the rulemaking proceedings.

Taconite brought an action in the state trial court seeking a declaratory judgment that the regulation was invalid as applied to it. After taking evidence for six weeks, the trial court agreed and invalidated the regulation as applied to Taconite. Should this decision be affirmed? *See* Gelpe, "Exhaustion of Administrative Remedies: Lessons from Environmental Cases," 53 Geo.Wash.L.Rev. 1 (1984).

§ 11.2.5 PRIMARY JURISDICTION
NADER v. ALLEGHENY AIRLINES, INC.
426 U.S. 290 (1976).

[Ralph Nader purchased a ticket on Allegheny Flight 864 from Washington to Hartford, Conn. on the morning of April 28, 1972. Allegheny (like all airlines) overbooks its flights since there are usually no-shows; however, it did not disclose this practice to customers. Allegheny confirmed 107 tickets for Flight 864, but only 100 seats were available. Nader (who arrived 5 minutes before flight time) was "bumped" and had to fly to Boston and travel by car to his destination.

While the chances of being bumped are statistically small, it happens to about 80,000 passengers per year. Civil Aeronautics Board (CAB) rules neither authorized nor forbade overbooking but did require compensation to bumped passengers in the form of liquidated damages equal to the price of the ticket (with a $25 minimum and a $200 maximum). The rules stated that passengers could refuse these damages and pursue judicial remedies. At the time of this case, the CAB was conducting a rulemaking proceeding to consider further rules concerning overbooking.

Nader rejected Allegheny's offer of liquidated damages ($32.41) and sued for damages for common law fraud. The District Court entered a judgment for Nader, awarding him $10 in compensatory damages and $25,000 in punitive damages. The Court of Appeals reversed, remanding the award of punitive damages for further findings. It also held that the CAB should have an opportunity to pass on the issue of whether the failure to disclose overbooking violated § 411 of the CAB enabling act. The District Court was instructed to stay proceedings until the CAB resolved this question, either through adjudication or rulemaking. It characterized its holding as "but another application of the principle of primary jurisdiction, a doctrine whose purpose is the coordination of the workings of agency and court.]

POWELL, J.:

. . .

The question before us, then, is whether the Board must be given an opportunity to determine whether respondent's alleged failure to disclose its practice of deliberate overbooking is a deceptive practice under § 411 before petitioner's common-law action is allowed to proceed. The decision of the Court of Appeals requires the District Court to stay the action brought by petitioner in order to give the Board an opportunity to resolve the question. If the Board were to find that there had been no violation of § 411, respondent would be immunized from common-law liability.

A

Section 1106 of the [CAB enabling] Act provides that "[n]othing contained in this chapter shall in any way abridge or alter the remedies now existing at common law or by statute, but the provisions of this chapter are in addition to such remedies." The Court of Appeals found that "although the saving clause of section 1106 purports to speak in absolute terms it cannot be read so literally." In reaching this conclusion, it relied on *Texas & Pacific R. Co. v. Abilene Cotton Oil Co.,* 204 U.S. 426. In that case, the Court, despite the existence of a saving clause virtually identical to § 1106, refused to permit a state-court common-law action challenging a published carrier rate as "unjust and unreasonable." The Court conceded that a common-law right, even absent a saving clause, is not to be abrogated "unless it be found that the preexisting right is so repugnant to the statute that the survival of such right would in effect deprive the subsequent statute of its efficacy; in other words, render its provisions nugatory."

But the Court found that the continuance of private damages actions attacking the reasonableness of rates subject to the regulation of the Interstate Commerce Commission would destroy the purpose of the Interstate Commerce Act, which was to eliminate discrimination by requiring uniform rates. The saving clause, the Court found, "cannot in reason be construed as continuing in shippers a common law right, the continued existence of which would be absolutely inconsistent with the provisions of the act. In other words, the act cannot be held to destroy itself."

In this case, unlike *Abilene*, we are not faced with an irreconcilable conflict between the statutory scheme and the persistence of common-law remedies. In *Abilene* the carrier, if subject to both agency and court sanctions, would be put in an untenable position when the agency and a court disagreed on the reasonableness of a rate. The carrier could not abide by the rate filed with the Commission, as required by statute, and also comply with a court's determination that the rate was excessive. The conflict between the court's common-law authority and the agency's ratemaking power was direct and unambiguous. The court in the present case, in contrast, is not called upon to substitute its judgment for the agency's on the reasonableness of a rate—or, indeed, on the reasonableness of any carrier practice. There is no Board requirement that air carriers engage in overbooking or that they fail to disclose that they do so. And any impact on rates that may result from the imposition of tort liability or from practices adopted by a carrier to avoid such liability would be merely incidental. Under the circumstances, the common-law action and the statute are not "absolutely inconsistent" and may coexist, as contemplated by § 1106.

B

Section 411 of the Act allows the Board, where "it considers that such action .. would be in the interest of the public," "upon its own initiative or upon complaint by any air carrier, foreign air carrier, or ticket agent," to "investigate and determine whether any air carrier . . . has been or is engaged in unfair or deceptive practices or unfair methods of competition . . . ." Practices determined to be in violation of this section "shall" be the subject of a cease-and-desist order. The Court of Appeals concluded—and respondent does not challenge the conclusion here—that this section does not totally preclude petitioner's common-law tort action. But the Court of Appeals also held, relying on the nature of the airline industry as "a regulated system of limited competition," and the Board's duty to promote "adequate, economical, and efficient service," "at the lowest cost consistent with the furnishing of such service," that the Board has the power in a § 411 proceeding to approve practices that might otherwise be considered deceptive and thus to immunize carriers from common-law liability.

We cannot agree. No power to immunize can be derived from the language of § 411. And where Congress has sought to confer such power it has done so expressly, as in § 414 of the Act, which relieves those affected by certain designated orders (not including orders issued under § 411) "from the operations of the 'antitrust laws.'" When faced with an exemptive provision similar to § 414 in *United States Navigation Co. v. Cunard S.S. Co.*, 284 U.S. 474 (1932), this Court dismissed an antitrust action because initial consideration by the agency had not been sought. The Court pointed out that the Act in question was "restrictive in its operation upon some of the activities of common carriers . . ., and permissive in respect of others."

Section 411, in contrast, is purely restrictive. It contemplates the elimination of "unfair or deceptive practices" that impair the public interest. Its role has been described:

> 'Unfair or deceptive practices or unfair methods of competition,' as used in § 411, are broader concepts than the common-law idea of unfair competition. . . . The section is concerned not with punishment of wrongdoing or protection of injured competitors, but rather with protection of the public interest.

As such, § 411 provides an injunctive remedy for vindication of the public interest to supplement the compensatory common-law remedies for private parties preserved by § 1106.

Thus, a violation of § 411, contrary to the Court of Appeals' conclusion, is not coextensive with a breach of duty under the common law. We note that the Board's jurisdiction to initiate an investigation under § 411 is expressly premised on a finding that the "public interest" is involved. The Board "may not employ its powers to vindicate private rights." Indeed, individual consumers are not even entitled to initiate proceedings under § 411, a circumstance that indicates that Congress did not intend to require private litigants to obtain a § 411 determination before they could proceed with the common-law remedies preserved by § 1106.

Section 411 is both broader and narrower than the remedies available at common law. A cease-and-desist order may issue under § 411 merely on the Board's conclusion, after an investigation determined to be in the public interest, that a carrier is engaged in an "unfair or deceptive practice." No findings that the practice was intentionally deceptive or fraudulent or that it in fact has caused injury to an individual are necessary.

On the other hand, a Board decision that a cease-and-desist order is inappropriate does not represent approval of the practice under investigation. It may merely represent the Board's conclusion that the serious prohibitory sanction of a cease-and-desist order is inappropriate, that a more flexible approach is necessary. A wrong may be of the sort that calls for compensation to an injured individual without requiring the extreme remedy of a cease-and-desist order. Indeed, the Board, in dealing with the problem of overbooking by air carriers, has declined to issue cease-and-desist orders, despite the determination by an examiner in one case that a § 411 violation had occurred. Instead, the Board has elected to establish boarding priorities and to ensure that passengers will be compensated for being bumped either by a liquidated sum under Board regulations or by resort to a suit for compensatory damages at common law.

In sum, § 411 confers upon the Board a new and powerful weapon against unfair and deceptive practices that injure the public. But it does not represent the only, or best, response to all challenged carrier actions that result in private wrongs.

C

The doctrine of primary jurisdiction "is concerned with promoting proper relationships between the courts and administrative agencies charged with particular regulatory duties." *United States v. Western Pacific R. Co.,* 352 U.S. 59. Even when common-law rights and remedies survive and the agency in question lacks the power to confer immunity from common-law liability, it may be appropriate to refer specific issues to an agency for initial determination where that procedure would secure "[u]niformity and consistency in the regulation of business entrusted to a particular agency" or where

"the limited functions of review by the judiciary [would be] more rationally exercised, by preliminary resort for ascertaining and interpreting the circumstances underlying legal issues to agencies that are better equipped than courts by specialization, by insight gained through experience, and by more flexible procedure." *Far East Conference v. United States,* 342 U.S. 570.

The doctrine has been applied, for example, when an action otherwise within the jurisdiction of the court raises a question of the validity of a rate or practice included in a tariff filed with an agency, particularly when the issue involves technical questions of fact uniquely within the expertise and experience of an agency—such as matters turning on an assessment of industry conditions. In this case, however, considerations of uniformity in regulation and of technical expertise do not call for prior reference to the Board.

Petitioner seeks damages for respondent's failure to disclose its overbooking practices. He makes no challenge to any provision in the tariff, and indeed there is no tariff provision or Board regulation applicable to disclosure practices. Petitioner also makes no challenge . . . to limitations on common-law damages imposed through exculpatory clauses included in a tariff.

Referral of the misrepresentation issue to the Board cannot be justified by the interest in informing the court's ultimate decision with "the expert and specialized knowledge" of the Board. The action brought by petitioner does not turn on a determination of the reasonableness of a challenged practice—a determination that could be facilitated by an informed evaluation of the economics or technology of the regulated industry. The standards to be applied in an action for fraudulent misrepresentation are within the conventional competence of the courts, and the judgment of a technically expert body is not likely to be helpful in the application of these standards to the facts of this case.

We are particularly aware that, even where the wrong sought to be redressed is not misrepresentation but bumping itself, which has been the subject of Board consideration and for which compensation is provided in carrier tariffs, the Board has contemplated that there may be individual adjudications by courts in common-law suits brought at the option of the passenger. The present regulations dealing with the problems of overbooking and oversales were promulgated by the Board in 1967. They provide for denied boarding compensation to bumped passengers and require each carrier to establish priority rules for seating passengers and to file reports of passengers who could not be accommodated. The order instituting these regulations contemplates that the bumped passenger will have a choice between accepting denied boarding compensation as "liquidated damages for all damages incurred . . . as a result of the carrier's failure to provide the passenger with confirmed reserved space," or pursuing his or her common-law remedies. The Board specifically provided for a 30–day period before the specified compensation need be accepted so that the passenger will not be forced to make a decision before "the consequences of denied boarding have occurred and are known." After evaluating the consequences, passengers may choose as an alternative "to pursue their remedy under the common law."

III

We conclude that petitioner's tort action should not be stayed pending reference to the Board and accordingly the decision of the Court of Appeals on this issue is reversed. The Court of Appeals did not address the question whether petitioner had introduced sufficient evidence to sustain his claim. We remand the case for consideration of that question and for further proceedings consistent with this opinion.

JUSTICE WHITE added a brief concurring opinion.

FOREE v. CROWN CENTRAL PETROLEUM CORP.
431 S.W.2d 312 (Tex.1968).

[Defendant, a "common purchaser" of oil, refused to extend its pipeline to plaintiff's oil field. The Texas Railroad Commission investigated plaintiff's claim of discrimination but never reached a final decision because another pipeline became available and the Commission considered the case moot. Plaintiffs sued under § 11c of Art.

6049a which provides that "[W]hen any person . . . is discriminated against by a common purchaser in favor of the production of said common purchaser, a cause of action for damages . . . shall lie against said common purchaser and said person . . . may bring suit for same in any court of competent jurisdiction . . . ." The trial court granted defendant's motion to dismiss on the basis of primary jurisdiction, and the Court of Civil Appeals affirmed.]

. . .

We find no express provision in Art. 6049a or related statutes which denies to a complainant his statutory right to prosecute a suit for damages in the absence of a final and subsisting Commission order finding discrimination. Indeed, the plain wording of Sec. 11c, Art. 6049a, seems clearly to authorize such a suit without regard to Commission action. If, therefore, an order of the Commission finding discrimination is prerequisite to the right to sue for and recover damages, it must be made so by the judicially created doctrine of "primary jurisdiction". According to one writer, "Questions of primary jurisdiction arise only when the statutory arrangements are such that administrative and judicial jurisdiction are concurrent for the initial decision of some questions". Davis, Administrative Law Doctrines, 28 Tex.L.R. 376 (1950). That is the situation here.

The statutes confer no jurisdiction upon the Railroad Commission to award damages or statutory penalties; liability for these exactions is to be determined exclusively by the courts. On the other hand, the courts are not vested with original jurisdiction to order that common carrier pipelines be extended and connected to particular wells; that jurisdiction is confided to the Commission by Secs. 7, 8b and 11d, Art. 6049a, upon findings that the extension is "reasonable and required in the public interest and that the expense involved will not impair the ability of such common carrier * * * to perform its duty to the public". In both forums, a preliminary finding of discrimination is prerequisite to the granting of relief. Jurisdiction of the courts and the Commission is thus concurrent on the issue of discrimination. In such situations, the general rule, as stated by Davis in Administrative Law Text, (1950), at 352, is as follows:

> The theory seems reasonably clear that the test for applying the principle of primary jurisdiction is not whether some parts of the case are within the exclusive jurisdiction of the courts but whether some parts of the case are within the exclusive jurisdiction of the agency. Because the purpose of the doctrine is to assure that the agency will not be by-passed on what is especially committed to it, and because resort to the courts is still open after the agency has acted, the doctrine applies even if the agency has no jurisdiction to grant the relief sought. Thus, the doctrine was applied in Thompson v. Texas, Mexican Railway [328 U.S. 134 (1946)], even though the suit was for damages and even though the ICC could not award damages. When an agency cannot grant the

relief sought, the court may stay the judicial proceeding pending the administrative determination; this is what was done in the Tex–Mex case.

There are exceptions to the general rule.

We had occasion in Gregg v. Delhi–Taylor Oil Corp., 344 S.W.2d 411 (1961), to review the problem of primary jurisdiction of administrative agencies in considerable depth. In that case, we held that although clothed with extensive powers to make rules and regulations to prevent waste of oil and gas and to protect correlative rights of owners of interests therein, the Railroad Commission did not have primary jurisdiction to prevent a trespass by one operator upon the property of another. The rationale of our holding that the courts had original jurisdiction to ascertain whether a trespass was being committed and to enjoin it was that the questions presented were "primarily judicial in nature". . . .

The cause of action for damages in the instant case illustrates another necessary exception to the general rule, to wit: when the administrative agency is powerless to grant the relief sought and has no authority to make incidental findings which are essential to the granting of the relief. We have purposely stated the exception narrowly because we do not have before us a case in which the administrative agency is powerless to grant the relief sought, but does have authority to make incidental findings which are essential to the granting of the relief. The effect incidental findings, in the latter situation, should have on judicial action in granting or denying relief which only the courts can give need not be decided. We will save the problem for another case and another day.

Art. 6049a and related conservation statutes confer broad powers upon the Railroad Commission to hold hearings, make findings, promulgate rules and regulations and enter orders to prevent or to terminate discriminatory practices by common carriers and common purchasers of oil and gas. In none of the statutes, however, do we find authority for the Commission to hold hearings and make findings of discrimination except as incidental to the power to take official action, i.e., to promulgate rules and regulations or to enter and issue orders. In other words, no authority is conferred upon the Commission to make findings of discrimination in a vacuum or as a mere agent of a trial court. It follows, therefore, that the Commission does not have authority, and cannot have exclusive primary jurisdiction, to make findings of discrimination in a particular case when the alleged discrimination no longer exists and official action by the Commission is thereby mooted. That is the situation here. . . .

[The] mootness of the Commission's order and its incidental finding of discrimination did not destroy petitioners' cause of action for damages. Their suit stood on the court's docket for trial of the issue of discrimination and the amount of their damages. The court of civil appeals erred in affirming the take-nothing judgment on the ground that a final and subsisting Commission order finding discrimination was prerequisite to petitioners' right to sue for and recover damages.

Notes and Questions

1. *The two faces of primary jurisdiction.* Note that the issue presented in final order, ripeness, and exhaustion of remedy cases is the timing of judicial review of agency action. In primary jurisdiction cases, the issue is not the timing of judicial *review* of agency action. Instead, these cases present the problem of concurrent *trial* jurisdiction. When both a court and an agency have jurisdiction to try a case, the question is: who goes first? In general, where an agency has delegated authority over a matter, the agency has primary jurisdiction over that matter, even where, as in *Foree*, the statute appears to vest concurrent original jurisdiction in the courts.

Primary jurisdiction cases are of two different kinds. If a court finds that the agency should go first, and the agency proceeding will dispose of *all* the issues in the case, the court dismisses the action. The matter returns to court only upon judicial review of the agency action. This is primary jurisdiction of the whole case. If the court finds that the agency cannot dispose of the entire case, the court stays the action, remands to the agency, and retains jurisdiction to try the remaining issues after the agency is done. This is primary jurisdiction of an issue or issues.

Were *Nader* and *Foree* examples of primary jurisdiction over the whole case or primary jurisdiction over issues? In a case of primary jurisdiction over issues, why couldn't a court simply ask the agency to express its views by filing an amicus brief instead of sending the case to the agency? Why would a plaintiff oppose a judicial decision to send a matter to an agency?

2. *Rationale for primary jurisdiction.* Why should a court, which has jurisdiction over a matter, decide that the entire case, or some of the issues, should be tried by an agency? The *Nader* case indicates that there may be three reasons for doing so:

     i. A need for uniform results;

     ii. A need for the agency's expertise;

     iii. The possibility that agency approval of a challenged practice may immunize that practice from judicial challenge, or at least alter the legal status of the practice.

Why were these rationales for primary jurisdiction unpersuasive in *Nader?* In *Foree?*

Should the doctrine of primary jurisdiction apply when the agency lacks authority to provide the remedy sought by plaintiff in the court in which it filed suit? Was that the problem in *Foree?* Or is this no problem—the case comes back to court after the agency has done its job in order that the appropriate remedy can be decreed. Could *Nader* be explained in part by the inability of the CAB to provide the money damage remedy sought by plaintiff?

Could *Nader* be explained by the fact that there was no clear procedural mechanism by which the plaintiff could invoke agency process to resolve his problem? Compare *Foree* with *Ricci v. Chicago Mercantile Exch.,* 409 U.S. 289 (1973) (primary jurisdiction applies despite fact that statute gave petitioner no means by which to require agency to consider his case and despite fact that agency lacked authority to settle dispute).

Could *Nader* be explained by the fact that the bodies of law to be applied by the CAB and by the court are quite distinct (as opposed to *Foree* where both court and agency would have to analyze the economics of the oil pipeline business)?

Could it be explained by the fact that the CAB's special expertise would not have been particularly helpful in analyzing the issues before the court? *See School Committee v. Greenfield Educ. Ass'n,* 431 N.E.2d 180 (Mass.1982) (legal and constitutional issues for court, technical issues for agency); *Great Northern Ry. v. Merchants Elevator Co.,* 259 U.S. 285 (1922). In the *Great Northern* case, the only issue was the construction of a railroad tariff. Neither party claimed that the words had any special meaning, and it was not necessary to take evidence on railway custom and practice. Since the ICC's expertise would not be helpful in such a case and the issue was purely legal, primary jurisdiction was inapplicable. *Compare United States v. Western Pacific R. Co.,* 352 U.S. 59 (1956). In *Western Pacific,* the Court held that primary jurisdiction applied to an issue of railway tariff construction; ICC expertise was needed to decide whether napalm bombs without fuses were "incendiary bombs" or "gasoline in steel drums," the former having a much higher rate than the latter.

Should the doctrine of primary jurisdiction apply in a *criminal* case when the defendant argues that agency expertise is needed to resolve technical issues? *Compare United States v. General Dynamics Corp.,* 828 F.2d 1356 (9th Cir.1987) (primary jurisdiction should not apply in a criminal case for defrauding the government on a defense contract) *with United States v. Yellow Freight Sys. Inc.,* 762 F.2d 737 (9th Cir. 1985) (case remanded to ICC to resolve tariff construction issues).

3. *Primary jurisdiction and antitrust.* The most difficult and important primary jurisdiction cases concern the conflict between regulation and antitrust. The antitrust philosophy is that the public interest is best served by unrestrained competition and free markets. The regulation philosophy is that unrestrained competition is contrary to the public interest; a regulatory scheme relies on an agency rather than the market to set prices, license competitors or routes, or otherwise restrain competition.

Some observers believe that competition essentially is dead in this country and that the nation thus simply should accept increased regulation of industry. Other observers have more faith in the future of competition, however, and thus oppose the potentially anticompetitive effects of exclusive agency jurisdiction. Indeed, the commentators appear diametrically opposed as to whether regulation or competition is to be preferred.

Botein, "Primary Jurisdiction: The Need for Better Court/Agency Interaction," 29 Rutgers L.Rev. 867, 872 (1976).

As the *Nader* case observes, an agency frequently has statutory power to immunize a particular business practice from antitrust scrutiny. Similarly, a statute which creates a regulatory scheme may exempt certain practices from the antitrust laws or require a relaxed application of the antitrust laws. In such cases a court will ordinarily allow the agency to go first. If the agency declares the conduct immune from antitrust, there is nothing left for the court to do (except to judicially review the agency's determination). If the agency declines to immunize the practice (or holds that it is not within a statutory exemption), the antitrust action can proceed. Often that antitrust action will be informed by the agency's conclusions concerning the role of the challenged practice in the regulatory scheme.

The many cases on the antitrust-regulation conflict are confusing and difficult to reconcile. Each conflict between antitrust and regulation presents a unique problem. In part, the area is difficult because of the need to construe the scope of ambiguous statutory grants of antitrust immunity. Compare the Court's construction of § 411 in *Nader*. Sometimes statutes do not explicitly confer antitrust immunity, but the Court nevertheless implies immunity because the regulatory scheme is so pervasive that the antitrust laws would disrupt that scheme. Similarly, courts often consider the murky question of whether the antitrust law should be accommodated to the regulatory scheme at issue even if no absolute immunity is granted. In other cases, the Court construes the statute tentatively, remands to the agency for application of its expertise, and makes the final decision on antitrust immunity or antitrust-regulation reconciliation on judicial review of the agency's decision.

The antitrust-regulation cases are also difficult because they force the justices to take sides on the philosophical conflict mentioned above. If the court sends the matter to the agency, the result is likely to be immunity from the antitrust laws; if the court keeps the case, the result is likely to be an application of the antitrust laws and enhanced competition. Of course, even if a case is sent to an agency which seeks to confer antitrust immunity, a reviewing court might ultimately hold that the agency's accommodation of antitrust and regulatory goals is invalid and that the agency lacked power to confer immunity.

4. *Private rights of action.* In addition to his claim for common law fraud, Nader also won a judgment in the district court against Allegheny on the theory that § 404(b) of the Act prohibited an airline from bumping a passenger with a confirmed reservation. This statute provided:

No air carrier . . . shall . . . give . . . any undue or unreasonable preference or advantage to any particular person . . . or subject any particular person . . . to any unjust discrimination or any undue or unreasonable prejudice or disadvantage . . .

The Court of Appeals reversed for further findings under § 404, and the issue of its applicability was not presented to the Supreme Court. The Act provides that the CAB can enforce § 404 and also provides for criminal penalties, but leaves open the question of whether victims of prejudice or discrimination by airlines have a "private right of action" to sue the airline in federal court for damages. The courts have upheld private lawsuits under § 404. *See Fitzgerald v. Pan American World Airways,* 229 F.2d 499 (2d Cir.1956) (singer Ella Fitzgerald alleged that she had been bumped from a flight because of racial discrimination).

The problem of whether a prohibitory statute gives rise to an implied private right of action by a victim against the party who caused the harm is difficult and recurrent. In *Cort v. Ash,* 422 U.S. 66 (1975), the Court set forth a four-factor test to analyze whether Congress intended to create a private right of action under statutes imposing public duties that are silent with respect to private rights.

    i. Is the plaintiff one of the class for whose special benefit the statute was enacted?

    ii. Is there evidence of legislative intent to create such a remedy or deny it?

    iii. Is it consistent with the underlying purposes of the legislative scheme to imply such a remedy?

    iv. Is the cause of action one traditionally relegated to state law so that it would be inappropriate to infer a cause of action based solely on federal law?

5. *Problem.* The FCC heavily regulates interstate telephone service under the Communications Act. That Act requires telephone companies to file with the FCC tariffs setting forth their rates and conditions of service and requires the tariffs to be adhered to until changed. The FCC must disapprove any such tariff if it is not "just and reasonable." Several years ago, AT&T filed Tariff 132 with the FCC. It prohibited the attachment of any device not furnished by AT&T to an AT&T phone. It also allowed AT&T to remove such a device or to terminate service to the user. The FCC accepted Tariff 132 as filed but did not consider its validity.

Carter invented a device (a Carterphone) which could be attached to a telephone and would allow someone miles away to converse over that phone. Citing Tariff 132, AT&T (which marketed a different type of remote communicating device) threatened to terminate phone service to anyone who attached a Carterphone to an AT&T phone. Carter sued AT&T in federal district court for violation of the antitrust laws.

AT&T's conduct in threatening termination of phone service to Carterphone users would normally be a violation of the Sherman Act (as an attempt to monopolize). The Communications Act contains no explicit antitrust exemption for regulated phone companies. Should the court

(i) proceed to decide the case,

(ii) dismiss the case, or

(iii) retain jurisdiction but stay the case pending an FCC decision? *See Carter v. AT&T,* 365 F.2d 486 (5th Cir.1966).

Appendix A

FEDERAL ADMINISTRATIVE PROCEDURE ACT UNITED STATES CODE, TITLE 5 CHAPTER 5—ADMINISTRATIVE PROCEDURE

Table of Sections

Sec.
551. Definitions.
552. Public information; agency rules, opinions, orders, records, and proceedings.
552a. Records maintained on individuals [Privacy Act omitted.]
552b. Open meetings [Sunshine Act omitted.]
553. Rule making.
554. Adjudications.
555. Ancillary matters.
556. Hearings; presiding employees; powers and duties; burden of proof; evidence; record as basis of decision.
557. Initial decisions; conclusiveness; review by agency; submissions by parties; contents of decisions; record.
558. Imposition of sanctions; determination of applications for licenses; suspension, revocation, and expiration of licenses.
559. Effect on other laws; effect of subsequent statute.
701. Application; definitions.
702. Right of review.
703. Form and venue of proceeding.
704. Actions reviewable.
705. Relief pending review.
706. Scope of review.
3105. Appointment of administrative law judges.
7521. Actions against administrative law judges.
5372. Administrative law judges.
3344. Details; administrative law judges.
1305. Administrative law judges.

§ 551. Definitions

For the purpose of this subchapter—

(1) "agency" means each authority of the Government of the United States, whether or not it is within or subject to review by another agency, but does not include—

    (A) the Congress;

    (B) the courts of the United States;

    (C) the governments of the territories or possessions of the United States;

    (D) the government of the District of Columbia; or except as to the requirements of section 552 of this title—

    (E) agencies composed of representatives of the parties or of representatives of organizations of the parties to the disputes determined by them;

    (F) courts martial and military commissions;

    (G) military authority exercised in the field in time of war or in occupied territory; or

    (H) functions conferred by sections 1738, 1739, 1743, and 1744 of title 12; chapter 2 of title 41; or sections 1622, 1884, 1891–1902, and former section 1641(b)(2), of title 50, appendix;

(2) "person" includes an individual, partnership, corporation, association, or public or private organization other than an agency;

(3) "party" includes a person or agency named or admitted as a party, or properly seeking and entitled as of right to be admitted as a party, in an agency proceeding, and a person or agency admitted by an agency as a party for limited purposes;

(4) "rule" means the whole or a part of an agency statement of general or particular applicability and future effect designed to implement, interpret, or prescribe law or policy or describing the organization, procedure, or practice requirements of an agency and includes the approval or prescription for the future of rates, wages, corporate or financial structures or reorganization thereof, prices, facilities, appliances, services or allowances therefor or of valuations, costs, or accounting, or practices bearing on any of the foregoing;

(5) "rule making" means agency process for formulating, amending, or repealing a rule;

(6) "order" means the whole or a part of a final disposition, whether affirmative, negative, injunctive, or declaratory in form, of an agency in a matter other than rule making but including licensing;

(7) "adjudication" means agency process for the formulation of an order;

(8) "license" includes the whole or a part of an agency permit, certificate, approval, registration, charter, membership, statutory exemption or other form of permission;

(9) "licensing" includes agency process respecting the grant, renewal, denial, revocation, suspension, annulment, withdrawal, limitation, amendment, modification, or conditioning of a license;

(10) "sanction" includes the whole or a part of an agency—

(A) prohibition, requirement, limitation, or other condition affecting the freedom of a person;

(B) withholding of relief;

(C) imposition of penalty or fine;

(D) destruction, taking, seizure, or withholding of property;

(E) assessment of damages, reimbursement, restitution, compensation, costs, charges, or fees;

(F) requirement, revocation, or suspension of a license; or

(G) taking other compulsory or restrictive action;

(11) "relief" includes the whole or a part of an agency—

(A) grant of money, assistance, license, authority, exemption, exception, privilege, or remedy;

(B) recognition of a claim, right, immunity, privilege, exemption, or exception; or

(C) taking of other action on the application or petition of, and beneficial to, a person;

(12) "agency proceeding" means an agency process as defined by paragraphs (5), (7), and (9) of this section;

(13) "agency action" includes the whole or a part of an agency rule, order, license, sanction, relief, or the equivalent or denial thereof, or failure to act; and

(14) "ex parte communication" means an oral or written communication not on the public record with respect to which reasonable prior notice to all parties is not given, but it shall not include requests for status reports on any matter or proceeding covered by this subchapter.

§ 552. Public information; agency rules, opinions, orders, records, and proceedings

(a) Each agency shall make available to the public information as follows:

(1) Each agency shall separately state and currently publish in the Federal Register for the guidance of the public—

(A) descriptions of its central and field organization and the established places at which, the employees (and in the case of a uniformed service, the members) from whom, and the methods whereby, the public may obtain information, make submittals or requests, or obtain decisions;

(B) statements of the general course and method by which its functions are channeled and determined, including the nature and requirements of all formal and informal procedures available;

(C) rules of procedure, descriptions of forms available or the places at which forms may be obtained, and instructions as to the scope and contents of all papers, reports, or examinations;

(D) substantive rules of general applicability adopted as authorized by law, and statements of general policy or interpretations of general applicability formulated and adopted by the agency; and

(E) each amendment, revision, or repeal of the foregoing.

Except to the extent that a person has actual and timely notice of the terms thereof, a person may not in any manner be required to resort to, or be adversely affected by, a matter required to be published in the Federal Register and not so published. For the purpose of this paragraph, matter reasonably available to the class of persons affected thereby is deemed published in the Federal Register when incorporated by reference therein with the approval of the Director of the Federal Register.

(2) Each agency, in accordance with published rules, shall make available for public inspection and copying—

(A) final opinions, including concurring and dissenting opinions, as well as orders, made in the adjudication of cases;

(B) those statements of policy and interpretations which have been adopted by the agency and are not published in the Federal Register; and

(C) administrative staff manuals and instructions to staff that affect a member of the public;

unless the materials are promptly published and copies offered for sale. To the extent required to prevent a clearly unwarranted invasion of personal privacy, an agency may delete identifying details when it makes available or publishes an opinion, statement of policy, interpretation, or staff manual or instruction. However, in each case the justification for the deletion shall be explained fully in writing. Each agency shall also maintain and make available for public inspection and copying current indexes providing identifying information for the public as to any matter issued, adopted, or promulgated after July 4, 1967, and required by this paragraph to be made available or published. Each agency shall promptly publish, quarterly or more frequently, and distribute (by sale or otherwise) copies of each index or supplements thereto unless it determines by order published in the Federal Register that the publication would be unnecessary and impracticable, in which case the agency shall nonetheless provide copies of such index on request at a cost not to exceed the direct cost of duplication. A final order, opinion, statement of policy, interpretation, or staff manual or instruction that affects a member of the public may be relied on, used, or cited as precedent by an agency against a party other than an agency only if—

(i) it has been indexed and either made available or published as provided by this paragraph; or

(ii) the party has actual and timely notice of the terms thereof.

(3) Except with respect to the records made available under paragraphs (1) and (2) of this subsection, each agency, upon any request for records which (A) reasonably describes such records and (B) is made in accordance with published rules stating the time, place, fees (if any), and procedures to be followed, shall make the records promptly available to any person.

(4)(A)(i) In order to carry out the provisions of this section, each agency shall promulgate regulations, pursuant to notice and receipt of public comment, specifying the schedule of fees applicable to the processing of requests under this section and establishing procedures and guidelines for determining when such fees should be waived or reduced. . . .

(B) On complaint, the district court of the United States in the district in which the complainant resides, or has his principal place of business, or in which the agency records are situated, or in the District of Columbia, has jurisdiction to enjoin the agency from withholding agency records and to order the production of any agency records improperly withheld from the complainant. In such a case the court shall determine the matter de novo, and may examine the contents of such agency records in camera to determine whether such records or any part thereof shall be withheld under any of the exemptions set forth in subsection (b) of this section, and the burden is on the agency to sustain its action.

(C) Notwithstanding any other provision of law, the defendant shall serve an answer or otherwise plead to any complaint made under this subsection within thirty days after service upon the defendant of the pleading in which such complaint is made, unless the court otherwise directs for good cause shown.

(D) [Repealed]

(E) The court may assess against the United States reasonable attorney fees and other litigation costs reasonably incurred in any case under this section in which the complainant has substantially prevailed.

(F) Whenever the court orders the production of any agency record, improperly withheld from the complainant and assesses against the United States reasonable attorney fees and other litigation costs, and the court additionally issues a written finding that the circumstances surrounding the withholding raise questions whether agency personnel acted arbitrarily or capriciously with respect to the withholding, the Civil Service Commission shall promptly initiate a proceeding to determine whether disciplinary action is warranted against the officer or employee who was primarily responsible for the withholding. The Commission, after investigation and consideration of the evidence submitted, shall submit its findings and recommendations to the administrative authority of the agency concerned and shall send copies of the findings and recommendations to the officer or employee or his representative. The administrative authority shall take the corrective action that the Commission recommends.

(G) In the event of noncompliance with the order of the court, the district court may punish for contempt the responsible employee, and in the case of a uniformed service, the responsible member.

(5) Each agency having more than one member shall maintain and make available for public inspection a record of the final votes of each member in every agency proceeding.

(6)(A) Each agency, upon any request for records made under paragraph (1), (2), or (3) of this subsection, shall—

(i) determine within ten days (excepting Saturdays, Sundays and legal public holidays) after the receipt of any such request whether to comply with such request and shall immediately notify the person making such request of such determination and the reasons therefor, and of the right of such person to appeal to the head of the agency any adverse determination; and

(ii) make a determination with respect to any appeal within twenty days (excepting Saturdays, Sundays, and legal public holidays) after the receipt of such appeal. If on appeal the denial of the request for records is in whole or in part upheld, the agency shall notify the person making such request of the provisions for judicial review of that determination under paragraph (4) of this subsection. . . .

(C) Any person making a request to any agency for records under paragraph (1), (2), or (3) of this subsection shall be deemed to have exhausted his administrative remedies with respect to such request if the agency fails to comply with the applicable time limit provisions of this paragraph. If the Government can show exceptional circumstances exist and that the agency is exercising due diligence in responding to the request, the court may retain jurisdiction and allow the agency additional time to complete its review of the records. Upon any determination by an agency to comply with a request for records, the records shall be made promptly available to such person making such request. Any notification of denial of any request for records under this subsection shall set forth the names and titles or positions of each person responsible for the denial of such request.

(b) This section does not apply to matters that are—

(1)(A) specifically authorized under criteria established by an Executive order to be kept secret in the interest of national defense or foreign policy and (B) are in fact properly classified pursuant to such Executive order;

(2) related solely to the internal personnel rules and practices of an agency;

(3) specifically exempted from disclosure by statute (other than section 552b of this title), provided that such statute (A) requires that the matters be withheld from the public in such a manner as to leave no discretion on the issue, or (B) establishes particular criteria for withholding or refers to particular types of matters to be withheld;

(4) trade secrets and commercial or financial information obtained from a person and privileged or confidential;

(5) inter-agency or intra-agency memorandums or letters which would not be available by law to a party other than an agency in litigation with the agency;

(6) personnel and medical files and similar files the disclosure of which would constitute a clearly unwarranted invasion of personal privacy;

(7) records or information compiled for law enforcement purposes, but only to the extent that the production of such law enforcement records or information (A) could reasonably be expected to interfere with enforcement proceedings, (B) would deprive a person of a right to a fair trial or an impartial adjudication, (C) could reasonably be expected to constitute an unwarranted invasion of personal privacy, (D) could reasonably be expected to disclose the identity of a confidential source, including a State, local, or foreign agency or authority or any private institution which furnished information on a confidential basis, and, in the case of a record or information compiled by criminal law enforcement authority in the course of a criminal investigation or by an agency conducting a lawful national security intelligence investigation, information furnished by a confidential source, (E) would disclose techniques and procedures for law enforcement investigations or prosecutions, or would disclose guidelines for law enforcement

investigations or prosecutions if such disclosure could reasonably be expected to risk circumvention of the law, or (F) could reasonably be expected to endanger the life or physical safety of any individual;

(8) contained in or related to examination, operating, or condition reports prepared by, on behalf of, or for the use of an agency responsible for the regulation or supervision of financial institutions; or

(9) geological and geophysical information and data, including maps, concerning wells.

Any reasonably segregable portion of a record shall be provided to any person requesting such record after deletion of the portions which are exempt under this subsection.

(c)(1) Whenever a request is made which involves access to records described in subsection (b)(7)(A) and—

(A) the investigation or proceeding involves a possible violation of criminal law; and

(B) there is reason to believe that (i) the subject of the investigation or proceeding is not aware of its pendency, and (ii) disclosure of the existence of the records could reasonably be expected to interfere with enforcement proceedings,

the agency may, during only such time as that circumstance continues, treat the records as not subject to the requirements of this section.

(2) Whenever informant records maintained by a criminal law enforcement agency under an informant's name or personal identifier are requested by a third party according to the informant's name or personal identifier, the agency may treat the records as not subject to the requirements of this section unless the informant's status as an informant has been officially confirmed.

(3) Whenever a request is made which involves access to records maintained by the Federal Bureau of Investigation pertaining to foreign intelligence or counterintelligence, or international terrorism, and the existence of the records is classified information as provided in subsection (b)(1), the Bureau may, as long as the existence of the records remains classified information, treat the records as not subject to the requirements of this section.

(d) This section does not authorize withholding of information or limit the availability of records to the public, except as specifically stated in this section. This section is not authority to withhold information from Congress.

(e) On or before March 1 of each calendar year, each agency shall submit a report covering the preceding calendar year to the Speaker of the House of Representatives and President of the Senate for referral to the appropriate committees of the Congress. . . .

(f) For purposes of this section, the term "agency" as defined in section 551(1) of this title includes any executive department, military department, Government corporation, Government controlled corporation, or other establishment in the executive branch of the Government (including the Executive Office of the President), or any independent regulatory agency.

§ 552a. Records maintained on individuals [Privacy Act omitted]

§ 552b. Open meetings [Sunshine Act omitted]

§ 553. Rule making

(a) This section applies, accordingly to the provisions thereof, except to the extent that there is involved—

> (1) a military or foreign affairs function of the United States; or

> (2) a matter relating to agency management or personnel or to public property, loans, grants, benefits, or contracts.

(b) General notice of proposed rule making shall be published in the Federal Register, unless persons subject thereto are named and either personally served or otherwise have actual notice thereof in accordance with law. The notice shall include—

> (1) a statement of the time, place, and nature of public rule making proceedings;

> (2) reference to the legal authority under which the rule is proposed; and

> (3) either the terms or substance of the proposed rule or a description of the subjects and issues involved.

Except when notice or hearing is required by statute, this subsection does not apply—

> (A) to interpretative rules, general statements of policy, or rules of agency organization, procedure, or practice; or

> (B) when the agency for good cause finds (and incorporates the finding and a brief statement of reasons therefor in the rules issued) that notice and public procedure thereon are impracticable, unnecessary, or contrary to the public interest.

(c) After notice required by this section, the agency shall give interested persons an opportunity to participate in the rule making through submission of written data, views, or arguments with or without opportunity for oral presentation. After consideration of the relevant matter presented, the agency shall incorporate in the rules adopted a concise general statement of their basis and purpose. When rules are required by statute to be made on the record after opportunity for an agency hearing, sections 556 and 557 of this title apply instead of this subsection.

(d) The required publication or service of a substantive rule shall be made not less than 30 days before its effective date, except—

(1) a substantive rule which grants or recognizes an exemption or relieves a restriction;

(2) interpretative rules and statements of policy; or

(3) as otherwise provided by the agency for good cause found and published with the rule.

(e) Each agency shall give an interested person the right to petition for the issuance, amendment, or repeal of a rule.

§ 554. Adjudications

(a) This section applies, according to the provisions thereof, in every case of adjudication required by statute to be determined on the record after opportunity for an agency hearing, except to the extent that there is involved—

(1) a matter subject to a subsequent trial of the law and the facts de novo in a court;

(2) the selection or tenure of an employee, except an administrative law judge appointed under section 3105 of this title;

(3) proceedings in which decisions rest solely on inspections, tests, or elections;

(4) the conduct of military or foreign affairs functions;

(5) cases in which an agency is acting as an agent for a court; or

(6) the certification of worker representatives.

(b) Persons entitled to notice of an agency hearing shall be timely informed of—

(1) the time, place, and nature of the hearing;

(2) the legal authority and jurisdiction under which the hearing is to be held; and

(3) the matters of fact and law asserted.

When private persons are the moving parties, other parties to the proceeding shall give prompt notice of issues controverted in fact or law; and in other instances agencies may by rule require responsive pleading. In fixing the time and place for hearings, due regard shall be had for the convenience and necessity of the parties or their representatives.

(c) The agency shall give all interested parties opportunity for—

(1) the submission and consideration of facts, arguments, offers of settlement, or proposals of adjustment when time, the nature of the proceeding, and the public interest permit; and

(2) to the extent that the parties are unable so to determine a controversy by consent, hearing and decision on notice and in accordance with sections 556 and 557 of this title.

(d) The employee who presides at the reception of evidence pursuant to section 556 of this title shall make the recommended decision or initial decision required by section 557 of this title, unless he becomes unavailable to the agency. Except to the extent required for the disposition of ex parte matters as authorized by law, such an employee may not—

(1) consult a person or party on a fact in issue, unless on notice and opportunity for all parties to participate; or

(2) be responsible to or subject to the supervision or direction of an employee or agent engaged in the performance of investigative or prosecuting functions for an agency.

An employee or agent engaged in the performance of investigative or prosecuting functions for an agency in a case may not, in that or a factually related case, participate or advise in the decision, recommended decision, or agency review pursuant to section 557 of this title, except as witness or counsel in public proceedings. This subsection does not apply—

(A) in determining applications for initial licenses;

(B) to proceedings involving the validity or application of rates, facilities, or practices of public utilities or carriers; or

(C) to the agency or a member or members of the body comprising the agency.

(e) The agency, with like effect as in the case of other orders, and in its sound discretion, may issue a declaratory order to terminate a controversy or remove uncertainty.

§ 555. Ancillary matters

(a) This section applies, according to the provisions thereof, except as otherwise provided by this subchapter.

(b) A person compelled to appear in person before an agency or representative thereof is entitled to be accompanied, represented, and advised by counsel or, if permitted by the agency, by other qualified representative. A party is entitled to appear in person or by or with counsel or other duly qualified representative in an agency proceeding. So far as the orderly conduct of public business permits, an interested person may appear before an agency or its responsible employees for the presentation, adjustment, or determination of an issue, request, or controversy in a proceeding, whether interlocutory, summary, or otherwise, or in connection with an agency function. With due regard for the convenience and necessity of the parties or their representatives and within a reasonable time, each agency shall proceed to conclude a matter presented to it. This subsection does not grant or deny a person who is not a lawyer the right to appear for or represent others before an agency or in an agency proceeding.

(c) Process, requirement of a report, inspection, or other investigative act or demand may not be issued, made, or enforced except as authorized by law. A person compelled to submit data or evidence is entitled to retain or, on payment of lawfully prescribed costs, procure a copy or transcript thereof, except that in a non-public investigatory proceeding the witness may for good cause be limited to inspection of the official transcript of his testimony.

(d) Agency subpenas authorized by law shall be issued to a party on request and, when required by rules of procedure, on a statement or showing of general relevance and reasonable scope of the evidence sought. On contest, the court shall sustain the subpena or similar process or demand to the extent that it is found to be in accordance with law. In a proceeding for enforcement, the court shall issue an order requiring the appearance of the witness or the production of the evidence or data within a reasonable time under penalty of punishment for contempt in cases of contumacious failure to comply.

(e) Prompt notice shall be given of the denial in whole or in part of a written application, petition, or other request of an interested person made in connection with any agency proceeding. Except in affirming a prior denial or when the denial is self-explanatory, the notice shall be accompanied by a brief statement of the grounds for denial.

§ 556. Hearings; presiding employees; powers and duties; burden of proof; evidence; record as basis of decision

(a) This section applies, according to the provisions thereof, to hearings required by section 553 or 554 of this title to be conducted in accordance with this section.

(b) There shall preside at the taking of evidence—

(1) the agency;

(2) one or more members of the body which comprises the agency; or

(3) one or more administrative law judges appointed under section 3105 of this title.

This subchapter does not supersede the conduct of specified classes of proceedings, in whole or in part, by or before boards or other employees specially provided for by or designated under statute. The functions of presiding employees and of employees participating in decisions in accordance with section 557 of this title shall be conducted in an impartial manner. A presiding or participating employee may at any time disqualify himself. On the filing in good faith of a timely and sufficient affidavit of personal bias or other disqualification of a presiding or participating employee, the agency shall determine the matters as a part of the record and decision in the case.

(c) Subject to published rules of the agency and within its powers, employees presiding at hearings may—

(1) administer oaths and affirmations;

(2) issue subpenas authorized by law;

(3) rule on offers of proof and receive relevant evidence;

(4) take depositions or have depositions taken when the ends of justice would be served;

(5) regulate the course of the hearing;

(6) hold conferences for the settlement or simplification of the issues by consent of the parties;

(7) dispose of procedural requests or similar matters;

(8) make or recommend decisions in accordance with section 557 of this title; and

(9) take other action authorized by agency rule consistent with this subchapter.

(d) Except as otherwise provided by statute, the proponent of a rule or order has the burden of proof. Any oral or documentary evidence may be received, but the agency as a matter of policy shall provide for the exclusion of irrelevant, immaterial, or unduly repetitious evidence. A sanction may not be imposed or rule or order issued except on consideration of the whole record or those parts thereof cited by a party and supported by and in accordance with the reliable, probative, and substantial evidence. The agency may, to the extent consistent with the interests of justice and the policy of the underlying statutes administered by the agency, consider a violation of section 557(d) of this title sufficient grounds for a decision adverse to a party who has knowingly committed such violation or knowingly caused such violation to occur. A party is entitled to present his case or defense by oral or documentary evidence, to submit rebuttal evidence, and to conduct such cross-examination as may be required for a full and true disclosure of the facts. In rule making or determining claims for money or benefits or applications for initial licenses an agency may, when a party will not be prejudiced thereby, adopt procedures for the submission of all or part of the evidence in written form.

(e) The transcript of testimony and exhibits, together with all papers and requests filed in the proceeding, constitutes the exclusive record for decision in accordance with section 557 of this title and, on payment of lawfully prescribed costs, shall be made available to the parties. When an agency decision rests on official notice of a material fact not appearing in the evidence in the record, a party is entitled, on timely request, to an opportunity to show the contrary.

§ 557. Initial decisions; conclusiveness; review by agency; submissions by parties; contents of decisions; record

(a) This section applies, according to the provisions thereof, when a hearing is required to be conducted in accordance with section 556 of this title.

(b) When the agency did not preside at the reception of the evidence, the presiding employee or, in cases not subject to section 554(d) of this title, an employee qualified to preside at hearings pursuant to section 556 of this title, shall initially decide the case unless the agency requires, either in specific cases or by general rule, the entire record to be certified to it for decision. When the presiding employee makes an initial decision, that decision then becomes the decision of the agency without further proceedings unless there is an appeal to, or review on motion of, the agency within time provided by rule. On appeal from or review of the initial decision, the agency has all the powers which it would have in making the initial decision except as it may limit the issues on notice or by rule. When the agency makes the decision without having presided at the reception of the evidence, the presiding employee or an employee qualified to preside at hearings pursuant to section 556 of this title shall first recommend a decision, except that in rule making or determining application for initial licenses—

(1) instead thereof the agency may issue a tentative decision or one of its responsible employees may recommend a decision; or

(2) this procedure may be omitted in a case in which the agency finds on the record that due and timely execution of its functions imperatively and unavoidably so requires.

(c) Before a recommended, initial, or tentative decision, or a decision on agency review of the decision of subordinate employees, the parties are entitled to a reasonable opportunity to submit for the consideration of the employees participating in the decisions—

(1) proposed findings and conclusions; or

(2) exceptions to the decisions or recommended decisions of subordinate employees or to tentative agency decisions; and

(3) supporting reasons for the exceptions or proposed findings or conclusions.

The record shall show the ruling on each finding, conclusion, or exception presented. All decisions, including initial, recommended, and tentative decisions, are a part of the record and shall include a statement of—

(A) findings and conclusions, and the reasons or basis therefor, on all the material issues of fact, law, or discretion presented on the record; and

(B) the appropriate rule, order, sanction, relief, or denial thereof.

(d)(1) In any agency proceeding which is subject to subsection (a) of this section, except to the extent required for the disposition of ex parte matters as authorized by law—

(A) no interested person outside the agency shall make or knowingly cause to be made to any member of the body comprising the agency, administrative law judge, or other employee who is or may reasonably be expected to be involved in the decisional process of the proceeding, an ex parte communication relevant to the merits of the proceeding;

(B) no member of the body comprising the agency, administrative law judge, or other employee who is or may reasonably be expected to be involved in the decisional process of the proceeding, shall make or knowingly cause to be made to any interested person outside the agency an ex parte communication relevant to the merits of the proceeding;

(C) a member of the body comprising the agency, administrative law judge, or other employee who is or may reasonably be expected to be involved in the decisional process of such proceeding who receives, or who makes or knowingly causes to be made, a communication prohibited by this subsection shall place on the public record of the proceeding:

(i) all such written communications;

(ii) memoranda stating the substance of all such oral communications; and

(iii) all written responses, and memoranda stating the substance of all oral responses, to the materials described in clauses (i) and (ii) of this subparagraph;

(D) upon receipt of a communication knowingly made or knowingly caused to be made by a party in violation of this subsection, the agency, administrative law judge, or other employee presiding at the hearing may, to the extent consistent with the interests of justice and the policy of the underlying statutes, require the party to show cause why his claim or interest in the proceeding should not be dismissed, denied, disregarded, or otherwise adversely affected on account of such violation; and

(E) the prohibitions of this subsection shall apply beginning at such time as the agency may designate, but in no case shall they begin to apply later than the time at which a proceeding is noticed for hearing unless the person responsible for the communication has knowledge that it will be noticed, in which case the prohibitions shall apply beginning at the time of his acquisition of such knowledge.

(2) This subsection does not constitute authority to withhold information from Congress.

§ 558. Imposition of sanctions; determination of applications for licenses; suspension, revocation, and expiration of licenses

(a) This section applies, according to the provisions thereof, to the exercise of a power or authority.

(b) A sanction may not be imposed or a substantive rule or order issued except within jurisdiction delegated to the agency and as authorized by law.

(c) When application is made for a license required by law, the agency, with due regard for the rights and privileges of all the interested parties or adversely affected persons and within a reasonable time, shall set and complete proceedings required to be conducted in accordance with sections 556 and 557 of this title or other proceedings required by law and shall make its decision. Except in cases of willfulness or those in which public health, interest, or safety requires otherwise, the withdrawal, suspension, revocation, or annulment of a license is lawful only if, before the institution of agency proceedings therefor, the licensee has been given—

(1) notice by the agency in writing of the facts or conduct which may warrant the action; and

(2) opportunity to demonstrate or achieve compliance with all lawful requirements.

When the licensee has made timely and sufficient application for a renewal or a new license in accordance with agency rules, a license with reference to an activity of a continuing nature does not expire until the application has been finally determined by the agency.

§ 559. Effect on other laws; effect of subsequent statute

This subchapter . . . [does] not limit or repeal additional requirements imposed by statute or otherwise recognized by law. Except as otherwise required by law, requirements or privileges relating to evidence or procedure apply equally to agencies and persons. Each agency is granted the authority necessary to comply with the requirements of this subchapter through the issuance of rules or otherwise. Subsequent [statutes] may not be held to supersede or modify this subchapter . . . except to the extent that it does so expressly.

§ 701. Application; definitions

(a) This chapter applies, according to the provisions thereof, except to the extent that—

(1) statutes preclude judicial review; or

(2) agency action is committed to agency discretion by law.

(b) For the purpose of this chapter—

(1) "agency" means each authority of the Government of the United States, whether or not it is within or subject to review by another agency, but does not include—

(A) the Congress;

(B) the courts of the United States;

(C) the governments of the territories or possessions of the United States;

(D) the government of the District of Columbia;

(E) agencies composed of representatives of the parties or of representatives of organizations of the parties to the disputes determined by them;

(F) courts martial and military commissions;

(G) military authority exercised in the field in time of war or in occupied territory; or . . .

(2) "person", "rule", "order", "license", "sanction", "relief", and "agency action" have the meanings given them by section 551 of this title.

§ 702. Right of review

A person suffering legal wrong because of agency action, or adversely affected or aggrieved by agency action within the meaning of a relevant statute, is entitled to judicial review thereof. An action in a court of the United States seeking relief other than money damages and stating a claim that an agency or an officer or employee thereof acted or failed to act in an official capacity or under color of legal authority shall not be dismissed nor relief therein be denied on the ground that it is against the United States or that the United States is an indispensable party. The United States may be named as a defendant in any such action, and a judgment or decree may be entered against the United States: *Provided,* That any mandatory or injunctive decree shall specify the Federal officer or officers (by name or by title), and their successors in office, personally responsible for compliance. Nothing herein (1) affects other limitations on judicial review or the power or duty of the court to dismiss any action or deny relief on any other appropriate legal or equitable ground; or (2) confers authority to grant relief if any other statute that grants consent to suit expressly or impliedly forbids the relief which is sought.

§ 703. Form and venue of proceeding

The form of proceeding for judicial review is the special statutory review proceeding relevant to the subject matter in a court specified by statute or, in the absence or inadequacy thereof, any applicable form of legal action, including actions for declaratory judgments or writs of prohibitory or mandatory injunction or habeas corpus, in a court of competent jurisdiction. If no special statutory review proceeding is applicable, the action for judicial review may be brought against the United States, the agency by its official title, or the appropriate officer. Except to the extent that prior, adequate, and exclusive opportunity for judicial review is provided by law, agency action is subject to judicial review in civil or criminal proceedings for judicial enforcement.

§ 704. Actions reviewable

Agency action made reviewable by statute and final agency action for which there is no adequate remedy in a court are subject to judicial review. A preliminary, procedural, or intermediate agency action or ruling not directly reviewable is subject to review on the review of the final agency action. Except as otherwise expressly required by statute, agency action otherwise final is final for the purposes of this section whether or not there has been presented or determined an application for a declaratory order, for any form of reconsideration, or, unless the agency otherwise requires by rule and provides that the action meanwhile is inoperative, for an appeal to superior agency authority.

§ 705. Relief pending review

When an agency finds that justice so requires, it may postpone the effective date of action taken by it, pending judicial review. On such conditions as may be required and to the extent necessary to prevent irreparable injury, the reviewing court, including the court to which a case may be taken on appeal from or on application for certiorari or other writ to a reviewing court, may issue all necessary and appropriate process to postpone the effective date of an agency action or to preserve status or rights pending conclusion of the review proceedings.

§ 706. Scope of review

To the extent necessary to decision and when presented, the reviewing court shall decide all relevant questions of law, interpret constitutional and statutory provisions, and determine the meaning or applicability of the terms of an agency action. The reviewing court shall—

(1) compel agency action unlawfully withheld or unreasonably delayed; and

(2) hold unlawful and set aside agency action, findings, and conclusions found to be—

(A) arbitrary, capricious, an abuse of discretion, or otherwise not in accordance with law;

(B) contrary to constitutional right, power, privilege, or immunity;

(C) in excess of statutory jurisdiction, authority, or limitations, or short of statutory right;

(D) without observance of procedure required by law;

(E) unsupported by substantial evidence in a case subject to section 556 and 557 of this title or otherwise reviewed on the record of an agency hearing provided by statute; or

(F) unwarranted by the facts to the extent that the facts are subject to trial de novo by the reviewing court.

In making the foregoing determinations, the court shall review the whole record or those parts of it cited by a party, and due account shall be taken of the rule of prejudicial error.

§ 3105. Appointment of administrative law judges

Each agency shall appoint as many administrative law judges as are necessary for proceedings required to be conducted in accordance with sections 556 and 557 of this title. Administrative law judges shall be assigned to cases in rotation so far as practicable, and may not perform duties inconsistent with their duties and responsibilities as administrative law judges.

§ 7521. Actions against administrative law judges

(a) An action may be taken against an administrative law judge appointed under section 3105 of this title by the agency in which the administrative law judge is employed only for good cause established and determined by the Merit Systems Protection Board on the record after opportunity for hearing before the Board. . . . [The actions covered include removal, suspension, and reduction in grade or pay.]

§ 5372. Administrative law judges

Administrative law judges appointed under section 3105 of this title are entitled to pay prescribed by the Office of Personnel Management independently of agency recommendations or ratings and in accordance with subchapter III of this chapter and chapter 51 of this title.

§ 3344. Details; administrative law judges

An agency as defined by section 551 of this title which occasionally or temporarily is insufficiently staffed with administrative law judges appointed under section 3105 of this title may use administrative law judges selected by the Office of Personnel Management from and with the consent of other agencies.

§ 1305. Administrative law judges

For the purpose of sections 3105, 3344, 4301(2)(D), and 5372 of this title and the provisions of section 5335(a)(B) of this title that relate to administrative law judges, the Office of Personnel Management may, and for the purpose of section 7521 of this title, the Merit Systems Protection Board may investigate, require reports by agencies, issue reports, including an annual report to Congress, prescribe regulations, appoint advisory committees as necessary, recommend legislation, subpena witnesses and records, and pay witness fees as established for the courts of the United States.

Appendix B

MODEL STATE ADMINISTRATIVE PROCEDURE ACT (1981)

Uniform Law Commissioners

Table of Sections

ARTICLE I. GENERAL PROVISIONS

Sec.
1–101. [Short Title.]
1–102. [Definitions.]
1–103. [Applicability and Relation to Other Law.]
1–104. [Suspension of Act's Provisions When Necessary to Avoid Loss of Federal Funds or Services.]
1–105. [Waiver.]
1–106. [Informal Settlements.]
1–107. [Conversion of Proceedings.]
1–108. [Effective Date.]
1–109. [Severability.]

ARTICLE II. PUBLIC ACCESS TO AGENCY LAW AND POLICY

2–101. [Administrative Rules Editor; Publication, Compilation, Indexing, and Public Inspection of Rules.]
2–102. [Public Inspection and Indexing of Agency Orders.]
2–103. [Declaratory Orders.]
2–104. [Required Rule Making.]
2–105. [Model Rules of Procedure.]

ARTICLE III. RULE MAKING

Chapter I. Adoption and Effectiveness of Rules

3–101. [Advice on Possible Rules before Notice of Proposed Rule Adoption.]
3–102. [Public Rule-making Docket.]
3–103. [Notice of Proposed Rule Adoption.]
3–104. [Public Participation.]

Sec.

3–105. [Regulatory Analysis.]

3–106. [Time and Manner of Rule Adoption.]

3–107. [Variance between Adopted Rule and Published Notice of Proposed Rule Adoption.]

3–108. [General Exemption from Public Rule-making Procedures.]

3–109. [Exemption for Certain Rules.]

3–110. [Concise Explanatory Statement.]

3–111. [Contents, Style, and Form of Rule.]

3–112. [Agency Rule-making Record.]

3–113. [Invalidity of Rules Not Adopted According to Chapter; Time Limitation.]

3–114. [Filing of Rules.]

3–115. [Effective Date of Rules.]

3–116. [Special Provision for Certain Classes of Rules.]

3–117. [Petition for Adoption of Rules.]

Chapter II. Review of Agency Rules

3–201. [Review by Agency.]

3–202. [Review by Governor; Administrative Rules Counsel.]

3–203. [Administrative Rules Review Committee.]

3–204. [Review by Administrative Rules Review Committee.]

ARTICLE IV. ADJUDICATIVE PROCEEDINGS

Chapter I. Availability of Adjudicative Proceedings; Applications; Licenses

4–101. [Adjudicative Proceedings; When Required; Exceptions.]

4–102. [Adjudicative Proceedings; Commencement.]

4–103. [Decision Not to Conduct Adjudicative Proceeding.]

4–104. [Agency Action on Applications.]

4–105. [Agency Action Against Licensees.]

Chapter II. Formal Adjudicative Hearing

4–201. [Applicability.]

4–202. [Presiding Officer, Disqualification, Substitution.]

4–203. [Representation.]

4–204. [Pre-hearing Conference—Availability, Notice.]

4–205. [Pre-hearing Conference—Procedure and Pre-hearing Order.]

4–206. [Notice of Hearing.]

4–207. [Pleadings, Briefs, Motions, Service.]

4–208. [Default.]

4–209. [Intervention.]

4–210. [Subpoenas, Discovery and Protective Orders.]

4–211. [Procedure at Hearing.]

4–212. [Evidence, Official Notice.]

4–213. [Ex parte Communications.]

4–214. [Separation of Functions.]

4–215. [Final Order, Initial Order.]

4–216. [Review of Initial Order; Exceptions to Reviewability.]

4–217. [Stay.]

4–218. [Reconsideration.]

Sec.

4–219. [Review by Superior Agency.]
4–220. [Effectiveness of Orders.]
4–221. [Agency Record.]

Chapter III. Office of Administrative Hearings

4–301. [Office of Administrative Hearings—Creation, Powers, Duties.]

Chapter IV. Conference Adjudicative Hearing

4–401. [Conference Adjudicative Hearing—Applicability.]
4–402. [Conference Adjudicative Hearing—Procedures.]
4–403. [Conference Adjudicative Hearing—Proposed Proof.]

Chapter V. Emergency and Summary Adjudicative Proceedings

4–501. [Emergency Adjudicative Proceedings.]
4–502. [Summary Adjudicative Proceedings—Applicability.]
4–503. [Summary Adjudicative Proceedings—Procedures.]
4–504. [Administrative Review of Summary Adjudicative Proceedings—Applicability.]
4–505. [Administrative Review of Summary Adjudicative Proceedings—Procedures.]
4–506. [Agency Record of Summary Adjudicative Proceedings and Administrative Review.]

ARTICLE V. JUDICIAL REVIEW AND CIVIL ENFORCEMENT

Chapter I. Judicial Review

5–101. [Relationship Between this Act and Other Law on Judicial Review and Other Judicial Remedies.]
5–102. [Final Agency Action Reviewable.]
5–103. [Non-final Agency Action Reviewable.]
5–104. [Jurisdiction, Venue.]
5–105. [Form of Action.]
5–106. [Standing.]
5–107. [Exhaustion of Administrative Remedies.]
5–108. [Time for Filing Petition for Review.]
5–109. [Petition for Review—Filing and Contents.]
5–110. [Petition for Review—Service and Notification.]
5–111. [Stay and Other Temporary Remedies Pending Final Disposition.]
5–112. [Limitation on New Issues.]
5–113. [Judicial Review of Facts Confined to Record for Judicial Review and Additional Evidence Taken Pursuant to Act.]
5–114. [New Evidence Taken by Court or Agency Before Final Disposition.]
5–115. [Agency Record for Judicial Review—Contents, Preparation, Transmittal, Cost.]
5–116. [Scope of Review; Grounds for Invalidity.]
5–117. [Type of Relief.]
5–118. [Review by Higher Court.]

Chapter II. Civil Enforcement

Sec.

5–201. [Petition by Agency for Civil Enforcement of Rule or Order.]

5–202. [Petition by Qualified Person for Civil Enforcement of Agency's Order.]

5–203. [Defenses; Limitation on New Issues and New Evidence.]

5–204. [Incorporation of Certain Provisions on Judicial Review.]

5–205. [Review by Higher Court.]

ARTICLE I

GENERAL PROVISIONS

§ 1–101. [Short Title]

This Act may be cited as the [state] Administrative Procedure Act.

§ 1–102. [Definitions]

As used in this Act:

(1) "Agency" means a board, commission, department, officer, or other administrative unit of this State, including the agency head, and one or more members of the agency head or agency employees or other persons directly or indirectly purporting to act on behalf or under the authority of the agency head. The term does not include the [legislature] or the courts [, or the governor] [, or the governor in the exercise of powers derived directly and exclusively from the constitution of this State]. The term does not include a political subdivision of the state or any of the administrative units of a political subdivision, but it does include a board, commission, department, officer, or other administrative unit created or appointed by joint or concerted action of an agency and one or more political subdivisions of the state or any of their units. To the extent it purports to exercise authority subject to any provision of this Act, an administrative unit otherwise qualifying as an "agency" must be treated as a separate agency even if the unit is located within or subordinate to another agency.

(2) "Agency action" means:

(i) the whole or a part of a rule or an order;

(ii) the failure to issue a rule or an order; or

(iii) an agency's performance of, or failure to perform, any other duty, function, or activity, discretionary or otherwise.

(3) "Agency head" means an individual or body of individuals in whom the ultimate legal authority of the agency is vested by any provision of law.

(4) "License" means a franchise, permit, certification, approval, registration, charter, or similar form of authorization required by law.

(5) "Order" means an agency action of particular applicability that determines the legal rights, duties, privileges, immunities, or other legal interests of one or more specific persons. [The term does not include an "executive order" issued by the governor pursuant to Section 1–104 or 3–202.]

(6) "Party to agency proceedings," or "party" in context so indicating, means:

   (i) a person to whom the agency action is specifically directed; or

   (ii) a person named as a party to an agency proceeding or allowed to intervene or participate as a party in the proceeding.

(7) "Party to judicial review or civil enforcement proceedings," or "party" in context so indicating, means:

   (i) a person who files a petition for judicial review or civil enforcement; or

   (ii) a person named as a party in a proceeding for judicial review or civil enforcement or allowed to participate as a party in the proceeding.

(8) "Person" means an individual, partnership, corporation, association, governmental subdivision or unit thereof, or public or private organization or entity of any character, and includes another agency.

(9) "Provision of law" means the whole or a part of the federal or state constitution, or of any federal or state (i) statute, (ii) rule of court, (iii) executive order, or (iv) rule of an administrative agency.

(10) "Rule" means the whole or a part of an agency statement of general applicability that implements, interprets, or prescribes (i) law or policy, or (ii) the organization, procedure, or practice requirements of an agency. The term includes the amendment, repeal, or suspension of an existing rule.

(11) "Rule making" means the process for formulation and adoption of a rule.

§ 1–103. [Applicability and Relation to Other Law]

(a) This Act applies to all agencies and all proceedings not expressly exempted.

(b) This Act creates only procedural rights and imposes only procedural duties. They are in addition to those created and imposed by other statutes. To the extent that any other statute would diminish a right created or duty imposed by this Act, the other statute is superseded by this Act, unless the other statute expressly provides otherwise.

(c) An agency may grant procedural rights to persons in addition to those conferred by this Act so long as rights conferred upon other persons by any provision of law are not substantially prejudiced.

[§ 1–104. [Suspension of Act's Provisions When Necessary to Avoid Loss of Federal Funds or Services]

(a) To the extent necessary to avoid a denial of funds or services from the United States which would otherwise be available to the state, the [governor by executive order] [attorney general by rule] [may] [shall] suspend, in whole or in part, one or more provisions of this Act. The [governor by executive order] [attorney general by rule] shall declare the termination of a suspension as soon as it is no longer necessary to prevent the loss of funds or services from the United States.

[(b) An executive order issued under subsection (a) is subject to the requirements applicable to the adoption and effectiveness of a rule.]

(c) If any provision of this Act is suspended pursuant to this section, the [governor] [attorney general] shall promptly report the suspension to the [legislature]. The report must include recommendations concerning any desirable legislation that may be necessary to conform this Act to federal law.]

§ 1–105. [Waiver]

Except to the extent precluded by another provision of law, a person may waive any right conferred upon that person by this Act.

§ 1–106. [Informal Settlements]

Except to the extent precluded by another provision of law, informal settlement of matters that may make unnecessary more elaborate proceedings under this Act is encouraged. Agencies shall establish by rule specific procedures to facilitate informal settlement of matters. This section does not require any party or other person to settle a matter pursuant to informal procedures.

§ 1–107. [Conversion of Proceedings]

(a) At any point in an agency proceeding the presiding officer or other agency official responsible for the proceeding:

(1) may convert the proceeding to another type of agency proceeding provided for by this Act if the conversion is appropriate, is in the public interest, and does not substantially prejudice the rights of any party; and

(2) if required by any provision of law, shall convert the proceeding to another type of agency proceeding provided for by this Act.

(b) A conversion of a proceeding of one type to a proceeding of another type may be effected only upon notice to all parties to the original proceeding.

(c) If the presiding officer or other agency official responsible for the original proceeding would not have authority over the new proceeding to which it is to be converted, that officer or official, in accordance with agency rules, shall secure the appointment of a successor to preside over or be responsible for the new proceeding.

(d) To the extent feasible and consistent with the rights of parties and the requirements of this Act pertaining to the new proceeding, the record of the original agency proceeding must be used in the new agency proceeding.

(e) After a proceeding is converted from one type to another, the presiding officer or other agency official responsible for the new proceeding shall:

(1) give such additional notice to parties or other persons as is necessary to satisfy the requirements of this Act pertaining to those proceedings;

(2) dispose of the matters involved without further proceedings if sufficient proceedings have already been held to satisfy the requirements of this Act pertaining to the new proceedings; and

(3) conduct or cause to be conducted any additional proceedings necessary to satisfy the requirements of this Act pertaining to those proceedings.

(f) Each agency shall adopt rules to govern the conversion of one type of proceeding to another. Those rules must include an enumeration of the factors to be considered in determining whether and under what circumstances one type of proceeding will be converted to another.

§ 1-108. [Effective Date]

This Act takes effect on [date] and does not govern proceedings pending on that date. This Act governs all agency proceedings, and all proceedings for judicial review or civil enforcement of agency action, commenced after that date. This Act also governs agency proceedings conducted on a remand from a court or another agency after the effective date of this Act.

§ 1-109. [Severability]

If any provision of this Act or the application thereof to any person or circumstance is held invalid, the invalidity does not affect other provisions or applications of the Act which can be given effect without the invalid provision or application, and for this purpose the provisions of this Act are severable.

ARTICLE II

PUBLIC ACCESS TO AGENCY LAW AND POLICY

§ 2-101. [Administrative Rules Editor; Publication, Compilation, Indexing, and Public Inspection of Rules]

(a) There is created, within the executive branch, an [administrative rules editor]. The governor shall appoint the [administrative rules editor] who shall serve at the pleasure of the governor.

(b) Subject to the provisions of this Act, the [administrative rules editor] shall prescribe a uniform numbering system, form, and style for all proposed and adopted rules caused to be published by that office [, and shall have the same editing authority with respect to the publication of rules as the [reviser of statutes] has with respect to the publication of statutes].

(c) The [administrative rules editor] shall cause the [administrative bulletin] to be published in pamphlet form [once each week]. For purposes of calculating adherence to time requirements imposed by this Act, an issue of the [administrative bulletin] is deemed published on the later of the date indicated in that issue or the date of its mailing. The [administrative bulletin] must contain:

(1) notices of proposed rule adoption prepared so that the text of the proposed rule shows the text of any existing rule proposed to be changed and the change proposed;

(2) newly filed adopted rules prepared so that the text of the newly filed adopted rule shows the text of any existing rule being changed and the change being made;

(3) any other notices and materials designated by [law] [the administrative rules editor] for publication therein; and

(4) an index to its contents by subject.

(d) The [administrative rules editor] shall cause the [administrative code] to be compiled, indexed by subject, and published [in loose-leaf form]. All of the effective rules of each agency must be published and indexed in that publication. The [administrative rules editor] shall also cause [loose-leaf] supplements to the [administrative code] to be published at least every [3 months]. [The loose-leaf supplements must be in a form suitable for insertion in the appropriate places in the permanent [administrative code] compilation.]

(e) The [administrative rules editor] may omit from the [administrative bulletin or code] any proposed or filed adopted rule the publication of which would be unduly cumbersome, expensive, or otherwise inexpedient, if:

(1) knowledge of the rule is likely to be important to only a small class of persons;

(2) on application to the issuing agency, the proposed or adopted rule in printed or processed form is made available at no more than its cost of reproduction; and

(3) the [administrative bulletin or code] contains a notice stating in detail the specific subject matter of the omitted proposed or adopted rule and how a copy of the omitted material may be obtained.

(f) The [administrative bulletin and administrative code] must be furnished to [designated officials] without charge and to all subscribers at a cost to be determined by the [administrative rules editor]. Each agency shall also make available for public inspection and copying those portions of the [administrative bulletin and administrative code] containing all rules adopted or used by the agency in the discharge of its functions, and the index to those rules.

(g) Except as otherwise required by a provision of law, subsections (c) through (f) do not apply to rules governed by Section 3–116, and the following provisions apply instead:

(1) Each agency shall maintain an official, current, and dated compilation that is indexed by subject, containing all of its rules within the scope of Section 3–116. Each addition to, change in, or deletion from the official compilation must also be dated, indexed, and a record thereof kept. Except for those portions containing rules governed by Section 3–116(2), the compilation must be made available for public inspection and copying. Certified copies of the full compilation must also be furnished to the [secretary of state, the administrative rules counsel, and members of the administrative rules review committee], and be kept current by the agency at least every [30] days.

(2) A rule subject to the requirements of this subsection may not be relied on by an agency to the detriment of any person who does not have actual, timely knowledge of the contents of the rule until the requirements of paragraph (1) are satisfied. The burden of proving that knowledge is on the agency. This provision is also inapplicable to the extent necessary to avoid imminent peril to the public health, safety, or welfare.

§ 2–102. [Public Inspection and Indexing of Agency Orders]

(a) In addition to other requirements imposed by any provision of law, each agency shall make all written final orders available for public inspection and copying and index them by name and subject. An agency shall delete from those orders identifying details to the extent required by any provision of law [or necessary to prevent a clearly unwarranted invasion of privacy or release of trade secrets]. In each case the justification for the deletion must be explained in writing and attached to the order.

(b) A written final order may not be relied on as precedent by an agency to the detriment of any person until it has been made available for public inspection and indexed in the manner described in subsection (a). This provision is inapplicable to any person who has actual timely knowledge of the order. The burden of proving that knowledge is on the agency.

§ 2–103. [Declaratory Orders]

(a) Any person may petition an agency for a declaratory order as to the applicability to specified circumstances of a statute, rule, or order within the primary jurisdiction of the agency. An agency shall issue a declaratory order in response to a petition for that order unless the agency determines that issuance of the order under the circumstances would be contrary to a rule adopted in accordance with subsection (b). However, an agency may not issue a declaratory order that would substantially prejudice the rights of a person who would be a necessary party and who does not consent in writing to the determination of the matter by a declaratory order proceeding.

(b) Each agency shall issue rules that provide for: (i) the form, contents, and filing of petitions for declaratory orders; (ii) the procedural rights of persons in relation to the petitions and (iii) the disposition of the petitions. Those rules must describe the classes of circumstances in which the agency will not issue a declaratory order and must be consistent with the public interest and with the general policy of this Act to facilitate and encourage agency issuance of reliable advice.

(c) Within [15] days after receipt of a petition for a declaratory order, an agency shall give notice of the petition to all persons to whom notice is required by any provision of law and may give notice to any other persons.

(d) Persons who qualify under Section 4–209(a)(2) and (3) and file timely petitions for intervention according to agency rules may intervene in proceedings for declaratory orders. Other provisions of Article IV apply to agency proceedings for declaratory orders only to the extent an agency so provides by rule or order.

(e) Within [30] days after receipt of a petition for a declaratory order an agency, in writing, shall:

(1) issue an order declaring the applicability of the statute, rule, or order in question to the specified circumstances;

(2) set the matter for specified proceedings;

(3) agree to issue a declaratory order by a specified time; or

(4) decline to issue a declaratory order, stating the reasons for its action.

(f) A copy of all orders issued in response to a petition for a declaratory order must be mailed promptly to petitioner and any other parties.

(g) A declaratory order has the same status and binding effect as any other order issued in an agency adjudicative proceeding. A declaratory order must contain the names of all parties to the proceeding on which it is based, the particular facts on which it is based, and the reasons for its conclusion.

(h) If an agency has not issued a declaratory order within [60] days after receipt of a petition therefor, the petition is deemed to have been denied.

§ 2–104. [Required Rule Making]

In addition to other rule-making requirements imposed by law, each agency shall:

(1) adopt as a rule a description of the organization of the agency which states the general course and method of its operations and where and how the public may obtain information or make submissions or requests;

(2) adopt rules of practice setting forth the nature and requirements of all formal and informal procedures available to the public, including a description of all forms and instructions that are to be used by the public in dealing with the agency; [and]

(3) as soon as feasible and to the extent practicable, adopt rules, in addition to those otherwise required by this Act, embodying appropriate standards, principles, and procedural safeguards that the agency will apply to the law it administers [; and] [.]

[(4) as soon as feasible and to the extent practicable, adopt rules to supersede principles of law or policy lawfully declared by the agency as the basis for its decisions in particular cases.]

§ 2–105. [Model Rules of Procedure]

In accordance with the rule-making requirements of this Act, the [attorney general] shall adopt model rules of procedure appropriate for use by as many agencies as possible. The model rules must deal with all general functions and duties performed in common by several agencies. Each agency shall adopt as much of the model rules as is practicable under its circumstances. To the extent an agency adopts the model rules, it shall do so in accordance with the rule-making requirements of this Act. Any agency adopting a rule of procedure that differs from the model rules shall include in the rule a finding stating the reasons why the relevant portions of the model rules were impracticable under the circumstances.

ARTICLE III

RULE MAKING

Adoption and Effectiveness of Rules

§ 3–101. [Advice on Possible Rules before Notice of Proposed Rule Adoption]

(a) In addition to seeking information by other methods, an agency, before publication of a notice of proposed rule adoption under Section 3–103, may solicit comments from the public on a subject matter of possible rule making under active consideration within the agency by causing notice to be published in the [administrative bulletin] of the subject matter and indicating where, when, and how persons may comment.

(b) Each agency may also appoint committees to comment, before publication of a notice of proposed rule adoption under Section 3–103, on the subject matter of a possible rule making under active consideration within the agency. The membership of those committees must be published at least [annually] in the [administrative bulletin].

§ 3–102. [Public Rule-making Docket]

(a) Each agency shall maintain a current, public rule-making docket.

(b) The rule-making docket [must] [may] contain a listing of the precise subject matter of each possible rule currently under active consideration within the agency for proposal under Section 3–103, the name and address of agency personnel with whom persons may communicate with respect to the matter, and an indication of the present status within the agency of that possible rule.

(c) The rule-making docket must list each pending rule-making proceeding. A rule-making proceeding is pending from the time it is commenced, by publication of a notice of proposed rule adoption, to the time it is terminated, by publication of a notice of termination or the rule becoming effective. For each rule-making proceeding, the docket must indicate:

(1) the subject matter of the proposed rule;

(2) a citation to all published notices relating to the proceeding;

(3) where written submissions on the proposed rule may be inspected;

(4) the time during which written submissions may be made;

(5) the names of persons who have made written requests for an opportunity to make oral presentations on the proposed rule, where those requests may be inspected, and where and when oral presentations may be made;

(6) whether a written request for the issuance of a regulatory analysis of the proposed rule has been filed, whether that analysis has been issued, and where the written request and analysis may be inspected;

(7) the current status of the proposed rule and any agency determinations with respect thereto;

(8) any known timetable for agency decisions or other action in the proceeding;

(9) the date of the rule's adoption;

(10) the date of the rule's filing, indexing, and publication; and

(11) when the rule will become effective.

§ 3–103. [Notice of Proposed Rule Adoption]

(a) At least [30] days before the adoption of a rule an agency shall cause notice of its contemplated action to be published in the [administrative bulletin]. The notice of proposed rule adoption must include:

(1) a short explanation of the purpose of the proposed rule;

(2) the specific legal authority authorizing the proposed rule;

(3) subject to Section 2–101(e), the text of the proposed rule;

(4) where, when, and how persons may present their views on the proposed rule; and

(5) where, when, and how persons may demand an oral proceeding on the proposed rule if the notice does not already provide for one.

(b) Within [3] days after its publication in the [administrative bulletin], the agency shall cause a copy of the notice of proposed rule adoption to be mailed to each person who has made a timely request to the agency for a mailed copy of the notice. An agency may charge persons for the actual cost of providing them with mailed copies.

§ 3–104. [Public Participation]

(a) For at least [30] days after publication of the notice of proposed rule adoption, an agency shall afford persons the opportunity to submit in writing, argument, data, and views on the proposed rule.

(b)(1) An agency shall schedule an oral proceeding on a proposed rule if, within [20] days after the published notice of proposed rule adoption, a written request for an oral proceeding is submitted by [the administrative rules review committee,] [the administrative rules counsel,] a political subdivision, an agency, or [25] persons. At that proceeding, persons may present oral argument, data, and views on the proposed rule.

(2) An oral proceeding on a proposed rule, if required, may not be held earlier than [20] days after notice of its location and time is published in the [administrative bulletin].

(3) The agency, a member of the agency, or another presiding officer designated by the agency, shall preside at a required oral proceeding on a proposed rule. If the agency does not preside, the presiding official shall prepare a memorandum for consideration by the agency summarizing the contents of the presentations made at the oral proceeding. Oral proceedings must be open to the public and be recorded by stenographic or other means.

(4) Each agency shall issue rules for the conduct of oral rule-making proceedings. Those rules may include provisions calculated to prevent undue repetition in the oral proceedings.

§ 3–105. [Regulatory Analysis]

(a) An agency shall issue a regulatory analysis of a proposed rule if, within [20] days after the published notice of proposed rule adoption, a written request for the analysis is filed in the office of the [secretary of state] by [the administrative rules review committee, the governor, a political subdivision, an agency, or [300] persons signing the request].

The [secretary of state] shall immediately forward to the agency a certified copy of the filed request.

(b) Except to the extent that the written request expressly waives one or more of the following, the regulatory analysis must contain:

(1) a description of the classes of persons who probably will be affected by the proposed rule, including classes that will bear the costs of the proposed rule and classes that will benefit from the proposed rule;

(2) a description of the probable quantitative and qualitative impact of the proposed rule, economic or otherwise, upon affected classes of persons;

(3) the probable costs to the agency and to any other agency of the implementation and enforcement of the proposed rule and any anticipated effect on state revenues;

(4) a comparison of the probable costs and benefits of the proposed rule to the probable costs and benefits of inaction;

(5) a determination of whether there are less costly methods or less intrusive methods for achieving the purpose of the proposed rule; and

(6) a description of any alternative methods for achieving the purpose of the proposed rule that were seriously considered by the agency and the reasons why they were rejected in favor of the proposed rule.

(c) Each regulatory analysis must include qualification of the data to the extent practicable and must take account of both short-term and long-term consequences.

(d) A concise summary of the regulatory analysis must be published in the [administrative bulletin] at least [10] days before the earliest of:

(1) the end of the period during which persons may make written submissions on the proposed rule;

(2) the end of the period during which an oral proceeding may be requested; or

(3) the date of any required oral proceeding on the proposed rule.

(e) The published summary of the regulatory analysis must also indicate where persons may obtain copies of the full text of the regulatory analysis and where, when, and how persons may present their views on the proposed rule and demand an oral proceeding thereon if one is not already provided.

(f) If the agency has made a good faith effort to comply with the requirements of subsections (a) through (c), the rule may not be invalidated on the ground that the contents of the regulatory analysis are insufficient or inaccurate.

§ 3–106. [Time and Manner of Rule Adoption]

(a) An agency may not adopt a rule until the period for making written submissions and oral presentations has expired.

(b) Within [180] days after the later of (i) the publication of the notice of proposed rule adoption, or (ii) the end of oral proceedings thereon, an agency shall adopt a rule pursuant to the rule-making proceeding or terminate the proceeding by publication of a notice to that effect in the [administrative bulletin].

(c) Before the adoption of a rule, an agency shall consider the written submissions, oral submissions or any memorandum summarizing oral submissions, and any regulatory analysis, provided for by this Chapter.

(d) Within the scope of its delegated authority, an agency may use its own experience, technical competence, specialized knowledge, and judgment in the adoption of a rule.

§ 3–107. [Variance between Adopted Rule and Published Notice of Proposed Rule Adoption]

(a) An agency may not adopt a rule that is substantially different from the proposed rule contained in the published notice of proposed rule adoption. However, an agency may terminate a rule-making proceeding and commence a new rule-making proceeding for the purpose of adopting a substantially different rule.

(b) In determining whether an adopted rule is substantially different from the published proposed rule upon which it is required to be based, the following must be considered:

(1) the extent to which all persons affected by the adopted rule should have understood that the published proposed rule would affect their interests;

(2) the extent to which the subject matter of the adopted rule or the issues determined by that rule are different from the subject matter or issues involved in the published proposed rule; and

(3) the extent to which the effects of the adopted rule differ from the effects of the published proposed rule had it been adopted instead.

§ 3–108. [General Exemption from Public Rule-making Procedures]

(a) To the extent an agency for good cause finds that any requirements of Sections 3–103 through 3–107 are unnecessary, impracticable, or contrary to the public interest in the process of adopting a particular rule, those requirements do not apply. The agency shall incorporate the required finding and a brief statement of its supporting reasons in each rule adopted in reliance upon this subsection.

(b) In an action contesting a rule adopted under subsection (a), the burden is upon the agency to demonstrate that any omitted requirements of Sections 3–103 through 3–107 were impracticable, unnecessary, or contrary to the public interest in the particular circumstances involved.

(c) Within [2] years after the effective date of a rule adopted under subsection (a), the [administrative rules review committee or the governor] may request the agency to hold a rule-making proceeding thereon according to the requirements of Sections 3–103 through 3–107. The request must be in writing and filed in the office of the [secretary of state]. The [secretary of state] shall immediately forward to the agency and to the [administrative rules editor] a certified copy of the request. Notice of the filing of the request must be published in the next issue of the [administrative bulletin]. The rule in question ceases to be effective [180] days after the request is filed. However, an agency, after the filing of the request, may subsequently adopt an identical rule in a rule-making proceeding conducted pursuant to the requirements of Sections 3–103 through 3–107.

§ 3–109. [Exemption for Certain Rules]

(a) An agency need not follow the provisions of Sections 3–103 through 3–108 in the adoption of a rule that only defines the meaning of a statute or other provision of law or precedent if the agency does not possess delegated authority to bind the courts to any extent with its definition. A rule adopted under this subsection must include a statement that it was adopted under this subsection when it is published in the [administrative bulletin], and there must be an indication to that effect adjacent to the rule when it is published in the [administrative code].

(b) A reviewing court shall determine wholly de novo the validity of a rule within the scope of subsection (a) that is adopted without complying with the provisions of Sections 3–103 through 3–108.

§ 3–110. [Concise Explanatory Statement]

(a) At the time it adopts a rule, an agency shall issue a concise explanatory statement containing:

(1) its reasons for adopting the rule; and

(2) an indication of any change between the text of the proposed rule contained in the published notice of proposed rule adoption and the text of the rule as finally adopted, with the reasons for any change.

(b) Only the reasons contained in the concise explanatory statement may be used by any party as justifications for the adoption of the rule in any proceeding in which its validity is at issue.

§ 3–111. [Contents, Style, and Form of Rule]

(a) Each rule adopted by an agency must contain the text of the rule and:

(1) the date the agency adopted the rule;

(2) a concise statement of the purpose of the rule;

(3) a reference to all rules repealed, amended, or suspended by the rule;

(4) a reference to the specific statutory or other authority authorizing adoption of the rule;

(5) any findings required by any provision of law as a prerequisite to adoption or effectiveness of the rule; and

(6) the effective date of the rule if other than that specified in Section 3–115(a).

[(b) To the extent feasible, each rule should be written in clear and concise language understandable to persons who may be affected by it.]

(c) An agency may incorporate, by reference in its rules and without publishing the incorporated matter in full, all or any part of a code, standard, rule, or regulation that has been adopted by an agency of the United States or of this state, another state, or by a nationally recognized organization or association, if incorporation of its text in agency rules would be unduly cumbersome.

§ 3–112. [Agency Rule-making Record]

(a) An agency shall maintain an official rule-making record for each rule it (i) proposes by publication in the [administrative bulletin] of a notice of proposed rule adoption, or (ii) adopts. The record and materials incorporated by reference must be available for public inspection.

(b) The agency rule-making record must contain:

(1) copies of all publications in the [administrative bulletin] with respect to the rule or the proceeding upon which the rule is based;

(2) copies of any portions of the agency's public rule-making docket containing entries relating to the rule or the proceeding upon which the rule is based;

(3) all written petitions, requests, submissions, and comments received by the agency and all other written materials considered by the agency in connection with the formulation, proposal, or adoption of the rule or the proceeding upon which the rule is based;

(4) any official transcript of oral presentations made in the proceeding upon which the rule is based or, if not transcribed, any tape recording or stenographic record of those presentations, and any memorandum prepared by a presiding official summarizing the contents of those presentations;

(5) a copy of any regulatory analysis prepared for the proceeding upon which the rule is based;

(6) a copy of the rule and explanatory statement filed in the office of the [secretary of state];

(7) all petitions for exceptions to, amendments of, or repeal or suspension of, the rule;

(8) a copy of any request filed pursuant to Section 3–108(c);

[(9) a copy of any objection to the rule filed by the [administrative rules review committee] pursuant to Section 3–204(d) and the agency's response;] and

(10) a copy of any filed executive order with respect to the rule.

(c) Upon judicial review, the record required by this section constitutes the official agency rule-making record with respect to a rule. Except as provided in Section 3–110(b) or otherwise required by a provision of law, the agency rule-making record need not constitute the exclusive basis for agency action on that rule or for judicial review thereof.

§ 3–113. [Invalidity of Rules Not Adopted According to Chapter; Time Limitation]

(a) A rule adopted after [date] is invalid unless adopted in substantial compliance with the provisions of Sections 3–102 through 3–108 and Sections 3–110 through 3–112. However, inadvertent failure to mail a notice of proposed rule adoption to any person as required by Section 3–103(b) does not invalidate a rule.

(b) An action to contest the validity of a rule on the grounds of its noncompliance with any provision of Sections 3–102 through 3–108 or Sections 3–110 through 3–112 must be commenced within [2] years after the effective date of the rule.

§ 3–114. [Filing of Rules]

(a) An agency shall file in the office of the [secretary of state] each rule it adopts and all rules existing on the effective date of this Act that have not previously been filed. The filing must be done as soon after adoption of the rule as is practicable. At the time of filing, each rule adopted after the effective date of this Act must have attached to it the explanatory statement required by Section 3–110. The [secretary of state] shall affix to each rule and statement a certification of the time and date of filing and keep a permanent register open to public inspection of all filed rules and attached explanatory statements. In filing a rule, each agency shall use a standard form prescribed by the [secretary of state].

(b) The [secretary of state] shall transmit to the [administrative rules editor], [administrative rules counsel], and to the members of the [administrative rules review committee] a certified copy of each filed rule as soon after its filing as is practicable.

§ 3–115. [Effective Date of Rules]

(a) Except to the extent subsection (b) or (c) provides otherwise, each rule adopted after the effective date of this Act becomes effective [30] days after the later of (i) its filing in the office of the [secretary of state] or (ii) its publication and indexing in the [administrative bulletin].

(b)(1) A rule becomes effective on a date later than that established by subsection (a) if a later date is required by another statute or specified in the rule.

(2) A rule may become effective immediately upon its filing or on any subsequent date earlier than that established by subsection (a) if the agency establishes such an effective date and finds that:

(i) it is required by constitution, statute, or court order;

(ii) the rule only confers a benefit or removes a restriction on the public or some segment thereof;

(iii) the rule only delays the effective date of another rule that is not yet effective; or

(iv) the earlier effective date is necessary because of imminent peril to the public health, safety, or welfare.

(3) The finding and a brief statement of the reasons therefor required by paragraph (2) must be made a part of the rule. In any action contesting the effective date of a rule made effective under paragraph (2), the burden is on the agency to justify its finding.

(4) Each agency shall make a reasonable effort to make known to persons who may be affected by it a rule made effective before publication and indexing under this subsection.

(c) This section does not relieve an agency from compliance with any provision of law requiring that some or all of its rules be approved by other designated officials or bodies before they become effective.

§ 3–116. [Special Provision for Certain Classes of Rules]

Except to the extent otherwise provided by any provision of law, Sections 3–102 through 3–115 are inapplicable to:

(1) a rule concerning only the internal management of an agency which does not directly and substantially affect the procedural or substantive rights or duties of any segment of the public;

(2) a rule that establishes criteria or guidelines to be used by the staff of an agency in performing audits, investigations, or inspections, settling commercial disputes, negotiating commercial arrangements, or in the defense, prosecution, or settlement of cases, if disclosure of the criteria or guidelines would:

(i) enable law violators to avoid detection;

(ii) facilitate disregard of requirements imposed by law; or

(iii) give a clearly improper advantage to persons who are in an adverse position to the state;

(3) a rule that only establishes specific prices to be charged for particular goods or services sold by an agency;

(4) a rule concerning only the physical servicing, maintenance, or care of agency owned or operated facilities or property;

(5) a rule relating only to the use of a particular facility or property owned, operated, or maintained by the state or any of its subdivisions, if the substance of the rule is adequately indicated by means of signs or signals to persons who use the facility or property;

(6) a rule concerning only inmates of a correctional or detention facility, students enrolled in an educational institution, or patients admitted to a hospital, if adopted by that facility, institution, or hospital;

(7) a form whose contents or substantive requirements are prescribed by rule or statute, and instructions for the execution or use of the form;

(8) an agency budget; [or]

(9) an opinion of the attorney general[; or] [.]

(10) [the terms of a collective bargaining agreement.]

§ 3–117. [Petition for Adoption of Rule]

Any person may petition an agency requesting the adoption of a rule. Each agency shall prescribe by rule the form of the petition and the procedure for its submission, consideration, and disposition. Within [60] days after submission of a petition, the agency shall either (i) deny the petition in writing, stating its reasons therefor, (ii) initiate rule-making proceedings in accordance with this Chapter, or (iii) if otherwise lawful, adopt a rule.

Review of Agency Rules

§ 3–201. [Review by Agency]

At least [annually], each agency shall review all of its rules to determine whether any new rule should be adopted. In conducting that review, each agency shall prepare a written report summarizing its findings, its supporting reasons, and any proposed course of action. For each rule, the [annual] report must include, at least once every [7] years, a concise statement of:

(1) the rule's effectiveness in achieving its objectives, including a summary of any available data supporting the conclusions reached;

(2) criticisms of the rule received during the previous [7] years, including a summary of any petitions for waiver of the rule tendered to the agency or granted by it; and

(3) alternative solutions to the criticisms and the reasons they were rejected or the changes made in the rule in response to those criticisms and the reasons for the changes. A copy of the [annual] report must be sent to the [administrative rules review committee and the administrative rules counsel] and be available for public inspection.

§ 3–202. [Review by Governor; Administrative Rules Counsel]

(a) To the extent the agency itself would have authority, the governor may rescind or suspend all or a severable portion of a rule of an agency. In exercising this authority, the governor shall act by an executive order that is subject to the provisions of this Act applicable to the adoption and effectiveness of a rule.

(b) The governor may summarily terminate any pending rule-making proceeding by an executive order to that effect, stating therein the reasons for the action. The executive order must be filed in the office of the [secretary of state], which shall promptly forward a certified copy to the agency and the [administrative rules editor]. An executive order terminating a rule-making proceeding becomes effective on [the date it is filed] and must be published in the next issue of the [administrative bulletin].

(c) There is created, within the office of the governor, an [administrative rules counsel] to advise the governor in the execution of the authority vested under this Article. The governor shall appoint the [administrative rules counsel] who shall serve at the pleasure of the governor.

§ 3–203. [Administrative Rules Review Committee]

There is created the ["administrative rules review committee"] of the [legislature]. The committee must be [bipartisan] and composed of [3] senators appointed by the [president of the senate] and [3] representatives appointed by the [speaker of the house]. Committee members must be appointed within [30] days after the convening of a regular legislative session. The term of office is [2] years while a member of the [legislature] and begins on the date of appointment to the committee. While a member of the [legislature], a member of the committee whose term has expired shall serve until a successor is appointed. A vacancy on the committee may be filled at any time by the original appointing authority for the remainder of the term. The committee shall choose a chairman from its membership for a [2]–year term and may employ staff it considers advisable.

§ 3–204. [Review by Administrative Rules Review Committee]

(a) The [administrative rules review committee] shall selectively review possible, proposed, or adopted rules and prescribe appropriate committee procedures for that purpose. The committee may receive and investigate complaints from members of the public with respect to possible, proposed, or adopted rules and hold public proceedings on those complaints.

(b) Committee meetings must be open to the public. Subject to procedures established by the committee, persons may present oral argument, data, or views at those meetings. The committee may require a representative of an agency whose possible, proposed, or adopted rule is under examination to attend a committee meeting and answer relevant questions. The committee may also communicate to the agency its comments on any possible, proposed, or adopted rule and require the agency to respond to them in writing. Unless impracticable, in advance of each committee meeting, notice of the time and place of the meeting and the specific subject matter to be considered must be published in the [administrative bulletin].

(c) The committee may recommend enactment of a statute to improve the operation of an agency. The committee may also recommend that a particular rule be superseded in whole or in part by statute. The [speaker of the house and the president of the senate] shall refer those recommendations to the appropriate standing committees. This subsection does not preclude any committee of the legislature from reviewing a rule on its own motion or recommending that it be superseded in whole or in part by statute.

[(d)(1) If the committee objects to all or some portion of a rule because the committee considers it to be beyond the procedural or substantive authority delegated to the adopting agency, the committee may file that objection in the office of the [secretary of state]. The filed objection must contain a concise statement of the committee's reasons for its action.

(2) The [secretary of state] shall affix to each objection a certification of the date and time of its filing and as soon thereafter as practicable shall transmit a certified copy thereof to the agency issuing the rule in question, the [administrative rules editor, and the administrative rules counsel]. The [secretary of state] shall also maintain a permanent register open to public inspection of all objections by the committee.

(3) The [administrative rules editor] shall publish and index an objection filed pursuant to this subsection in the next issue of the [administrative bulletin] and indicate its existence adjacent to the rule in question when that rule is published in the [administrative code]. In case of a filed objection by the committee to a rule that is subject to the requirements of Section 2–101(g), the agency shall indicate the existence of that objection adjacent to the rule in the official compilation referred to in that subsection.

(4) Within [14] days after the filing of an objection by the committee to a rule, the issuing agency shall respond in writing to the committee. After receipt of the response, the committee may withdraw or modify its objection.

[(5) After the filing of an objection by the committee that is not subsequently withdrawn, the burden is upon the agency in any proceeding for judicial review or for enforcement of the rule to establish that the whole or portion of the rule objected to is within the procedural and substantive authority delegated to the agency.]

(6) The failure of the [administrative rules review committee] to object to a rule is not an implied legislative authorization of its procedural or substantive validity.]

(e) The committee may recommend to an agency that it adopt a rule. [The committee may also require an agency to publish notice of the committee's recommendation as a proposed rule of the agency and to allow public participation thereon, according to the provisions of Sections 3–103 through 3–104. An agency is not required to adopt the proposed rule.]

(f) The committee shall file an annual report with the [presiding officer] of each house and the governor.

ARTICLE IV

ADJUDICATIVE PROCEEDINGS

CHAPTER I. AVAILABILITY OF ADJUDICATIVE PROCEEDINGS; APPLICATIONS; LICENSES

§ 4–101. [Adjudicative Proceedings; When Required; Exceptions]

(a) An agency shall conduct an adjudicative proceeding as the process for formulating and issuing an order, unless the order is a decision:

(1) to issue or not to issue a complaint, summons, or similar accusation;

(2) to initiate or not to initiate an investigation, prosecution, or other proceeding before the agency, another agency, or a court; or

(3) under Section 4–103, not to conduct an adjudicative proceeding.

(b) This Article applies to rule-making proceedings only to the extent that another statute expressly so requires.

§ 4–102. [Adjudicative Proceedings; Commencement]

(a) An agency may commence an adjudicative proceeding at any time with respect to a matter within the agency's jurisdiction.

(b) An agency shall commence an adjudicative proceeding upon the application of any person, unless:

(1) the agency lacks jurisdiction of the subject matter;

(2) resolution of the matter requires the agency to exercise discretion within the scope of Section 4–101(a);

(3) a statute vests the agency with discretion to conduct or not to conduct an adjudicative proceeding before issuing an order to resolve the matter and, in the exercise of that discretion, the agency has determined not to conduct an adjudicative proceeding;

(4) resolution of the matter does not require the agency to issue an order that determines the applicant's legal rights, duties, privileges, immunities, or other legal interests;

(5) the matter was not timely submitted to the agency; or

(6) the matter was not submitted in a form substantially complying with any applicable provision of law.

(c) An application for an agency to issue an order includes an application for the agency to conduct appropriate adjudicative proceedings, whether or not the applicant expressly requests those proceedings.

(d) An adjudicative proceeding commences when the agency or a presiding officer:

(1) notifies a party that a pre-hearing conference, hearing, or other stage of an adjudicative proceeding will be conducted; or

(2) begins to take action on a matter that appropriately may be determined by an adjudicative proceeding, unless this action is:

(i) an investigation for the purpose of determining whether an adjudicative proceeding should be conducted; or

(ii) a decision which, under Section 4–101(a), the agency may make without conducting an adjudicative proceeding.

§ 4–103. [Decision Not to Conduct Adjudicative Proceeding]

If an agency decides not to conduct an adjudicative proceeding in response to an application, the agency shall furnish the applicant a copy of its decision in writing, with a brief statement of the agency's reasons and of any administrative review available to the applicant.

§ 4–104. [Agency Action on Applications]

(a) Except to the extent that the time limits in this subsection are inconsistent with limits established by another statute for any stage of the proceedings, an agency shall process an application for an order, other than a declaratory order, as follows:

(1) Within [30] days after receipt of the application, the agency shall examine the application, notify the applicant of any apparent errors or omissions, request any additional information the agency wishes to obtain and is permitted by law to require, and notify the applicant of the name, official title, mailing address and telephone number of an agency member or employee who may be contacted regarding the application.

(2) Except in situations governed by paragraph (3), within [90] days after receipt of the application or of the response to a timely

request made by the agency pursuant to paragraph (1), the agency shall:

    (i) approve or deny the application, in whole or in part, on the basis of emergency or summary adjudicative proceedings, if those proceedings are available under this Act for disposition of the matter;

    (ii) commence a formal adjudicative hearing or a conference adjudicative hearing in accordance with this Act; or

    (iii) dispose of the application in accordance with Section 4–103.

(3) If the application pertains to subject matter that is not available when the application is filed but may be available in the future, including an application for housing or employment at a time no vacancy exists, the agency may proceed to make a determination of eligibility within the time provided in paragraph (2). If the agency determines that the applicant is eligible, the agency shall maintain the application on the agency's list of eligible applicants as provided by law and, upon request, shall notify the applicant of the status of the application.

(b) If a timely and sufficient application has been made for renewal of a license with reference to any activity of a continuing nature, the existing license does not expire until the agency has taken final action upon the application for renewal or, if the agency's action is unfavorable, until the last day for seeking judicial review of the agency's action or a later date fixed by the reviewing court.

§ 4–105. [Agency Action Against Licensees]

An agency may not revoke, suspend, modify, annul, withdraw, or amend a license unless the agency first gives notice and an opportunity for an appropriate adjudicative proceeding in accordance with this Act or other statute. This section does not preclude an agency from (i) taking immediate action to protect the public interest in accordance with Section 4–501 or (ii) adopting rules, otherwise within the scope of its authority, pertaining to a class of licensees, including rules affecting the existing licenses of a class of licensees.

Formal Adjudicative Hearing

§ 4–201. [Applicability]

An adjudicative proceeding is governed by this chapter, except as otherwise provided by:

    (1) a statute other than this Act;

    (2) a rule that adopts the procedures for the conference adjudicative hearing or summary adjudicative proceeding in accordance with the standards provided in this Act for those proceedings;

(3) Section 4–501 pertaining to emergency adjudicative proceedings; or

(4) Section 2–103 pertaining to declaratory proceedings.

§ 4–202. [Presiding Officer, Disqualification, Substitution]

(a) The agency head, one or more members of the agency head, one or more administrative law judges assigned by the office of administrative hearings in accordance with Section 4–301 [, or, unless prohibited by law, one or more other persons designated by the agency head], in the discretion of the agency head, may be the presiding officer.

(b) Any person serving or designated to serve alone or with others as presiding officer is subject to disqualification for bias, prejudice, interest, or any other cause provided in this Act or for which a judge is or may be disqualified.

(c) Any party may petition for the disqualification of a person promptly after receipt of notice indicating that the person will preside or promptly upon discovering facts establishing grounds for disqualification, whichever is later.

(d) A person whose disqualification is requested shall determine whether to grant the petition, stating facts and reasons for the determination.

(e) If a substitute is required for a person who is disqualified or becomes unavailable for any other reason, the substitute must be appointed by:

(1) the governor, if the disqualified or unavailable person is an elected official; or

(2) the appointing authority, if the disqualified or unavailable person is an appointed official.

(f) Any action taken by a duly-appointed substitute for a disqualified or unavailable person is as effective as if taken by the latter.

§ 4–203. [Representation]

(a) Any party may participate in the hearing in person or, if the party is a corporation or other artificial person, by a duly authorized representative.

(b) Whether or not participating in person, any party may be advised and represented at the party's own expense by counsel or, if permitted by law, other representative.

§ 4–204. [Pre-hearing Conference—Availability, Notice]

The presiding officer designated to conduct the hearing may determine, subject to the agency's rules, whether a pre-hearing conference will be conducted. If the conference is conducted:

(1) The presiding officer shall promptly notify the agency of the determination that a pre-hearing conference will be conducted.

The agency shall assign or request the office of administrative hearings to assign a presiding officer for the pre-hearing conference, exercising the same discretion as is provided by Section 4–202 concerning the selection of a presiding officer for a hearing.

(2) The presiding officer for the pre-hearing conference shall set the time and place of the conference and give reasonable written notice to all parties and to all persons who have filed written petitions to intervene in the matter. The agency shall give notice to other persons entitled to notice under any provision of law.

(3) The notice must include:

(i) the names and mailing addresses of all parties and other persons to whom notice is being given by the presiding officer;

(ii) the name, official title, mailing address, and telephone number of any counsel or employee who has been designated to appear for the agency;

(iii) the official file or other reference number, the name of the proceeding, and a general description of the subject matter;

(iv) a statement of the time, place, and nature of the pre-hearing conference;

(v) a statement of the legal authority and jurisdiction under which the pre-hearing conference and the hearing are to be held;

(vi) the name, official title, mailing address and telephone number of the presiding officer for the pre-hearing conference;

(vii) a statement that at the pre-hearing conference the proceeding, without further notice, may be converted into a conference adjudicative hearing or a summary adjudicative proceeding for disposition of the matter as provided by this Act; and

(viii) a statement that a party who fails to attend or participate in a pre-hearing conference, hearing, or other stage of an adjudicative proceeding may be held in default under this Act.

(4) The notice may include any other matters that the presiding officer considers desirable to expedite the proceedings.

§ 4–205. [Pre-hearing Conference—Procedure and Pre-hearing Order]

(a) The presiding officer may conduct all or part of the pre-hearing conference by telephone, television, or other electronic means if each participant in the conference has an opportunity to participate in, to hear, and, if technically feasible, to see the entire proceeding while it is taking place.

(b) The presiding officer shall conduct the pre-hearing conference, as may be appropriate, to deal with such matters as conversion of the proceeding to another type, exploration of settlement possibilities, preparation of stipulations, clarification of issues, rulings on identity and limitation of the number of witnesses, objections to proffers of evidence, determination of the extent to which direct evidence, rebuttal evidence, or cross-examination will be presented in written form, and the extent to which telephone, television, or other electronic means will be used as a substitute for proceedings in person, order of presentation of evidence and cross-examination, rulings regarding issuance of subpoenas, discovery orders and protective orders, and such other matters as will promote the orderly and prompt conduct of the hearing. The presiding officer shall issue a pre-hearing order incorporating the matters determined at the pre-hearing conference.

(c) If a pre-hearing conference is not held, the presiding officer for the hearing may issue a pre-hearing order, based on the pleadings, to regulate the conduct of the proceedings.

§ 4–206. [Notice of Hearing]

(a) The presiding officer for the hearing shall set the time and place of the hearing and give reasonable written notice to all parties and to all persons who have filed written petitions to intervene in the matter.

(b) The notice must include a copy of any pre-hearing order rendered in the matter.

(c) To the extent not included in a pre-hearing order accompanying it, the notice must include:

(1) the names and mailing addresses of all parties and other persons to whom notice is being given by the presiding officer;

(2) the name, official title, mailing address and telephone number of any counsel or employee who has been designated to appear for the agency;

(3) the official file or other reference number, the name of the proceeding, and a general description of the subject matter;

(4) a statement of the time, place, and nature of the hearing;

(5) a statement of the legal authority and jurisdiction under which the hearing is to be held;

(6) the name, official title, mailing address, and telephone number of the presiding officer;

(7) a statement of the issues involved and, to the extent known to the presiding officer, of the matters asserted by the parties; and

(8) a statement that a party who fails to attend or participate in a pre-hearing conference, hearing, or other stage of an adjudicative proceeding may be held in default under this Act.

(d) The notice may include any other matters the presiding officer considers desirable to expedite the proceedings.

(e) The agency shall give notice to persons entitled to notice under any provision of law who have not been given notice by the presiding officer. Notice under this subsection may include all types of information provided in subsections (a) through (d) or may consist of a brief statement indicating the subject matter, parties, time, place, and nature of the hearing, manner in which copies of the notice to the parties may be inspected and copied, and name and telephone number of the presiding officer.

§ 4-207. [Pleadings, Briefs, Motions, Service]

(a) The presiding officer, at appropriate stages of the proceedings, shall give all parties full opportunity to file pleadings, motions, objections and offers of settlement.

(b) The presiding officer, at appropriate stages of the proceedings, may give all parties full opportunity to file briefs, proposed findings of fact and conclusions of law, and proposed initial or final orders.

(c) A party shall serve copies of any filed item on all parties, by mail or any other means prescribed by agency rule.

§ 4-208. [Default]

(a) If a party fails to attend or participate in a pre-hearing conference, hearing, or other stage of an adjudicative proceeding, the presiding officer may serve upon all parties written notice of a proposed default order, including a statement of the grounds.

(b) Within [7] days after service of a proposed default order, the party against whom it was issued may file a written motion requesting that the proposed default order be vacated and stating the grounds relied upon. During the time within which a party may file a written motion under this subsection, the presiding officer may adjourn the proceedings or conduct them without the participation of the party against whom a proposed default order was issued, having due regard for the interests of justice and the orderly and prompt conduct of the proceedings.

(c) The presiding officer shall either issue or vacate the default order promptly after expiration of the time within which the party may file a written motion under subsection (b).

(d) After issuing a default order, the presiding officer shall conduct any further proceedings necessary to complete the adjudication without the participation of the party in default and shall determine all issues in the adjudication, including those affecting the defaulting party.

§ 4–209. [Intervention]

(a) The presiding officer shall grant a petition for intervention if:

(1) the petition is submitted in writing to the presiding officer, with copies mailed to all parties named in the presiding officer's notice of the hearing, at least [3] days before the hearing;

(2) the petition states facts demonstrating that the petitioner's legal rights, duties, privileges, immunities, or other legal interests may be substantially affected by the proceeding or that the petitioner qualifies as an intervener under any provision of law; and

(3) the presiding officer determines that the interests of justice and the orderly and prompt conduct of the proceedings will not be impaired by allowing the intervention.

(b) The presiding officer may grant a petition for intervention at any time, upon determining that the intervention sought is in the interests of justice and will not impair the orderly and prompt conduct of the proceedings.

(c) If a petitioner qualifies for intervention, the presiding officer may impose conditions upon the intervener's participation in the proceedings, either at the time that intervention is granted or at any subsequent time. Conditions may include:

(1) limiting the intervener's participation to designated issues in which the intervener has a particular interest demonstrated by the petition;

(2) limiting the intervener's use of discovery, cross-examination, and other procedures so as to promote the orderly and prompt conduct of the proceedings; and

(3) requiring 2 or more interveners to combine their presentations of evidence and argument, cross-examination, discovery, and other participation in the proceedings. . . .

§ 4–210. [Subpoenas, Discovery and Protective Orders]

(a) The presiding officer [at the request of any party shall, and upon the presiding officer's own motion,] may issue subpoenas, discovery orders and protective orders, in accordance with the rules of civil procedure.

(b) Subpoenas and orders issued under this section may be enforced pursuant to the provisions of this Act on civil enforcement of agency action.

§ 4–211. [Procedure at Hearing]

At a hearing:

(1) The presiding officer shall regulate the course of the proceedings in conformity with any pre-hearing order.

(2) To the extent necessary for full disclosure of all relevant facts and issues, the presiding officer shall afford to all parties the opportuni-

ty to respond, present evidence and argument, conduct cross-examination, and submit rebuttal evidence, except as restricted by a limited grant of intervention or by the pre-hearing order.

(3) The presiding officer may give nonparties an opportunity to present oral or written statements. If the presiding officer proposes to consider a statement by a nonparty, the presiding officer shall give all parties an opportunity to challenge or rebut it and, on motion of any party, the presiding officer shall require the statement to be given under oath or affirmation.

(4) The presiding officer may conduct all or part of the hearing by telephone, television, or other electronic means, if each participant in the hearing has an opportunity to participate in, to hear, and, if technically feasible, to see the entire proceeding while it is taking place.

(5) The presiding officer shall cause the hearing to be recorded at the agency's expense. The agency is not required, at its expense, to prepare a transcript, unless required to do so by a provision of law. Any party, at the party's expense, may cause a reporter approved by the agency to prepare a transcript from the agency's record, or cause additional recordings to be made during the hearing if the making of the additional recordings does not cause distraction or disruption.

(6) The hearing is open to public observation, except for the parts that the presiding officer states to be closed pursuant to a provision of law expressly authorizing closure. To the extent that a hearing is conducted by telephone, television, or other electronic means, and is not closed, the availability of public observation is satisfied by giving members of the public an opportunity, at reasonable times, to hear or inspect the agency's record, and to inspect any transcript obtained by the agency.

§ 4–212. [Evidence, Official Notice]

(a) Upon proper objection, the presiding officer shall exclude evidence that is irrelevant, immaterial, unduly repetitious, or excludable on constitutional or statutory grounds or on the basis of evidentiary privilege recognized in the courts of this state. In the absence of proper objection, the presiding officer may exclude objectionable evidence. Evidence may not be excluded solely because it is hearsay.

(b) All testimony of parties and witnesses must be made under oath or affirmation.

(c) Statements presented by nonparties in accordance with Section 4–211(3) may be received as evidence.

(d) Any part of the evidence may be received in written form if doing so will expedite the hearing without substantial prejudice to the interests of any party.

(e) Documentary evidence may be received in the form of a copy or excerpt. Upon request, parties must be given an opportunity to compare the copy with the original if available.

(f) Official notice may be taken of (i) any fact that could be judicially noticed in the courts of this State, (ii) the record of other proceedings before the agency, (iii) technical or scientific matters within the agency's specialized knowledge, and (iv) codes or standards that have been adopted by an agency of the United States, of this State or of another state, or by a nationally recognized organization or association. Parties must be notified before or during the hearing, or before the issuance of any initial or final order that is based in whole or in part on facts or material noticed, of the specific facts or material noticed and the source thereof, including any staff memoranda and data, and be afforded an opportunity to contest and rebut the facts or material so noticed.

§ 4–213.   [Ex parte Communications]

(a) Except as provided in subsection (b) or unless required for the disposition of ex parte matters specifically authorized by statute, a presiding officer serving in an adjudicative proceeding may not communicate, directly or indirectly, regarding any issue in the proceeding, while the proceeding is pending, with any party, with any person who has a direct or indirect interest in the outcome of the proceeding, or with any person who presided at a previous stage of the proceeding, without notice and opportunity for all parties to participate in the communication.

(b) A member of a multi-member panel of presiding officers may communicate with other members of the panel regarding a matter pending before the panel, and any presiding officer may receive aid from staff assistants if the assistants do not (i) receive ex parte communications of a type that the presiding officer would be prohibited from receiving or (ii) furnish, augment, diminish, or modify the evidence in the record.

(c) Unless required for the disposition of ex parte matters specifically authorized by statute, no party to an adjudicative proceeding, and no person who has a direct or indirect interest in the outcome of the proceeding or who presided at a previous stage of the proceeding, may communicate, directly or indirectly, in connection with any issue in that proceeding, while the proceeding is pending, with any person serving as presiding officer, without notice and opportunity for all parties to participate in the communication.

(d) If, before serving as presiding officer in an adjudicative proceeding, a person receives an ex parte communication of a type that could not properly be received while serving, the person, promptly after starting to serve, shall disclose the communication in the manner prescribed in subsection (e).

(e) A presiding officer who receives an ex parte communication in violation of this section shall place on the record of the pending matter all written communications received, all written responses to the communications, and a memorandum stating the substance of all oral communications received, all responses made, and the identity of each person from whom the presiding officer received an ex parte communication, and shall advise all parties that these matters have been placed on the record. Any party desiring to rebut the ex parte communication must be allowed to do so, upon requesting the opportunity for rebuttal within [10] days after notice of the communication.

(f) If necessary to eliminate the effect of an ex parte communication received in violation of this section, a presiding officer who receives the communication may be disqualified and the portions of the record pertaining to the communication may be sealed by protective order.

(g) The agency shall, and any party may, report any willful violation of this section to appropriate authorities for any disciplinary proceedings provided by law. In addition, each agency by rule may provide for appropriate sanctions, including default, for any violations of this section.

§ 4–214. [Separation of Functions]

(a) A person who has served as investigator, prosecutor or advocate in an adjudicative proceeding or in its pre-adjudicative stage may not serve as presiding officer or assist or advise a presiding officer in the same proceeding.

(b) A person who is subject to the authority, direction, or discretion of one who has served as investigator, prosecutor, or advocate in an adjudicative proceeding or in its pre-adjudicative stage may not serve as presiding officer or assist or advise a presiding officer in the same proceeding.

(c) A person who has participated in a determination of probable cause or other equivalent preliminary determination in an adjudicative proceeding may serve as presiding officer or assist or advise a presiding officer in the same proceeding, unless a party demonstrates grounds for disqualification in accordance with Section 4–202.

(d) A person may serve as presiding officer at successive stages of the same adjudicative proceeding, unless a party demonstrates grounds for disqualification in accordance with Section 4–202.

§ 4–215. [Final Order, Initial Order]

(a) If the presiding officer is the agency head, the presiding officer shall render a final order.

(b) If the presiding officer is not the agency head, the presiding officer shall render an initial order, which becomes a final order unless reviewed in accordance with Section 4–216.

(c) A final order or initial order must include, separately stated, findings of fact, conclusions of law, and policy reasons for the decision if it is an exercise of the agency's discretion, for all aspects of the order, including the remedy prescribed and, if applicable, the action taken on a petition for stay of effectiveness. Findings of fact, if set forth in language that is no more than mere repetition or paraphrase of the relevant provision of law, must be accompanied by a concise and explicit statement of the underlying facts of record to support the findings. If a party has submitted proposed findings of fact, the order must include a ruling on the proposed findings. The order must also include a statement of the available procedures and time limits for seeking reconsideration or other administrative relief. An initial order must include a statement of any circumstances under which the initial order, without further notice, may become a final order.

(d) Findings of fact must be based exclusively upon the evidence of record in the adjudicative proceeding and on matters officially noticed in that proceeding. Findings must be based upon the kind of evidence on which reasonably prudent persons are accustomed to rely in the conduct of their serious affairs and may be based upon such evidence even if it would be inadmissible in a civil trial. The presiding officer's experience, technical competence, and specialized knowledge may be utilized in evaluating evidence.

(e) If a person serving or designated to serve as presiding officer becomes unavailable, for any reason, before rendition of the final order or initial order, a substitute presiding officer must be appointed as provided in Section 4–202. The substitute presiding officer shall use any existing record and may conduct any further proceedings appropriate in the interests of justice.

(f) The presiding officer may allow the parties a designated amount of time after conclusion of the hearing for the submission of proposed findings.

(g) A final order or initial order pursuant to this section must be rendered in writing within [90] days after conclusion of the hearing or after submission of proposed findings in accordance with subsection (f) unless this period is waived or extended with the written consent of all parties or for good cause shown.

(h) The presiding officer shall cause copies of the final order or initial order to be delivered to each party and to the agency head.

§ 4–216. [Review of Initial Order; Exceptions to Reviewability]

(a) The agency head, upon its own motion may, and upon appeal by any party shall, review an initial order, except to the extent that:

(1) a provision of law precludes or limits agency review of the initial order; or

(2) the agency head, in the exercise of discretion conferred by a provision of law,

(i) determines to review some but not all issues, or not to exercise any review,

(ii) delegates its authority to review the initial order to one or more persons, or

(iii) authorizes one or more persons to review the initial order, subject to further review by the agency head. . . .

(d) The presiding officer for the review of an initial order shall exercise all the decision-making power that the presiding officer would have had to render a final order had the presiding officer presided over the hearing, except to the extent that the issues subject to review are limited by a provision of law or by the presiding officer upon notice to all parties.

(e) The presiding officer shall afford each party an opportunity to present briefs and may afford each party an opportunity to present oral argument.

(f) Before rendering a final order, the presiding officer may cause a transcript to be prepared, at the agency's expense, of such portions of the proceeding under review as the presiding officer considers necessary.

(g) The presiding officer may render a final order disposing of the proceeding or may remand the matter for further proceedings with instructions to the person who rendered the initial order. Upon remanding a matter, the presiding officer may order such temporary relief as is authorized and appropriate.

(h) A final order or an order remanding the matter for further proceedings must be rendered in writing within [60] days after receipt of briefs and oral argument unless that period is waived or extended with the written consent of all parties or for good cause shown.

(i) A final order or an order remanding the matter for further proceedings under this section must identify any difference between this order and the initial order and must include, or incorporate by express reference to the initial order, all the matters required by Section 4–215(c).

(j) The presiding officer shall cause copies of the final order or order remanding the matter for further proceedings to be delivered to each party and to the agency head.

§ 4–217. [Stay]

A party may submit to the presiding officer a petition for stay of effectiveness of an initial or final order within [7] days after its rendition unless otherwise provided by statute or stated in the initial or final order. The presiding officer may take action on the petition for stay, either before or after the effective date of the initial or final order.

§ 4–218. [Reconsideration]

Unless otherwise provided by statute or rule:

(1) Any party, within [10] days after rendition of an initial or final order, may file a petition for reconsideration, stating the specific grounds upon which relief is requested. The filing of the petition is not a prerequisite for seeking administrative or judicial review.

§ 4–219. [Review by Superior Agency]

If, pursuant to statute, an agency may review the final order of another agency, the review is deemed to be a continuous proceeding as if before a single agency. The final order of the first agency is treated as an initial order and the second agency functions as though it were reviewing an initial order in accordance with Section 4–216.

§ 4–220. [Effectiveness of Orders]

(a) Unless a later date is stated in a final order or a stay is granted, a final order is effective [10] days after rendition, but:

(1) a party may not be required to comply with a final order unless the party has been served with or has actual knowledge of the final order; . . .

(d) This section does not preclude an agency from taking immediate action to protect the public interest in accordance with Section 4–501.

§ 4–221. [Agency Record]

(a) An agency shall maintain an official record of each adjudicative proceeding under this Chapter.

(b) The agency record consists only of:

(1) notices of all proceedings;

(2) any pre-hearing order;

(3) any motions, pleadings, briefs, petitions, requests, and intermediate rulings;

(4) evidence received or considered;

(5) a statement of matters officially noticed;

(6) proffers of proof and objections and rulings thereon;

(7) proposed findings, requested orders, and exceptions;

(8) the record prepared for the presiding officer at the hearing, together with any transcript of all or part of the hearing considered before final disposition of the proceeding;

(9) any final order, initial order, or order on reconsideration;

(10) staff memoranda or data submitted to the presiding officer, unless prepared and submitted by personal assistants and not inconsistent with Section 4–213(b); and

(11) matters placed on the record after an ex parte communication.

(c) Except to the extent that this Act or another statute provides otherwise, the agency record constitutes the exclusive basis for agency action in adjudicative proceedings under this Chapter and for judicial review thereof.

Office of Administrative Hearings

§ 4–301. [Office of Administrative Hearings—Creation, Powers, Duties]

(a) There is created the office of administrative hearings within the [Department of _____], to be headed by a director appointed by the governor and confirmed by the senate.

(b) The office shall employ administrative law judges as necessary to conduct proceedings required by this Act or other provision of law. [Only a person admitted to practice law in [this State] [a jurisdiction in the United States] may be employed as an administrative law judge.]

(c) If the office cannot furnish one of its administrative law judges in response to an agency request, the director shall designate in writing a fulltime employee of an agency other than the requesting agency to serve as administrative law judge for the proceeding, but only with the consent of the employing agency. The designee must possess the same qualifications required of administrative law judges employed by the office.

(d) The director may furnish administrative law judges on a contract basis to any governmental entity to conduct any proceeding not subject to this Act.

(e) The office may adopt rules:

(1) to establish further qualifications for administrative law judges, procedures by which candidates will be considered for employment, and the manner in which public notice of vacancies in the staff of the office will be given;

(2) to establish procedures for agencies to request and for the director to assign administrative law judges; however, an agency may neither select nor reject any individual administrative law judge for any proceeding except in accordance with this Act;

(3) to establish procedures and adopt forms, consistent with this Act, the model rules of procedure, and other provisions of law, to govern administrative law judges;

(4) to establish standards and procedures for the evaluation, training, promotion, and discipline of administrative law judges; and

(5) to facilitate the performance of the responsibilities conferred upon the office by this Act.

(f) The director may:

(1) maintain a staff of reporters and other personnel; and

(2) implement the provisions of this section and rules adopted under its authority.

(B. & A.) State & Fed'l Admin.Law ACB—28

Conference Adjudicative Hearing

§ 4–401. [Conference Adjudicative Hearing—Applicability]

A conference adjudicative hearing may be used if its use in the circumstances does not violate any provision of law and the matter is entirely within one or more categories for which the agency by rule has adopted this chapter [; however, those categories may include only the following:

(1) a matter in which there is no disputed issue of material fact; or

(2) a matter in which there is a disputed issue of material fact, if the matter involves only:

(i) a monetary amount of not more than [$1,000];

(ii) a disciplinary sanction against a prisoner;

(iii) a disciplinary sanction against a student which does not involve expulsion from an academic institution or suspension for more than [10] days;

(iv) a disciplinary sanction against a public employee which does not involve discharge from employment or suspension for more than [10] days;

(v) a disciplinary sanction against a licensee which does not involve revocation, suspension, annulment, withdrawal, or amendment of a license; or

(vi) . . . .]

§ 4–402. [Conference Adjudicative Hearing—Procedures]

The procedures of this Act pertaining to formal adjudicative hearings apply to a conference adjudicative hearing, except to the following extent:

(1) If a matter is initiated as a conference adjudicative hearing, no pre-hearing conference may be held.

(2) The provisions of Section 4–210 do not apply to conference adjudicative hearings insofar as those provisions authorize the issuance and enforcement of subpoenas and discovery orders, but do apply to conference adjudicative hearings insofar as those provisions authorize the presiding officer to issue protective orders at the request of any party or upon the presiding officer's motion.

(3) Paragraphs (1), (2) and (3) of Section 4–211 do not apply; but,

(i) the presiding officer shall regulate the course of the proceedings,

(ii) only the parties may testify and present written exhibits, and

(iii) the parties may offer comments on the issues.

§ 4–403. [Conference Adjudicative Hearing—Proposed Proof]

(a) If the presiding officer has reason to believe that material facts are in dispute, the presiding officer may require any party to state the identity of the witnesses or other sources through whom the party would propose to present proof if the proceeding were converted to a formal adjudicative hearing, but if disclosure of any fact, allegation, or source is privileged or expressly prohibited by any provision of law, the presiding officer may require the party to indicate that confidential facts, allegations, or sources are involved, but not to disclose the confidential facts, allegations, or sources.

(b) If a party has reason to believe that essential facts must be obtained in order to permit an adequate presentation of the case, the party may inform the presiding officer regarding the general nature of the facts and the sources from whom the party would propose to obtain those facts if the proceeding were converted to a formal adjudicative hearing.

Emergency and Summary Adjudicative Proceedings

§ 4–501. [Emergency Adjudicative Proceedings]

(a) An agency may use emergency adjudicative proceedings in a situation involving an immediate danger to the public health, safety, or welfare requiring immediate agency action.

(b) The agency may take only such action as is necessary to prevent or avoid the immediate danger to the public health, safety, or welfare that justifies use of emergency adjudication.

(c) The agency shall render an order, including a brief statement of findings of fact, conclusions of law, and policy reasons for the decision if it is an exercise of the agency's discretion, to justify the determination of an immediate danger and the agency's decision to take the specific action.

(d) The agency shall give such notice as is practicable to persons who are required to comply with the order. The order is effective when rendered.

(e) After issuing an order pursuant to this section, the agency shall proceed as quickly as feasible to complete any proceedings that would be required if the matter did not involve an immediate danger.

(f) The agency record consists of any documents regarding the matter that were considered or prepared by the agency. The agency shall maintain these documents as its official record.

(g) Unless otherwise required by a provision of law, the agency record need not constitute the exclusive basis for agency action in emergency adjudicative proceedings or for judicial review thereof.

§ 4-502. [Summary Adjudicative Proceedings—Applicability]

An agency may use summary adjudicative proceedings if:

(1) the use of those proceedings in the circumstances does not violate any provision of law;

(2) the protection of the public interest does not require the agency to give notice and an opportunity to participate to persons other than the parties; and

(3) the matter is entirely within one or more categories for which the agency by rule has adopted this section and Sections 4-503 to 4-506 [; however, those categories may include only the following:

(i) a monetary amount of not more than [$100];

(ii) a reprimand, warning, disciplinary report, or other purely verbal sanction without continuing impact against a prisoner, student, public employee, or licensee;

(iii) the denial of an application after the applicant has abandoned the application;

(iv) the denial of an application for admission to an educational institution or for employment by an agency;

(v) the denial, in whole or in part, of an application if the applicant has an opportunity for administrative review in accordance with Section 4-504;

(vi) a matter that is resolved on the sole basis of inspections, examinations, or tests;

(vii) the acquisition, leasing, or disposal of property or the procurement of goods or services by contract;

(viii) any matter having only trivial potential impact upon the affected parties; and

(ix) . . . .]

§ 4-503. [Summary Adjudicative Proceedings—Procedures]

(a) The agency head, one or more members of the agency head, one or more administrative law judges assigned by the office of administrative hearings in accordance with Section 4-301 [, or, unless prohibited by law, one or more other persons designated by the agency head], in the discretion of the agency head, may be the presiding officer. Unless prohibited by law, a person exercising authority over the matter is the presiding officer.

(b) If the proceeding involves a monetary matter or a reprimand, warning, disciplinary report, or other sanction:

(1) the presiding officer, before taking action, shall give each party an opportunity to be informed of the agency's view of the matter and to explain the party's view of the matter; and

(2) the presiding officer, at the time any unfavorable action is taken, shall give each party a brief statement of findings of fact, conclusions of law, and policy reasons for the decision if it is an exercise of the agency's discretion, to justify the action, and a notice of any available administrative review.

(c) An order rendered in a proceeding that involves a monetary matter must be in writing. An order in any other summary adjudicative proceeding may be oral or written.

(d) The agency, by reasonable means, shall furnish to each party notification of the order in a summary adjudicative proceeding. Notification must include at least a statement of the agency's action and a notice of any available administrative review.

§ 4-504. [Administrative Review of Summary Adjudicative Proceedings—Applicability]

Unless prohibited by any provision of law, an agency, on its own motion, may conduct administrative review of an order resulting from summary adjudicative proceedings, and shall conduct this review upon the written or oral request of a party if the agency receives the request within [10] days after furnishing notification under Section 4-503(d).

§ 4-505. [Administrative Review of Summary Adjudicative Proceedings—Procedures]

Unless otherwise provided by statute [or rule]:

(1) An agency need not furnish notification of the pendency of administrative review to any person who did not request the review, but the agency may not take any action on review less favorable to any party than the original order without giving that party notice and an opportunity to explain that party's view of the matter.

(2) The reviewing officer, in the discretion of the agency head, may be any person who could have presided at the summary adjudicative proceeding, but the reviewing officer must be one who is authorized to grant appropriate relief upon review.

(3) The reviewing officer shall give each party an opportunity to explain the party's view of the matter unless the party's view is apparent from the written materials in the file submitted to the reviewing officer. The reviewing officer shall make any inquiries necessary to ascertain whether the proceeding must be converted to a conference adjudicative hearing or a formal adjudicative hearing.

(4) The reviewing officer may render an order disposing of the proceeding in any manner that was available to the presiding officer at the summary adjudicative proceeding or the reviewing officer may remand the matter for further proceedings, with or without conversion to a conference adjudicative hearing or a formal adjudicative hearing.

(5) If the order under review is or should have been in writing, the order on review must be in writing, including a brief statement of findings of fact, conclusions of law, and policy reasons for the decision if it is an exercise of the agency's discretion, to justify the order, and a notice of any further available administrative review.

(6) A request for administrative review is deemed to have been denied if the reviewing officer does not dispose of the matter or remand it for further proceedings within [20] days after the request is submitted.

§ 4–506. [Agency Record of Summary Adjudicative Proceedings and Administrative Review]

(a) The agency record consists of any documents regarding the matter that were considered or prepared by the presiding officer for the summary adjudicative proceeding or by the reviewing officer for any review. The agency shall maintain these documents as its official record.

(b) Unless otherwise required by a provision of law, the agency record need not constitute the exclusive basis for agency action in summary adjudicative proceedings or for judicial review thereof.

ARTICLE V

JUDICIAL REVIEW AND CIVIL ENFORCEMENT

CHAPTER I. JUDICIAL REVIEW

§ 5–101. [Relationship Between this Act and Other Law on Judicial Review and Other Judicial Remedies]

This Act establishes the exclusive means of judicial review of agency action, but:

(1) The provisions of this Act for judicial review do not apply to litigation in which the sole issue is a claim for money damages or compensation and the agency whose action is at issue does not have statutory authority to determine the claim.

(2) Ancillary procedural matters, including intervention, class actions, consolidation, joinder, severance, transfer, protective orders, and other relief from disclosure of privileged or confidential material, are governed, to the extent not inconsistent with this Act, by other applicable law.

(3) If the relief available under other sections of this Act is not equal or substantially equivalent to the relief otherwise available under law, the relief otherwise available and the related procedures supersede and supplement this Act to the extent necessary for their effectuation. The applicable provisions of this Act and other law must be combined to govern a single proceeding or, if the court orders, 2 or more separate proceedings, with or without transfer to other courts, but no type of

relief may be sought in a combined proceeding after expiration of the time limit for doing so.

§ 5–102. [Final Agency Action Reviewable]

(a) A person who qualifies under this Act regarding (i) standing (Section 5–106), (ii) exhaustion of administrative remedies (Section 5–107), and (iii) time for filing the petition for review (Section 5–108), and other applicable provisions of law regarding bond, compliance, and other pre-conditions is entitled to judicial review of final agency action, whether or not the person has sought judicial review of any related non-final agency action.

(b) For purposes of this section and Section 5–103:

(1) "Final agency action" means the whole or a part of any agency action other than non-final agency action;

(2) "Non-final agency action" means the whole or a part of an agency determination, investigation, proceeding, hearing, conference, or other process that the agency intends or is reasonably believed to intend to be preliminary, preparatory, procedural, or intermediate with regard to subsequent agency action of that agency or another agency.

§ 5–103. [Non-final Agency Action Reviewable]

A person is entitled to judicial review of non-final agency action only if:

(1) it appears likely that the person will qualify under Section 5–102 for judicial review of the related final agency action; and

(2) postponement of judicial review would result in an inadequate remedy or irreparable harm disproportionate to the public benefit derived from postponement.

[*Alternative A.*]

§ 5–104. [Jurisdiction, Venue]

(a) The [trial court of general jurisdiction] shall conduct judicial review.

(b) Venue is in the [district] [that includes the state capital] [where the petitioner resides or maintains a principal place of business] unless otherwise provided by law.

[*Alternative B.*]

§ 5–104. [Jurisdiction, Venue]

(a) The [appellate court] shall conduct judicial review.

(b) Venue is in the [district] [that includes the state capital] [where the petitioner resides or maintains a principal place of business] unless otherwise provided by law.

(c) If evidence is to be adduced in the reviewing court in accordance with Section 5–114(a), the court shall appoint a [referee, master, trial court judge] for this purpose, having due regard for the convenience of the parties.

§ 5–105. [Form of Action]

Judicial review is initiated by filing a petition for review in [the appropriate] court. A petition may seek any type of relief available under Sections 5–101(3) and 5–117.

§ 5–106. [Standing]

(a) The following persons have standing to obtain judicial review of final or non-final agency action:

(1) a person to whom the agency action is specifically directed;

(2) a person who was a party to the agency proceedings that led to the agency action;

(3) if the challenged agency action is a rule, a person subject to that rule;

(4) a person eligible for standing under another provision of law; or

(5) a person otherwise aggrieved or adversely affected by the agency action. For purposes of this paragraph, no person has standing as one otherwise aggrieved or adversely affected unless:

(i) the agency action has prejudiced or is likely to prejudice that person;

(ii) that person's asserted interests are among those that the agency was required to consider when it engaged in the agency action challenged; and

(iii) a judgment in favor of that person would substantially eliminate or redress the prejudice to that person caused or likely to be caused by the agency action.

[(b) A standing committee of the legislature which is required to exercise general and continuing oversight over administrative agencies and procedures may petition for judicial review of any rule or intervene in any litigation arising from agency action.]

§ 5–107. [Exhaustion of Administrative Remedies]

A person may file a petition for judicial review under this Act only after exhausting all administrative remedies available within the agency whose action is being challenged and within any other agency authorized to exercise administrative review, but:

(1) a petitioner for judicial review of a rule need not have participated in the rule-making proceeding upon which that rule is based, or have petitioned for its amendment or repeal;

(2) a petitioner for judicial review need not exhaust administrative remedies to the extent that this Act or any other statute states that exhaustion is not required; or

(3) the court may relieve a petitioner of the requirement to exhaust any or all administrative remedies, to the extent that the administrative remedies are inadequate, or requiring their exhaustion would result in irreparable harm disproportionate to the public benefit derived from requiring exhaustion.

§ 5–108. [Time for Filing Petition for Review]

Subject to other requirements of this Act or of another statute:

(1) A petition for judicial review of a rule may be filed at any time, except as limited by Section 3–113(b).

(2) A petition for judicial review of an order is not timely unless filed within [30] days after rendition of the order, but the time is extended during the pendency of the petitioner's timely attempts to exhaust administrative remedies, if the attempts are not clearly frivolous or repetitious.

(3) A petition for judicial review of agency action other than a rule or order is not timely unless filed within [30] days after the agency action, but the time is extended:

(i) during the pendency of the petitioner's timely attempts to exhaust administrative remedies, if the attempts are not clearly frivolous or repetitious; and

(ii) during any period that the petitioner did not know and was under no duty to discover, or did not know and was under a duty to discover but could not reasonably have discovered, that the agency had taken the action or that the agency action had a sufficient effect to confer standing upon the petitioner to obtain judicial review under this Act.

§ 5–109. [Petition for Review—Filing and Contents]

(a) A petition for review must be filed with the clerk of the court.

(b) A petition for review must set forth:

(1) the name and mailing address of the petitioner;

(2) the name and mailing address of the agency whose action is at issue;

(3) identification of the agency action at issue, together with a duplicate copy, summary, or brief description of the agency action;

(4) identification of persons who were parties in any adjudicative proceedings that led to the agency action;

(5) facts to demonstrate that the petitioner is entitled to obtain judicial review;

(6) the petitioner's reasons for believing that relief should be granted; and

(7) a request for relief, specifying the type and extent of relief requested.

§ 5–110. [Petition for Review—Service and Notification]

(a) A petitioner for judicial review shall serve a copy of the petition upon the agnecy in the manner provided by [statute] [the rules of civil procedure].

(b) The petitioner shall use means provided by [statute] [the rules of civil procedure] to give notice of the petiton for review to all other parties in any adjudicative proceedings that led to the agency action.

§ 5–111. [Stay and Other Temporary Remedies Pending Final Disposition]

(a) Unless precluded by law, the agency may grant a stay on appropriate terms or other temporary remedies during the pendency of judicial review.

(b) A party may file a motion in the reviewing court, during the pendency of judicial review, seeking interlocutory review of the agency's action on an application for stay or other temporary remedies.

(c) If the agency has found that its action on an application for stay or other temporary remedies is justified to protect against a substantial threat to the public health, safety, or welfare, the court may not grant relief unless it finds that:

(1) the applicant is likely to prevail when the court finally disposes of the matter;

(2) without relief the applicant will suffer irreparable injury;

(3) the grant of relief to the applicant will not substantially harm other parties to the proceedings; and

(4) the threat to the public health, safety, or welfare relied on by the agency is not sufficiently serious to justify the agency's action in the circumstances.

(d) If subsection (c) does not apply, the court shall grant relief if it finds, in its independent judgment, that the agency's action on the application for stay or other temporary remedies was unreasonable in the circumstances.

(e) If the court determines that relief should be granted from the agency's action on an application for stay or other temporary remedies, the court may remand the matter to the agency with directions to deny a stay, to grant a stay on appropriate terms, or to grant other temporary remedies, or the court may issue an order denying a stay, granting a stay on appropriate terms, or granting other temporary remedies.

§ 5–112. [Limitation on New Issues]

A person may obtain judicial review of an issue that was not raised before the agency, only to the extent that:

(1) the agency did not have jurisdiction to grant an adequate remedy based on a determination of the issue;

(2) the person did not know and was under no duty to discover, or did not know and was under a duty to discover but could not reasonably have discovered, facts giving rise to the issue;

(3) the agency action subject to judicial review is a rule and the person has not been a party in adjudicative proceedings which provided an adequate opportunity to raise the issue;

(4) the agency action subject to judicial review is an order and the person was not notified of the adjudicative proceeding in substantial compliance with this Act; or

(5) the interests of justice would be served by judicial resolution of an issue arising from:

(i) a change in controlling law occurring after the agency action; or

(ii) agency action occurring after the person exhausted the last feasible opportunity for seeking relief from the agency.

§ 5–113. [Judicial Review of Facts Confined to Record for Judicial Review and Additional Evidence Taken Pursuant to Act]

Judicial review of disputed issues of fact must be confined to the agency record for judicial review as defined in this Act, supplemented by additional evidence taken pursuant to this Act.

§ 5–114. [New Evidence Taken by Court or Agency Before Final Disposition]

(a) The court [(if Alternative B of Section 5–104 is adopted), assisted by a referee, master, trial court judge as provided in Section 5–104(c),] may receive evidence, in addition to that contained in the agency record for judicial review, only if it relates to the validity of the agency action at the time it was taken and is needed to decide disputed issues regarding:

(1) improper constitution as a decision-making body, or improper motive or grounds for disqualification, of those taking the agency action;

(2) unlawfulness of procedure or of decision-making process; or

(3) any material fact that was not required by any provision of law to be determined exclusively on an agency record of a type reasonably suitable for judicial review.

(b) The court may remand a matter to the agency, before final disposition of a petition for review, with directions that the agency conduct fact-finding and other proceedings the court considers necessary and that the agency take such further action on the basis thereof as the court directs, if:

(1) the agency was required by this Act or any other provision of law to base its action exclusively on a record of a type reasonably suitable for judicial review, but the agency failed to prepare or preserve an adequate record;

(2) the court finds that (i) new evidence has become available that relates to the validity of the agency action at the time it was taken, that one or more of the parties did not know and was under no duty to discover, or did not know and was under a duty to discover but could not reasonably have discovered, until after the agency action, and (ii) the interests of justice would be served by remand to the agency;

(3) the agency improperly excluded or omitted evidence from the record; or

(4) a relevant provision of law changed after the agency action and the court determines that the new provision may control the outcome.

§ 5–115. [Agency Record for Judicial Review—Contents, Preparation, Transmittal, Cost]

(a) Within [_____] days after service of the petition, or within further time allowed by the court or by other provision of law, the agency shall transmit to the court the original or a certified copy of the agency record for judicial review of the agency action, consisting of any agency documents expressing the agency action, other documents identified by the agency as having been considered by it before its action and used as a basis for its action, and any other material described in this Act as the agency record for the type of agency action at issue, subject to the provisions of this section.

(b) If part of the record has been preserved without a transcript, the agency shall prepare a transcript for inclusion in the record transmitted to the court, except for portions that the parties stipulate to omit in accordance with subsection (d).

(c) The agency shall charge the petitioner with the reasonable cost of preparing any necessary copies and transcripts for transmittal to the court. [A failure by the petitioner to pay any of this cost to the agency does not relieve the agency from the responsibility for timely preparation of the record and transmittal to the court.]

(d) By stipulation of all parties to the review proceedings, the record may be shortened, summarized, or organized.

(e) The court may tax the cost of preparing transcripts and copies for the record:

(1) against a party who unreasonably refuses to stipulate to shorten, summarize, or organize the record;

(2) as provided by Section 5–117; or

(3) in accordance with any other provision of law.

(f) Additions to the record pursuant to Section 5–114 must be made as ordered by the court.

(g) The court may require or permit subsequent corrections or additions to the record.

§ 5–116. [Scope of Review; Grounds for Invalidity]

(a) Except to the extent that this Act or another statute provides otherwise:

(1) The burden of demonstrating the invalidity of agency action is on the party asserting invalidity; and

(2) The validity of agency action must be determined in accordance with the standards of review provided in this section, as applied to the agency action at the time it was taken.

(b) The court shall make a separate and distinct ruling on each material issue on which the court's decision is based.

(c) The court shall grant relief only if it determines that a person seeking judicial relief has been substantially prejudiced by any one or more of the following:

(1) The agency action, or the statute or rule on which the agency action is based, is unconstitutional on its face or as applied.

(2) The agency has acted beyond the jurisdiction conferred by any provision of law.

(3) The agency has not decided all issues requiring resolution.

(4) The agency has erroneously interpreted or applied the law.

(5) The agency has engaged in an unlawful procedure or decision-making process, or has failed to follow prescribed procedure.

(6) The persons taking the agency action were improperly constituted as a decision-making body, motivated by an improper purpose, or subject to disqualification.

(7) The agency action is based on a determination of fact, made or implied by the agency, that is not supported by evidence that is substantial when viewed in light of the whole record before the court, which includes the agency record for judicial review, supplemented by any additional evidence received by the court under this Act.

(8) The agency action is:

(i) outside the range of discretion delegated to the agency by any provision of law;

(ii) agency action, other than a rule, that is inconsistent with a rule of the agency; [or]

(iii) agency action, other than a rule, that is inconsistent with the agency's prior practice unless the agency justifies the inconsistency by stating facts and reasons to demonstrate a fair and rational basis for the inconsistency;

(iv) [otherwise unreasonable, arbitrary or capricious.]

§ 5–117. [Type of Relief]

(a) The court may award damages or compensation only to the extent expressly authorized by another provision of law.

(b) The court may grant other appropriate relief, whether mandatory, injunctive, or declaratory; preliminary or final; temporary or permanent; equitable or legal. In granting relief, the court may order agency action required by law, order agency exercise of discretion required by law, set aside or modify agency action, enjoin or stay the effectiveness of agency action, remand the matter for further proceedings, render a declaratory judgment, or take any other action that is authorized and appropriate.

(c) The court may also grant necessary ancillary relief to redress the effects of official action wrongfully taken or withheld, but the court may award attorney's fees or witness fees only to the extent expressly authorized by other law.

(d) If the court sets aside or modifies agency action or remands the matter to the agency for further proceedings, the court may make any interlocutory order it finds necessary to preserve the interests of the parties and the public pending further proceedings or agency action.

[§ 5–118. [Review by Higher Court]

Decisions on petitions for review of agency action are reviewable by the [appellate court] as in other civil cases.]

Civil Enforcement

§ 5–201. [Petition by Agency for Civil Enforcement of Rule or Order]

(a) In addition to other remedies provided by law, an agency may seek enforcement of its rule or order by filing a petition for civil enforcement in the [trial court of general jurisdiction.]

(b) The petition must name, as defendants, each alleged violator against whom the agency seeks to obtain civil enforcement.

(c) Venue is determined as in other civil cases.

(d) A petition for civil enforcement filed by an agency may request, and the court may grant, declaratory relief, temporary or permanent injunctive relief, any other civil remedy provided by law, or any combination of the foregoing.

§ 5–202. [Petition by Qualified Person for Civil Enforcement of Agency's Order]

(a) Any person who would qualify under this Act as having standing to obtain judicial review of an agency's failure to enforce its order may file a petition for civil enforcement of that order, but the action may not be commenced:

(1) until at least [60] days after the petitioner has given notice of the alleged violation and of the petitioner's intent to seek civil enforcement to the head of the agency concerned, to the attorney general, and to each alleged violator against whom the petitioner seeks civil enforcement;

(2) if the agency has filed and is diligently prosecuting a petition for civil enforcement of the same order against the same defendant; or

(3) if a petition for review of the same order has been filed and is pending in court.

(b) The petition must name, as defendants, the agency whose order is sought to be enforced and each alleged violator against whom the petitioner seeks civil enforcement.

(c) The agency whose order is sought to be enforced may move to dismiss on the grounds that the petition fails to qualify under this section or that enforcement would be contrary to the policy of the agency. The court shall grant the motion to dismiss unless the petitioner demonstrates that (i) the petition qualifies under this section and (ii) the agency's failure to enforce its order is based on an exercise of discretion that is improper on one or more of the grounds provided in Section 5–116(c)(8).

(d) Except to the extent expressly authorized by law, a petition for civil enforcement filed under this section may not request, and the court may not grant any monetary payment apart from taxable costs.

§ 5–203. [Defenses; Limitation on New Issues and New Evidence]

A defendant may assert, in a proceeding for civil enforcement:

(1) that the rule or order sought to be enforced is invalid on any of the grounds stated in Section 5–116. If that defense is raised, the court may consider issues and receive evidence only within the limitations provided by Sections 5–112, 5–113, and 5–114; and

(2) any of the following defenses on which the court, to the extent necessary for the determination of the matter, may consider new issues or take new evidence:

(i) the rule or order does not apply to the party;

(ii) the party has not violated the rule or order;

(iii) the party has violated the rule or order but has subsequently complied, but a party who establishes this defense is not necessarily relieved from any action provided by law for past violations; or

(iv) any other defense allowed by law.

§ 5–204. [Incorporation of Certain Provisions on Judicial Review]

Proceedings for civil enforcement are governed by the following provisions of this Act on judicial review, as modified where necessary to adapt them to those proceedings:

(1) Section 5–101(2) (ancillary procedural matters); and

(2) Section 5–115 (agency record for judicial review—contents, preparation, transmittal, cost.)

§ 5–205. [Review by Higher Court]

Decisions on petitions for civil enforcement are reviewable by the [appellate court] as in other civil cases.

Index

References are to Pages

ABORTIONS
Suspending or revoking medical licenses, investigatory hearing, 142 et seq.

ACTIONS AND PROCEEDINGS
Adjudications, generally, this index
Judicial Review, generally, this index
Taxpayer actions, standing, 700, 701

ADJUDICATIONS
Generally, 9, 10
Administrative Law Judges, generally, this index
Advantages over rulemaking, 259, 260
Attorney general, separation of functions, 148
Communications between arbitrators and outside parties, 164 et seq.
Defined, 244
    Federal Administrative Procedure Act, 743
Delegation of adjudicatory power to agencies, 461 et seq.
Discovery, 206 et seq.
Evidence, 209 et seq.
Failure to request hearing, 131
Federal Administrative Procedure Act, 751, 752
Findings of fact and supporting reasons, 219 et seq.
Formal hearings, Model State Administrative Procedure Act, 785, 786
Institutional model of decision, 132 et seq.
Internal agency communications, 149 et seq.
Intervention, 192 et seq.
Judicial model of decision, 131 et seq.
Judicial Review, generally, this index
Model State Administrative Procedure Act, 783 et seq.
Official notice, 212 et seq.
Parties, 191 et seq.
Res judicata, 227 et seq.
Right to closed or open hearing, 209
Rulemaking-adjudication distinction, 93 et seq.
Separation of functions, 142 et seq.
Stare decisis, 234 et seq.
Statutory rights to a hearing, 106 et seq.
Suspension of employee or license, 74
Timing, 62 et seq.

ADJUDICATIVE FACTS
Defined, 98

ADMINISTRATIVE AGENCIES
Generally, 1
Application of rules, 248 et seq.
Defined,
    Federal Administrative Procedure Act, 743
    Model State Administrative Procedure Act, 764
Discretion, range of choice, 12
Federal agencies, 3
Information, power to obtain, 196 et seq.
Internal communications, 141 et seq.
Legitimacy, 14 et seq.
Political Control, generally, this index
Records on individuals, invasion of privacy, 559
Scope and limits of agency authority, 422 et seq.
Separation of functions, 141 et seq.
Standing, 692
State agencies, 3

ADMINISTRATIVE COURT
Generally, 186 et seq.
State courts, 190

ADMINISTRATIVE LAW
Generally, 2
Interest representation, 15

ADMINISTRATIVE LAW JUDGES
Generally, 175 et seq.
Absolute immunity, 656, 657
Agency internal communications, 150 et seq.
Appointment, 177 et seq.
    Exhaustion of remedies, 720 et seq.
Central panel, 176, 181 et seq.
Decisional independence, 184, 185
Disqualification, 153 et seq.
Federal Administrative Procedure Act, 759, 760
Selection, 177 et seq.
Selective certification, 179, 180
Separation of functions, 189
Specialization, 181 et seq.
Veterans preference, selection process, 179

ADMINISTRATIVE PROCEDURE
Adjudications, generally, this index
Command influence, 153
Declaratory rulings, 242, 243
Hearings, generally, this index
Internal agency communications, 142 et seq.
Political Control, generally, this index
Principal of necessity, 153
Procedural Due Process, generally, this index
Rulemaking, generally, this index
Summary judgments, 129, 130

ADMINISTRATIVE PROCEDURE ACTS
See, also, Statutes, generally, this index
Generally, 4 et seq.
Agencies, combination of functions, 148
Bias or prejudice, challenge, 162
Federal Administrative Procedure Act, 742 et seq.
Jurisdiction, judicial review, 631, 632
Model State Administrative Procedure Act, 761 et seq.
Parameters of judicial review, 633
Statutory rights to adjudicative hearing, 106 et seq.

ADMINISTRATIVE RULES REVIEW COMMITTEES
Generally, 498 et seq.
Model State Administrative Procedure Act, 781, 782

ADMINISTRATIVE SEGREGATION
Prisoners, 47 et seq., 77 et seq.

ADVERSE OR PECUNIARY INTEREST
Adjudicators, 153 et seq.

ADVERTISEMENTS
Children's television, rulemaking, bias of agency head, 357 et seq.

ADVISORY COMMITTEES
Federal Advisory Committee Act, 557 et seq.

AGENCIES
Administrative Agencies, generally, this index

AGENT AND PRINCIPAL
Estoppel, actions of agent, 237 et seq.
Federal Tort Claims Act, 638 et seq.

AID TO FAMILIES WITH DEPENDENT CHILDREN
Administrative proceedings, 24 et seq.

AIR POLLUTION
Construction of statutes by agency, judicial review, 589 et seq.

AIR POLLUTION—Cont'd
Motor vehicle inspection program, attorney fees, 659 et seq.

AIR TRAFFIC CONTROLLERS
Labor dispute, communications with outside parties, 164 et seq.

AIRLINES
Overbooked flights, primary jurisdiction, 729 et seq.
Rulemaking, circumventing hearing requirements, 122 et seq.

APPEAL AND REVIEW
Generally, 10, 11
Agency heads, power to reverse, 176
Judicial Review, generally, this index
Legislative and executive review, 11

APPOINTMENTS
Administrative law judges, 177 et seq.
Agency officials, 1, 3
Discharge of appointees by chief executive, 512 et seq.
Independent counsel, 510
Political control, chief executives, 509 et seq.

APPROPRIATIONS
Political control, 501, 502

ARIZONA
Executive review, proposed rules, 506

ARMED FORCES
Military Forces, generally, this index

ASSESSMENTS
Tax assessments, hearings, 94 et seq.

ATOMIC ENERGY ACT
Licenses and permits, radioactive waste, statutory right to hearing, 106 et seq.

ATTORNEY FEES
Freedom of information actions, 537
Recovery, 659 et seq.
Sunshine Act, 554
Veterans, fee limitation, 83 et seq.

ATTORNEY GENERAL
Adjudication, separation of functions, 148

ATTORNEYS
Privileges and immunities, agency investigations, 203
Representation, Model State Administrative Procedure Act, 786
Right to counsel, 92

AUTOMOBILES
Emissions inspection program, attorney fees, 659 et seq.

AUTOMOBILES—Cont'd
Passive restraints, standards, judicial review, 607 et seq.

BANKS AND BANKING
Data processing services, sale, standing, 686 et seq.
Regulation, state agency, liability for malfeasance, 640 et seq.

BENEFITS
Rulemaking, effective date, 387

BIAS OR PREJUDICE
Command influence, 153 et seq.
Rulemaking, agency heads, 357 et seq.

BOARDS AND COMMISSIONS
Administrative Agencies, generally, this index

BRANCHES OF GOVERNMENT
Political Control, generally, this index

BUILDING CODES
Delegation of legislative powers, 454, 455

BUSINESS AND COMMERCE
Trade secrets, disclosure, freedom of information, 549 et seq.

BUSINESS RECORDS
Disclosure, privileges and immunities, 203, 204

BUSINESS REPORTS
Agencies, power to obtain information, 197 et seq.

CALIFORNIA
Office of Administrative Law, executive review, 504, 505

CERTIFICATES AND CERTIFICATION
Administrative law judges, selective certification, 179, 180

CERTIORARI
Generally, 636, 637

CLEARANCE SYSTEM
Applications to proceed, 8

CODE OF FEDERAL REGULATIONS
Generally, 7, 384

COLLATERAL ESTOPPEL
Generally, 227 et seq.

COLLEGES AND UNIVERSITIES
Students, dismissal, academic due process, 83
Termination of employment, 38 et seq.

COMMODITY FUTURES
Regulation, public officials, tort liability, 647 et seq.

COMMODITY FUTURES TRADING COMMISSION
Delegation of adjudicatory authority to agency, 462 et seq.

COMPENSATION AND SALARIES
Delegation of authority, wage and price freeze, 437 et seq.
Unemployment Compensation, generally, this index

CONFERENCE ADJUDICATIVE HEARING
Model State Administrative Procedure Act, 798, 799

CONFERENCES
Separation of functions, 151, 152

CONFIDENTIAL OR PRIVILEGED INFORMATION
Agency disclosure, 207
Law enforcement files and manuals, 547
Private information, 547 et seq.

CONFLICT OF INTEREST
Adjudicators, 153 et seq.

CONGRESS
Political Control, generally, this index
Removal power, agency officials, 527 et seq.

CONSTITUTIONAL LAW
Agency creation, 3
Checks and balances, 420 et seq.
Delegation of legislative power, 431, 432
Due process clauses, 22
Legislative veto, separation of powers, 483 et seq.
Preclusion of judicial review, 671
Privileges and immunities, agency investigations, 203, 204
Separation of powers, 420 et seq.
Standing, 683
Tort liability of state and local government, 643 et seq.

CONTEMPT
Agency powers, 201

CONTESTED CASES
Adjudications, generally, this index
Defined, 115

CORPORATIONS
Records, disclosure, privileges and immunities, 203, 204

CORRECTIONAL INSTITUTIONS
Administrative proceedings, 47 et seq.
Cancellation of good time credits, 76

CORRECTIONAL INSTITUTIONS—Cont'd
Capital punishment, use of drugs, 673 et seq.
Deprivation of property, 61

COST–BENEFIT ANALYSIS
Administrative process, 11 et seq.
Rulemaking, 325 et seq.

COSTS
Recovery, 659 et seq.

COUNSEL
Attorneys, generally, this index

COURTS
Administrative common law, creation, 316
Administrative court, 186 et seq.
Judicial Review, generally, this index
Rulemaking, imposition of additional procedures, 312 et seq.

CREDIT UNIONS
Banking services, explanatory statement for rule, 370 et seq.
Standing to challenge rules, 689 et seq.

CRIMES AND OFFENSES
Delegation of authority, 471 et seq.
Licenses and permits, revocation, pending criminal proceedings, 75
Self incrimination, privileges and immunities, 203, 204

CROSS–EXAMINATION
Rulemaking, 304, 305

DAMAGES
Delegation of legislative authority to agencies, 476
Judicial review, 637 et seq.
Model State Administrative Procedure Act, 810

DATA PROCESSING
National banks, sale of services, standing, 686 et seq.

DECLARATORY JUDGMENTS
Judicial review, 633

DECLARATORY ORDERS
Model State Administrative Procedure Act, 769, 770

DECLARATORY RULINGS
Generally, 242, 243

DEFINITIONS
Adjudications, 9, 244
Adjudicative facts, 98
Contested case, 115
Ex parte communication, 165
Federal Administrative Procedure Act, 743, 744

DEFINITIONS—Cont'd
Formal adjudication, 106
Informal adjudication, 106
Legislative facts, 98
Legislative rules, 249
Legislative veto, 479
Liberty, 40 et seq.
Meetings, 555, 556
Model State Administrative Procedure Act, 764, 765
Nonlegislative rules, 249
Order, 246
Private rights, 466
Property, 40 et seq.
Public rights, 466

DELEGATION
Generally, 431 et seq.
Adjudicatory power to agencies, 461 et seq.
Crimes and offenses, 471 et seq.
Damages, 476
Fines and penalties, 471 et seq.
Legislative veto, 479 et seq.
Nondelegation doctrine, 431 et seq.
Private persons or entities, 459 et seq.
Safeguards, 445, 446, 455, 456
Standards, 440 et seq.
States, 451 et seq.

DENTISTS
License revocation, unprofessional conduct, 267 et seq.

DEPORTATION
Command influence, prejudice, 153
Rights to hearing, 114
Staff operations instructions, rulemaking exemption, 411 et seq.
Suspension, extreme hardship, legislative veto, 482 et seq.

DEPRIVATION OF LIFE, LIBERTY OR PROPERTY
Procedural Due Process, generally, this index

DISABILITY CLAIMS
Social security, 62 et seq.

DISABLED PERSONS
Denial of benefits, judicial review, 583 et seq.

DISCIPLINARY PROCEEDINGS
Correctional institutions, 47 et seq.

DISCLOSURE
Confidential or privileged information, 207
Documents, filing, application to proceed, 8
Freedom of information, 536 et seq.

DISCOVERY
Adjudications, 206 et seq.
Freedom of Information Act, 546, 547

DISCRETION

Abuse of discretion,
  Judicial review, 607 et seq.
  Orders, 264
Agency choices, 12
Agency powers, limits and structure, 23
Choosing rulemaking or adjudication, 261
  et seq.
Commitment to agency discretion, judicial
  review, 673 et seq.
Judicial review, 563
Standards of review, 221

DISCRIMINATION

Labor and employment, res judicata, 227 et
  seq.

DISQUALIFICATION

Adjudicators, 153 et seq.

DISTRICT COURTS

Federal district courts, jurisdiction, judicial
  review, 631, 632

DOCTORS

License to practice, adjudication, official
  notice, 213 et seq.
Suspending or revoking licenses, investigatory hearing, 142 et seq.

DOCUMENTS

Federal Advisory Committee Act, 558
Freedom of information, 536 et seq.

DRUG ENFORCEMENT AGENCY

Controlled substances, publication, 381 et
  seq.

DRUGS AND MEDICINE

Licenses and permits, 8
Prescription drugs, labeling, generic
  names, 711 et seq.

DUE PROCESS

Constitutional amendments, 22
Procedural Due Process, generally, this in-
  dex
Substantive due process, 44, 45

EDUCATION

Colleges and universities, termination of
  employment, 38 et seq.
Students,
  Corporal punishment, 61
  Disciplinary suspension, type of hearing,
    81

ELECTIONS

Agency officials, 1, 3

EMERGENCIES

Deprivation of liberty or property without
  prior hearing, 62

EMERGENCIES—Cont'd

Rulemaking, emergency rules, effective
  date, 386

**EMERGENCY ADJUDICATIVE PROCEED-
INGS**

Model State Administrative Procedure Act,
  799

EMPLOYMENT

Labor and Employment, generally, this index

ENVIRONMENTAL PROTECTION

Fines and penalties, delegation of judicial
  power, 476 et seq.

ENVIRONMENTAL PROTECTION AGENCY

Construction of statutes, judicial review,
  589 et seq.
Proposed regulation, validity, 251, 252
Sulfur dioxide emissions, ex parte communications, 348 et seq.

EQUAL ACCESS TO JUSTICE ACT

Attorney fees and other expenses, 665, 666

ESTOPPEL

Generally, 237 et seq.
Collateral estoppel, 227 et seq.

EVIDENCE

Adjudications, 209 et seq.
Admissibility, illegally seized, 197
Burden of persuasion, judicial review, 574,
  575
Discovery, adjudications, 206 et seq.
Judicial review, 562 et seq.
  Appellate court, taking evidence, 630,
    631
Model State Administrative Procedure Act,
  791, 792
Rulemaking, 304, 305

EX PARTE COMMUNICATIONS

Defined, 165
  Federal Administrative Procedure Act,
    744
Model State Administrative Procedure Act,
  792, 793
Rulemaking, 338 et seq.

EXECUTIVE BRANCH

Political Control, generally, this index

EXECUTIVE ORDERS

Agency creation, 3

EXECUTIVE PRIVILEGE

State secrets, 547

EXECUTIVE VETO

Agency rules, 503

EXEMPTIONS
Freedom of information, 539 et seq.
Open meetings, 556, 557
Rulemaking requirements, 395 et seq.

**EXHAUSTION OF ADMINISTRATIVE REM-
EDIES**
Generally, 704, 719 et seq.
Model State Administrative Procedure Act,
804, 805

EXPENSES AND EXPENDITURES
Freedom of information, 538

EXPERTS
Administrative law judges, specialization,
181 et seq.

**FEDERAL ADMINISTRATIVE PROCEDURE
ACT**
Generally, 742 et seq.

FEDERAL ADVISORY COMMITTEE ACT
Generally, 557 et seq.

FEDERAL AGENCIES
Administrative Agencies, generally, this,
index

**FEDERAL COMMUNICATIONS COMMIS-
SION**
Petition for rulemaking, denial, 391 et seq.

FEDERAL REGISTER
Rules, publication, 380 et seq.

FEDERAL TRADE COMMISSION
Oil companies, unfair competition, 705 et
seq.

FEES
Attorney Fees, generally, this index
Recovery, 659 et seq.

FILING
Rules, 386

FINAL ORDERS
Generally, 704 et seq.

FINANCIAL STATEMENTS AND REPORTS
Agencies, power to obtain information, 197
et seq.

FINES AND PENALTIES
Delegation of authority, 471 et seq.

FISH AND GAME
Licenses and permits, subsistence fishing,
judicial review, 587 et seq.

FOOD STAMPS
Notice of benefits, 99 et seq.

FOREIGN AFFAIRS
Rulemaking, exemptions, 400

FORMAL ADJUDICATION
Adjudications, generally, this, index
Defined, 106

FORMAL RULEMAKING
Generally, 307 et seq.

FORMALDEHYDE INSULATION
Regulation, judicial review, 615 et seq.

FREE SPEECH
Termination of employment, 45

FREEDOM OF INFORMATION
Generally, 536 et seq.
Exemptions, 539 et seq.
Invasion of privacy, exemption, 553

GOOD TIME CREDITS
Prisoners, liberty interests, 53

HANDICAPPED PERSONS
Denial of benefits, judicial review, 583 et
seq.

HAZARDOUS SUBSTANCES AND WASTE
Formaldehyde insulation, rule, judicial review, 615 et seq.

**HEALTH AND HUMAN RESOURCES, DE-
PARTMENT OF**
Legislative rule, application, 247, 248

HEARING EXAMINERS
Administrative Law Judges, generally, this
index

HEARINGS
See, also, Adjudications, generally, this
index
Generally, 10, 209 et seq.
Administrative Law Judges, generally, this
index
Aid to families with dependent children, 26
et seq.
Constitutional rights, 22 et seq.
Elements, 76 et seq.
Federal Administrative Procedure Act, 753
et seq.
Formal hearings, Model State Administra-
tive Procedure Act, 785, 786
Internal agency communications, 149 et
seq.
Investigatory hearings, due process, 55
Legislative committee hearings, 501
Statutory rights to a hearing, 106 et seq.
Students,
Disciplinary suspension, type of hearing,
81
Dismissal, academic due process, 83
Tax assessments, 94 et seq.

HEARINGS—Cont'd
Timing, 62 et seq.

HEARSAY
Admissibility of evidence, 212

HOMOSEXUALS
CIA employee, termination of employment, 679
Military forces, discharge from service, 219 et seq.

HOSPITALS
Medicare, rulemaking exemptions, 397, 398

HOTELS
Employees, wages and working conditions, statement of basis for rule, 360 et seq.

IMMIGRATION AND NATURALIZATION SERVICE
Staff operations instructions, rulemaking exemption, 411 et seq.
Suspension of deportation, legislative veto, 482 et seq.

IMMUNITIES
Privileges and Immunities, generally, this index

INDEMNIFICATION
Public officials, 658

INDEPENDENT AGENCIES
Political control, 524 et seq.

INDEPENDENT COUNSEL
Appointment, 510
Removal, 513 et seq.

INDIGENT PERSONS
Rulemaking, participation, 301, 302

INFORMAL ADJUDICATION
Adjudications, generally, this index
Defined, 106

INJUNCTIONS
Judicial review, 633

INMATES
Correctional Institutions, generally, this, index

INSPECTIONS
Agencies, power to obtain information, 196 et seq.

INTERPRETIVE RULES
Rulemaking exemptions, 405 et seq.

INTERVENTION
Adjudications, 192 et seq.
Model State Administrative Procedure Act, 790

INVASION OF PRIVACY
Administrative agencies, 9
Power to obtain information, 196 et seq.
Freedom of information, exemption, 553
Privacy Act, 559, 560

HEARINGS, DUE PROCESS, 55
Internal agency communications, 151

JOBS
Labor and Employment, generally, this index

JUDGES
Administrative Law Judges, generally, this index
Judicial Review, generally, this, index

JUDGMENTS AND DECREES
Administrative summary judgment, 129, 130
Declaratory judgments, 633
Res judicata, 227 et seq.
Stare decisis, 234 et seq.

JUDICIAL NOTICE
Generally, 212, 213

JUDICIAL REVIEW
Generally, 10, 11, 562 et seq.
Abuse of discretion, 607 et seq.
Administrative Law Judges, generally, this index
Agency inaction, 680, 681
Appellate courts, 630, 631
Arbitrary and capricious standard, 607 et seq.
Burden of persuasion, 574, 575
Certiorari, 636, 637
Clearly erroneous test, 562, 569 et seq.
Commitment to agency discretion, 673 et seq.
Construction of statutes by agencies, 586 et seq.
Damages, 637 et seq.
Declaratory judgments, 633
Discretion,
   Scope of review, 563
   Standards of review, 221
Evidence, appellate court, taking evidence, 630, 631
Exhaustion of administrative remedies, 704, 719 et seq.
Extraordinary or prerogative writs, 634 et seq.
Federal Administrative Procedure Act, 758, 759
Final orders, 704 et seq.
Finality statutes, 671
Findings of fact and supporting reasons, 224 et seq.
Hard look review, 621 et seq.
Implicit delegation, law-interpretive power of agency, determining, 594, 595

JUDICIAL REVIEW—Cont'd
Independent judgment on the evidence, 562, 582 et seq.
Injunctions, 633
Intervention, 194, 195
Investigations, 199
Jurisdiction, 629 et seq.
Lack of record, 620
Legal interpretations by agencies, 586 et seq.
Mandamus, 634 et seq.
Manifest weight of evidence test, 562
Mixed question of law and fact, 598 et seq.
Model State Administrative Procedure Act, 802 et seq.
Non-prejudicial error, 606
Petitions, filing, 631
Preclusion, 667 et seq.
Prejudicial error, 606
Primary jurisdiction, 704, 705, 729 et seq.
Questions of law, de novo review, 593
Reasonable interpretation, affirming, 595
Record, 619
Regulatory analysis, 330, 331
Reports, required filing, standards of review, 198 et seq.
Ripeness, 704, 711 et seq.
Rulemaking record, 372 et seq.
Scintilla test, 563
Scope of review, 562 et seq.
   Application of law to facts, 598 et seq.
   Federal Administrative Procedure Act, 759
   Model State Administrative Procedure Act, 809, 810
Sovereign immunity, waiver, 632
Standing, 683 et seq.
Statutory preclusion of review, 563
Substantial evidence test, 562 et seq.
Timing, 703 et seq.
Trial courts, states, 630
Trial de novo, 562, 578 et seq.
Venue, 632
Weight of interpretion by agency, 596, 597

JURISDICTION
Judicial review, 629 et seq.
Model State Administrative Procedure Act, 803
Primary jurisdiction, 704, 705, 729 et seq.

JURY TRIAL
Delegation of adjudicatory authority to agency, 470 et seq.

LABOR AND EMPLOYMENT
Discharge for cause, 56 et seq.
Discrimination,
   Freedom of information, disclosure, 547 et seq.
   Res judicata, 227 et seq.
Notice of charges against employee, 73
Reinstatement of employee, protest of safety conditions, 74

LABOR AND EMPLOYMENT—Cont'd
Representation election, agency discretion, 275 et seq.
Right-privilege doctrine, 43
Suspensions, 74
Teachers, termination of employment, 38 et seq.
Unfair labor practices, disqualification, arbitrators, 154 et seq.

LABOR DISPUTES
Air traffic controllers, communications with outside parties, 164 et seq.
Plant relocation, stare decisis, 234 et seq.
Representation election, agency discretion, judicial review, 261 et seq.
Steel mills, Presidential seizure, 507

LABOR UNIONS
Records, disclosure, privileges and immunities, 203, 204

LAW CLERKS
Separation of functions, 152

LAW ENFORCEMENT
Administrative agencies, 9

LAWYERS
Attorneys, generally, this, index

LEGISLATIVE FACTS
Defined, 98

LEGISLATIVE REVIEW
Generally, 11

LEGISLATIVE RULES
Generally, 249

LEGISLATIVE VETO
Generally, 479 et seq.

LEGISLATURE
Political Control, generally, this, index

LIABILITY
Federal Tort Claims Act, 638 et seq.
Public officials, 644 et seq.

LIBERTY
Defined, 40 et seq.
Deprivation. Procedural Due Process, generally, this, index

LICENSES AND PERMITS
Generally, 8
Defined,
   Federal Administrative Procedure Act, 744
   Model State Administrative Procedure Act, 764
Dentists, revocation, unprofessional conduct, 267 et seq.

LICENSES AND PERMITS—Cont'd

Federal Administrative Procedure Act, 756, 757

Medical licenses, suspending or revoking, investigatory hearing, 142 et seq.

Nuclear power plants, safety and environmental review, 312 et seq.

Nuclear regulatory commission, statutory right to hearing, 106 et seq.

Revocation, pending criminal proceedings, 75

Suspension, 74

Television station, application, party in interest, 193

LIVESTOCK AGENTS

Rates and charges, responsibility of decisionmaker, 133 et seq.

LOCAL GOVERNMENT

Administrative procedure acts, applicability, 6

Torts, liability, 640 et seq.

MANDAMUS

Generally, 634 et seq.

MEDICARE

Hospitals, rulemaking exemptions, 397, 398

Payments to allopathic family physicians, 667 et seq.

MEETINGS

Sunshine Act, 554 et seq.

MENTAL INSTITUTIONS

Transfer of prisoners, liberty interests, 53

MILITARY FORCES

Homosexuals, discharge from service, 219 et seq.

Rulemaking, exemptions, 400

Veterans, generally, this, index

MODEL STATE ADMINISTRATIVE PROCEDURE ACT

Generally, 761 et seq.

MOTOR VEHICLES

Emissions inspection program, attorney fees, 659 et seq.

Passive restraints, standards, judicial review, 607 et seq.

NATIONAL LABOR RELATIONS BOARD

Company union, jurisdiction, 719, 720

Freedom of information, exemption, memoranda, 539 et seq.

Termination of employment, insubordination, judicial review, 564 et seq.

NEGOTIATED RULEMAKING

Generally, 286 et seq.

NOTICE

Discharge from employment, 73

Federal Advisory Committee Act, 558

Food stamps, benefits, 99 et seq.

Official notice, 212 et seq.

Prisoners, cancellation of good time credits, 76

Proposed rules, Model State Administrative Procedure Act, 772, 773

Rulemaking, 283, 284, 291 et seq.

Welfare determinations, hearings, 30

NUCLEAR POWER PLANTS

Construction permits, safety and environmental review, 312 et seq.

Licenses and permits, 8

NUCLEAR REGULATORY COMMISSION

Licenses and permits, radioactive waste, statutory right to hearing, 106 et seq.

OCCUPATIONAL HEALTH AND SAFETY ADMINISTRATION

Employees accompanying inspectors, rulemaking exemption, 405 et seq.

Inspections, instructions to staff, rulemaking exemption, 401 et seq.

Standards, toxic materials, delegation of power, 440 et seq.

OCCUPATIONAL SAFETY AND HEALTH REVIEW COMMISSION

Generally, 189 et seq.

OFFENSES

Crimes and Offenses, generally, this, index

OFFICE OF ADMINISTRATIVE HEARINGS

Model State Administrative Procedure Act, 797

OFFICIAL NOTICE

Generally, 212 et seq.

OIL PIPELINES

Extending, primary jurisdiction, 734 et seq.

OMBUDSMEN

Agencies, oversight functions, 501

OPEN MEETINGS

Sunshine Act, 554 et seq.

OPTOMETRISTS

Conflict of interest, disqualification, 160

ORDERS

Defined, 246

    Federal Administrative Procedure Act, 743

    Model State Administrative Procedure Act, 765

Final order rule, 704 et seq.

Retroactive treatment, 246

Rule-order dichotomy, 254 et seq.

ORDINANCES
Employees, discharge, 59
Tax assessments, hearings, 94, 95

PAPERWORK REDUCTION ACT
Generally, 205

PAROLE AND PROBATION
Prisoners, liberty interests, 53

PARTIES
Adjudications, 191 et seq.
Third party standing, 702

PARTNERSHIPS
Records, disclosure, privileges and immunities, 203, 204

PASSPORTS
State department, delegation of authority, 423 et seq.

PERMITS AND LICENSES
Licenses and Permits, generally, this index

PETITIONS
Judicial review, 631
Model State Administrative Procedure Act, 780, 805, 806
Rules, adoption, amendment or repeal, 388 et seq.

PHYSICIANS AND SURGEONS
License to practice, adjudication, official notice, 213 et seq.
Suspending or revoking licenses, investigatory hearing, 142 et seq.

POLITICAL CONTROL
See, also, Delegation, generally, this index
Generally, 420 et seq., 478 et seq.
Administrative rules review committees, 498 et seq.
Agencies as instruments of, 16 et seq.
Appointments, chief executive, 509 et seq.
Appropriations, 501, 502
Checks and balances, 420 et seq.
Discharge of appointees by chief executive, 512 et seq.
Executive control, 502 et seq.
Executive veto, 503
Independent agencies, 524 et seq.
Independent counsel, appointment, 510
Legislative and executive review, 478 et seq.
Legislative committee hearings, 501
Legislative power, delegation, 431 et seq.
Legislative veto, 479 et seq.
Legislators, direct contacts, 502
Limited sanctions, 533
Nondelegation doctrine, 431 et seq.
Ombudsmen, oversight functions, 501

POLITICAL CONTROL—Cont'd
Oversight committees, 498 et seq.
Policy monitoring, 531 et seq.
Sanctions, limits and political costs, 533 et seq.
Scope and limits of agency authority, 422 et seq.
Separation of powers, 420 et seq.
Ultra vires, agency actions, 422 et seq.

PREJUDICE OR BIAS
Command influence, 153 et seq.
Rulemaking, agency heads, 357 et seq.

PRIMARY JURISDICTION
Generally, 704, 705, 729 et seq.

PRINCIPAL AND AGENT
Estoppel, actions of agent, 237 et seq.
Federal Tort Claims Act, 638 et seq.

PRISONS AND PRISONERS
Correctional Institutions, generally, this index

PRIVACY ACT
Generally, 559, 560

PRIVATE RIGHTS
Defined, 466

PRIVATE SCHOOLS
Tax exemptions, standing, 693 et seq.

PRIVILEGED OR CONFIDENTIAL INFORMATION
Confidential or Privileged Information, generally, this index

PRIVILEGES AND IMMUNITIES
Generally, 203, 204
Executive privilege, state secrets, 547
Public officials, tort liability, 646 et seq.

PROBATION AND PAROLE
Prisoners, liberty interests, 53

PROCEDURAL DUE PROCESS
Generally, 22 et seq.
Agency created standards, 270
Bias or prejudice, 153 et seq.
Command influence, 153
Correctional institutions, 47 et seq.
Discharge for cause from employment, 56 et seq.
Interests protected, 37 et seq.
Social security, disability claims, 62 et seq.
Students, dismissal, academic due process, 83
Teachers, termination of employment, 38 et seq.
Variable due process, 93
Veterans, attorney fee limitation, 83 et seq.

PROCEEDINGS
Actions and Proceedings, generally, this index

PROCESS
Compulsory process, 207

PRODUCTION OF BOOKS AND PAPERS
Agencies, power to obtain information, 196

PROFESSORS
Termination of employment, 38 et seq.

PROPERTY
Defined, 40 et seq.
Deprivation. Procedural Due Process, generally, this index
Entitlements, 59, 60
Status or benefits, 60

PUBLIC HEALTH COUNCIL
Smoking in public area, delegation of authority, 425 et seq.

PUBLIC OFFICIALS
Absolute immunity, 656, 657
Qualified immunity, 657
Torts, liability, 644 et seq.

PUBLIC RIGHTS
Defined, 466

PUBLIC WELFARE
Administrative proceedings, 24 et seq.
Intervention, adjudications, 194, 195

PUBLICATION
Federal Administrative Procedure Act, 744 et seq.
Freedom of information, 536 et seq.
Model State Administrative Procedure Act, 767 et seq.
Rules, 379 et seq.

PUBLICITY
Press releases, pending investigations, 205, 206

RAILROADS
Rates and charges, freight cars, rulemaking procedures, 307 et seq.

RATEMAKING
Generally, 10
Treatment as order or rule, 246

RATES AND CHARGES
Check cashing, delegation of power, 451 et seq.

REAL ESTATE
Tax assessments, hearings, 94 et seq.

RECORDS
Agencies, power to obtain information, 196 et seq.
Business records, disclosure, privileges and immunities, 203, 204
Federal Advisory Committee Act, 558
Freedom of information, 536 et seq.
Judicial review, 619
Model State Administrative Procedure Act, 796, 808, 809
Rulemaking record, judicial review, 372 et seq.

REFORMING ADMINISTRATIVE PROCEDURE
Generally, 11 et seq.

REGULATORY AGENCIES
Generally, 1

REPORTS
Agencies, power to obtain information, 196 et seq.
Freedom of information, 536 et seq.

RES JUDICATA
Generally, 227 et seq.

REVIEW
Appeal and Review, generally, this index

RIGHT–PRIVILEGE DOCTRINE
Generally, 43

RIPENESS
Generally, 704, 711 et seq.

RULEMAKING
Generally, 7, 244 et seq., 282 et seq.
Actual notice, 295
Advantages over adjudication, 258, 259
Agency heads, role, 356
Authority to make legislative rules, 409, 410
Benefits, effective date, 387
Bias or prejudice, agency heads, 357 et seq.
Changes from proposed rule, explanation, 369
Circumventing hearing requirements, 121 et seq.
Congressional interference, 355
Constructive notice, 291 et seq.
Cost-benefit analysis, 325 et seq.
Courts, imposition of additional procedures, 312 et seq.
Cross-examination, 304, 305
Deferred effective date, publication requirement, 379 et seq.
Defined,
    Federal Administrative Procedure Act, 743
    Model State Administrative Procedure Act, 765
Efficiency, 285

RULEMAKING—Cont'd
Emergency rules, effective date, 386
Ex parte communications, 338 et seq.
Executive branch interference, 353, 354
Exemptions, 395 et seq.
Explanatory statement, 365 et seq.
Factual basis for proposed rule, notice, 296, 297
Fairness, 284
Federal Administrative Procedure Act, 750, 751
Filing of rules, 386
Foreign affairs, exemption, 400
Formal rulemaking, 299, 303 et seq.
Formulation of proposed rules, 286 et seq.
Good cause exemptions, 319 et seq.
Hybrid rulemaking, 299
Indigent persons, participation, 301
Informal rulemaking, 299 et seq.
Initiating proceedings, 286 et seq.
Interested persons, 300, 301
Interpretive rules, exemptions, 405 et seq.
Legislative veto, 493
Management and personnel of agencies, exemptions, 400 et seq.
Military or foreign affairs functions, exemptions, 400
Model State Administrative Procedure Act, 771 et seq.
Negotiated rulemaking, 286 et seq.
Non-legislative rules exemption, rationale, 416
Notice, 283, 284, 291 et seq.
Objectives, 282 et seq.
Oral proceeding, 300
Overregulation, prevention, 284
Petition for adoption, amendment or repeal of rules, 388 et seq.
Policy statements, exemption, 411 et seq.
Political influence, 338 et seq.
Politically responsible rules, 283
Proprietary matters, exemptions, 396
Public disclosure, ex parte communications, 346 et seq.
Public satisfaction, 284
Publication, 379 et seq.
Record, exclusivity, 372 et seq.
Regulatory analysis, 325 et seq.
Required rulemaking, 266
Rulemaking-adjudication distinction, 93 et seq.
Statement of basis, findings and reasons, 360 et seq.
Statement of purpose, notice, proposed rules, 296
Test results, notice, proposed rule, 296, 297
Time,
    Good cause exemptions, 324
    Proposed rules, period for comment, 292
Trial-type proceedings, 299, 303 et seq.
Unpublished rules, consequences, 385
Variance between proposed and final rule, 293, 294

RULEMAKING—Cont'd
Witnesses, 304, 305

RULES AND REGULATIONS
    See, also, Rulemaking, generally, this index
    Generally, 7, 246 et seq.
Code of federal regulations, 384
Defined,
    Federal Administrative Procedure Act, 743
    Model State Administrative Procedure Act, 765
Generic rules, validity, 128
Petition for adoption, amendment or repeal, 388 et seq.
Publication, 379 et seq.
Rule-order dichotomy, 254 et seq.

SANCTIONS
Role of administrative procedures, 17, 18

SCHOOL BOARDS
Conflict of interest, disqualification, 161

SCHOOLS AND SCHOOL DISTRICTS
Private schools, tax exemptions, standing, 693 et seq.
Students,
    Corporal punishment, 61
    Disciplinary suspension, type of hearing, 81

SCHOOLTEACHERS
Termination of employment, 38 et seq.

SEARCHES AND SEIZURES
Agencies, power to obtain information, 197
Pretrial detainees, liberty interests, 53

SELF INCRIMINATION
Privileges and immunities, agency investigations, 203, 204

SENTENCE AND PUNISHMENT
Agencies, power to adjudicate penalties, 474 et seq.
Commutation of life sentence, liberty interests, 53

SEWERS AND SEWAGE
Pollution abatement program, approval, right to hearing, 116 et seq.

SMOKING
Public areas, delegation of authority, 425 et seq.

SOCIAL SECURITY
Disability claims, 62 et seq.

SOVEREIGN IMMUNITY
Abandonment, estoppel, 239
Waiver, judicial review, 632

STANDARDS
Delegation of authority, 440 et seq.
Due process, agency created standards, 270

STANDING
Generally, 683 et seq.
Agencies, 692
Causation requirement, 701
Ideological plaintiffs, 699, 700
Injury in fact test, 686 et seq.
Judicial review, adjudications, intervention, 194, 195
Legal wrong test, 684, 685
Model State Administrative Procedure Act, 804
Non-economic injuries, 691
Remediability requirement, 701
Taxpayer actions, 700, 701
Third party standing, 702
Zone of interest test, 686 et seq.

STARE DECISIS
Generally, 234 et seq.

STATES
Administrative courts, 190
Contested case proceedings, right to hearing, 115 et seq.
Delegation doctrine, 451 et seq.
Incorporation by reference, federal guidelines, 457, 458
Interpretive rules, rulemaking exemptions, 410
Legislative veto, rulemaking, 495 et seq.
Notice, proposed rulemaking, 293
Open records, exemptions, 545
Preclusion of judicial review, 672, 673
Res judicata, adjudications, 231
Torts, liability, 640 et seq.
Trial courts, judicial review, 630
Trial de novo, judicial review, 581

STATUTES
Administrative procedure acts, 4 et seq.
Agency creation, 3
Attorney fees, 603, 604
Construction of statutes by agencies, judicial review, 586 et seq.
Delegation, vague standard, 271
Final order rule, 709
Finality statutes, 671
Hybrid rulemaking, 306
Incorporation by reference, federal guidelines, 457, 458
Rights to a hearing in adjudication, 106 et seq.
Substantial evidence standard, judicial review, 625

STAYS
Agency actions, 718
Model State Administrative Procedure Act, 795

STUDENTS
Corporal punishment, 61
Disciplinary suspension, type of hearing, 81
Dismissal, academic due process, 83

SUBPOENAS
Agencies, power to obtain information, 196
Defenses to enforcement, 201, 202
Model State Administrative Procedure Act, 790
Witnesses, 207

SUBSTANTIVE DUE PROCESS
Generally, 44, 45

SUMMARY ADJUDICATIVE PROCEEDINGS
Model State Administrative Procedure Act, 800 et seq.

SUMMARY JUDGMENT
Administrative summary judgment, 129, 130

SUNSHINE ACT
Generally, 554 et seq.

TARIFFS
Delegation of legislative power, 432

TAX ASSESSMENTS
Hearings, 94 et seq.

TEACHERS
Termination of employment, 38 et seq.

TELEVISION
Advertising, children's television, bias of agency head, 357 et seq.
Cable and subscription, ex parte communications, 339 et seq.
License application, party in interest, 193

TENURE
Generally, 38 et seq.
Implied contract, 46

TIME
Judicial review, 703 et seq.
Petitions, filing, Model State Administrative Procedure Act, 805

TORTS
Damages, judicial review, 637 et seq.
Federal Tort Claims Act, 638 et seq.

TRADE SECRETS
Disclosure, freedom of information, 549 et seq.

TRIAL
Jury trial, delegation of adjudicatory authority to agency, 470 et seq.

TRIAL COURTS
Judicial review, states, 630

TRIAL DE NOVO
Judicial review, 562, 578 et seq.
States, judicial review, 581

TRIAL–TYPE HEARINGS
Adjudications, generally, this index

ULTRA VIRES
Agency actions, 422 et seq.
Liability of public officials, 646

UNEMPLOYMENT COMPENSATION
Construction of law by agency, judicial review, 598 et seq.
Estoppel, actions of agent, 237 et seq.
Evidence, adjudications, 209 et seq.

VENUE
Federal Administrative Procedure Act, 758
Judicial review, 632
Model State Administrative Procedure Act, 803

VETERANS
Administrative law judges, selection, veterans preference, 179
Benefits, precluding judicial review, 670
Representation, attorney fee limitation, 83 et seq.

WARRANTS
Agencies, power to obtain information, 196

WELFARE
Administrative proceedings, 24 et seq.
Intervention, adjudications, 194, 195

WITNESSES
Prisoners, cancellation of good time credits, 76
Rulemaking, 304, 305
Subpoenas, 207

WORKERS' COMPENSATION
Denial of benefits, judicial review, 569 et seq.

†